www.euro.gov.uk

www.euromoney.com

www.europa.eu.int/institutions/index_en.htm

www.ex.ac.uk

www.exim.gov

www.experian.com

www.fanniemae.com

www.fcmstablevalue.com

www.fdic.gov

www.fdic.gov/bank

www.fdic.gov/consumers

www.federalreserve.gov

www.federalreserve.gov/fomc

www.federalreserve.gov/releases

www.federalreserveeducation.org

www.federaltaxreturn.com

www.fedmoney.com

www.fese.be

www.ffiec.gov

www.fhlbi.com

www.fidelity.com

www.fin.gc.ca

www.finaid.org/calculators

www.financial-planning.com

www.financialpowertools.com

www.finix.at

www.finpipe.com

www.finpipe.com/bndjunk.ht.

www.finpipe.com/derivglossary.htm

www.fitchratings.com

www.fool.com

www.forbes.com

www.forexnews.com

www.fortune.com

www.franklintempleton.com

www.frbatlanta.org/publica

www.frbdiscountwindow.org

www.freddiemac.com

www.ft.com

www.ftbusiness.com

www.ftc.gov

www.funds-newsletter.com

www.fxstreet.com

www.gcn.com

www.gecapital.com

www.gecommercialfinance.com

www.getsmart.com

www.ginniemae.gov

www.globalfindata.com

www.governmentguide.com

www.gpo.gov/usbudget

www.gsm.uci.edu

www.hrblock.com

www.hsbc.com

www.hsh.com

www.hud.gov

www.ibcdata.com

www.ideas.uqam.ca

www.ifebp.org

www.iiin.com/iiincompanies.html

www.imf.org

www.imfsite.org

www.imoneynet.com

www.ins.state.pa.us

www.interestcalculator.com

www.interestratecalculator.com

www.intermoney.com

www.in-the-money.com

www.investing.com

www.investing.wsj.com

www.investinginbonds.com

www.investopedia.com

www.investorhome.com

www.ire-net.com/pubs

www.iseoptions.com

www.jsc.nasa.gov

PowerWeb: ETHICS IN FINANCE

Welcome to PowerWeb! This site has been designed to enhance your course—giving you access to readings, up-to-the-minute news, research links, and more!

To access PowerWeb:

1. Use a Web browser to go to http://register.dushkin.com.

2. Enter your unique access code in the space provided. You must enter the <u>entire</u> code as it appears in the box below when you register.

3. Your unique access code is in the box below.

4. After you have entered the "unique access code," click on the "Register" button to continue the registration process.

THIS UNIQUE ACCESS CODE WORKS FOR BOTH SITES.

emykx-ccaf-jrsq-h2r8

Welcome to the **EDUCATIONAL VERSION** of Market Insight!

www.mhhe.com/edumarketinsight

Check out your textbook's website for details on how this special offer enhances the value of your purchase!

1. To get started, use your web browser to go to www.mhhe.com/edumarketinsight.

2. Enter your unique access code exactly as it appears in the box above.

3. You may be prompted to enter the unique access code for future use — *please keep this card.*

4. Your unique access code can be found in the box above.

*If you purchased a used book, this unique access code may have expired. For new password purchase, please go to **www.mhhe.com/edumarketinsight**.
Password activation is good for a 6 month duration.

ISBN 0-07-319549-9

Money and Capital Markets

Financial Institutions and Instruments in a Global Marketplace

Ninth Edition

Peter S. Rose

Texas A&M University

Milton H. Marquis

Florida State University

McGraw-Hill
Irwin

Boston   Burr Ridge, IL   Dubuque, IA   Madison, WI   New York   San Francisco   St. Louis
Bangkok   Bogotá   Caracas   Kuala Lumpur   Lisbon   London   Madrid   Mexico City
Milan   Montreal   New Delhi   Santiago   Seoul   Singapore   Sydney   Taipei   Toronto

To our families

PETER S. ROSE

MILTON H. MARQUIS

McGraw-Hill
Irwin

MONEY AND CAPITAL MARKETS:

Financial Institutions and Instruments in a Global Marketplace

Published by McGraw-Hill/Irwin, a business unit of The McGraw-Hill Companies, Inc., 1221 Avenue of the Americas, New York, NY, 10020.

Some ancillaries, including electronic and print components, may not be available to customers outside the United States.

This book is printed on acid-free paper.

1 2 3 4 5 6 7 8 9 0 VNH/VNH 0 9 8 7 6 5

ISBN 0-07-295739-5

Publisher: *Stephen M. Patterson*
Editorial coordinator: *Barbara Hari*
Executive marketing manager: *Rhonda Seelinger*
Lead producer, Media technology: *Kai Chiang*
Lead project manager: *Pat Frederickson*
Lead production supervisor: *Michael R. McCormick*
Senior designer: *Mary E. Kazak*
Senior media project manager: *Susan Lombardi*
Developer, Media technology: *Brian Nacik*
Cover design: *Brian Perveneckis*
Interior design: *Amanda Kavanaugh*
Cover image: *© Chris Gregerson Stock Photography*
Typeface: *10.5/12 Times Roman*
Compositor: *Cenveo*
Printer: *Von Hoffmann Corporation*

Library of Congress Cataloging-in-Publication Data

Rose, Peter S.
    Money and capital markets: financial institutions and instruments in a global
marketplace / Peter S. Rose, Milton H. Marquis.— 9th ed.
        p. cm.— (The McGraw-Hill/Irwin series in finance, insurance, and real estate)
    Includes index.
    ISBN 0-07-295739-5 (alk. paper)
    1. Finance—United States.   2. Money market—United States.   3. Capital market—United
States.   I. Marquis, Milton H., 1948–II. Title. III. Series.
HG181.R66 2006
332:0973–dc22   2004042323

www.mhhe.com

The McGraw-Hill/Irwin Series in Finance, Insurance, and Real Estate

Stephen A. Ross
Franco Modigliani Professor of Finance and Economics
Sloan School of Management
Massachusetts Institute of Technology
Consulting Editor

Financial Management

Adair
Excel Applications for Corporate Finance
First Edition

Benninga and Sarig
Corporate Finance: A Valuation
Approach

Block and Hirt
Foundations of Financial Management
Eleventh Edition

Brealey, Myers, and Allen
Principles of Corporate Finance
Eighth Edition

Brealey, Myers, and Marcus
Fundamentals of Corporate Finance
Fourth Edition

Brooks
FinGame Online 4.0

Bruner
Case Studies in Finance: Managing for Corporate
Value Creation
Fourth Edition

Chew
The New Corporate Finance: Where Theory Meets
Practice
Third Edition

Chew and Gillan
Corporate Governance at the Crossroads:
A Book of Readings
First Edition

DeMello
Cases in Finance
Second Edition

Grinblatt and Titman
Financial Markets and Corporate Strategy
Second Edition

Helfert
Techniques of Financial Analysis: A Guide to Value
Creation
Eleventh Edition

Higgins
Analysis for Financial Management
Seventh Edition

Kester, Ruback, and Tufano
Case Problems in Finance
Twelfth Edition

Ross, Westerfield, and Jaffe
Corporate Finance
Seventh Edition

Ross, Westerfield, and Jordan
Essentials of Corporate Finance
Fourth Edition

Ross, Westerfield, and Jordan
Fundamentals of Corporate Finance
Seventh Edition

Smith
The Modern Theory of Corporate Finance
Second Edition

White
Financial Analysis with an Electronic Calculator
Fifth Edition

Investments

Bodie, Kane, and Marcus
Essentials of Investments
Fifth Edition

Bodie, Kane, and Marcus
Investments
Sixth Edition

Cohen, Zinbarg, and Zeikel
Investment Analysis and Portfolio Management
Fifth Edition

Corrado and Jordan
Fundamentals of Investments: Valuation and
Management
Third Edition

Farrell
Portfolio Management: Theory and Applications
Second Edition

Hirt and Block
Fundamentals of Investment Management
Eighth Edition

Financial Institutions and Markets

Cornett and Saunders
Fundamentals of Financial Institutions Management

Rose and Hudgins
Bank Management and Financial Services
Sixth Edition

Rose and Marquis
Money and Capital Markets: Financial Institutions
and Instruments in a Global Marketplace
Ninth Edition

Santomero and Babbel
Financial Markets, Instruments, and Institutions
Second Edition

Saunders and Cornett
Financial Institutions Management: A Risk
Management Approach
Fifth Edition

Saunders and Cornett
Financial Markets and Institutions: A Modern
Perspective
Second Edition

International Finance

Beim and Calomiris
Emerging Financial Markets

Eun and Resnick
International Financial Management
Third Edition

Kuemmerle
Case Studies in International Entrepreneurship:
Managing and Financing Ventures in the Global
Economy
First Edition

Levich
International Financial Markets: Prices and Policies
Second Edition

Real Estate

Brueggeman and Fisher
Real Estate Finance and Investments
Twelfth Edition

Corgel, Ling, and Smith
Real Estate Perspectives: An Introduction to Real
Estate
Fourth Edition

Ling and Archer
Real Estate Principles: A Value Approach
First Edition

Financial Planning and Insurance

Allen, Melone, Rosenbloom, and Mahoney
Pension Planning: Pension, Profit-Sharing, and
Other Deferred Compensation Plans
Ninth Edition

Crawford
Life and Health Insurance Law
Eighth Edition (LOMA)

Harrington and Niehaus
Risk Management and Insurance
Second Edition

Hirsch
Casualty Claim Practice
Sixth Edition

Kapoor, Dlabay, and Hughes
Focus on Personal Finance: An Active Approach to
Help You Develop Successful Financial Skills
First Edition

Kapoor, Dlabay, and Hughes
Personal Finance
Seventh Edition

Williams, Smith, and Young
Risk Management and Insurance
Eighth Edition

The twenty-first century is still very young. The first decade of this new century hasn't yet reached its end, but already we can sense the unfolding of a new millennium and a new world. The war on terror rages around us on nearly every continent. And, despite the end of the Cold War more than a decade ago, the nuclear threat remains, this time in a new form and in new and more fanatical hands. Freedom and liberty and our most cherished institutions appear to be facing their greatest challenge since World War II, more than half a century ago. We have begun to wonder if anything really can be considered "safe" anymore.

Nowhere are these concerns for safety, freedom, and liberty more evident today than in the functioning of the global financial marketplace and its fabled institutions—the money and capital markets and the thousands of banks, insurance companies, security brokers and dealers, investment bankers, and investment companies that provide us with essential financial services. Collectively, these critical components of our financial system:

- Provide us with supplies of *credit* when we need borrowed funds to supplement our income and maintain our standard of living.

- Encourage *saving* for the future on the part of millions of businesses and households (individuals and families) so that we will have financial resources available when they may be most needed down the road (such as for retirement).

- Convert those savings into *investments* in the building and refurbishing of plant and equipment and the stocking of inventories of goods to sell so that economic activity continues to grow, provide more jobs, and enhance our standard of living.

- Provide a channel through which trillions of currency units (dollars, euros, pounds, yen, etc.) pass daily to effect *payments for purchases of goods and services* so that spendable funds flow rapidly and safely from buyers to sellers.

- Supply a vibrant marketplace through which we can *liquidate assets* in order to raise cash (liquidity) quickly to meet our spending needs.

- Offer *risk protection* in the form of insurance policies, derivatives, and other financial products to safeguard our well-being and protect what we own and value most highly.

- Serve as a *channel for public policy* through which governments work to regulate their economies and achieve critical economic goals, such as maximum employment for their citizens, stable prices and the avoidance of inflation, and sustainable economic growth into the future.

What an incredible array of jobs for one of society's great institutions—the money and capital markets and the financial system that surrounds them! How lucky we are to have such a vital set of markets and institutions to meet our needs for credit, savings, investment, making payments, providing liquidity and risk protection, and promoting a healthy, growing economy that generates jobs and avoids severe inflation.

Moreover, as recent global events have illustrated, how different our lives can become when the financial system of markets and institutions is significantly damaged or can no longer perform as efficiently or as assuredly as we have come to expect. For example, when the terrible tragedy of September 11, 2001, unfolded and the World Trade Center collapsed in New York City, not only were thousands of lives lost, but essential facilities for trading financial instruments and making payments suddenly were put out of commission. Frightened investors in stocks and bonds suddenly lost contact with professionals in the financial-service community and feared for the safety and security of their savings and investments. Payments that needed to be made to security traders and from those repaying old loans or seeking new loans were suddenly shut down or delayed. The New York Stock Exchange and other key financial markets around the globe temporarily closed or drastically slowed, contributing to a global recession and loss of jobs.

What is truly remarkable, however, is the *speed* with which the financial system of money and capital markets quickly righted itself and moved forward after the tragedy of 9/11. Financial-service businesses, including major banks and securities houses, that suffered huge losses of talented people, equipment, and funds, still fought their way back to full service to the public within a matter of days. Our money and capital markets proved to be far more resilient than most of us had imagined. Equally important, we learned anew that what happens in those markets impacts *all of us*—every individual and family, every business and governmental institution around the globe. More than ever before we recognize now how much we rely upon the vital services—credit, savings, investments, payments, liquidity, risk protection, and supporting the proper functioning of the economy—that emerge every day from the workings of our financial system.

Recent tragedies impacting the money and capital markets and the institutions that surround them have provided us with a key reason for this book and for other sources of information on the financial system. We have learned that we can ill-afford to lose the critical services that the money and capital markets provide. Neither can we afford to be ignorant or misinformed about the many roles that the financial system plays in our daily lives. If ever we needed an incentive to explore this book and other sources of information about our financial system, that need has been awakened. It is an adventure we need to undertake and there is no better time to begin than now!

Ways This Book Can Be Used

As *Money and Capital Markets* enters its ninth edition, we have incorporated many changes in our telling of the story of the financial system. The book is somewhat shorter—24 chapters now instead of 26 in the previous edition. Still, this text continues to be one of the most comprehensive overviews of the global financial system to be found anywhere in the field. The ninth edition continues to offer its readers and those who teach in this field several alternative routes through the vast panorama represented by the money and capital markets and the financial system. Every reader and every teacher can self-select the course of study they would like to pursue in order to learn about the financial system and the markets that drive that system. For example:

- *A Security Markets-Oriented Course.* Users of this text who would like to focus upon the security markets and the trading of financial instruments would be more likely to make use of Part One (especially Chapters 2–4 on financial assets, financial information, and trends in the financial marketplace), Part Two (Chapters 5–9 on interest rates and asset pricing), Part Three (Chapters 10–13 on the money market and its key institutions and traders), Part Four (especially Chapter 16 on mutual funds and investment banks), Part Five (including

Chapters 18–20 on government and corporate securities), Part Six (especially Chapter 22 on the mortgage market), and Part Seven (particularly Chapter 23 on the currency markets).

- *A Financial Institutions-Related Course.* In contrast, those who wish to know as much as possible about financial-service providers, including the great financial institutions represented by commercial banks, investment banks, insurance companies, mutual funds, pension funds, finance companies, and security brokers and dealers, would find it most helpful to center their attention around Part One (particularly Chapters 1, 2, and 4 on financial intermediation and trends in marketing financial services), Part Three (Chapters 10–13 dealing with key financial firms in the money market and central banking), Part Four (which, in Chapters 14–16, reviews the characteristics of all major financial institutions and, in Chapter 17, presents a detailed look at the regulation of financial institutions), Part Five (which examines the financial side of governments and businesses in the marketplace), Part Six (including Chapters 21 and 22 on consumer lending and borrowing and mortgage lending institutions), and Chapter 24, which explores the field of international banking.

- *A Policy and Regulations-Oriented Course.* For those who have the greatest interest in public policy and government regulation within the financial system, key portions of the book would include Part One (especially Chapters 3 and 4 on information sources and trends in financial institutions' regulation), Part Two (particularly Chapter 7 on yield curves and inflation and Chapter 8 on tax laws), Part Three (including Chapters 10–13 on central banking and the rules that surround the money market), Part Four (especially Chapter 17 on the regulation of financial institutions), Part Six (particularly Chapter 21 on households in the financial markets and new disclosure and privacy rules and Chapter 22 on federal government involvement in developing the home mortgage market), and Part Seven (including Chapter 23 on changing government policy regarding exchange rates and Chapter 24 on the important topic of regulating international banking firms).

- *An Internationally Focused Course.* The increasing globalization of our financial system has aroused great interest in a global view of the money and capital markets and of financial-service firms. While internationally focused material appears throughout this edition, certain sections and chapters do have a heavier emphasis on the international financial markets field. An internationally focused course would want to emphasize such portions of the text as Part One (Chapters 1–4, especially Chapters 3 and 4), Chapters 5, 7, and 9 from Part Two, Part Three on the money market and central banking around the globe, Chapters 14 and 17 on banking and regulations, and Chapters 23 and 24 on international transactions, currency values, and international banking.

- *A Financial Theory-Oriented Course.* For users most interested in the basic theoretical concepts of finance and the results of recent research in the finance field, several parts of the new edition deserve further examination. These include Part One (especially Chapters 1, 2, and 3), Part Two (particularly Chapters 5, 7, 8, and 9), Part Three (especially Chapters 10, 12, and 13), Part Five (particularly Chapters 18 and 20 on the effects of government borrowing and stock market efficiency), and Chapter 23 (which tracks the theory of currency exchange rates and international currency standards).

Key Features of the Ninth Edition

This edition of *Money and Capital Markets* provides a variety of helpful learning aids for the reader. For example:

- Each chapter begins with a statement of *learning objectives*—what the reader can expect to learn from the material covered in the chapter.

- Beside each list of learning objectives is a *key topics outline* of the most important concepts and issues to be explored in each chapter.

- In this new edition for the first time each chapter is divided into *numbered sections* so readers and teachers can more easily designate which sections they wish to assign and use for each class session and which sections they may wish to omit.

- *Key terms* are marked in bold where they are defined in the text and each key term is printed in the margin in bold near the spot where it is discussed, insuring that the reader does not miss them. As in the previous edition, all key terms are listed at the end of each chapter, along with the page numbers where they are discussed.

- At the back of the text, a *Money and Capital Markets Dictionary* lists all of the key terms, defines them, and indicates the chapter or chapters where they appear.

- Numerous *graphs, tables,* and *examples* appear in the text's pages in order to make key points more vivid and memorable.

- Several *boxes* reporting special events, pertinent issues, and key research studies bearing on the topics presented are positioned in each chapter. This box material falls into three general topic areas—*Financial Developments, Ethics in the Money and Capital Markets,* and *E-Commerce in the Financial Marketplace.* The e-commerce boxes reflect the ever-growing role of electronic equipment and computer networks in storing information and in providing vital services that the financial system must produce and deliver each day.

- *Web sites* are given a much more prominent place in this new edition. Throughout each chapter, URLs appear in the page margins and are printed in bold nearest the point in the text where they most apply. Toward the end of each chapter, a box labeled *Markets on the Net: The Most Important Web Sites for This Chapter* provides a listing of key Web sites and URLs.

- *Questions to Help You Study* appear at strategic points within each chapter to give the reader a pause for review to make sure he or she understands the key points and ideas just discussed.

- An expanded *Summary of the Chapter's Main Points*, arrayed by bullet points for the convenience of readers and teachers, appears near each chapter's conclusion, emphasizing the highlights and most important ideas and observations that were presented. This summary, along with the key terms and study questions mentioned earlier, helps the reader do a quick check to determine if any important items might have been missed along the way. The summary also provides a useful review before exams and can be used by teachers to guide classroom discussion.

- One of the greatest innovations in the ninth edition is the significantly expanded *problem section* that appears near the end of each chapter. In the section labeled *Problems and Issues,* many of the best of the problems from previous editions have been carried over into the new edition. Most chapters also provide a multi-part problem, involving both discussion and calculations, based on the extensive database supplied by *Standard & Poor's Market Insight, Educational Version* and covering hundreds of leading corporations (including top financial-service firms). In this same section, labeled *Standard & Poor's Market Insight and Web-Based Problems,* numerous new Web site–oriented problems appear, most of them having multiple parts and asking that the user not only explore the Web sites mentioned but also supply answers to key questions and make calculations from data gathered at the designated Web sites.

- Another significant innovation, completely new, is the creation of a *semester project,* devoted to a study of one of the most important financial markets today—the federal funds market. This semester-long project starts at the conclusion of Chapter 1 and proceeds through the first 14 chapters of the new edition. Each end-of-chapter segment requires those pursuing this semester-long project to gather data and information, answer questions, and solve numerical problems, enriching their understanding about how this important interbank market functions and why it is so important to all participants in today's financial marketplace. Readers are frequently reminded that the federal funds market has become a key barometer today for forecasting changes in money and credit policy and for predicting future changes in market interest rates.

- Finally, the *Selected References to Explore* section that concludes each chapter includes many of the most recent articles available to the public from a wide variety of government agencies and private journal sources. These selected references often deal with the hottest and most critical issues addressed in each chapter.

New Topics in the Ninth Edition

Many new issues and concepts appear in the ninth edition, including, to name a few:

- The *mutual fund scandal* that has resulted in billions of dollars in losses to fund investors, traceable to the effects of after-hours trading and other violations of trading rules and marked by recent huge cash settlements levied by regulators and law-enforcement authorities. (See especially Chapters 1 and 16.)

- The sharp expansion of *asset-backed securities (ABS)* issued in the corporate debt market, including both the advantages and the problems that ABS growth has created for leading corporations around the globe. (See Chapters 8, 19, and 22.)

- The increasingly sharp controversy over the effectiveness and possible threats to civil liberties represented by *recent terrorist legislation in the United States and Europe,* including the Bank Secrecy and USA Patriot Acts. (See, in particular, Chapter 17.)

- The impact on publicly traded corporations (including publicly owned financial-service providers) of the *Sarbanes-Oxley Accounting Standards Act,* which imposes tough new auditing rules and requires CEO and CFO certification of the accuracy and honesty of corporate financial reports. (See especially Chapter 17.)

- The rapid rise of *E-money* (including the use of credit and debit cards, computer networks, Web sites, etc.), supplanting checks as the number one route for making payments for purchases of goods and services in the United States and Europe. (See Chapters 1, 3, 14, 15, 18, and 22.)

- The development of the new *Basel II Agreement* on bank capital standards in leading nations around the globe and what this implies for the future of bank regulation and for bank risk-taking. (See, in particular, Chapter 17.)

- An expanded discussion of *credit derivatives,* which have recently experienced explosive growth as a key device to reduce potential losses from defaulted loans. (See especially Chapter 8.)

- The expanding controversy over the extent and impact of *outsourcing* and the *accounting treatment of stock options* by major corporations around the globe. (See, in particular, Chapters 20 and 23.)

- The development of *new interest-rate futures and option contracts,* including the popular federal funds contracts that provide a basis for gauging future changes in monetary policy and for anticipating trends in market interest rates. (See, in particular, Chapters 9 and 11.)

- The growing use of *transparency* and *inflation targeting* by major central banks around the world (including the Bank of Japan, the Bank of England, and the Bank of New Zealand) in an effort to reduce public confusion and uncertainty regarding central bank money and credit policies and their objectives. (See Chapters 12 and 13.)

- The development and implementation of *new discount window policies at the Federal Reserve banks,* including "no hassle" loans and conversion of the Fed's discount rate to a penalty rate at a fixed spread above the key federal funds interest rate. (See, in particular, Chapter 13.)

- An exploration of the widespread use today of *credit scoring techniques to evaluate borrowers' requests for loans*—their design, advantages for lenders and borrowers, and their possible limitations and weaknesses. (See especially Chapter 21.)

- The passage of *Check 21* into law, which allows the transmission of check images, and its potential consequences for the expansion and changing makeup of the payments mechanism inside the United States. (See, in particular, Chapter 4.)

- An expanded discussion of *GSEs* (government-sponsored enterprises)— especially the Federal Home Loan Bank (FHLB) System, the Federal National Mortgage Association (Fannie Mae), and the Federal Home Loan Mortgage Corporation (Freddie Mac)—their incredible growth in both assets and debt, and the current concern over the devastating effects that may unfold should any of these agencies move to the brink of failure. (See, for example, Chapters 11 and 22.)

- The rise of *financial holding companies (FHCs)* in the United States and around the world and the transformation of the banking community and financial-service conglomerates that this recently developed organizational form has made possible. (See especially Chapters 4, 14, and 17.)

- The alarming explosion of *identity theft*—the fastest growing crime of this new century—and the efforts of legislatures, regulators, private financial institutions, and consumers to slow the spread of this serious crime and preserve the confidence of the public in the markets for credit and payments services. (See, in particular, Chapter 21.)

- The changing role of *investment bankers* within the financial system and the shifting structure of their industry. (See, for example, Chapters 16, 19, and 20.)

- The rise and fall of *initial public offerings (IPOs)*—one of the most volatile of all markets—and their implications for corporate financing and business restructuring. (See especially Chapters 16 and 20.)

- The growing use of *mortgage lock-ins* and their advantages and disadvantages for borrowers and lenders in the huge home mortgage market. (See Chapter 22.)

- The continuing expansion of the *European Union* and the new nations that have joined this elite "club"—including their possible contribution toward the strengthening of Europe's collective economy and competition for trade with the United States. (See especially Chapters 4, 12, 13, 23, and 24.)

- The rise of *China* as a global power in trade and finance and the economic weaknesses China must still overcome (including repairing the troubled Chinese banking sector) if that nation is to continue to expand its economic and political influence in an increasingly competitive international marketplace. (See, in particular, Chapters 23 and 24.)

There are many more fascinating subjects also unique to this new edition, but the above list of topics should give you at least the flavor of the ninth edition.

Supplementary Materials to Help You Make Full Use of This Text

Useful supplemental materials serve to strengthen the effectiveness of this new edition in reaching its readers and in making the teacher's experience more rewarding and enjoyable. Among the key supplements are:

- **Instructor's Resource CD ROM** (ISBN 0072957409), which encompasses the following items:

  Instructor's Manual and Test Bank   This useful tool provides an outline of each chapter and lays out hundreds of questions and problems available for preparing tests and exams and for use in class discussions.

  Power Point Presentation System   This compilation of clear and concise slides provides both teachers and students with sharply focused ideas and illustrations of key points within each chapter. There are numerous graphs, charts, and examples as well as frequent listings of key points to be retained. The user can easily edit or rearrange each slide to meet his or her unique teaching or learning needs.

- **Text Web Site for the New Edition (www.mhhe.com/rose9e)**, which provides questions and problems for use by teachers and readers and contains an *Updates* section that tracks new developments in the money and capital markets since publication of the 9th edition.

Acknowledgment of the Many Professionals Who Have Helped to Make This Book Better Over Time

As this book has progressed through nine editions, it has benefited greatly from the criticisms and suggestions of numerous professionals—teachers, students, and financial market participants—over the years. These are people who care about their discipline and field and care about reaching those who seek to learn more and come to a deeper and richer understanding of the global financial marketplace and the place we occupy within this unique and massive institution. There have been so many contributors and helpers over the years that the authors are hesitant to write down a list for fear of omitting the worthwhile contributions and names of deserving professionals. We ask for your understanding in this regard and, if necessary, will be glad to make amends in future editions.

With this said, some of the most significant contributors through the various editions have been: James C. Baker of Kent State University; Ivan T. Call of Brigham Young University; Eugene F. Drzycimski of the University of Wisconsin System; Mona J. Gardner of Illinois Wesleyan University; Timothy Koch of the University of South Carolina; David Mills of Illinois State University; John O. Olienyk of Colorado State University; Colleen C. Pantalone of Northeastern University; Richard Rivard of the University of South Florida; Paul Bolster of Northeastern University; Robert M. Crowe, formerly of the American College at Bryn Mawr; Joseph P. Ogden of SUNY-Buffalo; Donald A. Smith of Pierce College; Oliver G. Wood, Jr., of the University of South Carolina; Larry Lang of the University of Wisconsin—Oshkosh; Jeffrey A. Clark of Florida State University; James F. Gatti of the University of Vermont; Gloria P. Bales of Hofstra University; Ahmed Sohrabian of California State Polytechnic University at Pomona; Thomas A. Fetherston of the University of Alabama at Birmingham; Mary Piotrowski of Northern Arizona University; Rick Swasey of Northeastern University; Owen K. Gregory of the University of Illinois at Chicago; Thomas Dziadosz of The American College; Tom Potter of the University of North Dakota; Lester Hadsell of State University of New York, Albany; John Hysom of George Mason University; Frank Ohara of the University of San Francisco; Robert Schweitzer of the University of Delaware; and Donald J. Smith of Boston University.

The authors also wish to add a special note of gratitude to those professionals who offered comments and suggestions during the construction of this latest (ninth) edition:

Jack Aber, Boston University

Bonnie Buchanan, University of Georgia

Samuel Bulmash, Stockton College

Krishnan Dandapani, Florida International University

John Halstead, Southern Connecticut State University

John Hysom, George Mason University

Bento Lobo, University of Tennessee at Chattanooga

Tim Michael, James Madison University

Walter Perlick, California State University at Sacramento

In addition, the authors express deep and sincere appreciation to the staff of professionals at McGraw-Hill/Irwin Publishers, particularly Steve Patterson, Meghan Grosscup, Barbara Hari, Michelle Driscoll, Rhonda Seelinger, Pat Frederickson, Kai Chiang, Mary Kazak, Michael McCormick, and Sue Lombardi. Their guidance and kindnesses throughout the revision and production process were invaluable and their support made this new edition possible.

A special "thank you" also goes to Professor Yee-Tien (Ted) Fu, Visiting Scholar at Stanford University, for his construction and revision of the Instructor's Manual, Test Bank, Power Point Presentation system, and online quizzes.

In addition to these outstanding contributors are many associations and institutions that have contributed to the content of this text in a wide variety of ways over the years. These include the American Council of Life Insurance, the *Canadian Banker* (official publication of the Canadian Bankers Association), the Chicago Board of Trade, the Credit Union National Association, the Insurance Information Institute, Moody's Investors Service, and Standard & Poor's Corporation.

The authors also gratefully acknowledge the support and patience of family and friends who made the completion of this new edition possible. Any shortcomings that remain belong to the authors, who, nevertheless, strive to make the text a better learning tool with each new edition.

A Note to the Student and Other Readers of This Text

The money and capital markets, along with the financial system that supports and surrounds them, are an exciting area for study. What happens daily in these markets and within the financial system as a whole has a powerful impact on our daily lives. Indeed, our ability to function as human beings and as professionals in our chosen careers is shaped, in so many ways, by the functioning of the financial system. Moreover, the money and capital markets and the financial system in which they do their work are constantly in a state of flux. Broad changes are forever remaking the financial marketplace as new institutions, new methods, new problems, and new services continually appear.

The rapidity of change that characterizes the financial system today means that we have no choice but to try to keep up with our unfolding financial world. Indeed, so rapid and sweeping are the changes going on in the money and capital markets that no book, no matter how many times it is revised, can serve as more than an *introduction*— indeed, an invitation—to learn about the often incredible goings-on within the financial marketplace.

Without question, you need to read this book and understand what it is trying to say. But reading this book cannot be the end of the road. You cannot stop here. A great American poet, Robert Frost, once declared that we "cannot stop here" for we have "promises to keep" and "miles to go before we sleep." For the sake of your own future success, personally and professionally, plan to enjoy what you discover in the pages that follow, but view this book as only the *first step* in what must be a lifetime journey of learning about the financial system and its effects on our everyday existence. Truly, each one of us has "promises to keep" to ourselves and others and "miles to go" before we can be satisfied with what we have accomplished.

As you begin each new chapter of this book, set your sights on true *mastery* of the subject. Make the most of the time you spend with this text. Plan for success and hit that target with determination and well-organized study techniques. How can you do that? How can you learn what you need to know in today's complex financial world?

First, begin with the *Learning Objectives* and the *Key Topics Outline* that open each chapter. These are really road signs, alerting you to the key questions and issues each chapter will address. They tell you what you should *expect to learn* in the pages that follow. It is a useful idea to review the list of Learning Objectives and the Key Topics Outline as you sit down to tackle each new chapter and then to revisit them when you are finished reading.

Have you touched base with each learning objective and each key topic as you read the material? If you are not sure of one or more of the learning objectives or key topics, go back and review the relevant portions of the chapter that apply to that particular topic or objective. Ask yourself if the learning objective or key topic you are focusing upon makes sense to you and if you now feel better informed about it than you did before.

Next, examine the list of *Key Terms* at the close of each chapter. There are page numbers telling you where each key term is defined and discussed. Return to the pages where any key terms appear that still seem to be a mystery to you. Let us suggest that you make a list of these key terms in your personal computer or in a notebook and accumulate them as the assigned chapters roll by. This is much more than an act of memorizing terms. Rather, this is reaching out to learn the "language" of the financial marketplace.

You want to make the language of the money and capital markets second nature to you so that, for everything you subsequently read and hear about the financial system, you will understand and be able to make that information work for you. You may even want to write out or type into the computer a definition of each key term and then double-check that definition against the meaning that appears in the *Money and Capital Markets Dictionary* at the end of the book.

In each chapter, *Questions to Help You Study* appear at various locations. These study questions encourage you to pause after reading several pages and ask yourself: Do I really understand what I just read? Try to answer each of these study questions, either verbally or, better still—if you have the time—by writing out a brief answer and then double-checking its accuracy by referring back to the relevant portion of the chapter you are working on. You may wish to store the answers you develop in your personal computer or in a paper file for future reference, particularly just before exams come along.

In each chapter of the ninth edition, several useful *Web sites* appear. In the margins of various pages in a chapter, important and often very interesting URLs appear in bold, giving you an opportunity to explore further the topics and ideas discussed. Near the conclusion of each chapter is a list of *The Most Important Web Sites for This Chapter.* Check out these Web sites and learn as much as possible about the subject matter of the chapter from a different perspective—from the point of view of the authors of these Web sites. Thus, by reading both the text and the material in many of the associated Web sites, you are following one of the most famous ideas about how we learn—the idea that "repetition is the key to learning."

At the end of each chapter there are two sets of problems to solve—one set is entitled *Problems and Issues,* which are relatively short and often require you to find some numerical answers, and a second set labeled *Standard & Poor's Market Insight and Web-Based Problems,* which are generally longer, multi-part problems that typically ask you to go to the World Wide Web, gather information, and come to some conclusions or make calculations. These two problem sets add another important dimension to your studies. Finance is about problem solving and the better you become at solving problems in this field, the greater your chances for success. As you work through each problem save the solutions and conclusions you reach for future reference, either in your computer or in a paper file.

Near the close of a majority of chapters (specifically, Chapters 1–14) there is a long problem set entitled *Semester Project: A Study of the Federal Funds Market.* This series of questions and problems asks you to devote part of your semester to learning about one of the most important markets in the United States' financial system—the market for interbank loans, known today as *federal funds.*

The Fed funds market has taken center stage in recent years because the U.S. central bank, the Federal Reserve, uses the federal funds interest rate on overnight loans between banks as its key operational target for monetary policy. The result is that the federal funds market conveys important clues to market participants about future Fed monetary policies and about the future course of market interest rates. Pursuing this semester project will teach you a great deal about how the financial markets work and about how to gauge the outlook for changing interest rates and credit conditions. Even if your instructor doesn't assign this project for your study this term, consider pursuing the project on your own to learn as much as you can about how the real financial world works.

Finally, on the last page of every chapter is a section entitled *Selected References to Explore.* These lists provide references to up-to-date, publicly accessible articles that discuss some of the key issues raised in each chapter. Many of the articles are printed on the World Wide Web at sites maintained by a publishing house or publishing agency listed with each article. These readings often provide greater depth than is available in this book on a given topic area or present a different point of view on what you have been studying. They are an excellent way to help you achieve mastery over your subject.

Finance in general and the money and capital markets, in particular, are moderately difficult disciplines to master. Yet, finance does have its challenges. Therefore, group study sessions are often helpful in tackling its hardest issues and problems. See if you can form a study group that periodically gets together and goes over some of the more difficult concepts and problems. Be a contributor to these sessions, and take the lead in explaining and helping others. *Teaching others* is one of the best ways to learn a new subject for yourself.

Always try to keep in mind that this book has two fundamental purposes: (1) to give you an arsenal of *analytical tools* that you can apply to any financial problem so as to make better financial decisions; and (2) to make you feel comfortable with the *language of the financial marketplace* so you can speak that language with comfort and maximum understanding. A truly successful course of study will develop *both* the tools and the language of the financial system and get you started along the road to mastery and personal success.

This course can be a foundation stone for many promising future careers. Perhaps you have considered becoming the financial manager or CFO of a large corporation, the head of the financial division of an important unit of government, a member of the legislature or of the Congress where financial issues are always among the main topics of discussion, a trader (dealer or broker) in securities or derivative contracts, a consultant or adviser to those who wish to enter the global financial marketplace, or an active investor in your own right, striving to build up your personal wealth and to prepare for a rewarding lifestyle. Wherever your career path leads you, superior knowledge and understanding of the financial marketplace will be an absolutely essential companion on your journey.

However, as you already know from prior experience with other challenging fields of study, mastering the money and capital markets and the financial system will *not* be easy. In the words of the poet, your future success in keeping the "promises" you have made and traveling successfully the many "miles to go" before you reach your goals will depend crucially upon the energy and enthusiasm, the commitment to excellence, and the hard work that you bring to this subject. By any measure, it is a challenge worthy of your best efforts. Good luck on your journey!

Peter S. Rose

Milton H. Marquis

January 2005

Brief Contents

Part Six

Consumers in the Financial Markets 641

Part Seven

The International Financial System 693

Contents

Part Four

Financial Institutions: Organization, Activities, and Regulation 419

Part Five

Governments and Businesses in the Financial Markets 543

Part Seven

The International Financial System 693

Part 1

The Global Financial System in Perspective

Try to imagine living in a world in which there are no financial institutions, no financial markets, and no financial assets. In such a world, there would be no opportunity to borrow against future income in order to purchase a home or an automobile, or to finance an education. Nor would you be able to save some of your current income (and, thereby, accumulate wealth over time) to handle the future expenses of a growing family or retirement. Businesses could not come up with the resources needed to produce the goods and services you like to consume. There would be no way to acquire insurance against sickness and death. Even the simple act of buying food would become extremely difficult, requiring you to barter simply to survive.

The financial system has emerged to fill these and many other critical needs that require some separation in time between the use of resources (such as capital and labor), the production of goods and services, and the actual consumption of those goods and services desired. Financial markets and institutions deal with these issues and provide for the smooth functioning of modern economies, enabling resources to find their way to their most highly valued use. In so doing, the financial system dramatically enhances the efficiency of the economy and raises our standard of living.

In order to set the stage for our study of the global financial system, Part One of *Money and Capital Markets* takes up essential topics—the linkage between financial and nonfinancial markets, the mechanism by which financial assets are created, valued, and traded, and the critical importance of public and private information in determining the value of a financial asset. Finally, any study of the financial system would be hopelessly ill-informed if it were not conducted against the backdrop of the fast-paced, ever-changing world of finance. Spurred on by technology and the creativity of those working in the financial marketplace, the financial system has rapidly evolved to better perform its traditional roles and meet new challenges. This rapid pace of change is unlikely to slow in the future, requiring all of us to learn how to adapt to a dynamic financial marketplace.

Chapter 1

Functions and Roles of the Financial System in the Global Economy

Learning Objectives

in This Chapter

- You will understand the functions performed and the roles played by the system of financial markets and financial institutions in the global economy and in our daily lives.

- You will discover how important the money and capital markets and the whole financial system are to increasing our standard of living, generating new jobs, and building our savings to meet tomorrow's financial needs.

What's in This Chapter?
Key Topics Outline

1.1 Introduction to the Financial System

This book is devoted to the study of the **financial system**—the collection of markets, institutions, laws, regulations, and techniques through which bonds, stocks, and other securities are traded, interest rates are determined, and financial services are produced and delivered around the world. The financial system is one of the most important creations of modern society. *Its primary task is to move scarce loanable funds from those who save to those who borrow to buy goods and services and to make investments in new equipment and facilities so that the global economy can grow and increase the standard of living enjoyed by its citizens.* Without the global financial system and the loanable funds it supplies, each of us would lead a much less enjoyable existence.

The financial system determines both the cost and the quantity of funds available in the economy to pay for the thousands of goods and services we purchase daily. Equally important, what happens in this system has a powerful impact upon the health of the global economy. When funds become more costly and less available, spending for goods and services falls. As a result, unemployment rises and the economy's growth slows as businesses cut back production and lay off workers. In contrast, when the cost of funds declines and loanable funds become more readily available, spending in the economy often increases, more jobs are created, and the economy's growth accelerates. In truth, the global financial system is an integral part of the global economic system. We cannot understand one of these systems without understanding the other.

1.2 The Global Economy and the Financial System

Flows within the Global Economic System

To better understand the role played by the financial system in our daily lives, we begin by examining its position within the global economy.

The basic function of the global economic system is to allocate scarce resources—land, labor, management skill, and capital—to their most highly valued use, producing the goods and services needed by society. The high standard of living most of us enjoy today depends on the ability of the global economy to turn out each day an enormous volume of food, shelter, and other essentials of modern living. This is an exceedingly complex task because scarce resources must be procured in just the right amounts to provide the raw materials of production and combined at just the right time with labor, management, and capital to generate the products and services demanded by consumers. In short, any economic system must combine inputs—land and other natural resources, labor and management skill, and capital equipment—to produce output—goods and services. The global economy generates a flow of production in return for a flow of payments.

We can depict the flows of payments and production within the global economic system as a *circular flow* between producing units (mainly businesses and governments) and consuming units (principally households). (See Exhibit 1.1.) In the modern economy, households provide labor, management skill, and natural resources to business firms and governments in return for income in the form of wages and other payments. Most of the income received by households is spent to purchase goods and services from businesses and governments. In 2003, for example, nearly 97 percent of the more than $9 trillion in total personal income received by individuals and families in the United States was spent on the consumption of goods and services or paid out in taxes to purchase government services. The remainder of personal income—a little more than 3 percent—was set aside as *savings*. The result of this spending is a flow of funds back to producing units as income, which stimulates them to produce more

Circular Flow of Income, Payments, and Production in the Global Economic System

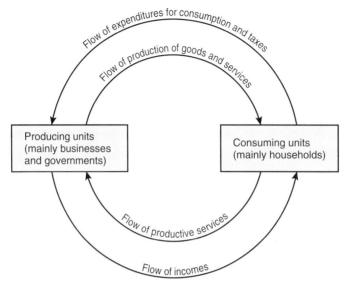

goods and services in the future. The circular flow of production and income is interdependent and never ending.

The Role of Markets in the Global Economic System

market

Most economies around the world rely principally upon *markets* to carry out this complex task of allocating scarce resources, making possible the production and sale of goods and services that are in demand by businesses and households. What is a **market?** It is an institution through which buyers and sellers meet to exchange goods, services, and productive resources. This exchange determines what goods and services will be produced and in what quantity.

The marketplace is *dynamic*. It must respond continuously not only to changes in consumers' tastes, but also to the introduction of new goods and services, often associated with new technology. Today, cell phones and DVDs are part of our everyday lives, yet they barely existed a short 10 years ago. How did the resources of the economy get redeployed to produce those new goods?

This shift in production was accomplished in the marketplace through changes in the *prices* of goods and services being offered. If the price of an item rises, for example, this stimulates business firms to produce and supply more of it to consumers. In the long run, new firms may enter the market to produce those goods and services experiencing increased demand and rising prices. A decline in price, on the other hand, usually leads to reduced production of a good or service, and in the long run some less-efficient suppliers may leave the marketplace.

Markets also distribute *income*. In a pure market system, the income of an individual or a business firm is determined solely by the contribution each makes to producing goods and services demanded by the marketplace. Markets reward superior productivity and sensitivity to consumer demands with increased profits, higher wages, and other economic benefits. Of course, in all economies, government policies also affect the distribution of income and the allocation of other economic benefits.

Types of Markets

There are essentially three *types of markets* at work within the global economic system: (1) factor markets, (2) product markets, and (3) financial markets (see Exhibit 1.2). In

EXHIBIT 1.2   **Three Types of Markets in the Global Economic System**

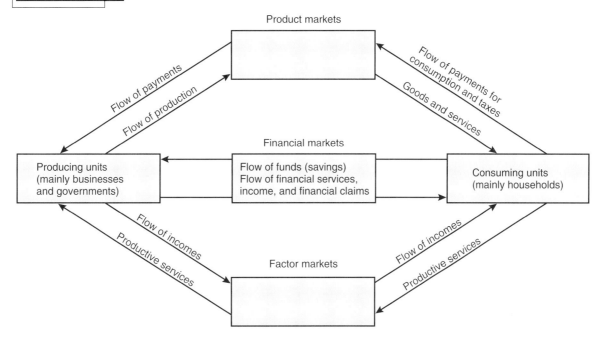

factor markets, consuming units sell their labor and other resources to those producing units offering the highest prices. The *factor markets* allocate factors of production— land, labor, managerial skills, and capital—and distribute income—wages, rental payments, and so on—to the owners of productive resources.

Consuming units use most of their income from factor markets to purchase goods and services in *product markets*. Food, shelter, automobiles, theater tickets, and clothing are among the many goods and services sold in product markets.

The Financial Markets and the Financial System: Channel for Savings and Investment

Of course, not all factor income is consumed. A proportion of after-tax income received by households each year—close to $280 billion in 2003—is earmarked for *personal savings*. In addition, business firms save billions of dollars each year to build up their reserves for future contingencies and for long-term investment. For example, in 2003, U.S. corporations earned nearly $470 billion in after-tax profits, of which almost $200 billion was set aside (undistributed) for possible future needs as *business savings*.

financial market   It is here that the third kind of market, the **financial market,** performs a vital function within the global economic system. The financial markets channel savings to those individuals and institutions needing more funds for spending than are provided by their current incomes. The financial markets are the heart of the global financial system, attracting and allocating savings and setting interest rates and the prices of financial assets (stocks, bonds, etc.).

savings   *Nature of Savings*   The definition of **savings** differs depending on what type of unit in the economy is doing the saving. For households, savings are what is left from current income after current consumption expenditures and tax payments are made.

In the business sector, savings include current earnings retained inside business firms after payment of taxes, stockholder dividends, and other cash expenses. Government savings arise when there is a surplus of current revenues over current expenditures in a government's budget.

Nature of Investment   Most of the funds set aside as savings flow through the global financial markets to support **investment** by business firms, governments, and households. Investment generally refers to the acquisition of capital goods, such as buildings and equipment, and the purchase of inventories of raw materials and goods to sell. The makeup of investment varies with the particular unit doing the investing. For a business firm, expenditures on *capital goods* (fixed assets, such as buildings and equipment) and *inventories* (consisting of raw materials and goods offered for sale) are investment expenditures. In contrast to businesses, for *households,* current accounting procedures in the United States stipulate that only the purchase of a home may be counted as an *investment.* All other household expenditures on durable goods (such as autos and furniture), as well as expenditures on nondurable goods (for example, food and fuel) and services (such as having your hair styled) are lumped together as *consumption spending* (i.e., expenditures on current account), rather than investment spending. Government spending to build and maintain public facilities (such as buildings, monuments, and highways) is another form of investment.

Modern economies require enormous amounts of investment to produce the goods and services demanded by consumers. Investment increases the productivity of labor and leads to a higher standard of living. However, investment often requires huge amounts of funds, far beyond the resources available to a single individual or institution. By selling financial claims (such as stocks and bonds) in the financial markets, large amounts of funds can be raised quickly from the pool of savings accumulated by households, businesses, and governments. The unit carrying out the investment then hopes to repay its loans from the financial marketplace by drawing on future income. Indeed, the money and capital markets make possible the *exchange of current income for future income* and the *transformation of savings into investment* so that production, employment, and income can grow, and living standards can improve.

Those who supply funds to the financial markets receive only *promises* in return for the loan of their money. These promises are packaged in the form of attractive financial claims and financial services, such as stocks, bonds, deposits, and insurance policies (see Exhibit 1.3). *Financial claims* promise the supplier of funds a future flow of income in the form of dividends, interest, or other returns. But there is no guarantee that the expected income will ever materialize. However, suppliers of funds to the financial system expect not only to recover their original funds but also to earn additional income as a reward for waiting and assuming risk.

The role of the financial markets in channeling savings into investment is absolutely essential to the health of the economy. For example, if households set aside savings and those funds are not returned to the spending stream through investment by businesses and governments, the economy will begin to contract. The amount of income paid out by business firms and governments will *not* be matched by funds paid back to

investment

To learn more about savings and investment see Bankrate.com at bankrate.com/brm

Information about savings and investment options in the money and capital markets may be found in such popular Web sites as businessweek.com; forbes.com; fortune.com; moneyline.com; kiplinger.com; and smartmoney.com

The Global Financial System

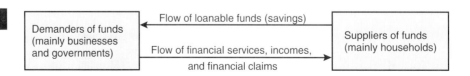

those same sectors by households. As a result, income payments will decline, leading, in turn, to reduced consumption spending. The public's standard of living will fall. Moreover, with less spending, the need for labor will be curtailed, resulting in fewer jobs and rising unemployment.

QUESTIONS TO HELP YOU STUDY

1. Why is it important for us to understand how the global financial system works?
2. What are the principal links between the financial system and the economy? Why is each important to the other?
3. What are the principal functions or roles of the global financial system? How do the money and capital markets fulfill those roles or functions?
4. What exactly is *savings*? *Investment*? Are these terms often misused by people on the street? Why do you think this happens?
5. How and why are savings and investment important determinants of economic growth? Do they impact our standard of living? How?

1.3 Economic Functions Performed by the Global Financial System and the Financial Markets

The great importance of the financial system in our daily lives can be illustrated by reviewing the different functions that it performs. The global financial system has *seven* basic economic functions that create a need for money and capital markets.

Savings Function

The global system of financial markets and institutions provides a *conduit for the public's savings.* Bonds, stocks, and other financial claims sold in the money and capital markets provide a profitable, relatively low-risk outlet for the public's savings, which flow through the financial markets into investment so that more goods and services can be produced (i.e., productivity will rise), increasing the world's standard of living. When savings decline, investment and living standards begin to fall in those nations where savings are in short supply.

Wealth Function

While current savings represent a *flow* of funds, accumulated savings built up over time represent a *stock* of assets that we often refer to as *wealth.* For those businesses and individuals choosing to save, the financial instruments sold in the money and capital markets provide an excellent way to *store wealth* (i.e., preserve the value of assets we hold) until funds are needed for spending. Although we might choose to store our wealth in "things" (e.g., automobiles), such items are subject to depreciation and often carry great risk of loss. However, bonds, stocks, and other financial instruments do *not* wear out over time and usually generate income; moreover, their risk of loss often is much less than for many other forms of stored wealth.

wealth   Incidentally, what is **wealth?** For any individual, business firm, or government, wealth (W_t) is the sum (Σ) of the values of all individual assets (A_i) held at any moment in time (t). That is,

$$W_t = \sum{}_i A_{it} \qquad\qquad (1.1)$$

Wealth is built up over time by a combination of current savings plus income earned on previously accumulated wealth. In symbols,

$$\Delta W_t = S_t + r_t \cdot W_{t-1} \qquad (1.2)$$

where ΔW_t represents the change in wealth in the current period, S_t is the volume of current savings, r_t is the current average rate of return on accumulated assets, and W_{t-1} is the value of all accumulated wealth (assets) held at the end of the preceding period $(t-1)$.

financial wealth

The portion of wealth held by society in the form of stocks, bonds, and other financial assets—that is, **financial wealth**—is created by the financial system and the money and capital markets within that system. The volume of financial wealth is huge and growing nearly every year. For example, in 2003 nearly $80 trillion in securities, deposits, and other financial assets were held by domestic businesses, households, and governments in the United States, while foreign investors held almost $8 trillion in financial instruments that were issued inside the United States during the same year. Individuals and families (households) alone held close to $30 trillion in stocks, bonds, and other financial assets.

net financial wealth

If we subtract total debts owed by U.S. businesses, households, and governments, which amounted to about $21 trillion in 2003, we obtain what is called **net financial wealth.** The total *net* financial wealth (financial assets − debts) held by U.S. individuals and institutions was nearly $65 trillion. Wealth holdings represent *stored purchasing power* that will be used in future periods as income to finance purchases of goods and services and increase society's standard of living. Therefore, income emerges from the wealth function of the global financial system. Income (Y_t) is created by the rate of return (r_t) that current wealth holdings (W_t) generate for their owners. Or,

$$Y_t = W_t \cdot r_t \qquad (1.3)$$

In turn, that wealth-created income leads to *both* increased consumption spending and to new saving, resulting in a higher standard of living for those who hold wealth in income-generating forms.

Liquidity Function

liquidity

For wealth stored in financial instruments, the global financial marketplace provides a means of converting those instruments into cash with little risk of loss. The world's financial markets provide **liquidity** (immediately spendable cash) for savers who hold financial instruments but are in need of money. In modern societies, *money* consists mainly of currency and deposits held in banks, credit unions, and other depository institutions and is the only financial instrument possessing *perfect liquidity*. Money can be spent as it is without the necessity of converting it into some other form. However, money generally earns the lowest rate of return of all assets traded in the financial system, and its purchasing power is seriously eroded by inflation. That is why savers generally minimize their holdings of money and hold other, higher-yielding financial instruments until they really need spendable funds. Of course, money is not the only means of making purchases of goods and services. In many lesser-developed economies, simple bartering—exchanging one good or service for another—performs many of the same services that money provides in a developed economy.

Credit Function

credit

In addition to providing liquidity and facilitating the flow of savings into investment to build wealth, the global financial markets furnish **credit** to finance consumption and investment spending. Credit consists of a loan of funds in return for a promise of future

More and more transactions in the money and capital markets today are being carried out with *E-money*—swiping a plastic card through an electronic reader or punching information into a computer networked to other computers. The rise of E-money within the economy and the financial system suggests that we are moving toward a faster, more efficient, and safer payments system in the future.

The *Internet* has enabled millions of customers to keep track of their checking, savings, and loan balances at the bank every day and place electronic orders for everything from stocks and bonds to sweaters and books. At the same time, *plastic cards* and *card readers* have literally taken over purchases made in gas stations, retail shops, and fast-food restaurants and are increasingly used for paying rent and other regular monthly bills. *Portable card-swiping devices*, operating much like cellular phones, are emerging to facilitate payments from anywhere on the planet.

Equally impressive are *debit cards* and *smart cards*, encoded with a customer's personal information and used to electronically subtract what is owed from a customer's checking or savings funds immediately. While *credit cards* are increasingly being used to pay for the largest purchases (such as clothing and appliances) or to take advantage of special offers (such as bonuses for airline travel), debit and smart cards have moved in to capture a growing share of small-size purchases in millions of stores and shops.

Europe appears to be leading the way toward an *E-money system*. However, the United States's payments system also is on the move with the writing of paper checks decreasing over the past decade (though Americans still write about 40 billion checks annually). The money and capital markets, like the rest of the economy, are being revolutionized by the rapid rise of *E-money* based payments technology.

payment. Consumers need credit to purchase a home, buy groceries, repair the family automobile, and retire outstanding debts. Businesses draw on their lines of credit to stock their shelves with inventory, construct new buildings, meet payrolls, and grant dividends to their stockholders. State, local, and federal governments borrow to construct buildings and other public facilities and to cover daily cash expenses until tax revenues flow in.

The volume of credit extended by the money and capital markets today is huge and growing. In the United States alone total credit funds raised in U.S. financial markets in 2003 amounted to more than $2.3 trillion—about double the amount raised in the money and capital markets only a decade before. Growth of the economy, inflation, and the tax deductibility of some interest payments all appear to have fueled this rapid growth in credit usage by businesses, households, and governments.

Payments Function

The global financial system also provides *a mechanism for making payments for purchases of goods and services*. Certain financial assets—including *currency, non-interest-bearing checking accounts (referred to as demand deposits), and interest-bearing checking accounts (referred to as negotiable order of withdrawal or NOW accounts)*—still serve as a popular medium of exchange in making payments all over the globe (especially in the United States). Also high on the payments list are plastic debit and credit cards issued by banks, credit unions, and retail stores. In the case of *debit cards,* a customer pays immediately for purchases by electronically debiting his or her account in a depository institution; in the case of *credit cards,* the customer receives instant access to short-term credit when contracting for purchases of goods and services. If present trends continue, electronic means of payment, including *computer terminals in homes, offices, and stores* and *digital cash* (accessed by an encoded plastic card) will eventually replace checks and other pieces of paper as the principal means of paying in the future. Indeed,

On September 11, 2001, the United States experienced one of the most devastating tragedies in its history when hijackers took control of four commercial airliners and crashed two of the four into the World Trade Center in New York City and one into the Pentagon in Washington, D.C. More than 3,000 people lost their lives.

The assault on the World Trade Center was an attack on a key trading center within the financial system—a place where major dealers in securities, large banks, and other financial-service institutions served clients around the globe. When the trade center collapsed, several financial firms faced severe disruption, losing their communications links and suffering death or serious injury to their employees.

Still the flexibility and resilience of the money and capital markets in adjusting to this terrible tragedy proved to be remarkable. Within a handful of days the New York Stock Exchange was reopened and major security, banking, and insurance firms found new space from which to serve their customers.

Of course, even with the remarkable "bounce back" of the financial system from terror, significant damages to the economy and financial system were felt. Lenders and investors became more concerned about *risk*. Stock prices around the globe fell for a time as investors sold riskier securities and fled into government bonds and insured bank deposits. Insurance companies braced for an unprecedented volume of financial claims related to deaths and destruction. Layoffs of workers rose and business sales fell.

These tragic events remind us of several key points. First, the economy and the financial system are intimately connected to each other—an external shock that affects one affects the other. Second, though a great institution, the money and capital markets are fragile and need the support of governments and the confidence of the public to operate efficiently and perform their essential functions. Third, the financial marketplace is now unquestionably global rather than belonging to a single nation—significant events in any nation, either good or bad, quickly spread around the world and eventually affect all markets.

electronic means of payment are growing rapidly today (especially in Europe), while checks and other paper-based means of payment are declining in volume.

Risk Protection Function

For further exploration of the many risks often present in the financial system and markets, see, for example, Standardandpoor.com; moodys.com; and cbot.com

The financial markets offer businesses, consumers, and governments *protection against life, health, property, and income risks.* This is accomplished, first of all, by the sale of insurance policies. Policies marketed by life insurance companies indemnify a family against possible loss of income following the death of a loved one. Property-casualty insurers protect their policyholders against an incredibly wide array of personal and property risks, ranging from ill health and storm damage to negligence on the highways. In addition to making possible the sale of insurance policies, the money and capital markets have been used by businesses and consumers to "self-insure" against risk; that is, holdings of wealth are built up as protection against future losses.

The financial system permits individuals and institutions to engage in both *risk sharing* and *risk reduction.* Risk sharing occurs when an individual or institution transfers risk exposure to someone willing to accept that risk (such as an insurance company), while risk reduction usually takes place when we diversify our wealth across a wide variety of different assets so that our overall losses are likely to be more limited.

Policy Function

Finally, in recent decades, the financial markets have been *the principal channel through which government has carried out its policy of attempting to stabilize the economy and avoid inflation.* By manipulating interest rates and the availability of credit, government can affect the borrowing and spending plans of the public, impacting the growth of jobs, production, and prices. As we will see later on, this task of economic stabilization has been given largely to central banks, such as the Federal Reserve System in the United States, the Bank of England, the Bank of Japan, and the new European Central Bank (the ECB).

QUESTIONS TO HELP YOU STUDY

6. What seven vital *functions* does the financial system of money and capital markets perform?

7. Why is each function of the financial system important to households, businesses, and governments? What kinds of lives would we be living today if there were no financial system or no financial markets?

8. What exactly do we mean by the term *wealth*? Why is it important?

9. What is *net financial wealth*? What does it reveal about each of us?

10. Can you explain what factors determine the current volume of financial wealth and net financial wealth each of us has?

1.4 Types of Financial Markets within the Global Financial System

The global financial system fulfills its various roles mainly through *markets* where financial claims and financial services are traded (though in some lesser-developed economies government dictation and even barter are used). These markets may be viewed as *channels* through which moves a vast flow of loanable funds that is continually being drawn upon by demanders of funds and continually being replenished by suppliers of funds.

The Money Market versus the Capital Market

The flow of funds around the world may be divided into different segments, depending on the characteristics of financial claims being traded and the needs of different investors. One of the most important divisions in the financial system is between the *money market* and the *capital market.*

money market
    The **money market** is designed for the making of short-term loans. It is the institution through which individuals and institutions with *temporary* surpluses of funds meet the needs of borrowers who have *temporary* funds shortages (deficits). Thus, the money market enables economic units to manage their liquidity positions. By convention, a security or loan maturing within one year or less is considered to be a money market instrument. One of the principal functions of the money market is to finance the working capital needs of corporations and to provide governments with short-term funds in lieu of tax collections. The money market also supplies funds for speculative buying of securities and commodities.

capital market
    In contrast, the **capital market** is designed to finance long-term investments by businesses, governments, and households. Trading of funds in the capital market makes possible the construction of factories, highways, schools, and homes. Financial instruments in the capital market have original maturities of *more than one year* and range in size from small loans to multimillion dollar credits.

    Who are the principal suppliers and demanders of funds in the money market and the capital market? In the money market, commercial banks are the most important institutional supplier of funds (lender) to both business firms and governments. Nonfinancial business corporations with temporary cash surpluses also provide substantial short-term funds to the money market. On the demand-for-funds side, the largest borrower in the U.S. money market is the Treasury Department, which borrows billions of dollars weekly. Other governments around the world are often among the leading borrowers in their own domestic money markets. The largest and best-known corporations and securities dealers are also active borrowers in money markets around the world. Due to the large size and strong financial standing of these well-known money market borrowers and lenders, money market instruments are considered to be high-quality, "near money" IOUs.

In contrast, the principal suppliers and demanders of funds in the capital market are more varied than in the money market. Families and individuals, for example, tap the capital market when they borrow to finance a new home. Governments rely on the capital market for funds to build schools and highways and provide essential services to the public. The most important borrowers in the capital market are businesses of all sizes that issue long-term debt instruments representing claims against their future revenues in order to cover the purchase of equipment and the construction of new facilities. Ranged against these many borrowers in the capital market are financial institutions, such as insurance companies, mutual funds, security dealers, and pension funds, that supply the bulk of capital market funds.

Divisions of the Money and Capital Markets

The money market and the capital market may be further subdivided into smaller markets, each important to selected groups of demanders and suppliers of funds. Within the money market, for example, is the huge *Treasury bill* market. Treasury bills—short-term IOUs issued by many governments around the world—are a safe and popular investment medium for financial institutions, corporations of all sizes, and wealthy individuals.

An interesting source of information on ongoing trends in financial services and the financial market-place is *The Economist* from London at economist.com

Somewhat larger in volume is the market for *certificates of deposit* (CDs) issued by banks and other depository institutions to raise funds in order to carry on their lending activities. Two other important money market instruments that arise from large corporations borrowing money are *bankers' acceptances* and *commercial paper.* In another corner of the money market, *federal funds*—the reserve balances of banks plus other immediately transferable monies—are traded daily in huge volume. Another segment of the money market reaches around the globe to encompass suppliers and demanders of short-term funds in Europe, Asia, and the Middle East. This is the vast, largely unregulated *Eurocurrency market,* in which deposits denominated in the world's major trading currencies—for example, the dollar and the Euro—are loaned to corporations and governments around the globe.

The capital market, too, is divided into several sectors, each having special characteristics. For example, one of the largest segments of the capital market is devoted to residential and commercial *mortgage loans* to support the building of homes and business structures, such as factories and shopping centers. In the United States, state and local governments sell their *tax-exempt (municipal) bonds* in another sector of the capital market. Households borrow in yet another segment, using *consumer loans* to make purchases ranging from automobiles to home appliances. There is also an international capital market for borrowing by large corporations represented by *Eurobonds* and *Euronotes.*

Probably the best-known segment of the capital market is the market for *corporate stock* represented by the major exchanges, such as the New York Stock Exchange (NYSE) and the Tokyo Exchange, and a vast over-the-counter (OTC) market, including electronic stock trading over the Internet. No matter where it is sold, however, each share of stock (equity) represents a certificate of ownership in a corporation, entitling the holder to receive any dividends paid out of current company earnings. Businesses also sell a huge quantity of *corporate notes* and *bonds* in the capital market each year to raise long-term funds. These securities, unlike shares of stock, are pure IOUs, evidencing a debt owed by the issuing company. Each of these financial instruments will be examined in detail in the chapters that lie ahead.

Open versus Negotiated Markets

open markets

negotiated markets

For interesting and often useful information about corporate stocks and bonds, see such sites as finance.yahoo.com; wsj.com; financenter.com; and bloomberg.com

Another distinction between markets in the global financial system focuses on **open markets** versus **negotiated markets.** For example, some corporate bonds are sold in the open market to the highest bidder and are bought and sold any number of times before they mature and are paid off. In contrast, in the negotiated market for corporate bonds, securities generally are sold to one or a few buyers under private contract.

An individual who goes to his or her local banker to secure a loan for a new car enters the negotiated market for auto loans. In the market for corporate stocks there are the major stock exchanges, which represent the open market. Operating at the same time, however, is the negotiated market for stock, in which a corporation may sell its entire stock issue to one or a handful of buyers.

Primary versus Secondary Markets

primary markets

secondary markets

The global financial markets also may be divided into **primary markets** and **secondary markets.** The primary market is for the trading of *new* securities. Its principal function is raising financial capital to support new investment in buildings, equipment, and inventories. You engage in a primary-market transaction when you purchase shares of stock just issued by a company or borrow money through a new mortgage to purchase a home.

Saving is vital to support the growth of *investment* in new capital equipment and new technologies so that economies can grow and increase the standard of living of their citizens. Although the national savings rate of the United States has remained fairly stable for much of the nation's history, the United States today posts one of the lowest savings rates in the world, with a savings-to-gross domestic product ratio well below that of Japan and Germany, for example.

One reason for low savings rates may simply be changing public attitudes toward saving itself. Older generations remember the Great Depression of the 1930s, with millions of people out of work. Younger savers, however, are more likely to have experienced periods of prosperity and low unemployment and see less need for savings protection.

Then, too, the U.S. government's Social Security and Medicare systems promise workers at least a minimal level of retirement income, reducing the apparent need for maximizing personal savings, at least in the minds of many savers. Moreover, when inflation rises, many consumers prefer to buy now rather than add to their savings.

The currently low U.S. savings rate may come back to haunt Americans in the future. For example, a relatively low savings rate coupled with a low investment rate make the economy more prone to inflation because, with less investment in new equipment, fewer goods and services can be produced as demands for goods and services increase. Living standards of individuals and families are likely to grow more slowly in the future. However, some economists believe that the U.S. savings rate will begin to rise in the future as the population ages because there will be more Americans concerned about building their savings for retirement. Let's hope they are right!

For further discussion of the importance of savings see bankrate.com/brm

In contrast, the secondary market deals in securities previously issued. Its chief function is to provide *liquidity* to security investors—that is, provide an avenue for converting financial instruments into cash. If you sell shares of stock or bonds you have been holding for some time to a friend or call a broker to place an order for shares currently being traded on the American, London, or Tokyo stock exchanges, you are participating in a secondary-market transaction.

The volume of trading in the secondary market is far larger than in the primary market. However, the secondary market does *not* support new investment. Nevertheless, the primary and secondary markets are closely intertwined. For example, a rise in security prices in the secondary market usually leads to a similar rise in prices on primary-market securities, and vice versa. This happens because many investors readily switch from one market to another in response to differences in price or yield.

Spot versus Futures, Forward, and Option Markets

We may also distinguish between *spot markets, futures* or *forward markets,* and *option markets.* A spot market is one in which assets are traded for immediate delivery (usually within one or two business days). If you pick up the telephone and instruct your broker to purchase Telecon Corporation stock at today's price, this is a spot market transaction. You expect to acquire ownership of Telecon shares today.

A *futures* or *forward market,* on the other hand, is designed to trade contracts calling for the *future delivery* of financial instruments. For example, you may call your broker and ask to purchase a contract calling for delivery to you of $1 million in government bonds six months from today. The purpose of such a contract would be to shift risk to some individual or institution willing to bear that risk by agreeing upon a delivery price today rather than waiting six months when government bonds might be priced much higher.

Finally, *options markets* also offer investors in the money and capital markets an opportunity to reduce risk. These markets make possible the trading of options on selected stocks and bonds, which are contracts that give an investor the right to either buy designated securities from or sell designated securities to the writer of the option at a guaranteed price at any time during the life of the contract. We will see more clearly how and why such transactions take place when we explore the financial futures and options markets in Chapter 9 and the forward markets for foreign currencies in Chapter 23.

1.5 Factors Tying All Financial Markets Together

Each corner of the financial system represents a market segment with its own special characteristics. Each segment is insulated from the others to some degree by investor preferences and by rules and regulations. Yet when interest rates and security prices change in one corner of the financial system, *all* of the financial markets likely will be affected eventually. This implies that, even though the financial system is split up into many different markets, there must be forces at work to tie all the financial markets together.

Credit, the Common Commodity

One unifying factor is the fact that the basic commodity being traded in most financial markets is *credit*. Borrowers can switch from one market to another, seeking the most favorable credit terms wherever they can be found. It is not uncommon, for example, for an oil company to finance the construction of a drilling rig through short-term loans from the money market when interest rates in the capital market are unusually high, but to seek long-term financing of the project later on when capital market conditions are more favorable. The shifting of borrowers between markets helps to weld the parts of the financial system together and to bring credit costs in different markets into balance with one another.

Speculation and Arbitrage

Another unifying element is profit seeking by demanders and suppliers of funds. *Speculators* in securities are continually on the lookout for opportunities to profit from their forecasts of future market developments. The speculator in the financial marketplace gambles that security prices or interest rates will move in a direction that will result in quick gains due to his or her ability to outguess the market's collective judgment. Many speculators are *risk seekers,* willing to gamble their funds even when the probability of success is low. Speculators perform an important function in the markets by leveling out the prices of assets, buying those they believe are underpriced and selling those thought to be overpriced.

arbitrage

For an overview of the concept of arbitrage, see especially finpipe.com/derivglossary.htm

Still another unifying force in the financial markets comes from investors who watch for profitable opportunities to **arbitrage** funds—transferring funds from one market to another whenever the prices of assets in different markets appear to be out of line with each other. *Arbitrageurs* help to maintain *consistent prices between markets*, aiding other buyers in finding the best prices with minimal effort.

Perfect and Efficient Markets

perfect market

There is some research evidence today suggesting that financial markets are closely tied to one another due to their near perfection and efficiency. What is a **perfect market?** It is one in which the cost of carrying out transactions is zero or nearly so and all market participants are *price takers* (rather than being able to dictate prices to the market). In such a market, there are no significant government restrictions on trading and the movement of funds; rather, competition among buyers and sellers sets the terms of trade. No financial market today is perfect, but several seem to come close to being so.

Some financial markets may also have another desirable characteristic: *The prices of financial instruments may accurately reflect their inherent value and fully reflect all available information.* Moreover, any new information supplied to the market may quickly be incorporated into a new set of prices. A market in which prices fully reflect the latest available information is an **efficient market.** No information that might affect prices or interest rates is wasted. Thus, no buyer or seller can expect to reap excess profits from collecting information that is readily available in the marketplace and trading on the basis of that information. As we will see in Chapters 3 and 20, numerous studies of the financial markets suggest that they approach fairly closely the ideal of a perfect and an efficient marketplace.

efficient market

For a discussion of the efficient markets concept see investorhome.com

Financial Markets in the Real World: Imperfection and Asymmetry

Unfortunately, as we will see in subsequent chapters, as nearly perfect and efficient as some financial markets may seem to be, there is still a great deal that is *imperfect* in our financial system. Not all financial-service markets are fully competitive, and collusion to fix prices or to bilk unsuspecting members of the public does occur quite frequently. For example, the *mutual fund scandal*—alleged illegal trading among the managers of some investment companies that resulted in losses to their customers amounting to billions of dollars—literally rocked the financial marketplace in 2003 and 2004. The scandal placed millions of small household investors in a real quandary. Were their savings and retirement plans really safe? Events of this magnitude remind us that the functioning and regulation of our financial marketplace still leave much room for improvement.

asymmetric
information

Moreover, we now realize that not all the information needed by purchasers of financial assets or services is readily or cheaply available. Increasingly, we are coming to an awareness of the importance of **asymmetric information** in our global financial system—that is, different participants in the markets often operate with different sets of information, some possessing special or inside information others do not possess. The result is that some market players may be able to earn excess profits by taking advantage of the special information they possess. Moreover, as we will see in Chapter 3, high-quality assets may be driven from the market when the asymmetrical distribution of information in the marketplace is severe.

1.6 The Dynamic Financial System

To learn more about possible inefficiencies, asymmetric information problems, and scandals in the financial marketplace, see especially the U.S. Securities and Exchange Commission at sec.gov/consumer

There is an old saying: "You cannot step into the same river twice, for rivers are ever flowing onward." That statement can be applied to the global financial system—it is rapidly changing into a *new* financial system. Powerful trends are under way to convert even smaller national financial systems into an integrated global system, at work 24 hours a day to attract savings, extend credit, and fulfill other vital roles. Satellites, computers, and other automated systems now tie together financial-service trading centers as widely dispersed as London, New York, Tokyo, Singapore, and Sydney. This process of integrating financial systems globally has been aided by gradual deregulation of financial institutions and services on the part of leading industrialized nations (such as the United States, Japan, and members of the European Economic Union). Many of these countries have begun to "harmonize" their regulations so that financial-service firms operate under similar rules no matter where they are located. The results have been increasingly intense competition for customers, the development of many new financial services, increased risk to financial firms and their customers, and a wave of mergers among financial institutions. One of the purposes of this book is to help you understand why these global trends are occurring and what they are likely to mean for all of us in the future.

QUESTIONS TO HELP YOU STUDY

11. Can you distinguish between the following institutions?
    Money market versus *capital market*
    Open market versus *negotiated market*
    Primary market versus *secondary market*
    Spot market versus *forward* or *futures market*

12. If we follow the money and capital markets around the world each day it soon becomes apparent that interest rates and security prices in different markets tend to move together, albeit with leads and lags. Why do you think this is so?

13. Can you explain what is meant by the term *perfect market*? An *efficient market*? What real-world elements might limit the perfection and efficiency of money and capital markets?

14. What is meant by the term *asymmetric information*? Why do you think this concept might be important to you and to other participants in the financial system?

1.7 The Plan of This Book

This text is divided into seven parts, each devoted to a particular segment of the financial system. Part One provides an overview of the global financial system—its role in the world's economy and basic characteristics. The vital processes of saving and investing, lending and borrowing, and creating and destroying financial assets are described. Part One surveys the principal sources of information available today on the workings of the worldwide financial marketplace and presents an overview of the financial system of the future.

Part Two examines forces that shape interest rates and the prices of financial instruments. Because the rate of interest is the key price in the financial system, this section begins in Chapter 5, which presents a variety of views about how interest rates are determined. Subsequent chapters address such important topics as the measurement of interest rates and financial asset prices, yield curves, duration, inflation, the risk of default, and taxes. Part Two concludes with a review of methods for hedging against interest rate and asset price changes, including swaps, futures, and options.

Part Three draws our attention to the money market and its principal institutions and instruments and to a government institution that often dominates the tone of the money market—the central bank. Chapters in this section examine the characteristics of Treasury bills, federal funds, repurchase agreements, bank certificates of deposit, commercial paper, federal agency securities, bankers' acceptances, and Eurocurrency deposits. Part Three also presents a thorough examination of the many roles and functions of the central bank within the financial system, including an in-depth look at the history, organizational structure, and policy tools of the Federal Reserve System as well as the policy tools used by other central banks around the world. Part Three concludes with a review of the goals and targets for implementing central bank monetary policy decisions.

In Part Four, the spotlight turns to private financial institutions—commercial banks, credit unions, savings and loan associations, money market funds, insurance companies, pension funds, mutual funds, investment banks, and other financial-service firms. The reader is presented with an overview of their characteristics, regulation, current problems, and management tools designed to deal with those problems.

Part Five turns to the role of governments (federal, state, and local) and business firms within the global financial system. The opening chapter of this section explores the fiscal and debt management policies of the U.S. government, followed by an overview of state and local government borrowing, spending, and taxation. Then Chapter 19 takes up the topic of business borrowing, including the pricing and marketing of corporate bonds and asset-backed securities. Part Five concludes with an exploration of the many facets of the corporate stock market.

The financial characteristics of consumers—individuals and families—are considered in Part Six. Chapter 21 looks at the types of consumer debt and savings instruments available today and reviews current laws that protect the financial services consumer. This section closes with an overview of the residential mortgage market—one of the largest of all financial markets. Chapter 22 explores the array of different types of home loans that have appeared in recent years and how this huge market has expanded lately under the umbrella of strong government support and aggressive private innovation.

Finally, Part Seven focuses upon the international financial system and future trends in global finance. Topics covered include international trade and the balance of payments, the markets for foreign currencies, hedging against currency risk, and international banking.

Throughout this text, there is a strong emphasis on the innovative character of modern financial systems and institutions. A veritable explosion of new services and trading techniques has occurred in recent years. Moreover, the pace of innovation in financial services appears to be accelerating under the combined pressure of increased competition, rising costs, and growing risks. As we will see in the pages that follow, these forces of innovation, competition, cost, and risk are profoundly reshaping the structure and the operations of our whole financial system today.

MARKETS ON THE NET: The Most Important Web Sites for This Chapter

Bankrate.com (bankrate.com/brm)
Chicago Board of Trade (cbot.com)
Derivatives Concepts A–Z (finpipe.com/derivglossary.htm)
Moody's Investors Service (moodys.com)
Securities and Exchange Commission (sec.gov)
Standard & Poor's Corporation (standardandpoors.com)

The Financial Times (ftbusiness.com)
The Wall Street Journal (wsj.com)
U.S. Bureau of Economic Analysis (bea.gov)
U.S. Bureau of the Census (census.gov)
U.S. Treasury Department (publicdebt.treas.gov)

Summary of the Chapter's Main Points

The opening chapter of *Money and Capital Markets* presents us with an introduction to the global financial system in which the money and capital markets play central roles. It also highlights the principal institutions that shape the character and functioning of the world's financial marketplace.

- The *financial system* produces and distributes financial services to the public. Among its most important services is a supply of *credit* which allows businesses, households, and governments to invest and acquire assets they need for daily economic activity. The financial system of money and capital markets determines both the amount and cost of credit available. In turn, the supply and cost of credit affect the health and growth of the global economy and our own economic welfare.

- Credit and other financial services are offered for sale in the institution we call a *market*. Markets allocate financial and physical resources that are scarce relative to demand.

- Another key role played by markets operating within the financial system is to stimulate an adequate volume of *savings* (i.e., funds left over after current consumption spending by households and earnings retained by businesses) and to transform those savings into an adequate volume of *investment* (i.e., the purchase of capital goods and the buildup of inventories of goods to sell). In turn, investment generates new products and services and creates new jobs and new businesses, resulting in faster economic growth and a higher standard of living. By determining interest rates within the financial system, the money and capital markets bring the volume of savings generated by the public into balance with the volume of investment in new plant and equipment and in inventories of goods and resources available for sale.

- One important way to view the financial system of money and capital markets is by examining its seven key functions or roles in meeting the financial needs of individuals and institutions, including generating and allocating savings, stimulating the accumulation of wealth, providing liquidity for spending, providing a mechanism for making payments, supplying credit to aid in the purchase of goods and services, providing risk protection services, and supplying a channel for government policy in helping achieve the nation's

www.mhhe.com/rose9e

economic goals (including maximum employment, low inflation, and sustainable economic growth).

- The markets that serve the financial system may be classified in several different ways, including *money markets,* supplying short-term loans (credit) of less than a year, and *capital markets,* supplying long-term loans (credit) lasting longer than a year. There are also *open markets* where anyone may participate as buyer or seller versus *negotiated markets* where only a few bidders seek to acquire assets. There are *primary* versus *secondary* markets; in the former, *new* financial instruments are traded in contrast to the latter where existing instruments are exchanged. Additional types of financial markets that make up the global financial system include markets that deal in the immediate purchase or sale of goods or services, called *spot markets,* and those that promise future delivery, known as *futures, forward,* or *option markets*

- While many different segments make up the money and capital markets around the globe, all these markets share the common purpose of supplying credit to answer global demands for borrowed funds and all encourage saving to make investment (and, therefore, economic growth) possible. Funds flow easily and, for the most part, smoothly from one segment of the marketplace to another, spurred by such forces as *arbitrage* and *speculation.* For example, *arbitrage* causes credit, savings, and investment to flow toward those market segments that offer the most favorable returns, helping different markets to price resources more consistently and eliminate price disparities for the same goods and services. Prices are also brought into balance from market to market by the force of *speculation,* which seeks out underpriced and overpriced services and goods.

- Finally, the money and capital markets have revealed themselves to be *efficient* institutions, gathering and quickly using all relevant information to price credit and other financial services. Some are nearly *perfect* markets where competition sets prices and allocates resources. However, important imperfections do exist within the financial system where competition is sometimes restricted and excess profits are sometimes earned by those who stifle competition or gain access to inside information not freely available to all due to *asymmetries* within the marketplace.

Key Terms Appearing in This Chapter

Problems and Issues

1. *None* of the following statements are correct. In each case, identify the error and correct the statement.

    a. A household's current savings includes its current purchases of corporate stock as well as prior holdings of corporate stock and its current investment includes the equity it currently has in its house.

    b. The change in a household's wealth over a quarter is given by its wealth at the beginning of the quarter plus its savings during the quarter.

    c. The ability of a household to borrow money from a bank to purchase a new PC is an example of the payments function of the financial markets, while the ability of the bank to make the loan is an example of the liquidity function.

    d. The ability of Treasury bills to retain their value over time is an example of the savings function of the economy, while the ability of a household to sell the Treasury bill on short notice with little risk of loss is an example of the liquidity function.

    e. The ability of the Federal Reserve to manipulate interest rates is an example of the policy function of the financial markets, while the ability of households to earn interest on those investments affected by the Fed's decision is an example of the risk-protection function of the financial markets.

2. George Wilkins checked the spreadsheet where he keeps track of his assets and liabilities and discovered that: (a) he owes $80,000 on his house, which he believes to be worth $150,000; (b) his car is worth $20,000 and he has two more payments of $1,000 each to make before he owns the car outright; (c) his stock portfolio has risen in value to $50,000; (d) he has a $10,000 balance in his bank account that is earning 2 percent annual interest; and (e) the value of his other belongings is about $45,000. He just received his monthly paycheck for $6,000 and needs to decide whether he should pay off his car or take a vacation. His monthly expenses are $3,000. He has two possible vacation choices: the Bahamas for $2,000 or the local beach for $1,000. Any money left over at the end of the month will be added to his bank account. Evaluate the following options for George:

    a. If he pays off his car, can he still take a vacation? If so, compute how much he saves and what his net wealth will be if his bank account is the only interest-bearing asset he owns (assuming no change in the value of his stocks during the month). Recompute his savings and net wealth if he decides *not* to take a vacation.

    b. If he only makes one monthly payment on the car, can he afford to go to the Bahamas? If so, what will his savings and net wealth be at the end of the month? If he does *not* take a vacation, what are his savings and net wealth for the month?

3. Classify the *market* in which each of the following financial transactions takes place as: (a) money versus capital; (b) primary versus secondary; (c) open versus negotiated; and (d) spot versus futures/forward.

    a. A three-year auto loan from a bank.

    b. A share of Google stock bought at its initial public offering (IPO).

    c. A six-month CD purchased from your local credit union.

    d. A contract for the delivery of hog bellies six months from today.

    e. A municipal bond purchased from a broker.

4. The household sector (individuals and families) recorded current income of approximately $3.35 trillion in a recent year and total consumption expenditures (including taxes) of $2.89 trillion in that same year. The household sector held about $24.36 trillion in the total value of its wealth (including stocks, bonds, bank deposits, accumulated retirement savings, houses, etc.) at the beginning of the year and earned an average rate of return of 4.5 percent on its wealth holdings during the year. Calculate the change (growth) in wealth for the household sector that occurred during the year.

5. Suppose that banks held total financial assets (loans, securities, and other financial instruments) of $3,786 billion, while the banking sector's total liabilities amounted to $3,631 billion. What is the banking system's *net* financial wealth? If the banking system began the year with total financial assets of $3,639 billion and saved $53 billion during the year, how much income was earned on previously accumulated assets? What was the banking system's *net* financial wealth at year-end?

Standard & Poor's Market Insight and Web-Based Problems

1. Your text defines the wealth of a business firm as the sum of all its assets. To determine its *net* wealth (or total equity) you have to subtract the firm's liabilities from its assets. Net wealth is the value of the firm and should be reflected in its market capitalization (or stock price times the number of shares outstanding). Firms in different industries will require different amounts of wealth to create the same market value (or market capitalization). In this problem you are asked to compare the wealth (total assets), net wealth (assets less liabilities), and market capitalization of a large firm in each of the following industries: Financial Services (Citigroup, ticker symbol C); Manufacturing (General Motors, GM); and High Tech (Microsoft, MSFT). Using the S&P Market Insight Web site, which is **mhhe.com/edumarketinsight,** key in each firm's ticker symbol and find its most recent balance sheet (under Excel Analytics) and market capitalization (under Financial Hlts). Are you surprised by how different these firms are in terms of the dollar value of assets required to create $1 of market value?

2. A large share of household wealth is held in the form of corporate stock. How much wealth does the entire stock market represent? To find an approximate answer, go to the Web site for Wilshire Associates at **www.wilshire.com** and click Indexes from the menu. Locate the information that explains how the Wilshire 5000 index is constructed. This index is weighted by the market capitalization of the firms included in it, such that if you add the right amount of zeros to the index, you obtain the total value of all the firms represented in the index. Why is this number a good approximation to the entire U.S. stock market? Now obtain a chart for the index. How much stock market wealth has been created or destroyed over the past 12 months? Determine how much stock market wealth was created or lost *per person* in the United States over this period. (Hint: You can find the U.S. population at **census.gov/main/www/popclick.html**). Compare this with the average after-tax annual income *per person* in the U.S. Use the disposable personal income figure that can be found under "Selected NIPA

Tables: Table 2.1" at **bea/gov.doc/bea/dn/nipaweb/index.asp** to make the comparison.

3. One of the world's most important financial markets that we will study throughout this book is the market for U.S. Treasury securities. It is important because it is one of the few default-free, highly liquid debt instruments available anywhere in the financial marketplace. To determine the size of this market go to the Treasury Department's Web site at **publicdebt.treas.gov** and find the *Monthly Statement of the Public Debt.* How much debt does the U.S. government owe *per person* in the United States? (See the previous problem on how to find the U.S. population figure.) How much of this debt is held by the public and how much by government agencies? Only a portion of this debt—termed "marketable"—is traded daily in the money and capital markets. The remainder is held by the buyer until it matures. How much of this public debt is "marketable"?

Semester Project: A Study of the Federal Funds Market

The following project on the money and capital markets may prove to be a very interesting one for you to work on and follow throughout the semester. This semester project focuses on what has become one of the most important marketplaces in today's financial scene—the **federal funds market.** This is not a market that your average man or woman on the street can participate in—yet it affects the lives of every one of us in *many* important ways.

The federal funds market is a market for *interbank loans.* It is centered in the United States but there is a parallel market worldwide—the Eurocurrency market—and several nations have their own versions of a domestic interbank loan market. The Fed funds market is crucial to the functioning of the payments system, the determination of short-term interest rates, the efficiency of the money and capital markets, and the conduct of monetary policy. We will have occasion to describe the many important aspects of this market throughout this text.

The information and questions below are designed to get you started on this semester project. Subsequent questions and issues to explore as you pursue this project appear at the end of Chapters 2 through 14. Moreover, Chapter 11, Section 11.3 discusses the basic characteristics of the federal funds market. You may want to read that section first as you begin this interesting journey.

First Project Assignment: Let's begin our journey by examining *how large* the Fed funds market is. In 2000 the total volume of transactions in Fed funds was $379.8 trillion! (You can find this information at **federalreserve.gov/pubs/bulletin/2002/0202lead.pdf.**) Note that the dollar figure just mentioned corresponds to more than $1 trillion traded per day. Transactions average approximately $3.5 billion each. Truly, this *is* a huge market!

Let's get an even better feel for just how big it is by comparing this market with the size of the U.S. government debt. To derive a comparative size measure visit the Web site of the U.S. Treasury Department at **publicdebt.treas.gov/opd/opdpenny.htm.** For a second size comparison find the total value of goods and services produced in the U.S. economy last year (Gross Domestic Product or GDP) by exploring the Web site of the Bureau of Economic Analysis, U.S. Department of Commerce at **bea.doc.gov.** Are you surprised by any of the numbers you are coming up with?

The next installment of this semester project appears at the conclusion of Chapter 2. The authors hope you enjoy this journey of discovery through a vitally important marketplace within today's financial system.

Selected References to Explore

Duca, John V. "The Democratization of America's Capital Markets." *Economic and Financial Review,* Federal Reserve Bank of Dallas, Second Quarter 2001, pp. 10–19.

Hilgert, Mariann A.; Jeanne M. Hogarth; and Sondra G. Beverely. "Household Financial Management: The Connection between Knowledge and Behavior." *Federal Reserve Bulletin,* July 2003, pp. 309–22.

Peach, Richard, and Charles Steindel. "A Nation of Spendthrifts? An Analysis of Trends in Personal and Gross Savings." *Current Issues in Economics and Finance,* Federal Reserve Bank of New York, September 2000.

Valderrame, Diego. "Financial Development, Productivity and Economic Growth." *FRBSF Economic Letter,* Federal Reserve Bank of San Francisco, June 27, 2003.

Chapter 2

Financial Assets, Money, Financial Transactions, and Financial Institutions

Learning Objectives

in This Chapter

- You will see the most important channels through which funds flow from lenders to borrowers and back again within the global system of money and capital markets.

- You will discover the nature and characteristics of *financial assets*—how they are created and destroyed by decision makers within the financial system.

- You will explore the critical roles played by *money* within the financial system and the linkages between money and inflation in the prices of goods and services.

- You will examine the important jobs carried out by *financial intermediaries* in lending and borrowing and in creating and destroying financial assets.

2.1   Introduction: The Role of Financial Assets

The financial system is the mechanism through which loanable funds reach borrowers. Through the operation of the financial markets, money is exchanged for financial claims in the form of stocks, bonds, and other securities. And through the exchange of money for financial claims, the economy's capacity to produce goods and services is increased. This happens because the global money and capital markets provide the financial resources needed for real investment. Although it is true that the financial markets deal mainly in the exchange of paper claims and computer entries evidencing the transfer of funds, these markets provide an indispensable conduit for the transformation of savings into investment, accelerating the economy's growth and developing new businesses and new jobs.

This chapter looks closely at the essential role played by the financial markets in converting savings into investment and how that role has changed over time. We begin by observing that nearly all financial transactions between buyers and sellers involve the creation or destruction of a special kind of asset: a *financial asset.* Moreover, financial assets possess a number of characteristics that make them unique among all assets held by individuals and institutions. In the next section, we consider the nature of financial assets and how they are created and destroyed through the workings of the global financial system.

2.2   The Creation of Financial Assets

financial asset   What is a **financial asset?** It is a *claim* against the income or wealth of a business firm, household, or unit of government, represented usually by a certificate, receipt, computer record file, or other legal document, and usually created by or related to the lending of money. Familiar examples include stocks, bonds, insurance policies, futures contracts, and deposits held in a bank or credit union.

2.3   Characteristics of Financial Assets

Financial assets do *not* provide a continuing stream of services to their owners as a home, an automobile, or a washing machine would do. These assets are sought after because they promise *future* returns to their owners and serve as a *store of value* (purchasing power). Their value rests on *faith* that their issuer will honor his or her contractual promise to pay.

A number of other features make financial assets unique. They *cannot be depreciated* because they do not wear out like physical goods. Moreover, their physical condition or form usually is *not* relevant in determining their market value (price). A stock certificate is not more or less valuable, for example, because of the size or quality of paper it may be printed on, because it may be frayed around the edges, or because of the type and format of the computer file in which it may appear.

Because financial assets are generally represented by a piece of paper (certificate or contract) or by information stored in a computer, they have little or no value as a commodity and their cost of transportation and storage is low. Indeed, the cost of the storage and transfer of funds and other bits of financial information declined sharply as the twenty-first century began due to rapid advances in computer and electronic technology, causing financial assets to grow faster than world trade and faster than the economic system as a whole. Finally, financial assets are *fungible*—they can be easily changed in form and substituted for other assets. Thus, a bond or share of stock often can be quickly converted into any other asset the holder desires.

2.4   Different Kinds of Financial Assets: Money, Equities, Debt Securities, and Derivatives

Although there are thousands of different financial assets, they generally fall into four categories: money, equities, debt securities, and derivatives.

money

Any financial asset that is generally accepted in payment for purchases of goods and services is **money.** Thus, checking accounts and currency are financial assets serving as payment media and, therefore, are forms of money. In the modern world, money—even the forms of money issued by the government—depends for its value only upon the issuer's pledge to pay as promised. **Equities** (more commonly known as *stock*) represent ownership shares in a business firm and, as such, are claims against the firm's profits and against proceeds from the sale of its assets. We usually further subdivide equities into *common stock,* which entitles its holder to vote for the members of a firm's board of directors and, therefore, determine company policy, and *preferred stock,* which normally carries no voting privileges but does entitle its holder to a fixed share of the firm's net earnings ahead of its common stockholders.

equities

debt securities

Debt securities include such familiar instruments as *bonds, notes, accounts payable,* and *savings deposits.* Legally, these financial assets entitle their holders to a priority claim over the holders of equities to the assets and income of an individual, business firm, or unit of government. Usually, that claim is fixed in amount and time (maturity) and, depending on the terms of the *indenture* (contract) that accompanies most debt securities, may be backed up by the pledge of specific assets as collateral. Financial analysts usually divide debt securities into two broad classes: (1) *negotiable,* which can easily be transferred from holder to holder as a marketable security, and (2) *nonnegotiable,* which cannot legally be transferred to another party. Passbook savings accounts and U.S. savings bonds are good examples of nonnegotiable debt securities.

derivatives

Finally, **derivatives** are among the newest kinds of financial instruments that are closely linked to financial assets. These unique financial claims have a market value that is tied to or influenced by the value or return on a financial asset, such as stocks (equities) and bonds, notes, and other loans (debt securities). Examples include futures contracts, options, and swaps. As we will see in future chapters, these particular instruments are often employed to manage risk in the assets to which they are tied or related.

2.5   How Financial Assets Are Created

How are financial assets created? We may illustrate this process using a rudimentary financial system in which there are only two economic units: a household and a business firm.

One of the most popular sites today for tracking the changing values of financial assets is *Money Magazine*'s money.com

Assume that this financial system is *closed,* so no external transactions with other units are possible. Each unit holds certain assets accumulated over the years as a result of its saving out of current income. The household, for example, has accumulated furniture, an automobile, clothes, and other items needed to provide entertainment, food, shelter, and transportation. The business firm holds inventories of goods to be sold, raw materials, machinery and equipment, and other assets required to produce its product and sell it to the public.

The financial position of these two economic units is presented in the form of balance sheets, shown in Exhibit 2.1. A balance sheet, of course, is a financial statement prepared as of a certain date, showing a particular unit's assets, liabilities, and net worth. *Assets* represent *accumulated uses of funds* made by an economic unit; *liabilities* and *net worth* represent the *accumulated sources of funds* that an economic unit has drawn upon to acquire the assets it now holds. The net worth (equity) account reflects total savings accumulated over time by each economic unit. A balance sheet

**Balance Sheets of
Units in a Simple
Financial System**

HOUSEHOLD
Balance Sheet

Assets		Liabilities and Net Worth	
Accumulated uses of funds:		Accumulated sources of funds:	
Cash	$13,000	Net worth (accumulated savings)	$20,000
Furniture	1,000		
Clothes	1,500		
Automobile	4,000		
Other assets	500		
Total assets	$20,000	Total liabilities and net worth	$20,000

BUSINESS FIRM
Balance Sheet

Assets		Liabilities and Net Worth	
Accumulated uses of funds:		Accumulated sources of funds:	
Inventories of goods	$ 10,000	Net worth (accumulated savings)	$100,000
Machinery and equipment	25,000		
Building	60,000		
Other assets	5,000		
Total assets	$100,000	Total liabilities and net worth	$100,000

must balance; total assets (accumulated uses of funds) must equal total liabilities plus net worth (accumulated sources of funds).

The household in our example holds total assets valued at $20,000, including an automobile, clothes, furniture, and cash. Because the household's financial statement must balance, total liabilities and net worth also add up to $20,000, all of which in this instance happens to come from net worth (accumulated savings). The business firm holds total assets amounting to $100,000, including a building housing the firm's offices, equipment, and inventory. The firm's only source of funds currently is net worth (accumulated savings), also valued at $100,000.

By today's standards, the two balance sheets shown in Exhibit 2.1 look very strange. Neither the household nor the business firm has any outstanding debt (liabilities). Each unit is entirely self-financed, because each has acquired its assets by saving and by spending within its current income, not by borrowing. In the terminology of finance, both the household and the business firm have engaged in **internal financing:** the use of current income and accumulated savings to acquire assets. In the case of the household, savings have been accumulated by taking some portion of each period's income and setting money aside rather than spending all income on current consumption. The business firm has abstained from paying out all of its current revenues in the form of expenses (including stockholder dividends), retaining some of its current earnings in its net worth account.

For most businesses and households, internally generated funds are still the most important resources for acquiring assets. For example, in the U.S. economy, well over half of all investments in plant, equipment, and inventories carried out by business firms each year is financed internally rather than by borrowing. Households as a group normally save substantially more than they borrow each year, with the savings flowing into purchases of real assets (such as homes and automobiles) and into purchases of stocks, bonds, and other financial assets.

internal financing

Suppose that the business firm in our rudimentary financial system wishes to purchase new equipment in the form of a drill press. Due to inflation and shortages of key raw materials, however, the cost of the new drill press has been increasing rapidly. Internal sources of funds are not sufficient to cover the equipment's full cost. What can be done? There are four likely alternatives: (1) postpone the purchase of the new equipment until sufficient savings can be accumulated, (2) sell off some existing assets to raise the necessary funds, (3) borrow all or a portion of the needed funds, or (4) issue new stock (equity).

Time is frequently a determining factor here. Postponement of the equipment purchase probably will result in lost sales and lost profits. A competing company may rush ahead to expand its operations and capture some share of this firm's market. Moreover, in an environment of inflation, the new drill press surely will cost even more in the future than it does now. Selling some existing assets to raise the necessary funds is a distinct possibility, but this may take time, and there is risk of substantial loss, especially if fixed assets must be sold. The third alternative—borrowing—has the advantage of raising funds quickly, and the interest cost on the loan is tax deductible.[1] The firm could sell additional stock if it hesitated to take on debt, but equity financing is often more expensive than borrowing and requires more time to arrange.

If the business firm decides to borrow, who will lend the funds it needs? Obviously, in this two-unit financial system, the household must provide the needed funds. The

external financing

firm must engage in **external financing** by issuing to the household securities evidencing a loan of money. In general, if any economic unit wishes to add to its holdings of assets but lacks the necessary resources to do so, it can raise additional funds by issuing financial liabilities (borrowing)—provided that a buyer of those IOUs can be found. The buyer will regard the IOUs as an asset—a financial asset—that may earn income unless the borrower goes out of business and defaults on the loan.

Suppose that the business firm decides to borrow by issuing a liability (debt security) in the amount of $10,000 to pay for its new drill press. Because the firm is promising an attractive interest rate on the new IOU, the household willingly acquires it as a financial asset. This asset is *intangible:* a mere promise to pay $10,000 at maturity plus a promised stream of interest payments over time. The borrowing and creation of this financial asset will impact the balance sheets of these two economic units. As shown in Exhibit 2.2, the household has purchased the firm's IOU by using up some of its accumulated cash. Its total assets are unchanged. Instead of holding $13,000 in non-interest-bearing cash, the household now holds an interest-bearing financial asset in the form of a $10,000 security and $3,000 in cash. The firm's total assets and total liabilities *increase* due to the combined effect of borrowing (*external finance*) and the acquisition of a productive real asset.

What would happen to the balance sheet shown in Exhibit 2.2 if the business firm in our small financial system decided to issue stock (*equities*), rather than debt, to finance the purchase of its new equipment? While selling stock is usually more expensive than borrowing, the dividend payments to stockholders are not usually a tax-deductible expense. And, while equity financing generally requires more time to arrange, it does have the advantage of making a business firm financially stronger because the owners (stockholders) are committing more of their funds to the firm, thereby giving it greater protection against failure. As Exhibit 2.3 shows, the household

[1]An added advantage associated with issuing debt is the *leverage effect.* If the firm can earn more from purchasing and using the new equipment than the cost of borrowing funds, the surplus return will flow to the firm's owners in the form of increased earnings, increasing the value of the company's stock. The result is positive financial leverage. Unfortunately, leverage is a two-edged sword. If the firm earns less than the cost of borrowed funds, the owners' losses will be magnified as a result of unfavorable (negative) financial leverage.

EXHIBIT 2.2

Unit Balance
Sheets Following
the Purchase of
Equipment and
the Issuance of
a Financial Asset
(a Debt Security)

HOUSEHOLD
Balance Sheet

Assets		Liabilities and Net Worth	
Cash	$ 3,000	Net worth (accumulated savings)	$20,000
Financial asset	10,000		
Furniture	1,000		
Clothes	1,500		
Automobile	4,000		
Other assets	500		
Total assets	$20,000	Total liabilities and net worth	$20,000

BUSINESS FIRM
Balance Sheet

Assets		Liabilities and Net Worth	
Inventories of goods	$ 10,000	Liabilities	$ 10,000
Machinery and equipment	35,000	Net worth	100,000
Building	60,000		
Other assets	5,000		
Total assets	$110,000	Total liabilities and net worth	$110,000

EXHIBIT 2.3

Unit Balance
Sheets Following
the Purchase of
Equipment and
the Issuance of
Stock to Pay for
That Purchase

HOUSEHOLD
Balance Sheet

Assets		Liabilities	
Cash	$ 3,000	Net worth (accumulated savings)	$20,000
Financial asset	10,000		
Furniture	1,000		
Clothes	1,500		
Automobile	4,000		
Other assets	500		
Total assets	$20,000	Total liabilities and net worth	$20,000

BUSINESS FIRM
Balance Sheet

Assets		Liabilities	
Inventories of goods	$ 10,000	Net worth (including the issuance	$110,000
Machinery and equipment	35,000	of new stock in the amount	
Building	60,000	of $10,000)	
Other assets	5,000		
Total assets	$110,000	Total liabilities and net worth	$110,000

in our rudimentary financial system would record its purchase of the firm's newly issued stock as a financial asset in the amount of $10,000. And, on the business firm's balance sheet, net worth would rise to $110,000, from $100,000. There would *not* be a liability account on the business's balance sheet because the household in this particular case is not a creditor, but rather a shareholder (part owner) of the business firm.

2.6   Financial Assets and the Financial System

This simple example illustrates several important points concerning the operation and role of the financial system within the economy. First, the act of borrowing or of issuing new stock simultaneously gives rise to the creation of an equal volume of financial assets. In the foregoing example, the $10,000 financial asset held by the household lending money is exactly matched by the $10,000 liability of the business firm borrowing money. This suggests another way of defining a financial asset: *Any asset held by a business firm, government, or household that is also recorded as a liability or claim on some other economic unit's balance sheet is a financial asset.* As we have seen, many different kinds of assets satisfy this definition, including stocks, bonds, bank loans, and deposits held with a financial institution.

For the entire financial system, the sum of all financial assets held must equal the total of all financial liabilities (claims) outstanding. In contrast, real assets, such as automobiles, are not necessarily matched by liabilities (claims) somewhere in the financial system.

This distinction between *financial assets* and *liabilities,* on the one hand, and *real assets,* on the other, is worth pursuing with an example. Suppose that you borrow $10,000 from the bank to purchase an automobile. Your balance sheet will now contain a liability in the amount of $10,000. The bank from which you borrowed the funds will record the transaction as a loan—an interest-bearing financial asset—appearing on the asset side of its balance sheet in the like amount of $10,000. On the asset side of your balance sheet appears the market value of the automobile—a real asset. The value of the real asset probably exceeds $10,000 since most banks expect a borrower to supply some of his or her own funds rather than borrowing the full purchase price. Let's say the automobile was sold to you for $15,000, with $5,000 of the cost coming out of your savings account and $10,000 from the bank loan. Then, your balance sheet will contain a new real asset (automobile) valued at $15,000, a liability (bank loan) of $10,000, and your savings account (a financial asset) will decline by $5,000.

Clearly, there are two equalities that hold not only for this transaction but whenever funds are loaned and borrowed in the financial system. First,

$$\begin{array}{ccc} \text{Volume of financial} & = & \text{Volume of liabilities} \\ \text{assets created for lenders} & & \text{issued by borrowers} \end{array} \tag{2.1}$$

$$\begin{array}{ccc} \text{In this case, a bank} & = & \text{A borrower's IOU of} \\ \text{loan of \$10,000} & & \$10,000 \end{array}$$

Second,

$$\text{Total uses of funds} = \text{Total sources of funds}$$

$$\begin{array}{ccc} \text{Purchase of \$15,000} & = & \text{Issuance of a \$10,000} \\ \text{automobile} & & \text{borrower IOU} + \$5,000 \\ & & \text{drawn from a savings} \\ & & \text{account} \end{array} \tag{2.2}$$

Every financial asset in existence represents the lending or investing of funds transferred from one economic unit to another.

Because the sum of all financial assets created must always equal the amount of all liabilities (claims) outstanding, the amount of lending in the financial system must always equal the amount of borrowing going on. In effect, *financial assets and liabilities (claims) cancel each other out across the whole financial system.* We illustrate this fact by reference to the balance sheet of any unit in the economy—business firm, household, or government. The following must be true for *all* balance sheets:

$$\text{Total assets} = \text{Total liabilities} + \text{Net worth} \qquad (2.3)$$

Then, because all assets may be classified as either real assets or financial assets, it follows that

$$\text{Real assets} + \text{Financial assets} = \text{Total liabilities} + \text{Net worth} \qquad (2.4)$$

Because the volume of financial assets outstanding must always equal the volume of liabilities (claims) in existence, it follows that the aggregate volume of real assets held in the economy must equal the total amount of net worth. Therefore, for the economy and financial system *as a whole:*

$$\text{Total financial assets} = \text{Total liabilities} \qquad (2.5)$$

$$\text{Total real assets} = \text{Net worth (i.e., accumulated savings)} \qquad (2.6)$$

This means that the value of all buildings, machinery, and other real assets in existence matches the total amount of *accumulated savings* carried out by all businesses, households, and units of government. We *are not* made better off in real terms by the mere creation of financial assets and liabilities. These are only pieces of paper or blips on a computer screen evidencing a loan or the investment of funds. Rather, society increases its wealth only by saving and increasing the quantity of its real assets, for these assets enable the economy to produce more goods and services in the future.

Does this suggest that the creation of financial assets and liabilities—one of the basic functions of the global financial system—is a useless exercise? Not at all. The mere act of saving by one economic unit does not guarantee that those savings will be used to build or purchase real assets that add to society's stock of wealth. In modern economies, saving and investment usually are carried out by different groups of people. For example, most saving is usually carried out by households (individuals and families), and business firms account for the majority of investments in productive real assets. Some mechanism is needed to ensure that savings flow from those who save to those who wish to invest in real assets, and the system of money and capital markets is that mechanism.

The *financial system* provides the essential channel necessary for the creation and exchange of financial assets between savers and borrowers so that real assets can be acquired. Without that channel for savings, the total volume of investment in the economy surely would be reduced. All investment by individual economic units would have to depend on the ability of those same units to save (i.e., engage in internal financing). Many promising investment opportunities would have to be forgone or postponed due to insufficient savings. Society's scarce resources would be allocated less efficiently than is possible with a system of financial markets. Growth in society's income, employment, and standard of living would be seriously impaired without a vibrant financial system at work.

QUESTIONS TO HELP YOU STUDY

1. Exactly what do we mean by the term *financial asset?*
2. How do financial assets come about within the functioning of the financial system?
3. Carefully explain why it is that the volume of financial assets outstanding must always equal the volume of liabilities outstanding.
4. What is the difference between *internal finance* and *external finance?*
5. When a business, household, or unit of government is in need of additional funding, what are its principal alternatives? What factors should these different economic units consider when they have to choose among different sources of funds?
6. What is the relationship between the process of creating financial assets and liabilities and the acts of saving and investment? Why is that relationship important to your financial and economic well-being?

2.7   Lending and Borrowing in the Financial System

Business firms, households, and governments play a wide variety of roles in modern financial systems. It is quite common for an individual or institution to be a lender of funds in one period and a borrower in the next, or to do both simultaneously. Indeed, financial intermediaries, such as banks and insurance companies, operate on *both sides* of the financial markets, borrowing funds from customers by issuing attractive financial claims and simultaneously making loans available to other customers. Virtually all of us at one point or another in our lifetimes will be involved in the financial system as both a borrower and a lender of funds.

A number of years ago, economists John Gurley and Edward Shaw pointed out that each business firm, household, or unit of government active in the financial system must conform to the following identity:

$$R - E \quad = \quad \Delta FA - \Delta D$$

Current income receipts − Expenditures out of current income	=	Change in holdings of financial assets − Change in debt and equity outstanding	**(2.7)**

If, on the one hand, our current expenditures (E) exceed our current income receipts (R), we usually make up the difference by (1) reducing our holdings of financial assets ($-\Delta FA$), for example, by drawing money out of a savings account; (2) issuing debt or stock ($+\Delta D$); or (3) using some combination of both. If, on the other hand, our receipts (R) in the current period are larger than our current expenditures (E), we can (1) build up our holdings of financial assets ($+\Delta FA$), for example, by placing money in a savings account or buying a few shares of stock; (2) pay off some outstanding debt or retire stock previously issued by our business firm ($-\Delta D$); or (3) do some combination of both of these steps.

EXHIBIT 2.4

Net Acquisitions of Financial Assets and Liabilities by Major Sectors of the U.S. Economy, 2003* ($ Billions)

Source: Board of Governors of the Federal Reserve System, *Flow of Funds Accounts.*

*Figures do not add exactly due to omitted groups and statistical discrepancies.

Major Sectors of the Economy	Net Acquisitions of Financial Assets during the Year	Net Increase in Liabilities during the Year	Net Lender (+) or Net Borrower (−) of Funds
Households	$770.9	$912.6	$−141.7
Nonfinancial business firms	709.3	540.1	169.2
State and local governments	70.0	141.6	−71.6
Federal government	−3.0	421.5	−424.5
International sector:			
Foreign investors and borrowers	810.5	234.6	575.9

deficit-budget unit

surplus-budget unit

balanced-budget unit

It follows that for any given period of time (e.g., day, month, or year), the individual economic unit must fall into one of three groups:

Deficit-budget unit (DBU): $E > R$; and so $\Delta D > \Delta FA$
(net borrower of funds)

Surplus-budget unit (SBU): $R > E$; and thus $\Delta FA > \Delta D$
(net lender of funds)

Balanced-budget unit (BBU): $R = E$; and, therefore, $\Delta D = \Delta FA$
(neither net lender nor
net borrower)

A *net lender of funds (SBU) is really a net supplier of funds to the financial system.* He or she accomplishes this function by purchasing financial assets, paying off debt, or retiring equity (stock). In contrast, a *net borrower of funds (DBU) is a net demander of funds from the financial system,* selling financial assets, issuing new debt, or selling new stock. The business and government sectors of the economy tend to be net borrowers (demanders) of funds (DBUs) in most periods; the household sector, composed of all families and individuals, tends to be a net lender (supplier) of funds (SBU) in most (though not all) years.

Net lending and borrowing sectors in the U.S. economy in 2003 reflected some of the patterns discussed above, but there were some important exceptions as well. For example, as shown in Exhibit 2.4, households during 2003 were significant net borrowers of funds in the financial system, declining to play their historic role as net lender. That is, U.S. households borrowed an amount from other sectors of the economy—recorded as their "Net Increase in Liabilities"—that was $141.7 billion *more* than the amount they loaned to other sectors—recorded as "Net Acquisitions of Financial Assets." The biggest borrowers in 2003 were governments. State and local governments combined were net borrowers to the tune of $71.6 billion, while the federal government sold off $3.0 billion in previously acquired financial assets to raise new money and then borrowed $421.5 billion on top of that!

If households and governments were net borrowers in the money and capital markets in 2003, who loaned them the money? As Exhibit 2.4 clearly shows, it was the business sector and foreign investors who supplied the funds that these domestic borrowers were seeking. Nonfinancial businesses made a significant contribution by lending $169.2 billion more than they borrowed. However, foreign investors were by far the largest contributors. Foreign participants active in U.S. financial markets sought out U.S. dollar-denominated assets, buying up corporate stock, government bonds, and thousands of other American financial instruments, resulting in total net lending to U.S. borrowers of $575.9 billion. Many of these overseas lenders of funds saw the

United States as a relatively safe haven for their money, in contrast to the turmoil that characterized many foreign markets at the time.

Finally, if we look across all sectors in Exhibit 2.4 we note that in 2003 total funds loaned exceeded total funds borrowed by about $107 billion. How could that be? Where did the excess funds go? Some of those excess funds went to sectors not shown in the exhibit—for example, borrowings by the financial institutions' sector of the economy. Still other funds flowed into "unrecorded transactions" (sometimes referred to as a "statistical discrepancy"). Many experts believe that some of these mysterious transactions probably reflect unreported money flows across national borders—money that is very hard to trace.

Of course, over any given period of time, any one household, business firm, or unit of government may be a deficit-, surplus-, or balanced-budget unit. In fact, from day to day and week to week, many households, businesses, and governments fluctuate from being deficit-budget units (DBUs) to surplus-budget units (SBUs) and back again. Consider a large corporation such as Ford or General Electric. Such a firm may be a net lender one week, supplying monies to deficit-budget units in the financial system for short periods of time through purchases of Treasury bills, bank Euro-deposits and CDs, and other financial assets. The following week, a dividend payment may be due company stockholders, bonds must be refunded, or purchases must be made to increase inventories and expand plant and equipment. At this point, the firm may become a net borrower of funds, drawing down its holdings of financial assets, securing loans by issuing liabilities, or selling equity (stock). Most of the large institutions that interact in the global financial marketplace continually fluctuate from one side of the market to the other. *One of the most important contributions of the global financial system to our daily lives is in permitting businesses, households, and governments to adjust their financial position from that of net borrower (DBU) to net lender (SBU) and back again, smoothly and efficiently.*

2.8 Money as a Financial Asset

What Is Money?

The most important financial asset in the economy is *money*—one of the oldest and most useful inventions in the history of the world. Metallic coins served as money for many centuries until paper notes (currency) first appeared in China during the Tang Dynasty over a thousand years ago (618–907 C.E.) and in Sweden in 1661. The federal government of the United States did not issue paper money until 1861 in the form of "greenbacks," named for the green ink on the back of each note. Many other assets besides currency and coin have served as money in earlier periods, including beads, seashells, cigarettes, and even playing cards.

All financial assets are valued in terms of money, and flows of funds between lenders and borrowers occur through the medium of money. Money itself *is* a financial asset, because all forms of money in use today are claims against some institution, public or private. For example, one of the largest components of the money supply today is the checking account, which is the debt of a bank or other depository institution. Another important component of the money supply is the sum of all currency and coin—pocket money—held by the public. The bulk of currency in use today in the United States, for example, consists of Federal Reserve notes, representing debt obligations of the 12 Federal Reserve banks. In fact, if the Federal Reserve ever closed its doors (a highly unlikely event!), Federal Reserve notes held by the public would be a first claim against the assets of the Federal Reserve banks. Other forms of money that are growing rapidly in popularity include credit and debit cards to allow instant borrowing or the withdrawal of funds from a bank deposit; stored-value ("smart") cards that are encoded via computer with a fixed amount of money available for spending; and digital cash available through

Money performs multiple functions in the financial system, serving as a medium of exchange, a store of value (purchasing power), a standard for valuing goods and services (unit of account), and a source of liquidity (spending power). These different functions of money have given rise to a variety of different definitions of the actual money supply available to the public, with each definition reflecting a different function that money performs for those who hold it. For example, in the United States the principal definitions of money in use today are:

M1 = Currency and coin held by the public and outside bank vaults, plus various kinds of payments accounts at depository institutions. M1 emphasizes the role of money as a medium of exchange. In 2004, M1 totaled just over $1.3 trillion in the United States.

M2 = M1 plus small savings and time deposits (less than $100,000) and share accounts at retail money market mutual funds. Thus, M2 adds in primarily short-term household savings to the money supply. In 2004, M2 amounted to just over $6.1 trillion.

M3 = M2 plus, for the most part, key financial instruments that business firms use to store their short-term savings (such as institutional money market shares, large time deposits, wholesale repurchase agreements, and foreign U.S. dollar-denominated deposits). In 2004, M3 reached nearly $9 trillion.

Clearly, each of the foregoing definitions reflects the many different roles money performs in the economy and financial system.

the Internet computer network from a variety of financial-service providers. As we will see in the accompanying box on alternative definitions of the money supply, some concepts of what money is today include savings accounts at banks, credit unions, and money market funds—all forms of debt, giving rise to financial assets.

The Functions of Money

Want to know more about the money supply and what makes it up? See especially frbatlanta.org/publica

Money performs a wide variety of important services. It serves as a *standard of value* (or *unit of account*) for all the goods and services we might wish to trade. Without money, the price of every good or service would have to be expressed in terms of exchange ratios with all other goods and services—an enormous information burden for both buyers and sellers. We would need to know, for example, how many loaves of bread would be required to purchase a quart of milk, or what quantity of firewood might be exchanged for a suit of clothes. To trade just 12 different goods and services, we would have to remember 66 different exchange ratios! In contrast, the existence of money as a common standard of value permits us to express the prices of all goods and services in terms of only one good—the *monetary unit.* In the United States and Canada that unit is the dollar; in Japan, the yen; and in China, the yuan. But whatever the monetary unit is called, it always has a constant price in terms of itself (e.g., a dollar always exchanges for a dollar). The prices of all other goods and services are expressed in multiples of the monetary unit.

The importance of money within the financial system is discussed further in encarta.msn.com

Money also serves as a *medium of exchange.* It is usually the only financial asset that virtually every business, household, and unit of government will accept in payment for goods and services. By itself, money typically has little or no use as a commodity (except when gold or silver, for example, is used as the medium of exchange). People accept money only because they know they can exchange it at a later date for goods and services. This is why modern governments have been able to separate the monetary unit from precious metals (such as gold and silver bullion) and successfully issue *fiat money* (i.e., pieces of paper or data stored in a computer file or on a plastic card) not tied to any particular commodity. Money's service as a medium of exchange frees us from the terrible constraints of barter, allowing us to separate the act of selling goods and services from the act of buying goods and services. With a medium of exchange, buyers and sellers no longer need to have an exact coincidence of wants in terms of quality, quantity, time, and location.

Money serves also as a *store of value*—a reserve of future purchasing power. Purchasing power can be stored in currency, in a checking account, or in a computer file until the time is right to buy. Of course, money is not always a good store of value. The value of money, measured by its purchasing power, can experience marked fluctuations. For example, the prices of consumer goods represented in the U.S. cost-of-living index roughly quadrupled between 1960 and 2004. If individuals or families had purchased in each of these years the identical market basket of goods and services represented in the cost-of-living index, they would have found that the purchasing power of each unit of their money had decreased by more than two-thirds during this period.

Money functions as the *only perfectly liquid asset* in the financial system. An asset is liquid if it can be converted into cash quickly with little or no loss in value. A liquid asset possesses three essential characteristics: *price stability, ready marketability,* and *reversibility.* An asset must be considered *liquid* if its price tends to be relatively stable over time, if it has an active resale market, and if it is reversible so that investors can recover their original investment without loss.

All assets—real and financial—differ in their *degrees of liquidity.* Generally, financial assets, especially bank deposits and stocks and bonds issued by major corporations, tend to be highly liquid; on the other hand, real assets, such as a home or an automobile, may be extremely difficult to sell in a hurry without taking a substantial loss. *Money is the most liquid of all assets because it need not be converted into any other form to be spent.* Unfortunately, the most liquid assets, including money, tend to carry the lowest rates of return. One measure of the "cost" of holding money is the income forgone by the owner who fails to convert his or her money balances into more profitable investments in real or financial assets. The *rate of interest* determined by the financial system is a measure of the penalty suffered by an investor for not converting money into income-earning assets.

2.9 The Value of Money and Other Financial Assets and Inflation

inflation

The value of money—its *purchasing power*—changes due to **inflation,** defined as a rise in the average price level of all goods and services. Inflation lowers the value or purchasing power of money and is a special problem in the money and capital markets because it can damage the value of financial contracts (such as a bond or a deposit). Financial loss due to inflation is particularly likely where the amount of price inflation has not been fully anticipated or if the people and institutions who agreed to a financial contract were simply not able to adjust fully to the inflation that subsequently occurred.

deflation

The opposite of inflation is **deflation,** where the average level of prices for goods and services actually declines. Less common than inflation, deflation benefits those whose income doesn't also decline with prices and, therefore, can buy more goods and services than they could in the past. Unfortunately, deflation may be accompanied by a troubled economy so that, even though living costs are less, many people may still find themselves with sharply reduced income (purchasing power).

price indexes

Today most economists measure inflation using popular **price indexes,** such as the Consumer Price Index (CPI), the Producer Price Index (PPI), or the Gross Domestic

Product (GDP) Deflator Index. The CPI, a cost of living index, measures the cost of a market basket of goods and services normally purchased by an urban family of four people. To determine this measure of the cost of living, the actual prices of designated items are collected from thousands of stores in cities across the United States each month, averaged, and combined into one index number which is never revised. The U.S. CPI is widely used to make cost of living adjustments (COLAs) in labor contracts, Social Security payments, and in other government and private programs. A number of other nations, especially in Europe, have begun in recent years to compile their own CPIs in order to monitor their cost of living and the effects of inflation on their economies.

The Producer Price Index, compiled by the U.S. Department of Labor, Bureau of Labor Statistics, measures the average change over time in the selling prices received by U.S. domestic producers for the products and services they turn out, including agriculture, mining, manufacturing, and a growing list of service industries. About 25,000 firms are sampled each month, primarily by mail, in order to gather close to 100,000 different producer prices.

The Bureau of Economic Analysis of the U.S. Department of Commerce also calculates a range of price indexes covering broad sectors of the American economy each quarter of the year. For example, there is a Consumption Chain Price Index covering the prices paid by U.S. households for newly produced consumer goods and services that are part of the annual U.S. gross domestic product (GDP). An even broader price index is the GDP deflator series, which gathers both business and consumer prices on goods and services produced each year by labor and property inside the United States.

We can use any of the foregoing indexes to measure percentage changes in price levels (and inflation) relative to some base year using the following relationship:

$$\Delta P = \frac{(PI_t - PI_{t-1})}{PI_{t-1}} \times 100 \tag{2.8}$$

where ΔP is the percentage change in prices or in the price index we are following between two time periods (t and $t-1$), PI_t is the price or price index in period t, and PI_{t-1} is the price index in some previous time period ($t-1$).

For example, suppose the U.S. CPI rises from 100 to 125 over a five-year period. We know that this cost of living index has climbed

$$\frac{(125 - 100)}{100} = 0.25 \text{ or 25 percent}$$

over the five-year period we are studying. Unless the value of our incomes and our investments in financial assets and other forms of wealth has also gone up at least 25 percent during the same time period, we would have suffered a decline in purchasing power and in the true value of our wealth in terms of the goods and services we can now buy.

What else can a price index tell us? In 2003 the U.S. Consumer Price Index (CPI) averaged just over 180. This index value was based on the base period 1982–84 when the CPI was set at 100. This means that between 1982–84 and 2003 consumer prices in U.S. urban communities climbed an average of about 80 percent (that is, $(180 - 100) \div 100$). We can use numbers such as these to help figure out what has happened recently to the purchasing power of the basic monetary unit.

For example, suppose we wish to know what has happened to the purchasing power of the U.S. dollar recently. We could use this relationship:

$$\begin{array}{l} \text{Purchasing power} \\ \text{of the U.S. dollar} \end{array} = \frac{1}{\begin{array}{c} \text{Cost of living index} \\ \text{where goods and services} \\ \text{are sold in U.S. dollars} \end{array}} \times 100 \tag{2.9}$$

To learn more about the Producer Price Index, see especially bls.gov

Additional information concerning personal consumption and GDP deflator price indexes may be found at bea.doc.gov

To learn more about U.S. inflation and how to adjust costs for inflation's effects see stats.bls.gov

As an illustration, if the American CPI stood at close to 180 in 2003 and was equal to 100 in 1982–84, the U.S. dollar's relative purchasing power would have fallen to

$$\frac{1}{180} \times 100 = 0.56$$

between 1982–84 and 2003. In other words, in 2003, one dollar bought only about 56 percent of what it would have purchased two decades earlier.

These dramatic changes in the purchasing power of money, even in the United States where inflation is relatively modest, give us a stern warning. We should get into the habit of thinking in terms of the **real** ("purchasing power adjusted") **values** of things—incomes, goods, services, financial assets such as bonds, stocks, bank deposits, and so on—rather than only in terms of their **nominal** (or face) **values**, which can be highly misleading in periods of significant inflation or deflation.

real value

nominal value

QUESTIONS TO HELP YOU STUDY

7. What do the following terms mean?
    Deficit-budget unit (DBU)
    Surplus-budget unit (SBU)
    Balanced-budget unit (BBU)

8. Which were you last year—a deficit-, surplus-, or balanced-budget unit? Why is it important to know?

9. Explain what *money* is. What are its principal functions within the system of money and capital markets? within the economy?

10. Does money have any serious limitations as a financial asset? What are these limitations?

11. Can you distinguish between *inflation* and *deflation?* What do they have to do with money, if anything?

12. Would you expect to find a relationship between money supply growth and inflation or deflation? What kind of relationship?

2.10 The Evolution of Financial Transactions

Financial systems are *never* static. They change constantly in response to shifting demands from the public, the development of new technology, and changes in laws and regulations. Competition in the financial marketplace forces financial institutions to respond to public need by developing better and more convenient financial services. Over time, the global system of financial markets has evolved from simple to more complex ways of carrying out financial transactions. The growth of industrial centers with enormous capital investment needs and the emergence of a huge middle-class of savers have played major roles in the gradual evolution of the financial system.

Whether simple or complex, all financial systems perform at least one basic function. They move scarce funds from those who save and lend (surplus-budget units) to those who wish to borrow and invest (deficit-budget units). In the process, money is exchanged for financial assets. However, the transfer of funds from savers to borrowers can be accomplished in at least three different ways. We label these methods of funds transfer: (1) direct finance, (2) semidirect finance, and (3) indirect finance. Most financial systems have evolved gradually over time from direct and semidirect finance toward greater reliance on indirect finance.

Direct Finance (Direct lending gives rise to direct claims against borrowers)

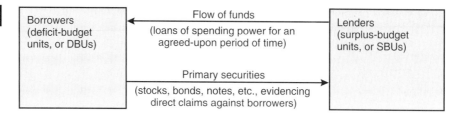

Direct Finance

direct finance

With the direct financing technique, borrower and lender meet each other and exchange funds in return for financial assets without the help of a third party to bring them together. You engage in **direct finance** when you borrow money from a friend and give him or her your IOU, or when you purchase stocks or bonds directly from the company issuing them. We usually call the claims arising from direct finance *primary securities* because they flow directly from the borrower to the ultimate lender of funds. (Exhibit 2.5 illustrates the process of direct financing.)

Direct finance is the simplest method of carrying out financial transactions and most financial systems in history started out using direct finance. However, it has a number of serious limitations. For one thing, both borrower and lender must desire to exchange the *same amount* of funds at the *same time*. More important, the lender must be willing to accept the borrower's IOU, which may be quite risky or slow to mature. Clearly, there must be a coincidence of wants between surplus- and deficit-budget units in terms of the amount and form of a loan. Without that fundamental coincidence, direct finance breaks down.

Another problem is that both lender and borrower must frequently incur substantial *information costs* simply to find each other. The borrower may have to contact many lenders before finding the one surplus-budget unit (SBU) with just the right amount of funds and a willingness to take on the borrower's IOU. Not surprisingly, direct finance soon gives way to other methods of carrying out financial transactions as money and capital markets develop.

Semidirect Finance

semidirect finance

Early in the history of most financial systems, a new form of financial transaction called **semidirect finance** appears. Some individuals and business firms become securities brokers and dealers whose essential function is to bring surplus-budget (SBU) and deficit-budget (DBU) units together, thereby reducing information costs (see Exhibit 2.6).

We must distinguish here between a broker and a dealer in securities. A *broker* is merely an individual or financial institution who provides information concerning possible purchases and sales of securities. Either a buyer or a seller of securities may contact a broker, whose job is simply to bring buyers and sellers together. A *dealer* also serves as an intermediary between buyers and sellers, but the dealer actually acquires the seller's securities in the hope of marketing them at a later time at a favorable price. Dealers take a "position of risk" because, by purchasing securities outright for their own portfolios, they are subject to losses if those securities decline in value.

Semidirect finance is an improvement over direct finance in a number of ways. It lowers the search (information) costs for participants in the financial markets. Frequently, a dealer will split up a large issue of primary securities into smaller units affordable by even buyers of modest means and, thereby, expand the flow of savings

EXHIBIT 2.6	Semidirect Finance (Direct lending with the aid of market makers who assist in the sale of direct claims against borrowers.)

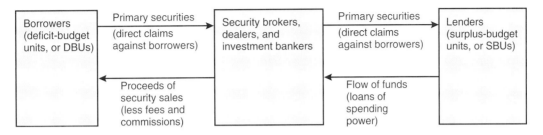

into investment. In addition, brokers and dealers facilitate the development of secondary markets in which securities can be offered for resale.

Despite the important contribution of brokers and dealers to the functioning of the global financial system, the semidirect finance approach is not without its limitations. The ultimate lender still winds up holding the borrower's securities, and, therefore, the lender must be willing to accept the risk and maturity characteristics of the borrower's IOUs. There still must be a *coincidence* of wants and needs between surplus- and deficit-budget units for semidirect financial transactions to take place.

Indirect Finance and Financial Intermediation

indirect finance

The limitations of both direct and semidirect finance stimulated the development of **indirect finance** carried out with the help of *financial intermediaries.* Financial intermediaries include commercial banks, insurance companies, credit unions, finance companies, savings and loan associations, savings banks, pension funds, mutual funds, and similar organizations. (See Exhibit 2.7.) Their fundamental role in the financial system is to serve both ultimate lenders and borrowers but in a much more complete way than brokers and dealers do. Financial intermediaries issue securities of their **secondary securities** own—often called **secondary securities**—to ultimate lenders and at the same time **primary securities** accept IOUs from borrowers—**primary securities** (see Exhibit 2.8).

EXHIBIT 2.7	Financial Intermediaries	

Major Financial Institutions Active in the Money and Capital Markets	Depository institutions:
	  Commercial banks
	  Nonbank thrifts:
	    Savings and loan associations
	    Savings banks
	    Credit unions
	    Money market funds
	
	Other financial intermediaries:
	  Finance companies
	  Government credit agencies
	  Mortgage companies
		Contractual institutions:
		  Life insurance companies
		  Property-casualty insurers
		  Pension funds
		Investment institutions:
		  Investment companies (mutual funds)
		  Real estate investment trusts

	Other Financial Institutions	
	Investment bankers Security brokers Security dealers	

EXHIBIT 2.8   Indirect Finance (The financial intermediation of funds)

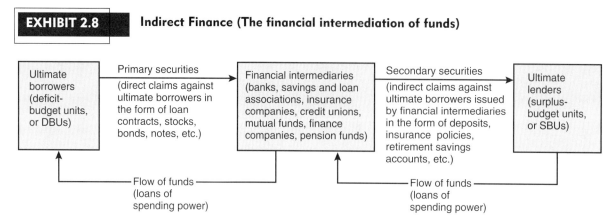

The *secondary securities* issued by financial intermediaries include such familiar instruments as checking and savings accounts, life insurance policies, annuities, and shares in a mutual fund. For the most part, these securities share several common characteristics. They generally carry *low risk of default.* For example, most deposits held in banks and credit unions are insured by an agency of government (in the United States, for amounts up to $100,000). Moreover, the majority of secondary securities can be acquired in *small denominations,* affordable by savers of limited means. For the most part, secondary securities are liquid and, therefore, can be converted quickly into cash with little risk of significant loss. Financial intermediaries in recent years have tried to make savings as convenient as possible through the mail and by plastic card, computer terminal, and telephone in order to reduce transactions costs to the saver.

Financial intermediaries accept *primary securities* from those who need credit and, in doing so, take on financial assets that many savers, especially those with limited funds and limited knowledge of the market, would find unacceptable. For example, many large corporations require billions of dollars in credit financing each year—sums that would make it impractical to deal directly with thousands of small savers. By pooling the resources of scores of small savings accounts, however, a large financial intermediary frequently can service the credit needs of several large firms simultaneously. In addition, many primary securities are not readily marketable and carry sizable risk of borrower default—a situation usually not acceptable to the small saver. By issuing its own securities, attractive to ultimate lenders (SBUs), and accepting primary securities from ultimate borrowers (DBUs), the financial intermediary acts to satisfy the financial needs of *both* surplus- and deficit-budget units in the economy.

One of the benefits of the development of efficient financial intermediation (indirect finance) has been to smooth out consumption spending by households and investment spending by businesses over time, despite variations in income, because intermediation makes saving and borrowing easier and safer. Financial intermediation permits a given amount of saving in the global economy to finance a greater amount of investment than would have occurred without intermediation.

Interestingly enough, finance theory suggests that in a perfect world with perfect competition and where the public has access to information at little or no cost, financial intermediaries probably would *not* exist. Rather, it is *imperfections* in the financial system (where, for example, some groups do not have access to relevant financial information or face prohibitive information costs) that help explain why

To learn more about the role of financial intermediaries in the economy see ny.frb.org

there are financial intermediaries and why they have grown to be such huge and important institutions within the financial system. Financial intermediaries overcome inefficiencies in the financial marketplace and reduce the cost to society of moving information and wealth among households, businesses, and governments, thereby providing access to economies of scale (information cost savings) that would otherwise not be available to smaller units in the economy. Financial intermediaries improve the real world efficiency of the money and capital markets in allocating the daily flow of capital toward its best possible uses. How well financial intermediaries work is a key determinant of which countries have the largest and strongest economies.

2.11 Relative Size and Importance of Major Financial Institutions

Financial intermediaries and other financial institutions differ greatly in their relative importance within any nation's financial system. Measured by total financial assets, for example, *commercial banks* dominate the United States's financial system (as shown in Exhibit 2.9) and most other financial systems around the globe. The more than $8 trillion in financial assets held by U.S. banks represent about one-quarter of the total resources of all U.S. financial institutions. By some measures banks appear to have lost some of their market share to some nonbank financial institutions (such as money market funds and credit unions), which may be less regulated or offer more flexible service options. In most countries, however, banks still represent the dominant financial institution.

Lagging well behind banks are *savings and loans associations*—another deposit-type financial intermediary active primarily in the U.S. mortgage market, financing the building and purchase of new homes. Very similar in sources and uses of funds to savings and loans are *savings banks,* which attract small savings deposits from individuals and families and make a wide variety of household loans. The fourth major kind of deposit-type financial intermediary, the *credit union,* was also created to attract small savings deposits from individuals and families and make loans to credit union members.

When the assets of all four deposit-type intermediaries—commercial banks, savings and loans, savings banks, and credit unions—are combined, they make up about one-third of the total financial assets of all U.S. financial institutions. The remainder of the sector's financial assets are held by a highly diverse group of nondeposit financial institutions. *Life insurance companies,* which protect policyholders against the risks of premature death and disability, are among the most important nondeposit institutions and rank fourth behind commercial banks in total assets. The other type of insurance firm—*property-casualty insurers*—offers a wider array of policies to reduce the risk of loss associated with crime, weather damage, and personal negligence. Among the most specialized of financial institutions are *pension funds,* which protect their customers against the risk of outliving their sources of income in the retirement years. Private pensions now rank second behind commercial banks in total assets held within the U.S. financial system. (See again Exhibit 2.9.)

Other important financial institutions include finance companies, investment companies, money market funds, and real estate investment trusts. *Finance companies* lend money to businesses and consumers to meet short-term working capital and long-term investment needs. *Investment companies* (mutual funds) pool the funds contributed by thousands of savers by selling shares and then investing in securities sold in the open

EXHIBIT 2.9

Total Financial Assets Held by U.S. Financial Institutions, Selected Years ($ Billions at Year-End)

Source: Board of Governors of the Federal Reserve System, *Flow of Funds Accounts: Financial Assets and Liabilities,* selected years.

*Figures are for the first quarter.

Financial Institutions	1970	1980	1990	2000	2004*
Financial intermediaries:					
Commercial banks	$489	$1,248	$3,340	$6,488	$8,044
Savings and loan associations and savings banks	252	794	1,358	1,219	1,557
Life insurance companies	201	464	1,367	3,204	3,849
Private pension funds	110	413	1,629	4,587	4,260
Investment companies (mutual funds)	47	64	602	4,457	4,890
State and local government pension funds	60	198	820	2,290	2,303
Finance companies	63	199	611	1,138	1,401
Property-casualty insurance companies	50	174	534	872	1,069
Money market funds	—	74	498	1,812	1,972
Credit unions	18	72	202	441	635
Mortgage companies	—	16	49	36	32
Real estate investment trusts	4	6	13	62	133
Other financial institutions:					
Security brokers and dealers	16	36	262	1,221	1,725

market and are particularly important in holding and investing the public's retirement savings. A specialized type of investment company is the *money market fund,* which accepts savings (share) accounts from businesses and individuals and places those funds in high-quality, short-term (money market) securities. Also related to investment companies are *real estate investment trusts,* one of the smallest members of the financial institutions sector, which invest mainly in commercial and residential properties. Finally, at the bottom of the list, size-wise, are *mortgage companies,* which facilitate the raising of credit to construct new businesses and homes.

2.12 Classification of Financial Institutions

depository institutions

contractual institutions

investment institutions

Financial institutions may be grouped in a variety of different ways. One of the most important distinctions is between **depository institutions** (commercial banks, savings and loan associations, savings banks, and credit unions); **contractual institutions** (insurance companies and pension funds); and **investment institutions** (mutual funds, and real estate investment trusts). Depository institutions derive the bulk of their loanable funds from deposit accounts sold to the public. Contractual institutions attract funds by offering legal contracts to protect the saver against risk (such as an insurance policy or retirement account). Investment institutions sell shares to the public and invest the proceeds in stocks, bonds, and other assets in the hope of providing higher returns to their shareholders.

2.13 Portfolio (Financial-Asset) Decisions by Financial Intermediaries and Other Financial Institutions

The management of a financial institution is called on daily to make *portfolio decisions* —that is, *deciding what financial assets to buy or sell.* A number of factors affect these critical decisions. For example, the *relative rate of return and risk* attached to different financial assets will affect the composition of each financial institution's portfolio. Obviously, if management is interested in maximizing profits and has minimal aversion to risk, it will tend to pursue the highest yielding financial assets available, such as corporate bonds and stocks. A more risk-averse institution, on the other hand, is likely to surrender some yield in return for the greater safety available from acquiring government bonds and high-quality money market instruments.

The *cost, volatility, and maturity of incoming funds* provided by surplus-budget units also have a significant impact on the financial assets acquired by financial institutions. Commercial banks, for example, derive a substantial portion of their funds from checking accounts, which are relatively inexpensive but highly volatile. Such an institution will tend to concentrate its lending activities in short- and medium-term loans to avoid an embarrassing shortage of cash (liquidity). On the other hand, a financial institution such as a pension fund, which receives a stable and predictable inflow of savings, is largely freed from concern over short-term liquidity needs. It is able to invest heavily in long-term financial assets. Thus, the *hedging principle*—the approximate matching of the maturity of financial assets held with liabilities taken on—is an important guide for choosing those financial assets that a financial institution wants to hold in its portfolio.

Decisions on what financial assets to acquire and what financial assets to issue to the public are also influenced by the *size* of the individual financial institution. Larger institutions frequently can take advantage of greater *diversification* in their sources and uses of funds. This means that the overall risk of a portfolio of financial assets can be reduced by acquiring financial assets from many different borrowers. Similarly, a larger financial institution can contact a broader range of savers and achieve greater stability in its incoming flows of funds. At the same time, through *economies of scale* (size), larger financial institutions can often sell financial services at lower cost per unit and pass those cost savings along to their customers.

Finally, *regulations and competition,* two external forces, play major roles in shaping the financial assets acquired and issued by financial institutions. Because they hold the bulk of the public's savings and are so crucial to economic growth, financial intermediaries are among the most heavily regulated of all business firms. Commercial banks are prohibited from investing in low-quality or highly volatile loans and securities in many countries. Insurance companies and pension funds must restrict asset purchases to those a "prudent person" would most likely choose. Most government regulations in this sector pertain to the assets that can be acquired, the adequacy of net worth, and the services that can be offered to the public. Such regulations are designed primarily to ensure the safety of the public's funds.

2.14   Disintermediation of Funds

disintermediation

One factor that has influenced the financial assets selected by financial institutions for their portfolios from time to time is the phenomenon of **disintermediation.** Exactly opposite from the intermediation of funds, disintermediation means the withdrawal of funds from a financial intermediary by ultimate lenders (SBUs) and the lending of those funds directly to ultimate borrowers (DBUs). In other words, disintermediation involves the shifting of funds from indirect finance to direct and semidirect finance (see Exhibit 2.10).

You engage in disintermediation when you remove funds from a savings account at the local bank and purchase common stock or other financial assets through a broker.

EXHIBIT 2.10

**Financial
Disintermediation**

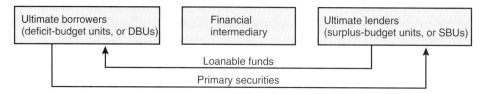

The phenomenon is more likely to occur during periods of high and rapidly rising interest rates, when the higher returns demanded by savers may outpace the interest rates offered by financial intermediaries. Disintermediation forces a financial institution to surrender funds and, if severe, may lead to losses of assets and ultimate failure. A good example is provided by savings and loan associations which, during the 1980s and early 1990s, lost billions of dollars in assets due to massive withdrawals of funds by worried depositors who feared the loss of their savings. Although intermediaries are forced to be more liquid and reduce their credit-granting activities during periods of disintermediation, there is no evidence that the *total* flow of credit through the financial system is necessarily reduced during such periods.

New Types of Disintermediation

Some authorities argue that new forms of disintermediation have appeared in recent years, some initiated by financial intermediaries themselves and some by their borrowing customers. For example, some banks in recent years have sold off some of their loans because of difficulties in raising capital. At the same time, some of their largest borrowing customers have learned how to raise funds directly from the open market (i.e., through direct and semidirect finance) rather than borrowing from a bank or other financial intermediary. These new forms of disintermediation have tended not only to slow the growth of some financial institutions but also to gradually reduce somewhat the overall importance of traditional financial intermediaries within the global financial system. A substantial volume of funds today flow through the financial system via direct and semidirect finance as well as through indirect finance.

2.15 Bank-Dominated versus Security-Dominated Financial Systems

While many lesser-developed financial systems are often referred to as *bank-dominated financial systems* because of the dominance of banks and similar financial intermediaries in supplying credit and attracting savings, many financial systems today are becoming *security-dominated financial systems,* in which traditional intermediaries play somewhat lesser roles in the lending and saving process and growing numbers of borrowers sell securities (such as stocks and bonds) directly to the public to raise the funds they need. For example, several nations in Asia today find themselves in transition from being heavily bank-dominated financial systems to increasingly security-oriented financial systems, though most of these countries have a long way to go in significantly reducing bankers' dominant position within their financial systems. In the long run, this trend toward more security-dominated financial systems may result in greater competition within the financial marketplace and, perhaps, higher returns for savers.

QUESTIONS TO HELP YOU STUDY

13. What is *direct finance? Semidirect finance? Indirect finance?*

14. In the evolution of the financial system, which came first—direct, indirect, or semidirect finance? Why do you think this is so?

15. What are the essential differences between *primary* and *secondary securities?* Why are these instruments important to the operation of the financial system?

16. In what different ways are financial institutions classified or grouped? Why are such classifications or groupings important in helping us understand what different financial institutions do and what kinds of financial assets they prefer to hold?

17. Which financial institutions are the *largest* within the financial system? Why do you think this is so?

18. What factors influence the particular financial assets each financial institution acquires?

19. What is *disintermediation* and why is it important? How has disintermediation changed in recent years?

20. Explain the difference between a *bank-dominated financial system* and a *security-dominated financial system.* Why might this distinction be an important one?

MARKETS ON THE NET: The Most Important Web Sites for This Chapter

Bondsonline (bondsonline.com)
Encyclopedia.com (encyclopedia.com/)
Federal Reserve Bank of Atlanta (frbatlanta.org)
Federal Reserve Bank of New York (ny.frb.org)
Moody's Investors Service (moodys.com)
Money Magazine (money.com)

New York Stock Exchange (nyse.com)
Standard & Poor's Corporation (standardandpoor.com)
The Bond Market Association (investinginbonds.com)
U.S. Bureau of Economic Analysis (bea.gov)
U.S. Bureau of Labor Statistics (bls.gov)

www.mhhe.com/rose9e

Summary of the Chapter's Main Points

The global financial system of money and capital markets performs the important function of channeling savings into investment. In that process a unique kind of asset in the economy—a *financial asset*—is created.

- Financial assets represent *claims against the income and assets* of individuals and institutions issuing those claims. There are three major categories of financial assets—*money, debt,* and *equities.* A fourth instrument, *derivatives,* is closely related to financial assets, deriving its value from these assets.

- *Money* is among the most important of all financial assets in the economy because it serves as a medium of exchange to facilitate purchases of goods and services, a standard for valuing all items bought and sold, a store of value (purchasing power) for the future, and a reserve of liquidity (immediate spending power). Despite all these advantages, money has a weakness—susceptibility to inflation (i.e., a rising price level), because its rate of return is normally so low. In contrast, the financial assets represented by *debt* or *equity* securities, and often by *derivatives* as well, carry greater average yields but, unlike money, may incur loss when converted into immediately spendable funds.

- The creation of financial assets occurs within the financial system through three different channels—direct, semidirect, or indirect finance. *Direct finance* involves the direct exchange of financial assets for money in which borrowers (deficit-budget units, or DBUs) and lenders (surplus-budget units or SBUs) meet directly with each other to conduct their business. *Semidirect finance* involves the use of a broker or dealer to help bring borrower and lender together and reduce information costs. *Indirect finance* refers to the creation of financial assets by financial intermediaries who accept *primary securities* from ultimate borrowers (DBUs) as their principal earning assets and issue *secondary securities* to ultimate savers (SBUs) to raise funds.

- *Financial intermediaries* (such as banks, pension funds, and insurance companies) have grown to dominate most financial systems today due to their greater expertise, efficiency, and capability in diversifying away some of the risks involved in lending money.

- One of the most serious management problems encountered by some financial intermediaries is *disintermediation*—the loss of funds from an intermediary to direct or semidirect finance. Much of the disintermediation experienced by modern intermediaries has occurred due to *financial innovation.* Borrowers have found new ways to obtain the funds they need without going through a financial intermediary.

- Finally, financial systems around the world appear to fall into one of two broad categories—*bank-dominated financial systems* and *security-dominated financial systems.* In bank-dominated systems the majority of financial assets arise from the banking system. When banks get into trouble the financial system itself may experience difficulties with risk exposure and slower growth. In security-dominated financial systems, by contrast, security brokers and dealers tend to be leaders in the financial system and often provide the greatest volume of funds to those in need of new capital. Security-dominated financial systems are heavily dependent upon direct and semidirect finance (i.e., the open market), while bank-dominated systems tend to rely upon financial intermediaries (indirect finance) for the raising of funds.

Key Terms Appearing in This Chapter

financial asset, 26	external financing, 29
money, 27	deficit-budget unit (DBU), 34
equities, 27	surplus-budget unit (SBU), 34
debt securities, 27	balanced-budget unit (BBU), 34
derivatives, 27	inflation, 37
internal financing, 28	deflation, 37

Problems and Issues

1. In a recent year, the various sectors of the economy listed below reported the following *net* changes in their financial assets and liabilities (measured in billions of dollars):

	Net Acquisitions of Financial Assets	Net Increase in Liabilities
Households	$434.6	$292.0
Farm businesses	2.7	−2.5
Nonfarm noncorporate businesses	8.7	35.0
Nonfinancial corporations	84.9	127.8
State and local governments	74.8	60.6
U.S. government	13.0	236.3
Foreign individuals and institutions	150.7	29.0
Federal Reserve System	32.0	31.2
Commercial banking	256.0	245.7
Private nonbank financial institutions	556.9	590.7

Using these figures, indicate which sectors were deficit-budget sectors and which were surplus-budget sectors for the year under study. Were there any balanced-budget sectors? For all these sectors *combined,* were more funds loaned or more funds borrowed? Why do you think there is a discrepancy between total funds loaned and total funds borrowed?

2. In this chapter, a number of different types of financial transactions were discussed: direct finance, semidirect finance, indirect finance (intermediation), and disintermediation. Examine each of the following financial transactions and indicate which type it is. (*Note:* Some of the transactions described below involve more than one type of financial transaction. Be sure to identify *all* types involved.)

    a. Borrowing money from a bank.

    b. Purchasing a life insurance policy.

    c. Selling shares of stock through a broker.

    d. Withdrawing money from a savings deposit account and lending it to a friend.

    e. Selling shares of stock to a colleague at work.

    f. Your corporation's contracting with an investment banker to help sell its bonds.

    g. Writing a bank check to purchase stock from your broker.

3. Each year in the United States, as the April income tax deadline nears, checking account balances go up nationwide as corporations and individuals get ready to

pay their taxes. If the majority of these funds were to come from household savings accounts in banks, what effect would this funds movement have upon M1? M2? M3? If, instead, most of these funds were drained from retail money market funds, what would happen to M1? M2? M3? Finally, if maturing large time deposits (CDs) were used, what would happen to M1? M2? M3?

4. ITT Corporation in the most recent period reported current sales receipts of $542 million, current operating expenditures of $577 million, and net new debt issued of $5 million. What change in holdings of financial assets must have occurred over the period? Was ITT a deficit-, surplus-, or balanced-budget unit in the most recent period? Explain why.

5. What would happen to the purchasing power of the U.S. dollar if the base period for the cost of living index were 1980 = 100 and the index reached the following levels in the indicated years?

    a. 1985—116

    b. 1990—127

    c. 1995—134

    d. 2000—151

    e. 2005—170

Standard & Poor's Market Insight and Web-Based Problems

STANDARD &POOR'S

1. The total volume of *primary securities* created by the banking system as a whole is referred to as *bank credit*. The total volume of *secondary securities* issued by the banking system is given by the banks' *total liabilities* minus any interbank lending, referred to as either "borrowings from other banks" or "federal funds purchased."

    a. Go to the Web site of the Federal Reserve System and find its H.8 statistical release: **federalreserve.gov/releases/h8/Current/.** Identify the total volume of primary and secondary securities for the banking system as a whole for the most recent quarter.

    b. Compute the *difference* between the total amount of credit created by the banking system in the form of primary securities and the banking system's liabilities in the form of secondary securities. What does this difference represent? What is this difference expressed as a percentage of total assets in the banking system?

    c. Go to Standard & Poor's Market Insight at **mhhe.com/edumarketinsight** and locate the annual balance sheets (look under "Excel Analytics") for two of the largest U.S. banks: Bank of America (BAC) and Wells Fargo (WFC). Identify the total amount of primary securities (investment securities plus loans, claims, and advances) and secondary securities (customer deposits plus short-term borrowings less federal funds purchased) for each bank. Perform similar calculations as in part (b) to determine what percentage of the total assets for each of these banks is the difference between primary and secondary securities on their books. Does this tell you anything about these very large banks relative to the banking industry as a whole?

2. Most major security brokerage houses engage in both *semidirect* and *indirect* financing in their roles as *financial intermediaries.*

    a. Identify which of these two types of financing should show up on the financial intermediary's balance sheet and which should not. Explain.

    b. How would you expect these two different types of financial transactions to show up on the financial intermediary's income statement?

    c. Go to Standard & Poor's Market Insight at **mhhe.com/edumarketinsight** and locate the annual balance sheet and income statement (under tab "Excel Analytics") for Lehman Brothers (LEH). Identify the *semidirect* and *indirect* finance activities on Lehman's financial statements. Explain. (*Note:* Lehman's financial statements are also available at **www.lehman.com.**)

Semester Project: A Study of the Federal Funds Market

We hope you enjoyed reading the introduction to this semester project about the federal funds market at the end of Chapter 1. In the discussion that follows, we introduce the second part of the Fed funds project and the questions we would like you to answer about that market. You will discover some of the most important reasons why we have a federal funds market today.

Earlier in this chapter we studied the important role played by *financial intermediaries* in the economy. You will recall that commercial banks are among the most important financial intermediaries, meeting the financial needs of both borrowers and lenders who otherwise would have to engage in a costly search process to find the terms of a loan contract agreeable to both parties. The federal funds market plays an important role in allowing banks in the United States to perform efficiently as intermediaries between borrowers and lenders. See if you can develop good answers to the questions that follow.

a. Consider a large, diversified economy like that in the United States, where there are "pockets" signifying both an excess demand for loans (potential borrowers) and an excess supply of funds (potential lenders). Now suppose (unrealistically) that banks must rely exclusively upon attracting local deposits in order to make loans in their local market areas and that there is no federal funds market. In this kind of world, how would you expect interest rates on loans of similar risk to vary across these local markets?

b. Now consider what would happen if a federal funds (interbank loan) market suddenly appeared. How would you expect interest rates on loans of similar risk to vary across markets? Explain how and why this would occur.

c. How would the introduction of a Fed funds market likely affect the overall volume of lending in the economy? Explain why you believe this would happen.

Selected References to Explore

Fitzgerald, Terry J. "Money Growth and Inflation." *Economic Commentary,* Federal Reserve Bank of Cleveland, August 1, 1999.

Gurley, John, and Edward S. Shaw. *Money in a Theory of Finance.* Washington, D.C.: Brookings Institution, 1960.

Revell, Jack. *The Recent Evolution of the Financial System.* New York: MacMillan, May 1997.

Valderrama, Diego. "Financial Development, Productivity, and Economic Growth." *FRBSF Economic Letter,* Federal Reserve Bank of San Francisco, June 27, 2003.

www.mhhe.com/rose9e

Chapter 3

The Financial Information Marketplace

Learning Objectives

in This Chapter

- You will be able to identify the most important sources of information about the money and capital markets and the financial system.

- You will discover why the efficient distribution of information within the financial system is so important and what can happen when relevant financial information is not readily available to all market participants.

- You will understand how any individual or institution active in the financial marketplace can keep track of the prices of financial assets and interest rates.

- You will learn about the *Flow of Funds Accounts of the United States* and discover what is meant by "social accounting."

3.1   Introduction: The Importance of Information in the Financial Marketplace

Every day in the money and capital markets, individuals and institutions must make important financial decisions. For those who plan to borrow, for example, key decisions must be made concerning the timing of a request for credit and exactly where the necessary funds should be raised. Lenders of funds must make decisions on when and where to invest their limited resources, considering such factors as the risk and expected return on loans and securities available in the financial marketplace. Government policymakers also are intimately involved in the financial decision-making process. It is the responsibility of government to ensure that the financial markets function smoothly in channeling savings into investment and in creating a volume of credit sufficient to support business and commerce.

Sound financial decisions require adequate and reliable *financial information.* Borrowers, lenders, and those who make financial policy require data on the prices and yields attached to individual loans and securities today and the prices and yields likely to prevail in the future. A borrower, for example, may decide to postpone taking out a loan if it appears that the cost of credit will be significantly lower six months from now than it is today. Moreover, because economic conditions exert a profound impact on the money and capital markets, the financial decision maker must also be aware of economic data series that reflect trends in employment, prices, and related types of information.

Where do financial decision makers go to find the data they need? We may divide the sources of information relied upon by financial decision makers into five broad groups: (1) debt security prices and yields, (2) stock prices and dividend yields, (3) information on security issuers, (4) general economic and financial conditions, and (5) social accounting data. In this chapter, we will discuss several of the most important sources of each of these different kinds of information.

3.2   The Great Debate over Efficient Markets and Asymmetric Information

Before we examine the principal sources of information available to financial market participants, however, we need to be aware of a great debate going on in the field of finance today concerning the availability and cost of information. One view, referred to as the **efficient markets hypothesis,** contends that information relevant to the pricing (valuation) of loans, securities, and other financial assets is readily available to *all* borrowers and lenders at *negligible cost.* The other view, called **asymmetry** or the concept of asymmetric information, argues that the financial marketplace contains pockets of inefficiency in the availability and use of information. Some market players—for example, professional lenders of funds, auditors, attorneys, journalists, or members of management and the boards of directors of corporations—may possess special information that enables them to get a more accurate picture of the value and risk of certain assets. These "insiders" allegedly can earn excess returns by selectively trading financial assets based on the special information they have been able to acquire—information that would be costly for others to obtain.

In this chapter, we briefly sketch out how these two contrasting views of the information marketplace—efficient markets and asymmetric information—differ in terms of the cost and availability of relevant information to decision makers in the financial marketplace and ultimately affect the prices (values) of all financial assets.

efficient markets hypothesis

asymmetry

The Efficient Markets Hypothesis (EMH)

What Is an Efficient Market?   The efficient markets hypothesis (hereafter EMH) suggests that *all* information that has a bearing on the market value of stocks, bonds, and other financial assets will be used to value (price) those assets. *An efficient market neither wastes information nor misuses information.* Under the terms of the EMH, the money and capital markets will not consistently ignore information that can earn profits, so there won't be any profitable trades of assets that are not made (at least not for very long) and there will be no systematic mispricing of assets.

For example, if an individual has savings to invest in stocks and bonds, he or she will seek out information on the financial condition of the business firms issuing those particular financial assets, the quality of their management and products, the strength of each firm's industry, and the condition of the economy in which each firm operates. Each individual investor will rationally use *all* of the available information relevant to valuing the stocks and bonds he or she might wish to buy. Because all investors are likely to be seeking the same information for the same reasons, the current market price of any financial asset will reflect all relevant information that investors as a group have been able to obtain regarding that asset's true value. Because all information available has been used to establish the value of financial assets, no single user of that same information can consistently earn "excess returns" or "abnormal returns" by trading on information available to all. Rather, in an efficient marketplace, each financial asset will generate an "ordinary," "normal," or "expected" rate of return commensurate with its level of risk.

If the EMH is correct, any temporary deviation of actual returns from expected returns (i.e., excess positive or excess negative returns) *should be quickly eliminated as investors react to temporary underpricing* (when a financial asset's actual return rises *above* its expected return) *or temporary overpricing of assets* (when a financial asset's actual return falls *below* its expected return) *and make changes in their asset portfolios.* Investors in the money and capital markets will react to financial assets they perceive to be *underpriced* (with positive excess returns) or *overpriced* (with negative excess returns) by buying or selling the temporarily mispriced assets. In short, the discovery of a financial asset whose expected return lies consistently above or below its "expected," "ordinary," or "normal" return would be a signal of possible market inefficiency, inconsistent with the EMH. This would be true because, according to the EMH, rational market participants use *all* relevant information available to value assets all the time. Because all financial asset prices instantaneously incorporate all relevant information concerning asset values in an efficient market, no excess returns from trading assets will be available.

Moreover, when *new* relevant information reaches the marketplace, the prices (value) of financial assets normally *will* change, and according to the EMH, they will change *quickly* as investors possessing this new information move rapidly to seize any profitable opportunities that appear, bidding up the prices of some assets and lowering the prices of others. And because market prices respond only to *new* information, which by its nature is unpredictable, the value of financial assets cannot be predicted consistently. If we could consistently predict asset values, this would be evidence of an inefficient market in which not all information is being fully utilized.

The essential contribution that the EMH makes to our understanding of the money and capital markets is to suggest that the current prices of all financial assets represent the *optimal use* of available information. And each asset's price, determined by demand-and-supply forces in the financial marketplace, is an optimal forecast of each asset's fundamental value.

In fact, a financial asset's current market price is the *best estimate* of that asset's expected fundamental value. However, each asset's fundamental value will vary with the state of the world (e.g., the condition of the economy, and the current concerns of asset buyers about risk) prevailing at the time the asset is being traded. Therefore, the current price of a financial asset equals its expected fundamental value given all possible states of the world recognized by buyers and sellers actively trading in the market. Under the terms of the EMH, the price of a financial asset must already embody *all* of the information relevant to the valuation of that asset, including all present and past information.

Different Forms of the EMH   In recent years, the EMH has been split into three different versions based on what each assumes to be true about the availability and cost of information. These three versions of the EMH are:

To examine the evidence for and against the efficient markets hypothesis see, for example, investorhome.com

1. *Weak form of the EMH,* which argues that the current prices of financial assets contain all information that buyers and sellers have been able to obtain on the past trading of those assets: their *price history and past volume of trading.* Moreover, this past price and trading information is publicly available and of negligible cost to obtain. No one buyer or seller of financial assets can earn excess profits beyond those that are "normal" or "expected" for the amount of risk taken on from trading on this historical price and volume information. If this were not true, investors would have figured out long ago how to profit from such historical data and asset prices would have been adjusted accordingly, eliminating further opportunities for exceptional returns.

2. *Semistrong form of the EMH,* which contends that the current prices of stocks, bonds, and other financial assets already reflect *all publicly available information* affecting the value of these financial instruments, including information about past prices and volume, the financial condition and credit rating of each issuer, any published forecasts, the condition of the economy, and all other relevant information. All buyers and sellers are rational and use all publicly available information to help them value financial assets. No one buyer or seller will, therefore, find opportunities for exceptional profits by trading on publicly available information.

3. *Strong form of the EMH,* which argues that the current prices of financial assets capture *all* the information—*both public and private*—that is relevant to the value of financial instruments. This includes the information possessed by "insiders," such as the officers, directors, and principal owners of a corporation issuing stocks and bonds or even accountants, attorneys, or journalists who work with the company and have access to its privileged information.

Repeated research studies tend to support the weak and semistrong forms of the EMH. Only limited opportunities for exceptional profits flowing from trading on past or present publicly available information appear to exist. The strong form of the EMH, however, has aroused the most controversy and resulted in mixed research findings, especially because of the existence of insider trading activities and because of the apparent presence of pockets of special information asymmetrically scattered throughout the financial system.[1]

Insiders and Insider Trading   The word "insiders" has come to have a sinister meaning for most of us. It smacks of something illegal or unfair. Someone has special knowledge or special privileges and can, at will, take advantage of that knowledge or

---

[1]For further discussion of research findings regarding the EMH, see Chapter 20 on the market for corporate stock.

privilege and profit from it, perhaps at our expense. Nowhere is the term "insider" more recognized and more often condemned than in the money and capital markets.

What Is Insider Trading?   The board of directors of a company, its officers or managers, and even many of its staff employees may know something about its condition that the public doesn't know, and as such, they may be able to benefit from that knowledge, perhaps by buying or selling the firm's stock in advance before the public becomes aware of what's really going on. Section 10(b)-5 of the U.S. Securities and Exchange Act of 1934 forbids any "manipulative or deceptive device" in trading securities and other financial assets, and Section 16(c) of the Securities and Exchange Act requires all trading by insiders to be reported to the Securities and Exchange Commission (SEC) within the first 10 days of the month following the particular month an insider trade has occurred. These insider trades are reported in the SEC's *Official Summary of Insider Transactions.* Recent federal laws have raised the maximum criminal penalties for insider trading up to a million dollars and have made it possible for judges to set jail terms for offenders of up to 10 years.

When Is Insider Trading Legal or Illegal?   Recent research suggests that **insider trading** frequently "works" in the sense that insiders often win exceptional ("abnormal" or "excess") returns on the trading of financial assets. For example, approximately one-half of the increase in the price of a firm's stock associated with the appearance of "new" information occurs *prior* to the release of that information to the public. These "early" price movements suggest that trading is taking place by insiders or by others privy to the "new" information before it becomes public knowledge.

insider trading

One of the most famous insider trading cases in history involved Michael Milken, a securities dealer and broker who worked with numerous companies to arrange their new bond and stock offerings and used some of the information he gained to earn millions of dollars in the financial markets. Ultimately, Milken paid fines in the hundreds of millions of dollars and went to prison for a time, eventually receiving a presidential pardon.

Actually, insiders can use privileged information legally if they provide that information to the public *before* they go into the money and capital markets to trade financial instruments. However, the number of insider trading cases prosecuted in court has been rising, despite doubts expressed by some experts that anyone is really consistently hurt by insider trading activity. In fact, insider deals may, under certain circumstances, actually be beneficial to the efficient functioning of the financial marketplace.

For example, consider managers who produce performance improvements for their company. Shouldn't they be able to benefit from trading in their firm's stock? Governments that penalize insider trading may actually discourage business managers from taking on risk and demonstrating their superior managerial capabilities. Other experts argue that businesses themselves, not the government, should decide if they want to permit or prohibit insiders from trading in their bonds, stocks, or other financial instruments. Moreover, they argue, insider-trading activity may actually *improve* market efficiency by encouraging more rapid information flows and quicker adjustments in the prices of financial assets to the appearance of *new* information. As a result, financial assets may be more correctly priced more quickly. This would tend to reduce risk to investors who hold ownership (equity) shares in a particular business.

The Concept of Asymmetric Information

What if, contrary to the efficient markets hypothesis, we lived in a world where *all* relevant information about the true value of financial assets was *not* readily available or was *not* costless to obtain? What would happen if some important information

ETHICS IN THE MONEY
AND CAPITAL MARKETS

What Is Legal and Illegal Insider
Trading in the Money
and Capital Markets?

Defining what types of insider activity are legal and what forms are illegal is one of the toughest distinctions to make, and many experts in the field flatly disagree. One problem is deciding who an "insider" really is. Certainly the board of directors, management, and employees of a company whose stocks, bonds, and other financial assets are publicly traded would qualify as privileged "insiders." These individuals are said to owe a *fiduciary duty* to their firm to act in their company's best interest and the best interests of its stockholders (owners). If these people personally benefit from inside information, they may be charged with breaching their fiduciary duty or with *misappropriating information* that belongs to their employer.

However, government lawyers often argue that outside consultants, investment bankers, and lawyers under contract to provide services to a firm also owe a fiduciary duty to that company and could be considered illegal "insiders," breaching their fiduciary duty if they use the information they receive to engage in related asset trading.

Beyond these particular groups of individuals, however, case law is badly split today. Generally speaking, those who clearly have a fiduciary duty because they are paid to work for a firm and benefit personally from using that firm's information to score profits in the market run the risk of prosecution. However, if you do *not* work for such a firm and still obtain insider information that you use to score trading profits, there may be no legal violation because there may be no fiduciary responsibility.

This happened to a print shop worker in the *Chiarella vs. the United States* case (1986) because of profit-generating information that Mr. Chiarella allegedly obtained while setting copy for the corporate clients of his printing firm. However, Mr. Chiarella went free because the Supreme Court found no evidence that he had a fiduciary duty to the firms whose reports he read.

On the other hand, you might be brought to trial on misappropriation of information if you are working for a company that has a relationship with another firm and just happen to overhear some nonpublic information and proceed to trade on it. This happened in the case of *James H. O'Hagan* vs. *the United States* (1996). Mr. O'Hagan allegedly found out about a proposed acquisition of Pillsbury—a case being worked on by attorneys in his law firm—and allegedly used that information to generate trading profits. Ultimately, the Supreme Court ruled that misappropriation of information had occurred with respect to the defendant's law firm. Unfortunately, the courts have mixed records on whether misappropriation of information or the existence of fiduciary duty can be broadly applied to individuals who are not employees or owners of a business firm.

pertinent to financial decision making were distributed *asymmetrically?* Suppose *some* individuals and institutions had access to pockets of important information concerning the true value and risk of financial assets and others did not.

The asymmetric view says that there *are* pockets of special information—a "lumpiness" in the supply of relevant information about financial assets. These pockets may include corporate insiders, journalists, security dealers, and financial analysts who possess unique analytical skills in spotting profitable trades. These possessors of special knowledge need not be operating illegally. Indeed, they may come by their unique talents in assessing value and risk through rigorous schooling and on-the-job training or by virtue of the special location they occupy within the financial system. For example, every year hundreds of corporations flock to college campuses to hire graduates whom they believe have the potential to become expert judges of the quality of financial assets.

Attempts by those armed with special information to exploit asymmetries in information could have great consequences for the financial marketplace as a whole. For example, with asymmetrically distributed information, there will be variations in both the quantity and the quality of information available. Unfortunately, most users of financial information cannot easily assess its quality at the time they must pay for it. Thus, considerable incentive exists in the money and capital markets for sellers of information to make wild claims about the quality and value of the information they are selling. It is not clear that the money and capital markets have yet developed an effective mechanism for policing the quality and truthfulness of information (as exemplified recently by the financial problems of such firms as Enron Corp. and Global Crossing), although, over time, those who provide misleading information may suffer a loss of reputation and eventually exit the industry due to lack of demand for their services. In short, the presence of imperfect or "bad" information may lead to market inefficiency, thwart the making of optimal decisions, and lead to more government intervention in the marketplace in an effort to fix the problems that asymmetrically distributed and poor quality information can create.

The asymmetric information theory does not necessarily contradict the weak and semistrong forms of the EMH. It concedes that the value of financial assets will capture all publicly available information. However, it is inconsistent with the strong form of the EMH in believing that some market participants have sufficient access to special (private) information that they can, at times, profit from, thereby earning excess returns. Moreover, where asymmetries are very strong, a financial market can misfire, misallocate resources, and even collapse.

Problems Informational Asymmetries Can Create: Lemons and Plums

Asymmetries can create many difficulties in the availability and distribution of information. One of the most familiar—often called the *lemons problem*—has confronted used car buyers ever since the automobile was invented. Everyone who has ever purchased a used car is aware of the risks involved in the process. The buyer does not know for sure whether the used automobile he or she is looking at is a real "lemon"—a continuing source of trouble and grief as repair bills mount—or if the car is a "plum"—a solid piece of transportation that runs and runs with few problems. The seller, in hopes of getting a higher price, has a strong incentive to misrepresent the car as a *plum*. Unless he or she is convinced this is true, the buyer will probably be unwilling to pay the full price for a plum due to the risk that the car will ultimately turn out to be a lemon. The seller possesses special ("inside") information built up by personal experience with the vehicle; the buyer cannot obtain this information except at considerable cost (such as by hiring a mechanic to do an inspection of the vehicle).

A similar problem confronts the loan officer of a bank. Dozens of customers come in every day asking for loans and claiming they will use the requested funds for a good (hopefully, profitable and legal) purpose that meets the lending institution's credit standards and promising that they will repay their loans on time. Clearly, the loan officer can't be sure without incurring substantial costs which of his or her customers is a lemon or a plum. Equally frustrating, some customers who were plums when they took out their first loan may now be lemons due to changing circumstances, such as the loss of a job or the failure of a business. This asymmetry problem helps explain why credit rating agencies have become so important to lending institutions that willingly pay the added expense required to have someone accumulate and evaluate the credit histories of borrowing businesses and households.

One more observation concerning the lemons problem is worth noting. Given the right circumstances, it can be shown that a market divided between lemons and plums can eventually become largely a market in which *only lemons are offered for sale*. This can happen because buyers will be unwilling to pay a premium price for plums if there is a substantial probability they will, in fact, be purchasing lemons. However, the seller, possessed of inside information, knows whether he or she owns a plum and will usually be unwilling to sell a plum for the price of a lemon. If there is no low cost way around this asymmetry problem, the ultimate result over time is that the plums will be driven from the market and only lemons will remain to be sold. *Lower-value assets will drive out higher-value assets.*

What can happen to used cars also can happen to financial assets, such as loans. Unless significant informational asymmetries can be overcome, lower-quality borrowers can drive away higher-quality borrowers who are unwilling to borrow at the higher interest rates that lower-quality borrowers must pay. This is a situation in which one price alone (such as the interest rate on a loan) cannot effectively separate the lemons from the plums. Something else is needed to insure that markets function efficiently, including independent audits, warranty contracts, loan commitment fees, and other devices.

Incidentally, if mispricing tends to drive higher-quality borrowers out of a particular market, where might those borrowing institutions go to get the funds they need? One way of escaping this dilemma is to turn to other markets where informational asymmetries may be less of an issue. As we noted in the previous chapter, a new form of *disintermediation* has occurred in recent years in which the largest, top-quality borrowers are avoiding traditional lending institutions, such as banks and insurance companies. Instead, they are going straight to the *open market,* selling their bonds, stocks, and other financial assets directly to global investors. In contrast, smaller borrowers with significant informational problems (such as unaudited financial statements) have frequently come to depend upon banks and other traditional lenders for the credit they need. In short, the existence of informational asymmetries has helped to restructure some of our most important marketplaces.

Problems Asymmetries Can Create: Adverse Selection

A related problem revolves around differences in the risk presented by different groups of customers who want to enter into contracts with financial institutions. In this case, information asymmetry exists *before* the parties to a contract reach an agreement. When an asymmetrical distribution of information is already present, it can drastically alter the nature of contracts that a business firm is willing to write in order to serve its customers.

For example, banks face an *adverse selection* problem with one of their most important services: checking accounts. To a banker, there are two principal categories of checking account customers: (1) those who hold high deposit balances and write few checks, giving the bank more money to lend while the low level of account activity keeps bank costs down, and (2) those customers who keep low balances in their account but write lots of checks, giving the bank few funds to invest while heavy account activity runs up bank costs. When a customer walks in to open a new account, the banker doesn't know what kind of checking account customer he or she will be. Only the customer has the "inside" information on what kind of checking account user he or she is likely to be.

If the banker sets a single, average price for all checking account customers in such an asymmetric situation, the bank runs the risk of being *adversely selected against* by its potentially most profitable customers. The preferred high-balance, low-activity customers will leave because the one price set by the bank is likely to be too high for them, but that price may be too low to cover the bank's operating costs in serving the less preferred low-balance, high-activity checking account customers. Another bank could simply enter the market with a checking account service that is cheaper and more attractive to high-balance customers and attract away the most profitable accounts. The first bank would be "adversely selected against" by those particular customers it most wanted to attract.

How does the first bank mitigate this problem of adverse selection? The most common technique used today is to set up a *conditional price schedule* in which the prices vary based on how much money each customer keeps on deposit and how many checks are written each month. The customer then chooses the most appropriate checking account plan. Such an array of different prices (rather than having only one price) for the same service, based on each customer's usage level and deposit balance, helps a bank to ensure that low-balance, high-activity customers will pay higher service fees and that low-activity, high-balance customers will pay lower fees. In effect, the customer "self-selects" his or her own checking account plan according to the "inside" information he or she possesses. Moreover, the customer's choice of any particular deposit plan signals to the banker what kind of customer he or she is likely to be.

Thus, in some situations the problem of asymmetric information can be mitigated by the use of *signaling:* letting participants in the marketplace who possess special or inside information take actions that will reveal the nature of that unique information to other potential participants. For example, an insider in a corporation who knows that his or her company is in trouble can signal the problem to the public by selling the company's stock. If the public happens to see insiders selling out, they too may begin to sell, driving the value of the company's stock lower in the financial marketplace.

Problems Asymmetries Can Create: Moral Hazard

moral hazard

Another problem in information asymmetry often arises *after* contracts are agreed to between buyers and sellers or principals and agents. One party to a contract may decide to pursue his or her own self-interest at the expense of other parties to the agreement. This is known as **moral hazard** and it often arises because of poorly drafted contracts or ineffective monitoring activity by the principal parties involved.

For example, the managers of a corporation, instead of managing the company for the benefit of the firm's stockholders, may grant themselves generous benefit packages and lavish offices, boosting their firm's expenses well beyond what is necessary to efficiently produce and sell the firm's products. Management may also conceal bad performance, take on excessive risk, misrepresent the outcomes of projects, or simply shirk in doing their jobs. The result is that management—the *agent* of the stockholders— optimizes its own well-being, while the stockholders—the *principals* in this instance— receive less than optimal returns on their stock. Because information on what is happening inside the firm is often difficult and expensive to obtain, the stockholders (principals) may not be aware for a long time (if ever) of the unnecessary expenses that their agent—the firm's management—is creating. (The act of running up operating costs higher than they need to be is often called *expense preference behavior.*) In this instance the agents are creating a "moral hazard" problem for a company's principals (its shareholders).

Moral hazard problems can lead to unexpected consequences. For example, elimination of moral hazard problems can be costly, both in discovering the problem and in rewriting the contract between principal and agent to get rid of the problem. Usually, moral hazard problems are dealt with by placing appropriate incentives in principal-agent contracts so that agents will want to act more in line with the interests of principals. For example, the board of directors of a corporation, representing its stockholders, might tie management salaries to the actual performance of the firm, such as its profitability or growth of sales, or to other performance measures linked to the firm's stock price.

Asymmetry, Efficiency, and Real-World Markets

No market in the real world in which we live is either completely efficient or completely asymmetric. Rather, all real-world markets have elements of *both* efficiency and asymmetry. Recent research has found some evidence that appears to be inconsistent with the pure efficient markets hypothesis. For example, there is evidence that

In this chapter we are exploring the damage that can be done to individuals and institutions in a situation where information is asymmetrically distributed. The classic case, as we saw earlier in this chapter, is the *lemons problem*—sellers have knowledge about the true worth of an asset, but buyers cannot access that information without incurring significant costs. As a result, quality items may be driven from the marketplace, leaving flawed merchandise for people to bid on.

The well-known global online marketer, eBay, which auctions off everything from autos to cordless drills, confronts this quality issue every day. eBay has attacked the "lemons" problem from several different directions. It warns sellers of the consequences of misrepresenting what they sell in terms of damage to their reputation, possible legal action, and possible loss of access to eBay's market. The firm cooperates with N.E.W. Customer Service in offering warranties to cover at least a portion of a buyer's loss. Moreover, claims that fully qualify may receive some reimbursement from eBay itself. Finally, eBay has set up an online dispute mechanism called *SquareTrade* where buyers and sellers may attempt to mediate their dispute.

None of the foregoing steps are without cost. However, as eBay has demonstrated, there are ways of dealing with an uneven distribution of quality information so that markets *can* function effectively.

some investors earn excess returns from trading the stock of *small firms*. Moreover, some market anomalies seem to run counter to a truly efficient market, such as unusually high stock returns on Fridays and unusually low stock returns on Mondays (known as the *weekend effect*). Stock prices also appear to display exceptionally high volatility in the short run, with some traders apparently buying on the basis of a stock's past performance (*momentum*) rather than buying on the basis of its fundamental value, temporarily driving its price higher, and then, subsequently, selling the stock as its price returns to its former level (a phenomenon called *mean reversion,* which also seems inconsistent with the efficient markets hypothesis). Perhaps real-world markets are split into segments: (1) a highly efficient segment, in which well-informed individuals and institutions (the "smart money") trade, and (2) a segment in which less-well-informed small investors trade, where information *is* asymmetrically distributed and the information that becomes public is of poorer quality.

We will see in the subsequent chapters of this book how financial market participants have moved to counter informational asymmetries by developing special kinds of expertise, forming special kinds of organizations (such as credit rating agencies, credit bureaus, and auditing firms), writing unique contractual agreements (such as detailed insurance and loan contracts that contain deductibles and commitment fees), using multiple prices for the same service to separate profitable from unprofitable clients, and striving continually to become more efficient and reduce operating costs. It is also useful to bear in mind that the possession of special or inside information does not always result in an advantage for its possessors. Research suggests that, at times, there may be a "curse of knowledge": *Some market participants may be so overloaded with information that they cannot effectively sort out what is relevant and what is irrelevant in order to make a profitable decision.*

Informational Asymmetries and the Law

One way to deal with market asymmetries is to pass laws and regulations designed to improve the flow of information between buyers and sellers and to protect the public against deception in valuing financial assets. For example, in 1933 the United States passed the Securities Act, requiring companies selling financial assets across state lines to submit a *prospectus* to a federal agency, the Securities and Exchange Commission (SEC), giving detailed economic and financial information on the firm's condition and prospects. Once the prospectus is approved, the SEC requires that the issuer of stocks, bonds, and other financial assets supply a prospectus to any investor interested in buying those instruments. Misrepresentation or fraud in a prospectus can trigger lawsuits by the SEC and by investors against a business firm selling financial assets, its directors, and any public accounting firms involved, as well as dealers handling the sale of those assets.

In 1934 the Securities Exchange Act was passed, requiring corporate insiders to follow guidelines in trading the financial instruments of firms with which they are affiliated in order to avoid excessive profit-taking from privileged information. This law also moved to outlaw fraud and misrepresentation in trading financial assets already issued, requiring assets traded on exchanges and trading firms themselves to register with the SEC and to provide detailed annual reports to the SEC and to their own shareholders. Shortly thereafter, the Maloney Act was passed, requiring trade associations, such as the National Association of Securities Dealers (NASD), to register with the SEC. Today, NASD tries to discourage cheating and deception of investors by enforcing an ethics code and by licensing dealers.

The Investment Company Act, passed in 1940, required mutual funds (investment companies) to register with the SEC and provide the shareholding public with reports on their activities and performance. The Investment Advisers Act, passed in the same year, required the registration of professional investment advisers, who also must report their procedures for analyzing and recommending investments. In 1970, the Securities Investor Protection Act set up the Securities Investor Protection Corporation (SIPC) to insure an investor against losses of up to $500,000 in securities and up to $100,000 in lost cash should his or her brokerage firm fail. The SIPC agrees to replace any assets lost due to the collapse of a brokerage firm, although it does not guarantee the value of those assets.

In the fall of 2000 the U.S. Securities and Exchange Commission passed Regulation FD (for Fair Disclosure). This required companies to disclose material financial information broadly rather than only to selected viewers (such as stockbrokers or security dealers). This supposedly gives *all* possible investors roughly equal access to market-moving information. Even more recently a settlement between the New York Attorney General's Office and major brokerage companies in 2003 restricted the exchange of privileged information between security brokers and their wealthiest clients who often pay large brokerage commissions and expect special treatment in return. At about the same time the SEC moved to block mutual funds from releasing inside information about the funds' portfolio strategies to hedge funds and other large investors. Rules such as these help to protect the public by giving them more equal access to pertinent information as an aid to sound financial decision making.

While the government regulations and controls recently put in place to mitigate the damaging effects of asymmetric information may be helpful in improving the efficiency of the financial markets, many observers think we have a long way to go in solving asymmetric information problems. They point, for example, to the case of Enron Corporation, a huge energy firm that filed for bankruptcy in 2001 and whose alleged insider dealings and questionable accounting practices cost investors billions in stock market losses and destroyed the retirement savings of many Enron employees. The accounting practices of major corporations need a closer look today to make sure that capital-market investors are getting the full amount of reliable and relevant information they need to make rational buy-sell decisions. The Sarbanes-Oxley Accounting Practices Act of 2002 makes chief executive officers (CEOs) and chief financial officers (CFOs) of public companies responsible when their firms dispense inaccurate or misleading information about the financial condition of the businesses they manage. Sarbanes-Oxley represents a step toward a more information-rich and information-reliable financial marketplace, but it is only a step in what is still a long road to travel. We turn now to look at some of the most important sources of financial information currently available to the public as a whole.

QUESTIONS TO HELP YOU STUDY

1. Why is the availability and reliability of financial information important to both borrowers and lenders of funds? What can happen when relevant information is missing?

2. Can you explain why financial information that is accurate and reliable is of great significance to government policymakers and regulators within the financial system?

3. Carefully explain what is meant by the term *efficient market*. Are there different *levels* of market efficiency?

4. Explain what is meant by *informational asymmetries*. What problems can these asymmetries create for participants in the money and capital markets?

5. What does it mean to say a financial asset is "temporarily overpriced" or "temporarily underpriced"? How can such a situation happen? Why is such overpricing or underpricing likely to be only temporary?

6. As you look at the real world around you, do you see examples of what seem to be efficient markets? Can you detect any real-world examples of what seem to be informational asymmetries? How did you identify these market situations?

7. What steps have been taken recently to promote greater accuracy and reliability of information concerning the financial marketplace and the valuation of financial assets?

3.3 Debt Security Prices and Yields: Sources of Information

Investors can get lots of information on investing in bonds through such sources as the Bond Market Association at investinginbonds.com

The concept of "efficient" markets assumes that information relevant to the valuation of *all* financial assets is readily available to the public *at low cost*. What kinds and what depth of information about the financial marketplace *does* the public receive? Let's begin with a look at some of the most popular information sources for debt securities, usually referred to as *bonds* and *notes*.

note

bond

Bonds and Notes   Bonds and notes are debt obligations issued by governments and corporations, usually in units (par values) of $1,000. A **note** is a shorter term written promissory obligation, usually not exceeding 5 years to maturity; a **bond** is a longer-term promissory note, at least 5 to 10 years to maturity and sometimes much longer. Although bonds and notes generally pay a fixed rate of return to their owner in the form of coupon income, their prices fluctuate daily as interest rates change. Therefore, although bonds and notes are often referred to as *fixed-income securities,* the investor may experience significant gains or losses on these instruments as their prices change if he or she chooses to sell the asset before it matures. Bonds and notes generally carry a set maturity date, at which time the issuer must pay the holder the asset's par value. These debt securities are generally identified by the name of the issuing company or governmental unit, their coupon (fixed interest) rate, and their maturity date.

Yield Series	1990	1992	1994	1996	1998	2000	2002	2004*
State and local government notes and bonds:								
Aaa-Moody's series	6.96%	6.09%	5.77%	5.52%	4.93%	5.58%	4.87%	4.42%
Bond buyer series	7.29	6.48	6.18	5.76	5.09	5.71	5.04	5.01
Corporate bonds:								
Seasoned issues, all industries	9.77	8.55	8.26	7.66	6.87	7.98	7.10	5.99
Moody's corporate bond indexes classified by rating:								
Aaa	9.32	8.14	7.97	7.37	6.53	7.62	6.49	5.54
Aa	9.56	8.46	8.15	7.55	6.80	7.83	6.93	5.91
A	9.82	8.62	8.28	7.69	6.93	8.11	7.18	6.08
Baa	19.36	8.98	8.63	8.05	7.22	8.36	7.80	6.44

EXHIBIT 3.1

Indicators of Average Bond Yields (Average Annual Yields in Percent)

Source: Board of Governors of the Federal Reserve System, *Federal Reserve Bulletin,* selected issues.

*2004 figures for January.

bid price

asked price

Bid and Asked Prices and Pricing Information Bonds and notes can be bought and sold through dealers who manage portfolio holdings of these securities. The dealers are referred to as "market makers" because each dealer creates a market for the securities that he or she holds by posting a **bid price,** the price at which the dealer is willing to purchase additional securities to add to his portfolio, and an **asked price,** the price at which the dealer is willing to sell from his portfolio.

Today traders require information regarding the prices and availability of debt securities on an up-to-the-minute basis. Computer networks report instant price quotations on the most actively traded bonds and similar financial instruments, supplemented by televised reports via channels such as the CNN Financial Network, Bloomberg, and CNBC. One of the most complete listings of daily price and yield quotations on bonds and notes appears in *The Wall Street Journal* (WSJ), published by Dow Jones & Company. In addition, most daily newspapers contain prices and yields on the most actively traded bonds.

Additional information on bond market investing and bond market behavior may be found in investinginbonds.com, bondsonline.com, and tradingedge.com

Recent changes in various bond yield indexes as reported in the *Federal Reserve Bulletin* and in the more recent monthly *Statistical Supplement to the Federal Reserve Bulletin* are shown in Exhibit 3.1. Note the fluctuations in bond yields, which reflect significant changes in economic and credit conditions during this period. This is why bond buyers pay a great deal of attention to announcements of new economic data each week, such as new information on auto sales, manufacturing employment, price inflation, or the construction of new homes. Any hint of softening in the economy or of reduced inflation often results in at least a short-term bond market price rally, pulling interest rates down and bond prices higher.

3.4 Stock Prices and Dividend Yields: Sources of Information

stocks

Of all the financial assets traded in the money and capital markets, **stocks** are among the most popular with active investors. Stock prices can be extremely volatile (especially the stock of smaller companies), offering the prospect of substantial capital gains if prices rise but also significant capital losses if prices tumble. Several corporations (such as General Electric and Verizon) pay dividends on their stock regularly, thus offering the buyer a relatively steady source of income as well as the opportunity for capital gains if prices go up. Unlike a bond, however, a share of stock is a certificate of ownership in a corporation, not a debt obligation. No corporation need pay dividends to its stockholders. In fact, some never have, preferring to retain all after-tax earnings in the business. In this section we summarize the kinds of public information that stock market investors have access to on a regular basis.

Price and Yield Information   As in the case of bonds, price and yield data on the most actively traded stocks are reported daily in the financial press as well as over television, radio, and the Internet. Most daily newspapers, along with *The Wall Street Journal* and other popular financial newssheets, list current stock prices. Each stock price quotation is identified by the abbreviated name of the company issuing it. High and low prices at which the stock has been traded during the past year and the most recent annual dividend declared by the issuing company are normally given. The dividend yield—the ratio of dividends to current price—often appears, along with the ratio of the stock's current price to the past 12 months of company earnings (the P-E ratio). Remaining entries in a financial newssheet may provide a summary of the previous business day's transactions in the markets on which that particular stock is bought and sold. The one-day sales volume, expressed in hundreds of shares, may also be shown, as well as the highest and lowest prices at which the stock was exchanged that day. The closing price for which the stock was traded in the last sale of the day is often reported, expressed in dollars and decimal fractions of a dollar.

Information on daily stock market developments for active investors may be found on the World Wide Web at such sites as moneycentral. msn.com/; fool.com; quote.com; nyse.com; and nasdaq.com

Stock prices for more than 1,700 companies in over 100 industries are provided by *The Value Line Investment Survey,* published weekly by Arnold Bernhard & Company of New York. Each company's business is described, and basic financial information, such as sales, net earnings, and long-term indebtedness, is provided for at least a decade. Individual stocks are also rated by *Value Line,* from those expected to be top performers down to those expected to be the poorest performers. Stock prices and basic financial data for individual companies are also presented in comprehensive reports compiled by Standard & Poor's Corporation (S&P). The performance of the shares issued by mutual funds is reported by Morningstar, which rates each mutual fund's recent performance using a star system of one to five. Five-star-rated mutual funds are considered by Morningstar to be among the best-performing and best-managed investment companies.

The stock market is watched closely by investors as a barometer of expectations in the business community. A rising trend in stock prices generally signals an optimistic assessment of future business prospects and expectations of higher corporate earnings. A declining market, on the other hand, is often a harbinger of adverse economic news and may signal a cutback in business investment and lower corporate earnings. Among the most important factors watched by stock traders are reports of corporate earnings, merger and dividend announcements, changes in corporate management, announcements of new products being introduced, changes in government policy that might affect interest rates (with the prospect of lower interest rates generally favorable for stocks), and apparent changes in the strength of the economy (as reflected in such data series as new orders to manufacturers of durable goods, new housing construction, the growth of business investment expenditures, changes in the level of business inventories, and measures of inflation).

For further information on stocks, bonds, and mutual funds see the Investment Company Institute at ici.org

Stock Price Indexes and Foreign Stock Prices   Many students of the financial markets follow several broad stock price indexes that reflect price movements in groups of similar quality securities. One of the most popular indexes is the Dow Jones Industrial Average of 30 stocks, including such major companies as General Motors and ExxonMobil. Dow Jones also reports a transportation average of 20 stocks (including such industry leaders as Federal Express) and a utility average of the shares of 15 leading utility companies (such as Pacific Gas and Electric). The utility average is of special importance to many investors because it appears to be highly sensitive to interest rate fluctuations, and some analysts regard it as a barometer of interest rate expectations.

To learn more about stock price indexes see such sources as That Money Show at pbs.org and through Standard & Poor's Corporation at stockinfo.standardpoor. com

Two of the most comprehensive stock market indicators available are Standard & Poor's 400 Industrial Stock Price Index and 500 Composite Stock Price Index, both of which include the most actively traded U.S. corporate equity shares. The S&P 500 includes the shares of 40 utility companies, 20 transportation firms, and 40 financial stocks not present in the S&P 400 industrial index. All five S&P stock series—the 400 Index, Utility Index, Transportation Index, Financial Stock Index, and the 500 Composite Index—are regarded as sensitive barometers of general stock price movements in the United States. An even broader price index than the S&P 500 Composite is the New York Stock Exchange Composite Index, which gives greatest weight to stocks having the highest market values. Considered an indicator of total market performance, the NYSE composite is often used to compare the performance of major institutional investors, such as investment companies and pension funds, against the market as a whole. Other broad market indicators include the NASDAQ Composite, which measures price movements in stocks sold over the counter rather than on the major exchanges, and the Wilshire 5000 Index, which is the broadest measure of stock market performance yet developed and includes more than 6,300 stocks—nearly all of them publicly traded stocks of corporations with U.S. headquarters that are traded on all major exchanges. The Wilshire is the best measure we currently have of overall stock market wealth in the United States.

Many newspapers and financially oriented magazines contain daily stock market diaries or summaries. Such summaries of recent market developments indicate both price movements and the volume of trading on the major exchanges. Examples may be found in *Barrons, Forbes, Fortune, Money,* and *The Wall Street Journal.* Market diaries or summaries usually report the total number of shares traded on a given day or week and the number of stocks advancing or declining in price.

You can track foreign stock price movements at such sites as stocksmart.com and finix.at

Finally, with the spreading globalization of markets, more and more savers and borrowers are turning to foreign markets to invest their savings and raise needed funds. Therefore, key information sources increasingly are reporting daily changes in security prices and interest rates in foreign trading centers, such as London, Frankfurt, Hong Kong, Singapore, Tokyo, and Sydney. To help foreign investors who deal predominantly in their own home currencies, there are also listings of currency exchange rates in various publications (such as the *Statistical Supplement to the Federal Reserve Bulletin, The Wall Street Journal,* and the *Financial Times*) so that they can translate a security's current price from one currency into another.

3.5 Information on Security Issuers

Want to know more about Moody's and Standard & Poor's? Try moodys.com or standardpoor.com

Moody's and Standard & Poor's Reports   Lenders of funds have a pressing need to secure accurate financial information on those individuals and institutions that seek to borrow funds or to sell their stock. Fortunately, financial information on many individual companies and other security issuers, particularly for the largest issuing institutions, is available from a wide variety of published sources.

Two of the most respected sources of information on major security issuers are Moody's Investors Service, Inc., and Standard and Poor's Corporation, both headquartered in New York City. In a series of annual publications, Moody's provides financial data on industrial corporations, financial institutions, utilities, and state and local units of government. The most widely known of Moody's annual publications include the *Industrial Manual, Bank and Finance Manual, Public Utility Manual,*

Transportation Manual, and *Municipal and Government Manual.* In the case of individual corporations, Moody's provides information on the history of each firm, names of key officers, and recent financial statements. In addition, Moody's assigns credit ratings to selected issuers of corporate and municipal bonds, commercial paper, and preferred stock as a guide for investors. These ratings are published in Moody's *Bond Record.* Standard & Poor's provides similar credit ratings for corporate and municipal bonds, assessing the likelihood of default on a security issue and the degree of protection afforded the buyer.

For further information about data and other types of information available from the SEC, see sec.gov

Securities and Exchange Commission (SEC) Reports   Even more extensive financial data are provided by the reports that corporations must file with the Securities and Exchange Commission (SEC). These SEC reports are available in many libraries on microfiche or microfilm. One company, Disclosure Incorporated, provides its subscribers with microfiche copies of more than 100,000 corporate documents filed each year by well over 10,000 companies. The most important of these corporate documents is the SEC's 10-K report, an annual statement that must be filed by most companies within 90 days after their fiscal year-end. These 10-K reports identify the principal products or services of each firm, provide a summary of its recent operations, note any securities outstanding, and list the names of key officers.

Company Histories   The backgrounds on thousands of businesses all over the world can be found by searching through a wide variety of private information sources. For example, *The International Directory of Company Histories* provides brief historical sketches of nearly 3,000 firms worldwide, while a service on CD-ROM called *Global Researcher SEC* provides information on the directors, officers, and leading shareholders for over 12,000 companies whose securities are traded in U.S. markets. A related CD-ROM source known as *Global Researcher Worldscope* provides financial data and news headlines for almost 15,000 firms that trade on leading stock exchanges around the world.

Learn more about Dun & Bradstreet at dnb.com

Dun & Bradstreet Ratings   Another useful source of data on individual business firms is Dun & Bradstreet, Inc. (D&B). This credit rating company collects information on approximately 3 million firms, making detailed financial reports available to its subscribers. Dun & Bradstreet also provides industrywide financial data so that the financial condition of an individual business borrower can be compared with that of other firms in the same industry. D&B's Key Business Ratios series includes key operating and financial ratios for more than 800 lines of business. Similar industrywide performance indicators are prepared and published in *Troy's Almanac* and in Risk Management Associates (RMA) *Annual Statement Studies* (which covers smaller firms in more than 400 lines of business). This information can be supplemented with news about individual industries and firms by checking *The Wall Street Journal Index,* the *New York Times Index,* and *Barron's Index.* Recently, a new Internet database called *Investext* was added, with financial reports and forecasts for more than 11,000 companies in over 50 different industries.

To discover more about information sources available from RMA, see especially pers.p.rmahq.org and the *Annual Statement Studies* link.

Financial Institutions   Information on banks and other financial institutions is available from a wide variety of sources, including trade associations in each industry and federal and state regulatory agencies. For example, the American Bankers Association, Life Insurance Association of America, Insurance Information Institute, and Credit Union National Association frequently provide annual reports or pamphlets describing recent industry trends. Studies of financial institutions' problems are found in specialized journals and magazines, such as the *Bankers Magazine, Financial*

Analysts Journal, Euromoney, The Economist, Forbes, Fortune, BusinessWeek, and the *Journal of Portfolio Management.*

Among key government agencies that provide annual reports and special studies of financial institutions' trends and problems are the Federal Deposit Insurance Corporation, Federal Reserve Board and Federal Reserve Banks, the Federal Home Loan Banks, and the Comptroller of the Currency. For example, the Federal Deposit Insurance Corporation (FDIC) has a detailed Web site that identifies all FDIC-insured depositories and provides financial data for each insured institution. Many government reports are available in university libraries or through the Superintendent of Documents in Washington, DC. There are also several popular directories that list the names of banks and other financial institutions and contain limited data on each institution, its address, and often the names of key officers. Among the most popular of these directories are *Moody's Bank and Finance Manual,* the *Thomson/Polk Bank Directory,* and *Qualisteam's List of Banks on the Internet.*

You can reach the Federal Deposit Insurance Corporation's Web site at fdic.gov, while the Comptroller of the Currency can be contacted at occ.treas.gov. The Federal Home Loan Banks are reachable at fhlbi.com

Credit Bureaus   Finally, information on individuals and families who seek credit is assembled and disseminated to institutional lenders by *credit bureaus.* The files of these bureaus include such information as the individual's place of residence and occupation, debts owed, and the promptness with which an individual pays his or her bills. Most credit bureaus maintain files on an individual's bill-paying record for up to seven years and may release that information only to lenders, employers, or licensing agencies who have a legitimate right to know the individual's credit standing. Individuals also have a right to see their credit files and verify their accuracy.

To discover more about what credit bureaus do, see The Consumer Data Industry Association at cdiaonline.org

3.6   General Economic and Financial Conditions

A number of different sources provide market participants with information on developments in the economy, prevailing trends in the money and capital markets, and actions by the government that may affect economic and financial conditions worldwide.

The Federal Reserve System   The Federal Reserve System releases large quantities of financial information to the public on request. Statistical releases available on a weekly, monthly, or quarterly basis cover such items as interest rates, money supply measures, industrial output, and international transactions. Information of this sort is summarized each month in the *Statistical Supplement to the Federal Reserve Bulletin,* published by the Board of Governors of the Federal Reserve System in Washington, DC. The Board also publishes the results of internal staff studies that examine recent financial trends or address major issues of public policy. Within the Federal Reserve System, the Federal Reserve banks scattered around the United States are also major suppliers of financial and economic information. Addresses for the Federal Reserve Board and all the Federal Reserve banks appear at the back of each quarterly *Federal Reserve Bulletin,* as well as on the Internet.

Learn more about the Federal Reserve Bulletin at federalreserve.gov

Other Domestic and International Sources of Information   A number of published sources regularly report on the status of the economy. Daily financial newspapers, such as *The Wall Street Journal* and the *Financial Times,* nearly always include important economic data. The U.S. Department of Commerce (USDC) maintains one of the most comprehensive collections of U.S. economic data available anywhere, including the latest statistics on consumer, government, and business spending, and on exports and imports. The USDC publishes several

For an excellent source of economic and financial data that can be easily downloaded into an Excel spreadsheet, see the Federal Reserve Bank of St. Louis's Web site: research.stlouisfed.org/fredII

For a comprehensive source of U.S. economic data, see doc.gov

convenient compilations of business data, including the annual *Statistical Abstract of the United States.*

Forecasts of *future* economic and financial developments are available from a wide variety of sources. For example, the Federal Reserve Bank of Philadelphia publishes the quarterly *Survey of Professional Forecasters,* which compiles a summary of the forecasts of leading economists regarding production, unemployment, inflation, and interest rates. Forecasts of annual capital spending based on repeated industry surveys are prepared by the U.S. Department of Commerce and McGraw-Hill Publications Company. Businesses often subscribe to the services of one or more of a number of economic consulting firms that prepare detailed forecasts of the nation's income and interest rates.

Important and interesting international Web sites include the International Monetary Fund at imf.org, the Bank for International Settlements at bis.org, the *Financial Times* at ft.com, and *Euromoney* at Euromoney.com

The growing internationalization of the financial markets has led to dramatic increases in new sources of information regarding foreign markets and institutions. Up-to-date security price and interest rate data are published in *The Wall Street Journal/Europe* from Brussels, and a corresponding *Asian Wall Street Journal* is issued from Hong Kong. *The Financial Times* of London is considered one of the finest daily newspapers in the world. *The Economist,* also published in London, deals with foreign business and political developments throughout the world. Of comparable quality is *Euromoney* (London), which monitors Europe's ongoing economic integration. For businesspersons interested in Asia and the Pacific Rim, such magazines as *Asiaweek,* the *Far Eastern Economic Review,* and *Asiamoney* offer greater understanding of Pacific economies and institutions.

QUESTIONS TO HELP YOU STUDY

8. If you needed to gather information for a possible stock or bond purchase, where would you go to get such information? What are the principal sources to check?

9. Suppose you wanted to evaluate the financial condition of a business firm. What major sources exist that could assist you in getting that kind of information?

10. Suppose you were planning to take a job with a particular company. What would you want to know about the company and where could you find that information?

11. If you wanted to gather information about the state of the U.S. economy, which information sources would likely be most helpful to you?

12. Where could you go to gather information about the global economy?

3.7 Social Accounting Data

Students of the economy and the financial markets also make use of social accounting systems to keep track of broad trends in economic and financial conditions. **Social accounting** refers to a system of record keeping that reports transactions between the principal sectors of the economy, such as households, financial institutions, corporations, and units of government. The two most closely followed social accounting systems in the United States are the National Income Accounts and the Flow of Funds Accounts.

social accounting

National Income and Product Accounts

National Income and Product Accounts

The **National Income and Product Accounts** (NIPAs) are compiled and released quarterly by the U.S. Department of Commerce. These accounts present data on the nation's production of goods and services, income flows, investment spending, consumption,

National Income and Product Accounts: The Components of U.S. Gross Domestic Product (GDP), 2004* ($ Billions, Current)

Source: U.S. Department of Commerce and the Board of Governors of the Federal Reserve System's *Flow of Funds Accounts.*

*Figures are for the first quarter of 2004 and annualized.

Personal consumption expenditures		$ 8,053.1
Durable goods	$ 955.9	
Nondurable goods and services	7,097.2	
Gross private domestic investment		1,818.6
Fixed investment	1,790.2	
Change in private inventories	28.4	
Net U.S. exports of goods and services		−528.5
Exports	1,134.4	
Imports	1,662.9	
Government consumption expenditures and gross investment		2,116.4
Federal	802.4	
State and local	1,314.0	
Gross domestic product (GDP)		$11,512.8

Data on the U.S. economy may be found at such Web sites as economagic.com. In addition, the American Economic Association sponsors a Web site that includes *Resources for Economists on the Internet,* which contains an extensive list of links to Web sites dealing with forecasting and consulting, at aeaweb.org/RFE/consult/index.html

Flow of Funds Accounts

and savings. Probably the best-known account in the NIPA series is gross domestic product (GDP)—a measure of the market value of all goods and services produced in the U.S. economy within the geographical boundaries of the United States. It is the most important barometer of overall U.S. economic activity. GDP may be broken down into the uses to which the nation's output of goods and services are put. For example, Exhibit 3.2, drawn from the U.S. Department of Commerce and the *Statistical Supplement to the Federal Reserve Bulletin,* indicates the size of the U.S. GDP and its major components for 2004.

The National Income and Product Accounts provide valuable information on the level and growth of the nation's economic activity, which have a profound impact on conditions in the money and capital markets. However, these accounts provide little or no information on financial transactions themselves. For example, one component of the NIPA system reports the annual amount of personal savings, but it does *not* show how those savings are allocated among purchases of bonds, stocks, and other financial assets. This task is left to the **Flow of Funds Accounts** prepared by the Board of Governors of the Federal Reserve System.

The Flow of Funds Accounts

Flow of funds data have been published quarterly by the Federal Reserve System since 1955. Monthly issues of the *Statistical Supplement to the Federal Reserve Bulletin* contain the latest summary reports of flow of funds transactions, and detailed breakdowns of financial transactions among major sectors of the economy are readily available on both a quarterly and an annual basis from the Federal Reserve Board in Washington, DC.

The basic purposes of the Flow of Funds Accounts are to: (1) trace the flow of savings by businesses, households, and governments into purchases of financial assets; (2) show how the various parts of the financial system interact with each other; and (3) highlight the interconnections between the financial sector and the rest of the economy.

Construction of the Flow of Funds Accounts takes place in *four* basic steps.

Constructing the Flow of Funds Accounts: Sectoring the Economy

The first step is to divide the economy into several broad *sectors,* each consisting of economic units (transactors) with similar balance sheets. Among the major sectors in

More information on the Federal Reserve's Flow of Funds Accounts may be found at such sites as federalreserve.gov/ releases

the current account series are the following:

- Households.
- Farm businesses.
- Nonfarm nonfinancial businesses.
- State and local governments and the U.S. government.
- Federally sponsored credit agencies, such as the Federal National Mortgage Association.
- Monetary authorities, including the Federal Reserve System and monetary accounts of the U.S. Treasury.
- Commercial banks.
- Nonbank financial institutions, including savings and loans, credit unions, insurance companies, mutual funds, pension funds, finance companies, and security dealers.
- Rest of the world (U.S. international transactions).

Constructing the Flow of Funds Accounts: Building Sector Balance Sheets
The second step in assembling the Flow of Funds Accounts is to construct *balance sheets* for each of the sectors listed above at the end of each quarter. Like any balance sheet for a business firm or household, sector balance sheets contain estimates of the total assets, liabilities, and net worth held by each sector at a single point in time. The assets held by each sector are divided into financial assets and tangible real (nonfinancial) assets.

An example of such a balance sheet—in this case, a partial balance sheet containing only the financial assets and liabilities for the household sector for the years 1980, 1990, 2000, and 2004—is shown in Exhibit 3.3. We note, for example, that U.S. households held total financial assets of nearly $35 trillion in 2004 (shown in line 1), more than five times their financial asset holdings in 1980. A substantial part of this total was represented by household deposits—checking (demand) accounts and time and savings deposits placed in commercial banks and savings institutions. These liquid financial assets totaled more than $5.5 trillion in 2004 (line 2). An even larger volume of financial assets held by households took the form of pension fund reserves (line 20), accumulated to prepare individuals and families for the retirement years. These reserves amounted to $9.4 trillion in 2004, followed by holdings of corporate stock (equities), which totaled almost $5.8 trillion in 2004 (line 16). Holdings of debt securities (credit market instruments), including U.S. Treasury notes and bonds, federal agency securities, state and local government bonds, mortgages, and similar assets, amounted to a little over $2 trillion (line 7) in 2004.

It is interesting that the total indebtedness of individuals and families in the United States is *far less* than their holdings of financial assets. Exhibit 3.3 indicates that the household sector's liabilities totaled just under $10 trillion in 2004 (line 24), or less than 30 percent of its total financial asset holdings. Most household indebtedness was in the form of home mortgages and home equity loans (line 26) and installment (consumer credit) debt obligations (line 27), which include automobile and education loans that are gradually retired in a series of payments stretching over months or years.

Sources of Balance Sheet Data
Where does information come from to build sector balance sheets in the Flow of Funds Accounts? It comes from a wide variety of public and private sources. For example, information on lending and borrowing by nonfinancial businesses is derived from such sources as the Securities and Exchange Commission and the U.S. Department of Commerce. Various trade groups provide financial data on their respective industries, such as Investment Companies Institute,

EXHIBIT 3.3

Statement of Financial Assets and Liabilities for the Household Sector, 1980, 1990, 2000, and 2004* ($ Billions, Outstanding at Year-End)

Source: Board of Governors of the Federal Reserve System's *Flow of Funds Accounts.*

Note: As used here, the term "households" includes personal trusts and nonprofit organizations as well as individuals and families. It excludes corporate entities.

*Figures for 2004 are for the first quarter, annualized.

Asset and Liability Items	1980	1990	2000	2004*
1. **Total Financial Assets**	**$6,602.2**	**$14,827.7**	**$33,937.0**	**$34,860.7**
2. Deposits	1,520.7	3,259.3	4,385.2	5,513.4
3. Foreign deposits	0.0	13.4	63.5	60.2
4. Checkable deposits and currency	219.5	412.4	225.3	274.4
5. Time and savings deposits	1,239.0	2,465.0	3,125.6	4,195.5
6. Money market fund shares	62.2	368.6	970.7	983.6
7. Credit market instruments	425.4	1,555.3	2,245.4	2,077.7
8. Open market paper	38.3	63.2	72.6	48.9
9. Treasury securities	160.0	471.2	594.6	446.4
10. Savings bonds	72.5	126.2	184.8	204.4
11. Other Treasury securities	87.5	345.0	409.8	242.0
12. Federal agency securities	5.3	68.9	423.5	379.2
13. Municipal securities	104.5	575.0	460.7	695.9
14. Corporate and foreign bonds	30.0	233.5	576.4	356.6
15. Mortgages	87.2	143.5	117.7	150.7
16. Corporate equities	875.4	1,781.4	7,650.1	5,828.2
17. Mutual fund shares	45.6	456.6	2,900.1	3,365.6
18. Security credit	16.2	62.4	412.4	507.2
19. Life insurance reserves	220.6	391.7	819.1	1,019.5
20. Pension fund reserves	970.4	3,376.3	9,067.3	9,422.8
21. Investment in bank personal trusts	265.3	551.7	1,095.8	955.0
22. Equity in noncorporate businesses	2,183.1	3,150.5	4,990.6	5,717.5
23. Miscellaneous assets	79.5	242.5	370.9	454.0
24. **Total Liabilities**	**1,453.0**	**3,719.3**	**7,403.5**	**9,834.8**
25. Credit market instruments	1,401.5	3,597.2	7,014.1	9,458.8
26. Home mortgages and home equity loans	932.0	2,504.1	4,837.4	6,897.8
27. Consumer credit	358.0	824.4	1,719.0	2,014.8
28. Municipal securities	16.7	86.6	143.0	187.3
29. Bank loans (not elsewhere classified)	27.8	17.9	74.1	92.7
30. Other loans and advances	52.1	81.7	119.8	119.3
31. Commercial mortgages	14.8	82.5	120.7	146.9
32. Security credit	24.7	38.8	235.1	199.1
33. Trade payables	13.8	66.8	134.7	155.7
34. Deferred and unpaid life insurance premiums	12.9	16.5	19.6	21.1

which provides data on mutual funds, and the Securities Industry Association, which provides selected information on gross offerings of securities. Inevitably, inconsistencies arise in classifying financial transactions due to differences in accounting procedures among the groups contributing data. Moreover, in an economy as vast and complex as that of the United States, some financial transactions fall between the cracks. To deal with problems in data consistency and coverage, the Federal Reserve includes a *statistical discrepancy* account that brings each sector into balance.

EXHIBIT 3.4		Changes in Asset and Liability Items		
Sources and Uses of Funds Statement for the U.S. Banking Sector, 2004* ($ Billions)	1. Gross saving	98.6	20. Customer liabilities on acceptances	−2.1
	2. Fixed nonresidential investment	26.9	21. Miscellaneous assets	345.6
	3. Net acquisition of financial assets	1,281.1	22. Net increase in liabilities	1,378.7
Source: Board of Governors of the Federal Reserve System's *Flow of Funds Accounts.*	4. Vault cash	14.1	23. Net interbank liabilities	−200.7
	5. Reserves at Federal Reserve	15.2	24. To monetary authority	−1.1
			25. To domestic banks	38.8
*Data are for the first quarter of 2004, annualized.	6. Checkable deposits and currency	2.9	26. To foreign banks	−238.3
	7. Total bank credit	905.3	27. Checkable deposits	−146.5
	8. Treasury securities	30.4	28. Federal government	−233.7
	9. Agency securities	380.2	29. Rest of the world	78.9
	10. Municipal securities	10.3	30. Private domestic	8.3
	11. Corporate and foreign bonds	72.7	31. Small time and savings deposits	306.4
	12. Total loans	416.5	32. Large time deposits	258.7
	13. Open market paper	0.0	33. Federal funds and RPs (net)	457.5
	14. Bank loans (other)	−24.2	34. Credit market instruments	186.0
	15. Mortgages	343.2	35. Open market paper	57.5
	16. Consumer credit	7.6	36. Corporate bonds	40.0
	17. Security credit	89.8	37. Other loans and advances	88.5
	18. Corporate equities	−0.1	38. Corporate equity issues	−0.6
	19. Mutual fund shares	−4.7	39. Taxes payable	3.1
			40. Miscellaneous liabilities	514.8
			41. Statistical discrepancy	169.3

Constructing the Flow of Funds Accounts: Preparing Sources and Uses of Funds Statements

sources and uses of funds statement

After balance sheets are constructed for each sector of the economy, the third step in the construction of the Flow of Funds Accounts is to prepare a **sources and uses of funds statement** for each sector. This statement shows changes in net worth and changes in holdings of financial assets and liabilities taken from each sector's balance sheet at the beginning and end of a calendar quarter or year.

An example of such a statement for the U.S. commercial banking sector for 2004 is shown in Exhibit 3.4. The first portion of the sources and uses statement (lines 1–21) shows changes in the banking sector's net worth (gross saving), real assets (net fixed investment in plant and equipment), and net acquisitions of financial assets. The second portion of the sources and uses statement (lines 22–41) reflects net borrowing as illustrated by an increase in the liabilities carried by U.S. commercial banks and their affiliates.[2]

We note, for example, that U.S.-chartered commercial banks increased their holdings of financial assets by just over $1,281 billion in 2004 (line 3). Bank loans to businesses, households, and other borrowers rose by about $416 billion (line 12) as the U.S. economy enjoyed a period of positive growth following a recession at the beginning of the

---

[2]All changes on a sources and uses of funds statement are shown *net* of purchases and sales. When purchases of an asset exceed sales of that asset, the resulting figure is reported as a *positive* increase in the asset. When sales exceed purchases, an asset item will carry a *negative* sign. A nonnegative liability item on the sources and uses statement indicates that net borrowing (i.e., total borrowings larger than debt repayments) has occurred during the period under study. If a liability item is negative, debt repayments exceed new borrowings during the period covered by the statement.

current decade. With the U.S. economy continuing its recovery in 2004, more individuals and businesses demanded bank credit to help them increase their standard of living and increase the economy's output of goods and services. Bank holdings of U.S. government and federal agency securities (including issues of mortgage-backed securities guaranteed by a federal government agency) also rose significantly, by more than $380 billion (line 9), reflecting bankers' search for higher-quality assets and the increased availability of government securities in the wake of large government budget deficits. U.S.-chartered commercial banks invested nearly $27 billion (line 2) in new plant and equipment (fixed nonresidential investment) during the year as the industry continued to automate many of its facilities and increase the number of branch offices.

Where did the banking sector get the funds it needed to make new loans and security purchases and increase its investment in new plant and equipment? The necessary funds came principally from a rise of about $306 billion in small-denomination (under $100,000 each) time and savings deposits (line 31), while the largest time deposits (each over $100,000 in amount) that banks sell—often called money-market CDs—rose by nearly $259 billion (line 32). Deposits in checking accounts by households and firms barely budged (line 30), while the federal government significantly cut back on its deposits at commercial banks by nearly $234 billion (line 28). This loss of funds was more than offset by the sizeable increase in federal funds and RPs (or short-term loans backed by government securities owned by the banks). The banking sector therefore drew on a wide range of sources in 2004 to support the industry's substantial increase in financial and real assets.

Banks often supplement their deposit growth with borrowing in the money market through such instruments as federal funds borrowings, security repurchase agreements, and sales of commercial paper in the open market. This particular source of bank funding increased $515 billion in 2004 (lines 33 and 35). U.S.-chartered banks also added to their savings (shown as gross savings) by nearly $99 billion (line 1), thereby opening up another source of cash that bankers could draw upon in the future to respond to their customers' service needs and help their industry grow.

Balancing Out a Sources and Uses of Funds Statement   As we have seen, sources and uses of funds statements in the Flow of Funds Accounts are derived from the aggregated balance sheets of each sector of the economy. Because balance sheets must always balance, we would also expect a sources and uses of funds statement to balance (except, of course, for discrepancies in the underlying data). In a sources and uses statement,

$$\begin{matrix} \text{Net investment} \\ \text{in plant and} \\ \text{equipment} \end{matrix} + \begin{matrix} \text{Net acquisitions} \\ \text{of financial} \\ \text{assets} \end{matrix} = \begin{matrix} \text{Net increase in} \\ \text{liabilities} + \text{Change in} \\ \text{current surplus} \\ \text{account} \end{matrix} \qquad (3.1)$$

financial investment

real investment

current borrowing

current savings

Net acquisitions of financial assets are frequently referred to as **financial investment;** net purchases of plant and equipment may be labeled **real investment.** Both are *uses of funds* for a sector or economic unit. Net increases in liabilities represent **current borrowing** in the current period, while changes in the current surplus account reflect **current savings.** These latter two items are *sources of funds.* Therefore, the relationship shown above may be written:

$$\begin{matrix} \text{Net real investment } + \text{ Net financial investment} \\ = \text{Net borrowing } + \text{ Net current saving} \end{matrix} \qquad (3.2)$$

or

$$\text{Total uses of funds} = \text{Total sources of funds} \qquad (3.3)$$

For each unit—business, household, or government—and for each sector of the economy, the above statement *must* be true—it is an accounting identity. For example, in the commercial banking sector in 2004 we have, as shown in Exhibit 3.4:

**SOURCES AND USES OF FUNDS STATEMENT
FOR THE BANKING SECTOR, 2004* ($ BILLIONS)**

Uses of Funds		Sources of Funds	
Net investment in plant and equipment (net increase in real assets)	$ 26.9	Net borrowing (net increase in liabilities)	$1,378.7
Net financial investment (net acquisitions of financial assets)	1,281.1	Net current saving (net change in net worth)	98.6
Statistical discrepancy	169.3		
Total uses of funds	$1,477.3	Total sources of funds	$1,477.3

Once the statistical discrepancy account is considered, total uses and total sources of funds should be equal for this and for all other sectors of the economy (except for small remaining discrepancies in column totals due to rounding error).

Constructing the Flow of Funds Accounts: Building a Flow of Funds Matrix for the Whole Economy   The final step in the construction of the Flow of Funds Accounts is to combine the sources and uses of funds statement for each sector into a flow of funds matrix for the entire U.S. economy. An example of such a matrix is shown in Exhibit 3.5, which lists borrowings by each major sector and total borrowings by all sectors combined. Another example appears in Exhibit 3.6, which shows funds raised by all sectors through the issuance of debt (credit market borrowing) and through the issuance of corporate equities (stock). The majority of funds sought by businesses, households, and governments in the financial marketplace clearly were raised by issuing debt instruments (primarily bonds and notes), as shown in Exhibit 3.6. The total of all debt instruments outstanding rose by just over $2.8 trillion (line 1 in Exhibit 3.6) in the year 2004 (as of the first quarter of that year, annualized).

Corporations were heavy borrowers of funds in the American economy, issuing nearly $411 billion in debt instruments (line 5 in Exhibit 3.6). Also among the heaviest borrowers were debtors taking on mortgage loans (both new home mortgages and commercial mortgages), who borrowed more than $1.1 trillion (line 8). Borrowings by governments at all levels ranked high in volume as well at around $767 billion (lines 3 and 4). Of course, borrowing—issuing debt—is not the only possible source of funds from the money and capital markets. Substantial funds also can be raised by issuing stock (corporate equities), which in 2004 totaled about $481 billion, including more than $64 billion in net new corporate equities and nearly $417 billion in shares offered by mutual funds (lines 10, 11, and 15 in Exhibit 3.6).

Exhibit 3.5 looks at borrowing in the economy from *both* the lenders' and borrowers' points of view. From Chapter 2 we know that what is borrowed by one sector just equals the credit extended to that sector by other sectors. For example, line 27 in Exhibit 3.5 shows that total funds *loaned* in U.S. credit markets during 2004 (through the first quarter, annualized) amounted to about $2.8 trillion. This amount exactly matches total net borrowing by all sectors reported in line 1 of Exhibit 3.5 and in line 1 of Exhibit 3.6 for the same time period.

EXHIBIT 3.5

Total Net Borrowing and Lending in Credit Markets and Borrowing by Sector ($ Billions)

Source: Board of Governors of the Federal Reserve System, *Flow of Funds Accounts.*

*Excludes corporate equities and mutual fund shares.

**Figures are for the first quarter of 2004, annualized.

		1993	2000	2004**
	Total Net Borrowing and Lending in Credit Markets*			
1.	Total net borrowing	930.6	1,704.0	2,801.5
2.	Domestic nonfinancial sectors	566.6	844.2	1,927.3
3.	Federal government	256.1	−295.9	466.0
4.	Nonfederal sectors	310.5	1,140.1	1,461.3
5.	Household sector	236.6	563.7	1,008.2
6.	Nonfinancial corporate business	34.4	357.2	187.6
7.	Nonfarm noncorporate business	−20.5	192.9	115.5
8.	Farm business	2.3	10.9	0.3
9.	State and local governments	57.7	15.5	149.7
10.	Rest of the world	69.8	57.0	68.4
11.	Financial sectors	294.2	802.8	805.7
12.	Commercial banking	13.4	60.0	186.0
13.	U.S.-chartered commercial banks	9.7	36.8	82.5
14.	Foreign banking offices in U.S.	−5.1	0.0	−0.0
15.	Bank holding companies	8.8	23.2	103.5
16.	Savings institutions	11.3	27.3	28.0
17.	Credit unions	0.2	0.0	−2.7
18.	Life insurance companies	0.2	−0.7	0.1
19.	Government-sponsored enterprises	80.6	234.1	36.1
20.	Federally related mortgage pools	84.7	199.4	95.1
21.	ABS issuers	85.2	183.0	135.2
22.	Finance companies	−1.4	81.9	133.7
23.	Mortgage companies	0.0	0.0	0.0
24.	REITs	1.7	2.7	54.2
25.	Brokers and dealers	12.0	15.6	51.9
26.	Funding corporations	6.3	−0.4	87.9
27.	Total net lending	930.6	1,704.0	2,801.5

EXHIBIT 3.6

Funds Raised in Credit and Equity Markets ($ Billions)

Source: Board of Governors of the Federal Reserve System, *Flow of Funds Accounts.*

*Figures are for the first quarter of 2004, annualized.

		1993	2000	2004*
	Credit Market Borrowing, All Sectors, by Instrument			
1.	Total net debt taken on	930.6	1,704.0	2,801.5
2.	Open market paper	−5.1	211.6	322.0
3.	U.S. government securities	421.4	137.6	597.3
4.	Municipal securities	66.3	23.6	170.1
5.	Corporate and foreign bonds	281.0	387.0	410.8
6.	Bank loans n.e.c.	−7.2	112.8	−24.2
7.	Other loans and advances	−8.9	120.8	89.1
8.	Mortgages	121.8	565.4	1,113.0
9.	Consumer credit	61.4	165.2	123.4
	Funds Raised through Corporate Equities and Mutual Fund Shares			
10.	Total net issues of stock	425.4	244.7	480.9
11.	Corporate equities	133.4	5.3	64.1
12.	Nonfinancial	21.3	−118.2	−104.0
13.	Foreign shares purchased by U.S. residents	63.4	106.7	78.2
14.	Financial	48.7	16.8	89.9
15.	Mutual fund shares	292.0	239.4	416.9

The flow of funds matrix reminds us that, for all sectors of the economy combined into one, the amount of saving must equal the total amount of real investment in the economy, and, therefore, the amount of borrowing in total must equal total financial investment (i.e., the total amount of financial assets acquired by all sectors).

Limitations and Uses of the Flow of Funds Accounts   It should be clear by now that the Flow of Funds Accounts provide a vast amount of information on trends in the financial system. These accounts provide indispensable aid in tracing the flow of savings through the money and capital markets. Estimates of flow of funds data can be used to help make forecasts of lending, borrowing, and interest rates. However, these social accounts have a number of limitations that must be kept firmly in mind.

First, the Flow of Funds Accounts present no information on transactions among economic units *within* each sector. If a household sells stock to another household, this transaction will *not* be picked up in the accounts, because both units are in the same sector. However, if a household sells stock to a business firm, this transaction *will* be captured by the flow of funds bookkeeping system.

Second, the Flow of Funds Accounts show only *net* flows between one point in time and another point in time. These accounts do *not* show any changes that occur *between* the beginning and ending points of the period under study.

Finally, all flow of funds data are expressed in terms of current *market values*. Therefore, these accounts measure not only the flow of savings in the economy but also capital gains and losses. This market-value bias distorts estimates of the amount of actual savings and investment activity that occur from year to year.

Despite these limitations, however, the Flow of Funds Accounts are among the most comprehensive sources of information available to students of the financial system. These accounts provide vital clues on the demand and supply forces that shape movements in interest rates and the prices of financial assets. The Flow of Funds Accounts indicate which types of financial assets are growing or declining in volume and which sectors finance other sectors. One of the principal uses of flow of funds data today is to forecast interest rates and build econometric models to simulate future conditions in the credit markets. Combined with other sources of information, Flow of Funds Accounts provide us with the raw material from which to make important financial decisions.

QUESTIONS TO HELP YOU STUDY

13. What is meant by the term *social accounting?* Why is such an accounting system needed?

14. Compare and contrast the Flow of Funds Accounts with the National Income and Product Accounts. What types of information does each system of accounts provide that could be useful for making financial decisions?

15. Why would information about the global economy be of significance to an investor in stocks, bonds, and other financial assets?

16. How are the Flow of Funds Accounts constructed?

17. What is a *sources and uses of funds statement?* Why is it important?

18. Discuss the principal limitations of flow of funds data. Why must a user of flow of funds information keep these limitations in mind?

MARKETS ON THE NET: The Most Important Web Sites for This Chapter

American Economic Association
(aeaweb.org/RFE/Consult/indx.html)
Comptroller of the Currency
(occ.treas.gov)
Dun & Bradstreet (dnb.com)
Federal Deposit Insurance Corporation
(fdic.gov)
Federal Reserve System
(federalreserve.gov)
FINIX European Stock Market Indexes
(finix.at)
International Monetary Fund (imf.org)

Investment Company Institute (ici.com)
Moody's Investors Service (moodys.com)
New York Stock Exchange (nyse.com)
The NASDAQ Stock Market (nasdaq.com)
Securities and Exchange Commission
(sec.gov)
The Bond Market Association
(investinginbonds.com)
The Financial Times (ft.com)
The Wall Street Journal (wsj.com)
U.S. Department of Commerce (doc.gov)

Summary of the Chapter's Main Points

This chapter examines the key role that *information* plays in the money and capital markets and the financial system. Among its key points are the following:

- An unimpeded flow of relevant, low-cost information is vital to the efficient functioning of the financial markets. If the scarce resource of credit is to be allocated efficiently and an ample flow of savings made available for investment, accurate financial information must be made readily available at low cost to all market participants.

- Two different types of markets operate within the financial system every day: an *information market* and a *market for financial assets.* The two different types of markets must work together in coordinated fashion to accomplish the desired result—directing the flow of scarce funds (coming primarily from savings) toward their most beneficial uses (primarily into investments that help to create jobs, expand the economy, and improve our standard of living).

- If the market for financial information is truly *efficient,* so that all relevant information for valuing financial assets is readily available at negligible cost, financial assets will be correctly priced based on their expected return and risk. Scarce resources will flow to those uses of funds promising the highest expected returns.

- When *asymmetries* exist in the flow and availability of information, however, the financial marketplace will operate imperfectly. Some market participants, armed with special information not available to all market participants, will earn *excess profits* (that is, they will generate returns that exceed the *normal* or *expected* rate of return for the amount of risk they take on).

- With imperfections in the quality and availability of information, scarce resources will be allocated less efficiently than otherwise might be the case. Research evidence to date suggests that most financial markets tend to be relatively efficient at some level but that important asymmetries (information imperfections) still remain.

www.mhhe.com/rose9e

- Some of the key problems informational asymmetries can create include (1) *the lemons problem*, in which vital information about the quality of assets is both costly and difficult to obtain, with the possible result that lesser-quality assets may drive superior-quality assets from the marketplace; (2) the *adverse selection problem*, in which sellers of some services (such as loans and insurance protection) have difficulty in correctly pricing what they offer because of inadequate information about the riskiness and other relevant characteristics of buyers, often resulting in multiple prices for the same service; and (3) the *moral hazard problem*, in which agents possessing superior-quality information (for example, the management of a corporation) may use it to their advantage at the expense of principals (for example, the stockholders of the same corporation), unless suitable arrangements can be worked out that better align the interests of both agents and principals.

- In this chapter, the principal focus has been on five categories of financial information available today: debt security prices and yields, stock prices and dividend yields, the financial condition of security issuers, general conditions in the economy and financial system, and social accounting data. This chapter gives the reader a broad overview of the kinds and quality of information currently available to the public. Knowing where to find relevant, up-to-date information is an essential ingredient in the process of solving economic and financial problems.

Key Terms Appearing in This Chapter

efficient markets hypothesis, 54
asymmetry, 54
insider trading, 57
moral hazard, 61
note, 64
bond, 64
bid price, 65
ask price, 65
stocks, 65
social accounting, 70

National Income and Product
   Accounts, 70
Flow of Funds Accounts, 71
sources and uses of funds
   statements, 74
financial investment, 75
real investment, 75
current borrowing, 75
current savings, 75

Problems and Issues

1. Construct sources and uses of funds statements for each sector and for the whole economy using the following information:

	Households ($ Billions)	Business Firms ($ Billions)	Banks and Other Financial Institutions ($ Billions)	Governmental Units ($ Billions)
Current saving	$428.8	$280.0	$35.0	−$35.0
Current real investment	332.5	350.0	17.5	—
Current financial investment	306.3	78.8	43.8	8.8
Current borrowing	210.0	148.8	26.3	43.8

Assume that the four sectors listed above are the only sectors in the economy and that there are no international transactions. Is there a statistical discrepancy? Where? Referring to the discussion in Chapter 2, which sectors are deficit-budget sectors (DBUs) and which are surplus-budget sectors (SBUs)? Are there any balanced-budget sectors (BBUs)?

2. Suppose that you are given the data listed below for the household sector of the economy. From this information, construct a statement of financial assets and liabilities for the household sector.

	($ Billions)		($ Billions)
Deposits in banks and savings institutions	$540	U.S. government securities	$110
Home mortgages	290	Credit extended by nonbank lending institutions	40
Installment loans extended by banks	110	Trade credit	5
Holdings of currency and coin	120	Corporate and foreign bonds	30
Security credit owed	10	Corporate equities	680
State and local government bonds	50	Life insurance reserves	130
Deferred and unpaid life insurance premiums	10	Pension fund reserves	420
Holdings of miscellaneous financial assets	50	Miscellaneous liabilities	35

3. At year-end 2005, suppose the corporate business sector posted net worth of $60 billion, total investment in plant and equipment of $75 billion, total holdings of financial assets of $131 billion, and total debt outstanding of $146 billion. The following year-end, 2006, suppose total corporate indebtedness climbed to $167 billion, holdings of financial assets fell to $120 billion, and net worth increased to $63 billion due to retained profits. Construct a sources and uses of funds statement for the corporate sector for 2006.

4. The following situations *may* be covered by *insider trading laws* in the United States. Examine each situation described and indicate whether, in your opinion, a violation of insider trading laws might have occurred. If you think a violation occurred, what kind of violation was it?

   a. The chief financial officer of Start Corporation reads an internal memorandum criticizing the firm's recent oil field development investments and picks up his phone to call his broker, placing an order to sell his holdings of the firm's shares when the market opens in the morning.

   b. Corren Professional Corporation, a CPA firm, assists Selkirk Industrial Corporation with its quarterly and annual financial reports. Jim Roberts, a CPA with Corren, after reviewing the latest information provided by Selkirk's CEO, calls a friend and suggests making certain stock and bond trades involving Selkirk's securities. Roberts will not benefit financially from these suggested trades and refuses to get involved.

   c. James Smith works for Cohen and Cooper, a local law firm, and while browsing in his firm's law library, he discovers a new report from a legal client of his colleague, Roscoe Adams, that predicts serious financial problems if the client proceeds with its recently drafted strategic plan. Smith subsequently discovers discreetly that the strategic plan is to be launched next week. He also learns that Roscoe is selling the client's stock short through his broker. Smith quietly advises Roscoe not to make the short sale and lets the matter drop.

> **d.** Samuel Joule learns from conversations with Sarah Conklin, a bartender at a local bar, that neighboring Locket Corporation has recently developed a warning device that may help prevent air collisions and may be worth tens of millions of dollars once announced to the public. Neither Joule nor Conklin works for Locket, though he has been dating Miss Conklin. Both of these individuals decide to purchase 1,000 shares of Locket's stock before Locket holds a press conference to announce the new air collision device. Joule and Conklin will use a bank loan to finance the purchase of Locket's shares. A wedding is planned if the transaction pays off.

5. In this chapter we discussed three different forms or levels of *market efficiency.* Refer to the appropriate forms of market efficiency in answering the following questions:

   a. Why is insider trading illegal?

   b. Why and how do small investors benefit from efficient markets?

   c. If you were a stock trader and markets were *not* efficient, how would this influence your trading activity? What does this tell you about *why* markets may be efficient?

   d. Consider the case of a day trader who looks only at the past history of stock prices in conducting his or her trades. How likely would it be for such a person to "beat the market"? What does this suggest about investing in the "entire market" (such as by purchasing shares in an index fund) rather than attempting to pick individual stocks?

Standard & Poor's Market Insight and Web-Based Problems

STANDARD &POOR'S

1. Go to the Internet and use the Standard & Poor's Market Insight database at **www.mhhe.com/edumarket** and the following Web sources— **www.federalreserve.gov, www.bea.gov**, and **www.bls.gov**—in order to obtain the following information:

   a. The latest stock price for IBM.

   b. The average yield on highly-rated long-term bonds.

   c. The interest rate on newly issued three-month U.S. Treasury bills.

   d. The size of the U.S. money supply (measured as M1 and M2).

   e. The annualized growth rate of the U.S. economy for the most recent quarter (real GDP).

   f. The size of the U.S. budget deficit (or surplus) for the last fiscal year.

   g. Total business fixed investment in the U.S. during the last calendar year.

   h. Total employment in the nonfarm business sector.

   i. The inflation rate in the United States for the past year, measured in terms of the growth rate of the CPI.

STANDARD &POOR'S

2. Track the performance of a stock issued by a company included in the Dow Jones Industrial Average (DJIA) Index (such as IBM or Microsoft) over the course of the semester and compare the performance of the stock you have selected relative to the performance of a broad stock-market index of your own choosing (such as the S&P 500 Stock Index, the Vanguard Total Stock Market

Index Fund, or the Wilshire 5000 Index). There is a wide variety of sources you might consult for the information you will need, including *The Wall Street Journal* **(www.WSJ.com),** the Standard & Poor's Market Insight database **(www.mhhe.com/edumarket),** the New York Stock Exchange **(www.nyse.com),** and other sources mentioned in this chapter.

At the end of each week, find the closing price of your stock and the stock index you have chosen. Keep a running account of the percentage gains and losses that you would have experienced had you (a) bought the stock, or (b) "bought the market" by buying an index fund representing a whole basket of stocks (such as an S&P 500 index fund). At the semester's end, compute the return you would have made had you invested $10,000 in your chosen stock or in your chosen index fund. Did your stock outperform or underperform the index fund? What information can you point to that seems to account for the over- or under-performance of your stock relative to the market?

Semester Project: A Study of the Fed Funds Market

At the end of the first two chapters we launched a semester project to learn about one of the most important markets in the financial system: the interbank loan or—as it is called in the United States—the federal funds market. In this installment of your semester project, we explore where you can go to obtain critical information regarding the Fed funds market.

One key source is the *Federal Reserve System* ("the Fed"). The majority of Fed funds transactions take place over an electronic funds transfer system (known as Fedwire) operated by the Federal Reserve. The Fed keeps track of all Fed funds transactions and computes an important interest rate known as the *effective federal funds rate,* which is the average interest rate on all brokered Fed funds transactions during each day. As we will discover later in this book, this is the interest rate the Fed attempts to "hit" when it conducts monetary policy. To examine how successful the Fed is in hitting its target for the Fed funds rate, the questions below ask you to *match up* the actual effective Fed funds rate on a daily basis with the Fed's target value for the funds rate.

a. First, go to the Federal Reserve's Web site (**www.federalreserve.gov/releases/ h15/data/m/fedfund.txt**) and obtain the actual value for the effective Fed funds rate over the past two years.

b. Next, identify the Federal Reserve's changing target for the funds rate from the official statements released after the Fed's periodic Federal Open Market Committee (FOMC) meetings by viewing **www.federalreserve.gov/ fomc'#calendars.**

c. Plot the actual values of the effective federal funds rate and the FOMC's announced targets over the past two years. What do you conclude from your graph about the Fed's ability to "hit" its target value for the Fed funds rate?

Selected References to Explore

Akerlof, George. "The Market for Lemons: Quality Uncertainty and the Market Mechanism." *Quarterly Journal of Economics* 84 (1970), pp. 488–500.

Ergungor, O. Emre, and Joseph G. Haubrich. "Information and Prices." *Economic Commentary,* Federal Reserve Bank of Cleveland, May 1, 2003, pp. 1–3.

Spence, Michael. "Signaling in Retrospect and the Informational Structure of Markets." *American Economic Review,* June 2002, pp. 434–459.

Stiglitz, Joseph, and Andrew Weiss. "Credit Rationing in Markets with Imperfect Information." *American Economic Review* 71 (1981), pp. 393–410.

Chapter 4

The Future of the Financial System and the Money and Capital Markets

Learning Objectives

in This Chapter

- You will explore the economic, demographic, social, and technological forces reshaping financial institutions, financial markets, and the financial system today.

- You will learn about recent trends in the financial system and how they may affect each one of us in the future, both personally and professionally.

- You will better understand how the problems the financial system faces today may well affect its future, leading to a new financial marketplace.

What's in This Chapter?
Key Topics Outline

4.1   Introduction: The Financial Markets in Change

The money and capital markets and the financial system that surrounds them are continually in transition, always moving toward something *new*. As we observed in the opening chapter, you cannot step into the same river twice, for rivers are ever flowing onward. So it is with the financial system and the money and capital markets. Today's financial system differs radically from that of a decade ago and will be still more different as we move forward into the future.

Powerful forces are reshaping financial institutions and financial services today. These forces for change include powerful new trends within the financial sector itself, major changes in the structure and functioning of the economy that surrounds the financial system, and new social and demographic trends that are altering the public's need for new financial services. In this chapter we focus upon these tidal changes that are refashioning the financial system that we see today and helping to build a new financial system for the future.

4.2   Financial Forces Reshaping the Money and Capital Markets Today

The money and capital markets that we see today will soon be very different as the financial marketplace continues to transform itself. Vast changes now under way within the financial system will demand that we continue to study the money and capital markets throughout our lives for our own personal benefit and for greater understanding.

financial innovation

One of the most important changes currently sweeping through the financial system is **financial innovation**—the development of many *new* financial services and instruments. Every year new financial services and instruments expand rapidly in variety and volume. Home equity credit lines, international mutual funds, currency and interest-rate swaps, loan securitizations, trust preferred stock, and many other exotic new services and financial instruments that we may have heard about (and will discuss later in this book) are only the vanguard of a wave of invention and change sweeping through the money and capital markets in every corner of the globe. Moreover, with

service proliferation

rapidly growing service innovation has come **service proliferation** as each financial institution expands the menu of services it is willing to offer customers.

competition

One of the causes of the ongoing rush to innovate and develop new services and techniques is the rise of intense **competition** among financial-service providers. Banks, insurance companies, securities dealers, mutual funds, and thrift institutions are locked in an intense struggle for the customer's business that is unparalleled in history. Many of these financial institutions are engaged in *mergers and acquisitions* aimed at creating financial giants out of numerous smaller financial-service providers—giant companies that are able to compete more effectively due to lower costs and offer one-stop financial-service shopping convenience for those customers that value that feature. Ultimately, these large firms win bigger shares of the financial-service marketplace. In

consolidation

short, a major trend toward the **consolidation** of smaller financial firms into fewer, but much larger financial-service providers is well under way as competitors seek any possible advantage over their rivals.

deregulation

The rise of greater financial-service competition has been fueled, in part, by **deregulation**—a trend set in motion over the years by several national governments. Major nations around the globe, especially the United States, Japan, and the countries of the European Union, are gradually freeing portions of the financial sector from the burden of so many government rules. As government regulations are being lightened or eliminated, the *private marketplace* is becoming more and more important in shaping how financial-service providers compete and perform in order to serve the public.

Financial-service competition is increasingly taking the place of government rules—a strategy of *privatization* of the financial sector driven by the expectation that the public will, ultimately, benefit in the form of more convenient services at lower cost.

The expanding competitive struggle in a deregulated financial marketplace has given rise to new services and new financial instruments, as well as new types of financial institutions—large, multiproduct, multimarket, technologically sophisticated, sales-oriented organizations designed to weather the risks inherent in today's volatile financial marketplace. As a result, financial institutions and financial-service industries have come to closely resemble each other and are organized in much the same ways.

convergence

Reflecting this trend toward **convergence** among financial firms and industries, traditional distinctions between one type of financial-service institution and another have become hopelessly blurred. Today many banks, thrifts, and credit unions clearly look like each other; the same is true for some of the largest investment banks and insurance companies. Increasingly, their service menus are mirror images of each other—a trend called **homogenization.** This has created a real challenge for marketing professionals, who must try to convince the public that their particular financial-service institution is truly different from its rivals.

homogenization

globalization

More financial institutions are establishing interstate operations and expanding their marketing programs to cover whole regions and, in many instances, the whole globe (usually referred to as **globalization**). The results are falling geographic barriers to international competition and strong pressure to consolidate smaller financial-service institutions into larger ones. More financial institutions are becoming *stockholder-owned corporations* in order to open up new sources of capital to fund their expansion. Under intense competitive pressure and rising costs, the number of independently owned financial institutions is declining—victims of merger or, in some cases, failure.

market broadening

Financial markets that have traditionally been local in character are expanding to become regional, national, and even international in scope. This **market broadening** reflects *recent advances in communications technology.* Such breakthroughs offer the prospect of reducing service delivery costs, improving employee productivity, bringing new financial services online more rapidly, and expanding the effective marketing area for both old and new services. For example, today many commercial and consumer loans are traded in national and international markets, providing new sources of liquidity for financial institutions making these loans and improving the availability of credit to the public.

As new financial-service markets develop, many of the larger businesses and governments will have less reason to borrow from traditional financial intermediaries and more reason to *sell debt and equity securities directly to investors in the open market.* Indeed, the role of the traditional financial intermediary in the channeling of savings into investment seems to be shrinking somewhat. Moreover, the development of a market for *securitized assets*—pools of loans—allows almost any large firm with a strong market reputation to package its loans and issue new securities against them, thereby generating more cash to make *new* loans and investments. Thus, there is less need for traditional loans from traditional financial institutions, although many banks and insurance companies have learned that they can benefit from this trend by selling advice on how to package new security offerings most effectively, acting as agents for such offerings, and issuing standby credit guarantees in case something goes wrong in the securitization process.

Of course, the trends we observe in today's financial system and among financial institutions is *not* a completely new story. Its roots lie deep in history. For example, today's trend toward deregulation of financial institutions counteracts the excesses of a much earlier era—the Great Depression of the 1930s—when comprehensive regulation of financial institutions promised *safety* but tended to stifle both competition and innovation. Furthermore, the current emphasis in the financial sector on new product development and research, frequent technological updating, elaborate marketing programs to sell financial services, and strategic planning is a carryover from manufacturing and industrial firms that have used such techniques for decades. There is a growing awareness that the challenges and techniques of managing a financial-service institution are *not* fundamentally different from those of managing any other business firm. The products are different, but the methods of control and decision making are essentially the same.

4.3 Social, Economic, and Demographic Forces Reshaping the Financial System

We must recognize that much of what is happening in the financial system of markets and institutions today is a response to broad social, economic, and demographic trends that span generations. These trends are affecting not just financial institutions but also governments, businesses, and households in every corner of society and every nation on the globe.

For example, fundamental changes in the age makeup of the population are having profound effects on savings habits, consumption, and borrowing decisions worldwide. The population is *rapidly aging,* due primarily to better medical care, nutrition, and changing attitudes about childbearing. The *life-cycle hypothesis*—developed by Modigliani and Ando (1960) and expanded later by others—suggests that, as individuals age, they reduce their expectations of lifetime income, mainly because their expected time in the labor force is decreasing. With retirement looming closer, personal savings rates should rise and, correspondingly, per-capita consumption spending should fall in real terms. Thus, the boom in recent years of runaway consumer borrowing and spending may soon be moderating, resulting in a more moderate-growth economy, lower average interest rates, and less inflation. The challenge faced by banks, insurance companies, and other service providers in the future will be to find better ways to accommodate the demands of older savers, including the greater need for retirement, tax, and estate planning.

The basic family unit is also changing, with *more single-parent households, a rising age at which first marriages occur,* and *a declining fertility rate in most industrialized countries.* However, in the United States, population growth estimates have recently been revised upward due to greater-than-expected immigration, an increase in fertility, and greater longevity related to improved medical care. A high divorce rate marks many industrialized nations, although married couples make up three-quarters of all U.S. households. But less than half of these have children living in the home. People living alone make up less than one-quarter of all households in the United States today, although their numbers appear to be rising. Also on the rise are dual-earner couples with above-average incomes, who are becoming one of the most important segments of the population in terms of their contributions to the economy.

More men are responsible for household chores and child care today, making them more conscious of the problems of household budgeting and the need to build savings capital. In contrast, women are entering the labor force in greater numbers and are also getting stronger educational backgrounds than at any other time in history. Today, a roughly *equal* proportion of young women and young men (ages 25 to 29) have completed at least four years of college. Moreover, in these younger age groups, the gap between the earnings of men and women has closed significantly, though not completely. In general, educational levels have risen so much that today almost half of the

- Aging population (with wealthier retirees and a growing volume of funds transfers over time to their heirs and to charities).

- Larger corporate customers going directly to the open market to raise funds, bypassing traditional financial institutions, such as banks and finance companies.

- Growing demands for retirement planning and long-term saving by millions of workers and their families not covered adequately by existing retirement plans.

- Increasing numbers of nontraditional families (including single-parent homes) who have credit-access problems and a need for lower-cost financial services.

- Growing need for financial planning programs to aid individuals and families in managing their retirement assets and their inheritances.

- Greater ethnic diversity in the populations of the world's leading countries, resulting in a range of different customer attitudes and philosophies about managing money and the need for a range of lower-cost financial services.

- More volatile job markets, with customers switching jobs and residential locations more frequently so that financial-service providers need greater product-line and geographic flexibility.

- Increased need for personal budgeting and debt management education for individuals, families, and smaller businesses as the volume of borrowing in the financial system continues to expand and debt burdens grow.

U.S. labor force (in the 25 to 64 age group) has been enrolled in college at one time or another. High school diplomas are becoming the minimal educational achievement an individual needs to avoid poverty.

For further discussion of recent demographic trends, see U.S. Bureau of the Census at census.gov

Although many of these demographic trends have slowed or paused recently, most demographers do not anticipate a significant *reversal* anytime soon, and so demands will continue to grow for new forms of housing, daycare facilities, flexible work schedules, and less expensive medical care. The result is a new matrix of financial-service needs, including demands for new savings instruments and loans that support retraining and relocation, provide college educations, and supply more venture capital to support new businesses that are struggling to be born.

Added to the demographic changes are broad *economic* movements. For example, manufacturing industries are being displaced by service industries in more developed economies (especially the United States). The computer has transformed the economy from a system primarily reliant on manufacturing to one centered increasingly upon the flow of *information*. The expansion of service firms is creating most of the new jobs, and these businesses have their own unique financing needs. Accelerated growth in automation, computer systems, telecommunications, and biotechnology is creating the need for new kinds of credit and risk protection that financial-service providers must respond to.

The broader and faster dissemination of information today is contributing to the *internationalization* of markets, which spurs competition and heightens the need for international cooperation among financial institutions and among the government agencies that regulate them. One of the most dramatic examples is the emergence of the European Union (EU), creating a common market with more than 400 million customers. (A similar trend toward establishing a "free trade zone" is under way among many nations in North and South America.) Banks, insurance companies, and other

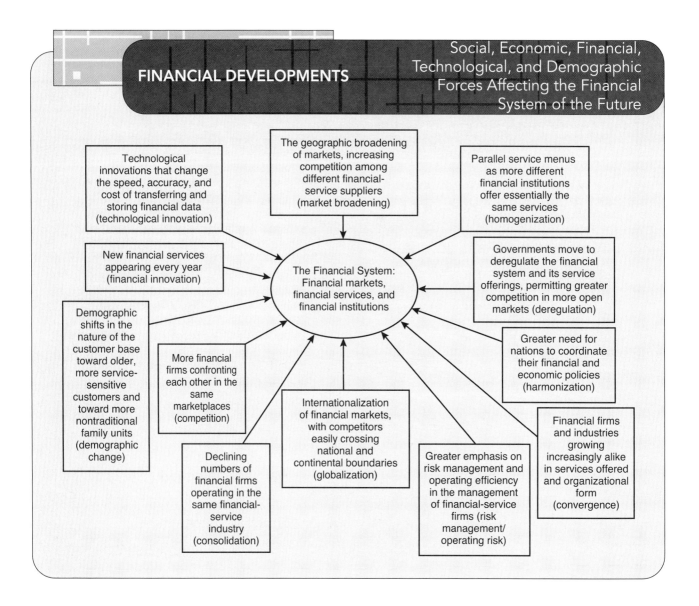

financial firms are licensed to offer their services throughout Western Europe, leading to the free and open marketing of financial services. These reforms have already set in motion a wave of mergers and joint ventures among leading European banks, insurance companies, and other firms in order to survive in a more open financial marketplace.

Similar developments loom on the horizon for Eastern Europe and the nations that comprise the former Soviet Union now that the Cold War has ended. Huge amounts of venture capital as well as funding for education are desperately needed in Russia and the other nations that belonged to the old Warsaw Pact in order to improve their living standards and retrain their workers to be competitive in a global marketplace. In one positive step taken early in the new century, several Eastern European nations were admitted as new members of the European Union (EU).

In Asia parallel changes are unfolding as expanding populations migrate to the cities to become part of a rapidly expanding industrial sector. Moreover, Asian economies, led by China, are opening their doors (in some cases, slowly) to foreign business ventures, including the banking and financial-service sector. However, if economic growth is to continue at its current rapid pace, this sector must expand and modernize along with the rest of the Asian economy.

Clearly, as the *internationalization* of economies and the *globalization* of the financial sector continue to proceed, along with steady advances in communications technology, there will be a wide range of possible benefits for the financial system and the public. More savings and investment opportunities will be opened. Investing in foreign corporations and institutions may eventually become less risky because more information will be available on their financial condition, and the markets serviced by these institutions will be better known and better understood. The result should be a more efficient allocation of scarce resources and increases in the real output of goods and services. Arbitrage opportunities due to discrepancies in prices between markets should be less frequent and shorter in duration.

However, increasing globalization of the financial and economic system will not be without its cost. Economic conditions within any one nation will become increasingly sensitive to foreign developments and harder for domestic policymakers to control or influence. Confirmation of security trades (*clearing*) and getting proper payment and timely delivery of securities bought and sold (*settlement*) will be more challenging in a globalized financial system, at least until advances in communications technology and international cooperation among governments and regulatory agencies catch up with rapidly advancing globalization.

So powerful are the foregoing trends that *none* can be ignored by the management and owners of financial-service firms today. The choice now for those who work in or use the services of the financial system is to either recognize and adapt to such trends or become a victim, rather than a beneficiary, of change.

QUESTIONS TO HELP YOU STUDY

1. Explain the meaning of the term *financial innovation*. How about *deregulation? Service proliferation? Consolidation? Convergence?*

2. Why are financial innovation and deregulation significant factors in today's money and capital markets? Are they also likely to be important to the future of the financial system?

3. What is meant by the term *market broadening?* Why is this phenomenon taking place inside today's financial marketplace?

4. Do you think *market broadening* will be an important force in shaping the future of the financial-service marketplace? Why?

5. Explain the reasoning behind the *life-cycle hypothesis*. How will the life-cycle idea affect the financial system of the future, in your opinion? Why?

6. What changes in the financial markets' *customer base* do you anticipate for the future? What are the implications of these projected changes for managers of financial-service institutions?

7. What is meant by the term *homogenization?* What do you think is motivating this trend toward service homogenization today?

4.4   The Challenges and Opportunities Presented by Recent Trends

There is little question now that the demographic, economic, and financial-service trends mentioned above will continue into the foreseeable future. But we must recognize that these trends have unleashed new problems of their own—great unresolved issues that must somehow be dealt with as we rush toward the future. We turn now to these critical issues for the future of the financial system in the sections that follow.

Dealing with Risk in the Financial System: Ensuring the Strength and Viability of Financial Institutions and Increasing Public Confidence

The money and capital markets and the financial institutions that operate within them depend heavily on *public confidence.* The financial system works to channel scarce loanable funds (credit) to their most productive uses only if individuals and businesses are willing to save and entrust their savings to financial institutions, and only if other businesses and individuals are willing to rely on the financial system to provide credit to support their consumption and investment. When *any* financial institution develops serious problems that reach public notice, the public's confidence in other financial institutions may be damaged as well. The result can be a smaller flow of savings through *all* financial institutions and restrictions on the availability of credit. Jobs and economic growth could be adversely affected.

The Consequences of Reduced Public Confidence

The close of the twentieth century and the opening of the twenty-first century brought new concerns on the part of the public regarding the strength and viability of both financial and nonfinancial businesses. Inaccurate and even illegal financial reporting on the part of companies such as Enron, Global Crossings, and other prominent firms weakened not only those particular firms but also some of their financial-service providers. At the same time, apparent misconduct on the part of several investment bankers and mutual fund managers led to deep public skepticism about the honesty and reliability of many financial institutions. As a result, financial-service customers today appear to be more sensitive to the risk of losing their funds and are, therefore, less loyal in dealing with any *one* financial institution. Financial-service *honesty* and *reliability* have become as important as price to many customers today.

Loss of public confidence not only produces adverse consequences for individual financial institutions but also damages the *efficiency* of financial market processes. A flight of funds from financial institutions reduces their size, threatening to make them less efficient in using resources. That portion of the public continuing to rely on the financial system is forced to pay higher prices for financial services that may be fewer in quantity and inferior in quality.

Ways to Promote Public Confidence in Financial Institutions and the Financial System

How can we ensure the continued viability of existing financial institutions and promote public confidence in them? Both government and the private sector may offer effective remedies.

To learn more about government insurance systems for financial institutions in the United States see, for example, fdic.gov and pbgc.gov

Government Insurance Systems   Governments have taken major steps over the years to ensure the safety of banks and other financial institutions in order to protect the public's funds. For example, during the 1930s, with thousands of banks failing, the U.S. Congress created the Federal Deposit Insurance Corporation (FDIC) to provide insurance coverage for small deposits (initially up to $2,500). Then, in 1980 in the wake of significant inflation (which had lowered the purchasing power of FDIC insurance payouts) and in anticipation of gradual government deregulation of the U.S. financial sector (which seemed to raise public concerns about deposit safety), the Congress increased federal deposit insurance coverage to a maximum of $100,000 per depositor. Recent proposals have come forward to increase FDIC deposit insurance coverage once again (perhaps as high as $200,000); however, these latest proposals have, thus far, met with strong opposition out of concern for moral hazard—a problem we discussed earlier in Chapter 3 and will review again shortly.

In the mid-1970s the U.S. Congress decided to copy the government-sponsored deposit insurance idea and extend similar protection to selected types of employee retirement plans. Following enabling legislation in 1974, the Pension Benefit Guaranty Corporation (PBGC) was set up to insure retirement income promised to the employees of businesses offering certain types of defined-benefit pension programs. It did not take long for similar proposals to be brought forward for public debate, including the possibility of offering government-sponsored insurance protection for certain kinds of insurance policies, annuities, and security investments.

There is, however, a serious concern today with the idea of further extending government-sponsored insurance in order to promote greater public confidence in financial institutions and the financial system. A government-provided insurance program, unless it is skillfully crafted, can do more harm than good. It can distort risk-taking decisions by the management of privately owned financial institutions. Federal deposit insurance, for example, has protected small depositors but led many banks and thrifts in prior decades to take on greater risk because, for most of the FDIC's history, insurance premiums were the same for *all* depository institutions, resulting in riskier depository institutions being subsidized by safer institutions. In brief, government-provided insurance can lead to a *moral hazard* problem in which agents (such as managers of an insured financial firm) take advantage of a guarantee underwritten by principals (in this case, the nation's taxpayers).

Of course, the potential moral hazard problem associated with government-subsidized insurance can be mitigated somewhat, perhaps, by using an insurance system modeled after some of those used by selected nations in the European Union. In several of these national insurance systems, no rescue fund is built up by the taxpayers or even by participating banks over time as happens with the FDIC in the United States. In other words, unlike the American deposit insurance system, there is *no* emergency reserve. Rather, when a failure occurs among the insured banks, the remaining banks are expected to provide the resources necessary to cover the losses of insured depositors. While this system may *reduce* moral hazard, it may not completely eliminate the problem, particularly if there is an implicit guarantee that government (in other words, the taxpayers) will rush in should the volume of failures threaten to swamp the current insurance system.

One solution mandated by the U.S. Congress for the FDIC (beginning in 1993) was to tie the size of government insurance premiums charged an insured bank or thrift institution directly to the amount of risk taken on by each insured institution—so that risk exposure to the insurance fund becomes the determinant of the cost of government-sponsored insurance to private financial institutions. Unfortunately, we aren't sure yet how to accurately measure the failure risk of an individual financial institution.

Ideally, we would like to have a *risk index* that correctly *ranks* insured financial institutions from most risky to least risky every time. This way we could be sure that the most risky financial-service firms are paying the highest insurance premiums. Our preferred risk index ought to tell us that if one financial firm is twice as risky as another, the former will pay insurance premiums twice as high as the latter. Moreover, the difference in risk premiums must be significant enough to modify the behavior of riskier financial institutions, providing a strong incentive for them to manage their affairs more prudently.

Unfortunately, no such ideal risk measure has yet been identified. Moreover, history indicates that private entrepreneurs possess great skill in finding loopholes in nearly all the regulatory formulas that have been devised.

Regulation of Capital   Another step governments can take to promote greater public confidence in financial institutions is to impose at least *minimum equity capital requirements* on financial-service firms. The stockholders' equity (net worth) in each financial institution provides a cushion to absorb losses until management can correct weaknesses. When a financial institution has insufficient capital to cover its current and anticipated risk exposure, it faces a *capital adequacy problem.* By imposing minimum equity capital requirements on a financial institution, regulators can force a financial firm's *stockholders* to accept a substantial share of the risks taken on by their firm. The bigger the stockholders' share of each financial institution's total capital, presumably the more watchful the stockholders will be over the firm's risk exposure and the policies pursued by its management. In this instance, the burden of controlling risk would be vested in a financial institution's stockholders, who must supply more high-cost capital if the institution suffers so many losses that it has a real capital adequacy problem.

For further discussion of trends in the financial system, see such sources as apra.gov.au and gcn.com/

Governments must be careful in imposing capital requirements on financial institutions, however. The international financial markets have become so competitive that if financial institutions in one nation face high minimum capital requirements while those in another nation face low or no capital requirements, the latter institutions will possess an unfair competitive advantage. Funds will tend to flow out of an area with burdensome regulations toward an area with less strict rules (often called *regulatory arbitrage*). This fact of international life led the 12 leading industrialized nations to adopt a revolutionary international agreement, known as the Basel Agreement on Bank Capital Standards, in July 1988 (discussed fully in Chapter 17). This regulatory agreement pledged bank supervisory authorities in all participating countries to require their banks to hold at least a minimum amount of capital (i.e., long-term funds provided mainly by the stockholders) relative to the size of their risk-exposed assets, thereby providing greater protection for depositors around the world. Important breakthroughs like the Basel Agreement which bring nations together to cooperate in global financial-sector regulation—sometimes referred to as **harmonization** of global regulatory rules—must continue in the future if public confidence in the global financial marketplace is to be maintained.

harmonization

Private Responses to the Safety Issue   Can the private financial sector satisfactorily ensure its own financial strength and stability? Is the *market* a competent police officer to control institutional risk taking and promote public confidence?

In theory at least, the private marketplace *is* its own regulator. Financial institutions choosing to accept greater risk in managing their customers' and their owners' funds must pay the penalty for risk that the market imposes: a higher cost for any funds raised and often a less reliable supply of funds. Thus, the financial markets will squeeze the earnings of riskier financial institutions through the mechanism of a rising cost of capital. This phenomenon is usually called *market discipline.*

One of the most important ways the private market is dealing with greater risk of failure today is by encouraging the development of *larger* financial institutions that diversify themselves geographically and by product line in order to spread risk over a greater number of markets and services. This development has been most evident, as we will see in Part Four of this text, in the recent rise of interstate banking in the United States and the emergence of highly service-diversified financial holding companies. This trend toward market-expanding operations has encompassed not only financial firms that have traditionally served broad regional, national, and international markets (such as insurance companies, money-center banks, and security brokerage firms) but also locally oriented financial institutions (such as credit unions and savings banks).

For a discussion of
risk management
techniques in the
modern world see
especially
ideas.uqam.ca and
finpipe.com/
derivglossary.htm

**risk-management
tools**

Developing Better Management Tools to Deal with Risk Ai
for private financial institutions to deal with risk in the financial system is i
and use better **risk-management tools.** Managers of successful financial ii
today must be intimately familiar with such risk-management tools as:

- *Interest rate SWAPs,* which permit institutions to trade interest payments for better matching of inflows and outflows of cash (discussed in Chapter 9).
- *Currency swaps,* which permit borrowers to trade currencies with each other and avoid exchange rate risk (discussed in Chapter 23).
- *Financial futures and option contracts,* which allow the setting of prices today for future security purchases or sales (discussed in Chapter 9).
- *Stress-testing of balance sheets,* through which financial firms employ computer simulations to better understand the risks inherent in their investment portfolio under various possible adverse sets of market conditions (discussed in Chapter 17).

Although these risk-management tools are useful, *new* tools must be added to the financial manager's arsenal in the future in order to identify and hedge effectively against the risks that will challenge tomorrow's financial-service institutions. Mere knowledge of existing risk-management tools does not guarantee that all risk exposures will be adequately dealt with, however. Continuing innovation in the risk-management field is absolutely essential to the future smooth operation of the financial system and to the continuing maintenance of public confidence in that system.

The Information Problem Unfortunately, relying *exclusively* on the private marketplace to ensure the strength of financial institutions is open to serious question. Given adequate information, an efficient market can correctly value individual financial institutions. But does the financial marketplace receive *all* of the information it needs to generate optimal decisions? The answer is probably *no.* Depository institutions, for example, still provide only limited information to buyers of the claims they issue against their earnings and assets. Key information regarding the quality of their assets (particularly their individual loans) is often known in detail only to government regulatory agencies.

Capital market investors can only *approximately* price the securities of financial institutions that do not fully disclose their financial condition and prospects. Serious consideration needs to be given to greater financial disclosure of the risk exposure of individual financial institutions, especially for the protection of the public's savings. In 1991, the U.S. Congress passed the FDIC Improvement Act, requiring regular full-scope, on-site examinations of each U.S.-insured depository institution. Moreover, federally insured depository institutions must supply regulatory agencies with annual reports, including an annual audit by an independent public accountant. The FDIC Improvement Act also called for more public disclosure of auditor information and of the market values of institutional assets and capital.

Similar legislation may be needed to promote disclosure among other, nondeposit-type financial institutions as well. In combination with a strong, risk-adjusted insurance program, increased public information about the true condition of financial-service firms could unleash the powerful economic force of *informed investing* to control risk taking by financial institutions more effectively, enhance the stability of the financial marketplace, and promote public confidence in the financial system.

QUESTIONS TO HELP YOU STUDY

8. How can we *reduce risk* in the financial sector?

9. Can we really *reduce risk* exposure or simply *shift* exposure to risk? Why?

10. What are the principal *types of risk* encountered by financial institutions?

11. In what ways can we promote and protect *public confidence* in the financial-service sector of the economy? Why is this important to the public and to financial institutions?

12. Can *publicly provided insurance* help to preserve and protect public confidence in our financial institutions? What are its advantages and possible disadvantages?

13. How can the private marketplace work to control a financial institution's assumption of risk and promote greater public confidence in individual financial firms and the financial system as a whole?

14. How might common capital rules among all financial institutions, improved risk-management tools, and greater disclosure to the public help promote public confidence in financial institutions and the financial system?

The Effect of New Technology on the Design and Delivery of Financial Services

The Information Revolution   Providing financial services to the public involves the analysis, storage, and transfer of *financial information.* A checking account, for example, conveys the information that an individual or a business firm has claim to assets managed by a depository institution or other financial institution offering a checkbook service. The writing of a check is a new information item, designating what amount of funds is to be removed from one account and transferred to another. The advent of computers and the Internet has taught us that information can be transferred in microseconds via computer through Web sites, and via wire, satellite, and other electronic networks that offer greater speed, lower cost, and greater accuracy. The technological revolution in information analysis, storage, and transfer is moving at an accelerating pace. Newer, smaller, and faster electronic-based communications systems appear every year, continually impacting the money and capital markets and the financial-service industry.

Recent Technological Advances   One area of continuing growth will be in *networking,* or *systems integration,* in which computers and other electronic devices are linked via a global communications network. The *Internet,* or *World Wide Web,* offers financial-service firms a low-cost channel through which to advertise their services and offer routine service packages that need not be personalized to the special needs of each customer. Leading financial firms today typically have extensive home pages on the Internet that describe the services they offer and their facilities. Web customers can file requests for transfers of funds, pay bills electronically, file loan applications, receive price or rate quotes, check on available balances, and, in many cases, carry out online purchases of certain goods and services. Once fully adequate safety measures are in place to protect the customer's privacy and funds, access to an even wider array of goods and services will be available instantly through the nearest networked computer, which can also offer digitized telephone communication through the internet.

For a good example of an extensive Web site maintained by a financial-service institution, see wellsfargo.com

Also beginning to have a real impact on financial-market transactions are *cellular* or *pocket telephones,* which allow financial-service customers to communicate from any location, 24 hours a day and even to bring up television clips conveying news, weather, and sports information as well as entertainment. Accompanying the development of full-service pocket telephones is the *pocket* or *handheld computer.* As faster and lighter computer chips are developed, pocket-size and palm-size PCs will be able to more rapidly merge information storage, information retrieval, telecommunications, and extensive computing power into one lightweight, eminently portable, information-gathering resource, available to almost everyone at low cost. Pocket and handheld computers will allow an increasing number of managers of financial-service firms, and more of their customers as well, to instantly record transactions, notes, and memos; fax documents; and send and retrieve data over wireless networks. Financial decision makers increasingly are being equipped with powerful new tools, permitting 24-hour market monitoring and decision making and the rapid implementation of financial decisions from anywhere.

New financial technologies are making it possible for customers to literally do away with their checkbooks. Growing numbers of depository institutions are offering telephone-bill-paying services as well as home and office personal computer (PC) links to a financial institution's computer through which the customer can authorize payments from his or her account with the touch of a button. Equally significant is the spread of "smart cards" encoded with "digitized cash" that allow the customer to pay for goods and services at the point of sale by merely presenting a plastic card. When inserted into a suitable terminal, the amount of a purchase is automatically subtracted from the remaining balance of "digitized cash." Smart cards have grown rapidly in Europe, but somewhat more slowly in the United States, though these cards seem to have a bright future almost everywhere.

These and other technological advances in information technology literally make every financial-service customer into a mobile "branch office." There may be less and less need to ever visit the brick-and-mortar office facilities of a financial institution. Fewer employees are also likely to be needed in the financial institutions sector. The financial-service business is in transition from a labor-intensive industry to a capital-intensive one that increasingly relies upon automation and electronic processing.

Public Attitudes and Cost   The adjustment of people and institutions to the unfolding technological revolution probably will be slower than the revolution itself. For example, many consumers and businesses still prefer the security and privacy of cash and checkbook transactions, even though checkbook volume in the United States has been falling since the mid-1990s. Personal communication between financial institutions and their customers will always be important in the delivery of some financial services, especially to older customers and smaller businesses. However, the cost of these traditional communication methods is rising, and their economic advantage over electronic methods continues to decline.

All financial institutions must be prepared for the continuing spread of new information technology. Otherwise, their competitors will wrest the "high ground" of new markets and new services away from them. But there are major challenges in this technological high ground for all financial institutions, including the following:

- Customer access to financial information and the transfer of financial information must be as user friendly and as nonthreatening as possible (especially for older customers, who grew up in an era when computers and electronic processing were less in evidence).

- Operating costs and service prices must be kept low relative to more conventional paper-based or in-person information systems so that there is sufficient economic incentive for the customer to use the most modern, cost-efficient delivery systems available.

- Adequate technological flexibility must be built in so that, as improved technologies for service production and delivery appear, they can be quickly pressed into service in order to keep each financial-service institution current and competitive. At today's rapid rate of technological innovation, new electronic systems and software packages become outdated within two to three years, on average.

- Finally, auditing and internal control programs must be strengthened to reduce the probability of loss due to computer error or computer fraud, which can drive away customers and endanger the viability of any financial institution (as illustrated by the system break-ins into Citigroup's operations that occurred in the former Soviet Union during 1997 and the more recent upsurge in identity theft around the world).

The Changing Mix of Financial-Service Suppliers in the Financial System

Who will offer the financial services of the future? When the customer wishes to purchase a life insurance policy, a retirement plan, or a checking account, who will be the most likely provider? One thing that is clear now is that the traditional walls between different financial-service industries have eroded so far that they are almost nonexistent today. For example, the cash management accounts and annuities that an insurance company sells to its customers are fully competitive with the cash-management and savings instruments offered by banks and securities firms. Going forward, most of the remaining vestiges of the traditional distinctions between one type of financial-service institution and another are likely to be swept away, as the service menus of different financial institutions look increasingly alike and different financial-service industries literally rush toward each other.

Price Sensitivity and Local Competition   Financial services will be purchased from the financial firm offering the lowest price and the best nonprice features. That low-cost supplier may differ from one market to another, depending on the level and intensity of competition in each financial marketplace. In smaller cities and rural communities, the local bank may turn out to be the most advantageous supplier of most financial services, as was the case in many local communities before elaborate regulatory restrictions were placed on the banking industry during the 1930s. Larger urban markets, in contrast, will continue to be characterized by multiple financial-service suppliers, usually locked in an intense competitive struggle. Moreover, financial-service firms will face a customer increasingly sensitized to differing terms of sale and more ready to transfer his or her business to the cheapest source for the quantity and quality of service desired.

Importance of Established Delivery Systems   Because cost control and productivity will be key factors for the future success of financial-service firms, financial institutions with extensive service delivery systems (including electronic delivery channels) already in place will have a competitive advantage. This feature will clearly favor financial-service institutions possessing established computer, telephone, and office networks. These cost and productivity advantages are likely to lead to still more mergers and consolidations among smaller financial-service companies so that service providers converge and consolidate into larger and larger producing units.

New Financial Institutions and Instruments   The future will usher in *new* financial institutions to deal with the newly emerging financial-service needs. For example, additional secondary (resale) markets for many loans will emerge so that lenders of funds can even more readily than today sell their older assets and gain the cash needed to make new loans and investments. Just as high-grade common stocks, bonds, and futures and options contracts are traded on national exchanges or in the open market today, freer and more open trading of many other financial instruments will eventually become a reality. The unfolding new markets will require new types of financial institutions and new financial services. A few of the newer financial instruments and services that appear to have good prospects for rapid development in the future include:

1. Loans to remodel residential dwellings (due to the aging of existing homes and greater availability of home equity credit).

2. Small business loans.

3. Credit risk derivatives (including credit swaps), which permit a lending institution to seek protection against loan defaults and depreciation in asset values (as discussed in Chapter 8).

securitization

Securitization   There will be a need for new institutions to facilitate the continuing trend toward **securitization** of many of the credit-related assets held by lending institutions and other corporations. The success of mortgage-backed securities over the past three decades demonstrates that a financial institution can more easily take some of the loans it has made and use them as collateral for borrowing money through the sale of securities. Today, there are loan-backed securities collateralized by such diverse assets as commercial and residential mortgage loans, mobile home loans, credit-card receivables, auto and boat loans, home equity loans, and computer equipment leases, to name just a few (see, for example, Chapters 8, 11, 22, and 24).

The future may bring even greater use of loan-backed securities because this device opens up additional funding sources for financial institutions and for many of their corporate customers, adding liquidity and diversification. Securitization is also likely to support the on-going shift of nonfinancial companies away from traditional types of credit obtained through a financial intermediary (such as a bank or savings and loan association) and toward self-financing and self-borrowing directly from investors in the open market. Banks, insurance companies, and other traditional intermediaries will have to continue their development of new services to offset the potentially damaging effects of this trend away from their traditional services on their future profitability.

Consolidations and Convergences within the Financial System

As we noted at this chapter's beginning, acquisitions and mergers have recently come to dominate the financial-service business, as the largest banks, insurance and finance companies, security dealers, and other financial firms have moved to expand in size in the fastest way possible, usually through megamergers involving multibillion-dollar institutions. These megamergers are generally of two types: (1) *consolidations,* which bring together financial firms serving the same industry, and (2) *convergences,* wherein firms from different industries combine their operations. Familiar examples include the *consolidation* of Bank of America with FleetBoston and JPMorgan Chase with Bank One in 2004, creating the second and third trillion-dollar banking organizations in the U.S. (following Citigroup). A good example of *convergence* was the 2002 acquisition of Household Finance—a consumer finance company—with HSBC Bank Plc—a British bank.

Many strong economic and technological forces are propelling these consolidating and converging changes, including a better-informed, more-demanding customer with growing funding needs, the globalization of financial transactions made possible by the rapidly changing technology of information and communication over great distances, and the development of many new financial instruments and services that only the largest financial-service companies can produce and deliver efficiently at low cost. Some of the key players in this race for market size and dominance argue that these financial-firm consolidation and convergence trends will bring about at least some of the following changes:

- Substantial operating cost savings (through the elimination of duplicate office facilities and other overlapping resources).

- Acceleration of revenue growth (as new services are developed and offered in both new and old markets in order to reach out to broader customer segments).

- Greater diversification and, therefore, reduction of risk by widening the service lines offered to the public and spreading out geographically into many different local markets, with each product and location possessing somewhat different cash-flow patterns over time.

- Increased professional expertise, developed by combining the best talents of two or more companies, so that customers get higher-quality services.

- Increased affordability of the latest information storage and transfer technology so that financial-service firms of a wide variety of types and sizes can remain up-to-date in developing new services and in reaching their customers, no matter how distant those customers may be.

- Greater efficiency in producing and selling a mix of services that can be jointly marketed and cross-sold so that the same customers are encouraged to buy more than one service from various parts of the same financial firm (i.e., one-stop shopping), helping to tie a larger proportion of customers more closely to the particular financial-service companies with which they trade.

However, other experts in the field warn that today's trend toward consolidation and convergence is definitely a "mixed blessing." There are key *disadvantages* that may prove to be as powerful as the alleged advantages of these major structural trends among financial-service institutions. These possible disadvantages include the following:

- Higher operating costs may result due to the greater complexities of managing and controlling a highly diversified, giant company that may have grown too fast, going well beyond the optimum (lowest) production cost point for its type of product mix or industry.

- There may be an overestimation of the public's real demand for "one-stop" financial shopping, because many consumers seem less interested in the convenience of receiving all their financial services from one supplier and more interested in shopping around for the best terms available for each major service that they buy, even if that requires trading with several different financial firms. This process has been enhanced by the growing volume of financial services being offered on the Internet.

- The possibility of damaging competition for the largest financial firms from smaller financial-service companies (including many newly chartered banks and other relatively small financial firms), which can provide more personalized financial services and superior individualized service quality (including making the most sensitive customers seem like valued clients, not simply a number in a computer file).

- The ability of smaller financial companies to compete effectively in the range of services they are able to offer, even against financial-service giants, by using *outsourcing*—that is, selling services provided to the offering firm by other suppliers (similar to the franchising concept in retailing)—in order to offer more service variety than a smaller firm operating exclusively on its own can provide.

The foregoing potential disadvantages of consolidation and convergence suggest that not every financial firm needs to be huge, national, or international in scope. Smaller, specialized financial-service companies may still be able to hold onto a solid niche in tomorrow's financial marketplace. This will be especially true if the smaller and more specialized firms can keep their operating costs under tight control and not be undersold by the more wealthy financial-service giants. Indeed, there is little evidence that economies of scale in financial services favor only the largest firms. Some of the best-run financial-service companies lie somewhere in the middle ground, being neither the largest nor the smallest suppliers of financial services.

QUESTIONS TO HELP YOU STUDY

15. What *technological changes* are likely to have the greatest impact on the production and delivery of financial services to the public in future years?

16. Why do you think *consolidation* and *convergence* are taking place today in the financial-service sector for the public? What are their consequences for the managers of financial institutions?

4.5   A New Role for Financial-Service Regulation in an Age of Financial-Service Consolidation and Convergence

The growing consolidation and convergence of financial-service companies pose major new challenges for the regulators and regulatory agencies charged with maintaining a safer and more stable financial system. Regulators cannot stop the powerful market forces that are bringing about the rise of massive financial-service conglomerates, such as Citigroup, HSBC Holdings, Bank America, or Deutsche Bank, because the financial-service industry is now worldwide and much of its growth is technologically driven, which recognizes no artificially erected boundaries. However, government regulators must find a way to make safety and soundness principles work and preserve at least something of the "safety net" that protects less financially sophisticated consumers from mistreatment and the loss of their savings.

This dual concern—letting markets and competition do their essential work to benefit consumers, while preserving safety and soundness to protect the most vulnerable customers—has led to the development of several different regulatory approaches, any one of which may come to dominate the future of government regulation of the financial-service business. For example, the recent Financial-Services Modernization (Gramm-Leach-Bliley) Act, passed in the United States in November 1999, now allows banks, thrifts, insurance companies, and securities firms to enter each other's backyard through a well-known type of financial structure, the *holding company,* where different affiliated firms offer different groups of services, but all are owned by one controlling company at the top of the organization. (See Exhibit 4.1.) Yet another possibility permitted under the new Gramm-Leach-Bliley Act is to allow one financial-service

Financial Holding Company Model

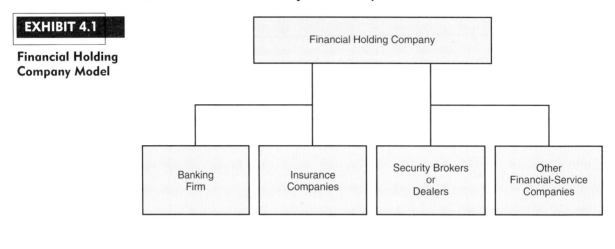

Subsidiary Model

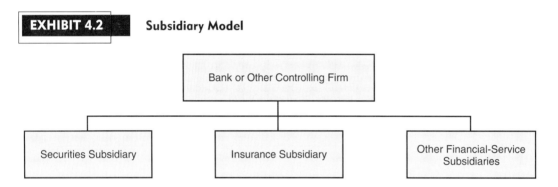

provider, such as a bank, insurance company, or security dealer, to sell other services through its own *subsidiary firms*. (See Exhibit 4.2.)

In the *financial holding company model,* each financial firm has its own capital and management and its own net earnings or earnings losses, which are independent of the earnings or losses of other affiliated companies belonging to the same holding company. With the *subsidiary model,* on the other hand, the earnings or losses of each subsidiary company also affect the parent firm. Nevertheless, regulators can develop walls of protection to shelter those financial firms they wish to insulate, such as by insisting upon stronger capitalization for one or more of the businesses belonging to the same parent company (especially any banks or other depository institutions that serve small savers) or by legally limiting transactions between more-regulated and less-regulated affiliates of the same holding company.

There are also different models that may be used in the future to help fashion new regulatory regimes—that is, to create new organizational structures for regulators that match the changing features of the financial-service industry. One such model—known as the *single regulator* approach—calls upon one regulatory agency to oversee an entire financial-service company with all of its component parts. The challenge here is that such a regulator has to know many different businesses well in order to do a good job of supervising the safety of complex financial institutions. Nevertheless, the "single regulator" strategy may work well in certain situations—for example, in the oversight of small banks, credit unions, and insurance companies. (See Exhibit 4.3.)

A different approach calls for *functional regulation*—letting specialized regulators oversee those financial firms about which they know the most and then pooling their

For further discussion of the Gramm-Leach-Bliley Act and its implications for financial institutions and their regulators see, for example, bankinfo.com and federalreserve.gov

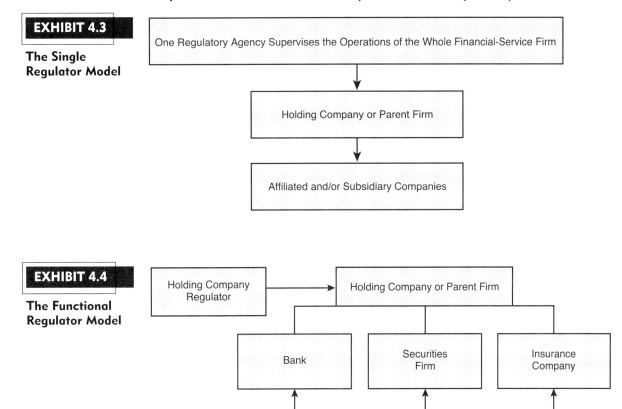

EXHIBIT 4.3

The Single Regulator Model

One Regulatory Agency Supervises the Operations of the Whole Financial-Service Firm

Holding Company or Parent Firm

Affiliated and/or Subsidiary Companies

EXHIBIT 4.4

The Functional Regulator Model

Holding Company Regulator

Holding Company or Parent Firm

Bank

Securities Firm

Insurance Company

Bank Regulator

Securities Regulator

State Insurance Commission

regulatory reports to get an overall picture of the condition of a large, complex financial company. For example, state insurance commissions could regulate and supervise a financial holding company's insurance affiliates or subsidiaries, while the Securities and Exchange Commission could oversee the activities of the securities dealers and brokers belonging to that same company, and the Comptroller of the Currency or the Office of Thrift Supervision could track the soundness of any commercial bank or savings bank that belongs to the large, complex financial firm we are describing. Finally, one regulatory agency (such as the Federal Reserve System) may act as overall or "umbrella" supervisor, receiving regulatory reports from the different regulatory agencies involved and making a general assessment of the strength or weakness of the entire financial-service company. (See Exhibit 4.4.)

Unfortunately, each of these regulatory models is somewhat cumbersome, may be costly to manage, and could lead to regulatory conflicts. In the case of the single regulator model, the same government agency must learn how to examine and supervise many different types of firms in different industries—a potentially costly endeavor— and could easily miss major problems or be misled. On the other hand, functional regulation may not allow any one supervisor to get an accurate picture of the true condition of the *whole* financial-service organization. This is one of the reasons the U.S. Congress, when it passed the Financial Services Modernization (Gramm-Leach-Bliley) Act in 1999, adopted a portion of *both* the single regulator model (with the Federal Reserve System normally serving as overall or "umbrella" regulatory supervisor for each financial-service company as a whole) and a form of functional regulation (with two or more different regulators looking at different units within the same financial-service company).

There is also the danger that some financial firms, if allowed to acquire many different types of companies without safeguards and checks on the quality of management they are hiring, will simply become "too big to fail," requiring governments and regulators to spread out (and possibly thin down) the government's safety net, which was originally set up to protect small savers. If the biggest financial-service providers are not allowed by government to fail, not only does this give financial companies an incentive to expand their size as fast as possible, it also does not fully allow the discipline of the marketplace to work effectively to control the assumption of risk by financial institutions. We may easily lose sight of the fact that the most vulnerable financial institutions are probably those that manage the public's savings deposits and carry out payments for businesses, households, and governments—two financial-service areas that we can ill afford to have break down due to reckless management and risk seeking because these services impact the whole economy and, if poorly done, threaten the public's confidence in the financial system.

We need more disclosure of information to the public on the true condition of financial institutions, and we also need more international regulatory cooperation (known as *harmonization*) to prevent global panics by investors and the public at large. We need to use recent technological advances to improve monitoring systems so that regulators can spot troubled financial firms earlier and have a chance to head off problems quickly. We need to have the owners of financial institutions bear more of their institutions' risk and encourage large account holders to play a bigger role in market disciplining poorly managed financial firms, stimulating the management and owners of financial-service companies to pay increasing attention to measuring and managing risk in order to protect the public from needless financial losses.

4.6 The Future of the Payments System

Tomorrow's economy and financial marketplace will depend crucially upon the continuing ability of the world's *payments system* to function efficiently, speedily, and accurately. Unless businesses that sell goods and services can be confident they will be paid accurately and promptly for what they sell, the economy will begin to slow down, production will fall, and unemployment will rise. A good example of partial payment system breakdown occurred in 2001 when the terrorist attacks of 9/11 caused several financial service firms to shut down temporarily. Ultimately, unless restored, the economy may collapse, because a well-functioning payments system is the essential lifeblood of a modern economy. A major breakdown in the flow of payments can result in economic disaster for millions of people who will lose their incomes and their standard of living.

There are, in reality, *two* payments systems continually at work in the economy today—one for *retail* (or small) payments flowing largely between individuals, families, and business firms; and one for *wholesale* (or large) transactions that flow mainly between banks, business firms, and agencies of government and typically pass through automated clearinghouses (ACHs), the Federal Reserve's wire network (Fedwire), and regional clearing institutions (such as the New York Clearinghouse, known as CHIPS). Technological change has affected *both* of these payments systems, as a growing volume of payments are being made today electronically through computers, via telephone, with plastic cards inserted in point-of-sale terminals in stores, through electronic wire networks between depository institutions, and through the Internet. By the opening of the twenty-first century, more than 3,000 U.S. banks had some form of interactive Internet sites, mostly to provide information and to initiate PC banking. The Internet continues to be mainly focused on information and shifting funds from one account to another, not upon the taking of deposits. In fact, less than a quarter of U.S. families do Internet or electronic banking today and only about half of these use the service on a regular basis. Nonetheless, the proportion of households active in electronic banking is increasing quite rapidly.

You can explore further the trends unfolding in the payments system through such sites as buscom.com

Thus, the retail payments system in the United States continues to lag behind the wholesale payments system in converting from expensive paper transactions to electronic systems. However, Smart cards (plastic wafers with an encoded computer chip aboard that lists how much is available to spend and identifies the account owner) are gaining ground (especially in Europe), as are online accounts inside the Internet, the use of automated teller machines, and telephone payments via verbal authorization or through the use of a credit card number. What the public must have for the future, if our financial system and economy is to avoid being overwhelmed by the cost of paper transactions, is a retail payments network that is fast, cheap, and convenient. Countries such as Norway have raised their use of electronic payments media to account for a majority of their daily payments from less than 10 percent of all their transactions a decade ago, and Denmark now operates a debit card system (called DanKort) that has reduced checks written by its citizens from 280 million a year in the 1980s to under 100 million annually in recent years. Meanwhile, the United States still remains a heavy user of paper, perhaps due to the fact that the prices of several financial services are often bundled together and U.S. customers frequently have no idea how much their paper-based checking account service really costs. Moreover, the U.S. banking system, through most of its history, has been dominated numerically by small depository institutions, making it difficult to bring together all banks within a single electronic payments system.

To be fair, however, we must note that the number of electronic payments in the United States has grown about fivefold in the past two decades and that these payments by wire have now begun to exceed the number of checks written each year. Moreover, the U.S. Congress passed new legislation in October 2003, known as the Check Clearing for the 21st Century Act or the Check 21 Act, for short, which no longer requires a check to be physically transported in order to be processed. Financial institutions can now truncate a check, make an image of it, use that image to create a *substitute check*, and process the substitute. Thus, using electronic means, checks can now be processed much faster and more cheaply than with the old paper-driven system in which the original check had to travel from the bank of deposit to the bank upon which the check was to be drawn. The Check 21 Act should sharply reduce the blizzard of paper that used to be needed to clear checks and move money.

Even with the help of the Check 21 Act, however, big problems still lie ahead for the American payments system, especially in the processing of wholesale payments where transactions typically exceed a trillion dollars a day. It is the *size* of individual wholesale transactions—many of these denominated in multimillions of dollars apiece—that poses a substantial threat for the future. If a few of these supersize transactions fail to *settle* (clear) because of credit risk (i.e., failure of one party to fully comply), liquidity risk (i.e., a temporary cash shortage on the part of one or more large transactors), Herstatt risk (where payments are made by one party but are not yet received by another), or unwinding risk (where payment instructions are subsequently reversed and, therefore, someone is left unpaid), the result could be a panicky chain reaction of failed payments transactions spreading around the globe. Eventually, the *whole* payments system could break down, like falling dominos, as institutions expecting payments do not receive them and, because of that, cannot meet all of their own promises to pay. To help head off such a calamity in the United States, the Federal

Reserve has set limits upon how much in total a payments-system participant can owe to everyone else who belongs to the same clearing system. It has also placed limitations upon the maximum payment a participant can accept from every other institution that is part of the same clearing system.

QUESTIONS TO HELP YOU STUDY

17. What exactly is meant by *functional regulation?* What are its advantages and disadvantages for financial institutions and their customers?

18. In what ways is regulation of the financial-service sector changing? What new types of regulation and deregulation can be expected in the future?

19. What is happening to the global *payments system* today? What changes in the payments system seem likely for the future?

20. Why was passage of the Gramm-Leach-Bliley (Financial Services Modernization) Act so important for American banks and other financial-service institutions?

4.7   The Future Need for Regulation of Financial Institutions

The recent trend toward *deregulation*—the removal of government restrictions on the freedom of the financial markets to trade and allocate resources—of the worldwide financial sector is likely to continue. Governments will be under continuing pressure to amend and relax regulations against product-line and geographic diversification and to lift or liberalize any restrictions placed on the cost of credit (interest rates) and currency prices. If governments do not act to free more completely the financial institutions they supervise from today's product-line and geographic restrictions, nonregulated financial institutions will move in and eventually drive out the more heavily regulated financial institutions from one market after another.

The more likely future developments in deregulation will be the following:

- Reduced barriers to geographic diversification in order to allow financial institutions to find new customers anywhere.

- Reduced restrictions on the portfolio choices made by financial institutions except as may be required to preserve public confidence in financial institutions and the financial system, allowing the private marketplace to play a larger role in shaping a financial-service firm's portfolio choices.

- Reorganization of regulatory agencies to avoid duplication and to minimize the burden of regulation upon financial institutions.

- Reduced barriers to product-line diversification (especially in securities underwriting and in merchant banking and other forms of equity financing).

- Greater reliance on firms' self-assessments of financial risk.

Within the United States, one of the most contentious regulatory debates will focus on the issue of what *new services* commercial banks and other depository institutions should be allowed to offer, consistent with the public's interest in a sound banking and financial system. For example, in the fall of 1999 the U.S. Congress lifted restrictions in place since the 1930s and allowed banks and financial-service holding companies the power to combine menus of banking, insurance, and security underwriting services under the same financial-service organization. The Gramm-Leach-Bliley Act also allowed regulators to expand the permissible list of financial services for banks and financial holding companies as market conditions change in the future. Thus, the United States recognized that financial-service institutions are not frozen in time and must adjust their service menus and service delivery methods to changing circumstances.

Overall, the pace of financial deregulation appears to be accelerating. For example, at the recent Uruguay Round of the General Agreement on Tariffs and Trade (GATT), with 105 nations participating, both Australia and the United States proposed a global free-trade agreement in financial services. In 1993 Mexico, Canada, and the United States crafted a free-trade agreement (NAFTA) parallel to the one signed by the United States and Canada in 1987. The move toward freer trade in financial services has been accompanied by banking and securities deregulation in Britain; recent liberalization of bank service offerings in Germany; and the licensing of European financial firms to offer their services throughout Western Europe as part of the continuing expansion of the European Union.

Regulations That Could Grow

But all regulations in the financial-service field will *not* be eliminated. Indeed, the regulation of financial institutions is shifting to a different ground. There will continue to be great concern over the safety of the public's savings and over maintaining public confidence in the smooth and efficient functioning of financial institutions and the money and capital markets in which they operate. But there is also likely to be continuing and possibly increasing regulatory attention to the issues of financial disclosure, customer privacy, social responsibility, and the importance of promoting a level playing field for financial service competitors.

Financial Disclosure   One important area of emphasis for the future will be **financial disclosure.** Financial institutions will be expected to divulge more completely their terms of service and their financial condition to investors and to the customers they serve in order to promote better financial decision making. Good examples of this trend in the United States in the recent past are the Competitive Banking Equality Act (1987), the Truth in Savings Act (1991), and the FDIC Improvement Act (1991). These laws require increased public disclosure of deposit terms and withdrawal penalties, as well as guaranteeing customers more rapid credit for their deposits so they will have quicker access to spendable funds and greater disclosure concerning the risks of losing one's home if it is used as collateral for a loan.

There is potential gain here as well as risk. With greater disclosure, more financial institutions will be subject to the risk of public disfavor. Ultimately the "discipline of the market" will be more completely unleashed to help ensure prudent management and to control risk taking. Increased disclosure will enable both investors in and customers of financial institutions to make more intelligent decisions about expected return and risk and make the most economical use of available resources.

Privacy Protection   The new century has ushered in a hotly debated issue centered around the disclosure of individuals' personal information (such as their social security number, driver's license number, deposit account numbers, etc.). Scores of proposed new laws have been introduced at federal and state levels to protect so-called "nonpublic information" about individuals and families.

One cause of this explosion in privacy legislation was "identity theft." Tens of thousands of credit card holders and other consumers were becoming victims each year of fraud and theft as their personal information was stolen and used to access their accounts in banks and other financial-service entities. Frequently before the thieves could be

---

Information on financial disclosure protection for the modern consumer may be found at such Web sites as consumerlaw.org and fdic.gov/consumers

financial disclosure

For further discussion of consumer privacy issues, see especially aba.com/Industry+ Issues/Issue . . . and ftc.gov

stopped, victimized consumers lost their access to credit, found that their credit reputation and rating had been severely damaged, or discovered that their savings had disappeared.

Under the terms of the Gramm-Leach-Bliley (Financial Services Modernization) Act banks and other covered financial-service entities were ordered to develop procedures to protect the privacy of their customers' nonpublic information. Moreover, customers were granted the authority to stop a financial institution from sharing their private information with nonaffiliated firms if those customers did so in writing or by some other acceptable method. However, the new law permitted companies that are part of the same overall organization to share private customer information with each other unless they voluntarily agreed not to do so.

The future is likely to bring much more debate over *privacy protection* for the customers of financial institutions. For example, several proposed new privacy laws call for requiring financial firms to protect consumer information and not share it *unless the customer grants permission to do so.* This would be a far more strict standard than the current rule which allows information sharing unless customers notify their financial-service institution that they wish to put a stop to this practice. While consumer groups tend to support such strict privacy legislation, many financial-service firms oppose these proposals because of the added cost and risk involved. Indeed, the debate over protecting the privacy of financial-service consumers is likely to persist far into the foreseeable future as consumer interests are balanced against the demands for efficiency, innovation, and cost control within the financial-service marketplace.

Social Responsibility

Social Responsibility   Another area of regulatory emphasis likely to grow in the future is the *social responsibility* of financial institutions. The financial-service industry will find itself under increasing regulatory scrutiny concerning the fairness of its use of resources and the distribution of its services, particularly access to credit. For example, are all loan customers subjected to the same credit standards? Is there any evidence that the age, race, religion, the neighborhood where someone lives or does business, or other irrelevant characteristics of a credit customer have entered into the decisions of what loans a financial institution has chosen to make or not make, resulting in illegal discrimination? Are some communities and neighborhoods losing convenient access to financial services as neighborhood financial-service facilities are closed, forcing some household residents and businesses to travel great distances in order to obtain the services they require? Are these closings due solely to economic factors or do they reflect hidden discrimination? How can the regulatory agencies who supervise these changes balance economic forces with social issues? Pressure will grow on *all* financial firms to make an "affirmative effort" to serve *all* of their customers, consistent with sound financial practice but with due regard for economic necessity and the fact that most financial-service firms are privately owned and must earn competitive returns for their owners in order to survive.

Promoting a Level Playing Field

Promoting a Level Playing Field   Finally, the *fair and equal regulatory treatment* of all financial institutions offering essentially the same services will continue to be a burning issue in future years. Bankers, who have labeled this the *level playing field* issue, will continue to be among its strongest advocates, pressing for more equal taxation of the earnings of different financial institutions and more equal powers to offer a full range of services in order to be competitive with all other financial-service firms. As long as some financial firms are taxed and regulated differently than other financial firms, the so-called level playing field issue will never go away. It will continue to be a bone of contention that divides the financial sector into the "more regulated" and the "less regulated" firms. Inevitably, financial-service businesses that are "more regulated" and see these added rules as a real burden will strive to bend or change the rules in order to close the gap between them and their less-regulated competitors.

QUESTIONS TO HELP YOU STUDY

21. What regulations in the financial sector are likely to grow in the future?
22. What is the *disclosure* issue and what is its significance?
23. What is *privacy protection* and why is it important to customers of financial institutions? To financial-service institutions themselves?
24. What does a *level playing field* mean to financial institutions and the public?

MARKETS ON THE NET: The Most Important Web Sites for This Chapter

American Bankers Association (aba.com/Industry+Issues)
Consumer Law (consumerlaw.org)
Federal Deposit Insurance Corporation (fdic.gov)
Federal Reserve System (federalreserve.gov)

Federal Trade Commission (ftc.gov)
FinPipe (finpipe.com/derivglossary.htm)
New York Stock Exchange (nyse.com)
Pension Benefit Guaranty Corporation (pbgc.gov)
Quote.com (quote.com)
U.S. Bureau of the Census (census.gov)

Summary of the Chapter's Main Points

The focus of this chapter is the future of the money and capital markets and the financial system that surrounds them. We have highlighted several powerful trends that are reshaping the financial marketplace today, including the following.

- Among the most important broad trends affecting the financial system today are *financial innovation* (i.e., the development of many new services and new service delivery mechanisms), *service proliferation* (as the service menu offered by most financial firms grows), *homogenization* (as the service menus of different financial institutions increasingly look alike), *deregulation* (as governments pull back somewhat and let the private marketplace play a bigger role in controlling the financial system), *market broadening* (as recent advances in communications technology allow financial firms to serve wider market areas, bringing more financial firms into direct competition with each other), *globalization* (as financial-service firms more frequently reach across national and continental boundaries), *consolidation* (as surviving financial firms grow larger in size but fewer in number through acquisitions and mergers), *convergence* (as financial-service providers from different industries make acquisitions and combine operations across traditional industry boundaries), and *competition* (as broader markets, better technology, and longer service menus bring more financial firms into intense rivalry with each other as they compete for the customers' business).

- This chapter also portrays the broad *social, economic,* and *demographic* trends that are restructuring financial institutions today. The chapter highlights major shifts in the character of the population—the consumers of today's and tomorrow's financial services. That population is not only growing older with a need for a somewhat different menu of services, but is also more focused on risk exposure and the need for long-term, relatively stable sources of income. Financial institutions must learn to better serve this older, most rapidly growing segment of the world's population.

- This chapter examines the broad *technological* and *economic* changes that are likely to make the financial markets look very different in the era ahead. Service-oriented industries are expanding, while manufacturing units are becoming less important, particularly in the United States and in Europe. Automation, telecommunications, and remarkable advances in biotechnology have opened up new areas for capital investment and accelerated economic growth, provided the financial system can generate more savings to fund them in the future.

- Each of the foregoing trends must be dealt with by the management and owners of financial institutions. These trends call for new managerial and technical skills, including greater knowledge of marketing and planning techniques, more sensitivity to older customers' financial needs, knowledge of how to integrate new technology into the financial-service business, and the capacity to deal with the information revolution.

- *Regulation* of the financial sector is changing in content and focus, with the *private marketplace* playing a larger role, disciplining financial firms to control risk and become more efficient. While many regulations may be reduced, eliminated, or at least simplified in the future, other rules governing the behavior of financial institutions may become more important and more complex in the future. Some of the regulations likely to become more significant in future years include *financial disclosure* rules, *privacy protection* for customers, rules to promote greater *social responsibility,* and regulatory changes designed to bring about a *level playing field* so that the rules of the game are essentially the same for *all* competing financial institutions.

- No one knows for sure what the financial system of the future will look like. However, it seems safe for us to predict fewer, but larger financial-service institutions and more highly diversified financial firms operating within an increasingly competitive financial marketplace.

- Financial institutions of the future will pay more attention to *risk management* and to training their employees to be more effective salespeople. Managers and their staffs inside financial firms will have to work harder to control expenses and improve productivity, and they will need to strive for greater reliability in serving the customer.

Key Terms Appearing in This Chapter

financial innovation, 86
service proliferation, 86
competition, 86
consolidation, 86
deregulation, 86
convergence, 87
homogenization, 87

globalization, 87
market broadening, 87
harmonization, 94
risk-management tools, 95
securitization, 99
financial disclosure, 107

Problems and Issues

1. Please describe how each of the following terms discussed in this chapter could affect the availability of financial services to the public:

deregulation	financial innovation	financial disclosure
consolidation	convergence	privacy protection
risk-management tools	homogenization	market broadening
globalization	harmonization	technological change

2. *Privacy protection* has become an important public policy issue in the financial-service industry. Why does this issue appear to be more important today than in the past? What are the costs and benefits of additional legislation and regulation designed to protect privacy? Is there evidence as to how these regulations benefit the public?

3. If you were managing a small bank or insurance agency in your local community, what future trends in financial services and institutions would likely have the greatest impact on your institution? Why? What responses could you make to each trend you have listed?

> ## Standard & Poor's Market Insight
> ## and Web-Based Problems

STANDARD
&POOR'S

1. This chapter points out the many ways the financial-service industry seems to be changing and suggests what changes we should look for in the future. The purpose of this exercise is for you to get a very current view of how and why some of these changes in the financial system may be taking place—whether the changes discussed in the chapter have slowed or accelerated. Perhaps new changes are taking place in the industry that were not described in this chapter.

   First, go to Standard & Poor's Market Insight database at **mhhe.com/edumarketinsight** and click the "Industry" tab. Locate the industry group (GISC sub-Industry Group) "Diversified Banks" and look under the "S&P Industry Surveys" tab to obtain the most recent banking survey. Then, go to the section labeled "Industry Trends" and try to identify the following: (1) the pace of bank merger activity; (2) the effects of recent banking legislation on the structure of the industry; and (3) the effect that new technology or financial innovation is having or is likely to have on the industry in the near future.

2. One of the interesting consequences of the growing internationalization of markets is the migration of more and more workers across national borders—most of whom send at least a portion of their paychecks back home to families and friends. This trend has spawned a huge volume of relatively small, individual remittances flowing across geographical boundaries (especially between Mexico and the United States). What problems has this created for the financial system and for the workers and families involved? See, for example, **usinfo.state.gov/regional/ar/mexico/02093002.htm.**

www.mhhe.com/rose9e

Semester Project: A Study of the Fed Funds Market

We continue our semester project begun at the end of Chapter 1—a study of the important *federal funds market*—by looking at the rapidly changing system of making payments in the economy. Early in our history, the principal means of making payments consisted of writing checks and dispensing currency and coin and, beginning in the twentieth century, employing the federal funds market (especially where large payments were involved and speed of payment was an important consideration). Today, checkbook volume is falling, supplanted increasingly by debit cards, credit cards, the Internet, and the like, as well as the expansion of the federal funds (interbank loan) market.

Faced with these great technological challenges, the check-clearing system itself is changing. In 2003 the U.S. Congress passed the Check Clearing for the 21st Century Act (referred to today as simply Check 21). Go to the Web site labeled **compliance-headquarters.com/Deposit_Ops/Deposit_Articles/check_21_act.html** and to other Web sources to answer the following questions about the changing check-clearing system and its possible links to the federal funds market:

  a. What is "check truncation"?
  b. What is a "substitute check"?
  c. What costs are banks likely to incur as they prepare for the changes Check 21 may bring? What benefits might they receive?
  d. In what ways does the operation of the federal funds market compete with and act as an important supplement to the check-clearing system? How might Check 21 impact the use of the federal funds market?

Selected References to Explore

Baily, Martin Neil, and Robert Z. Lawrence. "Do We Have a New E-conomy?" *American Economic Review* 91 (May 2001), pp. 308–12.

Federal Deposit Insurance Corporation. "Checks and Balances: New Rules, New Strategies for Bank Customers in the 21st Century," *FDIC Consumer News,* Summer 2004, pp. 1–4.

Kwan, Simon. "Banking Consolidation." *FRBSF Economic Letter,* Federal Reserve Bank of San Francisco, June 18, 2004.

Litan, Robert E., and Alice M. Rivlin. "Projecting the Economic Impact of the Internet." *American Economic Review* 91 (May 2001), pp. 313–17.

Mester, Loretta J. "Changes in the Use of Electronic Payments," *Business Review,* Federal Reserve Bank of Philadelphia, Third Quarter 2003.

Modigliani, Franco, and Albert Ando. "The Permanent Income and the Life Cycle Hypothesis of Saving Behavior." In *Proceedings of the Conference on Consumption and Saving,* The University of Pennsylvania, 1960, pp. 49–174.

Strahan, Philip E. "The Real Effects of U.S. Banking Deregulation." *Review,* Federal Reserve Bank of St. Louis, July/August 2003, pp. 111–28.

Part 2

Interest Rates and the Prices of Financial Assets

There is an old adage that says, "It takes money to make money!" When it comes to saving and investing, this is certainly true. But how much money can you make? The smart investor will have done his or her homework and have a pretty good idea. However, this same smart investor also knows there are few sure bets in the world. As Humphrey Bogart said in *The African Queen*, "You pays your money and you takes your chances." It is the smart investor who understands how much "chance" is being taken, and just what the nature of this "chance" is. The purpose of Part Two of this book is to help you become a smart investor—which is a status worth achieving because, quite literally, it pays!

How much money can an investor expect to earn? The answer depends on which financial asset he or she chooses to buy. But regardless of the choice made, when the asset is acquired, the investor gives up his or her ability to consume the amount of that investment today. A smart investor must be compensated fully for that loss of consumption power, even if there is no risk that the investment will turn sour. The amount of this compensation per dollar invested is referred to as the "risk-free real interest rate" and it plays a central role in determining the price of *every* financial asset. How the economy arrives at this fundamental interest rate is the subject of Chapter 5.

Understanding the risk-free real interest rate is only the first step toward becoming a smart investor. There are literally thousands of interest rates in the financial marketplace! And to complicate matters, there is no single way to compute an interest rate. The smart investor must understand exactly how the interest rate he or she has been quoted was computed and how to compute the right interest rate that he or she really needs to know when evaluating any investment. Chapter 6 develops the tools you will need to understand and compute the various interest rates in common usage in the financial marketplace today.

Chapters 7 and 8 are devoted to analyzing the "chances" investors take when they "pays their money." Should you invest in short-term or long-term assets? How can inflation turn a good investment into a loser? What other risks does the investor face and how do these risks differ across different financial assets? The smart investor must decide not only how much and what types of risk to accept, but also how much compensation for risk he or she requires in order to make the investment. Of course, many risks are unavoidable. Chapter 9 describes the rapidly growing number of special financial assets—referred to as *financial derivatives*—that enable these risks to be transferred from one investor to another. Therefore, smart investors also may choose to hedge the risks they face when they "takes their chances" in the financial marketplace.

Chapter 5

The Determinants of Interest Rates: Competing Ideas

Learning Objectives

in This Chapter

- You will see the important roles that *interest rates* play within the economy.
- You will explore the most important ideas about what determines the level of interest rates and asset prices within the financial system.
- You will be able to draw up a list for easy reference of the key forces that economists believe set market interest rates and asset prices in motion.

What's in This Chapter?
Key Topics Outline

Interest Rates: Nature and Roles within the Financial System

The Classical Theory of Interest: Assumptions and Conclusions

The Substitution Effect and Investment Demand

Liquidity Preference Theory: Demand and Supply of Cash Balances

Central Banking and Interest Rates

The Credit Theory of Interest Rates: Demand and Supply of Loanable Funds

Rational Expectations and the Public's Changing Outlook for Interest Rates

5.1   Introduction: Interest Rates and the Price of Credit

In the opening chapter of this book, we described the money and capital markets as one vast pool of funds, depleted by the borrowing activities of households, businesses, and governments and replenished by the savings these sectors supply to the financial system. The money and capital markets make saving possible by offering the individual saver a wide menu of choices where funds may be placed at attractive rates of return. By committing funds to one or more financial instruments (assets), the saver, in effect, becomes a lender of funds. The financial markets also make borrowing possible by giving the borrower a channel through which securities (IOUs) can be issued to lenders. And the money and capital markets make investment and economic growth possible by providing the funds needed for the purchase of machinery and equipment and the construction of buildings, highways, and other productive facilities.

rate of interest

price of credit

Clearly, then, the acts of saving and lending, borrowing and investing are intimately linked through the entire financial system. And one factor that significantly influences and ties all of them together is the **rate of interest.** The rate of interest is the price a borrower must pay to secure scarce loanable funds from a lender for an agreed-upon time period. Some authorities refer to it as the **price of credit.** But unlike other prices in the economy, the rate of interest is really a *ratio* of two quantities: the money cost of borrowing divided by the amount of money actually borrowed, usually expressed on an *annual percentage* basis.

Interest rates send *price signals* to those who ultimately supply funds to the economy through saving and lending and to those who ultimately demand funds by borrowing to make capital investments in the economy. Higher interest rates provide incentives to increase the supply of funds, but at the same time they reduce the demand for those funds. Lower interest rates have the opposite effects. Since (as we saw in Chapter 2) the total amount of funds supplied by the financial system must just equal the total amount borrowed—that is, quantity supplied equals quantity demanded, then whether an increase in interest rates increases the total amount of funds available in the economy depends on whether the supply response of savers and lenders is greater or less than the demand response of borrowers. In this chapter, we will discuss the forces that are believed by economists and financial analysts to underlie the supply and demand factors that ultimately determine market interest rates in the financial marketplace.

5.2   Functions of the Rate of Interest in the Economy

The *rate of interest* performs several important functions in the economy:

- It helps guarantee that current savings will flow into investment to promote economic growth.
- It allocates the available supply of credit, generally providing loanable funds to those investment projects with the highest expected returns.
- It brings the supply of money into balance with the public's demand for money.
- It is an important tool of government policy through its influence on the volume of saving and investment. If the economy is growing too slowly and unemployment is rising, the government can use its policy tools to lower interest rates in order to stimulate borrowing and investment. On the other hand, an economy experiencing rapid inflation has traditionally called for a

government policy of higher interest rates to slow borrowing and spending and encourage more saving.

In the pages of the financial press, the phrase "the interest rate" is frequently used. In truth, there is no such thing as "*the* interest rate," for there are thousands of different interest rates in the financial system. Even securities issued by the same borrower often carry a variety of interest rates. In Chapters 7 and 8, the most important factors that cause interest rates to vary among different loans and securities and over time will be examined in detail. In this chapter, we focus upon those basic forces that influence the level of *all* interest rates.

risk-free rate of interest

To uncover these basic rate-determining forces, however, we must make a simplifying assumption. We assume in this chapter that there *is* one fundamental interest rate, known as the *pure* or **risk-free rate of interest,** which is a component of *all* interest rates. While the pure or risk-free rate of interest exists only in theory, the closest real-world approximation to this pure rate of return is the market interest rate on government bonds. It is a rate of return presenting little or no risk of financial loss to the investor and representing the opportunity cost of holding idle cash because the investor can always invest in government bonds of lowest risk and earn this minimum rate of return.

Once we explain the pure rate of interest in this chapter, the interest rates we normally see in the real world will be explored in the chapters that follow. Only the government can borrow at approximately the risk-free rate of interest. Other borrowers in the real world must pay higher interest rates for borrowed funds than the risk-free rate due to several different risk factors—for example credit or default risk, maturity or term risk, marketability risk, and so on. In Chapters 7 and 8 we will add these risk factors onto the pure or risk-free rate of interest to determine the level of and changes in real-world interest rates that we see every day.

First, however, we must examine the forces that determine the pure or risk-free interest rate itself. In this chapter we present the four most popular views—the classical theory, the liquidity preference theory, the loanable funds theory, and the rational expectations theory of interest—about how the fundamental pure or risk-free rate of interest is determined. We will also note which of these views about interest rates is the most widely followed today by practitioners and active investors "on the street," keeping in mind, however, that there are some important truths to consider in every one of the interest-rate theories discussed in this chapter.

5.3 The Classical Theory of Interest Rates

classical theory of interest rates

One of the oldest theories concerning the determinants of the pure or risk-free interest rate is the **classical theory of interest rates,** developed during the nineteenth and early twentieth centuries by a number of British economists and elaborated on by Irving Fisher (1930) and others more recently. The classical theory argues that the rate of interest is determined by two forces: (1) the supply of savings, derived mainly from households, and (2) the demand for investment capital, coming mainly from the business sector. Let us examine these rate-determining forces of savings and investment demand in detail.

Saving by Households

What is the relationship between the rate of interest and the volume of savings in the economy? Most saving in modern economies is carried out by individuals and families. For these households, saving is simply abstinence from consumption spending. *Current savings, therefore, are equal to the difference between current income and current consumption expenditures.*

In making the decision on the timing and amount of saving to be done, households typically consider several factors: the size of current and long-term (permanent) income, the desired savings target, and the desired proportion of income to be set aside in the form of savings (i.e., the propensity to save). Generally, the volume of household saving rises with income. Higher-income families and individuals tend to save more and consume less relative to their total income than families with lower incomes.

Although income levels probably dominate saving decisions, interest rates also play an important role. Interest rates affect an individual's choice between current consumption and saving for future consumption. The classical theory of interest assumes that individuals have a definite *time preference* for current over future consumption. A rational individual, it is assumed, will always prefer current enjoyment of goods and services over future enjoyment. Therefore, the only way to encourage an individual or family to consume less now and save more is to offer a higher rate of interest on current savings. If more were saved in the current period at a higher rate of return, future consumption would be increased. For example, if the current rate of interest is 10 percent and a household saves $100 instead of spending it on current consumption, it will be able to consume $110 in goods and services a year from now.

The classical theory considers the payment of interest a reward for *waiting*—the postponement of current consumption in favor of greater future consumption. Higher interest rates increase the attractiveness of saving relative to consumption spending, encouraging more individuals to substitute current saving (and future consumption) for **substitution effect** some quantity of current consumption. This so-called **substitution effect** calls for a *positive* relationship between interest rates and the volume of savings. Higher interest rates bring forth a greater volume of current savings. For example, if the rate of interest in the financial markets rises from 5 to 10 percent, the volume of current savings by households might increase from $100 to $200 billion.

Saving by Business Firms

Not only households but also businesses save. Most businesses hold savings balances in the form of retained earnings (as reflected in their equity or net worth accounts). In fact, the increase in retained earnings reported by businesses each year is a key measure of the volume of current business saving, which supplies most of the money for annual investment spending by business firms.

The critical element in determining the amount of business savings is the level of business *profits*. If profits are expected to rise, businesses will be able to draw more heavily on earnings retained in the firm and less heavily on the money and capital markets for funds. The result is a reduction in the demand for credit and a tendency toward lower interest rates. On the other hand, when profits fall but firms do not cut back on their investment plans, they will be forced to make heavier use of the money and capital markets for investment funds. The demand for credit rises, and interest rates may rise as well.

Although the principal determinant of business saving is profits, interest rates also play a role in the decision of what proportion of current operating costs and long-term investment expenditures should be financed internally from retained earnings and what proportion should be financed externally from borrowing in the money and capital markets. Higher interest rates in the money and capital markets typically encourage firms to use internally generated funds more heavily in financing their projects. Conversely, lower interest rates encourage greater use of external funds from the money and capital markets.

Saving by Government

Governments also save, though usually less frequently than households and businesses. In fact, most government saving (i.e., a budget surplus) appears to be unintended saving that arises when government receipts unexpectedly exceed the actual amount of expenditures. Income flows in the economy (out of which government tax revenues arise) and the pacing of government spending programs are the dominant factors affecting government savings. However, interest rates can play a role in that higher interest rates raise interest payments owed on the government's debt. These higher expenditures tend to increase government deficits (or reduce budget surpluses) and, thereby, reduce government savings.

The Demand for Investment Funds

Business, household, and government savings are important determinants of interest rates according to the classical theory of interest, but they are not the only ones. The other critical rate-determining factor is *investment spending,* most of it carried out by business firms.

Certainly, businesses, as the leading investment sector in the economy, require huge amounts of funds each year to purchase equipment, machinery, and inventories, and to support the construction of new buildings and other physical facilities. The majority of business expenditures for these purposes consists of *replacement investment;* that is, expenditures to replace equipment and facilities that are wearing out or are technologically obsolete. A smaller but more dynamic form of business capital spending is labeled *net investment:* expenditures to acquire new equipment and facilities in order to increase output. The sum of replacement investment plus net investment equals *gross investment.*

Replacement investment usually is more predictable and grows at a more even rate than net investment. This is due to the fact that such expenditures are financed almost exclusively from inside the firm and frequently follow a routine pattern based on depreciation formulas. Expenditures for new equipment and facilities (net investment), on the other hand, depend on the business community's outlook for future sales, changes in technology, industrial capacity, and the cost of raising funds. Because these factors are subject to frequent changes, it is not surprising that net investment is highly volatile and a driving force in the economy. Changes in net investment are closely linked to fluctuations in the nation's output of goods and services, employment, and prices.

The Investment Decision-Making Process   The process of investment decision making by business firms is complex and depends on a host of qualitative and quantitative factors. The firm must compare its current level of production with the capacity of its existing facilities and decide whether it has sufficient capacity to handle anticipated demand for its product. If expected future demand will strain the firm's existing facilities, it will consider expanding its operating capacity through net investment.

Most business firms have several investment projects under consideration at any one time. Although the investment decision-making process varies from firm to firm, each business generally makes some estimate of net cash flows (i.e., revenues minus all expenses, including taxes) that each project will generate over its useful life. From this information, plus knowledge of each investment project's acquisition cost, management can calculate its expected net rate of return and compare that expected return with anticipated returns from alternative projects, as well as with market rates of interest.

One common method for performing this calculation is the *internal rate of return (IRR) method,* which equates the total cost of an investment project with the future net cash flows (NCF) expected from that project discounted back to their present values. Thus,

$$\text{Cost of project} = \frac{\text{NCF}_1}{(1+r)^1} + \frac{\text{NCF}_2}{(1+r)^2} + \cdots + \frac{\text{NCF}_n}{(1+r)^n} \qquad (5.1)$$

where each NCF represents the expected annual net cash flow from the project and r is its expected internal rate of return. The internal rate of return method performs two functions: (1) it measures the annual yield the firm expects from an investment project, and (2) it reduces the value of all future cash flows expected over the economic life of the project down to their present value to the firm. In general, if the firm must choose among several investment projects, it will choose the one with the *highest* expected internal rate of return.

Although the internal rate of return provides a yardstick for selecting potentially profitable investment projects, how does a business decide how much to spend on investment at any point in time? How many projects should be chosen? It is here that the money and capital markets play a key role in the investment decision-making process.

Suppose a business firm is considering the following projects with their associated expected internal rates of return:

Project	Expected Internal Rate of Return (annualized)
A	15%
B	12
C	10
D	9
E	8

How many of these projects will be adopted? The firm must compare each project's expected internal return with the cost of raising capital—the interest rate—in the money and capital markets to finance the project.

Assume that funds must be borrowed in the financial marketplace to complete any of the above projects and that the current cost of borrowing—the rate of interest—is 10 percent. Which projects are acceptable from an economic standpoint? As shown in Exhibit 5.1, projects A and B clearly are acceptable because their expected returns exceed the current cost of borrowing capital (10 percent) to finance them. The firm would be indifferent about project C because its expected return is no more than the cost of borrowed funds. Projects D and E, on the other hand, are unprofitable at this time.

It is through changes in the cost of raising funds that the financial markets can exert a powerful influence on the investment decisions of business firms. As credit becomes scarcer and more expensive, the cost of borrowed capital rises, eliminating some investment projects from consideration. For example, if the cost of borrowed funds rises from 10 to 13 percent, only project A in our earlier example would appear to be economically viable. On the other hand, if credit becomes more abundant and less costly, the cost of capital for the individual firm will tend to decline and more projects will become profitable. In our example, a decline in the cost of borrowed funds from 10 to $8\frac{1}{2}$ percent would make all but project E economically viable and possibly acceptable to the firm.

Investment Demand and the Rate of Interest

This reasoning explains, in part, why the demand for investment capital by business firms was regarded by the classical economists as *negatively* related to the rate of interest. At low rates of interest,

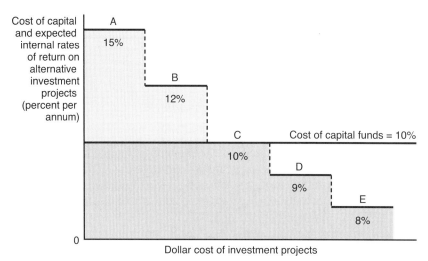

EXHIBIT 5.1

The Cost of Capital and the Business Investment Decision

more investment projects become economically viable and firms require more funds to finance a longer list of projects. On the other hand, if the rate of interest rises to high levels, fewer investment projects will be pursued and fewer funds will be required from the financial markets. For example, at a 12 percent rate of interest, only $100 billion in funds for investment spending might be demanded by business firms in the economy. If the rate of interest drops to 10 percent, however, the volume of desired investment by firms might rise to $200 billion.

The Equilibrium Rate of Interest in the Classical Theory of Interest

The classical economists believed that interest rates in the financial markets were determined by the interplay of the supply of saving and the demand for investment. Specifically, the equilibrium rate of interest is determined at the point where the quantity of savings supplied to the market is exactly equal to the quantity of funds demanded for investment. In Exhibit 5.2, the volume of saving in the economy is shown

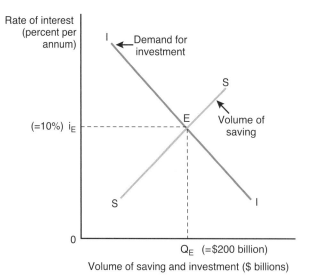

EXHIBIT 5.2

The Equilibrium Rate of Interest in the Classical Theory

to increase with the rate of interest (S-curve), and the demand for investment is shown to fall as the rate of interest rises (I-curve). Equilibrium occurs at point E, where the equilibrium rate of interest is i_E and the equilibrium quantity of capital funds traded in the financial markets is Q_E.

To illustrate, suppose the total volume of savings supplied by businesses, households, and governments in the economy at an interest rate of 10 percent is $200 billion (S-curve). Moreover, at this same 10 percent rate, businesses would also demand $200 billion in funds for investment purposes (I-curve). Then 10 percent must be the equilibrium rate of interest, and $200 billion is the equilibrium quantity of funds that would be traded in the money and capital markets.

The market rate of interest moves toward its equilibrium level. However, supply and demand forces change so fast that the interest rate rarely has an opportunity to settle in at a specific equilibrium level. At any given time, the interest rate is probably above or below its true equilibrium level but moving *toward* that equilibrium. If the market rate is temporarily above equilibrium, the volume of savings exceeds the demand for investment capital, creating an excess supply of savings. Savers will offer their funds at lower and lower rates until the market interest rate approaches equilibrium. Similarly, if the market interest rate lies temporarily below equilibrium, investment demand exceeds the quantity of savings available. Business firms will bid up the interest rate until it approaches the level at which the quantity saved equals the quantity of funds demanded for investment purposes.

The classical theory of interest rates helps us to understand some of the *long-term forces* driving interest rates. For example, some analysts argue that, in the future, interest rates on average could be relatively low compared to historic norms—a forecast that so far has turned out to be correct since the turn of the new century. These analysts pointed out that the populations of the United States and most other nations are aging, shifting heavily toward those age groups in which individuals spend less of their current income and save more (in part to prepare for retirement), pushing interest rates down. This viewpoint assumes that people's consumption and savings habits tend to follow a predictable *life cycle,* with younger workers borrowing heavily in anticipation of higher incomes in the future and older workers, who may have reached their maximum annual earnings, saving heavily in anticipation of lower incomes in the future. The money and capital markets make a vital contribution to this process, directing the savings of older individuals into the hands of younger people who desire to improve their current standard of living by borrowing.

Limitations of the Classical Theory of Interest

The classical theory of interest sheds light on the factors affecting interest rates. However, it has limitations. The central problem is that the theory ignores factors other than saving and investment that affect interest rates. For example, many financial institutions have the power to create money today by making loans to the public. When borrowers repay their loans, money is destroyed. The volume of money created or destroyed affects the total amount of credit available in the financial system and, therefore, must be considered in any explanation of interest rates. In addition, the classical theory assumes that interest rates are the principal determinant of the quantity of savings available. Today economists recognize that *income* and *wealth* are probably more important in determining the volume of saving. Finally, the classical theory contends that the demand for borrowed funds comes principally from the business sector. Today, however, both consumers and governments are also important borrowers. As we will see in the rest of this chapter, more

Data on interest rates may be found at a wide variety of sites on the World Wide Web such as bankrate.com and investinginbonds. com

recent theories about interest rates address a number of these limitations of the classical theory.

QUESTIONS TO HELP YOU STUDY

1. What are the functions or roles played by the rate of interest in the economy and financial system? Can you explain why each function is important to the well-being of individuals, businesses, and governments?

2. Explain the meaning of the term *pure* or *risk-free rate of interest*. Why is this interest rate important and what is its relationship to other interest rates?

3. If we could identify the forces shaping the risk-free or pure rate of interest, what advantage could this give us in explaining the many different interest rates we see every day in the real world?

4. In the classical theory of interest rates, what forces determine the market rate of interest? What assumptions does the classical theory of interest rest upon?

5. Explain why the supply curve in the classical theory of interest rates has a positive slope. Why does the demand curve in the classical theory have a negative slope?

5.4 The Liquidity Preference or Cash Balances Theory of Interest Rates

The classical theory of interest has been called a *long-term* explanation of interest rates because it focuses on the public's thrift habits—a factor that tends to change slowly. During the 1930s, British economist John Maynard Keynes (1936) developed a short-term theory of the rate of interest that, he argued, was more relevant for policymakers and for explaining near-term changes in interest rates. This theory is known as the **liquidity preference** (or *cash balances*) **theory of interest rates.**

liquidity preference theory of interest rates

The Demand for Liquidity

The liquidity preference theory contends that the rate of interest is really a payment for the use of a scarce resource—*money* (cash balances). Businesses and individuals prefer to hold money for carrying out daily transactions and also as a precaution against future cash needs even though money's yield is usually low or even nonexistent. Investors in fixed-income securities, such as government bonds, frequently desire to hold money or cash balances as a haven against declining asset prices. Interest rates, therefore, are the price that must be paid to induce money holders to surrender a perfectly liquid asset (cash balances) and hold other assets that carry more risk. At times the preference for liquidity grows very strong. Unless the money supply is expanded, interest rates will rise.

In the theory of liquidity preference, only two outlets for investor funds are considered: *bonds* and *money* or *cash balances* (including bank deposits). Money provides perfect liquidity (instant spending power). Bonds pay interest but cannot be spent until converted into cash. If interest rates rise, the market value of bonds paying a fixed rate of interest falls; the investor would suffer a capital loss if those bonds were converted into cash. On the other hand, a fall in interest rates results in higher bond prices; the bondholder will experience a capital gain if his or her bonds are sold for cash. To the classical theorists, it was irrational to hold money because it provided little or no return. To proponents of liquidity preference, however, the holding of money (cash balances) could be a perfectly rational act if interest rates were expected to rise, because rising rates can result in substantial losses for investors in bonds.

FINANCIAL DEVELOPMENTS

Interest Rates in the Money and Capital Markets and the Net Present Value (NPV) Method for Making Investment Decisions

Our discussion of how interest rates affect business investment decisions focused upon the internal rate of return (IRR) method for comparing interest rates with the expected return on an investment project. Actually, the IRR method for evaluating investments is less widely used today than another method of investment analysis—the *net present value* (NPV) approach.

For example, suppose that we operate a business that is considering an investment project costing $1,000 and generating expected net cash flows (cash revenues less cash expenses) of:

Year	Net Cash Flow
1	$100
2	200
3	300
4	400
5	500
6	600

after which the project becomes worthless. Thus, its internal rate of return (IRR) can be found from the formula:

$$\$1{,}000 = \frac{\$100}{(1+r)^1} + \frac{\$200}{(1+r)^2} + \frac{\$300}{(1+r)^3} + \frac{\$400}{(1+r)^4} + \frac{\$500}{(1+r)^5} + \frac{\$600}{(1+r)^6}$$

where the internal rate of return (r) turns out to be about 10 percent. If the going market rate on borrowed funds in the money and capital markets is 8 percent, this project is clearly acceptable because its expected internal rate of return exceeds the cost of borrowed funds.

Now suppose the firm believes that its stockholders demand a minimum required after-tax return of 12 percent. Then the proposed project's net present value must be:

$$NPV = -\$1{,}000 + \frac{\$100}{(1+.12)^1} + \frac{\$200}{(1+.12)^2}$$
$$+ \frac{\$300}{(1+.12)^3} + \frac{\$400}{(1+.12)^4} + \frac{\$500}{(1+.12)^5}$$
$$+ \frac{\$600}{(1+.12)^6} \approx \$304$$

This proposed investment project is acceptable because its NPV is *positive* (NPV > 0) at about +$304.

With IRR, the implied reinvestment rate of return for each project's cash flows is equal to the calculated internal rate of return and, therefore, is likely to be different for each proposed project. However, under the NPV method, the implied reinvestment rate is the *same* for *all* projects—investors' required rate of return (i.e., the minimum necessary return on the investment opportunity available to an investor to keep a business's stock price unchanged). Thus, NPV measures the true opportunity cost of a project for an investor whose goal is *value maximization* (i.e., maximizing the value of each business firm's stock).

As interest rates rise, offering investors higher returns on other investment alternatives of comparable risk, then investors will tend to raise the required return they demand from an investment project. Fewer projects will be acceptable. Conversely, when interest rates fall, investors' required rates of return will tend to decline. Investment spending will tend to rise. Clearly, interest rates in the money and capital markets play a vital role in determining the volume of investment and in attracting savings to make investment possible.

Motives for Holding Money (Cash Balances)   According to liquidity preference theory, the public demands money for three different purposes (motives). The *transactions motive* represents the demand for money (cash balances) to purchase goods and services. Because inflows and outflows of money are not perfectly synchronized in either timing or amount and because it is costly to shift back and forth between money and other assets, businesses, households, and governments must keep some cash in the till or in demand accounts simply to meet daily expenses. Some money also must be held as a reserve for future emergencies and to cover extraordinary expenses. This *precautionary motive* arises because we live in a world of uncertainty and cannot predict exactly what expenses or investment opportunities will arise in the future.

In the earliest versions of the theory, money demanded for transactions and precautionary purposes was assumed to be dependent on the level of national income, business sales, and prices. Reflecting money's role as a medium of exchange, higher levels of income, sales, or prices increase the need for cash balances to carry out transactions and to respond to future opportunities. However, neither the precautionary nor the transactions demand for money was assumed to be affected significantly by changes in interest rates, but remained fixed in the short term. In the longer term, however, transactions and precautionary demands were assumed to change as income changed.

Short-term changes in interest rates were attributed to a third motive for holding money or cash balances—the *speculative motive*—that stems from uncertainty about the future prices of bonds. To illustrate, suppose an investor has recently purchased a corporate bond for $1,000. The company issuing the bond promises to pay $100 a year in interest income. To simplify matters, assume the bond is a *perpetual security*. This means the investor will receive $100 a year for as long as the security is held. The annual rate of return (or yield) on the bond, then, is 10 percent ($100/$1,000). Suppose now that the interest rate on bonds of similar quality rises to 12 percent. What happens to the price of the 10 percent bond? Its price in the marketplace will *fall* because its annual promised yield at a price of $1,000 is *less* than 12 percent. The 10 percent bond's price will approach $833 because at this price the bond's $100 annual interest payment gives the investor an approximate annual yield of 12 percent ($100/$833). In the reverse situation, if interest rates were to decline—say, to 9 percent—the 10 percent bond would experience a rise in its market price.

If investors expect rising interest rates, many of them will demand money or near-money assets (such as deposits in a bank, credit union, or money market fund) instead of bonds because they believe bond prices will fall. As the expectation that interest rates will rise grows strong in the marketplace, the demand for cash balances as a secure store of value increases. We may represent this speculative demand for money by a line or curve that slopes downward and to the right, as shown in Exhibit 5.3, reflecting a *negative* relationship between the speculative demand for money and the level of interest rates. At low rates of interest, many investors believe that interest rates are soon to rise (i.e., bond prices are going to fall), and,

EXHIBIT 5.3

Speculative Demand for Money or Cash Balances

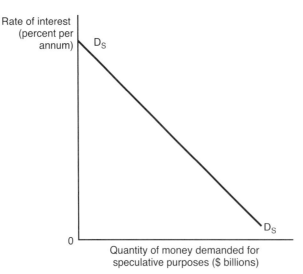

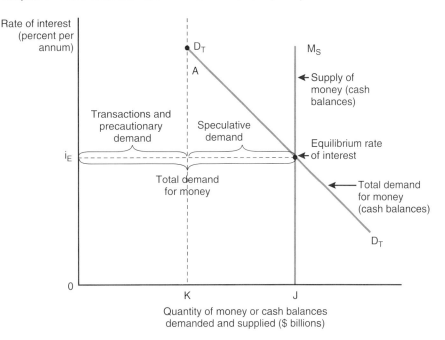

EXHIBIT 5.4

The Total Demand for Money or Cash Balances and the Equilibrium Rate of Interest in the Liquidity Preference Theory

therefore, more money is demanded. At high rates of interest, on the other hand, many investors will conclude that interest rates soon will fall and bond prices will rise, so the demand for cash balances decreases while the demand for bonds increases.

From another vantage point, when interest rates are high, the opportunity cost (loss) from holding idle cash increases. Thus, high interest rates encourage investors to reduce their cash balances and buy bonds. In contrast, when interest rates are low, the opportunity cost of holding idle cash is also low, but the expected capital loss from holding bonds is high should interest rates rise. Thus, there is more incentive to hold money rather than bonds when interest rates are low.

Total Demand for Money (Cash Balances)   The total demand for money or cash balances in the economy is simply the sum of transactions, precautionary, and speculative demands. Because the principal determinant of transactions and precautionary demand is income, not interest rates, these money demands are fixed at a certain level of national income. Let this demand be represented by the quantity $0K$ shown along the horizontal axis in Exhibit 5.4. Then, any amount of cash demanded in excess of $0K$ represents speculative demand. The total demand for money is represented along curve D_T. Therefore, if the rate of interest lies at the moment at i_E, Exhibit 5.4 shows that the speculative demand for money will be KJ and the total demand for money will be $0J$.

The Supply of Money (Cash Balances)

The other major element determining interest rates in liquidity preference theory is the supply of money. In modern economies, the money supply is controlled, or at least closely regulated, by government. Because government decisions concerning the size of the money supply presumably are guided by the public welfare, not by the level of interest rates, we assume that the supply of cash balances is *inelastic* with respect to

One way that government policy attempts to stimulate a weak economy—a period of slow or no growth and high unemployment—is to lower short-term interest rates. The usual impact of this policy action is to stimulate investment demand by businesses, which spurs production, leading producers to hire additional workers. As a result, output (real gross domestic product, or GDP) tends to rise and unemployment declines.

During the Great Depression of the 1930s, when economic activity fell sharply, this policy appeared to be ineffective in many countries around the world. The problem was that lower interest rates did not stimulate demand for goods and services, no matter how low the government reduced interest rates. This condition came to be known as the *liquidity trap*. An economic condition that is generally believed to be necessary for a liquidity trap to occur is falling prices (*deflation*).

Since the time of the Great Depression there has been little evidence of a liquidity trap anywhere in the world—that is, until very recently in Japan. Beginning in the early 1990s, the Japanese economy—the world's second largest, after the United States—began to stagnate after several decades of impressive growth. With falling prices, attempts to stimulate the Japanese economy by lowering short-term interest rates were not particularly successful. Economic stagnation and deflation continued for more than a decade, even though short-term interest rates had been driven essentially to *zero*. (Only after more than a decade of decline did the Japanese economy finally show some signs of a turnaround as the years 2003 and 2004 unfolded.)

The recent Japanese experience has led to a revival of interest in the liquidity trap. Government policymakers around the globe have become much more concerned about the possibility that their economies also might begin to experience deflation. Given the experience of the Japanese economy, policymakers elsewhere are now cognizant of the fact that new ways to stimulate a weak economy may be needed, if similar circumstances in their economies cause market interest rates to become an ineffective policy tool.

the rate of interest. Such a money supply curve is represented in Exhibit 5.4 by the vertical line M_S.

The Equilibrium Rate of Interest in Liquidity Preference Theory

The interplay of the total demand for and the supply of money or cash balances determines the equilibrium rate of interest in the short run. As shown in Exhibit 5.4, the equilibrium rate is found at point i_E, where the total quantity of money demanded by the public (D_T) equals the quantity of money supplied (M_S). Above this equilibrium rate, the supply of money exceeds the quantity demanded, and some businesses, households, and units of government will try to dispose of their unwanted cash balances by purchasing bonds. The prices of bonds will rise, driving interest rates down toward equilibrium at i_E. On the other hand, at rates below equilibrium, the quantity of money demanded exceeds the supply. Some decision makers in the economy will sell their bonds to raise additional cash, driving bond prices down and interest rates up toward equilibrium.

Liquidity preference theory provides some useful insights into investor behavior and the influence of government policy on the economy and financial system. For example, the theory suggests that it is rational at certain times for the public to hoard money (cash balances) and at other times to "dishoard" (spend away) unwanted cash. If the public disposes of some of its cash by purchasing securities, this action increases the quantity of loanable funds available in the money and capital markets. Other things being equal, interest rates will fall. On the other hand, if the public tries to "hoard" more money (expanding its cash balances by selling securities), less money will be available for loans. Interest rates will rise, other factors held constant.

Liquidity preference theory illustrates how central banks, such as the Federal Reserve System and the European Central Bank (ECB), can influence interest rates in the financial markets, at least in the short term. For example, if higher interest rates are desired, the central bank can contract the size of the money supply and interest rates will tend to rise (assuming the demand for money is unchanged). If the demand for money is increasing, the central bank may be able to bring about higher interest rates by ensuring that the money supply grows more slowly than money demand. In contrast, if the central bank expands the money supply, interest rates may decline in the short term (provided the demand for money does not increase).

Limitations of the Liquidity Preference Theory

For further information about the European Central Bank and the Federal Reserve, see ecb.int/ and federalreserve.gov

Like the classical theory of interest, liquidity preference theory has limitations. It is a short-term approach to interest rate determination unless modified because it assumes that income remains stable. In the longer term, interest rates are affected by changes in the level of income and by inflationary expectations. Indeed, it is impossible to have a stable equilibrium interest rate without also reaching an equilibrium level of income, saving, and investment in the economy. Also, liquidity preference considers only the supply and demand for the stock of money, whereas business, consumer, and government demands for credit clearly have an impact on the cost of credit. A more comprehensive view of interest rates is needed that considers the important roles played by *all* actors in the financial system: businesses, households, and governments.

QUESTIONS TO HELP YOU STUDY

6. What are the origins of the *liquidity preference theory of interest?* What assumptions underlie this important idea about what determines market rates of interest?

7. The demand for money is a critical element in the *liquidity preference theory of interest*. What are the three main components of the demand for money?

8. What factors appear to determine the *transactions demand* for money? How about the *precautionary motive* for demanding and holding money? The *speculative motive?*

9. What makes up the *total demand* for money? What is the shape of the relationship between the total demand for money and the market rate of interest?

10. What determines the equilibrium interest rate under the liquidity preference theory of interest? What forces cause the equilibrium interest rate to move?

11. What are the principal limitations of the liquidity preference theory of interest?

5.5   The Loanable Funds Theory of Interest

loanable funds theory of interest rates

A view that overcomes many of the limitations of earlier theories is the **loanable funds theory of interest rates.** It is the most popular interest-rate theory among practitioners and those who follow interest rates "on the street." The loanable funds view argues that the risk-free interest rate is determined by the interplay of two forces: the demand for and supply of *credit* (loanable funds). The demand for loanable funds consists of credit demands from domestic businesses, consumers, and governments, and also borrowing in the domestic market by foreigners. The supply of loanable funds stems from domestic savings, dishoarding of money balances, money creation by the banking system, and lending in the domestic market by foreign individuals and institutions.

The Demand for Loanable Funds

Consumer (Household) Demand for Loanable Funds   Domestic consumers demand loanable funds to purchase a wide variety of goods and services on credit. Recent research indicates that consumers (households) are not particularly responsive to the rate of interest when they seek credit but focus instead principally on the nonprice terms of a loan, such as the down payment, maturity, and size of installment payments. This implies that consumer demand for credit is relatively *inelastic* with respect to the rate of interest. Certainly a rise in interest rates leads to some reduction in the quantity of consumer demand for loanable funds, whereas a decline in interest rates stimulates some additional consumer borrowing. However, along the consumer's relatively inelastic demand schedule, a substantial change in the rate of interest must occur before the quantity of consumer demand for funds changes significantly.

Domestic Business Demand for Loanable Funds   The credit demands of domestic businesses generally are more responsive to changes in the rate of interest than is consumer borrowing. Most business credit is for such investment purposes as the purchase of inventories and new plant and equipment. A high interest rate eliminates some business investment projects from consideration because their expected rate of return is lower than the cost of borrowed funds. On the other hand, at lower rates of interest, many investment projects look profitable, with their expected returns exceeding the cost of funds. Therefore, the quantity of loanable funds demanded by the business sector increases as the rate of interest falls.

Government Demand for Loanable Funds   Government demand for loanable funds is a growing factor in the financial markets but does not depend significantly upon the level of interest rates. This is especially true of borrowing by the federal government. Federal decisions on spending and borrowing are made by Congress in response to social needs and the public welfare, not the rate of interest. Moreover, the federal government has the power both to tax and to create money to pay its debts. State and local government demand, on the other hand, is slightly interest elastic because many local governments are limited in their borrowing activities by legal ceilings. When open market rates rise above these legal ceilings, some state and local governments are prevented from borrowing money from the public.

Foreign Demand for Loanable Funds   In recent years, foreign banks and corporations, as well as foreign governments, have increasingly entered the huge U.S. financial marketplace to borrow billions of dollars. This huge foreign credit demand is sensitive to the spread between domestic lending rates and interest rates in foreign markets. If U.S. interest rates decline relative to foreign rates, foreign borrowers will be inclined to borrow more in the United States and less abroad. At the same time, with higher foreign interest rates, U.S. lending institutions will increase their foreign lending and reduce the availability of loanable funds to domestic borrowers. The net result, then, is a *negative* or *inverse relationship* between foreign borrowing and domestic interest rates relative to foreign interest rates.

Total Demand for Loanable Funds

The total demand for loanable funds is the sum of domestic consumer, business, and government credit demands plus foreign credit demands. This demand curve slopes downward and to the right with respect to the rate of interest (see Exhibit 5.5 on page 131). Higher rates of interest lead some businesses, consumers, and governments to curtail their borrowing plans, while lower rates bring forth more credit demand. However, the demand for loanable funds does not determine the rate of interest by itself. The supply of loanable funds must be added to complete the picture.

The Supply of Loanable Funds

Loanable funds flow into the money and capital markets from at least four different sources: (1) domestic saving by businesses, consumers, and governments; (2) dishoarding (spending down) of excess money balances held by the public; (3) creation of money by the domestic banking system; and (4) lending to domestic borrowers by foreigners. We consider each of these sources of funds in turn.

Domestic Saving   The supply of domestic savings is the principal source of loanable funds. As noted earlier, most saving is done by households and is simply the difference between current income and current consumption. Businesses, however, also save by retaining a portion of current earnings and by adding to their depreciation reserves. Government saving, while relatively rare, occurs when current revenues exceed current expenditures.

income effect

For a discussion of savings goals and how to achieve them, consult such sources as the National Endowment for Financial Education (NEFE) at nefe.org

There is evidence that some business and household saving may be goal oriented: the so-called **income effect.** For example, suppose an individual wishes to accumulate $100,000 in anticipation of retirement. Interest rates subsequently rise from 5 to 10 percent. Will this individual save more out of each period's income or less? Probably *less,* because the higher interest rates will enable the saver to reach the $100,000 goal with less sacrifice of current income. At higher interest rates, savings accumulate faster. On the other hand, a lower interest rate might lead to a greater volume of saving because a business firm or household then must accumulate savings at a faster rate to achieve its savings goal.

Clearly, then, the income effect would have the opposite result for the volume of saving than the substitution effect described earlier in our discussion of the classical theory of interest. The substitution effect argues for a *positive* relationship between the rate of interest and the volume of savings, while the income effect suggests a *negative* relationship between interest rates and savings volume. Thus, these two effects pull aggregate saving in opposite directions as interest rates change. It should not be surprising, therefore, that the annual volume of saving in the economy is difficult to forecast.

wealth effect

Recent research using econometric models has suggested the importance of another factor—the **wealth effect**—in influencing savings decisions. Individuals accumulate wealth in many different forms: real assets (e.g., automobiles, houses, land) and financial assets (e.g., stocks, bonds). What happens to the value of financial assets as interest rates change? If rates rise, for example, the market value of many financial assets will fall until their yield approaches market-determined levels. Therefore, a rise in interest rates will result in decreases in the value of wealth held in some financial assets, forcing the individual to save more to protect his or her wealth position. Conversely, a decrease in interest rates will increase the value of many financial assets, increasing wealth and necessitating a lower volume of current saving.

For businesses and individuals heavily in debt, however, the *opposite* effects may ensue. When interest rates rise, debt that was contracted in earlier periods when interest rates were lower seems less of a burden. For example, a home mortgage taken by a family when interest rates in the mortgage market were 5 percent seems a less burdensome drain on income when rates on new mortgages have risen to 10 percent. Therefore, a rise in interest rates tends to make those economic units carrying a large volume of debt relative to their financial assets feel better off. They may tend to save *less* as a result. A decrease in interest rates, on the other hand, may result in *more* saving due to the wealth effect.

The *net* effect of the income, substitution, and wealth effects leads to a relatively *interest-inelastic* supply of savings curve. Substantial changes in interest rates usually are required to bring about significant changes in the volume of aggregate saving in the economy.

Dishoarding of Money Balances   Still another source of loanable funds is centered on the public's demand for money relative to the available supply of money. As noted earlier, the public's demand for money (cash balances) varies with interest rates and income levels. The supply of money, on the other hand, is closely controlled by the government. Clearly the two—money demand and money supply—need not be the same. The difference between the public's total demand for money and the money supply is known as *hoarding.* When the public's demand for cash balances exceeds the supply, *positive hoarding* of money takes place as some individuals and businesses attempt to increase their cash balances at the expense of others. Hoarding *reduces* the volume of loanable funds available in the financial markets. On the other hand, when the public's demand for money is less than the supply available, *negative hoarding* (*dishoarding*) occurs. Some individuals and businesses will dispose of their excess cash holdings, *increasing* the supply of loanable funds available to others in the financial system.

Creation of Credit by the Domestic Banking System   Commercial banks and nonbank thrift institutions offering payments accounts have the unique ability to create credit by lending and investing their excess reserves (a process described in Chapters 12 and 14). Credit created by the domestic banking system represents an additional source of loanable funds, which must be added to the amount of savings and the dishoarding of money balances (or minus the amount of hoarding demand) to derive the total supply of loanable funds in the economy.

Foreign Lending to the Domestic Funds Market   Finally, foreign lenders provide large amounts of credit to domestic borrowers in the United States. These inflowing loanable funds are particularly sensitive to the difference between U.S. interest rates and interest rates overseas. If domestic rates rise relative to interest rates offered abroad, the supply of foreign funds to domestic markets will tend to rise. Foreign lenders will find it more attractive to make loans to domestic borrowers. At the same time, domestic borrowers will turn more to foreign markets for loanable funds as domestic interest rates climb relative to foreign rates. The combined result is to make the net foreign supply of loanable funds to the domestic credit market *positively* related to the spread between domestic and foreign rates of interest.

Total Supply of Loanable Funds

The total supply of loanable funds, including domestic saving, foreign lending, dishoarding of money, and new credit created by the domestic banking system, is depicted in Exhibit 5.5. The curve rises with higher rates of interest, indicating that a greater supply of loanable funds will flow into the money and capital markets when the returns from lending increase.

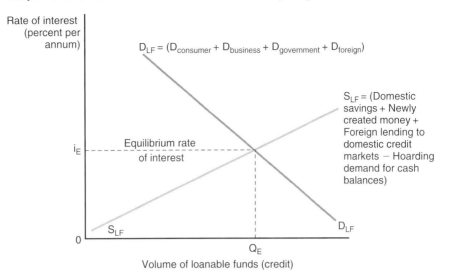

EXHIBIT 5.5

Total Demand and Total Supply of Loanable Funds and the Equilibrium Rate of Interest in the Loanable Funds (Credit) Theory

The Equilibrium Rate of Interest in the Loanable Funds Theory

The two forces of supply and demand for loanable funds determine not only the volume of lending and borrowing going on in the economy but also the rate of interest. *The interest rate tends toward the equilibrium point at which the total supply of loanable funds equals the total demand for loanable funds.* This point of equilibrium is shown in Exhibit 5.5 at i_E.

If the interest rate is temporarily *above* equilibrium, the quantity of loanable funds supplied by domestic savers and foreign lenders, by the banking system, and from the dishoarding of money (or minus hoarding demand) exceeds the total demand for loanable funds, and the rate of interest will be bid down. On the other hand, if the interest rate is temporarily *below* equilibrium, loanable funds demand will exceed the supply. The interest rate will be bid up by borrowers until it settles at equilibrium once again.

The equilibrium depicted in Exhibit 5.5 is only a *partial* equilibrium position, however. This is due to the fact that interest rates are affected by conditions in *both* the domestic and world economies. For the economy to be in equilibrium, planned saving must equal planned investment across the whole economic system. For example, if planned investment exceeds planned saving at the equilibrium interest rate shown in Exhibit 5.5, investment demands will push interest rates higher in the short term. However, as additional investment spending occurs, incomes will rise, generating a greater volume of savings. Eventually, interest rates will fall. Similarly, if exchange rates between dollars, yen, and other world currencies are not in equilibrium with each other, there will be further opportunities for profit available to foreign and domestic lenders by moving loanable funds from one country to another.

Only when the economy (including the markets for goods and services and the labor market), the money market, the loanable funds market, and foreign currency markets are *simultaneously* in equilibrium will interest rates remain stable. Thus, a completely *stable* equilibrium interest rate over the long run will be characterized by the following set of circumstances:

1. Planned saving = Planned investment (including business, household, and government investment) across the whole economic system (i.e., equilibrium in the economy, including the markets for goods and services and for labor).

EXHIBIT 5.6

Changes in the
Demand for and
Supply of
Loanable Funds

A. Effects of increased supply of loanable funds with demand unchanged

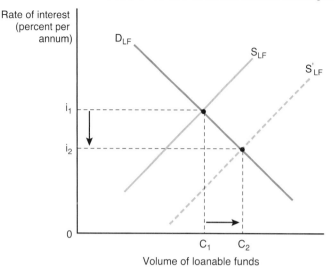

B. Effects of increased demand for loanable funds with supply unchanged

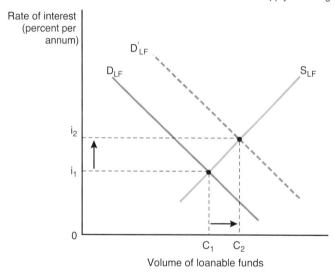

2. Money supply = Money demand (i.e., equilibrium in the money market).

3. Quantity of loanable funds supplied = Quantity of loanable funds demanded (i.e., equilibrium in the loanable funds market).

4. The difference between foreign demand for loanable funds and the volume of loanable funds supplied by foreigners to the domestic economy = The difference between current exports from and imports into the domestic economy (i.e., equilibrium in the balance of payments and foreign currency markets).

This simple demand-supply framework is useful for analyzing broad movements in interest rates. For example, if the total supply of loanable funds is increasing and the total demand for loanable funds remains unchanged or rises more slowly, the volume of credit extended in the money and capital markets must increase. Interest rates will fall. This is illustrated in Exhibit 5.6A, which shows the supply schedule sliding outward and to the right when S_{LF} increases to S'_{LF}, resulting in a decline in the equilibrium rate of interest from i_1 to i_2. The equilibrium quantity of loanable funds traded in the financial system increases from C_1 to C_2.

What happens when the demand for loanable funds increases with no change in the total supply of funds available? In this instance, the volume of credit extended will increase, but loans will be made at higher interest rates. Exhibit 5.6B illustrates this. The loanable funds demand curve rises from D_{LF}, to D'_{LF}, driving the interest rate upward from i_1 to i_2.

QUESTIONS TO HELP YOU STUDY

12. What are *loanable funds?* Why is this term important?

13. What factors make up the total *demand* for loanable funds? The total *supply* of loanable funds? List and define each of these demand and supply factors.

14. Explain how the equilibrium loanable funds interest rate is determined. Draw a picture of what the equilibrium rate of interest might look like.

15. Suppose the demand for loanable funds increases relative to the supply. What happens to the equilibrium rate of interest? Suppose, on the other hand, the supply of loanable funds expands with loanable funds demand unchanged. What does the equilibrium loanable funds interest rate look like under these circumstances?

16. What does it take to have a *permanently stable equilibrium interest rate* under the loanable funds theory of interest? How does this differ from a *temporary* or *partial* equilibrium loanable funds rate?

17. What are the principal *limitations* of the loanable funds theory of interest?

5.6   The Rational Expectations Theory of Interest

rational expectations theory of interest rates

In recent years, a fourth major theory about the forces determining interest rates has appeared: the **rational expectations theory of interest rates.** This theory builds on a growing body of research evidence that the money and capital markets are highly efficient institutions in digesting *new information* affecting interest rates and security prices.

For example, when new information appears about investment, saving, or the money supply, investors begin immediately to translate that new information into decisions to borrow or lend funds. So rapid is this process of the market digesting new information that asset prices and interest rates presumably incorporate the new data from virtually the moment they appear. As we saw in Chapter 3, in a perfectly efficient market, it is impossible to win excess returns consistently by trading on publicly available information.

This expectations theory assumes that businesses and individuals are *rational agents* who attempt to make optimal use of the resources at their disposal in order to maximize their returns. Moreover, a rational agent will tend to make *unbiased* forecasts of future asset prices, interest rates, and other variables. That is, he or she will make no systematic forecasting errors and will easily spot past patterns in forecast errors and correct them quickly.

If the money and capital markets are highly efficient in the way we have described, this implies that interest rates will always be very near their equilibrium levels. Any deviation from the equilibrium interest rate dictated by demand and supply forces will be almost instantly eliminated. Security traders who hope to *consistently* earn windfall profits from correctly guessing whether interest rates are "too high" (and therefore will probably fall) or "too low" (and therefore will probably rise) are unlikely to be successful in the long term. Interest rate fluctuations around equilibrium are likely to be random and rapid. Moreover, knowledge of *past* interest rates—for example, those that prevailed yesterday or last month—will *not* be a reliable forecast of where those rates are likely to be in the future. Indeed, the rational expectations theory suggests that, in the absence of new information, the *optimal forecast* of next period's interest rate would probably be equal to the current period's interest rate because there is no particular reason for next period's interest rate to be either higher or lower than today's interest rate until new information causes market participants to revise their expectations.

Old news will *not* affect today's interest rates because those rates already have impounded the old news. Interest rates will change only if entirely *new and unexpected* information appears. For example, if the federal government announces for several weeks running that it must borrow an additional $10 billion next month, interest rates probably reacted to that information the first time it appeared. In fact, interest rates probably *increased* at that time, because many investors would view the government's additional need for credit as adding to other demands for credit in the economy and, with the supply of funds unchanged, interest rates would be expected to rise. However, if the government merely repeated that same announcement again, interest rates probably would *not* change a second time; it would be old information already reflected in today's interest rates.

Imagine a new scenario, however. The government suddenly reveals that, contrary to expectations, tax revenues are now being collected in greater amounts than first forecast and therefore no new borrowing will be needed. Interest rates probably will fall immediately as market participants are forced to revise their borrowing and lending plans to deal with a new situation. How do we know which *direction* rates will move? Clearly, the path interest rates take depends on *what market participants expected to begin with*. Thus, if market participants were expecting increased demand for credit (with supply unchanged), an unexpected announcement of reduced credit demand implies lower interest rates in the future. Similarly, a market expectation of less credit demand in the future (supply unchanged) when confronted with an unexpected announcement of higher credit demand implies that interest rates will rise.

We can illustrate the foregoing points by modifying the loanable funds theory of interest so that its demand and supply schedules reflect not just actual demand and supply but also the *expected* demand for and supply of loanable funds. For example, referring to Exhibit 5.7, suppose D_0 and S_0 reflect the *actual* supply and demand for loanable funds in the current period, while D_F reflects the *actual* demand for loanable

EXHIBIT 5.7

Expected Demand for and Supply of Loanable Funds under the Rational Expectations Theory

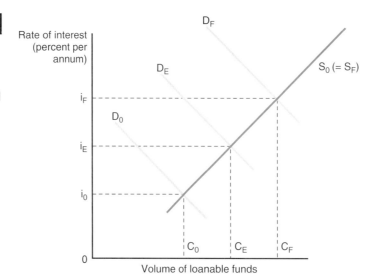

funds that will prevail in the next (future) time period. The supply of loanable funds is assumed to be the same in both time periods ($S_0 = S_F$).

Now imagine that during the current period, the government makes an unexpected announcement of its increased need to borrow more money in future period F due to an unusually large budget deficit. The result is a new expected demand for loanable funds curve D_E, projected to prevail in the next (future) period F but as viewed by borrowers and lenders today in time period 0. In this case, the equilibrium interest rate in the current period will not be i_0, but rather i_E, where the expected demand curve (D_E) intersects the actual supply curve S_0. The equilibrium quantity of loanable funds traded in the current period then will be C_E not C_0. This is because, according to the rational expectations theory, borrowers and lenders will act as rational agents, using all the information they possess (including expected events, such as the government announcing it will need to borrow more money in a future period) to price assets *today*. When the future period arrives, the equilibrium interest rate will rise to rate i_F and the quantity of loanable funds traded then will be C_F. The equilibrium rate moves upward because the demand for loanable funds in period F is more than the expected future loanable funds demand as seen by market participants in period 0.

Suppose, on the other hand, that actual loanable funds demand in period F moves upward and beyond D_0 but by a smaller amount than was anticipated by investors in the market in period 0. Demand schedule D_F would then fall somewhere between D_0 and D_E. The equilibrium interest rate (with the supply curve unchanged) would be *lower* than i_E, lying somewhere between i_0 and i_E.

But this is a startling conclusion! Actual demand *increased* (above D_0, but not to D_E) in the next period with supply held constant. Still, the equilibrium interest rate *fell*! How could this be? Clearly, it makes sense only when we assume that the real world works the way the rational expectations theory says it should. *To know which way interest rates will go, we must know what the market expects to begin with.* In this example, demand for loanable funds rose but not as high as the market expected. Therefore, interest rates will *decline,* other factors held constant.

The rational expectations view argues that forecasting interest rates requires knowledge of the public's *current set of expectations.* If new information is sufficient to alter those expectations, interest rates and asset prices *must* change. If correct, this portion of the rational expectations theory creates significant problems for government policymakers. It implies that policymakers cannot cause interest rates to move in any particular direction without knowing what the public already expects to happen and, indeed, cannot change interest rates and asset prices at all unless government officials can convince the public that a new set of expectations is warranted. Moreover, because guessing what the public's expectations are is treacherous at best, rational expectations theorists suggest that *rate hedging*—using various tools to reduce the risk of loss from changing interest rates—*is preferable to rate forecasting.* Indeed, to be a consistently correct interest rate forecaster under the rational expectations theory you must know (1) what market participants expect to happen and (2) what new information will arrive in the market before that information actually arrives. That's a tall order!

A growing number of studies today imply that at least some elements of the rational expectations/efficient markets view *do* show up in actual market behavior. For example, studies by Mishkin (1978) and others find that past interest-rate movements are *not* significantly related to current rates of return on bonds or stock—validating at least one of the theory's predictions. Other studies (e.g., Rozeff, 1974) have found that past information on economic conditions and money supply movements also appears to bear little correlation to today's interest rate levels or to observed changes in current interest rates. However, *unanticipated* growth in the money supply, income, and the price level *do* appear to be correlated with some bond and stock returns, especially with short-term interest rates. Moreover, adjustments in interest rates and asset prices to *new* information appear to be very rapid.

Nevertheless, the rational expectations view is still in the development stage. One key problem is that we do not know very much about how the public forms its expectations—what data are used, what weights are applied to individual bits of data, and how fast people learn from their forecasting mistakes. Moreover, several characteristics of real-world markets seem at odds with the assumptions of the expectations theory. For example, the cost of gathering and analyzing information relevant to the pricing of assets is not always negligible, as assumed by the theory, tempting many lenders and borrowers of funds to form their expectations by rules of thumb (trading rules) that are *not* fully rational. Although rationally formed expectations appear to exist in large auction markets (such as the markets for government securities or for listed common stock), it is not clear that such is the case for other financial markets, such as those for consumer loans. Thus, not all interest rates and security prices appear to display the kind of behavior implied by the rational expectations theory.

QUESTIONS TO HELP YOU STUDY

18. Can you explain what is meant by *rational expectations?*

19. What, then, is the *rational expectations theory of interest rates?* How does it differ from the other interest-rate determination theories, discussed in this chapter?

20. What *assumptions* underlie the rational expectations view of interest?

21. What are the implications of the rational expectations theory for those who try to *forecast* changes in market rates of interest? Based on this view of interest rates what would you recommend to interest-rate forecasters?

MARKETS ON THE NET: The Most Important Web Sites for This Chapter

Bank Rate.com (bankrate.com)
Bond Market Association (investinginbonds.com)
CNN/Money (cnnfn.com)
European Central Bank (ecb.int)

Federal Reserve System (federalreserve.gov)
National Endowment for Financial Education (nefe.org)

Summary of the Chapter's Main Points

This important chapter focuses on the leading ideas today of what determines the level of and changes in market interest rates and asset prices. Its specific target is the *pure* or *risk-free rate of interest* (such as the interest rate attached to a government bond). Each theory of interest attempts to account for changes we see every day in this pure or risk-free market interest rate.

- The chapter explores the critical roles played by interest rates in the functioning of the money and capital markets and the economy. These fundamental interest-rate roles include: (a) generating an adequate volume of savings in order to fund investment and growth in the economy; (b) directing the flow of credit in the economy toward those investment projects carrying the highest expected rates of return; (c) bringing the supply of money (cash balances) into alignment with the demand for money; and (d) serving as a tool of government economic policy so that the nation can better achieve its broad economic goals of full employment and avoidance of serious inflation.

• The *classical theory* of interest rates emphasizes the roles of savings and investment demand in determining market interest rates. The supply of savings is assumed to be positively related to the market interest rate, while the demand for investment is negatively related to the level of interest rates. The equilibrium interest rate in this long-run interest rate model is established at the point where the total supply of savings and the quantity of investment demand are in balance with each other.

• The *liquidity preference theory of interest* looks at the demand and supply for money (cash balances), fixing the equilibrium interest rate in the money market at the point where the quantity of money in supply matches the total demand for money. Demand for money consists of demands for cash balances for transactions purposes, precautionary savings, and speculation about the future course of interest rates and asset prices. The supply of money is heavily influenced by actions of the government, principally the central bank.

• The popular *loanable funds theory of interest* brings together elements of *both* the classical and liquidity preference theories, focusing upon the total demand for credit (loanable funds) and the total supply of credit (loanable funds). The aggregate demand for loanable funds includes credit demands from *all* sectors of the economy—businesses, consumers, and governments. The aggregate supply of loanable funds includes domestic and foreign savings, the creation of money by the banking system, and the hoarding or dishoarding of cash balances by the public. The equilibrium loanable funds interest rate tends to settle at the point where total demand for credit matches total credit supply.

• The *rational expectations theory of interest* focuses on the *expected* supply of credit relative to the *expected* demand for credit. This view of interest rates and asset prices assumes that the money and capital markets are highly efficient in the use of information in determining the public's expectations regarding future changes in interest rates and asset prices. Interest rates and asset prices incorporate all relevant information very quickly and change only when relevant *new* information appears. Forecasting market interest rates is presumed to be virtually impossible on a consistent basis because forecasters must know what new information is likely to arrive before that information appears and must assess how that new information will influence interest rates and asset prices when it does arrive.

• Collectively, the different views discussed in this chapter help guide us toward those fundamental forces that shape the level of and changes in market rates of interest, as well as the prices of assets. These include such critical forces as domestic and foreign savings, the demand for investment, the money supply, the demand for cash balances, and government economic policy (including the workings of central banks around the world). This chapter sets the stage for future chapters in Part Two of this text, where we attempt to discover what factors cause one interest rate to differ from another (including inflation, the term or length of a loan, credit or default risk, and several other important causal elements).

Key Terms Appearing in This Chapter

rate of interest, 115
price of credit, 115
risk-free rate of interest, 116
classical theory of interest rates, 116
substitution effect, 117
liquidity preference theory of interest
    rates, 122

loanable funds theory of interest
    rates, 127
income effect, 129
wealth effect, 129
rational expectations theory of interest
    rates, 133

Problems and Issues

1. The economy moves through business cycles, with periodic *expansions*, when economic activity is higher than average, and economic slow-downs, which, if severe enough, can lead to a *recession*. During expansion periods the volume of loanable funds available from the financial system tends to increase and real interest rates tend to rise. With this information in mind, explain the following:

   a. Why does the *demand* for loanable funds tend to increase during expansions?

   b. Why does the *supply* of loanable funds tend to increase during expansions?

   c. Does the supply of loanable funds tend to increase by *more* or *less* than the demand for loanable funds during economic expansions? How do you know?

2. Construct a supply of savings schedule (with all schedules and axes correctly labeled) that illustrates the *income effect*. Do the same to illustrate the *wealth effect* and the *substitution effect*. Explain the differences you observe.

3. Suppose the going market rate of interest on high-quality corporate bonds is 12 percent. FORTRAN Corporation is considering an investment project that will last 10 years and requires an initial cash outlay of $1.5 million but will generate estimated revenues of $500,000 per year for 10 years. Would you recommend that this project be adopted? Explain why.

4. A government securities dealer has purchased a 10-year bond bearing a coupon rate of 9 percent. The bond was purchased at par ($1,000). Interest rates on *new* bonds with comparable terms rise to 11 percent. What will happen to the 9-percent bond's market price? What price will it approach? Answer these same questions in the case in which bond rates decline to 7 percent. Explain the price changes you have calculated.

5. The statements listed below were gathered from recent issues of financial news sheets. Read each statement carefully and then (*a*) identify which theory or theories of interest rate determination are implicit in each statement and (*b*) indicate which *direction* interest rates should move if the statement is a correct analysis of the current market situation. Use appropriate supply-demand diagrams, where possible, to show the reasoning behind your answers to part (*b*).

   a. The factor which is likely to dominate interest rate changes in the weeks ahead is a tighter credit policy at the Federal Reserve.

   b. The White House unexpectedly disclosed today that budget negotiations with Capitol Hill have broken down. Market analysts are fearful of the effects on the bond and stock markets when trading begins tomorrow morning.

www.mhhe.com/rose9e

c. Corporate profits have declined significantly in the quarter just concluded, following a year of substantial growth. Financial experts expect this negative trend to continue for at least the next six months.

d. Personal consumption expenditures are rising rapidly, fueled by an unprecedented level of borrowing. Personal savings are up in real dollar terms, but the national savings rate dropped significantly this past year and further declines are expected. Economists believe this recent change in the savings rate explains the current trend in interest rates.

6. Suppose that total savings and business investment demand in the economy behave as shown in the table that follows (dollars are in billions):

Total Investment Demand for Funds	Volume of Total Savings Expected	Alternative Market Interest Rates
$170	$ 80	5%
155	96	6
142	103	7
135	135	8
128	178	9
111	207	10
92	249	11
86	285	12

According to the classical theory of interest, what equilibrium interest rate will prevail given the above schedules of planned saving and investment? What could cause the equilibrium rate to change?

7. Suppose the total demand for money is described by the following equation:

$$MD = 30 - 2i$$

where i is the prevailing market interest rate. The total supply of money is described by the following equation:

$$MS = 3 + 7i$$

According to the liquidity preference theory of interest rates, what is the equilibrium rate of interest?

8. INLAC Company, Ltd, is examining two investment projects as a part of its expansion plan for the coming year. These two projects are *not* mutually exclusive. The cost of project A is $9,870, while project B is expected to cost $17,850. INLAC's cost of capital (required rate of return) is 12 percent. Expected annual cash flows are projected as follows:

Year	Project A	Project B
1	$3,310	$6,525
2	3,310	6,525
3	3,310	6,525
4	3,310	6,525
5	3,310	6,525

Each project will last an estimated 5 years with no remaining significant scrap value. Determine the IRR and the NPV for each of these two projects. What should INLAC decide about each proposed project, assuming the above figures are truly accurate?

Standard & Poor's Market Insight and Web-Based Problems

STANDARD
&POOR'S

1. Financial institutions are a principal source of loanable funds in the economy. While commercial banks account for the single largest share of credit (loanable funds) creation in the financial system, savings and loan associations and other thrift institutions also play an important role in this credit creation process. This exercise asks you to examine the amount of credit contributed to the economy by one of the largest publicly held savings and loans.

   Go to Standard & Poor's Market Insight database at **mhhe.com/edumarketinsight** and locate the most recent annual balance sheet (look under "Excel Analytics") for Washington Mutual (WM). Identify the total amount of credit created by this thrift in the form of primary securities (Investment Securities plus Loans/Claims/Advances) and secondary securities (Customer Deposits plus Short-term Borrowings less Federal Funds Purchased). What percentage of Washington Mutual's total assets does this credit represent? What is the major use of the credit created by this thrift institution?

2. Why do explanations of interest-rate movements differ among investment professionals? Examine at least two of the most popular accounts of daily interest-rate changes. (Examples include **cnnfn.com** and **bondsonline.com.**) How does each source explain the most recent movements in market rates? Why are there differences among the "experts" about why market interest rates are changing?

Semester Project: A Study of the Federal Funds Market

In the questions sketched out below we continue our semester-long project devoted to the federal funds market. We learned in Chapters 2 and 5 that banks are one of the principal financial intermediaries in our financial system, bringing together demanders of loanable funds with suppliers of those funds. In performing this intermediation function, banking firms often need to exchange funds among themselves so that those banks facing high demand can receive funds from banks with an excess supply of funds. The purpose of this exercise is to examine what happens in the Fed funds market when there is an unusually high demand for loanable funds and to see what the central bank (in this case, the Federal Reserve) can do to alleviate this situation.

Consider the following scenarios:

a. Christmas season appears and shoppers are out in force. What would you expect to happen to the demand for short-term funds?

b. Suppose the supply of funds is fixed. Graph the supply and demand schedules for Fed funds that you would expect to see *before* the Christmas season begins and then *after* that season gets into full swing. What should happen to the equilibrium Fed funds rate? Illustrate this change on your graph.

c. Suppose the central bank has the ability to change the supply of Fed funds at will. What should it do if it wishes to keep the funds rate fixed before, during, and after the holiday season? Illustrate these three situations in a graph. (You have just identified one of the biggest challenges the Federal Reserve faces in its conduct of monetary policy!)

d. Go to the Web site **federalreserve.gov/releases/h15/data/d/fedfund.txt** and obtain daily effective Fed funds rates for the days between December 20th and January 5th for each of the past 10 years. Examining these data, try to determine how well the Federal Reserve was able to keep the Fed funds rate from experiencing wide swings during the Christmas season.

e. What would you expect to happen around tax time in April of each year? Why?

Selected References to Explore

Fisher, Irving. *The Theory of Interest*. New York: Macmillan, 1930.

Guo, Hui. "A Rational Pricing Explanation for the Failure of the CAPM." *Review*, Federal Reserve Bank of St. Louis, May/June 2004, pp. 23–33.

Keynes, John M. *The General Theory of Employment, Interest and Money*. New York: Harcourt Brace Jovanovich, 1936.

Marquis, Milt. "What's Behind the Low U.S. Personal Saving Rate?" *FRBSF Economic Letter*, Federal Reserve Bank of San Francisco, March 2002, pp. 1–3.

Mishkin, Frederick. "Efficient-Markets Theory: Implications for Monetary Policy." *Brookings Paper on Economic Activity* 3 (1978), pp. 707–52.

Rozeff, Michael S. "Money and Stock Prices: Market Efficiency and the Lag in Effect of Monetary Policy." *Journal of Financial Economics* 1 (September 1974), pp. 245–302.

www.mhhe.com/rose9e

Chapter 6

Measuring and Calculating Interest Rates and Financial Asset Prices

What's in This Chapter?
Key Topics Outline

Measures of Interest Rates and Prices on Stocks and Bonds

Measures of the Rate of Return on Financial Assets

The Yield to Maturity and Holding-Period Yields

The Relationship between Interest Rates and Asset Prices

Interest Rates Quoted by Institutional Lenders: Simple Interest, Add-on Rate, Discount Method, the APR

Home Mortgage Loan Rates

Compounding Interest

The APY on Deposits

Learning Objectives

in This Chapter

- You will explore the important relationships between the interest rates on bonds and other financial instruments and their market value or price.
- You will be introduced to the many different ways lending institutions may calculate the interest rates they charge borrowers for loans.
- You will be able to determine how interest rates or yields on deposits in banks, credit unions, and other depository institutions are figured.

6.1   Introduction to Interest Rates and Asset Prices

In the preceding chapter we discussed several theories regarding what determines the rate of interest. While these theories help us understand the forces that cause market interest rates to change over time, they provide little or no information about how interest rates should be *measured* in the real world. As a result, many different interest-rate measures have been developed for the different types of financial assets, leading to considerable confusion, especially for small borrowers and savers. In this chapter, we examine the methods most frequently used to measure interest rates and the prices of financial assets in the money and capital markets. We also take up the relationship between the prices of financial assets and market interest rates and how they impact each other.

6.2   Units of Measurement for Interest Rates and Asset Prices

Calculating and Quoting Interest Rates

interest rate

The **interest rate** is the price charged a borrower for the loan of money. This price is unique because it is really a *ratio* of two quantities: the total required fee a borrower must pay a lender to obtain the use of credit for a stipulated time period divided by the total amount of credit made available to the borrower. By convention, the interest rate is usually expressed in *percent per annum*. Thus,

$$\begin{array}{l}\text{Annual} \\ \text{rate of} \\ \text{interest on} \\ \text{loanable} \\ \text{funds (in} \\ \text{percent)} \end{array} = \frac{\begin{array}{c}\text{Fee required by the} \\ \text{lender for the} \\ \text{borrower to obtain credit}\end{array}}{\begin{array}{c}\text{Amount of credit made} \\ \text{available to the} \\ \text{borrower}\end{array}} \times 100 \qquad (6.1)$$

For example, an interest rate of 10 percent per annum on a $1,000, one-year loan to purchase a computer implies that the lender of funds has received a borrower's promise to pay a fee of $100 (10 percent of $1,000) in return for the use of $1,000 in credit for a year. The promised fee of $100 is in addition to the repayment of the loan principal ($1,000), which must occur sometime during the year.

Interest rates are usually expressed as *annualized percentages,* even for financial assets with maturities shorter than a year. For example, in the federal funds market, commercial banks frequently loan reserves to each other overnight, with the loan being repaid the next day. Even in this market the interest rate quoted daily by lenders is expressed in percent per annum, as though the loan were for a year's time. However, various types of loans and securities display important differences in how interest fees and amounts borrowed are valued or accounted for, leading to several different methods for determining interest rates. Some interest-rate measures use a 360-day year, while others use a 365-day year. Some employ compound rates of return, with interest income earned on accumulated interest, and some do not use compounding.

Basis Points

Interest rates on securities traded in the open market rarely are quoted in whole percentage points, such as 5 percent or 8 percent. The typical case is a rate expressed in hundredths of a percent: for example, 5.36 percent or 7.62 percent. Moreover, most interest rates change by only fractions of a whole percentage point in a single day or week. To deal with this situation, the concept of the basis point was developed. A **basis point** equals 1/100 of a percentage point. Thus, an interest rate of

basis point

10.5 percent may be expressed as 10 percent plus 50 basis points, or 1,050 basis points. Similarly, an increase in a loan or security rate from 5.25 percent to 5.30 percent represents an increase of 5 basis points.

Prices of Stocks and Bonds

The prices of common and preferred *stock* are measured today in many markets in terms of dollars and decimal fractions of a dollar (or other currency unit). This is a relatively recent development because stocks used to be quoted in the marketplace in standard fractions—for example, at a price of $40¼ per share. Today, however, such a stock's market price will usually be expressed as $40.25 or whatever its prevailing market value happens to be. An example of a typical stock price quotation as it often appears in financial newspapers and magazines is shown below. In this case the shares issued are common stock issued by Wells Fargo Corporation (stock symbol: WFC), one of the largest banking firms in the world.

EXAMPLE OF A STOCK PRICE QUOTATION AS TYPICALLY REPORTED IN THE FINANCIAL PRESS EACH DAY

STOCK LISTING	YTD %Chg.	52 week range High	Low	Yield Div.	%	PE Ratio	Volume (in 100s)	Closing Bid	Net Change
Wells Fargo (WFC)	−2.5	59.18	43.27	1.80	3.1	16x	36,315	57.41	−0.43

We notice from the data above that stock market investors are given several useful pieces of information about the trading of Wells Fargo's stock as of the close of trading the previous day. This information includes the percentage change in its price thus far in the current year or year-to-date (YTD), which in this instance, is a decline of 2.5 percent. During the past 52 weeks the stock ranged in market value at the close of each day from a high of $59.18 per share to a low of $43.27 per share. The most recent (annualized) shareholder dividend payment was $1.80 per share, which represented a dividend yield—or ratio of current (annualized) dividends to current price—of 3.1 percent when yesterday's trading ended. The concluding price bid was $57.41—a decline of 43 cents over the previous day's closing value. The stock's ratio of current market price to earnings over the previous 12 months (or "price multiple") was 16—a high "price-earning (P/E) ratio" by historical standards. Nearly $4 million in Wells Fargo shares were traded in yesterday's market.

Bond prices are expressed in points and fractions of a point, with each point equal to $1 on a $100 basis or $10 for a $1,000 bond. For example, a U.S. government bond priced at 97 points is selling for $97 on a $100 basis or for $970 for each $1,000 in face value. Fractions of a point are typically measured in 32nds, sixteenths, eighths, quarters, and halves of a point, though some bonds today use decimals instead.

EXAMPLE OF A BOND PRICE QUOTATION AS TYPICALLY REPORTED IN THE FINANCIAL PRESS EACH DAY

Bonds Listed	Current Yield	Volume Traded	Closing Price	Net Change
ATT 8⅝ 31	8.3	85	103½	−½

An example of a typical bond price quotation as it often appears in the newspaper or in magazines each day is shown for some bonds issued by American Telephone and Telegraph Corporation (ATT). In this instance the AT&T bonds are long-term debt scheduled to reach maturity in the year 2031 and bear an annual coupon (promised) interest return of 8⅝ percent (or 8.625%) of their face value. Their current yield—or ratio of annual interest income to current market price—was 8.3 percent on the trading day these statistics were recorded. The volume of these AT&T bonds trading hands on the day represented here amounted to $85,000. The closing price on this bond was $103.50 on a $100 basis or $1,035 for a bond bearing a face value of $1,000. This latest closing price represented a drop in market value from the previous day of $0.50 per $100 or $5 on a $1,000 face-value bond.

Many security dealers who act as "market makers" for financial assets will own and manage a portfolio of the assets they trade. Instead of quoting one price for the asset, they quote *two* prices. The higher of the two is the *asked* price, which indicates what the dealer will *sell* the security for. The *bid* price is the price at which the dealer is willing to *purchase* the security. The difference between bid and asked prices—known as the *spread*—provides the dealer's return for creating a market for the security. Generally, the longer the maturity of a security or the less liquid its market, the greater the spread between its bid and asked prices. This is due, at least in part, to the added risks associated with trading in long-term or infrequently traded securities. For example, short-term securities may trade with a spread as low as $312.50 for a sale of $1 million in securities while long-term or less liquid bonds may be trading on spreads of about $2,500 for every $1 million sold. For small transactions, a commission fee is usually added to cover the cost of executing the transaction. On large sales, however, dealers often forgo commissions and quote a *net* price.

6.3 Measures of the Rate of Return, or Yield, on a Loan, Security, or Other Financial Asset

The interest rate on a loan or other financial asset is the annual rate of return promised by the borrower to the lender as a condition for obtaining a loan. However, that rate is not necessarily a true reflection of the yield or rate of return actually earned by the lender during the life of the asset. Some borrowers, for example, will default on all or a portion of their promised payments. The market value (price) of the financial asset may rise or fall, adding to or subtracting from the saver's or lender's total rate of return (yield) on the transaction. Thus, the interest rate measures the "price" the borrower has promised to pay for a loan, but the actual *yield,* or rate of return, from the lender's or saver's viewpoint may be quite different. In this section, a number of the most widely used measures of the yield or rate of return on a loan or other financial asset are discussed.

Rate of Return on a Perpetual Financial Instrument

perpetuity rate

One of the easiest rate of return or yield measures to follow and understand is the **perpetuity rate**—the return on a financial instrument that never matures, but promises a fixed income to its holder every year *ad infinitum*. The British government has issued a perpetual bond from time to time, known as a *consol,* that it is not required to eventually be paid off. Rather, it must pay interest income annually as long as the bond remains outstanding. The annual rate of return on such a bond is simply

$$\text{Annual rate of return on a perpetual financial instrument} = \frac{\text{Annual cash flow promised}}{\text{Current price or present value}} \tag{6.2}$$

For example, if this bond promises interest payments of $100 per year and currently sells for $1,000 (its price or present value), its annual rate of return must be

$$\text{Annual rate of return on a perpetual financial instrument} = \$100/\$1,000 = 0.10, \text{ or } 10 \text{ percent}$$

Conversely, this simple formula can be rearranged to read

$$\begin{array}{c}\text{Present value (current price)}\\\text{of a perpetual instrument}\end{array} = \frac{\text{Annual cash flow promised}}{\text{Annual rate of return}} \qquad \textbf{(6.3)}$$

Thus, with a $100 promised annual cash flow and an expected 10 percent annual rate of return, the current price (present value) of this instrument must be $100/0.10, or $1,000.

The formula for a perpetual financial instrument reminds us of several key points regarding value and rate of return for financial assets (especially bonds and similar debt securities). First, an infinite stream of fixed payments does have a *finite value,* measured by a financial asset's current price (or present value). Second, there is an *inverse* (or *negative*) relationship between the current price and the rate of return or yield on a financial asset, especially for bonds and other debt instruments. We will explore this last point in greater detail later in this chapter.

Coupon Rate

coupon rate

One of the best-known measures of the rate of return on a bond or other debt security is the **coupon rate.** The coupon rate is the contracted interest rate that the bond issuer agrees to pay at the time a bond is issued and often is set close to prevailing interest rates on comparable financial assets at the time a bond is sold (unless the debt security is a zero coupon instrument). If, for example, a company issues a bond with a coupon rate printed on its face of 9 percent, the borrower has promised the lender an annual interest payment of 9 percent of the bond's par value. Most bonds are issued with $1,000 par values, and interest payments are semiannual.

The amount of promised annual interest income paid by a bond is called its *coupon.* The annual coupon may be determined from the formula

$$\text{Coupon rate} \times \text{Par value} = \text{Coupon} \qquad \textbf{(6.4)}$$

Thus, a bond with par value of $1,000 bearing a coupon rate of 9 percent pays an annual coupon of $90, or $45 every six months.

The coupon rate is *not* an adequate measure of the return on a bond or other debt security unless the investor purchases the financial asset at a price equal to its par value, the borrower makes all of the promised payments on time, and the investor sells or redeems the instrument at its par value. However, the prices of bonds and other debt securities fluctuate with market conditions; rarely does a bond trade exactly at par, for example.

Current Yield

current yield

Another popular measure of the return on a financial asset is its **current yield.** This is simply the ratio of the annual income (dividends or interest) generated by the asset relative to its current market value. Thus, a share of common stock selling in the market for $30 and paying an annual dividend to the shareholder of $3 would have a current yield calculated as follows:

$$\text{Current yield} = \frac{\text{Annual income}}{\text{Market price of asset}} = \frac{\$3}{\$30} = 0.10, \text{ or } 10\% \qquad \textbf{(6.5)}$$

Frequently, the yields reported on stocks, bonds, and selected other assets in the financial press are current yields. Like the coupon rate, the current yield is usually a poor reflection of the rate of return actually received by the lender or investor. It ignores the stream of actual and anticipated payments and the price at which the investor will be able to sell or redeem an asset.

QUESTIONS TO HELP YOU STUDY

1. Interest rates are often called the most important "price" within the financial system. Why do you think this is so?
2. What is different about interest rates, or *the price of credit*, from other prices in the economy?
3. What exactly is a *basis point?* Why is it an important interest-rate measure?
4. How are bond and stock prices usually measured today?
5. In your opinion, are the coupon rate and the current yield good measures of the rate of return on a bond or other financial instrument? Why or why not?

Yield to Maturity

yield to maturity

The most widely accepted measure of the rate of return on a bond or other debt security is its **yield to maturity.** It is the rate of interest the market is prepared to pay for a financial asset in order to exchange present dollars for future dollars. Specifically, the yield to maturity is the annualized rate of interest that equates the purchase price of a financial asset (P) with the present value of *all* of its expected net cash inflows (income) until the asset reaches its maturity date. In general terms,

$$P = \frac{I_1}{(1 + y)^1} + \frac{I_2}{(1 + y)^2} + \cdots + \frac{I_n}{(1 + y)^n} \tag{6.6}$$

where y is the yield to maturity (or YTM) and each I represents expected income from the asset, presumed to last for n periods (usually several years), when it finally matures and is paid off and retired. The I terms in the above formula include both receipts of income and repayments of principal over the life of a bond or other debt security.

Equation 6.6 above helps us calculate yields to maturity particularly for instruments whose life is measured in years and whose income payments (I) flow in once a year. In this case y in the above formula measures the *annualized yield to maturity*.

But what about financial instruments that pay out income to the investor more frequently than once a year? For example, most bonds pay interest semiannually and some instruments pay out quarterly or monthly during the year. In this instance the yield-to-maturity formula in equation 6.6 needs to be modified to include the parameter k—a measure of the number of times during the year that income (such as interest payments) is paid to the holder of a financial instrument. The yield formula now becomes

$$\text{Purchase price} = \frac{I_1/k}{(1 + y/k)^1} + \frac{I_2/k}{(1 + y/k)^2} + \cdots$$
$$+ \frac{I_{nk}/k}{(1 + y/k)^{nk}} + \frac{\text{Final price}}{(1 + y/k)^{nk}}$$

For example, if we have a 20-year government bond paying $50 interest twice each year, then k must equal 2 and there would be 40 periods (nxk = 20x2) in which the investor would expect to receive $50 in interest income. As the above formula shows we would have to divide the annualized yield to maturity (y) by k and discount the expected cash flows from the instrument over nxk, rather than n, time periods.

To illustrate the use of this formula, assume that an investor is considering the purchase of a bond due to mature in 20 years (with 40 semiannual interest-crediting periods), and carrying a 10 percent annual coupon rate, or 5 percent every six months. This asset is available for purchase at a current market price of $850. If the bond has a par value of $1,000, which will be paid to the investor when the asset reaches maturity, the bond's yield to maturity may be found by solving the equation:

$$\$850 = \frac{\$50}{(1 + y/2)^1} + \frac{\$50}{(1 + y/2)^2} + \cdots \\ + \frac{\$50}{(1 + y/2)^{40}} + \frac{\$1,000}{(1 + y/2)^{40}} \tag{6.7}$$

In this instance, y is close to 12 percent—a rate higher than its 10 percent annual coupon rate because the bond is currently selling at a *discount* from par.

Suppose this same $1,000, 10 percent annual coupon bond were selling at a *premium* over par. For example, if this 20-year debt instrument has a current market price of $1,200 and pays interest twice each year its yield to maturity could be found from the following equation:

$$\$1,200 = \frac{\$50}{(1 + y/2)^1} + \cdots + \frac{\$50}{(1 + y/2)^{40}} + \frac{\$1,000}{(1 + y/2)^{40}} \tag{6.8}$$

To calculate yield to maturity and other yield measures on bonds and other financial instruments see, for example, investopedia.com/calculator

In this case, y equals almost 8 percent. Because the investor must pay a higher current market price than par value (the amount the investor will receive back when the bond matures), this bond's yield to maturity must be *less* than its coupon rate.

From these two examples, it should be clear that the *value of a bond or other debt security depends on the size of its promised rate of return (coupon rate) relative to prevailing market interest rates on other financial assets of comparable quality and terms.* If a debt security's coupon rate equals the current market interest rate on comparable instruments, that security will trade at par. If the bond's coupon rate is less than the prevailing market rate, it will sell at a *discount* from par. Finally, if the coupon rate exceeds the current interest rate in the market, the bonds or other debt securities will sell at a *premium* above their par value.

The yield to maturity has a number of significant advantages as a measure of the rate of return or yield on a financial asset. In fact, security dealers typically use the yield to maturity in quoting rates of return on bonds and other debt securities to investors. Unlike the current yield, this return measure considers the time distribution of expected cash flows from a financial asset. Of course, the yield-to-maturity measure does assume that the investor will hold a financial instrument until it reaches maturity and is retired. Moreover, yield to maturity is *not* an appropriate measure for most stocks, the majority of which are perpetual instruments, or even for some bonds, because the investor may sell them prior to their termination date or the bonds may pay a variable return. Another problem is that this measure assumes that all cash flowing to the investor can be reinvested at the computed yield to maturity.

Holding-Period Yield

A slight modification of the yield-to-maturity formula results in a return measure for those situations in which an investor holds a financial asset for a time and then sells it to another **holding period yield** investor in advance of the asset's maturity. This so-called **holding-period yield** is simply

$$P = \frac{I_1}{(1 + h)^1} + \frac{I_2}{(1 + h)^2} + \cdots + \frac{I_m}{(1 + h)^m} + \frac{P_m}{(1 + h)^m} \tag{6.9}$$

where h is the annualized holding-period yield and the investor's holding period covers m time periods. Thus, the holding-period yield is simply the rate of discount (h) equalizing the market price of a financial asset (P) with all net cash flows between the time the asset is purchased and the time it is sold (including the selling price, P_m). If the asset is held to maturity, its holding-period yield equals its yield to maturity.

If income from an asset comes in more than once a year (i.e., k times during each year of the investor's holding period) we would divide each expected annual income flow (I) and the annualized holding-period yield (h) by k. We must also multiply the number of time periods (m) that make up the investor's holding period by k in order to help us find the correct annual holding-period yield (h).

Understanding the Concepts of Yield to Maturity and Holding-Period Yield

It is often helpful in understanding the concepts of yield to maturity and holding-period yield to look at an example of how we determine and interpret these two rate of return measures. Suppose, for example, that an investor is thinking about the purchase of a corporate bond, $1,000 in face or par value, with a promised annual (coupon) rate of return of 10 percent. Assume the bond pays interest of $50 every six months. Currently the bond is selling for $900. Assume that this is a five-year bond that the investor plans to hold until it matures, when it is redeemed at par by the issuer of the bond. We have

$$\$900 = \frac{\$50}{(1 + y/2)^1} + \frac{\$50}{(1 + y/2)^2} + \frac{\$50}{(1 + y/2)^3} + \cdots$$
$$+ \frac{\$50}{(1 + y/2)^9} + \frac{\$50}{(1 + y/2)^{10}} + \frac{\$1,000}{(1 + y/2)^{10}} \tag{6.10}$$

present value

It is useful at this point to consider what each term in Equation 6.10 means. Both the yield-to-maturity and holding-period-yield formulas are based on the concept of **present value:** Funds to be received in the future are worth *less* than funds received today. Present dollars may be used to purchase and enjoy goods and services today, but future dollars are only *promises* to pay and force us to postpone consumption until the funds actually are received. Equation 6.10 indicates that a bond promising to pay $50 every six months for a five-year period in the future plus a lump sum of $1,000 at maturity is worth only $900 in present value dollars. The yield, y/2, serves as a rate of discount reducing each payment of future dollars back to its present value in today's market. The further into the future the payment is to be made, the larger the discount factor, $(1 + y/2)^n$, becomes.

Turning the concept around, the purchase of a financial asset in today's market represents the investment of present dollars in the expectation of a higher return in the form of future dollars. The familiar *compound interest formula* (discussed later in this chapter) applies here. This formula

$$FV = P(1 + y)^t \tag{6.11}$$

indicates that the amount of funds accumulated t years from now (FV or future value) depends on the principal originally invested (P), the investor's expected rate of return or yield (y), and the number of years the principal is invested (t). Thus, a principal of $1,000 invested today at a 10 percent annual rate will amount to $1,100 a year from now [i.e., $1,000 \times (1 + 0.10)^1$]. Rearrangement of the compound interest formula gives

$$P = \frac{FV}{(1 + y)^t} \tag{6.12}$$

Equation 6.12 states that the present value of FV dollars to be received in the future is P if the promised interest rate is y. If we expect to receive $1,100 one year from now and the promised interest rate is 10 percent, the present value of that $1,100 must be $1,000.

Each term on the right-hand side of the yield-to-maturity and holding-period-yield formulas is a form of Equation 6.12. Solving Equation 6.10 for the yield to maturity of a bond simply means finding a value for y, which brings both right- and left-hand sides of the yield formula into balance, equating the current price (P) of a financial asset with the stream of future dollars it will generate for the investor. When all expected cash flows are not the same in amount, an electronic calculator or computer software may be used to find the solution. Fortunately, in the case of the bond represented in Equation 6.10, the solution is not complicated. Rewrite Equation 6.10 in the following form:

$$\$900 = \$50\left[\frac{1}{(1 + y/2)^1} + \frac{1}{(1 + y/2)^2} + \cdots + \frac{1}{(1 + y/2)^{10}}\right]$$
$$+ \$1,000\left[\frac{1}{(1 + y/2)^{10}}\right] \qquad (6.13)$$

This indicates that the bond will pay an annuity of $1 per year (multiplied in this case by $50) for five years (10 six-month periods) plus a lump sum of $1 (multiplied here by $1,000) at the end of the fifth year. Using a programmable calculator and entering the price (present value or PV) of the instrument (which is $900 in this case), the expected periodic interest payments (PMT = $50 semiannually), and the final value or payment ($1,000 in this example) tells us that y, the yield-to-maturity measure, is 12.83 percent. The investor interested in maximizing return would compare this yield to maturity with the yields to maturity available on other assets of comparable risk and liquidity.

Note that if the bond in this example had been a 10-year bond, but identical in every other way, then the investor with a five-year time horizon for his or her investment would receive a holding-period yield, h, of precisely the same 12.83 percent annualized yield-to-maturity, *if* he or she were able to sell the bond at precisely its par value. This result can be verified by setting $P_m = \$1,000$ in Equation 6.9 and solving for h.

Calculating the Holding-Period Yield on Stock

The reasoning we used to determine the yield to maturity and the holding-period yield on bonds can also be applied to calculate the holding-period yield on corporate stocks (equities)—a perpetual instrument unless the issuing company goes bankrupt! To illustrate, suppose an investor is considering the purchase of shares of common stock issued by General Electric Corporation, currently selling for $40 per share. He plans to hold the stock for two years and then sell out at an expected price of $50 per share. If dividends of $2 per share are expected each year, what holding-period yield does the investor expect to earn? Following the form of Equation 6.10, we have

$$\$40 = \frac{\$2}{(1 + h)^1} + \frac{\$2}{(1 + h)^2} + \frac{\$50}{(1 + h)^2} \qquad (6.14)$$

An electronic calculator programmed to determine holding-period yields tells us that the expected annualized holding-period yield on GE's stock is 16.5 percent.

The Bank Discount Rate

bank discount rate

An alternative to the yield-to-maturity (YTM) and holding-period-yield (HPY) measures of rate of return is the **bank discount rate.** It is widely used for short-term loans and securities traded daily in the money market on which there is no intermediate (coupon) payment made before the loan or asset matures. The bank discount rate is a much simpler measure of rate of return than either the yield to maturity or holding-period yield because (1) it does not require the compounding of interest income, (2) it uses par or face value (rather than market price) as an investment base, and (3) it rests on the assumption of a 360-day (rather than a 365-day) year. The discount rate (DR) measure is simply

$$DR = \frac{(\text{Par of face value } - \text{ Purchase price})}{\text{Par or face value}} \times \frac{360 \text{ days/year}}{\text{Days to maturity}} \quad \textbf{(6.15)}$$

As an example, suppose we are interested in purchasing a U.S. Treasury bill scheduled to mature in 180 days, at which time we would receive the par value of $100. There is no intermediate (coupon) payment to be received between now and the maturity date. If it is currently selling on the open market for a price of $98, then its discount rate (DR) yield is:

$$DR = \frac{(100 - 98)}{100} \times \frac{360}{180} = 0.04, \text{ or 4 percent}$$

It is quite easy to convert the discount rate (DR) calculated above into an equivalent yield-to-maturity (YTM) measure of rate of return if we employ the following formula:

$$\begin{aligned}\text{YTM-equivalent} \atop \text{return measure} &= \frac{(\text{Par or face value } - \text{ Purchase price})}{\text{Purchase price}} \\ &\times \frac{365 \text{ days/year}}{\text{Days to maturity}}\end{aligned} \quad \textbf{(6.16)}$$

For example, in the case of the 180-day Treasury bill with a 4 percent DR that we discussed above, the YTM equivalent is:

$$\text{YTM-equivalent} \atop \text{return measure} = \frac{100 - 98}{98} \times \frac{365}{180} = 0.0414, \text{ or } 4.14\%$$

Notice that, when computing the equivalent yield to maturity, we use the asset's purchase price as the investment base rather than its face value (as was done in calculating the bank discount rate). Similarly, a 365-day year is used in calculating the yield-to-maturity equivalent return rather than the 360 days associated with the DR measure. The result of these two differences is that the YTM-equivalent rate is always somewhat higher than the DR. We will encounter the popular bank discount rate of return (DR) measure again in Part Three of this text, where money market instruments are discussed in detail.

QUESTIONS TO HELP YOU STUDY

6. Explain the meaning of the interest rate measure known as the *yield to maturity*.

7. What *assumptions* underlie the calculation of the yield to maturity?

8. How does the *holding-period yield* differ from the yield to maturity?

9. Why are yields on bonds and other debt securities typically quoted on a yield-to-maturity basis, while stock yields are usually expressed as current yields or holding-period yields?

10. What is the *bank discount rate* (DR) and where is it normally used? How does this rate of return measure differ from the yield-to-maturity and holding-period-yield measures?

6.4 Yield-Asset Price Relationships

Interest Rates and the Prices of Debt Securities   The foregoing yield or rate of return formulas illustrate a number of important relationships between the prices of financial assets and yields or interest rates that prevail in our financial system. One of these important relationships is expressed as follows:

> The price of a financial asset (especially for a bond or other debt security) and its yield or rate of return are *inversely related*—a rise in yield implies a decline in price; conversely, a fall in yield is associated with a rise in the financial asset's price.

To reinforce this fundamental principle, we should remind ourselves that investing funds in financial assets can be viewed from two different perspectives—the borrowing and lending of money or the buying and selling of financial assets. As noted in Chapter 5, the equilibrium rate of interest from the lending of funds can be determined by the interaction of the supply of loanable funds with the demand for loanable funds. Demanders of loanable funds (borrowers) supply financial assets in the form of debt securities to the financial marketplace, and suppliers of loanable funds (lenders) demand debt securities and other financial instruments as an investment that will generate future income. Therefore, the equilibrium rate of return or yield on a debt security or similar financial instrument and its equilibrium price are determined at one and the same instant. In fact, they are simply different aspects of the same phenomenon—the borrowing and lending of loanable funds.

This point is depicted in Exhibit 6.1, which shows demand and supply curves for both the rate of interest (yield) and the price of financial assets (such as the price of bonds or similar financial instruments evidencing a loan of money). The supply of loanable funds curve (representing lending) in the interest-rate diagram (Exhibit 6.1A) is analogous to the demand for financial assets curve (also representing lending) in the price of financial assets diagram (Exhibit 6.1B). Similarly, the demand for loanable

| EXHIBIT 6.1 | **Equilibrium Asset Prices and Interest Rates (Yields)** |

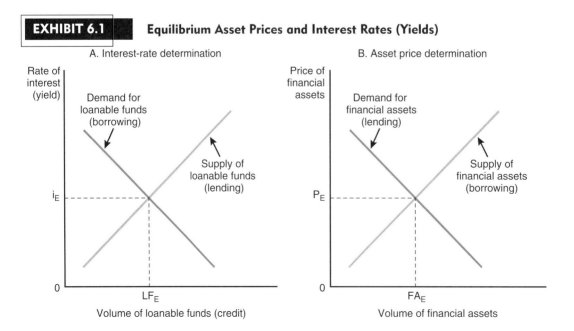

funds curve (representing borrowing) in the interest-rate diagram (Exhibit 6.1A) is analogous to the supply of financial assets (also representing borrowing) in the price of financial assets diagram (Exhibit 6.1B).

We note that in Exhibit 6.1B borrowers are inclined to issue a larger volume of financial assets (such as bonds and other debt securities) at higher asset prices, while lenders are inclined to demand more financial assets at lower prices. In Exhibit 6.1A, on the other hand, borrowers are inclined to demand a smaller quantity of loanable funds at higher interest rates, while lenders are inclined to supply fewer loanable funds at lower interest rates. The *equilibrium interest rate* (or yield) in Exhibit 6.1A is determined at point *i*, where the demand for loanable funds equals the supply of loanable funds. Similarly, in Exhibit 6.1B, the equilibrium price for financial assets lies at point *P*, where the demand for and supply of financial assets are equal. Only at the equilibrium interest rate and equilibrium asset price will *both* borrowers and lenders be content with the volume of lending and borrowing taking place within the financial system.

The *inverse* relationship between interest rates and financial-asset prices can be seen even more clearly when we allow the demand and supply curves depicted in Exhibit 6.1 to move. This movement is illustrated in Exhibit 6.2. For example, suppose that, in the face of continuing inflation, business firms and households accelerate their borrowings, increasing the demand for loanable funds. As shown in the upper left-hand portion of Exhibit 6.2, the demand for loanable funds curve slides upward and to the right with the supply of loanable funds curve unchanged. This increasing demand for loanable funds also means that the supply of financial assets (principally in the form of bonds and other debt securities) must expand, as shown in the upper right-hand portion of Exhibit 6.2 by a shift in the supply curve from *S* to *S'*. Both a new *lower* equilibrium price for financial assets and a *higher* equilibrium interest rate for loanable funds result.

Conversely, suppose that businesses and households decide to save more, expanding the supply of loanable funds. As shown in the lower left-hand portion of Exhibit 6.2, the supply of loanable funds curve slides downward and to the right from *S* to *S'*. But with more savings available, the demand for financial assets curve must rise, as businesses and households look for more financial assets to buy as investments for their savings. Therefore, as shown in the lower right-hand portion of Exhibit 6.2, the asset demand curve slides upward and to the right, from *D* to *D'*. The result is a *rise* in the equilibrium price of financial assets (especially the prices of bonds and other debt securities) and a *decline* in the equilibrium interest rate.

Interest Rates and Stock Prices   While the previous discussion describes well the inverse relationship that exists between interest rates and the prices of many financial assets—especially the prices of bonds and other debt securities—we should also note that interest rates and corporate stock (equity) prices frequently move in opposite directions as well (though by no means is this always the case). For example, if interest rates rise, bonds and other debt instruments now offering higher yields become more attractive relative to stocks, resulting in increased stock sales and declining equity prices (all other factors held equal). Conversely, a period of falling interest rates often leads investors to dump their lower-yielding bonds and switch to equities, driving stock prices upward. Then, too, lower market interest rates tend to lower the overall cost of capital for businesses issuing stock, resulting in a rise in stock prices (provided that expected corporate dividends do not fall).

What actually happens to stock prices when market interest rates change can often be understood by tracking changes in two fundamental factors that appear to influence *all* stock prices—the stream of shareholder dividends a company is expected to pay in

EXHIBIT 6.2   Effects of Changing Supply and Demand on Asset Rates (Yields) and Prices

A. Effects of an increase in the demand for loanable funds (credit): higher interest rates and lower asset prices

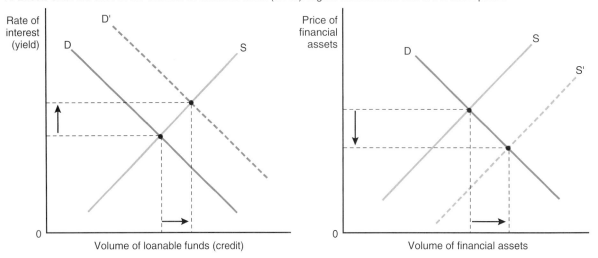

B. Effects of an increase in the supply of loanable funds (credit): lower interest rates and higher asset prices

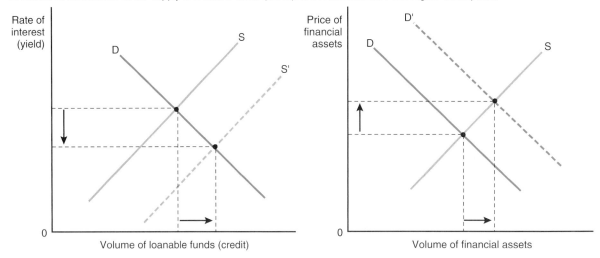

current and future time periods [$E(D)$] and the minimum rate of return required by a company's stockholders (r). Thus, a corporation's stock price per share (SP) is:

$$SP = \sum_{t=0}^{\infty} E(D_t)/(1 + r)^t \qquad\qquad (6.17)$$

Clearly, a rise in expected dividends [$E(D)$] or a fall in the required risk-adjusted rate of return for the company's stockholders (r) leads to higher stock prices per share (SP), other factors held equal. However, there are *no* guarantees surrounding the stock price–interest rate relationship we have just described because *both* expected dividends and the required risk-adjusted rate of return (r) may change at the same time, offsetting one another and leaving stock prices unchanged or causing them to move in an unexpected direction.

The formula stated above for determining the price of a company's stock is a general formula that takes into account the possibility that the dividends paid by a corporation to its shareholders may vary in timing and amount as the months and years go by. However, for many companies in recent years dividends have tended to grow at a relatively constant rate from period to period, often shaped by corporate management to convey the image of company stability. If corporate dividends do grow at a constant rate, the formula for corporate stock prices becomes much simpler and easier to follow:

$$SP = D(1 + r) / (r - g) \qquad (6.18)$$

where *D* represents the expected dividend to be paid in the first period and *g* is the expected constant annual growth rate of dividends in the future. As before, *r* is the rate of discount (cost of capital), which reflects the perceived risk of investing in the company's stock.

To illustrate the use of the above formula, suppose a company expects to pay a dividend of $2.50 per share in the initial period and to increase the amount of its future annual dividend payments by 5 percent each year. If the discount rate associated with the company's stock is 12 percent, then its current stock price will be:

$$SP = \$2.50(1 + 0.12) / (0.12 - 0.05) = \$40.00 \text{ per share}$$

Clearly, it is substantially easier to estimate the equity value for those companies—often the largest firms today—that pay a steady and predictable dividend rate.

6.5   Interest Rates Charged by Institutional Lenders

In this chapter, we have examined several different measures of the rate of return, or yield, on financial assets. Our list is not complete, however, for institutional lenders of funds—banks, credit unions, insurance companies, and finance companies, to name the most important—often employ very different methods to calculate the rate of interest charged on their loans. Six popular methods for calculating institutional loan rates are discussed on the following pages.

The Simple Interest Method

simple interest method

The widely used **simple interest method** assesses interest charges on a loan for only the period of time the borrower actually has use of the borrowed funds. The total interest bill *decreases* the more frequently a borrower must make payments on a loan because the borrower has less money to work with each time the repayment of part of a loan is made to the lender. This definition of a *simple interest loan* follows the U.S. government's Truth-in-Lending law passed originally in 1968.

For example, suppose you borrow $1,000 for a year at simple interest. If the interest rate is 10 percent, your interest bill will be $100 for the year. This figure is derived from the formula

$$I = P \times r \times t \qquad (6.19)$$

where *I* represents the interest charge (in dollars), *P* is the principal amount of the loan, *r* is the annual rate of interest, and *t* is the term (maturity) of the loan expressed in years or fractions of a year. (In this example, $1,000 \times 0.10 \times 1 = \$100$.)

If the $1,000 loan is repaid in one lump sum at the end of the year,

$$\frac{\text{Principal} + \text{Interest}}{\$1,000 + \$100} = \frac{\text{Total payment}}{\$1,100}$$

Suppose, however, that this loan principal is paid off in two equal installments of $500 each, every six months. Then you will pay

First installment:	$\dfrac{\text{Principal} + \text{Interest}}{\text{\$500} + \text{\$50 (i.e., 6 months' interest on \$1,000 at 10\%)}}$	= Total payment = \$ 550
Second installment:	$500 + $25 (i.e., 6 months' interest on $500 at 10%)	= \$ 525 = $1,075

Clearly, you pay a lower interest bill ($75 versus $100) with two installment payments instead of one. This happens because with two installment payments you effectively have use of the full $1,000 for only six months. For the remaining six months of the year you have use of only $500.

A shorthand formula for determining the total payment (interest plus principal) on a simple interest loan with a single lump-sum payment at maturity is

$$\text{Total payment due} = P + P \times r \times t = P(1 + r \times t) \qquad \textbf{(6.20)}$$

For example, borrowing $1,000 for six months at a 10 percent loan rate means the borrower owes:

$$\text{Total payment due} = \$1,000 + \$1,000 \times 0.10 \times 6/12 = \$50$$

The simple interest method is still popular today with many credit unions and banks.

Add-On Rate of Interest

add-on rate

A method for calculating loan interest rates often used by finance companies and banks is the **add-on rate** approach. In this instance, interest is calculated on the full principal of the loan, and the sum of interest and principal payments is divided by the number of payments to determine the dollar amount of each payment. For example, suppose you borrow $1,000 for one year at an interest rate of 10 percent. You agree to make two equal installment payments six months apart. The total amount to be repaid is $1,100 ($1,000 principal + $100 interest). At the end of the first six months, you will pay half ($550), and the remaining half ($550) will be paid at the end of the year.

If money is borrowed and repaid in one lump sum (a single payment loan), the simple interest and add-on methods give the same interest rate. However, as the number of installment payments increases, the borrower pays a higher effective interest rate under the add-on method. This happens because the average amount of money borrowed declines with the greater frequency of installment payments, yet the borrower pays the *same* total interest bill. In fact, the effective rate of interest nearly doubles when monthly installment payments are required. For example, if you borrow $1,000 for a year at 10 percent simple interest but repay the loan in 12 equal monthly installments, you have only about $500 available for use, on average, over the year. Because the total interest bill is still $100, the interest rate exceeds 18 percent.

Discount Loan Method

discount loan method

Many commercial loans, especially those used to raise working capital, are extended on a discount basis. This so-called **discount loan method** for calculating loan rates determines the total interest charge to the customer on the basis of the amount to be repaid. However, the borrower receives as proceeds of the loan only the *difference* between the total amount owed and the interest bill. For example, suppose you borrow $1,000 for one year at 10 percent, for a total interest bill of $100. Using the discount method, you actually receive for your use only $900 (i.e., $1,000 − $100) in net loan proceeds. The effective interest rate, then, is

$$\frac{\text{Interest paid}}{\text{Net loan proceeds}} = \frac{\$100}{\$900} \times 100 = 11.11\% \qquad (6.21)$$

Some lenders grant the borrower the full amount of money required but add the amount of discount to the face amount of the borrower's note. For example, if you need the full $1,000, the lender under this method will multiply the effective interest rate (11.11 percent) times $1,000 to derive a total interest bill of $111.11. The face value of the borrower's note and, therefore, the amount that must be repaid becomes $1,111.11. However, the borrower receives only $1,000 for use during the year. Most discount loans are for terms of one year or less and usually do not require installment payments. Instead, these loans generally are settled in a lump sum when the note comes due.

Home Mortgage Interest Rate

One of the most confusing of all rates charged by lenders is the interest rate on a home mortgage loan. Many home buyers have heard that under the terms of most mortgage loans, their monthly payments early in the life of the loan go almost entirely to pay the interest on the loan. Only later is a substantial part of each monthly payment devoted to reducing the principal amount of a home loan. Is this true?

Yes, and we can illustrate it quite easily. Suppose that you find a new home you want to buy and borrow $100,000 to close the deal. The mortgage lender quotes you an annual **home mortgage interest rate** of 12 percent on the loan. If we divide this annual interest rate by 12 months, we derive a monthly mortgage loan rate of 1 percent. The lender tells you that your monthly payment will be $1,100 each month (to cover property taxes, insurance, interest, and principal on the loan). This means that the first month's payment of $1,100 will be divided by the lender as follows: (1) $1,000 for the interest payment (or 1% per month × $100,000); and (2) $100 to be applied to the principal of the loan, insurance premiums, taxes, and so forth. For simplicity, let's assume the $100 left over after the $1,000 interest payment goes entirely to help repay the $100,000 loan principal. This means that next month your loan now totals just $99,900 (or $100,000 − $100). When you send in that next monthly payment of $1,000, the interest payment will drop to $999, and, therefore, $1,100 will now be left over to help reduce the loan principal. Gradually, the monthly interest payment will fall and the amount left over to help retire the loan's principal will rise. After several years, as the mortgage loan's maturity date gets near, each monthly payment will consist mostly of repaying the loan principal itself.

How do mortgage lenders figure the amount of the monthly payment new home buyers must make on their home loan? The usual formula is

home mortgage interest rate

To broaden your understanding about home mortgage interest rates you may find the Web site bankrate.com useful.

$$\text{Total amount borrowed} \times \frac{\left[\dfrac{\text{Loan interest rate}}{12}\right] \times \left[1 + \dfrac{\text{Loan interest rate}}{12}\right]^{t \times 12}}{\left[1 + \left(\dfrac{\text{Loan interest rate}}{12}\right)\right]^{t \times 12} - 1} \qquad (6.22)$$

where t stands for the number of years the money is borrowed by the home buyer, and the annual interest rate charged on the mortgage loan is divided by 12 to restate that interest rate on a monthly basis.

To see how this formula works, suppose a family takes out a $50,000 loan for 25 years at an interest rate of 12 percent to buy its new home. In this case, the required payment on the home mortgage loan each month would be

$$\$50,000 \times \frac{\left[\dfrac{0.12}{12}\right] \times \left[1 + \dfrac{0.12}{12}\right]^{25 \times 12}}{\left[1 + \dfrac{0.12}{12}\right]^{25 \times 12} - 1} = \frac{\$9,894.23}{18.7885} = \$526.62$$

Actually, the easiest way to calculate required home mortgage payments is by using an electronic calculator or computer software. Typically, just three pieces of data are needed—the number of payments to be made (usually designated on the calculator as N), the annual interest rate on the loan (the I/Y button on many calculators), and the amount the home buyer plans to borrow (usually designated as PV).

Annual Percentage Rate (APR)

The wide diversity of rates quoted by lenders is often confusing and discourages shopping around for credit. With this in mind, the U.S. Congress passed the Consumer Credit Protection Act in 1968. More popularly known as *Truth in Lending*, this law requires institutions regularly extending credit to consumers to tell the borrower what interest rate he or she is actually paying and to use a prescribed method for calculating that rate.[1] Specifically, banks, credit unions, and other lending institutions are required to calculate an **annual percentage rate (APR)** and inform the loan customer what this rate is *before* the loan contract is signed. The APR, which measures the yearly cost of credit, includes not only interest costs but also any transaction fees or service charges imposed by the lender. The APR for loans is equivalent to the yield to maturity for bonds.

Today, financial calculators and financial functions in spreadsheet programs (such as Excel) allow loan officers and their customers to easily determine the APR attached to their loans. To illustrate how the APR is determined for a loan, suppose you borrow $1,000 at 10 percent simple interest but must repay your loan in 12 equal monthly installments. The amount of each required monthly payment (PMT) can be figured as follows:

$$\begin{aligned} \text{Required monthly} \atop \text{loan payment} &= \frac{\text{Interest owed} + \text{Loan principal}}{\text{Number of payment periods}} \\ &= \frac{\$100 + \$1000}{12} = \$91.67 \end{aligned} \tag{6.23}$$

We can enter in the calculator the number of payment periods, N (in this case, 12); the amount or present value (PV) that the lender is granting to you, the borrower, for the term of the loan (in this case, PV = −$1,000 the day the loan begins); the amount to be repaid each month (in this case, PMT = $91.67 as determined above); and the future value (FV) of the loan (which at the end of the loan's term is $0 because you are expected to completely pay back what you borrowed). The calculator tells us that the APR (the annual percentage rate or I/Y) is very close to 18 percent in this example.

Competition among home mortgage lenders has intensified with the growing use of the Internet by borrowers. At some sites—for example, lenderscompete—several different lenders may bid for a borrowing customer's loan.

annual percentage rate (APR)

---

[1]See Chapter 21 for a discussion of consumer credit laws.

For further
information about the
APR see Consumer
Credit and Credit
Protection Laws at
federalreserve.gov

Congress hoped that introduction of the APR would encourage consumers to exercise greater care in the use of credit and to shop around to obtain the best terms on a loan. It is not at all clear that either goal has been realized completely, however. Many consumers appear to give primary weight to the size of installment payments in deciding how much, when, and where to borrow. If their budget can afford principal and interest charges on a loan, many consumers seem little influenced by the reported size of the APR and are often not inclined to ask other lenders for their rates on the same loan. Consumer education is vital to intelligent financial decision making, but progress in that direction has been slow. However, there is some evidence that with growing use of the Internet a greater proportion of borrowers are shopping around for credit today.

Compound Interest

compound interest

Some lenders and loan situations require the borrower to pay **compound interest** on a loan. In addition, most interest-bearing deposits at banks, credit unions, savings and loans, and money market funds pay compound interest on the balance in the account as of a certain date. The compounding of interest simply means that the lender or depositor earns interest income on both the principal amount and on any accumulated interest. Thus, the longer the period over which interest earnings are compounded, the more rapidly does interest earned on interest and interest earned on principal grow.

The conventional formula for calculating the future value of a financial asset earning compound interest is simply

$$FV = P(1 + r)^t \qquad (6.24)$$

Many different Web
site sources discuss
compounding of
interest—for
example, see
finaid.org

where FV is the sum of principal plus all accumulated interest over the life of the loan or deposit, P is the asset's principal value, r is the annual rate of interest, and t is the time expressed in years. For example, suppose $1,000 is borrowed for three years at 10 percent a year, compounded annually. Using an electronic calculator to find the compounding factor, $(1 + r)^t$, gives

$$FV = \$1,000(1 + 0.10)^3 = \$1,000(1.331) = \$1,331$$

which is the lump-sum amount the borrower must pay back at the end of three years. The amount of accumulated compound interest on this loan must be

$$\text{Compound interest} = FV - P = \$1,331 - \$1,000 = \$331 \qquad (6.25)$$

The World Wide Web
has made it possible
to search wide
geographic areas for
the best deposit and
loan rates available in
the marketplace. See,
for example,
money.cnn.com/pf/
banking/

Increased competition in the financial institutions' sector has encouraged most deposit-type institutions to offer their depositors interest compounded more frequently than annually, as assumed in the formula above. To determine the future value of accumulated interest from such a deposit, two changes must be made in the formula: (1) the quoted annual interest rate (r) must be divided by the number of periods during the year for which interest is compounded, and (2) the number of years involved (t) must be multiplied by the number of compounding periods within a year. For example, suppose you hold a $1,000 deposit, earning a 12 percent annual rate of interest, with interest compounded monthly, and you plan to hold the deposit for three years. At the end of three years, you will receive back the lump sum of

$$FV = P(1 + r/12)^{t \times 12} = \$1,000(1 + 0.12/12)^{3 \times 12}$$
$$= \$1,000(1.431) = \$1,431 \qquad (6.26)$$

Total interest earned will be $1,431 − $1,000, or $431. Compounding on a more frequent basis increases the depositor's accumulated interest and, therefore, the deposit's future value.[2]

The Annual Percentage Yield (APY) on Deposits

annual percentage yield (APY)

The annual percentage yield (APY) is discussed on the Web at **federalreserve.gov** under the Truth in Savings Act.

In 1991 the U.S. Congress passed the Truth in Savings Act in response to customer complaints about the way some depository institutions were calculating their customers' interest returns on deposits. Instead of giving customers credit for the average balance in their deposit accounts, some depository institutions were figuring a customer's interest return on the amount of the *lowest* balance in their account. The U.S. Congress responded to this practice by requiring depository institutions to calculate the *daily average* balance in a customer's deposit over each interest-crediting period and to use that daily average balance to determine the customer's **annual percentage yield (APY)** from the deposit account.

For example, suppose a customer deposits $2,000 in a one-year bank savings account for six months (180 days) but then withdraws $1,000 to help meet personal expenses, leaving $1,000 for the remainder of the year (185 days). Then the customer's daily average balance would be:

$$\text{Daily average balance} = \frac{\$2,000 \times 180 \text{ days} + \$1,000 \times 185 \text{ days}}{365 \text{ days}} = \$1,493.15$$

Suppose the bank credits the customer's account with $100 in interest. If the account has a term of 365 days (a full year) or has no stated maturity, then the customer's annual percentage yield can be calculated from the simple formula:

$$\text{APY} = 100 \,[\text{Annual interest earned/Daily average balance}] \qquad \textbf{(6.27)}$$

In this case,

$$\text{APY} = 100 \,[\$100/\$1,493.15] = 6.70 \text{ percent}$$

On the other hand, if the deposit account runs for *less than* a year, a depository institution subject to the provisions of the Truth in Savings Act must use the formula:

$$\text{APY} = 100 \left[\left(1 + \frac{\text{Amount of interest earned/Daily average balance}}{} \right)^{365/\text{days in term}} - 1 \right] \qquad \textbf{(6.28)}$$

For data on credit card plans and the interest rates and other terms they impose on customers, see the credit card analyzer at **creditcardanalyzer. com**

For example, suppose that a customer opens a savings account with a maturity of 182 days (six months) and leaves $1,000 in the account for the whole period. Suppose too that at the end of the deposit's term the bank credits the customer with $30.37 in interest earned. Then, the annual percentage yield (APY) that must be reported to the customer under the Truth in Savings Act would be

$$\text{APY} = 100[(1 + \$30.37/\$1,000)^{365/182} - 1] \approx 6.18 \text{ percent}.$$

Whenever a customer opens a new deposit account in the United States, he or she must be informed about how interest will be computed on his or her account, what fees will

---

[2]Many financial institutions quote deposit rates compounded *daily*. In this case, the annual interest rate (r) is divided by 360 for simplicity and the number of years (t) in the formula is multiplied by 365. Thus, the formula for *daily* interest rate compounding is

$$FV = P(1 + r/360)^{t \times 365}$$

be charged that could reduce the customer's interest earnings, and what must be done to earn the full APY promised on the deposit.

QUESTIONS TO HELP YOU STUDY

11. Explain why debt security prices and interest rates are inversely related. Illustrate this inverse relationship with a diagram.

12. Explain the meaning of the following terms and, where a formula is involved, explain the components of each formula:

    a. Simple interest

    b. Add-on interest

    c. Discount loan method

    d. APR

    e. Compound interest

    f. APY

13. How is the monthly payment that a home mortgage borrower must meet determined? Why is it that payments made early in the life of a typical home mortgage go largely to pay interest rather than repay principal?

MARKETS ON THE NET: The Most Important Web Sites for This Chapter

Bankrate.com (bankrate.com)

Compare Interest Rates (compareinterestrates.com)

Federal Reserve System (federalreserve.gov)

Financial Power Tools (financialpowertools.com)

Interest Rate Calculator (interestratecalculator.com)

Local Bank Rates on Loans and Savings (digitalcity.com)

The Credit Card Analyzer (creditcardanalyzer.com)

Investopedia.com (investopedia.com/calculator)

Summary of the Chapter's Main Points

Interest rates and asset prices are among the most important ingredients needed to help make sound financial decisions. Over the years, a number of methods have been developed to aid in the measurement and calculation of interest rates and asset prices within the financial system.

- Two of the most widely used and conceptually sound measures of the rate of return on a financial asset are the *yield to maturity* and the *holding-period yield.* Both take into account the size and timing of all payments expected to be received from a financial instrument and consider the *time value of money* (that is, payments to be received sooner are more valuable than payments to be received later).

- In contrast, other interest-rate or return measures, such as the *coupon rate* (or annual rate of return set by contract) or the *current yield* (annual interest payments or dividends divided by the price of a financial instrument) do *not* consider the present value of any income or principal payments received by the holder of a financial instrument.

- In this chapter, we have highlighted one of the fundamental principles of finance: the *inverse relationship between the prices of financial assets, particularly bonds and other debt securities, and interest rates.* Falling bond prices, for example, are associated with rising interest rates in the money and capital markets.

- Often we observe *stock prices* falling during a period of rising interest rates as well, although this need not always be so because stock prices are sensitive to several other factors besides interest rates (such as the condition of the economy, business profits, and dividend payments to stockholders).

- Banks and other lending institutions often calculate the loan rates they quote borrowers according to different interest-rate measures. Examples include the *simple interest rate* (where interest owed is adjusted for repayments of the principal of a loan) and the *add-on interest rate* (where interest owed is added to the principal of a loan and divided by the number of payments called for in a loan agreement). Other loan-rate measures include the *discount loan method* (where interest is deducted at the beginning of a loan) and the *APR* (or annual percentage rate), which adjusts interest owed for repayments of loan principal. The *APR* is subject to regulation so that lenders must calculate it the same way and borrowers can more meaningfully compare one loan agreement against another in order to find the best deal available.

- Interest rates or yields on deposits today are increasingly quoted as the *annual percentage yield* or *APY*. Regulations require that depositors receive APY information when taking out a new deposit or renewing an existing deposit so that the depositor can make an informed financial decision.

- Most depository institutions today pay *compound interest* on their deposits— that is, interest is earned on accumulated interest as well as on the principal invested in a deposit. Increasingly deposits accrue compound interest on a daily or other, more frequent basis than in the past.

- One of the more complicated interest rate and loan payment methods is the procedure used to figure loan rates and payment amounts on *home mortgage loans*. Under most home mortgage contracts, payments made early in the life of such a loan go largely to pay interest; only after several years are substantial portions of home mortgage payments directed to help repay the loan principal.

Key Terms Appearing in This Chapter

Problems and Issues

1. Suppose a 10-year bond is issued with an annual coupon rate of 8 percent when the market rate of interest is also 8 percent. If the market rate rises to 9 percent, what happens to the price of this bond? What happens to the bond's price if the market rate falls to 6 percent? Explain why.

2. Preferred stock for XYZ corporation is issued at par for $50 per share. If stockholders are promised an 8 percent annual dividend, what was the stock's current yield at time of issue? If the stock's market price has risen to $60 per share, what is its new current yield?

3. You plan to borrow $2,000 to take a vacation and want to repay the loan in a year. The banker offers you a simple interest rate of 12 percent with repayment of principal in two equal installments, 6 months and 12 months from now. What is your total interest bill? What is the APR? Would you prefer an add-on interest rate with one payment at the end of the year? If the bank applied the discount method to your loan, what are the net proceeds of the loan? What is your effective rate of interest?

4. An investor is interested in purchasing a new 20-year government bond carrying a 10 percent annual coupon rate with interest paid twice a year. The bond's current market price is $875 for a $1,000 par value instrument. If the investor buys the bond at the going price and holds to maturity, what will be his or her yield to maturity? Suppose the investor sells the bond at the end of 10 years for $950. What is the investor's holding-period yield?

5. Calculate the bank discount rate of return (DR) and the YTM-equivalent return for the following money market instruments:

   a. Purchase price, $96; par value, $100; maturity, 90 days.

   b. Purchase price, $97.50; par value, $100; maturity, 270 days.

6. You have just placed $1,500 in a bank savings deposit and plan to hold that deposit for eight years, earning $5\frac{1}{2}$ percent per annum. If the bank compounds interest daily, what will be the total value of the deposit in eight years? How does your answer change if the bank switches to monthly compounding? Quarterly compounding?

7. You decide to take out a 30-year mortgage loan to buy the home of your dreams. The home's purchase price is $120,000. You manage to scrape together a $20,000 down payment and plan to borrow the balance of the purchase price. Hardy Savings and Loan Association quotes you a fixed annual loan rate of 12 percent. What will your monthly payment be? How much total interest will you have paid at the end of 30 years?

8. A depositor places $5,000 in a credit union deposit account for a full year but then withdraws $1,000 after 270 days. At the end of the year, the credit union pays her $300 in interest. What is this depositor's daily average balance and APY?

9. A commercial loan extended to CIBER-LAND Corporation for $2.5 million assesses an interest charge of $350,000 up front. Using the discount loan method of calculating loan rates, what is the effective interest rate on this loan? Suppose that instead of deducting the interest owed up front, the company's lender agrees to extend the full $2.5 million and add the amount of interest owed to the face amount of CIBER's note. What, then, is the loan's effective interest rate?

10. The Pine family borrows $1,500 for a year at an 11 percent simple interest rate, but the loan is to be repaid in 12 equal monthly installments. What is the loan's APR?

www.mhhe.com/rose9e

> ## Standard & Poor's Market Insight and Web-Based Problems

1. The expression for computing the per-share stock price for a firm that is expected to have a constant dividend growth rate (given in the text as Equation 6.18) is:

$$SP = D(1 + r) / (r - g)$$

where *SP* is the firm's per-share stock price, *D* is the current dividend per share, *r* is the required rate of return for the investor to purchase the stock, and *g* is the expected constant dividend growth rate.

    The above equation can be useful in understanding how the financial markets arrive at stock values for well-established firms operating in different markets. For example, consider IBM and American Electric Power (AEP)—both leaders in their industries and expected to experience relatively stable growth. We can use Equation 6.18 and data from the market to compute the market's expectation of earnings growth, which will be reflected in dividend growth, for these two companies.

a. Assume the markets demand a 6 percent return for investing in either IBM or AEP. Go to Standard & Poor's Market Insight database at **www.mhhe.com/business/finance/edumarketinsight/** or use other appropriate Web sites for these two companies and find their current stock price and dividend. Use Equation 6.18 to compute the market's expectation of dividend (earnings) growth for these two firms. Which is larger? See if you can explain why by discussing the nature of the businesses these two companies are engaged in.

b. Equation 6.18 is derived from the more general expression for stock prices given by Equation 6.17 in the text. While Equation 6.18 can provide a useful guideline for market pricing equities issued by large, well-established firms like IBM and AEP, it often runs into trouble when used to estimate stock values for new start-up firms or for established companies changing their business plan. To see this, try to repeat the process you followed in (*a*) for Amazon.com (AMZN) and eBay (EBAY). What seems to be wrong? Can you explain why this equation fails to provide a reasonable estimate of the expected growth for these firms?

2. As described in the text, the *PE ratio* is the current price of a firm's stock divided by its most recent (quarterly) per-share earnings. One problem with the PE ratio is that its numerator is *forward-looking,* while its denominator is *backward-looking.* One way to make better use of the PE ratio as an investor guide is to compare its current value with the long-term average for the same company and/or a firm's industry group.

    For example, you could compare the current PE for Wells Fargo Corporation (WFC) with its average PE over the most recent 10-year period in order to get an idea of whether its near-term earnings prospects appear to have improved relative to past years (i.e., whether the firm's current PE is above its long-run average) and whether its current earnings prospects are strong relative to its industry (i.e., whether its current PE ratio lies above the industry average).

a. Choose a company from each of the following industry groups and determine whether the chosen firms' earnings prospects appear to be better or worse than they have been in the past 10 years and whether they are expected to be a strong performer in their industry. Consult S&P's Market Insight database at **www.mhhe.com/business/finance/edumarketinsight/** or other appropriate Web sources for:

(1) Industry group: Banking; sub-group: Diversified banking.

(2) Industry group: Metals: Precious; sub-group: Gold.

(3) Industry group: Airlines; sub-group: Airlines.

b. For each industry group read the "Industry Survey" at the S&P site by navigating the Web page. Identify the industry sub-group under the "Industry" tab at the top of the Web page.

c. Use the "Company" tab to find your selected firm using its stock symbol. To find the recent history of the firm's PE and an earnings projection for the firm and its industry, select the "S&P Stock Reports" tab and choose "Stock Report" and "Industry Outlook." Report your findings.

Semester Project: A Study of the Fed Funds Market

At the end of Chapter 5 we presented another installment of the semester-long project on the *federal funds market,* examining the unusual conditions in the funds market around the Christmas holiday season—a period when the demand for short-term funds is often exceptionally strong. In this segment of the project we view the funds market in more "normal" times.

Suppose that a bank or other depository institution finds itself temporarily flush with cash, holding approximately $10 million in excess liquid funds. Management would like to lend out this excess cash and earn additional interest income. In order to prevent its competition (principally other depository institutions) from being able to monitor its borrowing and lending activity in this market, the bank employs the services of a *Fed funds broker.* Nearly 80 percent of all federal funds transactions are brokered trades. The broker puts the funds up for "sale," indicating that funds can be borrowed overnight and specifying what the cost will be by posting an "asked rate" (i.e., the interest rate that another depository institution would have to pay for this overnight loan). The asked rate is based on a par value of 100 and is quoted in the form of a *bank discount rate* (discussed earlier in this chapter).

Suppose the broker's quoted asked rate is 1 percent. Then:

a. Compute the yield to maturity (YTM) the lending bank would realize on this loan.

b. Because this is to be an overnight loan, what actual dollar amount of interest will the borrowing bank have to pay if the par value of the loan is $10 million?

Selected References to Explore

Sundaresan, Suresh. *Fixed Income Markets and Their Derivatives.* New York: International Thomson, 1997.

Trainer, Richard D. C. *The Arithmetic of Interest Rates.* New York: Federal Reserve Bank of New York, 1980.

Chapter 7

Inflation and Deflation, Yield Curves, and Duration: Impact on Interest Rates and Asset Prices

Learning Objectives in This Chapter

- You will discover what *inflation* is all about and how inflation can impact interest rates and the prices of financial assets.

- You will understand why there is greater concern today about the prospect of *deflation*—the reverse of inflation—and how it might affect the economy and financial system.

- You will see how *yield curves* arise and view the controversy over what determines the shape of the yield curve.

- You will discover how yield curves can be a useful tool for those interested in investing their money and in tracking the health of the economy.

- You will explore the concept of *duration*—a measure of the maturity of a financial instrument—and see how it can be used to assist in making investment choices and in protecting against the risk of changes in interest rates.

What's in This Chapter? Key Topics Outline

7.1   Introduction

In Chapter 5 we examined demand and supply forces believed to determine the rate of interest on a financial asset. We know, however, that there is not just one interest rate in the financial system, but thousands. And many of these rates differ substantially from one another. For example, early in 2004 six-month maturity U.S. Treasury bills were being auctioned at an annual interest rate of just over 1 percent, while long-term Treasury bonds were offering investors a 5.40 percent annual return. The market yield on high-quality corporate bonds averaged almost 7 percent. At the same time, major banks were quoting average loan rates to their most financially sound (prime) customers near 4 percent. Meanwhile, investors in the market for state and local government (municipal) long-term bonds were being promised an annual rate of return of close to 5 percent.

Why are all these interest rates so different from one another? Are these rate differences purely random, or can we attribute them to a limited number of factors that can be studied and perhaps predicted? Understanding the factors that cause interest rates to differ among themselves is an indispensable aid to the investor and saver in choosing financial assets for a portfolio. It is not always advisable, for example, to reach for the highest yield available in the financial marketplace. The investor who does so may assume an unacceptable level of risk, have his or her securities called in by the issuer in advance of maturity, pay an unacceptably high tax bill, accept a rate of return whose value is seriously eroded by inflation, or suffer other undesirable consequences. Without question, the intelligent saver and investor must have a working knowledge of the factors affecting interest rates and be able to anticipate possible future changes in those factors. In this chapter and the next, we address these important issues.

7.2   Inflation and Interest Rates

inflation

One of the most serious problems confronting several economies around the globe in recent years has been **inflation.** Inflation is defined as *a rise in the average level of prices for all goods and services.* Some prices of individual goods and services are always rising while others are declining. However, inflation occurs when the *average* level of all prices in the economy rises.[1] Interest rates represent the "price" of credit. Are they also affected by inflation? The answer is *yes,* though there is considerable debate as to exactly *how* and by *how much* inflation affects interest rates.

The Correlation between Inflation and Interest Rates

To be sure, the apparent correlation in recent years between the rate of inflation in the United States and both long-term and short-term interest rates appears to be fairly strong. Exhibit 7.1, which reports two popular measures of the rate of inflation—the Consumer Price Index and the GDP deflator—and a key money market interest rate— the yield on six-month commercial paper—suggests a fairly close association between inflation and interest rates. For example, between 1980 and 2000, both inflation and U.S. interest rates generally declined, before rising slightly as the decade of the 1990s ended. Then, in the wake of terrorist attacks and a weakening U.S. economy, interest rates sank to 40-year lows as the new century opened, and the annual rate of U.S. inflation also dropped to one of the lowest levels since the 1940s.

In summary, then, interest rates and inflation appear to be at least moderately correlated with one another. But is there really a *causal* connection between them?

---

[1] See Chapter 13 for a discussion of the nature, causes, and recent public policy responses to inflation.

EXHIBIT 7.1	**Inflation and Interest Rates (Annual Rates, Percent)**		
	Rate of Inflation Measured by Percentage Change in		**Interest Rate on Prime Commercial Paper (Six-Month Maturities)**
Year	**Consumer Price Index**	**GDP Deflator**	
1960	1.6%	1.7%	3.85%
1970	5.9	5.4	7.72
1980	13.5	8.8	12.29
1990	6.2	4.0	7.83
2000	3.4	2.1	6.35
2003	2.3	1.7	1.15
2004*	3.6	2.6	1.99

Source: U.S. Department of Commerce and Board of Governors of the Federal Reserve System.

Note: 2004 inflation measures are for first quarter of the year. The 2004 interest rate applies to directly-placed commercial paper issued by General Electric Corporation in September.

Nominal and Real Interest Rates

nominal interest rate

real interest rate

inflation premium

To explore the possible relationship between inflation and interest rates, several key terms must be defined. First, we must distinguish between nominal and real interest rates. The **nominal interest rate** is the published or quoted interest rate on a financial asset. For example, an announcement in the financial press that major commercial banks have raised their prime lending rate to 10 percent per annum indicates what nominal interest rate is now being quoted by banks to some of their best loan customers. In contrast, the **real interest rate** is the return to the lender or investor measured in terms of its actual purchasing power. In a period of inflation, of course, the real rate will be lower than the nominal rate. Another important concept is the **inflation premium,** which measures the rate of inflation *expected* by lenders and investors in the marketplace during the life of a particular financial instrument.

These three concepts *are* related. Obviously, a lender of funds is most interested in the *real rate of return* on a loan; that is, the purchasing power of any interest earned. For example, suppose you loan $1,000 to a business firm for a year and expect the prices of goods and services to rise 10 percent during the year. If you charge a nominal interest rate of 12 percent on the loan, your *real* rate of return on the $1,000 loan is only 2 percent, or $20. However, if the actual rate of inflation during the period of the loan turns out to be 13 percent, you have actually suffered a real decline in the purchasing power of the monies loaned. In general, lenders will attempt to charge nominal rates of interest that give them desired *real* rates of return on their loanable funds based upon their expectations regarding inflation.

The Fisher Effect

Among the more interesting Web sites linking interest rates and inflation are globalfindata.com and economist.com

In a classic article written just before the end of the nineteenth century, economist Irving Fisher (1896) argued that the nominal interest rate was related to the real interest rate by the following equation:

$$\begin{array}{c}\text{Expected}\\\text{nominal}\\\text{interest rate}\end{array} = \begin{array}{c}\text{Expected}\\\text{real}\\\text{rate}\end{array} + \begin{array}{c}\text{Inflation}\\\text{premium}\end{array} + \begin{array}{c}\text{Expected}\\\text{real}\\\text{rate}\end{array} \times \begin{array}{c}\text{Inflation}\\\text{premium}\end{array} \qquad (7.1)$$

Clearly, if the expected real interest rate is held fixed, changes in expected nominal rates will reflect shifting inflation premiums (i.e., changes in the public's views on expected inflation). The cross-product term in the above equation (Expected real rate × Inflation premium) is often eliminated because it is usually quite small except in countries experiencing severe inflation.[2]

Does Equation 7.1 suggest that an increase in expected inflation *automatically* increases expected nominal interest rates? Not necessarily. There are several different views on the matter. Fisher argued that the expected real rate of return tends to be relatively stable over time because it depends on such long-term factors as the productivity of capital and the volume of savings in the economy. Therefore, changes in the expected nominal interest rate are most likely to reflect changes in the inflation premium, not the expected real rate, at least in the short run. The expected nominal rate will rise by close to the full amount of the expected increase in the rate of inflation. For example, suppose the expected real rate is 3 percent and the expected rate of inflation is 10 percent. Then the expected nominal rate would be close to

$$\text{Expected nominal interest rate} = 3\% + 10\% = 13\% \qquad \textbf{(7.2)}$$

According to Fisher's hypothesis, if the expected rate of inflation now rises to 12 percent, the expected real rate will remain essentially unchanged at 3 percent, but the expected nominal rate will rise to 15 percent.

Fisher effect   If this view, known today as the **Fisher effect,** is correct, it suggests a method of judging at least the *direction* of future interest rate changes. To the extent that a rise in the actual rate of inflation causes investors to expect greater inflation in the future, higher nominal interest rates will soon result. Conversely, a decline in the actual inflation rate may cause investors to revise downward their expectations of future inflation, leading eventually to lower nominal rates. This will happen because, in an efficient market, lenders will seek full compensation for the risk of expected changes in the purchasing power of their money.

Alternative Views about Inflation and Interest Rates

While the Fisher effect is among the most popular explanations of the link between inflation and interest rates, several alternative views of the inflation-interest rate connection have emerged over the years.

The Harrod-Keynes Effect of Inflation   The Fisher effect conflicts directly with a view of the inflation-interest rate phenomenon developed originally by British economist Sir Roy Harrod. It is based upon the Keynesian liquidity preference theory of interest rates discussed in Chapter 5. Harrod argues that the *real* rate *will* be affected by inflation but the nominal interest rate may not be. According to the liquidity preference theory, the nominal interest rate is determined by the demand for and supply of money. Therefore, unless inflation affects either the demand for or supply of money, the expected nominal interest rate must remain unchanged regardless of what happens to inflationary expectations.

What, then, is the link between inflation and interest rates according to this view? Harrod argues that a rise in inflationary expectations will lower the *real* rate of interest. In liquidity preference theory the real rate measures the inflation-adjusted return on bonds. However, conventional bonds, like money, are *not* a hedge against inflation, because their rate of return is usually fixed by contract. Therefore, a rise in the expected rate of inflation lowers investors' expected real return from holding bonds. If

---

[2] For example, if inflation is running 5 percent a year and the real rate of interest is 3 percent, the cross-product term in Equation 7.1 is only 0.05 × 0.03, or 0.0015. Equation 7.1 is derived from the relationship (1 + Nominal rate) = (1 + Real rate) × (1 + Inflation premium).

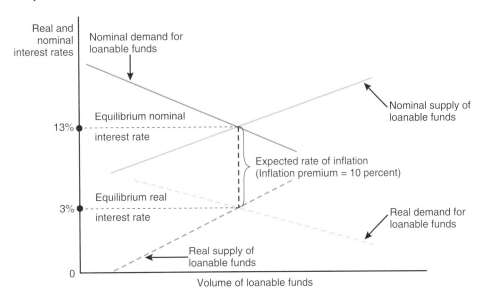

EXHIBIT 7.2

The Impact of Fully Anticipated Inflation on Real and Nominal Interest Rates

the nominal rate of return on bonds remains unchanged, the expected real rate *must* be squeezed when there are expectations of more rapidly rising prices.

Harrod-Keynes effect

This so-called **Harrod-Keynes effect** does not stop with bonds, however. There are two other groups of assets in the economy that, unlike bonds, may provide a hedge against inflation: *common stocks* and *real estate*. Inflationary expectations often lead to rising prices for homes, farmland, and commercial structures and occasionally to rallies in the stock market. Proponents of the Harrod-Keynes view argue that an increase in the rate of inflation causes the demand for these inflation-hedged assets to increase. Real estate and stock prices rise and, therefore, their nominal rates of return will fall until an equilibrium among the returns on bonds, real estate, and other assets is achieved. Thus, the Fisher and Harrod-Keynes effects take off in opposite directions.

Anticipated versus Unanticipated Inflation   One of the most obvious weaknesses of the Fisher effect was its failure to distinguish between *anticipated* (or expected) and *unanticipated* (or unexpected) inflation. For example, Fisher assumed that inflation is *fully anticipated*. As an example, suppose that both borrowers and lenders of funds expect an inflation rate for the next year of 10 percent and the real interest rate is 3 percent. We can illustrate this using Exhibit 7.2, which shows two sets of demand and supply curves for loanable funds: a set of *real* demand and supply curves intersecting at a 3 percent real interest rate, and a set of *nominal* demand and supply curves intersecting at a point just high enough to fully reflect the expected inflation rate (in this example, 10 percentage points higher than the real rate). The nominal supply and demand curves for loanable funds both shift upward just enough to ensure that the going nominal interest rate on a one-year loan is 3 percent plus 10 percent, or 13 percent. Lenders will be unwilling to lend money at any rate lower than 13 percent because they expect the prices of the goods and services they plan to purchase to increase by 10 percent during the life span of the loan.

Suppose, however, that all or a portion of the increase in inflation is *unanticipated*. In this case, there is no way to be certain about what the equilibrium nominal interest rate will be, for the nominal rate may not fully reflect the amount of inflation expected. The simple one-for-one change in the expected nominal rate in response to changing inflationary expectations may not be exactly correct. However, if unanticipated inflation—

once it is observed—is expected to persist, then the nominal interest rate should adjust accordingly.

The Inflation-Risk Premium

Recent research has also suggested that the Fisher effect may have left out a key term in the inflation-interest rate equation. The correct formula may look more like this:

$$\begin{array}{l}\text{Nominal} \\ \text{interest rate}\end{array} = \begin{array}{l}\text{Real} \\ \text{interest rate}\end{array} + \begin{array}{l}\text{Expected} \\ \text{inflation rate}\end{array} + \begin{array}{l}\text{Inflation-} \\ \text{risk premium}\end{array} \quad (7.3)$$

inflation-risk premium

The newly added term—the **inflation-risk premium**—represents compensation paid to a lender for that component of inflation that is *not expected*. Thus, the last term in the above equation represents uncertainty about what the actual inflation rate will turn out to be during the life of any particular financial instrument. For example, suppose the real rate is currently 3 percent, the expected rate of inflation is about 4 percent, and lenders are demanding an inflation-risk premium of 1 percent to compensate them should inflation rise faster than anticipated. The nominal interest rate must therefore be close to 8 percent.

The inflation-risk premium generally rises with the maturity of a nominal financial instrument because the longer the period until final payment of a loan, the greater the likelihood of unexpected inflation occurring. It is more difficult to forecast inflation over a lengthier period of time. Moreover, the longer the period before the final payment on a loan, the greater the cost of any inflation forecasting error a lender might make. Thus, the inflation-risk premium on a one-year loan might be half of a percentage point, but it might be closer to 1 percent on a 10-year bond. Recent research by Shen (1998) for the United Kingdom suggests that the inflation-risk premium can be sizeable—a percentage point or more added to the nominal rate of return on inflation-risk-exposed financial assets.

The Inflation-Caused Income Tax Effect

Finally, one factor affecting the link between inflation and interest rates that neither Fisher nor any of his contemporaries figured in was *income taxes*. As the old saying goes, nothing is more certain in life than death and taxes! And, surprisingly, something called the **inflation-caused income tax effect** may actually widen movements in nominal interest rates, resulting in nominal rates increasing by *more* than any given change in expected inflation. The heart of this argument is that lenders and investors not exempt from income taxes make lending and investing decisions on the basis of their expected real rate of return *after taxes*. If an investor desires to protect his or her expected real after-tax rate of return, then the expected nominal rate has to increase by a *greater* amount than any rise in the expected inflation rate because otherwise real after-tax returns will decline when expected inflation increases.

inflation-caused income tax effect

To see the validity of this argument, we observe that

$$\begin{array}{l}\text{Expected after-} \\ \text{tax real rate of re-} \\ \text{turn earned by a} \\ \text{taxpaying} \\ \text{investor}\end{array} = \begin{array}{l}\text{Expected} \\ \text{nominal} \\ \text{rate}\end{array} - \left[\begin{array}{l}\text{Expected} \\ \text{nominal} \\ \text{rate}\end{array} \times \begin{array}{l}\text{Taxpayer's} \\ \text{income tax} \\ \text{bracket rate}\end{array}\right] - \begin{array}{l}\text{Inflation} \\ \text{premium}\end{array} \quad (7.4)$$

Suppose an investor is in the 28 percent income tax bracket, so that a little more than a quarter of any additional income he or she earns is taxed. Moreover, suppose the current expected nominal interest rate on a one-year taxable financial asset this investor is interested in buying is 12 percent, and the inflation premium (expected inflation rate) over the coming year is 5 percent. Then this investor's expected real after-tax return from the asset must be

$$\text{Expected after-tax real rate of return earned by a taxpaying investor} = 12\% - [12\%\ (0.28)] - 5\% = 3.64\% \qquad \textbf{(7.5)}$$

Now suppose the expected rate of inflation rises from 5 to 6 percent. By how much must the *expected nominal rate* on the taxable financial asset rise to yield this investor the *same* expected real return after taxes? The answer must be that the nominal rate must rise to 13.39 percent, for

$$\text{Expected after-tax real rate of return earned by a taxpaying investor} = 13.39\% - [13.39\%\ (0.28)] - 6\% = 3.64\% \qquad \textbf{(7.6)}$$

Thus, a change of 1 percent in expected inflation required a 1.39 percent change in the expected nominal rate to leave this taxed investor in the same place in terms of a real (purchasing-power) return from his or her investment.

The arithmetic shown above works both ways: a *reduction* in expected inflation by 1 percent requires a 1.39 percent *decline* in the nominal rate to leave the expected real after-tax return where it is. While investors in lower tax brackets would not require as numerically large a change in expected nominal rates to leave after-tax real returns unaltered, inflation tends to force most investors into higher and higher tax brackets as both prices and nominal incomes rise (unless, of course, government tax schedules are indexed to change with inflation).

Conclusions from Recent Research on Inflation and Interest Rates

With all of the foregoing *possible* effects from inflation, what actually happens to nominal interest rates when the expected rate of inflation changes? As Fisher (1896) originally suggested, the inflation-nominal interest rate relationship appears to be *positive: Higher rates of inflation ultimately lead to higher nominal interest rates in most cases.* However, on average, nominal interest rates appear to rise by somewhat *less* than any given increase in the expected inflation rate and decline by somewhat *less* than any given decrease in the expected inflation rate. This happens probably because inflation not only affects interest rates but also the wealth and incomes of businesses and households, among other things, setting in motion a host of changes in the economy and financial system. However, most of the change in expected inflation (perhaps 60 to 90 percent) appears to find its way into the nominal interest rate, suggesting that *the Fisher effect frequently tends to dominate other forces affecting the link between expected inflation and nominal interest rates.*

The relationship between interest rates and inflation is discussed in numerous Web sites, including interestratecalculator. com and finpipe.com

Still, the reader should retain a healthy skepticism about research in this field. The topic of inflation and interest rates is plagued by numerous *measurement problems.* For example, there are no direct, widely accepted measures of the two key actors in the drama—the expected real rate and the expected rate of inflation. Because the underlying theory speaks of *expected* inflation and the *expected* real interest rate, there is the obvious problem of measuring people's expectations. We cannot, as a practical matter, survey all investors, and the results of such a survey would soon be irrelevant anyway, because expectations can change fast. Note, too, that we cannot automatically derive the expected real interest rate merely by subtracting the current inflation rate from the current nominal rate; this gives us a measure of the actual (ex post) real rate at a single point in time, not necessarily the *expected* real rate.

The Nature and Impact of Price Deflation

What Is Deflation?   For the past 50 years and more, *inflation—a rising* average level for the prices of goods and services—has been a key economic and financial problem. However, as the twenty-first century began, there was growing concern that **deflation**—a falling average level of prices—might eventually replace inflation as a significant economic problem for the future. Indeed, the world's second largest economy, Japan, had by that time experienced falling prices for more than a decade, accompanied by rising unemployment and domestic nominal interest rates hovering close to zero. (Between 1993 and 2002, Japan's average annual inflation rate was −0.2 percent.) Nor has Japan been entirely alone. In the United States, the price level for manufactured goods *fell* early in the twenty-first century. However, the price level for services rose so that, overall, the U.S. still experienced moderate inflation rather than deflation.

deflation

Possible Impacts of Deflation   If inflation tends to result in rising interest rates, what can we say about deflation? Would it lead to *falling* interest rates? We cannot say for sure because periods of deflation—at least during the past century—have been relatively rare. The last time the United States experienced a sustained deflation was during the Great Depression of the 1930s. Nominal prices of goods and services fell nearly 25 percent. At the same time, the production of goods and services dropped almost 40 percent in real terms. More recently, consumer prices and manufacturers' output fell slightly in the wake of the September 2001 terrorist attacks.

Were these economic developments—a falling price level and declining real output—connected somehow? Perhaps, because deflation *may* be damaging to production and to people's financial well-being. For one thing, deflation *may* be accompanied by higher real interest rates as nominal interest rates drop toward zero. Relatively higher real interest rates that are unaccompanied by new, more productive technology tend to slow investment spending and retard the development of new jobs. Real economic output may decline as factories come to produce less and business profits fall. At the same time, lenders may gain at the expense of borrowers because the former's purchasing power rises. If deflation causes nominal interest rates to approach zero, a central bank like the Federal Reserve System might have to change how it conducts monetary policy in order to strengthen the economy.

However, none of this is certain. For example, the U.S. experienced an average annual deflation rate of 1 percent during the last quarter of the nineteenth century, but it still recorded positive economic growth during that same period. This relationship between falling prices and higher output can occur in an economy during a time of rapid technological change, when the productivity of new capital equipment is rising rapidly. Improved productivity causes real interest rates to rise as the returns to investment by businesses increase. Firms respond by expanding investment and output. At the same time, the greater productivity of capital enables firms to produce goods and services more efficiently and at lower cost, thus driving down the prices they charge. The result is that the economy experiences both deflation and rapid economic growth.

In summary, price *deflation* may coincide with lower output (production) of goods and services, fewer jobs, and benefits that go primarily to lenders at the expense of borrowers, or it may be a by-product of rapid technological change that generally benefits nearly all individuals living and working in the economy. In any case, wrenching changes in the economy associated with deflation—as occurred during the Great Depression of the 1930s—are much less likely today, as businesses and financial systems are better positioned to deal with *both* inflation and deflation, in part because of the development of so many new risk management tools (such as financial futures and option contracts). It probably would take a major deflationary period—like the one that impacted the United States during the Great Depression or Japan's more recent experience—to cause serious economic and financial-market disruption. However, we cannot speak with certainty about this subject because we have only limited experience with deflation thus far.

7.3   Inflation and Stock Prices

The discussion so far has centered on the public's expectations about the prices of goods and services and their possible impact on interest rates attached to bonds and other debt securities. However, another interesting question centers on the relationship between expectations of inflation and *stock prices*. Does greater inflation cause the prices of corporate stock (equities) to rise? Common stock, for example, is widely viewed as a powerful hedge against inflation—a place to park your money if you want to preserve the purchasing power of your savings over the long haul.

Unfortunately, the facts often contradict what everybody "knows." For example, the stock market rose to unprecedented highs in the mid-1980s and again in the late 1990s, suggesting that inflation was also on the rise. Yet, the U.S. inflation rate actually *fell* during these periods. One useful way to view this issue is to decide what factors determine the prices of corporate stock and see if those factors are likely to be affected by inflation.

In basic terms, the stock price per share of any corporation is positively related to the *dividends* investors expect the company to pay to shareholders in future periods and is negatively related to the *risk* attached to that stream of expected dividends, as we saw in Chapter 6. That is,

$$\text{Price per share of corporate stock} = \sum_{t=0}^{\infty} \frac{E(D_t)}{(1 + r)^t} \tag{7.7}$$

where $E(D_t)$ are expected dividend payments in each period t, and r is the rate of discount applied to those expected dividends to express them in terms of their present value. The riskier the corporation's dividend stream, the higher the required rate of discount, r, because investors demand a higher rate of return to compensate them for the added risk of holding stock (which promises no specific rate of return).

Clearly, if a rise in expected inflation raises stock prices, it must increase the amount of dividends shareholders expect each company to pay them [$E(D)$], or lower the perceived risk of holding stock (r), or both. On the other hand, stock prices will tend to fall if more inflation causes investors to lower their dividend expectations, increases the perceived risk to stockholders, or both. Is there any research evidence on which way the inflation-stock price relationship goes?

There are several conflicting views. One line of argument says that if inflation is fully expected by all investors, nominal (published) stock prices may rise but *real* stock prices may not change at all. This is because corporate revenues and expenses may grow equally fast and the size of each firm's net income and dividend payments may *not* be affected at all (assuming the company's board of directors does not change the dividend rate). On the other hand, if the rate of inflation is only partly expected but is expected to persist, then the amount of unexpected inflation may be captured by company stockholders, as opposed to debt holders, in the form of increased earnings and real stock prices may rise. Conversely, if the company's depreciation expenses on worn-out equipment are inadequate to offset the rising cost of new equipment in a period of inflation, current before-tax corporate income will be overstated, resulting in higher taxes against the firm, lowering its after-tax income and reducing stockholder dividend

Nominal contracts are formal agreements that fix the terms in current (nominal) dollars under which a business firm will compensate its employees, creditors, and other suppliers of productive resources and the prices at which it will deliver its product or service to customers. Examples include business contracts with labor unions that fix wage rates, the issue of bonds at a fixed interest cost, or the valuing of business inventories and the depreciation of capital equipment using prespecified formulas. A business firm can be hurt by inflation, experiencing a fall in its stock price, if actual inflation turns out to be different from what it expected when it agreed to a nominal contract. However, some nominal contracts can benefit a firm experiencing inflation, particularly if the company correctly anticipated future price changes or, by using well-structured nominal contracts, managed to hold down its expenses or enhance its revenues. For example:

If a business firm enters into nominal contracts that:	Then, if inflation turns out to be *greater than expected*:	However, suppose inflation turns out to be *less than expected*. Then:
A. Fix its expenses at a constant level or constant rate of growth (e.g., borrowing money at a fixed rate or paying employees a guaranteed wage) based on its current expectations for inflation.	Business revenues may grow faster than expenses, increasing profits; the firm's stock price may *rise*.	Business expenses may increase faster than revenues, reducing profits; the firm's stock price may *fall*.
B. Fix its revenues at a constant level or constant rate of growth (e.g., selling to customers at a guaranteed price for the coming year) based on its current inflationary expectations.	Business expenses may grow faster than revenues, reducing profits; the firm's stock price may *fall*.	Business revenues may grow faster than expenses, increasing profits; the firm's stock price may *rise*.

payments. In this instance, more rapid inflation would tend to *lower* stock prices. For example, a study by Ammer (1994) finds a *negative* relationship between stock prices and inflation for several countries.

nominal contracts

Recently the concept of **nominal contracts** has emerged to help explain the inflation-stock price connection. What are nominal contracts? They are agreements between parties, such as a company and its workers or customers, that fix prices or costs in terms of current dollar (nominal) values for a stipulated time period. For example, corporations and labor unions may agree to increase wages 10 percent a year until current labor-management contracts expire or pledge to deliver their products to customers at a fixed price during the coming year. Corporate rules for valuing inventories or calculating depreciation expenses are other examples of nominal contracts. If inflation subsequently rises faster or slower than a company expected when it entered into its current nominal contracts, its profits may be squeezed or enhanced and its stock price may decrease or increase depending upon the circumstances. Thus, *the impact of inflation on stock prices may vary from firm to firm and from industry to industry, depending upon the actual rate of inflation and the terms of existing nominal contracts.*

An alternative view—called the *proxy effect*—argues for a *negative* relationship between inflation and stock prices but claims that relationship is *spurious*, not real. For example, changes in expected inflation are inversely related to fluctuations in expected output in the economy. If the public comes to believe that living costs will rise and the nation's economic output will decline at about the same time, then real stock prices may fall due to a more pessimistic outlook for business profits. However, it is the expected decrease in the economy's output, not the expected change in living costs (inflation), that leads to a decline in stock prices. Research evidence on these newer views is decidedly mixed. The issue of stock prices and inflation awaits further research to find the right answers.

7.4 The Development of Inflation-Adjusted Securities

TIPS

In 1997 the U.S. Treasury offered a possible way for investors buying government securities—considered one of the safest of all conventional debt obligations—to gain some protection against inflation. The Treasury began to issue inflation-indexed bonds called **TIPS** (Treasury Inflation Protection Securities), following the lead of such nations as Brazil and Great Britain, who experimented with inflation-indexed securities in earlier years.

Five- and 10-year TIPS were sold initially in the Treasury's experiment with these newly designed instruments. The Treasury also sells "I bonds" that are inflation-adjusted as part of its savings bond program. Investors buying these innovative new bonds can literally separate out inflation risk exposure from interest-rate risk exposure because TIPS adjust the payment of income to the investor to the actual amount of inflation experienced during the life of the bonds.

The inflation measure used to adjust the investor's return from TIPS is the Consumer Price Index (CPI), published by the U.S. Bureau of Labor Statistics and designed to reflect changes in the cost of living each month for an urban family of four. Thus, the real value of the interest payments from a TIPS will be constant in purchasing power for those goods and services included in the CPI. This happens because the bond's nominal (face) value will increase at the same rate as the actual CPI inflation rate.

For example, suppose the rate of inflation in the CPI is zero right now and the U.S. Treasury issues a new TIPS that has a nominal (face) value of $1,000 and promises a real annual coupon rate of 3.5 percent for five years. If inflation remains at zero, this bond will pay $35 a year in real interest income and, at maturity, when it is redeemed by the U.S. Treasury, its nominal value will remain at $1,000. Suppose, however, that inflation suddenly increases to 4 percent (annual rate) the day after the bond is issued and remains at that level for all five years of the bond's life. Then, the Treasury will calculate the bond's nominal value from the following formula:

Information regarding the nature of and the advantages and disadvantages attached to inflation-adjusted securities may be found at the U.S. Treasury site, savingsbond.com

$$\begin{matrix} \text{TIPS} \\ \text{inflation-adjusted} \\ \text{nominal value at maturity} \end{matrix} = \begin{matrix} \text{Original} \\ \text{face} \\ \text{value} \end{matrix} \left[1 + \begin{matrix} \text{Annual} \\ \text{rate of} \\ \text{inflation} \end{matrix} \right]^{\substack{\text{Time to maturity} \\ \text{in years}}} \quad (7.8)$$

In this example, the TIPS bond would have an inflation-adjusted nominal value at the end of its first year of:

$$\begin{matrix} \text{TIPS} \\ \text{inflation-adjusted nominal value} \\ \text{at the end of the first year} \end{matrix} = \$1,000 \, (1 + .04)^{1 \text{ year}} = \$1,040.00$$

If the inflation rate remains at 4 percent over the next four years until the above bond reaches maturity, this TIPS would have a nominal value at the end of five years of:

$$\begin{matrix} \text{TIPS} \\ \text{inflation-adjusted nominal value} \\ \text{at the end of 5 years} \end{matrix} = \$1,000 \, (1 + .04)^{5 \text{ years}} = \$1,216.65$$

The TIPS bond holder's annual nominal interest payment can be found from the simple formula:

$$\begin{matrix} \text{TIPS} \\ \text{inflation-adjusted} \\ \text{nominal value} \end{matrix} \times \begin{matrix} \text{Promised} \\ \text{coupon} \\ \text{rate} \end{matrix} = \begin{matrix} \text{Annual nominal} \\ \text{interest payment} \\ \text{from a TIPS} \end{matrix} \qquad \textbf{(7.9)}$$

If the bond's promised (coupon) rate is 3.5 percent, as in the example above, by the end of the bond's first year the amount of nominal interest earned by an investor would be:

$$\$1,040 \times .035 = \$36.40$$

instead of just $1,000 × 0.035, or $35, for a conventional bond whose principal is *not* adjusted for inflation. By the fifth year, when the TIPS described above reaches maturity, it will pay in annual nominal interest:

$$\$1,216.65 \times .035 = \$42.58$$

In summary, with an annual inflation rate of 4 percent a year, the inflation-adjusted bond just described would have increased its nominal principal and interest payments each year as follows:

Period	Actual Annual Rate of Inflation (%)	TIPS's Principal Nominal Value at the End of Each Year	Nominal Interest Payment to the TIPS Bond's Holder at Year-End	Nominal Interest Payment from a Conventional (Non-Inflation-Adjusted) Bond
First year	4%	$1,040.00	$36.40	$35
Second year	4	1,081.60	37.86	35
Third year	4	1,124.86	39.37	35
Fourth year	4	1,169.86	40.95	35
Fifth year	4	1,216.65	42.58	35

We must hasten to add, however, that even though the foregoing gains look impressive, the TIPS investor's real rate of return (that is, what he or she can actually buy with the earnings received) has *not* changed. The investor's *real* interest return must be:

$$\begin{matrix} \text{Actual real rate} \\ \text{of return on} \\ \text{the TIPS} \end{matrix} = \begin{matrix} \text{Nominal rate} \\ \text{of return on} \\ \text{the TIPS} \end{matrix} - \begin{matrix} \text{Actual} \\ \text{annual CPI} \\ \text{inflation rate} \end{matrix} \qquad \textbf{(7.10)}$$

Or, in the example above:

Actual annual real rate of return on the 5-year TIPS bond = 7.5% − 4% = 3.5%

The nominal return on the TIPS rises to 7.5 percent if inflation persists for five years at a 4 percent annual rate because *both* the face value of the bond and its interest earnings are adjusted upward. In contrast, if the markets fully anticipated this 4 percent inflation rate, then a conventional bond would have to fall in value to about

$$\begin{matrix} \text{Adjusted real value} \\ \text{of a conventional} \\ \text{bond under inflation} \end{matrix} = \frac{\text{Face value of conventional bond}}{\left[1 + \begin{matrix} \text{Actual} \\ \text{annual rate} \\ \text{of inflation} \end{matrix} \right]^{\text{Years to maturity}}} \qquad \textbf{(7.11)}$$

$$= \frac{\$1,000}{(1 + .04)^5} = \$821.93$$

in order to remain competitive in the market with TIPS and other inflation-adjusted assets available for purchase. The result for the conventional bond is an inflation-caused loss of $178.07 (or $1,000 − $821.93) if the investor sells the conventional bond prior to its maturity. Moreover, by the fifth year the investor's *real* annual interest income from the conventional bond would have dropped to only $28.77 [or $35/(1 + .04)^5] with inflation running at 4 percent a year. In contrast, as we saw in the table above, by holding a TIPS instead, this investor would receive a principal payment of $1,216.65 at the end of five years, gaining an additional $216.65 in nominal principal over a five-year period, or an average gain in principal of $43.33 per year. (Remember, however, that the investor's real principal value of the bond held at the end of five years would still be just $1,000, assuming a 4 percent annual inflation rate.) The TIPS's nominal price gain of $216.65 (or $1,216.65 − $1,000) plus its additional nominal interest revenues (which over five years will result in a total of $22.16 in additional interest income) would result in a nominal yield of about 7.5 percent.

Thus, Treasury inflation-index bonds (TIPS) are a relatively safe type of asset whose remaining risks include the danger that the real interest rate prevailing in the market will change (i.e., exposure to real interest rate risk). For example, real interest rates may rise and erode the real value of any bond; however, these new inflation-adjusted bonds make the management of risk more efficient by at least limiting an investor's overall risk exposure. The coupon (interest) income and the principal payment from these indexed bonds are both fixed in terms of purchasing power.

We should note, however, that not all inflation risk is eliminated by TIPS because rising inflation can drive an investor into a higher tax bracket, resulting in an after-tax rate of return that may be significantly less than the full inflation-adjusted real interest income from these special bonds. Moreover, TIPS are subject to market risk if an investor wishes to sell them ahead of their maturity date. However, Shen (1998) has demonstrated that the overall market risk for inflation-indexed bonds appears to be smaller than that for conventional bonds. Still, most investors in the financial markets have been lukewarm in their response to TIPS, possibly because these innovative instruments appeared during a period when inflation was relatively low inside the U.S.

Exhibit 7.3 illustrates the interesting relationship over time between the yields on inflation-adjusted versus non-inflation-adjusted Treasury securities and the public's expectations regarding future inflation. The difference between the nominal market yield on TIPS and the nominal market yield on non-inflation-adjusted Treasury securities of the same maturity gives us an approximate financial market forecast of future inflation. Theory suggests that when the public comes to expect faster inflation, TIPS and other inflation-adjusted financial assets will become more valuable. Their prices will rise and their yields will fall relative to the yields on ordinary financial assets not bearing an inflation-adjustment mechanism.

QUESTIONS TO HELP YOU STUDY

1. What is *inflation?* Why is it important?
2. Explain how inflation affects interest rates. What is the *Fisher effect?* What does it assume?
3. Explain how nominal contracts may cause inflation to affect the stock prices of some firms differently than it affects the stock prices of other firms.
4. What is meant by *deflation?* How does deflation appear to impact interest rates and the economy? Which nation has experienced deflation on a significant scale in recent years?
5. What are *TIPS?* What advantages do they offer investors? Any disadvantages?

EXHIBIT 7.3

Relationship between Inflation and Yield Spreads for Inflation-Adjusted versus Unadjusted Securities

Source: Federal Reserve Bank of Cleveland, Research Department, *Economic Trends,* August/December 2003.

Note: Inflationary expectations are based upon the monthly University of Michigan Household Survey.

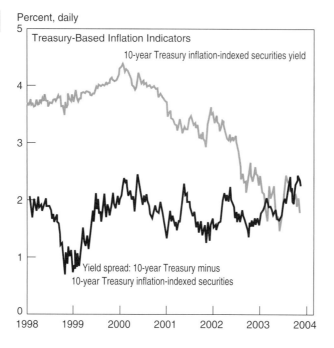

7.5   The Maturity of a Loan

maturity

One of the most important factors causing interest rates to differ from one another is differences in the **maturity** (or term) of securities and loans. Financial assets traded today in the world's financial markets have a wide variety of maturities. In the federal funds and U.S. government securities markets, for example, some loans are overnight or over-the-weekend transactions, with the borrower repaying the loan in a matter of

EXHIBIT 7.4

A Variety of Yield Curves for U.S. Treasury Securities

Source: U.S. Treasury Department and Federal Reserve Bank of Cleveland, Research Department, *Economic Trends*, June 2001.

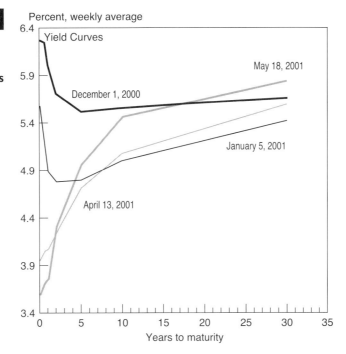

hours. At the other end of the spectrum, bonds and mortgages used to finance the purchase of new homes often stretch out 25 to 30 years, and some large corporations have recently issued 100-year bonds. Between these extremes lie thousands of financial assets issued by large and small borrowers with a tremendous variety of maturities.

The Yield Curve and the Term Structure of Interest Rates

yield curve

The relationship between the rate of return (yield) on financial instruments and their maturity is called the *term structure of interest rates*. This term structure may be represented visually by drawing a **yield curve** for all financial assets having the same credit quality. An example of the yield curve for U.S. government securities as it appeared during a period when the relationship between short-term and long-term interest rates was changing significantly is shown in Exhibit 7.4. We note that yield to maturity (measured by the annual percentage rate of return) is plotted along the vertical axis, and the horizontal scale shows the length of time (term) to final maturity (measured in years).

The yield curve considers only the relationship between the maturity or term of a financial asset and its yield at one moment in time (all other potentially influential factors held constant). For example, we cannot draw a yield curve for assets bearing different degrees of credit risk or subject to different tax laws because both risk and tax laws affect relative yields along with maturity. We may, however, draw a yield curve for U.S. government securities of varying maturity, for example, because they all have minimal credit risk, the same tax status, and so on. Similarly, yield curves could be constructed for all corporate bonds or for all municipal bonds having the same credit rating.

Types of Yield Curves

To follow the daily yield curve, see investinginbonds.com

Several different types of yield curves have been observed, but most may be described as upward sloping, downward sloping, or horizontal (flat). An upward-sloping yield curve indicates that borrowers must pay higher interest rates for longer-term loans than for shorter-term loans. A downward-sloping yield curve means that longer-term financial assets presently carry lower interest rates than shorter-term assets. Exhibit 7.4 illustrates a wide variety of yield curve shapes that prevailed as the twenty-first century began. Each shape of the yield curve has important implications for lenders, borrowers, and the financial institutions that serve them.

The Unbiased Expectations Hypothesis

unbiased expectations hypothesis

What determines the shape or slope of the yield curve? One view is the **unbiased expectations hypothesis,** which argues that investor expectations regarding future changes in short-term interest rates determine the shape of the curve. For example, a rising yield curve is presumed to be an indication that investors expect short-term interest rates to rise above their current levels in the future. A declining yield curve suggests declining short-term interest rates in the future. Finally, a horizontal yield curve implies that investors in the market expect interest rates to remain essentially unchanged from their present levels.

If the unbiased expectations hypothesis is true, the yield curve becomes an important *forecasting tool*. It suggests the direction of future movements in short-term interest rates as viewed by the financial marketplace today.

Many economists believe that the yield curve is a useful *economic indicator*. For example, economic history suggests that an upward-sloping yield curve is associated with a growing economy, rising incomes, and declining unemployment. In contrast, a negatively sloped yield curve appears to be associated frequently with a recession in the economy, declining output, and rising unemployment.

Assumptions of the Expectations Hypothesis   The unbiased expectations hypothesis assumes that investors act as *profit maximizers* over their planned holding periods and have no maturity preferences. All financial assets in a given risk class, regardless of maturity, are perfect substitutes for each other in the minds of investors. Under this theory, all investors are *risk neutral*. That is, they do not care about the character of the distribution of possible returns from an asset, only about its expected (mean) return. Each investor will seek those individual assets or combinations of assets offering the highest expected (mean) rates of return. For example, it is immaterial to investors with a planned 10-year investment horizon whether they buy a 10-year bond, two 5-year bonds, or a series of 1-year bonds until their 10-year holding period terminates. Each investor will pursue the investment strategy that offers the highest expected rate of return or yield over the length of his or her planned holding period. Profit-maximizing behavior on the part of thousands of investors interacting in the marketplace ensures that holding-period yields on all financial assets move toward equality.

Once equilibrium is achieved, and assuming no transactions costs, the investor should earn the *same* yield from buying a long-term asset as from purchasing a series of short-term assets whose combined maturities equal that of the long-term asset. If the rate of return on long-term financial assets rises above or falls below the return the investor expects to receive from buying and selling a series of short-term assets, forces are quickly set in motion to restore equilibrium. Investors at the margin will practice *arbitrage* (moving funds from one market to another) until long-term yields once again are brought into balance with short-term yields.

The Role of Expectations in Shaping the Yield Curve

How can a factor as intangible as *expectations* determine the shape of the yield curve? Expectations are a potent force in the financial marketplace because *investors act on their expectations.*

For example, if interest rates are expected to rise in the future, this can be disturbing news to investors in long-term bonds. As we noted in Chapter 6, rising interest rates mean falling prices for bonds and other debt securities. Moreover, the longer the term of a bond, the more sensitive tends to be its price to changes in market interest rates. Faced with the possibility of falling bond prices, many investors will sell their long-term bonds and buy short-term financial assets or hold cash instead. As a result, the prices of long-term bonds will plummet, driving their interest rates (yields) higher. At the same time, increased investor purchases of short-term assets will send the prices of these assets higher and their yields lower. With rising long-term interest rates and falling short-term interest rates, the yield curve will gradually assume an upward slope.

The yield curve's prophecy of rising interest rates will have come true simply because investors responded to their expectations by making changes in their asset portfolios.

Illustration of the Expectations Hypothesis Forecasting Future Interest Rates   How is it that the shape of the yield curve provides information about what the market expects interest rates to do in the future?

Suppose you are planning to invest $1,000 in government bonds for the next two years until you need these funds for spending. You have only two options for an investment strategy. You can:

1. Adopt a *buy-and-hold* strategy, buying a two-year bond that today is promising a 7 percent return for each of the two years of your investment horizon; or

2. Adopt a *roll-over* strategy, buying a one-year bond now which promises a 6 percent return and then, a year from today, rolling over your funds into a second one-year bond.

Notice that the yield curve is *positively sloped*. Two-year bonds are carrying a 7 percent annual yield, while one-year bonds are promising a 6 percent annual return. According to the expectations hypothesis, the yield curve must be forecasting a *rise* in the one-year bond rate a year from now. But, *how much* will it rise?

Answer: from 6 percent to 8 percent! How do we know? We know this because in a fully competitive and efficient financial marketplace you ought to get the *same* yield with either of the above investment strategies. The buy-and-hold strategy promises a 7 percent annual return. The roll-over strategy promises a 6 percent return the first year and, therefore, must be forecasting an 8 percent return in year two. This way the average rate of return for the roll-over strategy over the two-year holding period will also be (6% + 8%) / 2, or 7 percent.

Clearly, only if there is an 8 percent return on a one-year bond in the second year will *both* investment strategies lead to the same average holding-period return of 7 percent. The yield curve has given us a market forecast. Interest rates will rise in the second year.

Relative Changes in Long-Term Interest Rates versus Short-Term Interest Rates

One assumption of the expectations hypothesis does help to explain an interesting phenomenon in the financial markets. Long-term rates tend to change gradually over time, while short-term interest rates are highly volatile and often move over wide ranges. The expectations hypothesis, like many other views of the yield curve, rests on the premise that the expected long-term interest rate may be represented as a *geometric average* of a series of interest rates on current and future (forward) short-term loans whose combined maturities equal that of the long-term loan. In terms of conventional symbols,

$$(1 + {}_tR_n)^n = (1 + {}_tR_1)(1 + {}_{t+1}r_{1t}) \cdots (1 + {}_{t+n-1}r_{1t}) \qquad \textbf{(7.12)}$$

where

The construction of yield curves is explored at such Web sites as mathematicalfinance. com and at pvlinton.com/ securiti.htm

$_tR_n$ = The rate of interest prevailing at time t on a long-term loan covering n periods of time

$_tR_1$ = The one-period loan rate prevailing at time period t

$_{t+1}r_{1t}$ = Forward interest rate as quoted at time t on a one-period loan to start in time period $t+1$

$_{t+2}r_{1t}$ = Forward interest rate as quoted at time t on a one-period loan to start in time period $t+2$

.
.
.

$_{t+n-1}r_{1t}$ = Forward interest rate as quoted at time t on a one-period loan to start in time period $t+n-1$

The unbiased expectations hypothesis presumes that each of the forward rates— $_{t+1}r_{1t}, _{t+2}r_{1t}, \ldots, _{1+n-1}r_{1t}$—is equal to the future interest rate the market expects to exist in each future time period from $t+1$ through $t+n-1$. Equation 7.12 illustrates a fundamental principle in the expectations theory: *An investor expects the same holding-period yield regardless of whether he or she purchases one long-term financial asset or a series of short-term assets whose combined maturities make up the maturity of the long-term asset. This is true because all markets are presumed to be perfectly competitive without significant barriers between them and all financial assets, whatever their maturity, are presumed to be perfect substitutes for each other in the minds of investors.*

The rate of interest on a 20-year bond, for example, may be viewed as equivalent to the geometric average of the interest rate on a current one-year loan plus the rates expected to be attached in future periods to a series of 19 separate one-year loans, together adding up to 20 years. Experience teaches us that an *average* changes much more slowly than the individual components making up that average. If the long-term interest rate is really a geometric average of current and expected future short-term rates, then this helps to explain why, in real-world markets, long-term interest rates tend to be less volatile than short-term interest rates.

Policy Implications of the Unbiased Expectations Hypothesis

The unbiased expectations hypothesis has important implications for *public policy*. The theory implies that changes in the relative quantities of long-term versus short-term financial assets do *not* influence the shape of the yield curve *unless* investor expectations also are affected. For example, suppose the U.S. Treasury decided to refinance $100 billion of its maturing short-term IOUs by issuing $100 billion in long-term bonds. Would this government action affect the shape of the yield curve? Certainly, the supply of long-term bonds would be increased, while the supply of short-term assets would be reduced. However, according to the expectations theory, the yield curve itself would not be changed *unless* investors altered their expectations about the future course of short-term interest rates.

To cite one more example, the Federal Reserve System buys and sells government securities frequently in the money and capital markets to promote the economic goals of the United States. Can the Fed (or, for that matter, any other central bank around the world) influence the shape of the yield curve by buying one maturity of financial assets and selling another? Once again, the answer is "no" *unless* the central bank can influence the interest-rate expectations of investors. Why? The reason lies in the underlying assumption of the unbiased expectations hypothesis: *Investors regard all financial assets, whatever their maturity, as perfect substitutes*. Therefore, the relative amounts of long-term assets versus short-term assets simply should *not* matter.

The Liquidity Premium View of the Yield Curve

The strong assumptions underlying the unbiased expectations hypothesis coupled with the real-world behavior of investors have caused many financial analysts to question that theory's veracity. Securities dealers who trade actively in the financial markets frequently argue that other factors besides interest rate expectations also exert a significant impact on the character and shape of the yield curve.

For example, in recent years, most yield curves have sloped *upward*. Is there a *built-in bias* toward positively sloped yield curves due to factors other than interest rate expectations? The *liquidity premium view* of the yield curve suggests that such a *bias* exists.

Long-term financial assets tend to have more volatile market prices than short-term assets. Therefore, the investor faces greater risk of capital loss when buying long-term financial instruments. This greater risk of loss will be important to an investor who is *risk averse* (not risk neutral as in the expectations theory). To overcome the risk of capital loss, investors must be paid an extra return in the form of an interest rate (term) premium to encourage them to purchase long-term financial instruments. This additional rate or yield premium for surrendering liquidity—known as the **liquidity premium**—would tend to give yield curves a bias toward a *positive slope*.

liquidity premium

Why then do some yield curves slope downward? In such instances, expectations of declining interest rates plus other factors simply overcome the liquidity premium effect. The liquidity premium view does not preclude the important role of interest rate expectations in influencing the shape of the yield curve. Rather, it argues that other factors, such as liquidity and price risk, play an important role as well.

The liquidity argument may help explain why yield curves tend to *flatten out* at the longest maturities. (Note that this flattening out at the long-term end of the maturity spectrum is characteristic of all the yield curves shown in Exhibit 7.4.) There are obvious differences in liquidity between a 1-year and a 10-year bond, but it is not clear that major differences in liquidity exist between a 10-year bond and a 20-year bond, for example. Therefore, the size of the required liquidity (or term) premium may decrease for securities bearing longer maturities.

7.6 The Segmented-Markets and Preferred Habitat Arguments

The Possible Impact of Segmented Markets on the Yield Curve

A strong challenge to the expectations and liquidity premium explanations of the yield curve appeared several years ago in the form of the **market segmentation argument,** or *hedging pressure theory*. The underlying assumption is that all financial assets are *not* perfect substitutes in the minds of investors. *Maturity preferences* exist among some investor groups, and those investors will not stray from their desired maturity range unless induced to do so by higher yields or other favorable terms on longer- or shorter-term assets.

market segmentation argument

Why might some investors prefer one asset maturity over another? Market segmentationists find the answer in a fundamental assumption concerning investor behavior, especially the investment behavior of financial intermediaries, such as mutual funds, pension funds, and banks. These investor groups, it is argued, often act as *risk minimizers* rather than profit maximizers as assumed under the expectations hypothesis. They prefer to *hedge* against the risk of fluctuations in the prices and yields of financial assets by balancing the maturity structure of their assets with the maturity structure of their liabilities.

For example, pension funds tend to have stable and predictable long-term liabilities. Therefore, these intermediaries prefer to invest in bonds, stocks, and other long-term financial assets. Commercial banks, on the other hand, have volatile money market liabilities and thus prefer to confine the majority of their investments to short-term assets. These investor groups often employ the *hedging principle* of portfolio management: correlating the maturities of their liabilities with the maturities of their assets to ensure the ready availability of liquid funds when those funds are most needed. This portfolio strategy reduces the risks of fluctuating income and loss of principal.

The existence of maturity preferences among investor groups implies that the financial markets are *not* one large pool of loanable funds but rather are segmented by maturity into a series of submarkets. Thus, the market for financial assets of medium maturity (for example, 5- to 10-year bonds) attracts different investor groups than the market for long-term (over 10-year) assets. Demand and supply curves within each maturity range are held to be the dominant factors shaping the level and structure of interest rates within that maturity range. However, interest rates prevailing in one maturity range are little influenced by demand and supply forces at work in other maturity ranges.

The segmented-markets or hedging-pressure theory does *not* rule out the possible influence of expectations in shaping the term structure of interest rates, but it argues that other factors related to maturity-specific demand and supply forces are also important.

Policy Implications of the Segmented-Markets Theory

The segmented-markets theory, like the expectations theory, has significant implications for public policy. *If* markets along the maturity spectrum are relatively isolated from each other due to investor maturity preferences, government policymakers can alter the shape of the yield curve merely by influencing supply and demand in one or more market segments.

For example, if a positively sloped yield curve were desired, the government could flood the market with long-term bonds. Simultaneously, the government could purchase large quantities of short-term securities. The expanded supply of bonds would drive long-term interest rates higher, while government purchases of short-term securities would push short-term interest rates down, other factors held equal. Therefore, the government could alter the shape of the yield curve merely by shifting the supplies available of different maturities of financial assets relative to the demand for those assets. This conclusion directly contradicts the unbiased expectations hypothesis.

The Preferred Habitat or Composite Theory of the Yield Curve

During the 1960s and 1970s, an expanded model of the determinants of the yield curve appeared that attempted to combine the expectations, liquidity premium, and market segmentation arguments into a single theory. This composite view argues that investors **preferred habitat** seek out their **preferred habitat** along the scale of varying maturities of financial assets that matches their risk preferences, tax exposure, liquidity needs, regulatory requirements, and planned holding periods. Normally, an investor will not stray from his or her preferred habitat unless rates of return on longer- or shorter-term assets are high enough to overcome each investor's preferences. The result is that markets for financial assets are divided into distinct submarkets by these multifaceted investor preferences. Thus, according to the preferred habitat theory, factors other than expectations alone play a role in shaping the character of the yield curve.

Proponents of preferred habitat argue that investors derive their expectations about future interest rates on the basis of *historical experience*—the recent trend of interest rates and what history suggests is a "normal" range for rates. In the short term, the majority of investors expect current interest-rate trends to persist into the future; thus, rising interest rates in recent weeks often lead to the expectation that rates will continue to rise in the near term. However, investors generally expect that, given sufficient time (months or years), interest rates will return to their historical averages. An important implication here is that more recent movements in interest rates are linked to *past* interest rate behavior—a conclusion that tends to contradict the expectations and efficient markets theories of how the financial markets operate.

Research Evidence on the Yield Curve

Which view of the yield curve is correct? A number of research studies (e.g., Campbell, 1986) seem to reject the unbiased expectations hypothesis and find that the yield curve does *not* have significant predictive power in forecasting interest rates. However, these findings are contradicted by other research studies (e.g., Longstaff, 1990) that find evidence consistent with the unbiased expectations hypothesis. Some of these studies find significant forecasting power from the yield curve in predicting changes in interest rates, inflation, and the economy.

For example, Fama and Bliss (1987) found that one-year forward interest rates could forecast changes in the one-year interest rate two to four years in advance. Moreover, there is some evidence that yield curves can provide useful forecasts of inflation over periods of one year or longer.

This longer-term forecasting power of the yield curve may be due to the tendency of interest rates to move back toward their historic mean levels over a sufficiently long period of time (known as *mean reversion*). Although all investors clearly do not regard all maturities of financial assets as perfect substitutes, there are sufficient numbers of traders in the financial marketplace who do *not* have specific maturity preferences. These investors are guided principally by the relative expected returns on different assets. Their beliefs and actions may bring about the results predicted by the expectations theory.

Nevertheless, there is evidence that nonexpectational factors, especially the demand for liquidity, do affect the shape of the yield curve. Studies by Van Horne (1965) and others point to the existence of a liquidity premium attached to the yields on longer-term securities, compensating investors for added risk. Moreover, liquidity premiums appear to get smaller as we move toward longer asset maturities, and these premiums are also sensitive to the business cycle, rising in recessions and falling in business expansions. Also, term premiums do *not* appear to increase or decrease *uniformly* as maturity increases or decreases.

Recent research has delved more deeply into the issue of what kinds of events cause the yield curve's overall shape to change. Statistically, yield curves may change along any of at least three different dimensions: *level, slope,* or *curvature.*[3] As Exhibit 7.5A suggests, a change in the *level* of the yield curve means that interest rates all along the curve move roughly in parallel, shifting the whole curve up or down. Macroeconomic forces, such as increased inflation, a weaker economy, or significant technological change, may have their greatest impact on a yield curve's level.

---

[3] See especially Dai and Singleton (2000) and Wu (2003).

EXHIBIT 7.5   **The Level, Slope, and Curvature of Yield Curves**

A. Shifts in the *level* of the yield curve

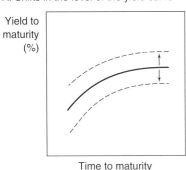

B. Changes in the *slope* of the yield curve

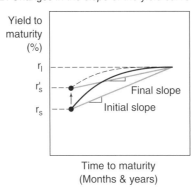

C. Changes in the yield curve's *curvature*

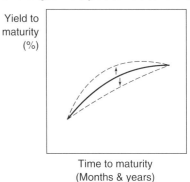

In contrast, the curve's *slope* or steepness changes when shorter-term interest rates rise or fall by greater amounts than longer-term interest rates. One measure of the slope of a yield curve is the longest-term interest rate (r_l) minus the shortest-term interest rate (r_s) contained in the curve divided by the difference in their terms to maturity. When this interest rate (or yield) spread is positive, the yield curve is generally upward sloping. Statistical evidence from U.S. data suggests that shifts in Federal Reserve monetary policy are one of the major influences on the curve's slope. This effect is captured in Exhibit 7.5B which depicts the central bank tightening money and credit conditions by raising short-term interest rates from r_s to r'_s. If long-term interest rates initially do not change (as shown) or change by a lesser amount than short rate (as is usually the case), then the average slope of the curve declines. In this example, the initial slope is seen to be steeper than the final slope.

Finally, as Exhibit 7.5C depicts, the *curvature* of a yield curve may change when interest rates in the middle of the maturity spectrum are impacted, such as by a shift in economic conditions of moderate length. This development would tend to give the yield curve a greater or lesser " hump" along its midsection. These various dimensions of a yield curve—its level, slope, and curvature—suggest that these curves are far more complex and more intimately connected with the economy and government policy than was once thought.

7.7   Uses of the Yield Curve

The controversy surrounding the determinants of the yield curve should not obscure the fact that this curve can be an extremely useful tool for borrowers and lenders.

Forecasting Interest Rates   If the expectations hypothesis is correct, the yield curve gives the investor a clue concerning the future course of interest rates. If the curve has an upward slope, for example, the investor may be well advised to look for opportunities to move away from long-term financial assets into investments whose market price is less sensitive to interest rate changes. A downward-sloping yield curve, on the other hand, suggests the likelihood of near-term declines in interest rates and/or a rally in bond prices if the market's forecast of lower rates turns out to be true.

One version of the yield curve—the so-called *yield spread* between long-term and short-term government securities—has been found in the United States to aid in the prediction of real growth in the economy and to seemingly forecast coming recessions in economic activity. According to several researchers a flattening of the yield curve conveys a strong signal that a recession is about to occur. For example, a study by Stojanovic and Vaughan (1997) finds that an inverted yield curve—where short-term interest rates are higher than long-term interest rates—has preceded U.S. economic recessions since 1960 and has generally out-predicted other widely used forecasting data series, such as common stock prices and the U.S. Commerce Department's Index of Leading Economic Indicators. In general, the *smaller* the interest rate spread between long- and short-term interest rates, the *greater* the probability of a recession in the United States over the next four quarters. Moreover, recent studies, (e.g., Bonser-Neal and Morley, 1997) of Australia, Canada, Japan, the United States, and the nations of Western Europe suggest that the yield spread seems to predict growth in GDP (gross domestic product) for these nations over the next year or so with greater accuracy than other popular economic indicators.

Uses for Financial Intermediaries

Uses for Financial Intermediaries   The slope of the yield curve is critical for financial intermediaries, especially banks, credit unions, and savings and loan associations. A steepening yield curve is generally favorable for these institutions because they borrow most of their funds by selling short-term deposits and lend a major portion of those funds long term. The more steeply the yield curve slopes upward, the wider the spread between borrowing and lending rates and the greater the potential profit for a financial intermediary. However, if the yield curve begins to flatten out or slope downward, this should serve as a warning signal to managers of these institutions.

A flattening or downward-sloping yield curve squeezes the earnings of financial intermediaries and calls for an entirely different portfolio management strategy than an upward-sloping curve. For example, if an upward-sloping yield curve starts to flatten out, portfolio managers of financial institutions might try to lock in relatively cheap sources of funds by getting long-term commitments from depositors and other funds-supplying customers. Borrowers, on the other hand, might be encouraged to take out long-term loans at fixed rates of interest. Of course, the institution's customers also may be aware of impending changes in the yield curve and resist accepting loans or deposits with terms heavily favoring financial intermediaries.

Detecting Overpriced and Underpriced Financial Assets

Detecting Overpriced and Underpriced Financial Assets   Yield curves can be used as an aid to investors in deciding which assets are temporarily overpriced or underpriced. This use of the yield curve derives from the fact that, in equilibrium, the yields on all financial assets of comparable risk should come to rest along the yield curve at their appropriate maturity levels. In an efficiently functioning market, however, any deviations of individual assets from the yield curve will be short lived, so the investor must act quickly.

If a financial asset's rate of return lies *above* the yield curve for financial assets comparable of risk, this sends a signal to investors: The asset is temporarily *underpriced* relative to other assets bearing the same maturity. Other things equal, this is a *buy* signal some investors will take advantage of, driving the price of the purchased asset upward and its yield back down toward the curve. On the other hand, if an asset's rate of return is temporarily *below* the yield curve, this indicates a temporarily *overpriced* financial instrument, because its yield is below that of financial assets bearing the same maturity. Some investors holding this asset will *sell,* pushing its price down and its yield back up toward the curve.

Indicating Trade-Offs between Maturity and Yield

Indicating Trade-Offs between Maturity and Yield   Still another use of the yield curve is to indicate the current trade-off between maturity and yield confronting the investor. If an investor wishes to alter the maturity of her portfolio, the

A prime example of "riding the yield curve" appeared in the wake of the September 11, 2001, terror attacks in New York and Washington, DC. A steep, positively sloped yield curve prevailed in the financial markets before the attacks, offering the opportunity for substantial profits if active investors played their cards right! In the aftermath of the attacks many investors expected that the yield curve would become *even steeper* than it already was. Short-term interest rates were expected to move lower while long-term interest rates were expected to head skyward.

In times of crisis many investors come to believe the yield curve will turn steeper because a crisis often creates greater uncertainties about the long run. Result: Investors will tend to move toward shorter-term assets, driving their prices up and interest rates down, and sell off longer-term assets, pushing their prices down and their associated interest rates higher. Long-term investors simply demand an extra yield premium before they will hold longer-term financial instruments. The yield curve may tilt sharply upward.

In the fall of 2001 sophisticated institutional investors (such as government security dealers) borrowed heavily to buy short-term assets whose prices were expected to rise, and sold off longer-term bonds, whose prices dropped for a time.

What might lead investors toward such expectations about the future course of interest rates and asset prices? One factor is *monetary policy* and another is *inflation*. If a crisis threatens to slow down the economy and create substantial unemployment, the central bank (e.g., the Federal Reserve System) is likely to push short-term interest rates lower. With easier credit conditions setting in, fears begin to rise in the investment community that inflation will accelerate. Because inflation tends to hurt long-term bond holders the most, they quickly begin to sell off their holdings. Long-term interest rates rise and the prices of these instruments decline. The yield curve becomes steeper for a time, offering profit opportunities to those who understand what is happening.

yield curve indicates what gain or loss in rate of return may be expected for each change in the portfolio's average maturity.

With an upward-sloping yield curve, for example, an investor may be able to increase a bond portfolio's expected annual yield from 7 percent to 9 percent by extending the portfolio's average maturity from 1 to 10 years. However, the prices of longer-term bonds are more volatile, creating greater risk of capital loss. Longer-term assets tend to be less liquid than short-term assets. Therefore, the investor must weigh the gain in yield from extending the maturity of his or her portfolio against added price and liquidity risk. Because yield curves tend to flatten out for the longest maturities, the investor bent on lengthening the maturity of a portfolio eventually discovers that gains in yield get smaller for each additional unit of maturity. At some point along the yield curve, it no longer pays, in terms of extra yield, to further extend the maturity of an investor's asset portfolio.

Riding the Yield Curve   Finally, some active investors, especially dealers in government securities, have learned to "ride" the yield curve for profit. If the curve is positively sloped, with a slope steep enough to offset transactions costs, the investor may gain by timely portfolio switching.

For example, if a security dealer purchases U.S. Treasury bills six months from maturity, holds them for three months and converts the bills into cash, and then buys new six-month bills, he can profit in two ways from a positively sloped yield curve. Because the yield is lower (and the price higher) on the three-month than the six-month bills, the dealer experiences a capital (price) gain on the sale. Moreover, the purchase of new six-month bills replaces a lower-yielding asset with a higher-yielding one at a lower price. Riding the yield curve can be risky, however, because yield curves are constantly changing their shape. If the curve suddenly gets flatter or turns down, a potential gain can be turned into a realized loss. In this case, riding the yield curve may be less profitable than a simple "buy and hold" strategy. Experience and good judgment are indispensable in using the yield curve for profitable investment decision making.

QUESTIONS TO HELP YOU STUDY

6. Explain the meaning of the phrase *term structure of interest rates*. What is a *yield curve?* What *assumptions* are necessary to construct a yield curve?

7. Explain the difference between the *expectations, market segmentation, preferred habitat,* and *liquidity premium* views of the yield curve. What does each theory assume?

8. What are the implications for investors and for public policy of each of the yield-curve ideas mentioned in the preceding question?

9. What *uses* does the yield curve have? Why is each possible use of potential value to borrowers and lenders of funds?

10. What conclusions can you draw from recent research regarding the determinants of the yield curve? Which theory of the yield curve appears to be most supported by recent research studies?

7.8 Duration: A Different Approach to Maturity

The Price Elasticity of a Bond or Other Debt Security

Theories of the yield curve remind us that longer-maturity financial assets tend to be more volatile in price. For example, for the same change in interest rates, the price of a longer-term bond generally changes more than the price of a shorter-term bond. A popular measure of how responsive a bond or other debt security's price is to changes in interest rates is its **price elasticity.** Thus:

price elasticity

$$\begin{array}{l} \text{Price elasticity of} \\ \text{a debt security} \\ \text{(E)} \end{array} = \dfrac{\begin{array}{c} \text{Percentage change} \\ \text{over time in a} \\ \text{security's price} \end{array}}{\begin{array}{c} \text{Percentage change} \\ \text{over time in a} \\ \text{security's yield} \end{array}} = \dfrac{\dfrac{P_1 - P_0}{P_0}}{\dfrac{y_1 - y_0}{y_0}} \qquad (7.13)$$

where P_0 and y_0 represent a debt security's price and yield at some initial point in time, while P_1 and y_1 represent the security's price and yield at a subsequent point in time. Price elasticity is generally measured from a debt security's par value and coupon rate and is larger for downward price movements than for upward price movements.[4] The price elasticity attached to a bond or other debt security must be negative, because rising interest rates (yields) result in falling debt security prices, and conversely.

For example, suppose we are interested in purchasing a 10-year bond, par value of $1,000, promising its holder a 10 percent coupon rate. Assume the bond pays interest of $100 once each year. Our discussion of the principles of bond pricing in Chapter 6 reminds us that if interest rates on comparable securities sold in the open market are currently at 10 percent, this bond will sell for exactly $1,000. If interest rates fall to 5 percent, this 10 percent bond will carry a price of about $1,389.70, and if rates climb to 15 percent, the bond's price will drop close to $745.10. What is the

---

[4] That is, for the same change in yield, capital gains generally are larger than capital losses on the same financial asset.

price elasticity of this bond, measured from par? From Equation 7.13, we have for the *downward* movement in interest rates from 10 to 5 percent:

$$\begin{array}{c}\text{Price elasticity}\\ \text{of 10 percent}\\ \text{bond (E)}\end{array} = \dfrac{\dfrac{(\$1{,}389.70 \ - \ \$1{,}000)}{\$1{,}000}}{\dfrac{5\% \ - \ 10\%}{10\%}} = \dfrac{0.3897}{-0.5} = -0.779 \quad \textbf{(7.14)}$$

On the other hand, for an upward movement in interest rates from 10 to 15 percent, this bond's elasticity is -0.510. (The reader should verify this.) Clearly, E is greater in absolute terms for a downward movement in interest rates (from 10 to 5 percent) than it is for a rise in interest rates (from 10 to 15 percent).

Higher price elasticity means that an asset goes through a greater price change for a given change in market rates of interest. And, as we noted above, longer-term debt securities generally carry greater price risk (their price elasticity, E, is larger) than shorter-term debt securities. However, this relationship between maturity and price elasticity is *not* linear (i.e., not strictly proportional). It is *not* true, for example, that 10-year bonds are twice as price elastic (and price volatile) as 5-year bonds. One important reason for this nonlinear relationship is that the price volatility and elasticity of a debt security depend upon the size of its *coupon rate*—the annual rate of return promised by the borrower—as well as upon its maturity.

The Impact of Varying Coupon Rates

The lower a debt security's annual coupon (promised) rate, the more volatile (and elastic) its price tends to be. Investors buying lower coupon securities generally take on greater risk of price fluctuations. In effect, a debt security promising lower annual coupon payments behaves as though it has a longer maturity even if it is due to mature on the same date as a security carrying a higher coupon rate. With a low coupon (promised) rate, the investor must wait longer for a substantial return on her funds because a greater proportion of the low-coupon security's total dollar return lies in the final payment at maturity when the bond's face value is returned to the investor. And the further in the future cash payments are to be received, the more sensitive is the present value of that stream of payments to changes in interest rates.

coupon effect

The relationship we have been describing is called the **coupon effect.** It says simply that the prices of low-coupon securities tend to rise *faster* than the prices of high-coupon securities when market interest rates decline. Similarly, a period of rising interest rates will cause the prices of low-coupon securities to fall *faster* than the prices of high-coupon securities. Thus, the potential for capital gains and capital losses is greater for low-coupon than for high-coupon securities.

An Alternative Maturity Index for a Financial Asset: Duration

Knowledge of the impact of varying coupon (promised) rates on security price volatility and elasticity resulted in the search for a new index of maturity other than straight calendar time (years and months)—the maturity measure used in conventional yield curves. What was needed was a measure of the term of a bond that would allow financial analysts to construct a *linear* (strictly proportional) relationship between maturity and price volatility or elasticity, regardless of differing coupon rates. Such a measure would have the property, for example, that a doubling of maturity would mean a doubling of price elasticity, thereby giving us a direct measure of the price risk faced by an investor. This maturity measure is known as **duration** and has the very practical interpretation in its simplest terms as the average expected length of time required for

duration

the investor in the financial asset to recover her initial investment. A financial asset's duration (D) is computed as follows:

$$D = \frac{\text{Present value of interest and principal payments from a security weighted by the timing of those payments}}{\text{Present value of the security's promised stream of interest and principal payments}} = \frac{\sum\limits_{t=1}^{n} \dfrac{I_t(t)}{(1+y)^t}}{\sum\limits_{t=1}^{n} \dfrac{I_t}{(1+y)^t}} \qquad (7.15)$$

In the duration formula above, I represents each expected payment of principal and interest income from the asset and t represents the time period in which each payment is to be received. The discount factor, y, is the yield to maturity, with final asset maturity reached at the end of n periods. Duration reflects the price elasticity of a financial instrument with respect to changes in the instrument's yield to maturity. As the formula indicates, D is a *weighted average* measure of maturity in which each payment of interest and principal is multiplied by the time period in which it is expected to be received by the investor.

We can explain the use of duration through an example. Let us imagine that an investor is interested in purchasing a $1,000 par-value bond that has a term to maturity of 10 years, a 10 percent annual coupon rate (with interest paid once a year), and a 12 percent yield to maturity based on its current price of $887.10. Then its duration must be

$$\text{Duration (D)} = \frac{\dfrac{\$100(1)}{(1.12)^1} + \dfrac{\$100(2)}{(1.12)^2} + \cdots + \dfrac{\$100(10)}{(1.12)^{10}} + \dfrac{\$1,000(10)}{(1.12)^{10}}}{\dfrac{\$100}{(1.12)^1} + \dfrac{\$100}{(1.12)^2} + \cdots + \dfrac{\$100}{(1.12)^{10}} + \dfrac{\$1,000}{(1.12)^{10}}} \qquad (7.16)$$

or

$$D = \frac{\$5,810.90}{\$887.10} = 6.55 \text{ years}$$

There is a simple way to calculate D that has the added value of making it easy to check your figures. Using the example above of the 10-year bond with a 12 percent yield to maturity, we can set up the following table:

To learn more about calculating and using duration see, for example, investopedia.com/calculator

Period	Expected Cash Flows from Security	Present Values of Expected Cash Flows (at 12% Rate of Discount)	Time Period Cash Is to Be Received (t)	Present Value of Expected Cash Flows × t
1	$ 100	$ 89.30	1	$ 89.30
2	100	79.70	2	159.40
3	100	71.20	3	213.60
4	100	63.60	4	254.40
5	100	56.70	5	283.50
6	100	50.70	6	304.20
7	100	45.20	7	316.40
8	100	40.40	8	323.20
9	100	36.10	9	324.90
10	100	32.20	10	322.00
10	1,000	322.00	10	3,220.00
		$887.10		$5,810.90

Then, as above, the duration of this bond must be

$$D = \frac{\text{Sum of present values of (cash flow} \times t)}{\text{Sum of present values of cash flow}} = \frac{\$5,810.90}{\$887.10} = 6.55 \text{ years}$$

Note that the denominator of the ratio above ($887.10) is the same value as the bond's current price.

A number of duration's features are evident from this example. For example, duration is always *less* than the time to maturity for a coupon-paying security.[5] Duration increases with a longer stream of future payments, but the rate of increase in D decreases as time to maturity increases. The larger an asset's yield to maturity, y, the lower its duration.

Duration reflects the amount and timing of *all* payments expected during the life of a financial asset, unlike the conventional measure of maturity—calendar time—which shows only the length of time until the final cash payment. As described earlier, duration can be thought of as an index of the average amount of time required for the investor to recover the original cash outlay used to buy the asset. Assets bearing higher values of D are more volatile in price and, therefore, carry increased price risk. Low-coupon bonds, for example, have longer durations and, therefore, display more price risk than high-coupon bonds.

The Convexity Factor

convexity

The relationship between a financial asset's change in market price and its change in yield or interest rate is called **convexity.** Research has shown that convexity increases with a financial asset's duration. Moreover, an asset's change in market price for any given change in interest rates will vary with the prevailing level of market interest rates.

In general, a financial asset's change in price is greater at lower market interest rates than it is at higher market interest rates. Thus, an asset's price risk tends to be greater at lower rates of interest than it is at higher interest rates. Moreover, the convexity of a financial asset tends to decline as that asset's promised rate of return (coupon rate) increases. In summary, the market prices of financial assets change in different ways depending upon their durations, promised rates of return (coupons), and the level of interest rates in the financial marketplace.

Uses of Duration

Estimating Asset Price Changes   Because duration is directly related to the price volatility of a financial asset, there is a useful approximate relationship between changes in market interest rates and percentage changes in asset prices. This relationship may be written:

To learn more about duration, see finpipe.com or contingencyanalysis. com

$$\begin{array}{c}\text{Percent change in}\\\text{the price of an}\\\text{asset (such as a}\\\text{debt security)}\end{array} \approx -D\left[\frac{\Delta r}{1 + r}\right] \times 100 \qquad (7.17)$$

---

[5] See Chapter 6 for a discussion of yield to maturity and calculating discounted present values such as required in the above duration formula. Any security carrying installment payments of principal and/or interest will have a duration shorter than its calendar maturity. Only for zero-coupon bonds or for any loan in which principal and accumulated interest are paid in a lump sum at maturity will duration and maturity be the same.

where D is duration and Δr is the change in interest rates. For example, consider the bond in the example above, whose duration was calculated to be 6.55 years. The bond's price at the coupon rate of 10 percent is $1,000, and at an r of 12 percent, its price is $887.10. Thus, if the interest rate changes from 10 to 12 percent, the bond's approximate percentage decline in price would be

$$\text{Percent change in bond's price} \approx -6.55 \times \left[\frac{.02}{1 + 0.10}\right] \times 100 = -11.91\% \quad \textbf{(7.18)}$$

In this instance, if interest rates rise by two percentage points, the bond's price declines by almost 12 percent (measured from the bond's par value and coupon rate). An investor who expects interest rates to rise would find this information helpful in deciding whether to continue holding this bond. In general, investors concerned about the risk of loss due to rising interest rates tend to move toward financial assets of shorter duration, while falling interest rates usually lead investors toward assets of longer duration.

Portfolio Immunization   Today, duration has aroused great interest among portfolio managers. The reason is its possible usefulness as a device to insulate (or, in the terminology of finance, *immunize*) asset portfolios against both market risk and/or reinvestment risk that can result from changing market interest rates. In theory, **portfolio immunization** against interest rate changes can be achieved by simply acquiring a portfolio of assets whose average duration equals the length of the investor's desired holding period. If this is done, the effect is to hold the investor's total return *constant* regardless of whether interest rates rise or fall. In the absence of borrower default, the investor's realized return can be no less than the return he has been promised by the borrower. Only if the future course of interest rates were known for certain would portfolio immunization be a less than optimal strategy.

Let's consider an example of how portfolio immunization with duration works. Suppose we are interested in purchasing a bond with a $1,000 par value that will mature in two years. The bond has a coupon rate of 8 percent, paying $80 in interest at the end of each year. Interest rates on comparable bonds also are currently at 8 percent but may fall to as low as 6 percent or rise as high as 10 percent. The buyer knows he or she will receive $1,000 at maturity, but in the meantime this buyer must face the uncertainty of having to reinvest the annual $80 in interest earnings from this bond at 6 percent, 8 percent, or 10 percent, depending on whether interest rates rise or fall.

Suppose interest rates decline to 6 percent. This bond will earn $80 in interest payments for year one, $80 for year two, but only $4.80 (or $80 × 0.06) when the $80 interest income received the first year is reinvested at 6 percent during year 2. With interest rates falling to 6 percent, the investor will earn only $1,164.80 in total over the two-year period:

portfolio immunization

First year's interest earnings		Second year's interest earnings		Interest earned reinvesting the first year's interest earnings at a 6 percent interest rate		Par value of security returned to investor at maturity		Total return
$80	+	$80	+	$4.80	+	$1,000	=	$1,164.80

$$\textbf{(7.19)}$$

On the other hand, what if interest rates rise to 10 percent after the first year? Again, the investor holding this bond earns $80 interest in each of the next two years but will also earn $8 in interest when he reinvests the $80 in interest income received at the end of the first year at the new rate of 10 percent ($80 × .10). In this case, the investor's total return from the bond will be $1,168 after two years:

$$\underset{\$80}{\underset{\text{earnings}}{\underset{\text{interest}}{\text{First year's}}}} + \underset{\$80}{\underset{\text{earnings}}{\underset{\text{interest}}{\text{Second year's}}}} + \underset{\$8.00}{\underset{\text{interest rate}}{\underset{\text{at a 10 percent}}{\underset{\text{interest earnings}}{\underset{\text{first year's}}{\underset{\text{reinvesting the}}{\text{Interest earned}}}}}}} + \underset{\$1,000}{\underset{\text{maturity}}{\underset{\text{to investor at}}{\underset{\text{security returned}}{\underset{\text{Par value of}}{}}}}} = \underset{\$1,168.00}{\underset{\text{return}}{\text{Total}}}$$

Clearly, the bond buyer's earnings could drop as low as $1,164.80 (with a 6 percent interest rate) or rise as high as $1,168 (with a 10 percent interest rate). Is there a way to avoid this kind of fluctuation in earnings and stabilize the total return received regardless of what happens to interest rates? Yes, if the buyer finds a bond whose *duration matches his or her planned holding period*. For example, suppose the buyer finds a $1,000 bond that also carries an 8 percent coupon rate whose maturity exceeds two years but whose duration is exactly two years, matching the buyer's planned holding period. This means that, at the end of two years, the buyer will have to *sell* the bond at the price then prevailing in the market because it will not have reached maturity yet.

What will happen to the buyer's total earnings with a bond whose duration is exactly two years? First, if interest rates fall to 6 percent, the bond will earn $80 interest at the end of year 1 and another $80 at the end of year 2, but as before, only $4.80 will be earned when the first year's interest income is invested during the second year at the low rate of 6 percent ($80 × 0.06). However, the bond's market price will *rise* to $1,001.60 due to the drop in interest rates. Therefore, the investor will receive in two years a total of $1,166.40 in cash:

$$\underset{\$80}{\underset{\text{earnings}}{\underset{\text{interest}}{\text{First year's}}}} + \underset{\$80}{\underset{\text{earnings}}{\underset{\text{interest}}{\text{Second year's}}}} + \underset{\$4.80}{\underset{\text{interest rate}}{\underset{\text{at a 6 percent}}{\underset{\text{interest earnings}}{\underset{\text{first year's}}{\underset{\text{reinvesting the}}{\text{Interest earned}}}}}}} + \underset{\$1,001.60}{\underset{\text{holding period}}{\underset{\text{investor's planned}}{\underset{\text{at the end of the}}{\underset{\text{selling bond}}{\underset{\text{received when}}{\text{Market price}}}}}}} = \underset{\$1,166.40}{\underset{\text{return}}{\text{Total}}}$$

$$(7.20)$$

Suppose instead that interest rates rise to 10 percent. Clearly, interest earnings will go up, but the bond's market price will be lower because of the rise in interest rates. In this case, the investor also receives a total return of $1,166.40:

$$\underset{\$80}{\underset{\text{earnings}}{\underset{\text{interest}}{\text{First year's}}}} + \underset{\$80}{\underset{\text{earnings}}{\underset{\text{interest}}{\text{Second year's}}}} + \underset{\$8.00}{\underset{\text{interest rate}}{\underset{\text{at a 10 percent}}{\underset{\text{interest earnings}}{\underset{\text{first year's}}{\underset{\text{reinvesting the}}{\text{Interest earned}}}}}}} + \underset{\$998.40}{\underset{\text{holding period}}{\underset{\text{investor's planned}}{\underset{\text{at the end of the}}{\underset{\text{selling bond}}{\underset{\text{received when}}{\text{Market price}}}}}}} = \underset{\$1,166.40}{\underset{\text{return}}{\text{Total}}}$$

In the foregoing example, *the buyer earns identical total earnings whether interest rates go up or down!* This happens because, with duration set equal to the buyer's planned holding period, a fall in the reinvestment rate (in this case, down to 6 percent) is completely offset by an increase in the bond's price (in this instance, the bond's market value climbs from $1,000 to $1.001.60). Conversely, a rise in the reinvestment rate (up to 10 percent in the second case) is counterbalanced by a fall in the bond's market price (down to $998.40). The bond buyer's total return is fully protected regardless of the future path followed by interest rates.

Of course, there is a price to be paid for reducing risk exposure. Duration, like any interest rate hedging tool, is *not* free. Suppose in the example above that the bond buyer had chosen not to worry about duration and just purchased a bond with a calendar maturity of two years. Suppose also that interest rates rose to 10 percent during the second year. Clearly, this investor would have earned a larger total return ($1,168) without using portfolio immunization. *The cost of immunization is a lower, but more stable, expected return.*

Limitations of Duration

All this sounds easy: *To protect the return from a portfolio of assets against changes in interest rates, merely select a portfolio whose duration equals the time remaining in your planned holding period.* In practice, it does not work out quite this easily. For example, it is often difficult to find a collection of assets whose average portfolio duration exactly matches the investor's planned holding period. As time passes, the investor's planned holding period grows shorter, as does the average duration of the investor's portfolio. However, these two items—the remaining holding period and the duration of the investor's portfolio—are not likely to decline at the same speed. Therefore, an investor must constantly make portfolio adjustments to ensure that duration still equals the remaining length of the investor's planned holding period. And because many bonds are callable in advance of their maturity, bondholders may find themselves with a sudden and unexpected change in their portfolio's average duration.

Another problem with duration matching arises if the slope of the yield curve changes during the investor's planned holding period. In general, different patterns of interest rate movements require somewhat different measures of duration—a complex problem. Because the future path of interest rates cannot be perfectly forecast, immunization with duration cannot be perfect without developing a complicated model that takes into account a wide range of factors. Thus, there is always some risk associated with the use of conventional measures of duration due to uncertainty about future interest-rate movements. This type of risk is often called *stochastic process risk*.

Immunization using duration seems to work well because the largest single element seen in most interest rate movements is a parallel change in *all* interest rates (a factor that explains about 80 percent of the variability we see in interest-rate movements over time). Thus, the assumption of duration models that interest rates tend to move in parallel (i.e., the slope of the yield curve does not change significantly over time) is not exactly true, but it represents a reasonably close approximation of what we often see in real-world markets over time. Thus, there is evidence that investors can achieve reasonably effective immunization by *approximately* matching the duration of their portfolios with their planned holding periods. The duration model, in other words, seems to be robust under a variety of different market conditions.

QUESTIONS TO HELP YOU STUDY

11. What is the *coupon effect?* How does it relate to the *price elasticity* of a financial asset?

12. What is the relationship between the coupon rate on an asset and the volatility of its price as interest rates change?

13. Explain the meaning and importance of the concept of *duration*.

14. What is *portfolio immunization?* How does it work?

15. What are the *limitations* of duration and the portfolio immunization technique?

MARKETS ON THE NET: The Most Important Web Sites for This Chapter

Central Bank Web Sites
(bis.org/cbanks.htm)
European Central Bank (ecb.int)
Federal Reserve System
(federalreserve.gov)
Global Financial Data (globalfindata.com)
Interest Rate Calculator
(interestratecalculator.com)

The Economist (economist.com)
The Bond Market Association
(investinginbonds.com)
The Financial Pipeline (finpipe.com)
U.S. Savings Bonds Online
(savingsbond.com)
Investopedia.com
(investopedia.com/calculator)

Summary of the Chapter's Main Points

While theories of how interest rates are determined usually focus upon a single interest rate in the economy, there are in fact thousands of different interest rates confronting savers and borrowers every day. This chapter has focused our attention upon two major factors that cause interest rates to differ from security to security and from loan to loan: (a) *inflationary expectations;* and (b) the *maturity, term,* or *duration* of a financial instrument.

- One key factor affecting interest rates is *expectations about inflation.* If lenders expect a higher rate of inflation to prevail during the life of a financial instrument they will demand a higher nominal return before making a loan. The *Fisher effect* argues that the expected nominal interest rate attached to a loan or security is the sum of its expected real rate plus the inflation premium (or expected rate of inflation). Fisher believed that the real rate would be relatively stable; therefore, changes in the nominal interest rate were due largely to changes in inflationary expectations.

- More recent research suggests that the relationship between inflation and interest rates may not be quite as simple as implied by the Fisher effect. For example, the *Harrod-Keynes effect* suggests that changes in the expected inflation rate may result, not in changes in the nominal rate, but changes in the real rate of return instead. Moreover, the economy, the structure of tax rates investors face, and the public's spending and investment habits may significantly impact the linkages between inflation and interest rates. For example, the *taxation* of interest income may force the expected nominal interest rate to increase by more than expected inflation so that savers can protect their after-tax return.

- Deflation—a fall in the average price level for all goods and services—tends to push nominal interest rates lower and raise real rates. Thus, periods of deflation may slow investment activity and job creation.

- There is great controversy today surrounding the possible linkages between *inflation* and *stock prices*. Rising inflation doesn't necessarily lead to rising stock prices. The stock-price impact from inflation may depend on *nominal contracts*—that is, whether the revenues and expenses of a stock-issuing corporation are favorably or unfavorably affected by inflation as a result of agreements the company has entered into concerning the wages and salaries paid to its workforce, the goods sold to its customers, and borrowing costs. Inflation doesn't affect all stocks the same way because different businesses and individuals are involved in different nominal contracts shaping their cash inflows (revenues) and outflows (expenses).

- This chapter explores the usefulness of the *yield curve* in explaining interest-rate movements. The yield curve visually captures the relationship between the annual rate of return on financial instruments and their term to maturity. Yield curves have sloped upward most frequently in recent years, with long-term interest rates higher than short-term rates. However, yield curves can slope downward or become relatively flat (horizontal).

- Why does the yield curve change its shape? The *unbiased expectations hypothesis* contends that yield curves reflect predominantly the interest-rate expectations of the financial marketplace. A rising yield curve suggests that market interest rates are expected to rise, while a declining yield curve points to lower expected interest rates in the future.

- Other viewpoints on the yield curve stem from the *liquidity premium, market segmentation,* and *preferred habitat* theories. For example, the *liquidity premium view* contends that the greater risk associated with longer-term financial instruments results in these longer-maturity assets bearing higher average returns, giving an upward bias to the slope of yield curves.

- The *market segmentation* and *preferred habitat* views of the yield curve suggest that the supply of financial assets of different maturities available to investors can affect the yield curve's shape. For example, a sudden increase in the supply of longer-term financial instruments may cause long-term asset prices to fall and their yields to rise, tipping the yield curve toward an upward slope.

- Regardless of which view may be valid, yield curves can play a key role in the management of financial institutions, which borrow a substantial portion of their funds at the short end of the maturity spectrum and lend heavily at longer maturities. Yield curves can provide an indication of the marketplace's overall forecast of future interest rates, with upward-sloping curves implying rising interest rates and downward-sloping curves implying falling interest rates in the future.

- Yield curves may help identify underpriced or overpriced assets whose yields will lie above or below the curve at any moment in time. Moreover, some security traders "ride the yield curve," taking advantage of opportunities to sell short-term securities bearing the lowest yields and purchasing longer-maturity securities bearing higher interest rates.

www.mhhe.com/rose9e

- In recent years financial analysts have become somewhat dissatisfied with one of the two key factors making up the yield-curve relationship—the *term to maturity* or number of months and years until a financial asset is due to be retired. An alternative measure of the maturity of a financial instrument—*duration*—has become popular in recent years because it is a weighted average measure of the maturity or length of a financial instrument, capturing both the size and the timing of all cash payments from an income-generating asset or portfolio of assets. Duration has grown in popularity among portfolio managers because it can be used to help *immunize* a single asset or an asset portfolio against possible losses due to changing market interest rates.

- Duration also is linked to the price volatility (or *price elasticity*) of a financial instrument in a directly proportional way. Duration connects the percentage change in price of a financial asset to the change in its interest return or yield. Longer-term assets tend to have longer durations and, therefore, greater price instability than do shorter-term assets.

Key Terms Appearing in This Chapter

inflation, 168
nominal interest rate, 169
real interest rate, 169
inflation premium, 169
Fisher effect, 170
Harrod-Keynes effect, 171
inflation-risk premium, 172
inflation-caused income tax effect, 172
deflation, 174
nominal contracts, 176
TIPS, 177

maturity, 180
yield curve, 181
unbiased expectations hypothesis, 182
liquidity premium, 185
market segmentation argument, 185
preferred habitat, 186
price elasticity, 191
coupon effect, 192
duration, 192
convexity, 194
portfolio immunization, 195

Problems and Issues

1. According to the Fisher effect, if the real interest rate is currently 3 percent and the nominal interest rate is 8 percent, what rate of inflation is the financial marketplace expecting? Explain the reasoning behind your answer. If the nominal rate rises to 11 percent and follows the assumptions of the Fisher effect, what would you conclude about the expected inflation rate? The real rate?

2. An investor buys a U.S. Treasury bond whose current yield to maturity as reported in the daily newspaper is 10 percent. The investor is subject to a 33 percent federal income tax rate on any new income received. His real after-tax return from this bond is 2 percent. What is the expected inflation rate in the financial marketplace?

3. Calculate the price elasticity of a 15-year bond around its $1,000 par value and 10 percent coupon rate if market interest rates on comparable bonds drop to 6 percent. The market price of the bond at a 6 percent yield to maturity is $1,392. Suppose now that the yield to maturity climbs to 14 percent. If the bond's price falls to $751.80, what is the bond's price elasticity?

4. Calculate the value of duration for a four-year, $1,000 par value U.S. government bond purchased today at a yield to maturity of 15 percent. The bond's coupon rate is 12 percent, and it pays interest once a year at year's end. Now suppose the market interest rate on comparable bonds falls to 14 percent. What percentage change in this bond's price will result?

5. A bank buying bonds is concerned about possible fluctuations in earnings due to changes in interest rates. Currently the bank's investment officer is looking at a $1,000 par-value bond that matures in four years and carries a coupon rate of 12 percent. Market interest rates are also currently at 12 percent, but the bank's officer believes there is a significant probability that interest rates could drop to 10 percent or rise to 14 percent during the first year and stay there until the bond matures. What would be this bond's total earnings for the bank over the next four years if interest rates rise to 14 percent? Fall to 10 percent? Remain at 12 percent? What will happen to total earnings if the bank's investment officer finds another bond whose maturity is reached in five years but whose duration is four years—the same as the bank's planned holding period?

6. The 10-year Treasury bond rate is currently trading at 6.08 percent, while the one-year bond rate carries a yield to maturity of 5.35 percent. What is the current yield spread between these instruments? What is this yield spread forecasting for the economy in the period ahead? Explain.

   Suppose the 10-year T-bond rate falls to 5.57 percent, while the one-year T-bond yield rises to 6.04 percent. What change in the yield spread has occurred? What is the expected outlook for economic conditions following this particular change in the yield spread? Can you explain why?

7. Synchron Corporation borrowed long-term capital at an interest rate of 8.5 percent under the expectation that the annual inflation rate over the life of this borrowing was likely to be 5 percent. However, shortly after the loan contract was signed, the actual inflation rate climbed to 5.5 percent, where it is expected to remain until Synchron's loan reaches maturity. Other factors held constant, what is likely to happen to the market value per share of Synchron's common stock? Explain your reasoning.

8. A four-year TIPS bond promises a real annual coupon return to investors of 4 percent and its face value is $1,000. While the annual inflation rate was approximately zero when the bond was first issued, the inflation rate suddenly accelerated to 3 percent and is expected to remain at that level for the four-year term of the bond. What will be the amount of interest paid in nominal dollars each year of the bond's life? What will be the face (nominal) value of the bond at the end of each year of its life?

9. A TIPS issued five years ago for $1,000 with a 10 percent coupon rate and maturing today had the following inflation history:

Year in Life of the TIPS Bond	Actual Inflation Rate (Measured by the CPI)
1	2%
2	3
3	4
4	3
5	2

   How did the nominal principal value and nominal interest payment associated with this bond change over its lifetime?

Standard & Poor's Market Insight and Web-Based Problems

STANDARD
&POOR'S

1. Interest rates on short-term and long-term debt instruments and the prices of stocks are significantly affected by overall changes occurring in the U.S. and world economies. To obtain a professional overview of important market events that have occurred recently or appear to be on the horizon, go to S&P's Market Insight database at **www.mhhe.com/business/finance/edumarketinsight/,** click on the "Trends and Projections" tab, and download the most recent report you find.

   a. After reading the report, return to the site. Go to the *Investment Policy Committee (IPC) Notes* and read their recommendations for allocating investment portfolios between cash, bonds, and domestic and foreign stocks. Explain how this committee's suggestions for asset allocation link to the economic and financial conditions discussed in the "Trends and Projections" file.

   b. What are the implications of the interest-rate projections you found at the S&P site for the shape of the yield curve? Suppose you held both 10-year U.S. Treasury bonds and three-month T-bills. In what ways would you be thinking about readjusting your portfolio?

   c. Now check out the list the S&P site provides on the best (5 STARS) and worst (1 STAR) stock picks. Regarding the reports and recommendations you accessed, are you able to identify anything that might affect these stock-pick recommendations?

2. During the late 1970s the inflation rate in the United States was in double digits. In response, the Federal Reserve decided to raise short-term interest rates dramatically to bring it down.

   a. What would you expect the yield curve to look like after this policy change?

   b. Visit the Fed's Web site at **federalreserve.gov** and click on the "Economic Research and Data" tab; then click on the "Statistics: Releases and Historical Data" tab and obtain historical data on "Selected Interest Rates" from the H.15 release. From these data construct a Treasury yield curve for April 1980 and for the most recent month you can find.

   c. Search the Internet for data on the current inflation rate (measured by the CPI) in the United States and the U.S. inflation rate in 1980. Does this information help to explain the shapes of the yield curves for these two time periods?

www.mhhe.com/rose9e

Semester Project: A Study of the Fed Funds Market

Continuing our semester-long study of a critical financial marketplace—the federal funds (interbank loan) market—we note that a bank or other depository institution in need of short-term funds can borrow from another institution that has funds to lend in the Fed funds market. However, most depository institutions have several alternative sources of funds they can draw upon. For example, if a banker finds that these alternative sources are cheaper, his institution's demand for federal funds will decline, helping to lower the Fed funds rate. This ability to switch from one money market source to another causes the Fed funds rate to be linked to other short-term interest rates within the financial system. With this point in mind, see if you can answer the following questions:

a. Based on this chapter's discussion of yield curves, how would you interpret the implications of a steeply upward-sloping yield curve for the future path of the federal funds interest rate? Why? What if the yield curve becomes inverted or downward-sloping?

b. According to today's financial news (for example, from *The Wall Street Journal* or from the Web at **bloomberg.com/markets/rates/**), what does the yield curve look like today? What would you say today's financial marketplace is expecting to happen to the Fed funds rate in the near future? Does the yield curve you uncovered have any implications for the future course of monetary policy conducted by the Federal Reserve?

c. Would you expect Fed funds traders to be concerned about the prospects for inflation? Why or why not?

Selected References to Explore

Ammer, John. "Inflation, Inflation Risk, and Stock Returns." *International Finance Discussion Paper 464,* Board of Governors of the Federal Reserve System, April 1994.

Bonser-Neal, Catherine, and Timothy R. Morley. "Does the Yield Spread Predict Real Economic Activity? A Multi-Country Analysis." *Economic Review,* Federal Reserve Bank of Kansas City, Third Quarter 1997, pp. 37–53.

Campbell, J. Y. "A Defense of Traditional Hypotheses about the Term Structure of Interest Rates." *Journal of Finance* 41 (1986), pp. 183–93.

Dai, Q., and K. Singleton. "Specification Analysis of Affine Term Structure Models." *Journal of Finance* 55 (October 2000), pp. 1943–78.

Fama, Eugene F., and R. R. Bliss. "The Information in Long Maturity Forward Rates." *American Economic Review* 72 (1987), pp. 680–92.

Feroli, Michael. "Monetary Policy and the Information Content of the Yield Spread," *Finance and Economics Discussion Series,* Z.11, Federal Reserve Board, Washington, D.C., 2004.

Fisher, Irving. "Appreciation and Interest." *Publication of the American Economics Association,* August 1896.

Fuhrer, Jeffrey, and Geoffrey M. B. Tootell. "What Is the Cost of Deflation?" *Regional Review,* Federal Reserve Bank of Boston, Fourth Quarter 2003, pp. 2–5.

Haubrich, Joseph G. "Interest Rates, Yield Curves, and the Monetary Regime." *Economic Commentary,* Federal Reserve Bank of Cleveland, June 2004.

Longstaff, Francis A. "Time Varying Premia and Traditional Hypotheses about the Term Structure." *Journal of Finance* 41, no. 4 (September 1990), pp. 1307–14.

www.mhhe.com/rose9e

Sack, Brian, and Robert Elsasser. "Treasury Inflation-Indexed Debt: A Review of the U.S. Experience." *FRBNY Economic Policy Review,* May 2004, pp. 47–63.

Shen, Pu. "How Important Is the Inflation Risk Premium?" *Economic Review,* Federal Reserve Bank of Kansas City, Fourth Quarter 1998, pp. 35–47.

Stojanovic, Dusan, and Mark D. Vaughn. "Yielding Clues about Recessions: The Yield Curve as a Forecasting Tool." *Economic Review,* Federal Reserve Bank of Boston, 1997, pp. 10–21.

Van Horn, James. "Interest-Rate Risk and the Term Structure of Interest Rates." *Journal of Political Economy,* August 1965, pp. 344–51.

Wu, Tao. "What Makes the Yield Curve Move?" *FRBSF Economic Letter,* Federal Reserve Bank of San Francisco, no. 2003-15 (June 6, 2003).

Chapter 8

The Risk Structure of Interest Rates: Defaults, Prepayments, Taxes, and Other Rate-Determining Factors

What's in This Chapter?
Key Topics Outline

Marketability and Liquidity

Default-Risk Premiums Attached to Interest Rates

Credit Ratings, Bankruptcies, and Junk Bonds

Call Privileges and Call Risk

Prepayment and Event Risk

Taxation of Asset Returns and Tax-Exempt Assets

Convertibility

The Structure of Interest Rates

Learning Objectives

in This Chapter

- You will see the effect of several different features of financial assets—such as their marketability, liquidity, default risk, call privileges, prepayment risk, convertibility, and taxability—on their interest rates and prices.

- You will learn why we have thousands of different interest rates within the global economy.

- You will discover how the "structure of interest rates" is built and why that rate structure is constantly changing.

- You will see more clearly why it is so difficult to accurately forecast interest rates and financial asset prices.

8.1   Introduction

In the preceding chapter, we examined two factors that cause the value of financial assets and, therefore, the interest rate or yield on one financial asset to be different from the interest rate or yield on another. These factors included the maturity or term of a loan or security and expected inflation. In this chapter, we focus on a different set of elements influencing relative asset prices and interest rates: (1) marketability, (2) default risk, (3) call privileges, (4) taxation of security income, (5) prepayment risk, and (6) convertibility. The impact of each of these factors is analyzed separately, but it should be noted that yields on financial assets and their prices are influenced by several factors acting *simultaneously.* For example, the market yield on a 20-year corporate bond may be 8 percent, while the yield on a 10-year municipal bond may be 6 percent. The difference in yield and value between these two assets reflects not only the difference in their maturities but also any differences in their degree of default risk, marketability, callability, and tax status. To analyze differentials in yield and price between various financial assets, therefore, we must understand thoroughly *all* of the factors that shape interest rates and asset values in the global money and capital markets.

8.2   Marketability

One of the most important considerations for an investor is *whether a market exists for those assets he or she would like to acquire.* Can an asset be sold quickly, or must the investor wait some time before suitable buyers can be found? This is the question of **marketability,** and financial instruments traded around the world vary widely in terms of the ease and speed with which buyers can be found.

marketability

For example, Treasury bills, notes, and bonds have one of the most active and deepest markets in the world. Large lots of marketable Treasury securities in multiples of a million dollars are bought and sold daily, with the trades taking place in a matter of minutes. Small lots (under $1 million) of these same securities are more difficult to sell. However, there is usually no difficulty in marketing even a handful of Treasury securities. Similarly, common stock actively traded on the New York, London, Frankfurt, or Tokyo exchanges typically can be moved in minutes, depending on the number of shares being sold. In active markets like these, negotiations are usually conducted by telephone or E-mail and confirmed by wire. Frequently, payment for any securities purchased is made the same day by wire or within one or two days by check or draft.

For thousands of lesser-known financial assets not actively traded each day, however, marketability can be a problem. Stocks and bonds issued by smaller companies usually have a narrow market, often confined to the local community or region. Trades occur infrequently, and it is often difficult to establish a consistent market price. A seller may have to wait months to secure a desired price or, if the security must be sold immediately, its price may have to be discounted substantially.

Marketability is positively related to the *size* (total sales or total assets) and *reputation* of the institution issuing the securities and to the number of similar securities outstanding. Not surprisingly, stocks and bonds issued in large blocks by the largest corporations and governmental units tend to find acceptance more readily in the global financial markets. With a larger number of similar assets available, buy-sell transactions are more frequent, and a consistent market price can be established.

Marketability is a decided advantage to the asset purchaser (lender of funds). In contrast, the issuer of assets is not particularly concerned about any difficulties the purchaser may encounter in the resale (secondary) market unless lack of marketability significantly influences asset sales in the primary market. And where marketability is a problem, it does influence the yield the issuer must pay in the primary market. In fact, there is a *negative* relationship between marketability and yield. More marketable assets generally carry *lower* expected returns than less marketable assets, other things being equal. Purchasers of assets that can be sold in the secondary market only with difficulty must be compensated for this inconvenience by a higher promised rate of return.

8.3 Liquidity

liquidity

Marketability is an important component of another feature of financial assets that influences their interest rate or yield: their degree of **liquidity.** A liquid financial asset is *readily marketable.* In addition, its price tends to be *stable* over time and it is *reversible,* meaning the holder of the asset can usually recover her funds upon resale with little risk of loss. Because the liquidity feature of financial assets tends to lower their risk, liquid assets carry lower interest rates than illiquid assets. Investors strongly interested in maximum profitability try to minimize their holdings of liquid assets. Examples of highly liquid assets, bearing relatively low rates of return, include most bank deposits, shares in money market mutual funds, and marketable U.S. Treasury securities.

As noted recently by Fleming (2003), measuring the liquidity of assets is a challenging task and research on that issue is continuing. One of the more popular measures of liquidity today is the *bid-ask spread*—the difference between the offer (bid) price at which an asset will be purchased and the price for which it is to be sold. For example, a security dealer like Goldman Sachs or Merrill Lynch may offer to buy (bid) $1,000 par-value Treasury bonds at a price of $950 and pledge to sell them (ask) for $960. In general, the narrower the bid-ask spread, the more liquid is the asset in question because one of the dominant characteristics of a liquid market is low transactions cost. Other commonly used measures of liquidity include trading volume, frequency of trades, and average trade size, with more liquid instruments generally registering higher in trading volume, trading frequency, and average daily trade size.

8.4 Default Risk and Interest Rates

default risk

Another important factor causing one interest rate to differ from another in the global marketplace is the degree of default risk carried by individual assets. Investors in financial assets face many different kinds of risk, but one of the most important is **default risk**—the risk that a borrower will not make all promised payments at the agreed-upon times. All debt except some government securities is subject to varying degrees of default risk. If you purchase a 10-year corporate bond with a $1,000 par value and a coupon rate of 9 percent, the issuing company promises in the indenture (bond contract) to pay you $90 a year (or more commonly, $45 every six months) for 10 years plus $1,000 at the end of the 10-year period. Failure to meet *any* of these promised payments on time puts the borrower in default, and the lender may have to go to court to recover the monies owed.

The Premium for Default Risk

The promised yield on a risky asset is positively related to the risk of borrower default as perceived by investors. Specifically, the promised yield on a risky asset is composed of at least two elements:

$$\text{Promised yield on a risky asset} = \text{Risk-free interest rate} + \text{Default-risk premium} \qquad (8.1)$$

EXHIBIT 8.1

The Relationship between Default Risk and the Promised Yield on Risky Assets

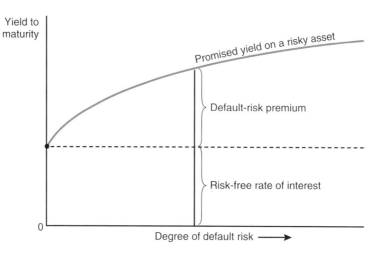

or

$$\text{Default-risk premium} = \text{Promised yield on a risky asset} \\ - \text{Risk-free interest rate} \qquad (8.2)$$

The *promised yield* on a risky debt security is the yield to maturity that will be earned by the investor if the borrower makes all promised payments when they are due. As Exhibit 8.1 illustrates, the higher the degree of default risk associated with a risky debt security, the higher the default-risk premium on that security and the greater the required rate of return (yield) that must be attached to that asset as demanded by investors in the global financial marketplace. Any adverse development that makes a borrower appear riskier, such as a downturn in the economy or serious financial difficulties, will lead the market to assign a higher default-risk premium to his debt security. And if the risk-free rate remains unchanged, the financial asset's promised risky yield must rise and its price must decline.

The Expected Rate of Return or Yield on a Risky Asset

Increasingly in recent years some of the largest business firms on the planet have been forced into default and subsequently declared bankruptcy. Among the leading U.S. bankruptcy filers in modern history are firms such as the following:

WorldCom, Inc. (2002), with $103.9 billion in assets.

Enron Corp. (2001), with $63.3 billion in assets.

Conseco, Inc. (2002), with $61.4 billion in assets.

Texaco, Inc. (1987), with $35.9 billion in assets.

Global Crossing Ltd. (2002), with $30.2 billion in assets.

UAL Corp. (2002), with $25.2 billion in assets .

Pacific Gas and Electric Company (2001), with $21.5 billion in assets.

Kmart Corp. (2002), with $14.6 billion in assets.

Not even governments have been exempt from default and ultimate bankruptcy, including Argentina, Russia, and Orange County, California. Volatile changes in business and consumer spending, interest rates, and commodity prices frequently have led to serious miscalculations by both large and small businesses and governments with sometimes fatal results. For this reason, many investors around the globe today have learned to look at the *expected* rate of return, or yield, on a risky asset as well as its *promised* yield.

expected yield

The **expected yield** is the weighted average of all possible yields to maturity from a risky asset. Each possible yield is weighted by the probability that it will occur. Thus, if there are *m* possible yields from a risky asset:

$$\text{Expected yield} = \sum_{i=1}^{m} p_i y_i \qquad (8.3)$$

where y_i represents the ith possible yield on a risky asset and p_i is the probability that the ith possible risky yield will be obtained. Assessing these possible outcomes (yields) and the likelihood of their occurrence (probabilities) is the job of the financial analyst.

Let's take a simple example to illustrate how the expected yield on an asset might be determined. Suppose a corporate bond traded in today's market appears to have possible yields of 6 percent, 8 percent, and 10 percent, with probabilities of 50 percent, 30 percent, and 20 percent, respectively. Then, its *expected yield* would be:

Expected yield on a bond = 6% (0.50) + 8% (0.30) + 10% (0.20) = 7.40%

While this bond's current *expected* yield is 7.40 percent, the yield *promised* by its issuer may be quite different.

Anticipated Loss and Default-Risk Premiums

For a risk-free asset held to maturity, the expected yield equals the promised yield. However, in the case of a risky asset, the promised yield may be greater than the expected yield, and the yield spread between them is usually labeled the *anticipated default loss.* That is,

Anticipated default loss on a risky asset = Promised yield
− Expected yield   (8.4)

The concept of *anticipated default loss* is important because it represents each investor's view of what the appropriate default-risk premium on a risky asset should be. Let's suppose that an investor carries out a careful financial analysis of a company in preparation for purchasing its bonds and decides that the firm is a less risky borrower default-wise than perceived by the market as a whole. Perhaps the market has assigned the firm's bonds a default-risk premium of 4 percent; the investor believes, however, that the true anticipated loss due to default is only 3 percent. Because the market's default-risk premium exceeds this investor's anticipated default loss, she would be inclined to *buy* the company's bonds. As she sees it, the risky asset's promised yield (including its market-assigned default-risk premium) is too high and, therefore, its price is too low. To this investor, the company's bonds appear to be a bargain—a temporarily underpriced financial asset.

Consider the opposite case. An investor calculates the anticipated default loss on bonds issued by a government toll road project. He concludes that a default-risk premium of 5 percent is justified because of a significant number of uncertainties associated with the future success of the project. However, the current promised yield on the risky asset is only 10 percent, and the risk-free interest rate is 6 percent. Because the market has assigned only a 4 percent default-risk premium, and the investor prefers a 5 percent default-risk premium, it is unlikely that he will purchase the bond. As the investor views this bond, its promised risky yield is too low and, therefore, its price is too high.

Among the more interesting credit rating agencies with Web sites to explore are **fitchratings.com, dufflic.com, jcr.co.ip/homepagee. htm,** and **bankwatch.org**

Major financial institutions, especially insurance companies, banks, and pension funds, employ a large number of credit analysts for the express purpose of assessing the anticipated default loss on a wide range of assets they would like to acquire. These institutions believe they have a definite advantage over the average investor in assessing the true degree of default risk associated with any particular asset. This high level of technical expertise may permit major institutional investors to take advantage of underpriced assets where, in their judgment, the market has overestimated the true level of default risk.

Factors Influencing Default-Risk Premiums

What factors influence the default-risk premiums assigned by the market to different assets? For many years, privately owned rating companies have exercised a dominant influence on investor perceptions of the riskiness of individual security issues. Among the most widely consulted investment rating companies are Moody's Investors Service—a division of Dun & Bradstreet—and Standard & Poor's Corporation—a subsidiary of McGraw-Hill, Inc. Both companies rate individual security issues according to their perceived probability of default (based on the borrower's financial condition and business prospects) and publish the ratings as letter grades. A summary of the letter grades used by these companies for rating corporate and municipal bonds is shown in Exhibit 8.2.

For nearly a century, Moody's and Standard & Poor's (S&P) have regularly assigned credit ratings to thousands of companies selling bonds and other forms of debt. Other rating agencies—for example, Fitch and Duff & Phelps—often issue their ratings when someone requests a "second opinion" concerning a new bond issue. The Securities and Exchange Commission has labeled Moody's, S&P, Fitch, and Duff & Phelps as "nationally recognized" raters for U.S. corporate bonds, while Thomson Bank Watch and IBCA are nationally recognized as credit-rating agencies that evaluate debt instruments issued by financial institutions. Recently, newer credit rating agencies (such as Japan Credit Rating Agency (JCR)) have appeared all over the globe to match the growing globalization of the money and capital markets.

The economic basis for the rise of credit rating companies has to do with economies of scale in collecting credit information. Presumably, large rating agencies can do credit evaluations more economically and conveniently than can small investors who lack the necessary data and market contacts. Allegedly, large credit rating companies

EXHIBIT 8.2 Bond-Rating Categories Employed by Moody's Investors Service and Standard & Poor's Corporation	Quality Level of Bonds	Moody's Rating Categories	Standard & Poor's Rating Categories	Default-Risk Premium
	High-quality or high-grade bonds	Aaa	AAA	Lowest
		Aa	AA	
		A	A	
	Medium-quality or medium-grade bonds	Baa	BBB	
		Ba	BB	
		B	B	
	Lowest grade, speculative, or poor-quality bonds	Caa	CCC	
		Ca	CC	
		C	C	
	Defaulted bonds and bonds issued by bankrupt companies	—	DDD	Highest
		—	DD	
		—	D	

have lower agency costs (because investors have developed confidence in the rating agencies' independence and competence at assessing the degree of risk exposure investors may face with any particular bond issue).

While theory might lead us to suspect that all credit agencies assign about the same ratings along equivalent credit risk scales, research by Cantor and Packer (1996) suggests that this is not always true. Even the same level of rating at two different credit agencies does not necessarily imply the same level of perceived default-risk exposure. Moreover, Moody's and Standard & Poor's tend to assign lower credit ratings, on average, than other, less well known agencies, like Fitch and Duff & Phelps. One explanation may be that Moody's and S&P have tougher credit standards, or it may be that those bond issuers requesting third and fourth credit ratings expect to get a higher rating from a third or fourth credit reviewer and, thereby, save on their borrowing costs. When ratings are different, either the highest rating or the second-highest rating is often generally recognized in the market as the correct risk level, no matter which agency happens to assign the one rating chosen as "representative." Larger debt issuers also tend to get third or even fourth ratings because they face lower percentage rating costs.

Moody's investment ratings range from Aaa, for the highest-quality securities with negligible default risk, to C, for those securities deemed to be speculative and carrying a significant prospect of borrower default. Quality ratings assigned by Standard & Poor's range from AAA, for high-grade ("gilt-edged") securities, to those financial instruments actually in default (D) or issued by bankrupt firms. Bonds falling in the four top rating categories—Aaa to Baa for Moody's and AAA to BBB for Standard & Poor's—are called *investment-grade issues.* Laws and regulations frequently require commercial banks, insurance companies, and other financial institutions to purchase only those securities rated in these four categories. Lower-rated securities are referred to as *speculative issues.*

Exhibit 8.3 illustrates how the yields on bonds bearing different degrees of default risk (for example: 10-year U.S. Treasury notes versus Baa corporate securities) change relative to each other with the progression of time, fluctuations in the economy, and other factors. Exhibit 8.4 compares market yields on long-term U.S. Treasury bonds with those on corporate bonds in the four top rating categories, Aaa to Baa. It is interesting to note that these yield relationships are all in the direction theory would lead us to expect. For example, the yield on Aaa corporate bonds—the least risky securities rated by Moody's and Standard & Poor's—is consistently lower than the yield attached to lower-rated (Baa) bonds. This suggests that investors in the marketplace tend to rank securities in the same relative default risk order as the credit rating agencies do. This

EXHIBIT 8.3

The Behavior of Interest Rates Attached to Risky versus Riskless Capital Market Securities

Source: Federal Reserve Bank of St. Louis, *Monetary Trends,* December 2003.

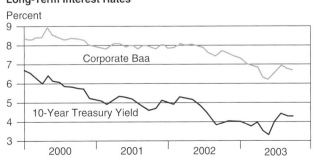

EXHIBIT 8.4

Market Yield on Rated Corporate Bonds and Long-Term U.S. Treasury Bonds, 1990–2004

*Corporate bond ratings are from Moody's Investors Service.

**2004 interest rates are averages for the month of January.

Source: Board of Governors of the Federal Reserve System, *Federal Reserve Bulletin,* selected issues.

Type of Bond	Average Yields (Percent per Annum)							
	1990	1992	1994	1996	1998	2000	2002	2004**
Long-term U.S. Treasury bonds	8.74%	7.52%	7.41%	6.80%	5.69%	6.03%	5.41%	5.05%
Aaa corporate bonds*	9.32	8.14	7.97	7.37	6.53	7.62	6.49	5.54
Aa corporate bonds*	9.57	8.46	8.15	7.55	6.80	7.83	6.93	5.91
A corporate bonds*	9.82	8.62	8.28	7.69	6.93	8.11	7.18	6.08
Baa corporate bonds*	10.36	8.98	8.63	8.05	7.22	8.36	7.80	6.44

seems to be an appropriate strategy, because there appears to be a high (though by no means perfect) correlation between the ratings assigned by the credit agencies and the actual default record of corporate bonds.

Recent research has found that there is a pronounced association between market-assigned default-risk premiums and fluctuations (cycles) in business activity (recessions versus expansions or boom periods). For example, the yield spread between Aaa- and Baa-rated securities rises during economic recessions and decreases during periods of economic expansion. The correlation is not perfect, though. Fluctuations in output and income do not always influence the default-risk premium on one security versus another in the same way or to the same degree. However, when economic and financial conditions suggest to investors that uncertainty has increased and that business prospects are less robust, the market generally translates these opinions into higher default-risk premiums.

Several studies in recent years have addressed the question of what factors influence default-risk premiums on securities and what factors rating firms use to evaluate default risk. Among the factors identified for corporate securities are variability in company earnings, the period of time a firm has been in operation, and the amount of leverage employed (i.e., volume of debt relative to equity capital).[1]

A company with volatile earnings runs a greater risk of experiencing periods when losses will exceed the firm's ability to raise funds. The longer a firm has been operating without default, the more investors come to expect continued successful performance. Greater use of financial leverage in the capital structure of a firm offers the potential for greater earnings per share of stock, because debt is a relatively cheap source of funds (especially when measured on an after-tax basis). However, financial leverage is a two-edged sword. As the proportion of borrowed funds rises relative to equity, the risk of significant declines in net earnings increases.

---

[1]We do not know for sure what factors credit rating agencies use to assign default-risk ratings, but we do know that they consider at least three levels of factors: (1) condition of the economy, (2) industry conditions, and (3) borrower-specific factors, including coverage ratios (earnings before interest and taxes to interest and principal payments owed), leverage ratios (debt-to-equity ratios), liquidity indicators (such as the ratio of current assets to current liabilities) and profitability measures (such as return on assets and return on equity). Studies of corporate bankruptcy have found some of these factors—especially liquidity, earnings, debt exposure, and stock prices—to be effective discriminators between corporations eventually declaring bankruptcy and healthy firms. Moreover, when a credit rating agency downgrades a firm's credit rating, the affected company's stock returns tend to fall immediately following the announcement.

Inflation and Default-Risk Premiums

Earlier, in Chapter 7, we saw that inflation can cause interest rates to rise as investors in the financial markets demand to be compensated with higher nominal returns when expected inflation or uncertainty about future inflation goes up. However, *inflation also appears to affect the size of default-risk premiums on risky securities.* Default-risk premiums (often called "quality spreads") tend to be higher and more volatile when inflation is high and volatile. Greater uncertainty about inflation tends to produce a "flight to quality" in the financial markets, and investors simply become more cautious about buying default-risk-exposed financial instruments. This is one of the many ways in which high and volatile price inflation can disrupt the efficient functioning of a market-oriented economy.

Yield Curves for Risky Securities

As we saw in Chapter 7, yield curves on low-default-risk securities (such as U.S. government and high-grade corporate bonds) have a tendency to display a positive slope—they *rise* with advancing maturity. In contrast, there is some evidence that the yield curves on high-default-risk instruments often have a downward (negative) slope or may have a significant bow or hump in them as maturity increases. If so, this unusual yield-curve shape *may* be traceable to the fact that bonds issued by poorer-quality borrowers are generally at their riskiest when first issued and appear to improve in quality (i.e., decline in default risk) the longer the issuer survives and manages to make the required payments. In other words, each required payment that is successfully made seems to lower the risk that subsequent payments will be missed.

While some studies tend to support this version of financial theory, recent work by Helwege and Turner (1997) tends to find the opposite—that the yield curve for most speculative-grade bond issues *rises* with advancing maturity just as it does for debt issued by low-risk borrowers. This is one area where additional research is needed to help us identify the true yield-curve, default-risk relationship.

The Volatile History of Junk Bonds

junk bonds

The decades of the 1980s and 1990s ushered in the rapid growth and development of **junk bonds**—long-term debt securities whose full repayment is judged to be significantly less certain than is true for bonds rated investment quality, as shown in the following table:

To discover how credit ratings are assigned and how buyers of financial assets can find out about changes in companies' credit ratings, see Moody's Investors Service at **moodys.com/** and Standard & Poor's Corporation at **standardpoor.com**

Junk versus Investment-Grade Corporate Bonds	
Investment-grade bond issues	All those debt securities rated:
	Aaa, Aa, A, or Baa by Moody's Investors Service
	AAA, AA, A, or BBB by Standard & Poor's Corporation
Junk Bonds	All those debt securities rated:
	Ba, B, Caa, Ca, or C by Moody's Investors Service
	BB, B, CCC, CC, C by Standard & Poor's Corporation

The term *junk bonds* arose years ago when several companies that were trapped in serious financial problems with low credit ratings ("fallen angels") were forced to issue inferior-quality bonds to stay alive. More recently, new companies and small established companies also have been able to reach the bond market, which previously was closed to them, by issuing these speculative-grade securities. Junk bonds also have been issued to facilitate mergers and, in the opposite situation, to prevent corporate takeovers. Some junk bonds are "zeros," which pay no interest, and others are "pics,"

Corporate and state and local government (municipal) debt securities sold in the financial markets generally must carry a credit rating assigned by one or more rating agencies. The two most widely respected credit rating agencies over the years have been Moody's Investors Service and Standard & Poor's Corporation, both head-quartered in New York City.

Other prominent security rating companies operating today include Fitch Investors Service, Thomson Bank Watch, and Duff & Phelps Credit Rating Co. in the U.S., as well as the Canadian Bond Rating Service, Dominion Bond Rating Service, IBCA, Ltd., and Nippon Investor Service Inc. The ratings assigned by these firms are generally regarded in the investment community as an objective evaluation of the probability that a borrower may *default*.

Each rating assigned to a security issue is a reflection of at least three factors: (1) the character and terms of the particular security being issued; (2) the ability of the issuer to make timely payments; and (3) the degree of protection afforded investors if the issuer is liquidated, reorganized, or declares bankruptcy. The rating agencies focus principally on (1) the past and probable future cash flows of the issuer as an indication of the institution's ability to service its debt, (2) the volume and composition of outstanding debt, and (3) the

stability of the issuer's cash flows over time. Other factors influencing quality ratings are the value of assets pledged as collateral and the securities' priority of claim against the issuer's assets.

The rating agencies stress that their evaluations are not recommendations to buy or sell or an indication of the suitability of any particular asset. The agencies do not act as financial advisers to the businesses or units of government whose securities they rate, which helps to promote objectivity in assigning ratings. Fees are assessed for ratings based on the time and effort involved. These fees are usually paid by the security issuer or the underwriter.

While credit rating agencies have a good record ranking the default-risk exposure of most security issuers, the interpretation of the ratings seems to vary with time and across different rating agencies. Because the number of credit-rating companies seems to be growing, there is some fear that security issuers in the future will "shop around" even more than they do today for the best ratings they can get. Fortunately, credit-rating firms have a strong incentive to preserve their reputation for publishing accurate ratings. Otherwise, security issuers and investors will tend to avoid agencies that lose their reputation for quality and objectivity.

Developments in the "junk bond" market may be followed through such sources as **encyclopedia.com, finpipe.com/bndjunk. htm,** and **speculativebubble.com**

which pay interest not in cash but in the form of new bonds—both ideal for companies with low or uncertain earning power. Such low-rated bonds may trade at interest yields of 4 or 5 percentage points or more over yields on comparable government securities.

The number of individual investors and financial institutions interested in purchasing junk bonds grew rapidly during the 1980s due to few actual defaults on these bonds. At the same time, a leading investment banking firm, Drexel Burnham Lambert, Inc., pioneered new techniques to sell junk bonds that rapidly expanded the scope of the market. Many investors discovered that a diversified portfolio of junk bonds (e.g., about 12 different issues) appeared to lower overall portfolio risk to a level comparable to many higher-rated bonds. Thus, the yields offered on junk bonds appeared to be higher than their actual degree of default risk. Moreover, the development of an active market for junk bonds gave many small and new firms access to another source of financing besides borrowing from banks and finance companies. Certainly, the tax deductibility of interest expenses on corporate debt and the more recent development of sophisticated hedging instruments (such as swaps, credit derivatives, financial futures, and options) to combat market risk encouraged private corporations to make greater use of junk securities in order to raise new capital.

On the negative side, however, the rapid growth of junk bonds has aroused concern among government policymakers over possible declines in the credit quality of corporate debt. For example, insurance company regulators from New York state acted to limit junk bond investments by insurance firms selling policies in that state, a move soon followed by other insurance regulators across the United States. The use of junk bonds to finance hostile takeovers and the failure of hundreds of savings and loans that had purchased junk securities finally captured the attention of the U.S. Congress. Passage of the Financial Institutions Reform, Recovery, and Enforcement Act of 1989 outlawed further purchases of junk bonds by federally supervised depository institutions. In 1990, Drexel Burnham Lambert—at one time the king of junk bond dealers—declared bankruptcy as junk bond prices plummeted.

Moreover, a recession in the U.S. economy in 1991 resulted in a wave of defaults by firms that had previously issued junk bonds, climbing up to a default rate as high as 11 percent, though by 1994 the mean default rate on junk bonds had dropped back to less than 2 percent. However, in 2001 a recession in the economy sent junk bond interest rates and business bankruptcies rising again. Research by Fons (1991) and Helwege and Kleimen (1996) suggests that junk bond default rates vary over time due to (1) the strength of the economy (with default rates dropping when the economy is strong); (2) the proportion of lower-rated bonds issued each year (with more lower-rated issues tending to increase the average default rate); and (3) an "aging effect" (with defaults more likely within the first three years of a junk bond issue).

Higher relative yields available on junk bonds coupled with a reduced supply of these securities sparked a market rally in junk bond prices and an upward surge in new offerings as the new century was beginning. Much of the price gain appeared to be due to the emergence of junk bond mutual funds that often buy half or more of available new junk issues. The rise in new junk bond offerings can be traced to more borrowing companies bypassing rigid and expensive bank loans as a source of credit. In addition, the formation of the European Union (EU) has recently acted as a spur to international junk bond offerings, as firms move to expand and take advantage of a huge new common market, using a common currency with sharply reduced trade barriers.

The Junk-Bond Spread and the Economy

The behavior of yields on junk bonds has attracted the attention of economists trying to forecast changes in the strength or weakness of the economy. They have recently begun to focus on the so-called *junk-bond spread:*

$$\text{Junk-bond spread} = \text{Junk-bond yields} \\ - \text{Average yield on Aaa-rated coporate bonds} \qquad (8.5)$$

The basic argument concerning this measure of economic conditions is that a rise in the junk-bond spread indicates a growing fear among bond market investors that marginal-quality corporate borrowers are more likely to default on their debts. Thus, greater risk among corporate borrowers signals a weakening economy. In contrast, a decline in the junk-bond spread suggests fewer corporate bond defaults and, therefore, an improving economy.

There is some anecdotal evidence favoring the junk-bond-spread concept. For example, during the year 1999—a period of economic expansion in the United States—the yield spread between Ba corporate bonds—the highest quality junk bond issues—and Aaa (top-quality) corporate bonds was only about three-quarters of a percentage point (75 basis points). Capital market investors were pricing the risk of corporate business failures fairly low. In contrast, by August of 2001—when the U.S. economy was in a recession—this junk-bond-yield spread was more than a full percentage point (100 basis points), as capital market investors began to express concern that a weakening economy might sink a number of weaker companies. More research is needed on this so-called "economic forecaster," however, before we can confidently accept its predictions about business conditions and the strength of the economy.

The buyers of bonds and other financial instruments must be ever watchful of *default risk*—failure to pay interest owed or to pay back the principal of a loan—which can occur in unexpected places and raise critical ethical issues involving corporate stockholders, managers, employees, and the public. A dramatic example of the dangers of lending funds to risky borrowers occurred when Enron Corporation became one of the largest corporate bankruptcies in U.S. history in 2001.

In the case of Enron—holding about $60 billion in assets—the ship went down fast with a jolting effect on the financial markets and on many individual investors. Enron was one of the largest energy companies in the United States, involved not only in the marketing and distribution of natural gas and other energy resources around the globe but also in trading derivatives that allowed producers and consumers to reduce the risk of energy price fluctuations. For years Enron scored one market success after another, generating excess returns for its shareholders, many of whom were employees and officers of the company.

Unfortunately, a combination of events threw Enron into bankruptcy court as 2001 drew to a close. The company had begun borrowing heavily to support its trading activities and the pile-up of corporate debt, coupled with the sell-off of many of its most valuable assets, made Enron vulnerable to adverse movements in energy prices. Slumping energy prices in the recession of 2001 wreaked havoc with Enron's revenues and asset values and, as the marketplace became aware of its growing financial troubles, the firm's borrowing costs soared. At the same time, investors in the market became aware of questionable accounting practices at the company which tended to inflate the value of its assets and overestimate its gains from market trading activities. Enron's bankruptcy threatened huge losses for many of its employees who had invested their personal savings and pension monies in the firm's stock. Remarkably, Enron's credit rating remained at investment grade until five days before it filed a federal bankruptcy petition, suggesting its problems were well concealed from the public until the last moment.

8.5 New Ways of Dealing with Default Risk: Credit Derivatives

credit derivatives

Rising concern over defaults and business bankruptcies in the 1980s and 1990s led to new techniques for protecting lenders against default risk. These so-called **credit derivatives** are financial contracts that provide at least some positive rate of return to the beneficiaries of each contract.

Among the most popular of these default-risk-protection instruments are *credit swaps,* in which two or more investors in risky loans and securities agree to exchange at least a portion of their expected payments due from borrowers. For example, a swap dealer may draw up an agreement involving two lenders, located in different regions, who pledge to deliver all or part of a $50 million stream of loan payments expected from their customers. Because the contracting lenders serve different market areas, each lender, in effect, is no longer completely dependent on his or her local loan market for revenue. As illustrated in the diagram below, each has geographically diversified its sources of revenue to a greater extent than before.

Diagram for a Credit Swap Arrangement

Credit Swap Dealer

Sends payments received from loans

Sends payments received from loans

Lender or Investor in Loans

Lender or Investor in Loans

Another example of a credit derivative is the *total return swap*. Under this arrangement a swap dealer may provide assurance that parties to this swap receive a minimum rate of return on the credit they have extended to borrowers. For example, the dealer may guarantee a lender a rate of return on its loans at least 2 percentage points higher than the prevailing market yield on long-term Treasury bonds. There is still risk here due to fluctuating interest rates, but the lender's credit risk attached to its loans has been reduced (unless, of course, the guarantor fails).

Under a so-called *credit option* an investor in risky assets may protect itself against such risks as rising borrowing costs or a decline in value of the risky assets it holds in its asset portfolio. For example, a risk-exposed lender may contact a swap dealer about an option contract that pays off if a loan begins to lose value. If the covered loan pays out as expected, the option becomes worthless and the lender loses the option fee that he or she paid. Alternatively, a financial institution about to borrow a large amount of funds and fearing a drop in its credit rating may seek an option contract that reimburses the institution if its borrowing cost rises above some maximum amount (often determined by a maximum "base rate spread" of the risky loan rate over the prevailing riskless rate on government bonds).

Credit derivatives help to reduce default risk by shifting that risk to someone else willing to accept it in return for a fee. They have opened up the money and capital markets to a wider range of risky borrowers. However, this is a comparatively young financial marketplace that remains largely untested. Standardization of credit derivative contracts is under way, but many legal issues are open to controversy. Some credit-risk contracts have provisions that are vague about what represents a true default on a loan contract and, therefore, may result in confusion about what must be paid and when. Then, too, the market, though rapidly growing, is still relatively small and no one is sure that it can withstand a major downturn in the economy.

A Summary of the Default Risk–Interest Rate Relationship

In summary, careful study of the relationship between default risk and interest rates points to a fundamental principle in the field of finance: *default risk and expected return are positively related.* The investor seeking higher expected returns must also be willing to accept higher risk of ruin. Default risk is correlated with both *internal* (borrower-specific) factors associated with a loan and *external* factors (especially the state of the economy and changing demands for industry products and services).

QUESTIONS TO HELP YOU STUDY

1. What does the term *marketability* refer to? Why is it important to the saver and the issuer of a loan or security?

2. What is the relationship between marketability and yield on a financial instrument?

3. Explain the meaning of the term *default risk*. What factors appear to have the most influence upon the degree of default risk displayed by a financial asset?

4. In what ways are security *ratings* designed to reflect default risk?

5. Exactly what are *junk bonds?* Why are they issued? How does their actual yield compare to their degree of default risk? Why do you think this is so?

6. What are *credit derivatives?* What are their principal advantages and disadvantages?

8.6 Call Privileges and Call Risk

call privilege

Some corporate bonds, mortgages, municipal revenue bonds, and federal government bonds carry a **call privilege.** This provision of a bond contract (indenture) grants the borrower the option to retire all or a portion of a bond issue by buying back the bonds in advance of their maturity. Bondholders usually are informed of a call through a notice in a newspaper of general circulation, while holders of record of registered bonds are notified directly. Normally, when the call privilege is exercised, the security issuer will pay the investor the *call price,* which equals the securities' face value plus a call penalty. The size of the *call penalty* is set forth in the indenture (contract) and generally varies inversely with the number of years remaining to maturity and the length of the call deferment period. In the case of a bond, one year's worth of coupon income is often the minimum call penalty required.

Calculating the Yields on Called Financial Assets

Bonds and selected other financial assets may be callable immediately, or the privilege may be deferred (postponed) for a time. In the corporate sector, bonds usually are not eligible for call for a period of 5 to 10 years after issue (known as a *call deferment period*) to give investors at least some protection against early redemption. Of course, calling a callable asset in advance of its final maturity can have a significant impact on the investor's effective yield, resulting in substantial *call risk.*

To demonstrate this, we recall from Chapter 6 that the yield to maturity of any financial asset is that discount rate, y, which equates the security's price, P, with the present value of all its future cash flows, I_t. In symbols:

$$P = \frac{I_1}{(1 + y)^1} + \frac{I_2}{(1 + y)^2} + \cdots + \frac{I_n}{(1 + y)^n} \tag{8.6}$$

where n is the number of periods until maturity. Suppose that after k periods (with $k < n$), the borrower exercises the call option and redeems the called asset. The investor will receive the call price (C) for the asset, which can be reinvested at the current market interest rate, i. If the investor's planned holding period ends in time period n, the expected holding-period yield (h) can be calculated using the formula:

$$P = \frac{I_1}{(1 + h)^1} + \frac{I_2}{(1 + h)^2} + \cdots + \frac{I_k}{(1 + h)^k} + \frac{i \times C_{k+1}}{(1 + h)^{k+1}}$$

$$+ \frac{i \times C_{k+2}}{(1 + h)^{k+2}} + \cdots + \frac{i \times C_n}{(1 + h)^n} + \frac{C}{(1 + h)^n} \tag{8.7}$$

Using summation signs, this reduces to

$$P = \sum_{t=1}^{k} \frac{I_t}{(1 + h)^t} + \sum_{t=k+1}^{n} \frac{i \times C_t}{(1 + h)^t} + \frac{C}{(1 + h)^n} \tag{8.8}$$

The first term in Equation 8.8 gives the present value of all expected cash flows (I) from a callable instrument until it is actually called in time period k. The second term captures the present value of income received by the investor after he or she reinvests at interest rate i the call price (C) received from the security issuer. The third and final term in the equation shows the current discounted value of the call price the investor expects to receive when the holding period ends in time period n.

As an example, let's suppose that a corporate bond, originally offering investors an 8 percent coupon rate for 10 years and issued at $1,000 par, is called five years after its issue date when going market interest rates on investments of comparable risk are 6 percent. What is this bond's 10-year holding-period yield (h) if its call price equals par ($1,000) plus one year's worth of coupon income ($80)? We have:

$$1,000 = \sum_{t=1}^{5} \frac{\$80}{(1 + h)^t} + \sum_{t=6}^{10} \frac{\$1,080 \times .06}{(1 + h)^t} + \frac{\$1,080}{(1 + h)^{10}} \qquad (8.9)$$

The reader, using an electronic calculator, should verify that h, the 10-year holding-period yield, is 7.94 percent in this example. Thus, the investor holding this bond would receive 0.06 percent *less* in yield than if the bond had *not* been called but had instead been held to maturity.

Equations 8.8 and 8.9 shows clearly that the investor in callable assets encounters two major uncertainties:

1. The investor does not know if or when the callable assets might be called (i.e., the value of k).
2. The investor does not know the market yield (reinvestment rate, i) that might prevail at the time the asset is called.

Therefore, how aggressively the investor chooses to bid for a callable instrument will depend upon:

1. The investor's expectations regarding future changes in interest rates, especially decreases in rates, during the term of the callable instrument.
2. The length of the deferment period before the asset is eligible to be called.
3. The call price (par value plus call penalty) the issuer is willing to pay to redeem the callable instrument.

Advantages and Disadvantages of the Call Privilege

Clearly, the call privilege (which is a type of *option*) is an advantage to the security issuer because it grants greater financial flexibility and the potential for reducing future interest costs. On the other hand, the call privilege is a distinct disadvantage to the security buyer, who may suffer a decline in expected holding-period yield if the security is called. The issuer will call in a security if the market rate of interest falls far enough so that the savings from issuing a new security at lower interest rates more than offset the call penalty plus flotation costs of a new security issue. This means, however, that the investor who is paid off will be forced to reinvest the call price in lower-yielding assets.

Another disadvantage for the investor is that call privileges limit the potential increase in a financial asset's market price. In general, the market price of an asset will not rise significantly above its call price. The reason is that the issuer can call in an asset at its call price, presenting the investor with a loss equal to the difference between the prevailing market price and the call price. Thus, callable securities tend to have more limited potential for capital gains than noncallable securities.

The Call Premium and Interest Rate Expectations

For all these reasons, financial assets that carry a call privilege generally sell at lower prices and higher interest rates than noncallable assets. Moreover, there is an inverse relationship between the length of the call deferment period and the required rate of interest on callable instruments. The longer the period of deferment and, therefore, the longer the investor is protected against early redemption and possible loss of yield, the lower the interest rate the borrower must pay. Issuers of callable assets must pay a *call premium* in the form of a higher rate of interest for the option of early redemption and for a shorter deferment period.

The key determinant of the size of the call premium is the *interest rate expectations* of investors in the marketplace. If interest rates are expected to rise, the risk that a callable asset will actually be called is low. Borrowers are unlikely to call in their securities and issue new ones at a higher interest rate. As a result, the yield differential between callable and noncallable instruments normally will be minimal. The same conclusions apply even if interest rates are expected to decline moderately but not enough to entice borrowers to call in already-issued financial assets and issue new ones.

Securities are most likely to be called when interest rates are expected to fall substantially. In this instance, security issuers can save large amounts of money—more than enough to cover the call penalty plus flotation costs of issuing new instruments—by exercising the call privilege. Thus, the call premium is likely to be significant, as investors demand a higher yield on callable issues to compensate them for increased *call risk.* For example, the yield spreads between callable bonds with long call deferments and those with short or no call deferments widen during such periods as investors come to value more highly the call deferment feature.

Research Evidence on Call Privileges and Call Risk

Is there evidence of an expected *inverse* relationship between interest rate expectations and the value of the call privilege? Research studies generally answer in the affirmative. For example, when interest rates are high, the call premium rises, because investors expect interest rates to fall in the future, resulting in more callable assets being called in. Call provisions also influence yield spreads between corporate bonds, some of which have the call privilege attached, and government bonds, which generally are *not* subject to call. For example, when interest rates are expected to fall, the spread between corporate and government bond rates tends to widen. Moreover, bonds carrying a call deferment have lower rates of return than bonds that are callable immediately.

Research also suggests that calling in bonds to save on interest costs may be a "zero sum game" between the bondholders and the stockholders of a company issuing callable bonds. Gains by stockholders (due to higher earnings from savings on interest costs) may be offset by losses for the bondholders (in the form of a lower effective holding-period yield). Generally, a call will occur when the owners of the issuing firm believe they will benefit at the expense of the firm's creditors. In an efficient market, with all participants possessing identical interest rate expectations, callable assets will sell at a price and yield just sufficient to compensate buyers for call risk. Therefore, in theory at least, management of the issuing firm should be indifferent between issuing callable or noncallable bonds. Under some circumstances, however, call provisions may be beneficial to the callable security issuer where management believes it has greater knowledge of the future course of interest rates than does the market as a whole, where a call provision prevents security holders from blocking beneficial investments that a security-issuing entity might make, or where a call privilege lowers the sensitivity of a callable asset's market value to changes in interest rates. Additional research is needed to clarify more precisely who the winners and losers are likely to be from transactions involving callable instruments.

In recent years, the proportion of corporate bonds issued with call privileges attached has declined significantly. One reason is the large number of shorter bond maturities, which means that issuing companies have less need to call in their outstanding bonds before they reach maturity. Then, too, there has been a virtual explosion in new financial instruments to hedge bond issues against interest rate risk, including financial futures, options, and swaps, also reducing the need for the interest rate protection afforded by the call privilege. Finally, the yield premium associated with issuing callable bonds, rather than noncallable bonds, appears to have increased over the years, discouraging many corporations from issuing bonds bearing a call feature. However, some institutions, such as the giant mortgage companies Fannie Mae (FNMA) and Freddie Mac (FHLMC), have issued large amounts of long-term callable debt to protect their income when market interest rates fall.

8.7 Prepayment Risk and the Yields on Loan-Backed Securities

A newer form of risk affecting the relative interest rates confronting modern investors arises when they acquire so-called *loan-backed securities,* such as mortgage passthroughs, collateralized mortgage obligations (CMOs), auto-loan-backed securities, and credit-card-backed securities. These instruments are usually created when a lending institution, such as a bank or mortgage company, removes a group of similar loans from its balance sheet and places them with a trustee (such as a security dealer) who, using the loans as collateral, sells securities to raise new capital for the lending institution. Each of these securities derives its value from the income-earning potential of the pool of loans that backs the securities. As the loans in the pool generate interest and principal payments, these payments flow through to holders of the loan-backed instruments.

Unlike ordinary bonds, which usually pay nothing but interest until they finally reach maturity, loan-backed financial instruments pay their purchasers a stream of income that includes *both* repayments of loan principal and interest. In this case, the purchaser may receive higher-than-expected repayments of principal early in the life of the pooled loans, possibly lowering his or her expected return from loan-backed securities. Investors in those loan-backed instruments that carry substantial **prepayment risk** will demand higher yields to compensate them for the risk associated with early prepayment of the loans backing the securities they hold.

Prepayment risk is especially troublesome for investors purchasing securities that are backed by pools of home mortgage loans. The pool of loans serving as collateral for these instruments generally consists of 25- and 30-year loans to purchase new homes. Many of these home loans will be retired early due to: (1) *refinancing of loans,* as homeowners try to get new, cheaper mortgage loans in order to lower their monthly mortgage payments as market interest rates fall; and (2) *home-owner turnover,* as families move and need to sell their homes or simply default on their loans.

The investor interested in purchasing loan-backed financial instruments needs to make certain assumptions about the likely prepayment behavior of the loans in the pool in order to decide what the true value of the loan-backed assets must be. Each package of pooled loans would have somewhat different characteristics due to variations in loan quality and location, the condition of the economy, and other factors. The current value of a loan-backed security can be determined from:

prepayment risk

$$\begin{array}{l} \text{Market value} \\ \text{(price) of} \\ \text{loan-backed} \\ \text{security} \end{array} = \frac{\begin{array}{c}\text{Expected}\\\text{cash flow}\\\text{including projected}\\\text{prepayments of}\\\text{loans in period 1}\end{array}}{(1 + y/m)^1} + \frac{\begin{array}{c}\text{Expected}\\\text{cash flow}\\\text{including projected}\\\text{prepayments of}\\\text{loans in period 2}\end{array}}{(1 + y/m)^2} + \cdots + \frac{\begin{array}{c}\text{Expected}\\\text{cash flow}\\\text{including projected}\\\text{prepayments of}\\\text{loans in period n}\end{array}}{(1 + y/m)^{m \times n}}$$

(8.10)

where y is the financial asset's yield to maturity, m is the number of times during a year that interest and principal payments occur, and n is the total number of years covered by the pooled loans. Note that each expected cash flow from a loan-backed instruments must be adjusted to reflect the risk that some loans will pay out early, increasing cash flows to an investor in these securities in the early years and, thus, reducing an investor's expected cash flow from these instruments in later years. The greater the prepayment risk, the higher the yield tends to rise and the lower the loan-backed security's price tends to go.[2]

One of the most popular devices today used to reduce prepayment risk from loan-backed instruments is to divide the loan-backed security issue into classes or *tranches* bearing different degrees of estimated prepayment risk. Each tranche promises a different rate of return based on a different maturity and risk profile. The shortest maturity tranches (usually designated Tranche A) receive principal payments from prepaid loans *first* until all Tranche A securities are paid off. Then loan prepayments flow to investors in Tranche B, who are willing to accept somewhat higher prepayment risk, until this second group is also paid off. The process of directed repayments continues until the entire loan-backed security issue is retired.

In short, the upper (shorter-maturity) tranches carry lower prepayment risk and, therefore, promise a lower rate of return, while the lower (longer-maturity) tranches reflect higher prepayment risk but promise a greater expected return. Different groups of investors prefer different tranches of loan repayments based on their portfolio characteristics, risk exposures, and regulations. For example, banks that face more volatile, short-term claims against them tend to prefer investing in shorter tranches, while insurance companies and pension funds with longer-term liabilities tend to seek out loan-backed securities in longer-maturity tranches.

QUESTIONS TO HELP YOU STUDY

7. What is a *call privilege?* Why is this privilege an advantage to a security issuer and a disadvantage to a buyer of financial instruments?

8. What types of *risk* are encountered by purchasers of callable *financial instruments?*

9. What is *prepayment risk?* What factors lead to an increase in prepayment risk?

10. How can a buyer of loan-backed assets reduce prepayment risk?

11. What is meant by the term *event risk* (see the nearby Financial Developments feature)? What factors appear to contribute to an increase in a corporation's stock price? A decrease in its stock price?

---

[2]Actually, the relationship between the value of a loan-backed instrument and changes in market interest rates is quite complicated. For example, when interest rates fall, investors in loan-backed instruments will experience quicker recovery of their invested funds, as more borrowers repay their loans early and the lower interest rates increase the present value of the loan-backed instruments' cash flow. On the other hand, with more loans paid off early, the investor loses future interest payments that will never be received, and the funds received by the investor will have to be reinvested at lower market interest rates, reducing future earnings from the instrument. Generally, a loan-backed asset will fall in value when lost interest payments and reduced reinvestment income offset the benefits from quicker recovery of principal and a lower discount rate applied to future cash flows.

Event Risk—Another Factor Affecting Interest Rates and Asset Prices

risk

Research in recent years has revealed another risk factor that often affects the market value of debt and equity securities issued by corporations and other units raising funds in the money and capital markets. This **event risk** factor consists of news announcements that reflect decisions by the management of a corporation or other fund-raising unit. Examples include announcements of new

stock or bond offerings, changes in corporate dividend payments, stock splits, mergers and acquisitions, replacement of old with new management, new product offerings, etc.

Financial research suggests that announcements of events like these tend to have fairly predictable impacts on asset values and borrowing costs. For example,

Event	Expected Market Response
Announcement of a new security issue	The issuer's security prices usually fall, at least temporarily.
Announcement of an increased stock dividend	The issuer's security prices usually rise, at least temporarily.
Announcement of a stock split	The issuer's security prices usually rise, at least temporarily.
Debt-equity swap (a company's bonds are replaced by stock)	The company's stock price usually falls, at least temporarily.

Many financial analysts believe that events such as the foregoing trigger changes in asset prices and interest rates for the affected institutions because they convey *new information* about the possible future performance of these institutions. For example, the management of a business firm possesses inside (asymmetric) information on the firm's true financial condition. Presumably, management draws on this inside information when it elects to go ahead with a new security offering, a change in dividends paid to stockholders, launching a new product, etc. Investors in the

marketplace regard announcements of such "events" as a revelation of how management views the firm's future prospects. The result is a reevaluation by investors of the value of a security issuer's stocks and bonds. Market prices and yields of those securities therefore will change with the appearance of new information.

Sources: See, for example, P. Asquith and T. A. Wizman, "Event Risk, Bond Covenants, and the Return to Existing Bondholders in Corporate Buyouts," *Journal of Financial Economics* 27 (September 1990), pp. 195– 213.

8.8 Taxation of Returns on Financial Assets

Recent Changes in Tax Laws

For information about tax policy and filling out U.S. tax forms, see especially **federal taxreturn.com** and **irs.gov**

Taxes imposed by federal, state, and local governments have a profound effect on the returns earned by investors on financial assets. The income from most securities—interest or dividends and capital gains—is subject to taxation at the federal level and by many state and local governments as well. Government uses its taxing power to encourage the purchase of certain financial assets and, thereby, redirect the flow of savings and investment toward areas of critical social need.

In 1986, the U.S. Congress enacted the Tax Reform Act, which resulted in major changes in personal and business tax rates in the United States, with major redistributive effects on the financial markets, the supply of savings, and the demand for loanable funds. Further changes were made in the federal tax code in 1990 and 1993 as the result of budget compromises between the president and Congress. The 1986 Tax

Reform Law had reduced both personal and corporate tax rates; however, tax rates on high-income individuals and corporations went up again during the 1990s. Capital gains tax rates (previously as low as 20 percent) were first increased, and then late in the 1990s were scaled back with passage of the 1997 Taxpayer Relief Act, designed to stimulate additional saving and investment. As a result, the longest-held investments faced considerably lower capital gains tax rates.

For example, short-term capital gains on assets held less than one year were to be taxed at the individual investor's ordinary marginal income tax bracket rate, which at the time could range as high as 39.6 percent for those with the highest taxable incomes. Thus, a top-tax-bracket investor, buying the stock of XYZ Corporation for $1,900 and later selling it during the same year for $3,100, would experience a taxable short-term gain of $1,200. This top-income-earner would have incurred a tax liability of $1,200 × 0.396, or $475.20.

However, long-term capital gains received after holding an asset for at least 18 months could be assessed no more than a 20 percent tax rate (and for assets held more than 12 months but less than 18 months, a maximum of 28 percent) up through the year 2000. After 2000, long-term capital gains tax rates were set at a maximum of 18 percent. Thus, the top-bracket taxpayer who previously owed $475.20 on the $1,200 gain described above then faced a maximum tax of only $1,200 × 0.18, or $216.00, if the $1,200 gain was a long-term capital gain. For investors in one of the lowest income tax brackets (15 percent), the capital gains tax rate would be as small as only 8 percent of any long-term gains received by these taxpayers.

The Taxpayer Relief Act of 1997 also endeavored to encourage individuals and families to save more by awarding tax exemptions to people (1) selling their homes; (2) setting aside savings for a college education; (3) buying a new home; (4) preparing for retirement; or (5) who might die with substantial accumulations of retirement savings left over and wish to pass more of those savings along to surviving loved ones or to other individuals or institutions. Estate taxes were substantially lowered, allowing tax-free transfers of up to a million dollars to a deceased person's beneficiaries by the year 2006.

Then, in the spring of 2001, The Economic Growth and Tax Relief Reconciliation Act was passed by Congress and signed into law by President George W. Bush. This sweeping new law was aimed at stimulating the economy and encouraging saving by lowering the tax rates carried by households (individuals and families) and allowing greater use of retirement and educational savings instruments (such as IRAs and Keoghs) than in the past. Among other major changes, the 2001 tax bill created a new low 10 percent tax bracket and gradually adjusted other income tax rates downward, increased the permissible tax credit for children, and called for a phaseout of estate taxes to be completed in 2010. However, most of these changes were stretched out over the first decade of the twenty-first century and the Tax Relief Act contained an unusual "sunset provision" which mandated that the new law's provisions would expire on December 31, 2010 unless extended in time by new legislation.

Finally, on May 28, 2003, President Bush signed the Jobs and Growth Tax Relief Reconciliation Act. Among the most important (though temporary) provisions of this latest federal tax law was a reduction in the ordinary federal income tax rates for individuals, with the top-bracket tax rate falling from 38.6 percent to 35 percent. Tax brackets were further adjusted to allow more households to qualify for the lowest tax rate of 10 percent (at least through 2004).

Particularly important for financial assets, both dividends on corporate stock and long-term capital gains on a wide range of assets were assigned lower tax rates. For example, the tax rate on *dividend income* was temporarily lowered (at least until 2009) to a top dividend tax rate of only 15 percent, whereas earlier dividend tax rates had ranged as high as 38.6 percent. One immediate consequence of this provision was to stimulate demand for dividend-paying stocks, driving their prices substantially higher. The top tax rate for *long-term capital gains* from assets held more than a year was pushed down to 15 percent (at least until 2009). Thus, for the $1,200 long-term capital gain described in the example above, the applicable tax would now be only $1,200 × 0.15, or $180 for a top-income-bracket investor. The same tax of $180 would apply to a top-tax-bracket investor receiving a $1,200 stock dividend. Thus, the U.S. Congress and the president sought to encourage long-term investment in an effort to stimulate a struggling economy.

Treatment of Capital Losses

For further discussion of the latest U.S. tax laws see, for example, such sources as tax planet.com/prez and taxes.about.com

Net losses on investments in financial assets are deductible for tax purposes within well-defined limits. For the individual taxpayer, a net capital loss is deductible up to the amount of the capital loss, the size of ordinary income, or $3,000, whichever is smaller. For example, suppose an investor experiences a net loss on securities held and then sold of $8,000. Suppose this person receives other taxable income of $20,000. How much of the capital loss can be deducted? What is this taxpayer's total taxable income? The maximum loss deduction in this case is $3,000, and therefore the taxpayer's net taxable income is $17,000 ($20,000 minus the $3,000 in deductible losses). Current federal law allows the taxpayer to carry forward into subsequent years the remaining portion of the loss ($5,000 in this example) until all of the loss has been deducted from ordinary income, but the loss cannot be carried backward.

Tax-Exempt Securities

tax-exempt securities

One of the most controversial tax rules affecting securities is the tax-exemption privilege granted investors in state and local government (municipal) bonds. The interest income earned on municipal bonds is exempt from federal income taxes.[3] **Tax-exempt securities** represent a subsidy to induce investors to support local government by financing the construction of schools, highways, airports, and other needed public projects. The exemption privilege shifts the burden of federal taxation from buyers of municipal bonds to other taxpayers.

What investors benefit from buying municipals? The critical factor here is the marginal tax rate (tax bracket) of the investor—the tax rate he or she must pay on the last dollar of income received during the tax year. For individual investors, these marginal tax rates range from zero for nontaxpayers to as high as about 35 percent for the highest income-earning taxpayers. (See Exhibit 8.5 for an example of recent tax rates for individuals and corporations.) The marginal tax rate for corporations is 15 percent on the first $50,000 in taxable profits up to as high as 39 percent on net income above $100,000 to $335,000 and up to 38 percent for corporations earning $15 million to about $18⅓ million annually. In recent years, marginal tax rates of approximately 20 to 30 percent have represented a break-even level for investors interested in municipal bonds. Investors carrying marginal tax rates above this range often receive higher after-tax yields from buying tax-exempt securities instead of taxable securities. Below this range, taxable securities often yield a better after-tax return.

---

[3]Although the interest income from municipals is federal income tax exempt, capital gains on municipals are generally taxable as ordinary income. In addition, most states do not tax income from their own bonds or from the bonds issued by local governments within their borders. Income from U.S. government securities is usually exempt from state and local taxes but not from federal taxes.

| EXHIBIT 8.5 | Examples of Recent Marginal Federal Income Tax Rates (Individual and Corporate Tax Brackets Shown) |

INCOME TAX BRACKETS AND TAX RATES FOR SINGLE AND MARRIED TAXPAYERS (2004)

INCOME TAX BRACKETS AND TAX RATES FOR CORPORATIONS PAYING TAXES (2000–2004)

Single Taxpayers' Taxable Incomes	Married Taxpayers' Taxable Incomes*	Marginal Tax Brackets (%)	Taxable Income Bracket	Base Amount Owed	Marginal Tax Rate Applied to Excess over Base
$0–$7,150	$0–$14,300	10%	Less than $50,000	$ 0	15%
$7,150–$29,050	$14,300–$58,100	15	$50,000–$75,000	7,500	25
$29,050–$70,350	$58,100–$117,250	25	$75,000–$100,000	13,750	34
$70,350–$146,750	$117,250–$178,650	28	$100,000–$335,000	22,250	39
$146,750–$319,100	$178,650–$319,100	33	$335,000–$10 million	113,900	34
$319,100 and over	$319,100 and over	35	$10 million–$15 million	3.4 million	35
			$15 million–$18.33$^1/_3$ million	5.15 million	38
			Over 18.33^1/_3$ million	6.416$^2/_3$ million	35

*Married taxpayers are assumed to be filing jointly.

Source: U.S. Treasury Department.

How would an individual figure his or her income tax? Suppose you are single and have taxable annual income (that is, gross income receipts less all exemptions and deductions allowable under tax law) of $25,000. Then you would owe:

Base amount owed + Excess income above preceding tax bracket × Marginal tax rate
$715 + ($25,000 − $7,150) × 0.15, or
$715 + $2,677.50
= $3,392.50 in total federal income taxes owed

What about a corporation? Suppose the company had annual net income (earnings) before taxes of $250,000. Then the company would owe federal taxes in the amount of:

Base amount owed + Excess earnings above preceding tax bracket × Marginal tax rate
$22,250 + ($250,000 − $100,000) × 0.39, or
$22,250 + $19,500
= $41,750 in taxes owed

Note: The taxable individual income brackets shown change each year as the inflation rate moves because the federal tax structure in the United States is indexed to inflation in order to at least partially prevent taxpayers from paying higher and higher taxes due solely to rising prices for goods and services. The above marginal tax rates do not reflect the Social Security Program's tax structure, which stands at 6.2 percent for up to $87,000 of annual earned income or 12.4 percent for a self-employed individual. There is also a 1.45 percent Medicare payroll tax levy against all of a person's annual earned income and, if you are self-employed, this Medicare tax rate jumps to 2.9 percent of annual earned income.

The Effect of Marginal Tax Rates on After-Tax Yields To illustrate the importance of knowing the investor's marginal tax rate in deciding whether to purchase tax-exempt assets, consider the following example. Assume the current yield to maturity on taxable corporate bonds is 12 percent, while the current tax-exempt yield on municipal bonds of comparable quality and rating is 9 percent. The after-tax yield on these two securities can be compared using the following formula:

$$\text{Before-tax yield} (1 - \text{Investor's marginal tax rate}) = \text{After-tax yield} \quad (8.11)$$

For example, for an investor in the 28 percent tax bracket (see Exhibit 8.5), the after-tax yields on these bonds are as follows:

Taxable Corporate Bond	Tax-Exempt Municipal Bond
12% (1 − 0.28) = 8.64%	9% before and after taxes

On the basis of yield alone, the investor in the 28 percent tax bracket would prefer the tax-exempt municipal bond.[4]

At what rate would an investor be *indifferent* as to whether securities are taxable or tax exempt? In other words, what is the break-even point between these two types of financial assets?

This point is easily calculated from the formula

$$\text{Tax-exempt yield} = (1 - t) \times \text{Taxable yield} \qquad (8.12)$$

where t is the investor's marginal tax rate. Solving for the break-even tax rate gives

$$t = 1 - \frac{\text{Tax-exempt yield}}{\text{Taxable yield}} \qquad (8.13)$$

Clearly, if the current yield is 8 percent on tax-exempt securities and 10 percent on taxable issues, the break-even tax rate is $1 - 0.80$, or 20 percent. An investor in a marginal tax bracket *above* 20 percent would prefer the yield on a tax-exempt security to a taxable one at these prevailing interest rates, other factors held equal.

The Bond Market Association provides a free online calculator to aid investors in comparing tax-exempt bond yields with yields on taxable securities at investinginbonds.com

Comparing Taxable and Tax-Exempt Securities The existence of both taxable and tax-exempt securities complicates the investor's task in trying to choose a suitable portfolio to buy and hold. To make valid comparisons between taxable and tax-exempt issues, the taxed investor must convert all expected yields to an *after-tax basis*.

In the case of the yield to maturity on a security, this can be done by using the following formula:

$$P_0 = \sum_{i=1}^{n} \frac{I_i(1 - t)}{(1 + a)^i} + \frac{(P_n - P_0)(1 - t_{cg})}{(1 + a)^n} + \frac{P_0}{(1 + a)^n} \qquad (8.14)$$

which equates the current market value (P_0) of the security to the present value of all after-tax returns promised in the future. If the security is to be held for n years, I_i is the amount of interest or other income expected each year, and t is the marginal income tax rate of the investor. If we assume the security will be sold or redeemed for price P_n at maturity, then ($P_n - P_0$) measures the expected capital gain on the instrument, which will be taxed at a rate, t_{cg}, which equals the taxpayer's ordinary income tax rate—up to a maximum of 15 percent under the most recent U.S. tax laws. Provided investors know their marginal income tax rate, the current price of the security, and the expected distribution of future income from the security, they can easily calculate discount rate a—the after-tax yield to maturity.

For example, consider the case of a $1,000 corporate bond selling for $900 (with par value of $1,000), maturing in 10 years, with a 10 percent coupon rate. If an investor

---

[4]The particular tax brackets favoring the purchase of municipals versus taxable securities change over time due to changes in tax laws and variations in the yield spread between taxable and tax-exempt securities.

in the 33 percent federal income tax bracket buys and holds the bond to maturity, her after-tax yield, a, could be found from evaluating the following:

$$\$900 = \sum_{i=1}^{10} \frac{\$100(1 - 0.33)}{(1 + a)^i} + \frac{(\$1,000 - \$900)(1 - 0.15)}{(1 + a)^{10}} + \frac{\$900}{(1 + a)^{10}}$$

In this instance, the reader should verify, using a financial calculator, that the after-tax yield, a, is close to 8.10 percent, assuming a 15 percent capital gains tax rate (t_{cg}).

Certainly, the tax-exempt privilege has lowered the interest rates at which municipals can be sold in the open market relative to taxable bonds and, therefore, the amount of interest costs borne by local taxpayers. For example, in April 2004, top-quality municipal bonds carried an average yield to maturity of about 4.69 percent, compared to 5.73 percent on comparable quality (taxable) corporate bonds—a yield spread of more than 1 percentage point or 110 basis points. However, the primary beneficiaries of the exemption privilege are investors who can profitably purchase municipals and escape some portion of the federal tax burden. Other taxpayers must pay higher federal taxes in order to make up for those lost tax revenues. By limiting the municipal market to these high tax-bracket investors, the tax-exempt feature has probably increased the volatility of municipal bond interest rates and made the job of fiscal management for state and local governments somewhat more difficult.

8.9 Convertible Securities

convertibility

Another factor that affects relative rates of return among different financial assets is **convertibility.** Convertible financial instruments consist of special issues of corporate bonds or preferred stock that entitle the holder to exchange these assets for a specific number of shares of the issuing firm's common stock. For example, Internet giant Amazon.com issued more than a billion dollars in 10-year convertible bonds in 1999, promising an annual interest return of 4.75 percent. Buyers were given the option, to be exercised at any time after issue, of exchanging each $1,000 bond for just slightly more than 6.4 shares of Amazon's common stock.

Convertibles are frequently called *hybrid securities* because they offer the investor the prospect of stable income in the form of interest or dividends plus capital gains on common stock once conversion occurs. While the timing of a conversion is most often at the option of the investor, an issuing firm often can "force" conversion of its securities by either calling them in or encouraging a rise in the price of its common stock (such as by announcing a merger offer) because conversion is most likely in a rising market.

Recent growth of convertible securities has led to the appearance of many new Web sites discussing convertibles. One example is convertbond.com

Investors generally pay a premium for convertible securities over nonconvertible securities in the form of a higher price (and, in the case of convertible bonds, a lower promised rate of interest). Thus, convertibles will carry a lower rate of return than other securities of comparable quality and maturity issued by the same company. This occurs because the investor in convertibles is granted a hedge against future market risk. If security prices fall, the investor still earns a fixed rate of return in the form of interest income from a convertible bond or dividend income from convertible preferred stock. On the other hand, if stock prices rise, the investor can exercise his or her option and share in any capital gains earned on the company's common stock.

Advantages for the Corporate Bond Issuer   Convertible bonds offer several significant advantages to the company that decides to issue them. Their most powerful issuer advantage is a *significantly lower interest cost* because, unlike conventional bonds, convertibles give the buyer potential access to capital gains and dividends from the stock that may replace the convertibles in the future.

An interesting illustration of this substantial interest-cost advantage appeared in the corporate bond market early in 2004. Among the 40 most actively traded corporate bonds in the United States at that time were two convertible issues: a Duke Energy Corp. convertible bearing a promised (coupon) rate of only 1.75 percent and a convertible issued by Walt Disney Corporation promising an interest return to the investor of only 2.25 percent. In contrast, the 38 other most actively traded corporate bonds carried promised (coupon) rates ranging from 3.5 percent to 8.75 percent. Similarly, among the 10 most actively traded junk bonds early in 2004 were those issued by Advanced Micro Devices and Amazon.com, bearing promised interest rates of 4.5 percent and 4.75 percent, respectively, while the remaining junk bonds on the most actively traded list promised investors interest returns ranging from 7.25 to 10.375 percent.

A second powerful advantage to issuers of convertible bonds is the ability to *avoid issuing more common stock*. For a time, convertibles allow a firm to delay selling new stock. This may be desirable because the added shares may dilute the equity interests of current stockholders and reduce their earnings per share.

Finally, a third important advantage is *tax savings*. Interest on convertible bonds is a tax-deductible expense in the United States and many other countries. Dividends on stock, on the other hand, are not deductible from federal income taxes, though recent tax legislation in the United States has somewhat reduced the tax burden associated with stock dividends.

Advantages for the Investor in Convertible Bonds   Key advantages for an investor buying convertible bonds include, as seen above, the receipt of at least some interest income, even when the value of the common stock of the issuing company is on the decline. Moreover, if the issuer's common stock is rising in price, the same company's convertibles also tend to increase in value.

Moreover, there is a floor under the price of a convertible bond—known as its *investment value*—below which its price normally will not fall. This is the price that would produce a yield on the convertible equal to the yield on nonconvertible bonds of the same quality. However, investors are often counseled by financial analysts not to buy convertibles unless they would be happy holding the issuing company's stock, because the issuer may call in the securities early, forcing conversion. This particular situation may present the investor with a substantially reduced rate of return.

8.10 The Structure of Interest Rates in the Financial System

As we conclude this chapter, it is important to gain some perspective on the fundamental purpose of this section of the book. In reality, Chapters 5, 6, 7, and 8 should be viewed as a unit, tied together by a common subject: what determines the level of and changes in interest rates and asset yields. In Chapter 5, we argued that there is *one* interest rate that underlies all interest rates and is a component of all rates. This is the *risk-free* (or pure) rate of interest, which is a measure of the opportunity cost of holding cash and a measure of the reward for saving rather than spending all of our income on consumption. All other interest rates are scaled upward by varying degrees from the risk-free rate, depending on such factors as inflation, the term (maturity) of a loan, the risk of borrower default, the risk of prepayment, and the marketability, liquidity, convertibility, and tax status of the financial assets to which those rates apply.

There is, then, a *structure* to interest rates whose foundation is the risk-free rate (as determined by the demand and supply for loanable funds described in Chapter 5).

EXHIBIT 8.6   An Example of the Structure of Interest Rates in the Financial System

During the month of January 2004: The long-term U.S. Treasury bond rate averaged 5.05% + 1.39% = 6.44%   while the Corporate Baa bond rate averaged:

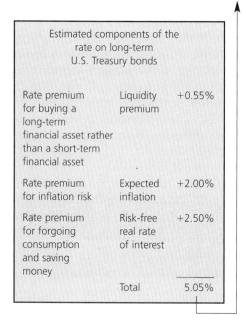

Estimated components of the rate on long-term U.S. Treasury bonds		
Rate premium for buying a long-term financial asset rather than a short-term financial asset	Liquidity premium	+0.55%
Rate premium for inflation risk	Expected inflation	+2.00%
Rate premium for forgoing consumption and saving money	Risk-free real rate of interest	+2.50%
	Total	5.05%

Estimated components of the rate or yield spread between corporate Baa bond rate and long-term Treasury bond rate		
Rate premium for accepting a less market-able financial asset	Premium for lower marketability	+0.14%
Rate premium for accepting risk financial asset might be called	Call risk premium	+0.25%
Rate premium for accepting risk of borrower default	Default-risk premium	+1.00%
	Total	1.39%

Source: Bond rates derived from *Statistical Supplement to the Federal Reserve Bulletin,* April 2004, Table 1.35; interest-rate components estimated by the authors.

interest rate structure   Perhaps one picture of that **interest rate structure** is worth a thousand words. Recently, the yield to maturity on long-term U.S. Treasury bonds was reported as close to 5.05 percent, while corporate Baa bonds were quoted at an average yield of about 6.44 percent. As Exhibit 8.6 indicates, each of these rates, like *all* interest rates, is a summation of rewards (premiums) paid to lenders of funds to get those investors to hold a particular financial asset. Each reward or premium is merely compensation for bearing some kind of *risk,* for example: (1) the risk of giving up liquidity and accepting greater market risk from buying a longer maturity asset, (2) the risk of inflation (loss of purchasing power) over the term of an asset, (3) the risk that the borrower will default on some or all of his promised payments, (4) the risk that some assets can be called in before they mature and the investor may have to reinvest her money at a lower interest rate, and (5) the risk of taking an asset with a weak resale market (low marketability). Each interest rate or yield that we see in today's market is the *sum* of all of these risk premium factors plus the real risk-free interest rate. And when interest rates change, that change may be due to a change in the risk-free rate or to a change in any of the risk premium factors cited above.

Truly, interest rates are a complex phenomenon, affected by many factors. We need to keep this complexity in mind as we proceed to the next chapter and take on the difficult task of trying to anticipate and forecast interest rate changes and discover how to hedge against possible losses due to interest rate movements.

QUESTIONS TO HELP YOU STUDY

12. What types of financial instruments are most favored by tax laws?

13. What portion of the income generated by municipal bonds is considered tax-exempt and what portion is taxable income? Why do you think the United States' laws are structured in this way?

14. Explain the relationship between a taxpayer's marginal tax rate and after-tax returns on corporate and municipal bonds. Would municipals be a worthwhile investment for you today? Explain why or why not.

15. What does *convertibility* refer to? Why are convertibles called *hybrid securities?*

16. Convertibles typically carry lower yields than nonconvertibles of the same maturity and risk class. Can you explain why?

17. What does *interest rate structure* refer to? What does the structure of interest rates tell us about the difficulties involved in forecasting interest rates?

MARKETS ON THE NET: The Most Important Web Sites for This Chapter

Duff & Phelps Credit Rating Co. (duffllc.com)
Federal Reserve Bank of Cleveland (clev.frb.org/research)
Federal Reserve System (federalreserve.gov/releases/)
Fitch Ratings (fitchratings.com)
High Yield or "Junk" Bonds (finpipe.com/bndjnk.htm)

Moody's Investors Service (moodys.com)
Standard & Poor's Corporation (standardpoor.com)
The Bond Market Association (investinginbonds.com)
Thomson Bank Watch (bankwatch.com)

Summary of the Chapter's Main Points

This chapter has focused our attention upon multiple factors that cause interest rates and prices to differ between one type of financial asset and another, including marketability, liquidity, default risk, call privileges, taxation, prepayment risk, and convertibility. Among the principal conclusions of the chapter are the following:

- *Marketability,* or the capacity to be sold readily, is positively related to an asset's price and negatively related to its rate of return or yield. More marketable financial instruments generally carry lower yields.

- *Liquid* financial instruments also tend to carry lower yields, but possess the advantages of ready marketability, stable price, and reversibility (i.e., the capacity to fully recover the funds originally invested).

- *Default risk*—the danger that a borrower will not make all promised payments at agreed-upon times—results in the promised yields of risky assets rising above the yields on riskless financial instruments. Potential buyers of these instruments compare their estimated (subjective) probability of loss from a risky asset to the market's assigned default-risk premium. For example, if a potential buyer anticipates less risk of loss than suggested by the market's assigned risk premium, he or she will tend to purchase the financial instrument in question because its risky yield appears to be too high and its price too low (i.e., the asset in question looks like a bargain).

- Default-risk premiums attached by the financial marketplace to the promised yields on risky assets tend to be heavily influenced by the *credit ratings* assigned by various credit rating agencies (such as Moody's Investors Service or Standard & Poor's Corporation) and by the condition of the economy. An expanding economy tends to result in lower default-risk premiums, while an economy trapped in a recession with rising business bankruptcies tends to generate higher default-risk premiums on risky assets.

- Many lower-rated companies with questionable credit ratings have issued speculative or *junk bonds* in large quantities in recent years. The rise of junk bonds has broadened the market for corporate debt, offering participating investors substantially higher yields than were previously available.

- Debt securities with *call privileges* attached tend to carry higher promised rates of return than financial instruments not bearing a call privilege. The right of a security issuer to call away the security he or she has previously issued and retire it in return for paying a prespecified price gives borrowers greater flexibility in adapting their capital structure to changing market conditions. Recently call privileges have been declining in use as corporate borrowers have discovered other ways of raising funds and protecting themselves against risk.

- The rapid growth of *loan-backed securities* (such as mortgage-backed instruments) has given rise to *prepayment risk*—the danger that loans used to back loan-backed securities may be paid back early, lowering an investor's expected yield from loan-backed instruments. The rapid expansion of loan-backed assets has made prepayment risk more important with time. Issuers of these instruments have sought to make them more attractive to buyers by creating different maturity classes (*tranches*) so that buyers can select how much prepayment risk they are willing to take on.

- *Event risk* has long been a significant factor in the pricing of corporate stock and debt securities. *Events* that appear to have an especially significant impact upon asset values include announcements of new security issues, stock dividends, stock splits, and management changes within a particular business firm.

- Financial assets generate interest or dividend payments and capital gains or losses—any or all of which may be subject to *taxation* at federal and state levels. Investors must be cognizant of continuing changes in tax laws and regulations. It is also important to be able to calculate tax-exempt yields versus taxable returns because some assets (such as municipal bonds) generate tax-exempt income and some investing institutions (such as credit unions and pension funds) are tax-exempt.

- Some corporate debt and stock instruments carry a *convertibility* feature which allows them to be exchanged for a certain number of shares of stock. Convertibles are often called "hybrid securities" because they offer not only relatively stable income (interest payments or fixed dividends) but also the prospect of substantial capital gains when converted into stock. Assets with convertibility features tend to sell at a higher price and a lower promised yield due to their potential for exceptional gains upon conversion.

- The chapter closes with an overview of the *interest rate structure* model, which aids us in understanding why there are so many different interest rates in the real world. Each different interest rate or yield is viewed in this model as the sum of the risk-free interest rate plus a series of risk premiums dependent on varying degrees of risk exposure. Among the risk premiums included in this model are liquidity and term (or maturity) risk, inflation risk, default risk, call risk, prepayment risk, and exposure to tax risk. Because these risk premiums can change at any time, interest rates themselves may change at any time and the causes of any particular interest-rate movement can be very complex.

Key Terms Appearing in This Chapter

marketability, 206
liquidity, 207
default risk, 207
expected yield, 209
junk bonds, 213
credit derivatives, 216

call privilege, 218
prepayment risk, 221
event risk, 223
tax-exempt securities, 225
convertibility, 228
interest rate structure, 230

Problems and Issues

1. A popular investment strategy for individuals about to retire is to pursue "laddered Treasuries." One example would be to purchase a fixed amount (perhaps $20,000) in 10-year U.S. Treasury notes each year for 10 years. Whenever a note matures, the investor "rolls over" that investment into another 10-year note of comparable size. In answering the following questions think about marketability, default risk, call provisions, and liquidity in addition to expected rates of return.

   a. Explain why this investment strategy would tend to provide a steady income. What could cause that income to vary over time?

   b. Why is this investment strategy preferable to investing in "laddered high-grade corporate bonds"? Do the corporate bonds have any advantages over the Treasuries?

   c. What could you say about the preferences of an individual who chooses laddered corporates over Treasuries?

   d. Under what conditions would the laddered-corporates portfolio be the better choice?

2. The market yield to maturity on a risky bond is currently listed at 14.50 percent. The risk-free interest rate is estimated to be 9.25 percent. What is the default-risk premium, all other factors removed? The promised yield on this bond is 15 percent. A certain investor, looking at this bond, estimates there is a 25 percent probability the bond will pay 15 percent at maturity, a 50 percent probability it will pay a 10 percent return, and a 25 percent probability it will yield only 5 percent. What is the bond's expected yield? What is this investor's anticipated default loss? Will the investor buy this bond?

3. A 10-year corporate bond was issued on January 1, 2002, with call privilege attached. The bond was sold to investors at $1,000 par value with a 10 percent coupon rate. The bond was called on January 1, 2005, at a call price paid to holders of par plus one year's coupon income. At the time, the prevailing market interest rate on securities of comparable quality was 8 percent. If a holder of this

www.mhhe.com/rose9e

bond reinvested the call price at 8 percent for seven years, calculate this investor's holding-period yield for the entire period of 10 years. How much yield did the investor lose as a result of the call?

4. Aaa-rated municipal bonds are carrying a market yield today of 5.25 percent, while Aaa rated corporate bonds have current market yields of 11.50 percent. What is the break-even tax rate that would make a taxable investor indifferent between these two types of bonds?

5. An investor purchases a 10-year U.S. government bond for $800. The bond's coupon rate is 10 percent and, at time of purchase, it still had five years remaining until maturity. If the investor holds the bond until it matures and collects the $1,000 par value from the Treasury and his marginal tax rate is 28 percent, what will his after-tax yield to maturity be?

6. A pool of credit-card loans is expected to pay the following stream of cash flows for each quarter of the year indicated:

Time Period	Expected Cash Flow Including Projected Prepayments
Year 1, quarter 1	$ 82 million
Year 1, quarter 2	80 million
Year 1, quarter 3	72 million
Year 1, quarter 4	60 million
Year 2, quarter 1	48 million
Year 2, quarter 2	36 million
Year 2, quarter 3	27 million
Year 2, quarter 4	18 million
Year 3, quarter 1	6 million
Year 3, quarter 2	1 million
Total expected cash flows	$430 million

If the yield to maturity on comparable quality instruments is 14 percent, what should be the market value (price) of each security issued against this particular pool of credit-card loans?

7. If the following *events* happen to Alvernon Way Corporation, what is likely to happen to the company's stock price, all other factors held constant?

a. Alvernon retires a bond issue with the issuance of new preferred stock.

b. Alvernon announces a dividend payment to holders of its common stock of $2.36 per share; security analysts had expected a dividend of $2.45 per share.

c. Alvernon is selling 270,000 new shares of common stock today.

d. Alvernon Class A common stock shares, currently priced at $140 per share, are splitting 2 for 1 next week.

e. Alvernon announces the development and marketing of a new medical device that promises significant relief for persons suffering from severe arthritis and stiffness of the joints.

f. Six weeks after receiving her largest salary bonus in history, Alvernon's chief operating officer announced early retirement today due to family and medical problems.

g. Alvernon has just been sued in federal court by the U.S. Department of Justice for alleged price fixing and antitrust violations.

Standard & Poor's Market Insight and Web-Based Problems

STANDARD
&POOR'S

1. As in most other industries, bank profits tend to fall during downturns in the economy. However, other factors also affect bank profitability, such as regulation and competition, as well as the portfolio decisions bank managers make. Certain financial ratios crudely measure the amount of financial risk facing any particular bank or nonbank firm.

   a. Visit S&P's Market Insight database at **mhhe.com/edumarketinsight** and obtain data on three "Financial Risk" measures reported there for the industry "Sub-Group: Diversified Banks." Compare these measures with the benchmark for that sub-group. In making your comparison, you will need to read the definitions for each of the financial risk measures. Which measures indicate that these banks are undertaking more financial risk than the benchmark against which they are being compared? Which suggest that these banks are undertaking less financial risk?

   b. Using the S&P Market Insight database select two large banks that are familiar to you. Check to see if they are included in the industry sub-group that you examined in part (a).

   c. Find the ticker symbol for the two banks that you chose in part (b) and go to the "Financial Highlights" for those particular banks. Obtain the same financial risk measures for those banks that you previously examined for the whole industry sub-group. Do the two banks you chose appear to be taking on more or less financial risk than the industry sub-group as a whole? Do all the financial risk measures paint a consistent picture of risk exposure? Or do the banks appear to be undertaking less financial risk according to some measures and more risk according to others?

2. The short-term market for corporate debt (commercial paper) is very sensitive to risk. Whenever the economy weakens, the issuance of commercial paper falls and the "price" of that risk increases as measured by the spread between the 90-day commercial paper rate and the three-month U.S. Treasury bill rate.

   a. Visit the Federal Reserve's Web site at **federalreserve.gov** and, after clicking on "Economic Research and Data," find "Selected Interest Rates." Construct the "risk spread" for the 90-day commercial paper rate minus the three-month T-bill rate and make a plot of the graph of this spread for the past 10 years using the G.13 monthly statistical release.

   b. Now locate the volume of "Nonfinancial Commercial Paper Outstanding" on the Fed's Web site. Plot this information for the same time period.

   c. Visit the National Bureau of Economic Research (NBER) Web site at **nber.com/cycles/cyclesmain.html** and locate the onset and end dates for any economic recessions that occurred in the U.S. economy over the past 10 years. Mark these dates on your graphs from parts (a) and (b) above.

   d. What are your conclusions regarding how the corporate debt (commercial paper) market responds to economic recessions?

Semester Project: A Study of the Fed Funds Market

Continuing the semester project we started in Chapter 1—an exploration of the many aspects of the important *federal funds* (or interbank loan) *market*—we now examine whether Fed funds interest rates carry significant risk premiums. In today's Fed funds market, a typical interbank loan transaction often involves a contract (frequently negotiated through a Fed funds broker) between some of the largest and most secure banks in the United States. Moreover, the maturity of these contracts is most often very short (in the majority of cases, overnight), although longer-term and continuing contracts do occur.

a. Based on what you know about federal funds, how do you think the Fed funds interest rate should compare with market rates on three-month U.S. Treasury bills and short-term uncollateralized notes (often referred to as *commercial paper*) issued by "blue chip" firms (those with the highest credit ratings)?

b. Visit the Federal Reserve Board's Web site at **federalreserve.gov** and, after clicking on "Economic Research and Data," find "Selected Interest Rates." Compare the three-month Treasury bill and six-month commercial paper rates with the "effective" Fed funds rate. Was your intuition about the relative size of these market rates correct? How large and stable are the spreads between these prominent money market interest rates and the funds rate?

c. What factors other than risk, if any, could account for the differences you observe in part (b)?

d. Is there no risk factor at all in the Fed funds market? Explain your answer.

Selected References to Explore

Cantor, Richard, and Frank Packer. "Municipal Ratings and Credit Standards: Differences of Opinion in the Credit Rating Industry." *Staff Report No. 12,* Federal Reserve Bank of New York, April 1996.

Fleming, Michael J. "Measuring Treasury Market Liquidity." *Economic Policy Review,* Federal Reserve Bank of New York, September 2003, pp. 83–108.

Fons, Jerome S. "Using Default Rates to Model the Term Structure of Credit Risk." *Financial Analysts Journal* L (1994), pp. 25–32.

Helwege, Jean, and Paul Kleimen. "Understanding Aggregate Default Rates of High Yield Bonds." *Current Issues in Economics and Finance,* Federal Reserve Bank of New York, May 1996, pp. 1–6.

Helwege, Jean, and Christopher M. Turner. "The Slope of the Credit Yield Curve for Speculative Grade Issues." *Research Paper No. 9725,* Federal Reserve Bank of New York, August 1997.

Weinberg, John A. "Accounting for Corporate Behavior." *Annual Report,* Federal Reserve Bank of Richmond, 2003.

www.mhhe.com/rose9e

Chapter 9

Interest-Rate Forecasting and Hedging: Swaps, Financial Futures, and Options

What's in This Chapter?
Key Topics Outline

The Business Cycle and Interest Rate Forecasting
Implied Forecasts
Hedging against Loss with Swaps: Features and Examples
Financial Futures Contracts: Types, Trading Hedges, and Their Effects
Option Contracts: Types and Possible Payoffs
Accounting for Derivatives: Their Costs and Risks

Learning Objectives

in This Chapter

- You will discover why financial analysts today usually choose hedging (protecting) against losses from changing interest rates and asset prices rather than attempting to forecast interest rates or the prices of financial assets (such as stocks and bonds).

- You will explore several of the most popular tools currently in use to protect borrowers and lenders from losses due to movements in market interest rates and asset prices, including interest rate swaps, financial futures, and option contracts.

9.1   Introduction

Thus far in Part Two we have looked at several of the most important factors that cause interest rates and asset prices to change over time. Included in our survey have been such powerful rate- and price-determining factors as savings, investment demand, inflation, default risk, taxes, call features, convertibility, and marketability. Yet even this impressive list of influential factors does not account for all of the changes in interest rates and asset prices we observe daily in the real world. Political developments at home and abroad, changes in government policy, changes in corporate earnings and business conditions, announcements of new security offerings, and thousands of other bits of information flood the money and capital markets daily and bring about fluctuations in interest rates and asset prices. In fact, for actively traded assets, demand and supply forces are continually shifting, minute by minute, so that investors interested in these assets must constantly stay abreast of the latest developments in the financial marketplace. It is no wonder that consistently accurate interest-rate and asset-price forecasting appears to be so difficult, if not impossible.

9.2   Interest-Rate and Asset-Price Forecasting

For many decades some economists and financial analysts believed that it was possible to forecast (predict) future levels of and changes in market interest rates and the prices of various financial assets (such as stocks and bonds). If this were true, what a tremendous advantage it would give to accurate forecasters—provided, of course, they could find others in the marketplace with whom to trade, whose own forecasts were not so accurate!

For example, if you knew when interest rates were likely to be at their lowest, you could wait for that low point and borrow more cheaply (that is, if you could find someone who believed that interest rates were going still lower and was willing to lend to you today). Likewise, if you knew when stock and bond prices were going to rise, you could position yourself to make a great deal of money—but you would need to find others in the marketplace who were not so optimistic and therefore willing to sell those assets to you. Therefore, to make money from your forecasts, your predictions must be consistently more accurate than those of other market participants. What a daunting challenge!

However, there are a *few* predictable aspects to interest-rate and asset-price movements that virtually all traders must account for. To ignore these regularities could be perilous; understanding the few regularities in rates and prices and how the financial markets account for them can significantly reduce the exposure of your investments to interest-rate and price movements and minimize market risk.

The Business Cycle and Seasonality   Economists often point out that market interest rates frequently *follow* the **business cycle**—the pattern of expansion (boom) and contraction (recession) periods in the economy. (See Exhibit 9.1.) *Market interest rates tend to rise when the economy is expanding toward its peak or highest point and fall when the economy is contracting toward the trough of a recession or its lowest point.* This is particularly true for short-term interest rates, which tend to move rapidly up or down with the business cycle, while long-term interest rates change more gradually and follow the business cycle less closely.[1] (See Exhibit 9.2.)

To understand how business cycles are defined in the United States see the National Bureau of Economic Research at nber.org/

business cycle

---

[1] We should note that this difference in the speed of up or down movements in long-term versus short-term market interest rates means that *yield curves* (discussed in Chapter 7) also tend to change with the business cycle. In particular, yield curves tend to slope upward (with long-term interest rates higher than

EXHIBIT 9.1

The Modern Business Cycle

To examine fluctuations over time in the economy and interest rates see the extensive collection of economic and financial data series at the Federal Reserve's site, **economagic.com/ fedbog.htm**

seasonality

The "ups and downs" of business activity—particularly fluctuations in businesses hiring new workers and making new investments—are known as *business cycles*. The downward phase of the business cycle is known as a *recession*—an event that has afflicted the U.S. economy about every 4 to 5 years since World War II. Today a recession is defined by the National Bureau of Economic Research as a widespread decline in economic activity (measured by such indicators as industrial production and employment) that lasts for more than a few months. Fortunately, recessions have averaged considerably shorter than the *expansion* ("up") phase of the cycle, lasting only about 11 months, on average. Interest rates, stock prices, and other financial data series are *strongly* affected by these cycles.

Another potentially useful time pattern among a few market interest rates is **seasonality.** At certain times of the year market rates appear to experience upward pressure and, at other times, seasonal pressures appear to pressure interest rates in the downward direction. For example, some short-term rates tend to feel upward pressure

EXHIBIT 9.2   **Interest Rates over the Course of a Business Cycle**

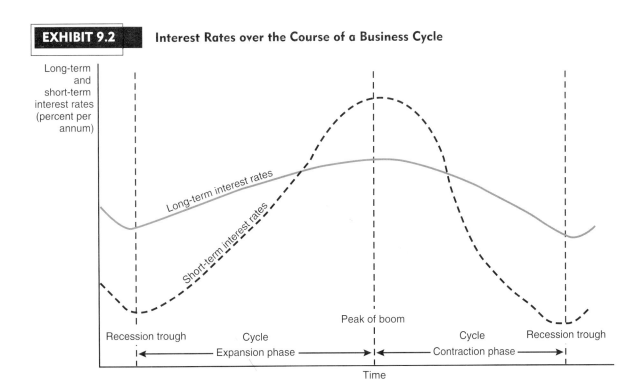

short-term rates) during periods of economic expansion and tend to slope downward (with higher short-term than long-term interest rates) in a recession. This implies that yield curves *may* have some forecasting power in predicting changes in the economy.

Another interesting aspect of interest-rate patterns is that the market *prices* of longer-term assets tend to be more volatile than the market *prices* of shorter-term assets. Thus, the maturity-asset price volatility relationship tends to be opposite that of the maturity-interest rate relationship. Investors in longer-term financial instruments usually face greater risk of capital loss (increased *principal risk*) due to price fluctuations than do investors in shorter-term assets. Of course, the investor in longer-term assets has the offsetting advantage of generally receiving a more stable rate of return (reduced *income risk*) than is true for investors in shorter-term assets.

in the second half of the year as businesses borrow more heavily to stock their shelves with goods for the fall and winter seasons. In contrast, certain long-term interest rates seem to experience upward pressure in the late spring and summer, possibly related to borrowing to support construction activity. However, seasonal patterns in interest rates and asset prices tend to be overshadowed by other forces, such as central bank monetary policy and political activities.

The Economy, Interest Rates, and the Daunting Challenge of Forecasting

The foregoing interest-rate patterns seem to suggest that if someone could forecast the changes about to occur in the economy, then surely interest rates and asset prices would follow a similar path. While we may not be able to make consistently accurate *point forecasts*—that is, predict the exact numerical value of an interest rate or asset price at a given future moment in time—we *might* be successful at making *directional forecasts*—predicting whether or not interest rates and asset prices will move higher or lower than they are today. In short, just read where the economy is going and asset values and interest rates will surely tag along!

Unfortunately, this forecasting strategy turns out to be a treacherous path because the economy itself can be so difficult to forecast, often changing direction or abruptly slowing down or speeding up. Moreover, the seasonal patterns discussed above tend to be overshadowed by other forces impacting the financial marketplace, such as changes in monetary policy, which are often unpredictable. Then, too, as we saw in Chapter 5, market interest rates are influenced by millions of borrowing and lending decisions made by millions of individual decision makers. We do not yet have a computer program big enough nor do we have sufficient, timely data at our disposal to track all of these millions of borrowing and lending decisions when they occur.

Recent research provides further evidence about the daunting challenge of trying to predict interest-rate and asset-price movements. This research points increasingly toward time patterns in market interest rates that come close to a *random walk*—that is, changes in interest rates may be described as random and, therefore, unpredictable on a consistent basis. However, over the very long run, interest rates do appear to exhibit *long-run mean reversion,* implying that there is some long-run average to which they will eventually return. Therefore, interest-rate changes may not be completely random. However, the tendency of interest rates to revert to the mean in the long run appears to be swamped by short-run changes and does not seem to provide very useful information for guiding short- or medium-term investments or market trading.

Implied Rate and Price Forecasting

implied forecasting

Nevertheless, some financial analysts and active market investors place considerable weight on what is called **implied forecasting.** This forecasting technique, which relies upon measures of the public's *expectations* to help predict the future, is a very important tool employed by many managers of large investment portfolios today.

For example, the prices of *financial futures contracts* (to be discussed later in this chapter) appear to reflect the public's expectations about whether future interest rates and asset prices are likely to be higher or lower than they are today. To illustrate, suppose a widely traded contract to deliver U.S. Treasury bonds to buyers in three months currently carries a delivery price of $88, but comparable T-bonds for delivery today are selling for $98. Clearly, there is an implied forecast in the financial futures market of a *decline* in bond prices (and, therefore, a rise in market interest rates) over the next three months.

In other words, expectations about future interest rates are embedded in the market prices of financial assets and are likely to be among the most accurate forecasts available to the average investor, provided the financial marketplace is efficient. However, there is *no guarantee* that any particular implied forecast will turn out to be right. Market inefficiencies may prevent interest rates and asset prices from fully adjusting to market forces. Moreover, the public's expectations are continually changing as new information bombards the marketplace daily.

QUESTIONS TO HELP YOU STUDY

1. Why are interest rates and asset prices so difficult to *forecast* accurately?

2. Suppose you could forecast market interest rates and asset prices correctly on a consistent basis. What obvious advantages would this give you?

3. How do long-and short-term interest rates behave over the course of the *business cycle?* Why do you think they behave this way?

4. How might knowledge of the business cycle of *expansions* and *recessions* be useful in anticipating the *direction* of interest-rate and asset-price movements?

5. What is *seasonality* and why is it often unreliable as an indicator of future movements in interest rates and asset prices?

6. What is an *implied forecast?*

7. Can you come up with an example of an *implied forecast?* Will this forecast necessarily turn out to be right? Why or why not?

9.3 Interest-Rate and Asset-Price Hedging Strategies

Volatile interest rates and asset prices in recent years, coupled with the difficulties inherent in interest-rate and asset-price forecasting, have led many individuals and institutions to search for ways to insulate themselves from these interest-rate and value changes.

If interest-rate and asset-price changes cannot be reliably forecast on a consistent basis, is it possible to at least *hedge* against (reduce) the damaging effects of increasing or decreasing interest rates and asset prices? The answer is "yes"—but only if skillfully done, using the right hedging tool at the right time.

Although several hedging methods have been developed, there is a "price" for employing this form of insurance against losses due to changes in asset values or interest rates. *Hedging tends to lower interest-rate and asset-price risk but also tends to reduce the profit potential that could be recovered from correctly forecasting the direction and magnitude of future interest-rate and asset-price changes.* In short, hedging tools tend to even out the hills and valleys in an investor's returns from investing in financial assets, but they also tend to limit possible gains as well as possible losses. Therefore, they are useful primarily to investors who are *risk averse* (more concerned with avoiding unexpected losses than with preserving a chance for surprisingly large gains).

In the sections that follow we look at the most popular methods used today for controlling interest-rate and asset-price risk: *interest rate swaps, financial futures,* and *option contracts.*

EXHIBIT 9.3

Using Interest Rate Swaps to Hedge against Fluctuating Interest Rates

The Swap Market

The situation:

Low-credit-rated (BB) borrower:
– Wants lower interest costs
– Prefers fixed-rate, long-term borrowing (such as by issuing bonds) to match the cash-flow characteristics of its long-term assets.

High-credit-rated (AAA) borrower:
– Wants lower interest costs
– Prefers flexible, short-term interest rate on its borrowings (such as a loan from a bank or finance company) to match the cash-flow characteristics of its short-term assets.

The swap agreement:

Low-credit-rated borrower gets a short-term loan from its bank at a floating interest rate but pays out the fixed interest cost on the long-term bonds issued by its swap partner.

Pays long-term interest rate

Pays short-term interest rate

High-credit-rated borrower issues long-term bonds carrying a fixed interest rate, but pays out a portion of the floating short-term interest rate owed by its swap partner.

Result: Both companies save on interest costs and better match the maturity structure of their assets and their liabilities. In reality, the two parties to the swap exchange only the *net difference* in their borrowing rates, with the party owing the highest interest rate in the market on the payment date paying the other party the interest-rate difference.

9.4 Interest Rate Swaps

What Are Swaps?

interest rate swap

Early in the 1980s a new interest-rate and value hedging tool—the **interest rate swap**—became popular. In an interest rate swap, two participating business firms independently borrow from two different lenders and then exchange interest payments with each other for a stipulated period of time. In effect, each company helps to pay off a portion of the interest cost owed by the other firm. The result is usually *lower* interest expense for both firms and a better *balance* between cash inflows and outflows for both firms. (See, for example, Exhibit 9.3.) Swaps give a borrowing company a powerful tool in managing its liabilities, helping to offset any maturity mismatches that may exist between its assets and liabilities.

Swaps were first used by multinational banks (such as J. P. Morgan Chase and Deutsche Bank) in the Eurocurrency markets beginning in 1982. These huge banks generally possess excellent credit ratings. This means that, if they wish to, multinational banks can borrow at low, fixed long-term interest rates. However, these international lending institutions may decide to "sell" their ability to borrow long term at low cost in exchange for what they want most: access to low-cost, short-term funds carrying floating interest rates in order to match their short-term, floating-rate assets. The development of interest rate swaps has made maturity matchups like this possible. The first domestic U.S. interest rate swap occurred when the Student Loan Marketing Association, a federal agency that guarantees college student loans, and ITT Corporation exchanged interest rate payments on some of their debt.

Most swaps today range from $25 to $100 million in dollar volume (usually called the *notional* amount of the swap because this dollar amount never changes hands). They usually cover periods ranging from about 3 years to 10 years and involve both fixed- and floating-rate loans, with the floating rate often tied to the London Interbank Offer Rate on Eurodollar deposits (LIBOR), the prime rate, or the market yield on Treasury securities.

How Swaps Work

The LIBOR rate that is the reference interest rate for most swaps is set daily by the British Bankers Association following a survey of leading banks. See bba.org.uk/

Swaps work because the interest-rate spreads related to default risk (called *quality spreads*) are generally greater in the long-term capital market than they are in the short-term money market. To see how swaps can simultaneously fulfill two goals—lower interest costs and better matching of the maturities of a firm's assets with the maturities of its liabilities—consider the following example. A top-rated corporation with a AAA credit rating can borrow in the long-term bond market at a 10 percent interest rate. However, this company prefers to borrow short-term money at a floating interest rate because it holds mainly short-term assets that roll over into cash just about the time its short-term borrowings come due. Because of the firm's top credit rating, it can borrow short-term funds at prime. Currently, the prime rate is 10 percent, but prime can rise or fall at any time.

A second company is interested in being the first company's swap partner, but this second firm has a credit rating no better than average. This firm has been told by its investment banker that it could issue long-term bonds at an interest rate of 11 percent. Alternatively, this lower-credit-rated firm could borrow short-term funds at prime plus 0.50 percent (making a current short-term loan cost of 10% + 0.50%, or 10.50%). However, the lower-rated firm would prefer to issue long-term bonds because it holds primarily long-term assets.

In summary, these two companies face the following situation:

The Two Parties to the Swap:	Could Borrow in the Long-Term Bond Market at	Could Borrow in the Short-Term Loan Market at	
Low-credit-rated borrower	11%	Prime rate + 0.50%	(9.1)
High-credit-rated borrower	10	Prime rate	
Quality spread	1%	0.50%	

In this case, *both* firms can save on interest costs if each company borrows in that financial market—long-term or short-term—in which it has the *greatest comparative interest cost advantage*.

A bank or securities dealer might aid these two firms by helping the top-rated firm sell long-term bonds in the open market at 10 percent, while the lower-rated company agrees to make the top-rated firm's bond interest payments. In the meantime, the lower-rated firm takes out a floating-rate bank loan in the same amount at an interest rate of prime plus 0.50 percent. The top-rated company agrees to pay this second firm a rate of prime less one-quarter of a percentage point (25 basis points), which would cover most of the lower-rated company's interest cost. If the prime rate remains at its current level of 10 percent, each firm would owe its swap partner the following:

- Low-credit-rated borrower pays the high-rated borrower the fixed 10 percent interest rate it owes on its long-term bonds.

- High-credit-rated borrower pays the low-rated borrower prime minus one-quarter point,—that is, 10 percent − 0.25 percent or 9.75 percent to cover the short-term loan rate.

- Low-credit-rated borrower saves 11 − 10, or 1 percent in long-term interest cost less 0.75 (that is, 10.50 – 9.75) percent additional cost on the prime rate loan, for a net savings of 0.25 percent.

- High-credit-rated borrower saves 0.25 percent in interest cost (prime less 0.25 percent).

Today, borrowers often negotiate swap agreements with lenders at the same time they reach an agreement on a loan. For example, if a borrower is granted a floating-rate loan based on the prime rate but fears that interest rates are going up, he or she can convert that floating-rate loan into a *synthetic fixed-rate loan* through a swap agreement. Although the swap and the loan are usually separate contracts, together they have the net effect of giving the borrower a fixed borrowing cost. As the diagram in Exhibit 9.4 shows, when the borrower pays a floating rate to the lender, the borrower also pays a fixed interest rate to the lender under a swap agreement. Simultaneously under the swap agreement, the lender sends the borrower a floating-rate payment. Therefore, the floating-rate payment from the borrower under the loan agreement is offset by the lender's floating-rate payment to the borrower under the swap agreement. What's left over is the borrower's fixed-rate payment to the lender under the swap.

Thus, a floating-rate loan agreement has been transformed by a swap into a fixed-rate loan, even though the borrower remains legally committed to make all the scheduled floating interest rate payments called for by the loan agreement.

Recently the International Swaps and Derivatives Association (ISDA) has begun to survey daily the fixed interest rates on swaps of varying maturity traded in the global marketplace. Not surprisingly, this new data source reveals that *the longer the term of a swap agreement, the higher the interest rate attached.* Thus, like most other financial instruments, swaps generally display an upward-sloping yield curve. Interest-rate risk increases with longer-term swap contracts and swap partners have had to find ways of dealing effectively with this form of risk exposure.

During the 1990s a new variety of swap contract appeared called the *index amortizing rate (IAR)* swap. An IAR swap, like most other swaps, is an over-the-counter contract calling for two parties to agree to exchange fixed-rate and floating-rate interest payments based upon a certain fixed principal (notional) value of a loan. However, unlike conventional ("plain vanilla") swaps, the principal or notional value of an IAR *decreases* over the swap's life at a rate that varies with changes in short-term interest rates. The pace at which the principal of the IAR swap decreases will be affected by an amortization schedule agreed upon by the two parties to the swap. The notional principal underlying the IAR swap will decline (amortize) more

EXHIBIT 9.4

The Synthetic Fixed-Rate Loan

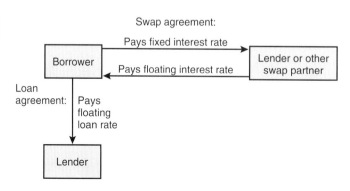

quickly if short-term interest rates fall and amortize more slowly if short-term interest rates rise. Actually not all swaps involve a fixed interest rate exchanged for a floating interest rate (now often called "coupon" swaps); the market has broadened to include "basis" swaps in which the parties exchange two different floating-rate payment streams (such as a three-month interest rate exchanged for a six-month rate).

Interest rate swaps have become much easier to arrange in recent years with the appearance of swap *brokers*. These financial firms—most often investment banks or commercial banks—usually charge a finder's fee of about $1/4$ of 1 percent of the principal (notional) amount of the swap to bring the two parties together under the swap agreement. Swap brokers charge more than this if they also are asked to administer the swap—that is, calculate the amount of interest owed by each party to the agreement, collect the monies owed, and distribute the required payments. The swap broker or another financial intermediary may also be asked to issue a *guarantee* in case either party to the swap cannot meet its obligation. These guarantees may cost from 1 to 15 basis points of the notional amount of the swap or more, depending on the credit record of each swap partner. In recent years, swap dealers have developed inventories of "unmatched" swaps—requests from customers who are willing to enter into swap agreements but need a counterparty to make the swap complete.

The Risks of Swapping

Swaps are never without risk. Either party to the agreement may go bankrupt or even steal the funds owed to its counterparty, leaving its swap partner exposed to interest-rate risk. Swaps help to cover interest-rate risk but do not necessarily reduce *credit* (*default*) *risk*. A few swaps call for one or both parties to post collateral, but this is usually not done. Unfortunately, without collateral requirements, it is easy for a swap partner to overdo the use of swaps and get itself into trouble. One dramatic example of this occurred during the 1990s, when several municipalities in Great Britain took on far more swaps than their revenues could accommodate. In fact, one local government near London faced a swap interest bill so huge that, had a British court not intervened and negated its swap agreements, it would have had to tax each of its citizens thousands of pounds merely to pay off the interest owed on all of its swaps! However, because the notional amount of a swap is not at risk, typically a swap is less risky than a bond.

Swaps are themselves subject to *interest-rate risk* due to the fact that shifts in market interest rates can alter the value of existing swap agreements and, therefore, affect a swap's replacement cost. *Rising* market interest rates result in greater risk of default on a swap than do stable interest rates. For example, Procter & Gamble Co. lost close to $160 million during the 1990s on interest rate swaps entered into on the assumption that interest rates would fall, but they rose instead. A swap can be hedged against interest-rate risk by entering into another swap agreement that is the mirror image of the first (a *matched pair*). Some companies use futures contracts or other hedging tools to counter interest-rate risk from their swaps rather than proliferating still more swaps.

One notable advantage of swaps is the largely unregulated character of the market. Swaps are private agreements with minimal government interference. There is no regulatory commission to restrict the use of this hedging tool. Some firms do not report the amount of swaps they have outstanding. This means that investors interested in buying their bonds or their stock may not know how much risk exposure these companies carry in the form of swap obligations. However, recently the Financial Accounting Standards Board (FASB) tightened up on its rules applying to swaps and other derivatives, asking corporations to report the fair-market value of derivatives on their balance sheets. Nevertheless, full disclosure by companies of

Information on swaps and other derivative instruments may be found at such sites as **finpipe.com/ derivglossary.htm**

As we have seen, the parties to an interest rate swap merely exchange interest payments. A swap partner that pays out a floating (variable) interest rate is said to be in a *short position*, sending a variable interest rate to its swap partner and receiving a fixed interest rate in return. In contrast, the swap partner that pays out a fixed interest rate and receives, in return, a floating interest rate is said to be in a *long position* in the swap market.

Counterparty to swap in a short position	Pays 3-month LIBOR rate* → Receives fixed interest rate ←	Financial intermediary in a hedged position	Receives 3-month LIBOR rate* → Pays fixed interest rate ←	Counterparty to swap in a long position

Financial intermediaries frequently occupy a *hedged position* between the counterparties to a swap, meaning that the hedged institution pays and receives both floating and fixed interest rates. In this case, the intermediary is often a swap dealer, aiding its customers with their interest-rate risk exposure. The dealer can make money on this hedged position in several different ways. A fee is often charged to bring these two counterparties together. Moreover, there may be a difference in the fixed interest rate or floating interest rate payments that

the dealer receives and pays out. For example, this swap intermediary may collect an annual fixed interest rate of 8 percent from the counterparty in the long position and pay out only a fixed interest rate of 7.75 percent to the counterparty in the short position. The hedged institution may pocket the 0.25 percent difference in interest rates received and paid out.

*London Interbank Offer Rate on short-term dollar deposits traded by international banks.

their commitments under swaps and other derivative obligations remains a problem as indicated by the recent collapse of Enron Corporation.

QUESTIONS TO HELP YOU STUDY

8. What is *interest-rate hedging?* What is its *goal?*
9. What are *interest rate swaps?* Why were these instruments developed?
10. What *risks* are associated with swap contracts? Can any of these risks be reduced?
11. When is a partner to a swap in *long position?* A *short position?* To what kinds of risk is each exposed?

9.5   Financial Futures and Option Contracts

Among the most innovative markets to be developed in recent years are the markets for *financial futures* contracts. In the financial futures markets, the risk of future changes in market prices or yields attached to various assets is transferred to someone else—an individual or an institution—willing to bear that risk. Financial futures are used in both the short-term money market and the long-term capital market to protect both borrowers and lenders against changing interest rates and shifting asset prices.

For a review of the history of futures and options see **cbot.com**

The Nature of Futures Trading

hedging

In the futures market, buyers and sellers enter into contracts for the delivery of assets at a specific location and time and at a price that is set when the contract is made. The principal reason for the existence of the futures market is **hedging**—the act of coordinating the buying and selling of a financial claim or other asset in order to protect it against the risk of future price fluctuations. In the futures market, investors interested in hedging trade futures contracts with investors interested in speculating (i.e., profiting from favorable market movements).

Hedging in futures does *not* reduce risk. It is a low-cost method of *transferring* the risk of unanticipated changes in prices or interest rates from one investor or institution to another. Ultimately, some investor must bear the risk of fluctuations in the prices and yields of financial assets. The hedger who successfully transfers risk through a futures contract can protect an acceptable selling price or a desired yield on a financial asset weeks or months ahead of the sale or purchase of that item.

Why Hedging Can Be Effective

The hedging process can be effective in transferring risk because prices in the spot (cash) market for assets are generally correlated with prices in the futures (or forward) market. Indeed, the price of a futures contract in today's market represents an estimate of what the spot (cash) market price will be on the contract's delivery date (less any storage, insurance, and financing costs). *Hedging essentially involves adopting equal and opposite positions in the spot and futures markets for the same assets.*

basis　　The relationship between the price or yield of a financial asset in the cash or spot market and its price or yield in the futures market is captured in the concept of **basis.** Specifically, in terms of prices,

$$\begin{array}{c}\text{Basis for a} \\ \text{futures contract}\end{array} = \begin{array}{c}\text{Spread between the cash (spot) price of a commodity} \\ \text{or financial asset and the futures (forward) price for that} \\ \text{same commodity or asset at the same point in time.}\end{array} \quad (9.2)$$

For example, if long-term Treasury bonds are selling in today's cash market for immediate delivery at a price of $98 per bond (assuming a $100 par value) but are selling in the futures market today for forward delivery in three months at $88 per bond, the basis for this T-bond futures contract purchased today is $98 − $88, or $10. We can also define basis in terms of interest rates; it is the difference between the interest rate attached to an asset in the cash market and the interest rate on that same asset in the futures market.

One important principle of futures trading is the *principle of convergence*. As the delivery date specified in a futures contract draws nearer, the gap (basis) between the futures and spot prices for the same asset narrows. At the moment of delivery, the futures price and spot price on the same asset must be identical (except for transactions costs), so that the basis of the futures contract becomes zero. Whether a futures trade ultimately turns out to be profitable depends on what happens to its basis now and when the contract ends. *It is changes in basis that create risk in the trading of futures contracts.*

Hedging through futures converts price or interest rate risk into basis risk. One useful measure of basis risk in financial futures is the *volatility ratio:*

$$\begin{array}{c}\text{Volatility ratio} \\ \text{for a} \\ \text{futures contract} \\ \text{(basis risk measure)}\end{array} = \dfrac{\begin{array}{c}\text{Percentage change in cash (spot)} \\ \text{price of an asset}\end{array}}{\begin{array}{c}\text{Percentage change in the price of the} \\ \text{futures instrument used for} \\ \text{hedging the asset}\end{array}} \quad (9.3)$$

The more stable the basis associated with a given futures trade—that is, the closer the volatility ratio is to 1—the greater the reduction of risk achieved by the futures trader. When cash and futures prices or interest rates move in parallel, basis risk is zero. The futures markets "work" to offset risk, because the risk of changes in basis is generally less than the risk of changes in the price or yield from an asset. A hedger trading in futures to combat risk strives to find a futures contract whose price volatility most closely tracks the price behavior of the cash-market instrument that needs to be protected, pushing the volatility ratio as close to 1 as possible.

The Purpose of Trading in Financial Futures

financial futures contracts

A securities dealer, bank, or other investor may sell **financial futures contracts** on selected financial assets in order to protect against the risk of falling prices (rising interest rates) and, therefore, a decline in the rate of return or yield from an investment. If the price of the asset in question does fall, the investor can lock in the desired yield, because a profit on the futures contract may offset the capital loss incurred when selling the asset itself. On the other hand, a rise in the market price of an asset (i.e., a fall in interest rates) may be offset by a loss in the futures market. Either way, the investor may be able to maintain his or her desired holding-period yield.

With a financial futures contract, for example, the seller agrees to deliver a specific asset at a fixed price at a specific time in the future. Delivery under the shortest contracts is usually in three months from today's date; a few contracts stretch out to 18 months or even two years. When the delivery date arrives, the security's seller can do one of three things: (1) make delivery of the asset if he or she holds it; (2) buy the asset in the spot (cash) market and deliver it as called for in the futures contract; or (3) purchase a futures contract for the same asset with a delivery date exactly matching the first contract. This last option would result in a buy and sell order maturing on the same day, canceling each other out ("zeroing out") and eliminating the necessity of making delivery. In reality, settlement of contracts generally occurs in the futures market by using offsetting buy and sell orders rather than making actual delivery.

Assets Covered by Financial Futures Contracts and Examples of Daily Price Quotations

Futures Contracts Most Commonly Traded   The number of different futures markets and the variety of futures contracts regularly traded have been expanding in recent years. Beginning in 1975 only one type of exchanged-traded financial futures contract (attached to a GNMA mortgage-backed security) was traded in the United States. By the opening of the twenty-first century, however, a wide variety of futures contracts were being traded on exchanges all over the world, including:

- Domestic and foreign government bonds and notes.
- Eurodollar and other Eurocurrency bank deposits.
- Federal funds loans, Treasury bills, and LIBOR-priced deposits.
- Common stock indexes (such as contracts tied to the Standard & Poor's 500 stock index, the Dow Jones Industrial Average, the Russell 2000 Index, and the New York Stock Exchange Composite Stock Index).
- Foreign currencies (such as the Euro, the Mexican peso, the Swiss franc, the Japanese yen, the British pound, and the Canadian dollar).
- Interest rate swaps (with contracts covering 2-, 5-, and 10-year swaps).

The Exchanges Where Futures Trading Occurs

To explore some interesting facts about futures and options exchanges, see such Web sites as **nyce.com, pacificex.com, amex.com,** and **belfox.be**

While the number of exchanges proliferated rapidly for a time, there is a strong trend today toward merging exchanges and for established exchanges to broaden their menu of services in order to lower operating costs and increase trading volume. Prominent and recent examples include the application of the German-Swiss EUREX to electronically trade financial futures in the United States and the sharing of building space by the New York Board of Trade and the New York Mercantile Exchange (an outgrowth of the problems created in New York City after the terrorist attacks of 9/11).

Another powerful driving force reshaping the exchanges is the transition from *pit trading*, in which brokers gather on the exchange floor and convey information with hand signals, to *electronic trading* via computers, which promises greater accuracy and speed. The most prominent example of this transition toward *exchange automation* involves the Chicago Board of Trade (CBOT), which has been in transition from pit trading to an electronic trading platform for at least a decade and has now formed a computer link with its rival, the Chicago Mercantile Exchange (CME), in order to settle transactions more efficiently.

Each exchange controls which contracts may be offered for sale, delivery dates and delivery methods, and the posting of prices. Each exchange also stands behind the transactions conducted through its facilities, paying off when the party to a contract fails to do so. Qualifications of traders and standards for admitting firms into exchange membership are monitored by each exchange's governing board. Overseeing the U.S. futures exchange industry are the Commodity Futures Trading Commission (CFTC) and the Securities and Exchange Commission (SEC).

Examples of Daily Price Quotations for U.S. Treasury Futures

The futures market for U.S. Treasury bonds is one of the most active markets for the forward delivery of an asset to be found anywhere in the world. Treasury bonds are a popular investment medium for individuals and financial institutions because of their

249

| **EXHIBIT 9.5** | **Examples of Daily Price Quotations on Financial Futures Exchanges** |

U.S. Treasury Bond Financial Futures Contracts
(in Denominations of $100,000; Prices in 32nds of 100 Percent)

Month When Maturity Is Reached	Opening Price	High Trading Price	Low Trading Price	Settlement Price	Change from Previous Trading Day	Lifetime Extreme Prices		Volume of Open Interest
						High Price	Low Price	
September	122–08	122–16	122–0	122–12	+4	125–01	118–2	950,655
December	122–04	122–10	121–31	122–04	+6	125–12	118–4	120,448

Estimated most recent trading volume: 320,000.
Previous day's trading volume: 366,580.

safety and liquidity. Nevertheless, there is substantial market risk involved with longer-term Treasury bonds and notes due to their lengthy maturities and relatively thin market. Because the market for U.S. Treasury bonds is thinner than for Treasury bills (which must mature within a year) and Treasury bond durations are longer, T-bond prices are more volatile, creating greater uncertainty for investors. Not surprisingly, then, U.S. Treasury bonds were among the first financial instruments for which a futures market was developed for hedging risk. Today there are parallel markets for contracts covering foreign government bonds centered on exchanges in London, Tokyo, and elsewhere around the globe.

All U.S. Treasury bonds delivered under a futures contract must come from the same issue. The basic trading unit is a $100,000 bond (measured at par) with a minimum maturity of 15 years and a coupon rate of 6 percent. Bonds with coupon rates above or below 6 percent are deliverable at a premium or discount from par in the months of March, June, September, and December. Delivery of Treasury bonds is accomplished by book entry, and accrued interest is prorated. Price quotes in the market are often expressed as a percentage of par value. The minimum price change that is recorded on published lists or in dealer quotations is $1/32$ of a point, or $31.25 per $100,000 face-value contract.[2]

Sample data on financial futures prices for U.S. Treasury bond contracts appear in many financial news sheets and on computer screens all over the world. As shown in Exhibit 9.5, the first column indicates the months when each futures contract matures. The next four columns show the opening price for the September and December T-bond contracts when trading began in yesterday's market. The September contract, for example, opened at a price of 122–08 (or $122 and $8/32$ on a $100 par value T-bond, or about $122,250 for a T-bond with a $100,000 face value). The September T-bond's futures price fluctuated during yesterday's trading from a high of $122,500 (or 122 and $16/32$) to a low of $122,000 (or 122 and $0/32$). Trading in the September bond contract closed (settled) at a price of 122 and $12/32$ (or $122,375 for a $100,000 par-value bond) at the end of the day. This settlement price was $4/32$ (or $125) higher than the previous trading day. During the life of this particular futures contract, the T-bond's futures price has fluctuated between a high of $125,031.25 (or 125 and $1/32$) and a low of $118,062.50 (or 118 and $2/32$). The final data column, labeled "Volume of Open Interest," reveals the number of outstanding September futures contracts—in this case, more than 950,000—not yet "zeroed out," indicating delivery of T-bonds must still be made when the contract matures unless the contract is canceled out before it reaches maturity. At the bottom of the

---

[2] See Chapter 6 on asset prices and interest rates for the meaning of 32nds and points and how bonds and other financial asset prices and yields are measured.

table information is often provided to interested investors on the volume of trading (number of contracts) for the most recent day and the preceding day.

Eurodollar Time Deposits

Futures trading in Eurodollar time deposits (or dollar denominated deposits in banks outside the U.S., which are described in Chapter 12) began in 1981 at the International Monetary Market (IMM) of the Chicago Mercantile Exchange (CME). The next year the London International Financial Futures Exchange (LIFFE) introduced a similar contract, and more recently, it introduced futures contracts on Euro-deposits based on leading international currencies traded on leading futures exchanges in Tokyo (TIFFE), Singapore (SIMEX), and Paris (MATIF). The Eurodollar futures market offers investors the opportunity to hedge against changing interest rates on commercial loans, bank deposits, and other short-term financial instruments. Eurodollar futures are settled in cash with the exchange clearinghouse if they are not "zeroed out" by an offsetting transaction before the contract matures. Prices are expressed as an interest-rate index equal to 100 minus the prevailing London Interbank Offer Rate (LIBOR) on short-term deposits (Eurodollar CDs) that day. In addition to the Eurodollar time deposit futures contract there are contracts for the delivery of Euros, Swiss Francs, Japanese yen, the British pound, Mexican pesos, and Canadian and Australian dollars designed to help guard against fluctuations in the value of these particular currencies.

Fed Funds and Other Money Market Futures Contracts

A type of futures contract being closely followed today is the 30-day *Fed funds futures contract*, trading in $5 million units at the Chicago Board of Trade. This device for hedging short-term money market borrowing costs and asset returns is priced at 100 minus the prevailing average Fed funds market interest rate during the delivery month named in the contract.

The Fed funds futures contract is a key contract in the financial system because it reflects the market's general outlook regarding Federal Reserve monetary policy and the likelihood of near-term changes in that policy. For example, if the index rate attached to Fed funds futures contracts rises, a likely reason for that rise would be the expectation in the marketplace that the U.S. central bank plans to tighten money and credit conditions in the near future. If we venture into the international money market, the interest rate risk associated with large commercial loans is often dealt with using one-month LIBOR futures contracts, which trade in $3 million units at the Chicago Mercantile Exchange and, like the federal funds contracts, are settled in cash.

Other current financial futures contracts bought and sold on the world's exchanges include Euribor deposit contracts, which are deposits denominated in a million Euros, and bonds issued by the governments of Canada, Germany, Great Britain, France, and Italy. Growing in popularity are futures contracts involving multiyear swap arrangements, sought after to hedge longer-maturity borrowing costs in the cash market. Finally, U.S. Treasury note contracts on U.S. and some foreign exchanges call for the delivery of T-notes ranging in maturity from 2 to 10 years.

Stock Index Futures

In February 1982, futures contracts on the index value of those common stocks making up the Value Line Stock Index were first offered by the Kansas City Board of Trade. Two months later, the Chicago Mercantile Exchange offered its own version of these "pin-stripe pork bellies" by opening trading in a contract tied to the Standard & Poor's (S&P) 500 stock index. And in May 1982, the New York Futures Exchange inaugurated trading in the New York Stock Exchange's (NYSE's) Composite Stock Price Index. Later Dow Jones Industrials, S&P Mid-Cap, Nasdaq 100, and Russel 2000 stock-index contracts were developed among others.

The advantage of these composite contracts is that they permit an investor to participate in the "action" of the stock market without buying individual stocks. The investor merely risks his cash on whether the stock or bond index will rise or fall in value. This is accomplished by buying or selling a futures contract a few points above or below the current stock index value. For example, one popular S&P 500 contract has a value based on the level of the S&P 500 stock index multiplied by $250. If the S&P 500 stock index stands at 1000, the S&P futures contract would have a value of 1000 × $250, or $250,000. If an investor purchased the S&P index contract at 1000 and then sold a similar contract later at 1010 for $252,500, he would receive a trading profit of $2,500 from the exchange clearinghouse. Current exchange rules require all stock index contracts to be zeroed out so that no exchange of stock occurs; the difference between buying and selling prices is settled in cash alone. Buyers of stock index futures bet on rising stock prices; sellers are usually forecasting declining stock prices.

> To learn more about the nature of financial futures, options, swaps and other derivatives, see such Web sources as encyclopedia.com

QUESTIONS TO HELP YOU STUDY

12. What is the basic purpose of futures and options trading in securities? Where is most futures and options trading carried out?
13. How do the spot (cash) markets differ from futures (forward) markets?
14. What is *basis?* Explain how the basis for a futures contract relates to trading risk.
15. For what specific kinds of securities is there now an active futures market? Who issues these securities?
16. How can investors hedge possible changes in U.S. monetary policy?

Types of Hedges in Futures

Basically *three* types of hedges are used in the financial futures market today: the *long hedge,* the *short hedge,* and the *cross hedge.* Each type of hedge meets the unique trading needs of a particular group of investors.

long hedge

The Long (or Buying) Hedge   A **long hedge** involves the *purchase* of futures contracts today before the investor must buy the actual asset (such as Treasury bonds) desired at a later date. The purpose of the long hedge is to guarantee (lock in) a desired yield in case interest rates decline before assets are actually purchased in the cash market.

As an example of a typical long hedge transaction, suppose that a bank or other institutional investor anticipates receiving $1 million 90 days from today. Assume that today is April 1 and funds are expected on July 2. The current yield to maturity on assets the investor hopes to purchase in July is 12.26 percent. We might imagine that these assets are long-term U.S. Treasury bonds, which appeal to this investor because of their high liquidity and zero default risk. Suppose, however, that interest rates are expected to decline over the next three months. If the investor waits until the $1 million in cash is actually available 90 days from now, the yield on Treasury bonds may well be lower than 12.26 percent. Is there a way to lock in the higher yield available now even though funds will not be available for another three months?

Financial futures and option contracts as well as swaps belong to a broad class of financial instruments called *derivatives*. These unique instruments depend for their value on one or more underlying securities or variables, such as stock prices, interest rates, or commodity prices. Recent experience has shown that derivatives pose their own special brand of risk for both buyers and sellers.

For one thing, derivatives involve at least two parties and either party may fail to deliver, exposing the other party to loss (*counterparty risk*). Other forms of risk associated with derivatives include *price risk* (as their market values change), *liquidity risk* (because traders may be prevented from carrying out risk-covering transactions), *settlement risk* (when assets are delivered before payment is received), *operating risk* (due to faulty internal controls on trading activity), *legal risk* (if customers sue to recover their losses), and *regulatory risk* (when regulations are changed or violated). Derivatives can become so complex that it's easy for a trader to become entangled in multiple contracts and lose track of his or her true position and exposure to loss.

Yes, if a suitable long hedge can be negotiated with another trader. In this case, the investor can *purchase* ("go long") 10 September Treasury bond futures contracts at their current market price. The number of bond futures contracts required can be figured as follows:

$$\frac{\text{Value of securities to be hedged}}{\text{Denomination of the appropriate futures contract}} = \frac{\$1 \text{ million}}{\$100,000} = 10 \text{ contracts} \qquad \textbf{(9.4)}$$

Cash payment on these contracts will not be due until September.

In many practical situations, the asset to be hedged and the time for risk protection will not exactly match available exchange traded futures contracts. These differences introduce uncertainty into the process of determining exactly *how many* futures contracts will be needed. A formula that takes some of these problems into account is the following:

$$\begin{array}{c}\text{Number of} \\ \text{futures} \\ \text{contracts} \\ \text{needed}\end{array} = \begin{array}{c}\text{Value of} \\ \text{securities or} \\ \text{loans to be} \\ \text{hedged} \\ \hline \text{Denomination} \\ \text{of futures} \\ \text{contracts}\end{array} \times \begin{array}{c}\text{Volatility ratio} \\ \text{of price} \\ \text{movements in} \\ \text{the cash (spot) asset} \\ \text{relative to the} \\ \text{price of} \\ \text{the futures} \\ \text{contract}\end{array} \times \begin{array}{c}\text{Days exposed to} \\ \text{risk in the cash} \\ \text{(spot) market} \\ \hline \text{Term of futures} \\ \text{contracts}\end{array} \qquad \textbf{(9.5)}$$

where the volatility ratio is the percentage change in market price of the cash (spot) asset relative to the percentage change in price of the desired futures contract over the most recent period. For example, if we wish to hedge $1 million in corporate bonds for 60 days with $100,000-denominated Treasury bond futures contracts covering 90 days and recent price movements of corporate bonds and T-bond futures have displayed a volatility ratio of 0.75, then

$$\text{Number of futures contracts needed} = \frac{\$1 \text{ million}}{\$100,000} \times 0.75 \times \frac{60}{90} \approx 5 \text{ contracts}$$

$$\textbf{(9.6)}$$

	Spot (or Cash) Market Transactions	**Futures (or Forward) Market Transactions**
EXHIBIT 9.6	April 1:	April 1:
An Example of a Long Futures Hedge Using U.S. Treasury Bonds	A portfolio manager for a financial institution wished to "lock in" a yield of 12.26 percent on $1 million of 20-year, $8^1/_4$ percent U.S. Treasury bonds at 68–14.	The portfolio manager purchases 10 September Treasury bond futures contracts at 68–10.
Source: Based on an example developed by the Chicago Board of Trade in an *Introduction to Financial Futures,* February 1981. Reprinted by permission of the Chicago Board of Trade.	July 2:	July 2:
	The portfolio manager purchases $1 million of 20-year, $8^1/_4$ percent U.S. Treasury bonds at 82–13 for a yield of 10.14 percent.	The portfolio manager sells 10 September Treasury bond futures contracts at 80–07.
	Results:	Results:
	Opportunity loss of $139,687.50 due to lower Treasury bond yields and higher bond prices.	Gain of $119,062.50 on futures trading (less brokerage commissions, interest cost on funds tied up in required cash margin, and taxes).

Suppose the price of T-bond futures contracts currently is 68–10, which is 68 and $^{10}/_{32}$, or $68,312.50 on a $100,000 face-value contract. Assume too that, as expected, bond prices rise and interest rates fall. At some later point, the investor may be able to sell these futures contracts at a profit, because their prices tend to rise along with rising bond prices in the cash market. Selling bond futures at a profit will help this investor offset the lower yields on Treasury bonds that will prevail in the cash market once the $1 million actually becomes available for investing on July 2nd.

The details of this long hedge transaction are given in Exhibit 9.6. We note that on July 1, the investor goes into the spot market and buys $1 million in $8^1/_4$ percent, 20-year U.S. Treasury bonds at a price of 82–13. At the same time, the investor sells 10 September Treasury bond futures at 80–07. Due to higher bond prices (lower yields) in July, the investor loses $139,687.50, because the market price of Treasury bonds has risen from 68–14 to 82–13. This represents an opportunity loss because the $1 million in investable funds was not available in April when interest rates were high and bond prices low. However, this loss is at least partially offset by a gain in the futures market of $119,062.50, because the 10 September bond futures purchased on April 1 were sold at a profit on July 2. Over this period, bond futures rose in price from 68–10 to 80–07. In effect, this investor will pay only $705,000 for the Treasury bonds purchased in the cash market on July 2. The market price of these bonds will be $824,062.50 (or 82 and $^{13}/_{32}$) per bond, but the investor's net cost is lower by $119,062.50 due to a gain in the futures market.

The Short (or Selling) Hedge   A financial device designed to deal with rising interest rates is the **short hedge.** This hedge involves the immediate *sale* of financial futures until the actual assets must be sold in the cash market at some later point. Short hedges are especially useful to investors who may hold a large portfolio of assets they plan to sell in the future but, in the meantime, must be protected against the risk of declining prices. We examine a typical situation in which a securities dealer might employ the short hedge.

Suppose the dealer holds $1 million in U.S. Treasury bonds carrying an $8^3/_4$ percent coupon and a maturity of 20 years. The current price of these bonds is 94–26 (or 94 and $^{26}/_{32}$ which is $948.125 per $1,000 par value), which amounts to a yield of 9.25 percent. However, the dealer is concerned that interest rates may rise. Any increase in interest rates would bring about lower bond prices and therefore reduce the value of the dealer's portfolio. A possible remedy in this case is to *sell* bond

short hedge

EXHIBIT 9.7

An Example of a Short Futures Hedge Using U.S. Treasury Bonds

Source: Based on an example developed by the Chicago Board of Trade in an *Introduction to Financial Futures,* February 1981. Reprinted by permission of the Chicago Board of Trade.

Spot (or Cash) Market Transactions	Futures (or Forward) Market Transactions
October 1:	October 1:
A securities dealer owns $1 million of 20-year, $8^3/_4$ percent U.S. Treasury bonds priced at 94–26 to yield 9.25%.	The dealer sells 10 Treasury bond futures contracts at 86–28.
October 31:	October 31:
The dealer sells $1 million of 20-year, $8^3/_4$ percent U.S. Treasury bonds at 86–16 to yield 10.29%.	The dealer purchases 10 Treasury bond futures contracts at 79–26.
Results:	Results:
Loss of $83,125 in spot (cash) market.	Gain of $70,625 on futures trading (less brokerage commissions, interest cost on cash margin maintained, and tax obligation).

futures to counteract the anticipated decline in bond prices. For example, suppose the dealer decides to sell 10 Treasury bond futures at 86–28 and 30 days later is able to sell $1 million of 20-year, $8^3/_4$ percent Treasury bonds at a price of 86 and $^{16}/_{32}$ for a yield of 10.29 percent. At the same time, the dealer goes into the futures market and *buys* 10 Treasury bond contracts at 79–26 to offset the previous forward sale of bond futures.

The financial consequences of these combined trades in spot and futures markets are offsetting, as shown in Exhibit 9.7. The dealer has lost $83,125 in the cash market due to the price decline in bonds. However, a gain of $70,625 (less brokerage commissions, interest on cash margins held, and any tax liability) has resulted from the fall in the futures price. This dealer has helped insulate the value of his asset portfolio from the risk of price fluctuations through a short hedge.

cross hedge

Cross Hedging Another approach to minimizing risk is the **cross hedge**—a combined transaction between the spot market and the futures market using *different types of assets* in each market. This device rests on the assumption that the prices of most financial instruments tend to move in the same direction and by roughly the same proportion. Because this is only approximately true in the real world, profits or losses in the cash market will not exactly offset losses or profits in the futures market because *basis risk is greater with a cross hedge.* Nevertheless, if the investor's goal is to minimize risk, cross hedging is usually preferable to a completely unhedged position.

As an example, consider the case of a bank that holds corporate bonds carrying a face value of $5 million and an average maturity of 20 years. The bank's portfolio manager anticipates a rise in interest rates, which will reduce the value of the bonds. Unfortunately, there is only a limited futures market for corporate bonds, and the portfolio manager fears that she cannot construct an effective hedge for these assets. However, futures contracts exist for U.S. Treasury bonds, providing a *short cross hedge* against the risk of a decline in the value of the corporate bonds.

Executing a Trade and the Cash Margin

Most trading in financial futures contracts takes place through a broker or dealer who may find another party interested in participating in the trade or, more commonly, will contact a trader affiliated with an organized futures exchange. The floor trader will attempt to place the customer's order, either *electronically* or via *open outcry* on the floor of the exchange, seeking a counterparty interested in the terms being offered. If a

Information on the trading and pricing of financial futures contracts appears in many places on the Web, including the National Futures Association at **nfa.futures.org,** the Commodity Futures Trading Commission at **CFTC.com,** and City Link at **citylink-uk.com**

trade is successful the customer will be asked to post a *cash margin* (equal to a specified percentage of the value of the contracts traded) with his or her broker.

What is the purpose of the *cash margin* that each investor must post? It protects the customers, brokers, and traders against market risk. At the end of each trading day, the exchange clearinghouse is required to *mark to market* (value) each contract outstanding based on its closing price that day. The cash margin covers the loss when a futures contract falls in price. If the price decline is more than a specified percentage of the margin, the investor may get a *margin call* to post additional cash or securities for protection.

Payoff Diagrams for Long and Short Futures Contracts

We can represent losses or gains from trading in futures and from taking long or short hedging positions by using payoff diagrams of the type shown in Exhibit 9.8. In these diagrams, the different possible prices of futures (F_t) are shown along the horizontal axis. The vertical axis records any profits or losses (not including taxes and transactions costs) that result when futures prices move up or down.

A 45° line is drawn through the original purchase price (F_B) of the contract marked on both horizontal and vertical axes. Because the line through F_B has an angle of 45°, this means that, along this line, a change of \$1 in the futures price, up or down, also results in a \$1 profit or loss to the holder of the contract. Note, too, that there is no profit or loss when the futures contract price equals its original, or base, purchase price, F_B.

As the left-hand diagram in Exhibit 9.8 illustrates, the buyer of a long hedge in futures scores a profit if the price of the underlying asset and the value of the associated futures contract rise. This happens if interest rates fall, causing subsequent futures prices to climb above their base price ($F_t > F_B$). On the other hand, suppose that futures prices

EXHIBIT 9.8   **Payoffs for Long and Short Futures Positions**

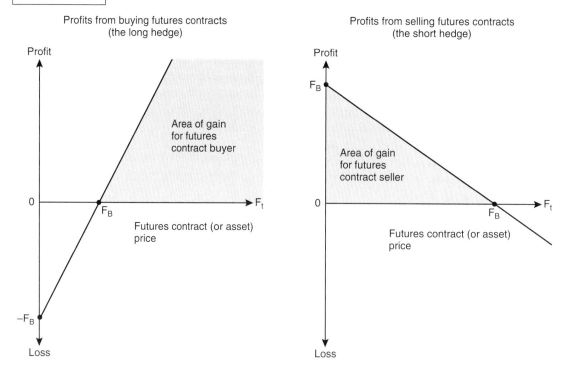

fall below the original purchase price, so that $F_t < F_B$ because interest rates have risen. Then the holder of a long hedge will suffer a loss.

The right-hand diagram in Exhibit 9.8 shows that the holder of a short futures position suffers losses when interest rates decline. In this case, the prices of the futures contract and of the assets named in that contract increase, forcing the holder of a short hedge to buy assets or futures at a higher price ($F_t > F_B$) to make delivery or to cancel out the short position. On the other hand, if interest rates rise, then the prices of futures (and the associated assets) eventually may drop below their original purchase price ($F_t < F_B$), handing the short hedger a profit.

Option Contracts on Financial Futures

option contract

In addition to financial futures contracts themselves, there is also active trading in options on financial futures contracts. An **option contract** is an agreement between a buyer and seller to grant the holder of the contract the right to buy or sell a futures contract or asset at a specified price on or before the day the contract expires. Options on farm commodities and on selected common stock have been traded for decades. There was an explosion of new options products in the 1980s, led by options on $100,000 Treasury bond futures introduced in October 1982. Then, in 1985, the International Monetary Market (IMM), a division of the Chicago Mercantile Exchange (CME), began trading option contracts on financial futures for Eurodollar deposits. As more investors began to take an interest in options trading, major exchanges around the world began developing many new option contracts on stock, foreign currencies, and financial futures contracts.

Basic Types of Option Contracts and Price Quotations   There are two

call options

basic types of option contracts. **Call options** give the contract buyer the right, but not the obligation, to buy ("call away") futures contracts or assets at a set price called the

strike price

strike price. The seller of the contract is called the *option writer.* Under the terms of U.S. or American options, the buyer may exercise the option and purchase the futures or assets specified from the writer at any time on or before the expiration date of the option. European options, on the other hand, can be exercised only on their expiration date. An option that is not used by its expiration date becomes worthless.

put options

Put options grant the contract purchaser the right, but not the obligation, to sell ("put," or deliver) futures contracts or securities to the option writer at a set (strike) price on or before the option's expiration date. Buyers of both call and put options

option premium

must pay an **option premium** for the privilege of being able to buy or sell futures or securities at a guaranteed price. By fixing the price of a financial transaction for a stipulated period, options provide an alternative way of hedging against market risk. Their principal advantage over futures contracts is that hedging with futures contracts limits the hedger's profits. Options, in contrast, can be used to limit losses while preserving the opportunity to make unlimited profits.

Recently more options and other securities have been traded electronically for greater speed and efficiency. A prominent example is the International Securities Exchange at **iseoptions.com,** which began trading options beginning in 2000.

Most options on financial instruments are traded today on organized exchanges such as the IMM or the Chicago Board Options Exchange (CBOE). Exchange-traded options are standardized contracts with uniform terms that enhance the marketability of options. The options exchange sets rules for trading and pricing options: The exchange clearinghouse keeps a record of all trades and guarantees performance on all exchange-traded options. In effect, the clearinghouse becomes the ultimate seller to all option buyers and the ultimate buyer for all option sellers.

Many option contracts are liquidated before they expire by each trader making an offsetting purchase or sale. For example, the buyer of a call option can "erase" his or her contract by selling a call option involving the same security with the same expiration

EXHIBIT 9.9

Examples of Daily
Price Quotations
on Option
Contracts

Strike (Exercise) Price	Call Options Settlement Prices		Put Options Settlement Prices	
	September	December	September	December
120	1–60	2–01	0–16	0–42
121	1–32	1–58	0–32	0–60
122	1–16	1–48	0–48	1–12

U.S. Treasury Bond Futures Options
(in Denominations of $100,000; Prices in 64ths of 100 Percent)

Estimated volume of trading: 120,000 contracts.

Open interest volume in call options: 485,776.

Open interest volume in put options: 250,715.

date and strike price. Put options are liquidated in the same fashion with the buyer (seller) of the put selling (buying) a comparable put on or before the expiration date.

Examples of Price Quotes on Options Contracts

One of the best-known exchange-traded options is the Treasury bond option contract, traded on the Chicago Board of Trade's Options Exchange in units of $100,000. The T-bond option contract's current price is quoted in points ($1 on a base of $100) and 64ths of a point. An example of the data most investors usually see on exchange traded options on their computers and in financial newspapers is shown in Exhibit 9.9.

Note, for example, that the option to *call* $100,000 U.S. Treasury bond futures contracts between now and their maturity date in September that carry a strike price of 120 (that is, $120,000 for a $100,000 futures contract) was trading at a market price of 1–60 (that is, 1 and $^{60}/_{64}$ for a $100 par value option, or $1,937.50 on a $100,000 face value call option contract). The prices of put options on T-bonds expiring in September and December appear in a companion table to the right of the table of call options. Trading volume information and the volume of uncancelled (open interest) options appear as a final item on many option price tables in the financial press.

As Exhibit 9.9 makes clear, the higher an option's strike price, the lower the call option's price (premium) tends to be, because there is less likelihood the call will be exercised. Moreover, call options expiring at a later date sell for higher premiums than those expiring sooner because there is more time in the case of the former options for security prices to change in a way that favors their exercise by the option buyer.

9.6 Options Offered on Exchanges Today

Just like financial futures contracts, there are numerous options calling for the delivery of equities, debt instruments, or financial futures. Exchange-traded put and call options have grown especially rapidly in recent years and are focused on instruments such as 30-day federal funds futures, Eurodollar and Euro deposit futures, Euro-denominated deposit futures, U.S. Treasury bills, notes, and bonds, and selected currency futures (including contracts for the delivery of Japanese yen, the British pound, the Swiss franc, and the European Union's Euro). There are also exchange-traded options on futures covering selected stock market indexes, such as the Dow Jones Industrial Average and the S&P 500 Stock Index, the S&P and the NASDAQ 100 stock indexes, and the New York Stock Exchange Composite Index.

Innovation is frequent in the options market; the exchanges are receptive to new instruments on a frequent basis. Recent examples include options on ETFs (which hold selected stock portfolios), LEAPS (which cover up to three years and are linked to any of about 450 stocks and 10 different stock indexes), and FLEX options (which permit professional investors to shape selected option contracts to match more closely their unique risk-management needs).

Uses of Options

Options have many uses. Their two most common ones involve (1) protecting a future investment's yield against falling interest rates by using call options and (2) protecting against rising interest rates by using put options.

Protecting against Declining Investment Yields   A major concern of most asset buyers is how to protect against falling yields and rising prices on bonds and other assets that will be purchased in the future. Options offer a way to prepare for a future investment, even if the investor doesn't yet have sufficient cash to make the investment, by carrying out a temporary transaction that helps guarantee future yields. An option contract enables an investor to set a maximum price for assets targeted for future purchase.

To learn more about options pricing and trading consider such sources as In the Money at **in-the-money.com** and CityLink at **citylink-uk.com**

For example, suppose a security dealer plans to buy $100 million in U.S. Treasury bonds in a few days and hopes to earn an interest yield of at least 7 percent. However, fearful of a substantial drop in interest rates before the dealer is ready to buy, he executes a call option on T-bond futures at a strike price of 120. If T-bond futures rise in value above 120 (i.e., fall below 7 percent in yield), the dealer probably will exercise the option because it is now "in the money." When the market price of a futures contract or asset rises above the strike price in the associated option contract, the buyer of the call option is said to be "in the money," because he or she can buy the futures contract or asset from the option writer at the strike price (in this case, at 120) and sell at a higher price (perhaps at 121) in futures or cash markets. The resulting profit (after paying the option's premium, taxes, and transactions costs) offsets the loss in yield on the planned investment due to a decline in market interest rates.

If interest rates go against the dealer's forecast, however, and rise instead, the call option will be "out of the money." Its strike price will be above the market's current price for the assets or futures covered by the option. In this case, the call will *not* be exercised, and the dealer will lose the premium he or she paid for the option. However, the fact that interest rates rose (and, therefore, Treasury bond prices fell) means the dealer can now purchase Treasury bonds at a cheaper price and a more desirable yield.

Incidentally, the profit on an exercised *call option* can be found by using the equation:

$$\text{Profit} = F - S - Pr - T \qquad (9.7)$$

where F is the current futures or asset price, S is the strike price agreed upon in the option contract, Pr is the premium paid by the call option buyer, and T represents any taxes owed as a result of the transaction. If the futures or asset price, F, rises high enough, the buyer can call away futures contracts or assets from the option writer at price S and still have some profit left over after paying the premium (Pr) and any taxes incurred (T). However, if the futures price, F, declines, the option will go unexercised and the buyer's loss will equal $-Pr$. The seller of the unexercised call will then reap a profit of $+Pr$.

Protecting against Rising Interest Rates   In contrast to lenders, who often worry about falling yields, borrowers' concerns usually are to keep borrowing costs from rising. Consider a bank, for example, that must borrow millions of dollars daily and fears rising money market interest rates. Perhaps market rates on deposits are currently at 8 percent and the bank fears a substantial rise in deposit interest costs to 9 percent. Accordingly, the bank's deposit manager purchases a put option on Eurodollar futures at a strike price of 92. If these futures fall below 92 in price due to rising interest rates, the bank's liability manager may decide to exercise the put option and sell Eurodollar futures to the option writer at the strike price. The manager will then liquidate the bank's futures position by buying equivalent futures contracts at the now lower market price and profit from the spread between the strike price of 92 and the current lower market price. This profit will at least partially offset the bank's higher borrowing costs.

On the other hand, if interest rates do not rise, the bank's deposit manager will not exercise the put option. This will mean losing the full amount of the option premium, but the bank's borrowing costs will stay low. In this instance, it paid a premium for interest rate insurance that turned out not to be needed.

The profit to the buyer of a *put option* can be calculated from the following equation:

$$\text{Profit} = S - F - Pr - T \tag{9.8}$$

where S is the strike price, F the market price of the futures or assets named in the option, Pr the premium paid for the option, and T taxes owed. If the futures or asset price, F, falls far enough below strike price S, the put buyer will show a profit $S - F$. On the other hand, if the futures or asset price rises, the put will go unexercised, and the buyer's loss will be measured by $-Pr$. The seller of the unexercised put will then experience a corresponding profit of $+Pr$.

Payoff Diagrams for Valuing Options

We can diagram how options are valued by looking first at the value of a put option to the investor who holds it (the option buyer) on the date or dates the option can be exercised. Exhibit 9.10 illustrates the relationship between a put option's value and the value of the underlying futures contract or asset named in the option. Point S marked on the horizontal axis in Exhibit 9.10 represents the strike price, the price at which the futures contract or asset can be sold by the option's holder.

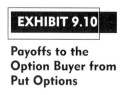

EXHIBIT 9.10

Payoffs to the Option Buyer from Put Options

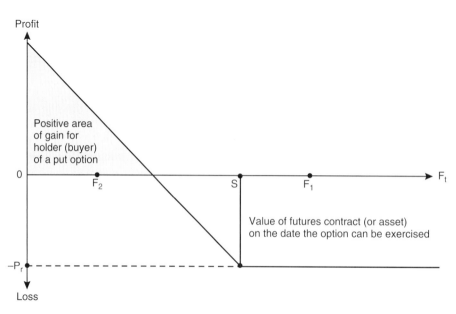

Suppose the futures contract or asset in question currently is selling for price F_1, which is more than its strike price, S (i.e., $F_1 > S$). In this case, the option has a current value of zero (actually less than zero because the option buyer had to pay premium Pr, which is lost if the option goes unexercised). The holder of the option would prefer to sell the futures contracts she holds at current market price F_1 rather than deliver them to the option writer for a price of only S. If current price F_1 is significantly larger than S, however, the option buyer may still reap a substantial gain despite losing the option premium.

In contrast, suppose that the futures contract has a current price of F_2, where $F_2 < S$. In this instance, with a market price lower than the strike price, exercise of the option results in a profit for its buyer. The option buyer will deliver the futures to the option writer and receive strike price S for a net profit per contract of $S - F_2 - Pr - T$. Clearly for the holder of a put option, when $S > F_t$, the option will normally be exercised for a profit and be "in the money" as long as $S - F_t$ exceeds the option premium, taxes, and transactions costs. When $S < F_t$, the option will expire unexercised; the profit will be zero or negative and clearly will be "out of the money." Only within the triangle in the upper left-hand corner of Exhibit 9.10 will the holder of a put option reap positive gains.

From the standpoint of the writer (seller) of a put option, the writer benefits if the option is *not* exercised. This happens if the market value of the futures contract or asset remains higher than the option's strike price, as at $F_1 > S$. Exhibit 9.11 shows the area of gain for the writer of a put option lies around and to the right of strike price S. In this region, the option currently is "out of the money" from the buyer's standpoint, and the writer pockets the premium paid by the option holder.

In the case of *call options*, the writer agrees to sell securities to the buyer of the option at a stipulated strike price. If, as shown in Exhibit 9.12, the market price of the underlying futures contract or asset rises above the strike price to F_1, the holder of the call option will exercise that option and call away the futures contract or asset from the option writer at strike price S. Exercise of this now "in the money" call option will enable the option buyer to resell each of the newly acquired futures contracts or assets for a profit of $F_1 - S - Pr - T$. If, on the other hand, the market value of futures contracts or assets falls *below* the option's strike price, as at F_2, the option holder would be better off purchasing the futures contracts or assets in the open market rather than exercising his or her option to buy at price S. The call will

EXHIBIT 9.11

Payoffs for Put Options to the Option Writer

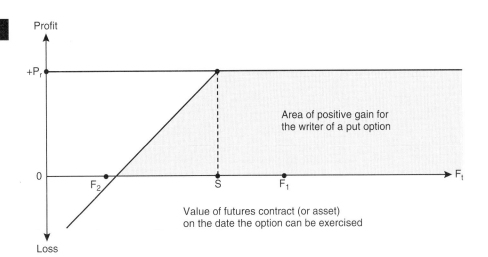

EXHIBIT 9.12

Payoffs to the Option Buyer from Call Options

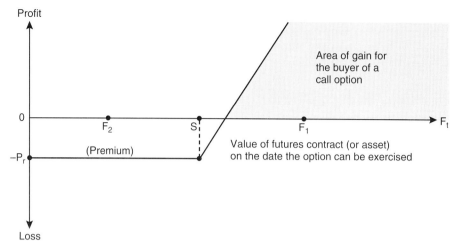

expire unused ("out of the money"), and the option buyer will suffer a loss due to the premium (Pr) he or she has paid. Thus, the area of positive gain to the holder of a call option generally lies to the right of the strike price in Exhibit 9.12 and in the upper right-hand portion of that diagram.

The writer of a call option, on the other hand, gains when the market value of the futures contract or asset falls below the strike price, as at $F_2 < S$ in Exhibit 9.13. At this price and at all prices below S, the call option is "out of the money" for the option buyer and will go unexercised, allowing the option writer to earn the option premium, Pr. However, if the futures' or asset's market value climbs above S, as at price F_1 in Exhibit 9.13, the writer must sell off from his portfolio of currently higher-valued assets to the option buyer at the low contract price S, taking a loss equal to $F_1 - S$. The call option clearly has become "in the money" for the option buyer. As shown in Exhibit 9.13, the region of positive gain for the writer of a call option lies in the upper left-hand portion of the price diagram (including price F_2). In contrast, futures or asset prices increasingly to the right of point S result in decreasing profits or increasing losses for the option writer.

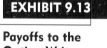

EXHIBIT 9.13

Payoffs to the Option Writer from Call Options

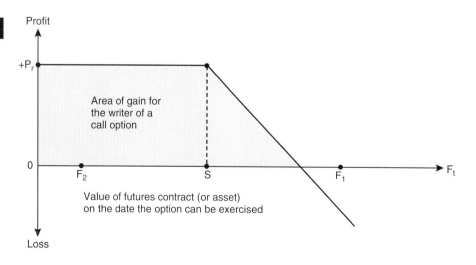

9.7 Risks, Costs, and Rules for Trading in Derivatives

Risks and Costs Associated with Futures and Options

Futures and options trading is not without its own special risks and costs. The risk of price and yield fluctuations can be reduced by negotiating these contracts, but the investor faces the risk of changing interest rates and asset prices between futures and spot markets (*basis risk*). It is rare that gains and losses from simultaneous trading in spot, futures, or options markets exactly offset each other, resulting in a perfect hedge. There is the risk of broker cash margin calls due to adverse price movements (*margin risk*), as well as possible problems in liquidating an open position in futures or options (*liquidity risk*). Moreover, there are substantial brokerage fees for executing trades and required minimum deposits in margin accounts that tie up cash in non-interest-bearing assets. The decision to trade financial futures and options contracts is, like everything else in life, a cost versus benefit issue.

Accounting Rules for Transactions Involving Derivatives

The rapid expansion of trading has led to new accounting rules to promote fuller disclosure of risk exposures and to permit management and outsiders to judge the effectiveness of hedging techniques. Late in the 1990s, the Financial Accounting Standards Board (FASB) issued FASB 133, followed subsequently by FASB 137 and 138. These new rules stipulate that the derivative positions of publicly traded companies should be reflected in the values of assets and liabilities shown on their balance sheets. Derivatives must be reported at their *fair value,* as determined by an instrument's discounted cash flows (as explained in Chapter 6). Any shift in the fair value of a derivative or in the value of the underlying asset or liability being hedged must be captured on the hedging institution's income statement.

FASB also addressed the accounting consequences of *cash-flow hedges,* which are designed to protect the investor against liabilities associated with such things as interest income expected from loans and interest costs associated with taking on liabilities. The portion of a cash-flow hedge that is *effective* should be reflected in a hedging institution's equity capital. The ineffective part of any cash-flow hedge, on the other hand, must be recorded on the hedger's income statement.

QUESTIONS TO HELP YOU STUDY

17. Define and explain the use of the following: (a) long hedge; (b) short hedge; and (c) cross hedge.

18. Which type of hedge named above works best in an environment of rising interest rates? Of falling interest rates? Illustrate both cases using a payoff diagram.

19. Explain the uses of the following instruments: (a) call options; and (b) put options.

20. What type of option contract is appropriate in an environment of rising interest rates? Falling interest rates? Illustrate using payoff diagrams.

21. What risks and costs are inherent in financial futures and options trading?

22. What is FASB 133 and how does it relate to the value and impact of derivatives on publicly traded companies?

> ## MARKETS ON THE NET: The Most Important Web Sites for This Chapter
>
> Chicago Board of Trade (cbot.com)
> Chicago Board Options Exchange (cboe.com)
> Chicago Mercantile Exchange (cme.com)
> Commodity Futures Trading Commission (CFTC.com)
> London International Financial Futures and Options Exchange (liffe.com)
>
> The American Stock Exchange (amex.com)
> The Brussels Exchange (belfox.be)
> The Financial Pipeline: Derivatives Concepts (finpipe.com/derivglossary.htm)
> The International Securities Exchange (iseoptions.com)
> The New York Board of Trade (nyce.com)
> The Pacific Exchange (pacificex.com)

Summary of the Chapter's Main Points

This chapter is devoted to the forecasting (predicting) and hedging (risk protection activities) associated with changing interest rates and changes in the prices of financial assets. Among its most important conclusions are:

- Interest rates appear to bear a close relationship to the *economy,* and especially to the *business cycle,* tending to rise in periods of economic expansion and fall in recessions.

- Short-term interest rates tend to change more rapidly than long-term interest rates, moving over a much wider range than long-term interest rates as economic conditions change.

- Several different methods of interest-rate forecasting have been employed in recent years, though none have been consistently successful. Most forecasting approaches today rely upon linkages between the economy and the financial system, and upon tracking the changing expectations of borrowers and lenders in the financial marketplace as reflected in such indicators as the prices and yields attached to financial futures contracts.

- The great difficulties inherent in forecasting interest rates have led many borrowers and lenders of funds to practice *hedging,* insulating themselves at least partially from the ravages of fluctuating interest rates and asset prices in the financial marketplace.

- In recent years one of the most popular of all interest-rate and asset-price hedging tools has been the *interest rate swap,* in which borrowing institutions exchange interest payments with each other. The net effect of a well-drawn swap agreement is to achieve a better balance between interest revenues and interest costs. Such transactions may also lower interest costs for participants in a swap agreement.

- During the 1970s and 1980s *financial futures* and *options contracts* on a variety of debt securities, stocks, and stock indexes began trading in the United States at the Chicago Board of Trade (CBOT) and the Chicago Mercantile Exchange (CME) and, subsequently, spread around the world on multiple exchanges, such as the London International Financial Futures and Options Exchange (LIFFE). Both futures and options are contracts calling for the future delivery of assets or cash at an agreed-upon price in an effort to set the price or yield on a future trade and, thereby, lessen the risk associated with future price and interest-rate fluctuations.

www.mhhe.com/rose9e

- Hedging with financial futures contracts and options transfers risk from one investor to another willing to bear that risk. The hedger contracts away all or a portion of the risk of asset-price and interest-rate fluctuations in order to lock in a targeted rate of return or asset value. This is accomplished by taking equal and opposite positions in the spot (cash) market and in the forward (or futures) market or by purchasing put or call options to deliver or take delivery of designated assets at a stipulated price on or before a specific date.

- If interest rates are expected to *fall* and an investor desires to lock in a current high yield on an asset, he or she would buy a contract calling for the future delivery of the security (or other financial asset) at a set price (i.e., take on a *long hedge*) or purchase a *call option* contract. An opposite set of buy-sell transactions in the futures market (i.e., a *short hedge*) or in the options market (i.e., a *put option*) would generally be used if interest rates were expected to *rise*.

Key Terms Appearing in This Chapter

business cycle, 238
seasonality, 239
implied forecasting, 240
interest rate swap, 242
hedging, 246
basis, 247
financial futures contracts, 248
long hedge, 252

short hedge, 254
cross hedge, 255
option contract, 257
call options, 257
strike price, 257
put options, 257
option premium, 257

Problems and Issues

1. In an interest rate swap transaction, a large corporation can borrow in the bond market at a current fixed rate of 9 percent and can also obtain a floating-rate loan in the short-term market at the prime bank rate. However, this firm wishes to borrow short term because it has a large block of assets that roll over into cash each month. The other party to the swap is a company with a lower credit rating that can borrow in the bond market at a long-term interest rate of 11.5 percent and in the short-term market at prime plus 1.50 percent. This lower-rated company has long-term predictable cash inflows, however. The higher-credit-rated company wishes to pay for its part in the swap an interest rate of prime less 50 basis points. The lower-rated company is willing to pay the underwriting cost associated with the higher-rated company's security issue, which is estimated to be 25 basis points. The swap transaction is valued at $100 million. What kind of interest rate swap can be arranged here? Which company will borrow short term and which long term? If the prime bank rate is currently 10 percent, who will pay what interest cost to whom? Explain what the benefit is to each party in this swap.

2. Suppose that a top-quality firm with an A-1 or AAA credit rating can borrow at a fixed coupon rate attached to its bonds of 12 percent. Moreover, this firm's bank is willing to extend it a LIBOR-based loan in London at a rate of 9.5 percent that will change weekly as LIBOR moves. Working through its principal banker, this top-rated company makes contact with a firm whose credit rating is considerably lower (rated only BB). The lower-rated firm has been informed by its investment

banker that it probably could sell bonds at a 14 percent coupon rate, and the finance company from which it receives short-term money has promised a LIBOR-based floating-rate loan of 11.25 percent. Could these two firms benefit from a swap under the interest rates given above? Which firm would save the most, and under what circumstances? Will the company with the lower credit rating have to offer the top-credit-quality firm an added inducement to participate in a rate swap? What inducements could be used to equalize the interest savings for both parties?

3. A large money center bank plans to offer money market CDs in substantial volume (at least $100 million) in six months due to a projected upsurge in credit deals from some of its most valued corporate customers. Unfortunately, the bank's economist has just predicted that money market interest rates should rise over the next year (with perhaps a full 1.5 percentage point increase within the next six months). Explain why the bank's management would be concerned about this development. Suppose management expects its corporate loan customers to resist any loan terms that would automatically result in loan rates being immediately adjusted upward to reflect rate increases in the money market. What futures market transaction would you recommend? What is the best options contract alternative for the bank?

4. An investment banking firm discovers that 90 days from today it is due to receive a cash payment from one of its corporate clients of $972,500. The firm's portfolio manager is instructed to plan to invest this new cash for a horizon of three months, after which it will be liquidated. Interest rates are attractive today at 10 percent, but a steep decline is forecast due to a developing recession. The portfolio manager decides to try to guarantee a 9 percent rate of return today on this planned three-month investment of cash.

    a. Describe what the manager should do today in the financial futures market. Then, indicate how he will close out the futures position eventually.

    b. What are the appropriate (buy-sell) steps for the manager if options on financial futures are to be used?

5. During the month just concluded, the prices of U.S. Treasury bonds fluctuated between a price of $95 (based on a $100 par value) and a price of $93. Treasury bond futures over the same period fluctuated between $92 and $88 (based on a $100 par value). How did the *basis* for T-bond futures contracts change over this period? What was the *volatility ratio* for T-bond futures for the month just ended? Now assume you wish to hedge for the next 30 days $25 million in Treasury bonds that you currently hold with $100,000 denomination T-bond futures contracts maturing in 90 days. Using the volatility ratio you calculated above, how many T-bond futures contracts will you need to buy to fully cover the $25 million in securities at risk?

Web-Based Problems

1. Interest rate swap contracts carry market interest rates that vary with the maturity of each swap and its degree of risk exposure. There is also a swap yield curve that is constructed each day and is carefully followed by thousands of institutions and individuals. This version of the yield curve reports the interest rates that a fixed-rate swap partner would pay based on representative swap rates and maturities as collected by survey each day. Consulting information sources such

as the International Swaps and Derivatives Association **isda.org/index.html**, the Chicago Board of Trade **cbot.com**, and the Federal Reserve System **federalreserve.gov**, see if you can construct a recent swap yield curve. How does it compare with a Treasury yield curve (as found in *The Wall Street Journal* at **wsj.com**, for example) covering the same range of maturities? What might explain any differences you observe?

2. Visit the Web sites of the leading financial futures and options exchanges in the world—in particular, the Chicago Board of Trade at **cbot.com**, the Chicago Mercantile Exchange at **cme.com**, and the London Financial Futures and Options Exchange at **liffe.com**. Make a list of the principal financial futures and options contracts (measured by trading volume) currently actively traded on these exchanges. Which contracts are the most popular and why? What kinds of risk exposure does each contract deal with? What types of institutions would most benefit from these particular contracts? Are there any new futures or options contracts under development?

Semester Project: A Study of the Fed Funds Market

Earlier in this semester project you learned that the key short-term interest rate in the economy is the *federal funds rate* and that the Federal Reserve keeps that rate close to a preannounced "target value." When the Fed changes its Fed funds "target," all other short-term interest rates respond. This fact of life in the financial marketplace creates a demand for a market that permits institutions that rely heavily on short-term funding to hedge against future changes in monetary policy that could increase their funding costs and threaten their profitability. In this case, the hedging market is the 30-day Fed funds futures market centered at the Chicago Board of Trade (CBOT). The terms of settlement in this market are based on the average effective Fed funds interest rate each month.

The *buyer* of a Fed funds futures contract on the CBOT exchange receives a certain quantity of cash ($5 million per contract) at the end of the month. These funds are purchased at a "discount" where the rate of discount continually adjusts to the market's changing expectation of what the average daily effective Fed funds rate will be for the month. At the conclusion of each day's trading activity, CBOT reports "Settlement Prices," equal to 100 minus the expected value of the effective funds rate at month's end.

   a. In this installment of the semester project, go to CBOT's Web site at **cbot.com** and click on "30 Day Fed Funds." The table you will find there lists futures contracts currently traded by their month of expiration, beginning with the current month.

   b. If the market has closed, go to the "Settle" column and compute what the market's expectation is for the average daily effective Fed funds rate for each month listed. If the market is still open when you arrive at the site, use the "Prev Settle" from the prior day's trades.

   c. Is the market expecting the Fed funds rate to rise, fall, or remain unchanged over the next few months? How do you know?

Selected References to Explore

Black, Fisher, and M. Scholes. "The Pricing of Options and Corporate Liabilities." *Journal of Political Economy* 81 (May–June 1973), pp. 637–54.

Haubrich, Joseph G. "Swaps and the Swaps Yield Curve." *Economic Commentary,* Federal Reserve Bank of Cleveland, December 2001, pp.1–4.

Lopez, Jose A. "Supervising Interest Rate Risk Management," *FRBSF Economic Letter,* Federal Reserve Bank of San Francisco, No. 2004–26, September 17, 2004.

Nosal, Ed, and Tan Wang. "Arbitrage: The Key to Pricing Options." *Economic Commentary,* Federal Reserve Bank of Cleveland, January 1, 2004.

Sundaresan, Suresh. *Fixed Income Markets and Their Derivatives.* Cincinnati: Southwestern Publishing, 1997.

www.mhhe.com/rose9e

Appendix

The Black-Scholes Model for Valuing Options

With the rapid growth of options around the world, analysts and investors began to take great interest in the question of how options should be valued or priced. However, establishing the true value of an option was a daunting task that went unresolved for many years because options are so unusual. For example, unlike most bonds and stocks, many options turn out to be completely valueless due to adverse movements in the price of the asset to which they apply.

Suppose you hold a *call option* allowing you to purchase General Electric (GE) stock at $40 per share from the option writer but GE's stock remains *below* $40 in the market for the entire term of your option. Then you won't exercise it because you can buy GE stock more cheaply in the open market. On the other hand, if GE stock climbs above $40, say to $45 per share, you *will* exercise the call option and earn $5 for every GE share you acquire. Should the stock's market value continue rising, your profit will grow. But you don't know which outcome—profit or no value at all—will surface during the term of your option.

Discounting an option's possible future cash flows in order to find its true value is hard to do because so much depends upon whether the underlying asset will rise or fall in price. If, in the example above, GE stock rises above $40 per share, there *will* be future cash flows after exercising the option. On the other hand, if GE stock declines below $40, there not only will be *no* positive cash flow at all, but cash flow will actually be *negative* because the investor must pay out a premium up front to acquire the option to begin with.

How is it possible to correctly price an option bearing such skewed and uncertain cash flows? A major breakthrough occurred when researchers Fisher Black and Myron Scholes (1973) developed a model to explain the price of a call option (*C*) using continuous-time mathematics. They discovered that the value of an option depends upon five key variables:

Rf = The *risk-free rate of interest* (such as that attached to default-free government securities), which is positively related to option prices.

P = The *current market value* (price) of the asset that is the subject of the option contract, which is positively related to the option's price.

σ = The *degree of volatility* in the value of the underlying asset, measured by the variance (σ^2) or standard deviation (σ) of its rate of return, which is also positively related to the price of the option.

S = The *strike price* specified in the option contract, which is negatively related to the price of the option.

t = The *length of time* between now and when the option expires, also positively related to the option's price.

The model that Fisher Black and Myron Scholes developed to explain the price of a call option (*C*) states that the call option's price can be found by using the following equation:

$$C = P \times Nr\,(Y_A) - Se^{-Rft} \times Nr\,(Y_B) \quad \textbf{(A.1)}$$

where

$$Y_A = [\ln(P/S) + Rft + \sigma^2 t/2]\sigma t^{1/2} \quad \textbf{(A.2)}$$

and

$$Y_B = [\ln(P/S) + Rft - \sigma^2 t/2]\sigma t^{1/2} \quad \textbf{(A.3)}$$

In the above formula, *ln* represents the log of a quantity relative to the base *e*, and *Nr* stands for the normal cumulative probability density function, measuring the probability that a normally distributed random variable will be equal to or less than *Y*. Many traders operating today on Wall Street use computer programs that calculate the expected value of an option as figured from the above formula and then buy or sell options or securities until option prices approach their expected levels. (See the accompanying box for an example of using the Black-Scholes formula to calculate an option's expected value.)

Reduced to nonmathematical terms, the preceding equation suggests that option prices depend on the expected value of the underlying asset named in the option and the expected value of the strike price on the day the option expires, both expressed in present value terms. The discount rate used is the risk-free interest rate because, Black and Scholes assumed, there are enough informed and technically sophisticated

269

investors to effectively reduce risk close to the risk-free rate of return by constructing an adequately hedged investment portfolio. In such a portfolio, movements in the value of options, futures, and assets will offset each other, leaving the value of the investor's total portfolio better protected against adverse price and rate movements (though there always remains some unhedgeable volatility risk).

Subsequent testing of the Black-Scholes model suggests that it performs reasonably well at calculating the true value of European options (which can be exercised only on a single day), making significant errors only when the underlying assets have especially large or small variability in rates of return or, in the case of options on stock, when a stock's dividend payments are significant.[1]

Pricing Options: An Example

To illustrate how to price an option using the Black-Scholes model, let's suppose that the current price of the asset in which we are interested is $100 with a standard deviation around its expected rate of return of 0.50, or 50 percent; that the option on this asset has a strike price of $95; and that the risk-free interest rate is currently 10 percent. If the option will expire in three months (0.25 years), what is its expected price?

The expected current price of a *call option* (*C*) on this asset can be found from:

$$\text{Expected call option price (C)} = P \times Nr(Y_A) - Se^{-Rf \times t} \times Nr(Y_B)$$

where P is the current market price, S the strike price, Rf the risk-free rate, and t the option's time to maturity. The terms $Nr(Y_A)$ and $Nr(Y_B)$ measure the probability the option will have value to the buyer (i.e., the probability the option will eventually be exercised because it is "in the money"). The higher the probability an option will be "in the money," the higher must be its price to the option buyer. Nr represents the normal distribution; the asset's return is assumed to be normally distributed.

We can calculate the probability that this option will pay off from:

$$Y_A = [\ln(P/S) + Rf \times t + \sigma^2 t/2]/\sigma t^{1/2}$$

Substituting in the figures from our example,

$$Y_A = (\ln[100/95] + [0.10 \times 0.25] + 0.25 \times (0.50)^2/2)/0.50 \times (.25)^{1/2} = 0.43$$

continued

---

[1] The Black-Scholes formula in Equation A.1 measures the expected value of a *call option* (*C*). We can find the expected value of the corresponding *put* option having the same strike price and time to maturity by solving:

$$\text{Expected value of put} = C + Se^{-Rf \times t} - P$$

where P is the price of the underlying security or futures contract and S, Rf, and t are the same as defined for Equation A.1.

The Black-Scholes option pricing model rests on some strong assumptions. It assumes there are no transactions costs or taxes, that the underlying asset does not pay out income during the life of an option, that the standard deviation of return is constant, that asset prices follow a continuous random process, that homogenous expectations exist among investors, and that the risk-free interest rate is constant over time and the same regardless of maturity. However, repeated testing suggests that even if these assumptions are violated, the option value estimates generated by the Black-Scholes model usually are remarkably close to real-world values.

concluded

We derive the second probability estimate in the equation, Y_B, from:

$$Y_B = Y_A - \sigma t^{1/2} = (0.43) - (0.50) \times (0.25)^{1/2} = 0.18$$

Next, we find the corresponding values from the assumed normal distribution of asset prices, represented by $Nr(Y_A)$ and $Nr(Y_B)$. These we can look up in a table for the cumulative normal distribution or by using appropriate software. A portion of such a table is given below:

Cumulative Normal Distribution Table

Y	Nr(Y)	Y	Nr(Y)	Y	Nr(Y)	Y	Nr(Y)
−0.50	.3085	−0.20	.4207	0.12	.5478	0.20	.5793
−0.40	.3446	−0.10	.4602	0.14	.5557	0.30	.6179
−0.30	.3821	0.00	.5000	0.16	.5636	0.40	.6554
−0.25	.4013	0.10	.5398	0.18	.5714	0.50	.6915

Checking the above table and interpolating if necessary for the normal probabilities associated with Y_A and Y_B gives:

$$Nr(0.43) = .6664$$

$$Nr(0.18) = .5714$$

Then, the expected value of the call option must be:

$$\text{Expected call option price (C)} = \$100 \times (.6664) - \$95 \times e^{-10 \times 0.25} \times (.5714) = \$13.70$$

Could we also find the value of a put option for this same asset? Assuming the same option strike price and maturity, the expected value of the corresponding put option would be:

$$\text{Expected put option price} = C + Se^{-Rf \times t} - P$$

Substituting in the calculated call option price (C) of $13.70, the asset's price (P) of $100, the strike price (S) of $95, the risk-free interest rate (Rf) of 10 percent, and 0.25 years time to maturity (t) from the example above, we get an expected put option price of:

$$\text{Expected put option price} = \$13.70 + \$95e^{(-.10 \times 0.25)} - 100$$

Checking the value of $e^{(-10 \times 0.25)}$ on a calculator gives:

$$\text{Expected put option price} = \$13.7 + \$95(0.9753) - \$100 = \$6.35$$

Part 3

The Money Market and Central Banking

When you think of "money" what comes to mind? Ferraris? Movie stars on opening night? South Beach? Those images suggest what money can *buy*! But where *is* the money that bought the Ferrari, the movie star's evening gown, or the time needed to get that South Beach tan? Typically, the actual dollars exchanged to acquire these symbols of wealth would continue to change hands long after those transactions were complete. For example, the car dealer who sold the Ferrari may have deposited the payment he received in his bank account. In turn, his bank may have purchased a Treasury bill with those funds and then issued a repurchase agreement against the T-bill to raise more money in order to cover a cash withdrawal by the movie star who purchased the evening gown. The salon that sold the gown may have deposited the proceeds of that sale in its money market fund, which in turn might have purchased a certificate of deposit (CD) from a bank that needed funds in order to make a vacation loan so the lady next door could lie contentedly in the white sand tanning her body at South Beach!

What makes all of this economic activity possible? It's not just money, but rather the institution we call "the money market." It's really not a single market, but rather a *collection* of markets. In the sequence of transactions discussed above there were exchanges of money for goods and services, but there were also exchanges of money for short-term financial instruments—the Treasury bill, the money market fund account, the bank CD, and the repurchase agreement—and for each of these financial instruments there are markets that are absolutely crucial to a smoothly functioning, vibrant economy. In Part Three we want to think about "money," not in terms of the goods and services it buys, but in terms of the markets that make so many of these purchases possible because of their great speed and efficiency. Speed, dexterity, and innovation are hallmarks of the money market. Its sole purpose is to bring together those individuals or institutions with temporary cash surpluses—that could be earning interest—with those who demand cash in order to make purchases or pay debts. The needs of individuals and institutions demanding and supplying cash are varied and the rich array of short-term financial instruments created to accommodate those needs lies at the heart of the money market. Our first goal in Part Three, which we pursue in Chapters 10 and 11, is to understand each of the more important financial instruments that comprise the money market.

Our second goal in Part Three is to examine a very important governmental institution in the money market—the *central bank*. The activities of the central bank are closely monitored and anticipated by the financial marketplace because of its ability to impact short-term interest rates. In Chapters 12 and 13 we examine the organization and activities of central banks, with particular emphasis on the U.S. central bank—the Federal Reserve System. Here we will gain an understanding of *how* the central bank can exercise its considerable influence over money market interest rates by altering the supply of money in the economy. The central bank's decision to change interest rates is actually made by just a handful of people. We will learn who these people are, how they are chosen, and, most importantly, why these policymakers may choose to alter short-term interest rates in order to affect the overall performance of the economy.

Chapter 10

Introduction to the Money Market and the Roles Played by Governments and Security Dealers

Learning Objectives

in This Chapter

- You will understand the many roles and functions performed by the money market in order to aid the financial system and the economy.

- You will also be able to determine who the key actors—individuals and institutions—are in the workings of the money market.

- You will examine the roles that governments and security dealers play in the functioning of the money market.

- You will discover how Treasury bills and repurchase agreements (RPs) arise through borrowing and lending in the money market.

What's in This Chapter?
Key Topics Outline

Nature and Characteristics of the Money Market

Key Borrowers and Lenders and the Structure of the Money Market

Money Market Investor Goals and Investment Risks

Government Involvement in the Money Market

Treasury Bills: Growth, Types, and Yields

Primary Security Dealers

Repurchase Agreements (RPs)

10.1   Introduction: The Market for Short-Term Credit

To the casual observer, the financial markets appear to be one vast cauldron of borrowing and lending activity in which some individuals and institutions are seeking credit while others supply the funds needed to make lending possible. All transactions carried out in the financial markets seem to be basically the same: borrowers issue securities (financial assets) that lenders purchase. When the loan is repaid, the borrower retrieves the securities and returns borrowed funds to the lender. Closer examination of our financial system reveals, however, that beyond the simple act of exchanging financial assets and funds, there are major differences between one financial transaction and another.

For example, an individual may borrow $100,000 for 30 years to purchase a new home, whereas another's financing need may be for a six-month loan of $3,000 to cover a federal income tax obligation. A corporation may enter the financial markets this week to offer a new issue of 20-year bonds to finance the construction of an office building, and next week it may find itself in need of funds for just 60 days to purchase raw materials so that production can continue.

Clearly, then, the purposes for which money is borrowed within the financial system vary greatly among individuals and institutions and from transaction to transaction. And the different purposes for which money is borrowed result in the creation of different kinds of financial assets, having different maturities, risks, and other features. In this chapter and the others in Part Three, we will be focusing on a collection of financial markets that share a common purpose in their trading activity and deal in financial instruments with similar features. Our particular focus is on the *money market*—the market for short-term credit.

In the money market nearly all loans have an original maturity of one year or less. Money market loans are used to help corporations and governments pay the wages and salaries of their workers, make repairs, purchase inventories, pay dividends and taxes, and satisfy other short-term, working capital needs. In this respect, the money market stands in sharp contrast to the capital market. The capital market deals in long-term credit—that is, loans and securities over a year to maturity, typically used to finance long-term investment projects. There are important similarities between the money and capital markets, as we will see in subsequent chapters, but there are also important differences that make each of these two markets unique.

10.2   Characteristics of the Money Market

What the Money Market Does

money market

The money market, like all financial markets, provides a channel for the exchange of financial assets for money. However, it differs from other parts of the financial system in its emphasis on loans to meet purely short-term cash needs (i.e., current account, rather than capital account, transactions). The **money market** is the mechanism through which *holders of temporary cash surpluses meet holders of temporary cash deficits*. It is designed, on the one hand, to meet the short-term cash requirements of corporations, financial institutions, and governments, providing a mechanism for granting loans as short as overnight and as long as one year to maturity. At the same time, the money market provides an investment outlet for those spending units (also principally corporations, financial institutions, and governments) that hold surplus cash for short periods of time and wish to earn at least some return on temporarily idle funds. The essential function of the money market is to bring these two groups into contact with each other in order to make borrowing and lending possible.

The Need for a Money Market

Why is such a market needed? There are several reasons. First, for most individuals and institutions, inflows and outflows of cash are rarely in perfect harmony with each other. Governments, for example, collect taxes from the public only at certain times of the year, such as in April in the United States, when personal and corporate income tax payments are due. Disbursements of cash must be made throughout the year, however, to cover the wages and salaries of government employees, office supplies, repairs, and fuel costs, as well as unexpected expenses. When taxes are collected, governments usually are flush with funds that far exceed their immediate cash needs. At these times, they frequently enter the money market as lenders and purchase Treasury bills, bank certificates of deposit (CDs), and other attractive financial assets. Later, however, as cash runs low relative to current expenditures, these same governmental units must once again enter the money market as borrowers of funds, issuing short-term notes attractive to money market investors.

Business firms, too, collect sales revenues from customers at one point in time and dispense cash at other points in time to cover wages and salaries, make repairs, and meet other operating expenses. The checking account of an active business firm fluctuates daily between large cash surpluses and low or nonexistent cash balances. A surplus cash position frequently brings such a firm into the money market as a net lender of funds, investing idle funds in the hope of earning at least a modest rate of return. Cash deficits force it onto the borrowing side of the money market, however, seeking other institutions with temporary cash surpluses. Clearly, then, the money market serves to bridge the gap between receipts and expenditures of funds, covering cash deficits with short-term borrowing when current expenditures exceed receipts and providing an investment outlet to earn interest income for units whose current receipts exceed their current expenditures.

To fully appreciate the workings of the money market, we must remember that *money* is one of the most perishable of all commodities. The holding of idle surplus cash is expensive, because cash balances earn little or no income for their owners. When idle cash is not invested, the holder incurs an opportunity cost in the form of interest income that is forgone. Moreover, each day that idle funds are not invested is a day's income lost forever. When large amounts of funds are involved, the income lost from not profitably investing idle funds for even 24 hours can be substantial. For example, the interest income from a loan of $10 million for one day at a 10 percent annual rate of interest amounts to nearly $2,800.[1] In a week's time, nearly $20,000 in interest would be lost from not investing $10 million in idle funds. Many students of the financial system find it hard to believe that investment outlets exist for loans as short as one day or even less. However, billions of dollars in credit are extended in the money market overnight or for only a few daylight hours to securities dealers, banks, and nonfinancial corporations to cover temporary shortfalls of cash. As we will see in the next chapter, one important money market instrument—the federal funds loan—is designed mainly for extending credit within a day or less or over a weekend.

To help find answers to issues raised as you read this chapter, you may enjoy checking out investopedia.com

---

[1]As we saw in Chapter 6, the amount of interest income from a simple interest loan may be calculated from the formula:
$$I = P \times r \times t$$
where *I* is interest income, *P* is the principal amount loaned, *r* is the annual rate of interest, and *t* is the maturity of the loan. In the example given above, we have
$$I = (\$10,000,000)(0.10)(1/360) = \$2,777.78$$
Note that for purposes of simplifying the calculation, we have assumed a 360-day year—a common assumption in determining yields on money market instruments.

Key Borrowers and Lenders in the Money Market

Who are the principal lenders of funds in the money market? Who are the principal borrowers? (See Exhibit 10.1 for an overview of the structure of the money market.) These questions are difficult to answer, because the same institutions frequently operate on *both* sides of the money market. For example, a large commercial bank operating in the money market (such as Citibank or the Bank of Montreal) will borrow funds aggressively through CDs, federal funds, and other short-term instruments while lending short-term funds to corporations that have temporary cash shortages. Frequently, large nonfinancial corporations borrow millions of dollars on a single day, only to come back into the money market later in the week as a lender of funds due to a sudden upsurge in cash receipts. Institutions that typically play *both sides* of the money market include large banks, securities dealers, finance companies, major nonfinancial corporations, and units of government. Even central banks, such as the Federal Reserve System, the European Central Bank (ECB), the Bank of England, or the Bank of Japan, may be aggressive suppliers of funds to the money market on one day and reverse themselves the following day, demanding funds through the sale of securities in the open market. One institution that is virtually always on the demand side of the market, however, is the government. The U.S. Treasury, for example, is among the largest of all money market borrowers.

The Goals of Money Market Investors

Investors in the money market seek mainly *safety* and *liquidity,* plus the opportunity to earn some interest income. This is because funds invested in the money market represent only temporary cash surpluses and are usually needed in the near future to meet tax obligations, cover wage and salary costs, pay stockholder dividends, and so on. For this reason, money market investors are especially *sensitive to risk.*

The strong *aversion to risk* among money market investors is especially evident when there is even a hint of trouble concerning the financial condition of a major money market borrower. For example, when the huge Penn Central Transportation Company collapsed in 1970 and defaulted on its short-term commercial notes, the short-term commercial paper market virtually ground to a halt because many investors refused to buy even the notes offered by top-grade companies. Similarly, during the 1980s, when the huge Continental Illinois Bank had to be propped up by government loans, the rates on short-term certificates of deposit (CDs) issued by other big banks surged upward due to fears on the part of money market investors that *all* large-bank CDs had become more risky. (See Exhibit 10.2 for a summary of the goals and instruments of the money market.)

Types of Investment Risk That Investors Face

What kinds of risk do investors face in the financial markets? And how do money market instruments rank in terms of these different kinds of risk?

market risk

First, all securities, including money market instruments, carry **market risk** (sometimes called *interest rate risk*), which refers to the danger that their prices will fall (and interest rates rise), subjecting the holder to a capital loss. Even Treasury notes and bonds decline in price when interest rates rise. However, most money market assets are debt instruments that carry a fixed rate of return if the asset is held to maturity. Therefore, market risk is only a problem if the investor's time horizon for his or her investment is shorter than the maturity of the asset.

reinvestment risk

Not only can security prices fall, but so can interest rates. This latter development increases an investor's **reinvestment risk**—the risk that earnings from a financial asset will have to be reinvested in lower-yielding assets at some point in the future. Even government securities carry reinvestment risk.

EXHIBIT 10.1   **The Money Market Landscape: Structure and Organization of the Short-Term Market**

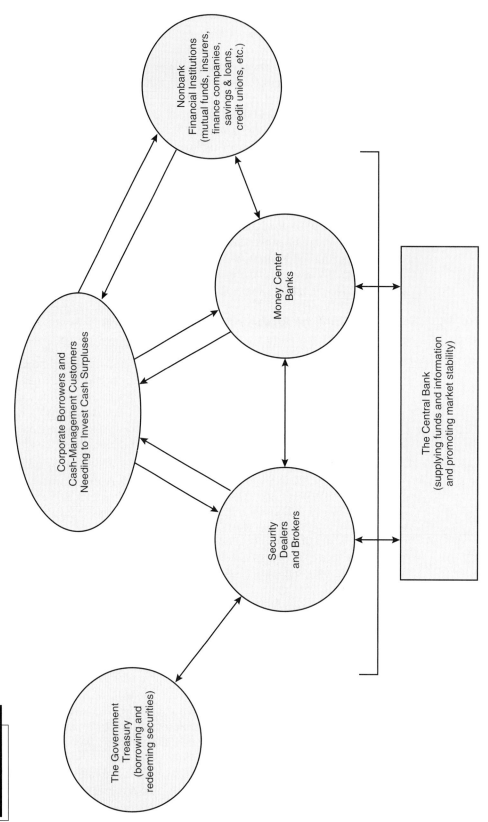

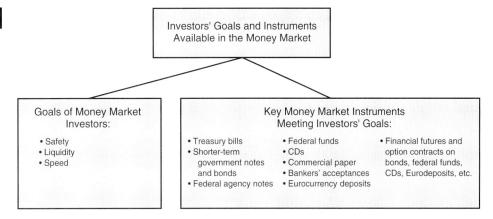

EXHIBIT 10.2

The Goals and Instruments of the Money Market

default risk

Securities issued by private firms and state and local governments carry **default risk.** For such securities, there is always some positive probability that the borrower will fail to meet some or all of his or her promised principal and/or interest payments (as happened to Orange County, California, in 1995, and to Enron Corporation and Argentina in 2001, for example, as discussed earlier in Chapter 8).

Lenders of funds face the possibility that increases in the average level of prices for all goods and services will reduce the purchasing power of their income. This is known **inflation risk** as **inflation risk** (sometimes called *purchasing power risk*). Lenders usually attempt to offset anticipated inflation by demanding higher contract rates on their loans.

currency risk

International investors also face **currency risk:** possible loss due to unfavorable changes in the value of foreign currencies. For example, if a U.S. investor purchases British Treasury bills on the London money market, the return from these bills may be severely reduced if the value of the British pound falls relative to the dollar during the life of the investment.

political risk

Finally, **political risk** refers to the possibility that changes in government laws or regulations will result in a diminished rate of return to the investor or, in the extreme case, a total loss of invested capital. For example, the windfall profits tax on U.S. petroleum companies levied by Congress during the 1980s generally reduced the earnings of petroleum stockholders. Investors in industries that are closely regulated, such as banking and public utilities, continually run the risk that new price controls, output quotas, or other restrictions will be imposed, reducing their earnings potential. In some foreign countries, facilities and equipment owned by U.S. corporations have been expropriated by national governments, resulting in total loss for the investors involved. A summary of each of the foregoing kinds of risk is shown in Exhibit 10.3.

Money market instruments generally offer more protection against such risks than most other investments. The prices of money market securities tend to be remarkably stable over time compared to the prices of bonds, stocks, real estate, and commodities such as wheat, oil, and gold. Money market instruments generally do not offer the prospect of significant capital gains for the investor, but neither do they normally raise the specter of substantial capital losses. Similarly, default risk is expected to be minimal in the money market. In fact, money market borrowers must be well-established institutions with impeccable credit ratings before their securities can even be offered for sale in this market.

liquidity

Few investments today adequately protect the investor against inflation risk. Money market securities are no exception. However, they do offer superior **liquidity,** allowing the investor to cash them in quickly, with little risk of loss of principal, when a promising inflation-hedged investment opportunity comes along.

EXHIBIT 10.3	Type of Risk	Definition
Types of Risk Confronting Investors in the Money and Capital Markets	Market risk	The risk to investors whose investment horizon is shorter than the maturity of a financial asset that the market price (value) of that asset will decline, resulting in a capital loss when sold. Sometimes referred to as *interest rate risk*.
	Reinvestment risk	The risk to investors whose investment horizon exceeds the maturity of a financial asset that they will be forced to place earnings from that maturing asset into a lower-yielding investment because interest rates have fallen.
	Default risk	The probability that a borrower will fail to meet one or more promised principal or interest payments on a loan or security.
	Inflation risk	The risk that increases in the general price level will reduce the purchasing power of earnings from a loan, security, or other investment.
	Currency risk	The risk that adverse movements in the price of one national currency vis-à-vis another will reduce the net rate of return from a foreign investment. Sometimes referred to as *exchange rate risk*.
	Political risk	The probability that changes in government laws or regulations will reduce an investor's expected return from an investment.

Currency risk concerns the international investor who frequently must convert one currency into another. That risk has increased dramatically in recent years due to the increase in foreign exchange rates that float with market conditions. Investors who purchase securities in foreign markets cannot completely escape currency risk, but they are probably less prone to such losses when buying money market instruments due to the short-term nature of money market assets. These assets also provide some hedge against political risk because they are short-term investments and fewer dramatic changes in government policy are likely over brief intervals of time. Moreover, the appearance of the Euro in the European money market has helped to reduce some forms of currency risk in one of the world's largest international markets for goods and services.

QUESTIONS TO HELP YOU STUDY

1. What exactly do we mean by the term *money market*?
2. Explain why there is a critical need within the financial system to have money market instruments available to anyone who can afford them.
3. What are the principal *goals* usually pursued by money market investors?
4. The money market is characterized by very large financial institutions. Who are the principal borrowers and lenders in this market?
5. Define the following types of *risk*: (a) market risk; (b) default risk; (c) inflation risk; (d) currency risk; and (e) political risk. Which of these risks are *minimized* by purchasing money market instruments? Does investing in the money market avoid *all* of the foregoing risks?

Money Market Maturities

Despite the fact that money market investments cover a relatively narrow range of maturities—one year or less—there are maturities available within this range to meet just about every short-term investment need. We must distinguish here between

original maturity

actual maturity

original maturity and actual maturity, however. The interval of time between the issue date of a security and the date on which the borrower promises to redeem it is the security's **original maturity. Actual maturity,** on the other hand, refers to the number of days, months, or years between today and the date the security is actually retired.

Original maturities on money market instruments range from as short as one day or a few hours on many loans to banks and security dealers to a full year on some bank deposits and Treasury bills. Obviously, once a money market instrument is issued, it grows shorter in actual maturity every day. Because there are thousands of money market assets outstanding, some of which reach maturity each day, investors have a wide menu from which to select the precise length of time they need to invest their cash.

Depth and Breadth of the Money Market

The money market is extremely *broad* and *deep,* meaning it can absorb a large volume of transactions with only small effects on security prices and interest rates. Investors can easily sell most money market instruments on short notice, often in a matter of minutes. This is one of the most efficient markets in the world, containing a vast network of securities dealers, money-center banks, and funds brokers in constant touch with one another and alert to any bargains. The slightest hint that a financial instrument is underpriced (i.e., carries an exceptionally high yield) usually brings a flood of buy orders, but money market traders are quick to dump or avoid overpriced financial assets. This market is dominated by active traders who constantly search their video display screens for opportunities to arbitrage funds; that is, they move money from one corner of the market with relatively low yields to another where investments offer the highest returns available. Overseeing the whole market are central banks (such as the European Central Bank and the Federal Reserve System) around the globe, who try to ensure that trading is orderly and that asset prices are reasonably stable.

There is no centralized trading arena in the money market as there is on a stock exchange, for example. The money market is a telephone and computer market, in which participants arrange trades over the phone or through computer networks and usually confirm their transactions by wire. Speed is of the essence in this market because, as we observed earlier, money is a highly perishable commodity. Each day that passes means thousands of dollars in lost interest income if newly received funds are not immediately invested. Most business between traders, therefore, is conducted in seconds or minutes, and payment is made almost instantaneously.

The Speed of Money Market Payments: Federal Funds versus Clearinghouse Funds

federal funds

How can funds move so fast in the money market? The reason is that money market traders usually deal in **federal funds.** These funds are mainly deposit balances of commercial banks and thrift institutions held at the regional Federal Reserve banks and at larger correspondent banks across the nation. For example, when a securities dealer that manages a portfolio of financial assets buys securities from an investor, it immediately contacts its bank and requests that funds be transferred from its account to the investor's account at another banking firm. Many of these transactions move via a public or private wire network (such as the Federal Reserve's electronic wire transfer network in the United States). In this case, the central bank or funds transfer firm removes funds from the reserve account of the buyer's bank and transfers these reserves to the seller's bank. The transaction is so quick that the seller of securities has funds available to make new investments, pay bills, or to use for other purposes the same day a trade is carried out or a loan is made. Federal funds are often called *immediately available* funds because of the speed with which money moves from one bank's reserve account to that of another.

Money markets around the world share several common characteristics. They reconcile cash imbalances for public and private individuals and institutions and do so at low levels of risk for both borrowers and lenders. Money markets transmit government economic policies, aiding governments in financing their deficits (fiscal policy) and in managing the growth of money and credit (monetary policy).

Each nation has its own money market, though some are poorly developed and others reach far beyond national boundaries to involve traders on many continents. There is an *international money market* that arches over domestic money markets all over the globe and ties them together. The heart of the international money market is the Eurocurrency market, where large bank deposits are traded outside the boundaries of the country where a particular currency is issued. No nation's money market today is unaffected by movements in interest rates and security prices in the international money market.

As Dufey and Giddy (1993) have observed, national money markets around the globe tend to fall into one of two types—those (such as the United States and Great Britain) that are *securities market dominated*, where most borrowing and lending is through open-market trading of financial instruments, and those that are *bank dominated*, where bank borrowing and lending is at the center of most transactions (as in Japan and China). However, worldwide deregulation of many financial institutions is under way, with the probable outcome that more money markets of the future are likely to become more security trading-oriented and less dominated by a few large financial institutions.

In developing countries, money markets are typically dominated by large banks because their securities markets usually are not well developed. Bank-dominated money markets have a potential weakness, however, as economic problems experienced in Asia during the late 1990s suggest. They can yield more easily to government pressure, resulting in many bad loans, and they may slow the development of long-term capital markets, which promote greater economic stability. Central banks, such as the Federal Reserve and the European Central Bank, are usually the single most important institution in money markets, regardless of whether they are security dominated or bank dominated.

Contrast this method of payment with that generally used in the capital market and by most businesses and households. When most of us purchase goods and services a check, credit card, or debit card is often the most desirable means of paying the bill.

clearinghouse funds

Funds transferred by check are known as **clearinghouse funds,** because, once the buyer writes a check, it goes to the seller's depository institution, which forwards that check to the deposit-type institution upon which it was drawn. If the two depositories are in the same community, they exchange bundles of checks drawn against each other every day through the local clearinghouse—an agreed-upon location where checks and other cash items are delivered and passed from one depository institution to another.

Clearinghouse funds are an acceptable means of payment for most purposes, but not in the money market, where *speed* is of the essence. It takes at least a day to clear many local checks and perhaps two to three days for checks moving between distant cities. For money market transactions, this is far too slow, because no interest can be earned until the check is collected. Clearinghouse funds also have an element of *risk,* because a check may be returned as fraudulent or for insufficient funds. Similar risks accompany credit and debit cards. Federal funds transactions, however, are both speedy and safe.

A Market for Large Borrowers and Lenders

The money market is dominated by a relatively small number of very large financial institutions. No more than a hundred banks in New York, London, Tokyo, Singapore, and a handful of other money centers are at the heart of this marketplace. These large institutions account for the bulk of federal funds trading through which many money market transactions are carried out. In addition, financial assets move readily from sellers to buyers through the market-making activities of major securities dealers and brokers. And, of course, governments and central banks around the world play major roles in this market as the largest borrowers and as regulators, setting the rules of the game. For example, the Federal Reserve System, operating principally through the trading desk at the Federal Reserve Bank of New York, is in the market frequently, either supplying funds to banks and security dealers or absorbing funds through security sales.

Individual transactions in the money market involve huge amounts of funds. *Most trading occurs in multiples of a million dollars.* For this reason, the money market is often referred to as a *wholesale market* for funds, as opposed to the *retail market* where most households and small businesses borrow and save their money.

QUESTIONS TO HELP YOU STUDY

6. What is the difference between the *actual maturity* and the *original maturity* of a financial asset? Why is this difference important in the money market?

7. How do money markets around the world differ from one another?

8. What danger do *bank-dominated money markets* face that may be less of a problem in *security-dominated money markets*?

9. What are *federal funds* and how do they differ from *clearinghouse funds*?

10. Which of these two types of funds—federal funds versus clearinghouse funds—are most important in the money market and why is this so?

11. Is the money market predominantly a wholesale or retail marketplace? How do you know?

12. What are the principal financial instruments traded in the money market? What common characteristics do these instruments possess?

10.3   Government Involvement in the Money Market

Thus far, Chapter 10 has presented an overview of the characteristics of the money market. For the remainder of this chapter and in the other chapters in Part Three we will focus on the key institutions that literally make the money market "go"— governments, security dealers, commercial banks, corporations, federal agencies, and central banks.

The Roles That Governments Play in the Money Market

Of all the institutions that trade for funds in the vast money market it is difficult to find one institution that is more important, directly or indirectly, to the proper functioning of the money market than the *governments* around the world. Governments set the rules of the money market "game" through regulation, and they consistently rank among the top issuers of money market debt. Moreover, working through central banks (like the Federal Reserve System)—institutions chartered by government—governments help to shape money market conditions and set the tone for daily borrowing and lending activities.

Selling Treasury Bills to Money Market Investors: The Anchor of the Money Market

Government is usually the most visible in the money market when it *borrows money.* Indeed, many money markets around the world have come into existence for the

EXHIBIT 10.4

U.S. Treasury Bills: Total Amount Outstanding and Their Proportion of the Marketable Public Debt of the United States, 1960–2004

Source: Board of Governors of the Federal Reserve System, *Federal Reserve Bulletin*, selected issues.

*2004 figures are for July 31, 2004.

End of Year	Total Volume of Bills Outstanding ($ Billions)	Marketable Public Debt of the United States ($ Billions)	T-bills as a Percent of the Total Marketable Public Debt
1960	$ 39.4	$ 189.0	20.8%
1970	87.9	247.7	35.5
1980	216.1	623.2	34.7
1990	527.4	2,195.8	24.0
2000	646.9	2,966.9	21.8
2004*	962.5	3,808.5	25.3

principal reason of giving governmental authorities a place to raise new cash quickly (other than resorting to taxes on their citizens). One of the largest of all borrowers in the U.S. money market is the U.S. Treasury Department, which enters the market every week to sell one of the world's most popular financial instruments—*Treasury bills*. Nor is the U.S. alone. Governments around the globe issue Treasury bills or their equivalent to raise short-term funds and meet their expenses.

U.S. Treasury bills

U.S. Treasury bills are direct obligations of the United States government, indicating that tax revenues or any other source of government funds can be used to repay holders of these financial instruments. By law, Treasury bills must have an original maturity of one year or less. T-bills were first issued by the U.S. Treasury in 1929 to cover the federal government's frequent short-term cash deficits.

In the United States the federal government's fiscal year runs from October 1 to September 30. However, individual income taxes—the largest single source of U.S. federal revenue—are not fully collected until April of each year. Therefore, even in those rare years when a sizable budget surplus is expected, the government is likely to be short of cash during the fall and winter months and often in the summer as well. During the spring, personal and corporate tax collections are usually at high levels, and the resulting inflow of funds can be used to retire some portion of the securities issued earlier in the fiscal year. T-bills are suited to this seasonal ebb and flow of government cash because their maturities are short, they find a ready market among investors, and their prices adjust readily to changing market conditions.

Volume of Bills Outstanding   The volume of U.S. Treasury bills outstanding, as shown in Exhibit 10.4, grew rapidly until the late 1990s. T-bills climbed over $760 billion in 1995 and then moved further upward to almost $780 billion the following year, compared to slightly over $200 billion in 1980. Subsequently, the volume of bills began to fall, only to rise sharply again as the new century began to unfold.

The major factors behind the growth of T-bills have been federal budget deficits, occasional economic recessions that reduced tax revenues, the rapid expansion of certain federal programs (such as national defense during the Cold War), and costly hot wars in various places around the globe (such as Vietnam and Iraq). Moreover, the global economy has grown rapidly in recent years, creating a greater need for liquid assets such as T-bills to aid banks and other investors in the efficient management of their cash positions.

Types of Treasury Bills   There are several different types of Treasury bills. *Regular-series bills* are issued routinely every week or month in competitive auctions. Bills issued in regular series carry original maturities of one month (4 weeks), three months (13 weeks), and six months (26 weeks). Today regular-series bills are auctioned weekly. The six-month bill provides the largest amount of revenue for the U.S. Treasury.

On the other hand, *irregular-series bills* are issued when the Treasury has an emergency need for cash. These instruments include strip bills and cash management bills. A package offering of bills requiring investors to bid for an entire series of different bill maturities is known as a *strip bill.* Investors who bid successfully must accept bills at their bid price each week for several weeks running. *Cash management bills,* on the other hand, usually consist simply of reopened issues of bills that were sold in prior weeks. During 2003 the U.S. Treasury announced that it would likely make greater use of cash management bills in the future as federal budget deficits continued to rise.

auction

How Bills Are Sold   U.S. Treasury bills are sold using the **auction** technique. The marketplace, not the U.S. Treasury, sets bill prices and yields. A new regular bill issue is usually announced by the Treasury on Thursday of each week (except for holidays) with bids from investors due the following Monday before 1 P.M. New York time. Interested investors complete a form tendering an offer to the Treasury for a specific bill issue at a specific price. These forms must be filed by the Monday deadline with one of the 37 regional Federal Reserve banks or branches or with the Treasury's Bureau of the Public Debt. The interested investor can appear in person at a Federal Reserve bank or branch to fill out a tender form, submit it by mail, or place an order in person or electronically through a security broker or depository institution. T-bills are now also traded online and are usually issued the Thursday following Monday's auction.

The Treasury entertains both competitive and noncompetitive tenders for bills. *Competitive* tenders typically are submitted by large investors, including banks and securities dealers, who bid for several million dollars' worth at one time. Although anyone can submit a bid for his or her own account, depository institutions and registered government security brokers and dealers (about 2,000 in number) may also bid on behalf of their customers. Institutions submitting competitive tenders bid aggressively for bills, trying to offer the Treasury a "price"—expressed as a discount rate of interest (DR)—high enough to win an allotment of bills. In contrast, *noncompetitive* tenders (normally less than about $1 million each) are submitted by small investors who agree to accept the price determined by the auction. Generally, the Treasury fills all noncompetitive orders for bills.

In the typical bill auction, Federal Reserve officials array all the bids received from the highest price bid to the lowest price. All competitive bids must be expressed as a DR or discount rate—a measure of a bill's rate of return that we will discuss shortly. For example, a typical series of bids in a Treasury auction might appear as follows:

Hypothetical Prices and Discount Rates Bid for Three-Month U.S. Treasury Bills	
Equivalent Treasury Bill Prices	**Treasury Bill Discount Rates Bid**
$96.460	3.540%
96.455	3.545
96.450	3.550
96.445	3.555
96.440	3.560
96.435	3.565
96.430	3.570

EXHIBIT 10.5	An Example of the Outcome of an Auction of U.S. Treasury Bills*	

	13 Week or 91-Day Bills	26 Week or 182-Day Bills
Volume of bills requested	$33.6 billion	$33.6 billion
Volume of bids accepted by the U.S. Treasury Department	$18.0 billion	$16.0 billion
Noncompetitive tender offers accepted by the U.S. Treasury Department	$1.4 billion	$1.1 billion
The bill price established in this auction	99.775 (on a $100 basis)	99.517 (on a $100 basis)
The discount yield established in this auction (DR)	0.890%	0.955%
Percentage of bids at the market's yield or rate of return	55%	69%
Investment or coupon-equivalent rate of return (IR)	0.907%	0.976%

*All successful Treasury bill bids are filled at a single price as determined by the bill yield that clears the market. A competitive bidder whose bid rate or yield is the highest rate or yield (lowest price) accepted may not receive the full amount of bills he or she requested. Competitive bidders who bid too low a price (i.e., filed too high a yield bid) may have their bids rejected depending upon the market-determined outcome of each Treasury auction.

Note in the table on page 285 that the column measuring possible T-bill prices expresses each bill's price as though it had a $100 par (face) value. In fact, the minimum denomination for U.S. Treasury bills is $1,000 and they are issued in multiples of $1,000 above that minimum. Once the volume of noncompetitive tenders is subtracted from the total amount of T-bills being auctioned, the highest competitive bidder receives bills and those who bid successively lower prices also receive bills until all available securities have been awarded. The lowest successful price bid, known as the "stop-out"(or market-clearing) price, becomes the common price that all successful bidders actually pay to the Treasury.

Many successful bidders choose to sell their bills immediately in the secondary market, giving unsuccessful bidders a chance to add to their own T-bill portfolios. Payments for bills won in the auction must be made in federal funds, cash, cashier's check, certified personal check, by redeeming maturing Treasury securities or coupon payments, or, when permitted by the Treasury, through crediting Treasury tax and loan accounts at banks.[2]

All bills today are issued only in *book-entry form*—a computerized record of ownership maintained at the Federal Reserve banks, through private depository institutions, and at the U.S. Treasury Department. The Federal Reserve manages the National Book-Entry System (NBES), which keeps records of Treasury security purchases for depository institutions, and the depository institutions, in turn, keep records on their customers' purchases. Alternatively, a purchaser of Treasuries can keep an electronic account with the U.S. Treasury Department's *Treasury Direct* system, showing all the buyer's holdings of Treasury obligations. Settlement of transactions involving purchases and sales of new bills or other Treasury securities takes place mainly through

---

[2]These so-called T&L accounts are Treasury deposits kept in thousands of the nation's depository institutions. The purpose of these accounts is to minimize the impact on the financial system of Treasury tax collections and debt-financing operations. As taxes are collected or securities are sold, the Treasury deposits the funds received in these T&L accounts and withdraws money from them as needed into its checking accounts held at the Federal Reserve banks.

depository institutions, led by a few large clearing banks that process a large volume of transactions daily.

Results of a Recent Bill Auction

A summary of the results from each T-bill auction is published in financial news sheets all over the world. The results of a recent U.S. Treasury bill auction are illustrated in Exhibit 10.5. In this particular example, two maturities of bills—13 and 26 weeks—were offered to the public, and both issues were heavily oversubscribed. More than $33 billion in 13-week bills and a similar amount of 26-week bills were requested by the public; however, the Treasury only awarded about $18 billion of the shorter-term bills and $16 billion of the 26-week bills.

Noncompetitive tenders in the amount of $1.4 billion for the 13-week issue and about $1.1 billion for the 26-week issue received their bills. The market-clearing auction price for the 13-week bill was $99.775 per $100 par value. The 26-week issue sold for an auction price of $99.517 for a $100-denominated instrument. This works out to a 0.890 percent discount rate of return (DR) on the 13-week bill and a 0.955 percent discount rate of return (DR) on the 26-week issue. On a yield-to-maturity (investment return [IR]) basis—a rate of return measure for bills we will also discuss shortly—the 13-week bill carried a market-clearing investment return of 0.907 percent, while the 26-week bill posted an investment (IR) yield of 0.976 percent.

QUESTIONS TO HELP YOU STUDY

13. Why did the volume of *Treasury bills* grow rapidly in earlier decades, then level off and decline, only to begin growing again recently?

14. Explain why Treasury bills are so popular with investors (savers) all over the world.

15. Why have governments found the Treasury bill such an effective instrument for raising new funds?

16. List and define the various *types* of Treasury bills. Why are there so many different types?

17. Explain how a Treasury bill *auction* works in the United States. Can you find some advantages stemming from this type of sale?

Calculating the Return on T-Bills

Treasury bills do not carry a promised interest rate but instead are sold at a discount from their par or face value. Thus, their yield is based on their appreciation in price between time of issue and the time they mature or are sold by the investor. Any price gain realized by the investor is treated for tax purposes not as a capital gain but as ordinary income received during the year the bill matures.[3] Bill yields are determined by the **bank discount method**—a rate of return measure we discussed earlier in Chapter 6, which ignores the compounding of interest rates, treats the par value as the investment base, and uses a 360-day year for simplicity.

bank discount method

---

[3]The income earned from investing in T-bills is *not* exempt from federal taxes, but it *is* exempt from state and local income taxes. Income from U.S. Treasury securities is subject to federal and state inheritance, gift, estate, and certain excise taxes, however.

The bank discount rate (DR) on bills is given by the formula:

$$DR = \frac{\text{Par value} - \text{Purchase price}}{\text{Par value}} \times \frac{360}{\text{Number of days to maturity}} \quad \textbf{(10.1)}$$

For example, suppose you purchased a Treasury bill for $97 on a $100 basis (par value) and the bill matures in 180 days. Then the discount rate on this bill would be

$$DR = \frac{(100 - 97)}{100} \times \frac{360}{180} = 0.06, \text{ or } 6\%$$

To learn more about calculating T-bill prices and rates of return see investopedia. com/calculator

Because the rate of return on T-bills is figured in a different way from the rate of return on most other debt instruments, the investor must convert bill discount yields to another interest-rate or yield measure in order to compare T-bill returns against those attached to government and corporate bonds. In Chapter 6 we referred to this particular yield measure as the YTM-Equivalent Return, which is used not only for T-bills but many other money market instruments as well. On the street, this yield measure is often called the "coupon-equivalent," "bond-equivalent," or "investment" return—frequently designated IR. Specifically,

$$IR = \frac{\text{Par value} - \text{Purchase price}}{\text{Purchase price}} \times \frac{365}{\text{Days to maturity}} \quad \textbf{(10.2)}$$

The IR on the bill discussed above having a purchase price of $97 is

$$IR = \frac{100 - 97}{97} \times \frac{365}{180} = 0.0627, \text{ or } 6.27\%$$

Notice that this IR formula explicitly recognizes that each bill is purchased at a discounted price, which should be used instead of par value as the basis for figuring the bill's true return. Because of the compounding of interest and the use of a 365-day year, the investment return (IR) on a bill is always higher than its discount rate (DR).

Several other formulas have become popular among investors for calculating yields on Treasury bills when the bills are *not* held to maturity. Both Equations 10.1 and 10.2 assume that the investor buys a T-bill and ultimately redeems it with the Treasury on its due date. But what if the investor needs cash right away and sells the bill to another investor in advance of its maturity? In this instance, we may use the following formulas:

$$\text{Holding-period yield on bill} = DR \text{ when purchased}$$
$$\pm \text{ Change in DR over the holding period} \quad \textbf{(10.3)}$$

where:

Key references for learning more about money market instruments and rules include: U.S. Treasury Department publicdebt. treas.gov

Federal Reserve Bank of New York ny.frb.org

Board of Governors of the Federal Reserve System federalreserve.gov

Federal Deposit Insurance Corporation fdic.gov

$$\begin{array}{l} \text{Change in DR} \\ \text{over the investor's} \\ \text{holding period} \end{array} = \frac{\begin{array}{c}(\text{Days to maturity when} \\ \text{purchased} - \text{Days held})\end{array}}{\text{Days held}} \times \begin{array}{c}\text{Difference in DR} \\ \text{on date purchased} \\ \text{and date sold}\end{array} \quad \textbf{(10.4)}$$

For example, suppose the investor buys a bill with 180 days to maturity at a price that results in a discount rate (DR) of 6 percent. As is typical, the bill's price begins to rise (and DR to fall) as it approaches maturity. Thirty days after purchase, the investor needs immediate cash and is forced to sell at a price that results in a DR of 5.80 percent. What is the investor's holding-period yield? Using Equation 10.4:

$$\text{Change in DR over the holding period} = \frac{180 - 30}{30} \times (6.00\% - 5.80\%)$$

$$= \frac{150}{30} \times 0.20\% = 1.00\%$$

U.S. Treasury bills and other U.S. government securities are traded 24 hours a day around the globe. But many people are not aware that governments in Europe, Asia, and the Americas also issue their own T-bills. For example, the Bank of Canada, acting as agent for the Canadian government, auctions bills to a select list of banks and dealers authorized to bid for themselves and their customers. In addition, Canada's provinces borrow through Provincial Bills, normally issued in denominations up to $100,000 (expressed in Canadian dollars).

In Europe, Treasury bills are issued by several governments and widely traded. Bills issued by the United Kingdom rank among the most popular in Western Europe. Leading central banks in Europe regularly trade in the bill market and monitor T-bill rates as a barometer of credit market conditions.

Treasury bills are a relatively recent government financing instrument in Japan, first appearing in 1986, but they are now sold regularly. Japan also issues Financing Bills to cover the emergency cash needs of the Japanese government. T-bills are considered to be in short supply in Japan because the Japanese government borrows principally through longer-term bonds, and an active secondary market for T-bills has been slow to develop. Similarly, in Korea the government issues Treasury bills irregularly, and thus, the secondary market for this money market instrument is not yet fully developed.

The Treasury bill market is one of the most important for the development of an efficient and fluid financial system in any nation. The bill market is a natural channel for government economic policy and can aid in the development of a strong central banking and financial market system.

Then, using Equation 10.3:

$$\text{Holding-period yield on bill} = 6.00\% + 1.00\% = 7.00\%$$

Because this T-bill rose in price, the investor experienced a gain that increased the bill's holding-period yield by 1 percent over the original discount rate of 6 percent.

Market Interest Rates on Treasury Bills

Due to the absence of default risk and because of the superior marketability of T-bills, the yields on these popular financial instruments are typically among the lowest in the money market. And because of the tremendous size of the bill market, conditions there tend to set the tone in other segments of the money market. A rise in T-bill rates, for example, often is quickly translated into increases in interest rates attached to other money market instruments.

Although the prices of Treasury bills tend to be relatively stable, yields on bills fluctuate widely in response to changes in economic conditions, government policy, and a host of other factors. This can be seen clearly in Exhibit 10.6, which gives annual averages for the secondary market yields on 3- and 6-month bills. T-bill rates typically fall during periods of recession and sluggish economic activity as borrowing and spending sag. Note, for example, the decline in bill yields in 1991–1992 and 2001–2004. These years were periods in which the economy reached the peak of a boom period and then dropped into a recession or near-recession. During periods of economic expansion, on the other hand, T-bill rates frequently surge upward, as happened, for example, between 1993 and 1997.

It is interesting to examine the shape of the *yield curve* for bills. As Exhibit 10.6 suggests, that curve usually *slopes upward*, with six-month bill maturities generally carrying the highest yields, and three-month bill maturities among the lowest yields. This is not always the case, however, as 1990 illustrates. Sometimes the bill yield curve seems to signal the onset of a recession by sloping downward or lying relatively flat.

Market Interest Rates on U.S. Treasury Bills, Three- and Six-Month Maturities (Annual Percentage Rates)

Source: Board of Governors of the Federal Reserve System; *Federal Reserve Bulletin,* selected monthly issues.

*Figures are averages for January of 2004.

Year	3-Month	6-Month
1990	7.50	7.46
1991	5.38	5.44
1992	3.43	3.54
1993	2.95	3.05
1994	4.25	4.64
1995	5.49	5.56
1996	5.01	5.08
1997	5.06	5.18
1998	4.78	4.83
1999	4.64	4.75
2000	5.82	5.90
2001	3.40	3.45
2002	1.61	1.75
2003	1.01	1.05
2004*	0.88	0.97

Investors in Treasury Bills

Principal holders of Treasury bills include commercial banks, nonfinancial corporations, state and local governments, and the Federal Reserve banks. Commercial banks and private corporations hold large quantities of bills as a reserve of liquidity until cash is needed. The most attractive feature of bills for these institutions is their ready marketability and stable price. The Federal Reserve banks conduct many of their open market operations in T-bills (or in repurchase agreements collateralized with T-bills) because of the depth and volume of activity in this market. The Fed purchases and sells bills in an effort to influence other money market interest rates, alter the volume and growth of bank credit, and ultimately affect the volume of investment spending and borrowing in the economy.

QUESTIONS TO HELP YOU STUDY

18. How are the yields on Treasury bills calculated?

19. How does the method for determining Treasury bill yields differ from the primary method used to calculate yields on most bonds? Why is this difference important?

20. What is the "normal" or "typical" shape of the yield curve for T-bills? What other shapes have been observed and why do you think these occur?

21. Who are the principal *buyers* of Treasury bills today? Make a list of the key factors that you believe motivate these investors to buy bills.

10.4 Primary Dealers in Government Securities

The money market depends heavily on the buying and selling activities of securities dealers to move funds from cash-rich units to those with cash shortages. Today, 23 **primary dealers** in government securities trade in both new and previously issued Treasury bills as well as Treasury bonds and notes. As shown in the primary dealer list below, these firms include such market leaders as Merrill Lynch, Goldman Sachs,

primary dealers

Due in part to competition and the nature of auction methods used by the U.S. Treasury Department prior to November 1998 to sell T-bills and other U.S. Government securities, the primary dealers for many years had a significant incentive to "corner" the government securities market and to "collude" and place common bids, so that all dealers received some share of all new securities issued and made a profit. In such a huge and competitive market, dealers could easily overbid, eliminating potential profits by either posting bid prices that were too high or by underbidding, receiving no securities from the government to meet their obligations to their customers. Thus, the dealers had a strong incentive to *share information* with each other on the size of the orders they planned to place with the government and on the prices they hoped to bid. In 1991 rumors swept through the financial markets that collusion was rampant. After several weeks of investigation, officials at the Federal Reserve and the Securities and Exchange Commission alleged that they had evidence of improper trading practices on the part of the old-line primary dealer, Salomon Brothers (now part of Citigroup Global Markets, Inc.).

It was alleged that Salomon cornered a $12-billion-plus auction of U.S. Treasury notes in May 1991, inflating the amount of its bid to the Treasury well beyond the 35 percent maximum share of a new issue normally allowed. When Salomon wound up with nearly 90 percent of the new Treasury notes, other dealers filed complaints that they were being "squeezed" by Salomon—forced to pay exorbitant prices to purchase the new notes in order to fill their own customers' orders. Subsequently, government investigators found evidence of manipulation of at least seven other government auctions. Moreover, the government wound up paying higher borrowing costs as a result of manipulation of the market.

In the wake of the Salomon scandal, the U.S. Treasury and the Federal Reserve Bank of New York quickly set up new rules by which government securities would be auctioned in the future. For one thing, customers purchasing large amounts of government securities through dealers were thereafter required to *verify in writing* the amounts they bid before they could receive any new securities. Any security dealer or broker registered with the SEC, not just primary dealers, could file bids on behalf of its customers without putting up a deposit or guarantee. The U.S. Treasury promised that it would move swiftly to automate the bidding process for government securities rather than relying on traditional handwritten bids. These steps were reinforced by the U.S. Congress when it enacted the Government Securities Act Amendments of 1993, broadening the U.S. Treasury's authority to regulate the government securities market.

In 1997 the Treasury Department set up large position-reporting rules and, from time to time, has conducted "test calls" in which major dealers whose net position in a particular Treasury instrument exceeds $2 billion have been required to report the extent of their holdings. The goal has been to discourage market manipulation and prevent one or a few dealers from putting a "squeeze" on other traders in government securities who may need to buy or borrow selected Treasury securities on behalf of themselves or their customers.

Perhaps the most important outcome of the Salomon scandal was a fundamental change in the way the Treasury auctions new securities. At the time of the scandal the auction method then in use was called a *first-price sealed-bid auction*, or English auction. Although it possessed the advantage of allowing the market to set the prices of Treasury securities, the English auction had definite weaknesses. It encouraged dealers to bid high to increase their probability of winning some of the auctioned securities. However, the higher the price that was bid, the lower the expected profit when any Treasury securities won in the auction were sold in the secondary market, because the highest bidders had to follow through on their commitment and pay the Treasury what they had bid even though other successful bidders were paying a lower amount for the same securities. Moreover, the high bidders could sell their securities for no more later in the resale market than those who bid less. In effect, dealers bidding the highest prices faced a real "winner's curse," because they incurred greater probability of loss when they attempted to resell the securities won in the auction to their customers. The first-price sealed-bid auction probably reduced the aggressiveness of competitive bidding by dealers and resulted in the Treasury getting a lower price for its securities.

Several experts suggested changes in the design of Treasury auctions. The winning recommendation was to set up a *Dutch* or *uniform-price auction*, in which bids are arrayed by price from highest to lowest but all the securities in the auction are sold for just *one price*—the highest bid just sufficient to sell out the whole issue, sometimes referred to as the "market clearing" or "stop-out" price. Thus, the price paid by every successful participant in a Dutch auction is identical and usually comes fairly close to the market consensus price, meaning less of a winner's curse. Dutch auctions tend to incite more aggressive bidding and to encourage more individuals and institutions to participate in Treasury auctions.

Morgan Stanley, Salomon Brothers, Inc., and Bear Stearns. Just over half are banks or securities affiliates of banks.

List of Primary Dealers Authorized to Trade with the Federal Reserve Bank of New York	
ABN AMRO Bank, N.V., New York Branch	Dresner Kleinwort Wasserstein Securities LLC
BNP Paribus Securities Corp.	Goldman, Sachs & Co.
Banc of America Securities LLC	Greenwich Capital Markets Inc.
Banc One Capital Markets, Inc.	HSBC Securities (USA) Inc.
Barclays Capital Inc.	J. P. Morgan Securities Inc.
Bear Sterns & Co., Inc.	Lehman Brothers Inc.
CIBC World Markets Corp.	Merrill Lynch Government Securities Inc.
Citigroup Global Markets, Inc.	Mizuho Securities USA Inc.
Countrywide Securities Corp.	Morgan Stanley & Co., Incorporated
Credit Suisse First Boston LLC	Nomura Securities International, Inc.
Daiwa Securities America Inc.	UBS Securities LLC
Deutsche Bank Securities Inc.	

Source: Primary Dealer List—Federal Reserve Bank of New York, January 14, 2004.

> The role of government security dealers in supporting the market for government securities is discussed in the publications of the Federal Reserve Bank of New York. See especially Primary Dealer Lists—Federal Reserve Bank of New York at ny.frb.org/markets/pridealers—listing.htm

The term *primary dealer* simply means that a dealer firm is qualified to trade securities directly with the Federal Reserve Bank of New York in order to assist the U.S. central bank in achieving its monetary policy objectives. To join the Fed's primary dealer list, the firm must agree to be available to trade securities at all times and to post adequate capital. Almost half of all primary dealer firms are controlled by corporations located outside the United States, including dealers with roots in Canada, Japan, France, Germany, and Great Britain. Many customers prefer to trade only with primary dealers. Moreover, achieving primary dealership status gives foreign dealers a solid foothold in U.S. markets. The primary dealers agree to "meaningfully participate" in trading with the Federal Reserve at any time the Fed wishes, to make "realistic" bids, and to trade continuously in the full range of government securities.

10.5 Dealer Borrowing and Lending Activities in the Money Market

Government security dealers supply a huge volume of T-bills and other securities daily to the financial marketplace. To do so, these dealers depend heavily on the *money market* for borrowed funds. Most dealer houses invest little of their own equity in the business. The bulk of operating capital is obtained through borrowings from commercial banks and other institutions. A major dealer firm carries hundreds of millions of dollars in securities in its trading portfolio, with 95 percent or more of that portfolio supported by short-term loans, some carrying only 24-hour maturities.

Demand Loans for Dealers

The two most heavily used sources of dealer funds are demand loans from the largest banks and repurchase agreements (RPs) with banks and other lenders. Every day major banks post interest rates at which they are willing to make short-term loans to dealers. Generally, one rate is quoted on new loans and a second (lower) rate is posted for renewals of existing loans. A **demand loan** may be called in at any time if the banks need cash in a hurry. Such loans are virtually riskless, however, because they usually are collateralized by U.S. government securities, which may be transferred temporarily to the lending bank or to its agent.

demand loan

Repurchase Agreements (RPs) for Dealers and Other Money Market Participants

repurchase agreement (RP)

A popular alternative to the demand loan is the **repurchase agreement (RP).** Under this agreement, the dealer sells securities to a lender but makes a commitment to buy back the securities at a later date at a fixed price plus interest. Thus, *RPs are simply a temporary extension of credit collateralized by marketable securities.* Some RPs are for a set length of time (*overnight* or *term RPs*), while others, known as *continuing contracts,* carry no explicit maturity date but may be terminated by either party on short notice. Larger banks provide both demand loans and RPs to dealers, and larger banks, in turn, borrow from dealers and other nonbank institutions through RPs in order to avoid deposit reserve requirements and prohibitions against their paying interest on demand deposit accounts. Moreover, nonfinancial corporations also have provided a growing volume of funds to dealers through RPs in recent years. Other lenders active in the RP market include state and local governments, insurance companies, and foreign financial institutions who find the market a convenient, relatively low-risk way to invest temporary cash surpluses that may be retrieved quickly when the need arises.

The typical RP loan transaction can be described easily through the use of T accounts (an abbreviated balance sheet) for a dealer and for the lender of funds. Exhibit 10.7 presents a typical example of such a loan. In this case, we assume a manufacturing company has a temporary $1 million cash surplus. The company is eager to loan its temporary cash surplus right away to avoid losing even a single day's interest, while the dealer wishes to borrow at the low-cost RP loan rate in order to purchase interest-bearing securities. The borrowing dealer and the lending company agree on a $1 million RP loan—the minimum loan usually made in this market—collateralized by Treasury bills, with the dealer agreeing to buy back the bills within a few days and to pay the interest on the loan. Normally, the securities that form the collateral for the RP are placed in a custodial account held by a third party. When the loan is repaid, the dealer's RP liability is automatically canceled and the securities are returned to the dealer.

There is evidence that this safety device of placing securities involved in an RP agreement into a separate custodial account has not always been scrupulously

---

EXHIBIT 10.7   **Example of a Typical RP Loan Transaction**

	Security Dealer		Manufacturing Company	
	Assets	Liabilities	Assets	Liabilities
a. Lender of funds—a manufacturing company—has a $1 million surplus in its cash account.			Deposit at bank + $1 million	
b. A security dealer and the company settle on an RP with the dealer using the borrowed funds to buy securities.	Securities held + $1 million	RP borrowing from manufacturer + $1 million	Deposit at bank − $1 million RP loan to security dealer + $1 million	
c. The RP agreement is concluded and the funds returned (plus interest).	Dealer's cash account − $1 million	RP borrowing from manufacturer − $1 million	Deposit at bank + $1 million RP loan to security dealer − $1 million	

followed in the past. Moreover, because the majority of outstanding RP loans are simply recorded as book entries at the Federal Reserve banks, verification of what has been done with the pledged securities can be difficult. The result is that if a government securities dealer goes out of business, a customer lending money under an RP to that dealer may have difficulty recovering the securities pledged as collateral behind the loan. Following the collapse of several dealer firms and the failure of several savings and loan associations that lost millions of dollars from inadequately collateralized security loans to those same dealers, federal authorities imposed stricter reporting requirements on the dealers. The Government Securities Act, passed in 1986, granted the U.S. Treasury additional oversight authority to protect the public from "unscrupulous" dealers. Under the act, new rules require written contracts between dealers and investors lending them money that describe where the securities in the RP are held. These written contracts also must specify whether other securities can be substituted for those held as loan collateral, and note that RPs are not protected by federal deposit insurance. The Securities and Exchange Commission and the federal banking agencies must enforce any rules for the government securities market that the Treasury Department writes.

Until recently, RPs were principally overnight transactions or expired in a few days. Today, however, there is a substantial volume of one- to three-month agreements, and some carry even longer maturities. The interest rate on RPs is the return that a dealer must pay a lender for the temporary use of money and is closely related to other money market interest rates. The RP (or repo) rate is based on the differences between the underlying security's current price and the agreed-upon future repurchase price. Usually, the securities pledged behind an RP are valued at their current market prices plus accrued interest (on coupon-bearing securities) less a small "haircut" (discount) to reduce the lender's exposure to market risk. The longer the term and the riskier and less liquid the securities pledged behind an RP, the larger the "haircut" will be to protect the lender in case security prices fall. Periodically, RPs are "marked to market," and if the price of the pledged securities has dropped, the borrower may have to pledge additional collateral.

Interest income from repurchase agreements is determined from the formula:

$$\frac{\text{RP interest}}{\text{income}} = \frac{\text{Amount}}{\text{of loan}} \times \frac{\text{Current}}{\text{RP rate}} \times \frac{\text{Number of days loaned}}{360 \text{ days}} \qquad \textbf{(10.5)}$$

For example, an overnight loan of $100 million to a dealer at a 7 percent RP rate would yield interest income of $19,444.44. That is,

$$\text{RP interest income} = \$100,000,000 \times .07 \times \frac{1}{360} = \$19,444.44$$

The interest rates on repurchase agreements (RPs) and other developments in the RP market may be traced through such Web sites as the Federal Reserve Bank of New York at ny.frb.org

Under a continuing contract RP, the interest rate changes daily, so the calculation above would be made for each day the funds were loaned, and the total interest owed would be paid to the lender when the contract is ended by either party. The current RP rate is usually close to the federal funds interest rate (which we will discuss in Chapter 11) as well as the prevailing Treasury bill rate.

A New Type of RP: The GCF Repo

As we have seen, repurchase agreements are very important in the operations of the primary dealers. Today RPs finance more than $2 trillion of dealers' security holdings annually. However, traditional RPs are somewhat inflexible and more costly than they need to be. In 1998, as described by Fleming and Garbade (2003), the Fixed Income

Clearing Corporation (FICC) and two dealer-clearing banking firms—J. P. Morgan Chase and the Bank of New York—stepped in to create a General Collateral Finance (GCF) Repo which subsequently has grown rapidly.

Prior to the appearance of GCF Repos, each RP transaction involving a particular dealer was settled independently of all other RP transactions, trade by trade. A dealer with multiple RPs outstanding could not settle the *net* amount owed to and received from all other parties in the market. Moreover, dealers had less flexibility in choosing the collateral they must pledge behind an RP (usually having to specify by 11 A.M. which securities they planned to deliver and post later that same afternoon). Significant changes in collateral pledged often resulted in the costly renegotiation of existing RP agreements. However, with the new GCF Repos, dealers working through a central clearinghouse—the FICC—are allowed to make changes in the securities they will ultimately deliver as collateral until late in the day (usually until 4:30 P.M.), thus giving the borrowing institution greater control over its collateral. Moreover, each dealer can *net* out the amount of its RP lending and borrowing activity with the FICC, resulting in a smaller volume of payments, fewer instruments actually changing hands, and reduced transactions costs and trading risks.

Sources of Dealer Income

The primary dealers take substantial risks to make a market for new Treasury bills and other financial instruments. To be sure, the securities they deal in are among the highest-quality instruments available in the financial marketplace. However, the prices of even top-quality securities can experience rapid declines if interest rates rise. Moreover, established dealer houses cannot run and hide but are obliged to stand ready at all times to buy and sell on customer demand, regardless of the condition of the market. In contrast to securities brokers, who merely bring buyers and sellers together, dealers take a *position of risk*, which means that they act as principals in the buying and selling of securities, adding any securities purchased to their own portfolios.

Dealers stand ready to buy specified types of securities at an announced *bid* price and to sell them at an announced *asked* price. This is called *making a market* in a particular financial instrument. The dealer hopes to earn a profit from such market-making activities in part from the positive spread between bid and asked prices for the same security. This spread varies with market activity and the outlook for interest rates but is narrow on bills (often about $50 per $1 million or less). Spreads range higher on longer-term securities, on small transactions, and on securities not actively traded due to greater risk and greater cost.

As we have seen, the dealers' holdings of securities are financed by borrowing, so their portfolio positions are extremely sensitive to fluctuations in interest rates. For this reason, dealers frequently shift from long positions to short positions, depending on the outlook for interest rates. A **long position** means that the dealers have purchased securities outright, taken title to them, and will hold them in their portfolios until a customer comes along. Long positions typically increase in a period of falling interest rates. A **short position,** on the other hand, means that dealers have sold securities they do not presently own to a customer. In doing so, they hope the prices of those securities will fall (and interest rates rise) before they must acquire the securities and make delivery. Obviously, if interest rates fall (and security prices rise), the dealer will experience capital gains on a long position but losses on a short position. On the other hand, if interest rates rise (resulting in a drop in security prices), the dealer's long position will experience capital losses, and the short position will post a gain.

In periods when interest rates are expected to rise, dealers typically reduce their long positions and go short. Conversely, expectations of falling rates lead dealers to increase their long positions and avoid short sales. By correctly anticipating interest-rate movements, the dealer can earn sizable *position profits*. Dealers also receive **carry income,** the difference between interest earned on securities they hold and their cost of borrowing funds. Generally, dealers earn higher rates of return on the securities they hold than the interest rates they pay for loans, but this is not always so. Because most dealer borrowings are short term, they normally are better off if the yield curve is positively sloped.

To help reduce exposure to risk, security dealers have recently diversified the revenue-generating services they offer. Some dealer firms now trade in foreign currencies, commodities (such as oil), security options, futures contracts, and swap contracts. Leading dealers—for example, Merrill Lynch & Co. and Citigroup Global Markets—offer cash management services in which they hold the funds of customers and invest them in securities, earning cash management fees from those same customers. Dealers have also tried to stabilize their income by acting much like banks and other financial intermediaries, simultaneously borrowing and lending money through a technique known as *matched book,* in which funds are borrowed through low-cost short-term RPs and then are loaned out through longer-term, higher-yielding RPs. (See, for example, Exhibit 10.8.) The yield spread between these "matched" RPs gives the dealer a net profit unless, of course, the slope of the yield curve suddenly changes and the dealer is forced to borrow short-term money at significantly higher interest rates.

Margin note: long position

Margin note: short position

Margin note: carry income

Dealer Positions in Securities

Dealer holdings of U.S. government and other securities are both huge and subject to erratic fluctuations. For example, in 1991 the dealers held a massive net long position in U.S. government securities of nearly $20 billion before falling to a sizable net short

EXHIBIT 10.8

Repurchase
Agreements (RPs)
as a Vehicle for
Dealers in
Securities and
Other Financial
Institutions to
Borrow and Lend
Money

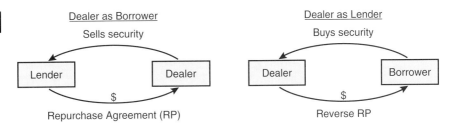

position of −$3.3 billion early in 1992. Early in 2004, on the other hand, the government security dealers held substantial net long positions in U.S. Treasury bills and federal agency securities but also held a huge short position in longer-term Treasury notes and bonds of more than $70 billion.

Why is there often such a tremendous difference in the size and direction of dealer portfolios from year to year? Interest rate movements and interest rate expectations explain a substantial proportion of the changes observed. For example, in 1991 and 1992 an economic recession drove short-term market interest rates sharply lower, holding out the lure of higher profits if the dealers could shift their holdings into a long position. Early in 2004, however, short-term interest rates were expected to rise from record lows and there was considerable fear among some market participants that a growing economy might eventually send long-term interest rates higher as well, creating losses on notes and bonds held in a long position.

Dealers make heavy use of interest-rate hedging tools today to further protect their portfolios from losses due to changes in interest rates. They are active participants in the *financial futures* markets and also are making increased use of *forward commitments,* in which a dealer sells securities but does not deliver to the customer until more than five business days have elapsed. A dealer often does not hold the securities to be delivered under the forward commitment but waits to acquire them near the promised delivery date. This strategy minimizes the risk of loss due to interest rate changes because the dealer is exposed to risk for only a brief period before delivery is made.

Dealer Transactions and Government Security Brokers

Trading among dealers and between dealers and their customers amounts to billions of dollars each day. Indeed, so large is the government securities market that the volume of trading often exceeds the total volume of trading on many of the world's stock exchanges. Government securities dealers trade among themselves usually through *brokers.* Government security brokers do not take investment positions themselves but try to match bids and offers placed with them by dealers and other investors. Each broker operates a closed-circuit TV network showing dealer prices and quantities available. These half-dozen interdealer brokers make price and trade information efficiently available and allow the dealers to remain anonymous in their trading.

Intense competition generally exists among government-security brokers. In 1992, for example, a "price war" broke out among leading brokerage houses in which commissions were cut by 50 percent or more and volume discounts were offered to the largest dealers. In some cases, dealers were told that if they placed a specified minimum volume of orders each month, any subsequent trades during that same month would be handled free of charge by the advertising broker. The principal motivation for the sudden appearance of "bargain" brokerage rates was a sharp decline in trading volume, related to a slowdown in the economy.

Dealerships are a cutthroat business in which each dealer firm is out to maximize its returns from trading, even if gains must be made at the expense of competing dealers. Indeed, market analysts housed within each dealer firm study the daily price quotations of competitors. If one dealer temporarily underprices securities (offering excessively generous yields), other dealers are likely to rush in before the offering firm has a chance to correct its mistake. It is a business with little room for the inexperienced or slow-moving trader and fraught with low margins and unstable earnings. For example, in 1982 two major firms—Drysdale Government Securities, Inc., and Lombard-Wall, Inc.—collapsed. These closings were soon followed by four more dealer failures: Lion Capital Group, RTD Securities, E.S.M. Government Securities, and Bevill, Bresler & Schulman Asset Management Corporation. In 1989 and 1990, several foreign-owned dealers, including Britain's National Westminster Bank PLC, Lloyds Bank PLC, Midland Bank PLC, and L.F. Rothchilds & Co., as well as Australia's Westpac Banking Corporaton, withdrew from the Fed's primary dealer list due to falling trading volume and declining profit margins. U.S. primary dealer Drexel Burnham Lambert also withdrew from that list in 1990 and filed for protection under the federal bankruptcy code. With soaring competition both at home and abroad, several primary dealers have posted substantial net losses in recent years. Moreover, government security prices and interest rates appeared to become somewhat less volatile as the twentieth century closed and the twenty-first century began. Unfortunately for the dealers, it is generally in periods of high price and rate volatility that these firms generate the most revenue, because the volume of security trading rises and there is more demand for interest rate risk protection at that time.

One of the most remarkable features of the dealer's business is how rapidly market conditions and the dealer's financial position can deteriorate. Large losses in tens of millions of dollars can be recorded in a few hours. Moreover, dealers may buy large quantities of bonds that are not yet issued (*when-issued securities*) without any money down and payment not due until delivery a week or so later, only to discover that within minutes the market values of these securities have dropped like a stone. Yet the dealers are *essential* to the smooth functioning of the financial markets, to the successful placement of billions of dollars in securities issued each year by the Treasury Department and by a host of federal and federally sponsored agencies, and to the successful pursuit of monetary policy by the central bank.

QUESTIONS TO HELP YOU STUDY

22. Explain why security dealers are essential to the smooth functioning of the securities markets and especially the money market.

23. What is a *demand loan?* How does it help security dealers obtain the financing they need?

24. What is a *repurchase agreement* (RP)? Explain what an RP's role is in financing the operations of security dealers.

25. In what different ways do security dealers generate *income* and make a profit?

26. To what types of *risk* is each form or source of dealer income subject? How might a dealer handle these different forms of risk exposure?

27. What causes the positions that dealers hold in securities to change over time?

MARKETS ON THE NET: The Most Important Web Sites for This Chapter

Bond Market Association
(bondmarket.com)
Browse Data of the Federal Reserve Board
(economagic.com/fedbog.htm)
U.S. Treasury Department Bureau of the
Public Debt (publicdebt.treas.gov)
Treasury Direct (Treasurydirect.gov)
Federal Reserve Bank of New York
(ny.frb.org)

Board of Governors of the Federal Reserve
System (federalreserve.gov)
Federal Deposit Insurance Corporation
(fdic.gov)
Primary Dealers—Federal Reserve
Bank of New York (ny.frb.org/markets/
pridealers-listing.htm)

Summary of the Chapter's Main Points

This chapter has presented, first of all, a broad overview of one of the most important components of any financial system, the *money market*. The chapter then explores the roles played by governments and security dealers in keeping the money market functioning efficiently.

- *Money markets* are defined as the collection of institutions and trading relationships that move short-term funds from lenders to borrowers and back again. All money market loans have an original maturity of *one year or less.* Thus, money market transactions typically consist of credit flows from lenders and borrowers that last for only hours, days, weeks, or months, unlike the *capital markets,* where credit transactions may cover many years.

- Most loans extended in the money market are designed to provide short-term working capital to businesses and governments so they can purchase inventories, pay dividends and taxes, and deal with other immediate needs for cash. Their short-term cash needs arise from the fact that inflows and outflows of cash are *not* perfectly synchronized. In the real world, even with the best planning available, temporary cash deficits and temporary cash surpluses are more often the rule rather than the exception.

- Money market investors are typically extremely conservative when it comes to placing their savings in financial instruments. They usually will accept little or no risk of borrower default, prefer financial instruments whose prices are stable, and usually require an investment from which their funds can be recaptured quickly (i.e., they prefer assets with high liquidity and marketability). The market's great sensitivity to risk helps explain why money market interest rates are among the lowest interest rates in the financial system.

- One of the most important of all institutions active in the money market is *government,* which sets the rules by which the money market operates and typically is among the largest of all money market borrowers. Indeed, the market for government securities sets the tone for the whole financial system in terms of interest rates, security prices, and the availability of credit to both governments and private borrowers. It is an indispensable tool for the government to finance its large volume of debt, and interest rates on government securities serve as reference rates for thousands of private loan contracts.

- Moreover, money market investors all over the globe rely upon government securities as a safe haven for their cash reserves. This is especially true of

www.mhhe.com/rose9e

Treasury bills, which are direct government debt obligations with an original maturity of a year or less. And it is in this same market today that most government economic policy changes begin.

- At the heart of the government security market are *security dealers* that actively make markets for a broad range of government, agency, and private security issues. These dealers actively raise funds to support their purchases of government and other securities from their customers. Among their most important funds sources are *demand loans* from banks and other lenders and *repurchase agreements* negotiated with financial and nonfinancial corporations. Demand loans can be canceled at any time by the borrower or the lender and carry daily posted interest rates. Repurchase agreements are collateralized loans, using high-quality securities (especially government IOUs) as collateral.

Key Terms Appearing in This Chapter

money market, 275
market or interest rate risk, 277
reinvestment risk, 277
default risk, 279
inflation (or purchasing power) risk, 279
currency risk, 279
political risk, 279
liquidity, 279
original maturity, 281
actual maturity, 281
federal funds, 281

clearinghouse funds, 282
U.S. Treasury bills, 284
auction, 285
bank discount method, 287
primary dealers, 290
demand loan, 292
repurchase agreement (RP), 293
long position, 296
short position, 296
carry income, 296

Problems and Issues

1. How much interest would be earned (on a simple interest basis) from a three-day money market loan for $1 million at an interest rate of 12 percent (annual rate)? Suppose the loan was extended on the third day for an additional day at the going market rate of 11 percent. How much total interest income would the money market lender receive?

2. From the following sets of figures, (1) calculate the bank discount rate (DR) on each T-bill and (2) convert that rate to the appropriate investment return (IR).
   a. A new three-month T-bill sells for $98.25 on a $100 basis.
   b. The investor can buy a new 12-month T-bill for $96 on a $100 basis.
   c. A 30-day bill is available from a U.S. government securities dealer at a price of $97.50 (per $100).

3. Calculate the holding-period yield for the following situations:
   a. The investor buys a new 12-month T-bill at a discount rate of $7\frac{1}{2}$ percent. Sixty days later, the bill is sold at a price that results in a discount rate of 7 percent.
   b. A large manufacturing corporation acquired a T-bill in the secondary market 30 days from its maturity but is forced to sell the bill 15 days later. At time of purchase, the bill carried a discount rate of 8 percent, but it was sold at a discount rate of $7\frac{3}{4}$ percent.

4. A dealer in government securities currently holds $875 million in 10-year Treasury bonds and $1,410 million in six-month Treasury bills. Current yields on the T-bonds average 7.15 percent, while six-month T-bill yields average 3.28 percent. The dealer is currently borrowing $2,300 million through one-week repurchase agreements at an interest rate of 3.20 percent. What is the dealer's expected (annualized) *carry income?* Suppose that 10-year T-bond rates suddenly rise to 7.30 percent, T-bill rates climb to 5.40 percent, and interest rates on comparable maturity RPs increase to 5.55 percent. What will happen to the dealer's expected (annualized) carry income and why? Should this dealer have moved to a long position or a short position before the interest rate change just described? Should the dealer alter his or her borrowing plans in any way? Explain your answer.

5. A government securities dealer is currently borrowing $25 million from a money center bank using repurchase agreements based on Treasury bills. If today's RP rate is 6.25 percent, how much in interest will the dealer owe the bank for a 24-hour loan?

6. Suppose that a dealer borrows cash through a $40 million RP from a manufacturing corporation for one day. If the dealer will have to pay $3,500 in interest on this loan, what is the current RP loan rate?

7. An automobile company, NISSAN, has a temporary cash surplus and lends its funds overnight through a repurchase agreement to a government securities dealer, earning $55,600 in interest income when the RP loan rate stood at 5.70 percent. What was the size of the loan that NISSAN granted to the securities dealer?

8. Ninety-one-day Treasury bills carry an investment return (IR) of 6.25 percent. What is their purchase price? What is their discount rate (DR)?

Standard & Poor's Market Insight and Web-Based Problems

STANDARD &POOR'S

1. Commercial banks and scores of other investors hold U.S. Treasury securities to reduce risk and add liquidity and marketability to their asset portfolios. However, these benefits come at a price—lower interest earnings—as Treasuries have among the lowest market yields of all debt instruments traded in the money and capital markets.

    a. Visit Standard & Poor's Market Insight database at **mhhe.com/edumarketinsight** and locate the annual balance sheet for a large commercial bank, such as Wachovia Corp (WB). Check "Excel Analytics."

    b. Compute the ratio of "Investment Securities: National Government" to total assets for the last five years. Has this figure varied much over the five years?

    c. For the most recent year, compute the ratio of "Investment Securities: Total" to total assets for this bank.

    d. Go to the Federal Reserve's Web site at **federalreserve.gov/Releases/H8/Current** and compute the ratio of the sum of "Securities in Bank Credit: Treasury and Agency Securities: Investment Account" plus "Securities in Bank Credit: Other Securities: Investment Account" to total assets.

    e. How much reliance does the bank that you selected place on investment securities (as calculated in part [c]) relative to the banking system as a whole (as determined in part [d])?

2. Visit one of today's sources of financial news (such as *The Wall Street Journal*) where you can find a complete listing of all U.S. Treasury securities along with the trading activity from the previous day. Identify the T-bills with 14, 91, and 182 days to maturity (or as close to these terms as you can find).

    a. Which of these U.S. Treasury securities have the lowest yield to maturity?

    b. Based on the information from part (a) how would you describe the slope of the yield curve over the maturity range covered by T-bills?

    c. Does your answer to part (b) suggest anything about how the slope of the yield curve in the less-than-one-year maturity range changed as a result of the previous day's trading activity?

    d. If there was a change reported in part (c) and if this change would have been due exclusively to a changed perception of future inflation by the financial markets, would the markets have raised or lowered their expectations for inflation?

3. Some of the largest government securities dealers are called "primary dealers" because they are authorized to deal directly with the Federal Reserve. However, these dealers also engage in many other types of transactions involving the purchase and sale of U.S. Treasury securities, federal agency securities, mortgage-backed securities, and corporate securities. (You will learn about each of these in the chapters that follow.) The purpose of this exercise is to understand how important these dealers are to the market for Treasuries—the principal market through which the Federal Reserve conducts monetary policy. In answering the following questions, you will consider both their outright purchases and sales from their portfolios and their RP transactions.

    a. Visit the Web site for the Federal Reserve Bank of New York at **ny.frb.org**, pull down the menu for "Markets," and click on "Primary Dealers."

    b. Go to the section on the "Weekly Release of Primary Dealer Transactions" and compute the ratio of total outright transactions in U.S. government securities to the total of all transactions listed for this group of dealers. What do you conclude about the relative importance of trading in U.S. Treasuries for primary dealers?

    c. Compute the ratio of outright transactions in Treasuries with nondealers ("other") to the total transactions of primary dealers with nondealers. How does this alter your view of the relative importance of trading in U.S. securities for primary dealers?

    d. Compute the ratio of total transactions within the primary dealer group to total transactions. What do you conclude about the need for dealers to trade with each other in order for the group as a whole to perform its particular role as financial intermediary more efficiently?

Semester Project: A Study of the Fed Funds Market

In its conduct of monetary policy, the Federal Reserve's chief policymaking unit—the Federal Open Market Committee (FOMC)—meets eight times per year in order to choose its "target" for the Fed funds rate. In normal times this target is expected to change only at the regularly scheduled meetings. In this installment of the semester project you will determine what the markets are expecting the average daily effective Fed funds rate to be for the portion of a month in which the FOMC *is* scheduled to meet, for those days *before* and *after* the meeting.

a. As you did at the end of Chapter 3, gather and retain the following information: (i) When does the FOMC next meet? (ii) What is the Federal Reserve's current target for the Fed funds rate? (iii) What are the actual values for the funds rate for the current month to date?

b. As you did at the end of Chapter 9, determine the effective funds rate for the whole month using data provided by the 30-day Fed funds futures market.

c. To illustrate the calculations needed to complete this part of the semester project, assume the following facts: Today is April 5th and the next scheduled FOMC meeting is April 15th; the current Fed funds target is 1 percent and the settle price for April 5 is 98.975 percent. You have uncovered the following data for the daily effective funds rate: April 1, 0.96 percent; April 2, 0.98 percent; April 3, 1.00 percent; April 4, 1.02 percent; and April 5, 1.01 percent. Compute the market's expectations of the average effective funds rate for those days *before* the FOMC meeting and denote this by x. This is just a weighted average of the effective funds rate for the days for which you have already gathered data (in our example, April 1–5) and the Federal Reserve's target rate that is expected to prevail until the FOMC meeting (in our example, from April 6–15). That is,

$$x = [(0.96 + 0.98 + 1.00 + 1.02 + 1.01) + 10 * (1.00)] / 15 = 0.998\%$$

Using the settle price for the month, compute the market's expectation for the average effective funds rate *after* the FOMC meeting and denote this by y:

$$(15/30) * 0.998\% + (15/30) * y = (100 - 98.975)\%, \text{ or } y = 1.052\%$$

d. Repeat the steps in part (c) using the actual data you gathered in parts (a) and (b) *unless* there is no FOMC meeting in the current month. If there is no meeting, compute the effective funds rate for the *whole* month.

Selected References to Explore

Duffey, Gunter, and Ian H. Giddy. "Money Markets in the Pacific Basin." *Working Paper 93–10,* Mitsui Life Financial Research Center, The University of Michigan, 1993.

Dupoint, Dominique, and Brian Sack. "The Treasury Securities Market: Overview and Recent Developments." *Federal Reserve Bulletin,* December 1999, pp. 785–806.

Fleming, Michael J. "The Round-the-Clock Market for U.S. Treasury Securities." *Economic Policy Review,* Federal Reserve Bank of New York, July 1997, pp. 9–32.

Fleming, Michael J., and Kenneth D. Garbade. "The Repurchase Agreement Refined: The GCF Repo." *Current Issues in Economics and Finance,* Federal Reserve Bank of New York, June 2003, pp. 1–7.

Keane, Frank. "Repo Rate Patterns for New Treasury Notes." *Current Issues in Economics and Finance,* Federal Reserve Bank of New York, September 1996, pp. 1–6.

Nandi, Saikat. "Treasury Auction: What Do the Recent Models and Results Tell Us?" *Economic Review,* Federal Reserve Bank of Atlanta, Fourth Quarter 1997, pp. 4–14.

Chapter 11

Commercial Banks, Major Corporations, and Federal Credit Agencies in the Money Market

Learning Objectives

in This Chapter

- You will discover several of the most important ways that *banks* and other depository institutions borrow and lend funds and supply other critical services needed in the money market.

- You will explore the nature and characteristics of one of the oldest of all money market instruments—*commercial paper*—and discover the important roles played by large corporations in both borrowing and lending funds in the money market.

- You will learn how *federal credit agencies*, by borrowing funds from the money market, provide financial aid to several sectors of the economy (including agriculture, home buyers, and small businesses).

- You will see *internationalization* at work in the money market, which now girdles the globe and helps to efficiently allocate scarce capital almost everywhere on the planet.

What's in This Chapter? Key Topics Outline

11.1   Introduction

In the previous chapter we examined the central characteristics of money market instruments and the critical roles played by governments and major securities dealers in the daily functioning of the money market. The purpose of this chapter is to explore the contributions to the global money market made by several other important institutions—*commercial banks, major corporations,* and *government-sponsored credit agencies.* As you will see, these institutions frequently work on both sides of the money market—often lending and borrowing short-term money at the same time. They are also among the most innovative and interesting of the thousands of participants trading in the money market every day.

11.2   The Roles Played by Banks in the Money Market

The single most important privately owned institution in most money markets is the *commercial bank.* Large money center banks, such as those headquartered in New York City, London, Paris, Tokyo, and a handful of other major cities around the globe, provide billions of dollars in funds daily through the money market to governments and corporations in need of cash. As we saw in the previous chapter, bank loans and repurchase agreements are a principal source of financing for dealers in securities, while banks also make large purchases of Treasury bills and other money market securities. Commercial banks support private corporations borrowing in the money market, both by purchasing their securities and by granting lines of credit to backstop a new security issue. Banks supply credit to support the movement of goods in domestic and international trade. And both large and small banks today readily lend their cash reserves to other financial institutions and to industrial corporations to cover short-term liquidity needs.

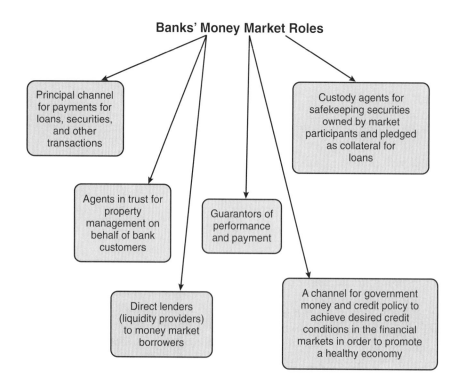

For banks to lend huge amounts of funds daily in the money market, they must also borrow heavily in that market. The owners (stockholders) supply only a minor portion of a commercial bank's total resources; the bulk of bank funds must be *borrowed.* The majority of bank borrowings come from *deposits,* but a growing portion of the industry's financing needs is supplied directly by the *money market.* However, bank managers today are often cautious in their use of money market borrowings. Such funds can be expensive to use at times, and their interest cost is more volatile than for most kinds of deposits. Many banks follow the strategy of maintaining a roughly equal balance between their lending and borrowing activities in the money market: The volume of short-term bank debt is counterbalanced by a nearly equal volume of short-term bank assets.[1]

In this chapter, we examine three of the most important money market sources of funds for banks and other deposit-type financial institutions: *federal funds, negotiable certificates of deposit (CDs),* and *Eurocurrency deposits.* We will also discuss a device used by international banks to fund the expansion of global trade—the *bankers' acceptance.*

11.3 Federal Funds Provided by the Banking System

federal funds

As we saw in the introductory chapter to the money market (Chapter 10), **federal funds** are among the most important of all money market instruments for one key reason: *Fed funds are the principal means of making payments in the money market.* By definition, federal funds are any monies available for immediate payment ("same-day money"). They are generally transferred from one depository institution to another by simple bookkeeping entries requested by online computer, by wire, or by telephone after a purchase of securities is made or a loan is granted or repaid.

The Nature of Federal Funds and Their Uses

The name *federal funds* came about because, early in the development of the market, the principal source of immediately available money was the reserve balance that each member bank of the Federal Reserve System had to keep at the Federal Reserve bank in its region of the United States. If one bank needed to transfer funds to another, it needed only to contact the Federal Reserve bank in its district, and funds were readily transferred into the appropriate reserve account—a transaction accomplished in seconds by telephone, telegraph, or, more recently, by computer.

Today, however, the Fed funds market is far broader in scope than just reserves on deposit with the Federal Reserve banks. For example, virtually all depository institutions keep funds with large correspondent banks in central cities; these deposits may be transferred readily by telephone, by computer, or by wire from the account of one bank to that of another. They also may be borrowed by the institution that holds the correspondent deposit, simply by transferring funds from the correspondent deposit to an account titled "Federal funds purchased" and reversing these entries when the loan matures. Savings associations and credit unions maintain deposits with commercial banks or with the Federal Reserve banks that also are available for immediate transfer to a customer or to another financial institution. Business corporations and state and

---

[1]The idea of maintaining a roughly *equal* balance between borrowing and lending in the money market follows one of the oldest concepts in the field of finance: the *hedging principle.* As discussed in Chapter 7, in a world of uncertainty, borrowers of funds can reduce their liquidity risk by matching the maturity of their assets and liabilities. This approach reduces the risk of borrowing when funds are not needed and lowers the risk of not having sufficient cash when bills come due.

local governments can lend federal funds by executing repurchase agreements with securities dealers, banks, and other funds traders. Securities dealers who have received payment for securities sold can turn around and make their funds immediately available to borrowers through the federal funds market. Without question, however, the most important of all borrowers in the Fed funds market are *commercial banks.*

Use of the Federal Funds Market to Meet Reserve Requirements

legal reserve requirement

Banks and other depository institutions *must* hold in a special legal reserve account liquid assets equal to a fraction of the funds deposited with them by the public. Banks are aided in this endeavor by the fact that their **legal reserve requirement** is calculated on a daily average basis over a two-week period, known as the *reserve computation period.* For example, the reserve computation period for *transaction deposits* (e.g., checking accounts) stretches from a Tuesday through a Monday two weeks later. The Federal Reserve calculates the daily average level of transaction deposits held by each depository institution over this two-week period and then multiplies that average by the required reserve percentage (3 percent for smaller banks and 10 percent for larger banks, for example) to determine the amount of legal reserves that must be held by each institution. These legal reserves must average the required amount over a two-week period known as the *reserve maintenance period.*

The manager of each depository institution's *money desk*—the department responsible for keeping track of the depository's legal reserve position—must adjust each institution's reserve balance at the district Federal Reserve bank to the right level over the two-week reserve maintenance period. The federal funds market is an indispensable tool for this kind of daily reserve management, especially for the largest and most aggressive banks which hold few reserves of their own. Indeed, many large U.S. banks today borrow virtually all of the legal reserves behind their deposits from the federal funds market.

Mechanics of Federal Funds Trading

The mechanics of federal funds trading vary depending on the locations of the buying (borrowing) and selling (lending) institutions. For example, suppose two commercial banks involved in a federal funds transaction are located in the heart of the New York money market. These banks could simply exchange checks. The borrowing bank could be handed a check drawn on the lending bank's reserve account at the Federal Reserve Bank of New York City. This check is payable immediately ("same-day money"), and therefore Fed funds would be transferred to the borrower's reserve account before the close of business that same day. The lender, on the other hand, may be given a check drawn on the borrower. This last check is "one-day money" (payable the following day) because it must pass through the New York clearinghouse for settlement. Thus, funds flow instantly to the borrowing bank's reserve account and are automatically returned to the lending bank's reserve account the next day or whenever the loan agreement terminates. In the past decade, this process has been streamlined somewhat by computers connected online. For example, the lending bank can simply contact the Federal Reserve Bank of New York's computer and ask it to electronically move funds from the lender's reserve account to the borrower's reserve account immediately, with the transaction usually reversed the next day. Interest on the Fed funds loan may be included when the funds are returned, paid by separate check, or settled by debiting and crediting the appropriate correspondent balances.

The federal funds market in the United States is not the only market for interbank loans. Banks in many other countries have established a market for making loans of reserves to each other. While the U.S. Fed funds market is efficient and works well, sometimes foreign interbank markets run into trouble with serious consequences for the rest of the economy. A dramatic example of how troubles in interbank lending can send tremors through a country's financial system occurred in Russia during the 1990s.

Newspaper stories and rumors spread through Russia's banking system to the effect that several Russian banks were not sound. Accordingly, many of Russia's more than 2,500 banks then in operation simply stopped extending loans to one another. Many Russian bankers indicated they could not get enough information on other banks to decide whether these banks were solvent enough to pay back their interbank loans. The overnight market for ruble-denominated deposits ground to a halt, and some banks offered interest rates as high as 1,000 percent in an effort to get a loan! Moreover, with bankers not trusting each other, the Russian public began to mistrust their banks, resulting in scores of depositors demanding to retrieve their funds.

Many observers were concerned that, should such an event continue, the Russian banking system might collapse. One possible solution was to have Russia's central bank grant loans to any banks in trouble. Only a few days into the crisis, the central bank began buying publicly held government bonds in order to flood the system with liquidity. However, over the longer term, reform of the Russian banking system to clarify regulations, install risk-management systems, and require banks to release more information about their true financial condition is needed.

If the transacting institutions are not both located within the same Federal Reserve district, the loan transaction proceeds in much the same way except that *two* Federal Reserve banks are involved. Once borrower and lender agree on the terms of a loan, the lending institution directly, or indirectly through a correspondent bank, contacts the Federal Reserve bank in its district, requesting an electronic transfer of federal funds. The Reserve bank then transfers reserves through the Fed's wire network (FEDWIRE) to the Federal Reserve bank serving the region where the borrowing institution is located. Funds travel the reverse route when the loan is terminated.

Incidentally, how do Fed funds borrowers and lenders contact each other to find out who has surplus funds to lend and who is short of funds? Computer networks and the telephone are the most common media for communicating between institutions in need of funds and those with surplus funds. In addition, a handful of *Fed funds brokers* active in the money market work to bring buying and selling institutions together, indicating via telephone and their computer network what funds are available and at what interest rate. In brief, there are three principal segments of the Fed funds market among banks today; (1) brokered funds; (2) nonbrokered direct loans among major banks; and (3) correspondent rebookings, where smaller banks loan their excess reserves through the deposits they hold at large correspondent banks in money centers.

Volume of Borrowings in the Funds Market

Commercial banks borrow billions of dollars each day in the federal funds market. The large banks in New York City, by virtue of their strategic location at the heart of the domestic money market, still account for a disproportionate share of all Fed funds transactions. However, the market has broadened considerably in recent years to include

EXHIBIT 11.1

Effective Interest Rates on Federal Funds Transactions, 1980–2004

Year	Average Daily Rate on Federal Funds	Year	Average Daily Rate on Federal Funds
1980	13.36%	1995	5.83
1985	8.10	2000	6.24
1990	8.10	2002	1.67
		2004*	1.00

Source: Board of Governors of the Federal Reserve System, *Federal Reserve Bulletin*, selected monthly issues.

*Average for January 2004.

both domestic and foreign banks in Atlanta, Chicago, San Francisco, and other major U.S. cities, as well as thousands of smaller banks in outlying areas.

Most federal funds loans are *overnight* (one-day) transactions or *continuing contracts* that have no specific maturity and can be terminated without advance notice by either party. One-day loans carry a fixed rate of interest, but continuing contracts often do not. There is a growing volume of loans lasting beyond one day. These longer-maturity interbank loans are usually called *term* federal funds and are being supplied increasingly by foreign banks, savings and loan associations, insurance companies, pension funds, and finance companies as a safe and profitable way to warehouse funds until they are needed for longer-term commitments.

Interest Rates on Federal Funds

The federal funds interest rate is highly volatile from day to day, although on an annual basis, it tends to move roughly in line with other money market interest rates (see Exhibit 11.1). The short-term volatility of the funds rate arises from substantial variations in the volume of funds made available by lenders each day and the size of daily cash deficits experienced by banks and other money market participants. The funds rate tends to be most volatile toward the close of the reserve maintenance period, depending on whether larger banks are flush with or short of reserves. There are also seasonal patterns, with the funds rate tending to rise around holiday periods, when loan demand and deposit withdrawals are often heavy.

Federal Funds and Government Economic Policy

The federal funds market is an easy and riskless way to invest excess reserves for short periods and still earn some interest income. It is essential to the daily management of bank reserves, because credit can be obtained in a matter of minutes to cover emergency situations. Fed funds are also critical to the whole money market, because these funds serve as the principal means of payment for securities and loans. Moreover, the funds market transmits the effects of Federal Reserve monetary policy quickly throughout the banking system because the Fed routinely sets target levels for the federal funds interest rate and raises or lowers these targets, depending on whether the Fed wishes to slow down borrowing and spending in the economy or speed it up. Using daily open market operations—buying and selling securities—the Fed is able to push the funds rate in the desired direction on any given day. There appears to be a particularly close relationship between the federal funds interest rate target and the Federal Reserve's inflation target. The U.S. central bank tends to raise the federal funds rate when inflation in the prices of goods and services rises to a level that the Fed finds unacceptable and tends to lower the funds rate when inflation declines.

Money market investors follow movements in the federal funds rate closely for clues as to which direction Federal Reserve monetary policy may be moving—toward

The Federal Funds Rate and the Rise of Sweep Accounts

Recently, the volume of legal reserves U.S. banks hold at the Federal Reserve banks has decreased substantially. Many banks have discovered a way to reduce their required reserve balances by rapidly switching funds out of customers' demand deposit accounts, which currently carry legal reserve requirements, into time and saving deposits, which carry *no* reserve requirements, often returning the funds to demand deposits the next day. These contractual switching arrangements—known as *sweep accounts*—not only reduce a bank's required legal reserves but also allow some customers to earn interest on checking account balances. More than $200 billion in sweep account arrangements were in place by the beginning of the twenty-first century, and, partly as a result, U.S. bank legal reserve balances fell by more than half.

Unfortunately, one consequence of the decline in required legal reserves was an apparent increase in the volatility of the federal funds interest rate because there were fewer reserves to be traded in the federal funds market. This increased volatility was of special concern because the federal funds rate is the Federal Reserve's prime instrumental target for achieving the goals of U.S. monetary policy. If the funds rate becomes too difficult to control, the Fed might have greater difficulty hitting its desired interest rate targets. The financial markets and the economy might become more difficult to control, and the public could become more confused about the central bank's true goals for money and credit policy.

It should be noted, however, that the apparent increased volatility of the federal funds interest rate has been relatively modest and bank managers seem to have adjusted well to the changing funds rate environment. In part, this is due to the improved technology of communications between the Fed and the banks that keep reserve balances at the Federal Reserve's regional banks. For example, in recent years, the Fed has made it possible for bankers to monitor on their computer screens, on a real-time basis, debits and credits to individual legal reserve accounts so that bank managers can see more clearly how their reserve position stands and can better anticipate surpluses and deficits. Moreover, as we will see in Chapter 13, recent changes in the Fed's policy for administering its discount (loan) window will likely put a ceiling on future movements in the Fed funds rate.

The key role of the federal funds market in aiding the central bank of the United States, the Federal Reserve System, in the conduct of monetary policy is discussed in several Web sites, especially the Intended Federal Funds Rate at federalreserve.gov/fomc

QUESTIONS TO HELP YOU STUDY

1. Define the term *federal funds*. Why are federal funds so important to the functioning of the money market?

2. Who are the principal *borrowers* active in the federal funds market? Why are they attracted to this market for the funds they require?

3. Who are the principal *lenders* active in the federal funds market? Why do they find this market a good place to lend money?

4. Describe the process of legal reserve position adjustment that depository institutions go through. What role does the federal funds market play in helping depository institutions manage their so-called *money* or *legal reserve position*?

5. Why has the federal funds market become so important to the United States' central bank, the Federal Reserve System, in carrying out the government's *monetary policy* operations?

tighter or looser credit conditions. As we saw earlier in Chapter 9, investors are now able to hedge against unexpected or adverse changes in the federal funds rate through two relatively new instruments traded at the Chicago Board of Trade: a federal funds futures contract and an options contract on Fed funds futures. The prices and interest rates attached to these two contracts are sensitive to changing market expectations regarding future changes in the Federal Reserve's target for the Fed funds rate. Money market investors can "lock in" a particular interest rate on short-term borrowings or loans and obtain a glimpse of the market's forecast for future funds rate movements.

11.4 Negotiable Certificates of Deposit (CDs) Issued by Banks

negotiable certificate of deposit (CD)

One of the largest of all money market instruments, measured by dollar volume, is the **negotiable certificate of deposit (CD)**. A CD is an interest-bearing receipt for funds left with a depository institution for a set period of time.[2] Banks and other deposit-type institutions issue many types of CDs, but true money market CDs are negotiable instruments that may be sold any number of times before reaching maturity and carry a minimum denomination of $100,000. The usual round-lot trading unit for money market CDs is $1 million.

The interest rate on a large negotiable CD is set by negotiation between the issuing institution and its customer and generally reflects prevailing market conditions. Therefore, like the interest rates on other money market securities, CD interest rates rise in periods of tight money, when loanable funds are scarce, and fall in periods of easy money, when loanable funds are more abundant.

The negotiable CD is one of the youngest of all U.S. money market instruments. It dates from 1961, when First National City Bank of New York (later Citibank) began offering the instrument to its largest corporate customers. Simultaneously, a small group of dealers agreed to make a secondary (resale) market for CDs of $100,000 or more. Other money center banks soon entered the competition for corporate funds and began to offer their own CDs.

The decision to sell this new money market instrument was an agonizing one for banks because CDs tended to increase the average cost and volatility of bank funds. However, commercial banks had little choice but to offer the new instrument or face the loss of billions of dollars in interest-sensitive deposits. The cash management departments of major corporations have become increasingly aware of the many profitable ways available to invest their short-term funds. Prior to the introduction of the negotiable CD, many bankers found that their biggest corporate customers were reducing their deposits and buying Treasury bills and other money market instruments. The CD was developed to attract those lost deposits back into the banking system.

Negotiable CDs are a real success story for most banks. Early in the twenty-first century, large ($100,000+) time deposits outstanding at banks and thrifts operating in the United States totaled more than $1 trillion. This compares with only about $100 billion in large CDs roughly two decades earlier.

Terms Attached to CDs and Who Buys Them

Negotiable CDs may be *registered* on the books of the issuing depository institution or issued in *bearer form* to the purchasing investor. CDs issued in bearer form are more convenient for resale in the secondary market because they are in the hands of the investors who own them. Denominations range from $25,000 to $10 million, although CDs actively traded in the money market carry a minimum denomination of $100,000.

---

[2]The minimum maturity permitted for CDs under federal regulation is seven days. There is no legal upper limit on CD maturities, however. Unlike T-bills, CDs must be issued at par and trade on an interest-bearing basis. Payment is made in federal funds on the day each CD matures.

Maturities range upward to around 18 months, depending on the customer's needs. However, most negotiable CDs have maturities of six months or less. CDs with maturities beyond one year are called *term* CDs.

Interest rates in the CD market are computed as a yield to maturity but are quoted on a 360-day basis (except in secondary market trading, where the bank discount rate is used as a measure of CD yields). The general formula to use is:

$$\text{Funds owed the depositor} = D + \frac{n}{360} \times D \times i \tag{11.1}$$

where D is the original deposit principal; i is the promised yield to maturity based upon a 360-day year; and n is the number of days that interest is earned. For example, if a business firm purchases a $100,000 negotiable CD for six months at an interest rate of 7.50 percent, it would receive back at the end of 180 days:

$$\$100{,}000 \times \left(1 + \frac{180}{360} \times 0.075\right) = \$103{,}750$$

To convert the yield on newly issued CDs to a true coupon-equivalent yield for a full 365-day year, that is, to determine the CD's true yield to maturity (YTM), we must multiply the 360-day-based yield (i) by the ratio 365:360. That is,

$$\text{YTM}_{\text{CDs}} = i \times \frac{365}{360} \tag{11.2}$$

For example, a 360-day yield (i) of 6.25 percent for a CD would mean a coupon-equivalent return (YTM) for that same CD of:

$$\text{YTM} = 6.25 \text{ percent} \times \frac{365}{360} = 6.33 \text{ percent}$$

In the secondary (resale) market, yields on negotiable CDs are figured by the bank discount rate (DR) method that we discussed earlier for Treasury bills in Chapter 10 and in Chapter 6. That is,

$$\text{DR}_{\text{CD}} = \frac{\begin{array}{c}(\text{Par value of CD} - \text{Purchase price}\\ \text{of CD in the secondary market})\end{array}}{\text{Par value of CD}} \times \frac{360}{n} \tag{11.3}$$

where n is the number of days until the CD matures or is sold in advance of its maturity to another investor. For example, a six-month CD bearing a 7.50 percent promised interest rate at maturity but sold three months (90 days) early for $98,200 would carry a discount yield (DR) of:

$$\text{DR}_{\text{CD}} = \frac{\$100{,}000 - \$98{,}200}{\$100{,}000} \times \frac{360}{90} = 7.20 \text{ percent}$$

As Exhibit 11.2 suggests, the yield on CDs normally is slightly above the Treasury bill rate due to greater default risk, a thinner resale market, and a state and local government tax exemption on earnings from Treasury bills. Because investors can easily *arbitrage* between short-term markets, moving funds toward the highest yields, the CD

Current yields available on negotiable CDs and the latest developments in the CD market can be followed daily via such Web sites as bankrate.com

Key Money Market Interest Rates over Time—Average Annual Interest Rates Attached to U.S. Treasury Bills, Money Market CDs ($100,000 or more), Federal Funds, Commercial Paper, Eurodollar Deposits, and Prime Bank Loans

Instrument	Annual Period						
	1984	1988	1990	1995	2000	2002	2004*
U.S. Treasury bills:							
Three-month	9.52%	6.67%	7.50%	5.49%	5.82%	1.61%	0.88%
Six-month	9.76	6.91	7.46	5.56	5.90	1.68	0.97
Federal funds	10.22	7.57	8.10	5.83	6.74	1.67	1.00
Bank certificates of deposit:							
Three-month	10.37	7.73	8.15	5.92	6.46	1.73	1.06
Six-month	10.68	7.91	8.17	5.98	6.59	1.81	1.12
Eurodollar deposits, three-month	10.73	7.85	8.16	5.93	6.45	1.73	1.05
Nonfinancial commercial paper, three-month	10.10	7.66	8.06	5.93	6.31	1.69	1.01
Prime bank loan rate	12.04	9.32	10.01	8.83	9.23	4.68	4.00

Source: Board of Governors of the Federal Reserve System, *Federal Reserve Bulletin,* and the Federal Reserve Board's Web site at **federalreserve.gov.**

Note: Bank CD rates are based upon weekly average rates quoted by five dealers. Treasury bill yields are those quoted in the secondary (resale) market on a bank discount basis extracted from daily closing bids. Commercial paper rates are quotes from leading dealer houses.

*Interest rates reported for 2004 are for January of that year.

interest rate hovers close to the average of current and future federal funds interest rates expected by investors to prevail over the life of the CD and is also close to the Eurodollar deposit rates posted in London each day. Of course, as Exhibit 11.2 also reminds us, the yield spread between CDs and other money market instruments varies over time, depending on investor preferences, the supply of CDs and other money market instruments, and the financial condition of issuing banks.

One of the most interesting developments in recent years has been the appearance of a *multitiered* (segmented) market for CDs. Investors have grouped issuing banks into different risk categories, and yields in the market are scaled accordingly. This development is a legacy of the collapse of such banking giants as Franklin National Bank of New York in 1974 and Continental Illinois Bank of Chicago in 1984. Faced with the spector of major bank failures, banks viewed as less stable by investors are usually compelled to issue their CDs at significantly higher interest rates.

CDs from the largest and most financially sound banks are rated *prime;* smaller banks or those viewed as less stable issue *nonprime* CDs at higher interest rates. As is true for any depositor in a U.S. insured bank, the holder of a CD is covered against loss by the Federal Deposit Insurance Corporation up to $100,000 if the issuing bank fails. Unfortunately, this insurance is of limited value to a corporation holding a million-dollar or larger CD. However, holders of large CDs do help to discipline their banks from taking on excessive risk by threatening to withdraw their funds if the banks with which they trade become too risky.

Buyers of CDs

The principal buyers of negotiable CDs include corporations, state and local governments, foreign central banks and governments, wealthy individuals, and a wide variety of financial institutions. The latter include insurance companies, pension funds, investment companies, savings banks, credit unions, and money market funds. Large CDs appeal to these investors because they are readily marketable at low risk, may be issued in any desired maturity, and carry a somewhat higher yield than that on Treasury bills. However, the investor gives up some marketability in comparison with T-bills because the resale market for CDs operates well below the average daily volume of trading in bills.

Most buyers hold CDs until they mature. However, prime-rate CDs issued by billion-dollar banks are actively traded in the secondary market. The purpose of the secondary market is principally to accommodate corporations that need cash quickly or see profitable opportunities from the sale of their deposits. Also, buyers of CDs who want shorter maturities or higher yields than are available on *new* CDs will enter the secondary market or redeem them in advance of maturity. Moreover, banks usually will not lend money on their own CDs as collateral because of the risk the borrower may default on the loan, in which case the bank would wind up owning its own CD and redeeming it before it matures.

New Types of CDs

Bankers have become increasingly innovative in packaging CDs to meet the needs of customers as the years have gone by. One notable innovation in CD history occurred in 1975, when the *variable-rate CD* was introduced. Variable, or floating-rate, CDs generally carry maturities out to five years, with an interest rate that is adjusted every 30, 90, or 180 days (known as a *leg* or *roll* period). The floating interest rate is usually tied to movements in the secondary-market yield on fixed-rate CDs, the prevailing federal funds interest rate, the prime bank rate, or the going market interest rate on Eurodollar deposits. A variable-rate CD may give the investor a higher return than normally would be obtained by continually renewing short-term CDs and is a popular investment for money market mutual funds.

Another innovation occurred in the 1970s when Morgan Guaranty Trust (now part of J.P. Morgan Chase) in New York City introduced the *rollover* or *roly-poly CD*. Because six-month CDs are the maximum maturity usually traded in the secondary market, Morgan offered its customers longer term CDs with higher rates, but in packages composed of a series of six-month CDs extending for at least two years. Thus, the roly-poly CD promised higher returns plus the ability to market some CDs in the package early to meet emergency cash needs. However, the bank's customer was still obligated to purchase the remaining certificates on each six-month anniversary date until the contract expired.

Recent years have ushered in still more CD innovations: for example, *jumbo CDs, Yankee CDs, brokered CDs, bear and bull CDs, installment CDs, rising-rate CDs,* and *foreign-index CDs. Jumbo CDs* are large ($100,000+), negotiable CDs issued by non-bank thrift institutions such as savings and loan associations and savings banks. *Yankee CDs* are issued in the United States by foreign banks (mainly Japanese, Canadian, and European institutions) that usually have offices in U.S. cities. *Brokered CDs* consist of CDs sold through brokers or dealers in maximum $100,000 denominations to qualify for federal deposit insurance. *Bear and bull CDs,* whose rates of return are linked to stock market performance, first appeared in the mid-1980s. *Installment CDs,* in contrast, allow customers to make a small initial deposit and then gradually build up the balance in the account to some target level. *Rising-rate CDs* are usually longer-term deposits whose promised yield increases over time with penalty-free withdrawals permitted on selected anniversary dates. Further innovations in CDs are likely in the future as banks struggle to adjust their fund-raising efforts in the face of increasingly stiff competition for funds.

QUESTIONS TO HELP YOU STUDY

6. What is a large *negotiable CD?*

7. When were CDs first offered in the money market? Why were CDs developed?

8. What factors appear to influence the interest rate offered on CDs issued by a depository institution?

9. What is meant by the term *multitiered market?*

10. What is the difference between a *prime-* and a *nonprime-rated* CD? Which carries the higher interest rate? Why?

11. What is a variable-rate CD? A Eurodollar CD? Is it likely that depository institutions will continue to develop and bring forward new types of CDs in the future? Why?

11.5 Eurocurrency Deposits in International Banks

Eurocurrency Market

Comparable to the domestic CD market, a chain of international money markets trading in deposits denominated in the world's most convertible currencies stretches around the globe. This so-called **Eurocurrency market** has arisen because of a tremendous need worldwide for funds denominated in dollars, Euros, pounds, and other relatively stable currencies. For example, as U.S. corporations have expanded their operations in Europe, Asia, and the Middle East, they have needed huge amounts of U.S. dollars to purchase machinery and other goods in the United States and to pay federal and state taxes. The same companies have also required large volumes of other national currencies to carry out transactions in the countries where they are represented. To meet these financial needs, international banks headquartered in the world's key financial centers began during the 1950s to accept deposits from businesses, individuals, and governments denominated in currencies other than that of the host country and to make loans denominated in those same currencies.

The nature and origins of the Eurocurrency markets are discussed in a wide range of publications prepared by the staff of the Federal Reserve Bank of New York at ny.frb.org, and for the Federal Reserve System as a whole at federalreserve. gov

One of the earliest sources of Eurocurrency deposits was the former Soviet Union, which, in the 1950s, moved huge amounts of dollar-denominated assets out of the United States in order to avoid sequestration (capture) of its funds by U.S. authorities. Anti-Soviet sentiment was then running very high in the United States, and a number of highly publicized spy trials and Congressional hearings had aroused the interest of the American public. A short time later, several large American banks themselves moved some of their dollar deposits abroad (especially to their Caribbean branch offices) to avoid restrictive U.S. banking regulations. Thus, the Eurocurrency market was born.

What Is a Eurodollar?

Eurodollars

Because the dollar remains the chief international currency today, the market for Eurodollars is the leading component of the Eurocurrency markets. What are **Eurodollars**? They are deposits of U.S. dollars in banks located outside the United States. The banks in question record the deposits on their books in U.S. dollars, not in their home currency. The majority of Eurodollar (and other Eurocurrency) deposits are held in Europe, and in Caribbean branch offices, but these deposits have spread worldwide.

Frequently, banks accepting Eurodollar deposits are foreign branches of U.S. banks. For example, in London—still the center of the Eurocurrency market today—branches of U.S. banks outnumber British banks and bid aggressively for deposits denominated in U.S. dollars. Many of these funds are then loaned to the banks' home offices in the United States to meet reserve requirements and other liquidity needs. The remaining funds are loaned to private corporations and governments abroad that need U.S. dollars. No one knows exactly how large the Eurodollar market is or how big the overall marketplace is for *all* Eurocurrency deposits. One reason is that the market is unregulated. Many banks refuse to disclose publicly their deposit balances in various currencies. Another reason for the relative lack of information on market activity is that Eurocurrencies are merely bookkeeping entries on a bank's ledger and not currencies. You cannot put Eurocurrency deposits in your pocket like bank notes or coins.

Eurodollars and other Eurocurrency deposits are continually on the move in the form of loans. They are employed to finance the import and export of goods, to supplement government tax revenues, to provide working capital for the foreign operations of multinational corporations, and to provide liquid reserves for the largest banks. In total, the Eurocurrency and Eurodollar markets represent the largest of all money markets worldwide, with total funds probably somewhere close to $5 trillion.

Some experts believe that Eurodollar growth in particular may slow appreciably or the volume of Eurodollar deposits may even decline as the European Union matures and the Euro grows in international prominence, creating a strong rival to U.S. dollars and dollar deposits. European central banks, for example, may have less need for U.S. dollar reserves as the European Community expands and may begin to dump some of their huge holdings of dollar-denominated assets, reducing the value of the U.S. dollar and U.S.-issued securities in international markets.

The Creation of Eurocurrency Deposits

To illustrate how Eurocurrency deposits arise, we trace through a simple but typical example. Our discussion is in terms of Eurodollars, but the reader should be aware that the process being described really applies to *any* type of Eurocurrency deposit.

Suppose a French exporter of fine wines ships cases of champagne to a New York importer, accompanied by a bill for $1 million. The importing firm pays for the champagne by issuing a check denominated in dollars and deposits it right away in a U.S. bank—First American Bank—where the French firm maintains a checking account. After this check clears, the results of the transaction are as follows:

French Exporter		First American Bank	
Assets	**Liabilities**	**Assets**	**Liabilities**
Demand deposit in U.S. bank +$1 million			Demand deposit owed French exporter +$1 million

Is the deposit shown above a Eurodollar deposit? *No,* because the deposit of dollars occurred in the United States, where the dollar is the official monetary unit. Suppose, however, that the French exporter is offered an attractive rate of return on its dollar deposit by its own local bank in Paris and decides to move the dollar deposit there. The Paris bank wants to loan these dollars to other customers who need to pay bills or make purchases in the United States. After the wine exporter and its Paris bank have negotiated the terms of the deposit and the funds are transferred, the French exporter receives a receipt for a dollar-denominated time deposit in its Paris bank. That bank, in return, now holds claim to the original dollar deposit in the United States. The Paris bank has at least one U.S. correspondent bank and asks to have the original dollar deposit transferred there. We show these transactions as follows:

French Exporter	
Assets	**Liabilities**
Demand deposit in U.S.bank −$1 million	
Time deposit in Paris bank +$1 million	

First American Bank	
Assets	**Liabilities**
Reserves transferred to U.S. correspondent bank −$1 million	Demand deposit owed French exporter −$1 million

U.S.Correspondent Bank	
Assets	**Liabilities**
Reserve received from First American Bank +$1 million	Demand deposit owed Paris bank +$1 million

Paris Bank	
Assets	**Liabilities**
Deposit in U.S. correspondent bank +$1 million	Time deposit owed French exporter +$1 million

Do we now have a Eurodollar deposit? *Yes*, in the form of a $1 million time deposit in a Paris bank. The wine exporter's deposit has been accepted and recorded on the Paris bank's books in U.S. dollars, even though the official monetary unit in France is the Euro. Let's follow this Eurodollar deposit through one more step. Assume now that the Paris bank makes a loan of $1 million to an oil company based in Manchester, England. The British company needs dollars to pay for a shipment of petroleum drilling equipment from Houston, Texas. By securing a dollar credit from the Paris bank, the British oil firm, in effect, receives a claim against dollars deposited in U.S. banks. The appropriate entries would be as follows:

Paris Bank	
Assets	**Liabilities**
Loan to British oil company +$1 million	
Deposit in U.S. correspondent bank −$1 million	

British Oil Company	
Assets	**Liabilities**
Demand deposit in U.S. correspondent bank +$1 million	Loan owed to Paris bank +$1 million

U.S. Correspondent Bank	
Assets	**Liabilities**
	Deposit owed to Paris Bank −$1 million
	Deposit owed to British oil company +$1 million

Note that we have assumed that the British oil company holds a deposit account in the same U.S. bank where the Paris bank held its deposits. This may not always be the case, but it was done here to reduce the number of accounting entries. If another U.S. bank were involved, we would simply transfer deposits and reserves to it from the U.S. correspondent bank that held the account of the Paris bank. The result would be exactly the same as in our example.

We must notice that, regardless of all the different transactions that took place, *the total amount of dollar deposits and U.S. bank reserves remained unchanged.* Funds were merely passed from U.S. bank to U.S. bank (especially through their Caribbean branches) as loans were extended and deposits made in the Eurodollar market. Thus, Eurodollar activity does *not* alter the total reserves of the U.S. banking system. In fact, the workings of the Eurocurrency markets remind us of a fundamental principle of international finance: *Money itself usually does not leave the country where it originates; only the ownership of money is transferred across international boundaries.*

The chain of Eurocurrency loans and deposits in our example above will go on unbroken as long as such loans are in demand and the funds are continually redeposited somewhere within the international banking system. Some economists believe that Eurobanks, like domestic U.S. banks, can create a multiple volume of deposits and loans for each Eurocurrency deposit they receive. However, this view has been disputed by a number of analysts who point out that major Eurobanks in their borrowing and lending activities are closer to nonbank financial institutions than to commercial banks. Eurobanks appear to closely match the maturities of their assets (principally loans) with the maturities of their liabilities (principally Eurocurrency deposits and money market borrowings); thus, funds raised in the Eurocurrency markets flow through Eurobanks back into those same markets. Rather than creating money, Eurobanks appear to function more as "efficient distributors of liquidity." If there is any actual credit or money creation in the Eurosystem, leading to a multiplication of deposits, the deposit multiplier must be close to one.[3]

Just as Eurocurrency deposits are created by making loans, they are also destroyed as loans are repaid. In our example, suppose the British oil company trades pounds for dollars with a foreign currency dealer and uses the dollars purchased to repay its loan from the Paris bank. At about the same time, the dollar time deposit held by the French exporter matures, and the exporter spends those dollars in the United States. As far as U.S. banks are concerned, total deposits and reserves remain unchanged. However, as a result of these transactions, all dollar deposits would now be held in the United States and, therefore, would have ceased to be Eurocurrency deposits.

---

[3]See Chapters 12, 13, and 14 for discussions of various aspects of the deposit multiplier. The granting of a Eurocurrency loan to a borrower does not give the borrower "money" in a strict sense. Eurocurrency deposits are not generally acceptable as a medium of exchange to pay for goods and services. They are more like regular time deposits (that is, bank CDs). The holder of a Eurocurrency deposit must convert that deposit into some national currency unit (such as Euros or U.S. dollars) before using it for spending. Thus, Eurocurrency deposits are not negotiable instruments. The Eurocurrency system does not create money in the traditional sense. A lender of Eurocurrency who needs liquid funds before a deposit matures must go back into the market and negotiate a separate loan.

Interest usually is paid only at maturity unless the Eurodeposit has a term of more than one year. Most deposit interest rates are tied to the London Interbank Offer Rate (LIBOR)—the rate at which major international banks offer term Eurocurrency deposits to each other. The rate is usually fixed for the life of the deposit, though floating rates tied to changes in LIBOR are not uncommon on longer-term deposits, with promised interest rates reset every three to six months at a spread over LIBOR.

Eurocurrency Maturities and Risks

Eurocurrency deposits are short-term time deposits (ranging from overnight to call money loaned for a few days out to one year) and therefore are true money market instruments. However, a small percentage are long-term time deposits, extending in some instances to about five years. Many Eurocurrency deposits carry one-month maturities to coincide with payments for shipments of goods. Other common maturities are 2, 3, 6, and 12 months.[4] The majority are interbank liabilities that pay a fixed interest rate.

Funds move rapidly in the Eurocurrency market from bank to bank in response to demands for short-term liquidity from corporations, governments, and Eurobanks themselves. There is no central trading location in the market. Traders thousands of miles distant may conduct negotiations by satellite, cable, computer networks, or telephone, with written confirmation coming later. Funds normally are transferred on the second business day after an agreement is reached through correspondent banks.

Eurocurrency deposits are known to be volatile and highly sensitive to fluctuations in interest rates and currency prices. A slight difference in interest rates or currency values between two countries can cause a massive flow of Eurocurrencies across national boundaries. One of the most famous examples of this phenomenon occurred in Germany during the 1970s when speculation that the German mark would be upvalued brought an inflow into Germany of billions in dollar deposits within hours, forcing the German government to cut the mark loose from its official exchange value and allow that currency to float upward.

Eurocurrency deposits are not without risk. There is *political risk* because governments may restrict or prohibit the movement of funds across national borders, as the United States did for a time during the Iranian crisis and more recently following the terrorist attacks on September 11th of 2001. There may be disputes between nations over the legal jurisdiction and control of deposits. *Default risk* may also be a factor because banks in the Eurobank system may fail; Eurocurrency deposits may be uninsured, or, because of their large size, only partially insured. This problem is compounded by the fact that it is usually more costly to secure information on the financial condition of foreign banks than on domestic banks. However, on the positive side, Eurobanks are among the largest and most stable banking institutions in the world. Moreover, most foreign nations have tried to encourage the growth of Eurocurrency markets through lenient regulation and taxation.

The Supply of Eurocurrency Deposits

Where do Eurocurrency deposits come from? The sources of Eurodollar deposits provide a good example of how and why this market continues to grow. For example, a major factor in the Eurodollar market's growth has been the enormous balance-of-payments deficits the United States has run in nearly every year since the 1950s.[5] U.S. firms building factories and purchasing goods and services abroad have transferred

---

[4]Banks active in the Eurocurrency market for liquidity-adjustment purposes use *short-date* deposits. Comparable to federal funds in the domestic U.S. money market, short dates represent deposits available for as long as 14 days, though generally they are weekend or two-day money, with some seven-day maturities as well. Short dates may carry fixed maturities or simply be payable on demand with minimal notice (such as 24 or 48 hours).

[5]See Chapter 23 for a discussion of the causes and effects of U.S. balance-of-payment deficits.

ownership of dollar deposits to foreign institutions. Domestic shortages of oil and natural gas have forced the United States to import about half or more of its petroleum needs, generating enormous outflows of dollars to oil-producing nations. The OPEC countries, for example, accept dollars in payment for crude oil and use the dollar as a standard for valuing most of the oil they sell. U.S. tourists visiting Europe, Japan, and the Middle East frequently use dollar-denominated traveler's checks or take U.S. currency with them and convert it into local currency overseas. Dollar loans made by U.S. corporations and foreign-based firms have added to the vast Eurodollar pool. Many of these dollar deposits have gravitated to foreign central banks, such as the Bank of England and the European Central Bank, as these institutions have attempted to support the dollar and their own currencies in international markets.

Eurodollars in U.S. Domestic Bank Operations

U.S. banks draw heavily on overnight Eurodollar deposits as a means of adjusting their domestic reserve positions. Thus, the manager of the money desk at a large U.S. bank, knowing the bank needs extra cash reserves today, can contact foreign banks holding dollar deposits and arrange a loan. The manager can also contact other U.S. banks with branches abroad (especially in the Caribbean) and borrow Eurodollars from them. Alternatively, if the money manager's own bank operates foreign branches accepting dollar deposits, these can be placed at the disposal of the home office. So rapid has been the growth of overnight Eurodollar loans inside the U.S. lately that, frequently, these interbank loans exceed the volume of federal funds loans between U.S. banks.

Eurodollar borrowing of bank reserves has been especially heavy during periods of rapidly rising interest rates in the United States. Such borrowings are extremely interest-rate sensitive, however. When U.S. money market rates fell precipitously from record highs during the 1980s and 1990s and domestic sources of reserves became much less expensive, American banks repaid their Eurodollar borrowings nearly as fast as they borrowed these international deposits in the earlier periods when market interest rates were at record highs.

Eurodollars often carry slightly *higher* reported interest rates than many other sources of bank reserves, such as domestic certificates of deposit, due to perceptions of higher risk, although this is not always the case. However, there are fewer legal restrictions on the borrowing of Eurodollars and other Eurocurrency deposits. For example, Eurodollar deposits have no reserve requirements or insurance fees today. In contrast, U.S. banks must, at times, pay assessments to the Federal Deposit Insurance Corporation on domestic nonbank deposits to cover the costs of deposit insurance.

For further discussion of the London Interbank Offer Rate (LIBOR), see the British Bankers Association at bba.com.uk/

In addition to meeting their own reserve needs from the Eurodollar market, U.S. banks have aided their corporate customers in acquiring Eurocurrency deposits. Direct loans in Eurocurrencies are made by U.S. banks, and these banks will readily swap Eurocurrencies at the customer's request. Although most Eurocurrency loans to nonbank customers are short-term credits to provide working capital, a sizable percentage in recent years has consisted of medium-term (one- to five-year) loans for equipment purchases, frequently set up under a revolving credit agreement. Both borrowers and lenders in the Eurocurrency market can more effectively hedge against interest rate risk on these international loans today due to the recent rapid growth of Eurocurrency interest rate futures markets centered in London, Chicago, and other leading international financial centers.

Eurodollar loan rates extended by major international banks and other leading lenders have two components: (1) the cost of acquiring Eurocurrency deposits (usually measured by the **London Interbank Offer Rate (LIBOR)** on three- or six-month Eurodeposits) and (2) a profit margin ("spread") based on the riskiness of the loan and the intensity of competition. Profit margins are low on Eurocurrency loans (often well below a single percentage point) because the market is highly competitive, lending costs are low, and the risk is normally low as well. Borrowers are generally well-known institutions with substantial net worth and solid credit standing. Loan transactions are usually carried out in large denominations, ranging from about $500,000 to $100 million or more.

Recent Innovations in the Eurocurrency Markets

Beginning in the 1980s, the Eurocurrency market witnessed rapid growth in medium-term credit arrangements between international banks and their corporate and governmental customers. These so-called *note issuance facilities* (NIFs) often span five to seven years and allow the customer to borrow in his or her own name by selling short-term IOUs (typically maturing in three to six months) to investors. The underwriting bank or banks backstop this customer paper either by purchasing any paper that remains unsold or by providing standby credit at an interest rate spread over LIBOR. The notes issued are usually denominated in U.S. dollars with par values of $100,000 or higher. With bank support, NIFs are roughly equivalent to Eurocurrency CDs and compete with them for investor funds.

Benefits and Costs of the Eurocurrency Markets

For the most part, the development of Eurocurrency trading has resulted in substantial benefits to the international community, especially to multinational corporations. The market ensures a high degree of funds mobility between international capital markets and provides a true international market for bank and nonbank liquidity adjustments. It has provided a mechanism for absorbing huge amounts of U.S. dollars flowing overseas and lessened international pressure to forsake the dollar for gold and other currencies. The market reduces the cost of international trade by providing an efficient method of economizing on transactions balances. Moreover, it acts as a check on domestic monetary and fiscal policies and encourages *international cooperation* in economic policies, because interest-sensitive traders in the market will quickly spot interest rates that are out of line and move huge amounts of funds from one point on the globe to another. Central banks, such as the Bank of England and the European Central Bank, monitor the Eurocurrency markets continuously in order to moderate inflows or outflows of funds that may damage their domestic economies.

The capacity of Eurocurrency markets to mobilize massive amounts of funds has occasionally brought severe criticism from regulators in Europe, the United States, and Asia. They sometimes see the market as contributing to instability in currency values. Moreover, the market can wreak havoc with any particular nation's monetary and fiscal policies designed to cure its domestic economic problems. This is especially true if a nation is experiencing severe inflation and massive inflows of Eurocurrency occur at the same time. The net effect of Eurocurrency expansion, other things being equal, is to push domestic interest rates down, stimulate credit expansion, and accelerate the rate of inflation (which may ultimately result in higher market interest rates). The ability of local authorities to deal with inflationary problems might simply be overwhelmed by a Eurocurrency glut. This danger is really the price of freedom, for an unregulated market will not always conform to the plans of government policymakers.

QUESTIONS TO HELP YOU STUDY

12. What is the *Eurocurrency market* and why is it needed?

13. Define the term *Eurodollar*. Can a U.S. bank create Eurodollars? How?

14. Describe the process by which Eurocurrency deposits are created. What happens to the total volume of domestic bank reserves and deposits in the process of creating Eurocurrency deposits?

15. Can Eurocurrency deposits be *destroyed*? How can this happen?

16. What are the principal *sources* of Eurocurrency deposits? Make a list.

17. What role do Eurodollar deposits play in *reserve management operations* of U.S. banking firms? What are the advantages of Eurodollar borrowings over other sources of reserves for banks? The disadvantages?

18. Evaluate the Eurocurrency markets from a social point of view. What are their major benefits and costs to the public and to market participants? In your opinion, should these markets be more closely regulated or should they remain relatively free of regulation?

11.6 Bankers' Acceptances

As the Eurocurrency markets remind us, the money market today is not confined within the boundaries of a single nation or even a single continent. Money flows around the globe in minutes or hours, seeking out those investments offering the highest expected returns for a given degree of risk. Moreover, world trade has expanded in recent years at a rapid pace, especially between the United States, Europe, Japan, China, India, Southeast Asia, and Central and South America. And, of course, the growth and development of world trade requires a concomitant expansion in both long- and short-term sources of financing. Long-term capital is needed to build new factories, transportation systems, and energy-producing and refining facilities, while short-term capital from the money market is needed to finance the export and import of goods and meet other near-term working capital needs. One of the oldest and most respected of these short-term financing vehicles is the *bankers' acceptance,* which we examine in this section.

The Nature of Acceptances

bankers' acceptance

A **bankers' acceptance** is a *time draft* drawn on a bank by an exporter or an importer to pay for merchandise or to buy foreign currencies. If the bank honors the draft, it will stamp "Accepted" on its face and endorse the instrument. By so doing, the issuing bank has unconditionally guaranteed to pay the face value of the acceptance at maturity, shielding exporters and investors in international markets from default risk. Acceptances carry maturities ranging from 30 to 270 days (with 90 days being the most common) and are considered prime-quality money market instruments. They are traded among financial institutions, industrial corporations, and securities dealers as a high-quality investment and source of ready cash. An illustration of a traditional bankers' acceptance, prepared for illustration by the Federal Reserve Bank of New York, is shown in Exhibit 11.3.

Why Acceptances Are Used in International Trade

Additional information on the nature of bankers' acceptances may be found in frb.org

Acceptances are used in the import and export trade because many exporters are uncertain of the credit standing of the importers to whom they ship goods. Exporters may also be concerned about business conditions or political developments in foreign countries.

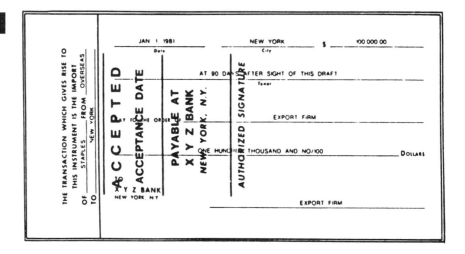

Nations experiencing terrorist violence or even civil war have serious problems in attracting financing for imports of goods and services because of the obvious risks of extending credit inside their territory. However, exporters usually are quite content to rely on acceptance financing by a well-regarded bank. Thus, an acceptance is a financial instrument designed to shift the risk of international trade to a third party willing to take on that risk for a known cost. Many banks are willing to take on such a risk because they are specialists in assessing credit risk and spread that risk over thousands of different loans.

How Acceptances Arise

Trade acceptances usually begin when an importer goes to a bank to secure a line of credit to pay for a shipment of goods from abroad. Once the line of credit is approved, the bank issues a letter of credit in favor of the foreign exporter. This document authorizes the exporter to draw a time draft for a specified amount against the issuing bank, provided that the exporter agrees to send appropriate shipping documents giving the issuing bank temporary title to the exported goods.

time draft

Because the letter of credit authorizes the drawing of a **time draft**—not a sight draft, which is payable immediately upon presentation—the exporter must wait until the draft matures (perhaps as long as six months) to be paid. Such a delay is unacceptable for most export firms, which must meet payrolls and satisfy other near-term obligations.

Moreover, the time draft generally is redeemed in the home currency of the issuing bank, and this particular currency may not be needed by the exporter. A French exporter holding a time draft from a U.S. bank, for example, would be paid in dollars on its maturity date, even though the exporter probably needs Euros to pay employees and meet other local expenses. Typically, then, the exporter *discounts* the time draft in advance of maturity through his or her principal bank. The exporter then receives timely payment in local currency and avoids the risk of trading in foreign currencies.

The foreign bank that has now acquired the time draft from the exporter forwards it (plus shipping documents if goods are being traded) to the bank issuing the original letter of credit. The issuing bank checks to see that the draft and any accompanying documents are correctly drawn and then stamps "Accepted" on its face. Two things happen as a result of this action: (1) a bankers' acceptance has been created and (2) the issuing bank has acknowledged an absolute liability, which must be paid in full at maturity. Frequently, the issuing bank discounts the new acceptance for the foreign bank that sent it and credits that bank's correspondent account for the proceeds. The acceptance may then be held by the issuing bank as an asset or sold to a dealer. Meanwhile, shipping documents for any goods that accompanied the acceptance are handed to the importer against a trust receipt, permitting the importer to pick up and market the goods. However, under the terms of the letter of credit, the importer must deposit the proceeds from selling those goods at the issuing bank in sufficient time to pay for the acceptance. When the time draft matures, the acceptance will be presented to the issuing bank for payment by its current holder. These stages in the life cycle of a bankers' acceptance are summarized below:

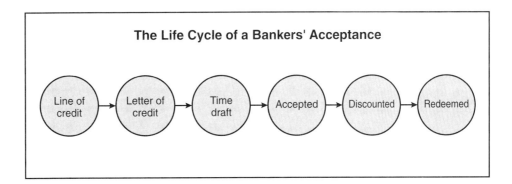

The Life Cycle of a Bankers' Acceptance

Line of credit → Letter of credit → Time draft → Accepted → Discounted → Redeemed

It should be clear that all three principal parties to the acceptance transaction financing international trade—the exporter, importer, and the issuing bank— benefit from this method of financing. The exporter receives good funds with little or no delay. The importer may delay payment for a time until the related bank line of credit expires. The issuing bank regards the acceptance as a readily marketable financial instrument that can be sold before maturity through an acceptance dealer in order to cover short-term cash needs.

However, there are costs associated with all these benefits. A discount fee is charged off the face value of the acceptance whenever it is discounted in advance of maturity. The accepting bank earns a commission (usually 50 to 100 basis points of the face amount), which may be paid by either exporter or importer, in addition to the fees associated with the original letter of credit.

The Growth and Decline of Acceptance Financing

Given the significant advantages of acceptance financing for exporters, importers, and banks, it is not surprising that the volume of bankers' acceptances outstanding grew rapidly, at least until the mid-1980s. The volume of U.S. dollar acceptances increased from less than $400 million in 1950 to just over $2 billion in 1960 and then tripled in 1970 to slightly more than $7 billion outstanding. However, even these rapid rates of growth look pale compared with the virtual explosion of acceptance financing during the 1970s and early 1980s. By December 1984, the volume of bankers' acceptances outstanding reached almost $80 billion—more than a tenfold increase in about 15 years.

Then the growth of acceptances in U.S. dollars leveled out and turned downward. Part of the reason for the turnaround was a slowing in trade as several leading export nations entered a recession at the beginning of the 1990s and subsequently their economies grew slowly. During the late 1990s, economic problems in Asia further dampened the need for traditional forms of trade financing. In addition, a wider variety of foreign currencies today are being readily accepted in payment for international purchases, and thus there is less need for dollar-denominated acceptances. Another factor has been greater use of direct bank loans bearing low money market interest rates for both exporters and importers. Moreover, many corporations involved in international trade have turned from banks toward the open market to borrow the funds they need, particularly through issues of bonds and commercial paper.

The majority of acceptances created by U.S. banks arise from four types of financial transactions: (1) the financing of imports into the United States; (2) the financing of exports from the United States; (3) the acquisition of dollars to add to foreign exchange reserves; and (4) the financing of goods stored in or transported between countries other than the United States. Acceptances arising from the last source are called **third-country bills** bills—the largest acceptance category. In fact, more than half of all dollar acceptances outstanding are accounted for by non-U.S. banks, primarily banks in France, Great Britain, Germany, Switzerland, Australia, Canada, and Japan.

Acceptances are *not* widely used inside the United States for purely domestic trade. A small amount of domestic acceptance financing is carried out to support the storage of staple commodities such as cotton and tobacco or the domestic shipment of goods. However, if a company can borrow at close to the prime interest rate, it will usually do so rather than use acceptance financing. It is usually much easier for a domestic firm to assess the financial condition of its domestic customers than to evaluate the credit standing of a foreign firm thousands of miles away. For this reason, suppliers of goods in the domestic market usually extend short-term credit (accounts receivable) directly to customers rather than insisting on the use of acceptances. Moreover, in domestic commerce, no exchange of foreign currencies is necessary, eliminating one important type of risk that motivated the development of acceptances.

Acceptance Rates

Acceptances do not carry a fixed rate of interest but are sold at a discount in the open market like Treasury bills. The prime borrower under an acceptance is charged a commitment fee for this line of credit, which is usually about $1\frac{1}{2}$ percent ($\frac{1}{8}$ of 1 percent per month) for top-quality customers. U.S. banks are limited in the dollar amount of acceptances they can create to 150 percent of their paid-in capital and surplus (or, by special permission from the Federal Reserve Board, up to 200 percent of their capital and surplus).

If the bank wishes to sell an acceptance in advance of its maturity, the rate of discount it must pay is determined by the current bid rate on acceptances of similar maturity in the open market. The yield on acceptances is usually only slightly higher than on Treasury bills because banks that issue them are among the largest and have solid international reputations. Acceptance rates hover close to negotiable CD rates offered by major banks because both acceptances and CDs are unconditional obligations of the issuing bank to pay. Adding to the stature of acceptances, depository institutions are permitted to borrow reserves from the Fed's discount window using certain types of acceptances as collateral.[6]

---

[6]The bankers' acceptance is one of the safest of all financial instruments. It is an irrevocable primary debt of the bank that stamps "accepted" on its face, as well as a contingent liability of the drawing firm and of any other bank, firm, or individual who endorses the document. Moreover, domestic banks are limited in the volume of acceptances they can have outstanding relative to the size of their capital. At the same time, the customer who has requested the initiating letter of credit that gives rise to the acceptance has guaranteed payment by the maturity date. Then too, any goods shipped under the letter of credit are nearly always insured and accompanied by trust and warehouse receipts specifying value and ownership.

Prominent Investors in Acceptances

Commercial banks regard acceptances as high-grade instruments suitable for liquidity management purposes. In addition, the essential safety of acceptances is recognized by the U.S. Treasury, which permits banks to use them as collateral to back the Treasury's tax and loan accounts (cash reserves) held in a majority of the nation's commercial banks. U.S. banks are also allowed to discount "eligible" acceptances with the Federal Reserve banks in order to borrow emergency funds. An acceptance is considered "eligible" by the Federal Reserve if it matures within six months and grows out of domestic or international trading or storage of goods. Smaller banks often participate in acceptance financing with money center banks to gain added income, spread out their risk, and accommodate their largest customers.

Other important investors in the acceptance market include industrial corporations, savings banks, money market mutual funds, local governments, federal agencies, and insurance companies. To many investors, acceptances are a close substitute for Treasury bills, negotiable CDs, or commercial paper in terms of quality, although the acceptance market is far smaller in trading volume.

Only a few dealers regularly trade acceptances, usually as an adjunct to their trading activities in Treasury bills, notes, and bonds. Trading is carried out purely on a negotiated basis, with most daily volume accounted for by swaps of holdings among accepting banks. Dealers call accepting banks and place bids for acceptances on behalf of their customers. Although a variety of denominations is available for both large and small investors, nonbank investors often find the menu of fresh offerings very limited. Nevertheless, an investor who is willing to accept the odd-lot denominations in which acceptances are issued may find the investment rewarding in terms of competitive rate of return and low risk.

QUESTIONS TO HELP YOU STUDY

19. What exactly is a *bankers' acceptance*? What is the meaning of the word "accepted"?

20. Explain why acceptances have been attractive to exporters and importers of goods moving between different countries. Why has the volume of acceptances declined in recent years?

21. Why are acceptances not as widely used inside the United States as they are in international markets?

22. Evaluate bankers' acceptances as an investment instrument. What are their principal advantages and disadvantages to savers interested in finding a secure financial asset that is readily marketable?

11.7 Evaluating the Money Market Costs of Funds Needed by Bankers

It is useful to conclude our discussion about banks' borrowing funds in domestic and foreign money markets by illustrating how a banker evaluates the choices among such sources as federal funds, negotiable CDs, and Eurocurrency deposits. Among other key factors, a banker must keep in close touch with money market developments each day, paying particular attention both to current money market interest rates and to forecasts about future interest rates.

Consider an example. Suppose that this past year federal funds were trading at an annual interest rate of about 4 percent and the average interest rate that New York money-center banks were paying to bring in deposits of large ($100,000) negotiable CDs from their customers was about 4.25 percent on three-month maturities. Similarly, international banks were selling three-month Eurodollar deposits at 4.30 percent.

Even though legal reserve requirements on domestic CDs had been set at zero several years earlier by the Federal Reserve Board, a bank raising money by issuing domestic CDs still might have been compelled to pay deposit insurance fees to the Federal Deposit Insurance Corporation (FDIC) equal to the full amount of the CD (not just the $100,000 portion covered by insurance). The U.S. deposit insurance fee has frequently been set at zero for the majority of banks in recent years, but let's assume for the purposes of illustration that the FDIC's current insurance fee on domestic deposits issued by financially sound money-center banks is 0.0004 cents per dollar (or 4 cents per $100) on any deposits received from the public.

Suppose a money-center bank needed to borrow $1 million for at least a day. Its daily cost of funds derived from each of these three sources would be:

Federal funds:

$$\$1 \text{ million} \times 0.0400 \times \frac{1}{360} = \$111.11 \tag{11.4}$$

Domestic negotiable CDs:

$$\overbrace{\$1 \text{ million} \times 0.0425 \times \frac{1}{360}}^{\text{Deposit interest Cost}} + \overbrace{\$1 \text{ million} \times 0.0004 \times \frac{1}{360}}^{\text{Deposit insurance cost}} = \$119.17 \tag{11.5}$$

Eurdollar deposits from the international money market:

$$\$1 \text{ million} \times 0.0430 \times \frac{1}{360} = \$119.44 \tag{11.6}$$

On this particular day in the money market, the cheapest funds source was *borrowing in the federal funds market*. However, because the domestic CD and Eurodollar deposit interest rates were fixed for three months in this instance (in contrast with the federal funds interest rate, which changes every day), if the Fed funds rate was expected to rise significantly, this borrowing bank might well decide to borrow at the currently more expensive CD or Eurodollar rates. Clearly, a banker borrowing in the money market must consider not only the level of current money market interest rates but also expected *future* interest rates and government regulations when choosing a source of funding.

11.8 Concluding Comment on Bank Activity in the Money Market

The money market has not always been as important a source of funds for banks and other depository institutions as it is today. Prior to the 1960s, even many of the largest money-center banks regarded borrowings from the money market as only a secondary source of funds. Bankers were aware that heavy dependence on money market borrowing would make their earnings more sensitive to fluctuations in interest rates. However, the force of competition intervened in the 1960s and 1970s. Major corporations began to seek out alternative investments for their short-term funds rather than holding most of their money in bank deposits. Bankers were forced to turn to the money market for additional funds. As we have seen in this chapter, the banking community approached the problem in several different ways. One was to offer a new financial instrument—the negotiable certificate of deposit—to compete directly for short-term corporate funds. Another approach was to draw more intensively on existing sources of money market funds, especially the federal funds market.

Prior to the 1960s and 1970s, the federal funds market was confined principally to the largest banks, which swapped reserves with each other. As bankers turned more and more to the funds market, however, it broadened tremendously. Thousands of small depository institutions in towns and rural areas across the United States began supplying their excess reserves to larger banks in the central cities, hoping to boost their earnings. In turn, the greater supply of Federal funds encouraged the largest banks to rely even more heavily on the money market and less on customer deposits as a source of reserves. The federal funds market had become an accepted innovation for both the smallest and largest financial institutions.

The rapid expansion of the CD and federal funds markets was just the beginning of banking's *money market strategy.* When the Federal Reserve became concerned over the rapid growth of CDs and federal funds and clamped down with tight-money policies, innovative financial managers were forced to find new sources of reserves or face a real cutback in their lending activities. Many turned to the Eurocurrency market, borrowing deposits from abroad, or to repurchase agreements backed by government securities to raise new funds.

liability management

All of these clever maneuvers form part of a technique called **liability management.** Bankers quickly came to realize that simply by varying the daily interest rates they were willing to offer on CDs, federal funds, Eurocurrency deposits, and other funds sources, they could gain a measure of control over their liabilities. If more funds were needed on a given day to accommodate customer loan demand, a bank active in the money market would simply offer a higher yield on the particular money market instrument it desired to use. If a smaller volume of funds was required at another time, the institution could lower its offer rate on money market borrowings.

To learn more about modern liability management see, for example, such Web sites as almprofessional.com and contingency-analysis.com

What is especially fascinating about liability management strategies is that they have had precisely the effects many analysts predicted from the start. The earnings of financial institutions *have* become more sensitive to fluctuations in interest rates; and in periods of rapidly escalating market interest rates, profit margins have often been squeezed. Whether this adverse impact on the earnings of banks and other money-market participants will continue into the future remains to be seen due to changing technology and the growing use of risk-management techniques. The great innovative abilities of these institutions, freed in recent years by deregulation, will do much to shape their earnings performance in the years ahead. But whatever the future holds, bankers have transformed the money market into a far larger and more dynamic institution than at any other time in history.

QUESTIONS TO HELP YOU STUDY

23. What factors influence a banker's choice among negotiable CDs, Eurocurrency deposits, and federal funds as important sources of borrowed reserves for banking institutions?

24. What exactly is meant by the term *liability management?* What changes has it brought to the depository institutions' industry?

11.9   Major Corporations in the Money Market: Commercial Paper

Each year leading corporations, such as American Telephone and Telegraph, General Motors, Marriott Corp., MCI Communications, and Philip Morris, borrow billions of dollars in the money market through the sale of unsecured promissory notes, known as *commercial paper*. Not long ago a survey of this short-term corporate debt market by the Federal Reserve System counted more than a thousand corporations in the United States (and a growing number of companies overseas) regularly selling their commercial notes to money market investors.

The Nature of Commercial Paper

commercial paper

Commercial paper is one of the oldest of all money market instruments, dating back to the eighteenth century in the United States. By definition, commercial paper consists of short-term, unsecured promissory notes issued by well-known companies that are financially strong and carry high credit ratings.[7] The funds raised from a paper issue normally are used for *current transactions*—to purchase inventories, pay taxes, meet payrolls, and cover other short-term obligations—rather than for *capital transactions* (long-term investments). However, a substantial number of paper issues today are used to provide "bridge financing" for such long-term projects as building pipelines and office buildings and manufacturing assembly lines. In these instances issuing companies usually plan to convert their short-term paper into more permanent financing when the capital market looks more favorable.

Commercial paper is generally issued in multiples of $1,000—in denominations designed to meet the needs of the buyer. It is traded mainly in the primary market. Opportunities for resale in the secondary market are more limited, although some dealers today assist their customers by redeeming a portion of the notes they sell. Because of the limited resale possibilities, investors are usually careful to purchase those paper issues whose maturity matches their planned holding periods, though resale opportunities (liquidity) have increased in recent years. The most common maturities are 7, 15, 30, 60, and 90 days and about 99 percent is issued in electronic not paper form.

Types of Commercial Paper

direct paper

There are two major types of commercial paper—direct paper and dealer paper. The main issuers of **direct paper** are large finance companies and bank holding companies that deal directly with the investor rather than using a securities dealer as an intermediary. These companies, which regularly extend installment credit to consumers and large working capital loans and leases to business firms, announce the rates they are

---

[7]As a further backstop to reduce investor risk, borrowers in the commercial paper market nearly always secure a *line of credit* at a commercial bank for a small fee or hold a compensating deposit at their bank. However, because the line of credit cannot be used to directly guarantee payment if the company goes bankrupt and the lender may renege on the credit line if the borrowing company has had a "material adverse change" in its condition, many issuers also take out irrevocable letters of credit prepared by their banks. Such a letter makes the bank unconditionally responsible for repayment if the corporation defaults on its paper. The lending institution usually charges a fee of $1/2$ percent to $1^1/_2$ percent of the amount of the guarantee it issues. Insurance companies and parent companies of paper-issuing firms also guarantee commercial paper. Early in the twenty-first century several major companies, including Tyco International Ltd., and Qwest Communications International, found themselves having to draw upon their backup bank lines of credit to pay their day-to-day bills when they ran into problems trying to sell their commercial paper in the money market.

currently paying on various maturities of their paper. For example, not long ago, the largest finance company borrowers in this market offered the following yields to interested investors:

Paper Maturity	Recent Direct or Finance Company Paper Yields (Percent)
1 month	1.04%
2 month	1.05
3 month	1.06

Source: Board of Governors of the Federal Reserve System.

Investors select their preferred maturities and buy the securities directly from the issuer. Interest rates may be adjusted during the day the paper is being sold to regulate the inflow of investor funds so that the borrowing companies achieve their funding goals.

Leading finance company borrowers in the direct paper market include General Motors Acceptance Corporation (GMAC), General Electric Capital Corporation (GE Capital), CIT Financial Corporation, and Commercial Credit Corporation. The leading U.S. bank holding companies that issue commercial paper are centered around the largest banks in New York, Chicago, San Francisco, and other major U.S. cities.[8] Today, about 50 financially oriented U.S. companies account for nearly all directly placed paper, with finance companies issuing approximately three-fourths of the total. All of these firms have an ongoing need for huge amounts of short-term money, possess top credit ratings, and have established working relationships with major institutional investors in order to place new paper rapidly.

Directly placed paper must be sold in large volume to cover the substantial costs of distribution and marketing. On average, each direct issuer will borrow at least $1 billion per month. Issuers of direct paper do not have to pay dealers' commissions, but these companies must operate a marketing division to maintain contact with active investors. Selected issuers, like New York's Citigroup, sell commercial paper in weekly auctions in which buyers bid and the issuing company accepts the highest price (lowest yield) bid. Sometimes direct issuers must sell their paper even when they have no need for funds in order to maintain a good working relationship with active investors. These companies also cannot escape paying fees to banks for supporting lines of credit, to credit rating agencies that rate their paper, and to agents (such as trust companies) that dispense required payments and collect funds.

The other major variety of commercial paper is **dealer paper,** issued by security dealers on behalf of their corporate customers. Also known as *industrial paper,* dealer paper is issued mainly by nonfinancial companies (including public utilities, manufacturers, retailers, and transportation companies), as well as by smaller bank holding

Additional information on commercial paper instruments and their market may be uncovered in several key Web sites, including federalreserve.gov/ releases, sec.gov, and economagic.com/ fedbog.htm

dealer paper

---

[8]Bank holding companies issue *both* direct and dealer paper, with the largest companies going the direct placement route. Much of this bank-related paper comes from finance company subsidiaries of large bank holding companies. Frequently, a holding company will issue paper through a nonbank subsidiary and then funnel the proceeds to one or more of its subsidiary banks by purchasing some of the banks' assets. This gives the affiliated banks additional funds to lend and may be especially helpful when a bank is having trouble raising funds.

companies and finance companies, all of which tend to borrow less frequently than firms issuing direct paper.

Industrial paper is used primarily to fund accounts receivable and inventory for the issuing companies and is usually closely connected to fluctuations in business inventory levels. The issuing company may sell the paper directly to the dealer, who buys it less discount and commission and then attempts to resell it at the highest possible price in the market. Alternatively, the issuing company may carry all the risk, with the dealer agreeing only to sell the issue at the best price available less commission, referred to as a *best efforts basis.* Finally, the open-rate method may be used in which the borrowing company receives some money in advance but the balance depends on how well the issue sells in the open market.

Not long ago dealers were posting the following short-term yields in the primary paper market:

Paper Maturity	Recent Nonfinancial or Dealer Paper Yields (Percent)
1 month	1.02%
2 month	1.03
3 month	1.04

Source: Board of Governors of the Federal Reserve System.

While we might expect the interest rates attached to direct (or finance company) paper to be *lower* than the interest rates on dealer (mainly nonfinancial) paper, because the latter is generally issued by smaller firms with somewhat greater risk exposure, the reverse—direct paper rates being slightly higher than dealer paper rates—has often been true in recent years. A key reason centers on the relative growth of the two types of commercial paper. Direct or finance-company paper has maintained a relatively high volume of new issues, while nonfinancial or dealer paper has recently declined in the volume of new offerings.

The Recent Track Record of Commercial Paper

As Exhibit 11.4 indicates, the volume of commercial paper nearly tripled between 1990 and 2000. Indeed, as Exhibit 11.5 shows, commercial paper issues have doubled, tripled, or quadrupled in volume in nearly every decade since 1960. By 2000, more than

EXHIBIT 11.4	**Volume of Commercial Paper Outstanding ($ Billions, End of Period)**						
Instrument	1984	1988	1990	1994	1998	2000	2004*
All issues	$237.6	$458.5	$562.7	$595.4	$1,163.0	$1,619.3	$1,348.7
Financial companies issuing paper							
Dealer placed—Total	56.5	159.8	214.7	223.0	614.1	989.9	1,014.4
Directly placed paper—Total	110.5	194.9	200.0	207.7	322.0	285.9	203.6
Nonfinancial companies issuing paper	70.6	103.8	147.9	164.6	227.1	343.4	130.7

Source: Board of Governors of the Federal Reserve System, *Federal Reserve Bulletin*, selected issues.

* Figures for 2004 are for the month of July.

EXHIBIT 11.5	**Year**	**Outstanding Volume of Paper in Billions of Dollars**
	1960	$4.5
Growth of Commercial Paper Issues in the United States	1970	33.4
	1980	124.4
	1990	562.7
	2000	1,619.3
	2004*	1,348.7

Source: Board of Governors of the Federal Reserve System, *Federal Reserve Bulletin*, selected issues.

*Figure as of July 2004.

1,200 companies had over $1.6 trillion in commercial notes outstanding. About one-fifth of the total was placed directly with investors by large finance companies and bank holding companies; the rest reached the market through the efforts of security dealers. Subsequently, however, paper volume fell in a recession-weakened economy as large corporations cut back on their borrowing and investment spending.

What factors explain the growth of commercial paper? One factor is the relative cost of other sources of credit compared to interest rates prevailing on commercial paper. For the largest, best-known corporations, commercial paper has often been a cost-effective substitute for bank loans and other forms of borrowing. This is especially true for nonfinancial companies issuing paper through dealers. These firms usually come to the paper market when it is significantly cheaper to borrow there than to tap bank lines of credit. In recent years, paper has also frequently been a cheaper funds source than issuing long-term bonds or selling stock, though in the first decade of the new century record low bond rates encouraged many companies to reduce their commercial paper issues and step up their borrowing through bonds. Also, many companies use the paper market today to participate in interest rate swaps, which are designed to hedge against losses from fluctuating interest rates.[9]

Another reason for the market's growth is the high quality of most commercial paper obligations. Many investors regard this instrument as a close substitute for Treasury bills and other money market instruments. As a result, market yields on commercial paper tend to move in the same direction and by similar amounts as the yields on other money market securities. This fact is shown clearly in Exhibit 11.2 earlier in this chapter, which compares market yields on commercial paper, Treasury bills, negotiable CDs, Eurodollar deposits, and federal funds and indicates that these interest rates tend to stay close to each other. We note that commercial paper yields are usually higher than market rates on comparable maturity Treasury bills due to the greater risk and lower marketability of paper and the fact that Treasury bills are exempt from state and local taxation.

credit enhancements   Still another key factor in the market's recent growth is the expanding use of **credit enhancements,** in the form of standby letters of credit, indemnity bonds, and other irrevocable payment guarantees. For example, a bank or other lending institution may issue a certificate that promises repayment of principal and/or interest on a customer's paper if the borrowing company fails to do so. The result is that such paper, often

---

[9]Chapter 9 contains an explanation of interest rate swaps.

called *documented notes,* usually carries the higher credit rating of the guarantor rather than the lower credit rating of the issuing firm. Through these guarantees, mortgage companies, utilities, and small manufacturers in large numbers have been attracted into a market that otherwise would be closed to them, still saving on interest costs even after paying the guarantor's fee.

Other groups recently entering the market include foreign banks and industrial companies, international financial conglomerates, and state and local governments (which offer *tax-exempt* commercial paper). Paper issued in the United States by foreign firms is called *Yankee paper* and frequently can be sold at lower interest costs in the United States than abroad. However, foreign borrowers in the U.S. market generally must pay higher interest costs than U.S. companies of comparable credit rating to compensate U.S. buyers for the added difficulty of gathering information on foreign borrowers and, in many cases, the lack of name recognition.

Maturities and Rates of Return on Commercial Paper

Maturities of U.S. commercial paper range from three days ("weekend paper") to nine months. Most commercial notes carry an original maturity of 60 days or less, with an average maturity ranging from 20 to 45 days. U.S. paper is generally not issued for maturities longer than 270 days because, under the provisions of the Securities Act of 1933, any security sold in U.S. markets for a longer term must be registered with the Securities and Exchange Commission. Yields to the investor are calculated by the *bank discount method,* just like Treasury bills. As in the case of T-bills, most commercial paper is issued at a discount from par; the investor's yield arises from the price appreciation of the security between its purchase date and maturity date.

For example, if a million-dollar commercial note with a maturity of 180 days is acquired by an investor at a discounted price of $980,000, the discount rate of return on commercial paper (DR_{CP}) is:

$$DR_{CP} = \frac{\text{Par value } - \text{ Purchase price}}{\text{Par value}} \times \frac{360}{\text{Days to maturity}}$$

$$= \frac{\$1,000,000 - \$980,000}{\$1,000,000} \times \frac{360}{180} = 0.04, \text{ or 4 percent} \qquad \textbf{(11.7)}$$

If this commercial note's rate of return were figured like that of a regular bond, its coupon-equivalent yield (or investment rate of return, IR_{CP}) would be

$$IR_{CP} = \frac{\text{Par value } - \text{ Purchase price}}{\text{Par value}} \times \frac{365}{\text{Days to maturity}}$$

$$= \frac{\$1,000,000 - \$980,000}{\$980,000} \times \frac{365}{180} = 0.0414, \text{ or 4.14 percent} \qquad \textbf{(11.8)}$$

This second formula helps an investor compare prospective returns on paper against the returns available on other securities available for purchase. In addition to discount paper, some corporations also sell interest-bearing (coupon) paper.

The commercial paper market in the United States has been copied abroad for many years now, though other countries have added their own special features. Among the leading national commercial paper markets today are those of Japan, France, Canada, and Sweden.

One of the most dramatic developments in the history of commercial paper markets has been the relatively recent development of the Japanese yen-denominated paper market. Yen-denominated commercial paper was first allowed to be offered in domestic Japanese markets by the Ministry of Finance in 1987. Many Japanese companies had threatened to move their short-term borrowing abroad unless the Japanese government relaxed its regulations. A year later, foreign businesses were given permission to sell "Samurai paper" inside Japan.

With so many U.S. companies operating in Canada and many Canadian firms having money market access inside the United States, the Canadian commercial paper market has relatively modest dimensions. Like U.S. paper, Canadian paper must be backed by a bank line of credit to catch the attention of money market investors. It has a broader range of maturities (usually from demand notes, cashable in 24 hours, out to about one year) than in the United States and also tends to be issued in larger denominations (usually $100,000 or more).

During the mid-1980s the *Europaper market* emerged. Europaper soared in volume because borrowing compa- nies were able to tap a larger reservoir of foreign cash. Many U.S. corporations having difficulty borrowing in the domestic market, often because of declining credit quality, turned to the Euromarket, which appeared to be less quality-conscious. The heaviest investors in Europaper are international banks, private corporations, and central banks.

Europaper is priced below face value and appreciates as maturity approaches. The interest rate quoted to investors is expressed as a discount rate (DR) like that attached to Treasury bills. For example, suppose we are interested in a $100 million Europaper issue with 90 days until maturity that bears a discount rate of 6 percent. The price the Europaper investor must pay is:

$$\text{Price of Europaper issue} = 100 - DR \times \frac{\text{Days to maturity}}{360 \text{ days}}$$

$$\text{Price} = 100 - 6 \times \frac{90}{360} = 98.50$$

In this instance, the $100 million Europaper issue would be priced today to sell at $98.5 million. There appears to be an active resale market for Europaper, which has an average maturity roughly double that of U.S. paper. The bulk of Europaper is sold through dealers with interest rates linked to Eurobank deposit rates.

The minimum denomination of commercial paper issues is usually $25,000, although among institutional investors, who dominate the market, the usual minimum denomination is $1 million. Payment is made at maturity on presentation to the particular bank listed as agent on the note. Settlement in federal funds is usually made the same day the note is presented for payment by its holder.

Changing Yields on Paper Issues

Because yields on commercial paper are open market rates, they fluctuate with the daily ebb and flow of supply and demand forces in the marketplace. In the wide swings between easy and tight money, between depressed and resurgent economic activity in recent years, commercial paper rates have fluctuated between extreme highs and lows. Indeed, the commercial paper market is highly volatile and difficult to predict. This is the reason that many corporations eligible to borrow there still maintain close working relationships with banks and other institutional lenders and employ interest-rate hedging techniques (such as financial futures contracts).

QUESTIONS TO HELP YOU STUDY

25. What do we mean by the term *commercial paper?*

26. Why is commercial paper attractive to such money market investors as banks, insurance companies, money market funds, and industrial companies?

27. Describe the functions that *dealers* perform in the functioning of the commercial paper market. In what market segment are they most active? Least active?

28. Why do some investors find commercial paper unsatisfactory for their needs?

29. Exactly how is the *rate of return* on commercial paper figured? Is the method used to determine paper's rate of return similar to the return calculation for any other money market instruments? Which ones?

Advantages of Issuing Commercial Paper

There are several financial advantages to a company able to tap the paper market for funds. Generally, interest rates on paper are lower than the interest rates on corporate loans extended by banks. For example, in recent years the bank prime rate has averaged almost three percentage points higher than the rate on three-month dealer paper has (See Exhibit 11.6.)

Moreover, the effective rate on many commercial loans granted by banks is even higher than the quoted prime rate, due to the fact that corporate borrowers usually are required to keep a percentage of their loans in a bank deposit. This *compensating balance* requirement is generally 15 to 20 percent of the amount of the loan. Suppose a corporation borrows $100,000 at a prime interest rate of 8.50 percent but must keep 20 percent of this amount ($20,000) on deposit with the bank granting the loan. Then the effective annual loan rate is 10.625 percent [or $8,500/($100,000 − $20,000)].

Another advantage of borrowing in the paper market is that interest rates there are often more flexible than bank and finance company loan rates. A company in need of funds can raise money quickly through either dealer or direct paper. Dealers maintain close contact with the market and generally know where cash may be found. Frequently, notes can be issued and funds raised the same day.

Generally, larger amounts of funds may be borrowed more conveniently through the paper market than from other sources, particularly bank loans. This situation arises due to federal and state regulations that limit the amount of money a bank can lend to a single

EXHIBIT 11.6			
Spread between the Average Prime Rate Quoted by Major U.S. Banks and the Three-Month Commercial Paper Rate, Selected Years			

Year	Bank Prime Lending Rate	Three-Month Commercial Paper Rate	Rate Spread in Percentage Points
1995	8.83%	5.93%	2.90%
1997	8.44	5.58	2.86
1999	8.00	5.18	2.82
2000	9.23	6.31	2.92
2002	4.67	1.69	2.98
2004*	4.00	1.02	2.98

Source: Board of Governors of the Federal Reserve System, *Federal Reserve Bulletin,* selected issues.

Note: The prime rate is the average of rates posted by major U.S. banks. The three-month commercial paper rate is the unweighted average of offer rates quoted by at least five dealers. The prime rate is averaged for each year.

*2004 Figures for January.

borrower. Corporate credit needs frequently exceed an individual bank's loan limit, and a group of banks (consortium) has to be assembled to make the loan. However, this takes time and often requires lengthy negotiations. The paper market is generally much faster than trying to hammer out a loan agreement among several parties, though some experts believe that the current consolidation of the banking industry worldwide, creating fewer, but much larger, banks, could limit the growth of the paper market in future years.

The ability to issue commercial paper gives a corporation considerable leverage when negotiating with banks and other lenders. For example, a banker who knows that a customer can draw on the paper market for funds is more likely to offer advantageous terms on a loan and be more receptive to future customer credit needs.

Possible Disadvantages from Issuing Commercial Paper

Despite the advantages, there are some risks for corporations that choose to borrow frequently in the commercial paper market. One of these is the risk of alienating banks and other institutional lenders whose loans might be needed when a real emergency develops. The paper market is sensitive to financial and economic problems. This fact was demonstrated convincingly in 1980 when Chrysler Financial, the finance company subsidiary of Chrysler Corporation, was forced to cut back its borrowings in the paper market due to the widely publicized troubles of its parent company, which sought and eventually received government assistance. However, the paper market appears to have strengthened and become so broad in recent years that it may be more tolerant of defaults and corporate failures. For example, in January and February 1997 when the huge auto lender Mercury Finance Company defaulted on more than $300 million in paper, there was little effect outside the automobile industry on the commercial paper market as a whole, though Enron's collapse in 2001 did depress this market for a time.

At times, it is difficult even for companies in sound financial condition to raise funds in the paper market at reasonable rates of interest. It helps to have a friendly banker available to supply emergency credit when this market turns sour. Another problem lies in the fact that commercial paper cannot usually be paid off at the issuer's discretion, but generally must remain outstanding until maturity. In contrast, many bank loans permit early retirement without penalty.

Who Buys Commercial Paper?

The most important investors in the commercial paper market include nonfinancial corporations, money market mutual funds, bank trust departments, small banks, pension funds, insurance companies, and state and local governments. In effect, this is a market in which corporations borrow from other corporations. These investor groups generally regard commercial paper as a low-risk outlet for their surplus funds, although recent financial problems and a few defaults among paper issuers have caused some investor groups, such as money market funds, to sharply cut back their purchases of lower-quality paper.

As the 1990s began, the U.S. Securities and Exchange Commission (SEC) became particularly concerned about the safety of money market funds and the risk to the savings of thousands of investors who, by that time, had placed nearly $500 billion with the money market fund industry. More than half the industry's assets had been invested in commercial paper, with an increasing proportion of these investments in lower-quality issues bearing higher but riskier yields. These lower-quality commercial notes are often acquired by more aggressive money fund managers interested in attracting more savings deposits by offering higher returns. Following several commercial paper defaults, the SEC ruled that money market funds could hold no more than 5 percent of their total assets in less than top-quality (not prime-rated) commercial paper, nor could they place any more than 1 percent of their assets in the paper of any one non-prime-rated corporate issuer. Money funds must inform investors that their shares are not insured or guaranteed by the U.S. government. The new rules appear to enhance the safety of savings held with money market funds, which now hold over a third of all paper outstanding, but they may also have placed a future restraint on the growth of the commercial paper market, making it more difficult for many companies, especially those with less-than-top credit ratings, to sell their paper.

Continuing Innovation in the Paper Market

master note

One important innovation in the direct paper market is the **master note,** most frequently issued to bank trust departments and other permanent money market investors by finance companies. Under a master note agreement, the investing firm agrees to take some paper each day up to an agreed-upon maximum amount. Interest owed is figured on the average daily volume of paper taken on by the investor during the current month. The prevailing interest rate on six-month commercial paper is generally used to determine the appropriate rate of return.

An extension of the paper market has appeared in the form of *medium-term notes* (MTNs). These 9-month to 10-year notes are issued by investment-grade corporations, normally carry a fixed interest rate, and are generally noncallable, unsecured obligations marketed through dealers. They are particularly suited to companies with substantial quantities of medium-term assets who wish to balance these assets with IOUs that are longer than the short maturities attached to conventional commercial paper. First sold by automobile finance companies in the 1970s, the MTN market has attracted industrial and utility companies and a secondary market has developed with several investment banking firms trading in these medium-length instruments.

Beginning in the 1980s, a new form of paper began to appear—*asset-backed commercial paper*—in which loans or credit receivables are pooled into packages and paper is then issued as claims against that pool (that is, the credit receivables are *securitized*). The loans or receivables are removed from the issuing company's balance sheet and placed in a *special-purpose entity* (SPE), which issues the paper and uses the proceeds to purchase the receivables. Among the most popular assets pooled to back these unique commercial paper issues are credit-card receivables, installment sales contracts, and lease receivables. Participants in these programs include banks, finance companies, and retail dealers. Banks find them a handy vehicle for assisting their corporate customers to obtain financing without having to loan them money and incur credit costs. A bank can earn fees for advising the paper-issuing customer, reviewing the quality of the assets to be pooled, and supplying credit enhancements (usually in the form of letters of credit, surety bonds, etc.) and liquidity enhancements (to help retire maturing paper in case of temporary cash shortfalls) for outstanding paper issues.

Asset-backed commercial paper gives issuing corporations a low and stable cost of financing that is often far cheaper than either direct financing through a bank or finance company or *factoring,* in which a company sells its accounts receivable to a lender at a sizable discount from their face value. For those asset-backed paper issues backed by credit and liquidity guarantees, any change of fortune at the customer's business should not appreciably affect the firm's actual funding costs. The SPE normally issues enough commercial paper to cover the discounted purchase price of the company's receivables and uses the proceeds from the paper issue to purchase the firm's receivables. The issuing customer usually services the underlying receivables, collecting interest and principal payments and passing the funds along to the SPE, or a bank chosen by the customer may service the receivables supporting the paper issue. The fact that paper is issued for less than the full nondiscounted value of the receivables generates a margin of value to protect investors.

Commercial Paper Ratings and Dealer Operations

Commercial paper is rated *prime, desirable,* or *satisfactory,* depending on the credit standing of the issuing company. Firms desiring to issue paper generally will seek a credit rating from one or more of several rating services, including such firms as Moody's Investors Service; Standard & Poor's Corporation; Fitch Investors Service; Duff & Phelps; Canadian Bond Rating Service; Japanese Bond Rating Institute; Dominion Bond Rating Service; and IBCA, Ltd.—with the first two rating companies especially prominent. Moody's assigns a rating of Prime-1 (P-1) for the highest-quality paper, with lower-quality issues designated as Prime-2 (P-2) or Prime-3 (P-3). Standard & Poor's assigns ratings of A-1+ or A-1, A-2, and A-3; Fitch uses F-1, F-2, or F-3. Any issue rated below P-2, A-2, or F-2 usually sells poorly or not at all.

Generally, commercial notes bearing credit ratings from at least two rating agencies are preferred by investors. The rating assigned to an issue often depends heavily on the liquidity position and the amount of backup lines of credit held by the issuing company. Moreover, there is evidence—for example, Crabbe and Post (1992)—that when a paper issuer's credit rating is lowered, large reductions occur in its volume of paper outstanding within a few weeks, reflecting declining demand for the downgraded issues. Eloyan, Maris, and Young (1996) found that a company's stock price tends to fall if its commercial paper is downgraded in quality or if its paper is placed on credit watch lists because of financial problems.

Dealers in Paper

The market is concentrated among a handful of dealers that account for the bulk of all trading activity. Top commercial paper dealers today include Citicorp (or Citigroup), the Credit-Suisse-First Boston Corporation, Morgan Stanley Dean Witter, and Merrill Lynch. Dealer firms charge varying fees to borrowing companies, depending on the size of an issue and how much paper the company has issued through the dealer recently. The dealer market has become more intensely competitive in recent years as many new foreign dealers have emerged. And dealer activities have further increased in the wake of passage of the Gramm-Leach-Bliley Act in 1999 that allowed U.S. financial holding companies to underwrite more securities through their affiliated securities firms. Dealers maintain inventories of unsold issues and repurchased paper, but they usually expect to turn over most of a new issue within 24 hours.

QUESTIONS TO HELP YOU STUDY

30. What are the principal *advantages* accruing to a company large enough to tap the commercial paper market for funds? Make a list of these advantages.

31. What are the principal *disadvantages* of commercial paper to an issuer? To buyers?

32. Who are the *principal investors* in commercial paper? Why do the types of investors you have named find commercial paper attractive?

33. How is commercial paper *rated*? Why does its rating matter?

34. Explain what *credit enhancements* are. What is *asset-backed* commercial paper? How have these devices aided growth of the paper market?

11.10 Credit Agencies in the Money Market

For nearly a century now, the federal government has attempted to aid certain sectors of the economy that appear to have an unusually difficult time raising funds in the

Government Agencies: Performing the Roles of a Financial Intermediary

money and capital markets. These "disadvantaged sectors" include agriculture, housing, small businesses, and college students. Dominated by smaller, less creditworthy borrowers, these sectors allegedly are pushed aside in the race for scarce funds by large corporations and governments, especially in periods of tight money.

Beginning in 1916, the federal government began to create special agencies or departments to make direct loans to or guarantee private loans extended to these disadvantaged borrowers. As the decades went by, such institutions as the Farm Credit System, the Small Business Administration, the Federal Home Loan Mortgage Corporation, and the Federal National Mortgage Association became familiar names to active investors worldwide who purchased these agencies' certificates, notes, and bonds. In turn, several of these agencies would buy selected assets from private lenders (creating a secondary market), giving these lenders additional capital for making new loans to disadvantaged borrowers. (See Exhibit 11.7.) Today, federal credit agencies are large enough and, with the government's blessing, financially strong enough to compete successfully for funds in the open market and channel those funds to areas of pressing social need.

Types of Federal Credit Agencies

government-sponsored agencies

There are two types of federal credit agencies: government-sponsored agencies and true federal agencies. **Government-sponsored agencies** are *not* officially a part of the federal government's structure but are quasi-private institutions. They are federally chartered but privately owned. In some instances, their stock is traded on major securities exchanges. The borrowing and lending activities of government-sponsored agencies are *not* reflected in the federal government's budget. This has aroused the ire of many fiscal conservatives who regard the credit-granting operations of government-sponsored agencies as a disguised form of government spending. Some critics contend that the agencies have been used to get around limits on federal spending. Because these agencies are omitted from the federal government's books, annual federal deficits look considerably smaller and conceal the full extent of federal deficit financing.[10] In

---

[10] Public concern over the growth of federal agency activities has increased in recent years. To the extent that agency borrowing and lending increase the total amount of credit available in the economy and add to aggregate spending for goods and services, they may add to inflationary pressures. Agency borrowing is not generally limited by restrictions that apply to direct debt obligations of the U.S. government. Moreover, there is a tendency to create a new agency each time a new problem rears its head, increasing the cost of government activities. For example, in 1987, the Financing Corporation (FICO) was established to bail out the failing Federal Savings and Loan Insurance Corporation (FSLIC), and in 1989, the Resolution Funding Corporation (REFCO) was created to support the liquidation of hundreds of failing savings and loans that the FSLIC could no longer handle.

The creation of these and many other special agencies has raised a number of significant issues concerning government involvement in the private sector of the economy. How many other firms should the federal government guarantee against failure in the future? Upon what basis are such guarantees to be made? What happens to the efficiency of the market system when some firms are not allowed to fail?

EXHIBIT 11.8	Agencies of the Federal Government	
Principal Borrowers in the Federal Agency Market	Export-Import Bank (EXIM) U.S. Railway Association Farmers Home Administration (FMHA) General Services Administration (GSA) Government National Mortgage Association (GNMA, or Ginnie Mae)	Postal Service (PS) Tennessee Valley Authority (TVA) Federal Deposit Insurance Corporation (FDIC)

	Government-Sponsored Agencies	
	Banks for Cooperatives (BC) College Construction Loan Insurance Association (CCLIA, or Connie Lee) Federal Farm Credit Banks (FFCB) Federal Home Loan Banks (FHLB) Federal Home Loan Mortgage Corporation (FHLMC, or Freddie Mac) Federal Intermediate Credit Banks (FICB) Federal Agricultural Mortgage Corporation (FAMC, or Farmer Mac)	Federal Land Banks (FLB) Federal National Mortgage Association (FNMA, or Fannie Mae) Student Loan Marketing Association (SLMA, or Sallie Mae) Financing Corporation (FICO) Financing Assistance Corporation (FAC) Resolution Funding Corporation (REFCO)

federal agencies

contrast, true **federal agencies** are legally a part of the government's structure. They are owned and operated by the United States government. Their borrowing and lending activities are included in the federal budget. The more these federally-owned agencies borrow, the larger the government's budget deficit tends to become or, during any years that budget surpluses occur, those budget surpluses tend to decrease as federal agency borrowing grows. The principal government-sponsored and federal agencies that borrow regularly in the money and capital markets are shown in Exhibit 11.8.

financial intermediaries

In their borrowing and lending activities, federal and government-sponsored agencies act as true **financial intermediaries**. They issue attractively packaged notes and bonds to capture funds from savers, and they direct the resulting flow of funds into loans and loan guarantees to farmers, small business owners, home mortgage borrowers, and other sectors. The securities issued by government-sponsored agencies are usually *not* guaranteed by the federal government, but many investors believe that the government is "only a step away" in the event that any agency gets into serious trouble.[11]

---

[11] Government-sponsored agencies are permitted to draw on the U.S. Treasury for funds up to a specified limit with Treasury approval. However, neither the principal nor the interest on the debt of government-sponsored agencies is guaranteed by the federal government, although the issuing agency guarantees its own securities. In contrast, securities of agencies owned by the federal government are fully guaranteed by the credit of the U.S. government. The government-sponsored agencies generally have capitalization requirements which limit to some extent the rate of growth of their debt, but the sponsored agencies operate with considerably less capital per dollar of debt than do most private lending institutions, giving them a distinct advantage in the money and capital markets over most private borrowers.

The lower capitalization of government-sponsored agencies aroused concern as the new century began due to their heavier use of financial derivatives and apparent increases in their risk exposure. The financial condition of FNMA (Fannie Mae) and FHLMC (Freddie Mac) came under heavy scrutiny in the financial press as new regulations required greater disclosure of their current financial position. At about the same time, allegations of internal accounting irregularities, operating inefficiencies, and the charging of excessive fees for their services added to the new pressures placed on these agencies from federal rulemakers and from the financial marketplace. Some agencies suffered substantial investment losses as thousands of home buyers refinanced their mortgage loans when market interest rates fell to historic lows, thereby reducing the expected yields from mortgage-backed securities—the principal investments held by some of the most prominent federal agencies.

(Continued on next page)

Growth of the Agency Security Market

Armed with this implied government support, the agency market has soared in recent years, with the volume of outstanding securities climbing from about $2 billion during the 1950s to more than $2 trillion today. (See Exhibit 11.9.) Estimates place the total of all agency obligations—both those issued inside the federal government's huge structure and those issued from outside agencies, many having stock that is privately owned—at well over $5 trillion, or about $2 trillion less than the federal government's direct debt. On an average day, the leading federal agency borrowers (especially the federal mortgage-market agencies) borrow at an interest cost that is at least a third of a percentage point cheaper than for the largest and best-known private borrowers, due primarily to the federal government's implied financial support. Moreover, the government-sponsored agencies consistently have been profitable in recent years, though they do face both credit (default) risk and interest rate risk on the loans they issue or buy and the debt they sell.

Federal Financing Bank (FFB)

The agency market is dominated by the government-sponsored agencies, which have limited access to government coffers and must rely mainly on the open market to raise money. In contrast, the federal agencies, which are part of the federal government, are financed through the **Federal Financing Bank (FFB),** which borrows money from the Treasury. The FFB is closely supervised by the Treasury Department and, in fact, is staffed by Treasury employees.[12] All FFB debt is fully guaranteed by the United States government.

Money market borrowing is usually done by issuing discount notes, which, like Treasury bills and commercial paper, have no promised interest rate but are sold at a price below their par value. Dealers sell the notes for a small fee, with banks, mutual funds, insurance companies, thrifts, and pension funds purchasing most of them. The sponsored agencies also issue short-term coupon securities and variable-rate notes. Long-term borrowing in the capital market is usually accomplished by issuing debentures, either on a monthly basis or irregularly as the need for funds arises.

Longer-term agency securities are available in denominations as small as $1,000, while the shorter-term notes traded in the money market generally come in minimum denominations of $50,000 or more. They are subject to federal income taxes, but many are exempt from state and local taxes. However, state and local government estate, gift, and inheritance taxes do apply to agency obligations. Depository institutions may use agency securities as collateral for loans from the Federal Reserve's discount window and as collateral pledged to secure government deposits at banks and other depositories.

The heaviest agency borrowers in recent years, as indicated in Exhibit 11.9, have been the Federal National Mortgage Association (FNMA), the Federal Home Loan Banks (FHLB), the Federal Home Loan Mortgage Corporation (FHLMC), the Student Loan Marketing Association, and the Farm Credit Banks. These agencies account for well over three-quarters of the outstanding debt issued by all federal and government-sponsored

---

Recently OFHEO (the Office of Federal Housing Enterprise Oversight), chief federal regulator of Fannie Mae and Freddie Mac, reached an agreement with these two mortgage agencies, requiring Fannie and Freddie to increase their capital in order to control their risk exposure and possibly to slow their growth. OFHEO has also recently launched a broad investigation of Fannie and Freddie's accounting practices, how they value their assets, especially their mortgage-loan related assets, and how they compensate management.

[12] The U. S. Treasury has to add a certain amount to its regular borrowings each year to cover any FFB drawings. The FFB was created by Congress in 1973. Up to that time each federal agency did its own borrowing. As a result, the number of different agency issues was proliferating at a rapid rate, creating confusion among investors. Centralization of borrowing in one agency, it was hoped, would increase efficiency in the funding process, improve the marketability of agency securities, and give the U.S. Congress a more adequate measure of the growth of agency activities.

EXHIBIT 11.9	Agency	Total Debt Outstanding
	Federal agencies:	
Total Debt Outstanding of Federal and Government-Sponsored Agencies, 2003* **($ Billions)**	Export-Import Bank	$ NA
	Federal Housing Administration	0.2
	Postal Service**	—
	Tennessee Valley Authority	27.0
	Other agencies	0.1
	Total federal agency debt†	$ 27.3
	Government-sponsored agencies:	
	Federal Home Loan Banks	704.3
	Federal Home Loan Mortgage Corporation	565.1
	Federal National Mortgage Association	894.9
	Farm Credit Banks§	90.0
	Student Loan Marketing Association	55.1
	Resolution Funding Corporation§	30.0
	Other agencies	12.3
	Total government-sponsored debt†	$2,351.7
	Total agency debt outstanding	$2,369.0

Source: Board of Governors of the Federal Reserve System, *Federal Reserve Bulletin,* December 2003, Table 1.44.

*Data as of July 2003. NA means data not currently available.

**Off-budget agency.

† Figures may not reflect column totals due to rounding and unavailability of some data.

§ In January 1979, the Farm Credit Banks began issuing consolidated bonds to replace those securities previously issued by the Federal Land Banks, the Federal Intermediate Credit Banks, and the Banks for Cooperatives. The Resolution Funding Corporation was established by the Financial Institutions Reform, Recovery, and Enforcement Act of 1989.

agencies, and an active secondary market exists for the short-term debt of these agencies. Most agency borrowing goes to support, directly or indirectly, the housing market and agriculture.

The securities of all government-sponsored agencies are regarded as highly similar by investors. Comparable maturities tend to have about the same yield, regardless of the issuing agency. Each agency is able to borrow at interest rates below the average yield on its asset portfolio due to government support but pays a slightly higher interest rate than the U.S. Treasury. Most of this small difference in interest cost is due to the fact that agency securities are less marketable than Treasury IOUs. The Treasury issues a security homogeneous in quality and other characteristics, but the agency market is splintered into many pieces. The yields on agency securities are lower than yields on private debt issues, however, due to their superior credit standing.

Characteristics and the Marketing of Agency Securities

Agency securities are generally short to medium term in maturity (running out to about 10 years). However the most rapidly growing segment is the money market segment— agency securities under one year to maturity. Among the most active buyers of agency securities are banks, state and local governments, government trust funds, and the Federal Reserve System. The Federal Reserve has been authorized to conduct open market operations in agency IOUs since 1966. Fed buying and selling of these securities has helped to improve their marketability and stature among private investors. Major securities dealers who handle U.S. government securities also generally trade in agency issues.

Government-sponsored agencies have become innovative borrowers in recent years. For example, FNMA and SLMA have sold securities in foreign markets, some of these denominated in foreign currencies or sold in "dual currency" form in which interest is paid in a foreign currency and the principal is repaid at maturity in U.S. dollars. These agencies have also used interest rate swaps and currency swaps to protect themselves against the risk of fluctuating interest rates and currency prices.

QUESTIONS TO HELP YOU STUDY

35. Federal agencies active in the financial markets were usually set up to aid so-called *disadvantaged sectors* of the economy. Identify these sectors and give some examples.

36. What is the difference between a *government-sponsored agency* and a *federal agency?*

37. What are the principal investment characteristics of federal agency securities? Which groups of investors are attracted to them and why?

MARKETS ON THE NET: The Most Important Web Sites for This Chapter

ALM Professional (almprofessional.com)
Bank Rate.com (bankrate.com)
Board of Governors of the Federal Reserve System (federalreserve.gov/fomc)
British Bankers Association (bba.com.uk)
Browse Data of the Federal Reserve Board (economagic.com/fedbog.htm)

Federal Reserve Bank of Atlanta (frb.atlanta.org/publica)
Federal Reserve Bank of New York (ny.frb.org)
Securities and Exchange Commission (sec.gov)
Treasury Direct (Treasurydirect.gov)

Summary of the Chapter's Main Points

In this chapter we have examined some of the most important money market institutions, including commercial banks, major corporations, and federal credit agencies. Among the key points were the following:

- *Banks* are among the most important financial institutions in the money market, providing credit to security dealers, industrial firms, and other money market participants. Banks are also the principal channel for making payments in the money market, acting as guarantors of payments and as custodians for the safekeeping of financial instruments. Finally, banks serve as a key channel for government economic policy, particularly in regulating the supply and cost of money and credit.

- Two of the most important domestic sources of funds in the money market that support the activities of banks are federal funds and negotiable CDs (certificates of deposit). *Federal funds* represent "immediately available" money in the form of large-denomination deposits that can be wired the same day from lenders to borrowers and then back again. *Negotiable CDs* are savings deposits with fixed or variable interest rates that are issued in denominations of $100,000 or more.

- Other important sources of money market funding for banks are *Eurocurrency deposits,* which consist of bank time deposits denominated in a currency other than the currency of the country where the bank accepting these deposits is located. Thus, a deposit of U.S. dollars in Great Britain is a Eurodollar deposit. They are not immediately spendable funds but constitute a reservoir of liquidity that can be used as a basis for expanding the volume of credit available within the international financial system.

- Among the most important sources of Eurocurrency deposits are tourist travel abroad, balance-of-payments deficits with other nations, and investments made overseas. Banks also use Eurocurrency deposits to help supply liquid reserves to support bank lending and investing activities.

- One of the best-known and oldest of bank-issued money market instruments is the *bankers' acceptance,* which constitutes a time draft drawn against a bank. The accepting bank pledges payment upon a specific date in the future. Widely used for many years to fund exports and imports of goods in international markets, the volume of acceptances has recently been declining as other financial instruments have moved in to take over the same role. Moreover, information flows between countries are much more complete today, reducing some of the risk of foreign trade that acceptances were designed originally to deal with.

- Eurocurrency deposits, federal funds, and negotiable CDs, help banks meet the *legal reserve requirements* that the central bank (in the United States, the Federal Reserve System) imposes upon their deposit holdings. Bankers must continually compare the cost and availability of federal funds, CDs, Eurocurrency deposits, and other sources of bank funds in order to secure the reserves they require.

- Major corporations are active as both borrowers and lenders in the money market. One of the best known of their borrowing instruments is *commercial paper*. The commercial paper market has grown over the years as major industrial corporations and financial-service companies, facing growing demands for their products and services, have turned increasingly to the open market for capital. The commercial paper market has provided a relatively low cost, flexible vehicle for raising short-term cash.

- Commercial paper has offered several distinct *advantages* over other sources of corporate funds, including ready access to new funds, lower interest rates than on most other sources of capital, and leverage to use against other lenders of funds when seeking new financing. A borrowing company that can tap the paper market for funding can always threaten to go to that market if a lending institution refuses to make a loan on reasonable terms. However, the paper market also has some *disadvantages,* being highly volatile at times with a scarce supply of available credit.

- One of the most rapidly growing of all money market segments in recent years involves trading in the IOUs issued by *federal agencies,* such as the Federal National Mortgage Association or the Farm Credit System. These agencies were set up to provide credit or help develop a market for loans to disadvantaged sectors of the economy, such as farms and ranches, new home buyers, and small businesses.

- Federal and government-sponsored agencies act like financial intermediaries, borrowing and lending funds at the same time. They rely upon the government's implied or expressed guarantee to give them an advantage in the competition for funds, lowering their cost of financing. With the government's implicit or explicit backing, these agencies issue securities almost as attractive as U.S. Treasury securities to most investors, but with slightly higher yields than are available on direct government obligations.

www.mhhe.com/rose9e

Key Terms Appearing in This Chapter

federal funds, 307

legal reserve requirement, 308

negotiable certificate of deposit (CD), 312

Eurocurrency market, 316

Eurodollars, 316

London Interbank Offer Rate (LIBOR), 322

bankers' acceptances, 323

time draft, 324

third-country bills, 326

liability management, 329

commerical paper, 330

direct paper, 330

dealer paper, 331

credit enhancements, 333

master note, 338

government-sponsored agencies, 340

federal agencies, 341

financial intermediaries, 341

Federal Financing Bank (FFB), 342

Problems and Issues

1. A money-center bank is trying to decide which source of funding to rely upon to cover loans being made today. It needs to borrow $10 million in either the federal funds market or in the negotiable CD market. Funds are needed for at least a week, but the bank's money desk manager is most concerned about the next 24 hours. Federal funds are currently trading at 4.80 percent; rates on new negotiable CDs posted by leading banks have reached 4.70 percent. FDIC insurance fees are currently 27 cents per $100.

   Calculate the cost to the bank for each of these funds sources. If you were a banker facing this decision, which source would you prefer to use?

2. Glenwood National Bank is short of required legal reserves. The bank's money manager estimates it will need to raise an additional $50 million in funds to cover its reserve requirement over the next three days. Federal funds are trading today at 5.90 percent, and the bank's economist has forecast a federal funds rate of 6.15 percent tomorrow and 6.20 percent the next day. Negotiable CDs in minimum maturities of seven days have been trading in New York this morning at 5.85 percent, with a forecast of 5.90 percent tomorrow and 5.98 percent the next day. The FDIC charges 30 cents per $100 for insurance coverage.

   Calculate the lowest-cost source of funding for Glenwood National Bank and the next cheapest source for borrowing over the next three days (today, tomorrow, and the next day). What are the relative advantages and disadvantages of each of these funding sources?

3. If Sterling Corporation purchases a $5 million bank CD that matures in 90 days and promises an interest return of 6.25 percent, how much in total will Sterling receive back when this CD matures?

4. What is the coupon-equivalent yield to maturity (YTM) on a 30-day negotiable CD promising an annualized interest return (i) of 5.95 percent?

5. Calculate the bank discount rate (DR) attached to a 60-day, $1 million CD selling in the secondary market for $990,000.

6. J . P . Morgan Chase Bank is short cash reserves in the amount of $225 million—a condition expected to last for the next five business days—and is weighing (a) securing a loan in the domestic federal funds market, where the interest rate prevailing today is 5.45 percent; (b) issuing seven-day domestic negotiable CDs at a current market rate of 5.50 percent; or (c) tapping its foreign branch offices for 30-day Eurodollars at a market rate of 5.58 percent. The

estimated noninterest cost of all of these various funding sources is approximately the same, except that the domestic CDs currently carry an annual FDIC insurance fee of $0.04 per every $100 in deposits received from the public. Which source of funds would you recommend the bank make use of? What factors should the bank's funds management division weigh in making this borrowing decision?

7. A new issue of 90-day commercial paper is available from a dealer in New York City at a price of $97.60 on a $100 basis. What is the bank discount yield on this note if held to maturity?

8. A note traded in the commercial paper market will mature in 15 days. The dealer will sell it to you at $98.35 on a $100 basis. What is the note's discount rate of return?

9. Commercial paper was purchased in the secondary market 30 days from maturity at a bank discount yield of 9 percent. Ten days later, it was sold to a dealer at an 8 percent discount rate. What was the investor's holding-period yield?

10. What is the difference in basis points between the discount rate of return (DR) and the investment rate of return (IR) on a $10 million commercial paper note purchased at a price of $9.85 million and scheduled to mature in 25 days?

11. A commercial paper note with $1 million par value and maturing in 60 days has an expected discount return (DR) at maturity of 6 percent. What was its purchase price? What is this note's expected coupon-equivalent (investment return) yield (IR)?

12. Alamo Corporation requests a $20 million, 90-day loan from its bank, which proposes to make the requested loan at an interest rate of 6 percent and a compensating balance requirement of 10 percent of the amount of the loan. What will Alamo's effective loan rate be under these terms? Suppose 90-day commercial paper sold by dealers is currently trading at an interest rate of 6.0 percent. What is the interest rate spread between the effective loan rate quoted by the bank and the current commercial paper rate? Does the bank's proposed loan carry any advantages that borrowing through the commercial paper market won't necessarily provide Alamo Corporation?

13. What price would attach today to Europaper issued at par (100) with a maturity of 180 days and carrying a discount rate of 7 percent?

14. What is the appropriate discount rate for a 270-day Europaper issue priced at par (100) and expected to sell today at a discounted price of 96?

15. A bank is willing to issue a line of credit to fully back a $25 million issue of commercial paper for a fee of 1 percent. If any portion of the line is used, an interest rate of 8 percent will be assessed. The compensating balance requirement for the line of credit is 5 percent, while the portion of the line that is used carries a 20 percent compensating balance requirement. How much will the borrowing company pay for the full unused line? Suppose $1.5 million is actually drawn upon for unexpected expenses and the balance of the credit line is used merely to back the paper issue. How much will the borrowing firm pay in total bank charges?

16. What is the discount rate (DR) and the investment return (IR) on the following commercial notes?

	Face Value	Purchase Price	Maturity in Days
a.	$10,000,000	$ 9,750,000	60
b.	$22,500,000	$21,350,000	45
c.	$48,750,000	$46,975,000	30
d.	$60,175,000	$48,850,985	15

17. A German manufacturer of furniture sells a large order of home furnishings to an outlet store in Houston. The Houston firm pays for the shipment by wiring funds from its local bank through Fedwire to the German firm's account at J. P. Morgan Chase Bank in New York City. Subsequently, the German manufacturer decides to invest half of the funds received in a dollar deposit offered by Barclays Bank in London, where interest rates are particularly attractive. No sooner are the funds deposited in London than a Japanese auto company, shipping cars to the U.S. and Europe, asks the London bank for a loan to purchase raw materials in the United States.

Later, when the loan falls due, the Japanese firm will go into the currency market to purchase dollars in order to retire its Eurodollar loan at Barclays Bank, receiving a dollar deposit at a U.S. bank. When the loan is repaid, Barclays gains the dollar deposit in the United States and uses the deposit to pay off the German firm when its time deposit matures. The German firm chooses to deposit the funds received from Barclays in its demand deposit account at J. P. Morgan Chase Bank in New York City because it now needs to buy goods and services in the United States.

Construct T accounts that reflect the foregoing transactions. In particular, show the proper entries for: (1) payment by the Houston firm to the German furniture company; (2) deposit of the funds in London; (3) the loan to the Japanese automaker; (4) repayment of the loan; and (5) return of funds to the United States. Indicate which deposit is a Eurodollar deposit and if any Eurodollars are destroyed at any particular stage.

18. A company known as Standard Quality Importing ships videocassette recorders made in Japan to retail dealers in the United States and Western Europe. It decides to place an order with its Japanese supplier for 10,000 DVDs at $200 each after securing a line of credit from Guaranty Security Bank in Los Angeles. Guaranty issues a credit letter to the Japanese supplier promising payment in U.S. dollars 90 days hence. However, the Japanese firm needs the promised funds within seven days from receipt of the credit letter to make purchases of technical components from an electronics firm in Phoenix, Arizona. Explain and illustrate with T accounts and diagrams how a bankers' acceptance would arise from the foregoing transactions, how the Japanese supplier could receive the dollars she needs in timely fashion, and what would happen to the acceptance at the end of the 90-day period. Use T account entries to show the movement of funds from the importer to the Japanese supplier, to the electronics firm, and to money market investors.

19. Instel Corporation has been offered a $100 million, three-month loan at a fixed rate of 90-day LIBOR plus $3/_8$% margin or at the prevailing federal funds rate plus $1/_2$% margin with the loan rate adjusted every 24 hours to the federal funds rate prevailing at the close of business each day. These rates, along with prevailing yields on U.S. Treasury bills, are posted in London and New York as follows:

90-Day LIBOR rate on Eurodollar deposits	4.275%	3-month U.S. Treasury bill rate	4.12%
Federal funds rate	4.08	6-month U.S. Treasury bill rate	4.20
One-month (30 day) U.S. Treasury bills	4.05	1-year U.S. Treasury bill rate	4.30

Which set of loan terms would you recommend to Instel's treasurer? Why?

20. A British investor withdraws her million-dollar deposit from Citicorp Bank, N.A., and converts the deposit into a dollar-denominated, 30-day CD in a Belgian commercial bank at the going market rate (LIBOR) of 5.85 percent. Almost immediately, the Belgian bank makes a loan of $750,000 to an aluminum frames manufacturer at LIBOR plus 30 basis points for 21 days. When the CD matures and the deposit is returned to Citicorp, how much in interest income will the depositor receive? How much will the aluminum frame manufacturer pay in total interest expense for its 21-day bank loan? Show the proper accounting entries for all of the foregoing transactions (including the return of funds to the original depositor).

Standard & Poor's Market Insight and Web-Based Problems

STANDARD
&POOR'S

1. The use of commercial paper by commercial banks to raise short-term funds is restricted in the United States to large money-center banks. Therefore, when you analyze the banking system as a whole you get an incomplete picture of how important commercial paper is for individual U.S. banks.
   a. Visit the S&P Market Insight database at **mhhe.com/edumarketinsight** and locate the annual balance sheet for a large commercial bank (such as Bank One [ONE]). Check under "Excel Analytics."
   b. Using data for the last five years, compute the ratio of "Commercial Paper" to "Short-Term Borrowings—Total." Does commercial paper represent a very significant source of borrowed funds for this bank? Has this figure varied much over the five-year period?
   c. Compute the ratio of "Commercial Paper" to "Liabilities—Total." Does commercial paper represent a very significant source of short-term funds for this bank overall (i.e., when you consider all of the bank's liabilities—its deposits and other borrowings)?
   d. Compute the ratio of "Short-Term Borrowings" to "Liabilities—Total." Has this ratio varied much over the past five years for this bank? (Note that while short-term borrowings are not the major source of funds for most banks, they are quite important in day-to-day bank operations, as you will see in the next several chapters.)

2. The negotiable CD market represents an important source of short-term funds for many banks. Among the important assets of banks are Treasury bills and business loans extended to "blue chip" companies with excellent credit ratings.
   a. Go to the FRED II database maintained by the Federal Reserve Bank of St. Louis at **research.stlouisfed.org/fred2** and download historical data for the interest rates paid on six-month CDs and six-month T-bills as well as the information needed to construct a series for the prime bank lending rate (i.e., the rate banks charge their best corporate clients).
   b. On a single graph plot *two* interest-rate spreads: (i) the six-month T-bill rate minus the six-month CD rate and (ii) the prime lending rate minus the six-month CD rate.

www.mhhe.com/rose9e

   c. Do your results from part (b) indicate why a bank could not operate by raising money in the CD market and investing all of it in Treasuries?

   d. Is corporate lending profitable for banks when they rely on the CD market to raise funds? Why or why not?

3. The Eurodollar market has become an important vehicle for larger commercial banks to raise short-term funds in the money market. Using a spreadsheet program (such as Excel) to make the required computations easily:

   a. Visit the Federal Reserve's Web site at **federalreserve.gov/releases/h6/hist** and obtain a time series covering the last 20 years for the volume of Eurodollars held by domestically chartered U.S. commercial banks.

   b. Go to **federalreserve.gov/releases/h8/data.htm** and obtain data covering the same time period as in part (a) for seasonally adjusted Total Liabilities of all domestically chartered U.S. commercial banks.

   c. Form a ratio of Eurodollar deposits (from part [a]) to total liabilities (from part [b]) and graph the results.

   d. How has bank reliance on Eurodollars as a funds source changed in each of the past two decades? Can you suggest plausible reasons for the changes?

Semester Project: A Study of the Fed Funds Market

Continuing our semester project on the federal funds market, we note that when the Federal Open Market Committee (FOMC) changes its Fed funds interest rate target, it nearly always limits those changes to plus or minus 25 or 50 basis points, with the changes usually happening at regularly scheduled FOMC meetings. The money and capital markets trade on this knowledge; it is reflected in the prices reported each day from the 30-day Fed Funds Futures Market. In this exercise you will compute the probability of a change in the Fed funds target rate at the next upcoming FOMC meeting.

a. Using your results for this project from previous chapters, you should now have the following information at hand: today's date, the date of the next FOMC meeting, the current Fed funds target rate, the expected average effective funds rate for the days leading up to the FOMC meeting (denoted by x), and the expected average effective Fed funds rate following the upcoming FOMC meeting (denoted by y). Fill in any missing items now.

b. Compare the average expected Fed funds rate *after* the FOMC meeting with the current target rate. If it is within 25 basis points, assume the markets expect one of two possible outcomes—either (i) the FOMC will change the target rate by 25 basis points (by increasing the target rate if y > target or by decreasing the target rate if y < target) or (ii) the FOMC will leave the target rate unchanged.

c. If y is between 25 and 50 basis points different than the current Fed funds target, assume the markets expect the two possible outcomes to be either (i) a 25 basis point increase or decrease or (ii) a 50 basis point change in the target rate (with an increase expected if y > target and a decrease expected if y < target).

d. Let p denote the probability that the FOMC will change the target by 25 basis points if part (b) applies and 50 basis points if part (c) applies. Then $(1 - p)$ represents the probability that the FOMC *will not* change the target if part (b) applies and *will* change the target by only 25 basis points if part (c) applies. Compute p and $(1 - p)$ with today's data and explain what the numbers represent.

e. Using prior results from the example in Chapter 10's installment of this project, (in which $y = 1.025$ and the FOMC meeting date is scheduled for April 15), the calculations would appear as follows:

$$p*1.25\% + (1 - p)*1\% = 1.052\%, \quad \text{or } p = 0.208$$

In this example, there is a 21 percent chance that the FOMC will raise the target Fed funds rate from 1 percent to 1.25 percent versus a 79 percent chance it will leave the target rate unchanged at 1 percent.

Selected References to Explore

Balbach, Anatol B., and David H. Ressler. "Eurodollars and the U.S. Money Supply." *Review,* Federal Reserve Bank of St. Louis, June–July 1980, pp. 2–12.

Crabbe, Leland and Mitchell A. Post. "The Effect of SEC Amendments to Rule 2A–7 on the Commercial Paper Market." *Finance and Economics Discussion Series* 199, Board of Governors of the Federal Reserve System, May 1992.

Eloyan, Fayez A., Bryan A. Maris, and Philip J. Young. "The Effects of Commercial Paper Rating Changes and Credit-Watch Placement on Common Stock Prices." *The Financial Review* 31, no. 1 (February 1996), pp. 149–67.

www.mhhe.com/rose9e

Kuttner, Kenneth. "Monetary Policy Surprises and Interest Rates: Evidence from the Fed Funds Futures Market." *Journal of Monetary Economics* 47, no. 3 (2001), pp. 523–544.

Nosal, Ed. "How Well Does the Federal Funds Futures Rate Predict the Future Federal Funds Rate?" *Economic Commentary,* Federal Reserve Bank of Cleveland, October 1, 2001.

Winters, Drew B. "Commercial Paper: A Colossal Market." *National Economic Trends*, Federal Reserve Bank of St. Louis, October 2002.

Chapter 12

Roles and Services of the Federal Reserve and Other Central Banks around the World

Learning Objectives

in This Chapter

- You will explore the many different roles played and the functions performed by *central banks* around the world.

- You will see how and why the *Federal Reserve System* came to be established as the U.S. central bank and how the Fed is organized to carry out the many tasks it must perform, not only domestically but also as part of the global financial system.

- You will discover the importance of *central bank independence* from the dictates of governments in carrying out effective money and credit policy.

- You will understand the concept of *legal reserves* and how actions taken by the central bank influence the level and growth of legal reserves and, ultimately, deposits and loans.

What's in This Chapter?
Key Topics Outline

Roles and Functions of Central Banking

Goals Pursued by Central Banks around the World

Channels of Central Banking: Their Influence on the Economy and Financial Markets

The Fed and the European Central Bank: How Do They Compare?

History and Structure of the Federal Reserve System

Central Bank Independence and Transparency: Their Importance Today

Bank Reserves and Deposit and Money Multipliers

12.1   Introduction to Central Banking

central bank

One of the most important financial institutions in any modern economy is the **central bank.** Basically, a central bank is an agency of government that has important public policy functions in monitoring the operation of the financial system, controlling the growth of a nation's money supply, and enhancing the performance of its economy. Central banks ordinarily do not deal directly with the public; rather, they are "bankers' banks," communicating with commercial banks and securities dealers in carrying out their essential policymaking functions. (For a list of the world's leading central banks and their Web site addresses, see the nearby Financial Developments box.) The central bank of the United States is the **Federal Reserve System,** a creation of the U.S. Congress charged with issuing currency, regulating the banking system, and taking measures to protect the value of the dollar and promote full employment. In this and the following chapter, we examine in detail the nature and impact of central bank operations and the major problems of policymaking faced by central bank money managers today.

Federal Reserve System

12.2   The Roles of Central Banks in the Economy and Financial System

Control of the Money Supply to Avoid Severe Inflation

Central banks, including the Federal Reserve System, perform several important functions in a modern economy. (See Exhibit 12.1.) One of the most important of their functions is *control of the money supply in order to avoid severe inflation.*

What is money? Money is anything that serves as a *medium of exchange* in the purchase of goods and services. Money, however, has another important function—serving as a *store of value,* for money is a financial asset that may be used to store purchasing power until it is needed by the owner. If we define money exclusively as a medium of exchange, the sum of all currency and coin held by the public plus the value of all publicly held checking accounts and other deposits against which drafts may be made (such as NOWs and money market accounts) would constitute the money supply. If we define money as a store of value, on the other hand, then time and savings accounts at banks and nonbank financial intermediaries would also be considered important components of the money supply.

However we define money, the power to regulate its quantity and value in the United States was delegated by the Congress early in the 20th century to the Federal Reserve System. The Fed has become not only the principal source of currency and coin (pocket money) used by the U.S. public but also a key government agency helping the U.S. Treasury to stabilize the value of the dollar and protect its integrity in international markets. Why is control of the money supply so important? One reason is that changes in the money supply seem to be closely linked to changes in economic activity. In other words, there appears to be a statistically significant relationship between current and lagged changes in the

EXHIBIT 12.1

Roles Usually Played by Central Banks in the Financial System

- Market stabilization
- Control of the money supply
- Lender of last resort
- Supervisor of the banking system
- Protecting and improving the flow of payments

money supply and changes in nominal gross domestic product (GDP).[1] The implication of these studies is that, if the central bank can control the growth rate of money, it can influence the nominal growth rate of the economy as a whole.

Another important reason for controlling the money supply is that, in the absence of effective controls, money in the form of paper notes and bank deposits could expand virtually without limit. The marginal cost of creating additional units of money is essentially *zero*. It costs no more to print a $100 bill than to print a $1 bill. (Which is why you are unlikely to hear of very many counterfeit $1 bills floating around!) Therefore, the banking system or the government or both are capable of increasing the money supply well beyond the economy's capacity to produce goods and services. Such a situation has often been described as "too much money chasing too few goods" and leads to severe price inflation that can eventually slow overall economic activity.

It is not surprising that modern governments have come to rely so heavily on central banks as guardians of the quantity and value of their currencies. For example, the Federal Reserve System and other central banks enter the financial markets frequently in an attempt to control domestic price inflation in order to protect the purchasing power of the home currency. It is generally believed that by accomplishing this task, central banks make their most important contribution toward promoting growth in the economy's output and employment in the long run. Thus, it is often argued today that price level stability *must* be the principal long-run goal of central bank policy and, therefore, that central banks *must* pay close attention to how fast money and credit are allowed to expand in order to avoid severe inflation.

Stabilizing the Money and Capital Markets

For a review of the structure, laws, and performance of central banks around the world, see the Web site of the Center for the Study of Central Banks at law.nyu.edu/central-bankscenter

A second vital function of central banking is *stabilization of the money and capital markets.* The financial system must transmit savings to those who require funds for investment so the economy can grow. If the system of money and capital markets is to work efficiently, however, the public must have confidence in financial institutions and be willing to commit its savings to them. If the financial markets are unruly, with volatile fluctuations in interest rates and security prices, or if financial institutions are prone to frequent collapse, public confidence in the financial system might well be damaged. The flow of investment capital may dry up, resulting in a drastic slowing in the rate of economic growth and a rise in unemployment.

All central banks play a role in fostering the mature development of financial markets and in ensuring a stable flow of funds through those markets. Pursuing this objective, a central bank may, from time to time, provide funds to major securities dealers and/or depository institutions when they have difficulty financing their portfolios or providing an adequate supply of credit so that buyers and sellers may easily acquire or sell securities and borrowers interested in making investments can find adequate funding. When the money supply and interest rates rise or fall more rapidly than seems consistent with economic goals and the desired volume of saving and investment in the economy, a central bank may intervene in the financial marketplace.

Lender of Last Resort

Another essential function of many central banks is to serve as a *lender of last resort.* This means providing liquid funds to those financial institutions in need, especially when alternative sources of funds have dried up. For example, through its discount

---

[1]For example, see the references at the end of the chapter for the Federal Reserve Bank of San Francisco (2004) and Marquis (2002).

window, the Federal Reserve will provide funds to selected deposit-type financial institutions to cover their short-term cash deficiencies. The central bank's discount window can supply large amounts of emergency funds very quickly, as occurred, for example, in the wake of the September 11, 2001, terrorist attacks when the Federal Reserve moved rapidly to supply liquidity to the struggling U.S. economy. As we will see, before the Federal Reserve System was created, one of the weaknesses in the financial system of the United States was the absence of a lender of last resort to aid financial institutions squeezed by severe liquidity pressures.

Maintaining and Improving the Payments Mechanism

Finally, central banks have a role to play in *maintaining and improving the payments mechanism.* This may involve the central bank helping to clear checks, providing an adequate supply of currency and coin, wiring funds, and preserving confidence in the value of the fundamental monetary unit. A smoothly functioning and efficient payments mechanism is vital for business and commerce. If checks or electronic payments cannot be cleared in timely fashion (as happened in the immediate wake of the terrorist crisis in September 2001) or if the public cannot get the currency and coin it needs to carry out transactions, business activity will be severely curtailed. The result might well be large-scale unemployment and a decline in the nation's rate of economic growth.

12.3   The Goals and Channels of Central Banking

Central Banks' Goals

Central banking is *goal oriented.* Since World War II, the United States and other industrialized nations have accepted the premise that a government is responsible to its citizens for maintaining high levels of employment, combating inflation, and promoting sustained growth in the economy so that living standards rise and jobs are available for all who want to work.

Specifically, central banking in the United States and in most other nations today is directed toward:

1. *Achieving maximum sustainable output and employment,* and
2. *Promoting stable prices.*

Of these two key monetary-policy objectives, more and more central banks around the globe are directing their primary effort toward the *promotion of stable prices*—that is, their focus is on *avoiding severe inflation.* They recognize that monetary policy can have a very significant *long-run* impact on inflation, and that inflation can be very dangerous because it can reduce economic growth—by introducing mistakes in business and consumer planning, by misallocating the economy's scarce resources and redistributing its wealth (primarily from lenders to borrowers), and by increasing interest rates (especially long-term interest rates).

So strong has been the recent emphasis on *long-run price stability* as the principal target of central bank monetary policy that a growing number of nations have set *inflation-rate targets* or *target ranges.* By attaching specific numbers to their goal of promoting stable prices, many central banks now have a way to measure their progress in the fight against inflation. Examples of central banks and nations adopting specific inflation-rate targets or target ranges include Australia, Brazil, Canada, the countries that are members of the European Monetary Union, Hungary, Israel, South Korea, New Zealand, Poland, Sweden, Switzerland, and the United Kingdom. The majority of

Bank of England (bankofengland.gov)

Bank of Japan (boj.ur.jp)

Swiss National Bank (snb.ch)

Bank of Canada (bankofcanada.ca/en)

Banque Nationale de Belgique (Belgium) (bnb.be/)

European Central Bank (ECB) (ecb.int)

Deutsche Bundesbank (Germany) (bundesbank.de/)

Banca D'Italia (bancaditalia.it)

Reserve Bank of Australia (rba.gov.au/)

Banco Central do Brasil (bcb.gov.br/)

Federal Reserve System (federalreserve.gov)

Banque de France (banque-france.fr/)

Reserve Bank of New Zealand (rbnz.govt.nz/)

De Nederlandsche Bank NV (The Netherlands) (dnb.n/)

The People's Bank of China (pbc.gov.cn/english/)

these nations have established a *target range* for inflation that typically lies in the 1 to 3 percent annual rate range.

Notice that the United States is not on the inflation-target list above. Neither the U.S. Congress nor the Federal Reserve has yet specified a specific numerical inflation target beyond the generic phrase, "promoting stable prices." This does not mean that the Fed does not pay close attention to the U.S. inflation rate, but that, due to the lack of specific numerical guidelines, it is up to the judgment of Federal Reserve policymakers to determine what the term "stable prices" really means. To paraphrase a famous statement by Federal Reserve Chairman Alan Greenspan, *"Price stability exists when inflation is so low that it does not materially affect important economic decisions [such as savings and investment]."*

Moreover, it is important to note that, given the recent experience in Japan and in the manufacturing and commodity sectors of the U.S. economy, central banks also must be prepared to deal with *deflation*. If the inflation rate turns negative and average prices fall (as happened in Japan for much of the 1990s), central bankers must deal with a new set of economic problems. Deflation tends to redistribute wealth from borrowers to lenders, make credit more difficult to obtain, push stock and real estate prices lower, and slow productive investment and job growth. In summary, both inflation and deflation present potential pitfalls to the successful management of national and global economies by central banks.

Challenges in Achieving Central Bank Goals

Articles and speeches by central banking officials around the world are compiled by the Bank for International Settlements at bis.org/review

Through their influence over interest rates and the growth of the money supply, central banks are able to influence the economy's progress toward the above goals. Achievement of all central bank goals simultaneously has proven to be difficult, however. One reason is that the goals often *conflict*. Pursuit of price stability, for example, may require higher interest rates and restricted credit availability—policies that tend to increase unemployment and slow economic growth. Central bank policymaking is often a matter of accepting *trade-offs* (compromises) among multiple goals.

Central banking in most major nations today operates principally through the *marketplace*. Modern central banks operate as a balance wheel in promoting and stabilizing the flow of savings from surplus-spending units to deficit-spending units. They try to ensure a smooth and orderly flow of funds through the money and capital markets so that adequate financing is available for worthwhile investment projects. This means, among other things, avoiding panics due to sudden shortages of available credit or sharp declines in the

357

values of financial assets. However, most of the actions taken by the central bank to promote a smooth flow of funds are carried out through the marketplace rather than by government order. For example, the central bank may encourage interest rates to rise in order to reduce borrowing and spending and combat inflation, but it does not usually allocate credit to particular borrowers. The private sector, working through supply and demand forces in the marketplace, is left to make its own decisions about how much borrowing and spending will take place and who is to receive credit.

The Channels through Which Central Banks Work

It is useful at this point to give a brief overview of the channels through which modern central banks influence conditions in the economy and financial system. Central bank policy affects the economy as a whole by making the following adjustments:

1. Changes in the cost and availability of credit to businesses, consumers, and governments.
2. Changes in the volume and rate of growth of the money supply.
3. Changes in the financial wealth of investors as reflected in the market value of their stocks, bonds, and other security holdings.
4. Changes in the relative prices of domestic and foreign currencies (currency exchange rates).
5. Changes in the public's expectations regarding future money and credit conditions and currency values (see Exhibit 12.2).

EXHIBIT 12.2   **The Impact of Central Bank Policy: How Central Banks Influence the Economy and the Global Financial System**

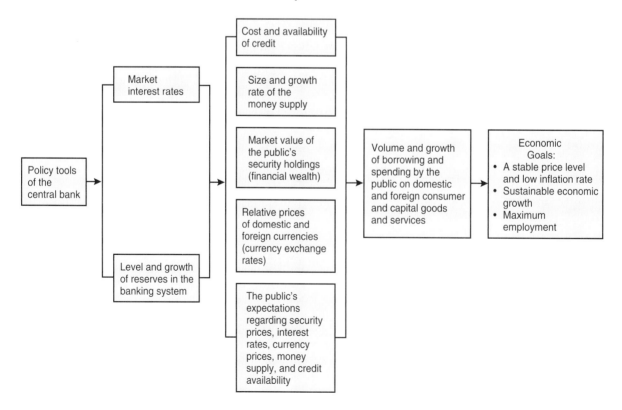

The central bank has a number of policy tools at its command to influence the cost of credit (interest rates); the value (prices) of financial assets; money supply volume and growth; the relative prices (exchange rates) of world currencies; and the public's expectations regarding future interest rates, currency prices, and credit conditions. In the United States, the principal policy tools used by the central bank are open market operations, changes in required reserves held by depository institutions, and changes in the discount rate on central bank loans. Many of these same tools are used by other central banks around the world, with a growing use of open market operations, which appears to be among the most popular monetary tools in nations around the globe.

Changes in interest rates, security prices, and bank reserves that result from the use of the central bank's policy tools influence, first of all, the cost and availability of credit. If borrowers find that credit is less available and more expensive to obtain, they are likely to restrain their borrowing and spending for both capital and consumer goods at home and abroad. This results in a slowing in the economy's rate of growth and perhaps a reduction in inflationary pressures. Second, if the central bank can reduce the rate of growth of the money supply, this policy may eventually slow the growth of income and production in the economy due to a reduction in the public's demand for goods and services.

Third, if the central bank raises interest rates and thereby lowers security prices, this will tend to reduce the market value of the public's holdings of stocks, bonds, and other securities. The result is a decline in the value of investors' financial wealth, altering the public's borrowing and spending plans and, ultimately, influencing employment, prices, and the economy's rate of growth. Fourth, the central bank can make changes in domestic interest rates relative to foreign interest rates, which will affect the exchange ratios (relative prices) in world markets between domestic and foreign currencies. If the price of the home currency falls relative to foreign currency prices, the home country's exports will become cheaper and more sought after abroad, stimulating domestic production and creating more jobs.

In recent years, economic research has suggested a fifth channel for central bank policy to affect the economy: *its impact on the public's expectations* regarding future credit costs, money supply growth, the value of loans and securities, and relative currency values. If central bank operations result in shifting public expectations, businesses and consumers will alter their borrowing, spending, and investing plans (unfortunately, not always in the direction the central bank wishes), which can have profound effects on the economy's rate of growth and the creation of jobs. We will have more to say about these important channels of central bank policy in Chapter 13.

QUESTIONS TO HELP YOU STUDY

1. What *functions* do central banks perform in a market-oriented economy? Explain why each function is important in the functioning of a market-oriented economic system.

2. What are the principal *goals* central banks pursue in order to carry out monetary policy?

3. To what extent are the principal goals of central bank monetary policy consistent or inconsistent with each other? What does a central bank do when the goals it wishes to pursue directly conflict with each other?

4. What are the principal *channels* through which central banks, including the Federal Reserve System, work to influence the economy and achieve their goals?

In 1998 a new central bank—the ECB, or European Central Bank—joined the world's financial institutions devoted to pursuing monetary policy and stabilizing economies. Formed as part of the European Union (EU), the new central bank, headquartered in Frankfurt, Germany, and representing all member nations of the EU as well as affecting the economic lives of more than 300 million European citizens, is reshaping the structure of interest rates on the European continent and assisting in the expansion of a common EU currency, the Euro. It has been aided in this task by the central banks of all EU countries, representing the new European System of Central Banks (ESCB). The principal goal of the ECB, as defined by the Masstricht Treaty, is to pursue *price stability*. The ECB is also assisting the European Monetary Institute and the central banks of EU member nations in developing a new electronic payments network comparable to the Federal Reserve's FEDWIRE, called TARGET—the Trans-European Automated Real-Time Gross Settlement Express Transfer—allowing cross-border payments to be processed in Europe's new currency.

The ECB faces multiple challenges as it operates in the 21st century. It must finalize the design and the powers of its organizational structure and governing council, learn how to use its policy tools effectively, establish credibility with international investors as well as its own citizens, and figure out how to maintain a uniform monetary policy for multiple European nations, each with a different mix of industries and varying social and political systems. It will supervise the achievement of uniform interest rates throughout its territory, though the central banks of EU member states retain the right to set their own nations' interest rate levels.

Each member state, regardless of its size, has only one vote on the ECB's Governing Council, which contains the governors of the member countries' central banks and is chaired by the ECB's president—a position comparable to the Chairman of the Board of Governors of the Federal Reserve System. The ECB is not as clearly dominated by its president as is the Fed with its Board chairman and, therefore, the ECB may be somewhat slower to respond to crises than is the Federal Reserve System. The ECB's Executive Board, which runs its daily operations, is appointed by the European Council of Ministers and confirmed by the European Parliament. In principle at least, the European central banking system could be one of the most independent central banks in the world, as its charter can be modified only by *unanimous* consent of all member nations.

12.4 History of the Federal Reserve System— Central Bank of the United States

The United States was one of the last major nations in the Western world to permanently charter a central bank, after two early attempts in 1791 and 1816 that ultimately failed. The Bank of England was established in 1694; the Bank of France and the central banks of Switzerland and Italy were founded during the eighteenth century. Most major industrialized nations early in their histories recognized the need for an institution that would provide a measure of stability and control over the growth of money and credit. Public officials in the United States were hesitant to permanently charter a central bank, for fear that it would possess great financial power and restrict the availability of credit to a growing nation. However, a series of economic and financial crises in the late nineteenth and early twentieth centuries forced the U.S. Congress to act, resulting in the creation of the Federal Reserve System.

Problems in the Early U.S. Banking System

To understand fully why the Federal Reserve System was created, we must understand the problems that plagued the U.S. financial system throughout much of this nation's early history. Many of these problems were born in the years prior to the Civil War, when the states, not the federal government, controlled the banking system. Unfortunately, with a few notable exceptions, the states generally did a poor job. Charters for new banks frequently were awarded by state legislatures and were therefore subject to political lobbying and influence peddling. If a new bank's organizers had the right political connections, a charter could be obtained by individuals with little banking experience and with minimal capital invested in the business.

Deposit banking was not as popular then as it is today. Most people preferred hard money (currency and coin) to deposits. As a result, banks made loans simply by printing and issuing their own paper notes, which circulated as currency. Because few controls existed, there was a tendency to issue these notes well beyond the financial strength of the bank making the loan. Frequently, charters were granted to "wildcat banks" that would issue a large quantity of notes and then disappear. Some banks, promising to redeem their notes in gold or silver coin, set up "redemption centers" in locations nearly impossible for the public to reach, such as in the middle of a swamp. Needless to say, there was a high failure rate among these poorly capitalized, ill-managed institutions, resulting in substantial losses to unlucky depositors.

Responding to these problems and also to the tremendous financial strain imposed by the Civil War, Congress passed the National Banking Act of 1863. This act authorized the establishment of federally licensed commercial banks, subject to regulations imposed by a newly created office, the Comptroller of the Currency, a part of the U.S. Treasury Department. Any group of businesspeople could organize a *national bank,* provided they could show that the new bank would be profitable within a reasonable period of time (usually within three years), meet minimum equity capital requirements imposed by the Comptroller's office, and not endanger the viability of banks already operating in the local area. Under the provisions of the National Banking Act, the chartering of commercial banks was, in the main, removed from the political sphere and made subject to carefully spelled-out rules. At the same time, Congress attempted to drive state-chartered banks into the national banking system by imposing a 10 percent tax on state bank notes. It was argued that most bankers would prefer the more liberal state regulations and avoid applying for national bank charters unless they were forced to do so.

To help finance the Civil War, Congress authorized national banks to issue their own notes as circulating currency. However, these notes had to be collateralized by U.S. government securities. Under the terms of the National Banking Act, federally chartered banks could issue notes up to 90 percent of the value of Treasury securities they deposited with the Comptroller of the Currency. The result was to create a money medium under federal control to help pay for the Civil War by creating a demand from banks for U.S. government securities. Even more important, the National Banking Act created a *dual banking system,* with both federal and state authorities having important regulatory powers over commercial banks. Unfortunately, these authorities were given overlapping powers, and in recent years competition between federal and state regulatory agencies has sometimes resulted in actions detrimental to the public interest.

Creation of the Federal Reserve System

Several festering problems (including some traceable to the provisions of the National Banking Act) resulted in the creation of the Federal Reserve System. For one thing, the new national bank notes proved to be unresponsive to the nation's growing need for a money or cash medium. The need for money and credit grew rapidly as the United States became more heavily industrialized and the Midwest and Far West opened up to immigration. Farmers and ranchers in these areas demanded an "elastic" supply of money and credit—adequate to their needs at relatively low cost. As we will soon see, the new Federal Reserve System would attempt to deal with this problem by issuing a currency of its own and by exercising closer control over the growth of money and credit.

As deposit banking and the writing of checks became increasingly popular, another serious problem appeared. The process of clearing and collecting checks was too slow and expensive. Then, as now, most checks written by the public were local in character, moving funds from the account of one local customer to that of another. These checks normally are cleared routinely through the local clearinghouse, which is simply a location where representatives of local banks meet daily to exchange checks drawn on each other's banks. For checks sent outside the local area, however, the collection process proved to be more complicated, with some checks passing through several banks before reaching their final destination.

To learn more about the history of the Federal Reserve System, see such Web sites as Fed101 at kc.frb.org/fed101 and the Federal Reserve Bank of Minneapolis at mpls.frb.org

Before the Federal Reserve System was created, many banks charged a fee (*exchange charge*) for the clearing and redemption of checks. This fee was usually calculated as a percentage of the par (or face) value of each check. Banks levying the fee were called *no-par* banks because they refused to honor checks at their full face value. To avoid exchange fees, bankers would try to route the checks they received only through banks accepting and redeeming them at par. Often this meant routing a check through scores of banks in distant cities until days or weeks had elapsed before the check was finally cleared. Such a delay was not just annoying, but also served as an impediment to commercial transactions. Exchange charges resulted in needless inefficiency and increased the true cost of business transactions far above their nominal cost. A new national check-clearing system was needed that honored checks at par and moved them swiftly between payee and payer. This responsibility too was given to the Federal Reserve System, which insisted that all checks cleared through its system be honored at full face (par) value.

A third problem with the banking and financial system of that time was recurring liquidity crises. Then, as now, money and bank reserves tended to concentrate in leading financial centers, such as New York City or San Francisco, where the greatest need for loanable funds existed. Bank reserves flowed into the major cities as smaller banks in outlying areas deposited their reserves with larger banking institutions to earn greater returns. However, when the pressures for agricultural credit increased in rural areas, many country banks had to sell securities and call in their loans to city banks in the nation's financial centers to come up with the necessary funds. Thus, when the reserve demands of country banks were larger than expected, security prices in leading financial centers plummeted due to massive sell-offs of bank-held securities. Panic selling by other investors soon followed, leading to chaos in the marketplace.

The banking system clearly needed a lender of ready cash to provide liquidity to those banks with heavy cash drains and to protect the stability of the financial system. A serious financial panic in 1907 finally led to the creation of the Federal Reserve System. In 1908, Congress created the National Monetary Commission to study the financial needs of the nation. The commission's recommendations were forwarded to Congress and ultimately resulted in passage of the Federal Reserve Act, signed into law by President Wilson in December 1913. The Federal Reserve banks opened for business as World War I began in Europe.

The Early Structure of the Federal Reserve

The first Federal Reserve System was quite different from the Fed of today. The original Federal Reserve Act reflected a mix of diverse viewpoints: an effort to reconcile competing political and economic interests. There was great fear that the Fed would have too much control over financial affairs and operate against the best interest of important segments of U.S. society. For example, small businesses, consumer groups, and farmers were concerned that the Fed might pursue restrictive credit policies, leading to high interest rates. In addition, it was recognized that the Federal Reserve would become a major financial institution wherever it was located. Any city that housed a Federal Reserve bank was likely to become a major financial center.

Responding to these various needs and interest groups, Congress created a truly "decentralized" central bank. Not 1 but 12 Federal Reserve banks were chartered, stretching across the continental United States. Each Reserve bank was assigned its own district, over which it possessed important regulatory powers. A supervisory board of seven members was set up in Washington, DC, to provide oversight of the actions taken by the 12 District banks. In practice, this supervisory board was ineffectual. The Federal Reserve District banks retained all of the essential decision-making authority within the early Fed's system and operated independently.

Goals and Policy Tools of the Fed

To deal with the financial problems of that day, the Federal Reserve Act permitted each regional Reserve bank to open a *discount window* where eligible banks could borrow reserves for short periods of time. However, borrowing banks were required to present high-quality, short-term business loans (commercial paper) to secure the loans they needed. The Fed's chief policy tool of the day was the *discount rate* charged on these loans, with each Reserve bank having the authority to set its own rate. By varying this rate, the Reserve banks could encourage or discourage banks' propensity to discount commercial paper and borrow reserves. Central bankers could promote easy or tight credit conditions and influence the overall volume of bank loans.

The Federal Reserve banks were given authority to issue their own paper notes to serve as a circulating currency, but these notes had to be 100 percent backed by Fed holdings of commercial paper plus a 40 percent gold reserve. Almost as an after-thought, Congress authorized the Reserve banks to trade U.S. government securities in the open market, known as *open market operations,* in order to give the Reserve banks a source of revenue to cover their operating costs. (Today these open market operations are the Fed's principal monetary policy tool.) Reserve requirements were imposed on deposits held by member banks of the system, but the Fed could not readily change these requirements.

Slowly but surely, economic, financial, and political forces combined to amend the original Federal Reserve Act and remake the character and methods of the central bank. The leading causes of change were war, economic recessions, and more recently, inflation. For example, to combat economic recession, fight wars, and pursue desired programs, the U.S. government issued billions of dollars in debt. As the debt began to grow, it seemed only "logical" to permit greater use of U.S. government securities in the Federal Reserve's operations. Banks were authorized to use government securities as backing for loans from the Fed's discount window. The Fed itself was called on to play a major role in stabilizing the market for U.S. government securities to ensure that the Treasury would have little difficulty in refinancing its maturing debt. Government securities were made eligible as collateral for the issue of new Federal Reserve bank notes.

More than any other historical event, however, it was the Great Depression of the 1930s that changed the character of the Federal Reserve. Faced with the collapse of the banking system and unprecedented unemployment—roughly a quarter of the U.S. labor force was thrown out of work during the 1930s—Congress entrusted the Fed with sweeping monetary powers as a result of the passage of the Banking Acts of 1933 and 1935. Significant changes also were made in the central bank's operating structure and lines of authority.

The seven-member Board of Governors in Washington, DC, became the central administrative and policymaking group for the Fed. Thereafter, any changes in discount rates charged by the Reserve banks had to be approved in advance by the Board of

Governors. The Board was granted authority to set minimum reserve requirements on deposits and maximum interest rates that banks could pay on those deposits. To control speculative buying of stocks, the Reserve Board was empowered to set margin requirements specifying what proportion of a security's market value the investor could borrow to buy that security. Recognizing that open market operations in U.S. government securities were rapidly becoming the Fed's main policy tool, a powerful policymaking body—the Federal Open Market Committee—was created in 1935 to oversee the conduct of open market operations. In summary, the Great Depression brought about a *concentration of power* within the Federal Reserve System so that the Fed could pursue unified policies and speak with one voice concerning monetary affairs.

12.5 How the Fed Is Organized Today

Board of Governors

The Federal Reserve System today has an organizational structure that resembles a *pyramid.* As Exhibit 12.3 shows, the apex of the pyramid is the **Board of Governors,** the Federal Reserve's chief policymaking and administrative group. At the middle level of the pyramid are the Federal Reserve District banks, which carry out system policy and provide essential services to banks and other depository financial institutions in their particular district and the Federal Open Market Committee. The bottom of the pyramid contains the member banks of the system, which the Fed supervises and regulates, and the manager of the System Open Market Account, who is responsible for buying and selling securities to achieve the goals of Fed monetary policy.

The Board of Governors

The key administrative body within the Federal Reserve System is the Board of Governors. The board consists of seven persons appointed by the president of the United States and confirmed by the Senate for maximum 14-year terms. Terms of office are staggered, with one board member's appointment ending every even-numbered year. When a member of the Federal Reserve Board resigns or dies, the president may appoint a new person to complete the remainder of the unexpired term, and that member may be reappointed to a subsequent full term. However, no member who completes a full term can be reappointed to the Board of Governors. The president designates one member of the board as its chairperson and another as vice chairperson, and both serve four-year terms in those positions. In selecting new board members, the president is required to seek a fair representation of the financial, agricultural,

See Board of Governors at federalreserve.gov for additional information about the Federal Reserve Board.

EXHIBIT 12.3

How the Federal Reserve System Is Organized

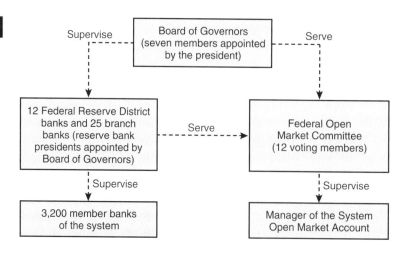

industrial, and commercial interests and geographical divisions of the country and may not choose more than one member from any one Federal Reserve district.

The powers of the Federal Reserve Board are extensive. The board sets reserve requirements on deposits held by depository institutions subject to its rules; reviews and determines the discount rate charged on loans to depository institutions; sets margin requirements on the public's purchases of securities; and provides leadership in the conduct of open market operations through the Federal Open Market Committee. Besides its monetary policy functions, the Board supervises the activities of the 12 Reserve District banks and has supervisory and regulatory control over member banks of the system. It regulates financial holding companies, foreign banks entering the United States, and the overseas activities of U.S. banks.

In principle, the Board is independent of both legislative and executive branches of the federal government. This independence is supported by terms of office much longer than the president's (up to 14 years) and by the fact that the Fed does not depend on the U.S. Congress for operating funds. The Federal Reserve supports itself from revenue generated by selling its services (such as clearing checks), making loans through the discount window, and earning interest on its considerable holdings of U.S. government securities. (In August 2004, the Fed held approximately 9 percent of the $7.3 trillion in U.S. government debt.) These monies are not retained by the Fed, because it is operated in the public interest and not for profit. All monies left over after expenses, dividends paid to member banks, and minimal allocations to equity reserves are transferred to the U.S. Treasury to help reduce tax collections from the private sector. For example, recently the Fed reported the following information about its sources of income and expense:

Income and Expense Statement for the Federal Reserve Banks	
Total income of the Federal Reserve banks in 2003	$23.792 billion*
Principal sources of the Fed's income:	
Interest income from securities held in the Fed's portfolio	$22.602 billion
Fees charged for Fed services (such as check clearings, wire transfers, etc.)	$887 million
Miscellaneous income from loans and other sources	$303 million
Expenses of operating the Federal Reserve System	$2.366 billion

*Of this amount, $21.997 billion was transferred to the United States Treasury Department.

The Federal Open Market Committee

Federal Open Market Committee (FOMC)

Aside from the Federal Reserve Board, the other key policymaking group within the system is the **Federal Open Market Committee (FOMC).** It has been called the most important committee of individuals in the United States because its decisions concerning the conduct of monetary policy and the cost and availability of credit affect the lives of millions of people. Membership on the FOMC consists of the seven members of the Federal Reserve Board and the presidents or first vice presidents of the Reserve banks. Only the seven members of the Board and five of the Reserve bank presidents or their representatives may vote when a final decision is reached on the future conduct of monetary policy, however. The president of the Federal Reserve Bank of New York is a permanent voting member of the FOMC, the presidents of the Chicago and Cleveland Federal Reserve banks alternate in filling one other voting seat, and the remaining three voting positions on the FOMC are rotated annually among the presidents of the nine remaining Federal Reserve

The Federal Open Market Committee—known as the FOMC—is widely followed by active investors around the globe. Greater understanding on why the FOMC is so important to interest rates and credit conditions may be found in such Web sites as federalreserve.gov/fomc and through the publications of the Federal Reserve Bank of New York at ny.frb.org

banks. Each Reserve bank representative occupying a rotating seat serves a voting term of one year.

By tradition, the chairperson of the Federal Reserve Board and the president of the New York Federal Reserve bank serve as chairperson and vice chairperson of the FOMC. The law stipulates that the FOMC will meet in Washington, DC, at least four times a year. In practice, however, the committee meets about eight times a year and more frequently if emergencies develop. Between regularly scheduled meetings, telephone conferences may occur, and the members of the FOMC may be asked to cast votes by telephone or telegram. FOMC meetings are *not* open to the public because confidential financial information frequently is discussed and also because the Fed wants to avoid sending false signals to the financial marketplace. Only Federal Reserve Board members, selected board staff, the Reserve bank presidents and their aides, and the manager and deputy manager of the System Open Market Account are permitted to attend FOMC meetings. A brief summary of the policy decisions taken at these meetings is immediately available to the public and minutes of FOMC meetings are released with a lag of approximately two months after a meeting is held.

The name Federal Open Market Committee implies that this committee's sole concern is with the conduct of Federal Reserve open market operations in securities. In fact, the FOMC reviews current economic and financial conditions and considers *all* aspects of monetary policy at its meetings. It also cooperates with the U.S. Treasury in protecting the dollar in the foreign exchange markets. Once a consensus is reached concerning the appropriate future course for monetary policy, a directive is given to the manager of the System Open Market Account (SOMA), who is a vice president of the Federal Reserve Bank of New York. The SOMA manager is told in general terms how open market operations should be conducted in the weeks ahead and what the FOMC's targets are, especially for the federal funds interest rate attached to overnight loans of reserves between banks. Decisions made by the FOMC and actions of the SOMA manager at the securities trading desk in New York are binding on the entire Federal Reserve System.

The Federal Reserve Banks

Federal Reserve bank

When the Federal Reserve System was created in 1913, the nation was divided into 12 districts, with one **Federal Reserve bank** in each district responsible for supervising and providing services to the member banks located there. Reserve banks were established in the cities of Atlanta, Boston, Chicago, Cleveland, Dallas, Kansas City, Minneapolis, New York, Philadelphia, Richmond, San Francisco, and St. Louis. In addition, 24 branches (later expanded to 25) were created to serve particular regions within the 12 districts.

Using computers and high-speed sorting machines, the regional Reserve banks route checks and other cash items drawn on financial institutions in one city and deposited in another city back to the institutions on which they were drawn for proper crediting of the amounts involved. Although the Fed processes only about 40 percent of all checks written in the United States, it still handles billions of checks and other paper items that reflect billions of transactions carried out by businesses and individuals each year. Recently, the volume of paper checks and other paper cash items handled by the Fed has been declining, however, as the public has been gradually switching to electronic means of payment and electronic *images* of checks now travel between many depository institutions rather than paper checks themselves.

The Federal Reserve maintains an electronic network (known as FEDWIRE), which transfers millions of dollars daily in money and securities among banking institutions in the United States that maintain reserves or clearing accounts with the Fed. Approximately 30 automated clearinghouses (ACHs) are operated by the Reserve banks and their branches to handle the direct deposit of payrolls, mortgage payments, and other funds transfer requests electronically. The Reserve banks fulfill requests from commercial banks and other depository institutions to both ship currency and coin to them at those times when the public needs more pocket money and store excess currency and coin when less pocket money is needed.

The Reserve banks serve as the federal government's *fiscal agent*. This involves keeping the financial accounts of the U.S. Treasury, delivering and redeeming U.S. government securities, and conducting auctions of newly issued U.S. government debt (centered in the Federal Reserve Bank of New York). The Reserve banks also accept deposits for federal income, excise, and unemployment taxes. In addition to serving as the federal government's fiscal agent, the Reserve banks closely supervise the activities of member banks within their districts. They conduct field examinations of all state-chartered member banks and supervise bank holding companies headquartered in their region.

The Reserve banks play a significant role in the conduct of money and credit policy. Each Reserve bank houses a research division to study regional economic and financial developments and conveys this information to the Board of Governors and to the Federal Open Market Committee. Only 5 of the 12 Reserve banks have voting seats on the FOMC, but all 12 Reserve bank presidents or first vice presidents attend FOMC meetings to report on conditions in their district and give their views on the appropriate course for monetary policy. The Reserve banks also administer the discount windows where loans are made to financial institutions in their district.

Each Federal Reserve bank is a corporation chartered by Congress. Officially, the Reserve banks are owned by the member banks of their districts, which select a majority of each bank's board of directors. Each Reserve bank president is nominated by that Reserve bank's board of directors, and the appointment is confirmed or denied by the Federal Reserve Board. Under federal law, the board of directors of each Federal Reserve bank must consist of nine directors, six elected by bankers in the district (with three of these directors representing bankers and three the general public or nonbank interests in the same district) and three directors selected by the Federal Reserve Board. The regional Reserve banks are closely controlled by the Federal Reserve Board, which not only reviews officer appointments but also may remove any officer or director of a Federal Reserve bank and examine, reorganize, or even liquidate a Reserve bank if this appears to be necessary to serve the public interest.

Although under the terms of the original Federal Reserve Act the Reserve banks could set the discount rate on loans to depository institutions, these rate changes must now be approved by the Federal Reserve Board in Washington. The regional banks are required to participate in all open market transactions on behalf of the system. These purchases and sales are carried out through the FOMC at the Federal Reserve Bank of New York, but the Reserve banks must provide the securities needed for open market sales and must also take their *pro rata* share of any security purchases the Federal Reserve System makes. As Exhibit 12.4 reveals, the Federal Reserve banks collectively held almost $711 billion in securities—their principal asset—and had issued $701 billion in Federal Reserve notes—the principal circulating currency of the United States and the principal liability of the Federal Reserve banks—in August 2004.

The Member Banks of the Federal Reserve System

member banks

The **member banks** of the Federal Reserve System consist of national banks, which are required to join the system, and state-chartered banks that agree to conform to the Fed's rules. Today, Federal Reserve member banks constitute a minority of all U.S. banks, about 40 percent of the total. There are about 2,000 national banks and about 900 state-chartered banks registered as members of the Federal Reserve System, compared to approximately 4,800 nonmember banks.

The issue of central bank independence from government has become a center of controversy in recent years. Studies by Alesina (1988) and Bade and Parkin (1987) found a significant negative correlation between the inflation rate experienced by leading industrial countries and the degree of independence from the political process enjoyed by their central banks. For example, between 1974 and 1990, Germany and Switzerland, whose central banks were operating under greater freedom from government control than most other nations, had average annual inflation rates of only about 3.5 percent, while Italy, whose central bank appeared to be more closely tied to the Italian government, experienced a 12.4 percent annual inflation rate during that period. Some researchers concluded that economies generally perform better where central banks enjoy greater independence from government because there is a strong political temptation to overissue money (thereby igniting inflation) in order to fund extravagant government programs.

The independence from government control enjoyed by central banks varies widely around the world. In the new European Central Bank, board members have eight-year terms, but the ECB has the additional protection that its charter cannot be changed without the unanimous vote of all member nations. In the United States, members of the Federal Reserve's Board of Governors can serve for up to 14 years, which limits the power of Congress or the president to alter Fed policy in the short run. Moreover, the Federal Reserve does not depend upon Congress for income—it generates its own revenues through security trading and service fees.

Several bills have been introduced in the U.S. Congress in recent years to restrict the freedom of action of the Fed. One proposal would expand the authority of the Government Accounting Office (GAO) to audit *all* phases of Federal Reserve operations. Another proposal would require congressional approval of anyone who wishes to serve as president of a Federal Reserve Bank.

Still another proposed change calls for denying Federal Reserve bank presidents any voting seats on the Federal Open Market Committee (FOMC), the Fed's chief policymaking body. There has even been a call for videotaping FOMC meetings as is now done for many congressional sessions and court trials. Recent presidential administrations have proposed stripping the Fed of its bank examination functions in order to allow it to concentrate on money and credit policy. For its part, the Fed has argued that these changes would render monetary policy less effective.

Some experts have argued that the whole structure of the Fed needs revamping in an age of electronics, with the banking system increasingly dominated by a few huge banks. They argue that some of the Federal Reserve banks are no longer needed and should be closed. The current geographic distribution of the Federal Reserve banks does not fully reflect the vast population shifts that have occurred in the United States since the Fed was founded in 1914. In an era of computers and satellite communications, the Fed's vast network of banks and branches *may* be an increasingly inefficient system. However, the Fed argues that many of its regional offices will likely always be needed to provide convenient services to local areas and to monitor regional conditions.

See, for example, Alberto Alesina, "Macroeconomics and Politics," in *NBER Macroeconomic Annual, 1988* (Cambridge, MA: MIT Press, 1988); and Robin Bade and Michael Parkin, "Central Bank Laws and Monetary Policy," Unpublished Mimeograph, Department of Economics, University of Western Ontario, 1987.

The structure of the Federal Reserve System is also discussed at some length at banx.com

Member banks must subscribe to the stock of the Reserve bank in their district in an amount equal to 6 percent of their paid-in capital and surplus accounts. However, only half of this amount must actually be paid, with the rest payable on call. Member banks are bound by Federal Reserve rules regarding capital, deposits, loans, branch operations, formation of holding companies, and policies regarding the conduct of officers and boards of directors. These banks are subject to supervision and examination by the Federal Reserve at any time. Moreover, member banks must hold reserves behind their deposits at levels specified by the Federal Reserve Board.

A number of important privileges are granted to member banks. Legally, they are "owners" of the Federal Reserve banks because they hold the stock of these institutions and elect six of their nine directors. A 6 percent annual dividend is paid to member banks on their holdings of Federal Reserve bank stock. Member banks may borrow reserves

Federal Reserve Board Chairman Alan Greenspan is once reported to have said, "Since I became a central banker, I have learned to mumble with great coherence."

In recent years, the Federal Reserve (along with selected other central banks around the world) has attempted to achieve greater **transparency** in its monetary policy deliberations and in the policy decisions that it makes. The Fed's aim is to make monetary policymakers' intentions about current and future policy clear ("transparent") to the public. The central bank believes that greater openness about what it is doing and why will help minimize the waste of resources caused by market players' decisions that may be misguided or may result from people trying to protect themselves against uncertain future monetary policies that they do not understand and cannot predict. In brief, if money and credit policy is truly "transparent," then borrowers and lenders should be informed enough that they come to expect the *same* policy actions as the policymaker does.

To achieve greater transparency, the Federal Reserve releases a brief statement to the press at the close of each of its FOMC meetings (which is immediately made available on the Web site of the Board of Governors of the Federal Reserve System at **federalreserve.gov**). The Fed's press release summarizes the decisions of the FOMC and the major issues of concern that could affect future policy decisions. These statements are *always* released, even if there is no change in the current stance of monetary policy. A transcript of the actual minutes of FOMC meetings is then made available with a lag of about two months following each policy meeting.

The Federal Reserve's move toward greater transparency has been mirrored by many other central banks around the world, including the Bank of England, the ECB, and especially the Bank of Japan (BOJ). The BOJ has adopted a very detailed approach to transparency since the Japanese government granted the bank greater independence just a few years ago. The Bank of Japan Law, passed in 1997, states that "after each Board meeting for monetary control matters, the chairman shall, without delay, prepare a document which contains an outline of the discussion at the meeting in accordance with the decisions made by the Board, and publish the document upon its approval at another Board meeting for monetary control matters." The Bank of Japan has pledged to release the minutes of its policy meetings, to announce to the public its key policy decisions right after each meeting, to publish reports on the Japanese economy each month, and to release schedules for its future policy meetings at least six months in advance. The BOJ's Web site at **boj.or.jp** provides daily reports of its account balances. Collectively, these recent changes suggest the BOJ has become one of the most transparent central banks in the world.

For further discussion, see Carl E. Walsh, "Transparency in Monetary Policy," *FRBSF Economic Letter*, Federal Reserve Bank of San Francisco, September 7, 2001, pp. 1–3.

EXHIBIT 12.4

The Balance Sheet of the Federal Reserve System

Source: Board of Governors of the Federal Reserve System, Release H.4.1(a), August 2004.

Note: End-of-month estimates: slight inaccuracies may exist because of rounding.

*Consolidated for all 12 regional Federal Reserve Banks.

The Federal Reserve System's Consolidated Assets and Liabilities, August 2004* ($ Billions)

Assets		Liabilities and Capital Accounts	
Gold and special drawing rights certificates	$ 13.2	Liabilities:	
		Federal Reserve notes	$700.9
Coins	0.7	Reverse repurchase agreements	20.6
Loans to depository institutions	0.3	Deposits from banks & thrifts	18.4
U.S. government and federal agency securities held	710.7	U.S. Treasury account	5.1
		Foreign and other accounts	0.4
Cash items in process of collection	7.6	Deferred availability cash items	6.5
		Other liabilities	2.4
Other assets	40.7	Capital:	18.9
Total assets	$773.2	Total liabilities and capital	$773.2

through the discount window of the Reserve bank in their district and use the Fed's check-clearing system to process checks and other cash items coming from distant cities. However, this is not an exclusive privilege, because nonmember banks and thrifts may also use the Fed's check-clearing facilities, provided that they agree to maintain a clearing account with the Reserve bank in the region. An intangible benefit of membership is the prestige that comes from belonging to the Federal Reserve System. Many bankers believe that membership in the system attracts large business deposits and correspondent accounts from smaller banks that otherwise might go elsewhere.

QUESTIONS TO HELP YOU STUDY

5. What major problems in the late nineteenth and early twentieth century led to the creation of the Federal Reserve System? How did the creation of the Fed help to solve these problems?

6. In what ways did the early Federal Reserve System differ from the Federal Reserve we see today?

7. What are the principal responsibilities assigned to the *Board of Governors of the Federal Reserve System?* To the *Federal Open Market Committee?*

8. What are the *Federal Reserve banks* expected to do in serving the public and the banking system?

9. What duties are assigned to the *manager of the System Open Market Account?*

10. What is meant by *monetary policy transparency?*

12.6 Roles of the Federal Reserve System Today

In the course of this chapter we have talked about the many roles the Federal Reserve plays in the financial system and how these roles have changed over time. In this section we pull together all of the Fed's responsibilities and roles to give a more complete view of how the central bank interfaces with the financial markets and the banking system.

The Clearing and Collection of Checks and Other Payments Media

As we saw earlier in this chapter, one of the earliest tasks of the Federal Reserve System was to establish a nationwide system for clearing and collecting checks and other cash items. When a depository institution receives a check drawn on another institution in a distant city, it can route this check through the Federal Reserve banks. The Fed credits an account called Deferred Availability Items on behalf of the institution sending in the check and routes that check or an electronic image of the check to the institution on which it was drawn for eventual collection. At the end of a specified period, the depository institution sending in the check will receive credit in its legal reserve account for the amount of that check. Eventually, the check or its image reaches the institution on which it was drawn and is deducted from that institution's reserve account.

Fed check-processing volume and Fed revenues from check-clearing services have been on the decline since the middle to late 1990s. Electronic means of payment (such as debit cards and point-of-sale terminals) have been growing even as check writing has declined and the Federal Reserve has begun closing some of its check-clearing facilities around the United States. Today, in the wake of The Check Clearing for the

21st Century Act (more popularly known as Check 21), the Fed is investing in electronic check-imaging equipment. The Check 21 law, which became effective in October 2004, permits the creation of new negotiable instruments—*substitute checks* that are reproductions of original checks through digital imaging and are the legal equivalents of traditional paper checks—that will further speed the modern payments process.

Issuing Currency and Coin and Related Services

Brief descriptions of Federal Reserve services may be found at kc.frb.org and frbservices.org

The Fed helps to promote an efficient payments mechanism not just through the clearing of checks but also by issuing its own currency in response to public need. Today, nearly all of the paper money in circulation consists of Federal Reserve notes, issued by all 12 of the Reserve banks and backed mainly by Federal Reserve holdings of government securities. These notes are liabilities of the Federal Reserve bank issuing them. In fact, Federal Reserve notes are a lien against the assets of the Fed, payable to the holder in the event the Reserve banks are ever liquidated. When the public demands more currency, financial institutions request a shipment of new currency and coin from the Federal Reserve bank in the region, which maintains an ample supply in its vault. Payment for the shipment is made simply by charging the legal reserve account of the institution requesting the shipment. In the opposite situation, when depository institutions receive deposits of currency and coin from the public beyond what they wish to hold in their vaults, the surplus is shipped back to the Reserve banks. Depository institutions receive credit for these return shipments through an increase in their legal reserve accounts at the Reserve bank.

Prior to 1981, most Federal Reserve services, including the clearing of checks and shipments of currency and coin, were provided free of charge. However, the Depository Institutions Deregulation and Monetary Control Act (DIDMCA) of 1980 required the Fed to assess fees for such services as transportation of currency and coin, check clearing, wire transfer of funds, the use of Federal Reserve automated clearinghouse facilities, and the safekeeping and redemption of government securities. All fees set by the Fed are to be reviewed annually and set at levels that, over the long term, recover the total costs of providing each service. A primary reason for requiring fees for Fed services was to enable private firms offering similar services to compete with the Fed on a more even footing.

Maintaining a Sound Banking and Financial System

Another important function of the Federal Reserve System today is to maintain a sound banking and financial system. It contributes to this goal by serving as a lender of last resort—providing loans of reserves to depository institutions that hold their legal reserve accounts with the Fed through the discount window of each Reserve bank. The window represents a source of funds that can be drawn on without taking reserves away from other banks, and it helps to avoid a liquidity squeeze brought about by sudden changes in economic and financial conditions (as occurred following the terrorist attacks in New York and Washington, DC, on September 11, 2001). The Fed also promotes a sound banking system by regularly examining member banks and bank holding company organizations, reviewing the quality and quantity of their assets and capital and making sure that federal and state laws are followed. These examinations have shifted in recent years to take advantage of modern technology to conduct continuous risk assessments of individual banking organizations and combine both on-site and off-site examinations.

Serving as the Federal Government's Fiscal Agent

fiscal agent

The Fed serves as the government's chief **fiscal agent.** In this role, it holds the Treasury's checking account and clears any checks written against that account.

The Fed supervises the thousands of Treasury Tax and Loan Accounts (TT&L) maintained in banks across the United States, which hold the bulk of the Treasury's cash balances until the Treasury needs these monies for spending. The Fed also makes recurring payments (for example, salary checks for government employees) for the federal government through its electronic network of automated clearinghouses. The Federal Reserve banks receive bids when new Treasury securities are offered and provide securities to the purchasers. They redeem maturing U.S. government securities as well. In general, the Fed is responsible for maintaining reasonable stability in the government securities market so that any new Treasury offerings sell quickly and the government raises the amount of money that it needs.

Providing Information to the Public

Another critical function that the Federal Reserve has performed particularly well in recent years is to provide *information* to the public. Each Reserve bank has its own research staff, and the Board of Governors maintains a large staff of economists who follow current economic and financial developments and recommend changes in policy. The Fed makes available on a daily, weekly, and monthly basis an impressive volume of statistical releases, special reports, and studies concerning the financial markets and the condition of the economy. This information function is one of the more important contributions of the central bank.

Carrying Out Monetary Policy

monetary policy

The most critical job of the Federal Reserve is to carry out **monetary policy.** Monetary policy may be defined as the use of various tools by the central bank to control the availability of loanable funds in an effort to achieve national economic goals, such as full employment and reasonable price stability. The policy tools reserved for the Federal Reserve include deposit reserve requirements, discount rates, open market operations, and margin requirements on purchases of securities. We will examine the Fed's policy tools in detail in Chapter 13.

QUESTIONS TO HELP YOU STUDY

11. List the principal *functions* of the Federal Reserve System today and explain why each of these functions is important.

12. What is the Federal Reserve's *primary job* (that is, its principal role or function)?

13. When we use the term *ECB*, what is meant?

14. How is the ECB *similar* to the Federal Reserve and in what ways is it *different* from the Fed?

15. Explain why the ECB is likely to be one of the world's most important central banks.

12.7   The Key Focus of Central Bank Monetary Policy: Interest Rates, Reserves, and Money

If the Federal Reserve's most critical job is *monetary policy*—regulating money and credit conditions in an effort to strengthen the economy—what target or targets does the Fed pursue in order to impact the money and capital markets and, ultimately, the economy as a whole?

Today the principal target of most central banks around the globe is *market interest rates,* pushing them higher in order to slow borrowing and spending in the economy and pushing them lower if the economy needs to grow faster. However, to impact market interest rates the Federal Reserve and other central banks must have a "lever" to pull—a device or tool to use over which the central bank has relatively close control.

The central bank's "lever"—its principal immediate monetary policy target—is usually *the volume of legal reserves available to the banking system.* In the United States, these consist mainly of deposits held at the Federal Reserve banks plus currency and coin held in bank vaults. These reserves are the raw material out of which banks and other depository institutions create credit and cause the money supply to grow. And because the growth of the money supply appears to be closely linked to changes in income, production, prices, and employment, the Federal Reserve and other central banks pay close attention on a daily basis to fluctuations in the quantity of reserves that depository institutions have at their disposal. The total supply of reserves can be changed directly by open market operations—the Federal Reserve's principal policy tool and a growing central bank tool worldwide—and by making loans to depository institutions through the central bank's credit or discount window. The Fed also can exert a powerful effect on the growth of money and credit by changing the legal reserve requirements applicable to deposits held by depository institutions.

Central banks like the Fed can nudge market interest rates in any desired direction by manipulating the legal reserve balances with which depository institutions work. When the supply of reserves is reduced relative to the demand for reserves, interest rates tend to rise as scarce funds are rationed among competing financial institutions. Conversely, an expansion in the supply of reserves usually leads to lower interest rates because of the increased availability of loanable funds. Why do these changes occur? What are the specific links between bank reserves and the money supply?

12.8 Reserve Composition and the Deposit and Money Multipliers

To answer the preceding questions, we need to look closely at what makes up the supply of reserves at depository institutions. All U.S. depository institutions offering selected kinds of deposits are required to hold a small percentage of those deposits in an asset account known as **legal reserves.** Legal reserves in the United States consist of the amount of deposits each institution keeps with the Federal Reserve bank in its district plus the amount of currency and coin held in its vault. (Other central banks often include other types of assets in their definitions of legal reserves—for example, government securities.)

legal reserves

Legal reserves may be divided into two parts: *required reserves* and *excess reserves.* In particular,

$$\text{Total legal reserves} = \text{Required reserves} + \text{Excess reserves} \qquad (12.1)$$

In the United States,

$$\text{Total legal reserves} = \begin{array}{c}\text{Deposits at the} \\ \text{Federal Reserve} \\ \text{banks}\end{array} + \begin{array}{c}\text{Vault cash held on the} \\ \text{premises of depository} \\ \text{institutions}\end{array} \qquad (12.2)$$

required reserves

excess reserves

Required reserves are those holdings of cash and deposits at the Fed that a depository institution *must* hold to back the public's deposits. **Excess reserves** are the amount of reserves left over after we deduct required reserves from total legal reserves. Excess reserves may be used to make loans, purchase securities, or for other purposes. Because legal reserve assets earn no interest income, most depository institutions try to keep their excess reserves close to zero. For example, the largest banks today frequently run reserve deficits and must borrow additional legal reserves in the money market to avoid costly penalties. The actual composition of legal reserves—that is, the exact proportion of deposits at the Federal Reserve versus vault cash—is left up to individual depository institutions to decide. Unlike larger depository institutions, the majority of small banks and other depositories meet their reserve requirements entirely with vault cash.

The Deposit Multiplier

The distinction between excess and required reserves is important because it plays a key role in the growth of money and credit in the economy. Depository institutions offering checkable (transaction) deposits have the unique ability to create and destroy deposits—which are the bulk of the money supply—at the stroke of a pen or, in today's world, the press of a computer key. Although an individual depository institution cannot create more deposit money than the volume of excess reserves it holds, the banking system as a whole can create a multiple amount of deposit money from any given injection of reserves by using its excess reserves to make loans and purchase securities.

deposit multiplier

How much in deposits can the banking system create if it has excess reserves available? The banking system's deposit-creating potential can be estimated using a concept known as the **deposit multiplier,** or coefficient of deposit expansion. The deposit multiplier indicates how many dollars of deposits (and loans) will result from any given injection of new excess legal reserves into the financial system. If we assume the existence of a very simple financial system in which the public makes all of its payments by writing a check or by swiping a debit card through an electronic reader, automatically transferring money out of its checkable deposit account, and does not convert any checkbook (transaction deposit) money into savings deposits and in which depository institutions do not wish to hold any excess reserves, then the transaction (checkable) deposit multiplier is

$$\frac{1}{\text{Reserve requirement on transaction deposits}} \qquad (12.3)$$

For example, if the Federal Reserve insists that depository institutions keep $0.12 in required reserves for each new dollar of transaction (checkbook) deposits they receive, the deposit multiplier must be 1/0.12, or 8.33.

Then how much in new deposit money can the banking system create under these circumstances? If all depository institutions continually make loans with any excess reserves they receive, the maximum amount of new deposits (and loans) that can be created by the entire banking system may be found from the following equation:

$$\frac{\text{Transaction deposit}}{\text{multiplier}} \times \frac{\text{Excess}}{\text{reserves}} = \begin{array}{c} \text{Maximum volume} \\ \text{of new deposits} \\ \text{and loans} \end{array} \qquad (12.4)$$

If banks and other depository institutions receive additional excess reserves in the amount of $1 million and the reserve requirement behind transaction deposits is 12 percent, we have the following:

$$1/0.12 \times \$1 \text{ million} = 8.33 \times \$1 \text{ million}$$
$$= \$8.33 \text{ million in new deposits and loans}$$

A *withdrawal* of reserves from depository institutions can work in the opposite direction, destroying deposits and loans. For example, a withdrawal of deposits by the public that causes depository institutions to have a $1 million deficiency in their required legal reserves would eventually lead to an $8.33 million *decline* in deposits, assuming a 12 percent reserve requirement.

Of course, the real world is quite different from the simple deposit expansion model outlined above. Leakages of funds from the banking system greatly reduce the size of the deposit multiplier, so that its actual value is probably somewhat less than 2. Among the most important leakages are the public's desire to convert some portion of new checkbook money into pocket money (currency and coin) or into other liquid assets, such as savings and time deposits and money market funds. Banks may also choose to hold substantial excess reserves rather than lend out all their excess funds, either because they cannot find enough qualified borrowers or because they wish to hold a protective "cushion" of reserves to meet unexpected withdrawals.

These various leakages of funds from transaction or checkable deposit balances suggest the need for a slightly more complex model of the deposit and loan expansion process. In this model, the deposit multiplier would be represented by the following expression:

$$\begin{array}{c}\text{Transaction deposit multiplier}\\\text{assuming drains of funds}\\\text{into cash and other liquid}\\\text{assets and excess reserves}\end{array} = \frac{1}{RR_D + LA + EXR} \qquad (12.5)$$

In this instance, RR_D represents the required legal reserve ratio for transaction (demand) accounts[2]; *LA* represents the amount of additional currency and coin and other liquid assets the public wishes to hold for each dollar of new transaction deposits they receive; and *EXR* stands for the quantity of excess reserves depository institutions desire to hold for precautionary purposes out of each dollar of new transaction deposits. The largest amount of transaction (checkable) deposits and loans that the banking system can create, assuming all of the above drains of funds occur, would be given by:

$$\frac{1}{RR_D + LA + EXR} \times \begin{array}{c}\text{Excess}\\\text{reserves}\end{array} = \begin{array}{c}\text{Maximum volume}\\\text{of new deposits}\\\text{and loans}\end{array} \qquad (12.6)$$

To illustrate the use of this formula, assume that depository institutions have just received an additional $1 million in excess reserves from some source outside the banking system. (One possible source is the central bank lowering deposit reserve requirements or buying securities from the public.) We further assume that, for each new dollar of transaction (checkable) deposits received, the public will convert $0.60 into cash and other short-term liquid assets (*LA* = 0.60). Further, suppose depository institutions elect to hold $0.05 of every new checkable deposit dollar received as excess

---

[2]Today only transaction deposits carry legal reserve requirements imposed by the Federal Reserve Board in the United States. Time and savings deposits at banks and other depository institutions carry zero reserve requirements, although the Federal Reserve Board retains authority to reimpose reserve requirements on nonpersonal (business) time deposits at any time that conditions seem to warrant that change. Such a reimposition of legal reserve requirements on time accounts seems unlikely, however, because the Fed decided some time ago that legal reserve requirements represented a heavy "tax" on bank reserves that, in some instances, threatened the competitiveness of deposits compared to other forms of liquid assets sold to the public. In Equation 12.5 and the equations that follow, time and savings deposits offered by banks and other depositories are included in the term *LA* (liquid assets).

reserves *(EXR = 0.05)* to protect against future contingencies. The reserve requirement on transaction deposits (RR_D) is assumed to be 10 percent. Thus, the maximum amount of new deposits and loans that depository institutions as a group can create with $1 million in excess reserves is calculated as follows:

$$\frac{1}{0.10 \; + \; 0.60 \; + \; 0.05} \times \$1 \text{ million} \; = \; \frac{1}{0.75} \times \$1 \text{ million}$$

$$= 1.33 \times \$1 \text{ million}$$

$$= \$1.33 \text{ million in new deposits and loans}$$

Clearly, the deposit multiplier is far smaller when we allow for the conversion of checkable deposits into currency, coin, and other liquid assets, and when banks and other depository institutions are unwilling to lend all of their excess reserves. This would appear to be good news for the central bank charged with controlling the growth of the money supply. A numerically small deposit multiplier implies that the banking system will not be able to significantly increase the size of the deposit money supply unless the supply of excess reserves is also greatly increased.

Unfortunately the existence of cash drains, time and savings deposits, and other reserve-absorbing factors, while reducing the size of the deposit multiplier, also make forecasting deposit flows much more difficult. The central bank must be constantly alert to shifts in the public's demand (preferences) for currency and coin and other liquid assets as well as to the changing demands of depository institutions for excess reserves. If the central bank cannot accurately forecast changes in the public's money preferences, control of the money supply and the supply of credit will be less precise, so that the achievement of economic goals will be more difficult for a central bank.

The Money Multiplier

money multiplier

Although the concept of the deposit multiplier is useful for some purposes, central bankers are usually more interested in a related concept known as the **money multiplier,** which defines the relationship between a measure of the money supply that is closely related to spending and income in the economy. The most important measure of the money supply is M2, which includes transaction deposits, currency and coin, and other liquid assets held principally by households (such as savings and time deposits and shares in money market funds) and the size of the total reserve base available to depository institutions. The money multiplier is defined as follows:

$$\text{Money multiplier} \; = \; \frac{1 \, + \, \text{LA}}{\text{RR}_D \, + \, \text{LA} \, + \, \text{EXR}} \qquad \textbf{(12.7)}$$

The terms *LA*, *EXR*, and RR_D are defined as they were in the deposit multiplier formula.

We note that the money multiplier differs from the deposit multiplier only in the addition of *LA*—the proportion of new transaction deposits the public desires to hold in the form of currency and coin and other liquid assets—to the numerator of the multiplier ratio. This change is made because these assets also form an important component of the money supply and must be accounted for in measuring how fast the money supply grows over time.

An important point to note about currency and coin is that fluctuations in the volume held by the public have a direct bearing on the reserves held by depository institutions, affecting both the size and rate of growth of transaction accounts and reserves. If the public desires to hold less pocket money, the excess currency and coin typically

The U.S. money supply and the monetary base are key indicators for the economy and the Federal Reserve System and are actively followed on such Web sites as stls.frb.org/research and federalreserve. gov/releases

monetary base

is redeposited in transaction accounts, increasing both reserves and demand deposits. Recognizing this important link between currency and bank reserves, economists have developed the concept of the **monetary base,** which is simply the sum of legal reserves plus the amount of currency and coin held by the public.

Why is the monetary base important? It is one of the principal determinants of the nation's money supply. Specifically,

$$\text{Money Multiplier} \times \text{Monetary base} = \text{Money supply}$$

or,

$$\frac{1 + \text{LA}}{\text{RR}_\text{D} + \text{LA} + \text{EXR}} \times \frac{\text{Monetary}}{\text{base}} = \frac{\text{Money}}{\text{supply}} \qquad (12.8)$$

We may use this formula as a device to estimate the size of the money multiplier. For example, at year-end 2003 the U.S. monetary base was about $750 billion and the M2 money-supply measure was $6,100 billion. The money multiplier was as follows:

$$\text{Money multiplier} = \$6,100 \text{ billion}/\$750 \text{ billion} = 8.13$$

On average, each $1 increase in the monetary base resulted in a rise in the M2 measure of the U.S. money supply of about $8.13. This is one reason the monetary base is often referred to as *high-powered money;* a change in the base, working through the money multiplier, produces a magnified change in the nation's money supply.

The monetary base–money multiplier relationship identifies the most important factors that explain changes in the money supply, and it also helps us understand how a central bank like the Federal Reserve System can influence the money and credit creation process. In the United States, the Fed is one of the principal determinants of the size of the monetary base, along with the public and the U.S. Treasury, since the monetary base includes most of the liabilities of the Fed. It can increase or decrease the total supply of reserves to change the size of that base. Alternatively, the Fed may choose merely to offset actions taken by the public or the Treasury to keep the size of the monetary base unchanged. Finally, the central bank can change the required reserve ratios behind deposits, which will affect the magnitude of the money multiplier. Occasionally, when the central bank wishes to exert a potent impact on economic and financial conditions, it makes changes in *both* the monetary base and the money multiplier. In the next chapter, we take a close look at the tools the Federal Reserve System uses to influence the size of the monetary base, the money multiplier, and, ultimately, the nation's supply and cost of money and credit.

QUESTIONS TO HELP YOU STUDY

16. What is/are the principal target(s) of monetary policy?

17. What are *legal reserves? Required reserves? Excess reserves?* Why are these concepts important?

18. Why are deposit-type intermediaries able to create money? What factors increase the deposits the banking system can create with any given injection of new reserves?

19. What factors *reduce* the *money-creating abilities of the banking system?*

20. In what ways can a central bank influence the *money and credit creation process?*

21. Why should a central bank like the Federal Reserve worry about money and credit growth?

MARKETS ON THE NET: The Most Important Web Sites for This Chapter

Bank of England (bankofengland.gov)
Bank of Japan (boj.ur.jp)
Board of Governors of the Federal Reserve System (federalreserve.gov)
Center for the Study of Central Banks (law.nyu.edu/centralbankscenter)
European Central Bank (ecb.int)
Federal Open Market Committee (federalreserve.gov/fomc)

Federal Reserve Services (frbservices.org)
Federal Reserve Bank of New York (ny.frb.org)
Federal Reserve Releases (federalreserve.gov/releases)
Reserve Bank of New Zealand (rbnz.govt.nz)

Summary of the Chapter's Main Points

In this chapter, we have examined the important roles played by *central banks* in the global financial system and the economy.

- Central banks function to control the money and credit supply, maintain stable conditions in the financial markets, serve as a lender of last resort to aid financial institutions in trouble, and maintain and improve the mechanism for making payments for purchases of goods and services.

- In most industrialized countries, central banking is *goal-oriented,* aimed principally at the major economic goals of reasonable stability in the prices of goods and services (i.e., the avoidance of significant inflation) and sustainable economic growth. In the Western world, central banks operate to achieve the foregoing goals principally by working in the *private financial marketplace,* influencing credit conditions but leaving to private borrowers and lenders the basic decision of whether to create credit, borrow, or spend.

- Central banks appear to influence the spending, saving, and borrowing decisions of millions of individuals and businesses through at least five interrelated *channels*—the cost and availability of credit, the volume and rate of growth of the money supply, the market value of assets held by the public, the relative prices of global currencies, and the public's expectations regarding domestic and international economic conditions.

- The central bank of the United States is the *Federal Reserve System.* Its chief administrative body is the *Board of Governors,* which controls such important policy tools as deposit reserve requirements, margin requirements on purchasing stocks and other securities, and changes in the discount rate on loans made by the Fed to depository institutions.

- Another important policymaking unit within the Federal Reserve System is the *Federal Open Market Committee (FOMC),* composed of the seven members of the Federal Reserve Board and the presidents of the 12 Federal Reserve banks, which oversees the use of the Fed's chief monetary policy tool—*open market operations.*

- The 12 *Federal Reserve District banks* represent the Fed's regional presence across the United States. These banks supervise private banks and financial holding companies within their individual districts, decide which depository institutions can borrow reserves from the Fed, and provide such services as clearing and collecting checks, shipping currency and coin, wiring funds to effect payments, and the safekeeping of securities.

- Each Federal Reserve bank also serves as a *fiscal agent* for the U.S. government and performs such services as dispensing and collecting the government's funds and selling and redeeming government securities.

- The Federal Reserve's most critical task in the financial markets today is the conduct of *monetary policy* in order to achieve the nation's economic goals. Today the Fed primarily targets market interest rates by manipulating the volume of reserves available to the banking system, which, in turn, affect the supply of deposits and money through the *deposit* and *money multipliers.* By creating or absorbing excess reserves available to depository institutions, the central bank can impact the growth and cost of money and credit and, ultimately, the economy as a whole.

Key Terms Appearing in This Chapter

central bank, 354
Federal Reserve System, 354
Board of Governors, 364
Federal Open Market Committee
  (FOMC), 365
Federal Reserve bank, 366
member banks, 367
transparency, 369

fiscal agent, 371
monetary policy, 372
legal reserves, 373
required reserves, 373
excess reserves, 373
deposit multiplier, 374
money multiplier, 376
monetary base, 377

Problems and Issues

1. As discussed in this chapter, the Federal Reserve has two policymaking groups: the Board of Governors and the Federal Open Market Committee (FOMC). Describe the composition of each of these groups, how their members are appointed, and the length of each member's term. What are the particular policy decisions that these two important groups are responsible for?

2. What special status is awarded to the president of the Federal Reserve Bank of New York (FRBNY) in the determination of U.S. monetary policy? Why is this so?

3. In the text it was stated that the FOMC meets eight times each year on preannounced dates in order to set monetary policy. What would happen if an emergency situation developed in the financial markets? Would the Federal Reserve have to wait until the next scheduled FOMC meeting?

4. Suppose the public wishes to hold $0.40 in pocket money (currency and coin) and other liquid assets and $0.15 in excess reserves for each new dollar of money received. If reserve requirements on transaction deposits are 3 percent, what is the size of the deposit multiplier? The money multiplier? Suppose $5 million in new excess reserves appear in the banking system. How much will be created in the form of new deposits and loans?

    Now suppose total legal reserves currently amount to $40 billion, while currency and coin and other liquid assets in public hands total $160 billion. The money supply is $525 billion. How large is the money multiplier?

www.mhhe.com/rose9e

5. Suppose the central bank injects $15 million in new reserves into the banking system and that the current legal reserve requirement on transaction deposits held by the banking system is 8 percent. Moreover, the banking system is perfectly efficient and there are no leakages of funds from that system except for the current legal reserve requirement. Set up an EXCEL spreadsheet that shows how much in total required reserves and new deposits can be created in this banking system as a result of the injection of the $15 million in new legal reserves.

   Now suppose the central bank subsequently withdraws $20 million in legal reserves from this same banking system. What level of deposits and legal reserves would ultimately result? Demonstrate on your EXCEL spreadsheet.

Standard & Poor's Market Insight and Web-Based Problems

1. As we discovered in this chapter, monetary policy operates through the banking system by altering the volume of bank reserves and, thereby, influencing the total quantity of money and credit in the economy and affecting short-term interest rates. However, the banking industry is highly concentrated, with the majority of bank assets held by a relatively small number of the largest banking firms. The purpose of this exercise is to gain insight as to how important the largest banks are in terms of transmitting monetary policy changes to the economy. We will focus here on one measure of the U.S. money supply—M1 (which includes mainly currency in the hands of the public, transaction deposits at depository institutions, and traveler's checks).

   a. Visit the Federal Reserve's Web site at **federalreserve.gov/releases** and look up the following information for December of last year from the Fed's H.6 release—M1 (from Table 1) and "Demand Deposits and Other Checkable Deposits: Total" (from Table 2).

   b. Using the data from part (a) compute the fraction of M1 that is represented by "Transaction Deposits," which are themselves made up of demand deposits and other checkable deposits.

   c. Visit another area in the Fed's Web site at **federalreserve.gov/releases/lbr/current/default.htm** and identify the top 10 commercial banks by size (based on "consolidated assets").

   d. For each of the 10 banks you listed in part (c), go to the S&P's Market Insight database at **mhhe.com/edumarketinsight** and find the annual balance sheets for these banking companies. Look under "Excel Analytics."

   e. For the latest year for which you have information, add up the total "Transaction Deposits" for all of the 10 top banks you have listed.

   f. Construct the ratio of transaction deposits for the top 10 banks (from part [e]) to transaction deposits for all depositories (from part [b]). This number indicates how dominant these top 10 banks are within an industry of close to 8,000 banking firms.

   g. Construct the ratio of transaction deposits for the top 10 banks (from part [e]) to M1 (from part [a]). This number indicates how important these top 10 banks are in determining the U.S. economy's money supply.

2. Traditionally, the most important measure of the U.S. money supply (for the purpose of providing information to the Federal Reserve on how it ought to conduct monetary policy) has been M2. The rationale is that M2 bears the closest long-term relationship with overall economic activity measured by nominal GDP (i.e., total expenditures on goods and services produced inside the United States). The ratio of nominal GDP to M2 is referred to as the "velocity" of M2 to capture how many times each dollar is spent ("turns over") on average during the year. (Note: This exercise is much easier to complete if you use a spreadsheet program such as Excel.)

   a. Visit the U.S. Commerce Department's Web site for its Bureau of Economic Analysis at **bea.gov/bea/dn/gpdlev.xls** and extract the annual data for "GDP in billions of current dollars" for the past 20 years.

   b. Go to the Federal Reserve's Web site at **federalreserve.gov/releases** and extract the data for M2 for the last month of each of the past 20 years from Table 1 of the H.6 release.

   c. Using the data from parts (a) and (b) construct a time series for the "velocity" of M2 over the past 20 years and produce a graph of M2 velocity versus time. Does this ratio appear to have a constant long-run trend that might provide a reliable indicator of economic activity that the Federal Reserve could use? If not, when does it appear to have been reliable and when does it appear to have gone awry? Can you explain why?

3. A directory of central banks around the world is available from the Center for the Study of Central Banks at **law.nyu.edu/centralbankscenter**. Which of the central banks listed maintain the most comprehensive Web sites (i.e., provide the most detailed information regarding their operations and organizational structure and the performance of their national economies)? What types of information do you believe a central bank's Web site should make available to the public? Why?

Semester Project: A Study of the Fed Funds Market

In this installment of our semester project, we explore the common belief that whenever the Federal Reserve changes its target for the effective Fed funds interest rate, other interest rates (especially those in the money market) adjust rapidly in the same direction and by roughly the same amount. To examine this commonly held belief, complete the following:

a. Visit the Federal Reserve's Web site at **federalreserve.gov** and click on "Monetary Policy." From there, click on "Policymaking: Federal Open Market Committee" and then "Meeting calendar, statements and minutes." Read through each of the statements that have followed the FOMC meetings held over the past 12 months and make note of when the FOMC announced a change in the Fed funds target rate.

b. Go to another area of the same Web site and extract the data for the weekly "selected interest rates" from the H.15 statistical release.

c. Observe what happens to the following short-term interest rates—the effective Fed funds interest rate, the three-month T-bill rate, and the six-month CD rate—in the three weeks leading up to and the week following the FOMC meetings in which you have identified a change in the FOMC's target for the Fed funds rate.

d. Based on what you observed in part (c), did interest rates change following the FOMC meeting? Was there any evidence of anticipation of the FOMC's decision that could have caused interest rates to change prior to the meeting? Or was the FOMC's announcement a complete surprise? (Hint: In answering this question, observe how the market interest rates you tracked changed after the FOMC meeting relative to the change in the Fed funds target rate.)

Selected References to Explore

Federal Reserve Bank of San Francisco. "U.S. Monetary Policy: An Introduction." *FRBSF Economic Letter,* Parts 1–4, January–February 2004.

Gavin, William T., and William Poole. "What Should a Central Bank Look Like?" *The Regional Economist,* Federal Reserve Bank of St. Louis, July 2003, pp. 5–9.

Marquis, Milton. "Setting the Interest Rate." *FRBSF Economic Letter,* Federal Reserve Bank of San Francisco, no. 2002–30 (October 11, 2002), pp. 1–3.

Santomero, Anthony M. "The U.S. Experience with a Federal Central Bank System." *Business Review,* Federal Reserve Bank of Philadelphia, Third Quarter 2002, pp. 1–13.

Walsh, Carl E. "Transparency in Monetary Policy." *FRBSF Economic Letter,* Federal Reserve Bank of San Francisco, no. 2001–26 (September 7, 2001), pp. 1–3.

Wheelock, David C. and Paul W. Wilson. "Trends in the Efficiency of Federal Reserve Check Processing Operations." *Review,* Federal Reserve Bank of St. Louis, September/October 2004, 86(5), pp. 7–19.

Chapter 13

The Tools and Goals of Central Bank Monetary Policy

What's in This Chapter?
Key Topics Outline

Learning Objectives

in This Chapter

- You will understand how the policy tools available to the Federal Reserve and other central banks around the world really work in carrying out a nation's money and credit policies and in affecting the cost and availability of loanable funds.

- You will explore the strengths and weaknesses of the monetary policy tools used by the Fed and other central banks to achieve their objectives.

- You will discover how the Federal Reserve System controls credit and interest rate levels inside the United States.

- You will see the various ways in which central bank policy actions affect a nation's economic goals, including control over inflation and sustaining adequate economic growth and maximum employment.

13.1 Introduction to the Tools and Goals of Monetary Policy

As we discussed in the preceding chapter, central banks like the Federal Reserve System have been given the task of regulating the money and credit system in order to achieve economic goals. Prominent among these goals are the achievement of maximum employment, a stable price level, and sustainable economic growth. As recent experience has demonstrated, these objectives are not easy to achieve and frequently conflict, at least in the short run. Still, the central bank has powerful policy tools at its disposal with which to pursue these economic goals. Our purpose in this chapter is to examine the policy tools available to the Federal Reserve, and many other central banks as well, in carrying out its task of controlling the supply of credit and affecting the cost of borrowed funds in order to achieve the nation's economic goals.

13.2 General versus Selective Credit Controls

general credit controls

selective credit controls

To change the volume of reserves available to depository institutions for lending and investing and to influence interest rates in the economy, the Federal Reserve System, along with other central banks, uses a variety of policy tools. Some of these tools are **general credit controls,** which affect the entire banking and financial system. Included in this list are reserve requirements, the discount rate, and open market operations. A second set of policy tools may be labeled **selective credit controls** because they affect specific groups or sectors of the financial system. Moral suasion and margin requirements on the purchase of listed securities are examples of selective credit controls.

13.3 General Credit Controls of the Fed

Reserve Requirements

Since the 1930s in the United States, the Federal Reserve Board has had the power to vary the amount of required legal reserves that member banks must hold behind the deposits they receive from the public, as we saw earlier in Chapters 11 and 12. With passage of the Depository Institutions Deregulation and Monetary Control Act (DIDMCA) in 1980, nonmember banks and other depository financial institutions (including credit unions and savings and loan associations) were required to conform

reserve requirements

to the deposit **reserve requirements** set by the Fed.

Early in the Fed's history, it was believed that the primary purpose of reserve requirements was to safeguard the public's deposits. Most recently, we have come to realize that their principal use is to give the central bank a powerful tool for affecting the supply of money and credit in the economy, particularly if emergency situations arise in the financial markets. Indeed, reserve requirements are probably the most potent policy tool the Federal Reserve System has at its disposal today. However, changes in reserve requirements are a little-used tool, as we will soon see, and, recently, reserve requirements have been reduced in the United States and eliminated in some other nations (for example, Canada, New Zealand, and the United Kingdom).

Effects of a Change in Deposit Reserve Requirements   A change in deposit reserve requirements—which acts very much like a "tax" on deposits—has at least *three* different effects on the financial system. First, it *changes the deposit multiplier* (or coefficient of expansion), which affects the amount of deposits and new loans the banking system can create for any given injection of new reserves. A change in reserve requirements also *affects the size of the money multiplier,* influencing the rate of increase in the money supply. If the Fed increases reserve requirements, the deposit multiplier and the money multiplier are *reduced,* slowing the growth of money, deposits, and loans. On the other hand, a decrease in reserve requirements increases the size of both the deposit multiplier and the money multiplier. In this instance, each dollar of additional reserves will lead to accelerated growth in money, deposits, and loans.

Second, a change in reserve requirements affects the *mix* between excess and required legal reserves. If reserve requirements are *reduced,* a portion of what were required reserves now becomes excess reserves. Depository institutions will soon convert all or a portion of these newly created excess reserves into loans and investments, expanding the money supply. Similarly, an *increase* in reserve requirements will mean that some depository institutions will be short required legal reserves. These institutions will be forced to sell securities, cut back on loans, and borrow reserves from other financial institutions to meet their reserve requirements. The money supply will grow more slowly and may even decline.

Third, *interest rates* also respond to a change in reserve requirements. A move by the central bank toward higher reserve requirements may soon lead to higher interest rates, particularly in the money market, as depository institutions scramble to cover any reserve deficiencies. Credit becomes less available and more costly. In contrast, a lowering of reserve requirements tends to bring interest rates down and increase investment spending and income.

An Illustration Exhibit 13.1 illustrates the effects of changes in reserve requirements. Suppose depository institutions are required to keep 10 percent of their deposits in legal reserves: $100 of legal reserves will then be needed to support each $1,000 in deposits. If there is sufficient demand for loanable funds, institutions will probably loan or invest the remaining $900. Suppose that the Federal Reserve increases reserve requirements from 10 to 15 percent. As a result, more legal reserves are necessary to support the same volume of deposits, and institutions have a $50 reserve deficit for each $1,000 of deposits. This deficit may be covered by selling financial assets, borrowing funds, or reducing deposits.

On the other hand, suppose required reserves are lowered from 10 to 8 percent. There are now $20 in excess reserves for each $1,000 in deposits, and that excess can be loaned or invested, creating new deposits. We should note that *total* legal reserves available to the banking system are *not* affected by changes in reserve requirements. A shift in reserve requirements affects only the *mix* of legal reserves between required and excess.

Current Levels of Reserve Requirements
In the United States, reserve requirements are imposed by the Federal Reserve Board on all depository institutions that are eligible for federal deposit insurance. Three types of deposits are, potentially at least, subject to legal reserve requirements:

1. *Transaction accounts,* which are deposits used to make payments by negotiable or transferable instruments and include regular checking accounts, NOW accounts, and any account subject to automatic transfer of funds.

2. *Nonpersonal time deposits,* which are interest-bearing time deposits—including savings deposits and money market deposit accounts (MMDAs)—held by businesses and governmental units, but not by individuals.

3. *Eurocurrency liabilities,* which are borrowings of deposits from banks and bank branches located outside the United States.

EXHIBIT 13.1	Effects of Changes in Reserve Requirements on Deposits, Loans, and Investments

With a 10 percent reserve requirement, $100 of reserves is needed to support each $1,000 of deposits.

Depository Institution			
Assets		**Liabilities**	
Loans and		Deposits	$1,000
investments	$ 900		
Legal reserves	100		
Required	100		
Excess	0		
	$1,000		$1,000

Increase in reserve requirements:

If required reserves are increased from 10 to 15 percent, more reserves are needed against the same volume of deposits. Any deficiencies (negative excess reserves) must be covered by liquidating loans and investments or by borrowing.

Depository Institution			
Assets		**Liabilities**	
Legal		Deposits	$1,000
reserves	$ 100		
Required	150		
Excess	−50		
Loans and			
investments	900		
	$1,000		$1,000

Decrease in reserve requirements:

If required reserves are reduced from 10 to 8 percent, excess reserves are created which can be loaned to the public or invested in other types of financial assets.

Depository Institution			
Assets		**Liabilities**	
Legal		Deposits	$1,000
reserves	$ 100		
Required	80		
Excess	20		
Loans and			
investments	900		
	$1,000		$1,000

As shown in Exhibit 13.2, the reserve requirements for 2004 transaction deposits—checkable or draftable accounts for making payments—are zero for banks holding total transaction deposits totaling $6.6 million or less (known as the *reserve requirement exemption* amount) and 3 percent for depository institutions with transaction accounts exceeding $6.6 million and up to $45.4 million. Transaction deposits exceeding $45.4 million are assessed a 10 percent reserve requirement.[1] Time and savings deposits and eurocurrency liabilities currently carry zero reserve requirements, although

---

[1] The Federal Reserve Board is empowered to vary reserve requirements on transaction accounts over $45.4 million between 8 and 14 percent. The $45.4 million dividing line (known as the *low reserve tranche*) is indexed and changes each calendar year by 80 percent of the percentage change in total transaction accounts of all depository institutions during the previous year ended June 30. In addition, the Garn-St Germain Depository Institutions Act of 1982 stipulated that some minimum amount of reservable liabilities (transaction accounts, nonpersonal time deposits, and eurocurrency liabilities) of each depository institution be subject to a zero reserve requirement, adjusted by the Federal Reserve Board each year by 80 percent of the percentage increase in total reservable liabilities. By 2003, this zero reserve requirement base had been expanded to $6.6 million.

EXHIBIT 13.2	Reserve Requirement Ratios for All Banking Firms in the U.S.	
Type of Deposit and Deposit Interval	**Percentage Reserve Requirement**	**Permissible Statutory Range %**
Net transaction accounts:		
$0–$6.6 million	0% of amount	—
Over $6.6 million and up to $45.4 million	3% of amount	3%
Over $45.4 million	$1,164,000, plus 10% of amount over $45.4 million	8–14
Nonpersonal time deposits	0% of amount	0–9
Eurocurrency liabilities	0% of amount	None

Source: Board of Governors of the Federal Reserve System, "Legal Developments," *Federal Reserve Bulletin,* December 2003, p. 497 and Table 1.15, p, A8.

Notes: Required reserves must be held in deposits with the Federal Reserve banks or in vault cash. Nonmember depository institutions may maintain their reserve balances with a Federal Reserve bank indirectly on a pass-through basis with certain approved depository institutions. Depository institutions subject to reserve requirements include commercial banks, savings banks, savings and loan associations, credit unions, agencies and branch offices of foreign banks, and Edge Act and Agreement corporations that offer checkable deposits or business time deposits. Edge Act and Agreement corporations are affiliates of banks and bank holding companies that deal mainly with international (off-shore) accounts.

the Federal Reserve Board could impose new reserve requirements on these deposits at any time. Average reserve requirements usually are higher on transaction accounts than on time and savings accounts because transaction balances are considered to be less stable than time and savings deposits.

Clearly, the largest *depository institutions* carry the heaviest reserve requirements. This is due to the fact that larger financial institutions hold the deposits of thousands of smaller deposit intermediaries. The failure of a large depository institution can send shock waves through the entire financial system and threaten the economic viability of many other institutions as well.

Changes in reserve requirements can be used to carry out major shifts in government economic policy. The reserve requirement tool is exceedingly powerful, so that even a small change affects hundreds of millions of dollars in legal reserves. Moreover, it is an inflexible tool. Required reserve ratios cannot be changed frequently because this would disrupt the banking system. Not surprisingly, changes in reserve requirements do not occur very often, averaging no more than once every three to five years since World War II. Since 1990, they have become even less frequent.

Today in the United States, legal reserves apply only to checkable-type deposits and are gradually fading in their impact on the banking system. Depository institutions have found innovative new ways (such as "sweep accounts" that temporarily move customer funds out of a deposit account subject to reserve requirements) to lower their required reserve levels. Indeed, most depositories now meet their reserve requirements by holding vault cash rather than keeping large balances at the Federal Reserve banks. Recently, the new European Central Bank (ECB) imposed a 2 percent reserve requirement on the short-term deposits and debt of financial institutions subject to its authority. Unlike the Federal Reserve, however, the ECB pays interest on required reserve balances.

Changes in the Federal Reserve's Discount Rate

discount rate

One of the oldest of all monetary policy tools is the **discount rate**—the interest rate that the Federal Reserve banks (and many other central banks as well) charge on loans they grant to other institutions (principally banks and security dealers). In the United

States, any depository institution that accepts transaction (payments) accounts or non-personal time deposits (mainly business CDs) and holds a legal reserve account at the Fed may request a loan from the discount window maintained by the Federal Reserve bank in its region. For the most part, these loans are regarded as *temporary credit* and a *backup source of funds* to the money market, where credit is usually much cheaper and easier to find.

For further discussion of recent changes in the Fed's discount rate policy, see especially federalrecerve.gov/pubs/bulletia/2002/02index.htm

On January 9, 2003, the Federal Reserve redesigned the discount windows of the Federal Reserve banks in an effort to streamline the Fed lending process, reduce administrative costs, lower the historic reluctance of depository institutions to seek Federal Reserve credit, and stabilize conditions in the marketplace for reserves (principally the federal funds market). The Fed also created two new types of loans, labeled *primary credit* and *secondary credit,* to replace older loan categories that used to be called "adjustment" and "extended" credit. A third loan category—known as *seasonal credit*—was retained.

Primary credit today is extended only to *sound* depository institutions—that is, those institutions with adequate capital and supervisory ratings in the top safety and soundness categories. A borrowing institution seeking primary credit no longer has to demonstrate, as it did in the past, that it has sought funds from other sources *before* coming to the Fed. These loans may be used for *any* lawful purpose, including the expansion of a depository institution's assets and to help finance the sale of federal funds to other institutions.

Secondary credit, on the other hand, is intended for borrowing institutions that do *not* qualify for primary credit. Moreover, the secondary-credit borrower may *not* employ the money it receives to expand its assets. For example, a depository institution requesting secondary credit cannot *arbitrage* funds, borrowing from the Fed at a cheaper interest rate and lending those funds to another borrower at a higher interest rate.

Seasonal credit is usually available only to relatively small depositories that show a clear pattern of seasonal (intrayear) fluctuations in their deposits and loans. For example, *farm banks* experience their greatest need for liquidity around planting and harvesting times in their local communities.

The Fed's discount rate on the loans described above is expressed in annual percentage terms. The board of directors of each Federal Reserve bank decides whether the discount rate in their district needs to be changed. However, the Federal Reserve Board in Washington, DC, must approve any discount rate change in any of the 12

EXHIBIT 13.3   **The Discount Rates Charged by the Federal Reserve Banks on Loans to Depository Institutions (percent per annum), February 2004**

Discount Rates at the Federal Reserve Banks by District	Types of Loans Available from the Discount Window		
	Primary Credit	Secondary Credit	Seasonal Credit
Boston, New York, Philadelphia, Cleveland, Richmond, Atlanta, Chicago, St. Louis, Minneapolis, Kansas City, Dallas, and San Francisco	2.00%	2.50%	1.05%

Source: Board of Governors of the Federal Reserve System, *Federal Reserve Bulletin,* December 2003, Table 1.14.

Notes: Primary credit loans are available from the Federal Reserve banks for very short terms as a backup source of liquidity to those depository institutions that are in generally sound financial condition in the judgment of the Federal Reserve bank granting the loan. Secondary credit may be extended to depository institutions not qualifying for primary credit, while seasonal credit is available to relatively small depositories with regular seasonal funds needs that cannot be satisfied through other lenders.

EXHIBIT 13.4

Types of Discount Window Loans Granted by the Federal Reserve Banks, May 2004 (in millions of dollars)

Primary Credit	Secondary Credit	Seasonal Credit	Total Discount-Window Loans
$9	$0	$103	$112

Source: Board of Governors of the Federal Reserve System, *Federal Reserve Bulletin,* August 2004, Table 1.12.

Federal Reserve districts. This procedure serves to prevent the existence of different discount rates from region to region of the nation for lengthy periods of time.

The most significant policy change recently made by the Fed involved setting the discount rate on primary and secondary credit *above* the target interest rate on federal funds. For example, in 2003 the Fed's Federal Open Market Committee (FOMC) set its target for the federal funds rate at 1 percent. Accordingly, the discount rate on primary credit was initially set at 1 percentage point (or 100 basis points) *above* the target federal funds rate and the rate on secondary credit was set at $1\frac{1}{2}$ percentage points (or 150 basis points) *above* the Fed funds rate target. Seasonal credit loan rates are usually much lower than either primary or secondary loan rates, however, and are usually based on prevailing market interest rates. (For a summary of recent discount-window loan rates, see Exhibit 13.3.)

In earlier times the discount rate was nearly always *less* than the federal funds rate, creating a great temptation for depository institutions to garner funds from the Reserve banks and relend those monies in the Fed funds market. To prevent this maneuver the Fed was forced to become a vigilant "watch dog." However, its actions tended to discourage many institutions from seeking *any* form of Federal Reserve credit, and borrowings at the discount window nearly ceased. With the changes instituted during 2003 the Fed hopes that depository institutions will be less reluctant to seek out discount-window loans, though borrowers will, in effect, be paying a penalty rate for the credit they receive. As illustrated in Exhibit 13.4, discount-window borrowing still remains small in volume—usually less than 1 percent of total legal reserves in the banking system—and seasonal credit tends to be the largest loan type by dollar volume, followed by primary credit.

The Fed's decision to create the new loan categories of primary and secondary credit and raise the discount rate *above* most other money market rates was motivated by several factors. One was the 9/11 terrorist crisis, during which time several leading banks and primary security dealers found themselves in desperate need of liquid funds and conventional funds sources dried up. The new discount-window policy ensures a "no hassle" supply of primary credit to sound depository institutions facing emergencies. Moreover, the fixed, positive spread between the discount rate and the federal funds rate target is expected to lower the volatility of the federal funds market rate, making it somewhat easier for the central bank to achieve its interest-rate targets. Indeed, under the newly revised policy, the primary credit rate is expected to serve as a *cap* for the prevailing market rate on federal funds because an attempt by the funds rate to rise above the discount rate would likely direct more borrowers to the Fed's discount window.

Borrowing and Repaying Discount Window Loans

Depository institutions that borrow regularly at the discount window keep a signed loan authorization form at the Federal Reserve bank in their district and keep U.S. government securities or other acceptable collateral on deposit there. When a loan is needed, the officer responsible for managing the borrowing institution's legal reserve position contacts the district Federal Reserve bank and requests that the necessary funds be deposited in that institution's reserve account.

In Exhibit 13.5, we illustrate the borrowing process by supposing that a depository institution has requested a loan of $1 million and the Fed has agreed to make the loan. The borrowing bank receives an increase in its account, Reserves Held at Federal

EXHIBIT 13.5

Borrowing and
Repaying Loans
from the Central
Bank

Borrowing from a Federal Reserve Bank:

Federal Reserve			Commercial Bank or Other Depository Institution		
Assets	**Liabilities**		**Assets**	**Liabilities**	
Discounts +$1 million and advances	Bank reserves	+$1 million	Reserves held at Federal Reserve bank	+$1 million	Bills payable	+$1 million

Repayment of Borrowings from the Fed:

Federal Reserve			Commercial Bank or Other Depository Institution		
Assets	**Liabilities**		**Assets**	**Liabilities**	
Discounts −$1 million and advances	Bank reserves	−$1 million	Reserves held at Federal Reserve bank	−$1 million	Bills payable	−$1 million

Reserve Bank, of $1 million. At the same time, the bank's liability account, Bills Payable, increases by $1 million. On the Federal Reserve bank's balance sheet, the loan is entered as an increase in Bank Reserves of $1 million—a liability of the Federal Reserve System—and also as an increase in a Fed asset account, Discounts and Advances. When the loan is repaid, the transaction is reversed.

Quite clearly, borrowings from the Fed's discount window *increase* the total reserves available to the banking system. Repayments of those borrowings cause total reserves to *fall*.

Effects of a Discount Rate Change

Most observers today believe that at least *three* effects follow from a change in the Federal Reserve's discount rate or in the lending rates of most other central banks. One is the *cost effect*. An increase in the discount rate may mean that it is more costly to borrow reserves from the central bank than to use some other source of funds. Other things being equal, loans from the discount window and the total volume of borrowed reserves may decline. Conversely, a lower discount rate may result in an acceleration of borrowing from the Federal Reserve and more reserves flowing into the banking system. Of course, the strength of the cost effect depends on the prevailing spread between the discount rate and other money market interest rates.

A second consequence of changes in the discount rate is called the *substitution effect*. A change in the discount rate may cause other interest rates to change as well. This is due to the fact that the central bank is one source of borrowed reserves, but it is certainly not the only source. An increase in the discount rate, for example, makes borrowing from the Fed less attractive, but borrowing from other sources, such as the Eurodollar market, may become relatively more attractive. Banks and other borrowers may shift their attention to these other markets, causing interest rates there to rise as well. A lowering of the central bank's discount rate, on the other hand, may cause a downward movement in market interest rates.

For a more detailed overview of the discount windows and discount rates of the Federal Reserve banks see especially frbdiscountwindow.org and chicagofed.org/discountwindow

The final possible effect of a discount rate change is called the *announcement effect.* The discount rate may have a psychological impact on the financial markets because the central bank's lending rate is widely regarded as an indicator of monetary policy. If, for example, the Federal Reserve raises its discount rate, some observers may regard this as a signal that the Fed is pushing for tighter credit conditions. Market participants may respond by reducing their borrowings and curtailing their spending plans.

Unfortunately, the psychological impact of the discount rate may work *against* the central bank as well as *for* it. It is possible, for example, that if the Federal Reserve raises its discount rate, borrowers will respond by accelerating their borrowings in an effort to secure the credit they need before interest rates move even higher. Such an action would tend to thwart the Fed's objective of slowing the growth of borrowing and spending.

Beginning in the middle of 1999, the Fed's discount rate was set up to follow the federal funds interest rate (discussed earlier in Chapter 11). Each time the target federal funds rate—the Federal Reserve's principal policy target today—was changed by the Federal Open Market Committee, the discount rate was moved in parallel fashion. As we noted earlier in this chapter, this policy was reinforced in 2003 when the spread between the discount rate on primary credit and the Fed's current target for the Fed funds rate was set at 1 percentage point (100 basis points). The result of this new policy has been to turn the discount rate and the discount window into a relatively passive tool in the conduct of U.S. monetary policy. This new minimal role for the discount rate (plus the very small amount of borrowing taking place through the discount window) has led to proposals to eliminate this policy tool. Yet, as the terrorist attacks in September 2001 demonstrated, access to the discount window can help to stabilize the economy in times of crisis and provide badly needed liquidity in a hurry. History teaches us that policy tools that may have little importance today can suddenly become important again in the future.

QUESTIONS TO HELP YOU STUDY

1. How does the *reserve requirement* tool affect the ability of deposit-type financial institutions to create money? What are the principal advantages and disadvantages of the reserve requirement tool?

2. How and why does a depository institution borrow from the central bank? Explain what may happen when a central bank changes its *discount* or *lending rate*. What are the principal advantages and disadvantages of the discount policy tool?

3. Why do you think reserve requirements and discount rates are not widely used policy tools at many central banks around the world? Are reserve requirements and the discount rate a general credit control or a selective credit control? Why?

Open Market Operations

open market operations

The limitations of the discount rate and reserve requirement policy tools have led the Federal Reserve (and many other central banks as well) to rely more heavily in recent years upon **open market operations** to accomplish their goals. By definition, open market operations in the United States consist of buying and selling U.S. government and other securities by the Federal Reserve System to affect the quantity and growth of legal reserves and, ultimately, general credit conditions. Open market operations are the most flexible policy tool available to the Fed, suitable for fine-tuning the financial markets when this is necessary. Other central banks around the world may use different types of securities to buy or sell in conducting their open market operations, especially if they lack a "deep" market for their government debt. Among the more common financial instruments traded by many central banks today are bank deposits, derivative securities, and central bank debt. Open market operations are rapidly becoming the most popular tool of leading central banks around the globe. Recently, the new European Central Bank (ECB) was granted the open market tool; it selects which financial instruments can be used and under what terms and conditions, but the ECB's operations must be carried out through the central banks of its member countries.

Effects of Open Market Operations on Interest Rates

The open market tool has two major effects on the banking system and credit conditions. First, it has an *interest rate effect.* For example, in the United States, the Fed typically buys or sells a large quantity (often exceeding a billion dollars worth) of government securities in the financial marketplace at any one time. If the Fed is *purchasing* securities, this adds additional demand for these securities in the market, which tends to increase their prices and lower their yields. In this case, interest rates decline. If the Federal Reserve is *selling* securities from its portfolio, this action increases the supply of securities available in the market, tending to depress their prices and raise their yields. In this case, interest rates tend to rise.

Effects of Open Market Operations on Reserves

The principal day-to-day effect of central bank open market operations is to change the level and growth of *legal reserves.* For example, a Federal Reserve *purchase* of government securities *increases* the reserves of the banking system and expands its ability to make loans and create deposits, increasing the growth of money and credit. In contrast, a *sale* of securities by the Federal Reserve *decreases* the level and growth of reserves and ultimately reduces the growth of money and credit. The impact of Federal Reserve open market operations on the reserve positions of depository institutions with accounts in the United States is illustrated in Exhibit 13.6.

Fed Purchases   In the top portion of Exhibit 13.6, we assume that the Fed is making *purchases* of U.S. government securities in the open market from either depository institutions, which keep their reserve accounts at the Federal Reserve banks, or from other institutions and individuals. If purchases are made from depository institutions, the Federal Reserve System would record the acquisition of securities in the System's asset account—U.S. securities—and pays for the securities acquired by increasing the reserve accounts of the selling institutions. Thus, reserves of depository institutions at the Fed *rise,* while institutional holdings of securities fall by the same amount. Note that *both* total and excess reserves rise in the wake of a Fed purchase, assuming that depository institutions have no reserve deficiencies to begin with. With these extra reserves, additional loans can be made and deposits created that will have an expansionary impact on the availability of credit in the economy.

An expansionary effect would also take place were the Federal Reserve to buy securities from an institution or individual other than a depository institution. Legal reserves would increase, but total deposits—a component of the money supply—would increase as well. Deposits would rise because the central bank would issue a check to pay for the securities it purchased and that check would be deposited in some financial institution, which would, in turn, present the check to the Federal Reserve for crediting to the institution's legal reserve account. Excess reserves would then have risen, making possible an expansion of deposits and loans on the part of depository

EXHIBIT 13.6	Central Bank Open Market Operations

The Federal Reserve Buys Securities

Open Market Purchase from a Bank or Other Deposit-Type Financial Institution:

Depository Financial Institution		Federal Reserve Bank		Effects
Assets	**Liabilities**	**Assets**	**Liabilities**	Total and excess legal reserves increase.
U.S. securities −1,000		U.S. securities +1,000	Reserves +1,000	
Reserves at Fed +1,000				

Open Market Purchase Not from a Depository Financial Institution:

Depository Financial Institution		Federal Reserve Bank		Effects
Assets	**Liabilities**	**Assets**	**Liabilities**	Total and excess legal reserves increase; deposits increase.
Reserves at Fed +1,000	Deposits +1,000	U.S. securities +1,000	Reserves +1,000	

The Federal Reserve Sells Securities

Open Market Sale to a Bank or Other Deposit-Type Financial Institution:

Depository Financial Institution		Federal Reserve Bank		Effects
Assets	**Liabilities**	**Assets**	**Liabilities**	Total and excess legal reserves decrease.
U.S. securities +1,000		U.S. securities −1,000	Reserves −1,000	
Reserves at Fed −1,000				

Open Market Sale Not to a Depository Financial Institution:

Depository Financial Institution		Federal Reserve Bank		Effects
Assets	**Liabilities**	**Assets**	**Liabilities**	Total and excess legal reserves decrease; deposits decrease.
Reserves at Fed −1,000	Deposits −1,000	U.S. securities −1,000	Reserves −1,000	

institutions. Note, however, that the rise in excess reserves is *less* in this case than would occur if the Fed bought securities only from depository institutions that maintain reserve accounts with the Federal Reserve banks. This is due to the fact that some of the new legal reserves created by the Fed purchase must be pledged as required reserves behind the newly created deposits. Therefore, Federal Reserve open market purchases of securities have *less* of an effect on total credit and deposit expansion if the Fed's transaction involves only nondeposit financial institutions and individuals.

Fed Sales   Central bank *sales* of securities *reduce* the growth of reserves, deposits, and loans. For example, as shown in the bottom half of Exhibit 13.6, when the Federal Reserve sells U.S. government securities from its portfolio to a depository institution or to a dealer with an account at a depository institution, that institution must pay for those securities by letting the Fed deduct the amount of the purchase from its reserve account. Both total reserves and excess reserves *fall.* If deposit institutions were fully loaned up with no excess reserves available, the open market sale would result in a reserve deficiency. Some institutions would be forced to sell loans and securities or borrow funds in order to bring in additional reserves, thereby reducing the availability of credit.

Suppose the central bank were to sell securities to an individual or a nondeposit institution. As Exhibit 13.6 reveals, in this instance, *both* reserves and deposits fall. Credit becomes less available and usually more expensive.

How Open Market Operations Are Conducted in the United States

All trading in securities by the Federal Reserve System is carried out through the System's Trading Desk, located at the Federal Reserve Bank of New York. The Trading Desk is supervised by the manager of the System Open Market Account (SOMA), a vice president of the New York Fed. The SOMA manager's activities are, in turn, supervised and directed by the Federal Open Market Committee. In reality, the Fed does not trade with the public; rather all Fed security purchases and sales are made through a select list of primary U.S. government securities dealers who agree to buy or sell in amounts called for by the Trading Desk at the time the Fed wishes to trade. Many of these dealers are commercial banks that have securities departments. The rest are exclusively dealers in U.S. government and selected private securities.

Federal Reserve purchases and sales of Treasury bills, repurchase agreements, and other financial instruments normally are huge in volume. For example, during the month of April 2004, Fed purchases of repurchase agreements (RPs) exceeded $160 billion and its rollover of reverse RPs exceeded $440 billion. By the end of that month the Fed held securities in its own portfolio amounting to more than $700 billion (at face value), of which more than $250 billion were U.S. Treasury bills and better than $430 billion were Treasury notes and bonds. It also held in custody on behalf of foreign governments and official institutions nearly $1.2 trillion in marketable securities. Most of its portfolio is short in maturity, rolling over within a year, keeping Fed traders in New York busy much of the time.

The Policy Directive   How does the SOMA manager decide whether or not to buy or sell securities in the open market on a given day? The manager is guided, first of all, by a *policy directive* issued to the Federal Reserve Bank of New York following the conclusion of each meeting of the Federal Open Market Committee (FOMC). The SOMA manager attends each FOMC meeting and participates in its policy discussions. He or she listens to the views of each member of the Federal Reserve Board and the Reserve bank presidents, who describe economic conditions in their region of the country. The manager also receives the benefit of a presentation by staff economists of the Federal Reserve Board who analyze current economic and financial developments.

In recent years, with the issuance of a policy directive to the SOMA manager at the Fed's Trading Desk in New York, the FOMC has been releasing to the public a *Federal Open Market Committee Statement* regarding its planned course of action after each committee meeting (normally by 2:15 P.M. EST on the last day of an FOMC meeting). These policy statements reflect the central bank's efforts to be more *transparent* (i.e., to make more public disclosures) and to be more *accountable* to the public for what it does. An example of a recent policy statement is shown in Exhibit 13.7. This statement summarizes the Federal Reserve's view of current economic developments, particularly those that pertain to the growth of output in the economy and to movements in prices and employment. The FOMC specifies a target level for a key money market interest rate—the *effective federal funds rate*[2]—and where it has set the discount rate.

---

[2] See Chapter 11 for a discussion of the federal funds market and the determinants of the effective federal funds interest rate.

EXHIBIT 13.7

**Federal Open
Market Committee
Statement**

The Federal Open Market Committee decided on October 28, 2003, to keep its target for the federal funds rate at 1 percent.

The Committee continues to believe that an accommodative stance of monetary policy, coupled with robust underlying growth in productivity, is providing important ongoing support to economic activity. The evidence accumulated over the intermeeting period confirms that spending is firming, and the labor market appears to be stabilizing. Business pricing power and increases in core consumer prices remain muted.

The Committee perceives that the upside and downside risks to the attainment of sustainable growth for the next few quarters are roughly equal. In contrast, the probability, though minor, of an unwelcome fall in inflation exceeds that of a rise in inflation from its already low level. The Committee judges that, on balance, the risk of inflation becoming undesirably low remains the predominant concern for the foreseeable future. In these circumstances, the Committee believes that policy accommodation can be maintained for a considerable period.

Voting for the FOMC monetary policy action were: Alan Greenspan, Chairman; Ben S. Bernanke; Susan S. Bies; J. Alfred Broaddus, Jr.; Roger W. Ferguson, Jr.; Edward M. Gramlich; Jack Guynn; Donald L. Kohn; Michael H. Moskow; Mark W. Olson; Robert T. Parry; and Jamie B. Stewart, Jr.

Source: Board of Governors of the Federal Reserve System, *Federal Reserve Bulletin*, December 2003, p.493.

We note that the FOMC policy statement is extremely general in nature and recognizes the need for flexibility as market conditions change. Many factors other than Federal Reserve operations affect interest rates and credit availability. Consequently, the Federal Open Market Committee must be flexible and trust the SOMA manager's judgment in responding to daily conditions in the money market, which subsequently may be quite different from those anticipated when the FOMC held its last meeting.

The Conference Call   As an added check on the decisions of the SOMA manager, a conference call between staff economists at the Federal Reserve Board, a member of the FOMC, and the SOMA manager is often held each day before trading occurs. The SOMA manager updates those sitting in on the conference call on current conditions in the money market and then makes a recommendation on the type and volume of securities to be bought or sold that day. At this point, the conference call participants may make alternative recommendations. Usually, however, the SOMA manager's recommendation is taken and trading proceeds.

Types of Open Market Operations   There are four basic types of Federal Reserve open market operations. (See Exhibit 13.8.) The so-called *straight,* or *outright, transaction* refers to the sale or purchase of securities in which outright title passes to the buyer on a permanent basis. In this case, a permanent change occurs in the level of legal reserves, up or down. Thus, when the Federal Reserve wants to bring about a *once-and-for-all* change in reserves, it tends to use the *straight* or *outright* type of transaction—something that normally takes place only a few times during the year. One reason the Fed wishes to make occasional permanent additions to its portfolio of government securities is to account for the secular growth in the liquidity demands of a growing economy.

In contrast, when the Fed wishes to have a *temporary* effect on bank reserves, correcting temporary mismatches between the demand for and supply of reserves, it employs a *repurchase agreement* with a securities dealer. Under a repurchase agreement (RP)—today the most popular type of open-market operation—the Fed buys securities from dealers but agrees to sell them back after a few days.[3] The result is a

For a more complete overview of the structure and operations of the Federal Open Market Committee (FOMC) and the SOMA manager, see especially federalreserve.gov/fomc

---

[3] See Chapter 10 for an explanation of how these repurchase agreements are used as a source of funds for securities dealers.

EXHIBIT 13.8

Types of Federal Reserve Open Market Transactions

Outright or Straight Open Market Transaction
(permanent change in the level of reserves held by depository institutions)

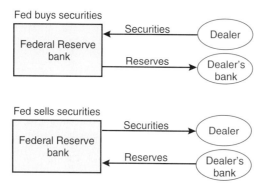

RP or Reverse RP Transaction
(temporary change in the level of reserves held by depository institutions)

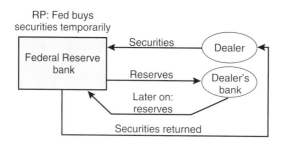

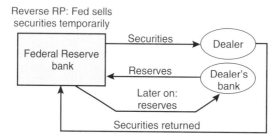

Runoff Transaction
(permanent reduction in the level of reserves held by depository institutions)

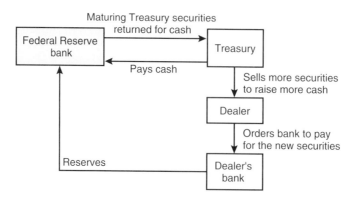

EXHIBIT 13.8

(Continued)

Agency Transaction
(may or may not affect the level of reserves held by depository institutions depending on the type of transaction)

A. First Type of Agency Transaction

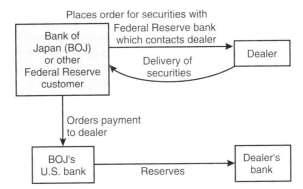

Net Effect: *No* change in total reserves held by all depository institutions as reserves merely shift from one depository institution to another; Fed acts only as a broker, contacting a dealer to complete the security transaction.

B. Second Type of Agency Transaction

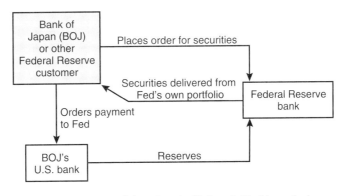

Net Effect: Total reserves of depository institutions fall in this particular transaction as payment for the securities acquired is made to the Fed; Fed acts as a security dealer.

temporary increase in legal reserves that will be reversed when the Fed sells the securities back to the dealers. Such RPs frequently are used during holiday periods or when factors are at work that have resulted in a temporary shortfall in reserves.

A good example of how the RP can be used to deal with temporary emergencies appeared in September 2001 when, in the wake of a terror attack on the United States, the Fed injected about $80 billion in additional liquidity into the U.S. financial system using repurchase agreements with primary security dealers. A week later, as market conditions stabilized, it withdrew most of these extra funds.

The Fed can also deal with a temporary excess quantity of reserves by using a matched-sale purchase (MSP) transaction, commonly called a *reverse RP.* In this instance, the Fed agrees to sell securities to dealers for a brief period and then to buy them back. Frequently, when deliveries are slowed by weather or strikes, the result is a sharp increase in the volume of uncollected checks (float), giving banks and other depository institutions millions of dollars in excess reserves until the unpaid items are

For a thorough description of how and why the Fed conducts open market operations as it does, see federalreserve.gov/pubs/bulletin/1997/199711/lead.pdf

cleared. The Fed can absorb these excess reserves using reverse RPs until the situation returns to normal. Incidentally, reverse RPs are used for the types of problems just described because the Fed is not allowed by law to use a simpler and less costly approach to the problem—borrowing from the public— in order to reduce the volume of reserves available to the banking system.

The third type of open market operation is the *runoff*. The Federal Reserve may deal directly with the U.S. Treasury in acquiring and redeeming securities. Suppose the Fed has some maturing U.S. Treasury securities and wishes to replace them with new securities currently being offered by the Treasury in its latest public auction. The amount of securities that the Fed takes will *not* then be available to the public, reducing the quantity of securities sold in the marketplace. Other things being equal, this would tend to raise security prices and lower interest rates.[4]

On the other hand, the Fed may decide *not* to acquire new securities from the Treasury to replace those that are maturing. This would mean the Treasury would be forced to sell an increased volume of securities in the open market to raise cash in order to pay off the Fed. At the same time, the Treasury would draw funds from its deposits held at private banks, reducing bank reserves, to redeem the Fed's maturing securities. Other things being equal, security prices would fall and interest rates rise. Credit market conditions would tighten up. Moreover, the Federal Reserve saves on transaction costs (in the form of dealer fees) by dealing directly with the Treasury and not conducting a regular open market transaction through private security dealers.

Finally, the Fed also conducts purchases and sales of securities on behalf of foreign central banks and other official agencies and institutions that hold accounts with the New York Federal Reserve Bank, known as *agency operations*. The Fed may buy or sell securities from its own portfolio to accommodate these foreign accounts or merely act as an intermediary between the foreign accounts and security dealers.

For example, suppose that the Federal Reserve Bank in New York has just received a request from the Bank of Japan to purchase U.S. government securities. That central bank has probably built up too much cash in its U.S. accounts and has decided to earn some interest on that cash by buying some U.S. Treasury bonds. To pay for the securities, the Bank of Japan transfers a portion of its deposit at a U.S. bank to its deposit account at the New York Fed. The Fed's Trading Desk may contact private dealers and make the purchase on behalf of the Bank of Japan, crediting the dealers' banks for the purchase price of the securities and reducing the Bank of Japan's deposits at the Fed. In this case, the total reserves of the U.S. banking system do *not change, falling initially* but then rising back to their original level.

However, the Fed may decide to sell the Bank of Japan securities from its *own* portfolio (that is "from System account"). In this case, bank reserves fall initially, as the Bank of Japan pays for its purchase, but do not rise again. The money received from this Fed sale is "locked up" within the Federal Reserve System and does not flow out to private banks. In general, sales of Federal Reserve-held securities to foreign accounts reduce U.S. bank reserves; purchases of securities from foreign accounts that go into the Fed's own security account increase U.S. bank reserves.

Goals of Open Market Operations: Defensive and Dynamic   In the use of any of its policy tools, the Federal Reserve, like other central banks, always has in mind the basic economic goals of maximum employment, a stable price level, and sustainable economic growth. However, only a portion of the Federal Reserve's daily open market

---

[4] The Fed is prohibited by law from purchasing government securities directly from the Treasury Department out of concern that such transactions could lead to government abuse of Federal Reserve credit and result in serious inflation in the economy.

Different central banks around the world often emphasize different policy tools. For example, the Bank of England (BOE) relies primarily upon purchases of British Treasury and commercial bills to affect interest rates and the availability of credit. The BOE also may make changes in the basic lending rate that it charges borrowing banks and securities houses.

The Bank of Canada (BOC) focuses its energies mainly on the buying and selling of short-term Treasury bills and repurchase agreements. The Canadian central bank also impacts reserves in the banking system by moving government deposits between the BOC and private banks within the Canadian system. Canada's central bank phased out its use of legal reserve requirements in 1994.

The European Central Bank (the ECB) may use a variety of open market instruments (including repurchase agreements, outright purchases and sales of securities, currency swaps, and the issuance of debt). The ECB also has the power to loan funds to financial institutions in need of liquidity and impose reserve requirements on short-term deposits and other forms of short-term debt. However, the use of the ECB's open market policy tool is somewhat dispersed because the central banks of the European Community's member states actually carry out open market operations.

The Bank of Japan (BOJ) uses security trading, primarily in commercial bills but also increasingly in Japanese government securities, to influence domestic credit conditions. The BOJ makes loans to banks through its discount window. In several other Asian countries—Indonesia, Korea, Taiwan, Hong Kong, and the Philippines—central banks issue and trade in their own IOUs in order to influence economic conditions.

Central banks do not change policy tools very often. However, with deregulation of financial markets and financial institutions becoming more alike all over the world, more central banks are choosing to work through the *private marketplace* to accomplish their goals, increasingly emphasizing the buying and selling of government and corporate financial instruments to change or maintain existing credit conditions. Such arbitrary, non-market-determined tools as interest rate and credit ceilings, currency (exchange-rate) controls, reserve requirements, and central bank loan or discount rates are increasingly being phased out or deemphasized. The discount (loan) windows of leading central banks today are more often used to relieve temporary stresses faced by individual financial institutions rather than to achieve broad policy goals—one of the reasons the Federal Reserve made major changes in its discount window policies, as discussed earlier in this chapter.

activity is directed toward those particular goals. The Fed is also responsible on a day-to-day basis for stabilizing the money and capital markets and keeping the financial markets functioning smoothly. These technical adjustments in market conditions are often referred to as *defensive* open market operations. Their basic purpose is to preserve the *status quo* and to keep the present pattern of interest rates and credit availability about where it is.

For example, suppose that the Fed believes that the current level of reserves held by the banking system—about $38 billion—is just right to hold interest rates and credit conditions where they are. However, due to changes in other factors affecting bank reserves (such as the public demanding more currency and coin from banks to spend over the holidays), total reserves in the system are expected to fall to $37 billion. The Fed is likely to buy about $1 billion in securities so that total reserves remain at $38 billion—a *defensive operation*.

In contrast, when the Federal Reserve is interested in the pursuit of broader economic goals, it engages in *dynamic* open market operations. These operations are designed to upset the status quo and to change interest rates and credit conditions to a level the Fed believes to be more consistent with its economic goals. For example, if the Fed believes the economy needs to grow faster to create more jobs, it may come to the conclusion that total reserves in the banking system must increase from $38 to $40 billion. In this case, the Fed's Trading Desk is likely to launch an aggressive program of buying securities until reserve levels reach $40 billion. Open market operations have now become *dynamic,* not merely defensive.

The fact that open market operations are carried out for a wide variety of purposes makes it difficult to follow a central bank's daily transactions in the marketplace and to draw firm conclusions about the direction of monetary policy. On any given day, the central bank may be buying or selling securities defensively merely to stabilize market conditions without any longer-term objectives in mind. The central bank is really a balance wheel in the financial system, supplying or subtracting reserves as needed to eliminate demand-supply mismatches on any given day. Although experienced central bank watchers find the daily pattern of open market operations meaningful, unless the investor possesses inside information on the motivation of central bank actions, it is exceedingly difficult to "read" daily open market operations. A longer-term view is usually needed, supplied in part by the FOMC's policy statement, to see the direction in which the central bank is trying to move the financial system.

13.4 Selective Credit Controls Used by the Fed

The discount rate, reserve requirements, and open market operations are often called *general credit controls* because each has an impact on the whole financial system. Another set of policy tools available to the Federal Reserve and other central banks, however, is more *selective* in its impact, focusing on particular sectors of the economy. Nevertheless, use of some of these selective tools can contribute toward the overall objectives of the central bank to achieve maximum employment, stabilize prices, and sustain economic growth.

Moral Suasion by Central Bank Officials

moral suasion

A widely used selective policy tool is known as **moral suasion**. This refers to the use of "arm-twisting" or "jawboning" by central bank officials to encourage banks and other lending institutions to conform with the spirit of its policies. For example, if the Federal Reserve wishes to tighten credit controls and slow the growth of credit, Fed officials issue letters and public statements urging financial institutions operating in the United States to use more restraint in granting loans. These public statements may be supplemented by personal phone calls from top Federal Reserve officials to individual lending institutions, stressing the need for more conservative policies. Some central banks, such as the Bank of Japan, use the moral suasion tool as an important supplement to their other policy tools.

Margin Requirements

margin requirements

A selective credit control still under the exclusive control of the Federal Reserve Board is the use of **margin requirements** on the purchase of stocks and convertible bonds and on short sales of those same securities. Margin requirements were enacted into law with passage of the Securities Exchange Act of 1934. This federal law limited the amount of credit that could be used as collateral for a loan. Regulations G, T, and U of the Federal Reserve Board prescribe a maximum loan value for marginable stocks, convertible bonds, and short sales. That maximum loan value is expressed as a specified percentage of the market value of the securities at the time they are used as loan collateral. The margin requirement on a regulated security, then, is simply the difference between its market value (100 percent) and the maximum loan value of that security.

For example, as shown in Exhibit 13.9, the current margin requirement on stock is 50 percent. This means that common and preferred stock can be purchased on credit with the stock itself used as collateral. However, the purchaser can borrow only up to

To learn more about security margin requirements, see such sources as nyse.com, speculative bubble.com, and nasdr.com

	Federal Reserve Margin Requirements on Stocks, Convertible Bonds, and Short Sales (Percent of Market Value and Effective Date)					
Security	March 11, 1968	June 8, 1968	May 6, 1970	Dec. 6, 1971	Nov. 24, 1972	Jan. 3, 1974
Margin stocks	70%	80%	65%	55%	65%	50%
Convertible bonds	50	60	50	50	50	50
Short sales	70	80	65	55	65	50

Source: Board of Governors of the Federal Reserve System, *Federal Reserve Bulletin,* January 2004, Table 1.36.

Note: Regulations G, T, and U published by the Board of Governors of the Federal Reserve System, in accordance with the Securities Exchange Act of 1934, limit the amount of credit to purchase or carry margin stocks when the securities to be purchased are used as collateral. Margin requirements specify the maximum loan value of the securities expressed as a percentage of their market value at the time a loan is made.

a maximum of 50 percent of the stock's current market value. He or she must put up the remainder of the stock's purchase price in cash money.

As Exhibit 13.9 suggests, margin requirements are not often changed. In fact, the current U.S. margin requirements on stocks, convertible bonds, and short sales of these securities have remained unchanged since January 1974. Most observers of the financial markets believe that the imposition of margin requirements was unnecessary. These requirements arose out of the turmoil of the Great Depression of the 1930s, when many believed that speculative buying and selling of stocks had contributed to the U.S. economy's sudden collapse. This was probably *not* the case, but margin requirements do ensure that a substantial amount of cash will be contributed by the buyer of securities, keeping borrowing against these securities within reasonable limits. One serious limitation of this selective tool is that it does *not* cover purchases of *all* types of stocks and bonds. For this reason, its future use as a tool of Federal Reserve monetary policy is likely to remain very limited.

For a further review of the Federal Reserve's credit controls and policymaking, see kc.frb.org/fed101

QUESTIONS TO HELP YOU STUDY

4. Why are *open market operations* increasingly the most popular monetary policy tool? What are the principal effects of open market operations on the financial system?

5. Describe the relationship between the SOMA manager and the FOMC. What is a *policy directive* and what is a *policy statement?* What policy target does the Federal Reserve use?

6. Explain the difference between an *RP* and a *straight* (or outright) open market transaction. Why is each used? What is a *runoff?* An *agency* operation?

7. Explain the difference between *defensive* and *dynamic* open market operations.

8. What is *moral suasion?* Do you believe this tool can be effective?

9. Explain how *margin requirements* affect the financial system. Why is this policy tool not frequently used?

13.5 Interest-Rate Targeting

The Federal Reserve and other central banks around the world have given increasing weight in recent years to targeting *the cost and availability of credit in the money market.* One reason is that central banks are charged with the responsibility of stabilizing conditions in the financial markets to assure a smooth flow of funds from savers (lenders) to borrowers. In addition, central banks must ensure that the government securities market functions smoothly so that adequate supplies of credit are available to security dealers and that the federal government can market its billions of dollars in debt securities without serious difficulty. But to what aspects of the money market does a central bank like the Federal Reserve pay the most attention today?

The Federal Funds Rate

As we saw earlier in Chapter 11, the money market indicator that usually feels the first impact from Federal Reserve policy moves is the *effective federal funds rate* or the *daily average interest rate on federal funds transactions.* Beginning in 1989 the Fed adopted a *federal funds interest rate targeting procedure*—the monetary policy approach it uses today. When the Fed sells securities, the supply of reserves available to depository institutions is reduced and, other things held equal, the Fed funds rate, which is the interest rate changed on overnight borrowings of reserves in the banking system, tends to rise. On the other hand, a Federal Reserve purchase of securities increases available reserves to depository institutions, which tends to push the Fed funds rate down.

Beginning in 1994, the Federal Reserve adopted a new policy of "openness" or "transparency" when it comes to announcing its target for the federal funds interest rate, letting the public know right away what the current funds rate target is and explaining its reasoning to the public if it is moving the funds rate target. For example, in January 2001, following a meeting of the Federal Open Market Committee, the Fed announced that it was dropping its target for the federal funds interest rate from 6 percent to $5\frac{1}{2}$ percent because the economy appeared to be slowing and inflation seemed to be under control. When the markets opened the next morning, the Fed funds rate moved quickly toward its new target level. A similar experience greeted the movement of the federal funds rate late in 2001 as the Federal Reserve battled a possible recession in the U.S. economy, made worse by tragic terrorist bombings in September of that year. On September 17, 2001, the Fed dropped the federal funds target rate 1/2 point to 3 percent in order to make it cheaper for individuals and institutions to raise more liquid funds and to increase public confidence as the New York Stock Exchange opened after the terrorist attacks of September 11th.

Finally, in November of 2002 the Federal Open Market Committee voted to lower the Fed funds interest-rate target—often called the "intended" federal funds rate—to 1 percent (the lowest level in 45 years). In order to justify such a move, the FOMC expressed concern about the possibility that deflation might replace inflation as the nation's number one economic problem and noted the existence of continuing weakness in the economy following the recession of 2001–2002. By mid-2004, however, there were signs of a U.S. economic recovery and the buildup of moderate inflationary pressures. Accordingly, the Federal Reserve nudged the federal funds rate upward and indicated the likelihood of a gradual rise in that interest rate—a policy it subsequently pursued.

How is the Federal Reserve's Trading Desk able to maintain the federal funds rate at or close to its announced interest rate target? Exhibit 13.10 provides us with an illustration of the process. Suppose the Fed has targeted a Fed funds rate of 5 percent and the funds rate currently sits at the 5 percent level, where the total demand for reserves by depository institutions (represented by schedule D in Exhibit 13.10) intersects the supply of total reserves (represented by schedule S), achieving an equilibrium rate of interest at E.

EXHIBIT 13.10	The Federal Reserve's Impact on the Federal Funds Interest Rate

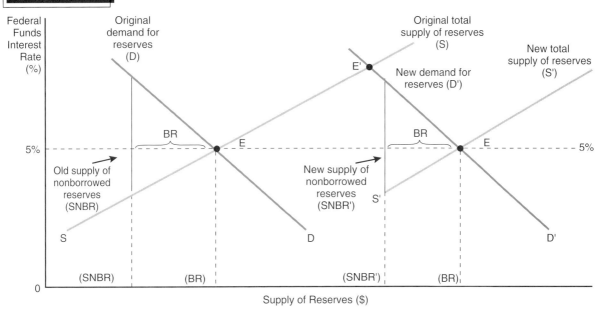

We note that the supply of total reserves consists of the sum of borrowed and nonborrowed reserves:

$$\text{Total reserves} = \text{Borrowed reserves} + \text{Nonborrowed reserves}$$

borrowed reserves

nonborrowed reserves

Borrowed reserves (labeled *BR* in Exhibit 13.10) are loans made to depository institutions by the Federal Reserve banks. **Nonborrowed reserves** are legal reserves that belong to depository institutions (labeled *SNBR* in Exhibit 13.10). Through open market operations the central bank impacts primarily nonborrowed reserves which, in turn, affect total reserves available to the banking system.

Now, suppose that depository institutions increase their demand for total reserves to *D'*. If the Federal Reserve does nothing to the supply of reserves, the Fed funds rate must rise above its current equilibrium 5 percent target level to accommodate the new higher level of demand for total reserves, perhaps rising to equilibrium level *E'*, well above the old 5 percent target for the Fed funds rate. If the Fed doesn't want this to happen, it will increase the supply of nonborrowed reserves by using open market operations, sliding the old schedule *SNBR* over to a new schedule, *SNBR'*. This action moves the supply of total reserves, *S*, over to a new schedule *S'*. If the amount of borrowed reserves doesn't change, we now have a *new* intersection of supply and demand for reserves, but the level of the Fed funds rate stays at the old equilibrium point *E*, and at the old 5 percent interest rate. Thus, *the Federal Reserve can keep the Fed funds interest rate at or near its desired level so long as the central bank is willing to offset changes in the demand for total reserves and in the demand for borrowed reserves by making appropriate adjustments in the supply of nonborrowed reserves through open market operations.*

One way to follow interest-rate targeting in the United States is to check frequently with such Web sites as federalreserve.gov/ fomc and economagic.com

Of course, the central bank cannot maintain the Fed funds rate exactly at its target level every hour of every day. This is because depository institutions are constantly changing their demands for reserves and their attitudes about borrowing reserves from the Federal Reserve banks. Moreover, interest rates are impacted by the public's expectations regarding inflation and by the total demand for and supply of credit within the financial system. The Fed's Trading Desk manager, acting on behalf of the FOMC, tries

FINANCIAL DEVELOPMENTS

Open Market Operations—The Lever
That Keeps Total Reserves of the
Banking System at the Level Desired

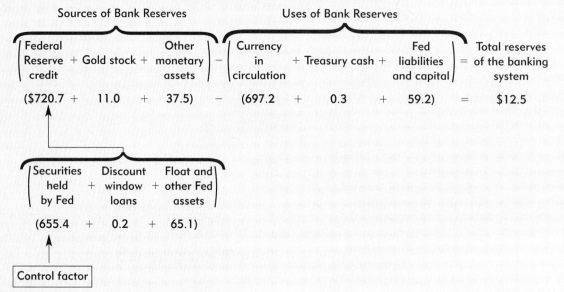

(Figures in $ Billions for September 2003)

Sources of Bank Reserves   Uses of Bank Reserves

$$\left(\begin{array}{c}\text{Federal} \\ \text{Reserve} \\ \text{credit}\end{array} + \text{Gold stock} + \begin{array}{c}\text{Other} \\ \text{monetary} \\ \text{assets}\end{array}\right) - \left(\begin{array}{c}\text{Currency} \\ \text{in} \\ \text{circulation}\end{array} + \text{Treasury cash} + \begin{array}{c}\text{Fed} \\ \text{liabilities} \\ \text{and capital}\end{array}\right) = \begin{array}{c}\text{Total reserves} \\ \text{of the banking} \\ \text{system}\end{array}$$

($720.7 + 11.0 + 37.5) − (697.2 + 0.3 + 59.2) = $12.5

$$\left(\begin{array}{c}\text{Securities} \\ \text{held} \\ \text{by Fed}\end{array} + \begin{array}{c}\text{Discount} \\ \text{window} \\ \text{loans}\end{array} + \begin{array}{c}\text{Float and} \\ \text{other Fed} \\ \text{assets}\end{array}\right)$$

(655.4 + 0.2 + 65.1)

Control factor

An example: The Fed's current target might be to keep total reserves around $12.5 billion in order to stabilize interest rates.

The Problem: Currency in circulation in the public's hands is expected to increase by $1 billion over the next two-week period, all other factors held constant. Bank reserves will fall and interest rates are likely to rise as the public withdraws this pocket money from banks unless the Federal Reserve acts.

Possible Solution: Use open market operations to purchase $1 billion in U.S. government securities (the Fed's open-market control factor) through the Trading Desk of the New York Federal Reserve Bank.

to project what the banking system's demand for reserves is likely to be in order to supply enough reserves through open-market operations to keep the federal funds rate at or close to its target level. Similarly, the Trading Desk manager must make further corrections through open-market operations when his or her forecasts are off the mark.

Fed Funds Targeting and Long-Term Interest Rates

Finally, one more important point about targeting the federal funds rate should be noted. Just because the Fed can manipulate the federal funds rate—a key money market interest rate—does not mean that long-term capital market interest rates will also respond in the same way to the Fed's activities in the financial marketplace. For example, when the Federal Reserve nudged the Fed funds rate *downward* in November of 2002 in order to bolster the sagging U.S. economy, the 10-year U.S. Treasury bond rate—a key capital market interest rate—hardly moved at all for three months, while nine months later it actually moved substantially higher, not lower, relative to its position when the Fed funds rate was lowered. Why do long-term interest rates sometimes move quite differently than the short-term federal funds rate?

One factor is *inflation*. When the central bank cuts short-term interest rates investors in the capital market may come to believe that prices will rise. Thus, easier monetary policy lowers short-term interest rates in the near term, but may lead longer-term investors to expect higher short-term interest rates in the future. Ultimately, higher inflationary expectations may push long-term interest rates upward as capital market investors seek compensation for the fear of greater inflation.

The key point to remember is that the central bank does *not* have direct control over longer-term interest rates. And, unfortunately, it is long-term interest rates that appear to have the greatest impact on investment spending in the economy and the creation of new jobs. The central bank must be patient. Short-term interest rates, like the Fed funds rate, react quickly to changes in central bank policy, but long-term interest rates may take several months to respond to what the central bank is trying to do. Monetary policy often operates with long and variable time lags.

13.6 The Federal Reserve and Economic Goals

For many years, the Federal Reserve System, along with other central banks around the world, has played an active role in the stabilization of the economy and the pursuit of economic goals. These goals include controlling inflation, maximizing employment, and promoting sustainable economic growth. In recent years, these goals have proven to be extremely difficult to achieve in practice. Nevertheless, the Fed and other central banks remain committed to them, with an ever-increasing emphasis on maintaining long-run price stability.

The Goal of Controlling Inflation

Inflation—a rise in the general price level of all goods and services produced in the economy—has been among the more serious economic problems of the world during the past half century, with many nations experiencing far higher annual rates of inflation than those currently prevailing in the United States. Moreover, inflation is *not* new; price levels have been generally rising since the beginning of the Industrial Revolution in Europe nearly 300 years ago. There is also evidence of outbreaks of rampant inflation during the Middle Ages and in ancient times.

What are the *causes* of inflation? During the 1960s and 1970s, war and government spending were certainly contributing factors. Soaring energy and food costs, higher home mortgage rates, and rapid increases in labor and medical care costs also played key roles until the 1980s brought a turnaround, as Exhibit 13.11 reveals. Another contributing factor was the decline in the value of the U.S. dollar in international markets. The dollar's weakness relative to other major currencies, such as the Japanese yen, raised the prices of imports into the United States and lessened the impact of foreign competition on domestic producers until the dollar strengthened significantly during the 1990s. With the opening of the twenty-first century inflationary pressures continued to be muted, owing principally to the continued resurgence of productivity growth in the United States that had begun in the mid-1990s. This greater productivity allowed businesses to increase the supply of goods and services without employing additional labor or capital in their production, thus keeping a lid on price increases. Later, when the economy dipped into recession in 2001, the demand for goods and services fell, and, for a brief period, the Fed switched its concern from inflation to deflation, which appeared to be a real threat for the first time since the Great Depression of the 1930s. However, once the economy regained its momentum, deflationary fears subsided. Nonetheless, this episode provided an important lesson for the Fed. It became aware that the conduct of monetary policy during deflationary times, when the economy is

The Federal Funds Futures Market— An Aid to Market Participants Trying to Guess Which Way the Central Bank Is Headed

Since early in 1994 the Federal Reserve has been setting target levels for the daily average federal funds interest rate. Moreover, when the Fed publicly announces a new target level for the effective federal funds rate, usually following a meeting of its Federal Open Market Committee (FOMC), the effective Fed funds rate moves quickly toward the new target level. This procedure of setting clear and explicit interest-rate targets and doing it right away has helped make it easier for investors to "tune in"on what the central bank is trying to do.

In October 1988 the Chicago Board of Trade (CBOT) began public trading of a federal funds futures contract in the amount of $5 million for 30 days and priced on the basis of 100 less the overnight federal funds rate for the delivery month. For example, if the prevailing federal funds interest rate is 5 percent, the contract's value is 100 − 5, or 95 (on a $100 basis). These futures contracts are usually traded for the current month out to about six or seven months ahead. The federal funds interest rate on these contracts may be readily found any time during the trading day through radio, television, or the Internet.

The futures contracts' funds rate is a *forecast* by the market of what the Federal Reserve is likely to do with its *target federal funds rate* in the near future. Thus, investors can put together a forecast of the decisions likely to be made by the FOMC to change that interest rate at little cost. The creation of the new futures contract and the Fed's willingness to be more open with its plans for the funds rate and with how it views the economy's condition has made monetary policy more *transparent* and more helpful to active market investors than ever before.

During 2003, CBOT opened daily trading on an *option contract* to buy or sell Fed funds futures. This put or call option for federal funds futures may well improve the accuracy of future market forecasts of the federal funds interest rate. Unlike the trading going on in Fed funds futures, which gives us some idea of the "average" Fed funds rate that the market as a whole currently expects, the newer options contract tells us something about the *range of opinion* in the financial marketplace regarding where the funds rate might be headed.

Recent research suggests that CBOT's various contracts for federal funds are a reliable and generally unbiased forecaster of what the actual funds rate is likely to do. The marketplace's prediction of the effective funds rate seems particularly accurate right before the next scheduled meeting of the Fed's chief policymaking group, the FOMC.

Sources: Ed Nosal, "How Well Does the Fed Funds Futures Rate Predict the Future Federal Funds Rate?" *Economic Commentary*, Federal Reserve Bank of Cleveland, October 1, 2001; and John B. Carlson, William R. Melick, and Erkin Y. Sahinoz, "An Option for Anticipating Fed Action," *Economic Commentary*, Federal Reserve Bank of Cleveland, September 1, 2003, pp. 1–4.

weak, may be very difficult, especially if the target federal funds rate has already been lowered close to zero.

Still another causal factor is *inflationary expectations:* the anticipation of continued inflation by businesses and households. Once underway, inflation may develop a momentum of its own, as consumers spend more and borrow more freely to stay ahead of rising prices, sending prices still higher. Businesses and labor unions begin to build inflation into their price and wage decisions, passing higher costs along in the form of higher prices for goods and services. The result may be a wage-price spiral in which each plateau of increased costs is used as a basis for justifying further price increases.

Inflation creates distortions in the allocation of scarce resources and hurts certain groups. For example, it tends to discourage saving and encourages consumption at a faster rate to stay ahead of rising prices. Moreover, the decline in the savings rate tends to discourage capital investment. Unfortunately, this means that the economy's growth in productivity (output per worker-hour) tends to slow, so that the supply of new goods and services cannot keep pace with rising demands, putting further upward pressure on prices. At the same time, workers often seek cost-of-living adjustments in wages and salaries, leading to an increase in labor costs. Some workers represented by strong unions or in growth industries may be able to keep pace with inflation, but other

EXHIBIT 13.11   **Measures of the Rate of Inflation in the United States (Compound Annual Rates of Change)**

	Period											
	1960–65	1965–70	1970–75	1975–80	1980–85	1985–90	1990–95	1996	1998	2000	2002	2004*
Consumer price index (CPI)	1.3%	4.2%	7.7%	8.9%	5.5%	4.0%	2.3%	2.9%	1.5%	3.4%	1.6%	3.6%
Producer price index, finished goods (PPI)	0.4	2.9	8.6	8.6	3.5	2.6	1.4	2.6	−0.9	3.7	−1.3	3.8
Implicit price deflator for gross domestic product	1.6	4.2	6.6	7.2	5.4	3.6	2.8	2.3	1.2	2.2	1.5	2.5

Source: Federal Reserve Bank of St. Louis, *Annual U.S. Economic Data;* U.S. Department of Commerce; and Board of Governors of the Federal Reserve System, *Federal Reserve Bulletin,* Table 2.15, selected issues.

*2004 figures are for the first quarter at annual rates.

groups, including retired persons and government employees, whose income is fixed or rises slowly, often experience a decline in their real standard of living when inflation is on the rise.

Central Bank Targeting of Inflation   Beginning in the 1990s several central banks around the world began setting *target inflation rates* to shoot at with their policy weapons. New Zealand was the first nation to establish a formal inflation-targeting regime. Canada followed in 1991, Great Britain in 1992, and Australia and Sweden in 1993. Before they joined the European Community, Spain and Finland adopted an inflation-targeting approach and the European Central Bank (ECB) soon declared that price stability was its primary goal. Other nations with inflation targets include Brazil, the Czech Republic, Hungary, Israel, South Korea, Poland, and Switzerland. In contrast, the United States has set no explicit inflation rate target, though it seeks to drive inflation so low that it doesn't affect business and consumer decisions.

Inflation targets vary among the nations that have set them—some are *point targets* and others are *inflation rate ranges.* For example, New Zealand's central bank has expressed its determination to keep inflation within a 0 to 3 percent annual rate range. (The New Zealand central bank's governor can be fired if he or she misses the target range!) Most other countries seek to hold inflation near 2 percent annually and the target inflation-rate range is normally somewhere close to 1 to 3 percent. The key inflation measure most widely used is some index of consumer prices, such as the Consumer Price Index (CPI). If the target or target range is missed, some nations give their central banks a specific time period to get the inflation rate back on track—for example, 18 months to two years.

The jury is still out on the success or failure of central bank inflation targeting. Certainly the central bank is the most likely institution to successfully pursue inflation targets successfully. But some central bankers are hesitant to set specific numerical inflation-rate targets, fearing a loss of flexibility and possible adverse consequences if the public becomes aware that the announced target has been missed. For example, might a missed inflation target lead to even greater inflation? More evidence is needed on the actual benefits and costs of inflation targeting.[5]

deflation

Deflation As suggested earlier, price stability can be disrupted by falling prices, or **deflation,** as well as by rising prices, or *inflation*. Deflation has plagued Japan for the past decade, during which time its economy—once the star performer among industrialized economies—has experienced an average annual growth rate of *zero* percent! In an effort to reinvigorate its economy, the Bank of Japan took monetary policy to its limits by driving interest rates to zero and then continuing to inject reserves into the banking system at a rapid pace—a policy that came to be known as *quantitative easing*. This policy has met with only limited success. Because it represents one of the few experiences over the past century of developed economies attempting to grapple with deflation, it is not surprising that this policy has caught the attention of central bankers around the world, who for so long have been struggling to reduce inflation rates down to the low single digits.

The Goal of Maximum Employment

The Employment Act of 1946 committed the United States government to *maximizing employment* as a major national goal. The Federal Reserve, as part of the government's structure, is committed to this goal as well. In recent years, the U.S. unemployment rate as determined from monthly surveys conducted by the U.S. Bureau of Labor Statistics has hovered mainly in the 4 to 7 percent range. (See Exhibit 13.12.) In terms of numbers of people, between 6 and 11 million workers have been actively seeking jobs but have been unable to find them. The nation's output of goods and services and its real standard of living are reduced by unemployment, which also may generate social unrest, increased crime, and higher tax burdens on those who are working.

Is it possible to have *zero* unemployment? What is *maximum employment*? In a market-oriented economy, where workers are free to change jobs and business people are free to hire and fire, some unemployment is inevitable. There is a minimum level of unemployment, known as *frictional unemployment,* which arises from the temporary unemployment of persons who are changing jobs in response to higher wages or better working conditions. *Full* or *maximum employment,* therefore, refers to a situation in which the only significant amount of unemployment is frictional in nature. In a fully employed economy, everyone actively seeking work finds it in a relatively short period. During the 1960s, the President's Council of Economic Advisers defined full employment as a situation in which only 4 percent of the civilian labor force is unemployed. Today the U.S. target seems to fall somewhere within the 4–6 percent unemployment range.

---

[5] Recent research (Federal Reserve Bank of St. Louis, 2004) suggests that inflation targeting has been most successful in those nations that previously had relatively high levels of inflation. To be successful, *credibility* with the public seems to be critical, along with a strong commitment on the part of a central bank to be honest and transparent in the goals it seeks and in its outlook for the economy. Moreover, inflation targeting tends to reduce the correlation between current and past inflation. Many experts argue that the Federal Reserve is unlikely to adopt inflation-targeting procedures any time soon because current U.S. law mandates that the Fed pursue multiple objectives, not just control over inflation, and the Fed, thus far, has been relatively successful in fighting inflation without an explicit targeting procedure.

EXHIBIT 13.12	1970	4.9%	1998	4.5
	1980	7.1	2000	4.0
U.S. Civilian Unemployment Rate (Percent of Civilian Labor Force)	1990	5.5	2002	5.8
	1992	7.4	2004*	5.6

Source: *Economic Report of the President* and *Federal Reserve Bulletin,* Table 2.11, selected issues.

Begining in 1994, a new unemployment survey was adopted that slightly increased the unemployment rate over previous levels.

*The 2004 figure is for February.

   Until recently, economists had raised their estimates of the amount of irreducible frictional unemployment. A key factor was the massive shifts that occurred in the composition of the U.S. labor force, especially the rapid increase in the number of adult women seeking jobs. Women 20 years of age and older, in fact, have accounted for more than half of the net increase in the U.S. labor force in recent years. This upward surge in women's employment may be attributed to a decline in fertility rates, more varied jobs available to women, and the erosion of family incomes due to inflation. Teenage participation in the labor force also has expanded under the pressure of inflation, the rising cost of college education, and the spread of vocational schools. Historically, these two groups (women and teenagers) have reported higher average unemployment rates than most other workers, moving in and out of the job market with greater fluidity than adult male workers due to family needs and schooling opportunities, thus tending to increase the average unemployment rate. Other groups also increasing in importance and who traditionally report higher average unemployment rates include nonwhite workers and unskilled laborers.

   In the most recent period the average unemployment rate inside the United States fell substantially to one of the lowest levels—about 4 percent—in modern history. One of the key factors in this period of declining unemployment, which lasted through much of the 1990s, was strong demand for consumer and business goods and services and a shortage of skilled workers. Another key force was demographics—a rise in the proportion of older workers who tend to experience less unemployment and greater job stability.

   Unfortunately, this downward movement in unemployment did not last as the U.S. economy subsequently entered a period of economic weakness and experienced the effects of terrorism as the twenty-first century began. Unemployment thus averaged higher for a relatively brief period. New high school and college graduates found it more difficult to find suitable employment and the United States appeared to be losing more of its jobs to other nations (*outsourcing*), especially to China, India, and Mexico. At the same time, *job tenure* (i.e., the average time spent in a particular job) moved downward as a growing proportion of American workers experienced greater uncertainty that their current jobs would last. In response, central banks, including the Federal Reserve, moved toward lower interest rates in order to stimulate the economy and generate more job opportunities.

The Goal of Sustainable Economic Growth

The Federal Reserve has declared that one of its important long-term goals is to *keep the economy growing at a relatively steady and stable rate*—that is, a rate high enough

Rates of Growth in Real U.S. GNP or Real GDP (Compounded Annual Rates of Change)

Time Period	Annual Rate of Change in Real GNP	Time Period	Annual Rate of Change in Real GDP
1960–69	3.9%	1996	3.9%
1970–79	3.5	1998	4.3
1980–89	3.0	2000	3.7
1990–95	2.1	2002	2.2
1996–2000	4.2	2004*	4.2

Source: Federal Reserve Bank of St. Louis, *National Economic Trends* and *Annual U.S. Economic Data,* various issues; and Board of Governors of the Federal Reserve System, *Federal Reserve Bulletin,* various issues.

*2004 figure is for the first quarter at an annual rate.

to absorb increases in the labor force and prevent the unemployment rate from rising but slow enough to avoid serious inflation. Most economists believe that this implies a rate of growth in GNP or GDP of about 3 to 4 percent annually on a real (inflation-adjusted) basis. Periodically, the economy grows more slowly than this or turns down into a recession, resulting in rising unemployment. (See especially Exhibit 13.13.) Although most economic recessions have been relatively brief they have averaged about two each decade.

Forecasting the actual starting point of each recession and its duration has proven to be an exceedingly difficult problem for the Federal Reserve. Each downturn in the economy springs from somewhat different causes, although most recessions involve a sharp cutback in business inventories. Fear of being caught with a large quantity of unsold goods leads to periodic cutbacks in new orders, throwing people out of work. At the same time, interest rates usually rise to peak levels before a recession begins, gradually choking off private investment in new capital goods and inventories. Central banks may respond by pushing market interest rates lower.

In the short run, a decline in the rate of economic growth should lead to a lower rate of inflation. This follows from the premise that recessions are marked by reduced demand for goods and services and falling incomes. Thus, in theory at least, a recession and slower economic growth may be short-term cures for severe inflation, although for those without jobs, they are certainly high-cost cures. Interestingly enough, some recent recessions have been accompanied by substantial inflation. Many observers believe there is some bias in the U.S. economy toward inflation, even during recessionary periods, that may be due to the rapid growth of service industries relative to the manufacturing sector, escalator clauses in wage contracts, and the expectation that government policy will always respond quickly to protect jobs whenever economic problems appear.

13.7   The Trade-Offs among Central Bank Goals

As we have seen in this chapter, the United States and other nations face some serious economic problems. Fortunately, inflation is less severe today in North America than in other parts of the world. For example, South America (particularly Argentina and Brazil) and Asia (especially China) are currently experiencing some of the severest price inflations seen in decades. But while inflation does not appear to be a major problem today inside the United States, the sluggish growth in new U.S.-based jobs and the struggle to maintain healthy economic growth are continuing challenges. Does this mean that the Federal Reserve System and other central banks around the world have failed to do their jobs?

Unfortunately, the problem is not that simple. For one thing, not every nation makes it clear to its central bank what its *priorities* are among different possible goals. Monetary policymakers may not be given a clear idea of which goals are most important to their governments and nations. There does appear to be a growing consensus, however, that the most feasible goal for a central bank is likely to be *controlling inflation* (i.e., maintaining reasonable price stability). As we saw earlier in this chapter, several nations (for example, Canada, New Zealand, Great Britain, and the European Union) have recently moved to spell out policy priorities for their central banks, particularly when it comes to controlling inflation.

Second, even in those cases where a central bank's goals have been spelled out, those goals may tend, in some cases, to *conflict* with one another. For example, controlling inflation in the prices of goods and services may require the central bank to slow down the domestic economy through restrictions on credit growth and higher market rates of interest. However, such a policy stance may generate more unemployment and subdue economic growth. In the short run, at least, central bankers may face some really hard choices among the multiple goals they are asked to pursue.

In the longer-run, however, many central bank goals may not necessarily be in direct conflict with each other. There is growing research evidence that the goals of maximum employment, sustainable economic growth, and price stability can be compatible with each other in the longer term. Indeed, according to the so-called Taylor curve (Chatterjee, 2002), the real trade-off that monetary policymakers may face over the long haul is a trade-off between variability in the rate of inflation and variability in the economy's level of output of goods and services. For example, monetary policymakers may be able to reduce variability in the economy's level of output and employment, but only at the cost of a more volatile rate of inflation. If this is true, monetary policymakers must decide what they most prefer—lower variability in output and jobs or lower variability in price increases (inflation). They must figure out which of these choices would have the greatest impact on the welfare of the populations they serve.

Unfortunately, we currently know relatively little about the comparative benefits and costs of fluctuations in inflation versus fluctuations in the economy's output and jobs. Clearly, more research is needed so that monetary policymakers can better see the consequences of the choices they make. It does appear that, in the long run, central banks can achieve a point of low unemployment (i.e., high availability of jobs) that can be maintained over fairly long periods of time without triggering serious inflation.

13.8   The Limitations of Monetary Policy

In addition to dealing with trade-offs among goals, central banks like the Federal Reserve find that they cannot completely control financial conditions, interest rates, or the money supply. Changes in the economy itself feed back on the money supply and the financial markets. It becomes exceedingly difficult, especially on a weekly or monthly basis, to sort out the effects of monetary policy from the impact of broad economic forces. Moreover, the structure of the economy itself is changing due to deregulation of interest rates and financial services, the increasing integration of global money and capital markets, and the breath-taking speed of new technological developments. As a result, international markets have come to exert a greater impact on the domestic economy and on central bank policymaking, while changes in domestic interest rates may not be as potent a factor affecting the economy as they were a decade ago. Central banks must learn how to deal with these changes in fundamental economic relationships.

QUESTIONS TO HELP YOU STUDY

10. What is *interest-rate targeting?* Which interest rate does the Federal Reserve focus upon in its conduct of monetary policy?

11. If the Federal Reserve wishes to put *upward* pressure on market interest rates, what would it be most likely to do? How would it proceed to push the federal funds rate in an upward direction? How would it *lower* the funds rate?

12. What are the principal economic *goals* of the Federal Reserve System? How could the Fed cause changes in the rate of inflation? In unemployment and economic growth?

13. Describe the *trade-offs* that appear to exist among key economic goals. How do these trade-offs appear to influence the central bank's ability to achieve economic goals?

14. What are the principal *limitations* of monetary policy?

www.mhhe.com/rose9e

MARKETS ON THE NET: The Most Important Web Sites for This Chapter

The Federal Reserve System (federalreserve.gov)
Bank of Canada (bankofcanada.ca/en)
Bank of England (bankofengland.gov)
Bank of Japan (boj.ur.jp)
European Central Bank (ecb.int)
Federal Open Market Committee (federalreserve.gov/fomc)

Interest-Rate Targeting (federalreserve.gov/fomc)
Reserve Bank of New Zealand (rbnz.govt.nz)
The Discount Window (frbdiscountwindow.org)

Summary of the Chapter's Main Points

The policy tools used by central banks, such as the Federal Reserve System, impact the quantity and rate of growth of legal reserves in the banking system and, in turn, the cost and availability of credit.

- The principal immediate target of Federal Reserve policy today is the *federal funds interest rate,* which, in turn, affects interest rates in both the money market and the capital market and, ultimately, the strength of the economy as a whole.

- The main policy tool used by the Federal Reserve to influence the cost and availability of credit is *open market operations*—the buying and selling of securities through the Trading Desk of the Federal Reserve Bank of New York. Open market *sales* tend to raise interest rates and restrict the supply of credit available, while open market *purchases* tend to lower interest rates and expand the supply of credit.

- The Fed, like many other central banks around the globe, has other policy tools at its disposal in the form of *deposit reserve requirements* and the *discount (loan) rates* of the individual Federal Reserve banks. An increase in reserve requirements or in the discount rate tends to tighten money and credit policy, slowing borrowing and spending, while a reduction in reserve requirements and discount rates tends to ease monetary policy, leading to an expansion of credit at lower cost.

- While open market operations, reserve requirements, and discount rates represent *general credit controls,* many central banks also have *selective credit controls* that impact specific groups or sectors of the financial system and the economy. The Federal Reserve's selective controls include moral suasion (or psychological pressure applied by central bank officials) and margin requirements (which restrict purchases of selected securities on credit).

- As open market operations have become the central tool of many central banks around the globe, different varieties of this important central bank tool have been developed. Examples include straight or outright open market operations (where actual title to security ownership changes hands), repurchase agreements (where only temporary transfer of security ownership occurs), runoff transactions (where the central bank demands cash for maturing securities), and agency transactions (where the central bank acts to buy or sell securities on behalf of a central bank customer, such as a foreign government or foreign central bank).

- Besides central bank monetary policy, actions of the public (such as demanding additional supplies of currency and coin) and operations of the government's treasury (such as collecting taxes) also impact interest rates and reserves in the financial system. The central bank must often act *defensively* to counteract these other sources of change in the financial marketplace, using its policy tools as a counterweight to the actions of the public and government.

- When the Federal Reserve decides to change the desired level of the federal funds interest rate, it uses open market operations to change the quantity of *nonborrowed reserves* held by depository institutions. Nonborrowed reserves plus borrowed reserves (loaned to depository institutions by the Federal Reserve banks) make up the supply of total reserves at the disposal of the banking system.

- The principal economic goals pursued by most central banks include the *control of inflation,* achieving *maximum employment,* and achieving *sustainable economic growth.* Unfortunately these policy goals may conflict, requiring the central bank to compromise, sometimes achieving only a portion of the goals it seeks.

Key Terms Appearing in This Chapter

general credit controls, 384	moral suasion, 400
selective credit controls, 384	margin requirements, 400
reserve requirements, 384	borrowed reserves, 403
discount rate, 387	nonborrowed reserves, 403
open market operations, 391	deflation, 408

Problems and Issues

1. Describe what is likely to happen to interest rates, deposits, and total bank reserves as a result of the transactions listed below:

   a. The Federal Reserve sells $50 million in securities outright to a bank.
   b. The Federal Reserve buys $85 million in securities outright from a bank.

www.mhhe.com/rose9e

c. The Federal Reserve sells $93 million in securities outright to a nonbank security dealer.

d. The Federal Reserve buys $42 million in securities outright from a nonbank security dealer.

e. The Federal Reserve sells $21 million in securities from its own portfolio to a foreign central bank.

f. The Federal Reserve buys $37 million in securities for its own portfolio that are being offered for sale by a foreign central bank.

g. The Federal Reserve declines the U.S. Treasury's offer to roll over $150 million in Treasury notes that are maturing in the Fed's own portfolio in exchange for new Treasury notes; instead the Federal Reserve demands cash from the Treasury.

2. Suppose the banking system's nonborrowed reserves total $48.3 billion, with total legal reserves standing at $51.2 billion. What must borrowed reserves be? This morning the Federal Reserve decided to undertake the sale of $500 million in government securities through open market operations. What will be the new level of nonborrowed reserves? If interest rates do not change, what will be the new level of total reserves? What must you assume to make this calculation? If interest rates do change, which way are they likely to move?

3. If the total supply of nonborrowed reserves equals $500 million and borrowed reserves are $50 million at the current equilibrium federal funds rate (FFR), and if the supply of total reserves is described by the following equation:

$$S = \$530 \text{ million} + 4 \text{ FFR}$$

What is the equilibrium federal funds rate (FFR)? What could the central bank do to increase the federal funds rate above its current equilibrium level? How could it reduce the funds rate below its current equilibrium level?

4. First National Bank of Elderidge borrowed $550,000 from the Federal Reserve Bank of St. Louis last Friday. The bank received short-term adjustment credit for three days and plans to repay its loan at the close of business Monday. Show the proper accounting (T-account) entries for this transaction when the loan was taken out on Friday and when it is repaid Monday afternoon. How much did total bank reserves rise when this loan was made? Are reserve requirements a factor here?

Standard & Poor's Market Insight and Web-Based Problems

STANDARD
&POOR'S

1. How closely do bank profits follow changes in the federal funds interest rate (which is closely regulated by the Federal Reserve System)? Draw a sample of banks from S&P's Market Insight, Educational Version database (such as Bank of America Corp., Bank One Corp., Bank of New York Co. Inc., Citigroup Inc., and J. P. Morgan Chase & Co.) and extract from Market Insight, starting in 2000, their profitability ratios (especially their return on assets [ROA] and their return

on equity capital [ROE]). Extract the effective federal funds rate over the same period from the Federal Reserve Board's H.15 release at **federalreserve.gov/releases/h15/update/**. What relationship, if any, between bank profits and the federal funds rate did you find? Should the relationship you found be of concern to the central bank? Why or why not?

2. The Federal Open Market Committee (FOMC) is sometimes called the single most important committee in America because of all the people who are affected by its decisions. Using the Web site **federalreserve.gov/fomc**, prepare a brief description of the makeup of this committee (i.e., who serves), what its principal tasks are, and the time schedule the committee maintains. Explain why you believe the FOMC is so important to many individuals, businesses, and governments.

3. How do the general and selective credit controls employed by the Bank of Canada at **bankofcanada.ca/en**, the Bank of England at **bankofengland.gov**, the Bank of Japan at **boj.uk.jp**, and the European Central Bank at **ecb.int** differ from those employed by the Federal Reserve System? Which credit control tool appears to be most important and most widely used among these prominent central banks?

4. Under current interest-rate targeting procedures used by the Trading Desk at the Federal Reserve Bank of New York, the only money market interest rate that is officially targeted is the federal funds rate. How closely do other money market interest rates follow the targeted Fed funds rate? Using either the interest-rate databank provided at **economagic.com** or through the Federal Reserve Board's H.15 release at **federalreserve.gov/releases/h15/update/**, determine how closely untargeted money market interest rates followed the targeted Fed funds rate on a weekly and a monthly basis over the past year. You can determine this possible interest-rate relationship either by preparing graphs comparing the funds rate and alternative money market rates (such as the CD, Eurodollar, and T-bill rates) or by calculating the correlations between these market rates.

www.mhhe.com/rose9e

Semester Project: A Study of the Fed Funds Market

In this installment of our semester-long project focusing on the *federal funds market,* our objective is to learn how the recently adopted changes to the Federal Reserve's discount window policy, described earlier in this chapter, serve to put a cap (upper limit) on the Fed funds interest rate and when that cap is effective. In your answers to this part of the project you will need to construct and then refer to a graph that illustrates activity in the market for bank reserves. Use the following steps to construct the graph with the Fed funds interest rate on the vertical axis and the volume of bank reserves on the horizontal axis.

a. Sketch a *demand schedule* for total bank reserves on your graph and explain the *slope* of the schedule you have drawn.

b. Visit the Federal Reserve's Web site at **federalreserve.gov** and obtain the policy statement from the Federal Open Market Committee's most recent meeting. What values did the FOMC choose for its target for the Fed funds interest rate and for the discount rate?

c. Now return to the Fed's Web site at **federalreserve.gov/releases/,** find the weekly H.3 release, "Aggregate Reserves of Depository Institutions and the Monetary Base," and find the total dollar volume of "Reserves of Depository Institutions" for the most recent week.

d. Choose a point in the middle of your demand schedule for bank reserves and indicate on the graph's axes that this point represents the demand for bank reserves you found in part (c) and the Fed funds target interest rate that you found in part (b).

e. Every day the Fed makes forecasts of what it believes the demand for bank reserves will be. For the purposes of this exercise, assume that the demand schedule drawn in part (d) coincides with the Fed's latest forecast. If the Federal Reserve could control the supply of bank reserves exactly through open market operations, the supply curve for bank reserves would be perfectly inelastic. Why? Show what this supply schedule would look like if the Fed wanted to "hit" its Fed funds rate target.

f. The Federal Reserve can only make its demand-for-reserves forecast with error. Illustrate this error on your graph by drawing two additional demand schedules—one where the demand for reserves is higher than forecast (at all interest rates) and one where the demand is lower (at all interest rates). Assign numerical values to those equilibrium interest rates that are equal to the Fed funds target rate plus and minus 2 percentage points.

g. Mark the level of the Fed's discount rate on your graph. Modify your reserves supply schedule to reflect the recently revised discount window policy in which the Fed supplies any amount of reserves demanded at the current discount rate. Based on what you have drawn, describe (in words) why the new discount rate is effective at putting a cap on the federal funds interest rate.

Selected References to Explore

Chatterjee, Satyajit. "The Taylor Curve and the Unemployment-Inflation Tradeoff." *Business Review,* Federal Reserve Bank of Philadelphia, Third Quarter 2002, pp. 26–33.

Federal Reserve Bank of St. Louis. "Inflation Targeting: Prospects and Problems." *Review,* July–August 2004.

Federal Reserve Bank of San Francisco. "U.S. Monetary Policy: An Introduction." *FRBSF Economic Letter,* Parts 1–4, January–February 2004.

Meyer, Laurence H. "Inflation Targets and Inflation Targeting." *Review,* Federal Reserve Bank of St. Louis, November–December 2001, pp. 1–13.

Nosal, Ed. "How Well Does the Federal Funds Futures Rate Predict the Future Federal Funds Rate?" *Economic Commentary,* Federal Reserve Bank of Cleveland, October 2001.

Stevens, Ed. "The New Discount Window." *Economic Commentary,* Federal Reserve Bank of Cleveland, May 15, 2003, pp. 1–4.

Wu, Tao. "Two Measures of Employment: How Different Are They?" *FRBSF Economic Letter,* Federal Reserve Bank of San Francisco, No. 2004–23 (August 27, 2004).

Part 4

Financial Institutions: Organization, Activities, and Regulation

Banking has sometimes been called a "confidence game." You place your money in a "demand deposit" account—perhaps earning a modest rate of interest—with the assurance that you can withdraw any of it at any time. The bank then turns around and loans the money out at a higher interest rate to households, businesses, and governments, who in turn agree to repay their loans in the future.

Suppose *all* of the banks' depositors wanted to withdraw *all* of their money and close their accounts. How would the bank pay up? The answer is that banks and similar depository institutions are counting on this event never happening! They expect *new* deposits to replace withdrawals, with only short periods of time during which withdrawals exceed deposits. During those brief intervals they use up their cash reserves or borrow or sell some of their marketable assets. On balance, however, the public's confidence that banks will be there tomorrow to honor their commitments to depositors is the essence of a *sound* banking system, and a sound banking system is essential to a vibrant, smoothly functioning economy.

In Part Four we will look at the inner workings of the major financial-service institutions in the global economy. We begin in Chapter 14 with *commercial banks*, which lie at the heart of the financial systems of most modern economies. The largest of these institutions now possess over a trillion dollars in assets and have operations that literally encircle the globe. However, banks are not alone in providing financial services. Nonbank financial institutions, including *savings and loans*, *credit unions*, *savings banks*, *money market funds*, *pension funds*, *insurance companies*, *finance companies*, and *mutual funds*, perform many of the same functions as commercial banks and are able to compete successfully (under somewhat different sets of rules) by specializing in terms of customer base or product offerings. The activities of nonbank financial institutions in the marketplace are described in Chapters 15 and 16.

Regulation of financial institutions has proven challenging. Inadequate regulation can create financial panic, while excessive regulation can induce significant losses for society by inhibiting economic activity. Chapter 17 describes how regulators have grappled with this trade-off most recently and how they have come to increasingly rely on the *marketplace itself* to structure rules that assure customers that the "confidence game" they are playing with their financial institutions is worth playing.

Chapter 14

The Commercial Banking Industry: Structure, Products, and Management

Learning Objectives

in This Chapter

- You will understand how important commercial banks are to the functioning of a modern economy and financial system.
- You will explore the structure of the United States' banking industry—one of the most important in the world.
- You will examine the content of bank financial statements and learn how to read them.
- You will see how banks create and destroy money and credit and why this activity is vital to the operation of both the economy and the financial system.

What's in This Chapter?
Key Topics Outline

The Organizational Structure of Modern Commercial Banking

Economies of Scale and Consolidation within the Banking Industry

Branch, Holding Company, and International Banking

Financial-Service Convergence and the Gramm-Leach-Bliley Act

Automation and the Changing Technology of Banking

Bank Balance Sheets and Income Statements

Money Creation and Destruction by Banks and Bank Accounting

14.1 Introduction to Banking

The dominant privately owned financial institution in the United States and in the economies of most major countries is the *commercial bank*. This institution offers the public both deposit and credit services, as well as a growing list of newer and more innovative services, such as investment advice, security underwriting, insurance, and financial planning. The name *commercial* implies that banks devote most of their resources to meeting the financial needs of business firms. In recent decades, however, commercial banks have significantly expanded their offerings of financial services to consumers and units of government around the world. The result is the emergence of a financial institution that has been called a *financial department store* because it satisfies the broadest range of financial service needs in the global economy.

The importance of commercial banks may be measured in a number of ways. They hold close to a quarter of the total assets of all financial institutions headquartered in the United States, as well as a major (often larger) share of financial assets abroad. Banks are still the principal means of making payments, through the checking accounts (demand deposits), credit cards, and electronic transfer services they offer. And banks are important because of their ability to create money from excess reserves made available from the public's deposits. The banking system can take a given volume of excess cash reserves and, by making loans and investments, generate a multiple amount of credit—a process explored later in this chapter.

Banks today are the principal channel for government monetary policy. In the United States, the Federal Reserve System implements policies to affect interest rates and the availability of credit in the economy mainly through altering the level and growth of reserves held by banks and other depository institutions. The same is true in Canada, Great Britain, the European Community, Japan, and many other nations. Today, commercial banks are the most important source of consumer credit (i.e., loans to individuals and families) and one of the major sources of loans to small businesses. Banks are major buyers of debt securities issued by federal, state, and local governments. For all of these reasons, commercial banks play a dominant role in the money and capital markets and are worthy of detailed study if we are to understand more fully how the financial system works.

14.2 The Structure of U.S. Commercial Banking

banking structure

The structure of U.S. banking is unique in comparison with other banking systems around the globe. The term **banking structure** focuses on the number and different sizes of commercial banks operating in thousands of local communities across the nation. Although the banking systems of most other nations consist of a few large banking organizations operating hundreds or thousands of branch offices, the U.S. system is dominated numerically by thousands of small commercial banks. For example, in the year 2004, nearly 7,800 commercial banking institutions were operating in the United States, compared to less than a dozen domestically chartered banks in Canada and less than three dozen domestically owned banks in the United Kingdom and Mexico.

Not surprisingly, most U.S. banks are modest in size compared to banks in other countries. Close to half of all U.S. commercial banks hold total assets of under $100 million each; only about 5 percent hold assets of a billion dollars or more and actively compete in global markets for loans and deposits. Smaller banks predominate in numbers, but the larger banks have a disproportionate share of the industry's assets. For example, the small handful of all U.S. banks with $1 billion or more in total assets hold more than four-fifths of all assets in the industry. Yet by 2004 only three U.S. banking organizations out of nearly 8,000 held a trillion dollars or more in total assets—Citigroup, Bank of America/Fleet Boston, and J. P. Morgan Chase/Bank One.

EXHIBIT 14.1

Number of Operating Commercial Banks and Branch Offices in the United States, Year-End 2003

Source: Federal Deposit Insurance Corporation, *Statistics on Banking*, 2003.

Type of Bank	Number of Banks	Number of Branch Offices
National banks	2,001	34,122
State-chartered member banks	935	13,383
Total member banks of the Federal Reserve System	2,936	47,505
Nonmember state-chartered banks	4,833	19,885
Total of all U.S.-insured commercial banks	7,769	67,390

state-chartered banks

national banks

Most commercial banks in the United States are chartered by the states rather than by the federal government. As shown in Exhibit 14.1, of the roughly 7,800 U.S. commercial banks in operation in the year 2003, just under three-quarters were **state-chartered banks.** The remaining banks, classified as **national banks,** were chartered by the federal government. National banks, on average, are larger and include nearly all of the nation's billion-dollar banking institutions. All national banks must be insured by the Federal Deposit Insurance Corporation (FDIC) and must also be members of the Federal Reserve System ("the Fed"). State-chartered banks may elect to become members of the Fed and also seek FDIC deposit insurance protection if they are willing to conform to the regulations laid down by these two federal agencies. The vast majority of U.S. banks (more than 98 percent) are FDIC insured, but only a minority have elected to join the Fed. Nevertheless, Fed member banks hold at least two-thirds of all bank deposits in the United States. (We will have more to say about the roles of the Federal Reserve, the FDIC, and other bank regulatory agencies in Chapter 17.)

A Trend toward Consolidation

consolidation

A number of structural changes have affected the banking industry in recent years. One of the most important is the drive toward **consolidation** of industry assets into fewer, but larger, banking organizations.

The United States is still essentially a nation of small banks. But great pressures are operating to form more large banking organizations in order to make more efficient use of resources. During the past 25 years the number of U.S. commercial banks has dropped from about 14, 000 to less than 7,800. Consequently, the average U.S. bank is substantially larger today than in the past.

Moreover, as noted in a recent study by Gunther and Moore (2004), the largest U.S. banks appear to be gaining market share rapidly, at the expense of small and medium-size banks. Adjusting for inflation, these researchers found that the share of the banking industry's assets accounted for by small banks (banks with less than a billion dollars in assets) fell from 23 percent to 13 percent between 1984 and 2003, while the largest U.S. banks (banks with more than $25 billion in assets) saw their industry share soar from 42 to 71 percent over the same period of time. In numbers, the small banks fell from about 11,000 in 1984 to about 6,000 in 2003. Almost simultaneously, the average profitability of the largest banks grew to outstrip the profitability of the industry's smallest banks— an outcome traceable to increased competition from bank and nonbank firms, new technology that reduced the advantage of banks having a local presence, and the development of services that could be offered over wider geographic areas.

Research studies suggest that, as banks grow, their costs increase more slowly than output, resulting in cost savings. For example, a 100 percent rise in deposit and loan accounts may result in only a 92 percent increase in the cost of bank operations. When automated bookkeeping and computer processing of accounts are used, substantial economies of scale characterize bank lending and the offering of checking accounts. Under pressure from a cost squeeze and increased competition from other financial institutions, many U.S. bankers view the strategy of growing into larger-sized banking organizations as a strong competitive response. However, scale economies resulting from bank growth appear to be modest. Once a bank reaches perhaps $500 million or so in total assets, its cost-of-production per unit of service appears to roughly level out. One reason given for this phenomenon is that, as banks become larger, they tend to multiply their service offerings and, thereby, increase their costs. For some large banks, this factor may outweigh the benefits of lower fund-raising costs and greater risk reduction from diversification across many different services and geographic areas.

Branch Banking

branch banking

The drive toward consolidation of banks into larger organizations is most evident in the long-term historical shift toward **branch banking.** Until the 1940s and 1950s, the United States was basically a nation of *unit banks*, each housed in only a single office. For example, in 1900 there were 12,427 banks, but only 87 of these had any branches. By 2003, however, there were less than 8,000 U.S. commercial banks, the majority of which were branch banking organizations. The number of branch offices has increased dramatically in recent years: In 1950 there were approximately 4,700 branch banking offices in operation; by 2003, the number of total U.S. full-service branches had climbed to more than 67,000, as shown in Exhibit 14.1.

The growth of branching has been aided by the liberalization of many state and federal laws to permit greater use of branch offices as a means of bank growth. As we will see more fully in Chapter 17, interstate bank expansion inside the United States continues to grow due, in part, to the passage of the Riegle-Neal Interstate Banking bill by the U.S. Congress in 1994, which allowed branching throughout the United States beginning in 1997. The spread of branching across the United States has also been aided by a massive population shift over the last three decades to suburban and rural areas and to the sunbelt states. Many of the nation's largest banks have followed their customers to distant markets through branching and mergers to protect their sources of funds and their earnings and have gradually spread across the nation. Recent research suggests that the development of interstate banking has had a *stabilizing* impact on the banking industry with somewhat less volatile revenues and earnings than in the past.

The principal trade association representing the U.S. banking industry is the American Bankers Association, which has a useful Web site about the industry at aba.com

Banks have also pursued greater geographic expansion through the establishment of branch offices because of the strong competitive challenge they face from a host of nonbank financial-service firms, including security brokers and dealers, mutual funds, insurance companies, credit unions, and dozens of other financial institutions. Many of these nonbank financial institutions (especially credit unions, mutual funds, and pension plans) appear to have gained market share at the expense of commercial banks, often by offering better returns and more flexible services. The rise of this form of outside competition has brought strong protests from the banking community for faster government deregulation of the industry and for permission to offer many new services. It also fueled the recently increased emphasis on retail branches, as exemplified by large-scale mergers, such as Bank of America with Fleet Boston and J. P. Morgan Chase with Bank One in order to consolidate hundreds of branch offices and reach thousands of new household and business clients, while broadening financial-service offerings as much as possible.

Bank Holding Companies

bank holding company

Paralleling the rapid growth of branch banking has been the growth of bank holding companies, which originated in the nineteenth century. A **bank holding company** is a

FINANCIAL DEVELOPMENTS

The Top Banks and Bank Holding
Companies in the United States,
Measured by Asset Size
(Ranked as of 12/31/03)

Top Banks in the U.S.	Total Assets in $ Billions	Top Bank Holding Companies in the U.S.	Total Assets in $ Billions
J.P. Morgan Chase Bank, NY	$628*	Citigroup Inc., NY	$1,264
Bank of America, Charlotte, NC	618	J.P. Morgan Chase & Co., NY	771*
Citibank, N.A., NY	582	Bank of America Corp., Charlotte, NC	736*
Wachovia Bank, Charlotte, NC	353	Wachovia Corp, Charlotte, NC	401
Bank One, N.A., Chicago, IL	257*	Wells Fargo & Co., San Francisco	388
Wells Fargo Bank, San Francisco	250	Bank One Corp., Chicago, IL	327*
Fleet National Bank, Providence, RI	192*	Taunus Corp., NY	291
U.S. Bank, N.A., Cincinnati, OH	189	FleetBoston Financial Corp., Boston	200*

*As 2004 began, J. P. Morgan Chase & Company of New York and Bank One of Chicago began the process of merging after regulatory approval, while Bank of America Corp. of Charlotte, North Carolina, and Fleet Boston Financial Corp. of Boston also announced merger plans.

Sources: Federal Financial Institutions Examination Council (ffiec.gov) and Board of Governors of the Federal Reserve System (federalreserve.gov).

The size, acquisitions, and recent performance of leading U.S. bank holding companies may be traced through the National Information Center of the Federal Financial Institutions Examination Council at ffiec.gov/nic

corporation organized to acquire and hold the stock of one or more banks. The company may also hold stock in nonbank business ventures. Holding companies have become popular as vehicles to avoid laws prohibiting the extension of branch banking and as a way to offer services that banks themselves cannot offer.

Bank holding companies have grown rapidly in the United States. In 1960 there were just 47 registered holding company organizations, controlling only about 8 percent of the total assets of U.S.-insured banks. By 2003, U.S. holding companies numbered close to 6,000 and held over 90 percent of U.S. bank assets, and that share continues to rise. In the international markets as well, holding companies have become the predominant bank organizational form because of their advantages in raising capital, spreading out their risk exposure, and allowing entry into new business opportunities.

The growth of nonbank business activities of holding companies has been rapid. Insurance agencies, finance companies, mortgage companies, consulting firms, and other businesses have been started or acquired in large numbers by bank holding companies in recent years. These ventures represent an attempt to diversify banking operations to reduce risk and gain access to a broader market. Unfortunately, many bankers have found that, often, they cannot effectively manage a highly diverse set of nonbank businesses. In recent years several large holding companies (e.g., Citigroup and Travelers) sold off some of their nonbank business ventures in an effort to cut costs and raise more capital for their banks.

International Banking

The growth of banking organizations at home has been paralleled by the growth of banks abroad. This expansion overseas has not been confined to the largest institutions in such established money centers as New York, Chicago, and San Francisco but also includes leading banks in regional financial centers such as Atlanta, Charlotte, and Miami. Several of the largest U.S. banks receive half or more of their net income from foreign sources, although several U.S. banks have reduced their overseas activity recently due to poorly performing international loans and high operating costs.

While branch banks and bank holding companies have dominated the expansion of banking inside the United States, bank expansion into international markets has taken place through a wide variety of unique organizational forms. *Representative offices,* the simplest form, represent the "eyes and ears" of a bank in foreign markets, helping to market each bank's services to both old and new customers, but these limited-service facilities cannot take deposits or book loans. In contrast, a *branch office* offers all or most of the services the home office provides, including the taking of deposits and the booking of loans. International banks sometimes find it less expensive to acquire an existing bank overseas with an established clientele than to set up their own branch office. The acquired institution becomes a *subsidiary* of the international bank, retaining its own charter and capital stock. Alternatively, a bank may establish a *joint venture* with a foreign firm, sharing expenses but gaining access to the expertise and customer contacts already made by the foreign company.

Banks today penetrate overseas markets for a wide variety of reasons. In many cases, their corporate customers expanding abroad demand access to multinational banking facilities. The huge eurocurrency market, which spans the globe, also offers an attractive source of bank funds when domestic funding sources are less available or more costly. Foreign markets frequently offer fewer regulatory barriers and less competition than may be found at home, but they also entail more risk (as in Argentina and Brazil).

Foreign banks have grown rapidly in the United States, with many of the largest Canadian, European, and Asian banks viewing the 50 states as a huge economically and politically stable common market. (See Exhibit 14.2 for a list of some of the world's largest banks and their principal financial-service competitors.) Moreover, foreign banks were able to offer some services, such as underwriting corporate securities or selling insurance, that U.S. banking organizations were restrained from offering until the Financial Services Modernization (Gramm-Leach-Bliley) Act was passed in 1999. Congress initially responded to this invasion by passing the International Banking Act in 1978, bringing foreign banks under federal regulation for the first time. Passage of the FDIC Improvement Act in 1991 also ushered in even greater regulatory control over foreign bank activity inside the United States, granting the Federal Reserve authority to close the U.S. offices of foreign banks if they are operated in an unsafe manner or are violating U.S. laws.

EXHIBIT 14.2		
Some of the Largest Banks around the Globe	Citigroup, United States	Bank of China
	Fuji/Dai-Ichi/Industrial Bank of Japan	Bank of America, United States*
	Bank of Tokyo—Mitsubishi	Bank One Corp., United States*
Sources: Board of Governors of the Federal Reserve System and various central banks.	Sanwa Bank, Japan	Barclays Bank, United Kingdom
	Sumitomo/Sakura Bank, Japan	Credit Agricole Mutuel, France
	Industrial and Commercial Bank of China	Dresdner Bank, Germany
*Note: J. P. Morgan Chase Bank and Bank One merged in 2004 as did Bank of America and FleetBoston Financial Corp.	ABN AMRO Bank, N.V., Netherlands	Banque Nationale de Paris, France
	HSBC Holdings PLC, United Kingdom	Hong Kong Bank
	Union Bank of Switzerland (UBS)	Royal Bank of Canada
	Deutsche Bank, Germany	Canadian Imperial Bank
	J.P. Morgan Chase Bank, United States*	Wells Fargo, United States
	Wachovia Corp., United States	Toronto–Dominion Bank, Canada
		FleetBoston Financial Corp., United States*

14.3   The Convergence Trend in Banking

Perhaps the most common characteristic of all international banks today is their striving to offer a full line of services to all customers. Thus, *commercial banks,* which specialize predominantly in lending and deposit taking, are combining with *investment banks,* which deal in securities issued by their customers. Several banks in Canada, Great Britain, and Western Europe long ago took an additional step to become *universal* and *merchant banks.* Universal banks, like Germany's Deutsche Bank and Britain's Barclays Bank, provide not only deposit, loan, and security underwriting services but also consulting, insurance, real estate sales, and hundreds of other services. Merchant banks make private equity investments in businesses, investing some of their owners' capital in their customers' projects, thus becoming principals as well as creditors in business investment projects. As a result, merchant and universal banks tend to make longer-term investments than traditional banks and are active in both the money market and the capital market simultaneously.

In 1999, with passage of the Gramm-Leach-Bliley Act, leading banks in the United States began to move toward universal banking more aggressively, establishing *financial holding companies* (FHCs) and combining banking, securities, insurance, and other affiliates under one corporate umbrella. Nineteen of the 20 largest U.S. banks now belong to an FHC. Close to 600 large and small U.S. banks have created FHCs because their traditional deposits and loans are declining and they feel the need to find new services and new sources of revenue.

Thus, one of the most important structural changes occurring in banking today is **convergence.** This means that banking organizations are looking more and more like other financial-service providers, offering many of the same services as security firms, insurance and finance companies, and other service suppliers. In turn, the public is finding it much tougher today to distinguish banks from other financial-service businesses. Competition between bank and nonbank service companies is intensifying, forcing many bank and nonbank companies to consolidate into fewer, but much larger multiservice organizations.

convergence

Bank Failures

The rapid expansion of bank services has not protected some banks and banking systems from getting into serious trouble, however, due to declining economies and falling real estate and stock prices coupled with excessive government control over who does and does not receive loans. For example, recently banks in Japan, Korea, and other parts of Asia as well as in Russia were forced to grapple with financial crises, with many banks collapsing or being swept up into mergers to add vitally needed capital and more experienced management. More recently, Japan has been pasting together new bail-out plans (with the help of the International Monetary Fund and other public and private institutions) to stem the tide of bank failures and restore public confidence in its banking system. Bad loans and weak stock prices continue to threaten some banks in Asia, South America, and elsewhere with failure.

In contrast, for most of the history of the United States, the American banking industry has experienced an extremely low failure rate (only about 1 or 2 percent of the U.S. banking population failing each year, on average) due to extensive regulatory supervision, a relatively strong economy, and conservative management on the part of most banks. For example, in 2003, only three commercial banks (out of an industry population of almost 8,000) were closed, with the Federal Deposit Insurance Corporation taking control of their assets as receiver. The insured deposits and selected assets of these three failed U.S. banks were sold to other FDIC-insured banking firms.

Information about U.S. bank failures each year can be found at fdic.gov/bank

The reasons behind most bank failures are numerous. Many bankers today are willing to accept greater risk in their operations, in part because of intensified competition and government insurance of bank deposits. Moreover, a worldwide movement toward banking **deregulation** (which we will discuss more fully in Chapter 17) has given banks greater opportunities to market new services and expand geographically without such strict government controls, but it has also increased their opportunities for failure. Some analysts argue that even more important is the *volatility of economic and financial conditions*—especially the prices of many foreign currencies, which fluctuate with market conditions. Increased economic volatility can make bank earnings and stock prices more unstable and force bankers to devote more time to the control and management of risk. An additional factor in bank failure is crime—fraud, embezzlement, and outright theft—which banks and bank regulators are working to combat with stronger security measures.

As Walter (2004) observes, bank failures are often more difficult to resolve than the failures of other businesses and typically require some form of government regulation over the failure process in order to avoid misallocation of resources. Deposit insurance, designed mainly to head off depositor runs against healthy banks, reduces the incentive of most depositors to demand that a troubled bank either pay off its creditors or, at least, pay higher interest rates on its deposits. A troubled bank can continue to raise funds by selling government-insured deposits, no matter how bad its financial situation might be, thus increasing its reliance on the government's deposit guarantees and increasing the amount that the government must pay insured depositors when the bank's doors are finally closed.

Thus, the marketplace frequently does *not* set in motion the timely closure of problem banks and lets some uninsured depositors escape before failure occurs. This was one of the reasons the U.S. government enacted the Federal Deposit Insurance Corporation Improvement Act of 1991. Under the terms of this law, the FDIC was given broad new powers to resolve problem-bank situations, taking control even before a bank becomes insolvent. The Improvement Act limits the ability of the bank regulatory agencies to prop up a troubled bank with government loans when that bank really should be closed. Current rules require that problem banks either raise more capital from their stockholders or be turned over to a receiver (usually the FDIC) to sell off their assets.

Changing Technology

Banking today is passing through a technological revolution. Computer terminals and high-speed information processing are transforming the industry, stressing convenience and speed in handling such routine transactions as making deposits, extending loans, and paying for purchases of goods and services. Most of the new technology is designed to reduce labor and paper costs, making the banking industry less labor intensive and more capital intensive.

Among the most important pieces of technology in the industry are automated teller machines (ATMs). ATMs accept deposits, dispense cash, and accept payments on loans and other bills owed by customers. For many banking transactions, they perform as well as human tellers do, with the added advantage of 24-hour availability. Initially, ATMs were placed on bank premises, but their growth has extended widely to shopping centers, gasoline stations, airports, and train terminals. In these locations, they are known as *remote service units* (RSUs). As the 21st century began there were more than 350,000 ATMs in the U.S. alone.

Most ATMs promote lower transaction costs for the customer and reduce the need for conventional branch banking offices. Related to ATMs are point-of-sale (POS) terminals located in retail stores and other commercial establishments. Connected online to the bank's computer, POS terminals accept plastic credit and debit cards, permitting the customer to pay instantly for a purchase without the necessity of cashing a check.

deregulation

Another important piece of electronic banking machinery is the automated clearinghouse (ACH). An ACH transfers information from one financial institution to another and from account to account via computer tape. The majority of banks and other financial-service institutions offering payments services are members of about three dozen ACHs serving the United States. They are used principally for handling business payrolls and processing federal government transactions. Check truncation systems are being used alongside the ACH. Such a system transmits images of checks ("substitute checks") electronically from one financial institution to another, eliminating the need to transfer paper, as permitted by recent passage of the Check 21 Act.

Finally, banking over the *Internet* through home and office computers is expanding rapidly, allowing customers to quickly and easily enter their requests for information or to conduct remote financial transactions. A growing portion of bank Web sites are offering 24-hour, Web-based transactional services, such as bill paying, transferring funds, applying for new loans, and security trading. Several Internet-only ("virtual") banks have been started recently, seeking to take advantage of low overhead, convenience, and speed. Unfortunately, this form of banking model has not been highly successful despite the savings on brick and mortar over conventional banks. Reasons for the comparatively weak performance of Internet-only banking institutions include their lack of volume, restricted range of services, and relatively high operating costs. However, virtual banks may become competitive in the future as more and more customers go online with their transactions and as the cost of conventional banking transactions continues to rise.

To learn about possible careers in banking see especially aba.careersite.com

These recent technological changes have profound implications for bank costs, employment, and profitability. In the future, customers will have less need to enter a bank building. Their future banking needs may be met mainly by electronically transferring information rather than by requiring people to move from one location to another. The banker's principal function will be one of providing the necessary equipment and letting customers conduct their own transactions. This development implies fewer but more highly skilled bank employees and more equipment. Heavy investment in computers and money machines will result in substantial fixed costs, requiring a large volume of transactions and favoring the largest banking organizations. The new technology of banking should further intensify pressures for consolidation and convergence of the industry into banks smaller in number but much larger in size and scope of services. In the long run, technology will lower overall operating costs and save the industry billions of dollars.

QUESTIONS TO HELP YOU STUDY

1. In what ways are commercial banks of special importance to the money and capital markets and the economy?

2. Four dominant movements in the structure of U.S. banking in recent years have been:

   a. The spread of branch banking.

   b. The growth of holding companies.

   c. The rise of interstate banking.

   d. The convergence of bank and nonbank firms.

   Explain what has happened in these four areas and why.

3. What is *consolidation* in banking? What appears to be driving this trend?

4. How numerous are bank failures and what seem to be their most important causes? Why are bank failures different from the failures of other businesses and how are they resolved today?

5. What changes are under way in bank technology and why?

14.4 Portfolio Characteristics of Commercial Banks

Commercial banks are the financial department stores of the financial system. They tend to offer a wider array of financial services than any other financial institution, meeting the credit, payments, and savings needs of individuals, businesses, and governments. This characteristic of financial diversity is reflected in the basic financial statements of the industry—the balance sheet (or statement of condition) and the income and expense statement. Exhibit 14.3 provides a list of the principal uses of funds (assets) and the major sources of funds (liabilities and equity capital) for all FDIC-insured U.S. commercial banks as they appeared on a recent industry balance sheet.

Cash and Due from Banks (Primary Reserves)

primary reserves

All commercial banks hold a substantial part of their assets in **primary reserves,** consisting of cash and deposits held with other banks. These reserves are the banker's first line of defense against withdrawals by depositors and customer demand for loans. Banks generally hold no more cash than is absolutely required to meet short-term contingencies, however, because the yield on cash assets is minimal. The deposits held with other banks do provide an implicit return, however, because they are a means of "paying" for correspondent banking services. In return for the deposits of smaller banks, larger U.S. correspondent banks provide such important services as clearing checks and processing records by computer. Thousands of smaller banks across the United States invest their excess cash reserves in loans to other banks (called *federal funds*) with the help of their larger correspondents.

Investment Security Holdings and Secondary Reserves

Commercial banks hold securities acquired in the open market as a long-term investment and as a secondary reserve to help meet short-term cash needs. Many banks still hold sizable quantities of *municipal securities*—bonds and notes issued by state, city, and other local governments—because their interest income is tax exempt, although recent tax reform legislation has substantially limited the tax advantages of municipal notes and bonds for many banks. However, holdings of *U.S. Treasury obligations* and especially *debt obligations issued or guaranteed by federal agencies* (such as the Federal National Mortgage Association ["Fannie Mae"] or the Farm Credit System) are much larger in volume today than municipal securities in U.S. bank investment portfolios. Banks generally favor shorter-term government securities because these securities can be marketed readily to cover short-term cash needs and are free of default risk. In the most recent period banks have been shifting more heavily toward federal agency securities due to their higher yields and strong credit quality.

A related type of security purchased in large volume by banks are loan-backed securities, each representing an interest in a pool of previously made loans, which pay interest and principal to investors as the loans are paid out. Most loan-backed securities held by banks are backed by government-guaranteed real estate mortgages or credit-card receivables. By the turn of the century mortgage-backed securities accounted for more than half of all investment securities held by U.S. banks.

Commercial banks also hold small amounts of corporate bonds and notes, although they generally prefer to make direct loans to businesses as opposed to purchasing their securities in the open market. Under existing regulations, U. S. commercial banks are forbidden to purchase most types of corporate stock. However, banks do hold corporate stock as collateral for some of their loans and are allowed to invest in selected equities, such as the stock of small business investment companies, community development corporations, and the Federal Reserve banks.

EXHIBIT 14.3

Bank Report of Condition (Balance Sheet): Assets, Liabilities, and Capital of Insured Commercial Banks in the United States ($ Billions, Year-End Figures)

	1980		1990		2000		2003	
	Billions of Dollars	Percent of Total Assets	Billions of Dollars	Percent of Total Assets	Billions of Dollars	Percent of Total Assets	Billions of Dollars	Percent of Total Assets
Assets:								
Cash and deposits due from banks	$ 331.9	17.9%	$ 318.0	9.4%	$ 369.8	5.9%	$ 387.6	5.1%
Investment securities:								
U.S. Treasury securities	104.5	5.6	150.8	4.4	75.7	1.2	73.9	1.0
Federal agency securities	59.1	3.2	275.6	8.2	634.7	10.2	931.8	12.3
State and local govt. securities	146.3	7.9	83.5	2.5	92.6	1.5	110.2	1.4
Corporate bonds	13.4	0.7	85.9	2.5	233.5	3.7	149.4	2.0
Corporate stock	1.8	0.1	8.8	0.3	41.1	0.7	191.0	2.5
Investment totals	$ 325.0	17.5%	$ 604.6	17.8%	$1,077.6	17.3%	$ 1,456.3	19.2%
Total loans and leases, gross	1,016.5	54.8	2,110.2	62.3	3,819.1	61.2	4,761.8	62.6
Real estate loans	269.1	14.5	829.8	24.5	1,670.3	26.8	2,272.3	29.9
Commercial and industrial loans	391.0	21.1	615.0	18.1	1,048.2	16.8	870.6	11.5
Loans to individuals	187.4	10.1	403.5	11.9	609.7	9.8	720.4	10.1
Agricultural loans	32.3	3.2	33.3	1.0	48.1	0.8	46.3	0.6
Loans to depository institutions	81.2	8.1	51.2	1.5	120.5	1.9	142.5	1.9
All other loans and leases	55.5	5.5	177.4	5.2	322.3	5.2	659.7	8.7
Less: Unearned income	−21.0	−2.1	−13.7	−0.4	−3.0	−0.1	−4.1	−0.1
Allowance for loan and lease losses	−10.1	−0.5	−55.5	−1.6	−64.1	−1.0	−77.1	−1.0
Net loans and leases	1,006.4	54.2	2,054.6	60.6	3,752.1	60.4	4,680.6	61.6
Bank premises and equipment	26.7	1.4	51.4	1.5	75.7	1.2	83.4	1.1
Other real estate owned	2.2	0.1	21.6	0.6	3.2	0.1	4.6	0.1
Intangible assets	NA	NA	10.6	0.3	102.7	1.6	158.2	2.1
All other assets	163.4	8.8	328.5	9.7	857.6	13.5	831.8	10.9
Total assets	$1,855.7	100.0%	$3,389.5	100.0%	$6,238.7	100.0%	$7,602.5	100.0%
Liabilities:								
Total deposits	$1,481.2	79.8%	$2,650.1	78.2%	$4,176.6	66.9%	$5,028.9	66.1%
Demand deposits	431.5	23.3	463.9	13.7	679.3	10.9	523.8	6.9
Savings deposits	200.9	10.8	798.1	23.5	1,567.0	25.1	2,306.5	30.3
Time deposits	554.7	29.9	1,094.7	32.3	1,371.5	22.0	1,253.5	16.5
Other deposits	294.1	15.8	293.4	8.7	558.8	9.0	945.1	12.4
Borrowings in the money market	177.7	9.6	385.3	11.4	1,256.2	20.1	1,267.6	16.7
Subordinated capital notes and debentures	6.5	0.4	23.9	0.7	87.0	1.4	101.5	1.4
Other liabilities	82.7	4.5	111.5	3.3	189.4	3.0	512.4	6.7
Total liabilities	$1,748.1	94.2%	$3,170.8	93.5%	$5,709.1	91.5%	$ 6,910.4	90.9%
Equity capital:								
Preferred stock	$ 0.1	0.0*	$ 1.7	0.1	$ 3.4	0.1	$ 6.5	0.1
Common stock	21.7	1.2	30.9	0.9	31.2	0.5	30.3	0.4
Surplus	37.8	2.0	92.4	2.7	259.4	4.2	350.4	4.6
Undivided profits	48.0	2.6	93.7	2.8	236.9	3.8	304.9	4.0
Total equity capital	107.6	5.8	218.6	6.4	529.6	8.5	692.1	9.1
Total liabilities and capital	$1,855.7	100.0%	$3,389.5	100.0%	$6,238.7	100.0%	$7,602.5	100.0%

*Less than $50 million.

Source: Federal Deposit Insurance Corporation, *Historical Statistics on Banking, 1934–1992; Statistics on Banking,* selected years; and **fdic.gov.**

Recently, American banks have been under strong regulatory pressure to value their security holdings and selected other assets and liabilities at current market value rather than at book value on the day they were acquired. The long-range goal is to make bank balance sheets reflect more accurately the true condition of a bank so that capital-market investors and depositors can make a more informed judgment about the bank's true financial standing. Unfortunately, this step has done little, thus far, to improve the quality of information coming from bank financial reports.

Loans

The principal business of commercial banks is to make *loans* to qualified borrowers (or at least make it easier for their customers to find credit from some source with a bank perhaps agreeing to underwrite a customer's security issue or guarantee a loan from a third-party lender). Loans are among the highest yielding assets a bank can add to its portfolio, and they often provide the largest portion of traditional banks' operating revenue.

Banks make loans of reserves to other banks through the *federal funds market* and to securities dealers through *repurchase agreements*. Far more important in dollar volume, however, are direct loans to businesses and individuals. These loans arise from negotiation between the bank and its customer and result in a written agreement designed to meet the specific credit needs of the customer and the requirements of the bank for adequate security and income.

As shown in Exhibit 14.3, a substantial portion of bank credit is extended to commercial and industrial customers in the form of direct loans. Historically, commercial banks have preferred to make *short-term loans* to businesses, principally to support purchases of inventory. Recently, however, banks have lengthened the maturity of their business loans to include *term loans* (which have maturities over one year) to finance the purchase of buildings, machinery, and equipment. Moreover, longer-term loans to business firms have been supplemented in recent years by equipment leasing plans. These leases are the functional equivalent of a loan—that is, the customer not only makes the required lease payments while using the equipment but is also responsible for repairs and maintenance and for any taxes due. Lease financing carries not only significant cost and tax advantages for the customer but also substantial tax advantages for a bank, because it can depreciate leased equipment.

Commercial banks are also important lenders in the real estate field, supporting the construction of residential and commercial structures. In fact, real estate loans are, by volume, the most important bank loan category. Major types of loans in the real estate category include farm and real estate credit, conventional government-guaranteed (FHA and VA) single-family residential home loans, conventional and government-guaranteed loans on multifamily residences (such as apartments), and mortgage loans on nonfarm commercial properties. Today, commercial banks are the most important source of construction financing in the economy.

To learn more about trends in bank balance sheets (reports of condition) and other financial reports for the banking industry as a whole see fdic.gov/bank and for individual banking firms see fdic.gov/bank/individual

One of the most dynamic areas in bank lending today is the making of installment loans to individuals and families, particularly loans secured by a property owner's equity in his or her home (i.e., *home equity loans,* the interest costs of which may be tax deductible to the borrower). Home equity loans can be used to finance a college education, start a new business, or to cover a variety of other financial needs not related to housing. While banks began making home equity loans equal to a fraction of a home owner's equity, intense competition among lenders has resulted in some home equity loans and lines of credit today exceeding the value of the home owner's equity investment in a home, increasing lenders' risk. Banks also finance the purchase of automobiles, home furnishings, and appliances and provide funds to modernize homes and other properties and to pay for education and travel.

There is a growing concern today that consumer loans, particularly of the credit-card variety, have become more risky for banks due to higher default rates. Many banks and credit card companies have increased their issue of new credit cards explosively, democratizing debt in order to reach millions of new customers, many of whom represent serious risks for lenders. Intense competition has encouraged many banks to give credit cards to customers who may have little or no credit history, some of whom turn out to be poor credit risks.

Recently bankers have faced the necessity of closely examining the *quality,* not just the quantity, of their loans, especially in the wake of the terrorist attacks of 9/11. Recent events have demonstrated the great sensitivity of bank loan performance to changes in the economy. Problem loans reduce bank loan revenues, raise operating expenses, and force bankers to reexamine their relationships with customers and redesign the terms they are offering on loan contracts.

Deposits

To carry out their extensive lending and investing operations, banks draw on a wide variety of deposit and nondeposit sources of funds. The bulk of commercial bank funds—about two-thirds of the total—comes from *deposits.* There are three main types of deposits: demand, savings, and time. *Demand deposits,* more commonly known as *checking accounts,* are still a very important means of making payments because they are safer than cash and are widely accepted (although outside the United States smart cards, credit cards, and transfers by electronic means have generally outstripped demand deposits as payments media). *Savings deposits* generally are in small dollar amounts; they bear a relatively low interest rate but may be withdrawn by the depositor with no notice. *Time deposits* carry a fixed maturity, a penalty for early withdrawal, and usually offer the highest interest rates a bank will pay. Time deposits may be divided into nonnegotiable certificates of deposit (CDs), which are usually small, consumer-type accounts, and negotiable CDs that may be traded in the open market in million-dollar amounts and are purchased mainly by corporations all over the world.

During the past three decades, new forms of checkable (demand) deposits appeared, combining the essential features of both demand and savings deposits. These **transaction accounts** include negotiable orders of withdrawal (NOWs) and automatic transfer services (ATS). NOW accounts may be drafted to pay bills but also earn interest, while ATS is a preauthorized payment service in which the bank transfers funds from an interest-bearing savings account to a checking account as necessary to cover checks written by the customer. Two newer types of transaction accounts— money market deposit accounts (MMDAs) and Super NOWs—are designed to compete directly with the high-yielding share accounts offered by money market funds. They carry prevailing market rates on short-term funds and can be drafted via check, automatic withdrawal, or telephone transfer.

transaction accounts

In recent years banks have experienced a shift in their deposits toward more costly interest-bearing accounts, such as MMDAs. These newer deposits are generally *market-linked accounts,* the returns of which are tied to movements in market interest rates and security prices, reflecting prevailing credit conditions in the financial system. This shift toward more expensive, market-responsive deposits reflects the growing sophistication of bank customers, who have developed efficient cash management practices and insist on competitive returns on their funds.

Moreover, the cost of attracting customer funds has been further increased by the tendency of bankers to expand their services in an effort to offer their customers "one-stop" financial convenience. Thus, to retain old customers and attract new ones, many banks have developed or are working through franchise agreements to offer (1) security brokerage services so that customers can purchase stocks, bonds, and shares in mutual funds and pay by charging their deposit accounts; (2) insurance

Banks are the most important financial-service institutions helping people and businesses pay for their purchases of goods and services. Unfortunately, in the United States the process of clearing and collecting payments is surprisingly slow in a rapidly developing electronic age. When a business purchases goods and services from a supplier, for example, the supplier may not receive payment for several days. The term used for completing this payment is *final settlement*, which the parties to the transaction agree must occur within a specific time frame. In recent years innovations in the U.S. payments system have lowered the average time to final settlement from about five days to about three days.

But even three days is *much* longer than it takes for business-to-business transactions inside many European countries. The reason is that the U.S. payments system is still encumbered by the need to process vast numbers of checks which must be routed to thousands of different banks—a costly and time-consuming process. For example, in 2001, U.S. corporations processed 9.1 billion transactions worth $31.3 trillion. Eighty-two percent of these transactions involved paper checks. In contrast, during 1999, 95 percent of all noncash payments in Germany, the Netherlands, and Switzerland were processed electronically with great speed. The U.S. has been slow to catch up, but rapid change is sure to come, particularly in the wake of check imaging, check truncation, debit cards, and other electronic advances.

On the business payments horizon is the concept of *straight-through-processing* (STP). With STP the time to final settlement will be measured in minutes, not days. But there are stumbling blocks. For one thing, STP requires standardization of accounting practices between businesses, including a matching of purchase orders with invoices, and there must be mechanisms in place to deal with incomplete remittances and security issues. While more challenging to implement than was first thought, STP seems sure to win out eventually, creating an electronic business-to-business payments system that will be accurate, fast, inexpensive, and safe to operate.

For greater detail on the STP issue see especially **webservicearchitect.com/articles/santani06print.asp** and **ababj.com/electropayments.html**.

counters to make life, health, and property-casualty insurance coverage available (often through joint ventures with affiliated or cooperating nonbank firms); (3) account relocation services and real estate brokerage of homes and other properties for customers who move; (4) financial planning centers to aid customers with important personal and business decisions; and (5) merchant banking services that aid major corporations with their long-term equity financing requirements. These new services may have opened up new markets for banks, but they have also created new risks for bank management and demanded greater efficiency in bank operations.

Nondeposit Sources of Funds

nondeposit funds

One of the most significant trends in banking in recent years is greater use of **nondeposit funds** (borrowings), especially as competition for deposits increases. Principal nondeposit sources of funds for banks today include purchases of reserves (federal funds) from other banks, security repurchase agreements (when securities are sold temporarily by a bank and then bought back later), and the issuance of capital notes. Capital notes are of particular interest because many of these securities may be counted under current regulations as "capital" for purposes of determining how much a bank can lend (i.e., its *loan limit*). Both state and federal laws limit the amount of money a commercial bank can lend to any one borrower to a fraction of the bank's capital. To be counted as capital, however, capital notes must be subordinated to deposits, so that if a bank is liquidated, the depositors have first claim to its assets.

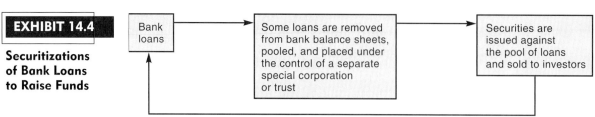

EXHIBIT 14.4

Securitizations of Bank Loans to Raise Funds

Proceeds of security sales flow back to the bank
as a new source of funds

Recently banks have turned to new nondeposit funds sources, including floating-rate CDs and notes sold in international markets, sales of loans, securitizations of selected assets, and standby credit guarantees. The floating-rate securities tend to be longer-term borrowings of funds, stretching out beyond one year, with an interest rate that is adjusted periodically to reflect changing conditions in international markets. Larger banks (such as J. P. Morgan Chase and Citibank) have expanded their sales of short-term business loans from their books, usually selling these credits in million-dollar blocks to raise new funds. Better-quality loans have been packaged into asset pools and *securitized*—that is, used as collateral for bank security issues that are sold to investors through a security dealer. (See Exhibit 14.4.) The bank se-

securitized assets   cures additional funds to make new loans and investments from these **securitized assets,** which have included packages of auto, credit-card, home mortgage, and other loan types. The packaged loans generate interest and principal payments, which are passed through to investors who purchased the securities backed by these loans.

standby credit letters   Finally, many large banks today are issuing **standby credit letters** on behalf of their customers who borrow from another lender or sell securities in the open market. As illustrated in Exhibit 14.5, standbys contain the bank's pledge to pay (guarantee) if its customer cannot pay a third party. They generate fee income for the bank without using up scarce funds or booking more assets that would require a bank to pledge more capital behind them.

Many of these activities are *off-balance-sheet transactions*—not recorded on a bank's balance sheet and using up little or no bank capital. However, securitizations, standby credits, and other off-balance-sheet activities help banks provide services to their customers and earn *fee* (noninterest) *income*—the fastest growing form of bank

EXHIBIT 14.5

Bank Standby Letters of Credit Issued on Behalf of Their Customers

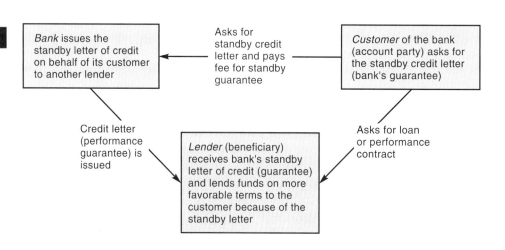

revenue. The result is an expansion in bank net earnings without booking additional assets on the bank's balance sheet.

Equity Capital

Equity capital (or net worth) supplied by a bank's stockholders provides only a minor portion (only about 9 percent, on average) of total funds for most banks today. In fact, while the ratio of equity capital to bank loans and deposits has risen recently, it previously had been in decline for several decades due to falling profit margins, inflation, and efforts by bank managers to employ greater financial leverage. This concerned many financial experts because one of the most important functions of equity capital is to keep a bank open in the face of operating losses until management can correct its problems. Recently, federal law has mandated minimum capital-to-asset ratios for banks, and many banks have expanded their equity capital positions. There is also a set of cooperative international capital regulations for major banks in the United States, Great Britain, Japan, and the nations of Western Europe, imposing minimum capital requirements on all banks in leading industrialized countries based on the degree of risk exposure that each of these banks faces.[1]

Revenues and Expenses

The majority of bank revenues come from interest and fees on loans, as shown by the industry's statement of earnings and expenses presented in Exhibit 14.6. Interest and dividends on investment security holdings are the second most important source of bank revenues after loans. Other minor sources of income include earnings from trust (fiduciary) activities and service charges on deposit accounts.

Bank expenses have risen rapidly in recent years, threatening to squeeze the industry's operating income. Greater competition from bank and nonbank financial institutions has resulted in increases in the real cost of raising funds, and the expense of upgrading computers and automated equipment has placed an added drain on bank revenues. Interest on deposits and other borrowed funds is the principal expense item for many commercial banks, along with the salaries and wages of their employees. Recently, however, interest expenses on bank deposits and other borrowings have declined in percentage terms, as banks have carried on a growing share of their service operations off of their balance sheets.

A careful perusal of the statement of earnings and expenses (Report of Income) for all U.S. insured banks in Exhibit 14.6 shows an interesting arrangement of revenue and expense accounts. First, bankers record all of their bank's interest income from loans and security investments. Then the total interest paid out on borrowed funds is subtracted to derive each bank's net interest income or *interest margin.* The interest margin measures how efficiently a bank is performing its function of borrowing and lending funds. For many banks this margin is the principal determinant of their profitability.

Of increasing importance in the industry, however, is the *noninterest margin,* which is the difference between total noninterest income (such as service fees on deposits) and noninterest expenses (such as employee salaries, wages, and benefits). The noninterest margin is growing in importance as a determinant of bank profits because commercial banks are developing more and more new services that generate noninterest fees, such as security underwriting services, guaranteeing the loan a customer has

To more fully understand the many facets of the commercial banking industry, see the Web sites of several leading banks, including Citibank at citibank.com; J. P. Morgan Chase at jpmorganchase.com; Wells Fargo Bank at wellsfargo.com; and Capital One at capitalone.com

You can track recent trends in U.S. bank earnings and expenses through FYI and Bank Trends, two publications appearing on the Federal Deposit Insurance Corporation's Web site at fdic.gov

---

[1]See Chapter 17 for a fuller discussion of the Basel Agreement on bank capital requirements.

EXHIBIT 14.6   **Bank Report of Income (Earnings and Expense Statement): Income and Expenses of Insured Commercial Banks in the United States, 1980, 1990, 2000, and 2003**

	1980		1990		2000		2003	
	Billions of Dollars	Percent of Total Operating Income	Billions of Dollars	Percent of Total Operating Income	Billions of Dollars	Percent of Total Operating Income	Billions of Dollars	Percent of Total Operating Income
Total interest income:	$176.4	92.5%	$320.5	85.4%	$428.0	73.7%	$335.8	64.3%
Interest and fees on loans	127.0	66.7	234.4	62.4	319.4	55.0	254.4	48.7
Lease income	1.4	0.7	4.4	1.2	10.8	1.7	8.9	1.7
Income from investment securities	23.1	12.1	51.1	13.6	68.5	11.8	56.8	10.9
Trading account income	NA	NA	5.4	1.4	9.4	1.6	7.9	1.5
Income from federal funds loans and security RPs	8.8	4.6	12.5	3.3	13.5	2.3	5.1	1.0
Other interest income	16.3	8.5	12.7	3.4	17.2	3.0	2.7	0.5
Total interest expense:	$120.1	63.0%	$205.0	54.6%	$224.2	38.6%	95.8	18.4%
Interest on deposits	34.9	18.3	161.5	43.0	151.7	26.1	63.1	12.1
Interest on federal funds and security RPs	16.8	8.8	22.7	6.0	27.4	4.7	8.1	1.6
Interest on subordinated capital notes and debentures	0.5	0.3	1.8	0.5	5.9	1.0	4.2	0.8
Interest on other borrowed funds	4.4	2.3	18.9	5.0	39.2	6.8	20.4	3.9
Net interest income	$ 56.3	29.5%	$715.5	30.8%	$203.8	35.1%	$240.0	46.0%
Total noninterest income:	14.3	7.5	54.9	14.6	152.8	26.3	186.5	35.7
Service charges on deposits	3.2	1.7	11.4	3.0	23.8	4.1	31.7	6.1
Other noninterest income	11.2	5.9	43.4	11.6	129.0	22.2	154.8	29.6
Total noninterest expense:	46.7	24.5	115.8	30.8	215.8	37.2	246.0	47.1
Employee salary and benefits	24.7	13.0	51.8	13.8	88.5	15.2	107.8	20.6
Occupancy expenses	7.4	3.9	17.4	4.6	26.8	4.6	31.3	6.0
All other noninterest expenses	14.6	7.7	46.6	12.4	100.5	17.3	106.8	20.4
Net noninterest income	−32.4	−17.0	−60.9	−16.2	−63.0	−10.8	−59.5	−11.4
Provision for loan and lease losses	4.5	2.4	−32.1	8.6	29.3	5.0	37.8	7.2
Pretax net operating income	19.5	10.2	22.6	6.0	111.5	19.2	145.8	27.9
Securities gains (or losses)	−0.9	−0.5	0.5	0.1	−2.3	−0.4	5.6	1.1
Applicable income taxes	4.7	2.5	7.7	2.1	38.0	6.5	49.2	9.4
Net extraordinary items	0.0*	0.0**	0.6	0.2	−0.3	0.1	0.4	0.0**
Net income after taxes	$ 14.0	7.3%	$ 16.0	4.3%	$ 71.2	12.3%	$102.6	19.6%

NA means "not available."

*Less than $50 million.

**Less than 0.05 percent.

Source: Federal Deposit Insurance Corporation.

gotten from another lender, managing pension plans for corporations, and so forth. Because bankers face stiff competition for funding, they have little influence over the interest expenses on their borrowed funds. Accordingly, they work especially hard to minimize their *noninterest expenses,* particularly employee costs, by substituting automated equipment for labor.

QUESTIONS TO HELP YOU STUDY

6. What are the principal *uses* of commercial bank funds? Major *sources* of funds?

7. What new sources and uses of funds have been developed in banking recently?

8. Explain how *securitization* of loans helps a bank raise new funds.

9. What benefits do *standby credit letters* provide for banks and their customers?

10. What are a bank's principal *revenue* and *expense* items?

11. What is the *net interest margin*? The *noninterest margin*? Why are they important?

14.5   Managing Commercial Bank Performance Today

As preceding pages of this chapter suggest, bank management is one of the toughest challenges in the financial-services marketplace today. Banks are buffeted by powerful forces—competition, regulation, technological change, and shifting economic conditions—and these forces sometimes overwhelm their defenses, causing them to fail. In response, bank managers have developed several fundamental principles to guide their decision making.

Managing Bank Assets, Liabilities, Revenues, and Expenses

One of the greatest challenges bank managers face is making new loans and properly monitoring those loans already on the books. This challenge is a stiff one because loans are usually a bank's number-one asset and number-one revenue generator. Moreover, most of a bank's risk exposure is usually concentrated in its loan portfolio. Top-performing banks today routinely prepare *written loan policies,* designed to guide individual loan decisions and shape the whole loan portfolio the way management and the stockholders would prefer. Written loan policies help to train new loan officers and assist management in determining how well its policies are being followed.

In addition to making loans, banks also extend credit to their customers by purchasing a customer's securities (principally stocks and bonds), which bankers place in their *investment portfolio*. Bank investment portfolios provide a source of income that supplements loan income and stabilizes overall revenue and earnings. Because risk is normally heaviest in the loan portfolio, bank investments are generally positioned in safer assets to help offset loan risk. Moreover, investments in marketable securities can be drawn upon for cash when the bank faces significant liquidity pressures. An investments officer must consider several different factors when deciding which securities to add to a bank's investment portfolio, including their expected after-tax rate of return, how that expected return correlates with returns from other assets the bank holds, the credit rating of the securities under review, and the projected liquidity (cash) needs of the institution.

Perhaps more than any other business, banks are challenged by continuing liquidity (cash) requirements. They must raise cash at a reasonable cost at precisely those times cash is needed and often in huge volume. Banks are "liquidity sensitive" because many of their deposits are payable immediately upon customer demand. A bank's liquidity manager must invest surplus cash right away to avoid loss of income and cover cash deficits as soon as they arise.

Beginning in 2003, the FDIC made it easier to understand the important linkages between local economic conditions and bank performance through its FDIC State Profiles databank at fdic.gov

In order to meet a bank's liquidity needs, two different strategies are usually employed: asset conversion or liability management. With *asset conversion,* assets from the bank's portfolio of loans and securities are *sold* to raise new cash. Most banks hold sizeable quantities of Treasury bills and other easily cashable assets to cover possible liquidity deficits. However, this strategy has shortcomings. It requires banks to surrender income when assets are sold and forces them to "store" liquidity in low-yielding assets that tend to reduce earnings.

In contrast to the asset conversion strategy, with *liability management* the necessary amount of liquidity is *borrowed.* Borrowing only occurs when there is an actual need for cash and the amount borrowed can be varied simply by changing the terms offered to those institutions with surplus cash. However, borrowing liquidity can be costly and that cost is often volatile. Therefore, most banks use a combination of asset conversion and liability management.

Finally, the bank's liquidity management team must pay special attention to the largest depositors and to those customers with large outstanding credit lines. The cash needs of these particular customers must be carefully monitored since they are likely to have the greatest impact upon the bank's cash position. By discovering ahead of time when a large deposit will be withdrawn or when a credit line will be tapped for money, bank managers can make good decisions on when and where to raise new cash.

Monitoring the Performance of a Bank

For interesting discussions about how to understand and analyze bank performance, see especially the FDIC's FYI at fdic.gov/bank/analytical/fyi

Today, banks are closely watched by their customers, by regulators, and by investors in the money and capital markets. The performance of a bank is evaluated not only relative to the institution's own goals but also relative to the performance of the bank's competitors. Four dimensions of bank performance tend to be the most closely followed in the industry:

1. The market value or stock price of a banking institution.
2. The rate of return or profitability ratios of a bank.
3. The bank's risk exposure along several different dimensions.
4. The operating efficiency of the institution.

The principles of financial management teach that a bank's *stock price* is usually the single best indicator of how well the firm is performing because its shareholders must be satisfied they are earning a competitive return on their capital. However, many banks around the world either do not have stockholders or have stock that is so infrequently traded that a realistic value cannot be determined. This is why many banks pay close attention to measures of *profitability,* such as the *return on assets* (ROA) and the *return on equity capital* (ROE)—the ratios of net after-tax income divided by total assets or equity capital.

Other important performance indicators include the *net interest margin,* which reflects the "spread" between interest revenue from loans and investments and interest expense associated with deposits and other borrowings divided by bank size. Another key indicator is the *ratio of equity capital* (or *net worth*) *to total assets.* If the risky assets a bank holds decline in value by more than the volume of its owners' equity (net worth), the institution may become insolvent. Similarly, the banker must monitor the proportion of all loans outstanding that are judged to be *uncollectible* and must be *charged off as worthless.* If these *loan-loss ratios* rise significantly, management must respond quickly to strengthen the bank's equity capital and improve its loan quality.

To aid bankers in monitoring their institutions' performance, several government and private agencies provide comprehensive data on bank performance and construct peer groups so that a banker can compare the performance of his institution to the performance of other similar banks. Among the most popular of these sources are the UBPRs (Uniform Bank Performance Reports) compiled by the Federal Financial Institutions Examination Council (FFIEC) inside the United States. This information is supplemented by numerous credit-rating agencies that monitor the riskiness of banks around the world.

Exhibit 14.7 provides an example of peer-group average performance ratios for all U.S.-insured banks as prepared by the FDIC and the FFIEC. Notice, for example, that in 2003 the banking industry's average return on assets (ROA) was 1.41 percent and its average return on equity (ROE) stood at 15.53 percent. The average net interest margin was 3.86 percent and the ratio of equity capital to total assets averaged just over 9 percent. A bank manager would want to compare her institution against these and other group performance measures to see if her bank lies above or below industry standards. How well has the industry been doing lately? Quite well in terms of ROA and ROE—both of which are substantially above historical averages—while net worth (equity) relative to total assets has held fairly steady at just slightly less than 10 percent. However, there have been performance weaknesses as well. For example, toward the bottom of Exhibit 14.7 we note that *noncurrent* (delinquent) *loans* exceeded 1 percent of total loans and loans "charged off" as worthless also approached 1 percent of all loans outstanding. These problems in the industry's loan portfolio are probably related to the U.S. economy's relatively slow recovery from the previous recession. Bankers recently have had to become more sharply focused on the issues of loan quality and risk.

Finally, notice that bank performance depends heavily upon the *type of bank* we are talking about. The right-hand side of Exhibit 14.7 groups U.S. banks according to their *asset concentration*—that is, those product lines that most characterize what each bank does. What is remarkable is how different in performance the different types of banks tend to be. For example, *credit-card-oriented banks* tended to achieve the highest profitability ratios—well above the industry average. However, credit card banks also reported the biggest loan-loss problems and were compelled to hold more equity capital relative to their assets to deal with greater risk exposure. In contrast, banks devoted primarily to commercial and mortgage lending posted much lower profitability ratios, but they also enjoyed fewer loan losses and less risk exposure. Performance measurement must always take into account differences in bank size, location, and especially the product-line focus each bank adopts as its principal service mission.

In the U.S., several rating agencies assess the safety and soundness of banks and selected other financial institutions and their customers, such as IDC Financial Publishing (idcfpgevepc.com), Sheshunoff Information Services (sheshunoff.com) and Veribank (veribank.com).

To compare the performance of banks against peer groups of banking firms see especially the Uniform Bank Performance Reports (UBPRs) available through ffiec.gov

---

QUESTIONS TO HELP YOU STUDY

12. How do banks control *risk* in their loans and in their investment portfolios?

13. Why are banks so sensitive to *liquidity risk?* How do they raise cash to meet liquidity needs?

14. What are the most popular measures of *bank performance?* What do they measure?

14.6 Money Creation and Destruction by Banks and Bank Accounting

Commercial banks differ from many other financial institutions in one critical respect: *Banks have the power to create money in the form of new checkable deposits, credit card lines, debit cards, and other immediately spendable funds.* The banking system creates and destroys billions of dollars in money each day.

EXHIBIT 14.7 Key Performance Measures for Commercial Banks in the United States, 2003 (Average Level of Performance for Peer Groups of Banking Institutions)

| Dollar Amounts in Billions Fourth Quarter 2003 | Commercial Banks | Asset Concentration Group | | | | | | | | |
		International Banks	Agricultural Banks	Credit Card Lenders	Commercial Lenders	Mortgage Lenders	Consumer Lenders	Other Specialized <$1 Billion	All Other <$1 Billion	All Other >$1 Billion
Number of FDIC-insured	7,769	6	1,765	36	4,250	1,033	158	530	1,313	91
Number of FDIC-supervised	4,833	0	1,223	11	2,497	409	80	281	775	42
Total assets	7,602	$1,448	$129	$348	$2,923	$1,658	$147	$61	$173	$2,190
Total loans	4,429	572	79	267	1,959	1,135	121	16	96	1,189
Domestic deposits	4,288	367	107	105	2,068	997	71	45	142	1,311
Net income (QTR)	26.595	4.390	0.338	3.826	8.855	5.365	0.389	0.497	0.403	7.065
Percent profitable (QTR)	90.0%	100.0%	89.6%	91.7%	90.7%	90.8%	88.0%	81.7%	90.9%	90.1%
Average return on assets (QTR)	1.41	1.22	1.06	4.65	1.22	1.28	1.07	3.28	0.94	1.31
Average return on equity (QTR)	15.53	16.66	9.86	28.18	13.26	14.29	14.31	20.11	8.96	14.73
Net interest margin (QTR)	3.86	3.06	4.05	8.78	3.93	3.21	4.83	3.03	3.85	3.48
Equity to assets	9.10	7.39	10.64	16.04	9.24	9.10	7.30	16.74	10.44	8.87
Noncurrent loan rate—total loans*	1.19	2.24	1.15	2.03	0.88	0.95	1.07	0.97	1.06	0.95
Real estate loans	0.86	1.30	1.03	0.40	0.75	0.97	1.20	0.85	1.02	0.63
C&I loans	2.10	4.23	1.87	1.28	1.40	1.30	2.06	1.61	1.64	2.18
Consumer loans	1.52	2.59	0.87	2.18	0.63	0.29	0.76	1.12	0.89	0.73
Coverage ratio**	145.79	102.23	132.89	236.49	166.49	75.65	158.24	182.42	130.24	158.47
Net charge-off rate—all loans (QTR)	0.91	1.36	0.43	5.31	0.48	0.13	2.76	0.52	0.45	0.56
Real estate loans (QTR)	0.25	0.10	0.17	0.17	0.16	0.05	2.55	0.12	0.15	0.34
C&I loans (QTR)	1.12	1.56	1.27	5.87	1.00	0.20	2.70	1.12	1.14	0.94
Consumer loans (QTR)	3.08	3.29	0.80	5.86	1.47	1.32	2.99	1.87	1.44	1.44

*Nonaccruing loans and loans past due 90+ days.

**Loss reserve as a percentage of noncurrent loans.

Source: Federal Deposit Insurance Corporation.

money creation

Money creation by banks is made possible because the public readily accepts claims on bank deposits (mainly checks, credit and debit cards, and computer entries) in payment for goods and services. In addition, the law requires individual banks to hold only a fraction of the amount of deposits received from the public as cash reserves, thus freeing up a majority of incoming funds for making loans and purchasing securities.

legal reserves

As we saw previously in Chapters 12 and 13, vault cash and deposits at the Fed constitute a U.S. bank's holdings of **legal reserves**—those assets acceptable for meeting legal reserve requirements behind the public's deposits. In turn, each bank's legal reserves may be divided into required reserves and excess reserves. *Required reserves* are equal to the legal reserve requirement percentage ratio times the volume of deposits subject to reserve requirements. For example, if a bank holds $50 million in checkable (transaction) deposits and the law requires it to hold 3 percent of its transaction accounts in legal reserves, the reserve requirement for this bank would be $50 million $\times$ 3%, or $1.5 million.

excess reserves

On the other hand, **excess reserves** equal the difference between the total legal reserves actually held by a bank and the amount of its required reserves. For example, if a bank is required to hold legal reserves equal to $1.5 million but finds on a given date that it has $500,000 in cash on the premises and $1.5 million on deposit with the Federal Reserve bank in its region, this bank holds $500,000 in excess reserves.

The Creation of Money and Credit

The distinction between excess and required reserves is important because it plays a key role in the growth of bank loans and the creation of money by the banking system. To understand why, we need to make certain assumptions concerning how banks account for their transactions with customers and the regulations they face. To simplify the arithmetic, assume that one of the banking system's key regulators, the Federal Reserve, has set a basic legal reserve requirement of 20 percent behind the public's deposits. Therefore, for every dollar that the public deposits in the banking system, each bank must put aside in either vault cash or deposits at the Federal Reserve 20 cents as required reserves. Assume also that, initially, the banking system is "loaned up"—that is, bankers have loaned out all excess reserves available to them. In addition, assume that all bankers are profit maximizers and attempt to loan out immediately any excess funds available to earn the most income possible.

Suppose that a deposit of $1,000 is made from some source outside the banking system. For example, the public may decide to convert a portion of its currency and coin holdings ("pocket money") into bank deposits for greater convenience and safety. Suppose a deposit of $1,000 appears at Bank A as shown in Exhibit 14.8. This exhibit contains an abbreviated balance sheet (T account) for Bank A with changes in its assets shown on the left-hand side and changes in its liabilities and net worth shown on the right-hand side.

Under the assumed Federal Reserve regulations, Bank A is required to place $200 aside as required legal reserves (i.e., 20 percent of the $1,000 deposit), leaving excess reserves of $800. Because the $800 in cash earns no interest income, the banker will immediately try to loan out these excess reserves. Banks make loans today by a simple accounting entry. The borrower signs a note indicating how much is borrowed, at what rate of interest, and when the note will come due. In return, the banker creates a checking account in the borrower's name. In our example, assume that Bank A has received a loan request from one of its customers and decides to grant the customer a loan of $800—exactly the amount of excess reserves it holds.

Banks find that, when they make loans, the borrowed funds are withdrawn rapidly as borrowers spend the proceeds of their loans. Moreover, it is likely that most of the

Powerful trends are reshaping banking around the globe:

1. *Deregulation* of banking in the United States, Canada, Great Britain, Japan, and in many other nations around the globe, permitting private markets to determine bank prices and services instead of governments.

2. Increased *penetration of foreign markets* by major banks, securities firms, and other financial institutions in most countries, so that banking and financial services are increasingly becoming a global industry with few territorial boundaries.

3. Growing *proliferation of services* (i.e., financial innovation) as bankers respond to increased competition, including the spread of securities underwriting, insurance services, and real estate development and brokerage services.

4. A spreading *technological revolution* with more banking transactions carried out via teller machines,

satellites, "smart" cards, fax machines, the Internet and the World Wide Web, and other innovative devices instead of through human labor, transforming banking into an increasingly automated, fixed-cost, capital-intensive industry.

5. *Changing sources and uses of funds* as banking's customer base changes toward more financially sophisticated, more interest-sensitive depositors. New sources of bank funds include loan sales and securitized loans. Banks are doing more "off-balance-sheet" support of their customers' service needs, providing guarantees behind customer borrowings, financial advice, and consulting. These support services usually earn fee income for banks but avoid draining scarce bank capital.

6. Growing *international cooperation* between governments and regulatory agencies from different countries to promote uniform regulation and supervision of banks, regardless of country.

borrowed funds will wind up as deposits in other banks as borrowing customers write checks against their loan balances. For this reason, Bank A will not loan out any more than the $800 in excess reserves it currently holds. This way, when a borrower spends his or her funds and the money flows to other banks, Bank A will have sufficient funds in reserve to cover the cash letters demanding payment that it will receive from other banks.

Assume that the $800 loaned by Bank A eventually winds up as a deposit in Bank B. As indicated in Exhibit 14.8, Bank B must place $160 (20 percent) of this deposit in required reserves; it then has excess reserves of $640, which are quickly loaned out. As the new borrowers spend their funds, the $640 in loans will find its way into deposits at Bank C. After setting aside required reserves of $128, Bank C has excess reserves of $512. It too will move rapidly to loan out these funds if suitable borrowers can be found.

The pattern of these changes in deposits, loans, and reserves should now be clear. The results are summarized in the bottom portion of Exhibit 14.8. Note that the total volume of bank deposits has been considerably expanded by the time it reaches the third or fourth bank. Similarly, the total volume of new loans grows rapidly as funds flow from bank to bank within the system. By making loans whenever excess reserves appear, the banking system eventually creates money in the form of deposits and loans several times larger than the original volume of new funds received.

Destruction of Deposits and Reserves

Not only can banks expand deposits and money by a multiple amount, but they can also contract deposits and money by a multiple amount. This is illustrated in Exhibit 14.9, in which a depositor has withdrawn $1,000 from a transaction account

EXHIBIT 14.8

The Creation of Credit and Deposits by the Banking System

1. Bank A Receives New Deposit

Assets		Liabilities	
Required reserves	200	Deposits	1,000
Cash	800		

4. Loan Made by Bank B

Assets		Liabilities	
Required reserves	160	Deposits	800
Loans	640		

2. Loan Made by Bank A

Assets		Liabilities	
Required reserves	200	Deposits	1,000
Loans	800		

5. Deposit of Loan Funds in Bank C

Assets		Liabilities	
Required reserves	128	Deposits from Bank B	640
Cash	512		

3. Deposit of Loan Funds in Bank B

Assets		Liabilities	
Required reserves	160	Deposits from Bank A	800
Cash	640		

6. Loan Made by Bank C

Assets		Liabilities	
Required reserves	128	Deposits	640
Loans	512		

By making loans whenever there are excess reserves, the banking system will ultimately generate a volume of deposits several times larger than the amount of the initial deposit received by Bank A.

	Transactions within the Banking System		
Name of Bank	Deposits Received	Loans Made	Required Reserves
A	$1,000	$ 800	$ 200
B	800	640	160
C	640	512	128
D	512	410	102
—	—	—	—
—	—	—	—
Final amounts for all banks in the system	$5,000	$4,000	$1,000

at Bank A and has decided not to place the money on deposit in another bank. Recall that behind the $1,000 deposit, Bank A holds only $200 in required reserves. This means that when the deposit is withdrawn, that bank will have a net deficiency of $800. If Bank A is loaned up and has used all of its cash to make loans and investments, it will have to raise the necessary funds through the sale of securities or through borrowing.

Suppose that Bank A decides to sell securities in the amount of $800. As indicated in Exhibit 14.9, the sale of securities increases Bank A's legal reserves by the necessary amount. However, the individuals and institutions that purchase those securities pay for them by wiring funds or writing checks against their deposits in other banks, reducing the legal reserves of those institutions.

For example, assume that Bank B loses deposits of $800 and required legal reserves of $800 as Bank A gains these funds. Considering Bank A and Bank B together, total

EXHIBIT 14.9

**Deposit and Credit
Destruction in the
Banking System**

Depositor withdraws funds:

Federal Reserve Bank		Bank A	
Assets	Liabilities	Assets	Liabilities
	Member bank reserves −1,000	Required reserves −1,000	Deposits −1,000

If Bank A was loaned up when the withdrawal occurred, it will now have a reserve deficiency of $800 as indicated below:

Total reserves lost at Bank A when depositor withdrew funds	$1,000
Required reserves no longer needed due to deposit withdrawals	−200
Net reserve deficit at Bank A	$ 800

Bank A		Bank B	
Assets	Liabilities	Assets	Liabilities
Securities −800		Required reserves −800	Deposits −800
Required reserves from Bank B +800			

The sale of securities in the amount of $800 enables Bank A to cover its reserve deficit. However, assume that customers of Bank B bought those securities and that bank was already loaned up. Bank B now has a reserve deficiency of $640. Thus:

Total reserves lost at Bank B after deposit withdrawals to purchase Bank A's securities	$800
Required reserves no longer needed due to deposit withdrawal	−160
Net reserve deficit at Bank B	$640

deposits have fallen by $1,800. This deposit contraction has freed up $360 ($200 + $160) in required reserves. However, if Bank B is also loaned up and has a net reserve deficiency of $640, further contraction of deposits will occur as Bank B attempts to cover its reserve deficiency by drawing reserves from other banks. Ultimately, deposits will contract by a multiple amount as banks try to cover their reserve deficits by raising funds at the expense of other banks.

Implications of Money Creation and Destruction

This capacity of banks to create and destroy money and deposits has a number of important implications for the financial system and the economy. Creation of money by banks is one of the most important sources of credit funds in the global economy—an important supplement to the supply of savings in providing funds for investment so the economy can grow faster. Money created by banks is instantly available for spending and, therefore, unless carefully controlled by government action, can fuel inflation. As we saw earlier in Chapters 12 and 13, that is why the Federal Reserve System and other central banks around the globe regulate interest rates and the growth of credit principally by influencing the growth of bank reserves and deposits.

QUESTIONS TO HELP YOU STUDY

15. How are banks able to *create money?*
16. Is the ability of banks to create money of significance for the economy and the creation of new jobs?
17. What are the dangers of money creation by banks?
18. How do banks *destroy money?*
19. Why is money creation and destruction of importance in the pursuit of public policy?

MARKETS ON THE NET: The Most Important Web Sites for This Chapter

American Bankers Association Career Web Site (aba.careersite.com)

Board of Governors of the Federal Reserve System (federalreserve.gov)

Federal Deposit Insurance Corporation (fdic.gov)

Federal Financial Institutions Examination Council (ffiec.gov)

Financial Reports for Individual Banks (fdic.gov/bank/individual)

FYI and Bank Trends Publications (fdic.gov/bank/analytical/fyi)

Office of the Comptroller of the Currency (occ.treas.gov)

Summary of the Chapter's Main Points

The banking industry has undergone significant financial and structural changes in recent years as well as expanding the number of services that banks offer to the public.

- One key trend reshaping the global banking industry is *consolidation* into fewer, but larger, banks serving geographically broader markets. Banking is one of the leading industries in mergers and acquisitions each year.

- Inside the United States the growing importance of larger banks has been accomplished through the rapid expansion of branch banks, bank holding companies, and interstate banking firms. In Europe banking units are spreading throughout the European Union, crossing national boundaries and also investing in banking facilities inside the United States.

- Leading banks around the globe have reached out to become *universal banks,* offering not only traditional services (including checking and savings deposits and loans) but also securities underwriting, insurance policy sales and underwriting, real estate services, and longer-term corporate equity funding, generating new sources of revenue but also new risks for the banking community. Large banks increasingly are experiencing *convergence,* offering many of the same services as other financial industries, such as insurance companies and security firms. The result is the appearance of more complex, multiservice conglomerates and financial holding companies (FHCs).

- *Cost pressures* have encouraged banks not only to grow larger, but to automate as many of their services as possible. This has enabled many banks to reduce

www.mhhe.com/rose9e

the number of their employees and close many full-service branch offices, reducing the costs of financial-service production and delivery.

- A growing list of bank services are now being offered through automated teller machines (ATMs), through computer networks and the Internet, and via telephones, satellites, and cable television systems. In short, banking is becoming a more heavily *fixed-cost industry* (based on greater volumes of capital equipment), with a smaller proportion of variable costs (especially labor time).

- The industry's financial statements are undergoing changes paralleling the above-noted structural changes. More of a bank's resources today typically are devoted to loans and to fee-generating services (such as assisting customers with financial planning). At the same time, nondeposit borrowings and stockholders' equity capital have grown as sources of bank funds while deposits—the traditional main source of bank funding—have become somewhat less important as a key source of bank funding.

- There is greater interest today than ever before in measuring and tracking *bank performance*. The principles and techniques bank managers use to control their institution's risk exposure and operating costs while achieving competitive rates of return for their stockholders are increasingly of interest as well. Bank managers are especially sensitive to changes in the condition of their institution's loan portfolio, investment security portfolio, and liquidity (or cash) position, as well as the cost of raising new funds and the preservation of net worth to prevent the bank from becoming insolvent.

- Among the many different measures of bank performance in use today are return on assets (ROA), return on equity capital (ROE), the net interest margin, operating efficiency ratios, the ratio of equity capital to total assets as a measure of solvency risk, and the proportion of all loans that are delinquent or judged to be worthless.

- The performance of banks today is heavily influenced by their *asset concentration*—that is, by the product lines they offer to the public. Among the most profitable banks today are credit-card banks, while banks that concentrate their assets in commercial and mortgage loans tend to have somewhat lower returns but also less exposure to loan losses, fraud, and other risks common in the credit-card field.

- Finally, banks are still the most important institution in most financial systems around the globe. They also remain the leading financial institution in creating money. Banks create money both by offering checkable deposits and by granting loans (credit). However, more and more nonbank financial institutions are competing with banks in money and credit creation.

Key Terms Appearing in This Chapter

banking structure, 421
state-chartered banks, 422
national banks, 422
consolidation, 422
branch banking, 423
bank holding company, 423
convergence, 426
deregulation, 427

primary reserves, 429
transaction accounts, 432
nondeposit funds, 433
securitized assets, 434
standby credit letters, 434
money creation, 441
legal reserves, 441
excess reserves, 441

Problems and Issues

1. Given the following information on the revenues and expenses of First National Bank, determine the bank's net income after taxes for the year just concluded:

Salaries and employee benefits	$ 80,000	Applicable income taxes	$ 50,000
Interest on deposits	170,000	Occupancy costs	11,000
Interest on loans	320,000	Provision for loan losses	22,000
Income from U.S. Treasury securities	75,000	Miscellaneous expenses	8,000
Extraordinary items, net	-0-	Interest on municipal securities	86,000
Interest on nondeposit borrowings	30,000	Service charges on deposits	10,000
Net securities gains	-0-	Miscellaneous operating revenues	13,000

2. Construct the report of condition (balance sheet) for First National Bank for December 31 of the year just ended from the following information:

Equity capital	$ 50 million	Real estate loans	$ 60 million
Demand deposits	100 million	U.S. Treasury securities	25 million
Savings deposits	150 million	Commercial and	
Time deposits	200 million	industrial loans	300 million
Federal funds borrowings	12 million	Other liabilities	38 million
Cash and due from banks	20 million	Municipal securities	55 million
Other assets	50 million	Loans to individuals	40 million

3. See if you can fill in correctly the missing items from the balance sheet (report of condition) and the statement of earnings and expenses (report of income) of the bank whose financial accounts are listed below:

Balance Sheet		Statement of Earnings and Expenses	
Cash and interbank deposits	$ 11	Revenue sources:	
Investment securities	?	Domestic loan interest and fees	$?
Federal funds sold	8	Foreign loan interest and fees	6
Loans, gross	81	Income from security investments	4
Allowance for loan losses	(6)	Miscellaneous revenues	1
Unearned discount on loans	(1)	Total revenues	?
Net loans	?		
Premises and fixed assets	2	Expenses:	
Miscellaneous assets	5	Interest on deposits	?
Total assets	$110	Interest on nondeposit borrowings	1
Demand deposits	?	Salaries and wages	2
Savings deposits	20	Occupancy costs	1
Time deposits	65	Provision for loan losses	1
Nondeposit borrowings	12	Miscellaneous expenses	2
Total liabilities	?	Total expenses	15
Stockholder's equity capital	4	Net operating income	3
		Income taxes	?
		Net income (or loss) after taxes	1

4. Suppose you have been given the financial information below for a commercial bank:

Income taxes owed	$ 13	Interest on nondeposit borrowings	$ 8
Noninterest revenues from service fees	70	Salaries and wages	
Interest revenues from loans	129	of bank employees	27
Interest and dividends from		Overhead costs	3
investments in securities	26	Loan-loss provision	2
Dividends paid to stockholders	4	Securities gains (or losses)	0
Interest paid to depositors	64		

a. Calculate this bank's net interest income, net noninterest income, pretax net operating income, net income after taxes, undivided profits (or retained earnings), total revenues, and total expenses.

b. Suppose the above bank's return on assets (ROA)—the ratio of its net income after taxes to total assets—is 0.85 percent. What is the total of the bank's assets in dollars?

c. Suppose this bank's return on stockholders' equity capital (ROE)—the ratio of its net income after taxes to total equity capital—is 12 percent. What is the bank's total equity capital in dollars?

d. Suppose the above bank's total deposits equal 75 percent of its total liabilities. How many deposits in total dollar volume does the bank hold?

Standard & Poor's Market Insight and Web-Based Problems

1. The profits of large, diversified banking firms do not always mirror those of firms in other industries. Therefore, the market value of their stocks will not necessarily move in lockstep with the stock market as a whole. The purpose of this exercise is to see how well the "Diversified Banks" group of banking firms has performed recently relative to a broad measure of stock market value—*the S&P 500 stock index.*

a. Visit S&P's Market Insight database at **mhhe.com/edumarketinsight** and find the information stored there for the GIC sub-industry "Diversified Banks." Click on "Industry Profile."

b. Based on the "Pricing" table found there, have large bank stocks generally outperformed the market as a whole since the beginning of the year? Have they outperformed the market over the last three years? The past five years? By how much have they bettered or been beaten by the market's overall performance?

c. Based on the "Valuation" table, do larger banks appear to pay higher-than-average dividends than other firms in the market? Quantify your answer.

d. Given your answer to part (c) identify other information from the "Valuation" table that might indicate whether you should expect larger banks to have faster growth in earnings than the average firm in the market. Explain.

2. As one of the chief regulators of the banking system, the Federal Reserve must monitor the lending activities of commercial banks. The bank loan category typically carrying the greatest default risk is Commercial and Industrial (C&I) Loans. The Fed monitors these particular loans through a survey of Senior Loan Officers. The following will help you get an idea about the types of information this periodic survey provides.

    a. Visit the Fed's Web site at **federalreserve.gov** and click on "Surveys and Reports." Then click on "Senior Loan Officer Opinion Survey on Bank Lending Practices" and find the most current survey. Download the "Charts" (pdf) at the bottom of the report.

    b. Have banks tightened lending standards on C&I loans since the previous survey?

    c. Have banks raised interest rates on C&I loans since the previous survey?

    d. Referring to the graphs that you considered in parts (b) and (c), can you identify any patterns that suggest what happens to business lending during recessions?

Semester Project: A Study of the Fed Funds Market

One of the responsibilities of the Federal Reserve System is to provide for an efficient and safe payments system for the economy. Accordingly, the Fed operates an electronic transfer system, *Fedwire,* which includes interbank transactions in the federal funds market. Fedwire transfers have developed from a rudimentary system first established in 1918 to one of the largest and most efficient electronic funds transfer systems anywhere in the world. In this final installment of the semester project, provide answers to the items listed below:

a. Visit the Federal Reserve's Web site at **federalreserve.gov/paymentsystems/ coreprinciples** and scroll down to the "Brief History" section. Use a "bullet point" outline to capture the factors that fostered the development of the Fedwire system.

b. Explain why Fedwire plays a key role in the functioning of the Fed funds market and in the U.S. payments mechanism. Why is it especially vital to banking institutions?

c. Scroll down the page "8.2 Pricing Policy and Competition" and explain how the Fed charges for its payments services and why these services are not provided to participating banks free of charge.

Congratulations!!! You have completed the semester project on the Fed funds market. We hope you learned a lot along the way and will be able to use what you have learned in the future.

Selected References to Explore

Ennis, Huberto M. "Some Recent Trends in Commercial Banking." *Economic Quarterly,* Federal Reserve Bank of Richmond, Spring 2004, pp. 41–61.

Gilbert, R. Alton, and Gregory E. Sierras. "The Financial Condition of U.S. Banks: How Different Are Community Banks?" *Review,* Federal Reserve Bank of St. Louis, January/February 2003, pp. 43–56.

Gunther, Jeffrey W., and Robert R. Moore. "Small Banks' Competitors Loom Large." *Southwest Economy,* Federal Reserve Bank of Dallas, January/February 2004, pp. 1, 9–18.

Kwan, Simon. "Banking Consolidation." *FRBSF Economic Letter,* Federal Reserve Bank of San Francisco, June 18, 2004, pp. 1–3.

Santomero, Anthony M. "Banking in the 21st Century. "*Business Review,* Federal Reserve Bank of Philadelphia, Third quarter 2004, pp. 1–4.

Stackhouse, Julie L., and Mark D. Vaughn. "Navigating the Brave New World of Bank Liquidity." *The Regional Economist,* Federal Reserve Bank of St. Louis, July 2003, pp. 12–13.

Walter, John R. "Closing Troubled Banks: How the Process Works." *Economic Quarterly,* Federal Reserve Bank of Richmond, Winter 2004, pp. 51–68.

Chapter 15

Nonbank Thrift Institutions: Savings and Loans, Savings Banks, Credit Unions, and Money Market Funds

Learning Objectives

in This Chapter

- You will see how significant *thrift institutions* are in the functioning of a modern economy and financial system.

- You will discover what types of *services* thrift institutions offer to the public and who their principal competitors are.

- You will come to understand the principal differences between major types of thrift institutions as well as their principal similarities and why these differences and similarities are important.

What's in This Chapter?
Key Topics Outline

15.1   Introduction to Thrift Institutions

There is a tendency in discussions of the financial system to minimize the role of non-bank financial institutions and to emphasize the part played by commercial banks in the flow of money and credit. For many years, financial experts did not consider the liabilities of nonbank financial institutions—including deposits in savings and loan associations, savings banks, money market funds, and credit unions—as really close substitutes for bank deposits. It was argued that interindustry competition between commercial banks and other financial institutions was slight and, for all practical purposes, could be ignored. Today, however, an entirely different view prevails concerning the relative importance of nonbank financial institutions. We now recognize that these institutions play a vital role in the flow of money and credit within the financial system and that they are particularly important in selected markets, such as the home mortgage market and the market for personal savings.

In truth, many nonbank financial institutions are becoming increasingly like commercial banks and are competing for many of the same customers. Moreover, banks themselves are offering many of the services traditionally offered by nonbank financial firms, such as brokering securities and selling insurance (often through joint ventures with nonbank firms). Thus, both bank and nonbank financial institutions are rushing toward each other in the services they offer and the markets they serve—a phenomenon known as *convergence.* This is why financial analysts today stress the importance of studying the *whole* financial institutions' sector to understand how the financial system works. In this chapter and the next, we examine the major types of nonbank financial institutions that channel the public's savings into loans and investments.

15.2   Savings and Loan Associations

savings and loan
associations

Savings and loan associations (S&Ls) are among the largest of all thrift institutions, accepting deposits and extending loans and other services primarily to *household customers.* S&Ls emphasize longer-term loans to individuals and families in contrast to the shorter-term lending focus of most other deposit-type financial institutions. In particular, in the United States savings and loans are a major source of mortgage loans to finance the purchase of single-family homes and multifamily dwellings (such as apartments and duplexes). At the same time, savings and loans today are developing many new financial services to attract customers and boost their earnings.

The history of S&Ls looks much like a roller-coaster ride—periods of prosperity punctuated by periods of financial disaster. For example, hundreds of S&Ls failed during the 1980s and early 1990s, and many have since converted into commercial bank and savings bank charters, some becoming branch offices of other depository institutions. We will discuss some of the causes of the industry's periodic problems in the sections that follow.

Origins of S&Ls

The first U.S. savings and loans were started in 1831. Many were called *building and loan associations,* in which money was solicited from individuals and families so that certain members of the group could finance the building of new homes. The same individuals and families who provided loanable funds were also borrowers from the association. Today, however, savers and borrowers are frequently different individuals.

The history of the
S&L industry is traced
out in
encyclopedia.com

Savings and loan associations began essentially as a *single-product industry,* accepting savings deposits from middle-income individuals and families and lending those funds to home buyers. More recently, however, competition from commercial

mutuals

banks, credit unions, and mutual funds, coupled with deregulation and many failures, has forced savings and loans to diversify their operations and aggressively solicit new customers.

Many savings and loans are **mutuals** and, therefore, have *no stockholders*. Technically, they are owned by their depositors. However, a growing number of associations are converting or have converted to stock form. *Stockholder-owned S&Ls* can issue capital stock to increase their net worth—a privilege that is particularly important when a savings and loan is growing rapidly and needs an additional source of long-term capital. Stockholder-owned associations, on average, are much larger in size than mutuals.

How Funds Are Raised and Allocated

Savings and loans, like credit unions, are gradually broadening their role, with many choosing to offer a full line of financial services for individuals and families. Other S&Ls are branching out into business credit and commercial real estate lending.

Asset Portfolios   Residential mortgage loans dominate the asset side of the savings and loan business. Exhibit 15.1 shows the combined financial assets and liabilities of both savings and loans and savings banks (which we will discuss next in this chapter).

EXHIBIT 15.1		

Combined Financial Balance Sheet of Savings and Loans and Savings Banks, 2004* ($ Billions)

Source: Board of Governors of the Federal Reserve System.

*Figures are for first quarter of 2004.

Balance Sheet Item	Amount	Percentage of Total Assets
Assets:		
Checkable deposits and currency	$ 25.0	1.6%
Reserves held at the Federal Reserve banks	5.1	0.3
Time and savings deposits	3.0	0.2
Federal funds and security RPs	31.2	2.0
Corporate equities	28.2	1.8
U.S. government and federal agency securities	240.6	15.5
State and local government (tax-exempt) securities	6.5	0.4
Corporate and foreign bonds	65.1	4.2
Mortgage loans	927.5	59.6
Consumer credit	81.3	5.2
Loans to business firms and others	49.6	3.2
Miscellaneous assets	93.5	6.0
Total financial assets	$1,556.6	100.0%
Liabilities:		
Checkable deposits	$ 443.0	29.2%
Small time and savings deposits	218.3	14.4
Large ($100,000 +) time deposits	285.4	18.8
Borrowings through security repurchase agreements	74.1	4.9
Borrowings from the Federal Home Loan banks and other loans and advances	275.5	18.2
Corporate bonds	6.0	0.4
Investments by parent companies	9.6	0.6
Miscellaneous liabilities	203.7	13.4
Total liabilities	$1,515.6	99.9%

As revealed in the exhibit, direct mortgage credit (predominantly loans to purchase new homes) accounts for more than half of all industry assets. But the current era has brought rapid growth in other housing-related investments, such as mortgage-backed securities, mobile home loans, and home equity loans. Mortgage-backed securities include pass-throughs issued by the Government National Mortgage Association, participation certificates (PCs) issued by the Federal Home Loan Mortgage Corporation, and collateralized mortgage obligations (CMOs). Pass-throughs, PCs, and CMOs are investor shares in the earnings generated by pools of mortgage loans, backed by the issuing government agency or put together by a private lender. As discussed earlier in Chapter 14, these forms of *loan securitizations* allow S&Ls and other thrifts to package many of their housing-related loans, remove them from their balance sheets, and generate new sources of fee income. CMOs are a little more flexible than other types of loan-backed securities because they can be found in short, medium, and long maturities, helping S&Ls minimize their risk exposure from changing market interest rates and from mortgage loans being paid off early.

As we will see in Chapter 17, the savings and loan industry was first deregulated in the early 1980s and given broad new service powers, including checking accounts, credit cards and other consumer lending powers, commercial real estate loans, trust services, investments in mutual funds, and the power to invest in riskier corporate and government bonds. Predictably, many S&Ls went overboard, bought too many "junk" bonds, and launched into new services with very little preparation, while market interest-rate changes added to their losses. Hundreds collapsed, so that by the 1990s, new legislation pushed S&Ls back heavily toward the home mortgage market, where they reside today with the majority of their loans.

Liabilities of S&Ls   Savings deposits provide the bulk of funds available to the savings and loan industry. However, there has been a significant shift in deposit mix in recent years from those savings accounts earning the lowest interest rate to deposits earning higher and more flexible returns. Particularly important among the newer higher-yield savings deposit plans offered by the industry are money market deposit accounts, CDs, NOW and Super NOW accounts, and Keogh and IRA retirement accounts. **Money market deposit accounts (MMDAs)** and Super NOWs were authorized for banks and S&Ls in 1982. Both of these deposit accounts are draftable by check and carry interest rates that change with market conditions. One unfortunate side effect of these newer deposits is that savings and loans today are faced with a costlier and at times a more volatile deposit base.

Savings and loans also rely on several nondeposit sources of funds to support their loans and investments. One of the most important consists of advances (loans) from the Federal Home Loan Bank System, which provide extra liquidity in periods when deposit withdrawals are heavy or when loan demand exceeds incoming deposits. As we saw above, another rapidly growing source of funds is securitized assets, when mortgages or other S&L loans are packaged together into a pool of loans (often backed by the guarantee of a government agency), and debt securities are issued against these pooled assets and sold to investors to raise longer-term funds. Thrift institutions continue to make widening use of *securitized assets,* issued against a growing list of home mortgage and consumer installment loans, to supplement their deposit flows and keep funding costs down. The ability of an S&L or other loan-securitizing institution to remove securitized assets from its balance sheet tends to lower its total assets and improves its ratio of capital to assets, possibly lessening regulatory pressure on the institution to raise more capital.

Another popular nondeposit funds source is *loan sales*—sales of existing loans to investors in the secondary (resale) market. These sales of S&L assets tend to be

To learn more about savings and loans, take a look at the Web sites of some existing S&Ls, such as Atlantic Bank of New York at atlantic-bank-ny.com and Flatbush Savings and Loan Association of Brooklyn, New York, at flatbush.com

money market deposit accounts (MMDAs)

heaviest during periods when loan demand is high and deposit growth is sluggish, and they give savings and loans the opportunity to invest in new, higher-yielding loans. They also help S&Ls better diversify their assets and avoid an increased regulatory burden (such as government demands for raising more owners' capital). One danger, however, is that S&Ls and other lending institutions may sell their best-quality loans, leaving them with a riskier loan portfolio overall.

Equity capital or net worth (i.e., the retained earnings and reserves held by individual savings and loans) presently makes up only about 3 to 4 percent of total S&L funds sources but is very important to the public. The net worth account absorbs losses and keeps the doors open until management can correct any problems. Some S&Ls, particularly in those regions of the nation struggling with a weak real estate market, have had a net worth close to zero. In the early 1990s the federal government of the United States was empowered by Congress to close those banks and thrifts whose net worth had fallen close to zero. Since then, the S&L industry's net worth position has improved substantially.

Trends in Revenues and Costs

Federal Deposit Insurance Corporation (FDIC)

During the mid-1980s and early 1990s, savings and loans experienced one of the darkest periods in their long history. Many savings associations were unprofitable or had very little net worth. Dozens of ailing associations were helped into mergers by the **Federal Deposit Insurance Corporation (FDIC),** which purchased sizable amounts of questionable industry assets. The industry's former deposit insurance agency (the FSLIC) went bankrupt during the 1980s, to be replaced at the beginning of the 1990s by the Savings Association Insurance Fund (SAIF), managed by the FDIC. The SAIF continues to protect S&L deposits (up to $100,000) today. At the same time, Congress moved to authorize agency-assisted mergers in which troubled S&Ls could be merged with stronger associations or with other depository institutions (such as a commercial bank through its holding company).

One indication of the industry's recent roller-coaster ride (from disaster more than a decade ago to more recent success) is the track record of its assets, deposits, and net earnings in recent years:

	Trends in Assets, Deposits, and Net Income after Taxes of U.S. Savings and Loans and Savings Banks		
Year	Total Financial Assets Reported at Year-End ($ Billions)	Total Deposits Reported at Year-End ($ Billions)	Net Income after Taxes of U.S. Savings and Loans and Savings Banks ($ Millions)
1980	$ 792	$ 665	$ 781
1988	1,641	1,605	−12,057
1994	1,009	734	4,200
1996	1,032	721	6,802
2000	1,219	727	8,014
2003	1,474	925	18,050

Source: Board of Governors of the Federal Reserve System, *Flow of Funds Accounts;* Federal Deposit Insurance Corporation; and Office of Thrift Supervision.

As the preceding figures suggest, the industry's overall assets and deposits peaked in 1988 and then began to contract until near the end of the twentieth century—the result of large numbers of failures and the conversions of some S&Ls into other kinds of financial intermediaries (most notably, commercial and savings banks). By the mid-1990s, industry profitability began to improve, however, achieving a return on assets (ROA) of 1.29 percent in 2003, just slightly below the ROA for the commercial banking industry that same year. More than 90 percent of savings and loans reported positive profits at that time, with significantly fewer troubled loans on the books and increased core capital (i.e., capital paid in plus surplus) to protect against unexpected losses. Commercial bank holding companies have helped to strengthen the S&L industry by purchasing growing numbers of thrifts, converting many to commercial bank charters or turning them into branch offices of existing banks.

Trends in the performance of the savings and loan industry may be followed in several Web sites, such as ots.treas.gov

Recent industry earnings might have been even higher except for mandates from the U.S. government that thrifts help recapitalize the Savings Association Insurance Fund (SAIF) in order to bring its deposit insurance reserves up to the levels required by the U.S. Congress. Nevertheless, S&Ls continue to gather strength in the new century and are becoming quite innovative, developing many new fee-based income-generating services (including servicing outstanding home mortgage loans, selling loans in the secondary market, and offering credit card plans). Many S&Ls are directing their lending into newer areas—such as construction loans, commercial real estate loans, and consumer loans used for purposes other than buying a new home (including financing college educations, starting new businesses, or purchasing new or used automobiles). Moreover, these thrift institutions have turned increasingly to the Federal Home Loan Banks (FHLB)—a federal agency designed to help the thrift industry—and to new security issues to fund their operations when their deposits have tended to grow slowly.

What factors got the savings and loan industry into such serious trouble during the 1980s and 1990s? Might these same factors reappear and cause trouble again in the future? Why did the industry nearly collapse and so many S&Ls sink beneath the waves during this earlier period of crisis? One primary cause was the fact that savings and loans, historically, have issued mortgage loans carrying mostly fixed interest rates while selling deposits to the public whose interest rates closely mirror changing market conditions. In short, many S&L assets were interest-rate *insensitive* in earlier years (and many still are), while most of their liabilities have been (and still are) highly interest-rate *sensitive*. During periods of rapidly rising market interest rates, the industry's net interest margin—the difference between its interest earnings on assets and its interest costs on borrowed funds—has often been severely squeezed. Indeed, in several recent periods, short-term interest rates paid on deposits exceeded interest rates earned on long-term loans, and the industry's net interest margin turned *negative* for a time.

Other recent trends also hurt S&L profitability. The individuals and families whose savings provide the bulk of association funds have become more financially sophisticated, withdrawing deposits whenever high returns are available elsewhere or whenever there is even a hint of trouble in the industry. Unquestionably, the savings and loan industry has been damaged to some extent by the growth of money market funds—aggressive institutions that offer small savers higher and more flexible yields—and, more recently, by the public's keen interest in stock and bond mutual funds. At the same time, government rules have prevented S&Ls from introducing more flexibility into their investments so their revenues can grow as fast as their operating costs.

The pressures of competition and technological change have caused many savings and loans to merge or be absorbed by larger institutions. As a result, the number of independently owned associations in the United States has been declining for more than four decades. The S&L population decreased from about 6,300 in 1960 to only about 1,200 by the beginning of the new century. More savings and loans are likely to be absorbed into larger financial institutions (especially bank holding companies) in the future, and many are likely to have their thrift charters converted into bank charters in order to be

Savings and loan associations, savings banks, and credit unions face a common problem that, at several times in the past, has caused many of them to fail. *The maturities* (and, therefore, the expected streams of future cash payments) *of many of their assets and their liabilities do not match.* In particular, asset maturities are usually considerably longer than the maturities attached to their liabilities. For example, the majority of savings and loans' assets are home mortgage loans, which usually take years to pay out, while the bulk of their liabilities are savings deposits and checking accounts that are often turned into cash in a matter of hours, days, or weeks. This means that thrifts must be prepared to pay out large amounts of cash on short notice. Moreover, the interest costs on their borrowed funds (including interest owed on deposits) tend to change faster, up or down, than the interest revenues from their assets.

If we use what has become conventional terminology when talking about thrift institutions, their volume of *interest-rate-sensitive liabilities (ISL)* (consisting largely of short-term savings and checkable deposits) exceeds their volume of *interest-rate-sensitive assets (ISA)* (such as floating-rate loans or short-term loans about to mature). That is, for most thrift institutions, ISA < ISL. A liability or an asset is interest sensitive if its rate of return changes with market conditions. This difference in the thrifts' volume of interest-rate-sensitive assets and liabilities is called the GAP:

$$GAP = ISA - ISL$$

If rate-sensitive liabilities are larger than rate-sensitive assets, the GAP is *negative*, which is the usual situation for many thrift institutions.

The GAP concept tells us that a thrift with a negative GAP will lose interest income if interest rates rise. Interest costs attached to the thrifts' rate-sensitive liabilities will move upward faster than the revenues from rate-sensitive assets. The thrifts' net interest income (i.e., their interest revenues less interest expenses) will fall.

We can visualize this classic maturity mismatch problem faced by many thrift institutions by viewing the diagram below. Deposit rates, like most other short-term interest rates, change rapidly and move over a wide range, rising as the economy expands and inflation increases and falling as the economy slows down or inflation weakens. In contrast, the average rate of return on a thrift's long-term assets tends to change more slowly. Losses build up when short-term interest rates exceed long-term interest rates. We recall from Chapter 7 that this situation coincides with an "inverted yield curve"— often a harbinger of a slowdown in the economy.

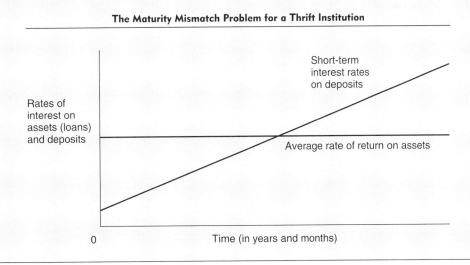

The Maturity Mismatch Problem for a Thrift Institution

Rates of interest on assets (loans) and deposits

Short-term interest rates on deposits

Average rate of return on assets

0   Time (in years and months)

able to offer a wider range of financial services. The leading S&Ls and savings banks headquartered in the United States today include Washington Mutual, Seattle at **wamu.com**, Golden State Bancorp, San Francisco at **goldenstatebancorp.com**, Golden West Financial Corp., Oakland at **worldsavings.com**, Sovereign Bancorp, Philadelphia at **sovereignbank.com**, Astoria Financial Corp, Lake Success at **astoriafederal.com**,

Greenpoint Financial Corp., New York City at **greenpoint.com**, Bank North Group, Inc., Portland at **banknorth.com**, and Commercial Federal Corp., Omaha at **comfedbank.com.**

Possible Ways to Strengthen the S&L Industry in the Future

If savings and loans are to continue to be competitive and remain successful thrift institutions in the future, they will need help from at least four sources: (1) sound decision making by S&L management to further diversify their activities by geographic area and by services offered, (2) careful management of the loan portfolio to put good loans on the books and minimize future loan losses, (3) better use of risk-management tools (such as financial futures, swaps, and options), and (4) a further relaxation of government regulations to permit the offering of new services and the merging of smaller associations into larger financial-service companies.

More aggressive S&Ls today are branching out in at least three different directions. Some have followed a *real estate model,* literally becoming mortgage banking firms. These savings associations are selling off their long-term mortgages and converting into real estate service organizations, managing and developing property and brokering mortgages. Many have become *family financial centers,* offering a full range of retail financial services to the consumer. Home mortgages continue to dominate their asset portfolios, but most S&Ls today offer adjustable-rate mortgages (ARMs), whose yields adjust more readily to changing market conditions, as well as fixed-rate mortgages (FRMs) and a wide variety of other consumer-oriented loans. Other S&Ls have adopted a *diversified model,* becoming holding company organizations with ownership and control over retail-oriented consumer banks, mortgage banking firms, commercial credit affiliates, and other businesses. Only time will tell which of these models can adapt successfully to the changing character of the financial marketplace. One hopeful sign recently has been the return to profitability of many S&Ls that survived the terrible debacle of the 1980s and 1990s and managed to direct their assets into better-quality investments and achieve greater operating efficiency.

savings banks

15.3 Savings Banks

Savings banks began in Scotland early in the nineteenth century and then took root in the United States approximately 150 years ago to meet the financial needs of the small saver. These institutions play an active role in the residential mortgage market, as do savings and loans, but they are more diversified in their investments, purchasing corporate bonds and common stock, making consumer loans, and investing in commercial mortgages.

In 1982 the U.S. Congress voted to allow savings and loan associations to convert readily into federally chartered savings banks, and savings banks to convert into S&Ls if they wished to do so. In 1989 Congress decided to allow S&Ls that qualify to become commercial banks. Recently, substantial numbers of S&Ls have converted to savings banks (along with a number of conversions to commercial bank charters) in an effort to lower their regulatory costs and further diversify their services. For this reason, the distinction between savings and loans, savings banks, and commercial banks is becoming very blurred. The public often cannot tell these depository institutions apart.

From their earliest origins, savings banks have designed their financial services to appeal to individuals and families. Deposit accounts often can be opened for amounts as small as $1, with transactions carried out by mail, electronically, or, in many instances, at 24-hour automated tellers in convenient locations. Savings banks in Massachusetts and New Hampshire were the first to develop the interest-bearing and checkable NOW account, one of the most important new consumer financial services of the past generation. Many savings banks advertise the availability of family financial counseling services, home equity loans, and travel planning, as well as a wide variety of savings instruments.

Number and Distribution of Savings Banks

The number of savings banks operating today is relatively small. The combined total of FDIC-insured savings and loans and savings banks fell from 3,626 in 1985 to only about 1,500 as the twenty-first century began. The U.S. Congress authorized the chartering of federal savings banks (FSBs) in 1978, which led to an increase for a time in the savings bank population. Unfortunately, many of these institutions failed in the economic dislocations of the late 1980s and early 1990s, along with hundreds of savings and loan associations. Savings banks today are scattered throughout the United States. Massachusetts leads the list, followed by New York. Other states in which savings banks are particularly important include California, Connecticut, Maine, New Hampshire, New Jersey, Pennsylvania, Rhode Island, Texas, and Wisconsin.

How Funds Are Raised and Allocated

Technically, savings banks are owned by their depositors. All earnings available after funds are set aside to provide adequate reserves must be paid to the depositors as owners' dividends. The industry's role in the financial system can be seen by looking at its financial balance sheet, which is shown for both savings and loans and savings banks combined in Exhibit 15.1. On the asset side, the key instruments are mortgages and mortgage-related instruments, which account for the majority of industry assets.

Most of the mortgage total represents direct mortgage loans to build single-family homes, apartments, shopping centers, and other commercial and residential structures. The remainder of the mortgage asset total is devoted primarily to mortgage-backed securities, such as Government National Mortgage Association (GNMA) pass-through securities (also known as Ginnie Maes), and similar mortgage-related securities backed by a pool of mortgages.[1]

A distant second in importance to mortgages are savings bank investments in nonmortgage loans (mainly consumer installment credit to finance purchases of furniture and appliances, autos, educational and medical services, and other household cash needs), corporate bonds, corporate stock, and government bonds. Also, many states have recently liberalized their regulations to allow savings banks to make increased purchases of common and preferred stock. Another factor favoring investments in stock has been the industry's growing federal tax burden. Because most of their stock dividend income is exempt from federal taxation or carries a very low tax rate, savings banks have taken greater interest in the stock market. State law and tradition, however, limit the growth of savings bank investments in the stock market.

The principal source of funds for savings banks is *deposits*. Savings deposits have no specific maturity but may be withdrawn at any time by the customer, and they generally carry the lowest rate of interest. Time deposits, on the other hand, have fixed maturities, and savings banks pay higher interest rates on these deposit accounts, depending on their maturity date.

Industry deposits have grown rapidly in recent years, reflecting the ability of savings banks to appeal to the financial needs of individuals and families. The larger savings banks have established extensive branch office systems and have been highly

---

[1] See Chapter 22 for a discussion of GNMA pass-throughs and other mortgage-related securities.

One of the more alarming developments in the financial institutions' sector as the twentieth century gave way to the twenty-first was the rapid rise of *subprime lending* by banks and thrift institutions. This form of credit consists mainly of consumer and small business loans extended to poor credit risks at lofty interest rates.

Subprime lending rests on the principle that if you as a lender price a loan correctly to account for its risk, you can still make money from such a loan despite the risks involved. The higher the degree of risk exposure (i.e., the lower the borrower's credit rating), the more the lender charges to compensate for risk exposure—sometimes well above a 20 percent interest rate. Some authorities refer to the highest-cost subprime loans as "predatory lending" because borrowers are more likely to default on such loans.

Unfortunately for some financial institutions over the past decade, loan losses outstripped revenue growth as loan defaults soared. Moreover, many high-risk borrowers were able to get their high-rate loans refinanced, paying off their subprime lenders sooner than expected. Subprime lending proved to be highly sensitive to economic conditions; a weaker economy generated a large volume of defaults among subprime loans and failures among lenders who granted them.

An added cause of problems in this field are so-called "loan residuals" in which certain loans are packaged together and securities representing claims against the pool of loans are sold to investors in the capital market. Because the loan package is, on the whole, less risky than individual loans would be, the lender is able to borrow more cheaply using securitized loans as collateral and profit from a more favorable interest-rate spread. This spread or "residual" is usually recorded on the lender's balance sheet as an asset, though it can be a volatile one. Higher interest rates often cause these "residual" assets to plunge in value.

Some of the largest depository institutions ran into trouble as a result of subprime lending, such as First Union Corp.'s Money Store, which was closed in 1998. These events suggest that a prolonged economic slump can create serious losses on subprime loans. For this reason, bank and thrift regulators have been discouraging highly risky subprime lending.

For a more in-depth look at the savings bank industry, you may wish to visit the Web sites of such popular institutions as American Federal Savings Bank at americanfsb.com and Washington Mutual Savings Bank at washingtonmutual.com

innovative in offering new services. Nearly all savings banks today offer checkable NOW accounts, money orders, loans against savings accounts, and home equity and home improvement loans. Many savings banks also offer life insurance policies to their customers when permitted by law.

Like savings and loan associations, savings banks have discovered that the customers they serve have become more financially sophisticated in recent years. Higher-yielding deposit accounts have grown much faster than lower-yielding savings plans. The most pronounced shift has been from regular passbook savings accounts to fixed-maturity time deposits and money market accounts that carry contract interest rates that float with conditions in the market. The net result of all of these changes has been to push up overall interest expenses, put pressure on savings bank earnings, and, at times, increase the volatility of their funds flows. Savings banks today must also be more concerned with changing electronic technology, which is forcing them to automate more of their routine services and make customer access to their facilities and services more convenient than ever before.

Current Trends and Future Problems

The savings bank industry faces a number of problems that will significantly affect its future as a conduit for savings and investment. One factor is increasing competition with savings and loan associations, credit unions, and commercial banks offering similar services. Because of the heavy concentration of savings bank assets in mortgage-related investments, savings banks are less flexible than commercial banks in adjusting to changing financial conditions and to the changing service needs of their customers.

Some have earnings problems due to inflexible asset structures and bad loans, coupled with higher fund-raising costs. On the other hand, many savings banks have countered this relative inflexibility in their asset structures with aggressive competition for funds and innovative new services. The future growth of this industry, like that of most other financial institutions, will depend heavily on the ability of savings banks to gain the necessary changes in government regulations to allow them to respond to changing financial market conditions.

QUESTIONS TO HELP YOU STUDY

1. How did *savings and loans* get started? How does the history of savings and loans compare with the history of savings banks? Which is the oldest institution?

2. What exactly are *mutuals*? How do these institutions differ from stockholder-owned depository institutions?

3. Why did the savings and loan industry get into serious trouble during the 1980s and 1990s?

4. What solutions have been developed to deal with the savings and loan industry's problems and to strengthen the industry's performance in the twenty-first century?

15.4 Credit Unions

credit unions

The characteristics and operations of **credit unions** have been a neglected area of research in the financial system. Recently, however, there has been a revival of interest in credit union behavior. One reason has been the rapid growth of this financial intermediary. For example, credit union assets have nearly tripled since 1990 (see Exhibit 15.2), though a combination of failures and mergers among smaller credit unions has recently slowed credit union growth somewhat. U.S. credit unions are the third-largest institutional supplier of nonmortgage installment credit to individuals and families, trailing only commercial banks and finance companies and outstripping installment credit extended by savings and loans and savings banks almost two-to-one. These institutions are household-oriented intermediaries, offering deposit and credit services to

---

EXHIBIT 15.2	Year	Number of Credit Unions in the United States	Number of Credit Union Members in the United States	U.S. Credit Union Assets ($ Millions)
Credit Unions in the United States and around the Globe	1950	10,586	4,617,086	$ 1,005
	1960	20,094	12,025,393	5,651
	1970	23,687	22,775,511	17,872
Source: Credit Union National Association, *Credit Union Report 2003;* World Council of Credit Unions, Inc., *2003 Statistical Report;* and Board of Governors of the Federal Reserve System, *Flow of Funds Accounts.*	1980	21,465	43,930,569	68,974
	1990	14,549	61,610,957	221,759
	2000	10,684	79,751,853	449,799
	2003	9,710	84,847,962	629,134

Credit Unions around the Globe:

Number of credit unions belonging to the World Council of Credit Unions, 2003: 40,421 CUs

Worldwide membership, 2003: 123,467,445 people

Worldwide assets (in U.S. dollars): $758.4 billion

individuals and families. Their long-run survival stems mainly from being able to offer low loan rates and high deposit interest rates to their customers and from their relatively low operating costs.

Credit unions are cooperative, self-help associations of individuals rather than profit-motivated financial institutions. Savings deposits and loans are offered only to members of each association and not to the general public. The members of a credit union are technically the *owners,* receiving dividends and sharing in any losses that occur. Each member gets one vote regardless of the size of his or her credit union account.

Credit unions began in nineteenth-century Germany in order to serve low-income individuals and families, working primarily in industrial jobs, by providing them with inexpensive credit and a ready outlet for their savings. The credit union movement began as a response to "loan sharking," where poorer households were charged extremely high interest rates for small cash loans. They came to the United States (beginning in the state of New Hampshire) in 1909. Early growth was modest until the 1950s, when these institutions broadened their appeal to middle-income individuals by offering many new financial services.

The credit union sector remains small compared to other major financial institutions, accounting for less than 10 percent of all consumer savings in the United States. However, worldwide, the industry's potential for future growth appears promising due to its innovative character and solid public acceptance. The credit union has become an aggressive competitor of banks and savings associations for both savings deposits and consumer installment loans. Beginning in 1978, credit unions were authorized to offer money market certificates, which can carry the same terms as the money market deposit plans sold by banks. In addition, many credit unions offer payroll savings plans by which employees can automatically set aside a portion of their salary in a savings account.

Credit union loans have kept pace with the growth of their deposits and today account for about 10 percent of all consumer installment loans in the United States and a substantial portion of these loans worldwide. Consumer loan rates charged by credit unions are fully competitive with loan rates charged by most other major consumer lenders. Moreover, credit unions frequently grant their borrowing members interest refunds up to 20 percent of the amount of a loan. Some credit unions provide life insurance free to their borrowing customers, a service charged for by most other lending institutions. Thus, credit unions often accept a smaller spread between their loan and deposit interest rates. This is possible because their operating costs are among the lowest of all financial-service firms. Frequently, the sponsoring employer or association provides free office facilities, and credit union members elect officers and directors who frequently serve with no compensation at all.

Interestingly enough, credit unions usually report one of the lowest default and delinquency rates on their loans of any lending institution in the financial system. Why? One reason is that they make fewer business loans than many competing financial institutions (especially banks), which, particularly during downturns in the economy, can be very risky credits. Another factor is something we are about to discuss—the common bond between credit union members which seems to encourage most borrowing members to repay their loans in a timely fashion.

Credit Union Membership

Credit unions are organized around a common affiliation or *common bond* among their members. Most members work for the same employer or for one of a group of related employers. Moreover, if one family member belongs to a credit union, other family members are eligible as well. Occupation-related credit unions account for about

To learn more about credit unions, you may enjoy viewing their Web sites—for example, take a look at the site of the American Credit Union of Milwaukee at americancu.org and the Chicago Post Office Employees Credit Union at my_creditunion.com

two-thirds of all U.S. credit unions. About one-fifth are organized around nonprofit associations, such as a labor union, a church, or a fraternal or social organization. Common area of residence, such as a city or state, and age (e.g., an association for retired persons) have also been used to get credit unions started. The Federal Credit Union Act permits these types of credit unions: (1) common bond (members from a single group); (2) community (members from a single area); and (3) multiple bond (members from several groups).

In recent years, credit unions have been allowed to define their members' common bond so liberally that millions of people have become eligible for credit union membership, and the industry in the United States has recently come under attack in court by bankers' groups for its lenient membership rules and special tax advantages. During its 1998 term, the U.S. Supreme Court voted to limit membership in federally chartered credit unions to members working for a single employer or to individuals residing in the same community—that is, individuals must share a single common bond. Recent legislation introduced in the U.S. Congress has now overridden key parts of that Supreme Court ruling, however, allowing most credit unions to keep their existing membership base and to merge multiple (unrelated) fields of membership.

Size of Credit Unions

There is a strong shift today toward fewer, but larger, credit unions. For example, the number of associations reached an all-time high in 1969 at almost 24,000 but now totals than fewer 10,000 in the United States, with the decline due primarily to mergers, failures, and a structural shift in the U.S. economy away from manufacturing industries (where credit unions have concentrated historically) toward more service industries (where credit union activity tends to be more subdued). With fewer credit unions but continued industry growth, the average-size credit union has risen substantially in recent years.

For example, although only about one-sixth of credit unions held more than $1 million in assets in 1970, today the average-size U.S. credit union falls in the $50 to $65 million asset-size range. The smallest credit unions are declining in number, while the largest credit unions are growing in number. Nevertheless, the average-size credit union remains very small compared to other kinds of depository institutions.

Still, worldwide membership in credit unions has not stopped its upward climb. Around the globe more than 120 million people belong to one or more of just over 40,000 credit unions scattered across close to 100 different countries. Inside the United States, credit union members grew from fewer than 5 million in 1950 to more than 84 million as the twenty-first century began. Nearly 100 percent of U.S. credit union deposits are either federally or privately insured.

New Services Offered

Credit unions are expanding the number of services they offer. Some sell life insurance. Others act as brokers for group insurance plans where state law permits. Many credit unions are active in offering 24-hour automated or telephone and Internet services, travelers checks, financial planning services, retirement savings, credit cards, home equity and first-mortgage loans, and money orders. Larger credit unions compete directly with banks for transaction accounts by offering **share drafts**—interest-bearing checkbook deposits. A substantial proportion of U.S. credit unions also offer credit cards and automated teller machines (many of which are linked nationwide through an electronic exchange network in order to accommodate members who travel). Several recently began to take loan applications via

share drafts

Financial institutions do battle not only within their market areas, fighting for the attention of customers, but also in courts and legislative bodies over differences in the rules and regulations they face. For example, when the set of rules applying to banks becomes more restrictive than the set of rules applying to credit unions, a phenomenon called "regulatory arbitrage" may occur. Credit unions may grow faster than banks. Bankers may fight back, both in the marketplace and through the legal process.

U.S. bankers fought back in the courts and by February 1998 had won a considerable victory in the U.S. Supreme Court, forcing future credit union membership to be limited more closely to traditional common-bond boundaries. However, U.S. credit unions appealed this court decision to their supporters in Congress and overturned much of it via new legislation—the Credit Union Membership Access Act. This bill, signed into law by President Clinton in August 1998, divides credit unions into several different groups:

1. Single-common-bond credit unions whose members share a common occupation or association.

2. Multiple-common-bond credit unions with members arising from more than one group having a common bond.

3. Community credit union members, living in or joining an organization that is part of a well-defined local area or neighborhood.

This latest credit-union law limits multiple-common-bond credit unions to 3,000 members except in cases where the National Credit Union Administration (NCUA) finds that achieving efficiency or safety and soundness requires a larger organization. Moreover, NCUA can approve larger multiple-common-bond unions if a particular area seems to be underserved. Existing credit union memberships are grandfathered under this most recent law, thereby allowing previously diverse credit unions to continue operating with their current members.

Credit unions can expand their membership if they are adequately capitalized, are capable of serving larger numbers of people, provide affordable services, are operating in safety, and would not harm existing credit unions. However, as they expand, credit unions must conform to capitalization (net worth) rules similar to those faced by banks and other thrift institutions, and the largest unions must have annual independent audits. Finally, credit unions were granted an avenue of escape from their industry if they so desire—they can convert themselves into other types of depository institutions.

Note: For more on credit unions, see especially No.s 96–843, 96–847, 1185.ct.927, and Willam R. Emmons and Frank A. Schmid, "Credit Unions Make Friends—But Not with Bankers," *The Regional Economist*, Federal Reserve Bank of St. Louis, October 2003.

fax and personal computers and offer preauthorized drafts as well as telephone and electronic bill paying.

U.S. credit unions are under intense pressure to develop new services and penetrate new markets due to increasing competition from other financial institutions and a decline in the demand for their historically most important credit service—automobile loans—where they face fierce competition from banks and finance companies (such as GMAC and Ford Motor Credit). In addition, because a larger proportion of family income today is spent on food, fuel, education, and other necessities, credit unions have been shifting many of their loans into these areas. First-mortgage loans to purchase new homes and second-mortgage loans to repair or improve existing homes, as well as home equity credit to fund a wide variety of household purchases, have grown rapidly and now account for about a third of all credit union loans. (See Exhibit 15.3.) Finally, loans to small businesses have recently been added to many credit union service menus, along with auto and equipment leases. As the new century began, credit unions' most rapidly growing loans included new auto and recreational vehicle loans, adjustable-rate first home mortgages, second home mortgage loans, and home equity loans.

EXHIBIT 15.3

Financial Assets and Liabilities Held by U.S. Credit Unions, 1980–2004 ($ Billions)

Source: Board of Governors of the Federal Reserve System, *Flow of Funds Accounts,* selected issues.

*Figures for 2004 are as of the first quarter.

Item	1980	1990	2000	2004*
Financial Assets:				
Checkable deposits and currency	$ 1.2	$ 4.8	$ 26.7	$ 50.4
Time and savings deposits	7.1	21.7	15.5	27.5
Federal funds loans and security RPs	0.7	14.6	4.0	4.3
U.S. government and federal agency securities	4.3	23.0	69.1	128.8
Home mortgage and equity loans	4.7	48.2	124.9	185.4
Consumer installment loans	44.0	93.1	184.4	207.7
Miscellaneous assets	5.7	9.3	16.3	30.3
Total financial assets	$67.7	$214.7	$440.9	$634.4
Liabilities:				
Checkable deposits/shares	$ 3.3	$22.2	$ 51.3	$ 70.3
Small time and savings deposits/shares	57.9	175.3	312.7	423.8
Large ($100,000+) deposits/shares	0.5	3.3	25.1	54.7
Loans from the Federal Home Loan banks and other advances	—	—	3.4	8.4
Miscellaneous liabilities	3.1	3.9	5.6	19.5
Total liabilities	$64.8	$204.7	$398.1	$576.7

Like banks, credit unions have a dual (federal and state) regulatory structure. First chartered only by the states, the federal government entered the picture in 1934 with passage of the Federal Credit Union Act, which issues charters of incorporation for federally supervised credit unions. A second layer exists in the industry today known as corporate credit unions (CCUs), that make loans to credit unions in need of financial help, process their checks, and professionally invest credit union funds.

Under current federal government rules in the United States, credit unions are permitted to make unsecured loans to members (including credit card loans) not exceeding five years to maturity and to grant secured loans out to 30 years. Their permissible investments in securities are limited to a list prescribed by either state or federal regulations. In the main, credit unions are permitted to acquire U.S. government securities; to hold savings deposits at banks, savings and loan associations, and federally insured credit unions; and to purchase selected federal agency securities. They rely heavily on U.S. government securities and on savings deposits to provide liquidity to meet deposit withdrawals and accommodate member credit needs. Credit unions pay dividends to their members, but they are considered *nonprofit associations,* doing business only with their owners, and, therefore, are classified as *tax-exempt mutual organizations.* Some of the leading credit unions in the U.S. include the Navy Federal Credit Union, Virginia at **navyfcu.org**, USA Federal Credit Union, California at **usafedcu.org**, Global Credit Union, Washington state at **globalcu.org**, Corporate One Federal Credit Union, Ohio at **corpone.org**, Municipal Credit Union, New York at **nymcu.org**, Lockheed Federal Credit Union, California at **secure.lockheedfcu.org**, and IBM Credit Union, Minnesota at **mmfcu.org**.

Up-to-date news about developments in the credit union industry may be found in cujournal.com and in the Credit Union Times at cutimes.com

A Strong Competitive Force

Credit unions represent stiff competition for commercial banks, savings banks, and other financial institutions serving consumers. Today, one of every four Americans belongs to a credit union—roughly double the proportion of a decade earlier. True, the total number of credit unions is down in some areas, such as in the United States, where a consolidation movement is under way. However, this industry has repeatedly demonstrated its capacity for service innovation and its ability to compete successfully for both consumer loans and savings accounts against some of the largest financial-service competitors in the world.

To learn more about the American Bankers Association's position on credit unions, see especially aba.com/ Industry+Issues/ Issues_CU_menu.htm

The American Bankers Association (ABA) has strongly objected to the many advantages under law that credit unions in the United States appear to possess compared to commercial banks. These advantages include an exemption from federal income taxes, while banks pay a substantial portion of their earnings (roughly a third in recent years) in federal taxes. Moreover, with the help of their trade associations (such as the Credit Union National Association) and their regulators (such as the National Credit Union Administration), credit unions appear to many bankers to have reached far beyond their original charters which called for providing small cash loans at reasonable interest rates and a safe outlet for family savings. Instead, credit unions today appear to be aggressive multiservice financial intermediaries, active in such diverse fields as small business loans, home mortgage and home equity loans, and auto and recreational vehicle lending, as well as providing such services as selling insurance and brokering stocks and bonds. Then, too, bankers must support their local communities with development loans and other services under the terms of the Community Reinvestment Act (CRA). In contrast, credit unions are generally exempt from this kind of direct community support. The ABA and other banking groups have filed lawsuits to limit the services credit unions can offer, restrict how far they can reach to attract new members, or make them follow the same rules for taxation and community support as bankers face. To date, credit unions have successfully resisted such changes.

To compare credit unions with banks and other thrift institutions, recent studies prepared by the U.S. Treasury Department may be helpful. Visit treasury.gov/ press/releases/ report3070.htm and treasury.gov/ press/releases/ report3071.htm

15.5 Money Market Funds

money market mutual fund

A fourth major nonbank thrift institution appeared on the scene as recently as 1974. In that year, the first **money market mutual fund**—a financial intermediary pooling the savings of thousands of individuals and businesses and investing those monies in short-term, high-quality money market instruments—opened for business. Taking advantage of the fact that interest rates on most deposits offered by commercial and savings banks were then restrained by government regulation, the money fund offered share accounts whose yields were free to reflect prevailing interest rates in the money market. Thus, the money fund represents the classic case of profit-seeking entrepreneurs finding a loophole around ill-conceived government regulations (many of which have since been repealed or eased). Leading money market funds today include such institutions as Merrill Lynch CMA Money Fund at **askmerrill.ml.com**, Fidelity Cash Reserves at **fidelityinvestor.com**, Prudential MoneyMart Assets at **prudential.com**, Touchstone Money Market Fund at **touchstonefunds.com**, Evergreen Money Market Fund at **evergreeninvestments.com**, Galaxy Prime Reserves at **valetaccount.com**, and Vanguard MMR Prime Portfolio at **Vanguard.FastTrack.Net**.

The most frequently asked questions about money market funds are answered by The Investment Company Institute at ici.org/aboutfunds

The growth of money market funds was explosive. As of year-end 1973, there were only 15 in existence, with assets totaling just $100 million. Money funds appeared to peak in 1982, when more than 200 of them held over $200 billion in assets (see Exhibit 15.4). Beginning in late 1982 and 1983, a decline in their assets set in as banks and other depository institutions fought back with Super NOWs and money market deposit accounts (MMDAs), both authorized by the U.S. government

EXHIBIT 15.4

Money Market Funds: Assets Held and Total Shares Outstanding, 1980–2004* ($ Billions)

Source: Board of Governors of the Federal Reserve System, *Flow of Funds Accounts; Financial Assets and Liabilities,* selected issues.

Note: Columns may not add to totals because of rounding.

*2004 figures are for first quarter of the year.

Item	1980	1990	2000	2004*
Financial Assets:				
Checkable deposits and currency	$ 0.2	$ 11.4	$ 2.2	$ −10.7
Time and savings deposits	21.0	21.0	142.4	158.2
Loans made through security RPs	5.6	59.0	183.0	269.0
Foreign deposits	6.8	27.1	91.1	73.2
U.S. government and federal agency securities	8.2	82.4	275.6	425.7
State and local government (tax-exempt) securities	1.9	83.6	244.7	306.7
Open-market paper	31.6	206.7	608.6	432.2
Miscellaneous assets	1.2	7.3	264.5	317.4
Total assets	$76.4	$498.4	$1,812.1	$1,971.9

If you are interested in further exploring the operation of money market funds, see, for example, Scudder Tax-Free Funds at scudder.com and the Franklin Tax-Exempt Money Fund at franklintempleton.com

in 1982 to carry unregulated interest rates. Subsequently, however, money market funds resumed their rapid growth, making share gains during the late 1980s, the 1990s, and into the twenty-first century. In fact, 2001 was the best year ever in money market fund history, with assets spiraling upward to a record of nearly $2.3 trillion late in that year before sliding back to about $2 trillion held in 989 money funds at year-end 2003. This recent growth pattern probably reflects several factors, including increased public concerns about saving and preparing for the retirement years and the public's concerns about risks in the economy and the financial sector, particularly after the recession and the terrorist attacks of 2001. Another factor boosting money funds are the comparatively light regulations tying the industry down. There are no legal interest-rate ceilings limiting what a money fund can pay to its shareholders and, unless a money fund happens to impose them, no penalties for early withdrawal of funds, as is required of customers by many banks and nonbank thrift institutions.

However, money market funds are not without their limitations. For example, during the 1980s a number of these thrift institutions reached out for riskier, but higher yielding, issues of commercial paper (i.e., short-term corporate notes) so they could offer high returns to savers. Unfortunately, massive losses soon occurred for some money funds. These losses on investments in commercial paper led the U.S. Securities and Exchange Commission (SEC) in 1991 to impose limits on money market fund investments in less than top-quality securities, restricting their investments in lower-quality financial instruments to no more than 5 percent of total assets. No more than 1 percent of a money fund's assets may be placed in securities coming from a single corporate issuer.

Moreover, future money market fund investments were restricted to securities that are rated in one of the two highest rating categories by at least two nationally recognized credit-rating companies (such as Moody's and Standard & Poor's). In the same year, the SEC allowed money funds to reach for somewhat longer-maturity financial instruments, allowing them to buy securities with maturities up to 13 months compared to a 12-month maximum under previous rules. However, the SEC reduced the permissible average maturity of a money fund's investment portfolio from a maximum of 120 days to a maximum of only 90 days. In 1996 the SEC tightened restrictions on money funds investing in risky derivative securities (such as futures or options) to reduce the risk that changing interest rates might threaten a money fund's stability and solvency. These new restrictions were accompanied by widely publicized reminders from the SEC to the general public that savings left with money market funds are *not* protected by federal insurance.

Trends in the money market funds industry can be followed via iMoneyNet at imoneynet.com

On the whole, however, money market funds hold high-quality assets—primarily U.S. Treasury bills and commercial paper—which helps explain why money market funds remain so popular with millions of investors. The interest-bearing securities they acquire generally carry low risk of borrower default and limited fluctuations in price. Contributing to the low-risk character of money fund investments is their short average maturity of only a few weeks or months. The short maturity of fund investments results in a highly liquid security portfolio that can be adjusted quickly to changing market conditions. Many funds declare dividends on a daily basis, crediting their earnings to customer accounts and often notifying the customer by mail monthly of any additional shares purchased with the dividends earned. Most are "no load" funds that do not charge their customers commissions for opening an account, purchasing additional shares, or redeeming shares for cash.

Another outstanding advantage of the money funds for many investors is the ease with which their accounts can be accessed. Most funds allow the customer to write checks to redeem shares, provided the amount of each check exceeds a designated minimum ($500 is common). The customer is issued a book of checks and can write and deposit checks in his or her local bank account, often receiving credit for the deposited check from the local bank the same day, even though it may take several days for the money fund check to be collected. Meantime, daily interest is still being earned on the monies waiting in the customer's share account. Most money funds also offer customers the option of purchasing or redeeming shares by wire or by telephone. Today, as was true when they began their operations during the 1970s, money market funds serve as: (1) cash-management vehicles where market rates of return can be earned on funds used for daily transactions; (2) tax-sheltering vehicles for those investors who choose shares in tax-exempt money market funds; (3) a temporary repository for liquid funds waiting for a major purchase or waiting for the appearance of higher-return investments expected to appear later in the marketplace; and (4) a haven of safety for savings when the rest of the financial marketplace appears to be too volatile and risky for a conservative saver to commit his or her funds immediately.

Many local newspapers and financial newssheets, as well as brokers' screens, report the current rates of return (yields) being posted by the largest money market funds, as well as the volume of assets currently held by each of these funds. We can see an illustration of a typical daily newspaper report on a couple of money market funds in Exhibit 15.5. Most money funds manage their assets with the goal of keeping their NAV (i.e., net asset value, or selling price) fixed at $1 per share. They carry no extra sales charge (that is, are not front-end loaded) and must stand ready to redeem the saver's shares for cash each business day. Shareholder dividends are earned every day in proportion to the number of shares each saver owns in the fund. All money market

---

EXHIBIT 15.5

An Example of Typical Money Market Fund Information Reported Daily by Security Brokers, Dealers, and in Daily Newspapers

Name or Abbreviation of Money Market Fund	Average Maturity of Fund's Portfolio in Days	Weekly Average Annualized Yield on the Fund's Assets	Millions of Dollars in Assets Held by the Fund (on the Date Indicated)
KPR Municipal Money Market Fund (KPRM)	54	2.97%	$ 878
Z.Row Money Market Assets (ZRMA)	43	4.68	1,651

funds must register with the Securities and Exchange Commission and abide by its rules in offering shares to the public.

Despite their numerous advantages for customers interested in professional management of their short-term funds, money market funds today possess some competitive disadvantages that must be overcome if their rapid growth is to continue. For one thing, their toughest competitors—commercial banks—today face fewer regulations than before, can invest in longer-term, higher-yielding assets than money funds, and have a broader customer base than is true of money market funds. Moreover, money-fund share accounts are *not* government insured, although many of the funds have attempted to deal with this problem by arranging for private insurance or by creating funds invested solely in default-free government securities, which attracted thousands of small investors during the 1980s and 1990s as concerns about risk in the banking system mounted. Moreover, the yield differential between posted yields on money market fund share accounts and money market deposits at banks has narrowed in recent years. The money market fund industry has recently shown itself to be vulnerable to *low* market interest rates, finding it difficult to pay shareholders a positive interest rate on their savings. With money market interest rates near zero early in the new century, operating expenses at many funds began to eat up interest from investments, resulting in significant losses. A handful of money funds closed early in the twenty-first century, while others raised their fees or cut operating expenses in order to survive.

Certainly the money market funds are not likely to go away. They are a potent competitor for both small individual savings accounts and businesses' liquid funds. However, barring further restrictive federal regulation of bank and thrift deposits, all bank and nonbank thrift institutions, including money market funds, will continue to compete for savings and transaction accounts on relatively equal terms, leading to intense competition and, perhaps, some failures among competing financial institutions in future years.

QUESTIONS TO HELP YOU STUDY

5. *Credit unions* are one of the fastest-growing financial intermediaries in the United States and in many other parts of the world as well. What explains this rapid growth?

6. What *services* do credit unions offer that compete with the services offered by banks and savings and loan associations? Why are bankers' groups concerned about the expansion of credit unions?

7. What advantages do credit unions have over banks? What disadvantages do they face?

8. How and why did *money market funds* begin to appear during the 1970s? What factors have contributed to their recent growth?

9. Exactly how are money market funds different from banks and credit unions in their behavior and the assets they hold?

10. If you are a small saver what advantages do money market funds appear to offer you relative to banks and credit unions? What are their disadvantages?

MARKETS ON THE NET: The Most Important Web Sites for This Chapter

Credit Union National Association (cuna.org)

Federal Deposit Insurance Corporation (fdic.gov)

Investment Company Institute (ici.org/aboutfunds)

Money Market Funds (encyclopedia.com)

National Credit Union Administration (ncua.gov)

Office of Thrift Supervision (ots.treas.gov)

Savings and Loan Industry (encyclopedia.com)

U.S. Treasury Department (treasury.gov/press/releases/report3070.htm)

World Council of Credit Unions (woccu.org)

Summary of the Chapter's Main Points

Thrift institutions—savings and loan associations, savings banks, credit unions, and money market funds—are among the most popular financial institutions within the financial system. They are especially well known to individuals and families (households)—their principal customer base. Among the key points in this chapter are:

- Thrift institutions began their history primarily to reach small savers (principally individuals and families) and help this group of customers achieve home ownership, a better education, satisfactory preparation for retirement, and other personal financial goals. Over time, however, thrifts have diversified their services and attempted to reach out to a broader customer base, including both households and some business enterprises.

- Some thrift institutions (particularly money market funds) have experienced fairly steady growth, while others (especially savings and loan associations) have experienced more volatile and somewhat more uncertain growth. Many of the more troubled thrift institutions have been merged into larger and healthier financial-service companies (including banks and financial holding companies) or have simply closed their doors.

- Nevertheless, thrift institutions have continued to be tough competitors with banks, often outbidding bankers for their customers' checking accounts, savings deposits, home mortgages, and personal installment loans. Unlike many other financial intermediaries they are primarily *local* service providers, though some thrifts have grown to become nationally and internationally known institutions.

- Like the banking industry (discussed in the previous chapter), the thrift industry is experiencing rapidly changing technology as it seeks to provide more electronic financial services in order to lower overhead and personnel costs and improve service.

- Thrifts have paralleled banks in a trend toward *consolidation*, contracting into smaller numbers. However, the average thrift institution has increased substantially in overall size. In turn, these larger thrifts have broadened their service menus and are reaching out to expand their beachfront within the global financial marketplace.

Key Terms Appearing in This Chapter

savings and loan associations, 452
mutuals, 453
money market deposit accounts (MMDAs), 454
Federal Deposit Insurance Corporation (FDIC), 455

savings banks, 458
credit unions, 461
share drafts, 463
money market mutual fund, 466

Problems and Issues

1. Stronghold Money Fund Assets is a relatively new *money market fund* with about $400 million in total financial assets and shares outstanding (each maintained at a value of $1.00 per share). Most of the fund's accounts represent the savings of high-income, interest-sensitive financial market investors. Stronghold's current distribution of financial assets is as follows:

U.S. Treasury securities	$170 million
Federal agency securities	115 million
Prime bank CDs	85 million
Prime commercial paper issues	30 million

Interest rates are expected to rise substantially in the money market over the next several weeks or months and Stronghold's management is concerned that its relatively low current yield (a seven-day average of 4.05 percent, one of the lowest yields among existing funds) may result in the loss of many of its more interest-sensitive share accounts. The fund's average maturity is currently 34 days, which is also substantially less than the industry's current average maturity of about 45 days.

What steps would you recommend to help Stronghold Money Fund prepare for an apparent impending change in money market conditions?

2. Identify the terms and concepts defined or described below as discussed in this chapter.

   a. Investment company investing only in short-term financial instruments.
   b. Interest-bearing checking accounts offered by a credit union.
   c. Nonprofit associations providing financial services only to their members.
   d. Depository institutions owned by their depositors.
   e. Insures deposits placed in U.S. banks and savings and loan associations.
   f. Deposits bearing market-sensitive interest rates and subject to withdrawal by check.
   g. A leading home mortgage lender in the United States.

Standard & Poor's Market Insight and Web-Based Problems

1. The differences between commercial banks and savings and loans have been narrowing in recent years, with regulations becoming increasingly uniform and product offerings becoming increasingly similar.

   a. Visit S&P's Market Insight database at **mhhe.com/edumarketinsight** and find the annual balance sheets for three of the nation's largest commercial banks and two of the nation's largest S&Ls listed in this chapter. Look under "Excel Analytics."
   b. For each bank and S&L, compute the ratios of "Commercial Loans" to "Loans/Claims/Advances—Customers—Total" and "Mortgages" to "Loans/Claims/Advances—Customers—Total." These ratios indicate what shares of the firms' total loan portfolios are made up of C&I and real estate loans, respectively.
   c. Compute the same ratios as in part (b), but for the three commercial banks combined and the two S&Ls combined.
   d. What choices have these individual firms made in terms of market focus? Is there a difference in market focus between the commercial banks and the S&Ls?

2. As part of the ongoing process of consolidation among depository institutions in recent decades, many savings and loans have converted their charters to a bank charter and/or have been merged with large commercial banks.

   a. Visit the Web site of the Office of Thrift Supervision at **ots.treasury.gov.** Click the tab "Data and Research" and then click "Thrift Industry Charts" and open the most recent set of charts (pdf-file). Go to the chart "Number and Assets."
   b. What appears to have happened to the total number of institutions in the industry over the past four years?
   c. What appears to have happened to the industry's size (as measured by total assets) over the past four years?
   d. What do your answers to parts (b) and (c) have to say about the average size of firms in the industry?

3. Historically, credit unions have been much smaller in size than most commercial banks or savings and loans and have focused their client base on consumer loans. However, as described in the text, the role of credit unions among depositories has been changing. The purpose of this exercise is to examine a few key features of the structure of federal credit unions and compare them with commercial banks.

    a. Visit the Web site of the National Credit Union Administration at **ncua.gov** and click on "Credit Union Data" under the tab "Data and Services." Then click "5300 Quarterly Data" and obtain the most recent consolidated balance sheet.

    b. Download the spreadsheet "Cbsfcu.xls."

    c. Under the heading "Consumer Loans," lump together the following assets on the consolidated balance sheet: (i) unsecured credit card loans; (ii) all other unsecured loans; (iii) new auto loans; and (iv) used auto loans. What share of total assets does this represent?

    d. Turn back to Exhibit 14.3 and compare the percentage that you computed in part (c) to the share of loans made by commercial banks listed as "loans to individuals." What do you conclude about the composition of credit unions' clients (and why they borrow from the credit union) versus those who are served by commercial banks? Is the difference suggested by the numbers pronounced or do the two institutions appear to be similar?

Selected References to Explore

Cohen, Andrew. "Market Structure and Market Definition: The Case of Small Market Banks and Thrifts." *Finance and Economics Discussion Series 2004–02,* Board of Governors of the Federal Reserve System, Washington, D.C., 2004.

Duca, John V. "How Low Interest Rates Impact Financial Institutions." *Southwest Economy,* Federal Reserve Bank of Dallas, November/December 2003, pp. 1, 8–12.

Emmons, William R., and Frank A. Schmid. "Credit Unions Make Friends—But Not with Bankers." *The Regional Economist,* Federal Reserve Bank of St. Louis, October 2003, pp. 4–9.

Investment Company Institute. *Mutual Fund Fact Book,* Washington, D.C., 2003.

Willis, Jonathan L. "What Impact Will E-Commerce Have on the U.S. Economy?" *Economic Review,* Federal Reserve Bank of Kansas City, Quarter II (2004), pp. 53–71.

World Council of Credit Unions. *Statistical Report 2003,* Madison, WI, 2004.

Chapter 16

Mutual Funds, Insurance Companies, Investment Banks, and Other Financial Firms

Learning Objectives

in This Chapter

- You will explore the many roles played by a variety of financial institutions ranging from mutual funds, insurance companies, and investment banks to finance companies, mortgage banks, and security dealers.

- You will discover the different *services* each of these nonbank financial institutions offers to the public.

- You will examine the principal *sources and uses of funds* that these nonbank institutions draw upon to carry out their daily activities.

- You will be able to understand more fully many of the problems faced by financial institutions operating in today's money and capital markets.

What's in This Chapter?
Key Topics Outline

Mutual Funds: Advantages for the Small Investor

New Types of Mutual Funds

Goals, Earnings, and Tax Status of Mutual Funds

Pension Funds: Objectives and Types of Retirement Plans

Pensions' Investment Strategies and Government Regulation (ERISA)

Life and Property-Casualty Insurers: Old and New Services Provided

Investment Policies and Insurable Risks

Finance Companies: Types of Companies, Asset Portfolios, and Funding Sources

New Consumer Options: Pawn, Title, and Check-Cashing Credit Providers

Investment Bankers, Mortgage Banks, REITs, Venture Capital and Leasing Companies

Trends Affecting All Financial Institutions

16.1 Introduction

We now turn to a highly diverse group of financial institutions that attract savings mainly from individuals and families and, for the most part, make long-term loans in the capital market. Included in this group are *mutual funds* (sometimes called investment companies), *pension funds* (or, as they are sometimes called, retirement plans), and *life* and *property-casualty insurers,* which today are among the leading institutional buyers of bonds and stocks. *Finance companies,* another member of this group of financial institutions, are active lenders to both business firms and consumers (households) and borrow heavily in the money market. Also included in this chapter is an overview of the *investment banking* industry, which underwrites new security offerings for corporations and governments around the world. As we will soon see, these institutions provide important services to participants in virtually every corner of the money and capital markets.

16.2 Mutual Funds (or Investment Companies)

mutual fund

investment companies

One of the most rapidly growing of all financial institutions over the past two decades is the **mutual fund** or, as it is more properly called, the investment company. **Investment companies** provide an outlet for the savings of thousands of individual investors, directing their funds into bonds, stocks, and money market securities. These companies are especially attractive to the small investor, to whom they offer continuous management services for a large and varied security portfolio. By purchasing shares offered by an investment company, the small saver gains greater diversification, risk sharing, lower transaction costs, opportunities for capital gains, and indirect access to higher-yielding securities that can be purchased only in large blocks. In addition, most investment company stock is highly liquid, because these companies stand ready at all times to repurchase their outstanding shares at current market prices. The majority of mutual fund shares are held by individuals and families rather than by institutional investors.

The Background of Investment Companies

Investment companies, first developed in Great Britain, made their initial appearance in the United States in the city of Boston in 1924, serving as a vehicle for buying and monitoring subsidiary corporations. Many were unsuccessful in the early years, and the Great Depression of the 1930s forced scores of these firms into bankruptcy. New life was breathed into the industry after World War II, however, when investment companies appealed to a rapidly growing middle class of savers. They were also buoyed by rising stock prices that attracted millions of investors, most of whom had only modest amounts to invest and little knowledge of how the financial markets work. The industry launched an aggressive advertising campaign that attracted more than 40 million shareholders during the 1960s alone.

Then the roof fell in as the long postwar bull market in stocks collapsed in the late 1960s and again during the 1970s. Small investors began to pull out of the stock market in droves. Many investment companies disappeared in this shakeout period, most of them consolidated into larger firms.

The future of the industry seemed in doubt until a new element appeared: *innovation.* Managers began to develop new types of investment companies designed to appeal to groups of investors with specialized financial needs. By tradition, investment companies had stressed investments in common stock, offering investors capital appreciation as well as current income. With the stock market performing poorly, these firms turned their focus increasingly to bonds and money market instruments. New *bond funds* directed the majority of the funds into corporate debt obligations or tax-exempt municipal bonds. Their principal objectives in recent years have been to generate current income and, in the case of the municipal bond fund, a higher after-tax rate of return for the investor. Capital appreciation is normally a secondary consideration to bond funds.

Money market funds, discussed in Chapter 15, emerged in 1974 with the announced intent of holding money market securities, mainly commercial paper and government bills. They were created in response to record-high interest rates and the desire of the small investor to skirt around federal interest rate ceilings on savings deposits offered by banks and thrift institutions. In addition, the money funds have offered investors professional management of their liquid funds.

The traditional stock-investing mutual funds began to grow rapidly again during the 1980s and 1990s. Although money market funds rescued the investment companies during the turbulent 1970s, equity-oriented mutual funds have outpaced the money market funds more recently, with money flowing in from individuals and institutions primarily for retirement purposes and from investors eager to take advantage of higher expected long-term yields on selected stocks versus the relatively low yields available on deposits and other short-term investment instruments. Moreover, several stock funds have outperformed the market as a whole by purchasing stocks from smaller, rapidly growing firms dealing in high-tech products, health care, and other specialty areas.

By the fall of 2000, at the height of the technology-driven "bubble" in the stock market, the assets of mutual funds of all types approached $5 trillion, compared to little more than $1 trillion in 1990. Nevertheless, many stock funds did *not* outperform the market and, when the stock market bubble burst, scores of funds plummeted in value. Their plight was further exacerbated by the onset of a recession in the U.S. economy and the slow recovery that followed. Thousands of investors were discouraged from placing their savings in the stock market and, therefore, turned away from many mutual funds. By mid-2002 mutual fund assets had fallen below $3.5 trillion. However, the market has since begun to rebound.

The increased volatility evident in the stock market as the new century unfolded—particularly in high-tech stocks—helped boost the popularity of so-called *index funds.* These innovative investment companies invest in a portfolio of stocks and other instruments that reflect the whole market or a large segment of that market. For example, some of these funds hold a basket of stocks that closely track the S&P 500 Stock Index, the Russell 2000 Index, or the Wilshire 5000 Index. Thus, index fund values tend to move synchronously with the overall market and minimize the investor's risk exposure from holding individual stocks. Index funds are also comparatively low operating-cost funds (i.e., a larger percentage of earnings generated tend to wind up in the hands of investors).[1]

The growing popularity of index funds subsequently led to the appearance of a related type of mutual fund—*exchange-traded funds* (ETFs). These baskets of stocks trade much like individual stocks and less like conventional mutual funds. Each ETF is linked to a particular stock index (such as the S&P 500 stock index), upon which its value is based, and trades *continuously* during normal trading hours. This means the price of an ETF changes frequently on any given day, unlike traditional mutual funds that usually trade at a single price established at the market's close each day. The current center of ETF trades is the AMEX—the American Stock Exchange at **amex.com**. The fact that ETFs trade continuously on an exchange makes them more attractive to active day traders and less susceptible to illegal trading practices like those experienced by regular mutual funds as the new century opened. By 2004 there were more than 140

---

[1]*Index funds* are based on the theory of efficient markets, which argues that in the long run, active money managers cannot beat the market as a whole. Thus, index funds tend to hold their investments longer and charge lower brokerage and service fees than do investment companies that turn over their security portfolios more rapidly. (See Chapters 3 and 21 for further discussion of market efficiency.)

Investment companies—among the fastest-growing major financial institutions in recent years—have also been a source of controversy among regulators and the public. These mutual funds provide savers with multiple benefits—easy access to the financial marketplace, professional asset management services, greater liquidity, and ready marketability.

While benefits such as these are appreciated by most investors, there is growing research evidence that many mutual fund investors *may* pay too much for the services they receive: One of the most significant fees paid by customers are *advisory fees*, which range between 0.50 and 0.60 percent of the "typical" mutual fund's total assets. Advisory fees compensate professional

managers for the research and investment decisions they carry out on behalf of the fund that hires them.

Of course, advisory fees are not the only charges fund investors often wind up paying. Many funds charge a *front-end* or *back-end load*, comparable to a brokerage fee or sales commission, which may range upwards of 5 to 8 percent of funds contributed. And there may be *administrative costs* and *trading fees* on top of that.

It does appear, however, that operating costs decline as a mutual fund grows so that investors may benefit more from investing in larger mutual funds—one reason industry mergers are soaring. In any event, knowing what fees and expenses a mutual fund charges or experiences is one of the wisest things an investor can do.

ETFs, holding over $170 billion in assets, compared to only about 30 ETFs and less than $13 billion in assets as the new century began.

To explore more fully the nature of investment companies (mutual funds) view the Web sites of two of the very largest families of funds at Fidelity (fidelity.com) and Vanguard (vanguard.com).

The 1980s and 1990s were marked by the rapid growth of *global funds*. These are stock and bond funds whose income-earning securities come from all over the world. These funds have access to security trading 24 hours a day through active exchanges in London, Tokyo, Singapore, Hong Kong, and other financial centers around the globe. Managers of these funds believe that higher returns are attainable with a balanced international portfolio, as opposed to a portfolio of domestic securities alone. Unfortunately, the risk attached to these global funds has often proven to be higher than expected (as in Asia and Japan, for example). Currently at least 80 percent of equity (stock) mutual funds are *domestic* in their focus rather than global. Another innovative investment company developed recently is the *vulture fund,* which purchases securities from firms in trouble in the hope of scoring exceptional returns should these firms recover or when their more valuable assets are liquidated.

A group of funds experiencing considerable popularity in recent years is the so-called *small-cap, mid-cap,* and *large-cap* investment companies. These mutual funds specialize in the stocks of companies that occupy different size groups. For example, the smallest-size firms in terms of total capitalization (i.e., the total market value of the firms' outstanding shares of stock) are called "small caps" while the largest companies are referred to as "large caps." There has been some research evidence in recent years that small- and mid-cap firms represent riskier investments but often provide higher average returns than do large-cap companies. In contrast, the large-cap funds frequently claim they offer more stable long-run returns than small-cap and mid-cap funds.

Finally, during the 1990s and early into the new century *hedge funds* became prominent. These mutual funds are really private partnerships that sell shares to only a limited number of investors in the hope of reaping large returns from pursuing high-risk investments. In this case, the word "hedge" refers to an investment strategy that splits the money being invested between those assets expected to increase in value if the market goes up and those assets believed to benefit if the market goes down. Many hedge funds gamble on the market's direction by betting that they know better than the market as a whole which way interest rates and security prices are likely to go. The high risk posed by these funds gave rise in the 1990s to public calls for closer regulation of investment company behavior, especially after the collapse of the huge Long-Term Capital Management hedge fund. The public outcry intensified after scandals rocked the mutual fund industry early in the new century and many investors demanded tighter industry rules.

Tax and Regulatory Status of the Industry

Investment companies have a favorable tax situation. As long as they conform to certain rules to qualify as an investment company (such as those spelled out in the Investment Company Act of 1940), they pay *no* federal taxes on income generated by their security holdings. However, no less than half of their resources must be devoted to securities and cash assets. Investment companies must maintain a highly diversified portfolio: A maximum of one-quarter of their total resources can be devoted to securities issued by any one business firm. Only a small portion of net income (no more than 10 percent) can be retained in the company. The rest must be distributed to shareholders. Investment companies and the securities they issue must be registered with the Securities and Exchange Commission.

Open-End and Closed-End Investment Companies

There are two basic kinds of investment companies. *Open-end investment companies*—often called *mutual funds*—buy back (redeem) their shares any time the customer wishes, and sell shares in any quantity demanded. Thus, the amount of their outstanding shares changes continually in response to public demand. The price of each open-end company share is equal to the *net asset value* of the fund—that is, the difference between the values of its assets and liabilities divided by the volume of shares issued.

Open-end companies may be either *load* or *no-load* funds. Load funds offer shares to the public at net asset value plus a commission to brokers marketing their shares. No-load funds sell shares purely at their net asset value. The investor must contact the no-load company or its representative directly, however. Whether load or no-load, open-end investment companies are heavily invested in common stock, with corporate bonds running a distant second. As Exhibit 16.1 shows, corporate stock represents approximately two-thirds of the mutual-fund industry's assets, with government bonds and corporate bonds accounting for most of the remaining assets.

Considering the mutual fund industry's heavy investment in stocks, it is not surprising to learn that more than half of the industry's population of just over 8,250 funds

EXHIBIT 16.1			
Financial Assets Held by Mutual Funds (Open-End Investment Companies)	**Asset Holdings**	**Amount in 2004*** **($ Billions)**	**Percent of Total Assets**
	Security repurchase agreements	$ 93.6	1.9%
	Corporate stock (equities)	3,246.3	66.4
	U.S. Treasury and federal agency securities	683.1	14.0
	State and local government (municipal) securities	295.2	6.0
	Corporate and foreign bonds	574.9	11.8
	Open-market paper	75.3	1.5
	Miscellaneous assets	1.9	0.0**
	Total financial assets held	$4,890.4	100.0%

Source: Board of Governors of the Federal Reserve System, *Flow of Funds Accounts.*

Note: Columns may not add to totals due to rounding error.

*Figures through the first quarter of 2004.

**Less than 0.05 percent.

in 2002 were stock (equity) funds. A quarter of all funds were bond-oriented funds and about 5 percent were hybrids (that is, combined stock and bond funds). Finally, nearly 1,000 funds (about 12 percent of the industry) were money market funds.

Closed-end investment companies sell only a specific number of ownership shares, which usually trade on an exchange. An investor wanting to acquire closed-end shares must find another investor who wishes to sell; the investment company itself does not take part in the transaction. These funds often attract investors by offering "double discounts," which consist of discounted prices on the stocks they hold and discounted share prices to buy into the fund itself. Closed-end companies issue a variety of securities to raise funds, including preferred stock, regular and convertible bonds, and stock warrants. In contrast, open-end companies rely almost exclusively on the sale of equity shares to the public in order to raise the funds they need.

Goals and Earnings of Investment Companies

Investment companies adopt many different goals. *Growth funds* are interested primarily in long-term capital appreciation and tend to invest mainly in common stocks offering strong growth potential. *Income funds* stress current income in their portfolio choices rather than growth of capital, and they typically purchase stocks and bonds paying high dividends and interest. *Balanced funds* attempt to bridge the gap between growth and income, acquiring bonds, preferred stock, and common stock that offer both capital gains (growth) and current income.

The majority of investment companies give priority to capital growth over current income, although funds stressing income, such as bond funds, money market funds, and option funds (which issue options against a portfolio of common stocks), have become more important in recent years. While most investment companies hold a highly diversified portfolio of securities, a few specialize in stocks and bonds from a single industry or sector (such as precious metals or oil and natural gas).

Keeping track of daily developments in the mutual fund industry can be done by following such Web sites as Mutual Fund Investor's Center at mfea.com, and the Mutual Fund Investing Newsletter at funds-newsletter.com

Policies and goals for investing funds are determined by an investment company's board of directors, which is elected by its shareholders. Its assets, however, are managed by an *investment advisory service* in return for an annual fee (usually 0.5 to 2 percent of a fund's assets). The contract between investment adviser and mutual fund must generally be approved by the fund's stockholders. Most funds have very few employees; most of their services (such as record keeping and investment advice) are "outsourced" to other firms. A mutual fund's price per share (or net asset value [NAV]) is often published in daily newspapers. As illustrated below, newspapers usually print the abbreviated name of the fund, its price or net asset value per share the preceding business day, the net change in price from the day before, and the change in yield occurring thus far in the current year. Thus:

Name	NAV per Share	Net Chg	Yield Chg
Balanced Equity Fund	$15.60	+0.08	+3.9

It is not at all clear that mutual funds hold a significant advantage over other investors in seeking the highest returns available in the financial marketplace. Moreover, there is evidence that, with the possible exception of index funds, these companies may roll over their portfolios too rapidly, which runs up the cost of managing the fund and tends to reduce investor earnings. Less frequent trading activity on the part of investment companies might well result in greater long-term benefits for the saver. Research evidence has been mounting for a number of years that security markets are relatively efficient. Overvaluation or undervaluation of securities is, at most, a temporary phenomenon. In this kind of environment, it is doubtful that investment companies are of significant benefit to the large investor, though they may aid the small investor in reducing information and transaction costs and opening up investment opportunities not otherwise available.

As the new century began, many investment companies began to raise their account fees and require customers to put up larger minimum investments, thereby increasing the burden on the small investor. The industry has cited declining investment volume and higher operating costs as a result of these adjustments. And, indeed, recent research evidence suggests that there are significant economies of scale in the investment-company industry, with larger funds reporting substantially lower operating costs per dollar of assets held.

To keep track of industry performance, an investor service—*Morningstar* at **morningstar.com**—provides online, up-to-date ratings of individual mutual funds in the form of a "reward-to-risk" ratio that allows investors to readily compare one fund against another. Examples of leading investment companies selling mutual-fund shares include The Growth Fund of America at **americanfunds.com**, USAA Income Stock at **maxfunds. com**, T. Rowe Price Equity Income Funds at **troweprice.com**, AIM Equity Constellation Fund at **aiminvestments.com**, Putnam Voyager Fund at **content.putnam.com**, Fidelity Magellan Fund at **fidelitynewsletter.com**, Janus Venture Fund at **janus.com**, and Vanguard 500 Index Fund at **vanguard.com**.

> To learn more about calculating mutual funds' operating expenses and how they may affect investors' returns see, for example, the SEC's Mutual Fund Cost Calculator at **sec.gov** or NASD's Mutual Fund Expense analyzer at **nsad.com**

Scandal Envelopes the Mutual Fund Industry

As the twenty-first century began, the mutual fund industry—which in the U.S. alone has attracted about 95 million investors—found itself confronted with a major public relations problem and the possible loss of thousands of customers. There was mounting evidence that the managers of several prominent funds had engaged in actions that were either illegal under federal and state law or represented a violation of several funds' own internal rules, reducing the potential returns to millions of investors.

Manager and trader transgressions included allegations of "late trading" and "market timing." Under the apparently widespread practice of *late trading,* some favored investors were permitted to buy and sell funds' shares at a price established hours earlier when the market closed. This procedure made it easy for these privileged investors to reap substantial trading profits, given that they already knew the per-share value of their transactions. In turn, some of the favored investors pledged to make substantial investments in those mutual funds that granted them late-trading privileges.

Other investment companies apparently permitted day traders to engage in *market timing* of their shares—a practice prohibited by most funds because it drives up fund expenses and, other factors held equal, lowers potential shareholder returns. Market timers rapidly turn over their holdings of mutual fund shares and other financial instruments, hoping to take instant advantage of daily rises and falls in market prices. They may buy and sell shares several times a day, depending upon market movements and the appearance of new information. In some cases, the "market timers" were affiliated with the funds whose shares they traded, giving them access to inside information.

These highly questionable and often illegal practices led to widespread calls for new legislation and for tighter regulation of the behavior of the mutual fund industry. Among the more popular recommendations from Congress and the public were proposed new rules calling for greater disclosure of:

1. All the fees borne by shareholders in each fund.

2. How the compensation of a fund's managers is determined.

3. How rapidly each fund's asset portfolio turns over and what this implies for an investor in the fund.

4. The fund's written policies and practices regarding late trading and market timing.

5. How broker-dealer commissions are determined and whether brokers and dealers are paid any incentives by a fund to promote the sale of the fund's shares among their customers.

6. The makeup of each mutual fund's board of directors (including information concerning which directors are independent of the fund itself).

In addition, the Securities and Exchange Commission (SEC) quickly proposed a new rule calling for banks, broker-dealers, and administrators of retirement plans to submit trading orders to mutual funds before 4 P.M. in the afternoon in order for their customers to receive that day's price. Under the proposed rule, any trading orders received after 4 P.M. would receive the next day's price. At this point in time, no one knows for sure how many criminal indictments and new regulations will emerge from this latest scandal on Wall Street. However, it seems clear that, for many investors, their long-standing trust in the management of mutual funds has been seriously damaged.

16.3 Pension Funds

pension funds

Pension funds protect individuals and families against loss of income in their retirement years by allowing workers to set aside and invest a portion of their current income. A pension plan places current savings in a portfolio of stocks, bonds, and other assets in the expectation of building an even larger pool of funds in the future. In this way, the pension plan member can balance planned consumption after retirement with the amount of savings set aside today.

Two main types of pension plans exist today. *Defined benefit* plans promise a specific monthly or annual payment to workers when they retire based upon the size of their salary during the working years and their length of employment. In contrast, *defined contribution* plans (such as a Keogh or 401(K) plan) specify how much must be contributed each year in the name of each worker but the amount to be received when retirement is reached will vary depending upon the amount saved and the returns earned on accumulated savings.

Defined-benefit pension programs have the advantage of guaranteed income if the employee remains with a particular employer for a relatively long period of time, but an employee who leaves early or is dismissed before retirement may get little or nothing. Under the defined contribution approach, however, the funds saved belong to the employee and are portable, provided the employee stays on the job long enough (usually 1 to 2 years) for the savings to be "vested" in his or her name. Defined benefit plans are declining as a percentage of all pension programs, while defined contribution plans are rising and now account for the majority of private pension programs. Leading pension funds include the California Public Employees' Retirement System at **calpers.ca.gov**, Ontario Pension Board at **opb.on.ca**, British Columbia Municipal Superannuation Fund at **pensionsbc.ca**, New York City Police Pension Fund at **myc.gov/nycppf**, TIAA-CREF Pension Plan at **tiaa-cref.org**, and Wisconsin Retirement System at **etf.wi.gov**.

Growth of Pension Funds

Pension funds have been among the most rapidly growing of all financial intermediaries. Between 1980 and 2000, the assets of all private and public pension funds multiplied more than 10 times over, reaching close to $8 trillion in the United States alone. (See Exhibit 16.2.) Approximately half of all full-time workers in private businesses and three-quarters of all civilian government employees are

EXHIBIT 16.2	Total Assets of Private and Public Pension Funds, Selected Years ($ Billions)						
Type of Pension Plan or Program	1940	1950	1960	1970	1980	1990	2000
Private pension programs:	$2.0	$12.1	$ 52.0	$138.2	$422.7	$2,324.8	$4,576.4
Insured plans	0.6	5.6	18.8	41.2	165.8	695.7	1,456.1
Noninsured plans	1.4	6.5	33.2	97.0	286.8	1,629.1	3,120.3
Government pension programs:	$4.3	$25.8	$ 56.1	$125.9	$289.8	$1,203.5	$3,288.2
State/local retirement systems	1.6	5.3	19.3	60.3	185.2	720.8	2,289.6
Federal civilian systems	0.6	4.2	10.5	23.1	75.8	247.5	416.7[*]
Railroad retirement program	0.1	2.6	3.7	4.4	2.1	9.9	14.9[**]
Social security program (OASDI)	2.0	13.7	22.6	38.1	26.5	225.3	567.0[**]
Total assets of all funds	$6.3	$37.9	$108.2	$262.0	$712.3	$3,528.3	$7,864.6

Note: Columns may not add to totals due to rounding.

[*]This 2000 figure is for the third quarter.

[**]Indicated figures are for 1996.

Source: Securities and Exchange Commission; Railroad Retirement Board; U.S. Department of Health and Human Services; the American Council of Life Insurance; and the Federal Reserve Board.

protected by pension plans other than the U.S. Social Security program (OASDI). About 200 million persons are insured by or are direct or indirect beneficiaries of the Social Security program. Social Security pays benefits to more than 50 million Americans each year.

Pension fund growth in the past has been spurred on by the relatively few retirees drawing pensions compared to the number of people working and contributing to a pension program. That situation is changing rapidly, however; individuals over 65 years of age now represent one of the fastest growing segments of the world's population. The growing proportion of retired individuals will threaten the solvency of many private pension funds and has already created significant future funding problems for various government programs (such as the U.S. medicare and medicaid programs) designed primarily to aid the elderly.[2]

Competition among employers for skilled management personnel has also spurred pension fund growth, as firms have tried to attract top-notch employees by offering attractive fringe benefits. This growth factor is likely to persist into the future due to a possible shortage of skilled entry-level workers as the population ages. Some experts foresee a real problem in this area, stemming from recent difficulties pension plans have had in keeping up with inflation and with the increasing number of retirees. Workers in the future are likely to demand better performance from their retirement plans and greater control over how their long-term savings are invested.

Recently, a highly controversial form of pension plan, a so-called *cash balance plan*, has appeared, especially at some of the largest companies, including IBM, AT&T, Xerox, Cigna, and Delta Airlines. These new plans appear to save employers money and to favor younger workers, while they may actually reduce older workers' benefits. With a cash balance plan, employers typically make a hypothetical contribution to an

---

[2]The present ratio of working adults to retired persons in the U.S. population is about 3:1. This ratio is projected to shrink to about 2:1 within little more than a generation. When the U.S. Social Security Act was passed in 1935, there were 11 working adults for each retired individual.

employee's retirement account equal to a percentage of the employee's annual salary and credit the employee's account with an annual interest credit based upon a reference interest rate (such as the U.S. Treasury bond rate). At retirement, the participating employee may receive periodic payments based on his or her accumulated funds, though many employees take a lump-sum payment when they retire.

Under many cash balance plans, you have to be a plan participant for at least five years in order to receive any benefits at all. When an employer converts from a traditional pension to a cash balance plan, that employer determines the accumulated value held in the old pension under each employee's name and may transfer all or only a portion of that accumulated value into the employee's new plan account. In short, employers have considerable discretion over how much built-up credit each employee receives upon conversion to a cash balance plan; older workers, in particular, seem most vulnerable to losing some of their accumulated retirement earnings and may have to work several additional years to catch up to where they were when their employer converted to a cash-balance-type pension. Clearly, the prime beneficiary of the cash balance plan is the *employer*, as the ultimate impact is usually to keep business costs down. Fortunately for most U.S. employees with employer-sponsored pension programs, federal law entitles covered employees to request and receive a periodic statement of vested benefits accrued to date. Such a request may be made once each year in writing. Once a request is received, the employer must reply within 30 days.

You can keep track of ongoing developments in the pension fund industry through such Web sites as that established by the International Foundation for Employee Benefit Plans at ifebp.org

Investment Strategies of Pension Funds

Pension funds are long-term investors with limited need for liquidity. Their incoming cash receipts are known with considerable accuracy because a fixed percentage of each employee's salary is usually contributed to the fund. At the same time, cash outflows are not difficult to forecast, because the formula for figuring benefit payments is stipulated in the contract between the fund and its members. This situation encourages pensions to purchase common stock, long-term bonds, and real estate and to hold these assets on a permanent basis. In addition, interest income and capital gains from investments are exempt from federal income taxes, and pension plan members are not taxed on their contributions unless benefits are actually paid out.

Although favorable taxation and predictable cash flows favor longer-term, somewhat riskier investments, the pension fund industry is closely regulated in many of its activities. The Employee Retirement Income Security Act (ERISA) requires all U.S. defined-benefit private plans to be *fully funded*, which means that any assets held plus investment income must be adequate to cover all promised benefits. ERISA also requires that investments must be made in a "prudent" manner, which is usually interpreted to mean that they be invested in highly diversified holdings of high-grade common stock, corporate bonds, and government securities along with some real estate investments.

Although existing regulations emphasize conservatism in pension investments, private pensions have been under intense pressure in recent years by management and employees of sponsoring companies to be more liberal in their investment policies. The sponsoring employer has a strong incentive to encourage its affiliated pension plan to reduce operating expenses and earn the highest possible returns on its investments. This permits the company to minimize its contributions to the plan. However, in 1985 the Financial Accounting Standards Board issued SFAS 87, which required *defined-benefit pension plans* to disclose their funding status more fully, asking businesses to make projections of their future pension obligations, publish estimates of how much in benefits employees will receive, and report any *unfunded* portion of pension benefits on each business's balance sheet as a liability. These accounting requirements have

Pension funds set aside current savings in a pool of earning assets in the hope of accumulating a larger amount of savings that will provide a stream of income during the retirement years. For example, suppose an employee is scheduled to retire in five years and has

$2,500 deposited in her retirement account this year. If the pension plan promises her a 6 percent annual yield on each dollar set aside for retirement, the $2,500 she sets aside today will be worth:

$$\text{Value of funds contributed today at retirement} = \text{Amount set aside today}\left(1 + \text{Promised rate of return}\right)^{\text{Years invested}}$$

$$= \$2,500(1 + .06)^5 = \$3,345.57$$

Suppose this same employee who plans to retire in five years has $2,500 contributed every year between now

and retirement and earns 6 percent on each dollar saved. Then her total savings pool at retirement will be:

$$\text{Total funds available at retirement} = \text{Amount of savings contributed each year} \times \text{Sum of compound interest factors for savings contributed each year up to retirement at interest rate } i$$

$$= \$2,500[(1 + .06)^5 + (1 + .06)^4 + \cdots + (1.06)^1]$$

$$= \$14,937.50$$

How much annual income can this employee look forward to in retirement from this pension plan? The answer depends on the annual annuity rate promised and whether the employee has access to (i.e., is vested with) all funds contributed in her name. Suppose this

employee is *vested* with the full amount shown above (i.e., a vesting ratio of 1.00) and is promised an annual annuity (income) rate of 5.5 percent based on her life expectancy. Then her expected annual retirement income from this one pension plan will be:

$$\text{Expected annual retirement income} = \text{Annual annuity rate} \times \text{Total funds available to employee at retirement} \times \text{Vesting ratio}$$

$$= 0.055 \times \$14,937.50 \times 1.0 = \$821.56$$

made some business firms offering pension plans look weaker and, along with strict government regulations, have caused many businesses to abandon their pension programs, leaving it to their employees to develop and manage their own retirement programs.

Pension Fund Assets

The particular assets held as investments by pension funds depend heavily on whether the fund is government controlled or a private venture. As shown in Exhibit 16.3, private funds currently devote the largest percentage of their investments to corporate stock, which represented about 40 percent of their assets in 2004. Corporate bonds ranked a distant second, accounting for about 9 percent of all private pensions' assets. With few liquidity needs, private pension funds held relatively small amounts of cash and bank deposits, although their holdings of U.S. government and federal agency securities have remained substantial (about 7 percent of their total assets) due to the relatively high yields and safety of these financial instruments. Many of the largest pension plans also hold substantial real estate investments for asset diversification and as a hedge against inflation.

EXHIBIT 16.3

Financial Assets Held by Private Pension Funds and State and Local Government Employee Retirement Funds

Source: Board of Governors of the Federal Reserve System, *Flow of Funds Accounts.*

*Figures are for the end of the first quarter of 2004.

**Less than 0.05 percent.

Assets Held by Private Pension Plans	Amount in 2004* ($ Billions)	Percent of Total Assets
Checkable deposits and currency	$ 7.4	0.2%
Time and savings deposits	130.0	3.1
Money market fund shares	75.4	1.8
Security repurchase agreements	35.6	0.9
Open market paper	42.4	1.0
U.S. Treasury and federal agency securities	301.0	7.2
Corporate and foreign bonds	383.2	9.2
Mortgage loans	17.9	0.4
Corporate stock (equities)	1,747.1	41.8
Shares in mutual funds	850.3	20.4
Miscellaneous assets	668.9	16.0
Total financial assets held	$ 4,175.9	100.0%

Assets Held by State and Local Government Pension Plans	Amount in 2004* ($ Billions)	Percent of Total Assets
Checkable deposits and currency	$ 9.6	0.4%
Time and savings deposits	1.0	0.0**
Security repurchase agreements	49.5	2.1
Open market paper	44.5	1.9
U.S. Treasury and federal agency securities	363.3	15.8
State and local government (tax-exempt) securities	0.7	0.0**
Corporate and foreign bonds	363.2	15.8
Mortgage loans	45.0	2.0
Corporate stock (equities)	1,334.3	57.9
Miscellaneous assets	92.4	4.0
Total financial assets held	$ 2,303.3	100.0%

Corporate stock recently has become more important in the portfolios of government pensions than among many private pension plans. As Exhibit 16.3 shows, state and local government pension programs held about 58 percent of their assets in corporate stock. Government pension plans also maintained significant holdings of corporate bonds and U.S. government and federal agency securities, each representing about 16 percent of their assets. The pressure of regulation falls more heavily upon government (public) pensions than upon private plans. As a result, the investments of government pensions tend to be somewhat more conservative, with heavier concentrations in higher-grade assets. However, both government and private pension plans have recently seen their total assets decline in value as stock prices weakened and became more uncertain and interest rates hovered around record lows. The net result of recent market movements has been to widen the gap between what many pensions have promised to pay their members (which is their principal liability) and the market value of their current asset holdings.

Indeed, as the stock market entered a period of increased volatility in this new century, some pension funds began to divert a larger portion of their incoming cash flow into bonds and other fixed-income investments and lighten up on their stock holdings. The industry began to look more seriously at bonds, not only because of the recent volatility in the stock market, but also because pension accounting standards are changing. In Europe (especially in the United Kingdom), many pension plans are required to record their assets at current market value. Similar proposals have appeared recently inside the United States. This growing movement toward "mark to market" in pension accounting will tend to make the balance sheets of pension-sponsoring companies significantly more volatile. A more volatile corporate balance sheet implies more risk and tends to reduce the stock prices of the companies involved, lowering the expected returns to stock investors.

Factors Affecting the Future Growth of Pension Funds

Most experts believe that pension fund growth may continue to be quite rapid in the future, particularly due to the uncertainty surrounding the U.S. Social Security program. With government and business playing a smaller role, individual workers will be compelled to rely more heavily upon their own resources to finance their retirement years. Still, there appear to be serious problems ahead for both the growth and the stability of pension plans. One concern is the rising proportion of pension beneficiaries to working contributors, related to the aging of the population. At the same time, the cost of maintaining pension programs has increased dramatically. The full funding of a defined benefit plan to cover all promised benefits may place extreme pressure on corporate profits, particularly if declining security markets or falling interest rates diminish investment returns.

Even more important is the rising cost of government regulation, which has imposed costly reporting requirements on the industry, granted employees the right to join pension programs soon after they are hired, and allowed pension plan members to acquire ownership and control more quickly of monies contributed on their behalf. These government regulations have forced many private pension plans to close. The control of others has been turned over to a financial institution—typically a bank trust department or life insurance company—that is better able to deal with the current rules. Many defined-benefit private pension plans are in weak financial condition, especially those connected to corporations that are in trouble. In addition, some of the

For further
information on the
activities of Penny
Benny, see especially
pbgc.gov

best pension plans have been terminated because their sponsoring employers wished to recapture their assets, the value of which had risen over the years.

Worse still, the pension insurance agency created by the U.S. Congress in 1974—the Pension Benefit Guaranty Corporation (known as PBGC or, more popularly, as "Penny Benny")—has recently reported sharply rising budget deficits. Penny Benny was set up to guarantee the pension benefits of employees with defined-benefit pension plans (which usually promise a fixed monthly payment to plan members). Unfortunately, more and more corporations have failed or sought financial relief from the courts by abandoning their costly pension programs and dumping them in Penny Benny's lap. Currently, Penny Benny insures the retirement plans of more than 44 million American workers and retirees. As Penny Benny has been compelled to take over more troubled companies' pension programs, especially in the declining manufacturing sector, the gap between what it owes workers and retirees and its available assets has widened significantly, reaching more than $10 billion in 2003. Unless the PBGC significantly reduces member benefits or charges companies with pension plans higher insurance fees, it may be compelled to turn to the U.S. Congress (and, ultimately, U.S. taxpayers) to be bailed out.

In short, the pension fund sector faces some serious problems that will require creative solutions in the future, including a redefining of the role of public and private institutions in assuring an equitable and adequate distribution of retirement monies to those who have earned them.

QUESTIONS TO HELP YOU STUDY

1. What advantages do *investment companies* (mutual funds) offer the small saver? Why has their growth been so erratic in recent years?

2. Define the following terms:

   a. *Open-end company*   d. *Money market fund*   g. *Global funds*
   b. *Closed-end company*   e. *Growth funds*   h. *Index funds*
   c. *Bond fund*   f. *Balanced funds*   i. *Hedge funds*

3. What is the principal function of *pension funds?* Explain why these institutions have been among the most rapidly growing financial institutions in recent years. Do you expect their growth to be faster or slower in the future? Why? What is the difference between a defined-benefit and a defined-contribution pension plan?

4. What are the principal assets acquired by pension funds? What factors guide their selection of assets to hold? What problems has the pension industry run into in recent years?

16.4 Life Insurance Companies

life insurance company

The recent rapid growth of mutual funds and pension funds contrasts sharply with the somewhat more moderate growth of one of the oldest financial-service firms—the **life insurance company.** Life insurers have been operating for centuries in Europe, and the life insurance company was one of the first financial institutions founded in the American colonies. The Corporation for Relief of Poor and Distressed Presbyterian Ministers and of the Poor and Distressed Widows and Children of Presbyterian Ministers, established in 1759, was the first U.S.-based life insurer.

Today life insurers have branched out to include not only traditional life insurance policies in their service menus, but also *health insurance* and *annuity plans.* Health

EXHIBIT 16.4		
The Principal Kinds of Insurance Policies and Annuity Plans Sold by Many Life Insurance Companies Source: American Council of Life Insurance.	Ordinary or whole life insurance	Insurance protection that covers the entire lifetime of the policyholder. Premiums build up cash values that may be borrowed by the policyholder.
	Term life insurance	Insurance coverage for a certain number of years so that the policyholder's beneficiaries receive benefit payments only if death occurs within the period of coverage.
	Endowment policy	A policy with benefits payable to the living policyholder on a specified future date or to the policyholder's beneficiaries if death occurs before the date specified in the policy.
	Group life insurance	Master insurance policy covering a group of people, usually all working for the same employer or members of the same organization.
	Industrial life insurance	Small-denomination life policies with premium payments collected monthly or weekly by a company agent.
	Universal life insurance	Insurance protection with premium payments whose amount and timing can be changed by the policyholder and including a savings account with a flexible rate of return.
	Variable life insurance	Insurance protection whose benefits vary in amount with the value of assets pledged behind the policy contract.
	Adjustable life insurance	A flexible form of insurance protection that permits the policyholder to alter some of the policy's terms, period of coverage, or face value.
	Credit life insurance	A policy pledged to pay off a loan in the event the borrower dies or becomes disabled before the debt is retired.
	Health insurance	Coverage of medical bills, the cost of hospitalization, and possible loss of income arising from accidents and disease.
	Fixed annuities	Pools of savings built up over time and expected to pay out a fixed stream of income payments beginning on a future date.
	Variable annuities	Savings plans invested in stocks and other assets that may appreciate in value over time and pay out an income stream whose size depends on the changing market value of invested savings.

insurance programs cover a portion of their policyholders' medical and dental bills, while annuity plans aid clients in building their long-term savings for college educations, new home purchases, and especially retirement funding. Many of the largest life carriers have now branched far afield from their origins, insuring damage to personal and business property, which places them in the territory of another insurance industry—*property-casualty insurers*—which we discuss in the next section of this chapter.

Life insurance companies offer their customers a hedge against the risk of financial loss that often follows death, disability and ill health, or retirement. Policyholders receive risk protection in return for the payment of policy premiums that are set high enough to cover estimated benefit claims against the company, all operating expenses, and a target profit margin. Additional funds to cover claims and expenses are provided by the earnings from investments made by life insurance companies in bonds, stocks, and other assets approved by law and government regulation. The principal kinds of life insurance policies sold by U.S. life insurers are listed in Exhibit 16.4.

The Insurance Principle

The insurance business is founded upon the *law of large numbers*. This mathematical principle states that a risk that is not predictable for one person can be forecast with reasonable accuracy for a sufficiently large group of people with similar characteristics. For example no insurance company can accurately forecast when any one person will die, but its actuarial estimates of the total number of policyholders who will die in any given year are usually quite accurate.

Life insurance companies today insure policyholders against three basic kinds of risk: *premature death,* the *danger of living too long and outlasting one's accumulated assets,* and *serious illness or accident.* Many policies combine financial protection against death, disability, and retirement with savings plans to help the policyholder prepare for some important future financial need, such as the purchase of a home or meeting the costs of a college education. Actually, most benefit payments are made to living, rather than deceased, policyholders, who receive annuity payments or health insurance benefits of various kinds.

Life insurance companies are among the leading sources of retirement (pension) benefit payments for older citizens, and today more than 60 million U.S. citizens are enrolled in pension programs managed by life insurers. Many life-insurer-managed pension plans consist of *fixed annuity accounts* or *variable annuity accounts.* The fixed annuities pay out a stable stream of income to the customer, based upon the amount saved, the expected rate of return on those savings, and the withdrawal rate agreed to between the annuitant and the insurance company. Variable annuities, in contrast, pay out a variable stream of income to the customer that changes over time as the value of the accumulated savings in the annuitant's account changes with market conditions.

Investments of Life Insurance Companies

Life insurers invest the bulk of their funds in long-term securities such as bonds, stocks, and mortgages, thus helping to fund real capital investment by businesses and governments. They are inclined to commit their funds long term due to the high predictability of their cash inflows and outflows. This predictability normally would permit a life insurance company to accept considerable risk in the securities it acquires. However, both law and tradition require a life insurer to act as a "prudent person." This restriction is imposed to ensure that sufficient funds are available to meet all legitimate claims from insurance policyholders or their beneficiaries at precisely the time those claims come due.

The life insurance industry and the current trends reshaping that industry can be followed through such Web sites as the U.S. Business Reporter at activemedia-guide.com and through the site *of Risk and Insurance Magazine* at riskandinsurance.com

Life insurance companies generally pursue *income certainty* and *safety of principal* in their investments. The majority of corporate securities they purchase are in the top four credit-rating categories.[3] Life insurers frequently follow a "buy and hold" strategy, acting as long-term holders of securities rather than rapidly turning over their portfolios. This investment approach reduces the risk of fluctuations in income and avoids having to rely as heavily on forecasting interest rates. We should note, however, that many life insurers have become more active traders in securities. Emphasizing performance more than permanence in their investments, larger life insurance companies have set up trading rooms to more closely monitor the performance of their investment holdings, selling out and reinvesting in higher-yielding alternatives when circumstances warrant. Because this active investment strategy creates additional risk, many larger insurers use financial futures, options, and other risk-hedging tools and more closely match asset and liability maturities to protect themselves against losses from fluctuating interest rates.[4]

Exhibit 16.5 shows the kinds of investments held by U.S. life insurance companies in 2004. The primary investment is in *corporate bonds* issued by both domestic and foreign companies. Several companies ran into trouble recently from heavy purchases of high-risk ("junk") corporate bonds as well as from poorly performing real estate investments. For example, during the 1990s Mutual Benefit Life Insurance Company and Executive Life Insurance Company were taken over by state regulators. Both firms were among the largest U.S. insurers ever to fail, due principally to losses on poor

---

[3]See Chapter 8 for an explanation of security ratings.
[4]See Chapter 9 for a detailed discussion of various interest-rate hedging methods, including financial futures, options, swaps, and other risk-protection tools.

EXHIBIT 16.5

Financial Assets and Liabilities of Life Insurers

Source: Board of Governors of the Federal Reserve System, *Flow of Funds Accounts.*

*Figures are for the end of the first quarter of 2004.

Asset and Liability Items Outstanding	Amount in 2004* ($ Billions)	Percent of Total Assets
Assets held:		
Checkable deposits and currency	$ 27.8	0.7%
Money market fund shares	144.2	3.7
Open market paper	79.5	2.1
U.S. Treasury and federal agency securities	345.1	9.0
State and local government (municipal) securities	21.5	0.6
Corporate and foreign bonds	1,616.1	42.0
Loans to policyholders	104.9	2.7
Mortgage loans	261.5	6.8
Corporate stock (equities)	966.9	25.1
Mutual funds shares	102.4	2.7
Miscellaneous assets	78.9	2.0
Total financial assets held	$3,848.8	100.0%
Liabilities outstanding:		
Loans and advances	$ 8.1	0.2%
Life insurance reserves	979.0	27.0
Pension fund reserves	1,784.2	49.2
Miscellaneous liabilities	851.9	23.5
Total liabilities outstanding	$3,623.2	100.0%

To understand the life insurance industry more fully, you can look in on a couple of the world's largest life insurers: Prudential Insurance at prudential.com and Metropolitan Life Insurance at metlife.com

quality assets. Industry regulators have recently restricted further purchases of junk bonds. Holdings of common and preferred stock, although smaller, have become significant in recent years. Life insurance companies have shown renewed interest in corporate stock due to the growing importance of variable annuity and variable life insurance policies in their sales programs.

Another important asset held by life insurance companies is *mortgage loans* on farm, residential, and commercial properties. Substantial changes have occurred in life insurer mortgage investments in recent years. The industry has frequently reduced its holdings of farm and residential mortgages on one- to four-family homes and increased its holdings of commercial mortgages, including loans on retail stores, shopping centers, office buildings, apartments, hospitals, and factories. The higher yields and shorter maturities of the latter loans explain much of the recent growth of commercial mortgage lending by the life insurance industry. However, life insurers continue to provide substantial indirect support to the residential mortgage market by making heavy purchases of federal agency securities, most of which come from government agencies aiding the home mortgage loan market.

Government securities play a secondary but still important role in the portfolios of life insurance companies. These securities serve the important function of providing a reservoir of *liquidity* because they may be sold with little difficulty when cash is required. U.S. life insurers buy mostly federal government securities rather than state and local government obligations. The industry has only a limited need for the tax-exempt income provided by state and local bonds because its effective tax rate is relatively low.

One asset whose importance increased dramatically in earlier years, though it has slowed recently, is *loans to policyholders.* The holder of an ordinary (whole life) insurance policy can borrow against the accumulated cash value of that policy, which increases each year. The interest rate on policy loans is stated in the policy contract and in some (especially older policies) is quite low. Policy loans tend to follow the business cycle, rising in periods when economic activity and interest rates are increasing, and declining when the economy or interest rates are headed down. Because of this cyclical characteristic, policy loans represent a volatile claim on the industry's resources. When policy loan demand is high, life insurance companies may be forced to reduce their purchases of bonds and stocks. In recent years, however, most new whole life policies have had floating loan rates tied to an index of corporate bond yields, and policyholder borrowing has settled into a relatively small percentage of industry assets.

Sources of Life Insurance Company Funds

The primary income source for life insurers comes from *premium receipts* from sales of various kinds of insurance policies. Premiums from sales of annuity plans and health insurance policies have actually grown faster than sales of traditional life insurance policies in recent years. Annual net income from investments in bonds, stocks, and other assets averages only about a third of premium receipts. The industry's net earnings after expenses roughly equal its net investment income each year, because most premiums from the sale of policies are ultimately returned to policyholders or their beneficiaries. This means that, on balance, the industry hopes to roughly break even from its insurance underwriting operations (with premiums flowing in approximately equal to benefits paid out) while earning its profits from its investment income.

This normal expectation of greater insurance-related income than insurance-industry claims and expenses sometimes goes awry when tragic events occur. A dramatic example of such an "exogenous shock" to the life insurance industry struck on September 11, 2001, when terrorist attacks on the United States resulted in great loss of life as well as huge property damage. Actually, life insurers often have built-in protections against such costly events should they decide to use them. For example, many life insurance policies exclude the payment of insurance claims resulting from acts of war unless, as happened frequently following the events of September 2001, the companies involved waive such exclusions.

Structure and Growth of the Life Insurance Industry

The majority of the approximately 1,600 U.S. life insurance companies are corporations owned by their stockholders. The rest are *mutuals*, which issue ownership shares to their policyholders. However, mutuals are bigger, on average, and typically were established much earlier than stockholder-owned companies. Most new insurance companies in recent years have been *stockholder owned*, and a substantial number of mutuals have converted to *stock* companies (such as Prudential Insurance) to gain greater financial flexibility and open up new sources of capital. Recently, several big life insurers have converted to stockholder form by creating mutual holding companies, attracting new stockholder capital and issuing stock options to their employees.

The U.S. life insurance industry's population reached a high of almost 2,350 in 1988 and has been falling ever since. Most recently, many of the biggest life insurers worldwide are merging with banks and securities firms, diversifying their services, and reaching across continents. Thus, the largest life insurers today are *converging* with other financial-service industries to form huge multiproduct businesses. The world's leading life/health insurance companies include ING Groep, Netherlands at **ing.com**; AXA, France at **axa-france.fr**; Nippon Life Insurance, Japan at **nissay.co.jp**; Assicurazioni Generali, Italy at **generali.com**; Aviva, United Kingdom at **aviva.com**; Sumitomo Life

Health insurance companies are often part of or closely related to life insurers. You can follow developments in the health insurance industry via such Web sites as the Healthcare Insurers at plunkettresearch.com

When insurance companies agree to provide risk protection to their customers, how do they decide how much to charge?

Consider an example. Suppose a life insurer has 100,000 policyholders, each 40 years of age with a $1 million life insurance policy. The company must set an annual premium so it will have sufficient cash to pay off the beneficiaries of any policyholders who die this year.

The first thing the insurer must do is determine the expected number of deaths this year. Actuarial science has produced mortality tables that predict how many individuals of any age are expected to die each year out of every 1,000 persons. If the expected death rate for 40-year-olds is 4 per 1,000, the expected number of deaths in the coming year from this group of 100,000 policyholders is:

$$\text{Expected deaths} = \frac{\text{Number of policyholders in age group}}{} \times \frac{\text{Expected mortality rate}}{}$$

$$= \frac{100}{\text{thousand}} \times \frac{4 \text{ per}}{\text{thousand}} = \frac{400 \text{ deaths}}{\text{expected}}$$

If each policyholder has a $1 million policy, the insurance company must prepare for expected claims of:

$$\text{Expected claims} = \text{Expected deaths} \times \frac{\text{Policy amounts promised}}{}$$

$$= 400 \times \$1 \text{ million} = \$400 \text{ million}$$

How much should the insurance company charge each policyholder in premiums? Suppose the 400 deaths expected will occur toward the end of this year. We want to determine how much to charge all policyholders at the beginning of this year to be ready for $400 million in claims at year's end. We need to estimate how much the insurance company will earn when it invests the premiums paid by its policyholders in stocks, bonds, and other financial assets. Let's suppose the company estimates it will earn an average of 8 percent on its asset portfolio in the coming year. Thus, to have $400 million available at year's end, the company needs the following amount from its policyholders at the beginning of the year: $400 million/$(1 + .08)^1$ = $370.4 million, or $3,704 per policyholder.

However, this calculation does not include operating costs (salaries of sales personnel, etc.), including the need to earn a normal profit for the company's stockholders. Suppose it will cost $2.6 million to service the insurance needs of policyholders this year. This operating cost is called the *loading*, which must be added to the net premium to drive the *gross premium* charged policyholders:

$$\text{Gross premium} = \frac{\$370.4 \text{ million} + \$2.6 \text{ million}}{100,000 \text{ policyholders}}$$

$$= \$3,730 \text{ per policyholder}$$

Insurance premium rates charged are also shaped by *competition*, which tends to hold premium rates down and encourages insurers to be more efficient.

Insurance, Japan at **sumitomolife.co.jp**; The Prudential, United Kingdom at **prudential. com**; MetLife Insurance, United States at **metlife.com**; and Aegon Company, Netherlands at **aegon.com**.

New Services

Life insurers are under increasing pressure to develop *new services* due to a long-term decline in their share of household savings and pressure on their earnings caused by new high-cost, more-automated service delivery systems. Many analysts argue that life insurance is becoming less attractive a product as the population ages, while retirement planning and retirement savings instruments (such as annuities) are likely to grow in importance. Increasing competition from other financial intermediaries, especially mutual funds, has also played a major role in encouraging the development of new services. Among recent developments are the offering of such innovative services as universal and adjustable life insurance, variable premium and variable life insurance, mutual funds, tax shelters, venture capital loans, corporate cash management systems, and deferred annuities.

Begun as far back as 1979, *universal life insurance* allows the customer to change the face amount of his or her policy and the size and timing of premium payments, as well as earn higher investment returns from any premiums paid in. Premium payments on a universal life insurance policy usually are invested in a money market fund. Another example of the newer and more flexible life insurance products emerging in recent years is *adjustable life insurance,* which permits the policyholder to change periodically from a whole life policy to term insurance (which offers protection only for a designated period) and back again to deal with changing circumstances. Adjustable policies allow the policyholder to increase or decrease the face value of a policy, the period of insurance protection, and the size of premium payments within limits spelled out in the policy contract. A variation of this idea is *variable premium life insurance,* which grants the policyholder lower premium payments when investments made by the life insurer earn a greater return. *Variable life insurance* pays benefits according to the value of assets pledged behind the policy rather than paying a fixed amount of money. There is normally a guaranteed minimum benefit for the policyholder's beneficiary, however—a form of inflation-hedged life insurance.

Life insurers have also been active in venture capital loans to help start new businesses and in offering professional funds management services to many businesses that have neither the time nor the experience to manage their own cash accounts. Life insurers have also found success in attracting *deferred annuity* accounts in which an individual will deposit funds with the insurer under an agreement to receive a future stream of income flowing from those deposited funds beginning on a stipulated future date. The insurer agrees to invest the funds in earning assets that will grow over time and escape taxation until the customer actually begins receiving income.

In recent years, insurance companies have found a way to supplement their cash inflows from insurance premiums by selling *guaranteed investment contracts* (GICs) to large institutional investors such as pension funds and state and local governments. Similar to deposits, GICs promise investors a fixed rate of return for a stipulated period. Many corporations and governmental units that have sold bonds in the open market have in turn purchased GICs with the proceeds of those bond issues. GICs have increased insurance company risk somewhat, however, because of their relatively high fixed cost.

One area of growing insurance needs is coverage for small businesses. New businesses are being formed today in large numbers, with more than 30 million uninsured persons currently working for them in the United States alone. The provision of life and health insurance for owners and employees of small firms has become a promising service area for those insurers able to correctly price the coverages they provide. Another area of need for the future is health and life insurance for individuals, such as retired citizens, who are no longer members of group insurance plans.

Without question, the new services offered by life insurers in future years will depend heavily upon favorable changes in government laws and regulations. One prominent example is expanded entry into Japan and China, two of the largest insurance and pension plan markets in the world, but this opportunity is dependent upon the willingness of the Japanese and Chinese governments to let more foreign financial firms come in. Life insurers must also continue to lower the cost of marketing and delivering their services, such as through increased use of telephone sales, automation, and joint-venture sales of policies through banks and stockbrokers. Correspondingly, the industry has made major cuts in its traditional vehicle for the delivery of services—local insurance agencies.

16.5   Property-Casualty Insurance Companies

property-casualty insurers

Property-casualty (P/C) insurers offer protection against fire, theft, bad weather, negligence, and other acts and events that result in injury to persons or property. So broad is the range of risk for which these companies provide protection that P/C insurers are referred to as *insurance supermarkets.* In addition to their traditional insurance lines—automobile, fire, marine, personal liability, and property coverage—many of these firms have branched into the health and medical insurance fields, clashing head-on with life insurers offering the same services. Others have merged with whole new industries and, thereby, reached out to large numbers of potential new customers with an expanded menu of new services.

Makeup of the Property-Casualty (P/C) Insurance Industry

The property-casualty insurance business has grown rapidly in recent years due to the effects of inflation, rising crime rates, and an increasing number of lawsuits arising from product liability and professional negligence claims. There were about 3,000 P/C companies in the United States as the twentieth century drew to a close, holding more than $900 billion in total assets. Stockholder-owned companies are dominant, holding about three-fourths of the industry's total resources. Mutual companies—owned by their policyholders—command roughly one-fourth of all industry resources.

The leading P/C insurers in the world today include Allianz, Germany at **allianz.com**; American International Group, United States at **aig.com**; Munich Re Group, Germany at **marclife.com/links/mrgroup.html**; State Farm Insurance Companies, United States at **statefarm.com**; Berkshire Hathaway, United States at **berkshirehathaway.com**; Zurich Financial Services at **zurich.com**; Allstate Insurance Company, United States at **allstate.com**; Millea Holdings Inc., Japan at **nni.nikkei.co.jp**; Swiss Reinsurance, Switzerland at **swissre.com**; and Royal & Sun Alliance, United Kingdom at **royalsunalliance.com**.

Property-casualty insurers are also grouped by whether they are *agency companies* or *direct writers.* Agency firms sell policies primarily through local agents who earn commissions on their sales of policies from many different insurance companies. Direct writers sell directly to the public (often via telephone or television) or have their own dedicated agents to promote their products. In recent years direct writers have captured a growing share of the insurance industry.

Changing Risk Patterns in Property/Liability Coverage

Property-casualty insurance is a riskier business than life insurance. The risk of policyholder claims arising from crime, fire, personal negligence, and similar causes is less predictable than is the risk of death. Moreover, inflation has had a potent impact on the cost of property and services for which this form of insurance pays. For example, the cost of medical care and repair of automobiles has increased at a significantly more rapid pace than the overall cost of living in recent years.

Equally important, basic changes now seem to be under way in the risk patterns of many large insurance programs, creating problems in forecasting policyholder claims and in setting new premium rates. Examples include a rapid rise in medical malpractice suits; a virtual explosion in product liability claims against manufacturers of automobiles, tires, home appliances, and other goods; a recent rise in civilian fire deaths and losses due to airplane crashes and weather damage; a rapid increase in terrorist-related losses; and the emergence of billions of dollars in claims from so-called *toxic torts,* arising from individuals suffering from illness or injury caused by exposure to asbestos, lead, nuclear radiation, and other hazardous substances.

Natural disasters have also proven to be exceptionally difficult for P/C insurers that are providing catastrophic insurance for floods, droughts, earthquakes, and hurricanes. One particular event that led to a major reassessment of the industry's exposure to such risks was Hurricane Andrew that devastated South Florida in 1992. This hurricane remains the largest single natural disaster in U.S. history with an estimated $20.3 billion in insured property losses.[5] These losses far exceeded the "worst case scenarios" of potential losses inflicted by a single storm and forced a number of P/C insurers into insolvency. Many other insurers began pulling out of the state until the Florida legislature intervened and forced a moratorium on insurance companies attempting to cancel existing policies. This action set in motion a series of legislative initiatives and reforms designed to assure that catastrophic hurricane insurance would continue to be provided to homeowners and businesses in the state at affordable rates. They included establishing the Florida Hurricane Catastrophe Fund (FHCF) to relieve financial stress on insurers in the aftermath of a hurricane disaster. The FHCF is financed by the insurance industry, but maintains a borrowing capacity based on low (tax-free) municipal bond interest rates to supplement the fund in extreme cases.

In addition, the Florida legislature passed stricter building codes to minimize structural damage from winds and tides, provided for funding to improve hurricane risk assessment models to better inform regulators about proper insurance rates, and set about to improve coordination of state and national emergency relief agencies to minimize post-hurricane damage due to flooding and tornadoes and the eventual loss of life. Nonetheless, with the predictions of hurricane forecasters that the Atlantic basin is currently in a period of heightened hurricane activity that is projected to last for at least another decade, the risk of unusual catastrophic insurance losses loom large, and the extraordinary hurricane season of 2004 that saw *four* hurricanes (Charley, Frances, Ivan, and Jeanne) make landfall in the state of Florida with combined insured property losses comparable to Andrew is evidence that these concerns are warranted.

To reduce risk, more P/C insurers have become *multiple-line companies,* diversifying into many different lines of insurance. Another risk-reducing device of growing importance is the *reinsurance* market, in which an insurer contracts with other companies to share some of the risks of its insurance underwriting in return for a share of the insurer's premium. The leading reinsurance firms today include Munich RE Group, Swiss RE Group, Berkshire Hathaway RE Group, and Employers RE Group.

One consequence of Hurricane Andrew and the devastating Northridge earthquake (in the Los Angeles area) in 1994 was the creation of a number of *monoline* reinsurance companies that specialize in property damage associated exclusively with wind and earthquake damage but that operate world-wide. In addition to these structural changes taking place within the industry, there have been a number of financial innovations, such as weather derivative and catastrophe bonds, that have been introduced to provide risk-sharing with investors outside the insurance industry.

It is interesting to compare the distribution of assets held by life insurance companies to those assets held by P/C companies. The net cash flows of the two industries—their annual premium incomes—are roughly comparable. Yet life insurers hold about six times the assets of P/C insurers. Much of the difference is explained by the fact that life insurance is a highly predictable business, whereas property and personal injury risks are not. Most life insurance policies are long-term contracts, and claims against the insurer are not normally expected for several years. In contrast, P/C claims are payable from the day a policy is written because an accident or injury may occur at any

Will my insurance company be around when I need it? One way to answer that question is to check with the company that provides quality ratings for insurance companies, A. M. Best Company, at bestweek.com

---

[5]In weather-related disasters, the collective droughts and heat wave over the central and eastern United States in 1988 were estimated to have resulted in $40 billion in property losses.

The terrorist attacks in September 2001 subjected insurance companies to one of the most panicky episodes in their history. The attacks on the New York City World Trade Center and the Pentagon cost more than 3,000 lives and millions of dollars in property damage. Fear of possible collapse ran through the insurance industry (with the stock prices of leading insurers falling precipitously) in the wake of these tragedies.

Because the terrorist attacks came from outside the normal purview of the financial system, this huge external shock to the insurance industry was completely unexpected. Insurance companies had no time to adjust the premiums they charge to cover the claims they faced and may encounter in the future. Many insurers feared they would have inadequate reserves to pay off a flood of policyholder claims.

Proposals were made to the U.S. government to backstop the industry and become an "insurer of last resort."

A number of insurers indicated that they had little choice but to include new *terror-exclusion clauses* in policies sold to the public. Reason: A number of leading *reinsurers*—companies that accept some of the risks taken on by primary insurance providers—declared that they would no longer underwrite terrorist-related risks. At the same time, several insurance companies debated whether or not to enforce a standard exclusion that has been included in many insurance policies for years—denial of any claims arising from "acts of war." Regardless, some companies have recently begun to offer anti-terror coverage and the insurance industry appears to have weathered the financial storm that the 9/11 tragedy created.

time. Therefore, although life insurers can stay almost fully invested, P/C insurers must be ready at all times to meet the claims of their policyholders. In addition, claims against P/C companies are directly affected by inflation, which drives up repair costs. Most life insurance policies, in contrast, pay the policyholder or beneficiary a fixed sum of money or an amount based upon the market value of investments that back the policies.

Investments by Property-Casualty (P/C) Companies

The majority of funds received by P/C companies are invested in corporate and foreign bonds, state and local government bonds, and common stock. P/C insurers, unlike most financial institutions, are subject to the full federal corporate income tax (except that policyholder dividends are tax deductible for the issuing company). Faced with a potentially heavy tax burden, these companies find tax-exempt state and local government bonds an attractive investment, but they also like the high yields and steady income promised by corporate bonds. As shown in Exhibit 16.6, industry holdings of state and local bonds represented about one-fifth of its total financial assets, with corporate and foreign bonds just a bit larger. Property-casualty insurers have placed less emphasis on purchases of municipal bonds in recent years, due in part to their sluggish earnings and recent changes in tax laws.

Another important asset—corporate stock, also representing close to a sixth of all industry assets—is intended to protect industry earnings and net worth against inflation. Other significant investments include U.S. government securities and federal agency securities, due primarily to their greater safety and liquidity.

Sources of Income

Like life insurance firms, P/C insurers plan to roughly break even on their insurance product lines and earn most of their net return from their investments. Achieving the break-even point in casualty insurance underwriting has been difficult, however, due

EXHIBIT 16.6

Financial Assets and Liabilities of Property-Casualty Insurers

Source: Board of Governors of the Federal Reserve System, *Flow of Funds Accounts.*

*Figures are for the end of the first quarter of 2004.

Asset and Liability Items Outstanding	Amount in 2004* ($ Billions)	Percent of Total Assets
Assets held:		
Checkable deposits and currency	$ 34.0	3.2%
Security repurchase agreements	56.2	5.3
U.S. Treasury and federal agency securities	197.0	18.4
State and local government (municipal) securities	208.7	19.5
Corporate and foreign bonds	227.1	21.3
Commercial mortgage loans	2.1	0.2
Corporate stock (equities)	186.9	17.5
Miscellaneous assets	156.5	14.6
Total financial assets outstanding	$1,068.5	100.0%
Liabilities outstanding:		
Taxes payable	30.3	4.4%
Miscellaneous liabilities	660.0	95.6
Total liabilities outstanding	$ 690.4	100.0%

In order to learn more about the problems and issues in the property/casualty insurance industry, see the Web sites of two of the largest P/C firms: State Farm Insurance Companies at statefarm.com and Allstate Insurance at allstate.com

to rising costs, increased litigation, the reluctance of state insurance commissions to boost policy premiums, and new forms of risk. In fact, property-casualty insurers have experienced billions of dollars in underwriting losses in recent years, and the recent terrorist attacks have added to their problems.

Business Cycles, Inflation, and Competition

Property-casualty insurance is an industry whose earnings and sales revenue reflect the ups and downs of the business cycle. This cyclical sensitivity, coupled with the vulnerability of P/C insurers to inflation, has created a difficult environment for insurance managers. Inflation pushes up the cost of claims, while intense competition holds premium rates down. Among U.S. P/C companies, a key challenge today is the rapid growth of foreign insurance underwriters who have entered the United States in large numbers, including such companies as Allianz, Munich Re Group, Zurich Financial Services, and Royalty Sun Alliance. Moreover, many U.S. corporations have started their own *captive* insurance companies. To improve their situation for the future, P/C insurers must become more innovative in developing new services and more determined to eliminate those services that result in underwriting losses, and they must reduce their operating costs. This will not be easy due to extensive regulations and public pressure for lower insurance rates.

QUESTIONS TO HELP YOU STUDY

5. Against what kinds of *risk* do life insurance companies protect their policyholders? What about property-casualty insurers?

6. Compare and contrast the asset portfolios of life insurance companies with the asset portfolios of property-casualty insurers. Explain any differences you observe.

7. What factors influence the *premiums* insurers charge their policyholders?

8. What is happening to the mix of services offered by life insurers and property-casualty insurance companies? Why?

One of the best examples of the struggles insurance companies have faced in recent years to preserve their profitability and capital is Lloyds of London (lloyds.com)—the three-centuries-old insurance market in which individual investors (called "names") underwrite the risks taken on by its clients in return for premiums and investment income. Lloyds has insured some unusual risks, including actress Elizabeth Taylor's eyes, while also underwriting the reward for corralling the Loch Ness monster! What is equally unusual about Lloyds is that its "names" (underwriters) pledge their entire net worth, if necessary, to cover their share of any losses that may occur.

Unfortunately from time to time the risks associated with a volatile economy, political upheaval as well as extremes in weather, environmental damage, and other sources of loss, have resulted in burgeoning claims that have threatened Lloyds's resources. One point in Lloyds's favor is that it requires full (100 percent) setting aside of reserves behind any possible claims, whereas most regular insurers set aside fewer reserves and count on other income (mainly investment earnings) to help cover any claims received. Moreover, Lloyds has imposed special levies on its members and, for the first time in its history, recently allowed corporate capital to come in. The venerable insurer has also turned more heavily to the reinsurance market (where policies are written to back up any excess risk presented by conventional insurance contracts). These recent steps by Lloyds illustrate how creative the managers of insurance companies must be to deal with the risks and intense global competition that confront the insurance industry today.

16.6   Finance Companies

finance companies

Finance companies are sometimes called *department stores of consumer and business credit.* These institutions grant credit to businesses and consumers for a wide variety of purposes, including the purchase of business equipment, automobiles, vacations, and home appliances. Most authorities divide firms in the industry into one of three groups—consumer finance companies, sales finance companies, and commercial finance companies.

Different Finance Companies for Different Purposes

Consumer finance companies make personal cash loans to individuals. The majority of their loans are home equity loans and loans to support the purchase of passenger cars, home appliances, and mobile homes. However, a growing proportion of consumer-finance-company loans centers on aiding customers with medical and hospital expenses, educational costs, vacations, and household expenses. Loans made by consumer finance companies are considered to be riskier than other consumer installment loans and, therefore, generally carry steeper finance charges than those assessed by most other lending institutions. Among the leaders in consumer finance are Household International at **household.com** and Beneficial Finance Corp. at **beneficial.com**.

Sales finance companies make indirect loans to consumers by purchasing installment paper from dealers selling automobiles and other consumer durables. Many of these firms are "captive" finance companies controlled by a dealer or manufacturer, whose principal function is to promote sales of the sponsoring firm's products by providing credit. Generally, sales finance companies specify in advance to retail dealers the terms of installment contracts they are willing to accept. Frequently they will give the retail dealer sample contract forms, which the dealer fills out when a sale is made. The contract is then sold to the finance company. Among the leading so-called "captive" finance companies are Ford Motor Credit Co. at **fordcredit.com** and GMAC Financial Services at **gmacfs.com**.

EXHIBIT 16.7

Financial Assets and Liabilities Held by Finance Companies

Source: Board of Governors of the Federal Reserve System.

*Figures shown are for end of first quarter of 2004.

**Financial assets held do not include receivables from operating leases granted by finance companies, such as consumer auto loans that are booked to operating income. The leased equipment is *not* a financial asset.

Asset and Liability Items Outstanding	Amount in 2004* ($ Billions)	Percent of Total Assets
Assets held:		
Checkable deposits and currency	$ 37.9	2.7%
Mortgage loans	206.2	14.7
Consumer credit	307.2	21.9
Business loans and advances	475.6	33.9
Miscellaneous assets	374.4	26.7
Total financial assets held**	$1,401.4	100.0%
Liabilities outstanding:		
Open market paper	$ 138.8	9.2%
Corporate bonds	761.8	50.6
Bank loans (not elsewhere classified)	60.5	4.0
Miscellaneous liabilities (including foreign direct investment in the United States and investments by parent companies)	363.5	24.1
Total liabilities outstanding	$1,505.8	100.0%

Commercial finance companies focus principally on extending credit to business firms. Most of these companies provide accounts receivable financing or factoring services to small- or medium-sized manufacturers and wholesalers. With accounts receivable financing, the commercial finance company may extend credit against the borrower's receivables in the form of a direct cash loan. Alternatively, a factoring arrangement may be used in which the finance company acquires the borrowing firm's credit accounts at an appropriate discount rate to cover the risk of loss. Most commercial finance companies today do not confine their credit-granting activities to the financing of receivables but also make loans secured by business inventories and fixed assets. In addition, they offer lease financing for the purchase of capital equipment and rolling stock (such as airplanes and railroad cars) and make short-term unsecured cash loans. Among the principal commercial finance companies today are GE Capital Corporation at **gecapital.com** and Morgan Stanley Dean Witter Credit Corp. at **morganstanley.com**.

We should not overdramatize the differences among these three types of finance companies. The larger companies are active in all three areas. In addition, most finance companies today are extremely diversified in their credit-granting activities, offering a wide range of installment and working capital loans, leasing plans, and long-term credit to support capital investment. Exhibit 16.7 shows that business loans are the most important financial assets held by finance companies, accounting for about one-third of their assets, followed by loans to individuals and families (consumers), accounting for slightly more than one-fifth of industry assets. Real estate mortgage loans are also significant, representing one of the fastest growing finance-company assets in recent years. Smaller amounts of funds are held in cash to provide immediate liquidity.

Growth of Finance Companies

Finance companies have been profoundly affected by recent changes in the character of competition among all financial intermediaries. The lack of an intensive network of branch offices has put many finance companies at a disadvantage in reaching the household borrower who values convenience. As a result, both banks and nonbank thrifts have been able to capture a larger share of the consumer loan market at the expense of finance companies. For example, data compiled by the Federal Reserve

Board show that finance companies held about 45 percent of consumer installment loans extended by financial institutions in 1950 but less than 15 percent as the twenty-first century opened, although captive finance companies of automobile firms (such as Ford Motor Credit) have done well vis-à-vis their competitors by offering discount-rate loans. By way of comparison, over the same time interval, credit unions have more than tripled their share of the consumer installment loan market. Despite the struggle of most finance companies to maintain their share of the financial-services market-place, some of these companies have grown tremendously, largely by merger. For example, GE Capital, which recently has made extensive acquisitions of consumer finance companies in Europe, ranks today as the largest nonbank financial firm in the world, with assets approaching $500 billion.

Many experts now believe that the fastest growing market for finance companies in future years will be in business-oriented, not consumer-oriented, financial services. Revolving credit, working capital loans, merger and acquisition loans, and equipment leasing are among the fastest growing forms of credit extended by finance companies today. Recently, finance companies have expanded their lending programs to include small- and medium- sized businesses, making loans to and accepting some of the stock of these firms. However, home equity lending to consumers has also grown rapidly in recent years.

Methods of Industry Financing

For a virtual tour of GE Capital, the world's largest finance company, see especially gecapital.com

Finance companies are heavy users of *debt* in financing their operations. Principal sources of borrowed funds include bank loans, commercial paper, and debentures (bonds) sold primarily to banks, insurance companies, and nonfinancial corporations. (See Exhibit 16.7.) The source of funds that these companies emphasize most heavily at any given time depends on the structure of interest rates. When long-term rates are high, these companies tend to emphasize commercial paper and short-term bank loans as sources of funds; when long-term rates are relatively low, bonds have been drawn on more heavily. The only source of industry funds that has not grown significantly in recent years is borrowings from parent companies, as finance companies have come to borrow more heavily in the open market rather than relying as heavily upon internally generated funds.

Recent Changes in the Character of the Finance Company Industry

The structure of the finance industry has changed markedly in recent years. As in the case of banks, credit unions, and savings and loans, the number of finance companies has been trending *downward,* although the average size of such companies has grown considerably. A survey by the Federal Reserve Board revealed that in 1960 there were more than 6,400 finance companies operating in the United States, but by the beginning of the new century, less than a thousand finance companies could be found, many of these operating as finance company subsidiaries belonging to holding companies. The industry is concentrated; the 20 top firms hold 70 percent or more of all receivables.

This long-term downtrend in the industry's total population of firms reflects a number of powerful economic forces at work. Rising cost pressures, the broadening of markets, the need to innovate, and intensified competition have encouraged finance companies to strive for larger size and greater operating efficiency. Many smaller companies have sold out to larger conglomerates. Despite their declining numbers, however, finance companies continue to be a potent force in the markets for business and consumer credit.

Indeed, relatively new forms of consumer-oriented finance companies have been emerging recently in the form of *pawnshop, rent-to-own, title loan,* and *check-cashing companies*—sometimes referred to as "fringe banks." These small finance firms invite customers to pledge their personal assets (such as an automobile, home, television set, or future paycheck) in return for a loan at a relatively high rate of interest (often the loan rates far exceed 100 percent). These businesses open up the financial system to a whole new tier of customers (mainly lower-income individuals and families) who are short of immediate cash and often have poor credit histories. The result is that pawnshop, rent-to-own, title loan, and check-cashing companies most frequently seem to serve those customers who have few other places from which they can borrow money.

16.7 Investment Banks

investment bank

If you are interested in a career in investment banking check out the site careers-in-finance.com

One of the most important institutions in the financial system (and also one of the riskiest) is the **investment bank.** These financial firms are not deposit-takers like the commercial and savings banks we discussed in the preceding two chapters. Rather, investment banks raise funds for and provide financial advice to corporations and government agencies around the world. The principal function of investment banks is to help market large volumes of *new* stocks, bonds, and other financial instruments issued by their corporate and governmental customers in order to raise new money.

The Underwriting Function of Investment Banks

These specialized "banks" are especially prominent in the offering of new corporate debt and equity securities, state and local (municipal) bonds and notes, and securities issued by various units of the federal government, including Treasury debt and agency securities issued by such institutions as Fannie Mae (the Federal National Mortgage Association), Freddie Mac (the Federal Home Loan Mortgage Corporation), and the Farm Credit Administration. They *underwrite* new offerings of these financial instruments, purchasing them from the original issuer and placing them in the hands of buyers, hopefully at a higher price than the price paid the issuer.

Security underwriting places investment banks at substantial *risk* because the market value of the securities being underwritten may fall, presenting the underwriter with substantial losses on resale. To mitigate these risks, often several investment bankers will band together to form a *syndicate* in order to bid for and market a new security issue, thereby spreading the risk exposure among multiple underwriters.

Other Investment Banking Services

Investment banks also deal with risk by offering a long menu of diverse services so that their revenue flows are not dependent on security underwriting alone. For example, they give advice on the best terms and times to engage in corporate mergers and acquisitions (including leveraged buyouts of companies) and when and where to venture into new markets, at home and abroad. Several are active traders in commodities and foreign currencies as well as debt and equity instruments. They manage assets for their customers (which include pension funds and major corporations) and set up hedge funds and other investment companies to attract their clients' investable funds.

Leading Investment Banks and the Convergence of Commercial and Investment Banking

Investment banking firms include some of the best-known names in the financial world—for example, Morgan Stanley at **morganstanley.com**, Goldman Sachs Group at **gs.com**, Merrill Lynch Capital Markets at **ml.com**, Credit Suisse Group at **credit-suisse.com/en/home.html**, Lehman Brothers at **lehman.com**, and Bear Stearns at **bearstearns.com**. Competition between these financial firms has become intense as markets have become global in their scope. In the wake of the repeal of the Glass-Steagall Act of 1933—which, for nearly 60 years, legally separated commercial and investment banking—many investment banks have been absorbed in recent years by commercial banking companies. Under the terms of the Gramm-Leach-Bliley (GLB) Act of 1999, investment banks may be acquired by holding companies centered around a commercial bank, be set up as subsidiary corporations of banks themselves, or acquire or start their own commercial banking affiliates.

The amalgamation of commercial and investment banking opens up a wider menu of services that bankers can sell to their major corporate customers. For example, the clientele of a combined commercial and investment banking firm may be offered conventional bank loans, if this traditional form of credit best meets a customer's financing needs or, alternatively, may be guided into the open market to seek out cheaper and more abundant funds through the sale of stocks, bonds, and other securities. Clearly, firms that operate simultaneously as both commercial and investment banks have a distinct advantage over their competitors in today's financial-service marketplace.

16.8 Other Financial Institutions

security brokers and dealers

In addition to the financial firms we have discussed thus far, a number of other financial-service institutions have developed over the years to meet the specialized needs of their customers. For example, **security brokers and dealers** provide a conduit for buyers and sellers of stocks, bonds, and other marketable financial instruments to adjust their holdings of these assets. For their part, *security dealers* stand ready to buy private and government securities from their clients and sell those same instruments to other clients who need to make adjustments in their investment portfolios. By standing ready to buy and sell particular assets, dealers literally "make a market" for the assets they trade. In contrast, *security brokers* do not "take a position of risk" as dealers do when they buy and hold assets from their customers. Rather, brokers merely bring buyers and sellers together and facilitate the exchange of assets.

Both brokers and dealers reduce information costs for buyers and sellers of financial instruments and help increase the liquidity of the instruments they trade. Brokerage commissions and dealer fees are charged to compensate these financial firms for the services they provide, although intense competition in this field (especially with the appearance of discount brokers) and the development of efficient computer software to support online trading have led to downward pressure on brokerage commissions and dealer fees and encouraged security brokers and dealers to develop and offer their customers an expanded menu of services today (including securities' research, cash management, and financial planning services). The leaders in this industry include such familiar names as Merrill Lynch at **ml.com**, Fidelity at **fidelity.com**, Paine Webber at **painewebber.com**, Charles Schwab at **charlesschwab.com**, and A. G. Edwards & Company at **agedwards.com**.

venture capital firms

To learn more about venture capital firms, see the Web site of the National Venture Capital Association at nvca.org

A rising but highly volatile financial-service industry today consists of **venture capital firms.** These businesses gather funds from private investors and other sources and then look for promising new businesses or rapidly emerging companies in which to invest. They often fund the development of innovative new products or services, such as new computer software or medicines, in the hope of earning exceptional returns if these new products or services succeed. Many large banks, insurance companies, and other traditional financial intermediaries have set up affiliated venture-capital companies to make these risky investments and hold the stock of promising new or rapidly growing businesses.

mortgage bank

A related type of dealer firm is the **mortgage bank.** Mortgage bankers commit themselves to take on new mortgage loans used to fund the construction of homes, office

Additional information about the mortgage banking industry is available from the Web site of the Mortgage Bankers Association at mbaa.org

real estate investment trusts (REITs)

Leasing companies

You can learn more about REITs from the National Association of Real Estate Investment Trusts at nareit.com. To explore trends in the leasing company industry, see such sites as The Association for Equipment Leasing and Finance at elaonline.com

buildings, and other structures. They carry these loans for a short time until the mortgages can be sold to a long-term (permanent) lender such as an insurance company or savings bank. As in the case with other dealer operations, the financial risks to the mortgage banker are substantial. A rise in interest rates sharply reduces the market value of existing fixed-rate mortgage loans, presenting the mortgage banker with a loss when it sells the loans out of its portfolio. The risk of rising interest rates and falling mortgage prices encourages mortgage banks to turn over their portfolios rapidly and to arrange lines of credit from lending institutions to backstop their operations. These firms also service the mortgage loans they sell to other lenders, collecting loan payments and inspecting mortgaged property. The leading mortgage bank and mortgage finance companies today are Wells Fargo Home Insurance Inc. at **wellsfargo-mn.com**, Chase Manhattan Mortgage Corp. at **chase.com**, National City Mortgage Company at **nationalcitymortgage.com**, Countrywide Financial Corp. at **countrywide.com**, General Motors Acceptance Corp. at **gmacfs.com**, and Ameriquest Mortgage Corp. at **ameriquest.com**.

Authorized by federal law in 1960, **real estate investment trusts (REITs)** are publicly held, tax-exempt corporations that must receive at least three-quarters of their gross income from real estate transactions (such as rental income, mortgage interest, and sales of property). They also must devote at least three-quarters of their assets to real estate property loans, cash, and government securities. REITs raise funds by selling stock and debt securities and invest most of their available funds in mortgage loans to finance the building of apartments, housing tracts, office buildings, shopping centers, and other commercial ventures.

Leasing companies represent still another kind of specialized financial institution that provides customers with access to productive assets, such as airplanes, automobiles, and equipment through the writing of leases. These leases allow a business or household to rent assets often at a lower cost than borrowing money and owning those same assets. The leasing company, on the other hand, benefits from the stream of lease payments and gains substantial tax benefits from depreciating the leased assets. Competition is intense in this industry because of the entry of scores of banks and bank holding companies, insurance and finance companies, and manufacturing firms that have either opened leasing departments or formed subsidiary leasing companies.

16.9 Trends Affecting All Financial Institutions Today

There are several major trends affecting virtually all financial institutions today. One of these trends is *increasing cost pressures* resulting from the considerable expense associated with raising funds for lending and investing and burgeoning land, labor, and equipment costs that have narrowed profit margins. Another trend is *consolidation,* in which each financial institution tries to expand its size to improve efficiency and ease its growing cost burden. A key result of the consolidation movement is declining numbers of independent financial institutions, while the remaining institutions average much larger in size and organizational complexity.

Still a third trend is *service diversification,* as all major financial institutions have invaded each other's traditional markets with new services in an effort to offset rising costs and protect thinning profit margins. Service diversification has led to a blurring of functions among the different institutions to such an extent that it is becoming increasingly difficult to distinguish between different financial institutions—a phenomenon known as *homogenization.*

Service diversification has led to *convergence* as banks, insurance companies, security firms, and other types of financial institutions rush toward one another and, increasingly, merge with each other to become large financial conglomerates. This convergence trend has been aided considerably by the passage of the Financial Services Modernization (Gramm-Leach-Bliley or GLB) Act passed in the United States in 1999. GLB permits banks, insurers, and securities firms (as well as selected other financial firms) to reach across industry boundaries and link up with each other.

The offering of many new services over wider market areas has been made possible by another trend in the financial institutions' sector: a *technological revolution,* particularly in the growing adoption of automated electronic equipment for making payments and transferring financial information. Increasingly, there is little need to walk into the offices of a financial institution, because many transactions can be handled more efficiently via home and office computers linked online to each financial institution's computer network.

The technological revolution has made possible a global financial system and unleashed a trend toward *global competition* in which all financial institutions find themselves increasingly in a common market, competing for many of the same customers. Distance and geography no longer shelter financial institutions from the forces of demand and supply in the financial system as they once did. Accompanying the rise of global competition is a drive toward *regulatory cooperation,* so that financial institutions headquartered in different countries face essentially the *same* regulatory rules. There is a trend toward harmonizing laws and regulations so that no one country's financial institutions operate at a competitive disadvantage vis-à-vis those of another country.

Many of the new services and technological innovations and the development of global competition have come into existence because of a trend toward *deregulation,* in which the content and prices of financial services increasingly are being determined by the marketplace rather than by government rules. Most of the deregulation movement, thus far, has centered in banking and among nonbank depository institutions as well as leading security dealers and brokers in Canada, the United States, Japan, Great Britain, Australia, and Western Europe. However, as depository institutions and securities firms continue to receive new service powers and expand their markets, it is quite likely that the whole panoply of financial institutions will seek to further loosen the regulatory rules that bind them today. It is hoped that the public will be the ultimate beneficiary in terms of more and better financial services at lower cost.

QUESTIONS TO HELP YOU STUDY

9. What role do *finance companies* play in supplying funds to the financial marketplace? How many different kinds of finance companies are there?

10. A growing sector within the general finance company industry consists of *small-loan companies,* which include *pawnshops, rent-to-own stores, title loan firms,* and *check-cashing companies?* What do these firms do? What kinds of customers do they serve?

11. What are *investment banks?* Why are they important to the economic and financial system? What risks do they face?

12. What is a *REIT?* A *mortgage bank?* A *leasing company?* Why do you think these specialized lenders came into being? Have they faced any serious problems of late?

13. What functions do security brokers and dealers perform within the financial system? Why are these security companies so important to the money and capital markets?

14. In the concluding section of this chapter, several major trends affecting all financial institutions today were discussed. Identify these trends. Which ones do you see as long-term trends likely to continue indefinitely into the future? Which may be short-lived (if any)? Explain your answer.

MARKETS ON THE NET: The Most Important Web Sites for This Chapter

A. M. Best Company (bestweek.com)

American Council of Life Insurers (acli.com)

Insurance Information Institute (iii.org)

Investment Company Institute (ici.org)

Lloyds of London (lloyds.com)

Morningstar (morningstar.com)

Mortgage Bankers Association of America (mbaa.org)

National Association of Real Estate Investment Trusts (nareit.com)

National Venture Capital Association (nvca.org)

Pension Benefit Guaranty Corporation (pbgc.gov)

Pension and Investments Newsletter (pionline.com)

Securities and Exchange Commission (sec.gov)

Summary of the Chapter's Main Points

This chapter examined the services offered by and the portfolio characteristics of a wide variety of different financial institutions, including mutual funds or investment companies, pension funds, life and property-casualty insurance companies, finance companies, security firms, mortgage banks, real estate investment trusts, leasing companies, venture capital firms, and financial conglomerates of various types.

- Several of the financial institutions discussed in this chapter—particularly *pension funds* and *insurance companies*—provide risk protection for their customers against death, ill health, negligence, loss of property, and the danger of outliving one's savings in retirement. In addition, pension funds, insurance companies, and most of the other financial-service institutions examined in this chapter make loans in the money and capital markets to businesses, individuals, and governments. They are predominantly *capital market institutions,* focused mainly upon providing long-term credit.

- Among the most rapidly growing financial institutions of the past decade have been *investment companies*—most often referred to as *mutual funds.* Investment companies sell shares to the public and use the proceeds of those sales to buy various types of stocks, bonds, and other securities. Shareholders in a mutual fund receive earnings based on the performance of the securities held by the company. Mutual funds have grown rapidly in recent years, in part because they offer small savers better access to the financial marketplace, provide professional funds management and portfolio diversification, and supply liquidity if a customer needs to quickly convert his or her investments into cash.

- Among the more rapidly growing sectors in this financial-service field are *finance companies,* which provide credit to businesses and households. Finance companies too are merging into fewer but larger firms with a growing menu of loans and other financial services. However, this financial-service industry is also developing numerous small-loan companies (in the form of pawnshops, title loan companies, rent-to-own stores, and check-cashing facilities) that cater to individuals and families, particularly those credit customers presenting greater risk of loan default.

- One of the most exciting and potentially rewarding financial-service industries is *investment banking.* Investment bankers assist corporations and governments in raising new capital by purchasing their clients' stocks, bonds, and other securities and reselling those same securities to other investors. In addition to

www.mhhe.com/rose9e

security underwriting services, investment bankers supply technical advice to businesses interested in pursuing mergers and acquisitions or entering into new product lines or new market areas.

- The chapter concludes its survey of major financial institutions with an overview of such key industries as *real estate investment trusts (REITs)* and *mortgage banks,* which serve the home loan industry and also provide funds for commercial building projects. Another key sector is *security brokers and dealers,* who make it possible for the public to buy and sell securities to adjust the quality and yield of their investment portfolios. Finally, financial support of businesses stemming from *leasing companies* and *venture capital companies* has been rising in recent years, particularly for new firms and rapidly growing enterprises that have limited sources of funding available to them.

- All of the financial institutions discussed in this chapter are undergoing major changes in the form of *consolidation* of smaller financial-service firms into larger financial-service providers. Not only are financial firms in the same industry growing larger, but many are reaching across industries and combining different service providers under one corporate umbrella—a phenomenon known as *convergence.* This convergence trend has been helped along by new government legislation (such as the Financial Services Modernization [Gramm-Leach-Bliley] Act passed in the United States in 1999).

- In an effort to lower production costs and reduce risk exposure, most financial institutions are diversifying their services—developing and adding new services in order to reduce the overall risk exposure to their revenues and net earnings. One result of this *service diversification* trend is to make more and more financial companies look alike (*homogenization*) because they are offering many of the same services as their neighbors.

- Changes in the *technology of information gathering and distribution* have had a greater impact on financial institutions than most other industries, permitting these institutions to serve their customers with greater accuracy and speed over wider geographic areas. New computer-based technology has allowed financial-service firms to reduce their personnel expenses and become less labor-intensive but more capital-intensive in their service production and distribution activities.

- More financial-service institutions have become *international* in their focus, reaching across national borders with their services. This trend toward *globalization* has contributed to the emergence of much larger financial institutions and broader financial service menus. Globalization has also encouraged government regulatory agencies in various countries to reach out to each other and cooperate in their oversight of the activities and performance of the financial-service sector.

Key Terms Appearing in This Chapter

Problems and Issues

1. The manager of a life insurance company is trying to decide what annual premium to charge a group of policyholders, each of whom has just reached his or her 40th birthday. A check of mortality tables indicates that, for every million persons born 40 years ago, 3 percent die, on average, sometime during their 40th year. If the company has 10,000 policyholders in this age bracket and each has taken out a $50,000 life insurance policy, estimate the probable amount of death benefit claims against the company. How much must be charged in premiums from each policyholder just to cover these expected claims? Suppose the company has operating expenses (plus a target profit) on sales to these policyholders of $500,000. What annual premium must be charged each policyholder to recover expenses and meet expected benefit claims?

2. A pension fund has accumulated $1 million in a retirement plan for James B. Smith, who retires this month at age 65. If Mr. Smith has a life expectancy of 75 years, what is the minimum size of the annual annuity check the pension plan will be able to send him each year (assuming that the value of the pension fund's investments remains stable)? Should he insist on receiving that size payment each year? Why or why not? What other kinds of information would be helpful in analyzing Mr. Smith's financial situation at retirement?

3. An employee has just joined SONY Corporation and a pension plan is set up in her name under which the company will contribute $5,000 per year and the employee herself will contribute $1,000 per year. How much will this year's contributed funds be worth in 10 years if the pension plan pledges a 7 percent annual return on each dollar saved? Suppose the employee plans to retire in 10 years. How much will be available in total at retirement if the company and the employee contribute the amounts noted above each year for the next 10 years and this employee owns (is vested with) the full amount of savings contributed to the pension plan? If the pension promises an annual annuity rate of 6 percent, given this employee's life expectancy, what annual retirement income can she expect?

4. Delbert Ray is planning to retire this year and draw upon the accumulated savings in his pension plan, which amount to $205,800. Mr. Ray is vested with 80 percent of the accumulated funds and, based on his life expectancy, has been promised an annual annuity (income) rate of 3.5 percent. What is Delbert Ray's expected annual retirement income from his pension plan?

5. What is the difference between the markets served by a property-casualty insurer, a life insurer, and a reinsurance firm? Which of them has the potential for the greatest risk exposure? Explain.

6. Some economists and financial analysts argue that "captive" finance companies, such as General Motors Acceptance Corporation (GMAC), have advantages over their principal regulated competitors—commercial banks, S&Ls, and credit unions—because the captives are not regulated as heavily. Others argue that because of their ties with parent companies, the captives have superior information about the value of the collateral for many of the loans they make. Explain the logic behind both of these arguments. Provide as much detail as you can in explaining how these two factors could enhance the competitive advantage of captive finance companies in the markets they serve.

Standard & Poor's Market Insight and Web-Based Problems

1. The property-casualty insurance industry has had its ups and downs in recent years with claims resulting from terrorism and natural disasters. The purpose of this exercise is to see what the current outlook is for this industry and to learn about the structure of property-casualty companies by focusing on one of the largest firms in the industry. Using S&P's Market Insight database at **mhhe.com/edumarketinsight**, complete the following:

    a. Click the "Industry" tab and locate the page for the GICS sub-industry group: "Property & Casualty." Under "S&P Industry Surveys" click on "Insurance: Property-Casualty." Read the brief "Current Environment" section and describe the following: (i) the current outlook for the industry, and (ii) the most serious problem(s) facing the industry.

    b. Click the "Companies" tab and locate the page for Allstate Corp. (ticker symbol ALL). Find its annual balance sheet under "Excel Analytics." First look at the fraction of the firm's investments that is maintained in financial assets: the ratio of "Short-Term Investments" plus "Investment Assets—Total" to "Assets—Total." Has this firm varied its allocation of investments to financial assets very much over the five years listed? Can you suggest some reasons why or why not?

    c. Now examine the structure of Allstate Corp's financial assets by recording: (i) its investments in money market assets ("Cash and Due from Banks"); (ii) its bond market investments ("Fixed Income Securities"); (iii) its stock market investments ("Equity Securities"); and (iv) its investments in mortgages ("Mortgage Loans"). Form ratios of these components to the sum of "Short-Term Investments" plus "Investment Assets—Total." Where does Allstate place most of its investments? Has the allocation of financial assets across these investment categories changed much over the five years shown? Why do you think this is so?

2. Auto loans represent an important share of all loans made by finance companies. This category includes loans for both new and used autos. The purpose of this exercise is to compare the average loan contracts for new and used autos that these companies offer. Complete the following:

    a. Visit the Federal Reserve's Web site at **federalreserve.gov** and click on "Economic Research and Data." On the next page, go to "Statistics: Releases and Historical Data" and find the most recent G.20 Finance Companies release.

    b. For each of the five years listed, compute the interest rate spread between the interest rate on used car loans and the interest rate on new car loans. Are you surprised at the size of this rate spread? What does your finding suggest about the relative risk associated with new car loans and used car loans? Has this spread changed much over the five years shown? Can you suggest reasons why?

    c. Is there much of a difference between new and used car loans in terms of: (i) maturity; (ii) the down payments; and/or (iii) the size of the loan? What might account for these differences?

3. Stock market mutual funds have become major investment vehicles for households over the past few decades. One advantage of these funds is the reduction in the

level of risk that an investor can achieve through portfolio diversification (i.e., by not having "all of your eggs in one basket"). Some mutual funds allow you to "buy the market" by investing in a portfolio of stocks that reflects a broad market index such as the S&P 500. To assess the possible advantages offered by some mutual funds over investing in individual stocks, choose a particular stock from the Dow Jones Industrial Average Index (such as IBM or Microsoft). Visit S&P's Market Insight database at **mhhe.com/edumarketinsight** or any of the stock-market tracking Web sites available and gather the information needed to answer the following questions:

a. Find the current price of the individual stock you have chosen (the closing price from the previous day) and the number of shares outstanding. Compute the total market value of the company in question (its share price times number of shares outstanding, often called its "market capitalization").

b. Find monthly data over the past three years for the (closing) company share price and (closing) value of the S&P 500 stock index. For the individual stock you picked, find the six-month period over the past three years for which your stock experienced *the greatest price appreciation* and compute the percentage increase.

c. Compare the gain you found in (b) to the percentage increase in the S&P 500 index over the same period. Would you have been better off owning the single stock you chose or picking a mutual fund that let you "buy the market" (in this case, the S&P 500 index)?

d. Now repeat the process you just went through for the six-month period that would have yielded *the smallest price appreciation or largest price decline* for the single stock you chose. Would you have been better off investing in the single stock you chose or in a market-tracking mutual fund (such as a fund mirroring the performance of the S&P 500 index)?

Selected References to Explore

Berlin, Mitchell. "That Thing Venture Capitalists Do." *Business Review,* Federal Reserve Bank of Philadelphia, January-February 1998, pp. 15–26.

Dynan, Karen R.; Kathleen W. Johnson; and Samuel Slowinski. "Survey of Finance Companies." *Federal Reserve Bulletin,* January 2002, pp. 1–14.

Engen, Eric M, and Andrew Lehnert. "Mutual Funds and the U.S. Equity Market." *Federal Reserve Bulletin,* December 2000, pp. 797–812.

Friedberg, Leora, and Michael T. Owyang. "Not Your Father's Pension Plan: The Rise of 401(K) and Other Defined Contribution Plans." *Review,* Federal Reserve Bank of St. Louis, January-February 2002, pp. 23–34.

Kwan, Simon. "Underfunding of Private Pension Plans." *FRBSF Economic Letter,* Federal Reserve Bank of San Francisco, no. 2003–16, June 13, 2003.

www.mhhe.com/rose9e

Chapter 17

Regulation of the Financial Institutions' Sector

Learning Objectives

in This Chapter

- You will explore the reasons why financial institutions represent one of the most regulated sectors in the modern world.

- You will discover the many types of *regulation* (government rule-making) affecting the behavior and performance of financial institutions.

- You will understand how regulation has influenced and shaped the structure of financial-service industries.

What's in This Chapter?
Key Topics Outline

17.1 Introduction to Financial Institutions' Regulation

Financial institutions are one of the most heavily regulated of all businesses in the world. Around the globe, these financial-service firms face stringent government rules limiting the services they can offer; the territories they can enter or not enter; the makeup of their portfolios of assets, liabilities, and capital; and even how they price and deliver their services to the public. As we will see in this chapter, a variety of reasons have been offered for heavy government intrusion into the financial institutions' sector, including protecting the public's savings and ensuring that consumers receive an adequate quantity and quality of reasonably priced financial services.

regulation

Many economists, financial analysts, and financial institutions have argued over the years that **regulation** has done more harm than good for both financial institutions themselves and for the public they serve. In particular, government restrictions allegedly have allowed nonregulated or less-regulated financial-service firms to invade the marketplace and capture many of the customers of highly regulated financial institutions, who are not sufficiently free to compete effectively. Moreover, regulations are often backward-looking, addressing problems that have long since disappeared, and they may compound this problem of "relevancy" by changing much more slowly than the free marketplace, inhibiting the ability of regulated financial institutions to stay abreast of new technologies and changing customer tastes. Other observers, however, argue that government regulations have achieved some positive results in the financial institutions' sector, reducing the number of failed financial-service firms, promoting more stable financial markets, and reducing the incidence of racial, religious, age, and sex discrimination in the public's access to financial services.

In this chapter we explore these and many other issues as we examine the variety of government regulations and regulatory agencies that oversee financial institutions today, assess the reasons for and the effectiveness of existing regulations, and explore recent efforts to deregulate the financial institutions' sector.

17.2 The Reasons behind the Regulation of Financial Institutions

Elaborate government rules controlling what financial institutions can and cannot do arise from multiple causes. One is a concern about the *safety of the public's funds,* especially the safety of the savings owned by millions of individuals and families. The reckless management and ultimate loss of personal savings can have devastating consequences for a family's future economic well-being and lifestyle, particularly at retirement. While savers have a responsibility to carefully evaluate the quality and stability of a financial institution before committing their savings to it, governments have long expressed a special concern for small savers who may lack the financial expertise and access to quality information necessary to be able to judge the true condition of a financial institution correctly. Moreover, many of the reasons that cause financial institutions to fail—such as fraud, embezzlement, deteriorating loans, or manipulation of the books by insiders—are often concealed from the public.

Related to the desire for safety is a government's goal of *promoting public confidence* in the financial system. Unless the public is confident enough in the safety and security of their funds placed under the management of financial institutions, they will withdraw their savings and thereby reduce the volume of funds available for productive investment to construct new buildings, purchase new equipment, set up new businesses, and create new jobs. The economy's growth will slow and, over time, the public's standard of living will fall.

Government rules are also aimed at ensuring *equal opportunity and fairness in the public's access to financial services*. For example, in an earlier era, many groups of customers—women, members of racial minority groups, the elderly, and those of foreign birth—found that their ability to borrow money on competitive terms was often severely restricted. Consumers of financial services were not well organized then, and the discriminatory policies of lending institutions seemed to change very slowly, particularly in markets where competition was subdued. While many economists believed that the potent force of competition generated by both domestic and foreign service suppliers would eventually kill off the vestiges of discrimination, other observers argued that such an event might take a very long time, particularly in those markets where financial firms colluded with each other and agreed not to compete.

Many regulations in the financial institutions' sector spring from the ability of some financial institutions to *create money* in the form of credit and debit cards, checkable deposits, and other accounts that can be used to make payments for purchases of goods and services. History has shown that the creation of money is closely associated with *inflation*. If uncontrolled money growth outstrips growth in the economy's production of goods and services, prices will begin to rise, damaging especially those consumers on fixed incomes, as their money balances can buy fewer and fewer goods and services. Thus, the regulation of *money creation* has become a key objective of government activity in the financial sector.

Regulation is often justified as the most direct way to aid so-called "disadvantaged" sectors in the economy—those groups that appear to need special help in the competition for scarce funds. Examples include new home buyers, farmers, small businesses, and low-income families. Governments often place high social value on subsidizing or guaranteeing loans made to—and supporting financial institutions that lend money to—these particular sectors of the economy.

Finally, the enforcement of government rules for financial institutions has arisen because *governments depend upon financial institutions for many important services*. Governments borrow money and depend upon financial institutions to buy a substantial proportion of government IOUs. Financial institutions also aid governments in the collection and dispersal of tax revenues and in the pursuit of economic policy through the manipulation of interest rates and the money supply. Thus, governments frequently regulate financial institutions simply to ensure that these important financial services will continue to be provided at reasonable cost and in a reliable manner.

What are we to make of these reasons so often posed for the extensive government regulations applied to many financial institutions? Few of them can go unchallenged. For example, while safety is important for many savers, no government can completely remove risk for savers. Indeed, in the long run, it may be more efficient and far less costly for governments to promote full disclosure of the financial condition of individual financial institutions and let competition in a free marketplace discipline poorly managed, excessively risky financial-service firms. Similarly, there is no question that discrimination on the basis of sex, race, religious affiliation, or other irrelevant factors is repugnant, but can we be more effective in eliminating discrimination by some method other than by struggling to enforce complicated rule books and by requiring endless compliance reports? Perhaps the same ends could be achieved by lowering the regulatory barriers to competition and by making it easier for customers hurt by discrimination to recover their damages in court.

Certainly the ability of financial institutions to create money needs to be monitored carefully, because excessive money growth can easily generate inflation and weaken the economy. But aren't there already enough tools available to control money growth?

For example, when money grows too fast, a central bank like the Federal Reserve System can use its powerful tools to slow money growth. And wouldn't it be more efficient to pay direct money subsidies to disadvantaged groups (such as new home buyers) rather than to reach these groups indirectly by regulating financial institutions and interfering with the free operation of the financial-services marketplaces? As for providing a reliable stream of financial services to governments, wouldn't profit-motivated financial institutions be likely to provide these services if it were profitable to do so?

In brief, there are no absolutely irrefutable arguments justifying the regulation of financial institutions. Much depends on your personal political philosophy regarding society's goals and whether those goals are each more likely to be achieved by an unfettered marketplace or by collective action through government laws and regulations. As we shall see shortly, there is a trend today toward gradually allowing private markets to discipline risk taking by financial institutions and to minimize the role of government. Progress toward **deregulation** of the financial sector is slow, however, and can easily be derailed if financial institutions abuse the new liberties that come their way.

deregulation

Does Regulation Benefit or Harm Financial Institutions?

For many years a controversy has been brewing as to whether government regulations help or hurt financial institutions. One of the earliest arguments on the positive side was propounded by economist George Stigler (1965), who suggested that regulated industries, far from dreading regulation, actually *invite* government intrusion, expecting to benefit from it. In the early history of the United States, for example, the railroads often prospered because government subsidized their growth and protected them from competition. Because regulators may prevent or restrict entry into an industry, the firms involved may earn excess profits ("monopoly rents") due to the absence of strong competitors. Therefore, the lifting of regulatory rules (deregulation) may bring about decreased profits for financial institutions.

A more balanced view of the benefits and costs of regulation has been offered by Edward Kane (1981). He suggests that, on the positive side, regulation tends to increase public confidence in the regulated industry. Thus, customers may trust their banks' stability and reliability more because they are regulated, increasing customer loyalty to regulated firms and helping to shelter them from risk. Moreover, regulation may lead to a curious form of "innovation," which Kane labels the *regulatory dialectic*. He believes that regulated firms are constantly searching for ways around government rules in order to increase the market value of their business. Once they find a regulatory loophole that attracts the regulators' attention, new regulations are imposed to close the gap. But this leads to still more "innovation" by regulated businesses in order to escape the new restrictions. The result is a continuing chain reaction: Regulations spawn innovative escapes that, in turn, give rise to new rules in a never-ending struggle between the regulators and the regulated.

Notice, too, that the so-called "innovation" brought on by the regulatory dialectic is not the most productive form of innovation from society's point of view. Instead of developing ways to lower costs and deliver financial services more efficiently to the public, financial institutions are spending their time and energy looking for regulatory loopholes—something they wouldn't do if the regulations weren't there in the first place. This "wasted" time and energy, Kane believes, places regulated firms at a disadvantage vis-à-vis their unregulated competitors. Other factors held equal, the market share of regulated firms begins to fall. Many economists believe that this has happened to commercial banks and other depository institutions in recent decades, as security brokers and dealers and mutual funds, facing fewer regulations, have

The growing specter of terrorism and the use of money-laundering techniques around the globe have given rise to new legislation and new regulations affecting banks, savings and loans, credit unions, check-cashing and money-order businesses, security and currency dealers, and thousands of other firms selling transaction-related services.

For example, the *Bank Secrecy Act*, passed by the U.S. Congress in October 1970, grants the Treasury Department authority to demand that financial-service institutions covered by the law keep records of their customers' transactions. Any *suspicious* financial activity is to be recorded in a Suspicious Activity Report (SAR) and forwarded to the Treasury's Financial Crimes Enforcement Network. Banks and other institutions mentioned in the law must maintain files on transactions that may "have a high degree of usefulness in criminal, tax, and regulatory investigations and proceedings."

A law with similar purposes and scope appeared following the terrorist attacks of 9/11 in the form of the *USA Patriot Act*, passed in the Fall of 2001. Banks and selected other financial firms must "know their customers" much better than in the past. They are required to verify the *identity* of customers opening a new account. Bank personnel now routinely check drivers' licenses, Social Security numbers, birth dates, taxpayer IDs, and other personal customer information and compare these against a list of known or suspected terrorists supplied by the U.S. government. Any suspicious items that emerge are to be reported to the U.S. Treasury Department.

These laws and their accompanying regulations have stirred up considerable controversy in both the United States and in Europe, where several similar laws have appeared. Law enforcement agencies argue that these newer, tougher rules are needed to keep up with criminal elements who engage in illegal monetary transactions and use the financial system as a vehicle to support drug trafficking, terrorism, and other dangerous and illegal acts. The most likely targets today are those individuals and businesses gathering funds inside the United States and moving those funds abroad to escape detection.

Opponents often object to the fact that information gathered under these rules can be used without a customer's permission or knowledge and without a court order. Those bearing the heaviest burdens from these government rules appear to be banks and other financial-service institutions who, in some cases, must develop extensive record-keeping and monitoring systems. Debate over the wisdom and effectiveness of these laws and regulations is likely to continue well into the future.

captured many of the commercial banking industry's biggest and most profitable customers, reducing the share of the financial-service marketplace controlled by depository institutions.

Thus, regulations are costly and can reduce the competitiveness of regulated financial institutions relative to nonregulated or lesser-regulated businesses. For example, a recent study of the banking industry by Ellihousen (1998) estimates that regulatory costs for this particular financial-service industry amounted to between 12 and 13 percent of all banks' noninterest costs, or about $15 to $16 billion per year. Moreover, some regulations, such as compliance with the disclosure rules regarding suspicious customer transactions under the Bank Secrecy Act, are particularly costly. Regulatory costs are labor intensive, particularly the costs of making sure each institution is in compliance with all the rules. Financial institution managers devote great amounts of time to regulatory compliance activities. However, there do appear to be economies of scale associated with regulatory compliance costs, so financial institutions tend to save somewhat on these costs as they grow larger. This cost factor may limit the entry of new institutions into the financial-service field, discourage the development of new services, and encourage consolidation of smaller financial-service companies into bigger ones. Regulators should be especially cautious about making frequent minor changes in regulatory rules, which appears to be a more costly practice than making major, but infrequent, rule changes.

On balance, then, regulation of financial institutions may be a "tale of two cities," delivering both the best of times and the worst of times. Regulation may increase regulated institutions' profitability and shelter them from risk, resulting in fewer failures, but perhaps at the price of less efficient financial firms. In return for greater stability and public confidence in financial institutions, customers may be less well served in terms of prices charged and quality of services delivered.

17.3 The Regulation of Commercial Banks

Due to their importance in the financial system, *commercial banks* are typically the most regulated of all financial institutions. Moreover, in the United States, banking is more heavily regulated than in most other industrialized countries. From the banking system's earliest history, there has been a fear of concentrated power in banking because bank credit and other banking services are so vital to the well-being of businesses and households.

Responsibility for regulating banks operating in the United States today is divided among three federal banking agencies and the 50 state governments. These regulatory agencies have overlapping responsibilities, so most banks are subject to multiple jurisdictions. The regulatory agencies responsible for enforcing banking's ground rules include the Federal Reserve System, the Comptroller of the Currency, and the Federal Deposit Insurance Corporation—all at the federal level—and the state banking commissions of the 50 states. Exhibit 17.1 provides a summary of the principal regulatory powers exercised by these federal and state agencies in the United States.

The Federal Reserve System (The Fed)

Federal Reserve System

The **Federal Reserve System** is responsible for examining and supervising the activities of all its member banks. When a member bank wishes to merge with another bank or establish a branch office, it must notify the Fed. The Fed must review and approve the acquisition of bank and nonbank businesses by bank holding companies operating inside the United States. The Federal Reserve is responsible for supervising U.S.-based international banking corporations, for overseeing the operations of member banks in foreign countries, and for regulating the activities of foreign banks inside the United States. The Fed also sets reserve requirements on deposits for all depository institutions.

Office of the Comptroller of the Currency (The OCC)

Comptroller of the Currency

The **Comptroller of the Currency**—also known as the Administrator of National Banks—is a division of the U.S. Treasury established under the National Banking Act of 1863. The Comptroller is the oldest federal regulatory agency in the United States and has the power to issue federal charters for the creation of new *national banks*. These banks, once chartered, are subject to an impressive array of regulations, most of which pertain to the kinds of loans and investments that may be made and the amount and types of capital each bank must hold. All national banks are examined periodically by the Comptroller's staff and may be liquidated or consolidated with another financial institution if deemed to be in the public interest.

Federal Deposit Insurance Corporation (FDIC)

Federal Deposit Insurance Corporation

The **Federal Deposit Insurance Corporation** insures deposits of commercial banks, savings banks, and savings and loans that meet its regulations. As a result of passage

EXHIBIT 17.1   Principal U.S. Bank Regulatory Agencies

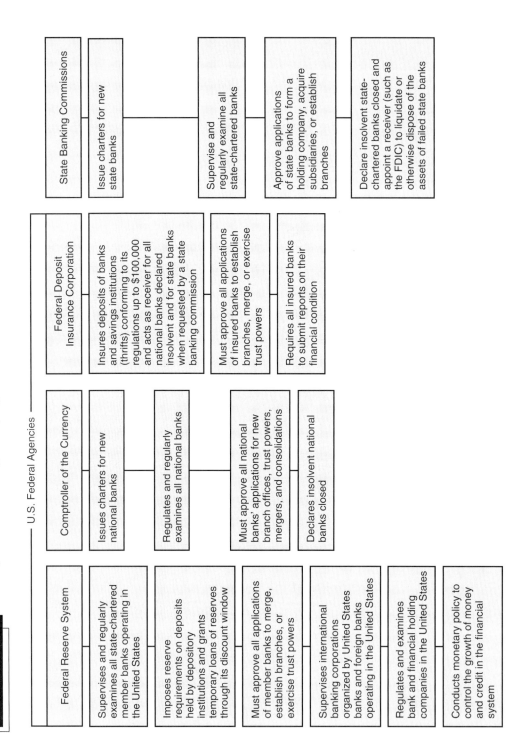

U.S. Federal Agencies

Federal Reserve System

Supervises and regularly examines all state-chartered member banks operating in the United States

Imposes reserve requirements on deposits held by depository institutions and grants temporary loans of reserves through its discount window

Must approve all applications of member banks to merge, establish branches, or exercise trust powers

Supervises international banking corporations organized by United States banks and foreign banks operating in the United States

Regulates and examines bank and financial holding companies in the United States

Conducts monetary policy to control the growth of money and credit in the financial system

Comptroller of the Currency

Issues charters for new national banks

Regulates and regularly examines all national banks

Must approve all national banks' applications for new branch offices, trust powers, mergers, and consolidations

Declares insolvent national banks closed

Federal Deposit Insurance Corporation

Insures deposits of banks and savings institutions (thrifts) conforming to its regulations up to $100,000 and acts as receiver for all national banks declared insolvent and for state banks when requested by a state banking commission

Must approve all applications of insured banks to establish branches, merge, or exercise trust powers

Requires all insured banks to submit reports on their financial condition

State Banking Commissions

Issue charters for new state banks

Supervise and regularly examine all state-chartered banks

Approve applications of state banks to form a holding company, acquire subsidiaries, or establish branches

Declare insolvent state-chartered banks closed and appoint a receiver (such as the FDIC) to liquidate or otherwise dispose of the assets of failed state banks

of the Financial Institutions Reform, Recovery, and Enforcement Act of 1989, the FDIC's insurance reserves are divided between the Bank Insurance Fund (BIF), backing commercial bank deposits; and the Savings Association Insurance Fund (SAIF), securing the deposits of savings and loans and savings banks. With passage of the Depository Institutions Deregulation and Monetary Control Act of 1980, each depositor is limited to a maximum of $100,000 in insurance coverage should a bank or savings institution fail. Under the terms of the FDIC Improvement Act of 1991, each participating bank is assessed a fee equal to a fraction of its eligible deposits to build and maintain the national insurance fund.[1]

If you're interested in the examination process and examination procedures used by the federal banking agencies, see the Web site maintained by the Federal Financial Institutions Examination Council, which coordinates examination standards by the various federal banking agencies, at **ffiec.gov**

One of the most important functions of the FDIC is to act as a check on state banking commissions, because few banks today—even those with state charters—open their doors without FDIC deposit insurance. The FDIC reviews the adequacy of capital, earnings prospects, the character of management, and the public convenience and needs aspects of each application before granting deposit insurance. This agency is also charged with examining insured banks that are *not* members of the Federal Reserve System. The FDIC acts as receiver for all failed national banks and for failed state-chartered banks when requested by a state banking commission. In most cases, an insolvent bank will be merged with or absorbed by a healthy one. If no suitable buyer can be found, the failed bank will be closed and the depositors paid off.

The savings and loan debacle of the 1980s, coupled with the failure of hundreds of banks during the late 1980s and early 1990s, eventually led to the realization that the federal deposit insurance system as originally created was flawed. Until the mid-1990s, each bank, no matter how risky, paid the *same* insurance premium per dollar of the public's deposits. Moreover, until passage of the Financial Institutions Reform, Recovery, and Enforcement Act (FIRREA) of 1989, there was lax enforcement of federal bank capital standards, which led to excessive risk exposure to the federal insurance fund. The result was the appearance of a "moral hazard" problem in which banks and savings and loans could attract low-cost deposits (due to the benefit of cheap insurance coverage) and then invest in highly risky assets, knowing the government would, in effect, underwrite their gamble. Because the FDIC's reserves began declining in the 1980s, numerous proposals were brought forward to strengthen the deposit insurance system. Finally, with the deposit insurance fund almost drained away, the FDIC Improvement Act of 1991 put Congress on record in favor of risk-adjusted deposit insurance premiums. The FDIC was ordered to charge riskier banks higher deposit insurance fees. Moreover, the FDIC was given authority to borrow additional funds through the U.S. Treasury Department.

Recently several bankers' associations and government policymakers have proposed raising the U.S. deposit insurance limit from $100,000 to $200,000. Supporting arguments include concern over inflation because the insurance limit of $100,000 was set back in 1980 and has not been increased since that time. Moreover, there is concern that banking risk may have increased with banks being allowed to affiliate more aggressively now with nonbank businesses. Opponents argue, on the other hand, that raising the insurance limit would not benefit small savers—the group it is principally designed to aid—and might well increase the "moral hazard" problem, making depositors even less inclined to monitor the risky behavior of their banks. This issue remains unresolved.

---

[1] Under the terms of the Financial Institutions Reform, Recovery, and Enforcement Act, the FDIC's insurance fund, which is invested in government securities, must hold assets that amount to a minimum of 1.25 percent of the amount of all insured deposits. Over 90 percent of all U.S. banks and thrifts have paid zero insurance fees for several years running because the FDIC's reserves have generally exceeded the 1.25 percent minimum required. Only a few banks and thrifts have paid significant FDIC insurance fees recently because of their weak capital positions and poor examination ratings.

State Banking Commissions

state banking commissions

State regulation of banks and other financial institutions is traceable through Web sites maintained by all state regulatory agencies—for example, banking.state.tx.us for the state of Texas and azbanking.com for the Arizona Banking Department.

The regulatory powers of the federal banking agencies overlap with those of the **state banking commissions** that regularly examine all state-chartered banks within their borders. The states also set rules prescribing the minimum amount of equity capital for individual state-chartered banks, issue charters for new state banks, and review and approve applications of state-chartered banks for establishing new branch offices and for mergers and acquisitions. Indeed, state regulatory authorities have played an important role in a number of the great issues surrounding banking in the United States over the past century and more, most notably in the rules that apply to the geographic expansion of banks across state lines.

Opening Competition across Political Boundaries

In the mid-nineteenth century (and until recently), banks operating in the United States were restricted by federal and state law and regulation against competing across geographic markets, which were generally defined by political boundaries. It was believed, until quite recently, that "too much competition" could lead to excess volatility in bank profits and introduce instability into the nation's banking system, thereby endangering the savings of depositors. In the early part of the twentieth century, the composition of bank depositors increasingly shifted from businesses to households and concerns over deposit safety mounted following a series of financial panics around the turn of the century and during the Great Depression of the 1930s. Many states passed laws effectively limiting the chartering of new banks, outlawing bank branching across city or county boundaries, and forbidding banking firms from crossing state borders.

Unfortunately, these geographic restrictions on bank expansion proved costly, with bank customers experiencing a reduction in the availability of loans and the variety of services offered, as well as an increase in loan rates and service fees. These geographic rules also became increasingly ineffective as innovative bankers spotted loopholes they could climb through and gradually cover larger and larger geographic markets. For example, many large banks formed *holding companies*—corporations controlling the stock of one or more banks—which acquired networks of smaller banks and nonbank businesses that offered bank-like services but were not subject to legally imposed geographic barriers.

Over time the geographic barriers to bank expansion have been gradually lifted through federal and state legislation (especially during the 1980s and 1990s). (See especially Exhibit 17.2.) The public's fear of possible bank instability has been dealt with more effectively and less costly through alternative regulatory measures—for example, providing increased security for depositors through deposit insurance systems, pursuing closer regulation of bank loan and investment activity, and requiring bank stockholders to bear greater risk of loss should their banks get into trouble. In addition, advances in communications technology and financial innovation have rendered many of the old restrictions simply obsolete.

To be sure, the process of deregulating the banking industry by allowing banks to compete more aggressively across wider geographic markets has been a slow one, proceeding state by state. However, the federal government finally stepped into the process in 1994, passing the Riegle-Neal Interstate Banking and Branching Efficiency Act (see Exhibit 17.3). This sweeping law granted banks the freedom to open branch offices across state lines and permitted banking organizations in any state to be acquired by holding companies (subject to restrictions in some states, such as required regulatory approval). Nearly all states chose to allow interstate banking subject to a variety of special conditions (such as protection from acquisition for newly chartered banks in a few states).

EXHIBIT 17.2	**Key Federal Laws That Have Affected the Structure and Regulation of the U.S. Banking Industry and Foreign Banks Operating in the United States over the Years**
National Bank Act (1863–1964)	Authorized federal chartering and supervision of banks by the Comptroller of the Currency.
Federal Reserve Act (1913)	Created the Federal Reserve System as central bank and guarantor of the banking system's liquidity.
Banking Act of 1933	Created the FDIC to insure the public's deposits and denied banks the power to underwrite corporate securities, separating commercial banking from investment banking.
Bank Holding Company Act (1956)	Required holding companies controlling two or more banks to register with the Federal Reserve Board; prohibited control by out-of-state holding companies of banks within a given state without that state's permission.
Bank Merger Act (1960)	Required mergers involving federally supervised banks to have the approval of their principal federal regulatory agency.
Bank Holding Company Act Amendments (1970)	Made holding companies controlling only one bank subject to Federal Reserve regulation; confined nonbank business ventures of bank holding companies to offering bank-related services.
International Banking Act (1978)	Brought foreign banks operating in the United States under federal regulation for the first time.
Depository Institutions Deregulation and Monetary Control Act (1980)	Granted nonbank thrift institutions broader deposit and credit powers like those possessed by banks, began the phaseout of federal deposit rate ceilings, and imposed uniform deposit reserve requirements on banks and thrifts.
Garn-St Germain Depository Institutions Act (1982)	Authorized banks and thrifts to offer money market deposit accounts and granted thrifts additional commercial and consumer lending powers.
Financial Institutions Reform, Recovery, and Enforcement Act (1989)	Restructured the federal supervisory agencies responsible for monitoring savings and loan associations, allowed bank holding companies to acquire savings and loans, and created two deposit insurance funds—one for banks (BIF) and the other for savings and loans (SAIF) under the FDIC.
Federal Deposit Insurance Corporation Improvement Act (1991)	Provided additional funding and borrowing authority for the FDIC; gave federal regulatory agencies the power to close an undercapitalized bank or thrift; required the FDIC to set deposit insurance fees based on a bank's risk exposure; and imposed new rules on foreign bank expansion inside the United States.
Riegle-Neal Interstate Banking and Branching Efficiency Act (1994)	Allowed holding companies to acquire banks in any state and banks to branch across state lines.
Financial Services Modernization (Gramm-Leach-Bliley) Act (1999)	Permitted financial-service providers to form financial holding companies (FHCs) offering banking, insurance, securities, and other services under one controlling corporation and regulated the sharing of private consumer information.

Information and data on bank mergers appears at multiple Web sites, such as clev.frb.org/research and at fdic.gov

One of the consequences of geographic deregulation has been sharply increased *consolidation* within the banking and thrift industries, including many megamergers that have created the first trillion-dollar banking organizations in U.S. history (such as Citigroup, Bank of America, and J. P. Morgan Chase). To be sure, the federal government moved to impose tighter controls over these mergers through passage of the Bank Merger Act of 1960 and its recent amendments, requiring regulatory approval of any proposed merger and allowing the U.S. Department of Justice to block mergers in the courts if competition, bank safety, or the availability of services to the public are being threatened. Nevertheless, in the wake of thousands of mergers and acquisitions, the U.S. banking industry is more concentrated today than ever before, with the 10 largest banks controlling close to 90 percent of all assets in the U.S. banking system. In more

| **EXHIBIT 17.3** | President Bill Clinton signed this nationwide bank holding company and interstate branching law on September 29, 1994. This sweeping banking law included the following provisions: |

The Riegle-Neal Interstate Banking and Branching Efficiency Act of 1994

1. Holding companies can acquire banks in any state even if state law prohibits such acquisitions.

2. However, no one banking organization can control more than 10 percent of nationwide deposits or more than 30 percent of the deposits in a single state unless a state chooses to waive this limit.

3. A banking organization can merge with banks in other states and convert those acquired banks into branch offices unless the state or states involved elect to "opt out" of interstate branching.

4. Branch offices established by national banks must conform to local laws requiring consumer protection, fair lending, and investments in local communities. Federal regulatory agencies must consider the views of local community organizations prior to closing an interstate banking organization's branch office situated in a low-income neighborhood.

5. Foreign-owned banks with subsidiary corporations based in the United States can acquire banks and branches across state lines to the same extent as U.S. banks.

than two-thirds of the 50 states, in excess of 15 percent of branch offices now belong to out-of-state depository institutions. (Bank of America alone has more than 5500 branches in at least 29 states and more than 500 U.S. banks operate out-of-state branch offices.)

In an effort to guard against excessive concentration in the industry, the Riegle-Neal law held that no one banking organization would be allowed to control more than 10 percent of nationwide deposits or more than 30 percent of all deposits in a single state (unless the state involved chooses to waive this upper limit). Finally, to prevent large interstate banking organizations from draining most of the deposits out of local markets, banks that expand across state lines are required to commit a substantial percentage of their incoming funds to locally based loans, so that branch offices controlled by interstate banks have loan-to-deposit ratios comparable to the average loan-to-deposit ratios in the states they enter.

Regulation of the Services Banks Can Offer

Even as banks have sought greater freedom to expand geographically, they have also fought for, but only occasionally won, new service powers in order to retain their existing customers and attract new ones. Unfortunately, regulations have been tight and sometimes unyielding in this area out of concern for bank safety (as service innovation can be highly risky) and because of a desire to protect certain nonbank financial institutions, such as credit unions and savings and loans, from tough bank competition.

Glass-Steagall Act   Probably the most influential law in American history in defining bank service powers was the **Glass-Steagall Act** (or Banking Act) of 1933. This sweeping law confined bank service powers essentially to the making of loans and the taking of deposits, while insurance services were largely relegated to insurance companies and home lending was centered in savings and loan associations and savings banks. U.S. bankers also lost an important service power they possessed in the decades before Glass-Steagall—the power to assist their largest corporate customers by purchasing corporate stock and then reselling it in the open market. Foreign banks continued to offer corporate bond and stock *underwriting services* to American companies, and U.S. banks were active in the security underwriting business overseas through a variety of affiliated organizations, but until recently they clearly lost customers to security dealers and foreign banks (principally from Canada and Western Europe) in domestic securities' underwriting, except where limited exceptions were granted from federal restrictions. Bankers avidly sought security underwriting powers because this business can be highly profitable and it complements traditional lending services.

Beginning in the late 1980s, the Federal Reserve Board began to permit individual banking organizations on a case-by-case basis to underwrite selected types of securities through separate subsidiaries. For example, individual institutions such as Bankers Trust of New York (part of Deutsche Bank), Citicorp (now Citigroup), and Security Pacific Corporation (now part of Bank of America) were granted authority to underwrite certain loan-backed securities and some forms of corporate debt. In September 1990, J. P. Morgan (now J. P. Morgan Chase) was extended the power to underwrite new issues of corporate stock. By 1998, about 40 U.S. and foreign banking corporations had been approved by the Federal Reserve Board to offer selected debt security underwriting services, while close to a dozen banking companies had received approval to underwrite corporate stock. However, tight restrictions were imposed upon all participating banks. For example, the underwriting of previously forbidden types of securities had to be carried out through a special subsidiary, not by the bank itself, and revenue generated from these previously forbidden underwriting activities could represent only a minor proportion of the total revenues of the underwriting subsidiary.

Despite such restrictions, however, U.S. banks' share of all corporate security underwriting activities grew quite rapidly and many bankers continued to ask for further expansion of their security underwriting powers. However, any proposed changes in the law faced stiff opposition from trade groups, representing those industries banks most wanted to enter, and from public interest groups concerned about consumer rights. There was also concern among bank regulators that affiliation with nonbank industries would stretch the so-called "federal safety net" (e.g., the protection provided by deposit insurance from the FDIC and low-interest loans from the Federal Reserve) to the breaking point.

The Gramm-Leach-Bliley (GLB) Act

Financial Services Modernization (Gramm-Leach-Bliley) Act

financial holding companies (FHCs)

Finally, in November 1999, the **Financial Services Modernization (Gramm-Leach-Bliley or GLB) Act** was passed, permitting banks to affiliate with security underwriting firms, insurance companies, and selected other types of businesses. This could be done by creating **financial holding companies (FHCs)** that own the shares of all of the above businesses or through a subsidiary structure in which a bank or other financial firm operates securities firms and other subsidiaries. This law opened up the United States for the first time in more than half a century to *universal* or *multidimensional* banking. However, surprisingly few financial-service providers rushed out to form FHCs right away—less than a fifth of the largest bank holding companies and a few securities houses, insurance companies, and smaller commercial banking organizations—though 19 of the 20 largest U.S. banks do currently belong to an FHC. Most financial institutions seem content with the organizational structures they already operate and many are waiting to see what the final rules for operating an FHC are going to look like in the near future.

As we saw earlier in Chapter 4, each business affiliated with an FHC is regulated and supervised by its *traditional functional regulator.* For example, the insurance company affiliate of an FHC would be regulated by a state insurance commission, while the securities affiliate would be supervised by the Securities and Exchange Commission (SEC). If the FHC contains a national bank, that bank's primary regulatory supervisor would be the Comptroller of the Currency. Supervision of the FHC as a whole, however, is the responsibility of the Federal Reserve. Any banks belonging to an FHC must be rated "well-capitalized" and "well-managed."

The long-standing debate over U.S. banks being allowed to offer security underwriting services is a reminder of the difficulties the banking industry has always faced when it tries to develop and offer any new services. Bankers have argued that new services could *reduce* bank risk, because the earnings generated by these new services may have a low positive, or even a negative, correlation with the earnings from traditional bank services. For example, during periods of rising short-term interest rates, when long-term interest rates are usually increasing at a slower pace, banks' borrowing costs are often rising more rapidly than their interest income on loans, thus squeezing their profit margins. However, at this same time, the earnings from securities underwriting services or the sale of insurance services could be on the rise, thereby reducing the overall volatility in bank earnings.

Moreover, they contend, unless banks can keep up with shifting public demand for financial services, they are in danger of becoming irrelevant to the workings of the financial system. Regulators, however, generally adopt a "go slow" approach in order to assess the risks involved for depositor safety. Bankers who wish to retain federal deposit insurance coverage must expect that regulations are likely to continue to be a significant hurdle to bank service innovation for the foreseeable future.

The Rise of Disclosure Laws in Banking

One of the most rapidly expanding areas of U.S. banking regulation today centers around *disclosure rules*—regulations requiring financial institutions to reveal certain information to customers (in an effort to encourage shopping around and avoid deception) and to regulators (to improve supervision of the banking industry). Among the most prominent examples are the Truth in Lending Act (1968) and the Truth in Savings Act (1991), which require disclosure of all the interest rates and fees associated with selling loans and deposits to individuals. Similarly, the Home Mortgage Disclosure Act (1975) requires banks to report to the public and to regulators the locations of both their approved and rejected applications for loans to purchase or improve homes as a check on possible discrimination in home lending. The FDIC Improvement Act (1991) requires banks and other depositories to notify customers and regulators in advance when branch offices are to be closed. Finally, the Community Reinvestment Act (1977) stipulates that bankers must make an affirmative effort to serve *all* segments of their trade territory, including low-income neighborhoods, and to disclose to the public their community service performance ratings. Regulators must review a bank's community service record before approving its request to offer new services, merge with or acquire other businesses, or set up new facilities.

A "reverse disclosure" law appeared in the U.S. in 1999 under the label of the Financial Services Modernization (GLB) Act. This new set of government rules permits customers of banks and selected other financial-service providers to stop the sharing of at least some of their *nonpublic personal information* with other businesses, except that customers must contact their financial institutions and indicate that they do not wish their personal data to be conveyed to others (such as to telemarketing firms). Otherwise, information sharing is generally permitted. Under a strict interpretation of the GLB Act, information sharing about customers can occur among affiliates of the *same company* and the customer involved cannot legally stop that. However, each covered financial-service provider must publish at least once a year a *privacy policy statement* and offer its customers the right to "opt out" of at least some personal information sharing. The firm issuing this statement can even decide not to share its customers' personal data with affiliates of the same company if it wishes to do so, thereby placing tougher restrictions on itself than the law requires.

These and other disclosure rules have aroused a storm of controversy. For most such rules, it is not clear that the benefits of greater disclosure outweigh the costs involved. For example, the U.S. Office of Management and Budget has estimated that U.S. bankers commit an average of at least 7.5 million hours each year just to comply with

For a review of the new rules on customer privacy and the sharing of personal information, see the Web site maintained by the Federal Trade Commission (FTC) at ftc.gov

the Truth in Lending Act mentioned above. Nor is it clear that the public pays much attention to these disclosure requirements.

The Growing Importance of Capital Regulation in Banking

In addition to the spread of interstate banking and the explosion in branching activity by banks in the United States, another major trend today that is reshaping the regulation of banks and other financial institutions globally centers upon their *capital*—the long-term funds invested in a financial institution, mainly by its owners. For example, when stockholders buy ownership shares in a bank, they have a claim against the bank's earnings and assets. However, a bank's stockholders bear all the risks of ownership. If the bank fails to generate sufficient earnings, the stockholders may receive no dividend income, and if the bank fails, they could lose everything.

Beginning in the 1980s, bank regulators in leading industrialized countries (including the United States, Canada, Japan, and the nations of Western Europe) came to the conclusion that regulatory control of risk taking by banks is best centered upon a bank's *owners*. When a bank chooses to take on more risk, its owners should be asked to increase their financial commitment to the bank by supplying more capital. Because stockholder capital is expensive to raise and could be lost completely if the bank fails, the owners of the bank are likely to monitor the bank's risk taking more closely, pressuring management to be more prudent in taking on added risk.

Basel I   This concept of making the owners more responsible for the consequences of risk taking by their banks led in June 1988 to the adoption of *minimum capital standards* for all banks in the leading countries of Western Europe, Canada, Japan, and the
Basel I Agreement   United States. The so-called **Basel I Agreement** (named for Basel, Switzerland,

523

Additional information regarding the terms of the Basel I Agreement on bank capital and its importance for the banking industry may be found at bis.org

where it was first adopted) stipulated that banks in all participating nations must have a minimum ratio of total capital to risk-weighted assets and other risk-exposed items of 8 percent. Risk-weighted assets are determined by classifying each of a bank's assets listed on its balance sheet into categories based on each asset's degree of risk exposure and then multiplying the volume of assets in each risk category by a risk weight ranging from 0 for cash and government securities to 1.00 for commercial loans and other higher-risk assets. Thus:

$$\begin{array}{l}\text{Total risk-weighted}\\\text{assets on a bank's}\\\text{balance sheet}\end{array} = \begin{array}{l}0 \times (\text{Cash and U.S. government securities}) + 0.20 \times (\text{Other}\\\text{types of government securities and interbank deposits}) +\\0.50 \times (\text{Residential mortgage loans, government revenue}\\\text{bonds, and selected types of mortgage-backed securities}) +\\1.00 \times (\text{Commercial and consumer loans and other assets}\\\text{of the highest risk exposure})\end{array}$$

The Basel I Agreement was unique in also including off-balance-sheet commitments that banks often make to their largest customers and often use to hedge themselves against risk, including credit commitments to grant future loans and futures, options, and swap contracts. The amount of each off-balance-sheet item is multiplied by a fractional amount known as its "credit-equivalent" value, which is, in turn, multiplied by a risk weight based on its assumed degree of risk exposure. The volume of risk-weighted off-balance-sheet items is then added to a bank's total risk-weighted on-balance-sheet assets. Thus:

$$\begin{array}{l}\text{Total risk-weighted}\\\text{on- and off-balance-}\\\text{sheet items}\end{array} = \begin{array}{l}\text{Total risk-weighted}\\\text{assets on a bank's}\\\text{balance sheet}\end{array} + \begin{array}{l}\text{Total risk-weighted}\\\text{off-balance-sheet}\\\text{items}\end{array}$$

To determine a bank's total capital, its longer-maturity liabilities and its equity (owners') capital are classified into two broad categories:

$$\begin{array}{l}\text{Tier-one, or}\\\text{permanent (core)}\\\text{bank capital}\end{array} = \begin{array}{l}\text{Tangible equity including common stock} + \text{Perpetual}\\\text{preferred stock} + \text{Surplus} + \text{Retained earnings} +\\\text{Capital reserves} - \text{Intangibles}\end{array}$$

$$\begin{array}{l}\text{Tier-two, or}\\\text{supplemental}\\\text{capital}\end{array} = \begin{array}{l}\text{Subordinated capital notes and debentures over}\\5 \text{ years to maturity} + \text{Limited-life preferred}\\\text{stock} + \text{Loan-loss reserves}\end{array}$$

The Basel I Agreement required each bank in all participating countries to achieve and hold the following *capital minimums:*

$$\frac{\text{Tier-one capital}}{\begin{array}{c}\text{Total risk-weighted on- and}\\\text{off-balance-sheet items}\end{array}} = \text{At least } 0.04, \text{ or } 4 \text{ percent}$$

$$\frac{\text{Total tier-one plus tier-two capital}}{\begin{array}{c}\text{Total risk-weighted on- and off-}\\\text{balance-sheet items}\end{array}} = \text{No less than } 0.08, \text{ or } 8 \text{ percent}$$

Thus, a bank with a 4 percent tier-one capital ratio and a 5 percent tier-two capital ratio would have a ratio of total capital to risk-weighted on- and off-balance-sheet items of 9 percent, 1 percent above the minimum required. However, if a bank had only a 3 percent tier-one capital ratio and a tier-two capital ratio of 5 percent, it would actually fall *below* the minimum 8 percent total capital ratio. This is because it would need to have at least a 4 percent tier-one capital ratio and could count toward meeting the Basel I capital requirements only an amount of tier-two capital up to the amount of its tier-one capital. Thus, this bank would be short 1 percent in tier-one capital and would have to work out a plan with its principal regulatory agency to raise the additional amount of required tier-one capital.

In the United States and selected other countries, a bank holding more than the required minimum amount of capital is allowed to expand its services and service facilities with few or no regulatory restrictions imposed. However, if bank capital drops below the minimum percentage of risk-exposed assets, regulatory restrictions become increasingly strict, restraining the bank's growth and subjecting its operations to greater supervision. This regulatory policy, called *prompt corrective action,* was adopted in the United States with passage of the FDIC Improvement Act of 1991. In addition, as we saw earlier, the FDIC Improvement Act required riskier, inadequately capitalized U.S. banks to pay higher fees for government deposit insurance.

Basel II It wasn't long before Basel I began to show signs of serious weakness as a vehicle for promoting bank safety and soundness. Regulators soon realized that Basel I's capital rules were failing on at least two grounds: (1) they failed to pick up important differences in risk exposure from bank to bank; and (2) they couldn't keep up with the rapid pace of innovation occurring in the banking industry, which tends to make old regulations obsolete in a hurry. A new regulatory system was required that would allow for adjustments in bank capital based on the relative amounts and types of risk that each bank actually faced.

Moreover, clever bankers were discovering loopholes in the Basel I system and taking advantage of them. For example, as we saw in the preceding numerical example regarding the capital minimums required by Basel I, bank assets and off-balance-sheet items were grouped into broad *risk categories*—so broad, in fact, that assets and off-balance-sheet items of significantly different risk often carried the *same* capital requirements. (For example, credit card loans and business loans carried the same risk weights under Basel I, despite significant differences in loss rates between these two types of loans.) Bankers quickly discovered that they could boost returns by shifting from lower-risk assets to higher-risk assets bearing the same Basel I risk weight and, therefore, the same capital requirements. Thus, banks were taking on additional risk without necessarily having to make additions to their capital in order to counter that added risk.

Accordingly, the Basel Committee on International Bank Capital Standards set to work on developing a *new* set of guidelines that have come to be known as the **Basel II Agreement.** This new approach, scheduled to take effect in 2007 or 2008, focuses primarily upon the largest banks in the world. Banks that qualify for the Basel II approach (most likely, about 20 of the largest international banks) will be allowed to develop their own internal models of risk assessment (known as the *internal-ratings-based* [IRB] approach) and use those models to calculate their own risk exposure and capital requirements. These models must be able to measure the "value at risk" (VAR) that each bank holds in its asset portfolio, which in turn must be subjected to "stress tests" that project how well the value of that portfolio will hold up when confronted with a wide range of possible market conditions (such as an interest-rate change of 200 basis points or a dramatic shift in the shape and slope of the yield curve).

Basel II recognizes that banks of roughly the same size may have quite different capital requirements based upon their own unique service menus and patterns of risk exposure and that the banks themselves are best able to assess that risk. For example, banks of comparable size and location may offer quite different menus of wholesale

Basel II Agreement

(business) and retail (consumer) banking services and hold widely varying amounts of such risky assets as corporate stock and securitized loans. Of course, the risk-assessment models developed by these banks and their calculation of minimum capital requirements are both subject to regulatory review to determine if the methods used are "reasonable."

Basel II considers a wider range of bank risk exposures than did Basel I. While Basel I was primarily directed at measuring credit (default) risk, Basel II brings in refined estimates of market risk exposure and adds new capital requirements for *operational risk* (i.e., the risk of losses banks can suffer from such events as crime and destructive weather, the breakdown of internal information systems, failed transactions processing, workplace hazards, etc.). Bank capital must be sufficient to offset *all* of these potential risk exposures. Basel II also places greater emphasis on increased public disclosure of banks' true risk situation, allowing the *marketplace* to play a greater role in disciplining banks that engage in reckless behavior.

This is not to say that Basel II solves all of the problems of modern banking regulation. Quite to the contrary, it faces significant problems of its own. For one thing, Basel II will place great demands on regulators to become better trained in their understanding of bank risk and in using the sophisticated tools available to deal with that risk. Moreover, not all of the components of bank risk are, as of yet, satisfactorily measurable. This means that a bank's total risk exposure will still remain something of a "hazy" estimate.

Moreover, the risk-determining models currently available cannot be satisfactorily applied inside the majority of banks—which are far smaller than the leading international money-center banks for which Basel II was developed. A compromise approach needs to be worked out for smaller banks; most likely, it will include many of the elements of Basel I.

The Unfinished Agenda for Banking Regulation

The tremendous changes in banking regulation in recent years—including the adoption of nationwide banking and universal banking with multiple financial services in the United States and the spreading internationalization of bank regulation as evidenced by the Basel I and II Agreements on bank capital—might lead us to think that there is little left to do in reshaping the future structure of bank regulation. Nothing could be further from the truth! Banking in the United States and in most other countries of the world remains heavily burdened by constraining government rules. Slowly, and along something of a zig-zag path, banking is experiencing an era of *deregulation*, as legal constraints are being lifted on a variety of banking activities.

More and more regulators of financial institutions are handing over a large share of the regulation and supervision of financial-service providers and the financial system to the *private marketplace*. If a financial institution is viewed as too risky, the marketplace will make it pay for that added risk by increasing its funding costs. Moreover, financial institutions' regulation is focusing increasingly upon the quality and comprehensiveness of the financial firm's *risk management systems*, making sure each financial-service provider understands the risk it faces and has adequate internal controls to deal with that risk. As we saw in the preceding section on the Basel Agreements, a key element in managing risk is making sure each financial institution has *adequate capital* (particularly the capital supplied by its owners) to protect itself from large and unexpected losses due to risk.

It seems clear that *market data* will be used much more heavily in the future to assess the condition and performance of banks and other financial-service providers. The marketplace will be used as a supplement to the work of regulatory supervisors in order to yield a more complete picture of the financial firm's risk exposure. Among the key market data items regulators will likely watch are:

1. A financial institution's stock price and stock price volatility (equity risk).
2. The market value and interest rate attached to senior debt instruments issued by a bank or other financial institution (such as subordinated notes and debentures).
3. The volume and interest cost attached to uninsured liabilities (such as deposits not covered by federal deposit insurance).
4. Changes in the proportion of uninsured liabilities (such as uninsured deposits) relative to other sources of funding for a financial firm.

In brief, *market-based information* seems to offer for the future a low-cost method of evaluating the condition and riskiness of banks and other financial-service firms that will aid supervisory and regulatory agencies in doing their job better. *Supervision of financial institutions in the future will rest primarily upon three main pillars: government examinations, capital requirements, and the discipline provided by the private marketplace.*

QUESTIONS TO HELP YOU STUDY

1. What are the principal *purposes* or *goals* of financial institutions' regulation?
2. What impact does *regulation* appear to have upon the availability and cost of financial services to the public? Upon financial institutions themselves?
3. What principal agencies are responsible for the regulation and supervision of commercial banks? What aspects of banking does each agency regulate and supervise?
4. How is the nature of government regulation of financial institutions changing today? What is the new focus of recent regulation? Why do you think this change is occurring?
5. What are the principal features of the Financial Services Modernization (Gramm-Leach-Bliley) Act? Why was it passed?
6. How will Gramm-Leach-Bliley likely affect the structure of the banking and financial-service industries? Why?
7. How will Gramm-Leach-Bliley affect the disclosure of financial information and the privacy rights of the customers of financial-service firms? Do you think additional legislation is needed in this field?
8. What are the *Basel I* and *Basel II* agreements? What is their purpose?
9. What types of *market data* will be used more intensively in the future to aid the regulators of banks and other financial institutions?

Information about credit union regulations may be found at the federal level through the National Credit Union Administration site at ncua.gov. If you are interested in state regulatory agency information, call up the particular state in question. If you want to find out about financial institutions' regulation in foreign countries, you may want to call up their names—for example, in Canada look at the Department of Finance at fin.gc.ca

17.4 The Regulation of Thrift Institutions

As we saw in Chapter 15, nonbank thrift institutions include credit unions, savings and loan associations, savings banks, and money market mutual funds. Like commercial banks, each of these institutions also faces an impressive array of federal or state regulations, or both.

Credit Unions

In the United States, credit unions are chartered and regulated at both the state and federal levels (see Exhibit 17.4). Today about three-fifths of all credit unions are chartered by the

EXHIBIT 17.4	Government Agencies That Regulate the Nonbank Thrifts (U.S. Federal and State Agencies)				
Nonbank Thrift Institution	Chartering and Licensing of Thrifts	Setting Up New Branches	Mergers and Acquisitions	Deposit Insurance	Supervision and Examination
Credit unions	National Credit Union Administration (NCUA)/state credit union or banking departments	No approval required	NCUA/state credit union or banking departments	NCUA Share Insurance Fund/state deposit insurance departments	NCUA/state credit union or banking departments
Savings and loan associations	Office of Thrift Supervision/ state banking or savings and loan departments	Office of Thrift Supervision/ Federal Deposit Insurance Corporation (FDIC)/state banking or savings and loan departments	Office of Thrift Supervision/ FDIC/state banking or savings and loan departments	FDIC's Savings Association Insurance Fund/state insurance departments	Office of Thrift Supervision/ state banking or savings and loan departments
Savings banks	Office of Thrift Supervision/ state banking departments	Office of Thrift Supervision/ state banking departments	Office of Thrift Supervision/ FDIC/state banking departments	FDIC/state insurance departments	FDIC/state banking departments
Money market funds	Securities and Exchange Commission (SEC)	No approval required	No approval required	No government insurance; some funds have private insurance	SEC for selected activities

Source: Federal Reserve Bank of New York, and the author.

National Credit Union Administration (NCUA)

federal government; the remainder are chartered by the states. Federal credit unions have been regulated since 1970 by the **National Credit Union Administration (NCUA)**—an independent agency within the federal government. Deposits are insured by the National Credit Union Share Insurance Fund (NCUSIF) up to $100,000. State-chartered credit unions may qualify for federal insurance if they conform to NCUA's regulations.

Credit unions, like banks, are closely regulated in the services they can offer the public, the investments they can make with their depositors' money, and the types of deposits they can sell. Fortunately for the industry, regulations have been liberalized in recent years through such federal deregulation laws as the **Depository Institutions Deregulation and Monetary Control Act (DIDMCA)** (1980), which gave U.S. credit unions the power to offer checkable deposits (share drafts) and home mortgage (real estate) loans in order to be able to compete effectively with commercial banks.

Depository Institutions Deregulation and Monetary Control Act (DIDMCA)

For further information on the current regulation of credit unions, see the National Association of State Credit Union Supervisors at nascus.org

Savings and Loans

Savings and loan associations are also regulated by and can receive their charter of incorporation from either state or federal government agencies. About half have charters from state authorities who supervise their activities and regularly examine their books, while the remainder have federal charters. Federal savings and loans are insured (up to a maximum of $100,000 per depositor) by the Savings Association Insurance Fund (SAIF) managed by the Federal Deposit Insurance Corporation (FDIC).

S&Ls chartered by the states also may qualify for insurance coverage from the FDIC. Both federally chartered and federally insured state associations are supervised and examined by the **Office of Thrift Supervision (OTS)** of the U.S. Treasury Department, and the FDIC also has certain S&L supervisory powers, such as regulating the capital positions of these savings associations. Qualified S&Ls can borrow emergency funds from the Federal Home Loan Banks and from the discount windows of the Federal Reserve banks.

Regulation of the savings and loan industry over the past two decades has resembled a roller coaster, with wide swings from deregulating the industry to imposing much tougher restrictions. For example, two major laws passed in the early 1980s—the Depository Institutions Deregulation and Monetary Control Act of 1980 and the **Garn-St Germain Depository Institutions Act** of 1982—granted federally supervised savings and loans major new service powers (such as credit cards and consumer installment loans) so they could compete directly with commercial banks. Then, after hundreds of S&Ls failed in the 1980s and early 1990s, in part because they sometimes moved too quickly to offer these new services, the federal government substantially tightened the rules surrounding savings and loan operations with passage of the **Financial Institutions Reform, Recovery, and Enforcement Act (FIRREA)** of 1989. No longer could S&Ls buy low-quality (junk) bonds, and the majority of their lending had to be focused on the housing industry. Designed to restore public confidence in savings and loans, this new law stipulated that to be a "qualified thrift lender" (QTL), eligible for special tax benefits and able to borrow funds at low cost from the Federal Home Loan Banks—a lender of last resort for the industry—S&Ls must hold a minimum of 70 percent of their total assets in real estate mortgage loans, mortgage-backed securities, and other qualifying assets.

This latter provision of the Financial Institutions Reform, Recovery, and Enforcement Act proved to be severely constraining on S&Ls that chose to remain in the thrift industry. Many converted to commercial or savings banks to enjoy more freedom and flexibility. In November 1991, these restrictive rules limiting S&L asset diversification were eased somewhat with passage of the FDIC Improvement Act, allowing savings associations to become qualified thrift lenders (QTLs) if a minimum of 65 percent of their portfolio assets were in mortgage-related investments or other qualified assets. Moreover, a portion of consumer loans and mortgage loans previously sold could be counted toward meeting the new requirements to qualify for special federal tax benefits as a QTL. (See Exhibit 17.5.)

The savings and loan industry was further jolted by tough new *regulatory forbearance* rules when the Financial Institutions Reform, Recovery, and Enforcement Act was passed in 1989 and when the FDIC Improvement Act (FDICIA) appeared in 1991. Prior to these laws, regulatory agencies often allowed insolvent S&Ls, banks, and other depository institutions to keep their doors open, and permitted them to pay higher and higher interest rates in an effort to keep the public's deposits invested in these troubled institutions. This form of regulatory forbearance drove up deposit costs for all depository institutions and, on occasion, drove some healthy banks and S&Ls to the point of failure. Moreover, if the regulators were eventually forced to close the insolvent institutions, the delay in taking action made it difficult to sell the failed institutions to healthy companies for enough money to recover all the costs involved. While regulatory forbearance was originally designed to save deposit insurance money, it often wound up costing the government's insurance fund more in the long run.

Congress put a stop to regulatory forbearance when the **FDIC Improvement Act (FDICIA)** was passed. Under this law, a bank or thrift can be closed if its ratio of

Office of Thrift Supervision (OTS)

Garn-St Germain Depository Institutions Act

Financial Institutions Reform, Recovery, and Enforcement Act (FIRREA)

S&Ls are among the world's leading institutions in residential mortgage lending, which presents its own regulatory challenges. For further information on regulation in this area, see the Web site of the American Association of Residential Mortgage Regulators at aarmr.org

FDIC Improvement Act (FDICIA)

EXHIBIT 17.5

Major Provisions of the Federal Deposit Insurance Corporation Improvement Act of 1991 Applying to Savings and Loan Associations, Other Thrifts, and Banks

Recapitalization of the FDIC and Protecting Federal Insurance Reserves

1. The Federal Deposit Insurance Corporation (FDIC) is empowered to borrow an additional $30 billion from the U.S. Treasury to be repaid from future insurance premiums. The FDIC may also borrow using the assets of failed institutions as collateral.

2. Federal regulators may close an undercapitalized bank or thrift institution that is not yet insolvent. Critically undercapitalized institutions (with capital/asset ratios below 2 percent) may be placed in receivership. Regulations become increasingly strict as a depository institution's capital position weakens and may include requiring a merger, restricting growth, and replacing management.

3. Riskier depository institutions will be assessed higher insurance fees. The FDIC must assess sufficient fees to bring federal insurance reserves up to at least 1.25 percent of all insured deposits.

4. The FDIC may prohibit undercapitalized depository institutions or those with no more than average capital from accepting deposits placed with them by security brokers unless the FDIC finds this is not unsafe.

New Rules on Services Offered and Foreign Banks

1. Misleading advertising of deposits is prohibited and any adverse change in deposit terms must be communicated to depositors 30 days prior to the change. Moreover, any insured depository institution must notify its customers and its principal regulator at least 90 days before closing any branch office.

2. Savings and loans may qualify for special benefits (e.g., tax benefits and borrowing from the Federal Home Loan Banks at low cost) if at least 65 percent of their total assets are in mortgage-related assets or other qualified assets.

3. The Federal Reserve Board must approve new offices and service activities of foreign banks and can revoke a foreign bank's license to operate in the United States if it is pursuing unsafe or illegal activities or is not adequately supervised by regulators in its home country.

4. Federal savings associations can loan up to 35 percent of their total assets to individuals and families.

5. Savings associations and banks can merge with each other, subject to regulatory approval.

---

tangible equity capital to total assets falls below 2 percent for more than 90 days. The troubled institution *must* be closed down or sold to a healthy firm if its undercapitalized condition lasts for more than 270 days. Thus, bank and thrift regulators do not have to wait until a depository institution has zero capital (i.e., is technically bankrupt) to close it, permitting the regulators to sell the troubled institution while it still retains enough value to interest potential buyers.

One final regulatory problem facing the savings and loan industry over the past decade centered upon SAIF—the federal Savings Association Insurance Fund administered by the FDIC. When Congress passed the Financial Institutions Reform, Recovery, and Enforcement Act of 1989, it mandated that all federal deposit insurance pools must be built up to a point where $1.25 in insurance reserves are available to cover each $100 in insured deposits by no later than 2006. The Bank Insurance Fund (BIF) reached the mandated insurance coverage goal in 1995, and bankers were told that their federal insurance fees would be reduced from about 24 cents per $100 of insured deposits to about 4 cents per $100. (Subsequently, adequately capitalized banks with acceptable examiner ratings had their insurance fees set at zero.) SAIF, on the other hand, was far away from the minimum-coverage goal, meaning savings and loans and other thrifts insured by SAIF would have to pay much larger federal insurance fees than commercial banks for a time. Eventually, Congress levied a special assessment against thrift institutions to bring their federal insurance reserves closer to required government standards and to level deposit insurance costs so that banks and thrifts faced more nearly equal insurance fees.

Savings Banks

To learn more about the regulation of savings associations, you may wish to examine the Web site of the Office of Thrift Supervision at ots.treas.gov at the federal level and, at the state level, the American Council of State Savings Supervisors at acsss.org

Savings banks, like savings and loans, can be chartered by either the states or the federal government. State and federal governments also share responsibility for insuring savings bank deposits (see again Exhibit 17.4). However, most savings banks have deposits insured by the Federal Deposit Insurance Corporation up to $100,000. Regulations are designed to insure maximum safety of deposits. This is accomplished principally through close control over the types of assets a savings bank is permitted to acquire. For example, state law and the "prudent person" rule enforced by the courts generally limit savings bank investments to first-mortgage loans, U.S. government and federal agency securities, high-grade corporate bonds and stocks, and municipal bonds. Investment powers are heavily restricted in this industry because it focuses upon small depositors who may not be able to evaluate the riskiness of these institutions. On the negative side, however, these strict regulations limit the flexibility of savings banks in responding to shifting customer service needs.

One regulatory issue involving savings banks that has rocketed into public prominence recently concerns the trend toward converting mutuals into stockholder-owned savings associations. As we saw in Chapter 15, the purpose of these mutual-to-stock conversions is to infuse new capital into these organizations and force them to become more profit and cost conscious and act in the interest of their owners. Unfortunately, these conversions have sometimes led to multi-million-dollar windfalls for the managements and boards of directors of mutuals, with few gains for the depositors—who, legally at least, own a mutual savings bank. Employees and trustees of these associations sometimes award themselves options to buy a major proportion of the converted savings banks' new stock. The management of the converting bank may pick an appraisal firm that underprices the initial stock offering. When trading begins in the new stock, its price rises rapidly to its true market value and insiders may score substantial capital gains.

Recently, U.S. regulators began to clamp down on these mutual-to-stock conversions. In the case of savings banks, the FDIC requires the submission of a conversion plan, which that agency can approve or disapprove in an effort to make sure that depositors are not cheated and that "insiders" in a mutual are not "unjustly enriched."

Money Market Funds

The final type of nonbank thrift institution is the *money market mutual fund.* Because this financial intermediary sells shares in pools of securities, it is primarily regulated by the U.S. Securities and Exchange Commission (SEC), which limits the majority of money market fund investments (95 percent or more) to top-quality securities and restricts the maximum and average maturity of money market fund security holdings. The SEC requires money funds to issue a prospectus to any potential buyer of their shares detailing the objectives of the fund, describing its recent performance, and revealing in what assets the shareholders' money has been invested. Today, in an effort to protect the small individual saver, money funds must remind their customers that their shares are *not* government insured and, therefore, may not always be able to maintain their par (usually $1.00) value.

17.5 The Regulation of Insurance Companies

While not quite as heavily regulated as commercial banks, insurance companies face tough regulations that are imposed primarily by state insurance commissions. The fundamental purpose of insurance company regulation is to ensure that the public is not overcharged or poorly served and to guarantee adequate compensation to insurance companies themselves. A new insurance company must be chartered under the rules of a particular home state (with most selecting states that have the most lenient rules, such as Arizona or Delaware). Once chartered, each company must submit periodic reports to state commissions, its agents must be licensed by the states, and the terms of its policies (including the premium rates it charges policyholders) must be approved.

Both the courts and state commissions insist that any investments of incoming policyholder premiums must conform to the common law standard of a "prudent person." While, as we saw in Chapter 16, speculative investments by insurance companies rose considerably in the 1980s, recent periods have ushered in a more conservative standard, with state insurance commissions inside the United States and regulators in other countries putting great pressure on insurance companies to significantly increase the quality of their asset portfolios and to maintain minimum levels of capital as protection against risk. Finally, federal law at the end of the twentieth century permitted banks and insurance companies to affiliate with each other inside the United States, similar to what other nations (especially those in Western Europe) have allowed for some time. To facilitate such mergers between banks and insurers, an increased number of insurers have recently converted from mutual to stockholder-owned companies.

17.6 The Regulation of Pension Funds

Because pension funds have risen rapidly to hold the bulk of the retirement savings of millions of workers, they have been subject to much heavier regulation by the courts and government agencies in recent years. Because employers—the principal creators and managers of pension plans—have an incentive to take on considerable risk in an effort to minimize the cost burden they must carry, many pension plans even today remain only *partially funded;* that is, the market value of their assets plus expected investment income does *not* fully cover all the benefits promised to pension plan members. While English common law requires pension plans to be "prudent" managers of their members' retirement savings, many pensions have branched out into riskier investments, including real estate projects and derivative securities contracts.

Responding to concerns about pension safety and employee accessibility, the U.S. Congress during the 1970s passed the Employee Retirement Income Security Act (ERISA), which requires full funding of all private pensions and prudent investment policies. ERISA granted employees the right to join a pension program, in most cases, after only one year on the job. More rapid *vesting* of accumulated benefits was also required so that employees can recover a higher proportion of their past contributions should they decide to retire early or move to another job. Trying to eliminate the danger that pensions may not have adequate funds to pay future claims against them, Congress now requires employers eventually to cover any past liabilities not fully funded at present. In addition, a federal agency, the Pension Benefit Guaranty Corporation (PBGC or "Penny Benny") was created to insure some vested employee benefits. Currently, Penny Benny insures the pension benefits of close to 40 million U.S. workers who belong to about 85,000 defined-benefit pension plans.

When it was founded, Penny Benny was expected to be self-supporting, receiving inflows of cash from insurance premiums, from its own investments, and from the assets received from companies turning their pension plans over to Penny Benny. By the early 1990s, however, Penny Benny had taken over more than 1,600 pension plans, and its liabilities were larger than its assets. Some experts fear a financial crisis in the future as the number of retired persons continues to increase, demanding an increasing volume of pension benefits.

Under the law, Penny Benny must insure all *defined benefit plans* (that is, those promising a fixed amount of income at retirement). This has meant that Penny Benny has become relatively less important with the passage of time because more and more pension programs are becoming *defined-contribution* retirement plans, in which no specific level of retirement benefits is promised. Nevertheless, to insure the pension plans for which it is responsible, Penny Benny assesses a flat insurance premium for each pension plan and does not charge riskier pension plans a higher insurance fee. This creates a "moral hazard," with riskier pensions being subsidized by safer ones. Moreover, Penny Benny currently has no legal authority to regulate pension funds, nor does it receive any substantial financial support from the government, having only a small line of credit with the U.S. Treasury.

Clearly, there is a pressing need for pension plan reform so that *all* pension plan members can have reasonable assurance of receiving their benefits. Recently proposed reforms include charging higher insurance premiums and placing a freeze on additional Penny Benny guarantees for those corporate pension plans that have been severely underfunded for a long period of time. Other recent reform proposals in the pension sector, particularly since the collapse of Enron Corporation, are aimed at providing greater protection for employees who have defined-contribution retirement plans. Of special concern are those pension plans heavily invested in their sponsoring company's own stock. Recent reforms, both actual and proposed, would require employers sponsoring a pension plan to more frequently update their employees on the condition and performance of their pension accounts, mandate greater diversification of pension-plan portfolios to promote increased risk protection for employees, provide easier access to investment advice for pension account holders, and allow employees to sell company stock more quickly when they feel the need to seek out other investment assets.

17.7 The Regulation of Finance Companies

As we saw in Chapter 16, finance companies rank among the most important lenders to consumers and businesses in recent years. The bulk of regulation of this industry is at the state level and focuses principally upon the making of consumer loans. Several states impose maximum loan rates so that finance companies are limited in the amount of interest they can charge consumers, which tends to limit the volume of credit extended to riskier households. The states, trying to protect consumers, also usually spell out the rules for installment loan contracts and the conditions under which automobiles, furniture, home appliances, or other household assets can be repossessed for nonpayment of a loan extended by a finance company.

New forms of small finance companies have, in recent years, spread across the United States, making the riskiest of consumer loans. These so-called "payday loan companies," "title loan companies," "rent to own" firms, and "check-cashing" outlets are regulated by state governments with some states placing ceilings on the loan rates they may charge and imposing minimum capital requirements on each small-loan company. Several other states have either outlawed these institutions or restricted their growth due to concerns that they may take advantage of troubled borrowers who often have to surrender their property when they cannot meet the high interest rates (frequently over 100 percent) that these firms often charge.

17.8 The Regulation of Investment Companies (Mutual Funds)

Investment companies (or mutual funds), which invest primarily in pools of stocks or bonds on behalf of individuals and institutional customers, are regulated predominantly by the federal government in the United States. Among the most important controlling

For additional information on the regulation of investment companies and other security-issuing and security-trading firms, see especially the Web site of the North American Association of Securities Administrators at nasaa.org

federal laws are the Investment Company Act and Investment Advisers Act, passed by the U.S. Congress in 1940. Registration of investment company ownership shares and the submission of periodic reports to the Securities and Exchange Commission (SEC) are mandatory under current U.S. law. The SEC requires mutual funds to provide their customers with a *prospectus* that describes each company's goals, performance, and financial condition. It is the SEC's duty to make sure the rights of investment company shareholders are fully protected, including the shareholders' right to elect at least two-thirds of an investment company's board of directors and the right to approve the choice of an investment advisory service that will manage the investment company's asset portfolio and make buy/sell decisions. In 2003 and 2004 the SEC crafted several new rules to promote fair dealing by mutual funds, including requiring that their boards be at least 75 percent independent and that funds have regulatory compliance officers.

17.9 An Overview of Trends in the Regulation of Financial Institutions

In this chapter we have tried to convey at least a sense of the great complexity of regulations that surround the financial institutions' sector and the rationale for those regulations. We have seen that regulation is rooted in the belief that financial institutions occupy a special place in the economy and that the behavior and performance of financial institutions can profoundly affect the welfare of businesses, governments, and households. Thus, regulation seeks to promote the safety and stability of financial institutions in order to preserve the confidence of the public and avoid institutional failures.

Unfortunately, the regulation of financial institutions has not proceeded at a measured pace over time. New regulations often have been piled on top of old regulations, in many cases set up to deal with problems that are no longer important in today's economy. Thus, regulations can become a costly burden that significantly increases financial institutions' operating costs and limits the cleansing effects of failure and competition. The research evidence suggests that the ultimate impact of regulation is to restrict the entry of new competitors, raising financial service prices but also reducing the likelihood of institutional failures.

The thrust of regulation is changing. It is seeking a lower profile as governments around the world seek to pull back from the financial marketplace somewhat and allow the management and owners of financial institutions to face more fully the competition of the marketplace and to respond directly to customers' demands rather than to regulators' demands alone. Instead of seeking to wall off and protect one type of financial institution from another, there is growing recognition that the distinctions between financial institutions are blurring and that, eventually, all financial firms must learn how to compete with one another and how to be efficient enough to survive without government support.

Regulators are letting *markets* do more of the regulation of financial firms and they are also learning how to *cooperate* more because the financial-service companies they oversee are becoming more alike and acquiring each other. In short, regulators must share more information with each other in order to be effective in the future. Indeed, there is a trend in Europe toward creating just one regulator to supervise *all* financial-service providers.

As financial-service industries are gradually being deregulated, the focus of regulation is moving away from control over services offered and geographic expansion to *controlling risk taking*. As we have seen in this chapter, more regulatory attention has recently been focused upon the amount of *capital* contributed by a financial institution's owners relative to the amount of risk accepted in a financial institution's assets and in its off-balance-sheet activities. Regulators increasingly are insisting that financial institutions have in place written plans describing their policies and

One of the most important regulators of mutual funds and other financial institutions in the United States is the **Securities and Exchange Commission (SEC)**, created by the Securities Exchange Act of 1934. The SEC requires that a mutual fund or other business selling new securities to the public provide a potential investor with a *prospectus* that truthfully describes the nature of operations of the offering company, its management and financial condition, the purpose of the new security offering, and any legal actions pending against the company. Security issuers must also file a *registration statement* with the SEC. Any false or misleading information in an SEC registration statement may subject the offending party to criminal penalties and lawsuits from investors who may have relied on such statements and lost money in the process.

The SEC also sets rules for the operation of securities exchanges, such as the New York Stock Exchange and the American Stock Exchange. Each exchange must set its own rules consistent with SEC guidelines and enforce those rules to ensure fair practices. If any exchange fails to effectively regulate itself, the SEC may step in to enforce securities laws. Passage of the Maloney Act of 1939 extended the SEC's power to regulate the over-the-counter securities market as well as the securities exchanges. The SEC limits the amount of debt a securities dealer can take on in an effort to protect the public against losses on security trading resulting from the failure of a dealer firm.

With passage of the Investment Advisers and Investment Company Acts of 1940, the SEC was granted power to regulate those who give investment advice for pay—investment advisers—and investment companies or mutual funds. A professional adviser must register with the SEC; however, the SEC doesn't usually investigate to determine if an adviser is competent or competitive.

For mutual funds, the Investment Company Act requires that these intermediaries invest no more than 5 percent of their assets in securities issued by any one firm, nor may they hold more than 10 percent of the voting shares of a single company (though these restrictions apply to only three-quarters of an investment company's portfolio in an effort to stimulate greater investments in small businesses). The SEC's Rule 126-1 requires mutual funds to disclose how they account for sales expenses and what impact brokerage commissions and operating expenses can have on an investor's return.

The SEC is governed by five commissioners, each appointed by the president of the United States for five-year terms. One of its most highly publicized activities is investigation of corporate *insider trading* activity. When insider activity places outside investors at a disadvantage, the SEC may stop such trading under the terms of the Insider Trading Act of 1988. Every stockholder that holds more than 10 percent of a corporation's outstanding shares and any officers and directors of that company must report their transactions in that firm's stock.

Securities and Exchange Commission (SEC)

procedures for managing exposure to a wide variety of risks, especially credit risk, interest rate risk, and currency and commodity risk.

At the same time, there is increasing regulatory interest in greater *public disclosure*—making sure the public is fully informed about the prices, service fees, risk exposures, and possible penalties they may pay for loans, deposits, and other key financial services. The fundamental idea is that an informed consumer will make better decisions regarding the use of financial services. Fuller disclosure stimulates competition as informed consumers shop around for the best terms available.

This issue moved closer to the front of the current regulatory agenda in 2001 when Enron Corporation filed for bankruptcy—at that time, the largest such filing in U.S. history—amid allegations of deceptive accounting practices, illegal insider trading, and lax oversight of its activities in the commodities and securities markets. Several authorities have recommended closer scrutiny of business accounting practices and increased regulation of corporations' use of off-balance-sheet transactions by such government agencies as the Securities and Exchange Commission (SEC) and the Commodities Futures Trading Commission (CFTC) in the United States.

For one of few times in the past century, the future path of government regulation of the financial sector is in doubt. We are beginning to evaluate more seriously the benefits and costs of letting governments set rules for financial institutions. We are asking more frequently: What purpose is served by both old and proposed new rules? Do the costs of both old and new regulations outweigh their benefits? How will market forces be distorted, and what will society gain or lose as a result of government interference with market forces? And, do we really need *multiple* regulatory agencies when financial-service firms are looking more similar to each other, offering many of the same services, and merging with each other in growing numbers? Shouldn't fewer numbers of financial institutions be matched by fewer regulators? On the other hand, does having multiple regulators actually bring some benefit, such as promoting competition among them and, thereby, minimizing the prospect of overzealous enforcement by one dominating government agency? It is answers to these questions that will form the guideposts to the future of financial institutions' regulation around the world.

QUESTIONS TO HELP YOU STUDY

10. Which particular government agencies regulate the following financial institutions: credit unions, savings and loan associations, savings banks, insurance companies, finance companies, investment companies, pension funds, and security brokers and dealers?

11. What *trends* are reshaping financial institutions' regulation today? Why has *capital regulation* become so important?

12. What new *disclosure rules* have recently appeared? Do you think these disclosure requirements help or hurt financial institutions? Why or why not?

13. Why might there be a need for *fewer* regulatory agencies in the financial sector today?

14. Based on your reading of this chapter, how has *globalization* of the financial sector impacted the regulatory agencies that oversee financial institutions? What do you think will happen in the future as the financial-service industry becomes more "globalized"?

In recent years, nations around the globe have often copied each other's regulations—in effect, learning from one another's mistakes and successes. For example, when Mexico and the nations of Asia got into trouble with bad loans and extensive numbers of failures in their banking systems, these countries selected recovery models that seemed to bear a close relationship to the recovery approach used by the United States to resolve its hundreds of bank and thrift institution failures during the 1980s and 1990s. Nevertheless, important differences still remain in how the regulation of financial institutions takes place around the globe.

One key difference lies in providing the public with deposit insurance coverage. Many nations have no formal deposit insurance plans at all. Others (e.g., Switzerland) have no fund that accumulates over time to prepare for future failures (as happens in the U.S. with the FDIC, for example). Rather, when a failure occurs the remaining solvent banks are asked to contribute sufficient funds to reimburse any depositors that have to be paid off.

Many *common* trends in the structure of financial-service industries do show up around the world, however.

For example, most financial systems are consolidating into fewer but larger financial firms, and banks seem to be losing market share to nonbank firms (such as security dealers, mutual funds, and pension funds). Yet some nations' financial systems (such as Germany and Japan) remain dominated by banks, which hold the bulk of the nation's financial assets, while in other countries security brokers and dealers are very important (as in Great Britain and the United States). In the latter nations, securities regulation and supervision has become as important a government activity as bank regulation.

Just as important differences exist in financial institutions' regulation from country to country, there is a definite trend toward greater *international cooperation* and more common rules (e.g., the Basel Agreement on Capital Standards for banks in industrialized countries). Some experts believe this *coordination* and *homogenization* of rules across nations will grow and may result ultimately in true multinational regulatory agencies that "level the playing field" so that leading financial institutions around the world all play by the same rules.

MARKETS ON THE NET: The Most Important Web Sites for This Chapter

Bank for International Settlements (bis.org)

Canadian Department of Finance (fin.gc.ca)

Conference of State Bank Supervisors (csbs.org)

European Union (europa.eu.int/inst-en.htm)

Federal Deposit Insurance Corporation (fdic.gov)

Federal Financial Institutions Examination Council (ffiec.gov)

Federal Reserve System (federalreserve.gov)

Federal Trade Commission (ftc.gov)

National Credit Union Administration (ncua.gov)

Office of the Comptroller of the Currency (occ.treas.gov)

Office of Thrift Supervision (treas.otc.gov)

Securities and Exchange Commission (sec.gov)

Summary of the Chapter's Main Points

Because financial institutions provide essential services to the public and can have a potent impact on the economy, regulation of the financial sector is extensive around much of the globe. Government rules encompass nearly every aspect

www.mhhe.com/rose9e

of the behavior and performance of financial institutions, including the services they offer, their management policies, their financial condition, and their ability to expand geographically.

- *Regulation* involves governments setting rules that bind financial institutions to obey laws and to protect the public interest. These rules are enforced by agencies and commissions that often operate at local or regional and federal levels.

- *Deregulation* is becoming a reality for many financial institutions as more and more governments eliminate some rules or ease some regulations to allow financial-service institutions to be governed more by the private marketplace and less by government dictation.

- Among the key bank regulatory agencies active in the United States are the Federal Reserve System, the Office of the Comptroller of the Currency, the Federal Deposit Insurance Corporation, and the 50 state banking commissions. The Federal Reserve oversees the member banks of the Federal Reserve System and financial holding companies (FHCs). The Comptroller of the Currency is responsible for the oversight of national (i.e., federally chartered) banks. The Federal Deposit Insurance Corporation supervises nonmember banks and insures the deposits of more than 98 percent of all banks selling deposits to the public inside the United States. The 50 state banking commissions supervise banks that have state charters of incorporation and often have regulatory responsibility for other types of financial institutions, such as state-chartered credit unions or savings and loan associations.

- Recent laws have dramatically changed the shape of financial-service industries. Examples include the Depository Institutions Deregulation and Monetary Control Act (1980), the Riegle-Neal Interstate Banking Act (1994), and the Financial Services Modernization (Gramm-Leach-Bliley) Act (1999). These laws have brought about such changes as giving more service powers to banks and thrift institutions so they can compete more freely with each other, permitting banks to branch across state lines, and allowing banking firms to affiliate with insurance companies, security firms, and other businesses just as financial firms have done in Europe for decades.

- Key regulatory agencies for nonbank financial institutions include the Office of Thrift Supervision, which supervises savings and loan associations; the National Credit Union Administration, which oversees federally chartered credit unions and supervises the credit union deposit insurance fund (NCUSIF); the Securities and Exchange Commission, which focuses principally on the behavior of security brokers and dealers and on the activities of corporations borrowing money in the open market; and boards or commissions present in each of the 50 U.S. states, which regulate insurance firms, finance and small-loan companies, and certain security firms and trust companies.

- The nature of government regulation of the financial sector is changing today, with the *private marketplace* gradually substituting for government rules. Today regulators are paying less attention to making and enforcing new rules and often find themselves pulling back to permit the discipline of the financial marketplace to play a greater role in controlling risk taking by financial-service firms. Regulators are also insisting that the owners of financial institutions (principally their stockholders) supply more of the capital these firms need to serve the public. The result is some shifting of financial institutions' risk from the public to the private owners of these businesses.

Key Terms Appearing in This Chapter

regulation, 511
deregulation, 513
Federal Reserve System, 515
Comptroller of the Currency, 515
Federal Deposit Insurance
    Corporation (FDIC), 515
state banking commissions, 518
Glass-Steagall Act, 520
Financial Services Modernization
    (Gramm-Leach-Bliley) Act, 521
financial holding companies
    (FHCs), 521
Basel I Agreement, 523
Basel II Agreement, 525

National Credit Union
    Administration (NCUA), 528
Depository Institutions Deregulation
    and Monetary Control Act
    (DIDMCA), 528
Office of Thrift Supervision (OTS), 529
Garn–St Germain Depository
    Institutions Act, 529
Financial Institutions Reform,
    Recovery, and Enforcement Act
    (FIRREA), 529
FDIC Improvement Act (FDICIA), 529
Securities and Exchange Commission
    (SEC), 535

Problems and Issues

1. A commercial bank has the following components in its capital account:

Common stock	$110	10-year subordinated debt	$25
Undivided profits	160	Loan-loss reserves	280
Perpetual preferred stock	15	Equity reserves	50
Surplus	35	Limited-life preferred stock	5

How much tier-one (or core) capital does this bank have? Tier-two capital?

2. First National Bank of Wimbley reports tier-one capital of $60 million and tier-two capital of $70 million. First National has assets of $10 million with a risk weight of zero, assets of $350 million with a 0.2 risk weight, assets of $680 million with a 0.5 risk weight, and assets of $1,010 million with a risk weight of 1.00. What is First National's total risk-weighted assets? Does the bank have enough tier-one capital under the terms of the Basel I Agreement? Enough total capital? Why or why not?

3. Indicate what type of financial institution is being described by each of the following items:

    a. SEC regulations require that at least two-thirds of this financial institution's board of directors must be elected by its stockholders.

    b. Insurance coverage is based upon the number of plan members.

    c. Regulated almost entirely by state commissions.

    d. Most of the regulation of this financial institution focuses upon its policies and procedures for making consumer loans.

    e. Deposits are insured by NCUSIF.

    f. This financial institution's principal regulatory agency is the OTS.

    g. All of these financial-service firms were originally mutual in form, but many have recently become stockholder-owned, filing conversion plans with their principal federal regulatory agency.

h. This financial institution must warn individual savers that their shares are not government insured and they may not always be able to maintain their fixed par value.

i. This financial service organization receives its corporate charter (certificate of association) from the Comptroller of the Currency.

j. This financial institution is chartered by the states but belongs to the Federal Reserve System.

Standard & Poor's Market Insight and Web-Based Problems

STANDARD
&POOR'S

1. As described in the text, there is a shift under way in the regulation of financial institutions toward more market-based solutions to regulatory issues. One of the most important aspects of this shift has been an increased emphasis on capital adequacy standards, with improved methods of assessing the overall level of risk inherent in a financial institution's asset holdings. The purpose of this exercise is to examine how well capitalized the largest commercial banks and savings and loan associations are relative to the tier-one and tier-two capital requirements described in this chapter.

   a. Visit the S&P Market Insight database at **mhhe.com/edumarketinsight** and find the annual balance sheets for three of the nation's largest commercial banks and two of the nation's largest savings and loans. (You may use any of the banks and savings and loans mentioned in this chapter if you wish.) Look under "Excel Analytics."

   b. For each of these financial institutions, list the "Risk-Adjusted Capital Ratio: Tier I" and "Risk-Adjusted Capital Ratio: Tier II" for each of the years that data are available.

   c. How well were these firms meeting the capital adequacy standards in the most recent year for which data are available?

   d. Which of these firms have become better capitalized and which have seen their capital adequacy position deteriorate recently? What might have caused this change?

2. An early indicator of potential problems at a depository institution is the volume of "nonperforming loans" on which borrowers are delinquent in their payments. Depository institutions are required by regulators to keep close track of these loans. The purpose of this problem is to examine the current significance of nonperforming loans at thrift institutions.

   a. Visit the Web site of the Office of Thrift Supervision at **ots.treasury.gov** and click the tab "Data and Research." Click on "Industry Performance" and then "Thrift Industry Charts" and open the most recent set of charts (pdf-file).

   b. Look up the chart containing "Loans 30–89 Days Past Due—Five Quarters." For this group of thrifts as a whole, list the six categories of loans in order from those having the highest percentage of "nonperforming loans" to those having the lowest percentage of "nonperforming loans." Compared to businesses, do households appear to be more or less consistent in paying their debts to these financial institutions?

    c. Which type of household loan has the best loan payoff record?

    d. Do you see any trends in the "nonperforming loans" in any loan category over the past year?

3. Each year banks "fail" and go into receivership. The Federal Deposit Insurance Corporation (FDIC) is the principal regulatory agency responsible for assuring minimal disruptions for borrowers, depositors, and local communities as a result of failed banks. The purpose of this exercise is to see how the FDIC goes about closing a failed bank.

    a. Visit the FDIC's Web site at **fdic.gov** and click the tab "Industry Analysis." Next click on "Failed Banks" and then click on "Failed Bank Information." Choose one of the banks listed as having failed over the past few years and click on the report.

    b. If you had deposits in that troubled institution, what would have happened to them?

    c. If you had a loan with that bank, what would have happened to it?

    d. If you had been a customer of the failed institution, do you think you would have had any major problems accessing your deposits or dealing with the repayment of your loan?

4. Credit unions must deal with delinquent or "nonperforming" loans that are held primarily by households. Many of these loans are "unsecured" (i.e., without specific collateral). However, a large proportion of the loans made by credit unions do have collateral in the form of new or used autos. Increasingly, credit unions are issuing mortgage loans secured by the borrower's home.

    a. Visit the Web site of the National Credit Union Administration (NCUA), which is the chief regulator of federally chartered credit unions, at **ncua.gov**. Click on "Credit Union Data" under the tab "Data and Services." Then click "5300 Quarterly Data" and obtain the most recent December consolidated balance sheet.

    b. Download the spreadsheet "Cbsfcu.xls."

    c. Go to the last page labeled on the tab "RATIOS."

    d. What is the percentage of total loans collectively held by federal credit unions that are labeled as "delinquent"?

    e. What is the percentage of total assets that the "delinquent" loans represent?

    f. One way to protect against the risk of loan delinquencies is to hold very safe assets. What is the largest category of "investment" assets held by federal credit unions? Are these generally safe assets? Explain.

Selected References to Explore

Ellihousen, Gregory. *The Cost of Banking Regulation: A Review of the Evidence*, Staff Study 171, Board of Governors of the Federal Reserve System, April 1998.

Federal Reserve Bank of Philadelphia. "New Basel Capital Accord." *Banking Legislation & Policy* 22, no. 3 (July–September 2003), pp. 4–5.

Jordan, Jerry L. "Effective Supervision and the Evolving Financial-Services Industry." *Economic Commentary,* Federal Reserve Bank of Cleveland, June 2001.

Kane, Edward J. "Accelerating Inflation, Technological Innovation and the Decreasing Effectiveness of Banking Regulation." *The Journal of Finance*, May 1981, pp. 355–67.

Kwan, Simon. "The Present and Future of Pension Insurance." *FRBSF Economic Letter,* Federal Reserve Bank of San Francisco, November 2003-25, August 29, 2003.

Lopez, Jose A. "Disclosure as a Supervisory Tool: Pillar 3 of Basel II." *FRBSF Economic Letter,* Federal Reserve Bank of San Francisco, 2003-22 (August 1, 2003).

Stigler, George J. "The Theory of Oligopoly." *Journal of Political Economy,* February 1965, pp. 44–61.

Weinberg, John A. "Competition Among Bank Regulators." *Economic Quarterly,* Federal Reserve Bank of Richmond, Fall 2002, pp. 19–36.

Part 5

Governments and Businesses in the Financial Markets

All parents wish for their children a better quality of life—better health, more wealth, and greater happiness—than they themselves have known. And history offers reasons to be optimistic that those wishes may come true. With each successive generation, people have led longer, healthier, and more prosperous lives than those who came before them. This track record is due, in part, to the continual striving of governments and businesses to efficiently transform new technology and new knowledge into a greater quantity and an increasing variety of higher quality goods and services than ever existed before. These efforts often involve planning, experimentation, and up-front expenditures that cannot be fully funded from the revenues that governments derive from taxes and user fees and the profits that businesses receive from sales. In these instances, governments and businesses—with a wide array of financing requirements—turn to the money and capital markets for funds. Without those markets, we would see very little improvement over time in either our own standard of living or the standard of living of our children.

Part Five of this book examines the many creative ways in which governments and businesses obtain the financing they require. First, we look at governments and ask: How large is the U.S. government's budget and on what is the money spent? How much of this spending is covered by borrowing? When and how does the U.S. government deliberately engage in deficit spending in order to stimulate the economy, thereby increasing the national debt? How does it manage the national debt? What are the special funding needs of state and local governments and how have these needs grown? How do their credit ratings and access to the debt markets differ from those of the federal government?

Next, we shift our focus to the wide range of debt instruments and equity issues that businesses use to fund their projects. When should a firm issue bonds to raise money and when should it sell stock? Does the intended use of the funds affect the method of financing selected? How important are the firm's financial statements to the source and cost of funds? How do new issues of debt and equity get placed in the financial marketplace? How are existing issues traded, and how do you know their true value?

In answering these and other questions, we learn that the complexity of the financing requirements among governments and businesses demands the highly flexible and innovative financial markets that we observe today in economic systems around the world.

Chapter 18

Federal, State, and Local Governments Operating in the Financial Markets

Learning Objectives

in This Chapter

- You will examine the many important roles played by the government's Treasury Department in supporting government programs and in pursuing the government's goals and objectives.

- You will be able to identify how the government raises new funds and how it manages to spend the funds that it raises.

- You will understand how the activities of the Treasury Department impact the money and capital markets and the economy.

- You will explore the various ways state, county, and city governments raise the funds needed to supply government services to the public.

- You will be able to describe the different instruments that state and local governments use to attract money and why these instruments are attractive to millions of investors.

What's in This Chapter?
Key Topics Outline

Sources and Uses of Federal Government Funds

Effects of Government Borrowing, Taxing, and Spending: Fiscal Policy

Debt Management: A Tool of Economic Policy

Size and Composition of the Public Debt

Types of Debt Securities Issued by States and Local Governments

The Key Characteristics of Municipal Debt

How State and Local Government Securities Are Marketed

18.1 Introduction to the Role of Governments in the Financial Marketplace

One of the most important institutions in any economy is the federal government's treasury or department of revenue. However, in the United States (and in most other nations as well), governments exist at several levels—federal or national, state, and local (e.g., cities and counties). And, the great majority of these governmental units are legally entitled to enter the money and capital markets at any time and borrow money. Moreover, the fund-raising activities of governments at all levels—borrowing money and raising revenue from taxes and fees—clearly impact the economy and affect market interest rates, asset prices, and overall credit conditions in the financial marketplace. In this chapter we look closely at two powerful sets of governmental institutions in the United States—the U.S. Treasury Department and the revenue departments of state and local units of government.

18.2 Federal Government Activity in the Money and Capital Markets

The Treasury Department in the Financial Marketplace

fiscal policy

debt management policy

In the United States, the Treasury Department exerts a powerful impact on the financial system because of two activities that it pursues on a continuing basis. One of these is **fiscal policy**, which refers to the taxing and spending programs of the government designed to promote high employment, sustainable economic growth, and other worthwhile economic goals. A second area in which the Treasury exerts an impact on financial conditions is **debt management policy,** which involves the refunding or refinancing of the federal government's debt in a way that may contribute to broad economic goals and minimize the burden of the debt upon the public and the economy. These Treasury policymaking activities may influence interest rates and the availability of credit for all sectors of the economy. In general, the Treasury pursues policies designed to achieve its economic goals without disturbing the functioning of the financial markets or unduly interfering with the operations of the Federal Reserve System, the nation's central bank.

The Fiscal Policy Activities of the U.S. Treasury

budget deficit

budget surplus

Congress dictates the amount of funds the federal government will spend each year for a variety of programs ranging from welfare to national defense. Congress also determines the tax rates that must be paid by individuals and businesses. Frequently, Congress votes for a higher amount of spending than can be supported by tax revenues. Alternatively, due to a slowdown in the economy, tax revenues may fall short of projections and not be sufficient to cover planned expenditures. Either way, the result is a **budget deficit**, requiring the U.S. Treasury to borrow additional funds in the financial markets. On the other hand, government revenues may exceed expenditures, resulting in a **budget surplus**, which the Treasury may use to build up its cash balances or to retire debt previously issued.

As shown in Exhibit 18.1, U.S. Treasury budget surpluses have been very infrequent. In fact, until 1998, the federal budget had been in surplus in only eight fiscal years since 1931. However, an agreement between the U.S. Congress and President Clinton led to more slowly growing federal expenditures, while a generally strong economy resulted in steadily advancing tax receipts. Federal budget deficits fell from

EXHIBIT 18.1

Federal
Government
Revenues,
Expenditures, and
Net Budget
Surplus or Deficit,
Selected Fiscal
Years,
1969–2005*

Fiscal Years	Total Revenues	Total Expenditures	Net Budget Surplus or Deficit
1969	$ 186.9	$ 183.6	$ +3.2
1970	192.8	195.6	−2.8
1980	517.1	590.9	−73.8
1990	1,031.3	1,251.8	−220.5
2000	2,025.2	1,788.8	+236.4
2004*	1,798.1	2,318.8	−520.7
2005*	2,036.3	2,399.8	−363.7

Sources: The President's Council of Economic Advisers, *Economic Report of the President,* selected years; and Board of Governors of the Federal Reserve System, *Federal Reserve Bulletin,* selected monthly issues.

*Estimates by the U.S. Department of the Treasury and the Office of Management and Budget.

Note: Figures based on the unified budget for fiscal years. Before 1977, fiscal years ran from July 1 through June 30. Thereafter, the federal government's fiscal year covered the October 1–September 30 period.

a peak of close to $300 billion in 1992 to only about $22 billion in fiscal 1997. A federal budget surplus finally emerged late in the 1990s and into the opening year of the twenty-first century.

Subsequently, however, sizeable federal budget deficits reappeared as a more slowly growing economy and tax cuts significantly lowered tax revenues. Moreover, as we move deeper into this century, sizeable federal budget deficits are likely to continue due, in part, to the growing financial burden imposed on federal, state, and local governments by the Social Security, Medicare, and Medicaid programs for the elderly and the disabled. These deficits will increase further if Congress and the president choose to enact more tax cuts and new federal spending programs in the future in an attempt to stimulate the economy.

Finally, it must be noted that, just like you and me, the government experiences periods of cash shortages in certain weeks and months, even during those fiscal years when the annual budget is in balance overall or even running a surplus. For example, during the year 2000—a year in which the U.S. Treasury posted the largest budget surplus in its history—federal receipts during the month of October trailed expenditures by $11 billion, requiring the Treasury to borrow money to fill this revenue gap. Subsequently, in December of the same year, federal receipts outstripped government spending by more than $30 billion, permitting the Treasury to pay back some of its earlier borrowings. In short, the Treasury will continue to need to borrow money every fiscal year in order to cover temporary cash shortages and refund outstanding debt, regardless of whether the federal budget is in surplus or running a deficit.

Sources of Federal Government Funds

What are the sources of revenue the federal government draws upon to fund its activities? The principal sources of federal revenue and spending programs are presented in Exhibit 18.2. On the revenue side, the bulk of incoming funds is derived from taxes levied against individual and family incomes. In fiscal 2003, for example, individuals were expected to pay close to $800 billion in income taxes, representing almost 45 percent of all federal revenues that year. Social Security taxes were forecast to supply more than $700 billion—about 40 percent of all federal revenues. Corporate income taxes were projected to contribute about 7 percent, and other taxes and fees for government services were expected to provide about 8 percent of all federal revenues.

EXHIBIT 18.2

Federal Government Revenues, Expenditures, and Net Budget Surplus or Deficit, 2003* (Estimates, $ Billions)

Budget Item	Amount	Percent of Total
On- and off-budget *receipts* by source:		
Individual income taxes	$ 793.7	44.5%
Corporation income taxes	131.8	7.4
Social insurance taxes and contributions	713.0	40.0
Other sources of revenue	144.8	8.1
Total revenues	$ 1,782.3	100.0%
On- and off-budget *expenditures* by function:		
National defense	$404.9	18.8%
International affairs	21.2	0.1
Health care	219.6	10.2
Income security programs	334.4	15.5
Social Security and Medicare	724.1	33.6
Net interest payments on the federal debt	153.1	7.1
Other expenditures**	300.3	13.9
Total expenditures	$ 2,157.6	100.0%
Net surplus (+) or deficit (−)	−$375.3	

Sources: President's Council of Economic Advisers, *Economic Report of the President*, selected years; and Board of Governors of the Federal Reserve System, *Federal Reserve Bulletin*, selected monthly issues.

*Figures for fiscal 2002–2003.

**Includes veterans' benefits, science, space and technology, energy, natural resources, and agriculture.

Note: Columns may not add to totals due to rounding.

During the 1970s and early 1980s, the share of federal revenues produced by personal income taxes declined. This was due to efforts by Congress to reduce withholding taxes and increase personal deductions against individual income taxes. Later, in the 1990s, personal income tax revenue rose or held steady as a proportion of all government receipts, reflecting Congress' desire to shift a greater share of the tax burden onto the more wealthy citizens. At the same time, payroll taxes for social insurance increased as Congress moved to rescue the Social Security system from deepening deficits. Corporate taxes were increased in an effort to offset declining personal tax rates and help to reduce budget deficits. As the twenty-first century began, however, a new presidential administration guided by George W. Bush sought to lower corporate and personal tax rates to stimulate the economy and increase saving and investment. Predictably, when the economy slowed and tax collections plummeted, federal budget deficits soared.

These changes in tax rates suggest that the federal government has attempted in recent years to make the tax structure more responsive to the nation's economic problems. When the economy headed down into a recession, or inflation pushed individuals into higher tax brackets, Congress generally responded (though often with considerable lags) and made appropriate income tax adjustments.

Federal Government Expenditures

The most recently compiled budget of the U.S. government is available from the Office of Management and Budget at gpo.gov/usbudget

The U.S. government today collects an enormous volume of revenue from its citizens. For example, federal revenues were almost $1.8 trillion in 2003. Where does the federal government spend this money?

Exhibit 18.2 indicates that slightly more than half of all federal spending goes for national defense and various income security programs, including Social Security, Medicare, and unemployment compensation. The latter programs are designed to sustain the spending power of individuals who are retired, ill or disabled, or temporarily unemployed. During the 1990s, the collapse of the Warsaw Pact in Europe and economic and political problems inside the states of the former Soviet Union stimulated the U.S. government to begin cutting back on spending for national defense (as a "peace dividend" from the end of the Cold War) and to shift more resources toward social programs and environmental protection (including more funds for medical research, improved educational opportunities for children, an upgrading of public housing and rental assistance programs, stronger antidrug programs, improved facilities for safeguarding air travel, and more aggressive efforts to clean up the environment). As the twenty-first century opened, however, a new and more conservative presidential administration took control and spending priorities began shifting again toward national defense, guarding against terrorism at home and abroad, and educational programs, with fewer monies likely to be directed toward other programs.

In recent years, several changes in tax and spending laws have taken place in an effort to make the U.S. government's fiscal policy a more effective tool for achieving the nation's goals. However, the truth is that fiscal policy has significant limitations and often it has proven ineffective. A major problem centers on *timing*. Fiscal policy often operates with long and variable lags. First, the legislature must agree on new tax and spending rules and then the Treasury and other government agencies must implement those rules. In the meantime, economic conditions may change greatly, making the new tax and spending rules obsolete. Many authorities today suggest that fiscal policy should be aimed, not at short-run objectives like dampening the business cycle, but at longer-range goals, such as promoting greater economic efficiency and greater equity in the allocation of the nation's scarce resources.

QUESTIONS TO HELP YOU STUDY

1. What exactly is *fiscal policy*? *Debt management policy?*

2. Explain how fiscal and debt management policy might be used to help fight inflation and unemployment. Can you see any weaknesses or potential problems with the use of these policy tools?

3. List (from largest to smallest) the principal sources of federal government revenue. What are the principal federal spending programs?

Effects of Government Borrowing on the Financial System and the Economy

What are the effects of government borrowing on the economy and the financial markets? If the federal government runs a *small* budget deficit, it is possible for the Treasury to cover this small shortfall in revenues by drawing upon its accumulated cash balances held at the Federal Reserve banks. However, when government deficits are large, substantial amounts of new debt securities must be sold to close the budget gap. The mechanics of how the Treasury *borrows* money from the public in the open market and then *spends* the borrowed funds may be illustrated quite easily with the T-accounts shown in Exhibit 18.3.

Suppose, as illustrated in Exhibit 18.3, the Treasury needs to borrow $20 billion, which it raises by selling bonds to the public. As the public pays for these attractive interest-bearing, low-risk securities, it writes checks against its deposits held with depository institutions. When the Treasury cashes these checks at its bank—the

	Federal Reserve Banks		Depository Financial Institutions	
EXHIBIT 18.3	Assets	Liabilities	Assets	Liabilities
The Sale of Securities by the Treasury to the Public		Legal reserves of depository institutions −20	Legal reserves of depository institutions −20	Deposits of the Public −20
		Government deposits +20		
The Treasury Spends the Borrowed Funds by Issuing Checks to the Public		Government deposits −20	Legal reserves of depository institutions +20	Deposits of the Public +20
		Legal reserves of depository institutions +20		

EXHIBIT 18.3

The Treasury Borrowing Money from the Public and Spending the Borrowed Funds

Federal Reserve—the legal reserves of depository institutions *fall,* as do deposits held by the public (other factors held constant), and the government has new deposit money to spend. Subsequently, the government spends the newly acquired money, writing checks totaling, in our example, $20 billion against its accounts at the Federal Reserve banks and distributing those checks to members of the public to whom it owes money. In this second round, deposits held by the public *rise* by $20 billion and the legal reserves of depository institutions climb by the same amount.

The likely impact of this sequence of government borrowing and government spending on the economy and the financial markets has been one of the most hotly debated issues in the history of economics and finance. The economy and the financial system are so complex, with so many changes going on at the same time, it is extremely difficult to make any dependable predictions about the ultimate outcome of government borrowing and spending.

For many years now, the conventional wisdom has been that new government borrowing, followed by the spending of those newly acquired government funds, may add to planned investment and consumption spending by businesses and households, tending to increase the economy's production and income levels, thus creating more jobs. However, it also has been argued that the additional borrowing and spending could eventually set in motion inflation, causing the prices of goods and services to increase and tending as well to force nominal interest rates upward. With higher interest rates, investment spending, production, and income might fall. We must be cautious here, however, because there is little solid evidence that government budget deficits cause inflation; indeed, current budget deficits appear to be more closely linked to past inflation rather than the other way around.[1]

---

[1] The T-accounts in Exhibit 18.3 illustrate the Treasury borrowing from the public. There is an alternative route to securing new funds, but it is highly dangerous and, in the United States anyway, restricted by law. This alternative method involves direct borrowing by the Treasury from the central bank, the Federal Reserve System. The Treasury sells government securities to the Federal Reserve banks and receives money in its checking account at the Fed. Initially there is no change in the public's deposits or in legal reserves. When the newly borrowed funds are spent, however, the public's deposit balances rise, as do reserves in the banking system. Financially speaking, this is a highly inflationary way for the government to borrow money. It is the equivalent of simply *printing money* and distributing it to the public, most likely causing prices to rise if the economy is near full production and employment and the central bank does nothing to offset this "monetizing" of the government's debt.

EXHIBIT 18.4	Federal Reserve Banks		Depository Institutions	
	Assets	Liabilities	Assets	Liabilities
The Treasury Collects a Net Surplus of Tax Revenues from the Public		Legal reserves of Depository Institutions −20 Government Deposits +20	Legal reserves of Depository Institutions −20	Deposits of the Public −20
The Treasury Buys Back Government Securities Held by the Public and Retires Them		Government Deposits −20	Legal reserves of Depository Institutions +20	Deposits of the Public +20

EXHIBIT 18.4

The Treasury Uses Its Surplus Funds to Pay Off and Retire Government Securities Held by the Public

Recent research into the impact of government borrowing and spending has introduced yet another argument: Interest rates and security prices in an *efficient market* simply may not respond at all to increased government borrowing and spending. This may happen, in part, because the government's borrowing and spending may have a "crowding out effect" on the private sector of the economy— that is, additional government borrowing and spending may discourage some private borrowing and spending. Thus, there may be little *net* gain in terms of economic activity or any significant changes in interest rates as a result of deficit spending by the government. With so many conflicting arguments about government borrowing and spending, this is definitely an area where more research and careful observation are needed.[2]

Incidentally, what happens when the government runs a budget surplus and uses a portion of that surplus to *retire debt*? Exhibit 18.4 summarizes the simple mechanics involved in such a debt-retirement transaction.

Suppose, as shown in Exhibit 18.4, that the Treasury collects $20 billion more in tax revenues than it spends, thus withdrawing a net $20 billion from the economy. The Treasury might save this surplus to apply to future cash needs, but if the surplus is sizeable, it more than likely will choose to hold so-called "reverse auctions"—buying back some of its debt from those who hold it, and retiring those securities. Indeed, this is what the U.S. government did as the twentieth century drew to a close. (For example, in the year 2000, the U.S. government used reverse auctions and other means to reduce the marketable public debt of the United States by just over $300 billion.)

Does debt retirement have any predictable effects on the economy and financial system? Once again, this field is filled with controversy and disagreement. Some economists and financial analysts argue that running budget surpluses and retiring the government's debt tends to slow economic activity as funds are transferred from tax

---

[2]While most studies find little or no connection between market interest rates and budget deficits, a new study by Laubach (2003) at the Federal Reserve finds a significant relationship. Specifically, this study found that an increase in the ratio of projected deficits to U.S. GDP by 1 percentage point produces a quarter point (i.e., 25-basis point) rise in long-term interest rates—some evidence for the "crowding out" effect.

payers (who may, on average, have a higher propensity to spend) to government security investors (who may have a higher propensity to save rather than spend), thereby slowing the economy. Others argue that the retirement of government debt simply makes more room for private borrowing and spending. If markets are truly *efficient* and the government is transparent about what it is doing with the public debt, there may be little impact at all. Clearly, we need to know much more about this subject before drawing any rock-solid conclusions.

QUESTIONS TO HELP YOU STUDY

4. Describe the possible impacts of *government borrowing* upon the financial system and the economy.

5. Describe the possible effects of *retiring government securities* on the financial system and the economy.

6. What is meant by the term *crowding-out effect?* What does recent research suggest about the link between government deficits, interest rates, and inflation?

Management of the Federal Debt

public debt

As we noted at the beginning of this chapter, one of the most important activities of any government's treasury is managing the nation's debt. In the U.S., the Treasury Department in Washington, D.C. manages the huge **public debt** of the United States. The U.S. public debt is the largest single collection of securities available in the financial system today. Securities issued by the Treasury are regarded by investors as having zero *default risk* because the federal government possesses power both to tax and to create money. The government, unless it is overthrown by war or revolution, can always pay its bills by taxing its citizens.

Government securities do carry *market risk,* however, because their prices fluctuate with changes in demand and supply. In fact, the longer the term to maturity of a government security, the more market risk it tends to possess.

The principal role of government securities in the financial system is to provide *liquidity.* Corporations, commercial banks, and other institutional investors rely heavily on government securities as a readily marketable reserve to be drawn upon when cash is needed quickly. Although private securities do carry higher explicit yields than government debt of comparable maturity, the greater liquidity of government securities represents an added (implicit) return to the investor.

The Size and Growth of the Public Debt

How much money does the federal government owe? As shown in Exhibit 18.5, the gross public debt of the United States had reached more than $7 trillion in 2004. On a per capita basis, the public debt amounts to more than $25,000 for every man, woman, and child living in the United States.

How did the federal debt become so large? Wars, economic depressions or recessions, and the rapid expansion of military expenditures and social programs have been among the principal causes. The federal government's debt began during the American Revolution as the United States needed money to fight for its independence. However, the central government's debt was relatively insignificant until the Great Depression of the 1930s when the administration of President Franklin D. Roosevelt chose to borrow heavily to fund government programs and provide more jobs. Even so, the public debt amounted to scarcely more than $50 billion at the beginning of World War II. The public

EXHIBIT 18.5			
The Public Debt of the United States, 2004 ($ Billions)	**Type of Securities**	**Amounts**	**Percent of Gross Public Debt**
	Interest-bearing public debt	$7,115.6	99.8%
	Marketable debt:	3,721.1	52.2
	Bills	985.0	13.8
	Notes	1,983.4	27.8
	Bonds	564.3	7.9
	Inflation-indexed notes and bonds	188.4	2.6
	Nonmarketable debt:	3,394.5	47.6
	State and local government series	155.7	2.2
	Foreign issues	6.7	0.1
	Savings bonds and notes	193.5	2.7
	Government account series	3,008.6	42.2
	Non-interest-bearing debt	15.4	0.2
	Total gross public debt	$7,131.1	100.0%

Sources: Board of Governors of the Federal Reserve and the U.S. Treasury Department.

Note: Columns may not add to totals due to rounding. Figures are for first quarter of 2004.

debt multiplied five times over during the war years, approaching $260 billion by the end of World War II. Embroiled in the most destructive and costly war in history, the U.S. government borrowed resources from the private sector to build planes, ships, and other war materials in enormous quantities.

For a brief period following World War II, it appeared that much of the public debt might be repaid. However, the Korean War intervened in the early 1950s, followed by a series of deep recessions when government tax revenues declined. The advent of the Vietnam War, along with costly Great Society programs and rapid inflation during the late 1960s and 1970s, sent the debt soaring (see Exhibit 18.6). Between 1970 and 1980, the public debt of the United States more than doubled; it then tripled to more than $3 trillion during the 1980–1990 period. Between 1990 and 2000, the federal government's debt expanded again, this time by more than $2 trillion. However, the total debt of the United States government began to decline in fiscal 2000 as budget surpluses emerged and some government debt could be repaid. Lower interest rates on the federal debt, the end of the Cold War, and a long-term economic boom extending through much of the 1990s made it possible for the federal budget to approach a surplus position as the new century began—a true federal budget surplus for the first time since 1969. However, the new budget surplus was soon threatened by a new economic recession in 2001, made worse by the terrorist attacks of 9/11, throwing the United States' federal budget back into a deficit as the early years of the twenty-first century unfolded.

How much government debt is simply too much? Opinions vary greatly on the answer to that question. For example, James Madison, fourth president of the United States, once

EXHIBIT 18.6				
The Public Debt of the United States in Selected Years, 1950–2004 ($ Billions at Year-End)	**Year**	**Total Gross Public Debt**	**Year**	**Total Gross Public Debt**
	1950	$225.4	1990	$3,364.8
	1960	287.7	2000	5,662.2
	1970	388.3	2004*	7,131.1
	1980	930.2		

Sources: Board of Governors of the Federal Reserve System and the U.S. Treasury Department.

Note: 2004 figures are for first quarter.

declared: "A public debt is a public curse." In contrast, Alexander Hamilton, the first U.S. Treasury Secretary under the Constitution, wrote: "A national debt, if it is not excessive, will be to us a national blessing." Who is right?

The answer depends, in part, on the standard used to gauge the size of the public debt. Measured against the national income (the earnings of individuals and businesses that can be taxed to repay the debt), the public debt is lower now than it was a generation ago. For example, in 2004, the gross public debt amounted to about 60 percent of the U.S. gross domestic product (GDP), compared to well over 100 percent at the end of World War II. Moreover, other forms of debt in the U.S. economy total as much or more than the public debt. For example, total mortgage debt outstanding in 2004 was more than $9 trillion and the combined debt of the private sector and state and local governments was roughly double that of the federal government. It should be remembered that U.S. government securities are at one and the same time both debt obligations of the government and also highly desirable marketable, liquid assets to the millions of investors who hold them.

Another issue to keep in mind about today's large federal debt and its possible burden on the economy and the financial marketplace concerns the difficulties we face in trying to accurately measure the true *size* of the debt. It turns out that the answer to the question—How big is the federal debt?—is not all that easy. For example, *inflation* increases the size of the debt because it tends to increase government deficits. In an inflationary period, the government typically must borrow more, but this does not necessarily mean that the burden of the debt has increased: Government may not be exerting a greater impact on the economy. Moreover, the size of the public debt is typically measured in terms of the *par value* of government securities outstanding. But when interest rates rise, the *market value* of government debt falls. Thus, a significant rise in interest rates will cause the value of that portion of the government's debt held by private investors to decline.

Accurate measurement of the burden imposed by government debt also means that we must consider the value of the *assets* held by government. Most national governments hold a reserve of gold and foreign currencies. We might also add the estimated value of government buildings, military hardware, highways, and airports. Thus, we may distinguish between *gross liabilities* of the federal government and its *net liabilities*— government debt minus government assets. Including all of the government's assets at their fair market value would yield substantially smaller net government liabilities. Of course, to be fair, we also have to consider the amount of debt owed by off-budget federal agencies (such as the farm credit agencies or the federal mortgage agencies), which amounts to just over one-third of the gross public debt. And *contingent liabilities* might be added to the government's debt total, such as deposit insurance like that offered by the FDIC to guarantee bank deposits or the Social Security Fund which must eventually pay retirement benefits to millions of citizens. Clearly, measuring the true size of the government's debt is a difficult job. For this reason, we must be careful before jumping to any hasty conclusions about how large or significant the debt is or what its impact on the economy and financial markets might be.

The Composition of the Public Debt   The U.S. public debt as it is traditionally measured consists of a wide variety of government IOUs with differing maturities, interest rates, and other features. A small amount—less than 1 percent—carries no interest rate at all. This *non-interest-bearing debt* consists of paper currency and coins previously issued by the U.S. Treasury Department. However, virtually all paper money in circulation today is in Federal Reserve notes, which are not officially a part of the public debt but are obligations of the Federal Reserve banks.

More than 99 percent of all federal debt securities are *interest bearing* and may be divided into two broad groups: marketable securities and nonmarketable securities. By definition, *marketable securities* may be traded any number of times before they reach maturity. In contrast, *nonmarketable securities* must be held by the original purchaser until they mature or are redeemed by the Treasury. It is marketable debt that has the greatest impact on the cost and availability of credit in the money and capital markets, and it is these securities over which the Treasury exercises the greatest control.

Marketable Public Debt   The marketable public debt totaled about $3.7 trillion in 2004, representing just over half of all interest-bearing U.S. government obligations. The marketable public debt today is composed of just three types of securities: Treasury bills, notes, and bonds. By law, a U.S. Treasury bill must mature within one year. In contrast, U.S. Treasury notes range in original maturity from 1 to 10 years, and Treasury bonds may carry any maturity, although generally, when issued, they have a maturity of more than 10 years.[3] With their greater liquidity and marketability, Treasury bills, notes, and bonds have been attractive savings outlets to individual and institutional investors for many years.

Nonmarketable Public Debt   The nonmarketable public debt consists mainly of Government Account series securities issued by the Treasury to various government agencies and trust funds (see again Exhibit 18.5). These agencies and trust funds include the Social Security Administration, the Tennessee Valley Authority, the Government National Mortgage Association, the Postal Service, and several smaller government agencies. As these governmental units accumulate funds, they turn them over to the Treasury in exchange for nonmarketable IOUs, thus reducing the federal government's borrowing activity in the open market. Another component of the nonmarketable debt is U.S. savings bonds sold to the general public in small denominations, which represent less than 2 percent of the public debt.

Holdings of U.S. dollars by foreign governments and foreign investors have remained at a relatively high level in recent years due to oil imports and the flow of U.S. capital to Europe, Asia, and the Middle East. Because large foreign holdings of dollars represent a constant threat to the value of the U.S. dollar in international markets, the Treasury periodically issues nonmarketable dollar-denominated securities to attract these foreign funds. To increase U.S. government holdings of foreign currencies that can be used to settle international claims, the Treasury can sell foreign-currency-denominated securities to investors abroad as well. The Treasury also issues special securities to state and local governments. These securities provide a temporary investment outlet for the funds raised by local governments when they borrow in the open market.

Investors in U.S. Government Securities   Who *holds* the public debt of the United States? Each month, the Treasury makes estimates of the distribution of its

---

[3]Both Treasury notes and bonds bear interest at a fixed interest rate payable semiannually, while bills do not carry a fixed interest rate but earn price gains instead as their market price rises over time. Treasury bonds may carry a call option, allowing the Treasury to redeem them early provided the Treasury gives at least four months' notice (though the U.S. government has issued only noncallable securities since 1985 and early in the 21st century the Treasury confined new marketable U.S. Treasury issues largely to notes rather than bonds). Notes and bonds have been issued in multiples of $1,000 and $5,000 depending upon maturity. Bills are available in multiples of $1,000. Payment for purchases of new Treasuries generally must be made in cash, immediately available funds, the exchange of eligible securities, or by check to the Federal Reserve banks or the U.S. Treasury.

EXHIBIT 18.7

Investors in the U.S. Public Debt, 2004* ($ Billions at End of First Quarter)

Sources: Board of Governors of the Federal Reserve System and the U.S. Treasury Department.

Investor Group	Amount Held in 2004*	Percent of Total Ownership
Federal government:		
U.S. government agencies and trust funds	$2,955.9	
Federal Reserve banks	674.1	
Total for federal government issues	$3,630.0	53.4%
Private investors:		
Depository institutions	$166.2	
Mutual funds	279.3	
Insurance companies	153.4	
State and local treasuries	339.4	
Individuals:		
Savings bonds	204.4	
Pension funds:		
Private pensions	108.1	
State and local government pensions	205.3	
Foreign and international	1,708.0	
Other miscellaneous investors*	N/A	
Total for private investors	$3,164.1	46.6%
Total for all investor groups	$6,794.1	100.0%

*The miscellaneous investor group includes holdings of Treasury securities by individuals, government-sponsored enterprises, brokers and dealers, bank personal trusts and estates, corporate and noncorporate businesses, and other investors. N/A indicates not available

securities among various groups of investors, drawing on data supplied by the Federal Reserve banks, government agencies, and private trade organizations. The results from a recent Treasury ownership survey are shown in Exhibit 18.7.

It is evident from the survey that a large portion of Treasury debt—almost half—is held by private individuals and institutions. Rather surprising to many observers, however, is the relatively large proportion of the federal government's debt—just over half—that is held by the government itself. For example, in 2004 U.S. government agencies and trust funds, including the Social Security Trust Fund and other federal departments, held about 40 percent of the total federal debt. In addition, the Federal Reserve banks held almost 10 percent of all public debt securities outstanding.

The sheer size of the government's holdings of its own debt is viewed with alarm by some analysts. A large volume of government debt held out of circulation in federal vaults tends to thin the market for government securities, reducing the volume of trading. Other factors held constant, interest rates and security prices become more volatile, discouraging some investment. This could be important, because the market for government securities is currently the anchor of the financial system.

Among private holders of the federal government's debt, pension funds, mutual funds, state and local governments, and individuals are at or near the top of the list. In 2004, for example, individual investors held about 3 percent of the public debt—the majority of these holdings in U.S. savings bonds. Pension funds held almost 5 percent, while mutual funds held about 5 percent of all Treasury-issued securities.

The proportion of the U.S. public debt held by foreign investors, including foreign central banks, governments, and other international investors, has risen in recent years to about one-quarter of all issues outstanding in 2004. The foreign contingent of investors is very important—they hold more than $1.7 trillion dollars in U.S. Treasuries and represent the single largest investor group holding U.S. Treasury securities outside of the federal government itself.

According to a recent U.S. Treasury survey, foreign investors held more than a trillion dollars in U.S. government securities of various kinds! Why are foreign and international investors such heavy buyers of United States government securities?

A key source of this trend favoring foreign investors has been U.S. trade deficits, with Americans paying for what they buy abroad by contributing dollars and dollar-denominated securities to foreign companies and individuals. Then, too, the United States appears to many foreigners to be a "safe haven" compared to many foreign markets. Many overseas territories are often in turmoil with weaker economies and, in some cases, unstable governments. By way of contrast, American businesses, bank deposits, stocks, and bonds look like havens of safety as well as good sources of profitability.

This story is not all positive, however. Some analysts fear that foreign investors may be more "fickle" than domestic buyers of government securities. Any sign of trouble inside the United States may send some foreign investors racing for the exits, dumping Treasuries along the way. The result could be a sharp decline in the value of the dollar in international markets and an upsurge in borrowing costs.

The bulk of foreign holdings of U.S. securities seems to be centered in Great Britain and Japan. Foreign holdings of government securities result, in part, from a rise in U.S. imports that lead foreign investors to build up dollar deposits in banks abroad. These investors have converted many of their dollars into purchases of Treasury securities in the money market and into foreign-currency-denominated securities purchased directly from the U.S. Treasury. Foreign holdings of U.S. Treasury securities have remained relatively high recently due to the development of active over-the-counter markets for longer-term Treasuries in London, Tokyo, and other financial centers. These overseas U.S. Treasury security markets have given Treasuries round-the-clock liquidity and are especially attractive to such investors as multinational corporations and others who find U.S. trading hours inconvenient. In the interdealer market, trading in Treasury bills worldwide starts at a minimum size of about $5 million, while T-notes and bonds trade in units of a million dollars. Daily trading in the resale market averages well over $100 billion, carried out through hundreds of brokers and dealers. Trading centered in Tokyo and London appears to generate some new information that subsequently affects the main market in New York.

QUESTIONS TO HELP YOU STUDY

7. Describe the types of securities that make up the *public debt* of the United States. What portions of this debt can the U.S. Treasury Department most closely control?

8. What problems exist when you try to measure the true *size* of the government's debt? Do you have any suggestions on how to deal with this measurement problem?

9. List the principal *holders* of the United States' public debt. What trends seem to be under way in the ownership of federal securities?

Methods of Offering Treasury Securities

Management of the public debt is a complicated task. Treasury debt managers are called on continually to make decisions about raising new money and refunding maturing securities. They must decide what kinds of securities to issue, which maturities will appeal to investors, and the form in which an offering of securities should be made.

auction method

The Auction Method   Today, the **auction method** is the principal means of selling Treasury notes, bonds, and bills. Although several different methods have been used over time, all such techniques have a number of features in common. Both competitive and noncompetitive tenders for new securities, whose dollar amount and maturity are announced about one week in advance, are invited from the public. Competitive bidders usually include money-center banks and securities houses. About 2000 security brokers and dealers are registered to trade in the U.S. government securities market. Noncompetitive bidders, including smaller financial institutions and individuals, average about 20,000 or more per Treasury auction. Noncompetitive bidders receive an allotment of securities at the average or prevailing auction price up to a maximum amount determined by the Treasury. As we have seen, federal agencies and trust funds purchase large amounts of Treasury issues. These agencies participate in virtually every auction but pay the price charged noncompetitive bidders. They receive a special allotment of securities in exchange for their maturing issues after the regular auction is concluded.

Types of Treasury Auctions   The Treasury has used several different auction methods over the years. Today, however, the auction method used most often for Treasury notes, bonds, and bills is known as a *yield auction.* The Treasury announces the amount of securities available and calls for yield bids accurate to three decimal places (e.g., 6.105%). Treasury bill bids must be based upon the discount rate (DR), discussed in Chapter 10. Investors submitting competitive bids for Treasury notes and bonds must express their offers on an annual percentage yield basis. Those bidding the lowest annual percentage yield (the highest price) normally will be awarded securities. Awards may continue to be made at successively higher yields (lower bid prices) until the issue is exhausted. Today, however, in what is called a *uniform price auction,* all successful bidders for federal government securities wind up paying *the same price*—the lowest price that ultimately clears the market of all available securities (the *stop-out price*).

Marketing Techniques   The Treasury places new securities *directly* with the investing public. New Treasury bills, notes, and bonds can be bought directly from the Treasury Department or from the Treasury's agents—the Federal Reserve banks—either in person, by mail, or online. Competitive tender offers are accepted from private and government investors at the Federal Reserve banks until 1 P.M. Eastern Standard Time, the day the new securities are sold. Individuals also may file bids for new Treasury securities with the Bureau of Public Debt in Washington, DC. Many investors place orders for new Treasury issues through a security broker or dealer, bank, or nonbank financial institution.

book-entry form

For a full description of the role and services provided by the TREASURYDIRECT System, see treasurydirect.gov

Book Entry   The marketable public debt is issued today only in **book-entry form.** This means that the investor does *not* receive an engraved certificate representing the Treasury's debt obligation but instead receives a statement of account. The investor's name and amount of securities purchased are recorded in an Account Master Record in the automated book-entry TREASURYDIRECT System maintained by the Bureau of the Public Debt or in what is called the *commercial book-entry system* maintained by financial institutions and government security brokers and dealers on behalf of their customers. Depository institutions are permitted to hold security safekeeping accounts at the Federal Reserve banks as part of the commercial book-entry system where their own security holdings and those of their customers are recorded. As interest is received or securities are sold or purchased, banks credit or debit their own or their customers' accounts and the TREASURYDIRECT System. Book entry is the safest form in which to hold any security because this method significantly reduces the risk of theft.

Other Services Offered Investors   To encourage greater participation in the government securities market and stimulate demand for new Treasury issues, both the Federal Reserve and the Treasury offer a number of other services to investors. For example, securities held in book-entry accounts at the Federal Reserve banks may be transferred by wire almost anywhere using the Fed's electronic wire transfer network. Interest and principal payments are electronically deposited on the due date into the deposit account each investor designates for that purpose. This device makes it easy to sell Treasury securities before maturity on a same-day basis.

Price Quotations on Treasury Securities   The widespread popularity of U.S. Treasury securities to investors around the world means that their prices and yields are closely watched every day. Newspapers carry price and yield information for Treasury bonds, notes, and bills, which usually include the following information:

Rate	Maturity	Bid	Asked	Change	Asked Yield
$6^1/_2$	Aug 08n	105:16	105:18	+13	5.73
$9^3/_8$	Feb 09	127:15	127:19	+16	5.75
$11^3/_4$	Nov 12–15	153:26	153:30	+22	5.92

Treasury security prices and yields are available from many Web sites, including Bloomberg at bloomberg.com and the Bond Market Association at investinginbonds.com

We note from the preceding that Treasury securities are usually listed in order of the dates they will mature, from the most recent to the most distant maturities. The promised coupon rates are shown under the column marked *Rate*. Thus, the first security in the list, which matures in August 2008, promises a $6^1/_2$ percent annual return, or $6.50 per year for each $100 in face value. The letter *n* next to the first entry indicates that the security in question is a Treasury note. The absence of *n* means that the security listed is a Treasury bond, as is the case with the $9^3/_8$ and $11^3/_4$ percent bonds maturing in the years 2009 and from 2012 to 2015.

The *bid* price in the next column (expressed in dollars and 32nds of a dollar) is the price for which a dealer is willing to *buy* the security. For example, the August 2008 note has a bid price of $105^{16}/_{32}$, or $105.50 on a $100 basis. The *asked* price is the price the security's current holder (usually a security dealer) is willing to sell it for. Any investor interested in purchasing the security in question will probably seek to buy it for a price somewhere between the current bid and asked prices. The column labeled *Change* indicates the change in bid price between yesterday's closing price and the day before's closing price, expressed in 32nds of a dollar. Thus, a change of +13 indicates a price rise yesterday of $^{13}/_{32}$ of a dollar, or $0.40625 per $100 par value security. The yield to maturity the purchaser would receive if he or she bought the security at yesterday's asked price is shown in the last column. For example, if the August 2008 note were purchased for 105:18, the investor buying at this price and holding the bond to its maturity date in August 2008 would receive a yield of 5.73 percent. Trading in new Treasury securities begins in the "when-issued" market several days before the new securities actually are issued and right after the Treasury releases information on the forthcoming auction date and the amount to be issued.

The Goals of Federal Debt Management

Over the years, the Treasury has pursued several different goals in the management of the public debt. These goals may be divided into two broad groups: (1) *housekeeping goals,* which pertain to the cost and composition of the public debt; and (2) *stabilization goals*, which have to do with the impact of the debt on the economy and the financial markets.

Minimize Interest Costs

The most important housekeeping goal is to keep the interest burden of the public debt as low as possible. The Treasury has not always been successful in the pursuit of this goal, however. Today, the interest burden of the public debt is the sixth largest category of federal expenditures after welfare payments, unemployment insurance, health care, Social Security payments, and national defense. This interest burden on the U.S. taxpayer increases when interest rates rise or the volume of debt increases faster than the nation's income.

Economic Stabilization

A much broader goal of debt management is to help stabilize the economy, promoting maximum employment and sustainable economic growth while avoiding rampant inflation. This may involve issuing *long-term* Treasury securities in a period of *economic expansion* and issuing *short-term* securities in a period of *recession*. The issuance of long-term securities may tend to increase long-term interest rates and therefore act as a brake on private investment spending, slowing the economy down. On the other hand, issuing short-term securities during a recession may take the pressure off long-term interest rates and avoid discouraging investment spending needed to provide jobs.

Unfortunately, the goal of economic stabilization often conflicts with other debt management goals, particularly the goal of minimizing the interest burden of the debt. If the Treasury sells short-term securities in a period of expansion when interest rates are high and then rolls over those short-term securities into long-term bonds during a recession when rates are low, this strategy tends to minimize the debt's average interest cost. The Treasury is able to lock in cheaper long-term rates. From a stabilization point of view, however, this can be exactly the wrong thing to do. The short-term debt may fuel inflation during an economic expansion, while long-term debt issued during a recession may drive up interest rates and reduce private investment. Treasury debt managers are confronted with tough choices among conflicting goals.

The Impact of Federal Debt Management on the Financial Markets and the Economy

What effect do Treasury debt management activities have on the financial markets and the economy? This is a subject of heated debate among financial analysts. Most experts agree that in the short run, the financial markets become more agitated and interest rates tend to rise when the Treasury is borrowing, especially when *new money* is involved. A mere exchange of new for old securities usually has minimal effects, however, unless the offering is very large.

The longer-run impact of Treasury debt management operations is less clear. Certainly the *liquidity* of the public's portfolio of securities changes. For example, suppose $10 billion in Treasury bonds are maturing next month. Treasury debt managers decide to offer investors $10 billion in 10-year notes in exchange for the maturing bonds. The bonds, regardless of what their original maturity might have been, are now short-term securities (with one-month maturities). If investors accept the new 10-year notes in exchange for the one-month bonds, the average maturity of the public's security holdings obviously has lengthened, all else being equal. Longer-term securities, as a rule, are less liquid than shorter-term securities.

Will this reduction in public liquidity affect spending habits and interest rates? The research evidence on this question is conflicting, with many studies finding little effect from debt management activities. However, there is some evidence that *lengthening debt maturities* tends to increase the public's demand for money and *raise interest rates.* In contrast, if the Treasury offers shorter-term securities, this tends to make the public's portfolio of securities more liquid and may reduce the demand for money. The result may be an increase in spending for goods and services and, for a time, *lower* interest rates.

Still another possible debt management impact is on the *shape of the yield curve.* *Lengthening* the average maturity of the debt tends to increase long-term interest rates relative to short-term rates. The yield curve assumes a *steeper positive slope,* favoring short-term investment over long-term investment. On the other hand, *shortening* the debt's maturity tends to reduce longer-term interest rates and raise short-term rates. The yield curve tends to *flatten out,* if positively sloped, or even turn down, favoring long-term investment over short-term investment. The net impact on total investment spending would depend on whether private investment is more responsive to short-term interest rates or long-term interest rates.

On balance, most authorities are convinced that the debt management activities of the Treasury do *not* have a major impact on economic conditions. The effects of debt management operations appear to be secondary compared to the more powerful impact of monetary and fiscal policy on the economy and financial markets. The optimal policy is probably one that makes Treasury refunding operations as unobtrusive as possible, especially when these operations might interfere with the monetary policy activities of the central bank. Nevertheless, debt management represents a policy tool that might be used by government in the face of serious economic problems.

QUESTIONS TO HELP YOU STUDY

10. Describe the current auction method or methods for selling U.S. Treasury securities.

11. List the principal *goals* of Treasury debt management. What is the essential difference between housekeeping goals and stabilization goals? To what extent could these goals conflict with each other?

12. Explain how changes in the maturity structure of the public debt can affect interest rates, the yield curve, spending and saving in the economy.

18.3 State and Local Governments in the Financial Markets

The Treasury is often joined in the marketplace by thousands of state and local governments also borrowing money. Indeed, the borrowing and spending activities of state and local governments have been one of the most dynamic, rapidly growing segments of the financial system in recent years. Pressured by rising populations and inflated costs, states, counties, cities, school districts, and other local units of government have been forced to borrow in growing numbers to meet increased demands for their services.

Despite the rapid growth in borrowing by state and local governments, many investors consider state and local debt obligations a highly desirable investment medium due to their high quality, ready marketability, and tax exemption feature. The interest income generated by state and local securities is exempt from federal income taxes, and most states exempt their own securities from state income taxes. As a result, these high-quality debt obligations—known as **municipals**—appeal to heavily taxed investors

municipals

such as top-income-bracket individuals and large corporations. In addition, an active secondary market permits the early resale of many higher-quality state and local government bonds.

Growth of State and Local Government Borrowing

The rapid growth of state and local government borrowing is reflected in Exhibit 18.8, which shows the total volume of municipal securities outstanding between the years 1940 and 2004. State and local government indebtedness grew slowly until the 1950s, when it nearly tripled. The volume of municipal debt doubled again during the 1960s and more than doubled during the 1970s and 1980s. By 2004, state and local debt outstanding had climbed to more than $1.6 trillion dollars.

What factors account for this strong record of growth in municipal borrowing? *Rapid population* and *income growth* are two of the most important causes. The U.S. population rose from less than 132 million in 1940 to an estimated 280 million by the beginning of the twenty-first century—a gain of nearly 150 million people. Rapid population growth implies that many local government services, such as schools, highways, and fire protection, must also expand rapidly. Tax revenues cannot provide all of the monies needed to fund these facilities and services.

Another factor pushing state and local borrowing higher is the *uneven distribution of population growth across the nation.* Beginning in the 1950s, a massive shift of the U.S. population out of the central cities into suburban areas began to take place. This demographic change was augmented during the 1970s, 1980s, and 1990s by a movement of population and industry into small towns and rural areas to escape the social and environmental problems of urban living, and toward the western and southern states in search of a warmer climate and new business opportunities. Smaller outlying communities were transformed into cities with a corresponding need for new streets, schools, airports, and freeways to commute back to the central cities for work, recreation, and shopping. The result was an upsurge in borrowing by existing local units of government and the creation of thousands of *new* borrowing units in the form of sewer and lighting districts, power and water authorities, airport and toll-road boards, and public housing authorities. Today, the United States has more than 83,000 state, county, municipal, and other units of local government. And the majority of them have the authority to issue debt, although most have constitutional prohibitions against budget deficits or limits on how much they can borrow.

Accompanying the growth and shift of the U.S. population has come an *upgrading of citizens' expectations* concerning the quality of government services. We expect much more from government today than we did a generation ago. Particularly noticeable is an increased demand for government services that directly affect the quality of life, such as better-designed schools, and improved medical and health care facilities.

EXHIBIT 18.8

Total Debt Issued by State and Local Governments in the United States, 1940–2004* ($ Billions)

Year	Debt Outstanding at Year-End	Year	Debt Outstanding at Year-End
1940	$ 20.3	1980	$ 302.8
1950	24.1	1990	848.6
1960	70.8	2000	1,270.6
1970	145.5	2004*	1,619.0

Sources: U.S. Department of Commerce: Board of Governors of the Federal System, *Flow of Funds: Assets and Liabilities Outstanding;* and the *Federal Reserve Bulletin,* selected issues.

*Figure as of the second quarter of 2004.

Instead of gravel roads and narrow highways, local citizens demand paved and guttered streets and all-weather, controlled-access highways. Many municipal governments are active in providing cultural facilities, such as libraries and museums, and are expected to play leading roles in controlling environmental pollution.

All of these public demands have had to be financed in an era of rising construction and labor costs, exacerbating the money burdens of local governments. Moreover, in the early 1990s, many local governments were faced with sluggish economic growth and the loss of a tax base upon which to build for the future, though later economic growth accelerated and many state and local governments racked up sizable budget surpluses until the 9/11 terrorist crisis and, especially, the economic recession of 2001–2002. State and local government revenue plunged and a serious budget crisis developed.

State and local governments are expected to continue to borrow heavily in future years, in part because the federal government seems intent on reducing its contributions to local funding and because of expected lower interest rates. In fact, the so-called "new federalism" marks an ongoing trend toward turning more and more social services over to the states to fund and manage. The states, in turn, seem to be passing more program responsibilities on to counties, cities, and other local governmental units, putting additional financial stress on these smallest units of government.

Sources of Revenue for State and Local Governments

Borrowing by state and local governments supplements their tax revenues and income from fees charged to users of government services. When tax and fee revenues fail to grow as fast as public demands, municipal borrowings rise. Moreover, when long-term capital projects are undertaken, long-term borrowing rather than taxation is often the preferred method of governmental finance.

As we study state and local governmental borrowing in the financial markets, it is useful to have in mind the principal sources and uses of state and local funds. Where do the majority of state and local government revenues come from? And where does most of the money go? Exhibits 18.9 and 18.10, drawn from a recent census of state and local units of government, provide some answers to these questions.

As expected, most state and local government *revenues* are derived from *local* sources of funds: the citizens these governments serve. About four-fifths of state and local government revenues normally are derived from local sources, according to a U.S. Department of Commerce census. However, intergovernmental transfers of funds, including state aid to local schools and federal aid to the states, also provide a significant share of total revenues. Local governments receive about a third of their revenues from state governments, on average.

Not surprisingly, *taxes* are the largest single revenue source for state and local governments. Property taxes are the mainstay of *local* government support, providing just over one-quarter of general revenues, followed by sales taxes. *State* governments, in contrast, rely principally upon sales and income taxes, each accounting for about 15 percent of state revenues. Selective sales taxes on alcoholic beverages, entertainment, gasoline, tobacco, and other specialized products and services are levied almost entirely at the state level and have increased significantly in recent years. User fees have also grown rapidly, with more than three-quarters of U.S. cities and counties increasing their charges and fees for government services and for access to public facilities in recent years. Income taxes are imposed almost exclusively at the state level and are levied mainly against individuals rather than corporations. Income taxes contribute about one-fifth of state government revenues. Most recently, property taxes have become more

EXHIBIT 18.9	**Sources of Revenue and Expenditures for State and Local Governments ($ Billions for Fiscal 2000–2001)**

Revenue Sources	Amounts	Percentage of Total	Expenditures by Function	Amounts	Percentage of Total
Property taxes	$ 263.7	16.0%	Education	$ 563.6	34.7%
Sales and gross receipts taxes	320.2	19.4	Highways	107.2	6.6
Individual income taxes	226.3	13.7	Public welfare spending	257.4	15.8
Corporate profits taxes	35.3	2.1			
Revenue from the federal government	324.0	19.7	All other state and local government spending (including expenses for public safety, housing, environmental cleanup and pollution prevention, administration, interest on debt, and general and miscellaneous expenditures)		
All other sources of revenue (including user fees and miscellaneous general revenues)	477.6	29.0		697.9	42.9
Total revenues	$1,647.2	100.0%	Total expenditures	$1,626.1	100.0%

Source: Economic Report of the President, 2002.

important as a source of local government funds, while income taxes have generally declined in the wake of a more slowly growing economy, a struggling stock market, and booming housing market.

Not shown separately in Exhibits 18.9 and 18.10 is the growing use of lotteries and taxation of gambling that close to 40 states have either set in motion or are seriously considering. State-run lotteries often dedicate net revenues from ticket sales to the support of a specific government service, such as education, which the public seems anxious to support. Lotteries have become a popular alternative to higher taxes or to slicing government services because they are a voluntary form of taxation, but they

EXHIBIT 18.10
State and Local Government Finances: Major Cash Inflows and Outflows
Source: U.S. Bureau of the Census, *Census of Governments.*

Cash Inflows:

- Taxes
  - Property
  - Sales
  - Income
  - Miscellaneous
- User fees
- Special assessments
- Intergovernmental transfers from federal and state governments
- Borrowings (net market value of municipal debt sold)

States, cities, counties, school districts, and other local governments

Cash Outflows:

- Schools and other educational facilities
- Transportation facilities (e.g., highways, airports, commuter systems, etc.)
- Social services (income supplements, medical support, housing, and public safety)
- Industrial development incentives
- Administration and employee payrolls
- Interest and debt repayments

incur high administrative costs and often contribute only a small portion of needed funds.[4]

Trends in state and local government spending for a single state can usually be dialed up by visiting an individual state's Web site—for example, for the state of Minnesota use auditor.leg.state.mn.us

State and Local Government Expenditures   Where do state and local governments *spend* most of their funds? As Exhibit 18.9 suggests, *education* is the single largest item on the budgets of local governmental units and usually ranks number one or two on state budgets as well. *Social services,* including public welfare and medical care, occupies second place in local government spending but often ranks first in some state budgets at about a quarter of total spending. *Transportation services,* especially highway construction and maintenance, often ranks third in state spending, but generally ranks lower for local governments. Overall, education, Medicare and general health care, public welfare, highway construction, sanitation, and correctional facilities represent close to two-thirds of state and local government spending today.

Some of the most important government services account for only a minor share of annual public budgets. For example, the cost of ensuring public safety—police and fire protection—generally accounts for less than 10 percent of local government expenditures, although recently expenditures for police departments and jail facilities have taken up an increased share of all local spending. Sewer and sanitation services, protection of the environment, and housing programs to aid the poor normally represent about 10 percent of local government costs but a much smaller share of state government spending.

The economic condition of states, metropolitan areas, and counties may be traced through a new FDIC Web site called RECON at fdic.gov

State and local government expenditures have grown rapidly in recent years. In 1997, expenditures by state and local units topped the $1.25 trillion level. This figure was five times larger than the level of state and local government spending in 1980. By 2001, spending by these governmental units reached more than $1.6 trillion. Local tax revenues have simply been inadequate to handle this kind of growth in current (short-term) and capital (long-term) expenditures. Moreover, there is a growing perception that many municipal facilities need modernizing. Accordingly, borrowing in the money and capital markets against future government revenues in order to accommodate local needs for renovation, modernization, and expansion of facilities has soared. In the 1990s, several states (led by New York) began aggressive infrastructure spending programs to create more jobs, taking over a portion of the fiscal function that traditionally has been the province of the federal government, and in the late 1990s into the turn of the new century, the federal government began to pass a bigger share of welfare and social programs back to the states.

Data revealing the fiscal condition of state and local governments in the United States are readily available through a key Web site of the U.S. Bureau of Economic Analysis at bea.doc.gov

State and local governments experienced a marked upward surge in revenues and most had substantial surpluses as the 1990s drew to a close and the twenty-first century began. In 1998, for example, the 50 states closed that fiscal year with a combined surplus of close to $25 billion, or about 6 percent of their annual expenses, even after several had made tax cuts in 1996 and 1997. Even New York City—with a long history of financial troubles—achieved a budget surplus of nearly $2 billion in 1998. Indeed, some states did so well with an expanding economy and rising tax collections that they were debating whether or not to award rebates to their

---

[4]As the 21st century began several local governments, especially large cities, made use of a clever devise known as a *sale and lease back*. For example, the city of Chicago sold its emergency center for close to $140 million to two banks, gaining substantial new revenues. For their part the banks involved were able to significantly reduce their taxes through depreciation of the newly acquired assets. Other cities (e.g., New York and Atlanta) were able to sell and lease back their subway and rail cars. The use of this government financing technique may be restricted in the future, however, due to proposed new federal legislation to protect the U.S. Treasury from losing substantial tax revenues.

The 1980s and 1990s ushered in a strong movement toward *privatization*—letting privately owned businesses produce and offer some local government services. Among the most common government services turned over to private suppliers in recent years have been the following:

Hospitals

Landfills

Stadiums, auditoriums, and other recreational facilities

Airports

Public transportation

Sewer systems

Natural gas (retail)

Water supplies

Electric power services

Fire protection

Libraries

Correctional facilities

By 1987, when the first census of U.S. governments to inquire about privatization took place, almost 40 percent of cities and towns with populations of at least 25,000 had contracted out to a private business at least one former government-provided service. Subsequent census reports suggested that the percentage of cities and towns over 25,000 in population with at least some privatized services had risen to about half of the total. Many state and local officials have seen privatization as a way to lower the cost of government, promote greater efficiency, and reduce taxes. The theory is that private competition replacing government monopolies should improve both service quality and cost. Some local governments see the private sourcing route as a way to offer services—stadiums or utilities, for example—that the local area could not otherwise afford.

Whatever the motivations have been, privatization lost some of its steam as the new century opened. No one knows for sure why this has occurred, but only a fraction of cities and towns previously involved in private outsourcing appear to still be doing so. One reason may be resistance from local government workers who fear loss of their jobs. Private production of government services seems to be seriously considered when a local community is facing a fiscal crisis and needs to stop providing some of its more costly services. However, when times improve, fewer local governments seem to be interested in the privatization route.

taxpayers or whether to retire debt or to expand their savings to deal with possible future emergencies. Some state governments decided to conserve their budget surpluses in order to protect their bond ratings and, thus, keep future borrowing costs as low as possible.

Then, in the year 2000 an economic slowdown began, with an actual decline in economic activity in 2001–2002. State and local sales and income tax revenues sagged for many states while the cost of social programs and of providing protection against possible future terrorism soared. Many states were forced to dip deeply into their previously accumulated surpluses and others raised taxes and increased borrowings (as in the case of California) in an attempt to cover their cash shortages.

The fiscal situation at the *local* level—cities, counties, and school districts—is often less "rosy" than for many states due to pressure from citizens for lower taxes and the prospect of cutbacks in federal financial aid. Many local governments face rising populations of jail inmates, school-age children, and aging and indigent individuals and families who need subsidized housing and health care. Added to these fiscal problems are many government employee retirement funds that are not yet fully funded, requiring local governments to set aside more funds or even borrow using pension-obligation bonds to insure that their employees receive the pensions they have been promised.

565

Motivations for State and Local Government Borrowing

State and local governments borrow money for several reasons. The first is to *satisfy short-term cash needs;* that is, meet payrolls, make repairs, purchase supplies, cover fuel costs, and maintain adequate levels of working capital. Most state and local governments use tax-anticipation notes (to be discussed later) and other forms of short-term borrowing as a supplement to tax revenues to meet these immediate cash needs. Frequently, the construction phase of a building project is financed from short-term funds, and then permanent financing is obtained by selling long-term bonds.

The second major reason for state and local government borrowing is to *finance long-term capital investment;* that is, to build schools, highways, and similar permanent facilities. Long-term projects of this sort account for the bulk of all municipal securities issued each year. Some governmental units try to anticipate future financial needs by borrowing when interest rates are low even though project construction will not begin for a substantial period of time. Funds raised through anticipatory borrowing are then "warehoused" in various investments (such as Treasury bills and notes) until actual construction begins.

In recent years, local governments have occasionally employed *advance refunding* of securities. Advance refundings occur when a governmental unit has been granted a higher credit rating on its bonds by a rating agency, such as Moody's Investors Service or Standard & Poor's Corporation. Bonds issued previously with lower credit ratings (higher interest rates) may be called in and new securities issued at lower cost. Any significant decline in market interest rates usually gives rise to more advance refunding activity by state and local governments—a practice that has sometimes led to alleged "pay to play" activities in which security underwriters have tried to persuade local government officials (by making contributions to local political campaigns) to refund outstanding debt and thereby generate more underwriting fees.

QUESTIONS TO HELP YOU STUDY

13. The market for state and local government debt has been among the most rapidly growing financial markets over the past half century. Why has this growth occurred?

14. Can you foresee any serious problems on the horizon as state and local governments work to deal with the rapid growth of public demands on their budgets?

15. What are the principal sources of *revenue* for state and local governments today? Where do they spend the bulk of their incoming funds?

16. For what principal reasons do state and local governments borrow money?

17. Why is the *economy* of special importance to state and local governments in planning their revenues and expenditures?

Types of Securities Issued by State and Local Governments

Many different types of securities are issued by state and local governments, and the variety of municipal securities available to investors is expanding rapidly. (See, for example, Exhibit 18.11.) One useful distinction is between short-term securities, which are generally issued to provide working capital, and long-term securities, used mainly to fund capital projects (such as the construction of new buildings or highways).

EXHIBIT 18.11

New Security Issues of Tax-Exempt State and Local Governments, 2003 ($ Billions)

Source: Board of Governors of the Federal Reserve System, *Federal Reserve Bulletin*, selected issues.

Types of Issue and Issuer or Use of Funds	2003	Use of Funds	2003
All issues	$384.1	Use of proceeds from new capital issues:	
Type of issue:			
General obligation	143.9	Education	$70.3
Revenue	238.2	Transportation	23.8
Type of issuer		Utilities and conservation	10.2
State governments	49.8	Social welfare	NA
Special districts	253.5	Industrial aid	22.4
Municipalities, counties and townships	78.8	Other purposes	97.7
Issues for new capital, total	264.5		

Note: Issues represented in the table are to raise new capital and refund outstanding debt.

tax-anticipation notes (TANs)

revenue-anticipation notes (RANs)

bond-anticipation notes (BANs)

Short-Term Securities   The most popular short-term securities issued by state and local governments are **tax-anticipation notes (TANs), revenue-anticipation notes (RANs),** and **bond-anticipation notes (BANs).**

Tax-Anticipation and Revenue-Anticipation Notes   These notes are used to attract funds in lieu of tax receipts or other revenues expected to be received in the near future. Governments, like businesses and households, have a daily need for cash to meet payrolls and purchase supplies. However, funds raised through taxes usually flow in only at certain times of the year. To satisfy their continuing need for cash between tax dates, state and local governments issue short-term notes with maturities ranging from a few days to a few months. Most of these short-term issues are acquired by local banks. When tax funds are received, the issuing government pays off the note holders and retires any outstanding securities.

Bond-Anticipation Notes   These short-term IOUs, also called *BANs,* are used to provide temporary financing of a long-term project until the time is right to sell long-term bonds. A school district, for example, may need to start construction on new school facilities due to pressure from rising enrollments. If market interest rates currently are too high to permit the issue of bonds, then construction can start from funds raised from bond-anticipation notes. Once the project is under way and interest rates decline to more modest levels, the school district then sells its long-term bonds and retires the bond-anticipation notes.

general obligation bonds

revenue bonds

Long-Term Securities   The most common type of municipal borrowing is through long-term bonds. There are two major types of municipal bonds issued today—**general obligation bonds** and **revenue bonds**—and both are used principally to finance construction.

General Obligation Bonds   These bonds, known as *GOs,* are the most secure form of municipal borrowing from the standpoint of the investor because they are backed by the "full faith and credit" of the issuing government and may be paid from *any* revenue source. State, county, and city governments, along with school districts, have the power to tax citizens to meet principal and interest payments on any debt issued. GOs are fully backed by this taxing power and often must be approved by public referendum before issue. The quality or level of risk of GOs depends on the economic base (income and property values) of local communities and the total amount of debt issued.

Revenue Bonds   In contrast, *revenue bonds* are payable only from a specified source of revenue, such as a toll road or a sewer project, and usually do not require a public referendum before they can be issued. These securities are not guaranteed or backed by the taxing power of government. Instead, revenue bonds depend for their value on the revenue-generating capacity of the particular project they support.[5]

---

[5]Some municipal bonds display characteristics of *both* GO and revenue securities. For example, a *special tax bond* is payable from the revenues generated by a special tax, such as a tax on gasoline. Many special tax bonds are backed by the full faith, credit, and taxing power of the issuing governmental unit, giving them the character of GOs. *Special assessment bonds* are payable only from assessments against property constructed or purchased from the proceeds of the bonds issued and arise from sewer and street construction or similar projects. Special assessment issues may take on the character of GOs when backed by the taxing power of the issuer. *Authority bonds* are issued by special governmental units set up by states, cities, or counties to construct and manage certain facilities, such as airports. Authority bonds may be either GOs or revenue issues.

Both general obligation and revenue bonds have grown rapidly over the past decade, and there has been a virtual explosion of different types of revenue bonds. Much of the growth of revenue issues is due to programs of the federal government designed to provide housing for low-income groups, improved medical facilities, and student loans, as well as efforts by local governments to modernize their facilities.

Types of Revenue Bonds   Among the best-known revenue issues are *student-loan revenue bonds* (SLRBs), which have been issued by some state government agencies that lend money to college students. The federal government guarantees 100 percent of the principal and interest of an SLRB, provided the issuing agency's loan-default ratio is low. If a high percentage of students default on their loans, federal guarantees are limited to only a certain portion (usually 80 to 90 percent) of principal and interest payments on the bonds.

In the housing field, several forms of state and local revenue bonds have been used. For example, *life-care bonds* have been issued by state and local development agencies to provide housing for the elderly. Frequently, nonprofit agencies organized by religious groups administer the property. Investor funds may be secured by lease rentals and mortgages against the property.

Construction of hospital facilities may be supported by *hospital revenue bonds.* These bonds have been issued by state authorities to build hospitals for lease to public or private operating agencies. Hospital revenue bonds have their principal and interest secured by lease rentals and a mortgage against hospital property.

An unusual type of municipal security that serves both public and private interests is the *industrial development bond* (IDB). These securities originally were used to finance plant construction and the purchase of land, which is then leased to a private company. More recently, IDBs have financed the construction of industrial parks, electric-generating plants, pollution control equipment, and other capital items. Their purpose is to attract industry into a local area and increase jobs and tax revenues. However, the use of public funds raised through the tax-exempt borrowing privilege for private purposes soon disturbed many members of Congress. The Deficit Reduction Act of 1984 listed several prohibited uses of IDB money, placed a ceiling on IDBs stemming from a single issuer, and restricted the total amount that could be issued from each state based upon its population. Accordingly, issuers of IDBs must plan much farther in advance and work to get their new issues approved and sold early in the new year before a local government's quota for IDB issues runs out.

Many local governments still borrow or use a portion of their current or expected future tax revenues to offer incentives for the development of new businesses in their area. Unfortunately, recent research evidence suggests that most businesses decide on which states and localities to enter based primarily upon such features as climate, energy costs, nearness to the firms' markets, and the availability of labor with the necessary skills—factors that are often beyond a local government's control—rather than being enticed by the financial incentives offered by many communities. (See, for example, Bradbury, Kodrzycki, and Tannenwald [1997].)

Innovations in Municipal Securities   The vast majority of state and local securities promise the investor a fixed rate of return. Unfortunately, this can reduce the attractiveness of GOs and revenue bonds in periods of rising interest rates and inflation. During such periods, several new municipal instruments that have been developed to deal with this "inflexibility" problem may be used. For example, some tax-exempt revenue bonds have been issued as *floaters*. In one case, U.S. Steel

Exhibit 18.12 illustrates the effect of this calculation with marginal tax rates ranging from 0 to 35 percent. For an investor in the top 35 percent tax bracket, the after-tax return on Aaa corporate bonds was 10 percent × (1 − 0.35), or 6.50 percent. Clearly, an investor in this high-income group would prefer to purchase municipal bonds yielding 7.75 percent rather than corporate bonds returning just 6.50 percent after taxes, other factors being equal. The same conclusion holds true for larger corporations and banks confronted with the top 35 percent federal tax rate.[6] Even for middle-bracket investors facing a moderate income tax rate (such as 28 percent), municipals often are attractive in terms of their after-tax return.[7]

Of course, the foregoing analysis focuses exclusively on after-tax rates of return, ignoring differences in liquidity and other features of taxable and tax-exempt securities. A corporation or an individual who needs to hold securities for liquidity purposes, for example, might well hold taxable issues, such as U.S. government securities, that can be converted into cash quickly and with little risk of loss, even though their after-tax yields may be lower than the yields on municipal bonds.

For income tax brackets below the top rung, taxable securities compare more favorably with municipals. For example, many small private investors whose applicable federal income tax rate may range from 10 to 15 percent find taxable securities more lucrative and purchase few municipals. In effect, the tax-exempt feature limits the demand for state and local government securities to high-income individuals and mutual funds that appeal to individuals as investors, property-casualty insurers, large nonfinancial corporations, and other higher tax-bracket investors. This limitation may represent a serious problem in future years when many local governments must raise an enormous volume of new funds to accommodate rapidly expanding populations.

The tax exemption feature is an advantage to municipal governments because it keeps their interest cost low relative to interest rates paid by other borrowers. These savings can be passed on to local citizens in the form of lower tax rates. Of course, the U.S. Treasury is able to collect less revenue from high-bracket investors as a result of the exemption privilege and must tax low-bracket taxpayers more heavily to make up the difference. Therefore, the *total* tax bill from all levels of government is probably little affected by the tax-exempt feature of municipals.

Exemption Contributes to Market Volatility

Because the market for municipal bonds is limited by the tax-exempt privilege to top-bracket investors, prices and interest rates on municipal bonds tend to be volatile. Prices of tax-exempt bonds tend

[6]Recent federal tax laws have sharply reduced the attractiveness of municipal securities to banks and other top tax-bracket investors. Successive tax laws have lowered the top corporate tax rate, forcing the after-tax yield on municipal bonds closer to the after-tax return on taxable securities. Federal tax reform, therefore, has made municipal bonds less attractive relative to all taxable securities. Many investors, especially individuals, still find municipals attractive, however, because they are one of only a few tax shelters left after federal tax reform. Banks, on the other hand, have significantly reduced their municipal holdings relative to taxable loans and U.S. government securities because federal laws have sharply reduced or eliminated, depending upon the issuer of the municipal securities, the tax deductibility of bank borrowing costs when banks purchase municipals. Overall, these tax law changes have resulted in a shift in the municipal market toward more *retail investors*— higher-income individuals and mutual funds appealing to individuals as investors—to whom the tax exemption feature of municipals is still an important tax shelter.

[7]The Economic Growth and Tax Relief Reconciliation Act of 2001 created additional tax brackets ranging from the lowest at 10 percent to a high of 39.1 percent in the year 2001. The top U.S. federal tax rate was lowered to 35 percent when the Jobs and Growth Tax Relief Reconciliation Act was passed in 2003.

to rise during periods when corporate and individual incomes are rising, because top-bracket investors have greater need to shelter their earnings from taxation at those times. However, a fall in individual or corporate earnings often leads to sharp reductions in the demand for municipal bonds. Prices of tax-exempt issues may plummet, and interest costs confronting borrowing governments may rise during those periods when corporate profits are squeezed. This makes financial planning in the state and local government sector more difficult.

Credit Ratings   A feature of municipal securities that makes them especially attractive to investors is their high credit rating. About 10 percent of all municipal securities are AAA-rated by Moody's Investors Service and Standard & Poor's Corporation; about half are AA- or A-rated. A relatively small proportion of all state and local government securities are rated BA or lower or carry no published rating. This means that most municipal issues are considered to be of *investment quality* rather than speculative buys.

Recently, Moody's Investors Service began to attach numerical modifiers to its standard A and B security ratings for municipal securities. These newer Moody's bond ratings for state and local government debt issues include the following:

Moody's State and Local Government Bond Rating Symbols

Aaa	Ba1
Aa1	Ba2
Aa2	Ba3
Aa3	B1
A1	B2
A2	B3
A3	Caa
Baa1	Ca
Baa2	C
Baa3	

In the above ratings, the modifier 1 means a new municipal bond issue ranks at the higher end of its rating category, 2 indicates a mid-range quality state and local security, and 3 implies the debt issue is judged to be at the low end of its rating class. Notice that the lowest-grade speculative municipal issues have *no* numerical modifiers.

Moody's began to apply the numerical modifiers to the ratings for state and local government debt because of several recent trends affecting the municipal sector, including:

1. A shift in the primary investor groups holding state and local bonds, as banks, for example, largely withdrew from heavy municipal bond holdings due to reduced tax incentives, while tax-exempt mutual funds and money market funds became major buyers of municipals. These latter institutions need finer grading and more accurate valuation of municipal bonds because they are frequently forced to liquidate their holdings of municipals quickly when mutual fund investors sell their shares.

2. Evidence of greater credit risk and volatility in the state and local government sector, including an increasing trend toward defaults as more and more local governments experience fiscal stress as the federal government moves to transfer more responsibilities to local governments and many local taxpayers resist new programs and higher taxes.

Factors Behind Setting Credit Ratings   In assigning credit ratings to municipals, Moody's and other rating services consider the past repayment record of the borrowing unit of government, the quality and size of its tax base, the volume of debt outstanding, local economic conditions, and future prospects for growth in the local economy. The fact that many municipal issues are backed by taxing authority or may draw on several different sources of revenue for repayment of principal and interest helps to keep the investment quality of tax-exempt municipal issues high. This is particularly important for regulated financial institutions that buy municipals. For example, regulations generally prohibit banks and other depository institutions from acquiring debt securities rated below BAA or BBB (so-called speculative issues). These restrictive rules encourage state and local governments to keep their credit ratings high in order to encourage more active participation by regulated financial institutions in bidding for new municipal securities.

Recent Credit Quality Problems   Until recently, state and local governments possessed almost unblemished credit records. No major defaults on municipal securities had occurred for nearly half a century. However, the turbulent economic and financial environment of recent decades has caused many investors to reassess the credit standing of municipals, especially the bonds and notes issued by some of the largest cities and those associated with special local government projects, such as operating public utilities or building toll roads. Nonetheless, there have been relatively few actual defaults on municipal bonds in recent years (though about 6,000 local government defaults have occurred in U.S. history as a whole) and, when they have occurred, investors usually have received back the principal value of their bonds (with some loss of interest).

The recent problems in the municipal bond market first surfaced in the dramatic financial crisis experienced by New York City during the 1970s. Soaring costs for municipal services, excessive reliance on short-term debt, and high unemployment combined to threaten that city with record high interest costs and financial default. In the wake of New York City's fiscal crisis, other northeastern U.S. cities—Chicago, Detroit, Philadelphia, and Washington, DC—also found their credit costs rising and investor resistance to buying their securities increasing. Then in 1978, Cleveland, Ohio, became the first major U.S. city to default on its debt since the Great Depression of the 1930s. This was followed by an even bigger debacle in 1983, to the tune of more than $2 billion, when a nuclear power consortium among several municipal governments—the Washington Public Power Supply System—fell into default under the weight of project delays and cost overruns.

More recently, as the 1990s began, several states and cities had the credit ratings on their bonds either lowered or placed on a "credit watch" list. The most dramatic example was the state of California, which faced projected annual budget deficits in the $5 billion range. Several of California's cities and other local governments appeared to be close to defaulting on their bonds. During the summer of 1995, Orange County, California, one of the largest urban areas in the United States, declared bankruptcy, with close to $800 million in unpaid obligations. The rapid growth in that county's population put its local government in a bind due to the soaring demand for public services. However, Orange County voters rejected several proposals to raise taxes. County officials, in dire need of revenue, then adopted an aggressive investment policy, including heavy investments in derivative securities, which lost about $2.5 billion when interest rates rose. Faced with numerous claims from creditors (including other local governments that had invested their funds with Orange County), county officials worked for nearly a year to hammer out a repayment plan to cover most of Orange County's debts.[8]

---

[8]See Chapter 8 for more discussion of the Orange County bankruptcy.

The Orange County debacle set the tone for credit quality issues as the twentieth century ended and a new century began. Following the lead of Orange County, a growing number of states, cities, and other local units of government have experienced a significant decline in their financial strength and stability. Not surprisingly, credit-rating agencies like Moody's and Standard & Poor's have begun putting increased numbers of states and municipal governments on their "credit watch" lists and several have recently had their credit ratings lowered. Many of these troubled governments are confronted with slow or no economic growth, a declining tax base, rising unemployment, aging populations, soaring health care costs for their employees and their citizens, and employee retirement plans that have become substantially underfunded, posing a serious drain on future government revenues. Probably the most dramatic example of these problems and their credit-quality consequences has centered on the city of Pittsburgh, Pennsylvania. In 2003, Standard & Poor's lowered Pittsburgh's credit rating five notches on its credit-quality scale—from investment grade to junk-bond status—affecting nearly $900 million of that city's outstanding debt. Nor was Pittsburgh alone—during the same year there were 10 downgrades of state government credit ratings scattered among six different states.

Orange County's financial collapse and Pittsburgh's sharp credit downgrade have reminded investors in municipals that local government failures are an ever-present possibility. Government bankruptcies are more likely in areas of economic decline or in localities where growth has far outstripped the ability of cities and counties to provide government services and citizens are unwilling to levy additional taxes or authorize the issuance of new debt. Another bankruptcy-threatening problem occurred as the new century began—power outages and rising energy costs that eroded the fiscal strength of some states (particularly California) until energy costs backed down. In 2003, California—faced with a mountain of debt approaching maturity—was forced to issue a record volume of new securities (more than $8 billion) to remain solvent. This fiscal crisis contributed to the recall of its governor for the first time in history.

Partly as a result of recent state and local government financial problems, the Securities and Exchange Commission (SEC) has amended its Rule 15c2-12 to bar security dealers from marketing new municipal security issues unless the issuers agree to provide annual financial reports and continuing disclosure of "material events" (such as delinquencies, defaults, modification of security holders' rights, credit rating changes, or sale of property backing a security issue) to designated national databanks. At almost the same time, the SEC approved a rule to severely limit the campaign ("pay to play") contributions that security dealers underwriting new municipal bond issues could make to local government officials and to those running for public office. The idea is to protect investors in municipals from the adverse consequences of political graft and corruption arising from state and local governments' borrowing money.

For an explanation of how municipal bond insurance works, see especially Municipal Bond Insurance at munibondadvisor.com/ BondInsurance.htm and the Municipal Bond Investors Assurance Corporation at mbia.com/tools/ services.htm

Insurance for Municipal Bonds   Investor concern over the quality of some municipal securities and the potential failure of some state and local government projects led to the creation of "sleep insurance" for selected municipal issues. First offered by Ambac Indemnity Corp. in the early 1970s and later by such companies as Municipal Bond Investors Assurance Corp. (MBIA), Financial Security Assurance, Inc., and Financial Guarantee Insurance Corporation, these insurance policies, which guarantee timely payment of principal and interest, now cover most top-rated state and local government bonds. Such insurance protection normally is requested and paid for by the bond issuer or the issuers' representative, not the investor purchasing the bonds. However, buyers of insured bonds usually receive lower yields compared to noninsured bonds. Therefore, issuers benefit from insurance policies because they can sell their bonds at lower interest cost. The rating agencies, such as Standard & Poor's Corporation and Moody's Investors Service, generally grant higher credit ratings to insured municipal securities. However, if the credit rating of the insurance company falls, the interest rates on municipal bonds insured by that particular company also tend to rise as investors become concerned about the insurer's ability to pay if the state or local government issuer cannot. Bond insurance has become more important in recent years as retail customers (individuals and mutual funds) have come to capture a larger share of purchases of new municipal securities.

One additional form of municipal "insurance" that has recently grown in popularity is the rise of bank credit lines and standby guarantee letters. These credit back-up contracts help to increase the salability of municipals by reassuring potential investors that a bank will provide the necessary liquidity if the issuing state or local government faces a cash shortage.

serialization

Serialization   Most municipal bonds are *serial* securities. **Serialization** refers to the splitting up of a single bond issue into several different maturities. Thus, an issue of $20 million in bonds to build a municipal auditorium might include the following securities:

Amount	Due in
$1 million	1 year
$1 million	2 years
$1 million	3 years
•	•
•	•
•	•
$1 million	20 years

Splitting a single issue of municipals into multiple maturities contrasts with the practice employed by most corporate borrowers and the federal government. Corporations, for example, generally issue *term* bonds in which all securities in the same issue come due on the same date. In effect, serialization of municipal bonds is a way of *amortizing* state and local debt.

Why is serialization so popular in the municipal field? Before serial bonds were widely adopted, state and local bonds were generally term securities. A sinking fund was created at the time of issue, and annual contributions were made to the fund until sufficient monies were accumulated to pay off the bond at maturity. However, sinking funds proved irresistible to unscrupulous politicians and to governments facing financial emergencies. Accumulated funds often disappeared, leaving virtually nothing to retire municipal debt when it came due. The serial feature seemed to offer an ideal solution to this problem.

Unfortunately, serialization has created as many problems as it has solved. For one thing, splitting a security into a number of different maturities reduces the liquidity and marketability of municipal securities. When a municipal issue is split into multiple maturities there is only a relatively small amount outstanding in any one maturity class. The potential volume of trading for particular maturities is, therefore, limited. Serialization also complicates the offering of new securities, because a number of different investor groups must be attracted into the bidding. For example, money market funds, banks, and individuals generally prefer the shorter-term (1- to 10-year) securities, and mutual funds and insurance companies often want only longer-term municipal bonds.

How Municipal Bonds Are Marketed

Keeping up with municipal prices and interest rates is easier today due to such sites as CNN/Money at cnnfm.com and the Bond Market Association at bondmarkets.com

The selling of municipals is usually carried out through a syndicate of banks and securities dealers. These institutions underwrite municipals by purchasing them from issuing units of government and reselling the securities in the open market at a higher price. Prices paid by the underwriting firms may be determined either by competitive bidding among several syndicates or by negotiation with a single securities dealer or syndicate. Competitive bidding normally is employed in the marketing of general obligation bonds; revenue bonds more frequently are placed through private negotiation.

In competitive bidding, syndicates (which may contain from two to upwards of a dozen or more underwriters) interested in a particular bond issue will estimate its potential reoffer price in the open market and what their desired underwriting commission must be. Each syndicate wants to bid a price high enough to win the bid but low enough so that the securities later can be sold in the open market at a price sufficient to protect the syndicate's commission. That is,

$$\text{Bid price} + \text{Underwriting commission} = \text{Market reoffer price}$$

The winning bid carries the lowest *net interest cost* (NIC) to the issuing unit of government. The NIC is simply the sum of all interest payments that will be owed on the new issue divided by its principal amount.

Bidding for new issues of municipal bonds is a treacherous business. Prices, interest rates, and market demand for municipals change rapidly. In fact, the tax-exempt securities market is one of the most volatile of all financial markets. This is due, in part, to the key role of mutual funds, banks, insurance companies, and individual investors in the municipal market, whose demand for municipals fluctuates with their net earnings, loan demand, and market conditions. Legal interest rate ceilings, which prohibit some local governments from borrowing when market interest rates climb above those ceilings, also play a significant role in the volatility of municipal trading. These combined factors render the tax-exempt market highly sensitive to the business cycle, monetary policy, and a host of other factors.

The specter of high interest rates often forces postponement of hundreds of millions of dollars in new security issues, and the onset of lower interest rates may unleash a flood of new security offerings. Still another problem is the unpredictability of federal tax reform legislation, which has reduced the volume and attractiveness of many municipal securities to investors from time to time. The nature of this large debt market can suddenly change, with serious consequences for many of its players. Still, the rewards of municipal bond underwriting can be substantial, even though only a handful of dealers make a continuous market for these securities. (Among the leading underwriters of state and local bonds today are Goldman Sachs, Bear Stearns, Lehman Brothers, Wachovia Securities, and Merrill Lynch.) For example, during 1998 one of the largest municipal bond underwritings in history took place: a staggered offering amounting to almost $7 billion in bonds issued to fund New York's takeover of the Long Island Lighting Company. In this instance, the team of underwriters involved expected to receive about $40 million in underwriting fees.

Problems in the Municipal Market

Problems and Proposals Regarding Tax Exemption   The municipal market has been plagued by a number of problems over the years, some related to its unique tax-exempt character. Many observers question the social benefit of the tax-exemption privilege. Although state and local governments can borrow more cheaply

In recent years the federal government has been passing more and more of its programs and activities along to the states, granting the states more power to implement federal programs and curtailing some of the old federal rules that limited what state and local governments could do. As a result, state and local government spending (net of federal aid) has recently risen to more than 10 percent of U.S. GDP, while net federal spending has fallen below that figure. This trend is called "devolution," with the federal government passing more of its responsibilities (such as welfare programs) to the states and local governmental units. This movement seems consistent with the move toward greater deregulation, decentralization, and free enterprise happening around the globe. The administration of President Clinton involved the states more proactively in rewriting federal program rules and standards, thus making it easier for many of the states to qualify for federal grants. A similar approach emerged in the George W. Bush administration.

There is substantial concern among some state and local authorities that local governments are not well prepared to pick up the *financial burdens* inherent in this "new federalism" approach. Many states and local governments already face a lack of financial resources and growing taxpayer resistance even before adding the burden of former federal programs tossed into their fiscal backyard. Some state and local governments may have to cut back on social services to their citizens that, in the past, used to help stabilize their economies. The result may be an overall shrinkage in government activity that may benefit some states (particularly states and local areas where individuals average higher private-sector incomes) but hurt other localities not as economically well off.

Overall, the quality of government service may eventually decline in the United States, though some researchers believe devolution is still desirable because it comes closer to what the original authors of the U.S. Constitution intended regarding federal powers versus state and local government powers. Some authorities believe the ultimate long-run solution may be to take advantage of the federal government's superior ability to collect revenues while using state and local governments' superior knowledge of local and regional service needs. This suggests that, from an efficiency point of view at least, the federal government should, perhaps, gather most tax revenues and give state and local authorities greater discretion in how, where, and for whom those revenues are to be spent.

as a result of tax exemption, the federal government must tax nonexempt groups more heavily to make up the lost revenue. Also, many important investor groups (such as pension funds) have little need for tax shelters and therefore display little interest in municipal bonds. Recently, commercial banks have drastically reduced their holdings of state and local government securities due to unfavorable tax treatment following the passage of federal tax reform laws. Now banks tend to concentrate their purchases of municipals in so-called "bank qualified" issues that are issued by smaller units of government and still promise significant tax benefits for the purchasing bank.

A number of proposals have been advanced over the years for improving the depth and stability of the municipal market and eliminating the tax-exempt feature. One interesting idea calls for reimbursing state and local governments for loss of the tax-exempt privilege by paying federal subsidies. A related idea calls for paying a subsidy directly to investors who choose to buy municipal securities. A federally sponsored *Urbank* was proposed a number of years ago that would issue its own bonds and direct the proceeds of bond sales to municipal governments. One criticism of this approach is the danger of increased federal controls over state and local government activities.

The Outlook for State and Local Governments   The outlook for state and local governments as the twenty-first century dawns is more encouraging than it has been in several years. Certainly there are serious problems with which to contend—for example, growing demands for new housing, medical, and recreational facilities for the elderly; demand for more equitable funding of schools located in poorer communities versus those situated in richer communities; the huge cost of defenses against possible future terrorist attacks; and a large prison population that will continue to require large-scale expenditures for adequate correctional facilities. Added to these demands are expensive *infrastructure* problems—water and sewer systems that are wearing out; city streets and bridges long ago worn down from adverse weather and heavy usage; deteriorating public buildings and highly expensive new building codes (such as currently apply to building new jails); and developing shortages of water and electrical-generating capacity.

Local government revenues will have to keep up with these demands for funds despite projected slower growth in the economy and the likelihood of less generous support from the federal government. States must plan for receiving fewer federal monies in the future; on the positive side, there are likely to be fewer federal restrictions on how local governments can spend federal money. At the same time, most states and localities are in hot pursuit of new industries to expand their economic base, which often means giving tax relief to new businesses and holding the line on the imposition of new taxes so that revenue sources are further reduced.

With slower economic growth and less federal support, more states will be under pressure to "pass the buck" to their local governments and force cities, counties, and school districts to deal with their own problems and find their own funding sources. Certainly, the need for local government services is not likely to fade, but the continued willingness of taxpayers to authorize new construction and new borrowing and the continued interest of large numbers of investors in buying state and local government debt securities (particularly through the purchase of shares in municipal-bond-oriented mutual funds) in order to support local governments' financial needs is a positive sign for the future growth of this challenging sector of the global financial marketplace.

QUESTIONS TO HELP YOU STUDY

21. What are the principal features of state and local government securities that have made them attractive to many groups of investors?

22. How has recent federal tax legislation impacted the market for municipals?

23. Describe how state and local government securities are marketed. What risks do syndicates face in this marketplace?

24. What key problems do you believe that state and local governments are likely to face in the years ahead? What factors seem to be the principal causes of these problems?

MARKETS ON THE NET: The Most Important Web Sites for This Chapter

Bond Market Association (investinginbonds.com)

Municipal Bond Insurance (munibondadvisor.com/BondInsurance.htm)

Office of Management and the Budget (gpo.gov/usbudget)

State and Local Governments on the Net (piperinfo.com)

U.S. Bureau of Economic Analysis (bea.doc.gov)

U.S. Bureau of the Census (census.gov)

U.S. Bureau of the Public Debt (publicdebt.treas.gov)

U.S. Treasury Department (treas.gov)

www.mhhe.com/rose9e

Summary of the Chapter's Main Points

In this chapter we examined the roles played by governments in the financial markets when they borrow money, levy taxes, and spend the funds they raise. We explored the fiscal policy and debt management practices of governments at all levels—federal or national, state, and local. Among the key points made in the chapter are the following:

- The chief fiscal agency of the United States is the U.S. Treasury Department. Other governments around the world have similar governmental departments which generally engage in two principal activities: (a) financing government expenditures through taxation, borrowing, and accessing other funds sources; and (b) managing the government's outstanding debt.

- The government affects the financial system and the economy through its taxing and spending activities, or *fiscal policy*. The government also can set in motion changes in the financial system and the economy through its *debt management policy*. This policy strategy involves changing the mix or composition of the government's debt (e.g., changes in the ratio of short-term to long-term government securities outstanding).

- If the government runs a *budget deficit,* with expenditures outstripping revenues, it will most likely be forced to borrow, issuing new debt. Market interest rates may tend to rise, while total income and spending may tend to move higher unless the central bank offsets the government's *fiscal policy* action or private borrowing and spending decline.

- On the other hand, the government may run a *budget surplus,* with revenues outpacing expenditures, and therefore may need to borrow less money. If the budget surplus is relatively large, a substantial portion of that surplus may be used to retire outstanding government debt. Income and market interest rates may tend to fall unless the central bank acts to offset the impact of the government's debt retirement program.

- The government also can use *debt management policy* to change conditions in the financial markets and the economy. For example, if the U.S. Treasury refunds maturing short-term securities by issuing new long-term securities, this action will tend to reduce the liquidity of the public's security holdings as the average maturity of the U.S. public debt increases. Short-term interest rates may tend to rise, while income (spending and production) may fall. In contrast, a government policy that emphasizes short-term borrowing may lead to more rapid economic growth and less unemployment, but possibly at the cost of greater inflation.

- The United States government carries one of the largest public debts in the world and, recently, due to a sluggish economy, record defense spending to fight terrorism, and costly social programs, that debt has been rising rapidly. With such a large and complex debt structure, U.S. Treasury debt managers must work to refund maturing government securities every week (in the case of short-term securities) and every quarter (in the case of longer-term securities) of the year. Their principal focus is on managing the *marketable* debt of the United States, represented by Treasury bills, notes, and bonds, which is sold to the public through security dealers. Today U.S. government agencies, the Federal Reserve System, and foreign investors hold a majority of the public debt of the United States.

- Fiscal policy and debt management policy, like monetary policy by the central bank, focus upon promoting maximum employment and sustainable economic growth and keeping inflation under control. But these different forms of public policy must be coordinated for maximum effectiveness; otherwise, the possible positive benefits of one policy may offset those of another.

- In addition to heavy borrowing by the U.S. Treasury Department, state and local governments in the United States also borrow billions of dollars each year to fund the construction of public facilities and to supply themselves with working capital to cover daily operations in providing government services to their citizens.

- The borrowings of these units of government are specially privileged under the U.S. Constitution and U.S. Treasury Department regulations. Their interest earnings are exempt from federal income taxation and many states also exempt the interest earnings on their own debt from state and local taxes. The tax-exemption feature makes these financial instruments (called *municipals*) uniquely attractive to investors occupying the highest tax brackets.

- Major factors driving state and local government borrowing have included rapid population and income growth, the upgrading of citizen expectations for publicly provided services, and a shifting of responsibility for funding many local services from the federal government to state and local units of government.

- Key revenue sources for state and local governments include sales and income taxes, property taxes, user fees, and funds transfers among governmental units. The largest categories of state and local government expenditures include education, social services, transportation services, health services, and construction spending.

- Many different types of securities are issued by states and local governments to borrow money. Short-term municipals include tax-anticipation notes (TANs), revenue-anticipation notes (RANs), and bond-anticipation notes (BANs). Each of these instruments is issued in the expectation that revenues to pay them off will subsequently appear.

- Long-term security issues include *general obligation (GO) bonds* and *revenue bonds*. The latter depend for their repayment on revenues generated by specific municipal projects, such as toll roads, toll bridges, and other revenue-generating ventures. There has been a tendency in recent years to develop many new types of state and local government securities such as securitized bonds and lottery bonds.

- Among the many significant features of municipal securities are their *tax-exempt* feature and their *subsidization* of high-tax-bracket investors—both of which tend to create a relatively volatile market. State and local obligations are also usually *serialized* or broken up into a range of maturities in order to appeal to a wider variety of potential buyers and minimize the risk of misusing public funds.

- State and local government securities are generally of high credit quality with low perceived default risk. However, in recent years a few notable failures have appeared, causing investors to rapidly move their funds to investments of higher quality. Recent failures also have spurred the expanded use of *municipal bond insurance,* even though it slightly lowers a municipal investor's expected yield.

- Municipals are generally marketed through security dealers under competitive bidding. However, there are some signs of taxpayer resistance to the continuing issuance of state and local debt obligations and the higher taxes that usually follow their sale in the money and capital markets.

www.mhhe.com/rose9e

Key Terms Appearing in This Chapter

fiscal policy, 545
debt management policy, 545
budget deficit, 545
budget surplus, 545
public debt, 551
auction method, 557
book-entry form, 557
municipals, 560

tax-anticipation notes (TANs), 568
revenue-anticipation notes
  (RANs), 568
bond-anticipation notes (BANs), 568
general obligation bonds, 568
revenue bonds, 568
tax-exemption privilege, 571
serialization, 576

Problems and Issues

1. It has often been noted that the U.S. government can pay for an increase in federal expenditures by one of three methods. It can raise taxes, issue debt, or print money. Explain in detail what the Treasury Department would have to do to employ the last of these methods.

2. Many state governments have complained in recent years about so-called "unfunded mandates" of the federal government, whereby social programs that were previously funded by the federal government or new social programs are required by federal legislation to be carried out by the states. Explain what would happen if the federal government cuts taxes to stimulate the economy at a time when additional unfunded mandates were being pressed upon the states. Would the federal tax cuts have the same beneficial effect on the economy as before?

3. Suppose that, due to an unexpected decline in federal income tax collections, the Treasury is compelled to borrow an extra $40 billion to cover planned expenditures in the current government budget. Based upon the discussion in this chapter, what would be some of the possible effects of this additional borrowing on the financial markets and the economy?

4. Now suppose that, due to drastic cuts in federal spending and strong economic growth, it now appears that the federal government will experience a $100 billion budget surplus in its cash account at the Federal Reserve. It will use the balance to retire $100 billion in government securities. Based on the discussion in this chapter, what would be some of the possible effects of this debt retirement operation on the economy and the financial markets?

5. Suppose the federal government's revenue and expenditure accounts in this fiscal year display the amounts shown (each item in billions of U.S. dollars):

Social security benefits	$400
Individual income tax collections	850
National defense	275
Net interest payments on the federal debt	250
Miscellaneous revenue sources	160
Income security programs	260
Social insurance taxes and contributions	600
International affairs	20
Corporate income taxes	200
Health care and Medicare	350
Miscellaneous expenditures	220

What were the government's total revenues and expenditures in this most recent fiscal year? Was the budget in surplus or in deficit? All other factors held constant, what are some of the possible effects of this year's government budget position on the economy's level of income and interest rates? Explain your reasoning in answering this final question.

6. Suppose the public debt of the United States consisted of the following types of security issues (all figures in billions of dollars):

Treasury bills	$ 750
Savings bonds and notes	180
Government account series	1,500
Federal government currency	6
Treasury bonds	600
Special notes issued to foreign investors	45
Treasury notes	2,200
Special bonds and notes sold to states and local governments	165

Calculate the following: *total marketable debt,* the *total nonmarketable debt,* the *total interest-bearing debt,* and the *gross public debt.*

7. Corporate bonds carrying an A rating are currently being priced to yield 8.62 percent. For an investor in the 28 percent income tax bracket, what yield must an A-rated municipal bond carry to make this investor indifferent as to the yield difference between the corporate and the municipal bond?

8. Sandoval County issued AA-rated bonds at a net interest cost of 6.85 percent. If annual interest payments promised on these bonds amount to $12.75 million, what was the principal amount of municipal bonds issued by Sandoval County?

9. Consider the case in which state and local governments across the United States collected or spent the following amounts classified as shown (all figures in billions of dollars for the most recent fiscal year):

Property taxes	$175	Individual income taxes	$70
Education	430	Corporate income taxes	15
User fees	25	Governmental administration	49
Highways	88	Interest on debt	104
Sales and gross receipts taxes	125	Intergovernmental funds transfers	
Public safety	80	from the federal government	150
Environment and housing	78	General and miscellaneous	
Miscellaneous general revenue	200	expenditures	75

What was the total revenue and total expenditures for all state and local governments? Was the state and local government sector running an overall deficit or surplus in its combined budget? Will borrowing likely be necessary to finish out the current fiscal year?

10. Identify the name for each of the types of state and local government securities described below:

a. Long-term debt payable only from revenues generated by a toll road.

b. Debt issued to support the construction of new business facilities.

c. Short-term borrowing that will later be replaced by long-term state or local government bonds.

d. Long-term securities issued under the Federal Housing Act to support the provision of low-income residential dwellings.

e. State or local government debt repayable from any revenue source.

f. Debt securities that can be sold back before maturity at face value to the issuer after a period of time has elapsed.

g. Short-term borrowing in lieu of expected local government tax receipts.

Standard and Poor's Market Insight and Web-Based Problems

1. Depository institutions rely on both Treasury securities and municipal bonds to balance out the level of risk in their asset portfolios (which regulatory agencies watch very closely) and add liquidity to their portfolios. The purpose of this exercise is to sample a few of the large depository institutions' balance sheets and see how heavily they depend on Treasury and municipal bonds.

  a. Visit S&P's Market Insight database at **mhhe.com/edumarketinsight** and look up the balance sheet of three of the nation's largest diversified banks and two of the nation's largest thrifts and mortgage finance companies. (Find the listing by clicking on the "Industry" tab and searching under "GICS Sub-Ind Constituents" for the categories, "Diversified Banks" and "Thrifts and Mortgage Finance.")

  b. From the most recent annual balance sheets (look under "Excel Analytics") for each of the companies that you have identified, determine what percentage of total assets ("Assets—Total") are represented by: (i) Treasuries and Federal Agency securities ("Investment Securities: National Government"), and (ii) municipal bonds ("Investment Securities: Local Government").

  c. From your results in part (b) does it appear that the large banks place a greater or lesser reliance on government debt as compared to thrifts and mortgage finance companies? Why or why not?

2. One of the more interesting sites on the World Wide Web is the Bureau of the Public Debt of the U.S. Treasury Department at **treas.publicdebt.gov** and the related site known as Treasury Direct at **treasurydirect.gov**. These sites contain a great deal of information about U.S. Treasury activities in the money and capital markets, about the changes in the public debt of the United States as time goes by, and about the government's revenue and expense budget. Using these two popular Web sites, research the following questions:

  a. What types of securities does the Treasury make available to investors? (Make a list.)

  b. In the latest Treasury auction, what was the volume of securities traded and what were their prices and yields?

  c. What are "strips" and how does the Treasury aid investors interested in these particular securities?

  d. What are Monthly Treasury Statements (MTS)?

  e. For the most recent month, how much revenue did the Treasury receive and how much did it spend?

3. Answer the following questions while again referring to the Treasury's popular Web sites, **publicdebt.treas.gov** and **treasurydirect.gov:**

    a. What is the size of the public debt of the United States right now?

    b. How big is that debt on a per capita basis?

    c. How has the volume of the public debt changed over time since the nation's founding under the Constitution?

    d. What is the Monthly Statement of the Public Debt and what does it contain? Can you see how this information might be useful to active buyers of Treasury securities?

4. The leading dealers in the world assisting state and local governments in raising new funds include such well-known financial institutions as Goldman Sachs at **gs.com**, Merrill Lynch at **ml.com**, Bear Stearns at **bearsterns.com**, and Lehman Brothers at **lehman.com**. Check out the official Web sites of these leading municipal dealers, viewing each Web site from two perspectives: (a) the viewpoint of the financial manager of a state or local government interested in seeking advice about raising new funds, and (b) the viewpoint of an investor possibly interested in buying municipal bonds and notes. From these two different perspectives, which dealer has the most helpful and inviting Web site and why do you think so? What recommendations would you offer to the Web-site managers and designers working for Goldman Sachs, Merrill Lynch, Bear Stearns, and Lehman Brothers? Explain the basis for your recommendations.

Selected References to Explore

Baxandall, Phineas. "Taxing Habits: The Economics of Sin Taxes." *Regional Review,* Federal Reserve Bank of Boston, First Quarter 2003, pp. 19–26.

Bradbury, Katherine L.; Yolanda Kodrzycki; and Robert Tannenwald. "The Effects of State and Local Public Policies on Economic Development: An Overview." *New England Economic Review,* Federal Reserve Bank of Boston, March/April 1997, pp. 1–47.

Daly, Mary. "Understanding State Budget Troubles." *FRBSF Economic Letter,* Federal Reserve Bank of San Francisco, no. 2003–23, August 15, 2003.

Jossi, Frank. "The Taxing Issue of E-Commerce." *Fedgazette,* Federal Reserve Bank of Minneapolis, November 2003, pp. 9–11.

Laubach, Thomas. "New Evidence on the Interest Rate Effects of Budget Deficits and Debt." *Finance and Economics Discussion Series,* Paper no. 2003–12, Board of Governors of the Federal Reserve System, May 2003.

Leduc, "Sylvian. "Deficit-Financed Tax Cuts and Interest Rates." *Business Review,* Federal Reserve Bank of Philadelphia, Second Quarter 2004, pp. 30–37.

Taylor, Lori. "The Sales Tax Crunch." *Southwest Economy,* Federal Reserve Bank of Dallas, May/June 2003, pp. 1–4.

Viard, Alan D. "The Federal Budget: What a Difference a Year Makes." *Southwest Economy,* Federal Reserve Bank of Dallas, January/February 2002, pp. 1, 6–10.

Chapter 19

Business Borrowing: Corporate Bonds, Asset-Backed Securities, Bank Loans, and Other Forms of Business Debt

Learning Objectives

in This Chapter

- You will examine the different ways business firms issue debt securities and negotiate loans in order to borrow funds in the money and capital markets.

- You will learn about the key factors that cause businesses to increase or decrease the volume of debt funds they seek to raise within the financial markets.

- You will see the often powerful impact that business borrowing has upon market interest rates and credit conditions inside the financial system.

What's in This Chapter?
Key Topics Outline

19.1   Introduction to Business Borrowing

Business firms draw on a wide variety of sources of funds to finance their daily operations and to carry out long-term investment. In 2003, for example, nonfinancial business firms in the United States raised just over $1.6-trillion in funds to carry out long-term investments, purchase inventories of goods and raw materials, and acquire financial assets. Of this total, just over $300 billion (about 20 percent) was supplied from the financial markets through issues of bonds, stocks, notes, and other financial instruments. In this chapter, we look at sources of borrowed (debt) funds used by businesses today. In the next chapter, we consider the advantages and disadvantages of stock (equity) as a source of business funding.

19.2   Factors Affecting Business Activity in the Money and Capital Markets

The funding demands of businesses are fueled by their desire to acquire new assets and replace existing assets (such as plant and equipment) that are wearing out. Specifically, at any point in time,

> *Total funding demands of business firms*
>
>   = *Desired increases in short-term assets* (inventories of goods and raw materials, credit (receivables) extended to customers, and holdings of marketable securities and other short-term assets)
>
>   + *Desired increases in long-term assets* (plant and equipment, construction of new homes and other facilities for sale, and the start-up or acquisition of other business firms)   (19.1)

These total funding demands from the business sector can be met from funds generated *inside* each firm (*internal financing*) in the form of undistributed profits and depreciation reserves and from funds generated from *outside* the individual firm (*external financing*) in the money and capital markets. Specifically,

> Total business funding demands − Undistributed profits and depreciation reserves from inside each firm
>
>   = *Business demands for external financing from the money and capital markets*   (19.2)

Many factors affect the extent to which business firms draw on the money and capital markets for external funds. One prominent factor is the *condition of the economy.* A booming economy generates rapidly growing sales, encouraging businesses to borrow in order to expand inventories and to issue stocks and bonds in order to purchase new plant and equipment. In contrast, a sagging economy normally is accompanied by declining sales and a reduction in inventory purchases and long-term investment. Other factors being equal, the need for external fund-raising declines when the economy grows more slowly or heads down into a recession. In contrast, rising demand for business goods and services is usually translated into rising demand for short- and long-term capital supplied from the financial marketplace.

Credit availability and *interest rates* also have powerful effects on business fund-raising activity in the money and capital markets. Rising interest rates that typically accompany a period of economic prosperity eventually choke off business borrowing and spending plans due to the increasing cost of carrying inventories, floating new securities, and renewing credit lines. Falling interest rates, on the other hand, can stimulate business borrowing and spending, leading to a restocking of inventories and an expansion of long-term investment financed by bonds, stocks, and direct loans.

A third factor in influencing how heavily businesses draw on the money and capital markets for financial support is the *level and expected growth of internally generated funds* (earnings and cash flow) for each firm. The financial markets are largely a *supplemental funds source* for most businesses, drawn upon to backstop internal cash flows when credit availability and economic conditions are favorable and when internally generated cash is inadequate to cover all desired business investments. Because business firms' earnings and cash flows tend to be volatile, it should not surprise us to learn that business fund-raising activity in the financial system is also highly volatile. Heavy business borrowings in one year to fill the *funding gap* between desired business capital spending and internally generated funds often are followed by a dearth of new security offerings and significant paydowns of outstanding loans the next year, particularly if internal funds have risen or if business expectations about the state of the economy have soured.

These marked fluctuations in business fund-raising in the financial markets result in wide swings in interest rates and security prices. Much of the volatility in stock and bond prices reported in the daily financial press may be attributed to the on-again, off-again character of financial market activity by the business sector. The key actors in this rapidly changing drama are, of course, the largest industrial corporations, which have the financial stature to tap both the open market and the negotiated loan markets for debt and equity funds. Skillful analysts often can read which way the wind is blowing as far as interest rates and security prices are concerned by watching what is happening to the current earnings and investment plans of major business corporations.

19.3   Characteristics of Corporate Notes and Bonds

corporate bond

corporate note

If a corporation decides to use long-term funds to finance its growth, the most popular forms of long-term financing are the **corporate bond** and the **corporate note.** This is especially true for the largest corporations whose credit standing is so strong that they can avoid dealing directly with an institutional lender such as a bank, finance company, or insurance company and sell their IOUs in the open market. Small companies without the necessary standing in the eyes of security investors usually must confine their long-term financing operations to negotiated loans with an institutional lender (such as a bank or finance company), an occasional stock issue, and heavy use of internally generated cash.

Principal Features of Corporate Notes and Bonds

A distinction needs to be drawn here between notes and bonds. By convention, a *note* is a corporate debt contract whose original maturity is five years or less; a *bond* carries an original maturity of more than five years. Both securities promise the investor an amount equal to the security's par value at maturity plus interest payments at specified intervals. Because both securities have similar characteristics other than maturity, we will use the word *bond* to refer to both notes and bonds in the discussion that follows.

indenture

Corporate bonds are generally issued in units of $1,000 and earn income that, in most cases, is fully taxable to the investor. These securities are known as *registered bonds* because the owner of these instruments must register with the issuing company in order to collect interest. Each bond is accompanied by an **indenture**, a contract listing the rights and obligations of the borrower and the investor. Indentures usually contain *restrictive covenants* designed to protect bondholders against actions by a borrowing firm or its shareholders that might weaken the value of the bonds by diminishing the firm's ability to meet its interest obligations to bondholders, thus increasing the risk of default. For example, restrictive covenants in an indenture may prohibit

For an interesting and
up-to-date look at the
market for corporate
bonds, see especially
the Bond Market
Association at
investinginbonds.com,
the CBS Market
Watch at
cbsmarketwatch.com,
and Financial Pipeline
at finpipe.com

increases in a borrowing corporation's dividend rate (which would reduce the ability of the firm to rely on internal financing), limit additional borrowing, restrict merger agreements, or limit the sale of the borrower's assets. These and other terms in a bond indenture are enforced by a third party—the trustee (often a bank trust department)—that represents investors holding the bonds. More restrictive indentures tend to lower interest costs for a borrowing company.

Recent Trends in Original Maturities of Corporate Bonds

The maturities attached to newly issued corporate bonds have fluctuated widely with changing economic conditions and shifts in interest rate expectations and the expectations for inflation. At the beginning of the twentieth century many railroads sold bonds with 100-year-plus maturities. During the 1950s and 1960s, corporations found a ready market for 20- to 30-year bonds, and telephone companies managed to sell 40-year bonds. Such long-term debt contracts are desirable from a borrowing company's point of view because they can lock in low interest costs for many years and make financial planning much simpler. However, the 1970s and 1980s ushered in a trend toward much shorter-maturity corporate debt issues (many in the 5- to 15-year range), due in part to rapid inflation and interest rates that soared to record levels. The development of sophisticated interest rate hedging tools (such as futures, options, and swaps) aided companies moving toward these shorter-maturity bonds because these tools help minimize damage from volatile shorter-term interest rates. Sharply lower interest rates and subdued inflation in the 1990s and into the twenty-first century, however, set in motion a swing back to longer maturity bonds. For example, two government agencies, the Resolution Trust Corporation (disbanded in 1996) and the Tennessee Valley Authority, issued 40- to 50-year bonds, while such companies as Walt Disney and Coca-Cola brought 100-year issues to market.

Call Privileges Attached to Corporate Bonds

A considerable proportion of corporate bonds that are outstanding today carry *call privileges,* allowing early redemption (retirement) of the bonds if market conditions prove favorable. The call privilege represents a way to shorten the average maturity of corporate bonds and gives the firm greater flexibility in financing its operations. However, it can be expensive when interest rates are high and expected to fall. Investors realize that the bond is likely to be called if interest rates fall and therefore demand a higher yield as compensation for the risk that the bond will be retired. However, most corporate bonds are issued today *without* a call privilege attached due to the added interest cost involved and the availability of hedging instruments such as futures and options.

Sinking Fund Provisions

Some corporate bonds are backed by *sinking funds* designed to ensure that the issuing company will be able to pay off the bonds when they come due. Periodic payments are made into the fund on a schedule usually related to the depreciation of any assets supported by the bonds. The trustee is charged with the responsibility of making sure the user places the right amount of money in the sinking fund each time a payment is due. Periodically, a portion of the bonds may be retired from monies accumulated in the sinking fund (often annually). Sinking funds tend to reduce borrowing costs.

Yields and Costs of Corporate Bonds

Yields on the highest-grade corporate bonds tend to move closely with yields on government bonds. In contrast, yields carried by lower-grade corporate bonds are more closely tied to conditions in the economy and to factors specifically affecting the risk position of each borrowing firm. Bonds issued by the largest U.S. companies are, with few exceptions, listed and traded on the New York or American stock exchanges, although the largest volume of corporate bond trading passes through dealers operating off the exchanges.

As we noted in Chapter 6, there are several different ways to measure the rate of return to the investor or the cost to the firm of issuing a debt security. From the point of view of the issuing company, one widely quoted measure of the cost of a bond is its *coupon rate*—the rate of interest the company promises to pay as printed on the face of the bond. However, the coupon rate may understate or overstate the true cost of a bond to the issuing company, depending on whether the bond was issued at a discount or at a premium from its par value. A better measure of the cost of issuing a bond is to compare the *net proceeds* from a bond sale available for the borrowing company's use to the present value of the stream of cash payments the firm must make to bondholders.

For example, suppose a corporation issues $1,000 par bonds, but flotation costs reduce the net proceeds to the company from each bond to $950.[1] If the bonds mature in 10 years and carry a 10 percent coupon rate, the before-tax cost, k, to the issuing company is figured as follows:

$$\text{Net proceeds per bond} = \frac{\text{Interest cost in year 1}}{(1+k)^1} + \frac{\text{Interest cost in year 2}}{(1+k)^2}$$
$$+ \cdots + \frac{\text{Interest cost in year 10}}{(1+k)^{10}}$$
$$+ \frac{\text{Principal payments in year 10}}{(1+k)^{10}} \qquad (19.3)$$

In this example:

$$\$950 = \frac{\$100}{(1+k)^1} + \frac{\$100}{(1+k)^2} + \cdots + \frac{\$100}{(1+k)^{10}} + \frac{\$1,000}{(1+k)^{10}}$$

The use of a financial calculator or computer software indicates that k in this example is 10.85 percent.

However, interest charges on debt are *tax deductible,* making the after-tax cost considerably less than the before-tax cost, especially for the largest and most profitable firms. For the largest corporations with annual earnings in the top tax bracket, the marginal federal income tax rate is 35 percent. Thus, a large company issuing the bond described above would incur an after-tax cost (k') of

$$k' = k(1 - t) \qquad (19.4)$$

where k is the before-tax cost and t is the firm's marginal tax rate. In this example,

$$k' = 10.85\%(1 - 0.35) = 7.05\%$$

Of course, if the firm were in a lower tax bracket, the after-tax cost of its debt would be higher. In the case of an unprofitable company (whose effective tax rate is zero), the after-tax cost of debt would equal its before-tax cost.

The before- and after-tax costs of debt vary not only with each firm's tax rate but also with conditions in the financial markets. During periods of economic expansion, when the supply of credit tends to become increasingly scarce relative to the demand for credit, the cost of borrowing may rise in order to allocate the available supply of

---

[1]The major elements of flotation cost for a new bond issue are the underwriting spread of the securities dealer who agrees to sell the issue, registration fees, paper and printing charges, and legal fees.

credit among many competing uses (unless, of course, an expanding economy contributes to lower default-risk premiums on corporate loans). In buoyant times, bonds often must be marketed at lower prices and higher interest rates. Conversely, during periods when the economy contracts into a recession, the cost of borrowing may tend to decline as the demand for credit cools down (unless, of course, default-risk premiums on corporate loans rise significantly). In depressed times, the prices of corporate debt securities may rise and their interest returns may fall.

There are, however, exceptions to the foregoing pattern. For example, sometimes the volume of borrowing increases markedly during business recessions as companies attempt to lock in the relatively low interest rates that may be available at that time. This happened during the 2000–2003 period when the global economy was in a recession and inflation was subdued. Business borrowing rates in the financial markets fell to 40-year lows and the market for long-term corporate debt was, at times, flooded with new debt security issues.

Signals Corporate Bond Issues May Send to the Financial Marketplace

Like the taking on of other types of debt or the issuing of new stock, firms choosing to sell corporate bonds to raise funds send "signals" to the financial markets that, in turn, can affect the value of their securities in the minds of investors. For example, the apparent *motivation* for a new bond issue can be critical. If a bond issue announcement appears to be driven by an unanticipated cash-flow shortage from the assets of the issuing company and the market is aware of this, bond and equity prices of the issuer may fall and its borrowing costs may rise. On the other hand, a new bond sold to expand and/or improve a firm's capitalization, to make a timely and well-considered acquisition, or for reasons other than unexpected cash deficits seems to send a *positive* signal to the market, and bondholders of the issuing firm may receive some positive abnormal returns. Where the financial markets cannot successfully discern the motivation for a new debt issue, equity and debt investors may experience some *negative* abnormal returns due, perhaps, to the implication that the assets the issuing company holds may be of lower value than first thought.

The Most Common Types of Corporate Bonds

debenture

Debentures   There are many different types of corporate bonds issued in the financial markets. Among the most common is the **debenture,** which is *not* secured by any specific asset owned by the issuing corporation. Instead, the holder of a debenture is a general creditor of the company and looks to the earning power and reputation of the borrower as the source of the bond's value.

Subordinated Debentures   A related form of bond is the *subordinated debenture,* frequently called a *junior security.* If a company goes out of business and its assets are liquidated, holders of subordinated debentures are paid only after all nonsubordinated creditors receive the monies owed them. Thus, there is greater risk with these instruments and a higher interest cost to the issuing firm.

mortgage bonds

Mortgage Bonds   Debt securities representing a claim against specific assets (normally plant and equipment) owned by a corporation are known as **mortgage bonds.** These bonds may be either *closed end* or *open end.* Closed-end mortgage bonds do not permit the issuance of any additional debt against the assets already pledged under the mortgage. Open-end bonds, on the other hand, allow additional debt to be issued against pledged assets, which may dilute the claims of current bondholders. For this reason, open-end mortgage bonds typically carry higher yields than closed-end bonds. Sometimes several mortgage bonds with varying priorities of claim are issued against the same assets. For example, the initial issue of bonds against a corporation's fixed assets may be designated first mortgage bonds, and later second mortgage bonds may be issued against those same assets. If the company were liquidated, holders of second mortgage bonds would receive only those funds left over after holders of the first mortgage bonds were paid off.

Income Bonds   Bonds often used in corporate reorganizations and in other situations when a company is in financial distress are known as *income bonds.* Interest on these bonds is paid only when income is actually earned, making an income bond similar to common stock. However, holders of income bonds do have a prior claim on earnings over both stockholders and holders of subordinated debentures. Some income bonds carry a cumulative feature under which unpaid interest accumulates and must be fully paid before the stockholders receive any dividends.

Equipment Trust Certificates   Resembling a lease in form, *equipment trust certificates* are used most frequently to acquire industrial equipment or rolling stock (such as railroad cars or airplanes). Title to the assets acquired is vested in a trustee (often a bank trust department), which leases these assets to the company issuing the certificates. Periodic lease payments are made to the trustee, who passes them along to certificate holders. Title to the assets passes to the borrowing company only after all lease payments are made. Both equipment trust certificates and mortgage bonds tend to post lower interest rates than other corporate bonds because they are backed by specific marketable assets.

Industrial Development Bonds   For many years now, state and local governments have been active in helping private corporations meet their financial needs. One of the most controversial forms of government-aided, long-term business borrowing is the **industrial development bond (IDB).** These bonds are issued by a local government borrowing authority to provide buildings, land, or equipment to a business firm. Because governmental units can borrow more cheaply than most private companies, the lower debt costs may be passed along to the firm as an inducement to move to a new location, bringing jobs to the local economy. The business firm normally guarantees both interest and principal payments on the IDBs by renting the buildings, land, or equipment at a rental fee high enough to cover debt service costs.

industrial development bond (IDB)

Innovations in Corporate Debt

Corporate bonds are traditionally called *fixed-income* securities because most pay a fixed amount of interest each year. This creates a problem for bondholders when interest rates rise, inflation increases, or both, because then the real market value of fixed-income securities falls. In recent years, repeated bouts with inflation or reduced quality ratings on corporate bonds have spurred companies to develop *new* types of bonds whose return to the investor is sensitive to changing inflation and changing bond values. New bonds have appeared with deferred interest payments and variable coupon (promised) rates of return to investors, in an attempt to help issuing companies with near-term cash shortages. Among the most interesting of these innovative securities are discount bonds, floating-rate bonds, commodity-backed bonds, and medium-term notes (MTNs).

Discount bonds are sold at a price below par and appreciate toward par as maturity approaches. Thus, the investor earns capital gains as well as interest, while the issuing corporation usually can issue discount bonds at a lower after-tax cost than conventional

zero coupon bonds

bonds. Some discount bonds, known as **zero coupon bonds,** pay no interest at all. First used by J.C. Penney in 1981, "zeros" pay a return based solely on their price appreciation as they approach maturity. However, the annual price increase is taxable as ordinary income, not as capital gains, under current IRS regulations.

Floating-rate bonds have their annual promised interest rate tied to changes in long-term or short-term interest rates. *Commodity-backed bonds* carry a face value tied to the market price of an internationally traded commodity, such as gold, silver, or oil. More recently, *inflation-linked corporate notes* have appeared. For example, shortly after the new century began, SLM Corporation—the student loan marketing company—issued a debt instrument promising investors an annual interest return 2.12 percent above the consumer price index (CPI). Other companies offering similar inflation-protected bonds included Merrill Lynch, Morgan Stanley, and Household International. Out of fear that inflation might eventually take off running, the issuers of these particular securities hedged themselves with derivatives to avoid the prospect of high future borrowing costs.

Medium-term notes (MTNs), carrying maturities of 1 to 10 years, exploded onto the corporate fund-raising scene during the 1980s and 1990s. Although they were developed as long ago as the early 1970s, MTNs outstanding rose to over $100 billion during the 1990s, compared to less than $1 billion in 1980. These securities are generally noncallable, unsecured, fixed-rate obligations. One advantage of MTNs for borrowing corporations is the ability to reduce exposure to interest rate risk, because MTNs give companies more opportunities to match the maturities of the assets they wish to acquire with the maturities of their liabilities.

One of the distinguishing hallmarks of U.S. corporate debt markets is their ability to provide funds to businesses at virtually every stage of their existence—from completely *new* ventures (where venture capital funds, pension plans, and even some banks provide start-up capital), to firms going public for the first time (i.e., initial public offerings, or IPOs, where venture capitalists and pension plans are often joined by insurance companies and wealthy individuals), to mature companies that have either routine long-term capital needs (often satisfied via the public sale of bonds to large numbers of investors and institutions), to companies with unusual financing needs (which may require the private sale of a new debt issue to a handful of sophisticated investing institutions). Most notable in recent years is the wider opening of corporate debt markets to small- and medium-size firms who can more easily sell lower-quality "junk" debt securities in the open (public) market than in the past, such as by getting *credit guarantees* from investment banks and other strong institutions in order to reduce the riskiness of the debt issues, and, thereby, broaden the group of investors interested in their new debt offerings.

For more information on the European corporate debt market, see especially the European Issues segment of the Bond Market Association's Web site at bondmarkets.com/research

One of the most exciting developments in the corporate bond market today is the rapid growth and development of Europe's corporate bond market, spurred on by that continent's new unity into one economy and one financial system. Differences in bond yields issued from different European Community (EC) member nations have recently declined, so that European bond dealers are finding that traditional arbitrage profits—switching between the bonds of different European countries—are sharply reduced. With the decline in interest-rate spreads, European bond dealers are looking for new ways to make money, such as by increasing the size of the European junk bond market and getting bond-issuing firms more interested in asset-backed bonds. At the same time, significant volumes of euro-denominated bonds are appearing in global financial markets in order to take advantage of public interest in the new EC international currency, the euro. Some U.S. companies, like Citigroup, offer European investors asset-backed securities, discussed in the next section of this chapter, while U.S. investors are increasingly seeking out European junk bonds because American investors are more used to buying high-risk bonds than are many European investors and U.S. interest rates in recent years have been among the lowest in modern history.

19.4 Asset-Backed Securities Issued by Corporations

To further explore the features of asset-backed securities see, for example, finpipe.com, key.com, and mortgage101.com.

asset-backed securities (ABS)

During the 1970s and 1980s, as borrowing costs for corporations soared along with inflation, both financial and nonfinancial corporations began searching for *new* ways to raise capital, expand their operations, and reduce some of their risk exposure. They received help from a major innovation in the home mortgage market, where housing lenders—in cooperation with federally sponsored mortgage agencies (including the Federal National Mortgage Association [FNMA], the Government National Mortgage Association [GNMA], and the Federal Home Loan Mortgage Corporation [FHLMC])—were successfully developing a new channel for corporate fund-raising called **asset-backed securities (ABS)**.[2] Groups of home mortgage loans, usually supported by guarantees issued by federal agencies, were being packaged by lenders, removed from the lenders' balance sheets, and placed in a separate trust account. Then, with the help of an investment bank or other securities firm, new securities backed by the packaged loans were sold in the open market to raise new capital. (See Exhibit 19.1.)

securitization

The process that gives rise to the creation of asset-backed securities, known as **securitization,** offers several potential *advantages* to those larger corporations able to use the device. For example, securitization may:

1. Reduce the cost of raising funds below the cost of either issuing traditional bonds or borrowing from a bank or finance company.

2. Grant companies greater control over their balance sheets, including the ability to take on *new* assets that may bear higher returns or lower risk than those assets that are being securitized and removed from a company's balance sheet.

3. Avoid the issuance of additional balance-sheet debt until a company is prepared to do so.

4. Improve the apparent financial strength of an issuing firm by increasing its ratio of equity capital relative to its total assets and liabilities.

5. Permit greater asset diversification, which may bring more stability to company earnings and reduce the overall cost of capital.

6. Provide a new source of company earnings in the form of servicing fees or residual income from the difference between the yield on securitized assets and the yield on securities issued against those assets.

Financial and nonfinancial companies not connected to the mortgage market soon discovered that this asset-backed fund-raising tool was also available to them. Investment banks, such as Bear Stearns and Goldman Sachs, for example, agreed to provide advice on how and when to establish a trust (or "special purpose entity") that would hold the pool of assets removed from a company's balance sheet, as well as advice on when to sell securities against the pooled assets. Moreover, commercial banks and other lenders (enhancers) agreed to make lines of credit available to backstop the expected cash flows from the packaged assets, to help insure that investors in the asset-backed securities receive the payments they are promised.

Over the past three decades corporations have intensively searched their balance sheets for income-generating assets that might be securitized to raise new money. To be attractive to most investors, the assets in question must be of high quality or adequately secured by credit guarantees, have a common purpose, and carry relatively

---

[2] For a detailed discussion of the roles played by the FNMA, the GNMA, and the FHLMC in the residential mortgage market, see especially Chapters 11 and 22.

EXHIBIT 19.1

Issuing Asset-Backed Securities to Raise New Funds for Corporations in Need of Capital

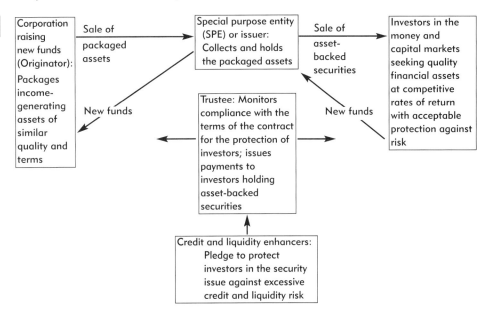

uniform terms. The more popular non-mortgage-related assets that have surfaced in recent years to back security issues include accounts receivable, business equipment leases, small business loans, credit-card loans, consumer automobile loans and leases, computer and truck leases, mobile home loans, farm loans, and energy loans.

As Exhibit 19.2 suggests, the use of asset-backed securities by a wide variety of financial-service and nonfinancial corporations has been explosive in recent years. Especially notable are the recent rapid increases in security issues backed by loans to large and small businesses, student loans, commercial and residential mortgages, and accounts receivable arising from credit sales of goods. Note also in Exhibit 19.2 that the majority of asset-backed securities are issued in the form of long-term corporate bonds, with the remainder issued in the form of commercial paper (i.e., short-term corporate IOUs nine months or less to maturity).

QUESTIONS TO HELP YOU STUDY

1. Explain what is meant by the statement: "The financial markets are a supplemental funds source for business." What factors appear to affect the volume of business fund-raising from the money and capital markets?

2. What *advantages* does the issuance of debt have over other sources of funds that a business firm might pursue? How about *disadvantages?*

3. Define each of the following terms having to do with business borrowing:

   Indenture   *Sinking fund*

   Call privilege   *Mortgage bond*

   Subordinated debenture   *Industrial development bond (IDB)*

   Income bond   *Debenture*

   Trustee   *Equipment trust certificate*

4. Explain how the *true cost* of a corporate bond may be determined.

5. How are *asset-backed securities* created?

6. What advantages do asset-backed securities offer an issuing corporation?

EXHIBIT 19.2

The Issue and
Growth of Asset-
Backed Securities
(ABS)

Source: Board of
Governors of the Federal
Reserve System, *Flow of
Funds Accounts,*
Statistical Release Z.1,
various quarterly issues.

Assets Backing Issued Securities	Year-End Volume in Billions of Dollars							
	1997	1998	1999	2000	2001	2002	2003	2004*
Loans to businesses and student loans	$62	$86	$83	$90	$108	$105	$104	$101
Residential (mortgage) loans**	302	439	441	480	559	622	763	823
Commercial mortgages	75	123	157	187	226	252	296	304
Consumer loans	317	389	448	521	600	637	629	617
Consumer leases***	11	13	10	7	7	6	6	5
Accounts (trade) receivable	128	166	187	220	246	270	291	296
Real estate investment trust assets	11	14	13	11	10	16	31	36
Percent of asset-backed securities issued as:								
Corporate bonds	76%	72%	67%	63%	62%	66%	70%	71%
Commercial paper	24	28	33	37	38	34	30	29

Note: Figures rounded to the nearest billion dollars.

*The dollar figures reported for 2004 are for the end of the first quarter of that year.

**Residential (mortgage) loans include single-family homes and multifamily dwellings.

***Receivables from operating leases, such as consumer auto leases.

19.5   Investors in Corporate Debt

Today the investor market for corporate bonds, asset-backed securities, and other forms of corporate debt is dominated by insurance companies, mutual funds, and pension funds (see Exhibit 19.3). Pension funds prefer buying corporate debt in the open market; insurance companies, on the other hand, frequently purchase their corporate securities directly from the issuing company in an off-the-market transaction. The stability of cash flows experienced by pension funds and insurance companies permits them to pursue corporate debt securities with long maturities and to lock in their higher yields.

One of the more dynamic investor segments in U.S. corporate securities includes *foreign* institutions, particularly leading security dealers, banks, and insurance firms, such as Credit Suisse and Deutsche Bank. Many purchases of U.S.-issued corporate debt instruments have been associated with foreign takeovers of U.S. companies and the desire of foreign investors to pursue safer investments in the United States in order to escape political and economic turmoil abroad and to take advantage of strong U.S. economic conditions relative to other parts of the globe. Then, too, the purchase of dollar-denominated assets such as corporate bonds gives foreign investors a way to store U.S. dollars at high yield until those dollars are needed either to buy U.S. goods or to purchase commodities sold in international markets that are denominated in dollars (such as oil).

Commercial banks are *not* among the heaviest investors in corporate bonds, though their investments in asset-backed securities, especially those backed by pools of residential mortgages, have grown rapidly due to their safety and relatively high yields. Generally, bankers prefer to deal personally with a business customer and grant a loan specifically tailored to the borrower's needs rather than to enter the impersonal bond market. Increasingly in recent years, commercial banks have become direct competitors with the corporate bond market through the granting of *term loans.* A term loan

EXHIBIT 19.3

Principal Investors in Corporate and Foreign Bonds, 2004*

Source: Board of Governors of the Federal Reserve System, *Flow of Funds Accounts: Financial Assets and Liabilities,* First Quarter 2004.

Investor Group	Amount	Percent of Total Bond Holdings
Households	$ 356.6	5.4%
Rest of the world (foreign investors)	1,616.6	24.3
Commercial banks	524.6	7.9
Savings institutions	65.1	1.0
Life insurance companies	1,616.1	24.4
Property-casualty insurance companies	227.1	3.4
Private pension funds	383.2	5.8
State/local government pension funds	363.2	5.5
Mutual funds	574.9	8.7
Security brokers and dealers and other investors	907.1	13.7
Totals	$6,629.5	100.0%

Note: Columns may not add to totals due to rounding.

*Figures are for the first quarter of the year at annualized rates.

has a maturity of more than one year. Responding to inflation and the rising cost of business equipment, bankers have gradually extended the maturity of term loans, with many falling in the 5- to 10-year maturity range. Interest rates on such loans often exceed the interest cost on corporate debt sold in the open market, however, especially when banks also insist that the borrowing firm keep funds on deposit with the bank.

One area of concern among investors in corporate debt in recent years has been an apparent decline in the overall credit quality of corporate debt securities. For example, a substantial proportion of all corporate bonds issued over the past two decades in the United States has been "junk bonds." Significant numbers of industrial bond issuers have seen their credit ratings reduced by credit rating agencies. As the danger of default has risen, capital market investors have demanded higher promised rates of interest on newly issued corporate debt and/or special covenants, allowing investors to redeem their holding of corporate debt instruments with the issuing companies at a fixed price if their credit rating is lowered or if the investors' position is weakened by restructuring of the issuing firm's capital.

Despite the rapid growth of bonds and other debt instruments in the United States in recent years, bond holdings by Americans have not come close to keeping up with Americans' stock holdings. For example, the percentage of savings invested in bonds by U.S. households fell from about 26 percent in 1990 to below 20 percent in 2003, while stock ownership rose from about 25 percent to more than 50 percent of U.S. savings over the same time period. Both individuals and institutional investors reduced their corporate bond holdings relative to stocks and other investments. In the meantime, foreign investors (especially from Europe, Japan, the Asian mainland, Canada, and Latin America) have accelerated their purchases of U.S. corporate bonds, whose superior yields and safety have made them particularly attractive to overseas investors worried about their own nation's economy. While the interest of foreign investors in U.S. bonds and other securities weakened somewhat after the September 2001 terrorist attacks, the U.S. bond market still looks much stronger than most overseas bond markets. In fact, with the relatively anemic performance of the stock market early in the new century, many pension funds and other major corporate security buyers were considering switching a substantial portion of their portfolios away from stocks and into bonds.

19.6   The Secondary Market for Corporate Debt

The resale (secondary) market for corporate bonds, asset-backed securities, and other corporate debt instruments is relatively limited compared to the larger resale markets for common stock, municipal bonds, and other long-term securities. Trading volume is generally thin, even for some debt instruments issued by the largest corporations. Part of the reason is the small number of individuals active as investors in this market. Individuals generally have limited investment time horizons (holding periods) and tend to turn over their portfolios rapidly when other attractive investments appear. In the past, the volume of secondary market trading in corporate debt instruments was also held back by the "buy and hold" strategies of many institutional investors, especially insurance companies and pension funds. Many of these firms purchased corporate debt instruments exclusively for interest income and were content to purchase the longest-term issues and simply hold them to maturity. However, under the pressure of volatile interest rates and inflation, many institutions buying corporate debt have shifted into a more aggressive strategy labeled *total performance*. Portfolio managers are more sensitive today to changes in prices and look for near-term opportunities to sell corporate securities and make capital gains. In fact, a number of insurance companies, pension funds, and mutual funds operate their own trading departments and keep constant tabs on developments in the corporate market.

Unlike the stock market, no one central exchange for the trading of bonds and other debt instruments dominates the market. Although corporate instruments are traded on all major exchanges, including the New York Stock Exchange (NYSE), most secondary market trading is conducted over the telephone and through electronic networks linking customers, brokers, and dealers. Dealers commit themselves to take on large blocks of securities, either from other dealers or from pension funds, insurance companies, and other clients. Dealers now try to close out positions taken in individual corporate debt instruments very quickly, frequently acting only as intermediaries in trades between buyers and sellers—without committing their own capital in order to avoid possible losses from changing market interest rates.

19.7   The Marketing of Corporate Debt

public sales

New corporate bonds, asset-backed securities, and other forms of corporate debt may be offered publicly in the open market to all interested buyers or sold privately to a limited number of investors. The first route, known as **public sales,** accounts for the largest portion of corporate security sales each year. Among smaller companies and those firms with unique financing requirements, however, a second route, known as **private or direct placements,** has often been popular.

private or direct placements

Public Sales

investment bankers

Public sales in the open market are handled principally by **investment bankers,** including such well-known investment houses as Bear Stearns, Goldman Sachs, and Citigroup, Inc.[3] Investment banks underwrite new issues of corporate securities and give advice to corporations on their financing requirements. An investment banking firm may singly take on a new issue of corporate securities or band together with other underwriters to form a *syndicate.* Either way, the investment banker's game plan is to acquire new corporate securities at the lowest possible price and sell them as

---

[3]For a more extensive discussion of the services provided by investment bankers, see especially Chapter 16.

quickly as possible in order to turn a profit. An investment banker may purchase the securities from the issuing company directly or merely guarantee the issuer a specific price for his securities. With either approach, it is the investment banker who carries the risk of gains or losses when corporate securities are marked for sale in the open market.

The largest issues of corporate securities sold in the open market are usually bid upon by several groups of underwriters. Competition among these syndicates can be intense. Investment bankers hope to acquire a new corporate security issue at the lowest possible bid price and place the securities with investors at a higher retail price, maximizing the *spread,* or return on invested capital. Unfortunately, each new corporate bond issue is always somewhat different from those that have traded before and may involve hundreds of millions or even billions of dollars. Moreover, a decision on what price to bid for new corporate securities must be made *before* the bonds are released for public trading; in the interim, prices may change drastically. If the underwriter bids too high a price, the investment bank may not be able to resell the securities at a price high enough to recover the cost and secure an adequate spread. To cite an example, a number of years ago, IBM Corporation offered $1 billion in notes and debentures through a collection of Wall Street underwriters. Unfortunately, just as the IBM issue was coming to market, bond prices tumbled (due, in part, to an announcement by the Federal Reserve suggesting that credit conditions might be tightened to deal with inflation). The underwriters suffered a massive loss on this particular corporate security issue.

Competition in the bidding process tends to narrow the underwriter's spread between bid and asked price. If several investment banking houses band together in a syndicate, a consensus bid price must be hammered out among the participants. Disagreements frequently arise within a syndicate, often due to different perceptions about the probable future direction of interest rates. Because dozens of underwriters may be included in a single syndicate, the task of reaching a compromise and placing a unified bid for a new corporate security issue may prove impossible. The old syndicate may break apart, with those bidders still interested in the issue hurriedly piecing together a new bid.

A number of factors are considered in pricing a new corporate debt issue. Certainly the credit ratings assigned by Moody's, Standard & Poor's Corporation, or other rating agencies are a key item, because many investors rely on such agencies for assessing the risk carried by a new corporate security. Another factor is the "forward calendar" of corporate security offerings, which lists new issues expected to come to market during the next few weeks. Obviously, if a heavy volume of new offerings is anticipated in the near term, prices will decline unless additional demand appears. Changes in government policy must be anticipated because that policy can have profound effects on corporate security prices. Other factors considered by investment bankers include the size of the issue, how aggressive other bidders are likely to be, and the strength of the "book," which consists of indications of advance investor interest in the new corporate security being offered.

Once the securities are received from the issuing company, the underwriters advertise their availability at the price agreed on by all members of the syndicate. *Delay* in selling new securities is one of the investment banker's worst enemies, because additional financing must be obtained to carry the unsold securities. Also, there is the added risk of price declines as time increases. To speed the process of selling new corporate instruments, many investment banking firms today have relationships with retail brokerage companies that maintain working agreements with large buyers, such as insurance companies, pension funds, and mutual funds.

The market for corporate bonds and other corporate debt securities is dominated by *giants*—leading companies borrowing money and leading investment banking houses assisting them in finding reliable funding at low cost. Most outstanding corporate bonds and notes are not heavily traded—at least compared to the huge daily volume of trading for government securities and many mutual funds. Among the relatively few corporate debt securities that are actively traded in considerable volume every day are:

Leading Fixed-Rate Corporate Bonds Traded in Today's Financial Markets

Issuing Company	Coupon Rate	Year Matures
Ford Motor Credit	7.00%	2013
General Motors	8.375	2033
AT&T Wireless	8.75	2031
Daimler Chrysler, NA	7.30	2012
Sprint Capital	8.35	2012
Ford Motor Co.	7.45%	2031
Goldman Sachs	5.25	2013
Citigroup Inc.	6.00	2033
Verizon Global	7.75	2030
Amerada Hess Co.	7.125	2033

Source: Web sites and financial reports of the issuing companies.

Note the generally *positive* relationship between promised yield (coupon rate) and maturity, with longer-term bonds generally posting higher rates of return. Other key factors in shaping investor returns are the issuer's credit rating, the size of the issue, and the specific terms accompanying each bond contract (indenture). Corporate bond yields are most frequently compared to rates of return on government securities, with the latter regarded as essentially default-free

financial instruments. Thus, a key indicator of the market's assessment of the current level of default risk on corporate bonds is the *yield spread* between corporate bonds and government securities that are comparable in maturity.

The Spread between the Market Yields on Aaa Corporate Bonds and 10-Year U.S. Treasury Bonds

	1997	1998	1999	2000
Aaa Corporate Bonds	7.27%	6.53%	7.05%	7.62%
U.S. Treasury (10-year) bonds	6.35	5.26	5.65	6.03
Corporate Treasury yield spread	0.92	1.27	1.40	1.59
	2001	**2002**	**2003**	**2004***
Aaa Corporate Bonds	7.08%	6.49%	5.70%	5.66%
U.S. Treasury (10-year) Bonds	5.02	4.61	4.29	4.01
Corporate Treasury yield spread	2.06	1.88	1.41	1.65

*Yields posted in January 2004.

Source: Board of Governors of the Federal Reserve System, *Statistical Supplement to the Federal Reserve Bulletin*, various issues.

Note how the corporate–Treasury yield spread rises in periods of economic recession (e.g., 2001–2002), when more businesses may be prone to failure, but drops lower in more prosperous periods (e.g., 1997–1999). The decision to offer new bonds or other corporate securities is usually made in consultation with an investment banker who may underwrite all or part of a new issue, thus accepting the market risk associated with purchasing and reselling the bonds. Leading underwriters of corporate debt instruments are listed below:

Leading Underwriters of Corporate Bonds and Notes around the Globe

Merrill Lynch & Co.	Citigroup, Inc.	Goldman Sachs Group
Lehman Brothers	Morgan Stanley	Credit Suisse Group
Deutsche Bank AG	J.P. Morgan Chase	Bear Stearns Group

Sources: Annual reports of issuing companies; Standard & Poor's Corporation's Market Insight, Educational Version (mhhe.com/edumarketinsight); and Board of Governors of the Federal Reserve System.

What happens to the market prices of securities sold by investment banking syndicates is the key determinant of the success or failure of the underwriting process. It takes only a small decline in retail price before the underwriter's profit is eliminated. Moreover, unfavorable price movements can damage the reputation of the investment banker with investors and the client companies that issue new securities. Clearly, investment banking is both risky and highly competitive.

Late in the 1990s an intense controversy with strong ethics overtones emerged concerning the pricing practices of dealers in the corporate security market. Some dealer firms appeared to be marking up the prices of corporate bonds sold to their customers well above the prevailing open-market price—sometimes with markups of 5 to 10 percent or more. One factor that facilitated these large markups was the delay in getting up-to-date information on actual trading prices. While many stocks are traded on both organized exchanges and through dealers who post new prices almost instantaneously, debt instruments are more frequently traded over the counter, where some dealers can quote a range of prices because the buyer may not be able to easily compare the price being offered against recent trades involving the same or similar securities.

Dealers often defend markups by pointing to the risks they face when they purchase blocks of corporate securities; the value of their holdings may drop suddenly when interest rates rise. An added problem is market diversity. Some securities may go for several hours or days without a transaction taking place, leaving the dealer with no current price to use as a reference point for pricing a new sale. Still, many investors would like to have a sales receipt that details *all* of the costs they are paying (including dealer markups). Borrowers sometimes report a similar information problem—a security issuer may be unable to get precise price quotes on securities sold in order to calculate the true cost of newly raised funds. Clearly, this information would be of great help to a business trying to decide whether to issue new debt or to explore other possible sources of funding.

Private Placements

In recent years, private placements of corporate bonds, asset-backed securities, and other corporate instruments with one or a limited group of well-informed investors have represented a fairly small, but still important proportion of public sales. For example, in recent years, private placements have accounted for less than 10 percent of public market sales of corporate bonds (though, by way of contrast, private placements of corporate stock recently have exceeded 50 percent of all public sales of stock). However, the ratio of private to public sales is sensitive to the changing composition of borrowing companies and to economic conditions. Usually, periods of rising interest rates and reduced credit availability bring more borrowing companies into the public market, and falling interest rates often bring a rise in private placements. For the largest corporations, public sales and private placements are *substitutes*. When interest rates are high or credit is tight in one of these markets, the largest borrowers shift to the other market. Most of the borrowers in the private market are small- and medium-sized corporations, however.

Private placements were significantly aided by a ruling of the U.S. Securities and Exchange Commission (SEC) known as Rule 144A. The SEC eliminated restrictions on the secondary trading of private placements by large institutional investors (known as QIBs, or qualified investment buyers). This step, in effect, created a secondary market for privately placed corporate securities, overcoming one of the historic barriers confronting investors who otherwise might be interested in privately placed securities. Revisions in Rule 144A have brought investment banks into the private placement arena to underwrite and distribute these securities. Privately placed corporate debt has become more liquid, bringing major new investors, such as mutual funds, into this market. The private-placement market has also been aided by the increasing presence of foreign investors and foreign issuers of private securities in U.S. markets and by the growing number of corporate mergers and divestitures. Much of the divestiture activity reflects companies attempting to downsize their operations in order to trim operating

601

costs or to raise scarce capital by selling marketable assets. Corporate mergers, in contrast, reflect the broadening of markets and the search for economies of scale in production and marketing.

Who buys privately placed bonds? Life insurance companies, finance companies, and pension funds, historically, have been the principal investors in this market. These institutions hope to secure higher yields and protection against call privileges by engaging in *direct negotiation* with borrowing corporations and by using due diligence and engaging in careful monitoring of any loans they grant. The avoidance of call privileges is of special benefit to life insurance companies and pension funds because these institutions prefer the stable income that comes from purchasing long-term debt instruments and holding them to maturity. In fact, institutional investors active in the private-placement market frequently impose extra fees in a sales contract containing an allowance for early retirement of a security by the issuing corporation. Investors other than life insurance companies and pension funds tend to play smaller roles in the private market due to their lack of expertise, small size, and the limited resale market for privately placed securities. In recent years, some life insurance companies have sharply curtailed their purchases of privately placed securities due to public pressure on insurers to strengthen their balance sheets and because many borrowers in the private-placement market have experienced lower credit ratings, presenting more risk to investors.

There are several advantages to the borrower from a private placement. One is the lower cost of distribution because there are no registration fees associated with the issuance of a prospectus as there would be with a public sale. Private placements are exempt from registration with the Securities and Exchange Commission (SEC). Generally, more rapid placement of corporate securities takes place in the private market because only a few buyers are involved and the loan is confidential. Special concessions can often be secured, such as a commitment for future borrowing. For example, a corporate borrower may negotiate a private sale of $50 million in traditional bonds to an insurance company but also may be granted a line of credit up to $2 million a year over the next five years. This kind of commitment is not usually possible in the impersonal public market, where the features of most corporate securities are highly standardized. Moreover, lenders in the private market try to tailor the terms of a loan to match the specific cash flow needs of borrowers. This may involve a conventional fixed-rate credit contract at the prevailing interest rate, a floating-rate loan that can be retired early if cash flows permit, or even a participating loan in which the lender charges a lower interest rate in return for a share of income from the project financed.

There is limited evidence that private placements may be more effective than public-sale corporate bond issues in keeping "agency conflicts" between borrowers and lenders under control (see Chapter 3). Due in part to the superior debt monitoring ability of the typical private-placement market buyer and the greater possibility of renegotiation of terms under a private sale as the conditions surrounding borrowers and lenders change, the private-placement market may minimize agency conflicts between lenders and borrowers, helping to protect the interests of both buyers and sellers. The advantages of the private-placement market make it particularly appealing to smaller businesses, privately held companies, and many foreign firms. However, predictably, private-sale borrowers usually pay higher costs for their issues than those companies (particularly very large firms) that can easily move back and forth, if they wish, between the public-sale and the private-sale markets.

One disadvantage is that interest costs generally are higher in private sales than in public sales. Moreover, private sale instruments are less liquid and often carry more risk of default. One indication of this is that privately placed debt issues tend to have more restrictive covenants in order to protect lenders. Still, the larger the size of a corporate issue, the smaller the cost differential between public and private placements tends to be.

QUESTIONS TO HELP YOU STUDY

7. Who are the *principal buyers* of corporate notes and bonds and other private debt instruments? Why are these groups of investors especially interested in acquiring these instruments?

8. Describe the important role that *investment bankers* play in the functioning of the corporate security market.

9. What are the principal types of *risk* that investment bankers take on? What factors must an investment banker consider in *pricing* a new corporate security issue?

10. Explain what is meant by a *private placement*. Who purchases privately placed corporate securities and why?

11. What are the principal *advantages* to a business borrower from offering debt in the private-placement market? Can you see any *disadvantages?*

19.8 The Volume of Borrowing by Corporations

The volume of borrowing through new issues of corporate bonds and other debt instruments has grown rapidly in recent years (see Exhibit 19.4). For example, annual offerings of new corporate debt securities approximately doubled in each decade of the 1970s and 1980s, and then increased more than eightfold between 1990 and 2000. In 2002 GE Capital brought to market the largest U.S. dollar-denominated corporate bond issue then recorded in history at $11 billion. During 2003, new bond issues of American corporations in total reached almost $1.7 trillion. Much of this growth in corporate borrowing could be traced to inflation in earlier years, which reduced the real cost of debt, the increased use of financial leverage to boost returns to corporate stockholders, the development of international capital markets, and relatively lower long-term interest rates that prevailed early in the twenty-first century. This track record suggests that the corporate debt market is very sensitive to economic conditions and to changes in the cost of long-term credit.

Another factor that has spurred the private security market's growth is a rash of corporate takeovers and merger proposals. Targets for these corporate raids have included such well-known companies as CBS, Firestone Tire, Fleet Boston Financial Corp., Hilton Hotels, Uniroyal, Pennzoil, and Paine Webber, to name just a few. Many of these mergers have been motivated by deregulation of key industries in recent years, including the airlines, commercial banking, and telecommunications; by more liberal antitrust rules followed by the U.S. government; and by the desire of many foreign investors to establish business operations inside U.S. territory.

Frequently, these proposed mergers include plans to offer millions of dollars in **junk bonds**—high interest-cost, low credit-rated (below investment grade) debt securities—as well as bank loans to finance the transaction. With the expanded use of debt, the credit ratings of scores of corporations have been reduced in recent years and several major corporate failures have occurred, with bankruptcy declared by several well-known firms, including Enron, Kmart, Polaroid, and WorldCom. Nevertheless, the growth of the *junk bond market* has been spurred by corporations' desire to restructure their capital, replacing stock with debt or replacing short-term securities

junk bonds

| EXHIBIT 19.4 |

The Growth of Corporate Bonds and Notes Issued by Companies in the United States ($ Millions)

Source: U.S. Department of Commerce and Board of Governors of the Federal Reserve System.

Year	New Issues of Corporate Bonds and Notes
1950	$ 4,920
1960	8,081
1970	30,321
1980	53,199
1990	114,500
2000	944,810
2003	1,692,260

Note: All figures in the exhibit represent gross proceeds of issues maturing in more than one year and are the principal amount or number of units multiplied by the offering price. Figures exclude secondary offerings, employee stock plans, mutual funds, intracorporate transactions, and Yankee bonds (sold by foreign corporations inside U.S. territory). Before 1987, the figures included only those issues that were underwritten.

with longer-term financial instruments. In addition, skilled dealer houses, led by Credit Suisse, Citigroup, Deutsche Bank, and Goldman Sachs, resurrected the junk bond market in a dramatic way as the twenty-first century opened.

In fact, the volume of corporate stock retirements, replaced in most cases by debt, broke all previous records during the 1980s and 1990s. A number of these retirements were carried out to discourage "hostile" takeovers or to participate in corporate mergers and acquisitions. The federal government's antitrust policy has taken a turn toward ease in recent decades, allowing more mergers and acquisitions to take place without government challenge. Then, too, many companies not well known to investors have been able to approach the long-term debt markets for funds for the first time, thanks to the rapid expansion of the market for junk bonds and the growing use of credit guarantees that permit lower-quality borrowers to successfully tap the open market for funds.

leveraged buyouts

Investors like to keep close track of bond market conditions in order to look for favorable trades. Several good Web sites to follow the market include cnnfn.com and bondmarkets.com

A substantial proportion of recent corporate takeovers has been in the form of **leveraged buyouts,** in which a single investor or small group of investors (frequently including senior management of the target company) buys the publicly owned stock of a business firm by borrowing 80 to 90 percent or more of the purchase price from banks and the bond market. In many leveraged buyouts (LBOs), the assets of companies that previously were publicly owned (that is, their stock was widely dispersed among thousands of investors) are conveyed to closely held private companies and partnerships. In these instances, the takeover group is counting on faster growth and improved profitability of the target company or on selling some of its assets to pay off the huge volume of acquisition debt.

These debt-funded mergers have generated much proposed federal and state legislation over the years to prevent "corporate raiders" from taking over some companies. Some targeted firms have developed *shark repellents* or *poison pills,* such as favorable deals for outside investors not affiliated with a corporate raider, revisions in corporate charters that make it more difficult for outsiders to take over the firm, and the taking on of heavy debt which makes the company less attractive as a takeover target. Surprisingly, research evidence shows that stockholders of companies targeted for acquisition benefit from takeover activity, even when the planned takeover is unsuccessful. Investors apparently believe that such takeovers will improve the efficiency and profitability of the target companies beyond what their existing management has been able to do and the stock of the target firm often rises in value, at least initially. Perhaps in recognition of this beneficial effect, along with efforts to clean up recent corporate scandals, fewer poison pills and other takeover defenses have been used in recent years. For example, familiar poison pill users like Circuit City and Goodyear Tire and Rubber have recently been dismantling some of their takeover defenses. The corporate market today appears to be more open to mergers and acquisitions than it has been in several years.

19.9 Bank Loans to Business Firms

The Volume of Bank Credit Supplied to Businesses

Commercial banks are direct competitors with the corporate debt security markets in making both long-term and short-term credit available to businesses. Unfortunately for many banks, growing numbers of corporations that once relied upon banking firms for the bulk of their funding have turned instead to selling securities in the open market, decreasing somewhat the relative importance of banks within the financial system. Still, the volume of bank credit made available to businesses remains enormous. For example, by July 2004 commercial and industrial loans extended by commercial banks operating in the United States totaled nearly $900 billion, or about a quarter of all U.S. commercial bank loans. Banks grant their loans to a wide variety of firms covering all major sectors of the business community. And bankers have come to play a key supporting role in the corporate debt market, issuing standby credit guarantees on behalf of borrowing companies to pay off their customers' debt if the borrowing companies cannot do so.

In recent years, the Federal Reserve Board has carried out periodic surveys of business lending practices by banks across the United States. These Federal Reserve surveys indicate that bank loans to business firms tend to be relatively short in maturity. For example, recent surveys suggest that short-term commercial and industrial loans average less than two months to maturity, while long-term business loans average just three to four years in maturity. The Federal Reserve surveys suggest that longer-term business loans carry *higher* average interest rates than do short-term business loans. This is due, in part, to the greater risk associated with long-term credit. In addition, yield curves have usually sloped upward in recent years, calling for higher rates on long-term loans. Moreover, the larger and longer-term a business loan is, the more likely its interest rate will *float* with market conditions. Clearly, banks become more determined to protect themselves against unexpected inflation and other adverse developments through floating interest rates as the maturity and size of a business loan increase.

The Prime, or Base, Interest Rate on Business Loans

prime bank rate

base rate

One of the best-known and most widely followed interest rates in the financial system is the **prime bank rate,** sometimes called a **base rate,** or *reference rate.* The prime rate is an annual percentage rate that banks may quote to their most creditworthy customers. Most prime loans are unsecured, but the borrowers often are required to keep a deposit at the lending bank equal to a specified percentage of the loan. This *compensating balance* may be 15 to 20 percent of the amount loaned. Even for a prime borrower, therefore, the true cost of a bank loan is often higher than the prime rate itself. Most prime loans are short-term—one year or less—loans taken out to finance purchases of business inventory and other working capital needs or to support construction projects.

Each bank must set its own prime or base rate. Beginning in the 1930s, however, a uniform prime rate began to appear, with differences in loan rates from bank to bank quickly eliminated by competition. Split primes do occur for some periods of time, however. A bank strapped for loanable funds may keep its prime rate temporarily above rates posted by other banks in order to allocate its more limited supply of credit. Similarly, a bank with ample funds to lend may post a prime temporarily below market to encourage its customers to borrow more frequently and in larger amounts.

Traditionally, the prime rate was set by one or more of the nation's leading banks, and other banks followed the leader. However, a major innovation in the market for prime loans occurred in 1971 when Citibank of New York (now a part of Citigroup) announced it would *float* its prime. Citibank's basic lending rate was pegged on a weekly basis at half a percentage point above the yield on 90-day commercial paper. Other leading banks soon followed, pegging their prime rates to prevailing yields on Treasury bills and other money market instruments. Linking the prime to such active money market rates as those attached to Treasury bills and commercial paper resulted in a more flexible base lending rate. The prime has come to reflect more accurately the forces of shifting credit demands, fluctuations in government policy, and inflation. A more flexible prime has enabled banks to better protect their interest margins—the difference between the return on loans and the cost of bank funds—and to make credit more readily available to customers willing to pay the price.

Many business loans today are priced at *premiums* above the prime or other base rate because only the most financially sound customers qualify for prime or below-prime loans. Nevertheless, commercial loan rates typically are tied to the base rate through a carefully worked out formula. One popular approach, *prime plus,* adds on a rate premium for default risk and often an additional premium for longer maturities (term risk). Thus, the banker may quote a commercial customer "prime plus 2," with a 1 percent premium above the base rate for default risk and another 1 percent premium for term risk. Other banks may use the *times-prime* method, which multiplies the base rate by a risk factor. For example, the business customer may be quoted a loan at 1.5 times prime. If the current prime is 10 percent, this customer pays 15 percent. If the loan carries a floating rate, then the interest rate in future periods can always be calculated by multiplying the base rate by 1.5.

Which of these prime-rate formulas the banker uses may depend on his or her forecast of interest rates. In a period of falling rates, interest charges on floating-rate loans figured on a times-prime basis decline faster than those based on prime plus. When interest rates are on the rise, times-prime pricing results in more rapid increases in business loan rates. Therefore, times-prime financing is more sensitive to the changing cost of bank funds over the course of the business cycle.

Other Examples of Base Rates for Business Loans

The prime bank rate is one example of a base rate for business loans, but it is by no means the only example in today's world. In fact, most commercial loan rates today are tied to base rates other than prime. This is frequently the case for large multinational corporations that have ready access to both domestic and international credit markets. For example, the *London Interbank Offer Rate* (*LIBOR*) on short-term Eurodollar deposits is often used as a base rate for the largest corporate loans. In some cases, the commercial paper rate, the federal funds interest rate, and the secondary market rate on bank CDs are also used as popular base rates.

Smaller numbers of borrowers today remain tied to the prime rate. Typically, borrowers in this category include less mobile customers with fewer alternative credit sources than many of the largest corporations. The largest businesses frequently can demand credit at interest rates significantly less than prime. These large loans are often made today at contract interest rates that are only a fraction of a percentage point (i.e., a few basis points) above a lender's actual cost of obtaining funds in the money market.

19.10 Commercial Mortgages

commercial mortgage

The construction of office buildings, shopping centers, and other commercial structures is generally financed with an instrument known as the **commercial mortgage.** Short-term mortgage loans are used to finance the construction of commercial projects, and longer-term mortgages are employed to pay off short-term construction loans, purchase land, and cover property development costs. The majority of long-term commercial mortgage loans are made by life insurance companies, thrift institutions, finance companies, and pension funds; in contrast, commercial banks are the predominant short-term commercial mortgage lender. Banks support the construction of office buildings and other commercial projects with loans secured by land and building materials. These short-term mortgage credits fall due when construction is completed, with permanent financing of the project then passing to insurance companies and other long-term lenders.

Additional information about the commercial mortgage market is available from such Web sites as REBUZ at rebuz.com and bondmarkets.com/research

Substantial volatility exists in the commercial mortgage market, due to multiple causes. One causal factor is the sensitivity of commercial construction borrowing to changes in market interest rates. For example, during the 2000–2004 period, commercial borrowing costs dropped to the lowest levels in decades and, partly in response, construction soared, led by the rapid expansion of retail store chains, multifamily dwellings (especially apartments and condos), and office space. Unfortunately, participants in this market have a tendency to overshoot with their investment plans, often frantically building up new facilities when market conditions appear promising, only to find themselves facing excess capacity and ruinously high vacancy rates (as occurred, for example, in some urban markets in 2003 and 2004).

In the past, most commercial real estate financing was provided through *fixed-rate mortgages.* Faced with inflation and a volatile economy, however, commercial mortgage lenders began searching for new financial instruments to protect their return. Many mortgage lenders today combine both debt and equity financing in the same credit package. The best-known example is the *equity kicker,* where the lending institution grants a fixed-rate mortgage but also receives a share of any net earnings from the project. For example, a life insurance company may agree to provide $50 million to finance the construction of an office building. It agrees to accept a 15-year mortgage loan bearing a 10 percent interest rate. However, as a hedge against inflation and higher interest rates, the insurance company may also insist on receiving 10 percent of any net earnings generated from office rentals over the 15-year period.

Another device used recently in commercial mortgage financing is *indexing.* In this case, the annual interest rate on a loan may be tied to prevailing yields on high-quality government or public utility bonds. Lender and borrower may agree to renegotiate the interest rate at certain intervals, such as every three to five years. There is also a trend toward shorter maturity commercial mortgage loans—many as short as five years—with the borrower paying off the debt or refinancing the unpaid principal with the same or another lending institution.

During the 1990s, asset-backed securitization entered the commercial mortgage market. Private mortgage lenders and federal mortgage agencies (such as the FNMA and the FHLMC) sought ways to free up their lending capacity by packaging large amounts of commercial real estate loans, taking them off the balance sheet, and then issuing securities against the packaged loans. Sellers of these securities (led by such well-known investment firms as Goldman Sachs and Prudential Insurance Company) frequently arranged guarantees from the security issuers, resulting in a growing portion of commercial mortgage-backed securities being rated "investment grade" and attracting major financial institutions (such as insurance companies and pension funds) as buyers. Nevertheless, securitized commercial mortgages have proven to be highly sensitive to changing economic conditions. For example, default rates on securitized loans, especially those connected to hotel, retail, and apartment mortgages, rose sharply in 2003 and 2004 following a global recession as the twenty-first century began.

QUESTIONS TO HELP YOU STUDY

12. What is a *leveraged buyout?* A *junk bond?* What are the dangers associated with these financial devices and instruments?

13. Supply a definition for each of the following terms:

    Term loan

    Floating rate

    Prime rate

    Compensating balance

14. For what purposes are *commercial mortgages* issued? What changes have occurred recently in the terms attached to these mortgage instruments?

15. What is an *equity kicker?* What are its principal advantages over a straight commercial mortgage loan?

MARKETS ON THE NET: The Most Important Web Sites for This Chapter

Bond Market Association (investinginbonds.com/)

Bond Market Association—European Issues (bondmarkets.com/)

CBS Marketwatch (cbs.marketwatch.com)

CNN/Financial (cnnfn.com)

Financial Pipeline (finpipe.com)

Mortgage 101 (mortgage101.com)

REBUZ—Commercial Mortgages (rebuz.com)

Summary of the Chapter's Main Points

This chapter focused upon businesses raising funds by borrowing in the open market and by seeking loans extended by banks and other financial institutions.

- The majority of funds drawn upon by business firms to meet their working capital and other investment needs normally come, not from the financial marketplace, but from *inside* the individual business firm. In most periods more than half of business capital requirements are supplied by earnings and noncash depreciation expenses (i.e., *internal cash flow*).

- Nevertheless, each year a significant portion of business investment needs is met by selling securities or negotiating new loans in the financial markets. The financial system is a backstop for the operations of business firms for those periods when internally generated cash fails to increase fast enough to support the growth of sales.

- The financial markets provide both short-term working capital to meet current expenses and long-term funds to support the purchase of buildings and equipment. The principal external sources of working capital include trade credit (accounts payable), bank loans and acceptances, short-term credits from nonbank financial institutions (such as finance companies), and sales of commercial paper in the open market.

- For businesses in need of long-term funding, the principal funds sources are the sale of traditional corporate bonds and notes, asset-backed securities, term loans from banks, the issuance of common and preferred stock, and commercial mortgages.

- Traditional corporate *bonds* have original maturities of more than five years; *notes* carry maturities of five years or less. There is a trend toward shorter maturities of corporate securities due to inflation and rapid changes in technology. Indexing of corporate bond rates to broader movements in the economy has also become more common.

- A wide variety of different bond and note issues have been developed to provide investors with varying degrees of security and risk protection, including debentures, zero coupon bonds, equipment trust certificates, mortgage bonds, and industrial development bonds. Each type of bond is accompanied by an *indenture,* spelling out the rights and obligations of borrowers and investors.

- The most dynamic sector of the corporate debt market in recent years has centered on *asset-backed securities (ABS)*—interest-bearing debt instruments that arise from a process called *securitization.* Loans, accounts receivable (credit sales), and other income-generating assets are pooled by a company and removed from its balance sheet. The pooled assets are placed in a separate trust account (a special purpose entity, or SPE) and securities, representing claims against the pooled assets, are then sold to investors in the open market who are promised income generated by the assets in the pool. The issuing corporation gains new funds and an opportunity to change the makeup of its balance sheet, possibly making its financial position appear stronger.

- Corporate debt securities are purchased by a wide range of investors today, but the dominant buyers are insurance companies, pension funds, mutual funds, and savings banks. New corporate securities may be offered publicly in the *open market,* where competitive bidding takes place, or in a *private sale* to a limited group of investors. Public sales account for the largest portion of annual long-term borrowings, but the private market appeals to many smaller firms unable to tap the open market for funds and to companies with unique financing needs or lower credit ratings. Public sales offer the advantage of competition, as investment bankers bid against each other to underwrite a new security issue.

- The corporate bond and asset-backed security market has faced competition in recent years from both domestic and foreign commercial banks making long-term business loans. These *term loans* are generally used to purchase equipment. Most such loans carry floating interest rates tied to the *prime lending rate,* or some other base rate (such as LIBOR).

- Commercial banks have always been a leading financial institution in extending both short-term and long-term loans to business firms. These loans support the construction of office buildings, shopping centers, and other commercial structures and provide working capital to support daily operations. Banks generally specialize in short-term mortgages that finance business construction, while long-term commercial mortgage financing is provided mainly by insurance companies, savings banks, and pension funds. Bankers' overall role in providing credit to the business sector has been declining somewhat in recent years as more firms turn to the open market to raise funds. However, banks have increasingly come to play a supporting role in guaranteeing and monitoring corporate debt.

Key Terms Appearing in This Chapter

corporate bond, 588
corporate note, 588
indenture, 588
debenture, 591
mortgage bonds, 591
industrial development bond (IDB), 592
zero coupon bonds, 593
asset-backed securities (ABS), 594
securitization, 594

public sales, 598
private or direct placements, 598
investment bankers, 598
junk bonds, 603
leveraged buyouts, 604
prime bank rate, 605
base rate, 605
commercial mortgage, 607

Problems and Issues

1. *None* of the following statements is correct. Identify what is wrong with the italicized portion of each statement and make appropriate corrections.

   a. Most businesses raise the majority of funds needed for their current operations and future growth by *issuing traditional corporate bonds, issuing corporate stock, or borrowing from banks.*

   b. Smaller businesses rely heavily on *commercial banks and publicly traded debt issues* to meet their borrowing needs.

   c. The explosive growth of medium-term notes (MTNs) in recent years is attributable in part to the fact that they offer the borrowing corporation the advantage of being noncallable, while also allowing for a better *maturity match between the firm's liabilities and the assets with which the MTNs are secured.*

2. Discuss access to the following sources of borrowings and the advantages and disadvantages of employing each for a large, publicly held corporation and a small, less established firm.

   a. Publicly placed traditional corporate bonds.

   b. Privately placed debt.

   c. Junk bonds.

   d. Securitization of accounts receivable.

   e. Bank loans.

3. What is the difference between *venture capital* and an *initial public offering (IPO)?* How would the groups of interested investors likely differ between the two?

4. A corporation sells $5,000 par-value bonds at par in the open market, bearing an 8 percent coupon rate. Costs of marketing the issue, including dealer's commission, amounted to $200 per bond. If the bonds are due to mature in 15 years, what is their before-tax cost to the corporation? If the issuing company is in the 35 percent tax bracket, what is the bonds' after-tax cost to the firm?

5. A corporation borrows $5 million from a bank at a 12 percent prime rate. If the bank requires the company to hold 15 percent of the amount of the loan on deposit as a compensating balance, what is the effective rate of interest on the loan?

6. A bank quotes one of its corporate customers a loan at prime plus four percentage points when prime is 12 percent. Another bank, posting the same prime rate, quotes this same customer a loan at $1\frac{1}{4}$ times prime. Which loan would you recommend the corporation take? Suppose both loans carry floating rates. Prime increases to 16 percent. Which loan is the better deal? Which would be the better deal if prime rises to 18 percent? Explain what is happening.

Standard & Poor's Market Insight and Web-Based Problems

1. It was stated in this chapter that the major source of funds for businesses needing to finance their ongoing operations and future growth is *internally generated funds.* For the most part, these funds come from earnings that the individual firm does not pay out as dividends to its shareholders. The *dividend policy* as well as the willingness of the firm to borrow varies from company to company, but also from industry to industry.
   a. Visit S&P's Market Insight database at **mhhe.com/edumarketinsight** and identify the industry groups ("GIC Sub-Ind.") for Microsoft, Ford Motor Company, American Electric Power, and Dow Chemical.
   b. For each of the above firms, identify its dividend policy by determining its dividend payout ratio (i.e., its annualized dividend divided by its share price), and rank the companies from high to low.
   c. For each of the four industry groups these companies represent, find the average debt-to-equity ratio and rank the industries from high to low.
   d. From your results in parts (b) and (c) discuss how these industry groups vary in their reliance on internally generated funds and determine whether the selected firms within those industry groups appear to be representative of their industry as a whole.

2. One of the forms in which households maintain their wealth is corporate debt. This exercise asks you to determine what share of the *net worth* (total assets less total liabilities) of all U.S. households is represented by corporate debt and how this share has changed over time.
   a. Visit the Federal Reserve's Web site at **federalreserve.gov** and click on the tab "Research and Statistics." From there, go to "Historical Data and Current Releases" and find the historical data for the quarterly "Flow of Funds Accounts."
   b. Go to the appropriate table in the "Flow of Funds" collection of tables (usually, L.100) and determine the share of "corporate and foreign bonds" to "net worth" from the available data for each final quarter for the years 1960, 1970, 1980, 1990, 2000, and the most recent quarter available.
   c. Discuss the numbers in part (b). Do corporate bonds appear to be a relatively large or small share of households' wealth holdings? Has that share been stable over time? What possible explanations do you have for the changes that you observe in the data?

Selected References to Explore

Bitler, Marianne P.; Alicia M. Robb; and John D. Wolken. "Financial Services Used by Small Businesses: Evidence from the 1998 Survey of Small Business Finances." *Federal Reserve Bulletin,* April 2001, pp. 183–205.

Culp, Christopher L., and Andrea M. P. Neves. "Financial Innovations in the Leveraged Commercial Loan Market." *Journal of Applied Corporate Finance* XI (Summer 1998), pp. 94–105.

Peristiani, Stavros, and Gijoon Hong. "Pre-IPO Financial Performance and Aftermarket Survival." *Current Issues in Economics and Finance* 10, no. 2, Federal Reserve Bank of New York (February 2004).

Prowse, Stephen D. "A Look at America's Corporate Finance Markets." *Southwest Economy,* Federal Reserve Bank of Dallas, September–October 1997, pp. 1–11.

Chapter 20

The Market for Corporate Stock

What's in This Chapter?
Key Topics Outline

The Stock Market and the Economy

Features of Common and Preferred Stock

Leading Stock Market Investors

The Exchanges and the Over-the-Counter (OTC) Market

The Third Market and Private Equity Issues

National and International Market Developments

Market Efficiency, and Technical and
   Fundamental Analysis

Learning Objectives

in This Chapter

- You will learn about the characteristics of common and preferred corporate stock.
- You will be able to compare and contrast the roles and functions of the organized stock exchanges and the over-the-counter market.
- You will explore the question of *market efficiency* and examine the evidence for and against the efficiency of the stock market.

20.1 Introduction to the Stock Market

In the preceding chapters, we focused almost exclusively on debt securities and the extension of credit. In this chapter, we examine a unique security that is not debt but *equity*. It is a certificate representing *ownership* of a corporation. Unlike debt, corporate stock grants the investor no promise of return. Rather, it grants only the right to share in the firm's assets and earnings, if any.

Corporate stock is unique in one other important respect. All of the securities markets we have discussed to this point are intimately bound up with the process of moving funds from ultimate savers to ultimate borrowers in order to support investment and economic growth. In the stock market, however, the bulk of daily trading activity involves the buying and selling of securities already issued rather than the exchange of financial claims for new capital. For example, in 2003 corporations in the United States issued more than $80 billion, net, in new shares of stock, but this volume of new shares was equal to only about 1 percent of the total amount of stock outstanding.

Despite the relatively small volume of new stock issues compared to shares already issued, the stock market continues to have a significant impact on the *expectations* of businesses when planning future investments. Stock trading indirectly affects employment, growth, and the general health of the economy.[1] In this chapter, we take a close look at the basic characteristics of corporate stock and the markets where that stock is traded.

If you are interested in keeping track of daily stock market movements, three quality Web sites for this purpose include cfonews.com, stockpickcentral.com, and msn.com

20.2 Characteristics of Corporate Stock

All corporate stock represents an ownership interest in a corporation, conferring on the holder a number of important rights as well as risks. In this section, we examine the two types of corporate stock issued today: common and preferred shares.

Common Stock

common stock

The most important form of corporate stock is **common stock**. Like all forms of equity, common stock represents a *residual* claim against the assets of the issuing firm, entitling the owner to share in the net earnings of the firm when it is profitable and to share in the net market value (after all debts are paid) of the company's assets if it is liquidated. By owning common stock, the investor is subject to the full risks of ownership, which means that the business may fail or its earnings may fall to unacceptable levels. However, the risks of equity ownership are limited, because the stockholder normally is liable only for the amount of his or her investment.

If a corporation with outstanding shares of common stock is liquidated, the debts of the firm must be paid first from any assets available. The preferred stockholders then receive their share of any remaining funds. Whatever is left accrues to common stockholders on a *pro rata* basis. Common stock is generally a *registered* instrument, with the holder's name recorded on the issuing company's books.

---

[1] One broad index of stock market prices—Standard & Poor's Composite Index—is considered to be a *leading indicator* of subsequent changes in economic conditions, especially of future developments in industrial production, employment, and total spending (GDP). Thus, the stock market often turns in its greatest gains in the deepest part of a recession and turns down before a boom is over. The stock market seems to provide a forecast of business capital spending plans and output, perhaps reflecting the fact that it captures the expectations of the business community.

The volume of stock a corporation may issue is limited by the terms of its *charter of incorporation*. Additional shares beyond those authorized by the company's charter may be issued only by amending the charter with the approval of the current stockholders. Some companies have issued large amounts of corporate shares, reflecting not only their need for large amounts of equity capital but also a desire to broaden their ownership base.

The *par value* of common stock is an arbitrarily assigned value, usually printed on each stock certificate, though some stock has no specified par value. Where present, par value is usually set low relative to the stock's current market value. Originally, par was supposed to represent the owner's initial investment per share in the firm. The only real significance of par today is that the firm cannot pay any dividends to stockholders that would reduce the company's net worth per share below the par value of its stock.

Common stockholders are granted a number of rights when they buy a share of equity in a business corporation. Stock ownership permits them to *elect the company's board of directors,* who, in turn, choose the officers responsible for day-to-day management of the firm. Common shareholders have a *preemptive right* (unless specifically denied by the firm's charter) which gives current shareholders the right to purchase any new voting stock, convertible bonds, or preferred stock issued by the firm in order to maintain their current *pro rata* share of ownership. For example, if a stockholder holds 5 percent of all shares outstanding and 500 new shares are to be issued, this stockholder has the right to subscribe to 25 new shares.

Although most common stock grants each stockholder one vote per share, nonvoting common is also issued occasionally. Some companies issue Class A common, which has voting rights, and Class B common, which carries a prior claim on earnings but no voting power. The major stock exchanges do not encourage publicly held firms to issue classified stock, but classified shares are used extensively by privately held firms whose stock is not traded on a major exchange.

A right normally granted to all common stockholders is the *right of access* to the minutes of stockholder meetings and to lists of existing shareholders. This gives the stockholders some power to reorganize the company if management or the board of directors is performing poorly. Common stockholders may vote on all matters that affect the firm's property as a whole, such as a merger, liquidation, or the issuance of additional equity shares.

Preferred Stock

preferred stock

The other major form of stock issued today is **preferred stock**. Preferred stock carries a stated annual dividend expressed as a percent of the stock's par value. For example, if preferred shares carry a $100 par value with an 8 percent dividend rate, then each preferred shareholder is entitled to dividends of $8 per year on each share owned, provided the company declares a dividend. Common stockholders receive whatever dividends remain after the preferred shareholders receive their annual dividend.

Preferred stock occupies the middle ground between debt and equity securities, including advantages and disadvantages of both forms of raising long-term funds. Preferred stockholders have a *prior claim* over the firm's assets and earnings relative to the claims of common stockholders. However, creditors must be paid before either preferred or common stockholders. Unlike creditors of the firm, preferred stockholders cannot press for bankruptcy proceedings against a company that fails to pay them dividends. Nevertheless, preferred stock is part of a firm's equity capital and strengthens a firm's net worth, allowing it to issue more debt in the future. It also is a more flexible financing arrangement than debt because firms may choose not to pay dividends to their shareholders if corporate earnings are inadequate.

Generally, preferred stockholders have no voice in the selection of management unless the corporation fails to pay dividends for a stipulated period. A frequent provision in corporate charters gives preferred stockholders the right to elect some members of the board of directors if dividends are passed for a full year. Dividends on preferred stock, like those paid on common stock, are *not a* tax-deductible expense. This makes preferred shares more expensive to issue than debt, especially for companies in higher tax brackets. However, IRS regulations specify that 70 percent of the stock dividends received by corporations from unaffiliated companies *are* tax deductible. This deductibility feature makes preferred stock attractive to companies seeking to acquire ownership shares in other firms and sometimes allows preferred shares to be issued at a lower net interest cost than debt securities. In fact, corporations themselves are the principal buyers of preferred stock.

Many preferred shares are *cumulative,* which means that the passing of dividends results in an arrearage that must be paid in full before the common stockholders receive anything. Some preferred shares are *participating,* allowing the holder to share in the residual earnings normally accruing entirely to common stockholders. To illustrate how the participating feature might work, assume that an investor holds 8 percent participating preferred stock with a $100 par value. After the issuing company's board of directors votes to pay the stated annual dividend of $8 per share, the board also declares a $20 per share common stock dividend. If the formula for dividend participation calls for common and preferred shareholders to share *equally* in any net earnings, then each preferred shareholder will earn an additional $12 to bring her total dividend to $20 per share as well. Not all participating formulas are this generous, and most preferred issues are *nonparticipating,* because participation is detrimental to the interests of the common stockholders.

Most corporations plan to retire their preferred stock, even though it usually carries no stated maturity. In fact, preferred shares usually carry *call provisions.* When interest rates decline, the issuing company may exercise the call privilege at the price stated in the formal agreement between the firm and its shareholders. Some preferred issues are *convertible* into shares of common stock at the investor's option. The company retires all converted preferred shares and may force conversion by simply exercising the stock's call privilege. New preferred issues are often accompanied by a sinking fund provision, whereby funds are accumulated for eventual retirement of preferred shares. A trustee is appointed to collect sinking fund payments from the company and periodically to call in preferred shares or purchase them in the open market. Although sinking fund provisions allow the issuing firm to sell preferred stock with lower dividend rates, payments into the fund drain earnings and may reduce dividend payments to common stockholders.

To learn more about the nature and characteristics of preferred stock, see especially QuantumOnline.com

In recent years, corporations have developed new types of *variable-rate preferred stock,* carrying a floating dividend rate that makes the stock a substitute for short-term debt. Many variable-rate preferred issues allow their dividend rate to be reset several times, which may be accomplished by a marketing agent or via a special auction. Some companies have issued *Dutch-auction* preferred shares, a process by which stock buyers submit interest rate bids and the highest-interest rate bid clears the auction. Frequently, the dividend rate has a ceiling rate based on a key market reference rate (such as the market yield on commercial paper). Many preferred shares issued recently have had an exchange option attached, giving the issuing company the choice of exchanging the preferred stock for debt securities. Not long ago another hybrid form of preferred stock, "MIPS" (monthly income preferred shares), appeared; MIPS are counted as equity but carry interest payments like debt. Thus, MIPS help to reduce the prominence of a company's debt and tend to lower its federal taxes. However, MIPS have recently come under attack in the wake of the failure of Enron Corporation, which made use of them.[2]

Yet another form of preferred equity that appeared in the mid-1990s is *convertible preferred*. Convertible preferred shares are sometimes called "toxic" or "death" spiral convertibles. Each share can eventually be exchanged for an unspecified number of common stock shares, with the number of new common shares depending upon the common stock's market price when conversion occurs. If the issuing firm is in trouble and its common stock is plunging in value, the preferred shareholders receive a growing share of the firm's ownership.

In summary, from the standpoint of the *investor*, preferred stock represents an intermediate investment between bonds and common stock. Preferred shares often provide more income than bonds (particularly in years of strong corporate earnings), but the investment is also usually at greater risk. Preferred prices tend to fluctuate more widely than bond prices for the same change in market interest rates. Compared to common stock, preferred shares generally carry a lower expected rate of return but are, in turn, often less risky. From the standpoint of *issuing corporations*, preferred shares also seem to lie between bonds and common stock, offering the advantages of equity (especially in the option to pay or not pay dividends and in strengthening the balance sheet), but also offering several of the advantages of debt (including limited life and relatively fixed financing costs in many cases).

To assess the risks associated with preferred stock, many investors consult FitchRatings.com

---

QUESTIONS TO HELP YOU STUDY

1. In what important ways does the stock market *differ* from the other securities markets we have described in earlier parts of this book?

2. What major differences do you see between corporate stock and corporate debt obligations (discussed in the previous chapter)?

3. What are the essential characteristics of *common stock*?

4. What priority of *claim* do common stockholders have in the event a corporation is closed and liquidated? What limits the volume of shares that a company may issue and have outstanding at any point in time?

5. Discuss the nature of *preferred stock*. In what ways are preferred shares similar to corporate debt and in what ways are they similar to common stock?

20.3 Stock Market Investors

Corporate stock is one of the most widely held financial assets in the world. Only one other financial asset—government securities—is held by as large and diverse a group of individuals and institutions as are common and preferred stock. One important source of information on stockholders in the United States is the Federal Reserve Board's Flow of Funds Accounts.[3] Exhibit 20.1 gives the names of major investor groups and their total holdings of common and preferred stock for the years 1980, 1990, 2000, and 2004.

---

[2]Regular preferred stock has become more attractive to investors in the United States lately because the dividend payments it generates are now subject to a low 15 percent tax rate (comparable to the low U.S. tax rate on capital gains). However, the majority of preferred shares currently traded in the U.S. are trust preferred shares that, for tax purposes, are treated as corporate debt, not stock. Thus, trust preferred shareholders receive interest, not dividend, payments and are subject to ordinary income tax rates (which range as high as 35 percent).

[3]See Chapter 3 for an explanation of the method of construction and the types of information contained in the Flow of Funds Accounts provided by the Federal Reserve Board.

| EXHIBIT 20.1 | Key Investors Buying Corporate Stock in the United States ($ Billions at Year-End; Market Values) |

	1980		1990		2000		2004**	
Groups of Investors	Amount	Percent of Total	Amount	Percent of Total	Amount	Percent of Total	Amount	Percent of Total
Households (individuals and families)	$ 875	58.6%	$1,781	50.3%	$ 7,650	43.4%	$5,828	36.9%
Rest of the world	75	5.0	244	6.9	1,626	9.2	1,655	10.5
Commercial banks	*	—	2	0.1	17	0.1	16	0.1
Savings banks	4	0.3	9	0.2	24	0.1	28	0.2
Life insurers	46	3.1	82	2.3	892	5.1	967	6.1
Property-casualty insurers	32	2.2	80	2.3	194	1.1	187	1.2
Pension funds:								
Private	232	15.5	606	17.1	1,956	11.1	1,747	11.1
Government	44	3.0	285	8.0	1,394	7.9	1,421	9.0
Investment companies (mutual funds)	42	2.8	233	6.6	3,227	18.3	3,246	20.6
Security brokers/dealers and other investors	143	9.6	241	6.8	651	3.7	687	4.4
	$1,495	100.0%	$3,543	100.0%	$17,627	100.0%	$15,783	100.0%

Source: Flow of Funds Accounts, compiled quarterly by the Board of Governors of the Federal Reserve System.

*Less than $1 billion.

**Figures are for first quarter 2004.

Note: Columns may not add to totals due to rounding.

From Exhibit 20.1 we see that direct holdings of stock by *households*—individuals and families—represent the largest share of investors in corporate stock in the United States. In 2004, households held nearly 40 percent of all corporate stock outstanding, down from close to 60 percent in 1980. The principal reason for this decline in the household group's market share is the phenomenal growth of *pension funds*—private and governmental—and *mutual funds,* each holding about 20 percent of all shares outstanding. For the most part, these funds represent indirect investments of households in the stock market that are managed on their behalf by *institutional investors.*

Unlike households, who tend to buy and hold stock for long periods, institutional investors actively trade shares of stock in an effort to keep their portfolios properly "balanced" based on their perception of the current economic climate. On any given day, the bulk of market transactions is conducted by institutional traders. The growth of pension funds reflects the great flexibility that households today have in directing where their retirement savings are to be invested, along with their desire to take advantage of higher expected returns in the stock market. The growth of mutual funds points to increased interest among middle-income investors, who invest in relatively small installments, seek out low or no brokerage commissions, wish to take advantage of the services of professional fund managers, and hope to lower the risk of their stock investments by buying into a diversified stock portfolio.

Among the remaining major investor groups holding corporate stock acquired in the United States are *foreign investors,* whose portion of the U.S. equities market climbed above 10 percent in 2004. American markets appeared less volatile and less vulnerable

One of the most popular ways of keeping track of stock market developments is to follow key *stock indexes*—weighted or unweighted averages of the prices of a group of stocks. There are hundreds of these indexes around the globe, including more than 50 major stock market indexes regularly published outside the U.S. in Asia, Europe, and the Americas. What is included in the best known of these market indicators?

Most are either price-weighted or size-weighted averages. A price-weighted index is merely the sum of all stock prices covered by the index, while a size-weighted index gives greater weight to the biggest companies (measured by the market value of each firm's capital). One of the oldest (founded in 1884) and best known is the Dow Jones Industrial Average (DJIA)—a price-weighted index of 30 leading U.S. corporations (including recently added Verizon, Pfizer, Home Depot, and Microsoft, which replaced AT&T, Kodak, Goodyear, and Sears), representing about one-fifth of the total value of publicly traded U.S. companies. The Dow 30 is accompanied by several sector indexes—for example, the DJ Transportation Average (including airline, railroad, and trucking companies) and the DJ Utility Average (largely devoted to electric and gas utilities).

Rivaling the Dow today are Standard & Poor's 500 and 100 stock indexes. The S&P 100 reflects the share values of 100 blue-chip, large-cap companies, while the S&P 500 includes 500 blue-chip industrial, utility, transportation, and financial stocks, accounting for about 70 percent of the U.S. market. Even broader are the Wilshire 5000, the Russell 2000, the New York Stock Exchange Composite Index, and the tech-heavy NASDAQ Composite Index. The NASDAQ Composite reflects all common shares for companies listed on the National Association of Security Dealers Automated Quotation (NASDAQ) system, which tracks more than 5,000 firms, weighted by the market value of their capitalization. The Wilshire 5000 encompasses just about every actively traded stock in the U.S. market, weighted by market capitalization. The Russell 2000 chooses two-thirds of the smallest firms from a population of 3,000, while the NYSE Composite Index tracks the performance of shares listed on the New York Stock Exchange (including more than 2,000 U.S. and foreign stocks, weighted by float-adjusted market capitalization). The NYSE also calculates index values for four sectors—industrial, transportation, utility, and finance-oriented shares.

to economic and political disaster than many of the markets overseas. Finally, *deposit-type intermediaries*—commercial and savings banks—collectively held less than 1 percent of available shares in 2004. State and federal laws severely limit savings bank investments in corporate stock and prohibit the majority of commercial banks from investing in most stocks for their own portfolios.

The fact that stocks generally carry greater risk than debt instruments for investors is reflected in higher expected returns on stocks. Exhibit 20.2 illustrates the relatively high historical returns that many investors have realized in the form of stock price appreciation. For example, the broad market indexes of the NYSE Composite and the S&P 500 grew approximately eightfold between 1980 and 2004, while the "blue chip" Dow Jones Industrial Average and the tech-heavy NASDAQ each experienced roughly a tenfold increase.

These incredible gains in stock values occurred despite an apparent "drag" on the market in the form of falling dividend payments to stockholders. Fewer companies paid dividends and those that did frequently lowered their dividend rates. Tax laws at the time favored retention of earnings inside corporations rather than paying out cash to shareholders. Then, too, many companies had a voracious appetite for spendable cash to update their computer systems and expand into new markets. Earnings per share fell sharply in the wake of dramatic price gains. However, that trend didn't slow down many investors who, in the words of Federal Reserve Board chairman, Alan Greenspan, seemed to be caught up in "irrational exuberance" regardless of the gradually souring corporate earnings and dividend picture.

619

EXHIBIT 20.2 Recent Movements in Stock Prices and Yields

New York Stock Exchange Indices

Years	Composite (12/31/02 = 5000)	(December 31, 1965 = 50)				Dow Jones Industrial Average	Standard & Poor's Composite Index (1941–43 = 100)	NASDAQ Composite (2/05/71 = 100)	Common Stock Yields	
		Industrial	Transportation	Utilities	Finance				Dividend-Price Ratio (D/P)	Earnings-Price Ratio (E/P)
1960	—	—	—	—	—	618.04	55.85	—	3.47%	5.90%
1970	483.4	48.03	32.14	74.47	60.00	753.19	83.22	—	3.83	6.45
1980	720.2	78.70	60.61	74.69	64.25	891.41	118.78	168.61	5.26	12.66
1990	1,939.4	225.78	158.62	181.20	133.26	2,678.94	334.59	409.17	3.61	6.47
2000	6,805.9	810.63	413.65	477.65	553.13	10,734.90	1,427.22	3,783.67	1.15	3.63
2003	5,456.5	634.11	437.37	238.05	566.74	8,993.59	965.23	1647.07	1.72	—
2004*	6,569.8	741.19	521.11	271.45	657.07	10,448.07	1,132.52	2,066.15	—	—

Sources: Board of Governors of the Federal Reserve System; and President's Council of Economic Advisors, *Economic Report of the President*, various annual issues.

Note: Index values reflect averages of daily closing prices. The NYSE figures include all stocks listed on that exchange. The Dow Jones Industrial Average sums the share prices of 30 leading companies, though the DJIA's composition has changed over time. Five hundred blue-chip stocks are included in the S&P Composite. Dividends are aggregate cash dividend payments (annual rate) divided by the aggregate market value of the underlying shares based upon Wednesday's closing prices. Earnings-price ratios are averages of quarterly earnings-to-price ratios.

*2004 figures; are for January.

Investors began to think, "Even an idiot can make a profit trading in stocks." Unfortunately for the unwary, stocks worldwide fell across a broad front in the year 2000, especially the shares of high-tech firms which dominated the NASDAQ Composite Index. The latter dropped about 60 percent between 2000 and 2003. Small investors by the millions headed for the exits as the new century opened and even major institutional investors sought shelter. Adding force to the decline was a global economic recession—the first downturn in a decade. The market would not resume its upward climb until 2003, when a recovering economy and stronger corporate earnings helped push stock prices higher. In this rebound, *small-cap stocks* (companies posting capitalization of less than $1.5 billion) led the way with a dramatic price rally.

Explaining Stock Values

Why do stock values change? Are there any stock-price models to help us understand what is happening in the market? Recent research suggests that much of the variability in stock prices, though not all, can be explained by a relatively simple valuation model:

$$S_0 = \sum_{t=0}^{\infty} \frac{E(D_t)}{[1 + (r + k)]^t} \qquad (20.1)$$

where S_0 equals today's ($t = 0$) market price per share of stock; $E(D_t)$ represents expected future dividend flows per share from the current period into the indefinite future, t (since stock is a perpetual instrument); r represents the default-free rate of interest; and k equals the premium for bearing equity risk, with the sum of these last two representing the current rate of discount applied to all expected future dividend flows by capital market investors based on their assessment of the risks involved. Stocks should not deviate very long from prevailing perceptions among capital market investors regarding their risk (k) and the cash flows they are expected to pay out over time, $E(D_t)$.

For example, suppose that General Electric stock is expected to pay annual dividends of $3 per share for 20 years, with the first dividend to be received one year from today (at date $t = 1$), discounted at a 10 percent annual rate to reflect the default-free interest rate and equity risk. Current holders of the stock believe they can sell it at the end of the 20-year period for $35 per share. Using computer software or a financial calculator, its market price per share will approach:

$$S_0 = \sum_{t=1}^{20} \$3/(1 + 0.10)^t + \$35/(1 + 0.10)^{20} = \$30.76 \text{ per share}$$

Note that the value of the last term in the equation above, showing the expected price of GE stock when it is sold in the future, is dependent on the flow of expected dividends in the years following the stock's sale. Thus, the value of *any* share of stock ultimately rests upon the expectations of the marketplace regarding the stock's discounted dividend flows to be received in the future.

If a corporation's dividend payments begin one year from today, at date $t = 1$, and are expected to grow at a constant rate, g, in the future, then Equation 20.1 can be reduced to[4]:

$$S_0 = D_1/(r + k - g) \qquad (20.2)$$

---

[4]Note that the dividend payment received one year from today, D_1, is equal to the currently observed dividend received at date $t = 0$, or D_0, multiplied by $(1 + g)$. If the owner of the stock today ($t = 0$) has claims over the current dividend, then Equation 20.1 must be modified to reflect that payment and it becomes (See Chapter 6):

$$S_0 = D_0(1 + r + k)/(r + k - g)$$

where D_1 represents the expected dividend to be paid initially and g is the expected growth rate for future dividends. In the example above, suppose General Electric paid a $3 dividend initially, but its future dividends are expected to grow at a constant rate of 7 percent annually. Then GE's stock price would approach a value of:

$$S = \$3/(0.10 - 0.07) = \$100 \text{ per share}^5$$

Over the past century there have been few decades in which stock prices did not rise. As shown below, average stock yields have significantly outdistanced bond yields and substantially beaten average long-run returns on other popular investments.

The Long-Run Return Premium Paid by Stocks over Other Investments	
Financial Instrument	**Long-Run Average Annual Real Rate of Return for the 1925–2001 Period**
Corporate stocks listed on the New York Stock Exchange	7.42%
Corporate bonds	2.64
U.S. government notes and bonds	1.85
U.S. Treasury bills	0.60

Source: New York Stock Exchange and Board of Governors of the Federal Reserve System.

Not only have corporate stocks responded positively to periods of strong economic growth and moderate inflation, but they have also increased in response to the growing urgency of millions of individuals preparing for their retirement years. Due to significant advances in medical technology and improved nutrition, people are living much longer today. As a result, they require greater growth in savings in order to sustain their income over a longer time span. For many investors, stocks may be an effective means of ensuring that savings keep up with inflation and may provide a decent long-run standard of living.

One of the fascinating, yet unanswered questions about corporate stock is, what outside factors are stock prices most sensitive to from a statistical point of view? Two obvious candidates are *inflation* and *market interest rates*. Many investors have believed for a long time that stocks are among the best long-term hedges against inflation, though, as we saw in Chapter 7, that is not necessarily true, particularly for stocks issued by companies having contracts that cause their costs to rise faster than their revenues when inflation strikes. More rapid inflation can throw a company's stockholders into higher tax brackets and increase investors' capital gains taxes, thereby lowering their after-tax returns from stock and reducing stock prices. Stock prices would also be expected, statistically, to be closely tied to movements in

---

[5]The stock-price formulas shown in Equations 20.1 and 20.2 give us some possible clues as to why stock prices often react sharply to unexpected changes in monetary policy by the Federal Reserve and other central banks. In particular, stock prices tend to *rise* when credit conditions ease (e.g., when the Fed lowers the federal funds rate) and tend to *fall* when credit conditions tighten (e.g., when the Fed raises the funds rate). For example, a hike in the funds rate is likely to increase the default-free interest rate (r), increasing the discount rate applied to future stock dividends and lowering stock prices. Another consideration is monetary policy's impact on corporate cash flows. A rising Fed funds rate, for example, may ultimately reduce a company's cash flows and its net worth, increasing its cost of external fund-raising. Gou (2004) observes that smaller companies' stock values seem to be more affected by unexpected changes in central bank policy than those of larger firms because smaller firms tend to have thinner cushions of retained earnings and, thus, are more susceptible to liquidity shortages, especially when the economy is weak.

FINANCIAL DEVELOPMENTS

Stock Dividend Yields—Is a Change Under Way?

According to some of the most popular stock-valuation models, stock prices depend upon two critical factors—the *expected stream of dividends* a share of stock will pay to its owner over time, and the *degree of risk* attached to that expected dividend stream. The expected dividend stream is *positively* related and the risk factor is *negatively* related to a stock's market value.

For the past 50 years, stock dividend yields have generally fallen. *A stock's dividend yield is determined by adding up its total per-share stockholder dividends for a year and then dividing by the current price of the stock.* Since reaching a peak at close to 9 percent during the 1950s, average dividend yields fell, dropping to about 1 percent as this new century dawned. Why? We are not sure, but higher stock prices (and the prospect of greater capital gains), the increased use of stock options for employee compensation, heavy taxation of dividends, and companies rushing to expand by retaining earnings have each played a role.

However, this trend may now be reversing. Recent corporate scandals (especially those involving excessive rewards for corporate insiders) and the poor choices made by many companies when reinvesting their earnings have recently combined to raise dividend yields. Another key factor is a new tax law passed in 2003 that lowers the maximum dividend tax rate for U.S. investors from 35 percent to 15 percent. Today the majority of S&P 500 companies are paying dividends and the number of dividend payers seems to be rising. Dividend-paying stocks have become more attractive to investors seeking a stable stream of future income.

market interest rates because: (1) interest-bearing debt securities compete with stocks for investors' money (so higher interest rates may pull money out of stocks and into bonds, for example); (2) interest rate levels affect the discount rate applied to future stock dividend streams and, thereby, should be inversely related to the level of stock prices; and (3) higher market interest rates make it more expensive for investors buying stock on margin to borrow funds and, therefore, tend to discourage the demand for those stocks not expected to be strong performers. However, a study by Golob and Bishop (1996) suggests that stock prices seem to follow inflation more closely than they do market interest rates. The inflation rate measured by the consumer price index appeared to explain more of the observed changes in stock earnings-price ratios than did market rates of interest.[6]

20.4 Characteristics of the Corporate Stock Market

organized exchanges

There are two main branches of the market for trading corporate stock. One is the **organized exchanges**, which in the United States include the New York Stock Exchange (NYSE) and the American Exchange (AMEX) plus exchanges dealing in stock futures and options (such as the Chicago Board of Trade, or CBOT) as well as regional exchanges scattered around the United States (including the Boston, Cincinnati, Pacific, and Philadelphia exchanges). Overseas, the Tokyo, Hong Kong, Singapore, Sydney, Paris, and London exchanges have also grown in importance as major centers

[6]Recent research suggests that stock prices and the proportion of investors' portfolios devoted to stock are influenced by several additional factors than those discussed above. For example, there appears to be a "home bias" in stock acquisitions as domestic investors tend to over-weight their portfolios with domestic stocks (and bonds as well) relative to foreign securities, contrary to what rational stock-value models would suggest. Accordingly, many foreign corporations in recent years have helped to offset the "home bias" of U.S. investors by cross-listing their stock on U.S. exchanges, increasing their financial disclosures, and committing to stronger corporate governance practices. See, for example, Sarker and Li (2002).

EXHIBIT 20.3

International Focus: Leading Stock Exchanges Active around the World in Recent Years

New York Stock Exchange	Brussels Exchange
American Stock Exchange	Sydney Exchange
Amsterdam Exchange	Hong Kong Exchange
Tokyo Exchange	Singapore Exchange
Osaka Exchange	Copenhagen Exchange
London Exchange	Shanghai Exchange
Frankfurt Exchange (DAX)	Taipei Exchange
Paris Bourse (MATIF)	Toronto Exchange
Mexico City Exchange	Wellington Exchange
Montreal Exchange	Swiss Stock Exchange

for trading corporate shares worldwide, propelled in part by the privatization of many state-owned businesses and massive stock investments by U.S. investors abroad. All of the exchanges around the globe (the most important in recent years are listed in Exhibit 20.3) use similar procedures for controlling membership and regulating purchases and sales.

Trading on the exchanges is governed by regulations and formal procedures designed to ensure competitive pricing and an active market for the stock of the largest, most financially stable companies. In contrast, the second branch of the equities market—the **over-the-counter (OTC) market**—involves trading of stock through brokers operating off the major exchanges. This market is more informal and fluid than exchange trading and includes the stocks and bonds of smaller companies, financial institutions, and foreign firms.

over-the-counter (OTC) market

The Major Organized Exchanges

American Exchanges   Among the best-known organized exchanges are the Big Board—The New York Stock Exchange (NYSE)—and the American Stock Exchange (ASE or AMEX). The NYSE and most other U.S. exchanges overlap in trading and function and are competitive markets for the most actively traded stocks. Each exchange provides a physical location for trading, and trading by member firms must be carried on at that location.

For example, the New York Stock Exchange has a trading floor of about 36,000 square feet that contains 20 trading posts, each staffed by a specialist and specialist clerks. Each NYSE-listed security is traded from one of these trading posts and is handled by one specialist. Prices are established by the auction method, with computer monitors set up around the trading floor to inform buyers and sellers what the last price was for each share traded. Surrounding the main floor are about 1,500 booths with brokers receiving customer orders for shares electronically or via telephone and then seeking out the specialist handling each stock requested. Exchanges like the NYSE permit the enforcement of trading rules in order to achieve the efficient and speedy allocation of equity shares at competitive prices.[7]

---

[7]As the 21st century opened the New York Stock Exchange began drafting a plan for its future, aimed at improving the speed, efficiency, and transparency of its operations and procedures. The initial draft plan submitted to the Securities and Exchange Commission in 2004 called for greater use of computers and electronic networking in order to replace some elements of the current human-based pricing and auction systems and some restrictions on the role played by specialists in influencing stock prices when they trade for their own accounts.

To be eligible for trading on an organized exchange, the stock must be issued by a firm *listed* with the exchange. A substantial number of major U.S. corporations are listed on several different exchanges. The listing qualifications demanded by the New York Stock Exchange are among the most comprehensive, which serves to limit NYSE trading to stocks issued by the largest domestic and foreign companies. While the NYSE's listing requirements vary with the location of a firm (foreign or domestic) and other factors, the NYSE generally requires a parent company to have more than a million shares available for public trading, before-tax annual earnings of at least $2.5 million, and worldwide capitalization of at least a billion dollars. Foreign companies may be listed on the NYSE if they qualify under domestic listing rules or satisfy so-called Alternative Listing Standards, which include the requirement that listed firms have at least 2.5 million shares traded and a billion dollars in average global capitalization. The basic intent of listing rules is to ensure that the listed firm has sufficient shares available to create an active market for its stock and discloses sufficient data so that investors can make informed decisions.

Even if a company meets all listing requirements, its stock must still be approved for admission by the exchange's board of directors, who are elected by firms with seats on the exchange. Corporations that are successful in listing their stock must disclose their financial condition, publish quarterly earnings reports, and help maintain an active public market for their shares. If trading interest in a particular firm's stock falls off significantly (as in the case of Enron Corporation in 2002), the firm may be *delisted.* Some companies may be granted "unlisted trading privileges" if their stock has been listed on another exchange. Recently, foreign firms have been admitted in large numbers to most major exchanges. Foreign companies with more than $5 million in assets and at least 500 shareholders whose stock is traded in the United States must register with the Securities and Exchange Commission, unless specifically exempted.

One of the most important advantages claimed for listing on an exchange is that it improves the *liquidity* of a corporation's stock. (A relatively large volume of shares can be sold without significantly depressing the price.) This feature is of special concern to large institutional investors (such as mutual funds and pension funds) that have come to dominate daily trading in the equities market, because these institutions trade in large blocks rather than a few shares at a time. Allegedly, a corporation can improve the market for its stock by becoming listed on a securities exchange.

Member firms of the exchange are the only ones that may trade listed securities on the exchange floor, either for their own account or for their customers. Most members own "seats" on the exchange and hold claims against the exchange's assets. Member firms are allowed to sell or lease their seats with the approval of the exchange's governing board.

Member firms fulfill a wide variety of roles on an exchange. Some act as *floor traders* that buy and sell only for their own account. Floor traders are really speculators whose portfolios turn over rapidly as they drift from post to post on the exchange floor looking for profitable trading opportunities. Other members serve as *commission brokers,* employed by member brokerage firms to represent the orders of their customers, or *floor brokers,* who are usually individual entrepreneurs carrying out buy and sell orders from other brokers not present on the exchange floor.

Some traders holding exchange seats are *specialists* who oversee trading in each stock. The specialist firms operating on the New York Stock Exchange act as *both* brokers and dealers, buying and selling for other brokers and for themselves when there is an imbalance between supply and demand for the stocks in which they specialize. For example, when sell orders pile up for the stocks for which a specialist firm is responsible, it moves in to buy some of the offered shares, creating a market and providing

To learn more about the major stock exchanges, go to their principal Web sites— for example, nyse.com and amex.com

An interesting recent innovation on several stock exchanges are ETFs, or Exchange-Traded Funds, which are similar to index mutual funds but can be traded like ordinary stocks. See, for example, Morningstar at morningstar.com and STREETTRACKS at streettracks.com

liquidity by trading for its own account. Specialists can help to create orderly and continuous markets and stabilize prices by agreeing to cover unfilled customer orders and by posting firm bid and ask prices to interested investors, though recently specialists on the NYSE have come under close scrutiny for alleged rule violations and possible trading irregularities. Finally, a few *odd-lot traders,* representing large brokerage firms dealing with the public, are also active on the exchange floor. Odd lots are buy or sell orders involving fewer than 100 shares that come primarily from individuals. The odd-lot trader purchases 100 or more shares—a *round lot*—and retains any extra shares not needed by customers.

Foreign Exchanges   Stock exchanges have emerged in every region of the globe, especially in Asia, Europe, and the Americas. Around the Pacific Rim, exchanges in Australia, China, Hong Kong, India, Singapore, and South Korea have become established leaders in the market for stocks. In Europe, exchanges in Austria, Belgium, France, Germany, Great Britain, and Switzerland have attracted the interest of global investors, as have exchanges in Russia and South Africa. In the Americas, Argentina, Brazil, Chile, and Mexico have active exchanges that publish their daily trading statistics for investors around the world.

For a closer look at several foreign exchanges, see especially fese.be

Among the most interesting of the exchanges outside the U.S. are those in Japan, which have recently swung from more than a decade of economic and financial disaster to some signs of recovery and are receiving renewed interest from the rest of the world. The largest Japanese exchange is the Tokyo Stock Exchange (TSE), which operates in two different sections. The First Section offers exchange services for shares of the largest corporations; the Second Section deals in the shares of smaller corporations. Most investors follow changes in Japanese stock prices by consulting the Nikkei Index, which tracks the average unweighted price of 225 shares traded each day on the TSE. A broader Japanese stock price indicator is the TOPIX, which reflects the current prices of all large-company stocks traded on the Tokyo Exchange. Rivaling the growth of the Tokyo exchange has been another exchange in Osaka, about 250 miles southwest of Tokyo. Osaka trades individual shares and futures contracts linked to the Nikkei index of 225 stocks.

Contributions of Exchanges   Stock exchanges are among the oldest financial institutions. The New York Stock Exchange, for example, was set up following an agreement among 24 Wall Street brokers in May 1792. Stock exchanges were opened in Tokyo and Osaka, Japan, in 1878. Exchanges provide a continuous market centered in an established location with rigid rules to ensure fairness in trading. By bringing together buyers and sellers, the exchanges appear to make stock a more liquid investment, promote efficient pricing of securities, and make possible the placement of huge amounts of financial capital.

The Over-the-Counter Market

The majority of securities bought and sold around the globe are traded over-the-counter (OTC), not on organized exchanges. There is no central trading location, but only an electronic communications network. The customer places a buy or sell order with a broker or dealer that is relayed via telephone, wire, or computer terminal to the dealer or broker with securities to sell or an order to buy. In this system of electronically linked marketmakers, brokers and dealers seek the best possible price, and the resulting competition to find the best deal brings together traders located hundreds or thousands of miles apart. The prices of actively traded securities quickly respond to the changing forces of demand and supply, so that many security prices appear to hover at or near competitive, market-determined levels.

For a look at the over-the-counter market, explore such Web sites as nasdaq.com and nasd.com

Many traders in the OTC market act as *principals* instead of brokers as on the organized exchanges. That is, they take "positions of risk" by buying securities outright for their own portfolios as well as for customers. These dealer firms handle the same stock so that customers can shop around. All prices are determined by negotiation with dealers acquiring securities at *bid* prices and selling them at *asked* prices.

The U.S. OTC market is regulated by a code of ethics developed and adopted by the National Association of Security Dealers (NASD), which recently merged with the American Stock Exchange (AMEX). NASD is a private organization that encourages ethical behavior among its member firms and their employees. It registers and supervises more than 5,000 brokerage firms and more than 650,000 securities representatives. Traders who break NASD's rules may be fined, suspended, or thrown out of the organization. NASD regularly issues alerts to the public regarding schemes and scams that occur all too frequently in the securities markets.

20.5   The Third Market: Trading in Listed Securities off the Exchanges

third market

The market for securities listed on a stock exchange but traded over the counter is known as the **third market**. Broker and dealer firms that are not members of an organized exchange are active in this market. The original purpose of the third market was to supply large blocks of shares to institutional investors. These investors engage mainly in *block trades,* defined as transactions involving 1,000 shares or more. Presumably, block traders possess the technical know-how to make informed investment decisions and then carry out transactions without assistance from a stock exchange. By trading with third-market broker and dealer firms, who, in effect, compete directly with specialists on the exchanges, a large institutional investor may be able to lower transaction costs and trade securities faster.

Historically, the third market has been a catalyst in reducing brokerage fees and promoting trading efficiency, stimulating the unbundling of commissions at many U.S. broker and dealer firms in order to more accurately reflect the true cost of each security trade. Many brokerage firms offer customers an array of peripheral services, such as research on market trends, security credit, and accounting for purchases and sales. However, the customer may pay for these services whether or not he or she uses them, and as the 1990s ended and the new century began, serious questions were being raised about the bias in broker/dealer market research services, which seemed to promote stocks that security firms wished to unload. The largest institutional investors have little need for such services, however, and they seek brokers and dealers offering their services at minimum cost. Numerous "discount" brokerage houses have appeared, and commissions charged institutional investors have dropped substantially, leading many institutional customers to abandon the third market and return to more traditional channels for executing their security orders.

20.6   The Private Equity Market

Just as there is a public market for the most popular stocks, led by the organized exchanges and over-the-counter trading, so is there a *private equity market* where new businesses, privately held companies and partnerships, troubled firms, and even larger publicly traded companies can find financing for their acquisitions and other investments as well as support for out-of-the-ordinary financial transactions.

Funding a company through a private sale of stock has several advantages. Privately conveyed shares are exempt from costly SEC registration requirements because the public does not become involved with these privately placed shares. Then,

Paralleling the stock market is a market for *stock options*. These contracts grant their holders the right (but not the obligation) to purchase (call away) shares of stock from or sell (put) shares of stock to another party at a designated "strike" price before the option expires. Options have a number of advantages over stock itself, including greater leverage which allows the option holder to control stock with only a limited investment (known as the option's *premium*).

For decades, many corporations have used options on their own stock as an inexpensive way to compensate their employees. Some employees are granted the right to acquire shares of their firm's stock at a favorable strike price after at least a year has elapsed. This enables many firms to retain their best employees without depleting their cash reserves. Moreover, stock options give employees an incentive to improve their company's performance. If the stock rises sufficiently in value, an employee can trade it for a profit.

Not having to expense employee stock options means businesses can report higher earnings, which tends to raise the value of their stock. Moreover, corporate directors and management who award themselves big option contracts may clear profits that sometimes reach into the millions of dollars. For many years, there were very lenient guidelines for businesses as to how to treat stock options on their books. The U.S. Accounting Principles Board in 1975 voted to treat stock options as business expenses, measured by their "intrinsic value" (i.e., the difference between the current stock price and the option's strike price). It was then possible to cancel out the expense and protect company earnings by setting an option's strike price equal to or higher than the current stock price. Most companies adopted this practice to protect their earnings. Then, in March 2004, the Financial Accounting Standards Board (FASB) proposed treating the value of any options granted employees as a company *expense*, effective in 2005. This would tend to reduce the income of option-issuing companies. However, FASB argued, financial reports would then more accurately reflect real earnings and the income reports of *all* companies would be more uniform, making it easier for investors to compare firms. Moreover, this step would bring U.S. stock-option accounting practices closer to international standards set down by the International Accounting Standards Board.

The subject of stock options (particularly employee stock options) has become highly controversial in the wake of recent corporate failures. See such Web sites as the Pacific Exchange at pacificex.com, Employee Stock Options at nceo.org, and Accounting for Stock Options at fed.org

too, like the private placements in the corporate debt markets, firms in need of greater equity capitalization but unable to successfully reach the public market, due perhaps to their small size, questionable credit ratings, or complicated financing requirements, often find private equities a reasonable solution to their problems. An added factor is the recent expansion of a new type of financial-service firm almost tailor-made for the private equity markets—the so-called *limited partnership*. Limited partnerships have recently grown as an important investment vehicle for wealthy individuals and institutional stock investors, and many of these partnerships have become skilled in arranging private equity deals that may return substantial rewards to members of the partnership. This form of partnership allows stock market investors to turn their long-term capital funds over to a professional funds manager who accepts most of the risks of the firm and makes the portfolio decisions that must be decided along the way.

These innovative partnership agreements can often force stock-issuing firms to put the interests of the partnership's stockholders first, unlike many publicly traded companies who have thousands of stockholders and whose managements, not the stockholders, often control the companies and may reap most of the benefits. Also, pension funds—among the very largest of all stock-buying institutions in today's global markets—have recently been allowed by regulation in many different jurisdictions to take greater positions in privately held stock. That step has brought huge amounts of new capital into private equity markets. Certainly, the rise of the private equity market has boosted the growth of new businesses. Venture capitalists have given tens of thousands of new firms the funds to get started and also allowed smaller companies to grow bigger by funding their buy-outs of other businesses.

20.7   Investment Banking and the Sale of New Stock

investment bankers

Whether offered in the private equity market or in the public market, the majority of new stock issues are sold today through **investment bankers**. These firms advise their corporate customers on the proper timing for issuing new stock and frequently purchase (underwrite) newly issued shares for resale to their investor clients (including pension and mutual funds, insurance companies, and wealthy individual investors). Among the leading stock underwriters in the global market today are such firms as Citigroup, Inc., UBS Warburg, Merrill Lynch & Co., Goldman Sachs Group, Morgan Stanley, and Lehman Brothers.

The *underwriting* of corporate stocks is among the riskiest of all ventures in the financial marketplace. As we saw earlier, stock values are highly sensitive to fluctuations in economic conditions and to changes in government policy. An investment banker must estimate the resale value of the stock he or she has pledged to buy, but that price can change dramatically in minutes, posing substantial gains or substantial losses that can never be fully anticipated.

IPOs

One of the most dynamic services offered by investment bankers in recent years has been **IPOs**, or *initial public offerings*—the issue of stock from companies that have never before sold ownership shares to the general public. Many of these fledgling corporations start out as small single proprietorships, partnerships, or family-owned companies. Subsequently, these businesses, if successful, find that private sources of funding are inadequate to sustain their future growth. Thus they turn to investment bankers to guide them into a larger funding arena. Other IPOs arise because a firm's private owners want to cash in on their firm's growth and financial success. A substantial number of IPOs in recent years have come from "high flyers"—principally high-technology customers with innovative new products or software. (The most famous of the recent "high flyers" was the IPO of Google Inc., Co-founded by a couple of students at Stanford University. Stanford's holdings of Google shares at the time of this IPO were valued at nearly $180 million.) Investment banks often tout these new offerings as "unprecedented opportunities" for profit and, indeed, during the prosperous period of the 1990s, numerous IPOs shot upward in price from the moment they first appeared.

Risk returned to this market in a big way as the new century began, however, and a business recession sent stock prices downward. With slower growth prospects, fewer companies came forward to raise new capital and investment bankers' commissions sagged. However, the IPO market appeared to rally in late 2003 and 2004 as the economy gained upward momentum and many new firms appeared.

So large have been recent IPO profits for many investment houses and their clients that an investigation of the industry began under the leadership of the Securities and Exchange Commission—the principal U.S. regulator of investment banking activities. Regulators soon unearthed a number of questionable, if not illegal, activities surrounding the IPO market. For example, some investment banking houses allegedly received kickbacks from large, wealthy investors in order to gain early access to new IPOs coming to market. Some investors claimed they were pressured to purchase IPOs at inflated prices or to buy other securities the banker was selling in order to get access to new IPOs. Hundreds of lawsuits involving some of the largest investment banks on Wall Street were soon filed by clients who claimed large losses due to market manipulation and preferential treatment for favored clients.

Recent events in the investment banking business serve as reminders of how risky this financial-service business really is. There is usually high *market risk* due to the exceptional price volatility of many stocks (especially shares issued by smaller companies). Also, there is substantial *regulatory risk* as the industry's practices have come under increased scrutiny in response to clients—both those seeking underwriting services and investors looking for new securities to add to their portfolios—who have begun to complain about the fairness of the security underwriting process.

QUESTIONS TO HELP YOU STUDY

6. What are the principal differences between trading in stocks *over the counter* and trading on an *organized exchange?* How would you rate these two markets in terms of their advantages for the small investor? the large investor?

7. Explain the possible link between economic conditions and the performance of the stock market. Why do stock price movements tend to lead changes in general economic conditions?

8. Who are the principal investor groups active in the stock market? How might the investment motives of these groups differ?

9. What are the essential differences among the following segments of the market for corporate stock?

   Organized exchanges

   Third market

   Over-the-counter market

   Private equity market

10. What services do *investment bankers* provide to what groups of clients? What *risks* do investment bankers face and why?

20.8 The Development of a Unified International Market for Stock

The National Market System

It is clear from the foregoing discussion that the stock market is fractured into several different parts, each with its own unique collection of brokers and dealers and, in some cases, its own unique collection of customers. However, one of the most significant developments in recent decades has been a movement to weld all parts of the equities market together into a single market for all traders and investors. In 1975, the U.S. Congress passed the Securities Act Amendments, which instructed the Securities and Exchange Commission—the federal government's chief regulatory agency for the capital markets—to "facilitate the establishment of a national market system for securities" in order to further the development of widespread trading in equities and bring greater competition to the stock market.

Although the 1975 amendments did not specify what the proposed *national market system* would eventually look like as the decades went by, the intent of Congress was to ensure that all investors would have ready access to information on security prices and could transact business at the best available price. Moreover, with greater mobility of funds from one exchange to another or between the exchanges and the over-the-counter market, the resulting increase in competition in stock trading might reduce the cost to corporations of raising new capital.

On October 19, 1987, the Dow Jones Industrial Average dropped by 508 points—the greatest one-day stock price fall in the history of the United States. The market's sudden "free fall" spread rapidly throughout the world, as stock prices in Western Europe and around the Pacific Rim tumbled, demonstrating how intimately tied together securities markets around the globe have become.

In order to head off future crashes, a number of "remedies" were set in place. The most highly publicized of these were **circuit breakers.** These devices would halt or slow trading during those periods when stock prices suddenly dropped. In April 1998 the Securities and Exchange Commission (SEC) and the Commodities Futures Trading Commission (CFTC) approved circuit breakers that would cause temporary trading halts if a decline of 10 percent, 20 percent, and 30 percent of the Dow Jones Industrial Average closing price occurred. Trading suspension points would be adjusted quarterly and their length would vary with the time of day that price declines occurred (for example, before or after 2 P.M. in the second quarter of 2004). These trading halts for the New York Stock Exchange were paralleled by a change in trading rules at the Chicago Mercantile Exchange (CME) for futures contracts. The CME installed "speed bumps"— 30-minute trading suspensions—if futures index prices dropped 2.5 percent and 5 percent during the course of a trading day. The "speed bumps" were to be reset on a quarterly basis according to index values for the preceding month. The basic idea was to prevent panic selling, which could gather momentum like an avalanche.

Unfortunately, when trading is halted the *liquidity* of investors' stock holdings virtually disappears unless buyers can be found off the exchanges in the over-the-counter market. When circuit breakers are tripped, investors may not be able to sell their shares even if they desperately need cash. Equally important, circuit breakers could make financial markets even *more* volatile, accelerating trading whenever stock prices fall. The reason is that panicky investors may rush to sell their stock out of fear that a circuit breaker will be invoked and they won't be able to sell their shares later on.

Moreover, it is not clear that shutting down a market for a brief period really prevents market crashes. When trading is *simultaneously* halted in stock and financial futures markets, many investors have no efficient substitute for protecting themselves against interest rate risk. On the other hand, the tripping of circuit breakers on a stock exchange will not necessarily trigger the breakers on financial futures exchanges. The result may be that investors will rush to those markets still open and set off a massive selling wave there as well. Moreover, in a world with alternative trading channels for stocks and bonds, the unilateral imposition of circuit breakers in any one nation will encourage security traders to shift their business elsewhere. If breakers are to be used at all, they need to be coordinated across all exchanges in fairness to all investor groups.

Suggested references: See especially the U.S. Presidential Task Force on Market Mechanisms (1988) in the references at the end of this chapter.

---

circuit breakers

After the Securities Act Amendments became law, the New York Stock Exchange announced that it would begin reporting daily trades of NYSE-listed stocks as they occurred on the exchanges. This meant that up-to-the-minute information on the latest stock trades would be reported on a *consolidated,* or *composite, tape* regardless of which exchange handled the transaction. However, no information was provided on the best bid and asked prices available. The Securities and Exchange Commission responded to this need by asking each U.S. stock exchange to make its quotations available to brokers and dealers everywhere.

The first major step in that direction was the development of an Intermarket Trading System (ITS). Brokers and specialists could then compare bid and ask prices on all the major U.S. exchanges for about 700 different stocks through a central computer system. In effect, ITS brought major U.S. equities markets into direct price competition with one another for trades in the most popular corporate stocks. Aiding the unified market's spread was a decision by the Securities and Exchange Commission, known as Rule 19c-3, which stated that new stock could be traded off the exchange by exchange member firms. Previously, a broker or securities dealer with membership on a particular exchange could not trade listed stocks anywhere but on the floor of that exchange. This decision brought the U.S. exchanges and OTC market into direct competition with each other for the trading of *new* stock.

NASD and Automated Price Quotations

As the 1980s began, the National Association of Security Dealers (NASD) moved to promote a broader market system by further automating price quotations on over-the-counter stock. Computer terminals with expanded capacity were set up to include a wide array of information on bid and asked prices offered by traders who might be hundreds or thousands of miles apart. At the same time, NASD and representatives of the ITS moved to link quotations and trading on the six major U.S. exchanges electronically with OTC quotations and trading through NASD's automated price quotation system (NASDAQ). NASDAQ today quotes prices for close to 5,000 financial instruments.

At about the same time, the Securities and Exchange Commission adopted new regulations aimed at improving the flow of stock price information to brokers and investors. Previously, the NASDAQ system for securities traded over the counter had carried only "representative" bid and asked prices. However, NASDAQ was soon required to display on its terminals the highest bid prices and the lowest asked prices present in the market. The new rule aided investors in determining what price brokers were actually paying to execute a customer purchase order or what the true sales price was when the customer placed his or her shares on the market. In theory, at least, the rule promoted competition among OTC brokers and made it easier for customers to negotiate low commission rates. Another SEC rule required that the consolidated tape carrying price quotations for stock listed on the major exchanges always include the *best* price available on *any* stock, regardless of which exchange is quoting that price.

Subsequently, NASD set up a so-called National Market System to shuttle information to investors immediately on completion of stock sales. NASD also set in motion a program for automated settlement of security trades, called the System of Automated Linkages for Private Offerings, Resales, and Trading (PORTAL). This system made possible purchases and sales of both unregistered domestic and foreign bonds and stocks. NASD's automated security price quotation system also set up computer telephone connections with the International Stock Exchange and the Singapore Stock Exchange, cross-listing and executing trades among a growing list of foreign securities. For example, a New York or London trader could instruct his Tokyo office to track stock prices while his home office was closed, and if stock prices reach a designated level, the overseas office would trade the securities involved according to guidelines received from the home office.

The Advent of Shelf Registration

The trend toward deregulation of the U.S. financial sector really began to exert its most potent impact on stock purchases and sales during the 1980s. On March 5, 1982, the SEC put Rule 415—the Shelf Registration Rule—into operation, allowing many large firms selling *new* corporate stocks and bonds to register an issue with the SEC and then sell securities from that issue at any time during the next two years. *Shelf registration* substantially reduced the cost of offering new stocks and bonds and gave offering companies greater flexibility in selecting when to enter the financial marketplace to sell new securities. Shelf registration increased competition in the underwriting of new security issues.

Global Trading in Equities

These developments in the United States leading toward a unified national market for corporate stock were joined during the 1990s and into the new century by movement toward a true international equities market in which the sun never sets on purchases and sales of stock somewhere. The trading of both U.S. corporate stock and shares of foreign companies on exchanges in Hong Kong, Singapore, Tokyo, Sydney and in other exchanges around the globe began to rival exchange trading in the United States and Western Europe. Satellite, cable, and wire communications networks now girdle the globe, allowing traders in distant financial centers to search for the best prices wherever they might be. U.S. and European trading firms can "pass the book" to their overseas branch offices as the sun moves west to keep abreast of the international stock and debt markets. Other traders have taken to hiring "all-nighters," who remain in the home office overnight to monitor market movements overseas and execute customer orders. Recent research suggests that stock markets in Europe, Asia, and the United States are becoming *cointegrated*, sending shock waves to each other as price movements occur, sometimes in remote corners of the globe.

As the 1990s began, the New York Stock Exchange announced plans for after-hours trading sessions via computer without fees and with minimal disclosure rules. These announcements represented an effort by the NYSE to lure back from overseas substantial numbers of pension funds, investment companies, and other large institutional investors that were trading elsewhere. Institutional trading of large blocks of stock inside the United States was given a boost recently when the U.S. Securities and Exchange Commission created Rule 144a, allowing financial institutions to trade large blocks of privately placed stocks and bonds without having to go through complicated disclosure procedures. The SEC also approved the launching of a system that made possible the trading of exchange-listed stocks after U.S. exchanges closed.

At about the same time, the National Association of Securities Dealers announced plans to extend the hours of operation of its automated quotations network to cover the hours when the London International Stock Exchange was open, supporting the growth of predawn stock trading inside the United States. Initially, NASDAQ International proposed to offer computer-screen trading of 400 to 500 stocks beginning at 3:30 A.M. EST in the United States. Not to be outdone, the American Stock Exchange, the Chicago Board Options Exchange, and Reuters Holdings PLC of Great Britain declared their intention to launch a system for night trading between 6:00 P.M. and 6:00 A.M. The Chicago Mercantile Exchange and Reuters announced plans for the Globex after-hours electronic order-entry and trade-maturity trading system involving purchases and sales of financial futures contracts, setting in motion an international partnership among futures exchanges in the United States and Western Europe. The Chicago Mercantile Exchange and the Singapore International Monetary Exchange also established a trading link, making it possible for identical futures contracts to be traded and closed out on either exchange. One of the areas of most rapid growth in the internationalization of the stock market is the cross-listing of stocks. For example, a U.S. corporation can request to have its stock listed on exchanges in London, Frankfurt, Tokyo, and other exchanges around the globe.

Paralleling the expansion of cross-listing is global stock underwriting in which only a portion of new stock issues may be sold in their country of origin. Today many large stock issues have underwriters from more than one nation, helping a corporate customer reach the widest possible range of international buyers.

The Development of ADRs

Further evidence of the growing links between U.S. and foreign stock markets emerged in the 1980s and 1990s with the development of new international financial instruments. For example, U.S. exchanges began trading **American depository receipts (ADRs)**. These are dollar-denominated claims on foreign shares of stock that are kept in safekeeping by U.S. financial institutions (usually by commercial banks and investment banking houses). In effect, ADRs are negotiable warehouse receipts for deposits of foreign stock that U.S. investors can trade without having to assume the risks of trading in foreign currencies. Among the most popular foreign firms whose ADRs have been traded regularly in the United States are Cifra and Telefonos de Mexico, British Petroleum, and Reuters Holdings in the United Kingdom.

ADRs do present some special risks of their own, however. For one thing, their underlying value is sensitive to fluctuations in foreign currency prices. A sharp decline in the value of the home country's currency, for example, can result in a significant loss of return from ADRs. Moreover, foreign stock prices tend to be more volatile than the prices of most actively traded U.S. equities. To be successful in the ADR market, U.S. investors must learn to become more aware of foreign business developments—information that often is difficult and costly to obtain, though the development of the World Wide Web (along with 24-hour television news services like CNN and Bloomberg) has aided international investors in staying abreast of new developments around the globe. Many U.S. investors have come to prefer *sponsored* ADRs, for which the foreign firm issuing the stock hires a U.S. company (such as a bank) to serve the interests of buyers and provide them with pertinent information about the foreign stock and its issuing company.

20.9 Valuing Stocks: Alternative Approaches

There are literally thousands of professional portfolio managers and stock market analysts who spend all of their time searching through information they hope will help them pick the winners in the stock market. They do not all use the same approach to placing a value on individual stocks. Some focus on trends in stock prices that might point to whether a stock is rising or falling and when it is about to reach a short-term peak or trough. Others look carefully at the issuing firm's financial statements and study its likely success in the current economic and political environment. While most small investors cannot hope to compete successfully in achieving the depth of knowledge these professional investors possess, the good news is that *competition among professional investors results in an efficient market*—one in which information that has value in terms of its ability to help forecast future stock price movements is quickly incorporated into those prices through the trading activities of professional investors. Because this information arrives randomly in the market, stock prices themselves also tend to behave in a nearly random fashion.

In its purest form, this characteristic of stock prices is referred to as a **random walk**—that is, successive changes in stock prices are as unpredictable as a sequence of numbers created by a random-number generator on a computer. The end result is that even the best-informed financial analyst has no greater ability to predict the future direction of stocks than does the average small investor. Therefore, a small investor who maintains a sufficient amount of diversification in his or her stock portfolio can do nearly as well as a professional portfolio manager. However, it is important to remember that this "leveling out" of the investor playing field is the result of the collective efforts of professionals who strive to correctly process all of the information in the marketplace that is relevant to the stocks they are following. The ability to quickly and correctly perceive the importance of new information to stock prices is what makes professionals successful and it is what they strive to achieve each day.

Technical and Fundamental Analysis

Professionals do not adhere strictly to the *random walk hypothesis* in conducting their trades—otherwise they would have nothing to do! Each trader performs his or her own analysis and no one trader looks at *everything*. Traders use the information that works for them in structuring their own trades or in making their stock recommendations.

One group tends to focus on patterns that emerge in *past* data. They draw charts reflecting prior upswings and downdrafts in stock prices and attempt to identify "resistance levels"—upper or lower barriers that stock prices have not been able to penetrate easily in the past. If a stock's price passes through one of these resistance levels, then these analysts are inclined to think it is likely to move further up, if it was an upper barrier, or down, if it was a lower barrier. They must then set new resistance levels and continue to monitor price movements in an effort to find the right time to buy or sell.

technical analysis

To learn about the principles of technical analysis see, for example, tradersfloor.com

This approach to stock selection is known as **technical analysis** and its adherents are often referred to as "techies" or "chartists." The "charts" that are followed by technical analysts can become extraordinarily detailed, incorporating such factors as the volume of trading, where a high trading volume that occurs when the market is rising may be interpreted as "momentum" that will carry stock prices higher. Some technical analysts—known as "contrarians"—track investor sentiment and find that when *too many* professional investors are optimistic, then the market is set for a *fall*. Usually, technical analysts follow their *own* collections of technical indicators that they believe have helped them make successful stock choices in the past.

To explore the nature of fundamental analysis in more detail see, in particular, greekshares.com/fundamental.asp

fundamental analysis

A second group of investors focuses attention on the financial performance of individual companies and tries to understand how well these companies are likely to perform in the current environment. Their task is to identify firms with strong balance sheets, meaning that the assets of the firm have good market value and are not overly diluted by the firm's liability and capital structure. For example, they do not want to see the firm carrying too much debt or exposed to too much interest rate (or other forms of) risk. This approach to stock selection is called **fundamental analysis**. In evaluating the "fundamentals" of a firm, these analysts must concern themselves with more than a business's financials. They may ask: Are we headed into a recession? Is the industry that this firm is a part of about to suffer a major setback or be enhanced by new technology? Is government considering tough new regulations for this industry? These factors can have major consequences for stock prices, but they are not easy to factor into those prices.

Private Information

Most studies examining how efficient the stock market is at incorporating relevant information into stock prices have concluded that it is very difficult to systematically exploit publicly available information for profit. There are some exceptions, however, which are referred to as *anomalies*.

For example, the observation that stock prices more often tend to rise, rather than fall, during the month of January is referred to as the "January effect." However, these anomalies are not completely reliable indicators. Otherwise, they would be akin to free money sitting on the table waiting for someone to pick it up!

Not all information important to the value of a stock is in the public domain. For example, corporate managers are often aware of decisions that the firm may be making or they may have information regarding the firm's recent performance that has not yet been made public. Respected financial news reporters are aware of the content of the columns they write or what they will say in television interviews before their reports are publicly known. These individuals are most likely to know whether and how that information will affect individual stock prices. Until this *private information* is made public, those who possess it can trade on this information for profit. Such "insider trading" is unethical and, in many cases, illegal. Once discovered, this type of trading activity is generally not tolerated because it creates an uneven playing field for investors that works to the disadvantage of *both* small investors and professionals who are not in possession of this private information.

QUESTIONS TO HELP YOU STUDY

11. What role do *circuit breakers* play in the equities market? What are their possible advantages and disadvantages?

12. What is the *national market system? Shelf registration?*

13. Why did *ADRs* develop? Why are they important?

14. What is the *random walk* hypothesis? Does research evidence tend to support or deny the validity of this hypothesis?

15. What is an *efficient market?* What are the consequences of market efficiency for the behavior of stock prices? Does recent research support the idea that the stock market is efficient?

16. What factors do *technical analysis* and *fundamental analysis* focus on in valuing stocks?

17. What advantages does private information give to the market participants who possess it?

MARKETS ON THE NET: The Most Important Web Sites for This Chapter

American Stock Exchange (amex.com)
Federation of European Securities
Exchanges (fese.be)
Morningstar (morningstar.com)
National Association of Security Dealers
(nasd.com)

NASDAQ (nasdaq.com)
New York Stock Exchange (nyse.com)
Pacific Stock Exchange
(pacificex.com)
Thomson Investors Network
(thomsoninvest.net)

Summary of the Chapter's Main Points

The market for corporate stock is the most widely followed of all securities markets, with millions of shares changing hands each day. In this chapter, the following points were made:

- Most stock trades involve *not* the creation of new funds—the raising of new capital—but rather the exchange of existing shares for money. Thus, most stock trading takes place in the *secondary market,* not the primary (or new issue) market.

- Trading in equity shares reveals a close correlation with *economic conditions*. Advancing stock prices appear to be a leading indicator, forecasting the growth of the economy, in part because business investment spending appears to be influenced by what is happening or is expected to happen to stock prices.

- Corporate stock can be divided into two major types: common stock and preferred stock. *Common stock* represents a residual claim against the assets of the issuing firm, entitling the owner to share in the earnings of the firm when it is profitable and to share in the market value of the company's assets if it is liquidated. *Preferred stock* carries a stated annual dividend expressed as a percent of the stock's par value.

- *Households*—individuals and families—are the dominant holders of corporate stock, followed by *pension funds, mutual funds,* and *insurance companies.*

- Stock prices are *positively* related to the *expected stream of dividends* paid by the firm that issued the stock and *negatively* related to the *discount rate* associated with that expected stream of dividends (measuring *equity risk*).

- The market for corporate equity shares normally is divided into two main parts—the *organized exchanges* and the *over-the-counter market*. Trading on the exchanges is governed by regulations and formal procedures to promote competition and to contribute toward improved liquidity of equity shares. The over-the-counter (OTC) market is less formal than the organized exchanges and generally involves broker-to-broker or dealer-to-dealer transactions on behalf of stock buyers and sellers.

- Other branches of the stock market have become important in recent years. These include a *third market,* in which exchange-listed stocks are traded over the counter; and a *private equity market,* where new businesses, privately held companies and partnerships, troubled firms, and even larger publicly traded companies can find financing for their long-term equity needs. The private equity market is involved in selling shares off the major exchanges, with trading taking place between stock issuers and limited partnerships, venture capital companies, and other specialized investors.

- The stock market has become *global* in scope, rising from a series of national markets due to advances in the technology of information and funds transfer.

- Competition for information among professional investors causes stock markets to be *efficient*—quickly incorporating new, publicly available information into the prices of stocks.

- Because new information arrives randomly, an informationally efficient stock market is characterized by stock prices that closely follow a *random walk*. Changes in stock prices appear to be essentially random and unforecastable.

- Some professional investors employ *technical analysis* when selecting stocks for their portfolios by charting patterns in the data; others rely on *fundamental analysis,* which calls for a detailed examination of a corporation's financial statements and other factors that could affect industry groups and the economy as a whole.

Key Terms Appearing in This Chapter

common stock, 614
preferred stock, 615
organized exchanges, 623
over-the-counter (OTC)
    market, 624
third market, 627
investment bankers, 629

IPOs, 629
circuit breakers, 631
American depository receipts
    (ADRs), 634
random walk, 634
technical analysis, 635
fundamental analysis, 635

Problems and Issues

1. From the standpoint of the firm and the investor, explain how the exercise of a "call provision" in a firm's preferred stock differs from the repurchase of a firm's common stock. Is the firm or the investor the beneficiary of the "call provision"? Explain. How does the call provision affect the preferred stock price?

2. Preferred stock is often referred to as a "hybrid security" that shares features of both a corporate bond and common stock. Is this comparison true? Explain. Compare preferred stock and corporate debt in terms of both default and market risk. Which should have the higher expected return?

3. Referring to Exhibit 20.1, explain the statement, "Institutional investors dominate share holdings." Do they dominate trading activity in the stock market? Explain.

4. Verizon shares of common stock are expected to sell for about $40 per share two years from now and dividend payments to Verizon shareholders over the next two years are expected to be about $4 annually. Reflecting Verizon's perceived equity risk, the discount rate to be applied to this expected cash stream of dividends is 12 percent. What price should be attached to each share of Verizon common under the foregoing assumptions?

5. Suppose that Verizon common shares, as discussed in the preceding problem, are expected to pay a $4 per-share annual dividend one year from today. Also assume that that dividend payment is expected to grow at a constant 5 percent annual rate into the future. If the discount rate reflecting equity risk remains at 12 percent, Verizon's stock price should approach what figure?

6. Suppose the indicator of equity risk associated with Verizon's shares of common stock (see problems 4 and 5) changes from 12 percent to 11 percent because investors expect Verizon's earnings stream to be more stable in the years ahead. What happens to the company's stock price per share under the assumptions given in problems 4 and 5?

7. A common stockholder of Milton Corporation is entitled to a *pro rata* share of any new stock issued by the company. If the firm plans to issue 500,000 new shares at a price of $3.50 per share and this particular stockholder currently holds 1.6 percent of all Milton's shares outstanding, how many new shares is this shareholder entitled to purchase? At what total cost?

8. Riter-Cal Corporation has preferred shares outstanding carrying a $35 par value and promising a 6 percent annual dividend rate. Daniel Smith holds 200 shares of R-C's preferred stock. What annual dividend can he expect to receive if the company's board of directors votes to pay the regular dividend? Suppose R-C's

preferred stock consists of *participating* shares, with preferred shareholders participating equally in net earnings with the firm's common stockholders. If the company declares a $10 per share common stock dividend, how much in additional per-share dividends will each of its preferred shareholders receive?

Standard & Poor's Market Insight and Web-Based Problems

STANDARD
&POOR'S

1. The airline industry has had a very difficult few years recently, especially since the events of September 11, 2001, when commercial airlines were used as vehicles for terrorist bombings. In this problem you will explore the current outlook for the airline industry. What problems have been overcome, what problems remain, and have there been any airline stocks that have managed to perform fairly well during these turbulent times?

    a. Visit the S&P Market Insight database at **mhhe.com/edumarketinsight** and identify the industry group ("GIC Sub-Ind.") for the airline industry. Read the brief "Current Environment" section and describe the following: (i) current outlook for the industry; and (ii) the most serious problem(s) facing the industry.

    b. Select seven different airlines and for each one go to its most recent balance sheet (look under "Excel Analytics") and obtain the following information: (i) its total assets, (ii) its market capitalization (stock price times the number of shares outstanding), and (iii) the firm's debt-to-equity ratio.

    c. From the information you obtained in parts (a) and (b) identify which of the airlines have been the most successful and the least successful in recent times. In detailing this answer, rely on the comparisons that you are able to make across the balance sheets of the firms from part (b) and consider how these differences relate to the information provided in part (a).

2. One of the significant controversies surrounding the use of stock options for employee compensation focuses upon how to value and account for these particular options. Using such key Web sites as Accounting for Stock Options at **fed.org**, Looks Smart at **lookssmart.com**, The Options Trader at **theoptionstrader.com**, and Employee Stock Options at **nceo.org**, explain why the employee stock option accounting issue has become so important. Also, discuss the merits and weaknesses of proposed solutions to this stock option valuation problem.

3. The Web site for CNN Money at **premium.money.comn.com/pr/subs/features/money 100/** publishes *Money Magazine*'s list of the top 100 mutual funds each year. Call up the latest list, known as The Money 100, and determine which fund has the highest one-year return, the highest three-year return, and the highest five-year return. Compare the expense ratio of these top performers to the average expense ratio for all other funds in The Money 100 list and for the class of funds (type or category assigned by *Money Magazine*) from which the top performers come. What makes up the expense ratio as reported in *Money Magazine*? Does there seem to be any relationship at all between the performance of mutual fund shares and each fund's expense ratio? Would you expect to find a performance relationship between a fund's rate of return and its expense ratio? Why or why not?

www.mhhe.com/rose9e

Selected References to Explore

Golob, John E., and David G. Bishop. "Do Stock Prices Follow Interest Rates or Inflation?" Research Working Paper 96-13, Federal Reserve Bank of Kansas City, 1996, pp. 1–21.

Guo, Hui. "Why Do Stock Prices React to the Fed?" *Monetary Trends,* Federal Reserve Bank of St. Louis, July 2004.

Haubrich, Joseph G. "Expensing Stock Options." *Economic Commentary,* Federal Reserve Bank of Cleveland, November 2003, pp. 1–4.

Leitner, Yaron. "Liquidity and Exchanges, or Contracting with the Producers." *Business Review,* Federal Reserve Bank of Philadelphia, First Quarter 2004, pp. 16–22.

McAndrews, James, and Chris Stefanadis. "The Consolidation of European Stock Exchanges." *Current Issues in Economics and Finance* 8, no. 6 (June 2002), Federal Reserve Bank of New York, pp. 1–6.

Sarker, Asani, and Kai Li. "Should U.S. Investors Hold Foreign Stocks?" *Current Issues in Economics and Finance*, Federal Reserve Bank of New York, March 2002.

Shiller, Robert. *Market Volatility*. Cambridge, Massachusetts: MIT Press, 1989.

U.S. Presidential Task Force on Market Mechanisms. *Report of the Presidential Task Force on Market Mechanisms,* Washington, D.C., January 1988.

Part 6

Consumers in the Financial Markets

Regardless of our jobs or professions, our social status or lifestyles, we are all *consumers* of financial services supplied by the money and capital markets. In fact, individuals and families (households) are among the most important borrowers of funds in today's marketplace. As consumers, households can finance their purchases of goods and services using current income, but when their expenditures exceed their income they must either borrow from the money and capital markets or liquidate some of their accumulated savings.

While we tend to stress most heavily the role of consumers as *borrowers* in the money and capital markets, consumers are also among the leading *lenders* within the financial system. When the household sector's current income exceeds its expenditures, the surplus income contributes to the amount of funds that flow to businesses and governments seeking to borrow money.

In this segment of the text, we examine the household sector as *both* a lender and a borrower of funds. We discover which financial services are most important to consumers today and how consumer preferences for various financial instruments and services have changed over time. We explore the fundamental financial characteristics of consumers—how they lend funds and what alternative sources of borrowing are available to them. And we learn more about the important consumer protection laws that have sheltered individuals and families for many years now whenever they venture into the treacherous and often murky waters of the financial marketplace.

In Part six, we also look at one of the largest of all financial markets—the market for residential mortgage loans—a marketplace that makes possible the "American dream" of home ownership. Purchasing a home is one of the most important and most difficult financial decisions that an individual will make during his or her lifetime. We will look into the factors that consumers should consider when borrowing to purchase a new home and the types of loans provided today by the residential mortgage market. We also will see how and why government has come to play such a major role in shaping who gains access to home mortgage credit and on what terms. Understanding the complexities of the mortgage market will enable you to become a wise consumer who avoids costly mistakes and reaps the substantial rewards of owning your own home.

Chapter 21

Consumer Lending and Borrowing

Learning Objectives

in This Chapter

- You will see the vital role played by *consumers*—households (individuals and families)—in supplying loanable funds to the money and capital markets through savings.

- You will learn about the important role consumers play as major *borrowers* of funds within the financial system and the laws that protect their rights.

- You will explore the principal characteristics and unique features of *consumer lending institutions*, including banks, credit unions, and finance companies.

21.1 Introduction to Consumer Lending and Borrowing

Among the most important of all financial markets are the markets providing savings instruments and credit to individuals and families (households). Many financial analysts have referred to the period since World War II as the *age of consumer finance* because individuals and families not only have become the principal source of loanable funds flowing into the financial markets today but also are one of the largest borrowing groups in the entire financial system. Moreover, the market for household financial services is the one market that *everyone,* regardless of profession or social status, will enter at various times during his or her lifetime. In this chapter, we examine the major characteristics of the consumer market for financial services, the principal lenders active in this market, and some important regulations applying to household borrowing and lending today.

21.2 Consumers as Lenders of Funds

Each of us is a consumer of goods and services every day of our lives. Scarcely a day passes that we do not enter the marketplace to purchase food, shelter, entertainment, and other essentials of modern living. We are also well aware, perhaps from personal experience, that consumers often borrow heavily in the financial marketplace to achieve their desired standard of living. U.S. households borrowed more than $750 billion in 2003, for example, and by the end of that year owed more than $9 trillion to various lending institutions.

What is not nearly so well known, however, is the fact that consumers as a group are also among the most important *lenders* of funds in the economy. Loanable funds are supplied by consumers when they purchase financial assets from other units in the economy. In 2003, gross savings by U.S. households reached $1.3 trillion, of which almost $900 billion flowed into bank deposits, bonds, stocks, and direct cash loans to others. The consuming public is among the chief sources of the raw material—loanable funds—that is exchanged in the money and capital markets.[1]

Financial Assets Purchased by Consumers

If consumers make loanable funds available to other units in the economy by purchasing financial assets, what kinds of financial assets do they buy? And what are the principal sources of borrowed funds for consumers? The Federal Reserve Board's Flow of Funds Accounts provide us with a wealth of information on the borrowing and lending habits of households. Exhibit 21.1 summarizes information contained in recent Flow of Funds reports on the kinds of financial assets acquired by households. One fact immediately evident is the wide diversity of financial assets purchased by individuals and families, ranging from those of very low risk and short maturity (such as bank deposits and government securities) to long-term, higher-risk investments (such as mortgages and corporate stock).

One of the most important household financial assets today is *corporate stock* (equities), led by a dramatic rise in holdings of shares in mutual funds (investment companies). The recent growth in households' common stock investments may reflect concern about a possible resumption of serious inflation. Then, too, many individuals and families are concerned that when they reach their retirement years, Social Security, Medicare, and other government retirement plans will simply be inadequate to cover living costs and health care expenses in their final years. Reflecting this same concern,

---

[1]Portions of this chapter were originally drawn from Rose (December 1978, June 1979, and September 1979).

EXHIBIT 21.1 Principal Financial Assets Held by U.S. Households, 1970, 1980, 1990, 2000, and 2004 ($ Billions)

Financial Assets Held	1970 Amount	1970 Percent	1980 Amount	1980 Percent	1990 Amount	1990 Percent	2000 Amount	2000 Percent	2004* Amount	2004* Percent
Demand deposits and currency	$ 112.5	4.4%	$ 219.5	3.3%	$ 412.4	2.8%	$ 225.3	0.7%	$ 274.4	0.8%
Time and savings accounts	419.4	16.4	1,239.0	18.8	2,465.0	16.6	3,125.6	9.2	4,195.5	12.0
Shares in money market mutual funds	—	—	62.2	0.9	386.6	2.5	970.7	2.9	983.6	2.8
U.S. government securities	77.5	3.0	160.0	2.4	471.2	3.2	594.6	1.8	446.4	1.3
State and local government securities	35.4	1.4	104.5	1.6	575.0	3.9	460.7	1.4	695.9	2.0
Open market paper	12.5	0.5	38.3	0.6	63.2	0.4	72.6	0.2	48.9	0.1
Corporate and foreign bonds	29.5	1.2	30.0	0.5	233.5	1.6	576.4	1.7	356.6	1.0
Mortgages	50.0	2.0	87.2	1.3	143.5	1.0	117.7	0.3	150.7	0.4
Corporate stock	572.5	22.4	875.4	13.3	1,781.4	12.0	7,650.1	22.5	5,828.2	16.7
Investment companies (mutual funds)	40.4	1.6	45.6	0.7	456.6	3.1	2,900.1	8.5	3,365.6	9.7
Life insurance reserves	130.7	5.1	220.6	3.3	391.7	2.6	819.1	2.4	1,019.5	2.9
Pension fund reserves	253.8	9.9	970.4	14.7	3,376.3	22.8	9,067.3	26.7	9,422.8	27.0
Security credit and other assets	823.3	32.2	2,549.5	38.6	4,089.3	27.6	7,361.8	21.7	8,072.6	23.2
Total financial assets	$2,557.5	100.0%	$6,602.2	100.0%	$14,827.7	100.0%	$33,937.0	100.0%	$34,860.7	100.0%

Source: Board of Governors of the Federal Reserve System.

*Figures for 2004 are first quarter only (annualized).

Note: Columns may not add to totals due to rounding.

pension fund reserves in total ranked at the top among all household assets, exceeding $9.4 trillion by the year 2004. Of course, many of the reserves held by pension plans are also invested in corporate stock, as are many *life insurance reserves.*

In third place among household holdings of financial assets are *deposits* in banks, savings and loan associations, credit unions, and other thrift institutions. These checkable demand deposits and time and savings deposits represented about 13 percent of the total financial asset holdings of U.S. consumers in 2004. Moreover, as Exhibit 21.1 reveals, the importance of deposits in consumer financial investments generally increased until the 1980s and early 1990s—when households became concerned about a rising tide of bank and thrift institution failures. At the same time, better yields appeared to be available from investments in *corporate stock* (including mutual funds) and *government and corporate bonds.*

There has also been a significant rise in household investments in small businesses, which are often owned and operated by an individual or a family. By 2000, household investments in the equity of unincorporated business firms (included under *Other assets* in Exhibit 21.1) totaled more than $2 trillion and then spiraled on up to nearly $6 trillion by 2004. When jobs become more difficult to find, more individuals and families organize their own businesses. At the same time, there is an ongoing trend toward early retirement and the launching of second careers by creating new businesses.

Recent Innovations in Consumer Savings Instruments

One of the most important of all trends affecting consumer savings and lending today is a veritable explosion of *new financial instruments.* Banks, brokerage houses, and other financial institutions began in the 1970s to compete aggressively for consumer savings, not only by offering higher returns where the law allowed but also by proliferating new services. Like a Baskin-Robbins ice cream store, financial institutions began to offer household customers 31 or more flavors of savings and transaction accounts as well as credit plans to meet a wide variety of personal financial needs.

NOW account

This trend toward financial service proliferation began with the introduction of the **NOW account** in New England in 1970. NOWs are checkbook deposits that, like any checking account, can be used to pay for purchases of goods and services. But when NOWs were first developed they broke new ground by paying *interest* on checkbook deposits—which federal law prohibited for regular checking accounts. NOWs were permitted nationwide beginning in 1981 as a result of passage of the Depository Institutions Deregulation and Monetary Control Act of 1980. This law also called for the gradual phasing out of federal interest rate ceilings on all bank and thrift institution deposits (other than commercial accounts), so that consumers could receive competitive, market-determined interest rates on their savings.

The Depository Institutions Deregulation and Monetary Control Act of 1980 (DIDMCA) also authorized two services that compete directly with NOWs. One of these—automatic transfer services (ATS)—permits the consumer to preauthorize a bank to move funds from a savings account to a checking account to cover overdrafts. The net effect is to pay interest on transaction balances at the savings account rate. Credit unions are permitted to offer their own version of the NOW account, known as the *share draft.* These checkbook plans often pay among the highest interest rates on liquid funds.

During the 1970s, money market mutual funds first appeared, offering consumers *share accounts* with low denominations (most allowing accounts to be opened for a few hundred dollars). Like NOWs, share accounts at money funds were developed originally to get around federal deposit interest rate ceilings and give smaller savers access to competitive rates of return on their funds. Later, several prominent brokerage houses began offering *consumer cash management services,* in which funds could be held in an interest-bearing money market fund until transferred into stocks, bonds, or other securities, or accessed via check or credit card. Closely related to these services is the *wrap account,* for which a security broker assembles for the consumer a suitable portfolio of stocks, bonds, and other assets and actively manages that portfolio in return for an annual fee.

Life insurance firms soon began offering a related service known as *universal life insurance,* in which savings contributed by the policyholder are placed in a money market fund, with the life insurer making periodic withdrawals to pay the premiums on the life insurance policy. The consumer is offered life insurance protection plus a higher return on savings.

In 1981, with passage of the Economic Recovery Tax Act of 1981, wage earners and salaried individuals were granted the right to make limited contributions each year, tax free, to an *individual retirement account (IRA)* offered by banks, brokerage firms, and other financial institutions or by employers with qualified pension or profit-sharing plans. Similarly, *Keogh Plan retirement accounts* were created to help self-employed persons prepare for retirement and may be offered by the same institutions that sell IRAs. As we noted in Chapter 8, tax-favored retirement accounts were supplemented further in the late 1990s when new types of accounts—for example, *Roth* and *Education IRAs*—were created to give household investors new tax-sheltered savings vehicles to prepare for retirement and to help offset the spiraling cost of a college education. The Roth IRA proved to be particularly popular because not only could the consumer invest monies and generate tax-sheltered earnings but, for qualified accounts, withdrawals could be made tax-free (unlike the conventional IRAs and Keogh plans). Legislation in 2001 and 2003 significantly expanded the amount of savings that could be placed in these tax-sheltered accounts.

Beginning in the late 1970s, flexible savings plans became popular as many consumers fought to stay ahead of inflation through savings instruments whose rates of return were sensitive to changes in the cost of living as well as to changing interest rates in the money and capital markets. *Money market certificates of deposit* were authorized by federal regulation in 1978 with interest rates that changed as market yields on U.S. government securities fluctuated. In 1982, the Garn-St Germain Depository Institutions Act allowed banks and thrift institutions to offer deposits competitive with shares offered by money market mutual funds, in the form of money market deposit accounts (MMDAs) and Super NOWs, each offering flexible interest rates but accessible via check to pay for purchases of goods and services. As the 1990s approached, several banks and savings associations, led by Chase Manhattan Bank (now J. P. Morgan Chase) of New York, introduced *market-index certificates of deposit* with returns linked to stock market performance.

Accompanying the development of more flexible-yield types of deposits, life insurance companies and pension programs began to offer new types of *life insurance policies* and *annuity accounts* that build up cash value and promise either a lump-sum payment or a stream of future income payments. The much older fixed-value insurance and annuity plans were supplanted in many markets by *variable-rate annuities* and *variable-rate insurance plans,* whose value depends on the market performance of the assets that make up these savings vehicles. With the right kinds of investments an individual or family can develop a sizeable reservoir of accumulated savings to protect their standard of living in the later stages of life.

During the 1990s, *corporate equities,* in the form of both individual corporate stocks and pools of shares held in *mutual funds,* exploded in popularity among household savers. Many individuals and families concluded that their long-range savings were not growing fast enough for their future needs (especially in meeting the challenges of saving for retirement, inflation, and future educational costs), particularly if those savings were held in deposits at banks and thrift institutions where promised interest yields were often very low. Equities, on the other hand, seemed to offer the promise of much larger long-term returns. Moreover, the pooling of equities in mutual funds appeared to lower the consumer's risk exposure to help offset the lack of federal insurance coverage. At the same time, the Securities and Exchange Commission (SEC) required mutual funds to clarify for the public their method of figuring their rates of return and required these funds to simplify their reports so that consumers could more easily understand what they were buying. The market for individual corporate stocks and shares in mutual funds sagged over the 2000–2002 period under adverse economic pressures, but it appeared to be stabilizing somewhat as the new century moved forward.

These recent innovations have been designed to bring individuals and families into the financial markets as more active lenders of funds. The newest financial services offer the consumer greater *financial flexibility*—easier access to liquid funds for transaction purposes and the ability to move funds more easily from one type of savings instrument to another. The newest savings instruments offer the potential for higher rates of return more closely tied to changing interest rates and security prices in the open market.

In recent years, a number of important groups and nonprofit associations have attempted to encourage individuals to save more and borrow less. See, for example, governmentguide.com and nefe.org

One interesting feature of the consumer financial services market worth remembering is that many households do *not* make a practice of purchasing *all* their financial services from one source. Instead, households tend to *bundle,* or *cluster,* their purchases of services from certain financial firms. One typical clustering centers around the purchase of a checking account. Usually, a specific depository institution will be chosen to hold a family's main checking account—in most cases, a bank, credit union, or savings and loan that is convenient. Savings accounts are often placed locally as well, although increasingly households have turned to distant financial firms, such as mutual funds, to help them invest their savings at the best yields. Credit services—home mortgages, credit cards, and installment loans—frequently are purchased from a separate financial firm, such as a finance company, savings association, or bank. The financial-service firms from which households purchase credit often are *local* firms, but frequently they will search both inside and outside the local area to find a loan on the best terms, particularly if the loan is large or the consumer is seeking a new credit card. Most households seem to regard checkable deposits (payments accounts), savings accounts, and credit as *separate* financial products for which they will seek out the best terms available.

QUESTIONS TO HELP YOU STUDY

1. Which sector of the economy usually provides the greatest amount of loanable funds for borrowers to draw upon? Does this sector primarily make direct loans or indirect loans to borrowers?

2. What is currently the most important *financial asset* held by U.S. households? Which financial asset is in second place in household (consumer) portfolios? Third place?

3. Define the following terms:

NOWs	Mutual funds
MMDAs	Fixed and variable-rate annuities
Roth IRAs	Share drafts
Home equity loans	Universal life insurance
ATS	Money market share accounts
IRAs	

   In what ways do the financial instruments and services listed above benefit consumers?

21.3 Consumers as Borrowers of Funds

We have noted that consumers provide most of the savings out of which financial assets are created in the money and capital markets. However, it is also true that consumers are among the most important borrowers in the financial system. Total credit market debt owed by U.S. households was about $10 trillion in 2004 (see Exhibit 21.2). This was only slightly less than the total amounts owed by the federal government and all state and local governments combined. In total, debt owed by households in America represents more than a quarter of all credit-market debt outstanding.

Is Consumer Borrowing Excessive?

Are consumers too heavily in debt today? Certainly, the total volume of household debt outstanding is huge in both absolute terms and relative to most other sectors of the economy. However, to judge whether consumer borrowing is really excessive, that debt should be compared to the financial assets consumers hold. These assets, presumably, can be drawn on to meet any interest and principal payments that come due on consumer borrowings. Exhibit 21.3 shows that, although the volume of consumer debt has increased rapidly in recent years, the volume of household financial assets has also tended to grow very fast. For example, in 2004, financial assets held by U.S. households exceeded their estimated liabilities by just over $25 trillion. Moreover, the absolute dollar size of that financial asset cushion has generally increased over the past three decades (as the third row of figures in Exhibit 21.3 demonstrates).

To gather data about the recent rapid growth of consumer debt and the current problems in the field of consumer debt see especially progress.org/cdebt.htm and economagic.com

When we measure the *ratio of consumer liabilities to financial assets,* however, the picture is not quite so optimistic. As shown in Exhibit 21.3 this liability-to-asset ratio rose from just over 10 percent in 1950 to nearly 30 percent in 2004. Whether the household liability–financial asset ratio stands at an "excessive" level depends, of course, on economic conditions and the educational level of consumers. If the average consumer today is better educated and more capable of managing a larger volume of debt, a relatively high ratio of liabilities to financial assets is probably not an alarming development. Moreover, the total wealth held by consumers includes not just their financial assets but also their real assets, such as homes, automobiles, and furniture. Although we have no really reliable measure of the value of real assets held by consumers, it is obvious that the current total wealth of all individuals and families (including both real and financial assets) far exceeds their current debt, on average.

The fact that households as a group hold more financial assets than liabilities does not mean that the recent buildup of consumer debt is completely innocuous, however. Recently, government policymakers have been especially concerned about a so-called *portfolio effect* that they believe might significantly slow the future growth of the U.S. economy. Consumer borrowings rose rapidly during the 1980s, 1990s and into the twenty-first century. The ratio of household debt-service payments to personal disposable income climbed to the highest levels in history. To the extent that U.S. households feel excessively burdened with this large debt accumulation and fearful about losing their jobs, they may cut back on their rate of consumption spending. Because consumer spending is the largest component of the nation's GDP (production and income), a slowdown of household spending can lead directly to slower economic growth. This concept of a household portfolio effect argues that consumers may alter their level of spending until they once again feel comfortable with the balance between their income, financial assets, and liabilities.

Of course, pulling in the opposite direction from the so-called portfolio effect discussed above may be the *wealth effect.* With the prices of many stocks, bonds, and other consumer-held assets rising at various times in recent years, household net worth increased substantially. This upsurge in consumer wealth caused many individuals and

EXHIBIT 21.2   The Principal Debt Obligations (Liabilities) of U.S. Households, 1970, 1980, 1990, 2000, and 2004 ($ Billions)

Debt (Liabilities) Outstanding	1970 Amount	1970 Percent	1980 Amount	1980 Percent	1990 Amount	1990 Percent	2000 Amount	2000 Percent	2004* Amount	2004* Percent
Home and other mortgages	$299.6	62.6%	$ 946.8	65.2%	$2,586.6	69.5%	$4,958.1	67.0%	$7,044.7	71.6%
Consumer installment credit	133.7	27.9	358.0	24.6	824.4	22.2	1,719.0	23.2	2,014.8	20.5
Other consumer credit	—	—	16.7	1.1	86.6	2.3	143.0	1.9	187.3	1.9
Bank loans n.e.c.**	6.1	1.3	27.8	1.9	17.9	0.5	74.1	1.0	92.7	0.9
Other loans	20.9	4.4	52.1	3.6	81.7	2.2	119.8	1.6	119.3	1.2
Security credit	6.9	1.4	24.7	1.7	38.8	1.0	235.1	3.2	199.1	2.0
Trade credit	6.5	1.4	13.8	0.9	66.8	1.8	134.7	1.8	155.7	1.6
Deferred and unpaid life insurance premiums	5.1	1.1	12.9	0.9	16.5	0.4	19.6	0.3	21.1	0.2
Other liabilities	18.5	3.9	51.5	3.5	122.1	3.3	389.4	5.3	376.0	3.8
Total liabilities	$478.7	100.0%	$1,453.0	100.0%	$3,719.3	100.0%	$7,403.5	100.0%	$9,834.8	100.0%

Source: Board of Governors of the Federal Reserve System.

*2004 figures are for first quarter only.

**Not elsewhere classified.

Note: Columns may not add to totals due to rounding.

EXHIBIT 21.3	The Household Sector as a Net Lender of Funds to the Rest of the Economy						
	Amounts Outstanding at Year-End ($ Billions)						
Item	1950	1960	1970	1980	1990	2000	2004*
Total financial assets held by households	$735.2	$1,348.6	$2,557.5	$6,602.2	$14,827.7	$33,937.0	$34,860.7
Total debts (financial liabilities) of households	76.3	223.4	478.7	1,453.0	3,719.3	7,403.5	9,834.8
Difference: Financial assets minus liabilities	$658.9	$1,125.2	$2,078.8	$5,149.2	$11,108.4	$26,533.5	$25,025.9
Ratio of household liabilities to financial assets	10.4%	16.6%	18.7%	22.0%	25.1%	21.8%	28.2%

Source: Board of Governors of the Federal Reserve System.

*2004 figures are as of the first quarter.

families to feel comfortable with heavier debt loads, believing they could sell off their higher-valued assets if trouble appeared on the horizon. Unfortunately, consumers may have overestimated the true value of their recent gains in wealth. If everyone tries to sell off their assets to repay debt, asset values will sink and many households will wind up poorer. Indeed, stock market declines early in the new century coupled with job layoffs did slow household spending somewhat, making some consumers feel poorer.

Categories of Consumer Borrowing

Consumer borrowing and savings activities have captured great interest lately and are frequently discussed on the Web. Two Web sites to explore are The Consumer Information Center at consumer.gov and MSN at msn.com

residential mortgage credit

installment credit

noninstallment credit

The range of consumer borrowing needs is enormous. Loans to the household sector support a more diverse group of purchases of goods and services than is true of any other sector of the economy. Consumers borrow *long term* to finance purchases of durable goods, such as single-family homes, automobiles, boats, and home appliances. They usually borrow *short term* to cover purchases of nondurable goods and services, such as medical care, vacations, food, and clothing. Financial analysts frequently divide the credit extended to consumers into three broad categories: (1) **residential mortgage credit**, used to support the purchase of new or existing homes; (2) **installment credit**, used primarily for long-term nonresidential purposes; and (3) **noninstallment credit**, generally used for short-term cash needs.

Which of these forms of consumer borrowing is most important? Exhibit 21.2 provides a clear answer. Far and away the dominant form of consumer borrowing is aimed at providing shelter for individuals and families through mortgage loans. Home mortgage indebtedness by U.S. households climbed above $7 trillion in 2004, representing about two-thirds of all household debt. Moreover, the volume of home mortgage credit flowing to households has grown rapidly in recent years with the attractiveness of home ownership as a tax shelter and with recent tax reforms that favor home-equity loans secured by the borrower's home (even though funds borrowed often go for non-housing-related expenditures).

Installment credit is the second major component of consumer debt in the United States. Installment debt consists of all consumer liabilities other than home mortgages that are retired in two or more consecutive payments, usually monthly or quarterly. Four major types of installment credit are extended by lenders in this field: automobile credit, revolving credit, mobile homes, and other installment loans. An incredibly wide variety of consumer goods and services is financed by this kind of credit, including the purchase of furniture and appliances, the payment of medical expenses, the purchase of automobiles, and the consolidation of outstanding debts. As shown in Exhibit 21.2, consumer installment debt totaled more than $2 trillion in 2004, more than five times the amount in 1980.

The final major category of consumer debt is *noninstallment credit,* which is normally paid off in a lump sum. This form of consumer credit includes single-payment loans, charge accounts, and credit for services, such as medical care and utilities. The total amount of noninstallment loans outstanding is difficult to estimate because many such loans are made by one individual to another or by department stores, oil and gas companies, and professional service firms that do not report their lending activities. Commercial banks, however, make a substantial volume of noninstallment loans to consumers and are considered the leading lender in this field.

21.4 Home Equity Loans

home equity loan

One new form of consumer borrowing that is closely related to residential mortgage credit is the **home equity loan**. Like traditional home mortgages, a home equity loan is secured by a borrower's home. However, unlike traditional home mortgages, many home equity loans consist of a prearranged revolving credit line the borrower can draw on for purchases of any goods or services he or she wishes to buy over the life of the credit line.

With a home equity line of credit, a consumer can literally write himself or herself a loan simply by writing a check or presenting a credit card for purchases made up to a stipulated maximum amount, known as the *borrowing base.* The borrowing base equals the difference between the appraised market value of the borrower's home and the unpaid amount of the mortgage against that home multiplied by a fraction (often 0.70, or 70 percent). Thus, a home currently valued at $100,000 with an outstanding mortgage loan against it of $40,000 would give the homeowner a base amount to borrow against of about ($100,000 − $40,000) × 0.70, or $42,000. Moreover, under current U.S. tax laws, the interest owed on a loan secured by the borrower's home that qualifies under all the rules laid down in the Internal Revenue Code represents a tax-deductible expense, encouraging consumers to substitute home equity loans for other types of credit whose interest cost is *not* tax deductible.[2]

Most home equity loan rates are linked to the bank prime interest rate (or other base interest rate, such as the U.S. government bond rate) plus an extra margin for risk (i.e., a floating loan rate). Federal law requires that a maximum (ceiling) interest rate be established for all such loans so that a home-equity borrower has some protection against extreme interest rate risk. Home equity loans cover 10 to 15 years in most cases, although a substantial proportion can be continued indefinitely. The Consumer Protection Act of 1988 prohibits a home equity lender from canceling a loan unless fraud, failure to pay, or other violations of the loan contract occur. Thus far, most home equity loans have been used to pay off other debts, make home improvements, buy automobiles, or finance an education.

Home equity credit has proved to be especially attractive to consumer lending institutions for a variety of reasons. These loans tend to have a lower rate of default

---

[2]U.S. tax laws state that the interest paid on home equity loans may still be tax deductible even if the home mortgage is taken out for reasons other than to buy or improve the borrower's principal residence. However, there are conditions that must be satisfied for tax deductibility, so homeowners should consult IRS regulations to make sure their home equity loan qualifies under current tax rules.

because borrowers feel more responsible when their home is pledged as collateral and that collateral tends to have a more stable value. Moreover, the cost of making home equity loans when amortized over the life of each loan is usually lower than the cost of a series of short-term loans made to the same customer. In addition, these loans typically carry interest rates that adjust to the market, whereas many other consumer loans have fixed interest rates. Finally, home equity credits help the lender build a working relationship with a customer better than most other types of consumer loans, creating more opportunities for the lender to sell that customer additional services. However, if the borrower cannot make the loan payments, his or her home may be repossessed and sold to pay back the lender. This risk of repossession may have increased in some instances because of a recent decline in the proportion of their homes that Americans actually own (i.e., the equity in the home relative to the home's market value), which has declined from about 70 percent in 1983 to only 54 percent in 2000. Many financial experts recommend that consumers use home equity credit with caution, particularly when their future employment prospects are uncertain.

21.5   Credit and Debit Cards

credit card

One of the most popular forms of installment credit available to consumers today comes through the **credit card**. Through this encoded piece of plastic, the consumer has instant access to credit for any purchase up to a prespecified limit. In the language of finance, the credit card has removed the "liquidity" constraint that restricted the spending power of millions of consumers, democratizing access to credit and spending power. More recently, another piece of plastic—the **debit card**—has made instant cash available, made check cashing much easier, and made possible rapid electronic payment for purchases of goods and services. The growth of credit and debit cards has been truly phenomenal. Current estimates suggest that there are well over one trillion credit and debit cards in use worldwide, and leading nonfinancial companies (such as General Motors and General Electric) have recently entered in large numbers as suppliers of credit-card services.

debit card

A wide array of new consumer financial services is being offered today through plastic credit- and debit-card programs. Such services include consumer revolving credit lines and preauthorized borrowing, the purchase of medical services and entertainment, and the payment of household bills using credit cards. In the future, customers will need to make fewer trips to their bank or other financial institution because transactions will be handled mainly over the telephone, through a conveniently located computer terminal, or through "smart cards" that have prepayment-encoded information (such as a credit line the cardholder can use for making purchases). The hometown financial institution will lose much of its convenience advantage for local customers. It will be nearly as convenient for the customer to maintain a checking, savings, or loan account in a city hundreds of miles away as to keep it in a local financial institution. In short, the ticket to many consumer financial services increasingly will be through a plastic credit or debit card and through a computer, with the capability to process financial data across great distances.

Credit Cards

Credit cards are used for very different purposes today, depending on the income and lifestyle of the user. Customers who use credit cards merely as a substitute for cash are referred to as *convenience users*. These people tend to be in upper income brackets and do not necessarily seek stores accepting their cards. Customers who maintain large outstanding credit card balances are referred to as *installment users* because they pay only a portion of their outstanding balance each month. These individuals frequently are in lower- and middle-income brackets and tend to be the most profitable credit-card customers for card-issuing firms.

One recent trend in credit cards that has benefited consumers but hurt many issuers is the heavy over-issue of credit cards. Recent mailings of millions of credit cards have resulted in sharply increased numbers of card customers—in effect, "democratizing" the service—and many of these consumers are heavily in debt, resulting in a substantial rise in the number of delinquent accounts. Moreover, to reach out for a bigger market share, many card issuers have recently cut their loan rates. Accordingly, thousands of borrowers have used their ability to borrow using cheaper-rate cards in order to pay off their accumulated debts run up earlier on higher-rate cards (known as "card surfing"). The net result has been to lower the profitability of many credit-card programs. While, historically, credit-card loan rates were among the "stickiest" interest rates in the financial system, these rates recently have become more flexible, and competition among card issuers has intensified. Something of a "shakeout" appears to be under way, with smaller credit-card programs consolidating into larger ones and other credit-card companies (such as Sears Roebuck) simply selling off their card receivables and moving into other product lines.

For both convenience users and installment users, the principal advantage of credit cards is *convenience*. The installment loan feature of the credit card is a major attraction because it functions as a revolving line of credit, granting loans at no cost for an average of about one month by taking advantage of interest-free grace periods. In addition, the card itself serves to identify the customer and makes pertinent information available when the privilege of using the card is exercised. Most merchants know that charge cardholders tend to have higher incomes and better payment records than the general population.

Recently, new cards have appeared that not only charge zero annual fees but also give customers rebates or discounts on purchases the more the card is used. A particularly popular feature is to grant "frequent flyer miles" with designated airlines based on the amount charged against the credit card. This feature encourages usage of the card. However, if wisely used, it can permit the credit-card customer to obtain flyer miles at no cost, provided the balance on the card is paid off during the "grace period," thus avoiding any interest expense.

Charge-offs (bad debts) from overusage of credit-card accounts has recently been rising. Part of the explanation lies in the fact that more households (including lower-income households) now have several credit cards, and there has been an increase in the proportion of families actually borrowing against their cards. With heavier debt burdens, the average credit-card account now appears to be somewhat riskier, resulting in growing bad debt in the credit-card field.

Debit Cards

Until recently, commercial banks were the only major financial institutions actively involved in the plastic card field. This situation changed rapidly during the 1970s and early 1980s, however, as nonbank financial institutions (principally credit unions, savings banks, and savings and loans) successfully invaded the plastic card market, first using debit cards and then, later, adding credit cards. While a credit card permits the customer to buy now and pay later, debit cards are merely a convenient way of paying *now*. A debit card enables users to make deposits and withdrawals from an automated teller machine and also to pay for purchases by direct electronic transfer of funds from their own accounts to the merchant's account. Debit cards are also used for identification and check-clearing purposes and to access remote computer terminals for information or for moving funds.

A closely related card to the debit card is a "smart card," which is encoded with the customer's account number and balance available for spending. It is a substitute for immediately spendable cash. "Smart cards" have not done particularly well in the United States to date, due, in part, to the risks involved and the availability of so many other payments media. These stored-value cards have been quite successful in Europe, however, and are expected to become more important worldwide in the new century.

Debit cards appear to have gained on both credit cards and checks in recent years as the preferred method of paying for goods and services sold in stores. Many consumers seem to like the discipline that debit cards bring to their lives because the money is automatically taken out of their checking account, usually the same day a purchase is made, and they have less temptation to spend more money than they have. Moreover, with debit cards the consumer has fewer checks to write.

Debit cards appear to be profitable for many small banks in the United States, who earn a fee for each transaction involving a debit card. In contrast, credit cards are profitable mainly for the largest banks because this is a service that appears to be characterized by strong economies of scale. Credit-card programs require high volume to overcome high operating costs, defaulted accounts, and credit-card fraud. Unfortunately, however, debit cards may have a legal drawback, possibly protecting the customer less if the card is lost or stolen. Federal law limits consumer losses on credit cards, but a debit card can be used to drain a customer's checking account before he or she realizes what's happening. However, some depository institutions have indicated a willingness to cover all or a portion of any losses in those cases where fraud can be verified.

QUESTIONS TO HELP YOU STUDY

4. How much money do U.S. households owe today? Do you believe consumers are too heavily in debt? Why or why not?

5. Into what broad categories is consumer borrowing normally divided? Which category is most important and why?

6. What is the difference between *credit cards* and *debit cards?*

7. Why is the distinction between *installment users* and *convenience users* of credit cards important? Which are you?

8. What advantage does a credit card grant its owner? A debit card? What are the principal disadvantages of each?

21.6 The Determinants of Consumer Borrowing

As we noted earlier, consumers represent one of the largest groups of borrowers in the financial system. Yet individual consumers differ widely in their use of credit and in their attitudes toward borrowing money. What factors appear to influence the volume of borrowing carried out by households?

Recent research points to a number of factors that bear on the consumer's decision of when and how much to borrow. Leading the list is the size of *individual or family income* and *accumulated household wealth.* Families with larger incomes and greater accumulated wealth tend to use greater amounts of debt, both in absolute dollar amounts and relative to their income. In part, the debt-income relationship reflects the high correlation between income levels and education. Families whose principal breadwinners have made a significant investment in education are most often aware of the advantages (as well as the dangers) of using debt to supplement current income. Moreover, there appears to be a high positive correlation between education and the income-earning power of the principal breadwinners in a family.

The *stage in life* in which adult income-earning members of a family find themselves is also a major influence on household borrowing. The *life cycle hypothesis* contends that young families just starting out tend to be heavy users of debt. The purchase of a new home, automobile, appliances, and furniture follow soon after a new family is formed. As children come along, living costs rise and a larger home may be necessary, resulting in additional borrowing. Young families are willing to take on these additional debts because they expect a stream of future income throughout their working lives, which are likely to go on for many years. Later, the family's income rises, children leave home, and saving increases, while borrowing falls relative to income because older families expect a shorter future income stream before retirement arrives and, therefore, work to pay off their debts and build up their savings.

Consumer borrowing is correlated with the *business cycle.* During periods of economic expansion, the number of jobs increases, and households become more optimistic about the future. New borrowings usually outstrip repayments of outstanding loans, and the total volume of household debt rises. When an economic expansion ends and a recession begins, however, unemployment rises and many households become pessimistic about the future. Some, fearing a drop in income or loss of a job, build up savings and cut back on borrowing. Loan repayments may rise relative to new borrowings, and total household debt declines[3].

In recent decades, *price expectations* have also influenced consumer borrowing, especially when the rate of inflation begins to accelerate. Postponing the purchase of an automobile, a new home, furniture, or appliances often means these goods may simply cost more in the future. If family incomes are not increasing as fast as consumer prices, it often pays to "buy now" through borrowing rather than to postpone purchases.

Fluctuations in *interest rates* also play a role in shaping the volume and direction of consumer borrowing. Interest rates rise as the economy expands and gathers momentum. At first, the rising rates are not high enough to offset strong consumer optimism, and household borrowing continues to increase. As the period of economic expansion reaches a peak, however, the rise in interest rates may become so significant that consumer borrowing begins to decline. The drop in borrowing leads to a decline in consumer spending, which may worsen the impending recession. Of course, as we saw earlier, interest rates are not the sole determinant of consumer borrowing. The size of debt payments and consumer income, the fate of a consumer's investments and wealth position, age, employment outlook, and a host of other factors shape how much and when consumers choose to borrow money.

21.7 Consumer Lending Institutions

Financial intermediaries—banks, savings and loan associations, credit unions, and finance companies—account for most of the loans made to consumers in the economy. However, as Exhibit 21.4 indicates, a growing share of consumer loans are being sold

---

[3]Not only does consumer borrowing tend to be pro-cyclical, but household saving also tends to move with the business cycle as well. These time patterns probably reflect the fact that households tend to use borrowing and saving as devices to *smooth out* their consumption spending over the course of the business cycle.

EXHIBIT 21.4

Leading Consumer Lending Institutions in the United States

Source: Board of Governors of the Federal Reserve System.

*2004 figures are as of first quarter.

Total Nonmortgage Loans at Year-End ($ Billions)			
Lending Institutions	1995	2000	2004*
Commercial banks	$ 502.0	$ 541.5	$ 624.7
Finance companies	152.1	220.5	307.2
Credit unions	131.9	184.4	207.7
Savings institutions	40.1	64.6	81.3
Nonfinancial businesses	85.1	82.7	67.1
Pools of securitized assets (no longer on the balance sheets of the original lenders)	211.6	521.3	617.0
Totals outstanding	$1,122.8	$1,615.0	$1,905.0

off the balance sheets of traditional lenders and placed in loan pools (securitizations), often under the guidance of security dealers. While many traditional consumer lenders have lost ground in terms of their share of all consumer loans outstanding, the loan pools have significantly gained market share. At the same time, the lenders pooling their loans and moving them off their balance sheets thereby gain new cash and the ability to make more loans.

Although each type of financial institution prefers to specialize in a few selected areas of consumer lending, there has been a tendency in recent years for institutions to diversify their lending operations across many different types of loans. One important result of this diversification has been to bring *all* major consumer lenders into direct competition with each other.

Commercial Banks

The single most important consumer lending institution is the *commercial bank*. Commercial banks approach the consumer in three different ways: by direct lending, through purchases of installment paper from merchants, and by making loans to other consumer lending institutions. Roughly half of all bank loans to consumers (measured by dollar volume) consist of mortgages to support the purchase, construction, or improvement of residential dwellings; the rest consist of installment and noninstallment credit to cover purchases of goods and services. In the mortgage field, commercial banks usually prefer to provide short-term construction financing rather than to make long-term permanent loans for family housing, though most banks make both types of loans.

Banks make a wider variety of consumer loans than any other lending institution. They grant almost half of all auto loans extended by financial institutions to consumers each year. However, most bank credit in the auto field is indirect—installment paper purchased from auto dealers—rather than being extended directly to the auto-buying consumer. Moreover, banking's leadership in auto lending has been challenged in recent years by finance companies and credit unions. Indeed, in many forms of consumer installment credit today, the lead of commercial banks is threatened by challenges from aggressive nonbank lenders who see the consumer market as a key growth area for the future.

Finance Companies

Finance companies have a long history of active lending in the consumer installment field, providing funds directly to the consumer through thousands of small loan offices and indirectly by purchasing installment paper from dealers. These active household lenders provide auto loans and credit for home improvements and for the purchase of appliances and furniture. Finance companies often face state-imposed legal limits on the interest rates they can charge for household loans and on loan size.

Other Consumer Lending Institutions

Other consumer installment lenders include credit unions, savings and loan associations, savings banks, and so-called "fringe banks" (such as check-cashing, payday, and title loan companies). Credit unions make a wide variety of loans for such diverse purposes as purchases of automobiles; vacations; home repair; and, more recently, mortgage credit for the purchase of new homes. Only the members of a credit union may borrow from that institution, however.

Also important in the consumer loan field have been savings and loans and savings banks, which experienced dramatic growth in consumer lending in the 1970s and early 1980s but more recently have faced slower growth due to limited capital and competitive pressures. Although these institutions have long been dominant in residential mortgage lending, they have moved aggressively to expand their portfolios of credit card, education, home improvement, furniture, appliance, and mobile home loans over the past decade. Much of the drive for expansion in the consumer credit field is due to recent federal deregulation of the services offered by savings institutions.

Finally, among the most rapidly growing consumer lenders in recent years have been fringe banks—small loan companies that lend primarily to distressed borrowers. Included here are such high-rate lenders as "check-cashing" companies, "title loan" companies, "payday lenders," "pawn shops," and "rent to own" shops. *Check-cashing firms* and payday lenders agree to accept a post-dated check from the borrowing customer which will be cashed later by the lender, in return for which the lender makes an immediate loan of cash to the customer. *Title loan companies* agree to take control of the title to a valuable asset (such as a borrowing customer's automobile) as collateral for making a loan. If the customer fails to repay the loan the lender keeps the title to the asset. *Pawn shops* accept assets that a customer may bring in, hold those assets, and extend the customer a loan based on a fraction of the assets' value. If the customer does not repay, the pawn shop retains the assets it has taken in and eventually sells them. Finally, *rent-to-own* stores provide customers with the use of furniture, home appliances, and other assets for rental fees that may subsequently be applied to the purchase price of those rented assets.

The loans made by these small-loan companies are normally very short term, covering only a few days or weeks, and are designed primarily to tide families over until the next payday arrives. Unfortunately, the loan rates charged are among the highest assessed by the consumer credit industry and loan defaults are frequent.

21.8 Factors Considered in Making Consumer Loans

Consumer loans are considered one of the most profitable uses of funds for many financial institutions. There is evidence, however, that such loans usually carry greater risk than most other forms of credit, and they tend to be more costly to make per dollar of loan. On the other hand, the lender often can offset these costs by charging higher interest rates.

Making consumer loans is a challenging dimension of modern financial management. It requires not only a thorough knowledge of household financial statements but also an ability to assess the character of the borrower. Over the years, many loan officers have developed decision "rules of thumb" as an aid to processing and evaluating consumer loan applications. For example, many consumer loan officers insist that

To learn more about "fringe banking" see addall.com/detail/ 0871541955.html and out-reach.missouri.edu/ ceupdate/scripts/1999/ 06/fringebanking.htm

household debt (exclusive of housing costs) should not exceed 15 to 25 percent of a family's gross income. For younger borrowers, without substantial assets to serve as collateral for a loan, a cosigner may be sought whose assets and financial standing represent more adequate security. The *duration of employment* of the borrower is often a critical factor, and many institutions deny a loan request if the customer has been employed at his present job for less than six months or a year.

The *past payment record* of a customer usually is a key indicator of *character* and the likelihood that the loan will be repaid in timely fashion. Many lenders refuse to make loans to consumers who evidence "pyramiding of debt"—frequent borrowing from one financial institution to pay another. Evidence of sloppy money handling, such as large balances carried on charge accounts or heavy installment payments, is regarded as a negative factor in a loan application. Loan officers are particularly alert to evidence of a lack of *credit integrity* as reflected in frequent late payments or actual default on past loans. The character of the borrower is a very important issue in the decision to grant or deny a consumer loan. Regardless of the strength of the borrower's financial position, if the customer lacks the willingness to repay debt, the lender has made a bad loan.

Most lenders believe that those who *own valuable property,* such as land or marketable securities, are a better risk than those who do not own such property. For example, homeowners are usually considered better risks than those who rent. Moreover, a borrower's chance of getting a loan usually goes up if he or she does other business (such as maintain a deposit) with the lending institution. If more than one member of the family works, this is often viewed as a more favorable factor than if the family depends upon only a single breadwinner, who may become ill, die, or lose a job. Having a telephone at home is another positive factor in evaluating a loan application because the telephone gives the lender an inexpensive way to contact the borrower. One way to lower the cost of a loan is for the consumer to pledge a bank deposit or other liquid asset as security behind the loan. The disadvantage here is that such a pledge ties up the asset pledged until the loan is repaid.

21.9. Credit Scoring Techniques

The rapidly changing world of information technology has had a significant impact on the processes used for evaluating consumer loan applications. Today advanced statistical techniques are employed to assemble information about applicants for consumer loans, analyze the information gathered, and develop a *numerical score* for each would-be borrower. Using that score, lenders can make a decision as to whether a borrower has scored high enough to qualify for a loan.

credit scoring techniques

For more information about FICO and other credit scoring systems, see especially myfico. fanniemae.com/faq/ 2310001s.jhtml p=FAQ, and hsh.com/pamphlets/ aboutfico.html

Today **credit scoring techniques** are used for a wide variety of loans and other financial services, including deciding who should receive credit cards, what their credit limit should be, what families should receive mortgage loans to help purchase new homes, and even who should receive auto insurance coverage and at what price.

Perhaps the most famous of the credit scoring systems in use today was developed by Fair Isaac Corporation (more widely known as FICO). Fair Isaac has developed sophisticated prediction techniques to prepare credit scores for thousands of consumers, distributing this information to credit bureaus, lenders, and even to consumers themselves who want to know their current score and how they might improve it. Indeed, consumers who can raise their credit score often can save a great deal of money by qualifying for lower loan rates and insurance premiums.

FICO and similar credit-scoring systems base the scores they calculate on a credit applicant's *payment history* (i.e., how much has been borrowed in the past and when amounts owed were repaid), the current volume and type of debt each consumer has outstanding, and the type of credit currently being requested. FICO assigns scores for most consumers that fall between 300 and 850, with the higher score indicating greater probability of repayment. However, under the FICO system each lending institution decides what minimum cut-off score applies. For example, some lenders say that a score below 450 is unacceptable, while others may insist on a minimum score of at least 650 before any loan can be granted.

Credit scoring systems have numerous advantages for both lenders and consumers. They allow the lender to handle a large volume of credit requests at comparatively low cost and offer the customer quick turnaround in receiving a "yes" or "no" decision regarding loan approval. On the downside, however, credit scoring systems must frequently be reevaluated to make sure they are contributing to good credit decisions at a statistically significant level and are not discriminating against borrowers on the basis of race, religion, sex, or other irrelevant factors.

QUESTIONS TO HELP YOU STUDY

9. Discuss the factors that influence the volume of borrowing by individuals and families. What role do you believe inflation plays in the borrowing and savings decisions of households today?

10. What factors do lending institutions usually consider when evaluating a consumer loan application? Why?

11. What are the principal types of *consumer lending institutions* in the financial system?

12. Many lenders contend that loans to individuals and families are among the riskiest loans made within the financial system. Do you believe this is true? What kinds of risk do consumer loans present to a lender? How can lenders help combat this risk exposure?

13. What is *credit scoring* and why is it used extensively today in evaluating consumer loan applications?

21.10 Financial Disclosure and Consumer Credit

Important new laws have appeared in recent years designed to protect the consumer in dealings with lending institutions. One major area of emphasis is *financial disclosure:* making all relevant information available to the customer before a commitment is made. Moreover, if all important information is laid out before an agreement is reached, this may encourage the consumer to shop around to find the cheapest and most convenient terms available. However, there is considerable debate today on whether consumer protection legislation has really accomplished its goals.[4]

Truth in Lending

Truth in Lending

In 1968, Congress passed a watershed piece of legislation in the consumer credit field—the Consumer Credit Protection Act, more widely known as **Truth in Lending**.

---

[4]It appears that many of the goals sought by recent consumer-oriented financial legislation have *not* been achieved. Many consumers do not shop for credit and appear more concerned about the affordability of monthly payments on a loan than with how one lender's interest charge compares with that quoted by another. Many consumers seem unaware of the rights and privileges granted them under recent federal financial legislation and see little practical benefit from these laws.

Shortly after the act was passed, federal regulatory agencies prepared new rules to implement and enforce the principles of Truth in Lending, such as the Federal Reserve Board's Regulation Z.

Truth in Lending simply requires banks and other lenders to provide sufficient information about a credit contract, in easily understood terms, so that the consumer can make an intelligent decision about purchasing credit. The law does not tell creditors how much to charge or to whom they may lend money. At the same time, consumers were granted certain rights. For example, they have the right to cancel or rescind a credit agreement within three business days if their home is included as part of the collateral for a loan. This *right of rescission* applies to the repair or remodeling of a home or the taking out of a mortgage on an existing home, where the credit requested is intended for personal or agricultural purposes and results in a debt obligation repayable in more than four installments.

The most widely known provision of Truth in Lending is the requirement that a lender must tell the customer the annual percentage rate of interest (APR) charged on a loan. Lenders must disclose the total dollar cost associated with granting a loan—known as the *finance charge*—that is the sum of all charges the customer must pay as a condition for securing the loan. These charges may include credit investigation fees, insurance to protect the lender, and points on a mortgage loan. Once the finance charge is determined, it must be converted into the APR by comparing it with the amount of the loan. The APR is really the ratio of the dollar finance charge to the unpaid balance of a loan, determined by the actuarial method. Because all lenders must quote the APR, computed by the same method, this makes it easier for the consumer to shop around and purchase credit from the cheapest source available.

The concept of Truth in Lending has been extended in a number of directions in recent years. One important dimension concerns *advertising*. A lender that advertises one attractive feature of a credit package to consumers must also disclose other relevant credit terms. For example, a car dealer that advertises low down payments must also disclose other aspects of the loan, such as how many payments are required, what the amount of each payment is, and how many months or years are involved before the loan is paid off.

Fair Credit Billing Act

Fair Credit Billing Act

In 1974, Congress passed the **Fair Credit Billing Act** in response to a torrent of consumer complaints about billing errors, especially on credit cards. Many individuals found that they were being billed for items never purchased or received, that some merchants would not respond when contacted about billing errors, and that finance charges were frequently assessed even though the consumer claimed no responsibility for charges listed on the billing statement.

The Fair Credit Billing Act requires a creditor to respond to a customer's billing inquiry within 30 days. In most cases, the dispute must be resolved within 90 days. The customer may withhold payment of any amounts in dispute, although he or she must pay any portions of a bill that are not in dispute. However, no creditor can report a customer as "delinquent" over amounts of a bill that are the subject of disagreement until the disparity has been resolved. A creditor who fails to respond to the customer's inquiry or makes no effort to settle the dispute may forfeit the disputed sum up to $50.

Fair Credit Reporting Act

Fair Credit Reporting Act

An extension of Truth in Lending occurred when the **Fair Credit Reporting Act** was passed by Congress in 1970. This law entitles consumers to have access to their credit files, which are kept by credit bureaus active in the United States and

Canada. These credit bureaus supply subscribing lenders with vital information on amounts owed and the payment records and credit ratings of individuals and families. They aid greatly in reducing the risks inherent in consumer lending. However, because the information credit bureaus supply has a substantial impact on the availability of credit to individuals and families, their activities and especially the accuracy of the information they provide have been brought under closer scrutiny in recent years.

Under the provisions of the Fair Credit Reporting Act, the consumer is entitled to review his or her credit file at any time. Moreover, he or she may challenge any items that appear in the file and demand an investigation. The credit bureau must respond, and if inaccuracies exist or if an item cannot be verified, it must be removed or the inaccuracies corrected. If the consumer determines that an item in the credit file is damaging and requires clarification, he or she may insert a statement of 100 words or less explaining the consumer's version of the matter. Data in the file are supposed to be shown only to properly identified individuals for approved purposes or on direct written request from the consumer. Information cannot be disclosed to anyone after a period of seven years unless the consumer is seeking a loan of $50,000 or more, purchasing life insurance, applying for a job paying $20,000 or more per year, or has declared personal bankruptcy. The consumer may sue if damaged by incorrect information in a credit file. Many financial analysts today recommend that consumers check their credit bureau report several months before applying for a major loan and, otherwise, at least once a year.

> To learn more about credit bureaus and credit ratings see especially equifax.com, experian.com, or transunion.com
>
> Are financial-service firms subject to federal restrictions on telemarketing, including the Federal Trade Commission's famous "Do-Not-Call" rule? Banks and insurance companies are subject to this rule, according to an FTC ruling in 2003. See especially ftc.gov/donotcall

Consumer Leasing Act

In 1976, Congress passed the *Consumer Leasing Act,* which requires disclosure by leasing companies of the essential terms of any lease involving personal property, such as an automobile. The customer must be told about all charges, any insurance required, the terms under which the lease may be canceled, any penalties for late payment, and any express warranties that go with the property.

Competitive Banking Equality Act

In 1987 President Ronald Reagan signed the *Competitive Banking Equality Act* into law. It requires depository institutions to disclose more fully to customers the terms on various *deposit services* they offer. One major change was the required disclosure of how many days a depositor must wait before a check that is deposited in an account becomes available for spending. Some depository institutions had previously delayed the granting of credit for some deposits for a week or even longer. The new law stipulated that no more than one business day usually can intervene between the day of deposit of a local check and the customer receiving credit for that deposit. Nonlocal checks must be credited to the customer's account in no more than four business days.

Fair Credit and Charge Card Disclosure Act

Reflecting concern over the rapid expansion of credit card debt, the *Fair Credit and Charge Card Disclosure Act* was passed in 1988. Credit-card issuers were required to notify consumers of the interest rates, fees, and other terms attached to these credit accounts, spelled out in easy-to-read format (known as the "Schumer Box" after its congressional sponsor). Card customers were to be supplied with a toll-free phone number and address to help get their credit-card questions answered.

Truth in Savings Act

A further effort to make sure that consumers are adequately informed about the deposit accounts they purchase was made in November 1991 when Congress passed the *Truth in Savings Act*. This law prohibits inaccurate or misleading advertising concerning deposit accounts. Each depository institution must maintain a publicly available schedule of information for each class of accounts offered and distribute that information to both new and established account holders. If depositors would be adversely affected by a change in the terms of a deposit, notice of that adverse change must be provided to the deposit holder at least 30 days before the change becomes effective. Moreover, the customer must receive interest on the *full* amount of the principal deposited in an account, not on just the amount that a depository institution claims is available for investing in earning assets.

The Financial Services Modernization (Gramm-Leach-Bliley) Act

Financial Services Modernization Act

In an effort to protect a household's personal financial information, the U.S. Congress passed the **Financial Services Modernization Act** (known also as *GLB* after its sponsors) in the fall of 1999. This new law requires financial-service firms to tell household customers, at least once a year, what their policies are in the handling of personal, nonpublic data. Consumers must be informed about any of their personal data that may be shared with other businesses (such as telemarketing firms, for example). Each consumer has to be offered the possibility to "opt out" of at least some information sharing. However, many consumer groups have recently complained that this law is too weak in protecting consumers' personal data and have demanded new privacy laws at federal and state levels.

Identity Theft

Useful information about stopping identity theft is available from the Federal Trade Commission at ftc.gov.

identity theft

Disclosure of information can be a great aid to consumers and lenders intent on making sound financial decisions. However, there are cases where disclosing too much information can be very damaging to consumers. Such is the case with the world's fastest growing crime today—**identity theft**—which has been fueled by the rapid expansion of the Internet.

The term "identity theft" refers to the stealing of someone's private information (such as his or her Social Security number, driver's license number, credit card account number, etc.), usually for the purpose of representing oneself as the person whose information has been stolen. Identity thieves use illegally obtained private information to access an individual's checking account, charge-card accounts, and other personal items in an effort to drain away the victim's money and credit lines. For a person victimized by identity theft, it may take months or even years to straighten out the damage to one's personal credit accounts and reputation. Moreover, because many lenders today have pledged to absorb some or all of their customers' losses when a credit card or deposit account number is stolen, the cost to financial-service providers of offsetting the damages from identity theft now approaches several billion dollars a year. This crime tends to drive up interest rates and results in higher financial-service fees for all consumers.

To learn more about dealing with *identity theft*, see especially ftc.gov. For information about how to file an identity theft complaint, contact the Identity Theft Clearinghouse, Federal Trade Commission, 600 Pennsylvania Ave., NW, Washington, D.C., 20580.

The Financial Services Modernization Act (discussed in the preceding section) was passed, in part, to create tougher laws to deal with identity theft. Stiffer criminal penalties were imposed to punish financial predators and various federal agencies (such as the Federal Trade Commission) were directed to increase public awareness of the dangers of identity theft and to instruct consumers on ways to protect their private information from thieves. Then, in 2003, the *Fair and Accurate Credit Transactions (FACT) Act* was passed, permitting consumers to initiate a "fraud alert" by contacting one of the national credit bureaus (who must then contact the remaining national credit bureaus) if identity theft is suspected and block the distribution of fraudulent information about a consumer.

Among the remedies for identity theft recommended by financial planners today are periodically checking your credit bureau report (at least once a year) for any unexpected transactions, destroying unwanted credit or debit cards, asking mail and telephone marketers to remove your name from their contact lists, and avoiding giving out over the telephone or via e-mail any personal data to people you don't know. None of these suggested steps completely removes the risk of having one's good name stolen, but they can reduce the *probability* of becoming a victim of identity theft.

21.11 Credit Discrimination Laws

The civil rights movement has had an impact on the granting of consumer loans. Among the most important civil rights laws involving consumer credit are the *Equal Credit Opportunity Act* of 1974 and its amendments in 1976, the *Fair Housing Act* of 1968, the *Home Mortgage Disclosure Act* of 1975, and the *Community Reinvestment Act* of 1977. The fundamental purpose of these laws is to *outlaw discrimination* in the granting of credit and other vital financial services. Today, lenders must be able to justify in terms of fairness and objectivity not only the loans that are made but also those that are not made.

Community Reinvestment Act and Financial Institutions Reform, Recovery, and Enforcement Act

Community Reinvestment Act

One of the most important and controversial pieces of financial legislation is the **Community Reinvestment Act**, signed into law by President Jimmy Carter in 1977. Under its terms, financial institutions are required to make an "affirmative effort" to meet the credit needs of low- and middle-income customers. Each commercial and savings bank must define its own "trade territory" and describe the services it offers or is planning to offer in that local area. Once a year, each institution must prepare an updated map that delineates the trade territory it will serve, without deliberately excluding low- or moderate-income neighborhoods. Customers are entitled to make written comments, which must be available for public inspection, concerning the lender's performance in meeting the credit needs of its designated trade territory. The basic purpose of the Community Reinvestment Act (CRA) is to prevent gerrymandering out low-income neighborhoods and other areas that a lender may consider undesirable.

In 1989, the *Financial Institutions Reform, Recovery, and Enforcement Act* was passed, requiring public disclosure of a bank's performance rating (known as a CRA rating) in meeting the credit needs of its local community. Moreover, the *FDIC Improvement Act* of 1991 required greater disclosure of the reasons why a depository institution received the particular community service (CRA) rating that it did. The CRA ratings currently assigned to financial institutions are O (outstanding), S (satisfactory), N (needs to improve), and SN (substantial noncompliance).

Equal Credit Opportunity Act

Equal Credit Opportunity Act

The **Equal Credit Opportunity Act** of 1974 forbids discrimination against credit applicants on the basis of age, sex, marital status, race, color, religion, national origin, receipt of public assistance, or good-faith exercise of rights under the federal consumer credit protection laws. Married women, for example, may receive credit under their

Thanks to the passage of numerous consumer protection laws at both federal and state levels in recent years, individuals and families have gained numerous new rights. To learn more about these consumer rights in the financial sector, see especially the Board of Governors of the Federal Reserve System at federalreserve.gov, the Federal Deposit Insurance Corporation at fdic.gov, and the Federal Trade Commission at ftc.gov

own signature, based on their own personal credit record and earnings, without having their husband's joint signature. Credit applicants must be notified, in writing, of the approval or denial of a loan request within 30 days of filing a completed application. The lender may not request information on the borrower's race, color, religion, national origin, or sex, except in the case of residential mortgage loans (where the government can gather such information in order to detect illegal discrimination). Under the FDIC Improvement Act of 1991, the regulatory agencies must refer loan discrimination violators to the U.S. Justice Department for possible prosecution.

Fair Housing and Home Mortgage Disclosure Act

Two other important antidiscrimination laws are the Fair Housing Act, which forbids discrimination in lending for the purchase or renovation of residential property, and the Home Mortgage Disclosure Act (HMDA). The latter requires financial institutions to disclose to the public the amount and location of their home mortgage and home improvement loans. HMDA was designed to eliminate *redlining,* in which some lenders would mark out areas of a community as unsuitable for home loans. Both HMDA and the Fair Housing Act require nondiscriminatory advertising by lenders. No longer can a consumer lending institution direct its advertisements solely to high-income neighborhoods to the exclusion of other potential customers. On written advertising, the Equal Housing symbol must be attached. Clearly, then, in advertising the availability of credit and in the actual granting of credit, the principles of civil rights and nondiscrimination apply.

Recent research evidence is mixed on the issue of whether discrimination in home mortgage lending or any other kind of financial service really exists. One study by Munnell, Tootell, Browne, and McEneany (1996) suggested that minority applicants in the city of Boston, for example, were about 40 percent more likely than white applicants to be rejected for home mortgage loans. Other recent studies question this finding because of mitigating factors and point out that minority lending has been growing faster than other forms of credit in recent years.

21.12 Consumer Bankruptcy Laws

Over the past two decades, the number of households filing for personal bankruptcy and relief from personal debts has soared. The right to declare bankruptcy is designed to give individuals and businesses a fresh start, helping them to work themselves out from under a crippling burden of debt. Bankruptcy is mentioned specifically in the U.S. Constitution which states that Congress shall have the power to "establish uniform laws on the subject of bankruptcy." Today, close to 1 percent of all U.S. households file for personal bankruptcy annually, which means that more than a million U.S. citizens enter some form of bankruptcy proceedings each year.

Consumers filing for bankruptcy primarily use one of two methods: Chapter 7 or Chapter 13. Filing for bankruptcy under Chapter 7 normally completely discharges all of a household's unsecured debts. The fact that a consumer has declared Chapter 7 bankruptcy can remain on the individual's credit record for as long as 10 years, however. Under the Chapter 7 method, the debtor submits a petition listing his or her assets and debts to a U.S. district court along with a filing fee. The court may decide not to free the debtor of certain debts, such as when a lender claims the debtor submitted a false financial statement, if any debts arose from illegal actions or from claims due to a drunk-driving incident, or if the petitioning debtor failed to reveal all of his or her debts when he or she borrowed money. Secured obligations—for example, home mortgage loans and auto credit—are usually still subject to being repaid by the bankrupt consumer or he or she will lose those assets because property that is used to secure debt can be repossessed by lenders under the terms of Chapter 7.

In contrast, a Chapter 13 bankruptcy filing usually sets in motion a new debt repayment plan. Such a filing normally disappears from the consumer's credit record after seven years. Under the terms of Chapter 13 the debtor asks a bankruptcy court to lift the burden on his or her earnings or property stemming from the total of all debts currently outstanding. Under this approach, the debtor pledges to make regular payments to a Chapter 13 trustee who will dispense these funds to the creditors involved. The petitioner hopes to keep all of his or her property (thus retaining more assets than under a Chapter 7 filing) but ultimately pay less than the total amount he or she owes. Filers under Chapter 13 must be in receipt of a regular source of income.

The bankrupt must agree to abide by a court-approved repayment plan. Debt used to purchase a home must be paid off on schedule, though any previously missed home mortgage payments can be rescheduled for repayment over a longer period if need be. In practice, most families using the Chapter 13 approach to bankruptcy ultimately do *not* fulfill their debt repayment plans and will not, then, be released from what they owe. Moreover, no debtor can escape via the bankruptcy code from what may be owed in child support payments, alimony to a former spouse, or income tax obligations.

An individual can file for bankruptcy no more frequently than once every six years. As a result, lenders often seek out recently bankrupt persons, knowing they must repay any new debts they take on and cannot escape paying by declaring bankruptcy for several years into the future. The cost of filing for bankruptcy generally ranges from $500 to $2,000, but if an individual can get rid of many thousands of dollars of debt simply by filing for bankruptcy, he or she can experience a substantial net monetary return. Moreover, current bankruptcy law prohibits an employer from firing a worker merely because he or she has sought bankruptcy protection. Many experts say that if you can't see a practical way to repay most of your obligations over a five-year period, then bankruptcy *may* be a viable option for you, though the bankruptcy option should generally be considered as a "last resort" and only after receiving competent professional advice. Some bankruptcy filers experience great difficulty in getting new loans, however, and a social stigma may attach to a bankrupt individual that could last a long time. Then, too, once the bankrupt person has "gone to the well," it will be years before one can use that option again.

Recent research evidence suggests that most consumer bankruptcies follow from the loss of a job, broken marriages, crippling or costly accidents (along with poor or no insurance coverage), sickness where the afflicted family has inadequate health insurance protection, family businesses that go under, the overuse of credit cards, gambling losses, and reliance on volatile or unpredictable sources of income. Added to these problems are aggressive loan advertising and lenient credit standards used by some lenders who often seem anxious to sign up new borrowers even though these customers cannot afford to take on more debt. One possibly effective long-run solution is to promote more personal financial education while people are still in school and through special community education programs for older adults. There is also a need to help families find ways of gaining access to affordable health and property/casualty insurance that will offset devastating personal losses from accidents and illnesses.

For further information about the proposed Bankruptcy Reform Act, see consumersunion.org

A proposed new Bankruptcy Reform Act has appeared in the U.S. Congress in recent years. This proposed new bankruptcy code would, if eventually passed, substantially restrict new bankruptcy filings and raise the cost and time involved in seeking bankruptcy protection for consumers. It would require bankrupt consumers to complete a financial education course and encourage the states to develop personal finance curricula in their elementary and high school programs. Some authorities believe that tougher bankruptcy rules, if finally passed into law, would tend to lower the cost of consumer credit for most borrowers, but would discourage borrowing by many high-risk consumers.

QUESTIONS TO HELP YOU STUDY

14. What is *Truth in Lending*? Describe the law's major provisions and explain why it was enacted in the first place.

15. What protections are offered to individual and family consumers under the *Fair Credit Billing Act*? the *Consumer Leasing Act*? the *Fair Credit Reporting Act*? the *Fair Credit and Charge Card Disclosure Act*? the *Financial Services Modernization Act*?

16. What are the principal purposes of the *Community Reinvestment Act*? the *Equal Credit Opportunity Act*? the *Fair Housing Act*? the *Home Mortgage Disclosure Act*? Assess the benefits and costs of these laws.

17. What changes in consumer rights and required disclosure of information to the consumer occurred when the *Financial Institutions Reform, Recovery, and Enforcement Act* was passed? With passage of the *Truth in Savings Act*? the *FDIC Improvement Act*?

18. Why have so many consumer *bankruptcies* occurred in recent years? How might these bankruptcies be prevented?

19. Why was a *new bankruptcy law* proposed as the twentieth century drew to a close? What unique provisions does the proposed new law contain?

MARKETS ON THE NET: The Most Important Web Sites for This Chapter

Consumer Information Center
(consumer.gov)
Equifax Credit Bureau (equifax.com)
Experian Credit Bureau (experian.com)
Federal Deposit Insurance Corporation
(fdic.gov)
Federal Reserve Board (federalreserve.gov)
Federal Trade Commission (ftc.gov)

FICO Scores and Reports (myfico.com)
Identity Theft Clearinghouse
(rn.ftc.gov/dod/widtpubl$.startup?Z-ORG-CODE=PU03)
National Endowment for Financial
Education (nefe.org)
Transunion Credit Bureau (transunion.com)

Summary of the Chapter's Main Points

One of the most remarkable developments in the financial system over the past century has been the awakening of the consumer as a leading borrower and lender of funds within the global financial system.

- *Households*—individuals and families—have become the principal sources of loanable funds in the money and capital markets in most years. They are also among the leading borrowing sectors in the financial system.

- Due to intense competition in the financial-service sector, new consumer-oriented financial services have appeared in profusion in recent years in an effort to attract and hold consumer accounts. Examples include NOWs, money market deposits, share accounts in money market mutual funds, universal life insurance policies, consumer cash management services, and home equity loans.

- While consumers are among the leading borrowing groups in the economy, overall their dollar holdings of financial assets far exceed their indebtedness, though their ratio of liabilities to financial asset holdings has risen in recent decades.

- Lenders to the household sector consider multiple factors in deciding whether or not to grant a loan, including the size and stability of a consumer's income, length of residence in current location, amount of installment debt outstanding, and any holdings of valuable assets (including stocks, bonds, and other assets of readily marketable value). Increasingly, *credit scoring* systems are being used to evaluate consumer loan requests, relying on computer processing and advanced statistical techniques to speed up and lower the cost of making consumer loan decisions.

- Important federal laws have been passed in the United States over the past four decades to accomplish two major objectives: (a) *disclose the terms* of loans and other financial services so the household customer can make an informed financial decision; and (b) *prevent discrimination* in gaining access to financial services (especially access to credit). Among the key pieces of federal legislation protecting consumers are the Truth in Lending Act, the Fair Credit Billing Act, the Fair Credit Reporting Act, the Equal Credit Opportunity Act, the Community Reinvestment Act, and the Truth in Savings Act. The Truth in Lending, Fair Credit Billing, Fair Credit Reporting, and Truth in Savings acts *promote greater disclosure* of the terms attached to loans, savings deposits, and other financial services, while the Equal Credit Opportunity Act and the Community Reinvestment Act focus mainly on *preventing discrimination* against consumers seeking access to financial services. Among the most recent laws passed are the Financial Services Modernization (Gramm-Leach-Bliley) Act and the Fair and Accurate Credit Transactions Act, which deal with protecting consumer *privacy* and stopping the rapid rise in *identity theft.*

- U.S. bankruptcy laws have been a center of controversy between consumers and lenders since the 1970s when a more liberal United States bankruptcy code was enacted and the numbers of household bankruptcies began to climb significantly. Fearing that debt relief rules for households might have become unbalanced in favor of the consumer, Congress debated a powerful new bankruptcy bill in the late 1990s and as the twenty-first century began. The proposed new law, if it ever passes, would raise the cost of consumer bankruptcies and demand that households seeking bankruptcy relief receive training in the hope of avoiding future financial problems.

Key Terms Appearing in This Chapter

NOW account, 645
residential mortgage credit, 650
installment credit, 650
noninstallment credit, 650
home equity loan, 651
credit card, 652
debit card, 652
credit scoring techniques, 658

Truth in Lending, 659
Fair Credit Billing Act, 660
Fair Credit Reporting Act, 660
Financial Services Modernization
  (Gramm-Leach-Bliley) Act, 662
identity thefts, 662
Community Reinvestment Act, 663
Equal Credit Opportunity Act, 663

Problems and Issues

1. Home equity loans to consumers are generally based on the *residual value* of a home (i.e., market value less the remaining balance on the outstanding home mortgage loan) and the fraction of that value (known as the *loan-to-value ratio*)

that the lending institution is willing to lend. The customer's borrowing base is the product of these two entities. Calculate the customer's borrowing base in the situations described below:

Appraised Value of Borrower's Home	Mortgage Loan Balance Outstanding	Lender's Required Loan-to-Value Ratio
a. $173,500	$ 67,800	75%
b. $64,150	$ 23,948	70%
c. $251,400	$111,556	80%
d. $789,000	$340,722	82%

2. Indicate which consumer-oriented law or laws passed in the United States apply in each of the situations described below:

   a. Matthew Crey is discussing with a bank loan officer the terms on a loan he needs to buy a car for his family.

   b. Robert and Mary Nash believe they were discriminated against when their loan to purchase a new home was denied.

   c. Sally Ferrel was denied a loan because of an adverse report from her credit bureau, which she believes is in error.

   d. Herbert Coleman has just received his credit card bill and finds several charges were made against his account that are not legitimate.

   e. Mary Eacher leased an automobile from a dealer for three years, but the lease was abruptly canceled even though Mary was making all required payments on time.

   f. First National Bank of Arden has just announced its latest CRA rating received from federal bank examiners.

   g. Earl and Susan Tolber believe they were denied a home improvement loan because their address is in a neighborhood where the local bank does not like to make such loans.

   h. Bill Gell decides to "opt out" of letting his bank and his insurance company share information about him with other businesses.

   i. Jean Shal has just been notified by her bank that it is going to reduce the interest rate on her certificate of deposit when it is renewed.

   j. John Saral is confused about the terms of a credit card and needs additional information from the card company.

3. Construct a balance sheet and estimate the annual take-home income of the Williams family from the information presented below:

Checking account balance	$ 2,860	Credit union deposit	$ 550
Credit card obligations	7,400	Bank loan	13,800
Department store debt	1,875	Estimated market value of	
U.S. savings bonds	3,460	Home	81,000
Unpaid life insurance premiums	625	Autos	23,780
Gas and oil credit card balances	289	Furniture and appliances	13,490
Home mortgage	68,500	Cash surrender value	
Mutual fund shares	15,430	of life insurance	3,770
Pension plan assets	47,995		
Annual take-home income— 0.28 of the family's total assets			

Would you grant this family a loan of $10,000 to fund the purchase of new kitchen appliances and repairs to the family automobile? Why or why not?

Standard & Poor's Market Insight and Web-Based Problems

1. Commercial banks are a principal provider of nonmortgage consumer credit. However, not all banks focus their business so exclusively on this type of lending, with some preferring to concentrate more on mortgage lending or business loans. This exercise asks you to select six of the largest U.S. banks and compare them with respect to the emphasis they place on consumer lending.

   a. Visit the S&P's Market Insight database at **mhhe.com/edumarketinsight** and look up the balance sheet of six of the nation's largest diversified banks. (You will find the listing by clicking on the "Industry" tab and searching under "GICS Sub-Ind. Constituents" for the GIC Sub-Ind." Category, "Diversified Banks.")

   b. From the most recent annual balance sheets (look under "Excel Analytics") for each of the companies you have identified, determine what percentage of total assets ("Assets—Total") are represented by: (i) consumer loans; (ii) mortgages; and (iii) commercial and industrial (business) loans.

   c. From your results in part (b) order the banks from high to low in terms of their reliance on consumer loans, mortgages, and commercial and industrial loans. Is there a significant difference between the highest and the lowest bank in each of the three categories? What does this suggest about specialization in lending within the banking industry?

2. A significant recent development in the financing of consumer loans has been the growth in securitization of many forms of consumer debt. A major category of consumer loans involves the purchase of new and used autos. Many lending agencies (such as commercial banks and credit unions) have found it profitable to be the originator of these loans, which they then package and sell as a single portfolio. The purpose of this exercise is to observe the growth in new and used auto loans carried by these firms.

   a. Visit the Federal Reserve's Web site at **federalreserve.gov/releases** and find the G.20 monthly release data on finance companies.

   b. From there, identify the dollar value of new and used auto loans ultimately financed by finance companies over the past 20 years and plot these data. Hint: Look under "Auto Loans," "Amount Financed (dollars)." You will need to obtain several "releases" in order to put together a complete data set.

   c. Now go to the Commerce Department's Bureau of Labor Statistics Web site at **bea.gov** and obtain data on the dollar value of all new autos sold in the U.S. in each of the past 20 years. There are various ways to navigate this informative Web site. One possibility is to click "National" on the Bureau's home page, then on successive pages click "Gross Domestic Product," "Interactive NIPA Tables," and "List of All NIPA Tables." From there, scroll down to Table 7.2.5B: Motor Vehicle Output. From that table, look for the data regarding final sales of domestic product, personal consumption expenditures, and new motor vehicles.

    d. Form the ratio of new car loans financed by finance companies to the dollar value of all new cars sold and plot this ratio. What do you observe?

3. Reliance on credit scoring systems to assess the creditworthiness of a loan applicant has become a routine practice among lending institutions. Use the Web sites **fico.com** and **freddiemac.com/knowyourscore** to answer the questions below:

    a. How do lending institutions benefit by using credit scoring systems?

    b. How do consumers benefit from having their credit score easily available to lenders?

    c. How might consumers be adversely affected by the credit scoring system?

    d. Are you able to determine your own credit score?

    e. Based on your current credit score, would you qualify for receiving a home mortgage loan? Explain.

    f. What could you do to raise your credit score?

Selected References to Explore

Bauer, Paul W. "What You Should Know about Identity Theft." *Economic Commentary,* Federal Reserve Bank of Cleveland, September 15, 2002, pp. 1–3.

Bernheim, B. Douglas; Lorenzo Forni; Jagadeesh Gokhale; and Laurence J. Kotlikoff. "How Much Should Americans Be Saving for Retirement?" *American Economic Review,* Papers and proceedings, May 2000.

Hilgert, Marianne A., and Jeanne M. Hogarth. "Household Financial Management: The Connection between Knowledge and Behavior." *Federal Reserve Bulletin,* July 2003, pp. 309–22.

Mester, Loretta J. "Is the Personal Bankruptcy System Bankrupt?" *Business Review,* Federal Reserve Bank of Philadelphia, First Quarter 2002, pp. 31–44.

Munnell, A., L. Browne, J. McEneaney, and G. Tootell. "Mortgage Lending in Boston: Interpreting HMDA Data." *American Economic Review* 86 (March 1996), pp. 25–53.

Rose, Peter S. "Bank Cards: The Promise and the Peril." *The Canadian Banker,* December 1978, pp. 62–7.

_____. "Social Responsibility in Banking: Pressures Intensify in the U.S." *The Canadian Banker,* June 1979, pp. 70–5.

_____. "Credit Discrimination under Attack." *The Canadian Banker,* September 1979, pp. 70–5.

Chapter 22

The Residential Mortgage Market

What's in This Chapter?
Key Topics Outline

Trends in Home Prices and Loan Terms

The Structure of the Mortgage Loan Market

Mortgage Lending Institutions and Their Preferred Market Segments

Government Reshapes the Mortgage Market: Lending, Guaranteeing, Making Markets

Mortgage-Linked Securities and Prepayment Risk

Innovations in Mortgage Instruments

Refinancing Existing Loans and Home Equity Borrowing

Learning Objectives

in This Chapter

- You will discover how the largest of all domestic financial markets in the United States—the *residential mortgage market*—functions in order to supply credit to build and buy homes, apartments, and other dwellings for individuals and families.

- You will come to understand the problems faced by lenders of residential mortgage money in designing new loan contracts that will protect them against inflation and other risks.

- You will discover what important jobs are performed by federal government agencies and government-sponsored mortgage firms, such as Fannie Mae (FNMA) and Ginnie Mae (GNMA), in supporting the development of the market for home mortgage loans.

22.1 Introduction to the Residential Mortgage Market

One of the most important goals for many families is to own their own home. Besides the psychic benefits of privacy and a feeling of belonging to the local community, home ownership confers important financial and economic benefits on those families and individuals both able and willing to make the investment. The market value of single-family residences has risen substantially faster than the rate of inflation over the long run, offering individuals and families of even modest means one of the few available hedges against inflation. Moreover, the interest cost on home mortgages is tax deductible in the United States, reducing significantly the *after-tax* interest rate levied on residential mortgage loans.

Unfortunately for families seeking home ownership, the residential mortgage market is often treacherous, swinging quickly from low interest rates and ample credit to high and rising rates with little credit available. In this volatile market, home ownership may become an impossible dream for thousands of individuals and families, though a greater proportion of U.S. households than ever before own their own homes today. The wide swings characteristic of the residential mortgage market also send reverberations throughout the economy. In fact, today the housing market appears to be playing a powerful *counter-cyclical* role, providing funds to households when they refinance their homes and thus boosting consumption spending and preventing downturns in the economy from becoming deeper than they otherwise might be.

22.2 Recent Trends in New Home Prices and the Terms of Mortgage Loans

We can get a glimpse of the tremendous pressures buffeting the market for residential mortgages today by looking at recent trends in the prices of new homes and the cost of financing them. Exhibit 22.1 provides recent data on the average terms quoted on a **conventional home mortgage loan** in the United States. A conventional mortgage loan is *not* guaranteed by the government but is purely a private contract between the home buyer and the lending institution. In this case, the lender of funds bears the risk that the home buyer will default on principal or interest payments associated with a mortgage loan, forcing foreclosure and resale of the home (although today most

conventional home mortgage loan

EXHIBIT 22.1	Item	1974	1980	1990	2000	2004**
	Primary market: Conventional mortgages on new homes					
Prices and Yields of Conventional Home Mortgage Loans	Purchase price ($000)	$40.10	$83.50	$153.20	$234.50	$288.0
	Amount of loan ($000)	29.80	59.30	112.40	177.00	211.0
	Loan/price ratio (percent)	74.30	73.30	74.50	77.40	75.6
	Maturity (years)	26.30	28.20	27.30	29.20	28.6
	Fees and charges ("points")	1.30%	2.10%	1.93%	0.70%	0.59%
	Contract interest rate (percent per year)	8.71	12.25	9.68	7.41	5.63
	Yield on FHA mortgages (percent per year)	9.22	13.95	10.17	7.45*	NA

Source: Board of Governors of the Federal Reserve System, *Federal Reserve Bulletin,* Table 1.53, various issues.

*FHA mortgage yield is for 1999.

**Figures for 2004 are averages for February.

The dream of home ownership has been satisfied for more people today than at any other time in American history. Many people think this is a good trend, both psychologically and financially, giving families an asset that is likely to appreciate in value and providing a borrowing base for raising funds in order to start a new business, send children to college, etc.

However, homes can be costly to maintain and difficult to sell (illiquid). Home ownership can also make it hard for a family to adequately diversify its assets, because a home often represents an individual family's single largest investment. Moreover, homes fluctuate in value with the economy and with changes in their age and condition. Many families having low or moderate income have literally "sunk" most of their wealth in a single asset whose value may plummet due to factors beyond their control. In some markets today homes have become more of a psychological boost to homeowners rather than a strong financial benefit.

In the long run, however, average home prices have tended to stay up with or even outstrip inflation, though housing values often have not performed quite as well as the stock market, on average, even though interest payments on home mortgage debt and property taxes can help to reduce a family's taxable income. However, housing values appear to be somewhat more stable than stock prices (often moving in the opposite direction), helping a family to diversify its investment returns and lower its overall risk exposure.

To examine recent data on the changing character of the mortgage market see, for example, HSH Associates Statistical Releases at hsh.com and Wholesale Access at wholesaleaccess.com

conventional loans are insured by private insurance companies). In contrast, mortgage loans issued through the Federal Housing Administration (FHA) or Veterans Administration (VA) are partially guaranteed as to principal and interest by the federal government and are primarily used to finance low and moderately priced housing.

As shown in Exhibit 22.1, the average purchase price of a conventional single-family residence in the United States has more than tripled over the past two decades. With housing prices and the demand for new homes rising, sellers and lending institutions have worked to accommodate more borrowers by increasing the average percentage of a new home's purchase price they are willing to lend, to as high as almost 80 percent in recent years. We note from Exhibit 22.1 that mortgage lenders are also willing to extend credit for longer periods. The average maturity of conventional home mortgage loans climbed to about 29 years in 2004. Extra fees and charges (known as "points" and usually calculated as percentages of the amount of a loan) levied by lenders as a condition for making home mortgage credit available have fallen recently. The average contract interest rate on conventional mortgage loans dipped to about 5.5 percent as the new century opened—the lowest level in decades. These low home-loan interest rates helped to boost U.S. home ownership so that about two-thirds of American households owned their own dwelling—the highest percentage in history.

Unfortunately, offsetting the relatively low home-mortgage loan rates of recent years have been record-high home prices. These high prices for new and existing homes have shut out scores of families from fulfilling a long-sought-after American dream—owning your own home. Several factors account for this dramatic long-term escalation in the price of home ownership. Certainly, inflation has played a key role in driving up building costs, and this increase has been passed on to the consumer. On the demand side, a substantial rise in the number of new family formations has occurred in recent years. Added to this has been a rapid increase in individuals living alone and in single-parent households. Therefore, although the U.S. birth rate has dropped to some of the lowest levels in history, the increase in new families and in single-adult households dramatically increased the demand for housing, especially for low- and medium-priced homes. Overall, real home prices have risen considerably faster than homeowner incomes, discouraging some potential home buyers.

EXHIBIT 22.2	Year	Amount
Total Mortgage Debt Outstanding in the United States at Year-End ($ Billions)	1950	$ 72.8
	1960	206.8
	1970	451.7
	1980	1,451.8
	1990	3,807.3
	2000	6,890.0
	2004*	9,617.5

Sources: Board of Governors of the Federal Reserve System, *Annual Statistical Digest*, 1971–1975, and *Federal Reserve Bulletin*, selected issues.

*Figures through the first quarter of 2004.

22.3   The Structure of the Mortgage Market

Volume of Mortgage Loans

A nice summary of unfolding trends in the home mortgage industry is available through the Web site of the Mortgage Bankers Association of America at mbaa.org

Mortgages are among the most important securities in the financial system. The total of all mortgages outstanding in the United States is now more than $9.5 trillion (see Exhibit 22.2). This total represents about two-thirds of the nation's gross domestic product (GDP) and makes the mortgage market the largest primary security market inside the United States.

Residential versus Nonresidential Mortgage Loans

residential mortgages

nonresidential mortgages

The mortgage market can be divided into two major segments: (1) **residential mortgages**, which encompass all loans secured by single-family homes and other dwelling units, and (2) **nonresidential mortgages**, which include loans secured by business and farm properties. Which of these two sectors is more important? As Exhibit 22.3 shows, loans to finance the building and purchase of homes, apartments, and other residential units dominate the U.S. mortgage market, accounting for about four-fifths of all mortgage loans outstanding. Mortgages on commercial and farm properties accounted for less than one-fifth of all mortgages issued. Because residential mortgages dominate the market, it should not be surprising that households are the leading mortgage borrower, accounting for about four-fifths of outstanding mortgage debt. The next largest group of mortgage borrowers—business firms—runs a distant second.

EXHIBIT 22.3	Type of Property	Amount	Percent of Total
Mortgage Loans Outstanding, 2004* ($ Billions)	Residential properties (one- to four-family and multifamily structures)**	$7,926.7	82.4%
	Nonresidential properties (commercial and farm)	1,690.8	17.6
	All properties	$9,617.5	100.0%

Source: Board of Governors of the Federal Reserve System, *Federal Reserve Bulletin*, selected issues.

*Figures are as of the first quarter of 2004.

**Note that not all residential loans go to just households but may include businesses and other units in the economy.

QUESTIONS TO HELP YOU STUDY

1. What has happened in recent years to new-home prices? To interest rates and other terms on conventional home mortgage loans? What are the *causes* of these trends?

2. Residential mortgages may be classified in several different ways. Describe the structure of the mortgage market as it relates to each of the following dimensions:

   Type of mortgage contract—conventional versus government guaranteed

   Residential versus nonresidential mortgages

   Type of mortgage borrower

3. What are the advantages and disadvantages of home ownership for the consumer?

4. How does the behavior of the home mortgage market reveal the problems that home buyers and mortgage lenders face as they operate in this huge financial market?

22.4 Mortgage-Lending Institutions

In the years before World War II, mortgages were one of the most widely held securities in the financial system, comparable to stock in the great diversity of investors who chose to add these securities to their portfolios. Individuals were then the dominant mortgage investors, with financial institutions in second place. However, the rapid growth of commercial banks, savings institutions, insurance companies, government agencies, and mortgage pools (where groups of loans are packaged together) as major mortgage lenders during the past half century has forced individual investors into the background.

Exhibit 22.4 shows the total amounts of mortgage loans held by various lender groups in 2004. Savings and loan associations, once the principal private mortgage-lending

EXHIBIT 22.4

Principal Lenders in the U.S. Mortgage Market, 2004*

Source: Board of Governors of the Federal Reserve System, *Federal Reserve Bulletin,* selected issues.

Note: Columns may not add to totals due to rounding.

*2004 Figures are for the first quarter of the year.

Lender Group	Volume of Mortgage Loans Held by Lender ($ Billions)	Percent of Total
Savings institutions (savings and loan associations and savings banks)	$ 927.5	9.6%
Commercial banks	2,329.5	24.2
Life insurance companies	261.5	2.7
Individuals and other private lenders	920.5	9.6
Mortgage pools or trusts:	4,636.5	48.2
Government National Mortgage Association	464.5	
Federal Home Loan Mortgage Corp.	1,166.7	
Federal National Mortgage Association	1,878.0	
Private mortgage conduits (including securitized loans)	1,127.2	
Federal and related agencies:	541.9	5.6
Government National Mortgage Association	0.5	
Federal Home Loan Mortgage Corporation	60.3	
Federal National Mortgage Association	240.7	
Farmers Home Administration	71.3	
Federal Land Banks	50.0	
Federal Housing and Veterans Administration	4.5	
Other agencies	114.6	
	$9,617.5	100.0%

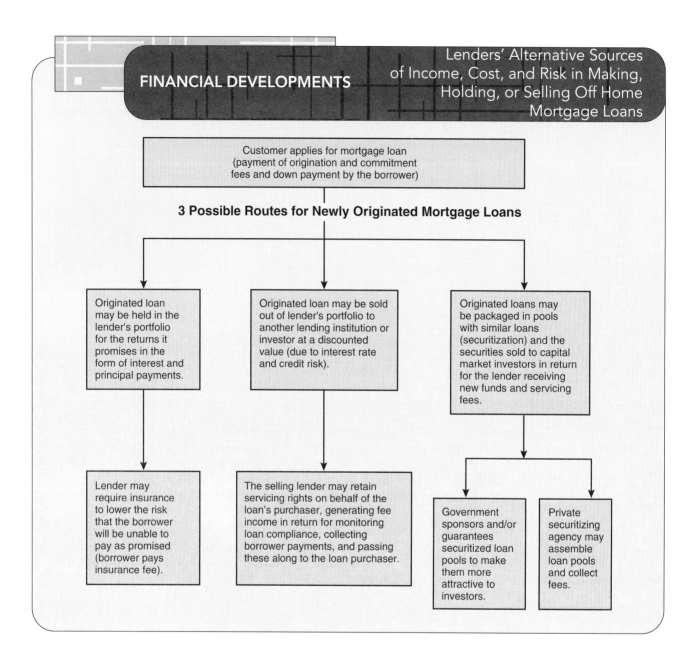

FINANCIAL DEVELOPMENTS

Lenders' Alternative Sources of Income, Cost, and Risk in Making, Holding, or Selling Off Home Mortgage Loans

Customer applies for mortgage loan (payment of origination and commitment fees and down payment by the borrower)

3 Possible Routes for Newly Originated Mortgage Loans

Originated loan may be held in the lender's portfolio for the returns it promises in the form of interest and principal payments.

Originated loan may be sold out of lender's portfolio to another lending institution or investor at a discounted value (due to interest rate and credit risk).

Originated loans may be packaged in pools with similar loans (securitization) and the securities sold to capital market investors in return for the lender receiving new funds and servicing fees.

Lender may require insurance to lower the risk that the borrower will be unable to pay as promised (borrower pays insurance fee).

The selling lender may retain servicing rights on behalf of the loan's purchaser, generating fee income in return for monitoring loan compliance, collecting borrower payments, and passing these along to the loan purchaser.

Government sponsors and/or guarantees securitized loan pools to make them more attractive to investors.

Private securitizing agency may assemble loan pools and collect fees.

It is interesting to explore the nature and structure of the mortgage market in other countries. For example, for a look at the Canadian mortgage market, see mortgagesincanada. com/residential

institution in the United States, have now dropped to less than 10 percent of all mortgage loans outstanding. Commercial banks now rank number one among private lending institutions, holding nearly one-quarter of all mortgage credit outstanding. In general, the relative share of the mortgage market accounted for by traditional private mortgage-lending institutions, such as savings and loans and insurance companies, has declined, while pension funds, finance companies, and government agencies have accounted for a growing share of outstanding loans. Noteworthy in this regard has been the rapidly expanding role of *mortgage pools:* lender-packaged groups of high-quality residential mortgages insured or guaranteed by a government agency and in which investors hold shares, entitling them to a portion of any interest and principal payments generated by the pool. We will have more to say about mortgage pools later in this chapter when we discuss the expanding role of the federal government in the mortgage market.

A mortgage loan is one of the most difficult of all financial instruments for which to establish a true value. Most mortgages generate multiple potential cash-flow streams—for example: (1) the payment of origination and commitment fees when a mortgage loan is first applied for; (2) the promise of a stream of periodic loan repayments plus loan interest; (3) the added compensation to a lender for the risk that a mortgage borrower will pay off his or her loan early or perhaps, ultimately, not at all; (4) the servicing income associated with collecting and recording amounts owed and monitoring compliance with the terms of a loan; and (5) the net returns or fees from securitization that arise when a mortgage loan is packaged with other, similar mortgage loans into a pool and income-generating securities are issued as claims against that pool of home loans.

Information for buyers and sellers in the home mortgage market is available through such sites as buyersresource.com, getsmart.com, and houses4sale-online.com

Different financial institutions operating in the mortgage market pursue one or more of the foregoing income sources. For example, many locally oriented banks, savings and loans, and other smaller depository institutions retain new mortgage loans in their asset portfolios and receive the resulting flow of borrower interest and principal payments, while other lenders may quickly sell any loans they make and instead pursue loan servicing, securitization, and other fee-generating services because of the greater geographic diversification, more predictable liquidity demands, and lower capital requirements involved with these supporting services. Each of these possible cash-flow sources from a mortgage loan has its own financial advantages and disadvantages in terms of sensitivity to default, interest rate, and liquidity risk, and possible changes in the size of cash flow expected to be received.

22.5 The Roles Played by Leading Financial Institutions in the Mortgage Market

Mortgage lenders tend to specialize in the types of loans they grant, and some are far more important to the residential market than to commercial mortgage lending. Moreover, even within the residential lending field, different institutional lenders will favor one type of mortgage (e.g., conventional versus government guaranteed) over another and also desire a certain range of maturities. Some lenders are organized to deal with home mortgage borrowers one at a time, while others may prefer to acquire large packages of mortgages associated with major residential building projects.

Savings and Loan Associations

Savings and loan associations (S&Ls) are predominantly *local* lenders, making the majority of their mortgage loans in the communities where their offices are located. Moreover, S&Ls often service the mortgage loans they make rather than turning that task over to a mortgage bank or trust company. Servicing a mortgage involves maintaining ownership and financial records on the mortgaged property, receiving installment payments from the borrower, checking on the mortgaged property to ensure that its value is maintained, and in the event of borrower default, foreclosing on the property to collect any unpaid balance on the loan.

Historically, S&Ls have preferred single-family home mortgages, which is where they started during the nineteenth century, lending to help families build their homes and encouraging individuals to save for the future. However, savings associations have diversified their portfolios in recent years to include many new kinds of mortgage-related assets, such as mobile home loans; mortgage credit for apartments and other multifamily housing units; and securities backed by pools of mortgage loans. S&Ls' attempts to diversify and increase long-term capital relative to their assets in order to lower their risk of failure have brought about a substantial decline in S&Ls' share of the total mortgage market. Thus, many S&Ls have had fewer funds to devote to new mortgage loans. Other savings associations have been purchased by bank holding companies and converted into banks with few mortgage loans or into mortgage companies that make only short-term loans in this market.

Commercial Banks

In contrast to savings and loans, *commercial banks* have expanded their market share of nearly every type of mortgage loan. Overall, they now rank first as lenders for the purchase of homes, condominiums, and apartments and in the commercial mortgage field. A large share of bank mortgage credit, however, goes for shorter-term loans to finance the *construction* of new commercial and residential projects, with other lenders usually taking on the long-term mortgage loans from these projects. Commercial banks have also shown a strong interest in financing upscale homes purchased by higher-income families in recent years—homes that command significantly higher prices and larger down payments. Finally, banks today are among the strongest supporters of the mortgage-backed securities market, devoting more than half of all their security holdings to these financial instruments which are backed by pools of mortgage loans.

Life Insurance Companies

Life insurance companies make substantial investments in commercial as well as residential mortgage properties. These companies search national and international markets for good mortgage investments instead of focusing only on local areas. They often prefer to purchase residential mortgages in large blocks rather than one at a time.

In the past, life insurers preferred government-guaranteed home mortgages. In recent years, however, the higher yields available on conventional mortgages have caused some shift of emphasis toward these more risky home loans. Despite the greater flexibility of conventional single-family home mortgages, however, life insurance companies have been gradually reducing their holdings of single-family home mortgages and emphasizing, instead, commercial and apartment mortgages. Commercial and apartment loans often carry "equity kickers" that permit the lending institution to receive a portion of project earnings as well as a guaranteed interest return.

Savings Banks

Another lender of importance in the residential mortgage market is the *savings bank,* which began in Scotland and, initially, concentrated in the eastern U.S. before spreading nationwide and then worldwide. These institutions invest in both government-guaranteed and conventional mortgage loans. Although single-family homes constitute the bulk of savings bank mortgage loans, their loans supporting multifamily units (including large apartment projects) have grown in recent years. Like life insurance companies, savings banks often prefer to acquire residential mortgages in large blocks, such as a whole subdivision, rather than loan by loan. Like savings and loan associations, savings banks have tended to lose mortgage market share to other private and governmental lenders.

Mortgage Bankers

Mortgage banking houses act as a channel through which builders or contractors in need of long-term funds can find permanent mortgage financing. In providing this service, mortgage bankers take on portfolios of mortgages from property developers, using mainly bank credit to carry their inventories of mortgages. Within a relatively short time span, these mortgages are placed with long-term institutional investors. Mortgage bankers supply important services to *both* institutional investors and property developers.

The developers receive a commitment for permanent financing, which allows them to proceed with planned real estate projects. Institutional investors, especially life insurance companies and savings banks, receive mortgages appropriately packaged to match the timing of their cash flows and risk-return preferences. The mortgage banker often secures servicing (loan management and monitoring) fees from institutional investors who purchase the mortgages he or she packages and sells.

22.6 Government Activity in the Mortgage Market

Federal Housing Administration (FHA)

FHA is a division of the Department of Health and Human Services (HUD) at hud.gov

Adequate housing for all citizens has been a major goal of the U.S. government for many years. One of the first steps taken by Congress to achieve this goal was the establishment of the **Federal Housing Administration (FHA)** in 1934. FHA has sought to promote home ownership by reducing the risk to private lenders on residential mortgage contracts, providing home loan insurance. At the same time, efforts have been made to encourage the development of an active secondary market for existing mortgage lenders in order to raise cash to make new loans and to attract new investors into the mortgage business. The combination of government guarantees and the development of a secondary market has led to greater participation in mortgage lending by *long-distance lenders,* such as insurance companies, pension funds, and savings banks. However, government agencies today dominate the mortgage market for low- and moderately priced loans.

The Impact of the Great Depression on Government Involvement in the Mortgage Market

Any attempt to understand how the mortgage market operates today must begin with the Great Depression of the 1930s and the enormous impact that economic calamity had on the market for property loans, especially in the United States. The Great Depression generated massive, unprecedented unemployment; for example, an estimated one-quarter of the U.S. civilian labor force was thrown out of work between 1929 and 1933. Few new mortgage loans were made during this period, and thousands of existing mortgages were foreclosed upon, forcing families to leave their homes. With so many forced sales, property values declined precipitously, endangering the financial solvency of thousands of mortgage lenders. The federal government elected to tackle the mortgage market's problems by moving in several directions at once.

Launching the Federal Home Loan Bank System

Federal Home Loan Bank (FHLB) System

In 1932 the first of the U.S. government agencies aimed at improving the availability of mortgage credit to households—the **Federal Home Loan Bank (FHLB) System**—was created. The FHLB was charged with supervising the activities of savings and loan associations and savings banks and extending loans to these depository institutions, which, at the time, were threatened with heavy withdrawals by panicky depositors. These loans helped to lower the liquidity risk associated with home mortgage lending, spurring private lending institutions to grant more affordable home loans. Prior to the creation of the FHLB System, most home mortgages carried relatively short maturities—for example, no more than five years—in contrast to the long-term (20- to 30-year) home loans most common today. Often, home loans during the 1930s carried a large balloon payment at the end or required the payment of a fee to further extend the loan. Most home buyers could not afford the high payments these shorter-term mortgages required.

The FHLB System was organized somewhat like the Federal Reserve System, with 12 regional home-loan banks supervised by a Federal Housing Finance Board.

The 12 FHL banks are owned by their members, which today include more than 8,000 commercial and savings banks, savings and loans, credit unions, and insurance companies. These institutions are eligible to borrow at the FHL bank in their region. Advances to member institutions may be made for terms as short as 24 hours and as long as 20 years or more.

Setting Up the Federal Housing Administration (FHA) and the Veterans Administration (VA)

In 1934 the National Housing Act was passed, setting up a system of federal insurance for qualified home buyers. The Federal Housing Administration (FHA) was authorized to guarantee repayment of as much as 90 percent of acceptable home loans up to a ceiling amount set by the FHA, encouraging lenders to lend more of a home's market value, charge lower interest rates, and accept longer-term mortgages. Shortly before the end of World War II, the **Veterans Administration (VA)** was created with passage of the Servicemen's Readjustment Act (1944). The VA was designed to aid military personnel returning to civilian life in finding adequate housing. Like the FHA, the VA offered to insure acceptable residential mortgages and helped to reduce the required down payment on a new home.

The Creation of Fannie Mae (FNMA)

The FHA-VA insurance program was an almost instant success and home mortgage lending grew rapidly following its inception. Federal government efforts to create a *resale* (secondary) *market* for residential loans took a little longer, however. In 1938, Fannie Mae—the **Federal National Mortgage Association (FNMA)**—was established for the purpose of buying and selling FHA-guaranteed mortgages in the secondary market. In 1948, FNMA was authorized to trade VA-guaranteed mortgages as well. And in 1968, Fannie Mae became a privately-owned mortgage company whose stock and debt securities could be publicly traded and that could purchase most insured and conventional home mortgage loans. The FNMA issues commitments to purchase a specific dollar amount of mortgages at a predetermined yield, significantly improving the resale potential of most residential mortgages.

Fannie Mae raises money for its mortgage-market ventures primarily by selling short-term notes and longer-term debentures. In addition, in 1981 the FNMA began to issue and guarantee securities backed by conventional mortgage loans purchased from private lenders. Today the majority of Fannie's mortgage-related assets are actually securities backed by various kinds of home mortgages. These FNMA mortgage-backed securities are marketed by lenders that deal directly with the FNMA or through security dealers.[1] Most recently Fannie Mae has branched out to purchase mortgage loans on manufactured housing (principally, mobile homes).

The FNMA holds some of the home mortgages it purchases in its portfolio and *securitizes* the remainder, bundling these loans into pools of similar quality and maturity. Fannie sells claims (securities) against the pooled loans as a way to raise new capital and purchase still more mortgage instruments. It guarantees these mortgage-backed

The VA home loan insurance program is discussed on the Veterans Administration's Web site at va.gov

Veterans Administration (VA)

Federal National Mortgage Association (FNMA)

To learn more about Fannie Mae's mortgage market activities, see fanniemae.com

---

[1]Fannie Mae is the world's largest mortgage bank and for a long time had a virtual monopoly in secondary market trading activities. Early in the 1970s, however, the Mortgage Guarantee Insurance Corporation (MGIC) was organized by a private group in Milwaukee, Wisconsin. Known as Maggie Mae, this corporation pledged to insure conventional home mortgage loans carrying down payments as low as 5 percent. Today, mortgage insurance, provided by a variety of private companies, is often required by lending institutions when the borrower makes a relatively small down payment on the purchase price of a home.

securities against default. Today well over half of U.S. single-family home loans have been placed into pools supporting the issuance of mortgage-backed securities.

The Creation of Ginnie Mae (GNMA)

You can explore the programs used by Ginnie Mae to promote affordable housing at ginniemae.gov

Government National Mortgage Association (GNMA)

Efforts by Congress to make the federal government's budget look better resulted in splitting Fannie Mae into two agencies in 1968. Fannie Mae itself became a private, shareholder-owned corporation devoted to secondary market trading. At the same time, loan programs requiring government subsidies or government credit were handed to a new corporation set up within the Department of Housing and Urban Development, known as the **Government National Mortgage Association (GNMA)**, or Ginnie Mae. In one portion of its program, Ginnie Mae purchases "assistance" mortgages to finance housing for low-income families and then sells these mortgages to FNMA or to private investors.

mortgage-backed securities

pass-throughs

GNMA Mortgage-Backed Securities   Far more important for the secondary market, however, is GNMA's **mortgage-backed securities** program. Backed by the full faith and credit of the U.S. government, Ginnie Mae agrees to *guarantee* principal and interest payments on securities issued by private mortgage institutions if those securities are backed by pools of government-guaranteed mortgages. These so-called **pass-throughs** are popular with institutional lenders and even individuals as safe, readily marketable securities with attractive rates of return. Mortgage lenders raise cash to make new loans by selling the pass-throughs against mortgages that they place in a mortgage pool.

The Federal Home Loan Mortgage Corporation (FHLMC)

Federal Home Loan Mortgage Corporation (FHLMC)

Additional information about Freddie Mac and its activities in the home mortgage market is available at freddiemac.com

To learn more about affordable housing issues see, for example, City Research at cityresearch.com

In 1970, the Emergency Home Finance Act gave birth to the **Federal Home Loan Mortgage Corporation (FHLMC)**, popularly known as *Freddie Mac*, and set up to compete with the FNMA. FHLMC, like Ginnie Mae, combines the mortgages it buys into pools and issues securities against them. Securities issued by Freddie Mac are guaranteed by that agency and have been very popular with investors, particularly savings associations and commercial banks. The creation of Freddie Mac reflected a desire by the federal government to develop a stronger secondary market for *conventional* home mortgages, of which it has purchased huge quantities.

FHLMC Mortgage-Backed Securities   To raise funds to support loan purchases, Freddie Mac sells mortgage participation certificates (PCs) and guaranteed mortgage certificates (GMCs). PCs represent an ownership interest in a pool of conventional mortgages bought and sold by Freddie Mac. FHLMC guarantees the investor's monthly interest and principal payments passed through from the mortgage pool. Guaranteed mortgage certificates (GMCs) are also claims against a pool of mortgages, but they are similar to corporate bonds in that interest is paid semiannually to investors.

Freddie and Fannie Face New Problems   Most recently, both Fannie Mae and Freddie Mac have come under sharp criticism and threats from the U.S. Congress to remove their long-standing special connection to the U.S. government. Fannie and Freddie's ties to the government are reflected in their (as yet, untapped) lines of credit with the U.S. Treasury Department. Investors in the financial markets appear to interpret this close tie-in between Fannie, Freddie, and the U.S. government as a result of the "too-big-to-fail" character of these mortgage-industry giants. If the U.S. government *has* effectively signaled to the marketplace that Fannie and Freddie are not allowed to fail, this tends to raise their credit rating, lower their borrowing cost, and benefit their stockholders because the perceived government tie grants them a competitive advantage over other mortgage-lending institutions.

Recent objections to Fannie and Freddie's government-related privileges have been spurred on by the rapid growth of both agencies, which have been aggressively expanding their market shares of both home mortgage loans and mortgage-backed securities. Bringing this controversy even closer to the boiling point, these government-sponsored enterprises (GSEs) appeared to be facing higher market risk as the new century began and mortgage interest rates approached record lows. Tens of thousands of home owners refinanced their mortgages to take advantage of the exceptionally low interest rates, reducing the expected return on Fannie and Freddie's asset portfolios and creating a bigger mismatch between the maturities of their assets and liabilities. Recent events appear to have made it more likely that Fannie and Freddie will be more closely regulated in the future, probably either by their present federal regulator—the Office of Federal Housing Enterprise Oversight (OFHEO)—or perhaps by a new regulatory agency. Recently OFHEO and Fannie Mae reached an agreement under which Fannie will increase its capital by 30 percent above current levels and carry out a "reaccounting" of its derivatives holdings.

Collateralized Mortgage Obligations (CMOs) and Real Estate Mortgage Investment Conduits (REMICs)

collateralized mortgage obligation (CMO)

real estate mortgage investment conduit (REMIC)

prepayment risk

Another recent innovation in fund-raising by FHLMC is the **collateralized mortgage obligation (CMO)**—a bond whose value is derived from a pool of mortgages packaged together to back (collateralize) the bond. CMOs differ from other mortgage-backed securities in that they are issued in several different maturity classes (*tranches*) based on a projected schedule for repaying the mortgage loans in back of each CMO. A similar instrument that also partitions the principal cash flow from a pool of mortgages or mortgage-backed securities into maturity classes is called a **real estate mortgage investment conduit (REMIC)**. Thus, CMOs and REMICs offer investors a range of different maturities from long-term to short-term and overcome at least some of the cash-flow uncertainty investors face when buying home mortgages themselves because a home owner may pay off his or her loan early—known as **prepayment risk**—resulting in a lower rate of return for the investor.[2] More recently, some mortgage-backed securities have been issued as "strips," in which the investor can receive either principal payments (POs,) from a pool of home mortgages or interest payments (IOs) from the pool, depending on the individual investor's preferences for maturity and risk. Strips make it easier for an investor to reduce interest rate risk using portfolio immunization because their maturity and duration are the same. During the 1990s, CMO trusts began to appear, offering even small investors a share in pools of collateralized mortgage obligations.

Impact of Securitized Mortgages

securitized mortgages

The development of the various types of **securitized mortgages**—debt securities backed by pools of outstanding mortgage loans—by Ginnie Mae, Fannie Mae, and other lending institutions have made mortgage securities more competitive with government securities and corporate stocks and bonds, allowing many mortgage lenders to invade national and international capital markets for funds. The mortgage-backed securities market has expanded tremendously, rising in volume from less than $25 billion in 1981 to more than $4 trillion as the new century opened. Foreign investors by the thousands have become active in

---

[2]For an extended discussion of prepayment risk and the use of portfolio immunization to reduce interest rate risk, see Chapter 7 and 8.

providing new capital to domestic mortgage markets, for example. They have also made it much easier to get old, low-yielding mortgages off lenders' books in order to make room for higher-yielding investments.

On the negative side, however, these new financial instruments have increased the sensitivity of mortgage interest rates to national and international market conditions. Home mortgage rates appear to be more volatile, on average, than in the past. The residential mortgage market has broadened geographically, but at the price of a somewhat less predictable credit market environment.

QUESTIONS TO HELP YOU STUDY

5. List the principal *mortgage lending institutions* in the United States. Which is most important? In what particular areas of the market?

6. Identify the following federal agencies and describe their roles or functions: FHA, VA, FHLB, FNMA, GNMA, and FHLMC.

7. How has the federal government's intervention over the past several decades changed the structure and operation of the home mortgage market? For what reason has all of this been done?

22.7 Innovations in Mortgage Instruments

Fixed-Rate Home Mortgages

fixed-rate home mortgages (FRMs)

Repeatedly in recent years, interest rates have climbed upward, only to fall back during brief recessions and then move upward again. Each upward movement in market interest rates forced mortgage lenders to cut back on the availability of funds for housing. In part, these cutbacks in mortgage funds were a response to the widespread use of **fixed-rate home mortgages (FRMs)**. FRMs return to the lender the same annual interest income (cash flow) regardless of what is happening to inflation or to interest rates. When depository institutions are forced to pay higher rates on their deposits to attract funds, their profits tend to be squeezed because the revenues from FRMs remain unchanged. Of course, these lending institutions are able to charge higher interest rates on *new* mortgage loans, but new loans normally are only a small fraction of an established lending institution's total loan portfolio. The bulk of that portfolio usually is in *old* mortgages, often granted during an era when interest rates were lower.

In short, the FRM amplified the normal up-and-down cycle of earnings for mortgage-lending institutions, leading to low or even negative earnings in periods of rising interest rates and to positive earnings in periods of falling rates. FRMs require the *lender* to bear the risk of interest-rate fluctuations. An alternative to the FRM was needed that both guaranteed lenders a satisfactory real rate of return on mortgage loans and made funds available to home buyers on reasonable terms.

Variable-Rate and Adjustable Mortgage Instruments

variable-rate mortgage (VRM)

The problems created by fixed-rate mortgages ushered in the development of several new mortgage instruments, led by the **variable-rate mortgage (VRM)**, which permits the lender to vary the contractual interest rate on a mortgage loan as market conditions change. Generally, the VRM loan rate is linked to a reference interest rate *not* determined by the lender. For example, the yield on 10-year U.S. Treasury bonds may be used as a reference rate so that, if Treasury bond yields rise, the homeowner pays a higher contractual interest rate. Alternatively, under a broader

adjustable mortgage instrument (AMI), the maturity of the mortgage loan may be lengthened or a combination of interest rate increases and maturity changes may be made as interest rates rise. In some cases, the loan principal can be increased along with interest rate increases, reducing the growth of the homeowner's equity—a process known as *negative amortization*. VRMs and AMIs shift the *risk* of interest rate fluctuations, partially or wholly, from the lender to the borrower.

Under most state and federal laws, changes in the interest rates attached to VRMs are limited as to frequency and amount. However, AMIs, with their options of varying monthly payments, the maturity of a mortgage loan, or the loan principal amount owed as interest rates change, generally face fewer legal restrictions. Many lenders offer *teaser rates* (i.e., loan rates that are temporarily below market levels) in order to get home buyers to commit to a VRM or an AMI instead of taking out a fixed-rate mortgage which bears greater interest rate risk for the lender.

Convertible Mortgages

The volatile interest rates of recent years led to the development of a combination variable-rate, fixed-rate home mortgage loan that some home buyers found attractive. This *convertible mortgage instrument* (CMI) starts out with an adjustable interest rate, but later the home buyer can switch to a fixed-rate mortgage if interest rates look more favorable. However, some loan contracts carry a mandatory holding period before conversion to a fixed-rate loan is permitted and also prohibit switching after a certain length of time has elapsed (such as five years). CMIs have initial adjustable interest rates that are usually lower than those on new fixed-rate mortgages and the switch to a fixed-rate loan in the future typically is cheaper than refinancing an old mortgage.

Another version of the CMI is the *balloon loan*. For example, a borrower may take out a five-year fixed-rate mortgage loan initially, but later on will probably have to refinance this five-year loan with a new longer-term loan because the first loan pays off only a fraction of a home's total cost. Borrowers under a balloon loan often hope to sell their homes before refinancing their mortgage becomes necessary—sometimes a risky proposition if the housing resale market weakens. Both FNMA and FHLMC agreed to begin purchasing balloon loans from lenders during the 1990s.

A very recent variation on the convertible mortgage appeared as the twenty-first century began—a *hybrid mortgage,* which offers a fixed interest rate initially (say, for the first five years). Then for the remainder of the loan the mortgage interest rate can be changed periodically (often once each year). These loans can be inexpensive at first, but they pose considerable borrower risk later on for those homeowners who plan to be in their homes a long time.

Interest-Only Mortgages

The growth of family home ownership and of home mortgage credit early in the 21st century threatened to slow drastically as the economy and job growth leveled out. Many households found themselves in financial trouble, and housing prices soared out of reach for many families. Leading mortgage bankers fought to keep the housing market rally going with some drastic innovations. One of the most risky loan types to emerge has been *interest-only mortgages.*

These unique loans offer borrowers the option of only paying the interest on their home mortgages, without retiring loan principal, for an initial time period. For example, the home buyer might pay a few hundred dollars in interest each month for the first five years of his or her loan. These initial loan payments typically are very low, making home ownership more affordable for scores of families. After the initial low-payment period, however, *both* principal and interest must be paid until the loan reaches maturity (normally in 30 years). Unfortunately for the home buyer, the required monthly payment eventually climbs sharply upward because the principal value of the loan must be retired in a shorter-than-usual time period (say, in 25 years rather than the full term of 30 years). Moreover, the majority of interest-only loans carry an adjustable interest rate. Should market interest rates rise, the home owner faces *both* greater principal payments and higher interest payments at the same time, often amounting to several thousand dollars each month. Particularly for families with weak credit ratings, the risk of losing their home can rise substantially. Careful explanation by mortgage lenders of *both* the advantages and the disadvantages of this unique form of residential mortgage loan appears to be a "must" when dealing with most home loan customers.

Reverse-Annuity Mortgages

A mortgage-financing device that may be of help to older families and retired individuals is the *reverse-annuity mortgage* (RAM). This financial instrument provides income to those who may have already paid off their mortgages but intend to keep their present home. The lender determines the current value of the home and pays the borrower a monthly annuity, amounting to a percentage of the property's value. The loan is secured by a gradually increasing mortgage on the borrower's home. Repayment of the loan occurs when the annuity holder dies, with the loan being discharged against the deceased's estate, or when the home is sold.

Epilogue on the Fixed-Rate Mortgage

It is interesting that, with all the new mortgage instruments developed in recent years, fixed-rate mortgages (FRMs) continue to hold a major share of the residential loan market. This is true even though FRMs usually carry a higher interest rate than adjustable mortgages, at least initially, and higher origination fees and prepayment penalties. One reason appears to be public mistrust of many of the new instruments, coupled with fear of inflation, which would push up the interest rate on a variable-rate loan. Another factor is competition. It is likely, therefore, that *both* FRMs and VRMs will continue to exist side by side in the home mortgage market, each serving the special needs of individual lenders and homeowners.

22.8 Pricing and Other Issues in Home Mortgage Lending

Pricing Home Mortgages and the Treasury Security Market

Whatever type of home mortgage loan we might be looking at today, a key reference interest rate that many mortgage lenders use to determine the appropriate loan rate on new home loans is the 10-year U.S. Treasury bond rate. A comparison of recent 10-year T-bond yields to home mortgage contract rates indicates that mortgage rates move closely with T-bond rates and maintain a yield spread of about 1.6 to 2 percentage points above them, as shown in Exhibit 22.5. That yield spread reflects differences in risk (including default risk, liquidity risk, and prepayment risk) between home mortgage loans and U.S. Treasury securities, the latter among the safest and most readily marketable financial instruments. The use of reference rates from the bond market as guides for home mortgage loan rates ties these two huge capital markets closer together.

EXHIBIT 22.5

Comparison of Home Mortgage Interest Rates and the Annual Yields on Ten-Year U.S. Treasury Bonds

	2001	2002	2003	2004***
Effective interest rate on loans for the purchase of newly built homes*	7.00%	6.44%	5.80%	5.42%
U.S. Treasury 10-year bond rate**	5.02	4.61	4.01	3.83
Yield spread between home mortgage loan rates and 10-Year Treasury bond rates	1.98 %	1.83%	1.79%	1.59%

Source: Board of Governors of the Federal Reserve System and Federal Deposit Insurance Corporation.

*The mortgage rates assume repayment of a 30-year home loan at the end of 10 years.

**The 10-year bond rate is the annual average yield from the U.S. Treasury's constant maturity series.

***2004 figures are averages for March.

Mortgage Lock-Ins, Loan Modifications, and Foreclosures

For most types of home mortgages the borrower wants to know before committing to the purchase of a home: What interest rate am I going to pay? Can I afford the monthly payments that the lender will require? And what if mortgage interest rates rise after I agree to buy that new home, endangering my ability to pay for it?

mortgage lock-ins

For more information on *mortgage lock-ins*, see pueblo.gsa.gov/cic-text/housing/lockins/lockins.txt

This is the purpose of **mortgage lock-ins**. When a borrower "locks in" a mortgage loan rate this means the home mortgage lender agrees to extend a loan offer at the prevailing mortgage interest rate for a specified period (usually 30 to 60 days and sometimes longer). This mortgage "lock-in" device is designed to protect borrowers from an increase in mortgage loan rates before the borrower takes possession of his or her new home.

However, what if market interest rates *fall* instead of rise? Can a borrower get his or her loan revised to capture the new and cheaper loan rate? Many "lock-ins" today grant the borrower additional flexibility by including a so-called "float down" option which usually costs extra. With a "float down" clause, if interest rates fall before the closing on the new home loan occurs, the lender will make the home mortgage loan available at a lower interest rate. Otherwise, if the borrower backs out of a loan agreement because interest rates have fallen, the lender may lose a substantial amount in loan fees. Sometimes, however, even without the floating rate feature, a lender will "give a little" if market interest rates fall, knowing the customer may be more likely to run to another lending institution unless there is some flexibility in setting up a new home loan.

What happens if the loan agreement is made and the borrower takes possession of a new home, only to discover he or she can no longer afford the payments? Usually the home owner will try to sell his or her home as quickly as possible, repay the mortgage with the proceeds of the sale, and move into cheaper housing. If this doesn't happen right away and several payments are missed, the lender is likely to *foreclose,* taking possession of the home and selling it to recover the loaned funds.

However, in recent years a new alternative to foreclosure has become popular—a *loan modification agreement.* Loan modifications are designed to assist troubled borrowers avoid foreclosure, remain in a home, and save the lender the costs of foreclosure, repossession, and the forced sale of a home. They may also result in additional fee income for the mortgage lender.

Loan modifications usually add any missed loan payments to the remaining balance the borrower still owes on a home and a new payment schedule is worked out. Many such agreements lower the required monthly mortgage payment somewhat by stretching out the maturity of the loan. Modification agreements have noticeably slowed foreclosures recently.

You may find it interesting to explore some of the most popular sites for finding lower-cost home mortgage loans. See, for example, elcan.com and lendingtree.com

Refinancing Home Mortgages

In recent years, many homeowners have found that it makes economic sense to convert their existing mortgage loans into *new* loans with lower interest costs because market interest rates have fallen substantially since the original loan was taken out. This happens most often to borrowers carrying a fixed-rate mortgage loan. However, many flexible-rate mortgages also allow the home buyer to convert during the early years of a home loan to a fixed-rate mortgage bearing a lower contract rate in return for a fee.

Is refinancing an existing mortgage loan a wise move for a home buyer? The answer hinges upon whether the savings outweigh the costs over a designated payback period. If mortgage interest rates have dropped at least a percentage point since the borrower took out the first mortgage loan, and the borrower plans to remain in the home long enough to fully recover the costs of refinancing (in many cases about three years), then refinancing through a cheaper new loan is often attractive. The costs of refinancing include the loss of some of the homeowner's interest deduction on federal tax returns due to the lower interest payments on the new loan and the fees ("closing costs") that must be paid in order to set up the new loan. Moreover, loan fees on refinanced property normally are not immediately tax deductible but must be written off gradually over the term of a new loan.

Other than falling interest rates, a strong housing market also can provide an incentive for some households to refinance their homes in order to capture some of the additional equity associated with rising home prices. For example, a homeowner may have paid the mortgage on her house down to 50 percent of the original purchase price of $100,000 or $50,000. However, in the interim (in a strong real estate market), the home may have doubled in value. In this case, the homeowner would actually own 75 percent of the house, now valued at $200,000. Her equity in the house would have risen to $150,000. In this case, the homeowner may elect to extract some of this gain in equity through a "cash out" refinancing of the existing home mortgage. For example, the new mortgage contract might be written for 50 percent of the home's current market value, or $75,000. Because the homeowner owes only $50,000 on the house, she can pay off the old mortgage contract and have $25,000 left over to spend for whatever purposes she desires. Cash-out refinancing can be combined with lower mortgage payments, provided interest rates have fallen, houses are appreciating, and the homeowner chooses to stretch out the maturity of the new mortgage contract.

All of these facets of home refinancing were taking place during the 2000–2002 period when the U.S. housing market was exceptionally strong and mortgage interest rates had fallen to historic lows. Canner, Dynan, and Passmore at the Federal Reserve Board (2002) examined U.S. home refinancing activity from January 2001 through March 2002 and discovered that households had extracted as much as $131 billion from the equity in their homes during this period and reduced their annual mortgage payments by about $18 billion. Most of the "cash-out" money was apparently used to make home improvements, purchase consumer goods, repay debts (especially credit card balances), and purchase selected other assets (such as stocks and bonds).

The ability of a homeowner to obtain refinancing depends critically upon a strong credit history and a significant amount of accumulated equity built up in the home to be refinanced. Increased volatility of interest rates tends to cause homeowners to postpone their plans to refinance their home mortgages. On the other hand, recent structural changes in the home mortgage market (such as greater convenience in finding lenders willing to refinance and in finding the best terms available for getting a new loan) have made it *much* easier for consumers to explore and possibly take advantage of refinancing opportunities.

Predatory Lending

predatory loans

One of the most controversial issues in the history of consumer lending centers on so-called **predatory loans**. Allegedly, some unscrupulous lenders attempt to mislead poorly informed, less well-educated borrowers into taking out high-cost loans, often with their home pledged as collateral. When the borrowers lured into this situation can no longer afford to make their payments, the lender usually either forecloses and takes their home or offers refinancing at an even higher cost to the borrower. Ultimately, the borrowing customer may be forced into bankruptcy.

For further information about the risks associated with predatory lending and how to prevent it, see fdic.gov/consumers/consumer/new

We know that predatory lending occurs. The current debate centers mainly on how to distinguish predatory from legitimate lending practices and how to protect the most vulnerable consumers. One solution is to educate the public about the risks associated with predatory loans—a process being pursued by such agencies as the Federal Deposit Insurance Corporation and the Federal Trade Commission in the United States. However, public education is a time-consuming and uncertain process.

In the interim, federal and state laws have appeared in an attempt to expose predatory lenders. For example, as discussed in Chapter 21, Truth in Lending laws require lenders to fully inform borrowers of all costs associated with a loan and give consumers the opportunity ("right of rescission") to cancel certain loan contracts (such as home equity loans) up to three business days after the loan agreement is signed where the borrower's home is at risk. A somewhat more vague law—the Home Ownership and Equity Protection Act—prohibits lenders from selling home equity loans to a consumer without regard to that customer's ability to repay the loan.

QUESTIONS TO HELP YOU STUDY

8. A number of new mortgage instruments have appeared in recent years. These new financial instruments include variable rate mortgages (VRMs), adjustable mortgage instruments (AMIs), interest only mortgages, and reverse-annuity mortgages (RAMs), in addition to the more conventional fixed-rate mortgages (FRMs). Describe how each of these home mortgage instruments works and what their advantages are.

9. What is a *mortgage lock-in?* Does it benefit the borrower or the lender? When might it not be a good idea?

10. What is a *loan modification agreement?* What is its purpose?

11. What are the advantages and disadvantages of home refinancings? Under what circumstances should a homeowner consider refinancing a home mortgage?

MARKETS ON THE NET: The Most Important Web Sites for This Chapter

A Consumer's Guide to Mortgage Lock-Ins (pueblo.gsa.gov/CIC/text/housing/lockins/lockins.txt)

Federal Deposit Insurance Corporation (fdic.gov/consumers/consumer/news)

Federal Home Loan Mortgage Corporation (freddiemac.com)

Federal National Mortgage Association (fanniemae.com)

Government National Mortgage Association (ginniemae.gov)

Interest Rate Calculator (interestratecalculator.com)

Mortgage Bankers Association of America (mbaa.org)

Summary of the Chapter's Main Points

This chapter has focused on one of the most important markets in the financial system—the market for residential home mortgage credit.

- *Home ownership* has grown in importance in recent years with a record number of households in the United States today (about two-thirds) owning their own homes. The value of homes as a tax-reducing investment and as a hedge against inflation has played a major role in this home ownership trend as has the drive toward more lenient borrowing terms, encouraged by government support of the home mortgage market.

- Among the leading home mortgage lending institutions today are *commercial banks, savings banks* and *savings and loan associations, life insurance companies,* and *mortgage banking firms.*

- U.S. federal government intervention in the home mortgage market began in earnest during the 1930s and 1940s with the creation of several major federal agencies, including the Federal Housing Administration (FHA), the Federal National Mortgage Association (FNMA), the Veterans Administration (VA), and the Government National Mortgage Association (GNMA). These agencies were directed to expand the supply of mortgage credit available and to make mortgages more affordable for a greater proportion of the U.S. population. This was accomplished through such devices as guaranteeing the repayment of selected home mortgages (through FHA and VA) and creating an active resale market for existing home loans (through FNMA and GNMA).

- Later the Federal Home Loan Mortgage Corporation (FHLMC) was created to assist in expanding the supply of home mortgage credit and to aid in the development of security-like mortgage instruments to broaden and deepen the market for mortgage credit.

- Among the most important of new mortgage-related securities developed in recent years to expand the depth and breadth of the residential mortgage market are mortgage-backed securities, collateralized mortgage obligations (CMOs), and real estate mortgage investment conduits (REMICs). Each is based on the notion of pooling together a group of similar home mortgage loans and issuing securities against that pool that will eventually be paid off by the principal and interest payments generated from the pooled loans.

- Mortgage-loan-backed-security instruments have been used to attract millions of new investors to the home mortgage market and to increase the liquidity of mortgage instruments. *Securitized mortgage instruments* have helped make the market for home mortgages a global capital market rather than a regionally isolated marketplace as it was before their invention.

- In order to encourage individuals and families to consider home ownership, many new home mortgage loans and other home financing devices have been developed, some of them making mortgage credit available on more lenient and affordable terms. Examples include variable-rate mortgages (VRMs), adjustable mortgage instruments (AMIs), convertible mortgages, reverse annuity mortgages, and home mortgage refinancings.

- Refinancing of existing home mortgages became popular in the 1990s and early in the new century with record low loan rates. Borrowers became more skilled in using "lock-ins" to protect the interest rate on a new loan from upward interest-rate pressures. However, explosive growth in mortgage lending brought in more high-risk borrowers in danger of losing their homes due to *predatory lending*.

- The home mortgage market today has become one of the largest markets for a single financial instrument on the planet. It has helped to make U.S. citizens among the best-housed individuals in the world and in the process has interconnected the market for home loans with those for bonds. No longer are mortgage-related instruments insensitive to the broad market trends that affect the global economy and the money and capital markets today.

Key Terms Appearing in This Chapter

conventional home mortgage
  loan, 672
residential mortgages, 674
nonresidential mortgages, 674
Federal Housing Administration
  (FHA), 679
Federal Home Loan Bank (FHLB)
  System, 679
Veterans Administration (VA), 680
Federal National Mortgage
  Association (FNMA), 680
Government National Mortgage
  Association (GNMA), 681
mortgage-backed securities, 681
pass-throughs, 681

Federal Home Loan Mortgage
  Corporation (FHLMC), 681
collateralized mortgage obligation
  (CMO), 682
real estate mortgage investment
  conduit (REMIC), 682
prepayment risk, 682
securitized mortgages, 682
fixed-rate home mortgage (FRMs), 683
variable-rate mortgage (VRM), 683
adjustable mortgage instrument
  (AMI), 684
mortgage lock-ins, 686
predatory loans, 688

Problems and Issues

1. John George owns a home that he purchased for $100,000 ten years ago with a 30-year fixed-rate mortgage at a 6 percent annual rate of interest. Today he owes $60,000 on the house, which has since doubled in value.

    a. If John George were to refinance his house today, his bank would write a new mortgage for 85 percent of the market value of his house, out of which he would be required to pay fees and points equal to 1 percent of the new mortgage. How much equity could he "cash out" of his house? If he financed the maximum the bank would allow, how much money would he receive in a direct payment from the bank?

    b. Assuming that the new home mortgage in part (a) carries an interest rate of 5 percent and the new loan is for 30 years, by how much would John's monthly mortgage payments change? (Use a financial calculator or go to **lendingtree.com** and use this Web site's online payment calculator.)

    c. What would the payments be on the new mortgage in part (a) if John George were to choose a 15-year mortgage contract at a 4.75 percent annual rate?

    d. What are the advantages and disadvantages of the new mortgage described in part (b) versus the loan described in part (c)?

2. FNMA ("Fannie Mae") and FHLMC ("Freddie Mac") were established by the U.S. Congress during the 1930s and the 1970s to "add liquidity" to the home mortgage market. Explain how they achieve this objective. How does this work to the benefit of consumers?

3. Unlike Fannie Mae and Freddie Mac, which are private firms, GNMA (Ginnie Mae) is a government agency. Why would it not be possible to "privatize" Ginnie Mae and allow it to continue to carry out the function it was originally set up to perform?

4. Which mortgage instruments meet the definitions provided below?

   a. A home mortgage loan under which some of the terms of the loan, such as the loan rate or maturity of the loan, varies as market conditions change.

   b. A mortgage loan that begins with an adjustable loan rate that can be switched later to a fixed loan rate.

   c. Debt securities backed by pools of mortgage loans.

   d. Mortgage-backed securities issued in a range of maturity classes so that prepayment risk can be more easily selected to match an investor's particular investment goals.

   e. Home mortgage loan carrying an interest rate that varies during the term of a loan, generally depending on the movement of interest rates in the open market.

   f. Provides income to those who have already paid off their mortgage but wish to receive a cash inflow (income) based on the value of the equity in their home.

Standard & Poor's Market Insight and Web-Based Problems

STANDARD &POOR'S

1. The purpose of this exercise is to gain an understanding of the government-sponsored agency Fannie Mae (the Federal National Mortgage Association) by comparing its business activities with those of one of the largest commercial banks in the U.S., Bank of America (BAC). The information is drawn from S&P's Market Insight Web site at **mhhe.com/edumarketinsight**.

   a. Visit the S&P Market Insight Web site and click the "Company" tab. For each ticker symbol, FNM and BAC, locate the two firms' respective business plans under "Long Bus. Des."

   b. From the information in part (a) describe how these two financial-service entities differ in terms of their perceived "mission," the markets they serve, and the geographic reach of their operations.

   c. Go to their most recent financial highlights ("Financial Hlts.") and identify the most significant differences between these two financial-service firms from the information provided. (Note: An explanation of each of the statistics listed, such as "Debt/Equity," can be found by clicking on that name.) Offer some plausible explanations for the observations you make with the help of the information gathered in part (b).

2. Exploring Web site information on *mortgage lock-ins* (for example, at **pueblo.gsa.gov/cic-text/housing/lockins** and other Web sources), explain the purpose of a mortgage lock-in and who it is supposed to benefit. List the

advantages and potential disadvantages of lock-ins for the home mortgage borrower.

3. Recently two mortgage industry leaders—Fannie Mae and Freddie Mac—have been at the center of a raging controversy. Using such Web sites as **fanniemae.com, freddiemac.com**, and **federalreserve.gov** explain the two sides of this controversy—that is, the point of view of the two mortgage agencies and the point of view of competing lenders and the public. The U.S. Congress is debating new legislation to tighten government oversight of Fannie and Freddie as well as other government-sponsored enterprises (GSEs). Based on your review of the arguments, what do you think this legislation should contain?

4. Suppose you are searching for a new home and need a mortgage loan to help finance it. Exploring Web sites such as **house4sale-online.com, interestratecalculator.com**, and **buyersresource.com**, along with other sites you uncover, describe the price range of homes for sale in your area. Using a mortgage rate calculator on the Web, which of these homes could you afford to take on with your current budget and income? With the personal income and budget you hope to have five years from now?

Selected References to Explore

Canner, Glenn; Karen Dynan; and Wayne Passmore. "Mortgage Refinancing in 2001 and Early 2002." *Federal Reserve Bulletin,* December 2002, pp. 409–81.

Duca, John V. "How Vulnerable Are Housing Prices?" *Southwest Economy,* Federal Reserve Bank of Dallas, no. 2 (March/April 2004).

Emmons, William R.; Mark D. Vaughan; and Timothy J. Yeager. "The Housing Giants in Plain View." *Regional Economist,* Federal Reserve Bank of St. Louis, July 2004, pp. 5–9.

Federal Deposit Insurance Corporation. "High-Cost 'Predatory' Home Loans: How to Avoid the Traps." *FDIC Consumer News*, Summer 2002.

Federal Reserve Bank of New York. "Policies to Promote Affordable Housing." *Economic Policy Review* 9, no. 2 (June 2003).

Part 7

The International Financial System

Today, no nation can view its financial system as being isolated from the global money and capital markets. In the financial marketplace of the modern era, trading of financial services and assets circles the globe, 24 hours a day, with few impediments to the exchange of information and the flow of capital from one spot on the planet to another. As the international sector has grown, international financial institutions and the global storage and transfer of financial data have grown and improved along with it. There is greater interest today almost everywhere in the promotion of trade between nations. But global trade depends heavily upon global financial services, especially the efficient transmission of payments and the extension of credit, wherever it is most needed.

Moreover, financial market participants in every corner of the globe follow daily financial developments. Today's lenders and borrowers and savers and investors increasingly recognize that the value of the assets—both financial and nonfinancial—that they hold is often sensitive to happenings half a world away. There are few places for financial market players to hide anymore.

In Part Seven, we turn initially to a key source of international financial information—a nation's balance of payments—and also examine the fundamental determinants of exchange rates between different national currencies (such as the dollar and the euro). We also explore how international banks are structured and what services they supply to their customers all over the globe. As you will see, despite all the great technological advances reshaping our world today, the international financial system still faces great risks even as it provides great benefits and essential financial services to businesses and consumers all over the globe.

Chapter 23

International Transactions and Currency Values

Learning Objectives

in This Chapter

- You will explore the functions and roles performed by the international markets within the global financial system.
- You will see how international payments for goods and services are made and how international borrowing and lending can be tracked through a nation's *balance-of-payments accounts*.
- You will come to understand how the values of *national currencies* (such as the dollar and the euro) are determined within the modern financial system.

What's in This Chapter?
Key Topics Outline

23.1 Introduction to International Transactions and Currency Values

In many ways, the world we live in is rapidly shrinking. Jet planes race across the Atlantic between New York and London in less than four hours, about the same time it takes a jetliner to travel across the United States. Broad-band transmissions and the Internet, fax machines, cell phones, and fiber optic cable move financial information from one spot on the globe to another in seconds. Orbiting satellites bring news of major international significance to home television sets and computer screens the moment an event takes place and make possible direct communication between those involved in international business transactions.

Accompanying these dramatic improvements in communication and transportation is enormous growth in world trade and international investment. For example, in 1965 total exports of goods and services worldwide reached $190 billion. By the twenty-first century, the estimated dollar value of world trade had climbed to close to $6 trillion, or more than half as much as the U.S. gross domestic product (GDP). Moreover, the United States itself has become increasingly dependent on world trade. For example, imports into the United States represented less than 5 percent of GDP in 1960 but had jumped to about 15 percent of GDP in 2003; U.S. exports climbed from 6 percent to about 10 percent of GDP over the same period. Thus, roughly a quarter of the value of production and spending in the U.S. economy stems from foreign trade. The international financial markets have had to grow rapidly just to keep up with the expansion in world trade.

Actually, international financial markets perform the same basic functions as domestic financial markets. They bring international lenders of funds in contact with borrowers, thereby permitting an increased flow of scarce funds toward their most productive uses. The volume of capital investment worldwide is made larger because of the workings of the global financial system. And with increased capital investment, the productivity of individual firms and nations is increased and economic growth in the international sector accelerates. The international financial markets also facilitate the flow of consumer goods and services across national boundaries, making possible an optimal allocation of resources in response to consumer demand on a global scale. With increased efficiency in resource use, the output of consumer goods and services is increased and costs of production are minimized.[1]

23.2 The Balance-of-Payments (BOP) Accounts

balance-of-payments (BOP) accounts

One of the most widely used sources of information concerning flows of funds, goods, and services between nations is each country's **balance-of-payments (BOP) accounts**. This annual statistical report summarizes all of the economic and financial transactions between residents of one nation and the rest of the world during a specific period of time. The BOP accounts reflect *changes* in the assets and liabilities of economic units—businesses, individuals, and governments—involved in international transactions. The major transactions captured in the BOP accounts include exports and imports of goods and services, income from investments made abroad, government loans and military expenditures overseas, and private capital flows between nations.

---

[1]These benefits from international trade and finance are most likely to occur if each nation follows the principle of *comparative advantage*. This principle argues that each country will have a higher real standard of living if it specializes in the production of those goods and services in which it has a comparative advantage in cost and imports those goods and services where it is at a comparative cost disadvantage. The principle of comparative advantage seems to work best in an environment of free trade that permits nations to specialize in their most efficient activities.

In a statistical sense, a nation's BOP accounts are always "in balance," because double-entry bookkeeping is used. For example, every payment made for goods and services imported from abroad simultaneously creates a claim on the home country's resources or extinguishes an existing liability. Similarly, every time a domestic business firm receives payment from overseas, it either acquires a claim against resources in a foreign country, or a claim that firm held against a foreign individual or institution is erased. In practice, however, imbalances frequently show up in the BOP accounts due to unreported transactions or inconsistencies in reporting. These errors and omissions are handled through a Statistical Discrepancy account.

The U.S. Balance of International Payments

The U.S. BOP accounts are published quarterly by the Department of Commerce. The quarterly figures are then *annualized* to permit comparisons across years. The transactions recorded in the balance of payments fall into three broad groups:

1. *Transactions on current account,* which include imports and exports of goods and services and unilateral transfers (gifts).

2. *Transactions on capital account,* which include both long- and short-term investment at home and abroad and usually involve the transfer of financial assets (bonds, deposits, etc.).

3. *Official reserve transactions,* which are used by monetary authorities (the Treasury, central bank, etc.) to settle BOP deficits, usually through transferring the ownership of official reserve assets to countries with BOP surpluses.

Transactions that bring about an inflow of foreign currency into the home country are recorded as *credits* (+). Transactions resulting in an outflow of foreign currency from the home country are listed as *debits* (−). Thus, credit (+) items in the BOP represent an increase in a nation's buying power abroad. Debit (−) items represent decreases in a nation's buying power abroad. If a country sells goods and services or borrows abroad, these transactions are credit items because they increase external buying power. On the other hand, a purchase of goods and services abroad or a paydown of a nation's international liabilities is a debit item because that country is surrendering part of its external buying power. A summary of the major credit and debit items making up the BOP accounts is shown in Exhibit 23.1.

The international transactions that made up the U.S. balance of payments from 1998 to 2003 are shown in Exhibit 23.2. These U.S. international transactions are subdivided into categories—the current account, the capital account, and residual items (including

EXHIBIT 23.1 **Principal Credit and Debit Items Recorded in a Nation's Balance of Payments (BOP)**	Credit Entries (Inflows of Funds, +)	Debit Entries (Outflows of Funds, −)
	Exports of merchandise	Imports of merchandise
	Services provided to citizens of foreign countries	Services provided to domestic citizens by foreign countries
	Interest and dividends due domestic citizens from business firms abroad	Gifts of money sent abroad by domestic citizens
	Remittances received from domestic citizens employed in foreign countries	Capital invested abroad by domestic citizens
	Foreign purchases of securities issued by domestic firms and units of government	Dividend and interest payments to foreign countries on investments made in the domestic country
	Repayments by foreigners of funds borrowed from domestic lending institutions	

EXHIBIT 23.2	U.S. International Transactions, 1998–2003 ($ Billions except as noted)					
Item	1998	1999	2000	2001	2002	2003
Trade in goods and services, net	$−165	$−263	$−378	$−363	$−422	$−497
Goods, net	−247	−346	−452	−427	−483	−548
Services, net	82	83	74	64	−61	51
Investment income, net	8	18	25	29	13	39
Compensation of employees, net	−5	−5	−5	−5	−5	−6
Unilateral transfers, net	−48	−47	−56	−47	−59	−67
Current account balance	$−210	$−297	$−413	$−386	$−474	$−531
Official capital, net	$−27	$55	$42	$23	$111	$251
Private capital, net	103	182	436	393	456	295
Financial account balance	$76	$237	$477	$416	$570	$546
Capital account balance	−1	−5	−1	−1	−1	−3
Statistical discrepancy	$135	$65	$−63	$−29	$95	$−12
Memo: Current account as percent of GDP	−2.4%	−3.2%	−4.2%	−3.8%	−4.5%	−4.8%

Note: Components may not sum to totals due to rounding.

Source: U.S. Department of Commerce, Bureau of Economic Analysis (BEA): U.S. international transactions accounts; and Board of Governors of the Federal Reserve System, *Federal Reserve Bulletin*, selected issues.

a sizeable statistical discrepancy due to unreported transactions)—that help us to understand how the BOP bookkeeping system works.

The Current Account

current account

One of the most publicized components of U.S. international transactions in recent years has been the **current account**. Its most important components include:

1. The *merchandise trade balance,* comparing the volume of goods exported to the volume of goods imported.

2. The *service balance,* comparing exports and imports of services.

3. *Net investment income,* measuring income from investments in assets purchased abroad less income from domestic assets purchased by foreigners.

4. *Compensation of employees,* tracking wages for domestic workers employed overseas relative to wages flowing to foreigners working in the domestic economy.

5. *Unilateral transfers,* reflecting the amount of gifts and grants made to foreigners by domestic citizens and institutions less gifts and grants from foreigners to units in the domestic economy.

The Merchandise Trade Balance in the Current Account Prior to the 1970s, the United States often reported a positive merchandise trade balance (surplus), with exports exceeding imports, due in part to substantial demand for U.S. agricultural products and for U.S. equipment overseas. However, since that time, a combination of factors, including rising oil prices, inflation, and the preferences of many Americans for foreign automobiles, TVs, and other goods, has turned what historically were trade surpluses for the United States into substantial trade deficits. (In other words, U.S. *sources* of external buying power have fallen short of U.S. *uses* of external buying power.) The United States's merchandise trade *deficit*—labeled "Goods, net" in Exhibit 23.2—reached nearly $550 billion in 2003, more than doubling in five years as the nominal value of imports into the United States rose significantly.

The Service Balance in the Current Account

If Americans typically have purchased a greater volume of goods from abroad in recent years than they have sold abroad, how has this deficit (debit balance) in the goods account been paid for? Historically, part of the needed funds has come from the *service balance*—sales of services sold to foreign entities less sales of services to U.S. individuals and institutions. Services normally included in the BOP accounts include insurance policies covering the shipment of goods overseas, international transportation services and hotel accommodations, entertainment, and medical care for persons traveling outside their home country. While still fairly substantial, net service income for the U.S. has declined in recent years, brought on, in part, by more U.S. citizens traveling abroad. Net revenues from U.S. services sold to foreigners amounted to just over $50 billion in 2003.

Investment Income in the Current Account

Americans have invested heavily in foreign ventures of many kinds—from banks to boutiques—generating substantial investment income flowing into the United States each year. However, as the new century dawned, investments of foreigners inside the United States continued to expand rapidly and these assets frequently paid out higher rates of return than many American investments abroad. Nevertheless, the difference between U.S. investment income received from abroad less foreign investment income received from the U.S. has remained positive, helping to mitigate America's current account deficit somewhat.

Compensation of Employees in the Current Account

The BOP's current account also reports the *net* amount of wages earned by U.S. residents working abroad relative to the wages paid to foreign workers currently employed inside the United States. The difference between these two income flows is labeled "compensation of employees, net". We note in Exhibit 23.2 that, during 2003, foreigners employed in the U.S. received $6 billion *more* in wages than U.S. residents at work overseas—one of the consequences of the large volume of investments foreigners have made inside the United States in recent years.

Unilateral Transfers in the Current Account

Another type of international transaction recorded in a BOP's current account, labeled *unilateral transfers,* consists mainly of gifts and grants from U.S. residents and institutions to foreigners less foreign gifts and grants to U.S. units. These transactions are called "unilateral" because they represent a *one-way flow of resources* with nothing expected in return. Typically, U.S. gift-giving far exceeds the return flow. For example, gifts and grants to foreigners from Americans were an estimated $67 billion larger than foreign gifts and grants flowing into the United States in 2003. Each gift and grant sent overseas represents the *use* of the contributing nation's external buying power and, therefore, is recorded as a debit ($-$) item in its BOP.

The Balance on Current Account

When we put the above components—trade in goods and services, investment income, compensation of employees, and unilateral transfers—together, we derive the *balance on current account*. The U.S. balance on current account in 2003 was a debit ($-$) item balance, estimated at just over $530 billion—a record number both in dollar terms and relative to the nation's total output of goods and services (the GDP).

What are some of the possible consequences of persistent current account deficits? A nation running current account deficits surrenders claims on its future income to foreign individuals and institutions. That is, a current account deficit generates net borrowing from abroad. In order to induce foreign investors to lend their funds to help cover a current account deficit, domestic market interest rates may need to be pushed higher, which *may*, in turn, slow domestic purchases of goods and services, increase unemployment, and lower domestic living standards.

The Capital Account

capital account

One of the most important institutions today in shaping global trading of goods and services is the World Trade Organization (WTO). See the Web site of this institution at wto.org

The flow of funds destined for investment in assets overseas is recorded in the **capital account**. The capital accounts in a nation's BOP are often divided into two major subcategories: *net private capital flows* between private individuals and institutions, and *net official capital flows,* involving governments, central banks, and government agencies of various kinds. Capital investment activity abroad also may be divided into (1) short-term capital flows, (2) direct investments, and (3) portfolio investments. *Short-term capital flows* reflect purchases of financial assets with maturities under a year (principally bank deposits, government notes and bills, and foreign currencies). In contrast, *direct investments* and *portfolio investments* represent long-term commitments of funds, involving the acquisition of foreign financial and nonfinancial assets having a maturity of more than a year.[2] For example, a U.S. automobile company building an assembly plant in Germany is making a direct investment abroad, while a U.S. security dealer purchasing the stock of a French company and holding it for two years is making a portfolio investment. When American citizens buy six-month British Treasury bills, they are making short-term capital investments overseas.

Of course, capital investments flow both ways. For example, in 2003, U.S. citizens and private organizations invested about $285 billion in capital assets overseas, while foreign individuals and private institutions invested just over $580 billion in U.S. assets of various kinds. The result was a *net private capital inflow* into the United States from abroad of $295 billion. U.S. banks, hotels, energy and insurance companies, and numerous other firms have all been acquisition targets for foreign investors. As a result of these heavy foreign capital flows into the United States in recent years, America's *net investment position*—holdings of foreign assets by U.S. individuals and institutions less holdings of U.S. assets by foreign individuals and institutions—went from positive to negative about two decades ago and has continued to head downward in recent years. On the positive side, this negative investment position has enabled the U.S. to finance a substantial portion of its merchandise trade deficit and has supported the creation of new U.S. businesses and additional jobs.

Official Transactions

When a nation has a BOP deficit, it must settle up with other nations by surrendering assets or claims to foreign accounts. *Official capital flows* usually consist of the movement of assets that are readily transferable in order to make international payments—for example, transferring the ownership of gold, convertible foreign currencies (such as the dollar, the euro, and the yen), deposits held in the International Monetary Fund

[2]What is the essential difference between *direct investment* and *portfolio investment?* The key factor is *control.* Portfolio investment involves purchasing securities (especially stocks and bonds) to hold in order to earn interest or dividend income. Direct investment, on the other hand, refers to the purchase of a loan or the acquisition of ownership shares in an attempt to control a foreign firm. The U.S. Department of Commerce defines direct investment as ownership of 10 percent or more of the voting stock or the exercise of other means of control of a foreign business enterprise by an individual or corporation. Ownership of less than 10 percent of a foreign firm's stock is usually referred to as portfolio investment.

(IMF) that may be readily transferred from the account of one IMF-member nation to that of another, and special drawing rights (SDRs or "paper gold"), which we will discuss later in this chapter.

When assets available for making international payments *increase,* this represents expanded external buying power by the nation experiencing the increase. On the other hand, a *decrease* in official capital represents a decline in external buying power by the nation experiencing the decrease. If a country has a credit (surplus) balance in its international accounts, its official capital position generally improves, indicating an excess of sales abroad over foreign purchases. Conversely, a nation experiencing a debit (deficit) balance in its international accounts usually finds its official capital position weakening. Such a decline may be temporarily offset, however, by borrowings through its central bank, treasury department, or other government agency.

In 2003, for example, with the United States experiencing a record BOP deficit, foreign governments and central banks increased their holdings of gold, currencies, and other official assets in the United States by just over $250 billion, net. As we noted earlier, most U.S. BOP deficits in recent years have financed themselves primarily through changes in official capital and through private capital inflows from abroad (especially purchases of U.S. stocks and bonds by foreign investors). This preference of foreign governments and foreign private investors for U.S. securities continued to grow over the past decade as the U.S. economy, despite a significant slowdown, looked relatively strong compared to many weaker economies abroad.

Disequilibrium in the Balance of Payments

For an exploration of some of the key issues surrounding balance-of-payments deficits see, for example, The International Monetary Fund at imf.org and the Hoover Institute for Public Policy Inquiry at imfsite.org

For several years now, the United States has displayed a *disequilibrium* position in its balance of payments. The U.S. has relied on foreign credit, foreign capital inflows, and its stock of gold, foreign currencies, and other official assets to settle U.S. BOP deficits. However, the amount of these financial devices is limited—no nation can go on indefinitely accumulating BOP deficits, borrowing abroad, and using up its official assets. Moreover, relying on foreign capital inflows can be dangerous, because the perceptions of foreign investors regarding the desirability of placing funds in the United States may change abruptly due to wars, stock market declines, and so on.

To this point, foreign central banks and foreign investors have regarded U.S. securities and dollar-denominated deposits as good investments and have been willing to extend an increasing volume of international credit to the United States. At some point, however, foreign governments and private investors *may* become satiated with dollar claims; at this point, the value of the U.S. dollar would tend to decline in international markets. U.S. purchases of goods and services abroad also would tend to decline because of the dollar's reduced buying power. The nation's standard of living would tend to fall until equilibrium in its balance-of-payments position was restored.

One factor that gives hope for the future lies in the capital account. As we noted earlier, in most of the years over the past several decades capital inflows into the United States have grown faster than U.S. investments abroad, making the United States the world's largest debtor nation. A major factor boosting foreign investment in the United States is the desire to avoid U.S. import restrictions by developing production facilities inside the United States (as many foreign automobile and electronics manufacturers have recently done, for example). Even more significant is the political stability of the United States, offering an attractive haven for international investors concerned about instability abroad. If this capital inflow continues to grow in the future, it will do much to alleviate the future international payments problems of the United States.

Japan contains the world's second largest economy—sandwiched (in terms of volume of output) between the United States and Germany—and, therefore, is large enough to substantially affect the economies of its major trading partners in Europe, Asia, and North America.

When Japan plummeted into a prolonged economic recession that began in 1990, its economic downslide sent ominous warnings across the planet. Of greatest concern to Japan's principal trading partners, such as the U.S., was evidence of plummeting prices for Japanese goods, services, and financial assets—*deflation*. For example, the value of Japanese stocks fell nearly 80 percent between 1989 and 2003, while the value of Japanese land dropped about 70 percentage points on average. That nation's unemployment rate nearly tripled and scores of Japanese banks failed due to a torrent of bad loans. Moreover, the Japanese government's debt soared to about 1.4 times that nation's GDP—more than double the U.S. government's debt-to-GDP ratio.

Concern arose throughout the global financial system that this adverse trend would infect other nations, including the United States. While Japan has had a trade *surplus* for close to half a century, the U.S.—the world's largest debtor nation—has depended critically upon Japan—the globe's biggest foreign investor—to help support the huge American trade deficit by its willingness to buy and hold billions of dollars in U.S. bonds and stocks.

Only with the dawn of the new century has Japan shown signs of a gradual economic and financial recovery, holding out the promise of renewed economic expansion as the new century unfolds.

QUESTIONS TO HELP YOU STUDY

1. Explain what is meant by the term *balance of payments*. Describe and list the principal components of a nation's balance-of-payments accounts.

2. Supply a brief definition of each of the following terms associated with the balance-of-payments accounts:

   Current account

   Merchandise trade balance

   Service transactions

   Official reserve assets

   Capital account

3. Describe and then discuss the major trends that have occurred in the following segments of the United States' balance-of-payments accounts in recent years:

   Merchandise trade balance

   Investments in overseas assets by U.S. residents

   Investments in United States assets by foreign residents.

4. When is a *balance-of-payments* deficit potentially a "bad" sign? In what sense can such deficits reflect possibly favorable trends.

23.3 The Problem of Different Monetary Units in International Trade and Finance

Businesses and individuals trading goods and services in international markets encounter a problem not experienced by those who buy and sell only in domestic markets. This is the problem of different monetary units used as the standard of value from country to country. Americans use the dollar as a medium of exchange and standard of value in domestic markets, while the European Union (EU) relies on the euro as its basic monetary unit. There are more than 100 different monetary units around the world. As a result, when goods and services are sold or capital flows across national boundaries, it is often necessary to sell one currency and buy another.

Unfortunately, the act of trading currencies entails substantial *risk*. Exporters and importers may be forced to purchase a foreign currency when its value is rising and the home country's currency is falling in value. Any profits earned on the sale of goods and services abroad may be outweighed by losses suffered in currency exchange. Differing monetary units also complicate government monetary policy aimed at curbing inflation and ensuring rapid economic growth. Repeatedly in recent years, massive flows of funds surged through foreign and domestic markets from speculative buying and selling of dollars, euros, and other currencies. These speculative currency flows increased the problems associated with economic recovery, the control of inflation, and balance-of-payments (BOP) deficits.

The Gold Standard

The problem of trading in different monetary units whose prices change frequently is one of the world's oldest financial problems. It has been dealt with in a wide variety of ways over the centuries. One of the most successful solutions prior to the modern era centered on *gold* as an international standard of value. During the seventeenth and eighteenth centuries, major trading nations in Western Europe made their currencies freely convertible into gold. Gold bullion could be exported and imported from one country to another without significant restriction, and each unit of currency was defined in terms of so many grains of fine gold. Nations adopting the **gold standard** agreed to exchange paper money or coins for gold bullion in unlimited amounts at predetermined prices.

gold standard

One advantage of the gold standard was that it imposed a common standard of value for all national currencies. This brought a measure of stability to international trade and investment, dampened interest-rate fluctuations, and stimulated the expansion of commerce and investment abroad. A second advantage was economic discipline. Tying currencies to gold regulated the growth and stability of national economies. A nation experiencing severe inflation or excessively rapid growth in consumption of imported goods soon found itself losing gold reserves to settle balance-of-payments deficits. Exports declined and unemployment rose. Eventually, the volume of imports was curtailed, and the outflow of gold slowed.

These advantages of stability and economic discipline were offset by a number of limitations inherent in the gold standard. For one thing, maintenance of that standard depended crucially on *free trade*. Nations desiring to protect their industries from foreign competition through export or import restrictions could not do so. Moreover, the growth of a nation's money supply was limited by the size of its gold stock. Problems of rising unemployment or lagging economic growth might call for expansion of the domestic money supply. However, such a policy could require a suspension of gold convertibility, taking a nation off the gold standard. Thus, the gold standard sometimes conflicted with national economic goals and limited the policy alternatives open to governmental authorities.

The Gold Exchange Standard

Although government policymakers were mainly concerned about the effects of the gold standard on domestic economies, investors and commercial traders found that gold bullion was not a convenient medium of exchange, especially in settling payments differences between nations. Gold is expensive to transport and risky to handle.

gold exchange standard

Moreover, the world's gold supply was limited relative to the expanding volume of international trade. These problems gave rise in the nineteenth century to the **gold exchange standard.** Institutions actively engaged in international commerce began to hold stocks of convertible currencies. Each currency was freely convertible into gold at a fixed rate but also was freely convertible into other currencies at relatively stable prices. In practice, transactions took place in convertible currencies, and gold faded into the background as an international medium of exchange.

Unfortunately, this monetary standard possessed many of the same limitations as the original gold standard. National currencies were still tied to gold, and growth in world trade depended upon growth in the international gold stock. The gold exchange standard collapsed during the economic chaos of the worldwide Great Depression in the 1930s.

The Modified Exchange Standard

modified exchange standard

Dissatisfaction with international monetary systems tied exclusively to gold resulted in a search for a new payments system. In 1944, Western countries convened at an international monetary conference in Bretton Woods, New Hampshire, to devise a stable money and payments system. The conference created a new mechanism called the Bretton Woods System, or **modified exchange standard**—and an agency for monitoring the exchange rate practices of member nations (known as the International Monetary Fund, or IMF, with headquarters in Washington, DC).

The IMF, which is headed by its Board of Governors with a representative from each member nation, establishes rules for settling international accounts between nations and grants short-term loans to member nations that lack sufficient international reserves to settle their BOP deficits. IMF balance-of-payments loans often are accompanied by strict requirements that a member nation receiving credit must adopt stern economic measures to curtail the growth of its imports and expand its sales abroad. The IMF's credit guarantee encourages banks and other nations to grant loans to a member nation in trouble. The funds loaned by the IMF come mainly from *quotas,* which each member nation must contribute in dollars or other official reserve assets. A companion organization to the IMF, the *World Bank,* also created under the Bretton Woods Agreement, makes loans to speed the long-term economic development of member nations.

For further details on the important international services provided by the World Bank and the International Monetary Fund, see worldbank.org and imf.org

The centerpiece of the Bretton Woods System was the linking of foreign currency prices to the U.S. dollar and to gold. The United States committed itself to buy and sell gold at $35 per ounce on request from foreign monetary authorities. Other IMF member nations pledged to keep their currency's price within 1 percent of its par value in terms of gold or the dollar. Central banks would use their reserves to buy or sell their own currency in the foreign exchange market. In practice, this usually meant that, if a foreign currency fell in value *below* par (the lower intervention point), a central bank would sell its holdings of dollars and buy that currency in the market, driving its price upward toward par. If the price of a nation's currency rose more than 1 percent *above* par (the upper intervention point), the central bank involved would sell its own currency and buy dollars, driving the currency's price down toward par. If a currency fell too far or rose too high, resulting in market disruption and threatening a massive loss of foreign exchange reserves, the country involved would simply revalue its currency, establishing a new par value relative to gold or the dollar.

Fundamentally, the success of the Bretton Woods System depended on the ability of the United States to maintain confidence in the U.S. dollar and protect its value. One of the weaknesses of the new system was that the U.S. dollar was in short supply early in the postwar period, though the system worked well at first because the dollar was the most stable monetary medium around. Later, however, the United States began to export large amounts of capital to Western Europe, Asia, and Central and South America. The result was sizable U.S. trade deficits that were dealt with by drains on the U.S. gold stock and by a buildup of dollar holdings abroad—an indication of fundamental problems developing in the U.S. and in the international payments system.

The Managed Floating Currency Standard

Inflation and other economic problems ultimately forced the abandonment of the Bretton Woods System during the 1970s. The first step in dismantling the old system was taken by the administration of President Richard M. Nixon in August 1971, when the U.S. dollar was devalued and the convertibility of foreign official holdings of dollars into gold suspended. Gold became a commodity only and not an international monetary medium. Soon, the largest IMF member nations were allowing their currencies to *float* in value, responding freely to demand and supply forces in the marketplace.

managed floating currency standard

In 1978, the **managed floating currency standard** was adopted by member nations of the IMF. Known as the Second Amendment to the International Monetary Fund's Articles of Agreement, the official rules under which today's international money system is supposed to operate allow *each nation to choose its own exchange rate policy, consistent with the structure of its economy and its goals*. There are, however, three principles that each member country must follow in establishing its exchange rate policy:

1. When a nation intervenes in the foreign exchange markets to protect its own currency, it must take into account the interests and welfare of other IMF member countries.

2. Government intervention in the foreign exchange markets should be carried out to correct disorderly conditions that are essentially short term in nature.

3. No member nation should intervene in the exchange markets in order to gain an unfair competitive advantage over other nations or to prevent necessary adjustments in a nation's balance-of-payments (BOP) position.

Nations that attempt to keep the exchange value of their currencies within a fixed range around the value of some other currency or basket of currencies are known as *peggers*. (For example, China over the last decade attempted to keep the yuan–dollar exchange rate at 8.3 yuan per U.S. dollar. The majority of pegging nations are developing countries that have strong commercial links with one or more industrialized trading partners. (Examples include Korea, Guatemala, Hong Kong, and Venezuela, which have, from time to time, connected the exchange rate on their currencies to the U.S. dollar.) Frequently, when a developing country has strong trade relations with more than one industrialized nation, it uses a basket (group) of major currencies to set the value of its own monetary unit in order to "average out" fluctuations in the value of its exports and imports.

special drawing rights (SDRs)

A few nations have, from time to time, pegged their currency's exchange rate to a basket of currencies assembled by the International Monetary Fund, known as **special drawing rights (SDRs)**. The SDR was originally created to help settle international claims arising from transactions between the IMF, governments of member nations, central banks, and various international agencies. SDRs are really "book entries" on the ledgers of the IMF, sometimes referred to as *paper gold*. Periodically, that organization issues new SDRs and credits them to the international reserve accounts of member nations based on each nation's IMF quota (contributions of currency and reserve assets to the IMF). To spend its SDRs, a nation or institution requests the IMF to

To learn more about SDRs—their history and current status— see especially imf.org

transfer some amount of SDRs from its own reserve account to the reserve account of another nation or institution. In return, the country or institution asking for the transfer gets deposit balances denominated in the currency of the country or institution receiving the SDRs. These deposit balances may then be used to make international payments. The value of SDRs today is based on a basket of currencies representing the IMF member nations with the largest volume of exports. Currently the value of SDRs is based on the euro, the U.S. dollar, the Japanese yen and the British pound.

Most of the developed nations *float*, rather than peg, their currencies. This means that the value of any particular currency is determined by demand and supply forces operating in the marketplace. Usually, a **managed float** is used, in which governments intervene on occasion to stabilize the value of their home currency. The United States has officially adopted a managed float policy, but in practice it often follows a "free" floating exchange rate policy, in which the open market determines the value of the dollar, with U.S. monetary authorities intervening only in emergencies. Most recently the United States has relied heavily on the strength of its economy to achieve a strong value of the dollar.

managed float

In theory at least, a system of floating currency values should help the United States and other nations experiencing BOP deficits today. For example, if Americans are importing more goods from abroad than they are able to sell to overseas customers, an excess supply of U.S. dollars should build up abroad. The result should be a decline in the dollar's market value vis-à-vis other world currencies, making U.S. exports cheaper and foreign goods sold in the United States relatively more expensive. Ultimately, U.S. exports and imports should become more evenly balanced.

QUESTIONS TO HELP YOU STUDY

5. Explain the meaning of *currency risk*. How does currency risk affect exporters, importers, and investors active in the international financial marketplace?

6. Why was the *gold standard* developed? What problems did it appear to solve and what problems did it create? What exactly is the difference between the gold standard and the gold exchange standard?

7. When and why was the so-called *modified exchange standard* created? Explain how this particular monetary system worked to stabilize the value of different currencies.

8. The international monetary system we have today has often been labeled the *floating currency standard*. Briefly explain what this term means. Can you anticipate any problems that might emerge with this standard for handling currency values and risk?

9. What are *SDRs* and what are they for?

10. Why do you think the U.S. dollar is such an important currency within the international financial system? Is the dollar's importance around the globe a matter of history, resources, economic strength, cultural values, or what?

23.4 Determining Foreign Currency Values in Today's Markets

As we saw in the preceding section, major international currencies have floated with relative freedom since the 1970s and into the twenty-first century, their values dependent primarily on demand and supply forces in the marketplace. With this newfound freedom for currency prices and the expansion of world commerce, the volume of currency trading and the number of financial institutions participating in that trading have exploded. This is especially evident in the London and New York money markets, where exchange brokers bring in currency trading orders from financial institutions worldwide.

However, as the international financial system has moved increasingly toward freely floating exchange rates, currency prices have become significantly more *volatile*. The risks of buying and selling currencies have increased markedly in recent years. Moreover, fluctuations in the prices of foreign currencies affect domestic economic conditions, international investment, and the success or failure of government economic policies. Governments, businesses, and individuals find that it is more important today than ever before to understand how foreign currencies are traded and what affects their relative values.

Consider the problem faced by a corporation headquartered in the United States and selling machinery overseas. This firm frequently negotiates sales contracts with a foreign importer months before the machines are shipped. In the meantime, the market value of the currency the U.S. company expects to receive in payment for its products may have declined precipitously, canceling out expected profits. Similarly, a U.S. importer bringing fine wines into domestic U.S. markets frequently must pay for incoming shipments in the currency demanded by a foreign exporter. The U.S. importer's profits could be significantly reduced if the value of the dollar declined relative to the values of currencies used by the importer to pay for goods purchased abroad. The same problems confront investors in foreign securities, who find that attractive interest rates available overseas must be protected from an erosion in value through suitable purchases and sales of foreign currencies. Knowledge of the foreign exchange markets is the *first step* toward successful international business and economic policy today.

Essential Features of the Foreign Exchange Market

foreign exchange markets

The **foreign exchange markets** are among the largest markets in the world, with annual trading volume in the hundreds of trillions of dollars. The purpose of the foreign exchange markets is to bring buyers and sellers of currencies together. It is an *over-the-counter market*, with no central trading location and no set hours of trading. Prices and other terms of trade are determined by negotiation using computer screens linked electronically all over the world. The foreign exchange market is *informal* in its operations; there are no special requirements for market participants, and trading conforms to an unwritten code of rules.

Exchange Rate Quotations

foreign exchange rates

spot market

forward market

currency futures and options market

The prices of foreign currencies expressed in terms of other currencies are called **foreign exchange rates**. There are three major markets for foreign exchange: (1) the **spot market**, which deals in currency for immediate delivery; (2) the **forward market**, which involves the future delivery of foreign currency; and (3) the **currency futures and options market**, which deals in contracts to hedge against future changes in foreign exchange rates. Immediate delivery is defined as one or two business days for most transactions. Future delivery typically means one, three, or six months from today.

Exhibit 23.3 cites some recent foreign exchange rates between the U.S. dollar and other major currencies. The exhibit shows, for example, that an American importer or investor could obtain pounds sterling (£) that could be used to buy British bonds or British goods and services at a cost of about $1.83 per pound ($1.83/£) in January 2004. Conversely, a British investor or importer seeking to make purchases in the United States would have to pay 0.548 pounds ($1/1.83 or 0.548/$) for each dollar needed. Clearly, the

EXHIBIT 23.3

Recent Foreign
Exchange Rates:
The U.S. Dollar vs.
Other Key
Currencies
(Figures Are
Currency Units per
U.S. Dollar Except
as Noted)

Country/Currency Unit	2004 Exchange Rate with U.S. Dollars ($)[*]	Country/Currency Unit	2004 Exchange Rate with U.S. Dollars ($)[*]
Canada/dollar	1.2958	Hong Kong/dollar	7.7663
China P.R./yuan	8.2770	Japan/yen	106.27
Australia/dollar	77.17[**]	United Kingdom/pound	182.55[**]
Switzerland/franc	1.2391	European Monetary Union/euro	1.2638[**]

Source: Board of Governors of the Federal Reserve System.

[*]Exchange rates are averages for January 2004.

[**]Exchange rate expressed in currency units per U.S. dollar except for the Australian dollar and British pound, which are expressed in U.S. cents per currency unit. The euro is reported in U.S. dollars per euro.

exchange rate between dollars and pounds is the *reciprocal* of the exchange rate between pounds and dollars, which is true as well for any other pair of currencies. Exhibit 23.4 illustrates the commonly accepted procedures for calculating exchange rates.[3]

Dealers and brokers in foreign exchange actually post not one, but *two,* exchange rates for each pair of currencies. That is, each trader sets a *bid* (buy) price and an *asked* (sell) price. For example, the dealer department in a New York bank might post a bid price for pounds sterling of £ = $1.83 US (or $1.83/£) and an asked price of £ = $1.86 US (or $1.86/£). This means that the dealer is willing to buy sterling at $1.83 per pound and sell it at $1.86. These two exchange rates are sometimes referred to as "double-barreled" quotations. The dealer makes a profit on the *spread* between the bid and asked prices, although that spread is normally very small.[4]

Dealers in the foreign exchange market continually watch exchange rate quotations in order to take advantage of any *arbitrage* opportunities. A *pure arbitrage* combines long (buying) and short (selling) positions such that the "investor" makes a zero net investment, incurs no risk, and realizes a profit. In the case of foreign exchange markets, arbitrage refers to the purchase of one currency in a certain market and the sale of that currency in another market in response to the price difference between the two markets. The force of arbitrage generally keeps foreign exchange rates from getting too far out of line in different areas around the globe.

Data on current and
forecasted foreign
exchange rates
(FOREX) may be
found in such
sources as
forexnewsletters.com/
and fxstreet.com

Factors Affecting Foreign Exchange Rates

The exchange rate for any foreign currency depends on a multitude of factors reflecting economic and financial conditions in the country issuing the currency. One of the most important factors is the status of a nation's *balance-of-payments (BOP) position.* When a country experiences a deficit in its balance of payments, it becomes a net demander of foreign currencies and may be forced to sell substantial amounts of its own currency to

---

[3]We note that in each quotation of a foreign exchange rate, one currency always serves as a unit of account (unit of value) and the other currency functions as the unit for which a price is stated. For example a quote of $1.83/£ tells us that one British pound costs $1.83. In this instance, the dollar serves as the unit of account, and the currency whose price is quoted is the pound. It is customary to place the symbol for the currency serving as the unit of account (in this case, $) in front of the stated number and the symbol of the currency whose price is being quoted (in this case, £) following the number.

[4]Dealers will usually quote the bid price first and the asked price second and, as a rule, only the last digits in the price will be quoted to the buyer or seller. Thus, the spot bid and asked rates on British pounds might be quoted by a currency dealer as 95/98 because it is assumed the customer is aware of current exchange rates and knows that the bid price being quoted is $1.8395 and the asked price is $1.8398.

EXHIBIT 23.4

How to Calculate Foreign Exchange Rates

Source: Based on a similar exhibit developed originally by the Public Information Center of the Federal Reserve Bank of Chicago.

Exchange Rate Conversion

Suppose the exchange rate between the European Monetary Union's new currency unit, the euro, and the U.S. dollar ($) is: euro/$ = 1.5000 or euro 1.50/$. What, then, is the $/euro exchange rate?

Answer: 1 ÷ 1.500 = $0.6667/euro

Exchange Rate Appreciation

Suppose the exchange rate between euros and the U.S. dollar rises from euro/$ = 1.000, or euro 1.00/$, to euro 1.50/$. How much has the U.S. dollar appreciated in percent?

Answer: 1.500 ÷ 1.000 = 0.50, or 50%

Suppose the euro–U.S. dollar exchange rate is euro/$ = 1.5000, or euro 1.50/$. If the dollar appreciates by 3 percent, what is the new euro–U.S. dollar exchange rate?

Answer: 1.5000 × 1.03 = 1.5450, or euro 1.545/$

Exchange Rate Depreciation

Suppose the exchange rate between euros and U.S. dollars rises from euro/$ = 1.000 to euro/$ = 1.500. How much has the euro depreciated, in percent?

Answer: Note that the $/euro exchange rate has changed from 1 ÷ 1.000 = $1.00/euro to 1 ÷ 1.500 = $0.6667/euro. The ratio of these two exchange rates is 0.6667 ÷ 1.000, or 0.6667. Then, 1 − 0.6667 = 0.3333. Therefore, an exchange rate depreciation of one-third has occurred.

Suppose the euro–U.S. dollar exchange rate is euro/$ = 1.50, or euro 1.50/$, and thus the U.S. dollar– euro exchange rate is $0.6667/euro. If the euro depreciates 5 percent, what is the new euro–U.S. dollar exchange rate?

Answer: Because 0.6667 × 0.95 = 0.6334, the new exchange rate is 1 ÷ 0.6334 = 1.5788, or euro $1.5788/$

Suppose, once again, the euro–U.S. dollar exchange rate is euro/$ = 1.5000. If the U.S. dollar depreciates 5 percent, what is the new euro–U.S. dollar exchange rate?

Answer: 1.5000 × 0.95 = 1.4250, or euro 1.4250/$

Cross-Exchange Rates

Suppose the euro–U.S. dollar exchange rate is euro/$ = 1.5000, or euro 1.5000/$, and the Japanese yen (¥)–U.S. dollar exchange rate is 1.000, or ¥1.000/$. What, then, is the yen/euro exchange rate?

Answer: 1.000 ÷ 1.500 = 0.6667, or ¥0.6667/euro

Suppose the euro–U.S. dollar exchange rate is euro/$ = 1.500, or euro 1.500/$, and the U.S. dollar–Japanese yen exchange rate is $/¥ = 1.000, or 1.00/¥ What, then, is the euro/¥ exchange rate?

Answer: 1.500 ÷ (1 + 1.000) = 0.75, or euro 0.75/¥

pay for imports of goods and services. Therefore, balance-of-payments deficits often lead to price depreciation of a nation's currency relative to the prices of other currencies.

Exchange rates also are profoundly affected by *speculation over future currency values*. Dealers in foreign exchange monitor the currency markets daily, looking for profitable trading opportunities. A currency viewed as temporarily undervalued quickly brings forth buy orders, driving its price higher vis-à-vis other currencies. A currency considered to be overvalued is greeted by a rash of sell orders, depressing its price, as speculators move in.

The market for a currency is also greatly influenced by *domestic political and economic conditions*. Wars, revolutions, inflation, recession, and labor strikes have all been observed to have adverse effects on the currency of a nation experiencing these problems. On the other hand, signs of rapid economic growth, rising stock and bond prices, and successful economic policies to control inflation and unemployment usually lead to a stronger currency in the exchange markets. Moreover, countries with higher real interest rates generally experience an increase in the exchange value of their currencies.

purchasing power parity

The theoretical link between each nation's currency value in the international markets and that nation's inflation rate is an important relationship that has been extensively studied by economists. The **purchasing power parity** theory argues that the exchange rate between two currencies will reflect differences in their countries' inflation rates. For example, if the annual inflation rate stands at 4 percent in the United States and only 1 percent in Great Britain, the value of the U.S. dollar will fall by about 3 percent on an annual basis relative to the value of the pound, reflecting relatively cheaper British goods. Of course, other factors may intervene to upset this expected relationship.

Overshadowing the currency markets is the ever-present possibility of *central bank intervention*. Major central banks around the world, including the Federal Reserve System in the United States, the Bank of England, the Bank of Japan, and the European Central Bank (ECB) representing the whole European Community, may decide on a given day that their currency is declining too rapidly in value relative to other key currencies. Thus, if the dollar falls precipitously against the euro, support operations by the Federal Reserve System in the form of heavy sales of euros and corresponding purchases of dollars may be employed to stabilize the currency markets. Usually, central bank intervention is temporary, designed to promote a smooth adjustment in currency values toward a new equilibrium level rather than to permanently prop up a weak currency. The reason is that, no matter how important central banks are, their resources compared to the resources of the whole foreign-exchange market are small—okay for making short-run adjustments, but not likely to be effective over a sustained period of time. Central bank intervention is not likely to have a lasting effect on currency exchange rates as long as capital is free to flow from nation to nation. This intervention does not appear to give any nation a lasting trade advantage either.

In the United States, the Treasury Department is the agency designated to pursue market intervention in order to protect the U.S. dollar in international markets. The Treasury must decide what to do about the value of the dollar, but it is usually the Federal Reserve System that carries out the buying and selling of currencies on the Treasury's behalf through the foreign exchange desk at the Federal Reserve Bank of New York. The Fed also buys large amounts of currencies for foreign central banks and government agencies abroad.

We must keep in mind that central bank intervention may affect not only relative currency values but also the reserves held by private banks and the money supply. This happens because the central bank generally pays for its purchases of currency by increasing the deposit balances of private banks participating in the transaction with it. Thus, a decision by a central bank to intervene in the foreign currency markets can have *both* currency market and money supply effects unless an operation known as **currency sterilization** is carried out. For example, any increase in bank reserves and deposits that results from a central bank currency purchase can be "sterilized" by using monetary policy tools that absorb reserves and deposits from the banking system.

> To learn more about the European Central Bank and the euro see such sites as ecb.int, euro.gov.uk/, and ecuactivities.be/

currency sterilization

Supply and Demand for Foreign Exchange

The factors influencing a currency's rate of exchange with other currencies may be expressed in terms of the market forces of demand and supply. Exhibit 23.5, for example, illustrates a demand curve and a supply curve for dollars ($) in terms of British pounds (£). Note that the demand curve for U.S. dollars is also labeled the supply curve for pounds. This is due to the fact that an individual or institution holding British pounds and demanding dollars would be supplying pounds to the foreign exchange market. Similarly, the supply curve for U.S. dollars is identical to the demand curve for British pounds because someone holding dollars and demanding pounds must supply dollars to the foreign currency markets in order to purchase pounds. We recall, too, that the price of dollars in terms of pounds is the reciprocal of the price of pounds in terms of dollars.

To illustrate how demand and supply forces operate in the foreign exchange markets, suppose the current exchange rate between dollars and pounds is £ = $1.65.

**Demand and
Supply of U.S.
Dollars in Terms
of British Pounds**

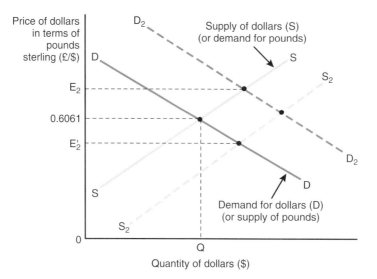

To purchase dollars, we have to pay 0.6061 pounds per dollar; to purchase British pounds costs us $1.65 per pound. This exchange rate between dollars and pounds is set in exchange markets by the interaction of the supply and demand for each currency. Exhibit 23.5 indicates that, at an exchange rate of 0.6061 pounds, the quantity of dollars supplied (S) is exactly equal to the quantity of dollars demanded (D).

If the price of dollars in terms of pounds were to fall temporarily *below* this exchange rate, more dollars would be demanded than supplied. Some buyers needing dollars would bid up the exchange rate toward the point where the demand for and supply of dollars were perfectly in balance. On the other hand, if the price of dollars were temporarily *above* 0.6061 pounds, more dollars would be supplied to the exchange markets. The price of dollars in terms of pounds would fall as suppliers of dollars willingly accepted a lower exchange rate to dispose of their excess dollar holdings. Only at that point where the exchange rate stood at 0.6061 pounds per dollar would quantity supplied equal quantity of dollars demanded. Only at that point would there be no reason for future changes in the exchange rate between the dollar and the pound unless changes occurred in the demand for or supply of either currency.

As we noted earlier, a number of factors affect the exchange rates between currencies, including a nation's balance-of-payments position, domestic political and economic developments, changes in real interest rates, and central bank intervention. Each of these factors leads to a shift in the demand for or supply of one currency vis-à-vis another, which brings about a change in their relative rates of exchange.

To illustrate the impact of shifts in currency demand and supply, suppose that consumers in Great Britain increase their demand for U.S. goods and services. As Exhibit 23.5 indicates, the demand curve for dollars would increase from D to D_2.

This is equivalent to an increase in the supply of British pounds seeking U.S. dollars. The equilibrium cost of dollars in terms of pounds, therefore, will rise to E_2. British importers will be forced to surrender a greater quantity of pounds per dollar in order to satisfy the demands of British consumers for U.S. goods and services. Other things being equal, the prices of imported goods from the United States will tend to rise.

The opposite effects would occur if U.S. consumers demanded a larger quantity of British goods and services. In this case, the supply-of-dollars (demand-for-pounds) curve slides downward and to the right from S to S_2, as shown in Exhibit 23.5. Reflecting the increased demand for pounds and associated sales of dollars for pounds

On January 1, 1999, the *euro* (€)—the single unit of currency adopted by the majority of nations forming the European Union (EU)—was introduced to the world. While euro currency was not issued to the public until 2002, deposits and other financial instruments denominated in euros were traded across the European landscape just before the new century began. Nations initially representing the "euro zone" included Austria, Belgium, Finland, France, Germany, Ireland, Italy, Luxembourg, the Netherlands, Portugal, Spain, and Greece.

May 2004 witnessed the addition of 10 new nations to the EU, including the Czech Republic, Estonia, Cyprus, Latvia, Lithuania, Hungary, Malta, Poland, Slovakia, and Slovenia. However, these nations were not immediately added to the euro zone. They first must meet *convergence criteria* (including the achievement of a "high

degree of price stability" and the elimination of "excessive deficits" in their government's financial position) before formally joining the euro-based financial system.

For businesses and households in Europe, the hoped-for benefits of being a part of the euro zone include the likelihood of lower prices for at least some goods and services due to greater cross-border competition, the elimination of currency risk inside the euro zone, and easier access to the financial markets in order to borrow money and thereby improve existing businesses and start new ones. Certainly, there is great potential in the growing euro zone. After bringing fully aboard the 10 new member states named in 2004, the euro zone will contain a population of more than 450 million, compared to a U.S. population of approximately 295 million.

by U.S. importers, the dollar's price in pounds sterling falls to E'_2. The market prices of British goods and services imported into the United States tend to rise.

One interesting financial institution playing a growing role in the expansion of the European Community (EC) and the euro is the European Bank for Reconstruction and Development at ebrd.com

What happens if a central bank, such as the Bank of England, European Central Bank, or the Federal Reserve, intervenes to stabilize the dollar–pound exchange rate at some arbitrary target level? The answer depends, among other things, on which side of the market the central bank enters to intervene, which currency is used as the vehicle for intervention, and the particular exchange-rate target chosen. For example, suppose that increased British demand for U.S. goods and services drove the dollar–pound exchange rate up to E_1, as shown in Exhibit 23.6. However, this upward surge in the dollar's value sharply reduced the purchasing power of the pound for dollar-denominated goods and services and threatened to have damaging effects on British foreign trade and industrial output. The Bank of England might intervene to force the

EXHIBIT 23.6

Effects of Central Bank Intervention to Stabilize the Dollar–Pound Exchange Rate

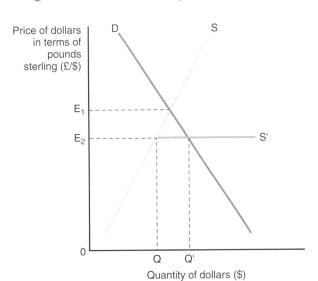

Quantity of dollars ($)

dollar–pound exchange rate down to E_2 by selling dollars out of its currency reserve and demanding pounds in the foreign exchange market. In effect, the supply-of-dollars curve would be "kinked" at the stabilization price, E_2. In order to peg the dollar–pound exchange rate at E_2, the central bank would have to spend $Q' - Q$ of its dollar reserves. Otherwise, the price of dollars would again rise toward E_1—the level dictated by demand and supply forces in the exchange markets. Conversely, if the dollar were falling to unacceptably low levels against the pound, the Bank of England or the Federal Reserve System might enter on the opposite side of the market, purchasing dollars with pounds and driving the dollar's price higher.

23.5 The Forward Market for Currencies

Knowledge of how the foreign exchange markets work and the ways in which currency risk can be reduced is indispensable for business managers today. Of course, the problem of fluctuating currency values is not so serious if payment for foreign goods, services, or securities must be made right away. Spot market prices of foreign currencies normally change by small amounts each day. However, if payment must be made weeks or months in the future, there is considerable uncertainty as to what the spot currency rate will be on any given future date. When substantial sums of money are involved, the rational investor or commercial trader will try to *guarantee* the future price at which currency can be purchased. This is the function of the *forward exchange market*.

Methods of Quoting Forward Exchange Rates

forward contract

Trading in the spot exchange market results in agreements to deliver a specified amount of foreign currency at an agreed-upon price, usually within one or two business days and sometimes on the same day. In contrast, a **forward contract** is an agreement to deliver a specified amount of foreign currency at a set price on some future date (usually within 1, 2, 3, 6, or 12 months). The actual delivery date is referred to by traders as the *value date*. In the event customers do not know when they will need foreign currency, an *option forward contract* may be used, which gives its holder the right but not the obligation to take delivery of foreign currency in the future.

There are several different ways of measuring and quoting forward exchange rates. Suppose the spot exchange rate on euros (€) is $1.16US and that dealers in foreign exchange are selling forward contracts for delivery of euros in six months at $1.14US. We may express the *forward* exchange rate for euros simply as $1.14US, or $1.14/euro—known as the *outright* rate.

Another popular method is to express the forward rate as a premium or discount from the spot rate, known as the *swap rate*. In the example above, euros are selling at a 2 cent *discount* in the forward market. Traders in the forward market appear to be signaling an expectation that the euro will fall in value over the next few weeks.

We may also express forward exchange rates in terms of an annualized percentage rate above or below the current spot price. To use the example above, $/€ spot = 1.16 and $/€ forward = $1.14. Then, the discount on forward euros (€) for delivery in six months is figured as follows:

$$\frac{\text{Forward rate } - \text{ Spot rate}}{\text{Spot rate}} \times \frac{12}{\text{Number of months forward}} \times 100 \quad \textbf{(23.1)}$$

$$= \frac{1.14 - 1.16}{1.16} \times \frac{12}{6} \times 100$$

$$= -.02 \times 2 \times 100$$

$$= -4\%$$

euros are selling at a 4 percent *discount* from their spot in the forward market. Because euros are selling at a discount from their spot price, forward dollars must be selling at a *premium* over spot.

Suppose we know the current spot rate between two currencies and the forward premium or discount. We want to know the actual forward exchange rate. The following will help determine that rate:

$$\text{Spot rate} + \frac{\text{Spot rate} \times [\text{Premium} (+) \text{ or discount} (-) \text{ expressed as an annual rate}] \times \text{Number of months forward}}{100 \times \text{Number of months in a year}} \quad (23.2)$$

Suppose the $/€ spot = 1.16 and forward euros for delivery in three months are selling at a 4 percent premium over spot. Using the formula above, we have:

$$1.1600 + \frac{1.16 \times 4.0 \times 3}{1,200} = 1.1716\text{\$/€ forward}$$

This means €/$ forward is 0.8535, or €0.8535/$.

23.6 Functions of the Forward Exchange Market

Contracts calling for the future delivery of currency are employed to cover a number of risks faced by investors and commercial traders. Some analysts group the functions of forward contracts into four categories: commercial covering, hedging an investment position, speculation, and covered interest arbitrage.

Commercial Covering

The export or import of goods and services usually requires someone to deliver payment in a foreign currency or to receive payment in a foreign currency. Either the payor or payee, then, is subject to currency risk, because no one knows for sure what the spot price will be for a currency at the time payment must be made. The forward exchange market can be used as a buffer against this risk.

To illustrate, suppose that a U.S. importer of cameras has agreed to pay 5,000 euros to a German manufacturer upon receipt of a new shipment. The cameras are expected to arrive dockside in 30 days. The importer has no idea what 5,000 euros will cost in U.S. dollars 30 days from now. To reduce the risk that the price of euros in terms of dollars may rise significantly, the importer negotiates a forward contract with his or her bank for delivery of 5,000 euros at $1.16/€ in 30 days.

When payment is due, the importer takes delivery of the euros (usually by acquiring ownership of a deposit denominated in euros) at the agreed-upon price and pays the German manufacturer. Because the price is fixed in advance, the risk associated with fluctuations in foreign exchange rates has been eliminated. Today, export and import firms routinely cover their purchases overseas with forward currency contracts or other currency risk hedging tools (to be discussed later in this chapter).

Hedging an Investment Position

Thousands of U.S. corporations have invested in long-term capital projects overseas, building manufacturing plants, warehouse and dock facilities, and office buildings. In recent years, a large return flow of long-term investments by foreign firms in the United States has occurred due to the underlying strength of the U.S. economy and a desire to avoid U.S. tariffs. Of course, the market value of these foreign investments may change drastically as the price of a foreign currency changes over time.

To illustrate, suppose a U.S. commercial bank constructed an office building in downtown London. When completed, the office facility had an estimated market value of £2 million. The current spot rate on pounds is, let us say, $1.40/£. The bank values the new building on its consolidated financial statement, therefore, at $2.8 million. However, suppose the pound has declined rapidly in value in recent months. Some market analysts expect pounds to be selling at $1.20/£ in the near future. In the absence of a hedged position, the bank would take a loss of $400,000 on its building. This is due to the fact that, at an exchange rate of $1.20/£, the office building will have a value of only $2.4 million.

Can this loss be avoided or reduced? Yes, provided the bank can negotiate a sale of pounds *forward* at a higher price. For example, the bank may be able to arrange with a dealer for the sale of £2 million for future delivery at $1.30US ($1.30/£). When this forward contract matures, if the spot price has fallen to $1.20/£, the bank can buy pounds at this rate and deliver them to the dealer at $1.30US as agreed. The result is a profit on the foreign exchange transaction of $200,000, partially offsetting the loss on the building from declining currency values.

Speculation on Future Currency Prices

A third use of the forward exchange market is speculative investment based on expectations concerning future movements in currency prices. Speculators will buy currency for future delivery if they believe the future spot rate will be *higher* on the delivery date than the current forward rate. They will sell currency under a forward contract if the future spot rate appears likely to be *below* the forward rate on the day of delivery. Such speculative purchases and sales carry the advantage of requiring little or no capital in advance of the delivery date. A speculator whose forecast of future spot rates turns out to be correct makes a profit on the spread between the purchase price and the sale price.

Covered Interest Arbitrage

One of the most common transactions in the international financial system arises when an investor discovers a higher interest rate available on foreign securities and invests funds abroad. When the currency risk associated with the purchase of foreign securities is reduced by using a forward contract, this transaction is often referred to as *covered interest arbitrage.*

To illustrate the interest arbitrage process, suppose that a British auto company is selling high-grade bonds with a promised annual yield of 7 percent. Comparable bonds in the United States offer a 5 percent annual return. The bonds are of good quality and there is probably little default risk, but there *is* currency risk in this transaction. The U.S. investor must purchase pounds in order to buy the British bonds. When the bonds earn interest or reach maturity, the issuing auto company will pay foreign and domestic investors in pounds sterling. Then the pounds must be converted into dollars to allow the U.S. investor to spend his or her earnings in the United States. If the spot price of sterling falls, the U.S. investor's net yield from the bonds will be reduced. For example, if the spot rate on pounds declines by 2 percent (on an annual basis), the interest gain from the British bonds will be offset by the loss on trading pounds. Clearly, a series of forward contracts is needed to sell pounds at a guaranteed price as the bonds generate a stream of cash payments.

The Principle of Interest Rate Parity

The foregoing example suggests an important rule regarding international capital flows and foreign exchange rates: *The net rate of return to the investor from any foreign investment is equal to the interest earned plus or minus the forward premium or discount*

With the opening of China to international markets and the rapid advances in worker skill levels in many less-developed nations, a number of U.S. businesses have found it advantageous to shift their production facilities offshore in an effort to reduce labor costs. This process—known as "outsourcing"—is a phenomenon that has been under way for many years. However, when outsourcing accelerates, as it appears to have done recently, it becomes a hotly debated issue. Segments of the economy that have experienced significant outsourcing include light manufacturing and various industries that rely heavily on advances in information technology, such as telemarketing, computer software, and account management (including financial-service accounts). India, in particular, has developed a well-trained labor force that has the additional advantage for U.S. markets of being trained in the English language.

While there are many examples of outsourcing among large multinational corporations (and there are probably more to come), it is unclear just how large an effect this phenomenon has had on employment inside the United States. Moreover, the jobs moving offshore seem likely to be *eventually* replaced with jobs fitting the skills of U.S. workers. However, there has been enough concern raised recently that the U.S. Department of Labor's Bureau of Labor Statistics (BLS) has begun to keep track of outsourcing in its regular surveys of U.S. businesses. The early evidence suggests that the net drain on job creation in the U.S. may not be that great. For example, in the first-reported BLS survey of U.S. companies, covering the first quarter of 2004, the jobs lost to outsourcing that were also associated with "mass layoffs"—defined as 50 or more workers losing their jobs in a single "event"—represented only about 2 percent of the total layoffs from those events. Moreover, these job losses have been offset to some extent by job creation within the U.S. due to the relocation of production facilities by non-U.S. businesses, which the BLS has not yet recorded.

It is too early to tell whether the current wave of outsourcing is unusually large and worthy of concern for U.S. trade policy. However, outsourcing will surely be watched closely in the years ahead.

For an expanded discussion, see "Extended Mass Layoffs Associated with Domestic and Overseas Relocations, First Quarter 2004," at the Bureau of Labor Statistics Web site bls.gov/mls/

interest rate parity

on the price of the foreign currency involved in the transaction. The theory of forward exchange states that the forward discount or premium on one currency relative to another is directly related to the difference in interest rates between the two countries involved. More specifically, the currency of the nation experiencing higher interest rates normally sells at a forward *discount* in terms of the currency issued by the nation with lower interest rates. And the currency of the nation with relatively low interest rates normally sells at a forward *premium* relative to that of the high-rate country. A condition known as **interest rate parity** exists when *the interest rate differential between two nations is exactly equal to the forward discount or premium on their two currencies.* When parity exists, the currency markets are in equilibrium and capital funds do not flow from one country to another. This is due to the fact that the gain from investing abroad at higher interest rates is fully offset by the cost of covering currency risk in the forward exchange market.

To illustrate the principle of interest rate parity, suppose interest rates in a foreign country are 3 percent above those in the United States. Then the currency of that foreign nation, in equilibrium, is likely to sell at a 3 percent discount in the forward exchange market. Similarly, if interest rates are 1 percent lower abroad than in the United States, in equilibrium, the foreign currency of the nations involved is likely to sell at a 1 percent premium against the U.S. dollar. When such an equilibrium position is reached, movements of funds between nations, even with currency risk covered, do not generate excess returns relative to domestic investments of comparable risk. Capital funds tend to stay in the domestic market rather than flowing abroad.

It is when interest rate parity does *not* exist, even temporarily, that capital tends to flow across national boundaries in response to differences in domestic and foreign interest rates. For example, suppose that interest rates in a foreign nation are 3 percent above U.S. interest rates on securities of comparable quality and the foreign currency involved is selling at a 1 percent discount against the dollar in the forward exchange market. In this case, investing abroad with exchange risks covered yields the investor a *net* added return of 2 percent per year. Clearly, there is a positive incentive to invest overseas.

Is this situation likely to persist for a long period of time? No, because the movement of funds into a country offering higher interest rates tends to increase the forward discount on its currency and lowers the net rate of return to the investor. Other factors held constant, the flow of funds abroad will subside, and capital funds will tend to stay at home.

QUESTIONS TO HELP YOU STUDY

11. What are the principal factors affecting the value of any particular foreign currency in the international exchange markets?

12. Distinguish between the *spot* and *forward markets* for foreign currencies. Why is it necessary to have two markets rather than one?

13. Describe the principal uses of *forward exchange contracts* today and give an example of each use.

14. What exactly are the *advantages* of a hedged position in one or more foreign currencies? What about the *disadvantages* (if any)?

23.7 The Market for Foreign Currency Futures

Forward contracts call for the delivery of a specific currency on a specified date in the future at a set price. The intent of buyer and seller in a forward contract is to actually *deliver* the currency mentioned in the contract. In recent years, an important variation of the forward currency contract has developed—*foreign currency futures*. These, too, are contracts calling for the future delivery of a specific currency at a price agreed on today, *but there is usually no intent to actually deliver the currencies mentioned in the contracts*. Rather, *currency futures are traded in the majority of cases to reduce the risk associated with fluctuating currency prices*. Today, currency futures contracts are traded in the United States (for example, at the Chicago Mercantile Exchange) and in a number of other world financial centers, principally on futures exchanges (unlike forward contracts, which are traded mainly in an unregulated dealer market). The most popular currency futures contracts today are for the future delivery of British pounds, Japanese yen, Canadian and U.S. dollars, Eurodollars, and euro currency units (€).

Currency futures are attractive to two groups: foreign exchange hedgers and foreign exchange speculators. The *hedgers*, who typically are banks, trading companies, and multinational corporations, seek to avoid damage to their profits from normal business transactions caused by unexpected changes in currency exchange rates. Usually, a hedger seeks out a *speculator* who hopes to profit from changes in relative currency rates by taking on the risk the hedger seeks to minimize. Two basic transactions take place on currency futures exchanges: the buying hedge and the selling hedge.

The Buying Hedge   Importers of goods typically use the *buying hedge*. In this case, a domestic importer who is committed to pay in a foreign currency when goods are received from abroad fears that currency may rise in price. He therefore *purchases* a futures contract, agreeing to take delivery of a currency at a set price as near as possible to the date on which the goods must be paid for. Because the price of this contract is fixed, the importer has "locked in" the value of the imported goods. As a final step, near the date the goods are paid for, the importer will "zero out" his futures contract purchase by *selling* a comparable currency futures contract, perhaps through a broker trading on the floor of a futures exchange. That is, the exchange's clearinghouse records each transaction taking place on the exchange and requires settlement only in the *net* trades for each trader. Therefore, it will automatically cancel out the importer's obligation both to take delivery of and to deliver a foreign currency.

How has the importer protected himself against loss due to currency risk? If a foreign currency rises in value during the life of a futures contract, the importer will experience reduced profits or increased losses on the imported goods themselves because the foreign currency has risen in value relative to his home currency. However, the market value of a currency futures contract also rises when the market value of the underlying currency increases. Therefore, the importer will be able to sell currency futures contracts at a higher price than the price for which they were originally purchased. The resulting profit in currency futures at least partially offsets the reduced gains or losses on the purchase of the imported goods.

The Selling Hedge   The opposite kind of hedge in currency futures is known as the *selling hedge*. This transaction is often employed by investors who purchase foreign securities and want to protect their earnings from a drop in currency values. In this instance, investors could hedge their expected earnings by *selling* futures contracts in the currency involved at the time the securities are acquired in the cash (spot) market. If contracts are sold in an amount that covers both principal and interest or dividends, investors have "locked in" their investment return regardless of which way exchange rates go. If the foreign currency involved has declined in price relative to the home currency when the security pays out cash or must be sold, a loss will be incurred in cash received, but investors will earn an offsetting futures market profit by *buying* futures contracts in an amount equivalent to those sold earlier.

23.8   Other Innovative Methods for Dealing with Currency Risk

The recent volatility of foreign exchange rates has given rise to an ever-widening circle of devices to deal with currency risk. For example, the *currency option* gives a buyer the right, though not the obligation, to either deliver or take delivery of a designated currency at a set price any time before the option expires. Thus, unlike the forward market, actual delivery *may* not occur, but unlike futures trading, no follow-up purchases or sales are needed to stop delivery. The advantage of the currency option is that it limits downside risk but not upside profits.

A related hedging instrument is the *option on currency futures. Call options* on currency futures give the buyer a way to protect against rising exchange rates by buying from another investor a currency futures contract at a fixed price, thus locking in a desired currency delivery price. On the other hand, *puts* on currency futures give a hedger protection against falling exchange rates by giving him or her the right to sell currency futures at a fixed price, regardless of how market prices change.

Another innovative device is the **currency swap**. In straight currency swaps, a company that has borrowed a foreign currency (such as yen) for a designated length of time immediately turns around and exchanges the yen for its home currency (say, dollars) with a counterparty. The counterparty may be a bank or other business firm with an exactly opposite situation, holding dollars but needing yen. As shown in Exhibit 23.7, when the loan comes due, the borrowing company reverses the transaction with the counterparty, swapping its home currency to get back the yen needed to pay off its foreign currency loan. In this case, there is no exposure to the risk of changing yen prices. The borrower has received an inflow of dollars at the beginning of the loan and

Additional information on the currency futures market is available from such Web sites as the Chicago Mercantile Exchange at cme.com and Business Jeeves at businessjeeves.com

currency swap

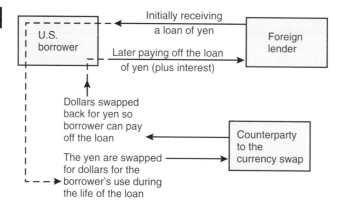

experienced a dollar outflow when the loan is paid off. The currency swap has merely facilitated the borrower's ability to borrow dollars from foreign markets without currency risk. The advantage of currency swaps is that they can be arranged with longer maturities and more suitable terms of settlement than most standard currency contracts. Central banks frequently use swaps to help defend currency prices.

Innovative new approaches to currency risk continue to emerge each year, and many old methods have been resurrected lately. For example, some multinational firms have expanded their use of *local loans*—that is, securing credit inside the countries where they have sales or production operations. Others have resorted to issuing *dual-currency bonds* with principal and interest payments denominated in two different currencies. Some exporters ship only if *prepayments* are made by a customer overseas that cover all or a substantial portion of the value of a shipment before it is made. Some companies simply *barter* (exchange) their goods or property directly so that no currency changes hands. *Selective currency pricing* is also employed, in which the seller invoices the buyer in a currency thought to be more stable or easier to hedge.

The ultimate economic response when other risk-reducing methods appear to be too costly or too risky is for a seller to use *risk-adjusted pricing* of goods and services traded across international boundaries. For example, goods sold to countries where currency risk is unacceptably high may be priced higher to compensate the seller for that added risk. Ultimately, individuals living in those countries where currency risk is unusually high are likely to wind up paying higher prices for goods and services.

23.9 Government Intervention in the Foreign Exchange Markets

The value of a nation's currency in the international markets has long been a source of concern to governments around the world. National pride plays a role in this case, because a strong currency, avidly sought by traders and investors in the international marketplace, implies a vigorous and well-managed economy at home. A strong and stable currency encourages investment in the home country, stimulating its economic development. Moreover, changes in currency values affect a nation's balance-of-payments position. A weak and declining currency makes foreign imports more expensive, lowering the standard of living at home. And a nation whose currency is not well regarded in the international marketplace may have difficulty selling its goods and services abroad, giving rise to unemployment at home.

The United States has pursued an "on-again, off-again" policy of supporting the dollar in international markets over the years, sometimes supporting the dollar vigorously and at other times merely "signaling" its target value for the dollar with occasional

To discover more about currency boards and dollarization see, for example, iie.com

vehicle currency

intervention. When the United States has intervened in the currency markets, it has done so mainly out of concern for the condition of the U.S. economy, particularly for the effects of inflation.

Another factor is the key role played by the U.S. dollar in the international financial system. The dollar is a **vehicle currency** that facilitates trade and investment between many nations. For example, international shipments of crude oil, regardless of their origin or destination, are more frequently than not valued in dollars. As noted in Chapter 11, the market for dollar deposits held in banks abroad—Eurodollars—is the world's largest money market, financing commercial projects and even providing operating funds for several foreign governments. For all of these reasons, the United States, as well as foreign governments and central banks, has intervened from time to time in the foreign exchange markets to stabilize currency values and insulate domestic economic conditions from developments abroad.

QUESTIONS TO HELP YOU STUDY

15. What is a *buying hedge* in currency futures? A *selling hedge?* Under what circumstances is each of these hedges likely to be employed?

16. Exactly what is meant by the phrase *interest rate parity?* How does it influence the flow of capital from one nation to another?

17. In recent years central banks have intervened in the foreign exchange markets from time to time to support one foreign currency or another. Why might central bank intervention in the currency markets be a necessity? What impact are central bank operations most likely to have in the short run and the long run?

18. What does the term *sterilization* refer to when talking about central bank intervention in the foreign currency markets?

19. What is the purpose of *currency swaps?* How exactly do they work?

20. Many new *currency hedging techniques and instruments* have appeared in recent years. List and define as many examples of these as you can.

MARKETS ON THE NET: The Most Important Web Sites for This Chapter

Chicago Mercantile Exchange (cme.com)
European Central Bank (ecb.int)
European Community Activities (ecuactivities.be/)
FOREX News (forexnews.com)

International Monetary Fund (imf.org)
The Euro (euro.gov.uk/)
World Bank (worldbank.org)
World Trade Organization (wto.org)

Summary of the Chapter's Main Points

The international financial system performs the same roles and functions that domestic money and capital markets do around the globe. It attracts savings and allocates capital for investment purposes toward the most promising projects, stimulating the international economy to grow.

- One of the most significant sources of information on world trade and the flow of savings (capital) between nations is provided by each country's *balance-of-payments (BOP) accounts,* which summarize economic and financial transactions between residents of a nation and the rest of the world. The principal components of a nation's balance of payments are the *current account* (which focuses primarily upon flows of merchandise and services between nations), the *capital account* (which traces long- and short-term capital flows between nations), and *official reserve transactions* (which are used by governments and central banks to aid in the settlement of balance-of-payments deficits).

- One of the most significant risks in the international financial system is *currency or foreign exchange risk*. Crossing national and regional borders with capital or merchandise usually is accompanied by transactions involving two or more different currencies whose relative values can change quickly, threatening losses on trade and in the value of capital investments.

- Reducing currency risk has been a continuing goal of nations, individuals, and businesses for centuries. Nations have resorted in the past to tying their currencies to assets (such as gold) recognized as having universal appeal and value. However, restrictions on the availability of gold and transaction costs as well as lack of flexibility in a nation's money and credit policy eventually led to a much more flexible currency standard, referred to today as the *managed floating currency standard*. Each nation chooses its own currency standard, taking into account the welfare of other nations.

- The exchange rate between one currency and another is determined by the foreign exchange (FOREX) market through the interplay of the demand and supply for each nation's currency. Currencies are traded over the counter in a relatively informal marketplace and prices are quoted as "double barrel" quotations—the price of one foreign currency expressed in terms of another.

- Foreign currency markets today are three-tiered, divided into *spot, forward,* and *futures and options markets*. While spot transactions involve immediate currency exchanges, forward, futures, and options markets are designed to hedge against currency.

- The supply and demand forces that shape foreign currency prices are influenced by a few powerful factors, including a nation's balance-of-payments position, speculation over future currency values, domestic economic conditions, and central bank policy.

- The *forward exchange market* is designed to protect against losses due to currency price fluctuations. The functions of forward currency contracts include (a) commercial covering designed primarily to affect export/import values; (b) hedging an investment position against loss in market values; (c) speculation about future currency values; and (d) covered interest arbitrage to help protect the yield on an investment instrument (such as a government bond).

- The principle of *interest rate parity* in international currency markets rests on the fact that the net return to the investor from any foreign investment is equal to the interest earned on the investment plus or minus the forward premium or discount on the price of any foreign currency involved in the transaction. The parity principle argues that the interest-rate differential between two nations is closely related to the forward discount or premium on their currencies.

- Foreign *currency futures contracts* call for the future delivery of a specific currency at a price agreed upon today and are designed to transfer currency risk to another investor willing to bear that risk. Importers of goods and services typically use a *buying hedge* in currency futures while a *selling hedge* is often employed by investors who purchase foreign securities and want to protect their earnings from a drop in currency values.

- Newer and more innovative methods for dealing with currency risk include *currency swaps*, where two parties exchange payments in different currencies; the use of *local loans* to avoid currency trading; *dual currency bonds*, with principal and interest payments made in at least two different currencies; the *bartering* of goods or property; and the *risk-adjusted pricing* of goods and services in order to take into account foreign exchange risk.

- Government intervention in foreign exchange markets has become less common today. However, most governments will intervene to change currency values when emergency shocks occur (such as terrorist attacks or a sudden plunge in the values of stock or bonds) that could damage a nation's economic welfare.

Key Terms Appearing in This Chapter

balance-of-payments (BOP)
   accounts, 695
current account, 697
capital account, 699
gold standard, 702
gold exchange standard, 703
modified exchange standard, 703
managed floating currency
   standard, 704
special drawing rights (SDRs), 704
managed float, 705
foreign exchange markets, 706

foreign exchange rates, 706
spot market, 706
forward market, 706
currency futures and options
   market, 706
purchasing power parity, 708
currency sterilization, 709
forward contract, 712
interest rate parity, 715
currency swap, 717
vehicle currency, 719

Problems and Issues

1. The U.S. balance of payments (BOP) is often described in terms of the current account or the merchandise trade deficit or surplus. What is the difference between the current account and the merchandise trade account? Which is the more comprehensive measure of international trade? Is it possible for the current account to be in deficit while the merchandise trade account is in surplus, or vice versa? Explain.

2. The print media regularly report the results of trading in the forward and futures markets for foreign exchange. What are the essential differences between these two markets? Explain what it means to "zero out" a position taken in the currency futures market. Why is it not possible to automatically "zero out" a position in the forward market?

3. Indicate whether each of the transactions below would represent a credit (+) or a debit (−) item in a nation's balance of payments (BOP).

   a. General Electric Corporation purchases electric switches from a supplier in Germany.

   b. Bell Helicopter sells new helicopters to a British oil field exploration company.

   c. Universal Studios makes the decision to begin building a new theme park in Singapore.

   d. George Elwin has just received a dividend check for the stock he holds in British Airways.

   e. Citigroup of New York agrees to provide insurance for goods shipped by the International Furniture Mart of Copenhagen to a London wholesale house.

   f. Carlos Mendoza sends his paycheck from southern California to his family in Mexico City.

4. Suppose the exchange rate between British pounds (£) and U.S. dollars ($) is $1.35 per pound. What is the correct way to write this pound–dollar exchange rate? The dollar–pound exchange rate?

5. Suppose the pound–dollar exchange rate is now 1.3500. Then, the U.S. dollar increases in value by 5 percent. What is the new pound–dollar exchange rate? What is the new exchange rate if the U.S. dollar appreciates by 10 percent?

6. If the pound–dollar exchange rate increases from £/$ = 1.3500 to 1.4000, by what percentage amount has the pound depreciated?

7. If the pound–dollar exchange rate is 1.4000 and the pound declines 10 percent in value, what is the new pound–dollar exchange rate?

8. Suppose the pound–dollar exchange rate is 1.4000 and the yen–dollar exchange rate is 2.3000. What is the yen–pound exchange rate?

9. Suppose the dollar–euro (€) spot exchange rate is 0.8620 and the three-month forward exchange rate for these two currencies is 0.8315. What then is the percentage discount on euros slated for delivery in three months?

10. You are asked to calculate the forward exchange rate on euros (€) versus the U.S. dollar. You find out that the current dollar–euro spot exchange rate is 0.8555 and that forward euros scheduled for delivery in six months are selling at a 3 percent premium over the spot rate. What is the euro–dollar forward exchange rate?

Standard & Poor's Market Insight and Web-Based Problems

1. Caterpillar Tractor Company (CAT) is a Fortune 500 multinational company with approximately 50 percent of its product sales outside the U.S. The success of its business plan is obviously very dependent upon events that occur around the globe. There are many other multinational companies in other industries that also must confront the challenges of trading in the international marketplace. The purpose of this exercise is to see what insight can be gained from an industry analysis and from knowledge of a multinational firm's business statements regarding its current status vis-à-vis conditions in the overseas markets that it serves.

   a. Visit S&P's Market Insight database at **mhhe.com/edumarketinsight**. Click the "Company" tab and locate the page for "ticker" CAT. Identify what industry group ("GICS Sub-Industry Group") CAT belongs to.

   b. Click on the "Industry Analysis" tab and learn what the status of the industry is as it relates to the international marketplace.

   c. Now return to the "Company" page for CAT and click "Stock Report" to obtain information on Caterpillar's business plan under "Business Summary."

Does the information you obtained in part (b) suggest that the international business climate is favorable to Caterpillar's business plan, considering the markets in which Caterpillar hopes to compete successfully?

   d. Would you choose to be a buyer of Caterpillar's stock? Why or why not? Does the current international outlook affect your decision in some significant way?

   e. Return to the "Company" page for CAT and click on "Wall St. Consen." Is your decision in part (d) consistent with the consensus view among professional investors on Wall Street?

   f. Pick another well-known multinational company from a different industry group and repeat this exercise. Is there a difference in the conclusions that you've drawn for Caterpillar versus the other company you selected? Do these differences relate to the industry group or to the geographic regions that are being serviced by the two firms, or both?

2. As noted in this chapter, the United States has been running merchandise and current account deficits consecutively for many years now. The purpose of this exercise is to examine the most recent U.S. data and see if these trends have continued and/or whether there are any noteworthy changes that may be under way.

   a. Visit the Web site of the Bureau of Economic Analysis at **bea.gov**, which is part of the U.S. Department of Commerce, and obtain data for "U.S. International Transactions," which regularly reports on the balance of payments (BOP) of the United States.

   b. Is the U.S. current account in deficit or in surplus, according to the latest figures? Has the deficit or surplus position widened or shrunk in the most recent year?

   c. What are the major components of the U.S. current account that would tend to produce a current account deficit? What are the major BOP components tending to mitigate the size of any potential current account deficit?

   d. Do a search on the Internet under "U.S. Current Account" and find news accounts of the most recently reported data. Do they offer any explanation for the facts that you described in parts (b) and (c)?

Selected References to Explore

Humpage, Owen F. "On the Rotation of the Earth, Drunken Sailors, and Exchange Rate Policy." *Economic Commentary,* Federal Reserve Bank of Cleveland, February 15, 2004, pp. 1–3.

Kamin, Steve B. "U.S. International Transactions in 2002." *Federal Reserve Bulletin,* May 2003, pp. 191–203.

Lambert, Michael J., and Kristin D. Stanton. "Opportunities and Challenges of the U.S. Dollar as an Increasingly Global Currency: A Federal Reserve Perspective." *Federal Reserve Bulletin,* September 2001, pp. 567–75.

Papaioannou, Stefan, and Kei-Mu Yi. "The Effects of a Booming Economy on the U.S. Trade Deficit." *Current Issues in Economics and Finance,* Federal Reserve Bank of New York, February 2001, pp. 1–6.

Parry, Robert T. "Globalization: Threat or Opportunity for the U.S. Economy?" *FRBSF Economic Letter,* Federal Reserve Bank of San Francisco, May 21, 2004, pp. 1–3.

Spiegel, Mark M. "The European System of Central Banks." *FRBSF Economic Letter,* Federal Reserve Bank of San Francisco, December 12, 2003.

Winnie, Mark A. "The European System of Central Banks." *Economic Review,* Federal Reserve Bank of Dallas, First Quarter 1999, pp. 2–14.

Chapter 24

International Banking

Learning Objectives

in This Chapter

- You will understand the important role that large *multinational banks* play in both domestic and foreign markets around the world.
- You will explore the types of physical facilities that multinational banks operate around the globe and be able to identify which financial *services* each banking facility offers.
- You will see how and why international banking is still so closely *regulated* in many areas of the world.

What's in This Chapter?
Key Topics Outline

24.1 Introduction to International Banking

No review of the international financial system would be complete without a discussion of the role of international banking institutions. Through these banking firms flow the majority of commercial and financial transactions that cross international borders. Along with British, Japanese, German, and Canadian banks, U.S. commercial banking institutions have led in the development of international banking facilities to meet the far-flung financial needs of foreign governments and multinational corporations. Until recently, the international activities of U.S. banks were concentrated principally in their foreign offices, due mainly to federal government controls over foreign lending. However, the gradual relaxation of government controls in recent decades, the high cost of maintaining a large network of foreign bank branches, political instability overseas, and improvements in communications technology have encouraged many international banks to offer more international services from their *domestic* offices.

The development of multinational banking over the past century has resulted in several benefits for international trade. One benefit to the public is greater competition in international markets, lowering the real prices of financial services. It also has tied together more effectively the various national money markets into a unified international financial system, permitting a more efficient allocation of the world's scarce resources. Funds flow relatively freely today across national boundaries in response to differences in relative interest rates and currency values. Although these developments have benefited both borrowers and investors, they also have created problems for governments trying to regulate the volume of credit, insure a stable banking system, and combat inflation.

24.2 The Scope of International Banking Activities

Multinational Banking Corporations

multinational corporation

To learn more about the field of international banking, including career possibilities, see, for example, the Guide to International Banking at bankinfo.com and Guide to Banking Law at hg.org/banking.html

The term **multinational corporation** usually is reserved for large nonfinancial corporations with manufacturing or trading operations in several different countries. However, this term is equally applicable to the world's leading banks, most of which have their home offices in Canada, the United States, Great Britain, Germany, France, Spain, and Japan but have established offices worldwide. These giant banks have accounted for most of the growth in multinational banking in recent decades.

Types of Facilities Operated by Banks Abroad

shell branches

representative offices

Edge Act and Agreement corporations

international banking facilities (IBFs)

Agency offices

Major banks around the world have used many vehicles to expand their international operations. All major banks have *international departments* in their home offices to provide credit, access to foreign currencies, and other services for their international customers, and many operate *full-service branch offices* in foreign markets as well. Others maintain simple booking offices, known as **shell branches**, on offshore islands such as the Bahamas to attract Eurocurrency accounts while avoiding domestic banking regulations. **Representative offices** help find new customers and give local customers a point of contact with the home office, but they cannot take deposits. U.S. banks and foreign banks active in the United States have set up **Edge Act and Agreement corporations** across state lines, which are special subsidiary companies that must, under Federal Reserve regulations, devote the majority of their activities to international banking. Many banking firms have also set up **international banking facilities (IBFs)** in the United States, consisting of computerized accounts maintained for international customers and subject to minimal U.S. regulations. **Agency offices**

Two of the most interesting multinational banks in the world are the Hong Kong and Shanghai Banking Corp. Limited and the Deutsche Bank. See their global Web sites at hsbc.com and deutschebank.com

provide specialized services, such as recordkeeping for business transactions and providing customers with liquid balances for spending as needed. In addition, multinational banks often make *direct equity investments* in foreign companies, either alone or as *joint ventures* with other financial firms.

Choosing the Right Kind of Facility to Serve Foreign Markets

Which kind of facility is adopted by a multinational bank to serve its customers depends on government regulations and the bank's size, goals, and location. Most banks begin with international departments in their home offices and then, as the volume of business grows, open up representative offices. Ultimately, full-service branches and investments in foreign businesses may be established. A recent trend toward legal liberalization of foreign trade and international lending has stimulated the growth of *home-based offices* that send officers to call on customers overseas or serve clients by satellite, the Internet, and other electronic channels. However, many multinational banks argue that successful international operations require an institution to have a stable presence overseas in the form of agencies, branches, representative offices, or even joint ventures with other banks.

Laws and regulations play a major role in determining the nature and location of multinational banking offices. For example, in some areas of the world, such as the Middle East, fears of political upheaval or outright expropriation of foreign-owned facilities have limited the entry of multinational banks.

For several of the largest U.S. banks, international operations yield from one-third to as much as one-half of their income, and a few receive more than half their earnings from international activities. Particularly noteworthy has been U.S. bank penetration of foreign consumer banking markets, such as the "money shops" operated by Citigroup in Europe. Personal financial services represent extremely attractive opportunities in many foreign markets, and U.S. banks hold a significant share of consumer loan and deposit markets abroad, especially in Europe, but also a growing market share in Central and South America and Asia.

24.3 Services Offered by International Banks

Multinational banks offer a wide variety of international financial services to customers. These services are described briefly below. Of course, the particular services offered by each bank depend on its size, location, the types of facilities it maintains overseas, and the regulations it faces.

Issuing Letters of Credit

letter of credit

Most banks enter the international sector initially to finance trade. In most cases, credit is needed to bridge the gap between cash expenditures and cash receipts and to reduce the risks associated with long-distance trading. In these situations, a **letter of credit** is often the ideal financing instrument.

A letter of credit is an international bank's future promise to pay for goods stored overseas or for goods shipped between countries. Such letters may be issued to finance exports and imports or to provide a standby guarantee of payment behind IOUs issued by a corporate customer. Through a letter of credit, the bank substitutes its own promise to pay for the promise of one of its customers. By substituting its promise, the bank reduces the seller's risk, facilitating the flow of goods and services through international markets. Occasionally, the seller becomes concerned about the soundness of the bank issuing the letter of credit. The seller may then ask his or her own bank to issue a *confirmation letter* in which that bank guarantees against foreign bank default.

Buying and Selling Foreign Exchange (FOREX)

Trading in foreign exchange is one of the riskier activities of international banks. For an illustration see forexnews.com

Major multinational banks have dealer departments that specialize in trading foreign currencies (FOREX). International banks buy and sell foreign currencies on a 24-hour basis to support the import and export of goods and services, the making of investments, the giving of gifts, and the financing of tourism. They also write forward contracts for the future delivery of foreign exchange, as we saw in Chapter 23.

Accepting Eurocurrency Deposits and Making Eurocurrency Loans

Eurocurrency deposits

Eurocurrency loans

International banks accept deposits denominated in currencies other than that of their home country. As we saw in Chapter 11, these **Eurocurrency deposits** are used to pay for goods shipped between countries and serve as a source of loanable funds for banks. Eurocurrency deposits also may be loaned to corporations and other large wholesale borrowers. The majority of **Eurocurrency loans** carry floating interest rates based on the London Interbank Offer Rate (LIBOR) for three-month and six-month Eurocurrency deposits. Eurocurrency credit normally goes to borrowers with impeccable credit ratings. One important innovation is the *syndicated Eurocurrency credit*, in which one or more multinational banks will put together a loan package accompanied by an information memorandum. Other banks can then participate in the loan without direct communication with the borrower.

For more information about the European Central Bank (ECB) and European Monetary Union (EMU), see ecb.int and cepr.org

Marketing and Underwriting of Both Domestic and Eurocurrency Bonds, Notes, and Equity Shares

Eurobond

For generations, leading international banks have assisted their customers in raising capital through the issuance of new securities—bonds and other forms of debt and equity shares. One of the most well known of these securities is the **Eurobond**—a debt security denominated in a currency other than that of the country or countries where most or all of the security is sold. For example, a U.S. automobile company may desire to float an issue of long-term bonds to raise capital for one of its subsidiaries operating in Greece. The company might issue bonds denominated in British pounds to be sold in Europe through an underwriting syndicate made up of banks and securities dealers. Alternatively, the borrowing company might issue bonds denominated in euros, which is now the largest corporate bond market in the world.

Multinational banks assist the Eurobond market in several ways. Major banks have established international clearing systems to expedite the delivery of Eurobonds. Banks and security brokers are the principal intermediaries through which Eurobonds find their way to the long-term investor. The borrower may contact a multinational bank and ask it to organize a syndicate to place a new Eurobond issue. At this point, a *consortium* is formed, embracing at least four or five U.S., British, Japanese, French, or German banks, and typically at least one bank located in the borrowing country as well. The consortium agrees to subscribe to the Eurobond issue at issue price minus commission and then organizes a large group of banks and securities dealers as underwriters. Sometimes more than 100 banks are included in the underwriting syndicate. Once formed, the underwriting group gives the borrower a firm offer for its bonds and, if accepted, works to place the issue with investors.

To further explore the market for Eurobonds, see such Web sites as finpipe.com and ISI Emerging Markets at securities.com

Multinational banks also assist their corporate and governmental customers with medium-term financing through note issuance facilities (NIFs). Under a standard NIF contract, a customer is authorized to issue short-term notes periodically (usually with three to six-month maturities) to interested investors over a designated time span

FINANCIAL DEVELOPMENTS

The New European Central Banking System: Regulating and Supervising Banks in Europe and Shaping European Monetary Policy

With the formation of the European Union (EU), the regulation and supervision of international banks selling their services in Europe and the money and credit policies of the European continent are now conducted and coordinated through a new system of central banking institutions—the European System of Central Banks, or ESCB, depicted in this box.

ECB, examines and supervises the banks headquartered in its home country.

Eleven countries adopted the *euro* as a common currency in 1999—Austria, Belgium, Finland, France, Germany, Ireland, Italy, Luxembourg, the Netherlands, Portugal, and Spain. Greece adopted the euro in 2001 but the three remaining original members of the EU—

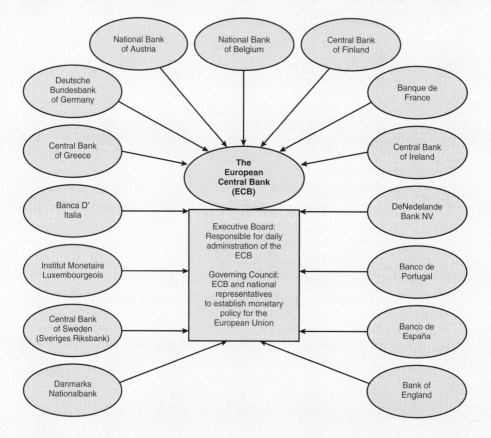

The ESCB is headed by the European Central Bank (ECB). Within the ECB itself there are two key decision-making groups—the Executive Board, which pursues a single monetary policy for all European member states, and the Governing Council, which includes the Executive Board plus the governors of the central banks from each member nation. While the ECB is charged to lead Europe's fight against inflation, it does not control exchange rates for the EU. That job is left to the EU's Council of Ministers. Each nation's central bank, not the

Denmark, Sweden, and Great Britain—elected to keep their own national currencies. In 2004, 10 additional nations were brought into the EU—Cyprus, the Czech Republic, Estonia, Hungary, Latvia, Lithuania, Malta, Poland, Slovenia, and Slovakia. (Bulgaria and Romania may be ready to join in 2007.) The central banks of these newest member states are members of the broader ECB system (though they cannot join the ECB's Governing Council until the euro becomes their national currency).

(perhaps five years). The bank or banks involved agree to provide backup funding (standby credit) at a spread over prevailing Euromarket interest rates. For an underwriting fee, the bank agrees to purchase any unsold notes or advance cash to the customers until sufficient market funding is obtained.

Securitizing Loans

Over the past two decades, leading multinational banks have unfurled a new source of funds for themselves and their customers: *securitization,* or the pooling of loans having similar purposes, quality, and maturities and the selling of financial claims (securities) against the pool of loans. Good examples are New York's Citigroup and J. P. Morgan Chase, which are among the leading packagers of consumer credit-card receivables, pooling the receivables that arise as households borrow on their credit cards and selling securities in the open market as claims against the income those receivables will ultimately bring in. International banks can earn income in several different ways from the securitization process: (1) by securitizing some of their own loans and pocketing the difference in interest earnings between the average yield on the pool of loans and the cost of issuing securities against the loan pool; (2) by agreeing to guarantee the income of investors from pools of securitized loans; (3) by retaining servicing rights on a pool of loans, collecting and recording the income received from the loans in return for a servicing fee; or (4) by acting as adviser or trustee for those customers that desire to securitize any loans or receivables they hold in order to generate new capital.

Advisory Services Provided by International Banks

In addition to the foregoing services, international banks offer extensive *advisory services* to their customers. These include analyses of foreign market conditions, evaluation of sales prospects and plant location sites, and advice on foreign regulations. International banks prepare credit reports on overseas buyers for exporters of goods and services and assist domestic firms interested in entering foreign markets.

Universal Banking Services and One-Stop Shopping

As the foregoing list of service offerings suggests, the world's largest banking firms, such as Citigroup and Deutsche Bank, are reaching out to diversify their services in many different directions, attempting to offer their customers "one-stop shopping" and becoming what European bankers have, for decades, referred to as "universal banks." Universal banking combines traditional banking, insurance, securities trading, real estate brokering, and a long list of other services under one corporate umbrella. Its alleged advantages include greater stability of revenues (cash flow) and profits, less risk of succumbing to market stress as declines in one service area may be offset by increased revenues from other services, and lower overall fund-raising costs.

Further information on recent developments in international banking can be found at such Web sites as bankinfo.com and finance.tfp.com

However, an international banking firm may not be able to manage all of its different service areas efficiently, resulting in lower rates of return and loss of market share. A prominent example appeared as the new century opened when Citigroup of New York, which had previously allied itself in the 1990s with Travelers Insurance Company of San Francisco to form one of the largest banking conglomerates in the world, announced that it would sell its Travelers property-casualty insurance affiliate and, slow the pace at which it was pursuing the goal of becoming a "one-stop" financial supermarket. Citigroup discovered that its insurance affiliate was earning a lower rate of return than its other businesses and dragging down its overall performance. Citigroup's experience suggests that international banks must proceed cautiously as they proliferate their services and avoid hasty acquisitions that may be difficult to control and reduce their competitive edge.

QUESTIONS TO HELP YOU STUDY

1. What exactly is a *multinational bank?*

2. What are the essential differences between the following types of *banking facilities:*

   International banking departments

   Edge Act and Agreement corporations

   Full-service branches

   Representative offices

   Shell branches

   International banking facilities (IBFs)

3. What factors appear to influence the types of *services* an international banking firm chooses to offer its customers?

4. What are the principal *services* offered by the international banking industry? Make a list of these services and briefly define what each is about.

24.4   Foreign Banks in the United States

Banks owned by foreign individuals and companies have entered the United States in great numbers in recent years. The reasons behind the expansion of foreign banking activities in the United States reflect growth in international trade and investments, the opportunity for profit in the huge U.S. market, and a search for safety when overseas markets are in turmoil. Originally, foreign-based banks penetrated U.S. markets for the same reasons U.S. banks established facilities overseas: *to follow their customers who had established operations in other countries.* Once in the United States, however, foreign banks found the possibility of attracting deposits and loans from major U.S. corporations and even from U.S. households irresistible.

The Growth of Foreign Bank Activity in the United States

To learn more about foreign banking in the U.S., see especially FRB: Foreign Banks in the U.S. at federalreserve.gov

The expansion of foreign bank operations inside the United States has been impressive. Today foreign banks are strong competitors with domestic U.S. banks, especially in the market for business loans. As of year-end 2003, 190 foreign banks from 54 nations operated just over 290 branch offices and nearly 135 representative offices in U.S. territory. At that time, foreign banks accounted for about 18 percent of total U.S. commercial banking assets. Clearly, foreign banks have become a competitive force to be reckoned with in the United States.

Federal Regulation of Foreign Bank Activity

Until the 1970s, no federal laws regulated foreign bank activity within U.S. borders. However, Congress has been monitoring foreign bank operations since 1966, when IntraBank, a Lebanese institution, collapsed and several U.S. banks suffered severe losses. Passage of the Bank Holding Company Act Amendments of 1970 marked an initial step toward federal regulation of foreign banking. Under the terms of these amendments, any corporation controlling one or more domestic banks became subject to supervision by the Federal Reserve Board. However, with foreign banks in the United States growing more rapidly than domestic banks, the pressure on Congress for more extensive regulation of foreign banks intensified. Proponents of restrictive legislation argued that foreign banks reduced the effectiveness of domestic monetary policy and that the lack of specific regulations applying to foreign banks was unfair to domestic banks, which must conform to an elaborate system of regulations.

International Banking Act (IBA)

Responding to these pressures, Congress passed the **International Banking Act (IBA)**, which became law in September of 1978. Under the terms of the IBA and subsequent regulations, U.S. branches and agencies of foreign banks with worldwide assets of $1 billion or more became subject to U.S. legal reserve requirements. Foreign banks that maintain U.S. offices were required to register with the Secretary of the Treasury. In total, the IBA proved to be a more lenient piece of legislation than many analysts had expected. It did not attempt to punish or discriminate against foreign banks relative to their U.S. counterparts. In fact, the act set in law the principle of *mutual nondiscrimination,* which permits foreign-owned banks to operate under the same conditions and to possess the same powers as domestic banks. It is a policy that avoids establishing two sets of banking regulations, one for domestic institutions and the other for foreign-owned banks.

Federal regulation of foreign banks was extended a step further in 1980 when the Depository Institutions Deregulation and Monetary Control Act was passed. (See Exhibit 24.1.) All foreign banking organizations offering services to U.S. residents became eligible for deposit insurance from the Federal Deposit Insurance Corporation and were required to conform to deposit reserve requirements set by the Federal Reserve Board. When a foreign bank opens an agency, branch, or loan production office in the United States, it must register as a bank holding company and conform with all holding company laws and regulations as administered by the Federal Reserve System. These new requirements even more firmly reflected Congress's intention to place all banks (foreign and domestic) on the same regulatory footing and in the same field of competition.

Finally, on the heels of the scandal involving the Bank of Credit and Commerce International (BCCI) of Luxembourg, which illegally attempted to acquire control of several U.S. banks, the Federal Reserve Board was granted even broader new powers to regulate the activities of agencies, branch offices, and subsidiaries of foreign banks inside U.S. territory. Under the terms of the Foreign Bank Supervision Enhancement Act passed by Congress in 1991, the Fed must approve any proposed bank agency, branch, or representative office to be set up in the United States. The Fed was empowered to *close* a foreign bank office if its home country fails to subject the parent bank to comprehensive supervision and regulation. Any foreign bank seeking to buy more than 5 percent of the stock of a U.S. bank or bank holding company must receive Federal Reserve Board approval. Moreover, small deposits (less than $100,000) can be accepted in the United States by foreign banks only through subsidiary companies that have FDIC insurance coverage and conform to all U.S. banking regulations.

24.5 Regulation of the International Banking Activities of U.S. Banks

A more significant problem than regulating foreign banking activities in the United States is the regulation, supervision, and control of U.S. banks offering their services overseas. Indeed, U.S. bank presence abroad is extensive. For example, at year-end 2003, nearly 75 American banks operated more than 835 branch offices in foreign countries. What limits should be placed on U.S. banks operating overseas? Who should enforce those limits?

EXHIBIT 24.1 **Purposes and Provisions of the International Banking Act (IBA) of 1978, the Foreign Bank Supervision Enhancement Act of 1991, and Other Recent U.S. Banking Laws Applying to International Banking Firms**	**International Banking Act of 1978** Purpose: To promote competitive equality between domestic and foreign banking institutions operating in the United States. Provisions: Limited the interstate branching of foreign banks. Provided for federal licensing of branches and agencies of foreign banks. Authorized the Federal Reserve Board to impose reserve requirements on the deposits of branches and agencies of foreign banks. Provided for foreign bank access to Federal Reserve services. Provided for federal deposit insurance for domestic branches of foreign banks. Subjected foreign banks operating branches and agencies to the prohibitions against nonbank business ventures in the U.S. Bank Holding Company Act. **Depository Institutions Deregulation and Monetary Control Act of 1980** Purpose: To further equalize deposit regulations and services that foreign banks can offer vis-à-vis domestic banks inside the United States. Provisions: All foreign banks selling services to U.S. residents were made eligible for FDIC insurance on their deposits but must also hold reserve requirements behind their deposits at levels specified by the Federal Reserve Board. **International Lending and Supervision Act of 1983** Purpose: To reduce the risks to international banks and their depositors from international lending. Provisions: U.S. banks must set aside special reserves against their foreign loans. Minimum capital requirements are imposed to protect depositors in these banks. **Foreign Bank Supervision Enhancement Act of 1991** Purpose: To give U.S. authorities greater control over foreign bank activities inside the U.S. and to limit risk to the FDIC insurance fund from foreign banks. Provisions: If foreign banks wish to accept deposits in the United States of less than $100,000, they must establish one or more U.S. banking subsidiaries and obtain FDIC insurance coverage for their deposits. Uninsured U.S. offices of foreign banks cannot accept deposits under $100,000. Prior approval of the Federal Reserve Board is required for the creation of new foreign bank branch, agency, or representative offices inside U.S. territory. Foreign banks operating inside the United States must be subject to comprehensive supervision by their home country and must not violate U.S. law or engage in unsound banking practices. Their U.S. operations may be closed by the Federal Reserve Board if found to be operated in an unsafe manner.

The *Federal Reserve Board* has been designated as the chief regulatory agency for U.S. international banking activities. A member bank of the Federal Reserve System choosing to expand its activities abroad through the creation of foreign branches or through investments in foreign firms must secure the approval of the Federal Reserve Board. In contrast, state laws govern the foreign operations of state-chartered banks. However, most state governments have exerted only nominal control over foreign banking activities.

Of prime concern to the Federal Reserve is the *protection of domestic deposits* and the *stability of the domestic banking system*. The Fed has argued that it is difficult to separate a bank's foreign operations from its domestic activities. If a foreign subsidiary gets into trouble, the danger exists that public confidence in the soundness of the controlling domestic bank will be undermined. For this reason, the Fed, in reviewing applications of U.S. banks to expand abroad, examines closely the condition of their domestic offices to determine if their home-based operations are adequately capitalized and if the bank has sufficient management skill to support both foreign and domestic operations.

The regulatory authorities would like to develop ways to insulate the foreign activities of U.S. banks from their domestic operations. Such insulation would grant wider latitude to banking activities abroad and at the same time shield domestic banks from the hazards associated with foreign operations. Legally, one bank subsidiary is not liable for the debts of another. However, in practice, a domestic bank might feel compelled to aid its affiliates operating in foreign markets. The practical, if not legal, links between foreign and domestic subsidiaries of multinational banks force regulators to keep close tabs on the foreign operations of all banks.

QUESTIONS TO HELP YOU STUDY

5. Explain why *foreign banks* have entered the United States in considerable numbers in recent years.

6. What federal government *regulations* apply to foreign banks operating in the United States today? Why did Congress pass laws to regulate foreign bank activity in the United States? What is the danger if laws of this type are made too restrictive?

7. What federal government agency is the chief *regulator* of foreign banks operating in the United States? Why do you think Congress picked this particular agency to play a leadership role in foreign bank regulation inside the United States?

8. What is meant by the principle of *mutual nondiscrimination?* What problems does this principle pose for regulators? What advantages does it have?

24.6 The Future of International Banking

Among the leading sources of information about the past, present, and future of international banking are the combined libraries of the World Bank and the International Monetary Fund at jolis.worldbankimflib.org, the Bank for International Settlements at bis.org, and the World Bank at worldbank.org

The future of international banking is clouded at this time due to the many cross-currents of economics and politics that pervade our world. Sluggish economic growth and high unemployment in some parts of the world (especially in Japan and in parts of western Europe), trade barriers, and political struggle and terrorism threaten the flow of international commerce and make bank lending across national boundaries risky. In this section, we take a brief look at these problems and their implications for the future of international banking.

The Risks of International Lending

Political and Currency Risk Lending funds in the international arena is riskier, on average, than is domestic lending. *Political risk*—the risk that government laws and regulations will change to the detriment of business interests—is particularly significant in international banking. Governments are frequently overthrown and confiscation of private property is a frequent occurrence in some parts of the world.[1] There is also *currency*

---

[1]Many financial analysts often lump political and other risks in international lending under the general term *country risk.* This is the possibility that governments borrowing money from multinational banks may be unable or unwilling to repay and that private borrowers may, because of law and regulation, be unable to make payment on their loans. For example, private borrowers may be prevented from paying due to *transfer risk,* a component of country risk in which a nation prohibits outflows of capital, dividends, or interest payments due to an internal shortage of foreign exchange. The other component of country risk—*political risk*—arises when loans cannot be repaid due to war, revolution, or changes in regulatory philosophy that adversely affect the ability of a borrower to fulfill a debt obligation.

risk—the risk associated with changing relative prices of foreign currencies. The value of property pledged behind an international loan falls if the currency of the home country is devalued, eroding the lender's collateral. Geography too works against the international lender. The large distances that frequently separate lender and borrower make it difficult for a bank loan officer to see that the terms of a loan are being followed.

The risks of international lending have become a greater concern in recent years because international banks have become the principal source of borrowed funds for developing countries as the United States and other industrialized countries have cut back on their foreign aid programs. Unfortunately, when international commodity prices declined, as they did until a recent recovery set in, numerous developing countries could not meet the terms of their loans. Many of these debts were rescheduled by agreement between international banks and debtor nations. Simultaneously, the International Monetary Fund and the World Bank moved to supply more funds to give these debtor nations time to adjust their domestic economies to a harsher economic climate.[2] As the twenty-first century approached, more and more developing nations in Asia, the Americas (especially Argentina), the former Soviet Union, and Africa began to experience credit problems. Some nations periodically threatened to repudiate their international debt (as in the case of Russia) or unilaterally alter the terms of their repayment (as in the case of Argentina). At the same time, some multinational banks began to scale down their international lending operations by selling old loans at deep discounts, which limited the availability of liquidity in international markets and slowed the growth of world trade.

Some banks pioneered *debt-for-equity swaps* in which they accepted shares of stock in some overseas projects as a substitute for holding loans. Debt-for-equity swaps also provided more flexible funding for developing countries, but most other troubled nations sought out restructuring of their existing loans. Some sought outright forgiveness of what they owed.

Geographic Distribution of International Bank Lending   Beginning in the late 1970s, U.S. bank regulators inaugurated semiannual surveys of foreign lending by U.S. banking organizations. The principal concern of these regulatory agencies was that U.S. multinational banks were overly committed to foreign loans, where the political and economic risks were unusually high. This might threaten the confidence of the public in the soundness of some of the world's largest banks. Recent surveys show that most loans extended by U.S. multinational banks are made to industrially developed nations (including Canada, western Europe, and Japan) and to countries in Central and South America, along with a growing loan commitment to China as it emerges as a major player in international trade. However, close to a third of all foreign loans typically are extended to lesser-developed countries, a number of which have been in serious financial difficulty at various times as the twentieth century gave way to the twenty-first (including Argentina, Brazil, and Russia).

---

[2] The relationship between lending activity by the IMF and the World Bank and parallel lending to the same customers by international banks has been a center of controversy in recent years. Some authorities believe that the IMF and the World Bank have actively contributed to international bank lending problems at times. They argue that IMF/World Bank loans have been regarded by some international bankers as a "stamp of approval" for their own extension of credit to troubled international borrowers. In short, loans extended by the IMF or the World Bank may create a "moral hazard" problem for the international banking system, encouraging unsound lending by international banks. Conversely, other observers argue that the IMF and the World Bank have followed lending policies that are too strict, imposing difficult, if not impossible, requirements ("conditionality") on nations asking for help and precipitating financial crises that otherwise might not have occurred. For a reasonably balanced discussion of this ongoing controversy, see especially Globalization.org at **globalization101.org/issue/imfworldbank/4.asp.**

An important government-sponsored international bank that facilitates international lending is the Export-Import Bank. See especially exim.gov and tradeport.org

Fortunately, loans to distant nations are mainly short term (maturity of one year or less), and many are made to banks themselves. On the whole, multinational banks appear to be relatively conservative lenders, directing their credits to large bank, corporate, and governmental borrowers situated mainly in Europe, more prosperous areas in Asia, and in rapidly growing Latin American markets. The bulk of such loans is concentrated among the largest international banks.

Public Confidence and Bank Failures

A persistent problem in international banking is the preservation of *public confidence* in the banking system. Essentially, this means protecting the major multinationals against failure. To avert serious financial difficulties among the world's largest banks, regulatory authorities in the United States and elsewhere look closely at the *capital positions* of multinational banks. Regulators have often urged a slower expansion of international loans and the avoidance of excessive credit exposure in loans to any one country, especially to non-oil-producing nations of the Third World. This is coupled with an insistence on adequate levels of equity capital. One of the first steps in this direction occurred in 1983 when the United States Congress passed the **International Lending and Supervision Act**. This law ordered bank regulatory agencies to prepare new rules requiring U.S. banks to:

International Lending and Supervision Act

1. Maintain special reserves against foreign loans in those instances where the quality of a bank's assets has been impaired by protracted borrower inability to repay loans.

2. Limit loan rescheduling fees charged troubled foreign borrowers.

3. Disclose a bank's exposure to foreign borrowers.

4. Hold minimum levels of capital as protection for an international bank's depositors.

5. Conduct feasibility studies of foreign projects involving mining, metal, or mineral processing before approving a loan to a customer.

Then, as we saw earlier in Chapter 17, in 1988 representatives from the Federal Reserve System, the Bank of England, the Bank of Japan, and the central banks of eight other countries signed the Basel Agreement. This historic international contract calls on central banks to monitor the capital positions of international banks under their jurisdiction and to impose minimum capital requirements on major banks around the world. The primary objective of this international capital standard is to ensure that banks from one nation do not have a competitive advantage over banks from other nations due to more lenient capital regulations. Beginning in 1993, all banks subject to the Basel Agreement were required to hold a ratio of core capital (mainly equity funds) to total risk-adjusted assets of at least 4 percent, and a ratio of total capital (core capital plus debt and other temporary forms of capital) to total risk-adjusted assets of at least 8 percent. Thus, the Basel Agreement reduced permissible leverage for banks that might handicap the ability of bankers to meet some international credit needs in the future. Moreover, banks accepting greater risk must hold more capital to preserve public confidence in their long-term viability. The Basel Agreement represents only the first step in a new era of international cooperation among regulators of banks, securities dealers, and other financial firms aimed at promoting stability in international markets and preserving the public's confidence in the global financial system and its leading banks.

As the new century approached, the initial Basel Agreement (now known as Basel I) was under revision and a new agreement (referred to as Basel II) was beginning

The high risks associated with international banking have pressured multinational banks to find ways of reducing their risk exposure. At the same time, the development of comprehensive trade agreements, such as the formation of the European Union (EU) and NAFTA, have brought banks previously isolated from one another into close contact and increased competition, increasing the risk of bank failure.

One of the principal ways international banks have dealt with these risk factors is by *merging* into larger, more diversified banking firms, in terms of both products and geographical location. Advances in communications technology have overcome barriers to management control and accelerated the "urge to merge." Nowhere has this merger trend been more evident than in Japan where the leading Japanese banks have engaged in dozens of recent mergers and acquisitions.

Examples include the recent combinations of Sanwa Bank with Tokai and Toyo Trust banks, the creation of Sumitomo Mitsui Bank Group from the merger of Sumitomo and Sakura banks, and the formation of the Mitsubishi Tokyo Financial Group, bringing together the Nippon Trust, Mitsubishi Trust, and the Bank of Tokyo–Mitsubishi. These combinations have created several of the largest banks on the planet. A more dramatic example is Mizuho Holdings, Inc., composed of Yasuda, Fuji, Dai-Ichi Kangyo, and Industrial banks with about $1.3 trillion in total assets.

In western Europe, huge mergers have taken place not only between banks, but also between banks, insurance companies, and security firms. Many of these largest combinations crossed national borders in the wake of the formation of the European Union, helping to tie together the financial systems of Germany, France, Italy, and other European countries. Examples include the recent merger of giant insurer Allianz AG of Munich with Dresdner Bank AG; the acquisition by Germany's Deutsche Bank AG of Bankers Trust Company of New York; and the alliance of Verisbank Group with the Bank of Munich.

Recently the European Commission, based in Brussels, was created to review and possibly block future mergers involving European financial and nonfinancial companies. The European Commission currently reviews larger mergers for evidence of "collective dominance," indicating excessive market concentration in a handful of companies. At some point, larger European financial-service firms may run into these competitive and regulatory barriers because banking there is already much more concentrated in the hands of the very largest banks than in the United States. Moreover, several European nations seem determined to shelter their domestic banks from being acquired by banking companies from other countries.

to emerge. This new set of capital rules, which may come into force as early as 2007, would be aimed principally at the largest banks in the world (approximately 20 of the leading international banks). Instead of using rigid formulas to determine how much capital each bank should hold (as in Basel I), each banking firm will be asked to develop its own internal models for determining its unique level of risk exposure and its corresponding need for capital. Moreover, each international bank will be required to "stress test" its asset portfolio under a variety of possible market conditions. The Basel II Accord is being designed to establish a *flexible* system for determining bank capital requirements that can be adjusted to shifting market conditions and to innovations that clever international bankers frequently devise.

The Spread of Deregulation: How Fast Should We Go?

As we saw in Chapters 14, 15, and 17, the United States began an aggressive program of *deregulating* domestic banking in the 1980s. Other nations—such as Great Britain with its Big Bang deregulation of banking and security dealer services in 1987—have also made significant strides toward lifting confining government rules and regulations, permitting their own banks as well as foreign banks operating within their borders to compete more equally. Unfortunately, the pattern of international banking deregulation

China, the world's most populous nation, is rapidly emerging as an economic leader around the globe. It has joined the World Trade Organization (WTO), agreeing to open its markets to foreign traders while sharply expanding its exports to the rest of the world. Unfortunately, the banking system of mainland China wrestles today with great problems and issues and, unlike the rest of the Chinese economy, is one of the weakest in the world.

Part of the reason for the problems experienced today by Chinese bankers can be attributed to the nation's *state-owned banks*. These cumbersome and inefficient organizations are saddled with huge amounts of bad loans and currently dominate China's domestic banking system. For example, four Chinese state-owned banks—the Bank of China, Industrial and Commercial Bank of China, China Construction Bank, and the Agricultural Bank of China—control about three-fifths of the more than $2 trillion in assets belonging to the Chinese banking system. They overshadow more than a hundred smaller domestic banks serving towns and cities across the nation. In addition, there are close to 200 foreign banks represented in China, but these banks account for less than 5 percent of the domestic industry's assets and offer principally foreign-currency-based services to their corporate clients trading with China.

Under the terms of admittance to the WTO, and assuming current plans hold, China must relax its restraints on foreign banking activity beginning in 2007. Some of the world's largest banks, led by such international giants as Great Britain's HSBC Holdings, Canada's Bank of Nova Scotia, American Express Morgan Stanley, and Citigroup from the United States, have selected the Chinese market as their key target in the new century. In response, the *Chinese Bank Regulatory Commission* is considering chartering new domestic, privately owned banks to compete with these foreign entrants, reaching out to the millions of Chinese families and smaller businesses that have few or no relationships with banks of any kind. For example, less than 5 percent of Chinese adults have credit card accounts. Interestingly enough, even as China works to expand opportunities for domestic and foreign banks it has also stiffened many of its banking rules—for example, at one point ordering Chinese banks to halve lending activity briefly and, recently, demanding that its banks adopt more prudent lending practices.

To follow recent developments in Chinese banking, see Chinadaily.com.cn and fpeng.peopledaily.com.cn

To learn more about China's Bank Regulatory Commission and some of its rules, see, for example, china.org.cn/english

has been spotty, with some nations (such as China and Japan) lowering regulatory barriers to competition slowly in order to protect domestic institutions. The real losers here are domestic consumers of financial services, who have fewer options and probably pay higher prices until government deregulation takes place. The key issue is how to allow government deregulation of financial services on an international scale to proceed rapidly without wholesale bank failures that destroy public confidence.

Finding the proper speed and scope for financial deregulation remains a challenging worldwide issue. Nevertheless, there is a growing trend toward relying more on the private marketplace and less on government rule-making in order to regulate global banking. Banks that have too little capital or accept greater than normal risks are likely to be punished by the private financial markets, especially when they attempt to raise new funds at reasonable cost.

An added complication was thrown into the debate over how fast and how far deregulation should go in freeing international banks from rigid government controls when the scandal involving the Bank of Credit and Commerce International (BCCI) Holdings, S.A., broke into the headlines in the early 1990s. This far-flung international bank holding company was based in Luxembourg, which, at the time, had few rules for holding company operations. Following revelations that BCCI violated U.S. holding company law by acquiring ownership interests in U.S. banks without approval of the Federal Reserve Board, further investigation uncovered possible money-laundering activities. U.S. investigators in the Department of Justice and at the Federal Reserve began to bring indictments and levy stiff fines against principals in the BCCI case. This case clearly points to a broader issue for international banking in the twenty-first century: the necessity for regulatory cooperation and for *harmonization* of banking regulations across nations so that no bank entrusted with the public's funds can find refuge in some corner of the world from some minimum level of public scrutiny that ensures respect for the law in business dealings. This is especially important in a world that is increasingly threatened by war and terrorism financed by powerful organizations active in nearly every continent of the globe.

24.7 Prospects and Issues for the Twenty-First Century

These recent trends suggest a somewhat different future for international banking than seemed likely in earlier years. Growth—limited by capital and the availability of experienced management—should be more gradual and loan quality more of a factor in future extensions of credit to businesses and governments abroad. However, continuing expansion of international banking activities in the United States, western Europe, the nations that emerged from the dissolution of the former Soviet Union, Asia (especially China, India, South Korea, Singapore, and Hong Kong), and Latin America can be anticipated as long as risk exposure can be held within acceptable limits.

Certainly, a number of critical questions must be answered for international banking to prosper and grow. For example, to what extent will the regulatory authorities of different nations *cooperate* to control foreign banking activities? How can we *harmonize* different banking rules from one country to the next to promote competition and innovation but also public safety? What is an appropriate capital position for banks engaged in foreign lending and for those subject to significant amounts of market risk in their on-balance-sheet and off-balance-sheet activities? Where must regulation end and the free play of market forces be allowed to operate in international banking?

And, what about the rise of strong competitors in the form of nonbank firms—security dealers and underwriters, finance companies, insurance companies, and the like? These firms today are offering parallel services to those offered by international banks, supplying credit, underwriting new security offerings, securitizing loans, offering long- and short-term savings instruments, and managing customer cash positions, but they are usually burdened with far fewer regulations. Leading international banks have begun to respond to these new competitors. For example, Deutsche Bank of Germany is a leading underwriter of corporate securities on the European continent and increasingly in the United States; France's BNP offers savers a product that looks very much like money market fund shares; and Citigroup, J. P. Morgan Chase, and Bank of America are leading securitizers of receivables emerging from credit-card loans, auto loans, and other forms of lending. As the opening of the twenty-first century beckons us forward into a new era, international banks must find innovative and efficient ways to adjust to the challenges posed by this "new competition" or suffer erosion of their current share of the international financial marketplace.

These perplexing issues have few clear answers. However, the importance of international banking and the penetration of domestic markets by foreign banking institutions demand that effective answers be found that strengthen the global financial system and provide a basis for its future growth and development.

QUESTIONS TO HELP YOU STUDY

9. What major problems have been encountered by the international banking community in recent years? How have these problems been dealt with?

10. What is *political risk?* Why is it important in international banking?

11. What is *currency risk?* What types of currency risk exposure are of special concern to international bankers?

12. What important principle about international banking was revealed by the global banking crisis of the 1990s?

13. How did the International Lending and Supervision Act affect international banks? How about the Basel Agreement? What are Basel I and Basel II?

14. Which nonbank financial-service firms are posing a strong competitive challenge to international banking today?

MARKETS ON THE NET: The Most Important Web Sites for This Chapter

Bank for International Settlements (bis.org)
European Central Bank (ecb.int)
European Monetary Union (europa.eu.int/euro/entry.html)
Export-Import Bank (exim.gov or tradeport.org)
Guide to Banking Law (hg.org/banking.html)

Guide to International Banking (bankinfo.com)
Foreign Banks in the U.S. (federalreserve.gov)
Foreign Exchange News (forexnews.com)
International Monetary Fund (imf.org)
ISI Emerging Markets (securities.com)
World Bank (worldbank.org)

Summary of the Chapter's Main Points

International banking firms—multinational banking companies that reach across national boundaries—offer financial services around the globe today. Their growth has proceeded at a pace mirroring the growth of international trade and global capital flows as international banks typically follow their largest customers overseas.

- International banks operate many different kinds of *service facilities* to provide financial services across national boundaries today. Among the best known of these facilities are (a) international banking departments, usually located within the headquarters of a single bank: (b) shell branches in offshore island locations, designed to minimize the burden of regulation in raising funds; (c) representative offices, which funnel service requests to the banks' central facilties; (d) Edge Act and Agreement corporations, which avoid or minimize some domestic regulatory restrictions; (e) international banking facilities (IBFs) that keep computerized records of offshore transactions; (f) full-service branches that offer most of the services available from the main bank office; and (g) agency offices, which assist customers with special transactions, including record keeping and cash-management services.

- Among the leading *financial services* provided by international banks are (a) letters of credit to help finance international trade; (b) buying and selling of foreign currencies for the bank and its customers; (c) issuing bankers' acceptances to facilitate trade financing or the purchase of currencies; (d) accepting Eurocurrency deposits and making Eurocurrency loans; (e) marketing and underwriting security sales to help customers raise new funds; (f) securitizing loans to help the bank and its customers generate new working capital and reduce balance-sheet risk; (g) cash management services to provide liquidity for customers as spending power is needed; (h) advisory services regarding potential foreign investments and foreign markets that bank customers might be interested in; and (i) miscellaneous other financially oriented services.

- *Foreign banks* have come to represent a substantial share of all banking assets in the United States and account for a relatively large share of business loans made within the American banking system. Foreign bank growth inside the United States has occurred, in part, due to foreign-bank customers entering the United States, the needs of foreign businesses to carry out security sales and other transactions within the U.S. in order to obtain capital and liquidity, and the continuing search of many bank customers for safety in the face of international risks. A bank that can cross national borders offers its customers the chance to enter new markets and diversify their business operations, thereby expanding potential revenues and possibly reducing risk exposure.

- *Government regulation* of foreign bank activities has expanded considerably in recent years, subjecting foreign banks to most of the same rules and regulations that domestic banks face. In the United States, recently passed federal laws have led to close supervision and regulation of foreign banks. One prime example is the Foreign Bank Supervision Enhancement Act passed in 1991, which appointed the *Federal Reserve Board* as the principal supervisor of foreign bank activities in the United States and requires the Board's approval of the expansion of foreign banking facilities inside U.S. borders. Moreover, the Federal Reserve can close a foreign-owned bank office if, in the Fed's opinion, it is not adequately supervised by its home country. The Federal Reserve is also the chief supervisor of U.S. banks' operations in overseas markets.

- The future of international banking presents significant risks today due to recent political and economic changes abroad and unanticipated movements in interest rates and currency prices. International banks also face greater lending risk because overseas loans, on average, are more risky than domestic loans due, in part, to the relative lack of information on the condition of foreign borrowers. In recent years, however, international banks have developed country risk profiles and other advanced tools to help lower the risks inherent in international lending.

- If international banks are to survive and prosper in the future, they must retain the public's confidence and control risk taking. One of the most important methods used to accomplish these goal in recent years has been to impose common capital rules on major banks in leading industrialized countries (through the Basel Agreement on Bank Capital Standards, signed by all participating industrialized nations in 1988 and recently modified to deal more effectively with changes in risk exposure among the world's leading banks).

- Today there is less emphasis in international bank regulation upon rigid standards and, instead, greater use of risk control models created by each bank to deal with its own unique risk exposures. Moreover, international banking rules are focusing today more and more on the *private marketplace* to impose discipline on bank behavior and risk taking. For example, international banks choosing to take on greater risk often find that the free market forces them to pay more for the capital they must raise in order to carry on their daily operations.

- International banking is likely to benefit in future years from greater *deregulation* as governments move to liberalize the rules limiting future bank expansion into new markets and allow private markets, rather than government dictum, to play a far greater role in shaping the service offerings and the performance of international banking corporations.

Key Terms Appearing in This Chapter

multinational corporation, 725
shell branches, 725
representative offices, 725
Edge Act and Agreement
   corporations, 725
international banking facilities
   (IBFs), 725
agency offices, 725

letter of credit, 726
Eurocurrency deposits, 727
Eurocurrency loans, 727
Eurobond, 727
International Banking Act (IBA), 731
International Lending and
   Supervision Act, 735

Problems and Issues

1. International banking activities have expanded rapidly over the past two decades.

   a. Describe the principal forces driving this expansion.

   b. What factors may be at work to slow the growth of at least some international banks?

   c. If you were investing in a U.S. bank that had extensive international operations, what factors would you need to consider?

2. Many countries around the world have moved to privatize and/or deregulate their banking systems. As this process continues, why is it essential that these countries strive to harmonize their banking laws? What role have the Basel Accords played in this respect? Why is the principal focus of those accords so crucial to the process of harmonization of banking laws?

3. A major money-center bank in the United States wishes to expand its presence in the unfolding European Union, where it currently services corporate customers but has no physical facilities. Based on the discussion in this chapter, what initial forms of facilities would you recommend to its management and why? What special problems can you anticipate given recent announcements by the European Union regarding changes in its monetary system and in its regulation of outside financial-service suppliers?

4. Which services typically offered by international banks:

   a. Involve the direct extension of credit to corporate customers?

   b. Aid customers in hedging against various forms of market risk?

c. Assist customers in making international payments?

d. Aid customers in restructuring their capitalization?

e. Help customers in obtaining additional capital from the open market or from other lending institutions?

5. Should the activities of foreign banks be regulated when they enter any particular domestic economy? Why or why not? What could be gained by the nation being entered and what dangers might follow? How would you propose to deal with the dangers or risks involved? Explain the reasons behind your recommendations.

6. If you were charged with evaluation of the *country risk* associated with the following nations, what factors would you want to examine?

    a. Brazil

    b. Korea

    c. China

    d. Japan

    e. Argentina

In each case, carefully explain why each factor that you specified relates to the risk exposure faced by an international bank making loans in each nation. What recent developments in each of the above nations suggest that a new assessment of country risk may be in order?

Standard & Poor's Market Insight and Web-Based Problems

1. Multinational banks serve essentially the same global marketplace but often differ substantially from bank to bank, in part because they are headquartered in different nations and are subject to different sets of laws and regulations. In order to get some idea as to how significant this "country effect" can be, compare the profitability, growth, and risk exposure of the following banks using information drawn from their individual Web sites and from S&P's Market Insight database at **mhhe.com/edumarketinsight**. The banks are: Barclays PLC (BCS) and HSBC Holdings (HSBC) from the United Kingdom; Deutsche Bank (DB) and Dresdner Bank AG (DXBC) from Germany; and Bank of America (BAC) and Bank One (ONE) from the United States. Do these banking firms—grouped by country of origin—appear to be more similar to each other in performance and financial condition than they do to banks headquartered in other nations? Do you see any evidence at all for a "country effect"?

2. Because of recent reforms in the regulation of the financial-service industry in Japan, non-Japanese banks and other financial-service providers are beginning to gain substantial access to the Japanese market. Describe the pros and cons of these ventures. To put together your answer, consult the Bank of Japan's Web site at **boj.jp** and read about the reforms to the Japanese banking system that were adopted in 1998. Have there been any significant reforms *since* 1998?

3. Explore the Web site of the Bank for International Settlements at **bis.org**, in order to explain the purpose of the BIS and describe the services it provides to the international banking sector. The BIS has been extensively mentioned in the news recently. Can you discover why?

4. Among the most visible of internationally oriented institutions are the World Bank at **worldbank.org** and the Export-Import Bank at **exim.gov**. What are the history and purpose of these two internationally focused organizations and what are their specific links to the international banking community?

5. Consulting such sites as **erisk.com, riskglossary.com**, and **euromoney.com**, explain the purpose of the original Basel Agreement. What changes in the original agreement will be brought about when Basel II replaces Basel I?

Selected References to Explore

Alm, Richard. "Five Years of the Euro: Successes and New Challenges. "*Southwest Economy,* Federal Reserve Bank of Dallas, July/August 2004, pp. 13–18.

Crystal, Jennifer S.; B. Gerald Dages; and Linda S. Goldberg. "Has Foreign Bank Entry Led to Sounder Banks in Latin America?" *Current Issues in Economics and Finance,* Federal Reserve Bank of New York, January 2002, pp. 1–6.

Curry, Timothy; Christopher Richardson; and Robin Heider. "Assessing International Risk Exposures of U.S. Banks." *FDIC Banking Review,* Federal Deposit Insurance Corporation, Washington DC, 1998, pp. 13–30.

Klein, Michael W. "European Monetary Union." *New England Economic Review,* Federal Reserve Bank of Boston, March/April 1998, pp. 3–12.

Zarazaga, Carlos E. J. M. "Do International Financial Crises Defy Diagnosis?" *Southwestern Economy,* Federal Reserve Bank of Dallas, 1999, pp. 10–12.

Money and Capital Markets Dictionary

A

actual maturity   The number of days, months, or years between today and the date a loan or security is redeemed or retired. *(Chapter 10)*

add-on rate   A method for calculating the interest charge on a loan when the interest bill is added to the principal amount of the loan. That sum is divided by the number of installment payments required to determine the amount of each payment needed to eventually pay off the loan. *(Chapter 6)*

adjustable mortgage instrument (AMI)   A home mortgage loan under which some of the terms of the loan, such as the loan rate or the maturity of the loan, will vary as market conditions change. *(Chapter 22)*

agency offices   Facilities operated in overseas markets by international banks in order to provide customers with selected services (such as cash management). *(Chapter 24)*

American depository receipts (ADRs)   Dollar-denominated claims on specific foreign shares of stock that are held in safekeeping by U.S. financial institutions, giving U.S. investors access to selected foreign stock without having to accept or make payments in foreign currencies. *(Chapter 20)*

annual percentage rate (APR)   The actuarially determined rate on a consumer loan that Truth-in-Lending law requires lenders to communicate to borrowers. *(Chapter 6)*

annual percentage yield (APY)   The annualized rate of return on a savings account that U.S. depository institutions must report to their customers. *(Chapter 6)*

arbitrage   The purchase of an asset in one market and the sale of that asset in another market in response to differences in price or yield between the two markets. *(Chapters 1 and 23)*

ask price   The price at which a dealer is willing to sell securities to the public. *(Chapter 3)*

asset-backed securities (ABS)   Financial claims backed by a pool of loans or other assets, such as home mortgages or credit-card loans. *(Chapter 19)*

asymmetric information   The concept that different participants in the financial markets often operate with different sets of information, some possessing special or inside information that others do not possess. *(Chapter 1)*

asymmetry   The financial marketplace contains pockets of inefficiency in the availability and use of information relevant to the value *(price)* of assets. *(Chapter 3)*

auction   A method used to sell assets in which buyers file bids and the highest bidders receive the assets. *(Chapter 10)*

auction method   The principal means by which U.S. Treasury securities are sold to the public. *(Chapters 10 and 18)*

B

balanced-budget unit (BBU)   An individual, business firm, or unit of government whose current expenditures equal its current receipt of income. *(Chapter 2)*

balance-of-payments (BOP) accounts   A double-entry bookkeeping system recording a nation's transactions with other nations, including exports, imports, and capital flows. *(Chapter 23)*

bank discount method   The procedure by which yields on U.S. Treasury bills, commercial paper, and bankers' acceptances are calculated; a 360-day year is assumed and there is no compounding of interest income. *(Chapters 6 and 10)*

bank discount rate (DR)   Rate of return measure used in the money market which is based on the par value of a financial instrument and assumes a 360-day year. *(Chapters 6, 10, and 11)*

bankers' acceptance   A time draft that a bank has agreed to pay unconditionally on the date the draft matures. *(Chapter 11)*

bank holding company   A corporation that owns stock in one or more commercial banks. *(Chapter 14)*

banking structure   The number, relative sizes, and types of banks in a given market or in the industry as a whole. *(Chapter 14)*

base rate   A loan rate used as the foundation for determining the size of the current interest rate to be charged a borrower, such as the prime rate or LIBOR. *(Chapter 19)*

Basel I Agreement   An agreement among the central banks of leading industrialized nations of Western Europe, Canada, the United States, and Japan, formally approved in 1988, that imposed common capital requirements upon all their banks in order to control bank risk exposure. *(Chapters 17 and 24)*

Basel II Agreement   Revisions to the Basel I Agreement allowing each bank in leading industrialized countries to determine its own risk exposure and required level of capital based, in part, on stress testing its asset portfolio. *(Chapters 17 and 24)*

basis   The spread between the cash (spot) price of a commodity or security and its futures (forward) price at any given point in time. *(Chapter 9)*

basis point   A measure of rate of return equal to one one-hundredth of a percentage point. *(Chapter 6)*

bid price   The price a securities dealer is willing to pay to buy securities from the public. *(Chapter 3)*

Board of Governors   The chief policymaking and administrative body of the Federal Reserve System, composed of seven persons appointed by the president of the United States and confirmed by the Senate for maximum 14-year terms. *(Chapter 12)*

bond   A debt obligation issued by a business firm or unit of government that covers several years, usually over five or ten years. *(Chapter 3)*

bond-anticipation notes (BANs)   Short-term securities issued by a state or local government to raise funds to begin a project that eventually will be funded using long-term bonds. *(Chapter 18)*

book-entry form   The method by which marketable U.S. Treasury securities are issued, with the buyer receiving only a receipt, rather than an engraved certificate, indicating that the purchase is recorded on the Treasury's books or recorded in another approved location. *(Chapter 18)*

borrowed reserves Legal reserves loaned to depository institutions through the discount windows of the Federal Reserve banks. *(Chapter 13)*

borrowing The change in liabilities outstanding reported by a sector or unit in the economy over a specified time period. *(Chapter 3)*

branch banking A type of banking organization in which services are sold through multiple offices, all owned and operated by the same corporation. *(Chapter 14)*

budget deficit A government's financial position in which current expenditures exceed current revenues. *(Chapter 18)*

budget surplus A government's financial position in which current revenues exceed current expenditures. *(Chapter 18)*

business cycle Fluctuations in economic activity, with the economy passing alternately through expansionary *(boom)* and recessionary *(depressed)* periods. *(Chapter 9)*

C

call options Grant the buyer the right to purchase a specified number of shares of a given stock or volume of debt securities at a specified price up to an expiration date. *(Chapter 9)*

call privilege The provision often found in a bond's contract (indenture) that permits the borrower to retire all or a portion of a bond issue by buying back the securities in advance of their maturity. *(Chapter 8)*

capital account A record of short-term and long-term funds flowing into and out of a nation and included in its balance-of-payments accounts. *(Chapter 23)*

capital market The institution that provides a channel for the borrowing and lending of long-term funds (over one year). *(Chapter 1)*

carry income The difference between interest income and interest cost experienced by a dealer in securities. *(Chapter 10)*

central bank An agency of government that has public policy functions such as monitoring the operation of the financial system and controlling the growth of the money supply. *(Chapter 12)*

circuit breakers Rules on a securities exchange that bring a halt to trading or that slow certain kinds of trades when prices decline beyond a prespecified limit. *(Chapter 20)*

classical theory of interest rates An explanation of the level of and changes in interest rates that relies on the interaction of the supply of savings and the demand for investment capital. *(Chapter 5)*

clearinghouse funds Money transferred by writing a check and presenting it for collection. *(Chapter 10)*

collateralized mortgage obligation (CMO) A type of mortgage-backed security offered in more than one maturity class in order to reduce prepayment risk to investors. *(Chapter 22)*

commercial mortgage A debt instrument used to provide financing for office buildings, shopping centers, and other business ventures involving the purchase or construction of land and buildings. *(Chapter 19)*

commercial paper A short-term debt security issued by a corporation that is not tied to any specific collateral but is secured only by the general earning power of the issuing corporation. *(Chapter 11)*

common stock A residual claim against the assets and earnings of the issuing corporation evidencing a share of ownership in that company. *(Chapter 20)*

Community Reinvestment Act A federal law passed in 1977 that requires depository institutions to designate the market areas they will serve and to provide services without discrimination to all neighborhoods within their designated market areas. *(Chapter 21)*

competition Rivalry between financial-service firms offering the same or similar services. *(Chapter 4)*

compound interest The payment of additional interest earnings on previously earned interest income. *(Chapter 6)*

Comptroller of the Currency Federal regulatory agency that charters national banks in the United States. *(Chapter 17)*

consolidation A trend among banks and other financial institutions in which smaller institutions are being combined through merger and acquisition into larger institutions. *(Chapters 14 and 17)*

contractual institutions Financial institutions that attract savings from the public by offering contracts that protect the saver against risk in the future, such as insurance policies and pension plans. *(Chapter 2)*

conventional home mortgage loan Credit funds extended to a home buyer by a private lender without a government guarantee behind the loan. *(Chapter 22)*

convergence The movement of different financial-service providers closer to each other in terms of services offered to the public. *(Chapters 4 and 14)*

convertibility A feature of some preferred stocks and bonds that entitles the holder to exchange those securities for a specific number of shares of common stock. *(Chapter 8)*

convexity The rate of change in an asset's price or value varies according to the level of market rates of interest. *(Chapter 7)*

corporate bond A debt contract (IOU) of a corporation whose original maturity is more than five years. *(Chapter 19)*

corporate note A debt contract (IOU) of a corporation whose original maturity date is five years or less. *(Chapter 19)*

coupon effect The size of a debt security's promised interest rate (coupon) influences how rapidly its price moves with changes in market interest rates. *(Chapter 7)*

coupon rate The promised interest rate on a bond or note consisting of the ratio of the annual interest income promised by the security issuer to the security's face (par) value. *(Chapter 6)*

credit A loan of funds in return for a promise of future payment. *(Chapter 1)*

credit card A plastic card that allows the holder to borrow cash or to pay for goods and services with credit. *(Chapter 21)*

credit derivatives Financial instruments designed to reduce a lender's exposure to default risk. *(Chapter 8)*

credit enhancements Financial devices, such as letters of credit from a bank, that upgrade the credit rating of a borrower and allow that borrower to obtain credit at lower cost. *(Chapter 11)*

credit scoring techniques Statistical models designed to evaluate a prospective borrower's default risk exposure based on variables reflecting the borrower's credit history and financial condition. *(Chapter 21)*

credit unions Nonprofit associations accepting deposits from and making loans to their members. *(Chapter 15)*

cross hedge The purchase of a futures contract for a different financial instrument than is being traded in the cash market. *(Chapter 9)*

currency futures and options market   Agreements that allow businesses or individuals acquiring or selling foreign currencies to protect themselves against future fluctuations in currency prices by shifting currency risk to someone else willing to bear that risk. *(Chapter 23)*

currency risk   Possible losses to a borrower or lender or to a holder of assets in foreign markets due to adverse changes in currency prices. *(Chapter 10)*

currency sterilization   An action taken by a central bank to offset the impact from government purchases or sales of currencies on bank reserves and deposits through the use of central bank policy tools. *(Chapter 23)*

currency swap   A contract designed to reduce the risk of loss due to changes in currency prices by exchanging one nation's currency for another that is of more use to a borrower. *(Chapter 23)*

current account   A component of a nation's balance-of-payments accounts that tracks purchases and sales of goods and services (trade) and gifts made to foreigners. *(Chapter 23)*

current borrowing   Net increases in liabilities on the balance sheet of an economic unit during the current period. *(Chapter 3)*

current savings   The change in net worth recorded by a sector or unit in the economy over the current time period. *(Chapter 3)*

current yield   The ratio of a security's promised or expected annual income to its current market price. *(Chapter 6)*

D

dealer paper   Short-term commercial notes sold by borrowing corporations and issued through security dealers who contact interested investors to determine whether they will buy the notes. *(Chapter 11)*

debenture   Long-term debt instruments secured only by the earning power of the issuing corporation and not by any specific assets pledged by the issuing firm. *(Chapter 19)*

debit card   A plastic card that is used to identify the owner of the card or to make immediate payments for goods and services. *(Chapter 21)*

debt management policy   The refunding or refinancing of the federal government's debt in a way that contributes to broad national goals and minimizes the burden of the debt. *(Chapter 18)*

debt securities   Financial claims against the assets of a business firm, individual, or unit of government, represented by bonds and other contracts evidencing a loan of money. *(Chapter 2)*

default risk   The risk to the holder of debt securities that a borrower will not meet all promised payments at the times agreed upon. *(Chapters 8 and 10)*

deficit-budget unit (DBU)   An individual, business firm, or unit of government whose current expenditures exceed its current receipts of income, forcing it to become a net borrower in the money and capital markets. *(Chapter 2)*

deflation   A fall in the average price level for all goods and services. *(Chapters 2 and 13)*

demand loan   A borrowing of funds (usually by a security dealer) subject to recall of those funds on demand by the lender. *(Chapter 10)*

deposit multiplier   A number that indicates what volume of new deposits will result from an injection of a given amount of excess reserves into the banking system. *(Chapter 12)*

depository institutions   Financial institutions that raise loanable funds by selling deposits to the public. *(Chapter 2)*

Depository Institutions Deregulation and Monetary Control Act (DIDMCA)   Law passed in 1980 by the U.S. Congress to deregulate interest rate ceilings on deposits and grant new services to nonbank thrift institutions as well as to impose common reserve requirements on all depository institutions. *(Chapters 15 and 17)*

deregulation   The lifting or liberalization of government rules that restrict what private businesses can do to serve their customers. *(Chapters 14, 17, and 4)*

derivatives   Financial instruments (such as swaps, financial futures, and options) whose value depends upon an underlying financial instrument (such as a stock or a bond). *(Chapters 2 and 9)*

direct finance   Any financial transaction in which a borrower and a lender of funds communicate directly and mutually agree on the terms of a loan. *(Chapter 2)*

direct paper   Short-term commercial notes issued directly to investors by borrowing companies without the aid of a broker or dealer. *(Chapter 11)*

discount loan method   A method for calculating the interest rate on a loan that deducts the interest cost up front from the face amount of the loan with the borrower receiving only the net amount remaining for his or her use. *(Chapter 6)*

discount method   A method for calculating the interest charge on a loan that deducts the interest owed from the face amount of the loan, with the borrower receiving only the net proceeds after interest is deducted. *(Chapter 6)*

discount rate   The interest charge (in annual percentage terms) set by the Federal Reserve banks for borrowing by depository institutions from the Reserve banks. *(Chapters 10 and 13)*

discount window   The department in a Federal Reserve bank that grants credit to depository institutions in need of short-term loans of legal reserves. *(Chapters 11 and 13)*

disintermediation   The withdrawal of funds from a financial intermediary by ultimate lenders (savers) and the lending of those funds directly to ultimate borrowers. *(Chapter 2)*

duration   A weighted average measure of the maturity of a loan or security that takes into account the amount and timing of all promised interest and principal payments. *(Chapters 7 and 9)*

E

Edge Act and Agreement corporations   Special subsidiaries of U.S. banking organizations authorized by federal law to offer international banking services. *(Chapter 24)*

efficient market   A competitive market in which the prices of financial instruments traded there fully reflect all the latest information available. *(Chapters 1, 3, and 20)*

efficient markets hypothesis   A theory of the financial markets that argues that security prices tend to fluctuate randomly around their intrinsic values, return quickly to equilibrium, and fully reflect the latest information available. *(Chapters 3 and 20)*

Equal Credit Opportunity Act   A federal law passed in 1974 forbidding lending institutions from discriminating in the granting of credit based on the age, race, ethnic origin, religion, or receipt of public assistance of the borrowing customer. *(Chapter 21)*

equities   Shares of common or preferred stock, with each share representing a certificate of ownership in a business corporation. *(Chapters 2 and 20)*

Eurobond   A long-term debt security denominated in a currency other than that of the country or countries where most or all of the security is sold. *(Chapter 24)*

Eurocurrency deposits   Deposits of funds in a bank denominated in a currency foreign to the bank's home country. *(Chapter 24)*

Eurocurrency loans   Loans made by a multinational bank in a currency other than that of the bank's home country. *(Chapter 24)*

Eurocurrency market   An international money market where bank deposits denominated in the world's most convertible currencies are traded. *(Chapter 11)*

Eurodollars   Deposits of U.S. dollars in foreign banks abroad or in foreign branch offices of U.S. banks or U.S. international banking facilities (IBFs). *(Chapter 11)*

event risk   The probability that changes inside a firm or other security-issuing individual or institution or external happenings will affect the value of the securities involved. *(Chapter 8)*

excess reserves   Cash and deposits at the Federal Reserve banks held by depository institutions that are in excess of their legal reserve requirements. *(Chapters 12, 13, and 14)*

expected yield   The weighted average return on a risky security composed of all possible yields from the security multiplied by the probability that each possible yield will occur. *(Chapter 8)*

external financing   Drawing upon sources of funding, such as the money and capital markets, that lie outside a business firm or other economic unit. *(Chapter 2)*

F

Fair Credit Billing Act   A federal law giving customers the right to question entries on bills sent to them for goods and services purchased on credit and giving them the right to expect that billing errors will be corrected as quickly as possible. *(Chapter 21)*

Fair Credit Reporting Act   A federal law that gives credit customers the right to view their credit record held by a credit bureau and to secure correction of any errors in that record. *(Chapter 21)*

federal agencies   Departments or divisional units of the federal government empowered to borrow funds in the open market in order to make loans to private businesses and individuals or otherwise subsidize private lending or borrowing. *(Chapter 11)*

Federal Deposit Insurance Corporation (FDIC)   Federal agency established in 1934 to insure the deposits of commercial banks and later expanded in 1989 to insure the deposits of savings associations as well. *(Chapters 14, 15, and 17)*

FDIC Improvement Act (FDICIA)   Passed by the U.S. Congress in 1991, this federal law provided additional capital and borrowing authority for the Federal Deposit Insurance Corporation (FDIC) and permitted regulatory authorities to restrict the activities of and even close undercapitalized banks. *(Chapters 15 and 17)*

Federal Financing Bank (FFB)   A unit of the federal government created in 1973 that borrows money through the U.S. Treasury Department and channels these funds to federal agencies. *(Chapter 11)*

federal funds   Funds that can be transferred immediately from their holder to another party for immediate payment for purchases of securities, goods, or services. *(Chapters 10 and 11)*

federal funds rate   The market interest rate attached to federal funds loans and a target interest rate for Federal Reserve monetary policy. *(Chapters 11 and 13)*

Federal Home Loan Bank (FHLB) System   U.S. federal agency created in 1932 to make loans to mortgage lenders and, thereby, increase the liquidity of home mortgage loans. *(Chapter 22)*

Federal Home Loan Mortgage Corporation (FHLMC)   A federal agency created in 1970 to improve the resale (secondary) market for home mortgages. *(Chapter 22)*

Federal Housing Administration (FHA)   An agency of the federal government established in 1934 to guarantee mortgage loans for low-priced and medium-priced homes, thereby reducing the risks of lending by financial institutions making qualified home loans. *(Chapter 22)*

Federal National Mortgage Association (FNMA)   A federal agency created in 1938 to buy and sell selected residential mortgages in the secondary market and encourage the development of a resale market for home loans. *(Chapter 22)*

Federal Open Market Committee (FOMC)   The chief body for setting money and credit policy within the Federal Reserve System, consisting of the seven members of the Federal Reserve Board and the presidents of the 12 Federal Reserve banks, only 5 of whom may vote. *(Chapters 12 and 13)*

Federal Reserve bank   One of 12 regional banks chartered by the U.S. Congress to provide central banking services to a specific region of the nation. *(Chapter 12)*

Federal Reserve System   The central bank of the United States, created by Congress to issue currency and coin, regulate the banking system, protect the value of the dollar, and promote maximum employment. *(Chapters 12, 13, and 17)*

finance companies   Financial-service firms that provide both business and consumer credit. *(Chapter 16)*

financial asset   A claim against the income or wealth of a business firm, household, or unit of government usually represented by a certificate, receipt, or other legal document. *(Chapter 2)*

financial disclosure   The provision of relevant information to the public to aid individuals and institutions in making sound financial decisions. *(Chapters 3, 4, 13, 17, 20, and 21)*

financial futures contracts   Contracts that call for the future delivery or sale of designated securities at a price agreed upon the day the contract is made. *(Chapter 9)*

financial holding companies (FHCs)   Corporations permitted under the terms of the Gramm-Leach-Bliley Act to acquire and control banks, insurance companies, security underwriters, and other financial firms, all under the sane corporate umbrella. *(Chapters 4, 14, and 17)*

financial innovation   A trend in the financial system toward developing new services and new service delivery methods. *(Chapter 4)*

Financial Institutions Reform, Recovery, and Enforcement Act (FIRREA)   Federal law passed in 1989 to bail out the U.S. savings and loan industry, strengthen the federal deposit insurance program, and liquidate the assets of failed thrift institutions. *(Chapters 15 and 17)*

financial intermediaries   Financial-service firms that simultaneously borrow funds through the issuance of secondary securities and lend funds by accepting primary securities from borrowers. Also referred to as indirect finance. *(Chapters 2, 11, and 14–16)*

financial investment   The net change in financial assets held by a sector or unit in the economy over a specified time period. *(Chapter 3)*

financial market   An institutional mechanism created by society to channel savings and other financial services to those individuals and institutions willing to pay for them. *(Chapter 1)*

Financial Services Modernization (Gramm-Leach-Bliley) Act   A 1999 law of the U.S. government permitting the formation of financial holding companies that bring banks, insurance companies, and securities firms together in the same organization and allow customers to protect their financial privacy. *(Chapters 4, 14, 17, and 21)*

financial system   The collection of markets, individuals, institutions, laws, regulations, and techniques through which bonds, stocks, and other securities are traded, financial services are produced and delivered, and interest rates are determined. *(Chapter 1)*

financial wealth   Portion of the wealth held by society or by an individual economic unit in the form of stocks, bonds, and other financial assets. *(Chapter 1)*

fiscal agent   A role of the Federal Reserve System in which it provides services to the federal government, such as clearing and collecting checks on behalf of the U.S. Treasury and conducting auctions for the sale of new Treasury securities. *(Chapter 12)*

fiscal policy   The taxing and spending programs carried out by government in order to promote maximum employment, price stability, and other economic goals. *(Chapter 18)*

Fisher effect   The theory of inflation and interest rates that says nominal interest rates respond one-for-one to changes in the expected rate of inflation over the life of a loan. *(Chapter 7)*

fixed-rate home mortgages (FRMs)   Mortgage loans that carry an unchanging loan rate. *(Chapter 22)*

Flow of Funds Accounts   A system of social accounts prepared quarterly by the Board of Governors of the Federal Reserve System that reports the amount of saving and borrowing in the U.S. economy by major sectors. *(Chapter 3)*

foreign exchange markets   Channels for trading national currencies and determining relative currency prices. *(Chapter 23)*

foreign exchange rates   The prices of foreign currencies expressed in terms of other currencies. *(Chapter 23)*

forward contract   An agreement to deliver a specified amount of currency, securities, or other goods or services at a set price on some future date. *(Chapter 23)*

forward market   Channel through which currencies, securities, goods, and services are traded for future delivery with the terms of trade set in advance of delivery. *(Chapter 23)*

fundamental analysis   A strategy for choosing stocks and other assets based upon an analysis of a security-issuer's financial statements and the financial condition of the issuing firm and its industry. *(Chapter 20)*

G

Garn-St Germain Depository Institutions Act   A law passed by the U.S. Congress in 1982 to further deregulate the depository institutions sector and to give federal deposit insurance agencies additional tools to deal with failing institutions. *(Chapters 15 and 17)*

general credit controls   Monetary policy tools that affect the entire banking and financial system, such as open market operations or changes in the Federal Reserve's discount rate. *(Chapter 13)*

general obligation bonds   Debt obligations issued by state and local governments and backed by the "full faith and credit" of the issuing government (i.e., may be repaid from any revenue source). *(Chapter 18)*

Glass-Steagall Act   The National Bank Act of 1933 that created the federal deposit insurance system and separated commercial from investment banking. *(Chapter 17)*

globalization   The spreading of financial services and financial institutions worldwide. *(Chapters 4, 23, and 24)*

gold exchange standard   A system for making international payments in which each national currency is freely convertible into gold bullion at a fixed price and also freely convertible into other currencies at relatively stable prices. *(Chapter 23)*

gold standard   A system of payments for purchases of goods and services in which nations agree to exchange paper money or coins for gold bullion at predetermined prices and allow gold to be exported or imported freely from one nation to another. *(Chapter 23)*

Government National Mortgage Association (GNMA)   A federal agency created in 1968 to assist the home mortgage market through such activities as purchasing mortgages to finance low-income family housing projects and guaranteeing principal and interest payments on securities issued by private mortgage lenders that are backed by pools of home mortgages. *(Chapter 22)*

government-sponsored agencies   Insitutions originally owned by the federal government but now privately owned with the authority to borrow from and lend money to private businesses and individuals or to issue loan guarantees. *(Chapter 11)*

H

harmonization   Regulatory cooperation among different nations. *(Chapters 4 and 17)*

Harrod-Keynes effect   The theory of the relationship between inflation and interest rates that argues that inflation affects real rates of return but not necessarily nominal rates of return. *(Chapter 7)*

hedging   The act of buying and selling financial claims or using other financial tools in order to protect against the risk of fluctuations in market prices or interest rates. *(Chapter 9)*

holding-period yield (HPY)   The rate of return received or expected from a financial asset or other investment over the period the asset or investment was held, including the price for which the asset or investment was sold to another investor. *(Chapter 6)*

home equity loan   Extension of credit to individuals who own their homes in which the borrowers' homes are pledged as collateral to support the loans and the amount of the loan is based on the difference between the market value of the home and the amount of any home mortgage debt outstanding (i.e., the owner's equity in a home). *(Chapter 21)*

home mortgage interest rate   The percentage cost of borrowed funds used to purchase a house or other residential dwelling. *(Chapter 6)*

homogenization   The tendency of different financial institutions to offer the same services. *(Chapter 4)*

I

identity theft   Using another person's name and nonpublic data (such as his or her Social Security number) to fraudulently obtain credit or personal assets. *(Chapter 21)*

implied forecasting   The market's expectation about future interest rates as indicated by the shape of the yield curve or by financial futures prices. *(Chapter 9)*

income effect   The relationship between interest rate levels and the volume of saving in the economy that argues that the advent of higher interest rates may induce savers to save *less* because each dollar saved now earns a higher rate of return. *(Chapter 5)*

indenture   A contract accompanying the issue of a bond or note by a corporation or other borrower that lists the rights, privileges, and obligations of the borrower and the investor who has purchased the bond or note. *(Chapter 19)*

indirect finance   Also known as financial intermediation, in which financial transactions (especially the borrowing and lending of money) are carried out through a financial intermediary. *(Chapter 2)*

industrial development bond (IDB)   Debt security issued by a local government to aid a private company in the construction of a plant and/or the purchase of equipment or land. *(Chapter 19)*

inflation   A rise in the average level of all prices of goods and services traded in the economy over any given period of time. *(Chapters 2 and 7)*

inflation-caused income tax effect   The presence of a progressive income tax structure tends to cause nominal interest rates to increase by more than the expected increase in inflation. *(Chapter 7)*

inflation premium   The expected rate of price inflation that, when added to the real interest rate, equals the nominal interest rate on a loan. *(Chapter 7)*

inflation (or purchasing power) risk   The probability that increases in the average level of prices for all goods and services sold in the economy will reduce the purchasing power of an investor's income from loans or securities. *(Chapter 10)*

inflation risk premium   Compensation paid to a lender for that component of inflation that is not expected. *(Chapter 7)*

insider trading   Buying or selling the securities of an issuing firm by an employee, director, or by someone under contract with the issuing firm in a fiduciary capacity who acts on the basis of private or privileged information about the issuing firm. *(Chapter 3)*

installment credit   All liabilities of a borrowing customer other than home mortgages that are retired in two or more consecutive loan payments. *(Chapter 21)*

interest rate   The price of credit, or ratio of the fees charged to secure credit from a lender to the amount borrowed, usually expressed on an annual percentage basis. *(Chapter 6)*

interest rate parity   A condition prevailing in international markets where the interest rate differential between two nations matches the forward discount or premium on their two currencies. *(Chapter 23)*

interest rate structure   The concept that the interest rate or yield attached to any loan or security consists of the risk-free (or *pure*) rate of interest plus risk premiums for the security holder's exposure to various forms of risk. *(Chapter 8)*

interest rate swap   A contract between two or more firms in which interest payments are exchanged so that each participating firm saves on interest costs and gets a better balance between its cash inflows and outflows. *(Chapter 9)*

internal financing   The use of saving by an economic unit, rather than debt, to support the acquisition of real and/or financial assets. *(Chapter 2)*

International Banking Act (IBA)   A U.S. law passed in 1978 to bring foreign banks operating in the United States under regulation. *(Chapter 24)*

international banking facilities (IBFs)   A domestically based set of computerized accounts recording transactions of a U.S. bank with its foreign customers. *(Chapter 24)*

International Lending and Supervision Act   A federal law passed in 1983 requiring U.S. banks to increase their capital and to pursue more prudent international loan policies. *(Chapter 24)*

investment   Expenditures on capital goods or on inventories of goods or raw materials that are used to produce other goods and services, causing future production and income to rise. *(Chapter 1)*

investment banks or bankers   Financial firms that assist their customers in raising funds by underwriting their security offerings. *(Chapters 16, 17, 19, and 20)*

investment companies   Financial intermediaries that sell shares to the public to raise funds and invest the proceeds in stocks, bonds, and other securities. *(Chapter 16)*

investment institutions   Financial intermediaries selling their customers financial assets in order to build up savings for retirement or for other customer uses. *(Chapter 2)*

IPOs   Initial public offerings of stocks and other securities as companies convert from privately held businesses to publicly held corporations. *(Chapter 20)*

J

junk bonds   Corporate debt securities bearing credit ratings below investment grade. *(Chapters 8 and 19)*

L

leasing companies   Financial-service firms that provide businesses and consumers access to equipment, motor vehicles, and other assets for a stipulated period of time at an agreed-upon leasing rate. *(Chapter 16)*

legal reserve requirement   A law or regulation that calls for a depository institution to hold certain assets (such as vault cash and reserves posted to an account at the central bank) as a reserve backing the institution's deposits and selected other liabilities. *(Chapters 11, 13, and 14)*

legal reserves   Deposits held at the Federal Reserve banks by depository institutions plus currency and coin held in the vaults of these institutions. *(Chapters 12, 13, and 14)*

letter of credit   An authorization to draft funds from a bank provided stipulated conditions are met. *(Chapter 24)*

leveraged buyouts   A form of corporate takeover in which the management of a company or other small group of investors buys the publicly owned stock of the firm, financing the transaction mainly with new debt that will be repaid from planned increases in company earnings. *(Chapter 19)*

liability management   The techniques used by banks to control the amount and composition of their borrowed funds by changing the interest rates they offer to reflect competition and the intensity of the bank's borrowing requirements. *(Chapter 11)*

life insurance companies   Financial-service firms selling contracts to customers that promise to reduce the financial loss to an individual or family associated with death, disability, or old age. *(Chapter 16)*

liquidity   The quality or capability of any asset to be sold quickly with little risk of loss and possessing a relatively stable price over time. *(Chapters 1, 8, and 10)*

liquidity preference theory of interest rates   An explanation of the level of and change in interest rates that focuses on the interaction of the supply of and demand for money. *(Chapter 5)*

liquidity premium   The added yield *(interest return)* that must be paid to investors to get them to buy and hold long-term instead of short-term securities. *(Chapter 7)*

loanable funds theory of interest rates   The credit view of what determines the level of and changes in interest rates that focuses on the interaction of the demand for and the supply of loanable funds *(credit)*. *(Chapter 5)*

London Interbank Offer Rate (LIBOR)   Short-term interest rate attached to Eurocurrency deposits traded between banks. *(Chapter 11)*

long hedge   The purchase of futures contracts calling for the delivery of securities or commodities to a counterparty on a specific future date at a set price. *(Chapter 9)*

long position   The purchase of assets outright from the seller in order to hold them until they mature or must be sold. *(Chapter 10)*

M

M1   The narrowest definition of the U.S. money supply, consisting of currency outside the U.S. Treasury, Federal Reserve banks, and the vaults of depository institutions; travelers checks of nonbank issuers; demand deposits at commercial banks (except the deposits of other banks, the U.S. government, and foreign banks and official institutions) less cash items in the process of collection and Federal Reserve float; and other checkable deposits (including NOW and ATS accounts at depository institutions, credit union share draft accounts, and demand deposits at thrift institutions). *(Chapter 2)*

M2   The definition of the U.S. money supply that includes M1 plus savings deposits (including money market deposit accounts); small-denomination time deposits (each less than $100,000) less individual retirement accounts (IRAs) and Keogh balances held at depository institutions; and balances kept with retail money market mutual funds less IRA and Keogh balances at money market mutual funds. *(Chapter 2)*

M3   The definition of the U.S. money supply that includes M2 plus balances held in institutional money market funds; large-denomination time deposits (each $100,000 or more); repurchase agreement (RP) liabilities of depository institutions (in denominations of $100,000 or more) on U.S. government and federal agency securities; and Eurodollars held by U.S. addresses at foreign branches of U.S. banks worldwide and at all banking offices in the United Kingdom and Canada. Large-denomination time deposits, RPs, and Eurodollars exclude amounts held by depository institutions, money market funds, the U.S. government, and foreign banks and official institutions. *(Chapter 2)*

managed float   An international monetary payments system in which the value of any currency is determined by demand and supply forces in the marketplace, but governments intervene on occasion in an effort to stabilize the value of their own currencies. *(Chapter 23)*

managed floating currency standard   System of currency valuation in which each nation chooses its own currency exchange rate policy. *(Chapter 23)*

margin requirements   The difference between the market value of a security and its maximum loan value as specified by a regulation enforced by the Federal Reserve Board. *(Chapter 13)*

market   An institutional mechanism for trading goods and services. *(Chapter 1)*

marketability   The feature of an asset that reflects its ability to be sold quickly to recover the purchaser's funds. *(Chapter 8)*

market broadening   A tendency for financial service markets to expand geographically over time due to advances in technology and increased customer mobility. *(Chapter 4)*

market risk (or interest rate risk)   The probability that the prices of securities or other assets will fall (due to rising interest rates), confronting the investor with a capital loss. *(Chapter 10)*

market segmentation argument   A theory of the yield curve in which the financial markets are thought to be separated into several distinct markets by the maturity preferences of various investors so that demand and supply for loans and securities in each market determine relative interest rates on long-term versus short-term securities. *(Chapter 7)*

master note   A borrowing arrangement between a corporation issuing commercial paper and an institution buying the paper in which the buying institution agrees to accept new paper each day up to a specified maximum amount. *(Chapter 11)*

maturity   Length of calendar time in days, weeks, months, and years before a security or loan comes due and must be paid off. *(Chapter 7)*

member banks   Banks that have joined the Federal Reserve System, consisting of all federally chartered *(national)* banks and any state-chartered U.S. banks that meet the Federal Reserve's requirements for membership. *(Chapters 12 and 14)*

modified exchange standard   A system of currency exchanges and international payments in which foreign currencies were linked to gold and the U.S. dollar, with the price of gold in terms of U.S. dollars remaining fixed. *(Chapter 23)*

monetary base   The sum of legal reserves in the banking system plus the amount of currency and coin held by the public. *(Chapter 12)*

monetary policy   The use of various tools by central banks to control the cost and availability of loanable funds in an effort to achieve national economic goals. *(Chapter 12)*

money   A financial asset that serves as a medium of exchange and standard of value for purchases of goods and services. *(Chapter 2)*

money creation   The ability of banks and other depository institutions to create a deposit, such as a checking account, that can be used as a medium of exchange (to make payments for purchases of goods and services). *(Chapter 14)*

money market   The institution set up by society to channel temporary surpluses of cash into temporary loans of funds, one year or less to maturity. *(Chapters 1 and 10)*

money market deposit accounts (MMDAs)   Deposits whose interest yields vary with market conditions and are subject to withdrawal by check. *(Chapters 14, 15, and 21)*

money market mutual fund   An investment company selling shares to the public and investing the proceeds in short-term securities, such as Treasury bills and other money market instruments. *(Chapter 15)*

money multiplier   The ratio of the size of the money supply to the total reserve base available to depository institutions. *(Chapter 12)*

moral hazard   When one party to an agreement or relationship uses their position of power or special knowledge to pursue their own self-interest and receives special benefits or rewards at the expense of the other party to the agreement or relationship. *(Chapter 3)*

moral suasion A monetary policy tool of the central bank in which its officers and staff try to persuade bankers and the public through speeches and written communications to conform more closely to the central bank's goals. *(Chapter 13)*

mortgage-backed securities Debt obligations issued by private mortgage-lending institutions using selected residential mortgage loans they hold as collateral; the mortgage loans generate principal and interest payments to repay holders of the mortgage-backed securities. *(Chapter 22)*

mortgage bank A financial-service firm that works with property developers to provide real estate financing and then places the long-term loans with long-term lenders such as insurance companies and savings banks. *(Chapter 16)*

mortgage bonds Long-term debt secured by a lien on specific assets, usually plant and equipment, held by the issuing corporation. *(Chapter 19)*

mortgage lock-ins Part of a home financing contract that fixes the mortgage loan rate for a designated period of time. *(Chapter 22)*

multinational corporation A large company with manufacturing, trading, or service operations in several different countries. *(Chapter 24)*

municipals Debt securities issued by states, counties, cities, school districts, and other local units of government. *(Chapter 18)*

mutual fund A type of investment company that sells as many shares of interest in a pool of assets as the public demands and invests the proceeds of those sales in a wide variety of assets, particularly such financial assets as stocks and bonds. *(Chapter 16)*

mutuals Depository institutions owned by their depositors, such as savings banks and some savings and loan associations. *(Chapter 15)*

N

national banks U.S. banking institutions that receive their charter of incorporation from the Comptroller of the Currency, an agency of the U.S. government. *(Chapter 14)*

National Credit Union Administration (NCUA) Federal regulatory agency that oversees the activities of federally chartered credit unions. *(Chapter 17)*

National Income and Product Accounts A system of social accounts compiled by the U.S. Department of Commerce that presents data on the nation's production of goods and services, income flows, spending, and saving. *(Chapter 3)*

negotiable certificate of deposit (CD) A marketable receipt issued by a bank or other depository institution to a customer acknowledging the deposit of customer funds for a designated period under a specified interest rate formula. *(Chapter 11)*

negotiated markets Institutional mechanisms set up by society to make loans and trade securities in which the terms of trade are set by direct bargaining between a lender and a borrower. *(Chapter 1)*

net financial wealth Portion of wealth held in financial assets less total debt owed. *(Chapter 1)*

net wealth Total assets minus total liabilities held by an economic unit. *(Chapter 1)*

nominal contracts Agreements between contracting parties that fix prices, interest rates, or costs in terms of current (nominal) values; a theory of how inflation may influence the prices of stocks issued by corporations. *(Chapter 7)*

nominal interest rate The published rate of interest attached to a loan or security that includes both a real interest rate component and the inflation rate (inflation premium) expected over the life of the loan or security. *(Chapter 7)*

nominal value The price of assets or other purchasable items measured in terms of their current market price or face value; the price of assets or other items not adjusted for the effects of inflation. *(Chapter 2)*

nonborrowed reserves The largest component of the total legal reserves of depository institutions, consisting of all those legal reserves owned by depository institutions themselves and not borrowed from the Federal Reserve banks. *(Chapter 13)*

nondeposit funds Borrowings in the open market by banks and other institutions in order to supplement monies raised by selling deposits. *(Chapter 14)*

noninstallment credit A loan that is normally paid off in a lump sum rather than in a series of installment payments. *(Chapter 21)*

nonresidential mortgages Loans secured by business and farm properties. *(Chapter 22)*

note A shorter-term debt obligation issued by a business firm, individual, or unit of government to borrow money with a time to maturity that usually does not exceed five years. *(Chapter 3)*

NOW account An interest-bearing checking account available to individuals and nonprofit institutions from banks and other depository institutions. *(Chapters 14, 15, and 21)*

O

Office of Thrift Supervision Federal agency that charters and supervises savings associations. *(Chapter 17)*

open market operations The buying and selling of selected assets by a central bank to affect the quantity and growth of the legal reserves of depository institutions and general credit conditions in order to achieve the nation's economic goals. *(Chapter 13)*

open markets Institutional mechanisms created by society to make loans and trade securities in which any individual or institution can participate. *(Chapter 1)*

option contract An agreement between contract writers and contract buyers to accept delivery of ("call") securities or place with buyers ("put") securities at a specified price on or before the date the contract expires. *(Chapter 9)*

option premium The fee that the buyer of an option contract must pay to the writer of the contract for the right to deliver or accept delivery of securities at a set price. *(Chapter 9)*

organized exchanges Locations where stocks, bonds, and other assets are traded according to the rules and regulations for trading established by members of the exchange. *(Chapter 20)*

original maturity The interval of time between the issue date of a security and the date on which the borrower promises to redeem it. *(Chapter 10)*

over-the-counter (OTC) market A mechanism for trading stocks and other assets through brokers or dealers operating off the major securities exchanges. *(Chapter 20)*

P

pass-throughs Securities issued against a pool of mortgage loans held by a financial institution. *(Chapter 22)*

pension funds Financial-service firms selling retirement plans to their customers in which savings are set aside in accounts established in the customers' names and allowed to accumulate interest until those customers reach retirement age. *(Chapter 16)*

perfect market   A market in which all available information affecting the value of financial instruments is freely available to everyone, transaction costs are minimal, and all participants are price takers rather than price setters. *(Chapter 1)*

perpetuity rate   Rate of return on a financial instrument that is perpetual (never matures). *(Chapter 6)*

political risk   The probability that changes in government laws or regulations will result in a lower rate of return to the investor or, in the extreme case, a total loss of invested capital. *(Chapters 10 and 24)*

portfolio immunization   An investment strategy that tries to protect the expected yield from a security or portfolio of securities by acquiring those securities whose duration equals the length of the investor's planned holding period. *(Chapter 7)*

predatory loans   High interest-rate loans granted to borrowers with weak credit ratings that substantially increase the likelihood these borrowers will default. *(Chapter 22)*

preferred habitat   The theory of the yield curve that claims investors prefer certain maturities of securities over other maturities due to differences in liquidity needs, risk, tax exposure, and other factors. *(Chapter 7)*

preferred stock   A share of ownership in a business corporation that promises a stated annual dividend. *(Chapter 20)*

prepayment risk   The probability that a loan or security (especially securities that draw their earnings from pools of loans) will be paid off ahead of schedule, lowering the investor's expected yield from the instrument. *(Chapters 8 and 22)*

present value   Funds received today are worth more than an equal nominal amount of funds promised in the future. *(Chapter 6)*

price elasticity   The ratio of changes in the price of a debt security to changes in its yield. *(Chapter 7)*

price idexes   A measure of the cost of a market basket of goods and services which provides an indicator of inflation or deflation in the whole economy or a sector of the economy. *(Chapter 2)*

price of credit   The rate of interest that must be paid to secure the use of borrowed funds. *(Chapter 5)*

primary dealers   Security firms that are recognized by the Federal Reserve System to buy and sell securities with the Fed. *(Chapter 10)*

primary markets   Institutional mechanisms set up by society to trade newly issued loans and securities. *(Chapter 1)*

primary reserves   Cash held in a bank's vault plus deposits held with other banks. *(Chapter 14)*

primary securities   The IOUs issued by borrowers from a financial intermediary and held by the intermediary as interest-bearing assets. *(Chapter 2)*

prime bank rate   Loan rate that many banks use as the base for pricing loans extended to their best customers. *(Chapter 19)*

private (or direct) placement   Placing securities with one or a limited number of investors rather than trying to sell them in the open market. *(Chapter 19)*

property-casualty insurers   Financial-service firms selling contracts to protect their customers against losses to persons or property due to negligence, crime, adverse weather changes, fire, and other hazards. *(Chapter 16)*

public debt   The volume of debt obligations that are the responsibility of the federal government and therefore of its taxpayers. *(Chapter 18)*

public sale   When securities are sold in the open market to any individual or institution willing to pay the price, usually through investment bankers. *(Chapter 19)*

purchasing power parity   The currency value of a nation with a higher rate of inflation will tend to fall relative to the currency value of a nation with a lower rate of inflation. *(Chapter 23)*

put options   Contracts granting the buyer the right to sell a specified number of equity shares or debt securities at a set price on or before the expiration date. *(Chapter 9)*

R

random walk   A theory of asset price movements that argues that the future path of individual asset prices is no more predictable than is the path of a series of random numbers. *(Chapter 20)*

rate of interest   The price of acquiring credit, usually expressed as a ratio of the cost of securing credit to the total amount of credit obtained. *(Chapters 5 and 6)*

rational expectations theory of interest rates   An explanation of the level of and changes in interest rates based on changes in investor expectations regarding future asset prices and returns. *(Chapter 5)*

real estate investment trusts (REITs)   Tax-exempt corporations that receive at least three-quarters of their gross income from real estate transactions and devote a high percentage of their assets to real property loans. *(Chapter 16)*

real estate mortgage investment conduit (REMIC)   A mortgage-backed security issued in a variety of maturities in an effort to reduce the purchaser's interest rate risk to an acceptable level. *(Chapter 22)*

real interest rate   The rate of return from a financial asset expressed in terms of its purchasing power (adjusted for inflation). *(Chapter 7)*

real investment   The net change in real assets held by a sector or unit in the economy over a specified period of time. *(Chapter 3)*

real value   The purchasing-power inflation-adjusted price of assets, services, or other items held or available for sale. *(Chapter 2)*

regulation   Government enforcement of rules that prescribe permissible and nonpermissible activities for businesses and consumers. *(Chapter 17)*

reinvestment risk   Probability that earnings from a loan or security will have to be reinvested in lower-yielding assets in the future. *(Chapter 10)*

representative offices   Facilities established in distant markets by a bank in order to sell the bank's services and assist its clients; these offices usually cannot accept deposits or make loans. *(Chapter 24)*

repurchase agreement (RP)   A loan (usually granted to a bank or security dealer) that is collateralized by high-quality assets (usually government securities). *(Chapter 10)*

required reserves   Holdings of cash and funds on deposit with the Federal Reserve banks by depository institutions that are required by law to backstop the public's deposits held by these same institutions. *(Chapters 12, 13, and 14)*

reserve requirements   The percentage of various liabilities (such as deposits received from the public) that must be held by depository institutions, either in vault cash or on deposit at the Federal Reserve banks. *(Chapter 13)*

residential mortgage credit   Loans provided to support the purchase of new or existing single-family homes and other permanent dwellings. *(Chapter 21)*

residential mortgages   Loans secured by single-family homes and other dwellings. *(Chapter 22)*

revenue-anticipation notes (RANs)   Short-term debt obligations issued by state and local units of government in lieu of expected future governmental revenues in order to meet near-term cash needs. *(Chapter 18)*

revenue bonds   Debt obligations issued by state and local governments that are repayable only from a particular source of funds, such as revenues generated by a toll road or toll bridge or from user fees derived by selling water or electric power. *(Chapter 18)*

risk-free rate of interest   The rate of return on a riskless asset, often called the *pure rate of interest* or the *opportunity cost of money. (Chapter 5)*

risk-management tools   Financial devices (such as *futures and options*) that permit a borrower or lender of funds to protect against the risks of changing prices and interest rates. *(Chapters 4 and 9)*

S

savings   The amount of funds left over out of current income after current consumption expenditures are deducted or, for a business firm, the current net earnings retained in the business instead of paid out to the owners. *(Chapter 1)*

savings and loan associations   A leading home mortgage lender in the United States, making predominantly local loans to finance the purchase of housing for individuals and families. *(Chapter 15)*

savings banks   Depository institutions that are owned by their depositors and can be chartered by the federal government and the states. *(Chapter 15)*

seasonality   Patterns in the behavior of interest rates, with rate increases during certain seasons of the year and decreases during other seasons. *(Chapter 9)*

secondary markets   Institutional mechanisms set up by society to trade or exchange loans and securities that have already been issued. *(Chapter 1)*

secondary securities   Financial claims, such as deposits, issued by a financial intermediary to raise loanable funds. *(Chapter 2)*

Securities and Exchange Commission (SEC)   Regulatory body of the federal government charged with monitoring the behavior of security brokers, dealers, and investment institutions. *(Chapters 3 and 17)*

securitization   The selling of shares or certificates representing an interest in a pool of income-generating assets (such as mortgage loans) as a method for raising funds by a financial institution. *(Chapters 4, 14, 19, and 22)*

securitized assets   Loans are packaged together in a pool and securities representing claims to the income generated by the pooled loans are sold to investors. *(Chapter 14)*

securitized mortgages   Securities issued against a pool of mortgage loans whose interest and principal payments are paid to security holders. *(Chapter 22)*

security brokers and dealers   Financial firms that provide a conduit for buyers and sellers to trade and adjust their asset portfolios. *(Chapters 2, 16, 19, and 20)*

selective credit controls   Monetary policy tools that affect specific groups or sectors in the financial system. *(Chapter 13)*

semidirect finance   Any financial transaction (especially the borrowing and lending of money) that is assisted by a security broker or dealer. *(Chapter 2)*

serialization   The splitting up of a single bond issue into several different maturities (used most often for state and local government bonds). *(Chapter 18)*

service proliferation   The development and spreading of new financial services so that more financial institutions offer more services. *(Chapter 4)*

share draft   Interest-bearing checking account offered by a credit union. *(Chapter 15)*

shell branches   Booking offices of multinational banks, usually set up offshore to attract deposits and avoid certain domestic banking regulations. *(Chapter 24)*

short hedge   The sale of futures contracts promising the delivery of securities or commodities to another party on a specific future date at a set price. *(Chapter 9)*

short position   Dealers and other investors promise to sell and deliver in the future assets they do not currently own, hoping asset prices will fall in the interim. *(Chapter 10)*

simple interest method   A method of figuring the interest on a loan that charges interest only for the period of time the borrower actually has use of the borrowed funds. *(Chapter 6)*

social accounting   A system of record keeping that reports economic and financial activity for the whole economy and/or between principal sectors of the economy. *(Chapter 3)*

sources and uses of funds statements   A financial report prepared for each sector of the economy in the Federal Reserve Board's Flow of Funds Accounts that shows changes in net worth and changes in holdings of financial assets and liabilities over a specific time period. *(Chapter 3)*

special drawing rights (SDRs)   An official monetary reserve unit developed by the International Monetary Fund to settle international claims between nations. *(Chapter 23)*

spot market   Channel through which currencies, securities, commodities, or other goods and services are traded for immediate delivery to the buyer once buyer and seller agree on the terms of trade. *(Chapters 1, 9, 10, and 23)*

standby credit letters   Contingent obligations issued by banks or other lending institutions promising to pay off the debt of a borrower if that borrower is unable to pay. *(Chapter 14)*

state banking commissions   Government boards that charter and supervise banks headquartered in a given state. *(Chapter 17)*

state-chartered banks   Banking firms whose charter of incorporation allowing them to open for business is issued by a state governmental body (such as a board or commission) in the United States. *(Chapter 14)*

stocks   Ownership shares in a corporation, giving the holder claim to any dividends distributed from current earnings. *(Chapters 2, 3, and 20)*

strike price   The price for securities specified in an option contract; also called the *exercise price. (Chapter 9)*

substitution effect   Positive relationship between rate of interest and volume of savings in the economy. *(Chapter 5)*

surplus-budget unit (SBU)   An individual, business, or unit of government whose current income receipts exceed its current expenditures and, therefore, is a net lender of funds to the money and capital markets. *(Chapter 2)*

T

tax-anticipation notes (TANs)   Short-term debt obligations issued by state and local governments to provide for immediate cash needs until tax revenues come in. *(Chapter 18)*

tax-exemption privilege   A feature bestowed by law on some financial assets (such as state and local government bonds) that makes the income they generate free of taxation at federal or state and local government levels, or both. *(Chapters 8 and 18)*

tax-exempt securities   Debt securities issued by state, city, county, and other local units of government or by other qualified borrowers whose interest income is exempt from federal taxation and from most state taxes as well. *(Chapters 8 and 18)*

technical analysis   A strategy for making buy/sell decisions on stock and other assets based on past patterns in prices and the volume of trading. *(Chapter 20)*

third-country bills   Bankers' acceptances issued by banks in one country that finance the transport or storage of goods traded between two other countries. *(Chapter 11)*

third market   Mechanism through which securities listed on a stock exchange are traded off the exchange in the over-the-counter market. *(Chapter 20)*

time draft   A bank's promise to pay a stipulated amount of funds upon presentation of the draft on a specific future date. *(Chapter 11)*

TIPS   Treasury inflation protection securities issued in order to help protect investors in U.S. government securities from lower rates of return due to inflation. *(Chapter 7)*

transaction accounts   Deposits (such as a checking account or other accounts offered by financial institutions) that can be used to make payments for purchases of goods and services. *(Chapters 12, 13, and 14)*

transparency   Policy used by some central banks today to make their policy goals and actions clear enough so that the public can develop accurate forecasts of where central bank policy is headed for the future. *(Chapters 12 and 13)*

Truth in Lending   A law passed by the U.S. Congress in 1968 that requires covered lenders to disclose fully all the relevant terms of a personal loan to the borrower and to report a standardized loan rate (known as the APR, or annual percentage rate). *(Chapters 6 and 21)*

U

unbiased expectations hypothesis   A theory of the yield curve that contends that the curve's shape is determined exclusively by investor expectations regarding future interest rate movements. *(Chapter 7)*

U.S. Treasury bills   A debt obligation, one year or less to maturity, issued by the United States government. *(Chapter 10)*

V

variable-rate mortgage (VRM)   Home mortgage loans carrying an interest rate that varies during the term of the loan, generally depending on the movement of interest rates in the open market. *(Chapter 22)*

vehicle currency   A monetary unit of a nation that is not only the standard of value (unit of account) for domestic transactions but is also used to express the prices of many goods and services traded between other nations as well. *(Chapter 23)*

venture capital firms   Financial firms that gather funds from individual and institutional investors and direct this capital into new or expanding businesses. *(Chapter 16)*

Veterans Administration   A U.S. federal agency set up in 1944 to provide benefits to individuals who have served in the U.S. military, including the promotion of home ownership among veterans by guaranteeing the repayment of their home loans. *(Chapter 22)*

W

wealth   Accumulated assets held by an economic unit as a result of saving. *(Chapter 1)*

wealth effect (of saving and interest rates)   Contends that the net wealth position of savers (the balance in their portfolios between debt and financial assets) determines how their desired levels of saving will change as interest rates change. *(Chapter 5)*

Y

yield curve   Relationship between short-term interest rates and long-term interest rates (that is, between yield to maturity and time to maturity of a debt security) as reflected in a smooth curve. *(Chapter 7)*

yield to maturity   The interest rate on a debt security that equates the purchase price of the security to the present value of all its expected annual net cash inflows (income) from now until its maturity date. *(Chapter 6)*

Z

zero coupon bond   A long-term debt security that generates no interest (coupon) payments prior to maturity and thus sells at a discount to its face value and tends to rise in value over the life of the bond. *(Chapter 19)*

Index

A

Abnormal returns, 55
Acceptance financing; *see* Bankers' acceptances
Acceptance rates, 326
Accountability, 394
Accounting rules
  derivatives, 263
  employee stock options, 628
Accounts payable, 27
Accumulated savings, 32
Actual maturity, 281
Add-on rate, 156
Adequate capital, 526
Adjustable life insurance, 488, 493
Adjustable mortgage instrument (AMI), 684
Adjustable-rate mortgages (ARMs), 458
Administrative costs, 477
Administrator of National Banks, 515
Advance refunding, 566
Adverse selection, 60–61
Advertising, 660
Advisory fees, 477
Advisory services, 729
After hours trading, 16
After-tax yields, 226–228
Agencies; *see* Federal agencies
Agency companies, 494
Agency conflicts, 602
Agency offices, 725
Agency operations, 398
Agency services, 12
Agency transaction, 397
Agent, 61
Akerlof, George, 84
Alesina, Alberto, 368
Alm, Richard, 743
American Bankers Association (ABA), 466
American depository receipts (ADRs), 634
American options, 257
American Stock Exchange (AMEX), 476, 535,
  623–624, 627
Ammer, John, 176, 203
Amortization, 576
Ando, Albert, 88, 112
Announcement effect, 391
Annual percentage rate (APR), 158–159, 660
Annual percentage yield (APY), 160–161
Annual Statement Studies, 68
Annualized percentages, 143

Annualized yield to maturity, 147
Annuity accounts, 646
Annuity plans, 487
Anomalies, 635
Anticipated default loss, 209–210
Anticipated vs. unanticipated inflation, 171–172
Arbitrage, 15, 182, 313, 388, 707
  covered interest, 714
  as unifying factor in financial markets, 15
Arbitrageurs, 15
Arm-twisting, 400
Arnold Bernhard & Company of New York, 66
Asked price, 65, 145, 296, 558, 627, 707
Asquith, P., 223
Asset-backed commercial paper, 338
Asset-backed securities (ABS), 594–595
Asset concentration, 439
Asset conversion, 438
Asset prices
  basis point, 143–144
  duration and price changes, 194–195
  forecasting and interest-rate and, 238–241
  hedging strategies, 241–242
  interest rates and, 143, 238–241
  stocks and bonds, 144–145
  supply and demand changes, 154
  units of measurement for, 143–145
  yield-asset price relationship, 152–155, 189
Assets, 27; *see also* Financial assets; Risky assets
  creation of financial assets, 27–31
Asymmetric information, 17, 54, 57–64
  adverse selection problem, 60–61
  concept of, 57–59
  efficiency and, 61–62
  laws and regulations, 62–64
  lemons and plums problems, 59–60, 62
  moral hazard problem, 61
  problems of, 59–64
  real-world markets and, 61–62
Asymmetry, 54
Auction, 285
  Salomon scandal, 291
  Treasury bill, 285–287
Auction method, 557
Auto-loan-backed securities, 221
Automated clearinghouses (ACHs), 104, 366, 428
Automated price quotations, 632
Automated teller machines (ATMs), 427
Automatic transfer services (ATS), 432, 645
Aversion to risk, 277

G

H

QUICK REFERENCE URL GUIDE

www.state.nh.us/nhdoj
www.statefarm.com
www.statelocalgov.net
www.stats.bls.gov
www.stern.nyu.edu
www.stls.frb.org
www.stocksmart.com
www.stomaster.com
www.streettracks.com
www.streetwatch.com
www.sysmod.com/eurofaq.htm
www.taxes.about.com/library
www.thestreet.com
www.thomson.com
www.toron.com
www.tradeport.org
www.tradingedge.com
www.transunion.com
www.treas.gov
www.treasurydirect.gov
www.trinity.edu/dwalz
www.va.gov
www.vanguard.com
www.veribank.com
www.wabash.edu/depart/economic
www.wamu.com
www.wdh.org
www.wellsfargo.com
www.wholesaleaccess.com
www.wocu.org
www.worldbank.org
www.worldbank.org/finance
www.wright.edu
www.wsj.com
www.wto.org
www.wwquote.com